Praise for Ted Landau's Previous Mac OS X Book

This book is the single best source of OS X troubleshooting tips and techniques that I have seen.

—Steve Becker, MacEase.com

Best single collection of problem-solving tips we've seen.

—John Nemerovski and David Weeks, mymac.com

I love this book; it's the best OS X book I've read since *Mac OS X: The Missing Manual.* My copy of this masterful work is already dog-eared, and I've had it only three weeks. A must addition to any OS X user's library. MacMice Rating: 5 out of 5.

—David Weeks, mymac.com

This is a book for the user, the frustrated user, the curious user, and the user who wants to get the very most from the system.

—thinksecret.com

Mac OS X Disaster Relief is extremely well-written, refreshingly down-to-earth.

—Ric Getter, *MacDirectory*

Landau covers almost every known Mac OS X bug…much valued.

—it-enquirer.com

If you only own one book on OS X, this should be it.

—Sherman Wilcox, amazon.com

This is one of those few books that is really worth five stars.

—amazon.com.uk

This is a tremendous book. You could call the book a survival guide to the latest phase of the computer age. Things always go wrong with computers (even Macs!), and this book is a great guide to getting out of trouble.

—amazon.com

This book should be on your shelf.

—Robert Pritchett, macnut.com

Mac OS X
Help Line

Panther Edition

Ted Landau

with Dan Frakes

 Peachpit Press

Mac OS X Help Line, Panther Edition

Ted Landau

Peachpit Press
1249 Eighth Street
Berkeley, CA 94710
510/524-2178
800/283-9444
510/524-2221 (fax)

Find us on the World Wide Web at www.peachpit.com.
To report errors, please send a note to errata@peachpit.com.

Peachpit Press is a division of Pearson Education.
Copyright © 2004 by Ted Landau

Editor: Clifford Colby
Production coordinator: Gloria Marquez
Copyeditor: Jill Simonsen
Proofreader: Elissa Rabellino
Compositor: Owen Wolfson
Indexer: Julie Bess
Cover design: Nathalie Valette with Mimi Heft

ISBN 0-321-19387-3

9 8 7 6 5 4 3 2 1

Printed and bound in the United States of America

To Bailey

Acknowledgments

My thanks go first to Dan Frakes, who has been an immeasurable help in writing this book. He wrote the primary drafts of two chapters ("Troubleshooting Networking: File Sharing and Internet" and "Troubleshooting the iApps") and generally served as a technical advisor. Without Dan, I'd probably *still* be working on this book.

My thanks also go to the people at TechTracker, who have graciously allowed me continued access to MacFixIt email, which has helped immensely in my quest to stay current with troubleshooting issues.

A very warm thanks to all of the staff at Peachpit (and a special nod to Cliff Colby, Nancy Ruenzel, Marjorie Baer, and Gary-Paul Prince). If there's a better bunch of people in the publishing industry, I have yet to find them. It's been a joy to work with them over the years. As long as they're willing to put up with me, I plan to stick with them.

I also want to express a heartfelt thank-you to my son, Brian. His enthusiasm and support for all things Macintosh, including my own accomplishments, have made him my unofficial partner. It would all have been far less fun without him.

Finally, I again offer my thanks to my wife, Naomi. Mere thanks are not enough to compensate for the constant support and patience she has given me through all the ups and downs of the past years. But it's a start.

Ted Landau
Email: ted@tlandau.com

Contents at a Glance

Contents

Chapter 11: Troubleshooting the iApps. 1011

Foreward

What's new in this edition?

For starters, the title is new: It's now called *Ted Landau's Mac OS X Help Line* instead of *Mac OS X Disaster Relief*. The inclusion of my name aside, the new title better describes the range of material the book contains. Although the emphasis remains on troubleshooting, this volume represents much more than a collection of specific problems and their solutions: It also explores the inner workings of Mac OS X, providing insights into such topics as permissions, packages, fonts, invisible files, the contents of the System folder, what exactly happens at startup, and using Terminal. I've always believed that the best troubleshooters are the ones who understand *why* things happen, not just what needs to be done to correct the problem. The new title better reflects this viewpoint.

What's changed in this edition *besides* the title? The short answer: Just about every page!

For starters, I used this revision as an opportunity to substantially reorganize the material in a way that should make it easier to find the specific help you need in a crisis. Of greater significance is the wealth of new information included in this edition. This edition has been completely updated to reflect all of the changes and new features in Panther (Mac OS X 10.3). Plus, it includes all of the information regarding Jaguar (Mac OS X 10.2) from the previous edition of *Mac OS X Disaster Relief* that is still relevant, together with dozens of new topics that emerged after the Jaguar edition was published. I've also included an entirely new chapter on troubleshooting Apple's i-software, such as iPhoto and iMovie (Chapter 11).

Now that Apple has taken to releasing a major Mac OS X update every year (!), writing an up-to-date book about Mac OS X has become increasingly difficult: By the time you finish one edition of your book, it's already time (perhaps even past time) to start working on the next.

So where does that leave this book in terms of Panther? I pushed hard to get *Mac OS X Help Line* published as soon as possible. This meant doing a good portion of the revision in advance of the official release of Panther. But I held off on the final revisions until months after Panther had gone public so as not to preclude coverage of troubleshooting information that only became apparent well after Panther was released. This book reflects the state of the art as of Mac OS X 10.3.3.

Although I was pleased with the previous editions of this book, I'm even more enthusiastic about this edition. As with software that improves and matures with each new upgrade, so has this book.

Why buy this book?

This was the question that kicked off the Foreward in the first edition. I answered it as follows:

> *Mac OS X is new. Mac OS X is different. Mac OS X is popular. In the computing world, whenever something new, different, and popular comes along, you can be certain that many books will be written about it. Such is the case with Mac OS X.*
>
> *So why should you buy this book—instead of or in addition to any other book on Mac OS X? The brief answer: If you want to know how to get Mac OS X working when something goes wrong, this book is the one you want. This book is not a general introduction to Mac OS X. Instead, its constant focus remains on troubleshooting—on providing how-to advice for solving problems.*

Mac OS X is no longer quite as new, but the basic premise remains. Although I include a good deal of basic information on Mac OS X in this edition, it remains primarily a troubleshooting book. In fact, if anything, this edition is more focused on troubleshooting: Now that Mac OS X has been around for a couple more years, I feel less compelled to spend time on the basics.

To keep this book from becoming a multivolume set, I've kept coverage of troubleshooting topics not specific to Mac OS X (for example, general hardware problems) to a minimum. This way, I have more room to cover the issues that *are* Mac OS X–specific. In fact, I believe these pages contain more Mac OS X troubleshooting information than you'll be able to find in any other single volume.

If you're a complete novice to the Mac universe, this probably isn't the first Mac OS X book you'll want to read—but it should be the second! And although it's not for novices, neither does it assume that you're an expert. This book is for the average Mac user—one who understands the basics of how to use a Mac and is motivated to know more.

For those who seek more general troubleshooting advice (regarding hardware problems, non-OS-specific networking problems, and so on) as well as information specific to Mac OS 9, I recommend my previous book *Sad Macs, Bombs, and Other Disasters* (Peachpit Press, 2000).

Mac OS X versions covered

It's hard enough to cover just the problems associated with the most recent versions of Mac OS X. To cover older-version problems (many of which have been fixed or made irrelevant by changes to the software) would require two volumes! For this reason, *Mac OS X Help Line* assumes you're using Panther.

Where differences exist between Jaguar and Panther, I often note them; however, I don't typically provide details on how things work in Jaguar. And anything specific to pre-Jaguar versions of Mac OS X is likely not covered at all. That said, if you're using an older version of Mac OS X, the similarities are great enough that, for the most part, you should be able to follow along with the text. Still, my advice remains: Upgrade to Panther!

Finally, in this edition, I've left out most advice that involved booting Mac OS 9 since this is no longer possible with the latest Mac hardware.

Sidebars

This book contains three main types of sidebars:

- **Take Note.** These sidebars contain background information that, although not directly related to the problem at hand (or able to fit easily fit into the flow of the main text), is still relevant to the main topic. For example, in a section where the main text refers to Xcode Tools software, a Take Note sidebar tells you exactly what's on this CD and how to obtain it. Consider these sidebars to be as essential as the main text.

- **Technically Speaking.** These sidebars cover more technical and/or advanced topics than the Take Note sidebars. You can usually skip them and still understand and apply the advice in the main text; however, if you do read them, you'll have an even more complete understanding of the topics at hand. They are, in essence, a bonus for more advanced users.

- **The Jaguar Way.** These sidebars summarize, for a particular topic, the ways in which Jaguar differs from Panther.

Cross-references

Often the same advice or information can be applied to several different situations, the coverage of which may be scattered across a number of chapters. To avoid doling out the same advice again and again, I frequently refer readers to information already covered elsewhere—hence the copious cross-references!

Still, too many cross-references can disrupt the flow, forcing you to thumb back and forth between chapters just to follow a thread. For this reason, I do sometimes repeat information.

Styled text

Sometimes my instructions for fixing problems include text or commands that you must type from the keyboard—particularly when I'm discussing the command-line interface of the Terminal application. To make these instructions as clear as possible, I've used the following text styles:

- **Monospaced text.** This indicates text that you input from the keyboard. For example:

  To move to the Applications directory, type `cd /Applications`.

  A few additional notes: A period that comes at the end of a command, if that command is at the end of a sentence, should not be included in what you type. Quotation marks in commands, however, *should* be typed. Unless otherwise indicated, all commands are to be typed on a single line, even if they take more than a line to print in this book. Assume that a space exists at the end of every printed line, where the command continues to the next line. Finally, assume that you need to press Return at the end of each command in order to run the command.

- **Monospaced bold text.** This indicates text the Mac generates in response to what you type. For example:

  After moving to the Applications directory, the command prompt on my Mac looks like this: `Yoda:/Applications tedmac$`.

- **Monospaced italicized text.** Used in conjunction with text that you type, text styled in this manner indicates that you should not type the text as written but rather substitute what the italicized text implies. For example:

  To view the contents of a text file in Terminal, you can type `cat` *filename*.

  Sometimes, especially if the italicized text is several words, they may be enclosed in brackets, such as `{name of application}`.

Getting more help: MacFixIt

Certain troubleshooting information, of necessity, could not or should not be covered in this book—in particular:

- Time-sensitive problems (for example, bugs that get fixed by updates released within weeks of their discovery)

- Problems not discovered until after the book was published

For these matters, I recommend the MacFixIt Web site (www.macfixit.com). This site—which I created six years ago (though I no longer own or produce its content) is devoted to Mac troubleshooting and provides extensive coverage of Mac OS X. You must pay an annual fee to access its archives (though the home page and forums remain free); however, I believe it offers the most comprehensive Mac troubleshooting information available on the Web.

My alternative choices for the latest in Mac OS X troubleshooting are Apple itself (especially its Apple Knowledge Base site, located at http://kbase.info.apple.com) and Mac OS X Hints (www.macosxhints.com).

Finally, I will be posting occasional online updates to this book at www.macosxhelpline.com.

Obtaining software mentioned here

Throughout this book, I mention products (mainly shareware utilities) that can assist you in troubleshooting Mac OS X. You can download all of this software from the Web; however, you don't have to search the Web to find each program. Instead, you can get the latest versions of all this software simply by going to the VersionTracker Web site (www.versiontracker.com), which includes links to just about every Mac program in existence.

In addition, you can obtain a list of *my* favorite Mac OS X utilities—which include most of the ones mentioned here—from my personal Web site: www.tlandau.com.

1

Why
Mac OS X?

Users familiar with Mac OS 9 understand that Mac OS X is not an incremental change in the Mac OS; it's more like a quantum leap. The first time a longtime Mac user boots Mac OS X, everything will seem different—sometimes just a bit different, but more often a lot different. System Preferences, Library folders, a Dock?

So why, you wonder, did Apple feel it necessary to abandon a successful operating system for uncharted territory? This chapter provides the answers.

In This Chapter
. . . .

Why Did Apple Need a New OS?

I still own Macintosh System Disk 1.0, which came with an original 1984 Mac. The single disk contained the first versions of MacWrite and MacPaint, as well as a System Folder. Its size? A single-sided 400 KB floppy disk!

Back in 1984, the Mac OS didn't include support for networking or the Internet; you could open only one application at a time; and QuickTime and PostScript did not exist. The only storage peripheral you could connect to your Mac was an external floppy drive.

Clearly, the most recent version of Mac OS 9 has come a long way from these System 1.0 roots. For starters, the System Folder alone now occupies more than 150 MB. And MacWrite and MacPaint no longer exist, having evolved into AppleWorks. We now have USB, FireWire, and Ethernet. Floppy disks have vanished. But the evidence of those 1.0 roots is still there.

As time passed, it became clear to Apple that continuing to improve an OS tied to the priorities (and technologies) of two decades past would require significant compromises. Mac OS updates too often depended on patches and add-ons that were not reliable. The original Mac OS was never intended to work in today's interconnected, multimedia-rich world. Trying to add essential new features while maintaining backward compatibility with previous Mac OS versions was becoming close to impossible. What Apple needed was a clean start.

Mac OS X *is* that clean start. Yes, Mac OS 9 and Mac OS X have many similarities, but underneath the hood, they are fundamentally different. For Mac OS X, these differences are both its greatest strength and its biggest weakness.

Mac OS 9: The upside

Apple's move to Mac OS X does not mean that Mac OS 9 has lost all of its appeal. It hasn't. For starters, Mac OS 9 retains a simplicity and common-sense approach that are the hallmarks of the Mac itself. When the Mac was first advertised as the computer for "the rest of us," Apple was talking about the ease of use of the Mac OS. Even a relative novice can figure out a good deal about how the OS works, with relatively little effort. Where are control panels stored? In the Control Panels folder, of course. How do you get a new item into the Apple menu? Drag it to the Apple Menu Items folder. What's the name of the extension that enables file sharing? File Sharing. It all just makes sense. (Well, it doesn't *all* make sense, but I'm speaking in generalizations here!)

Mac OS 9 is also remarkably portable. The entire OS is contained in a single System Folder. With some minor exceptions, you can use the Finder to copy a Mac OS 9 System Folder from one volume to another, and the new volume instantly becomes a bootable Mac OS 9 volume. In fact, a bare-bones System Folder with a System, Finder, and very little else are still all you need to start up a Mac from Mac OS 9.

This very simplicity provided the impetus for *Sad Macs, Bombs, and Other Disasters*—the premise being that even "the rest of us" could learn to troubleshoot our Macs.

Mac OS 9: The downside

Unfortunately, Mac OS 9 is also burdened with the limitations that existed 20 years ago. For one thing, it crashes more often than it should. Even worse, too many of its crashes require restarting the Mac, a time-consuming frustration. And diagnosing an extensions conflict can take hours. In addition, Mac OS 9 is too often plagued by out-of-memory errors, even when it seems that more than enough memory is installed. Getting on the Internet involves a tangle of extensions and control panels that can sometimes confound even experienced users.

The Mac was born in a time when the World Wide Web did not exist. In fact, even a local network was a rarity, other than in large institutions. As such, the original Mac OS had no security features or multiple-user support. Although Mac OS 9 now offers this support, it often doesn't work very well and is too easy to circumvent.

Mac OS X: The down- *and* upsides

The first Mac OS X upside is that it clearly addresses Mac OS 9's downsides! Mac OS X is more stable (you almost never need to restart it), and it handles memory and processor load more efficiently. This is due to such buzzword features as *protected memory* and *preemptive multitasking*. Its security and multiple-user features are so ingrained and feature-rich, in fact, that they drift toward becoming a downside, sometimes getting in the way of the single user who doesn't really need them.

The quality of Mac OS X's graphics and text displays is unmatched anywhere. (Just look at the Mac OS X icons for an example.) What's more, its advanced networking capabilities include simplified settings that sense how you're connected to the Internet and automatically change as needed! It also offers the potential for significantly greater application speed, including the capability to take advantage of multiple processors (should your Mac have them). Finally, you get software, such as iPhoto, that you won't find in any other Mac OS.

But Mac OS X also abandons some of the upsides of Mac OS 9. A standard Mac OS X installation, for example, involves thousands of files, many of which are invisible from the Finder. A peek inside the /System/Library folder reveals that Apple has abandoned the notion that the names of OS files should retain the common-sense appeal of Mac OS 9. Gone, too, is the portability of the Mac OS 9 System Folder: Creating a bootable Mac OS X volume is now a major exercise, requiring utilities other than the Finder. In fact, even just backing up Mac OS X is significantly more difficult than doing so with Mac OS 9.

Unix. For most Mac users, the biggest potential hurdle in mastering Mac OS X troubleshooting will be the Unix basis of Mac OS X's core functions. Unix uses a command-line interface (CLI)—which means it's an entirely text-based OS. You enter text via a command line and press Return. The OS then processes your command and gives you the appropriate feedback. If this arrangement sounds old-fashioned and quaint, that's because it is. It harks back to a style of computing that was in use before graphical user interfaces (GUIs) and mouse input were available. Unix dates back to the mammoth, clunky main-frame computers that were in use before desktop computing was born.

Thus, you might reasonably ask, "How does moving from Mac OS 9 to Unix represent a step forward?" Here's how:

- As an easily extensible operating system, Unix has done a good job of keeping pace with changes in the computer world. Although for better or worse, it retains its command-line interface (which some users actually find preferable for certain tasks), it's a much faster, sleeker, and more powerful OS than it was years ago.

- Unix is immensely popular for running multiple-user servers (such as those at universities, where a central server regulates traffic on a network of client computers). Because of its speed and stability, many Web sites also favor Unix (MacFixIt, for example, runs from a Unix server). Unix is even becoming increasingly popular on personal computers, primarily via its popular cousin Linux.

- By basing Mac OS X on Unix, Apple instantly acquired all the power and benefits of this mature OS. Mac OS X's Web Sharing feature, for example, is based on the Apache Web server included in Unix and far exceeds the Web sharing capabilities of Mac OS 9. If Apple had been forced to start from scratch in building all this functionality into Mac OS X, it probably would have taken another decade for the OS to reach the same level as Unix.

- Mac OS X is not merely a shell for Unix. Although some people have mischaracterized it as a graphical interface for accessing Unix, this is most certainly not the case. Mac OS X can do many things that would be otherwise impossible in Unix. (For example, AppleWorks could never run under Unix.) And although Mac OS X uses Unix for some of its core features, it expands upon those features extensively. It is this combination of Unix and the unique features of Mac OS X that make Mac OS X what it is today.

Still, in some cases, using Unix in Mac OS X *will* feel like a step backward. Unix can be intimidating for those who expect the Mac to work the way it always has. This is especially true for the typical user in Apple's prime markets: home users, small-office users, and students.

For this reason, Apple designed Mac OS X so that most users don't even need to know that Unix exists in Mac OS X. The OS succeeds at this most of the time. Running applications in Mac OS X seems to differ very little from doing so in Mac OS 9.

However, although Mac OS X succeeds in hiding its Unix underpinnings from the casual user, troubleshooters will need to become familiar with it. This doesn't mean you must become a Unix *expert* to be an expert Mac troubleshooter, but it does mean that you can't be an expert troubleshooter without at least a basic knowledge of Unix.

Unix exists as an operating system independent of Mac OS X. Numerous large books about Unix have been written, and there is no way I can provide a thorough background on Unix here. Instead, throughout the book I present specific "cookbook" examples, as appropriate. I also present a primer on Unix for Mac OS X troubleshooters in Chapter 10.

Bottom line: I applaud Apple's move to Mac OS X. I admit that I entered the Mac OS X swimming pool from the shallow end, taking my first steps rather tentatively—and wondering whether I would ever feel as comfortable as I did in Mac OS 9. The adjustment took some time, but now when I'm forced to use Mac OS 9, I can't wait to revert to Mac OS X. When I'm away from the operating system, I miss its elegant look, its stability, and its capability to do more at the same time with less hassle.

Now, thanks largely to the contributions of shareware software developers, I can have my cake and eat it, too. A host of utilities add back the Mac OS 9 features that I missed the most (for example, window-shading and the Application menu). More specific to troubleshooting, other utilities sidestep the need to work directly in Unix by providing graphic-based Mac-like alternatives that do the Unix work for you. In addition, upgrades to Mac OS X are expected to solve the most significant remaining issues, such as the difficulties in backing up a Mac OS X volume.

Since you're reading this book, I assume you've already made the move to Mac OS X. Don't worry: You made the right decision. Mac OS X is Apple's future. It's time to get on board.

A Brief History of Mac OS X

Now that you know *why* Apple decided to move to Mac OS X, it's worthwhile to take a brief look at *how* Apple made the move. As you will soon see, the road to Mac OS X was filled with detours, dead ends, delays, and surprises.

What we now call Mac OS X began as Mac OS 8—*not* the Mac OS 8 that was eventually released but a different OS entirely, which never saw the public light of day.

The original Mac OS 8 was intended to serve as a radical upgrade of what was then the current OS: System 7. (Back then, Apple used the word *System* to describe the OS.) Code-named Copland, Mac OS 8 included many of the critical features that are now part of Mac OS X, such as preemptive multitasking and protected memory (features that form the basis of Mac OS X's superior performance and stability).

After working on Mac OS 8 for several years, Apple finally announced it publicly in 1994, and development versions soon began to ship. CDs that took users on a demo tour of the new OS were handed out at Macworld Expos. The final-release version was scheduled for 1996.

Unfortunately, all of this was going on at the same time that Apple hit its financial nadir. During this period, Apple's sales and market share plummeted, and articles about the "death" of Apple began appearing in the media with the regularity of weather reports.

It was in this atmosphere that Apple took a hard look at the status of Mac OS 8 and realized it would require too much time and money to finish. The result: In 1996, Apple killed Copland.

In the meantime, the Mac OS 8 that *was* eventually released was a much more modest update. It added some significant new features to System 7 but was essentially the same OS.

Back at the drawing board, Apple realized it couldn't entirely abandon its plans for a new OS. But if not Mac OS 8, then what? The company had to do something fast. Apple had promised to announce its new strategy by January 1997. Having decided that it could no longer afford to design a new OS itself, Apple decided to purchase one. The focus quickly narrowed to two choices.

BeOS. On the surface, BeOS seemed to be the logical choice. Be Inc. had already released versions of BeOS that ran on Mac hardware. The compact, fast code often exceeded the capabilities of the Mac OS itself, and its user interface was sufficiently similar to the Mac OS so as not to be a shock to longtime Mac users. But BeOS had two strikes against it. First, many essential components (such as its printing and networking capabilities) were lacking. Second, Be, Inc., demanded more money than Apple was willing to pay. The latter turned out to be the decisive strike. Be was out.

NeXT. NeXT was the company Steve Jobs started after he left Apple in 1986. The original NeXT product was a combination of hardware and software, much like the Mac itself. By 1996, however, all that was left was the software, which was called NextStep and ran only on Intel processors. It eventually evolved into an open operating system called OpenStep, developed jointly with Sun Microsystems. OpenStep was a more mature OS than BeOS; it already had almost all of the features that Apple was looking for. The main problem was that it lacked the familiar Mac user interface. In fact, it didn't even run on Apple hardware. Nonetheless, Apple decided to tie its future to NeXT. In December 1996, the two companies announced their intention to merge.

The primary initial benefit of the merger was that Steve Jobs returned to Apple. This eventually led to the iMac and the subsequent "supercool" hardware that allowed Apple to rise from the ashes and become a profitable, thriving company again.

At the same time, work proceeded on converting OpenStep to the next-generation Mac OS. Initial plans centered on Rhapsody, the code name for a project that was largely a direct port of OpenStep to the Mac. The problem was that no existing Mac software would run in Rhapsody, so all Mac applications would have to be completely rewritten. Developers let it be known that they would abandon the Mac before doing this.

So Apple returned to the drawing board one more time. Rhapsody evolved into Mac OS X (a roman numeral X that was pronounced *ten*). In this version of the OS, existing Mac software would be able to run with just minor modifications—a process Apple called *Carbonizing* the software.

The Unix core, the Library-folder structure, and many of the development tools of Mac OS X have their origins in OpenStep. But the most distinctive feature of Mac OS X—the Aqua interface—came from Apple itself and was unveiled with great fanfare at Macworld Expo in January 2000. Apple also added the capability to run Mac OS 9 within Mac OS X via a feature dubbed Classic. With these pieces in place, Mac OS X had reached its final stages.

A public beta version of Mac OS X was released in September 2000. The official release, labeled Mac OS X 10.0, came in March 2001. This first release still had some significant limitations, such as no AirPort or DVD support. But these problems were largely addressed in Mac OS X 10.1, released in September 2001. This release was the first version of Mac OS X that was truly ready for prime time.

Almost a year later, in August 2002, Apple released Mac OS X 10.2, also known as Jaguar. This represented yet another quantum leap in the evolution of Mac OS X, introducing Sherlock 3, iChat, Ink, Rendezvous, and a significantly refined, bug-fixed interface.

In early 2003, Apple sounded the death knell for Mac OS 9: New Mac models would no longer be able to boot Mac OS 9. The only way to run Mac OS 9 software would be via Mac OS X's Classic mode.

By the middle of 2003, Apple had released iTunes 4 (and the iTunes Music Store), the Safari Web browser, and iChat AV—all now important components of Mac OS X.

In October 2003, Apple released its most recent major update to Mac OS X: Panther (Mac OS X 10.3). This version introduced numerous new and revised features, including these troubleshooting-related highlights:

- **Activity Monitor.** The former Process Viewer utility underwent such a major overhaul (with many added features) that Apple gave it a new name.

- **Exposé.** This new system preference allows you to instantly tile all your open windows so that you can locate and select the one you want.

- **Fast User Switching.** This is my favorite new feature in Mac OS X. It allows you to have multiple accounts logged in at the same time and (assuming you know the required passwords) to switch from one to the other without closing any of the open files. This is a boon to troubleshooting: When you need to determine whether a symptom only occurs with one account, this makes it a snap to do so.

- **Faxing capability.** This is now built into the Printing software.

- **FileVault.** This new security feature allows you to encrypt your entire home directory.

- **Font Book.** This new utility provides font-management options similar to the basic features found in third-party software such as Suitcase.

- **Restore.** This new feature of Disk Utility allows you to back up and restore a disk.

Apple also made dozens of smaller changes to the underpinnings of the OS: several preferences files have been relocated, Unix default settings have been modified, and so on. Although most of these changes are invisible to the typical user, they can have a significant impact on troubleshooting. Details on these and the rest of Panther's new features can be found throughout this volume. Clearly, Apple is keeping busy!

It's been a long road, but the hard part is over. It's now been 20 years since the introduction of the Macintosh, whose original OS set the standard for elegance and ease of use. Now Mac OS X is setting that standard all over again.

Mac OS X: The End of Troubleshooting?

In its ads, Apple touts Mac OS X stability, claiming that it never (or almost never) crashes. Apple makes a good point: Mac OS X is indeed incredibly stable. In Mac OS 9, it was not unusual to experience multiple system crashes each day, forcing you to restart your Mac every time. In Mac OS X, you can go weeks or even months without having to restart your Mac.

Similarly, many of the recommended maintenance tasks that were needed to keep Mac OS 9 running smoothly (such as rebuilding the Desktop, zapping the PRAM, running Disk First Aid) are either no longer needed or needed only rarely.

However, this *does not* mean that troubleshooting is less important in Mac OS X than in Mac OS 9. In fact, I would say that just the opposite is true.

As a relatively new OS, Mac OS X still suffers from some growing pains. There are more bugs and glitches in Mac OS X than you can easily count. And even though each new update fixes many of these bugs, the updates also introduce new ones—a cycle for which there's not yet an end in sight.

In addition, understanding how to troubleshoot Mac OS X is, if anything, more difficult than understanding how to troubleshoot Mac OS 9. Serious crash-and-burn problems may be less common in Mac OS X, but the number of more minor problems has multiplied dramatically. And these problems often have very specific cures (such as deleting or editing an obscure file), which makes it hard to create a *general* set of troubleshooting rules.

An install of Mac OS X includes tens of thousands of files. In addition to the main Library folders (especially /System/Library with all of its frameworks files), there are the invisible (to the Finder) Unix directories. This means that when something goes wrong, it can be a major effort just locating the source of the problem. It could be a plist or cache file that needs to be deleted. It could be a bug in a framework file, which will require another OS update to fix. A folder may have incorrect permissions that need to be modified. A Unix config file may need to be edited. Or you might need to modify a Unix variable via a command in Terminal. Often, users just give up and reinstall the entire OS.

Adding to the complexity, many problems affect only certain systems (such as G3 Macs or Macs with an attached USB floppy drive or Macs with a particular third-party application installed as a startup item). These things happened in Mac OS 9 as well, but they seem to be more common in Mac OS X.

More and more, troubleshooting Mac OS X is becoming a process of gathering and remembering specific fixes to specific problems, rather than learning a few general principles. Still, mastering general principles is an important first step to understanding how and why to apply specific fixes.

Again, none of this is meant to suggest that Mac OS X is trouble-prone. It's far more stable than Mac OS 9 and is a knockout winner in comparison with Windows. However, things can and do go wrong, and understanding why and what to do about them is not always simple—which is why I wrote this book. So enough introduction. Let's get to work …

2

Using Mac OS X: an Overview

If you're largely unfamiliar with Mac OS X, this chapter should bring you up to speed: you'll take a basic tour of the major features in the Mac OS X Finder, Dock, and Desktop.

Even if you are familiar with Mac OS X, however, don't be too eager to skip to the next chapter. This chapter also contains a variety of tips and technical information that even experienced Mac OS X users may not know.

This chapter is not intended as a comprehensive overview, but rather as a selective survey of the topics that are especially relevant to troubleshooting. Later chapters will make frequent reference to topics covered here.

In This Chapter

TAKE NOTE ▶ Mac OS X vs. Mac OS X Server

Mac OS X Server is a special version of Mac OS X that includes the software required to set up the operating system as a central server for a large network of client computers. It's the Mac OS X equivalent of what, in Mac OS 9, was referred to as AppleShare IP. For this book, I assume you're using the standard (client) version of Mac OS X, not the server version.

However, the distinction between Mac OS X client and server is really quite small. All of the software included in the client is also included in the server—and in exactly the same version. In fact, if you're willing to put a bit more effort into managing tasks, you can use the client as a server as well.

The primary differences between the two OS versions are that 1) Mac OS X Server includes some additional utilities (designed specifically for managing servers); and 2) some applications included with both client and server have options enabled when run in the server that are not enabled in the client. In the latter case, the key point is that the software is the same, even if you don't see the enabled option in the client. The software simply checks to see whether you're using the server before displaying the server-only option. For example, in the later versions of Jaguar, Disk Utility includes an option to enable journaling; however, the option is only visible if you are running Mac OS X Server (even though the utility is identical in both client and server).

The Dock

The first time you arrive at the Mac OS X Desktop, the predominant item will be the Dock—Mac OS X's primary navigational tool. Regardless of where you are in Mac OS X, you can almost always return to the Dock—either by clicking it directly or by clicking the Desktop background (which makes the Finder the active application and gets the Dock to emerge from behind any windows that may be hiding it).

Figure 2.1

The Dock.

Dock basics

The Dock itself is quite straightforward. Icons in the Dock represent applications, documents, and folders on your drive. The Dock is divided into two parts: All applications appear on the left side. On the right side are folders, documents, and anything else, along with the Trash. A line divides the two regions.

The Trash is where you place items when you want to delete them. You also use the Trash to eject, or unmount, media as well as to burn CDs. (When you're performing these actions, the Trash icon will change to an Eject or Burn icon.)

To launch an application or open a document, simply click it. If an application is currently running, a triangle appears below its icon. Clicking an already-open application makes it the active application, bringing all of its windows to the front.

While an application is opening, its icon bounces. Similarly, the icon for an open application bounces to alert you that it requires your attention. An email client's icon, for example, will bounce if it has received email in the background while you are working in another application. The bouncing will stop as soon as you make the email program the active one.

When you move the pointer over a Dock icon, its name pops up in text (helpful when the item's icon is not familiar to you). No clicking is needed for this feature.

Adding and removing items to and from the Dock

Adding items to the Dock. To permanently add an item to the Dock, simply drag its icon from its Finder window to the Dock. Keep in mind, however, that you cannot place an application icon on the *right* side of the Dock, nor can you place other types of icons on the left side of the Dock. Otherwise, you can put Dock icons pretty much where you want. You can even rearrange the icon order by dragging an icon to the desired location.

When you open an application whose icon does not appear permanently in the Dock, the icon appears there temporarily: When you quit the application, the icon disappears. However, if you move the application's icon into the Dock while the application is running, the Dock assumes you want it to reside in the Dock permanently. Thus, it will remain there even after you quit the application. You can also click-hold an application's Dock icon to bring up its menu, where you can select Keep in Dock.

Minimizing windows to the Dock. By clicking the yellow (minus) jewel button in a Finder or application/document window (discussed in "The Finder" later in this chapter), you can minimize a window to the Dock. This means the window moves from its location on the screen to become an icon in the Dock. The name of the window appears when you place the pointer over its minimized Dock icon, allowing you to tell what's what when you have several windows in the Dock. In addition, the icon for a window contains a mini-icon of the application that created the window. When you click the icon in the Dock, the window returns to its normal size. (An animation effect typically accompanies this movement.)

Removing icons from the Dock. To remove a "permanent" icon from the Dock, simply drag its icon off the Dock. You will see a "poof of smoke" animation before the Dock icon disappears. Don't worry: Removing a Dock icon does not delete it from your drive; it just removes its representation from the Dock. The Dock icon serves as a pointer to the actual item. The item still exists and can be accessed via the Finder.

Because all running applications appear in the Dock, you cannot remove the icon of an application that's running. If an application is not "permanently" part of the Dock, its icon will disappear from the Dock once the application quits; if you want to remove a permanent item from the Dock that is currently running, drag it off the Dock—you won't see the "poof," and the icon will remain until the application quits.

Dock menus

If you click an item in the Dock and hold down the mouse button (or Control-click the item, or right-click it if you have a multibutton mouse), a pop-up menu will appear. The menu itself depends on the nature of the item. At minimum, you should see a Show In Finder command; if you choose it, the Finder window containing the selected item will open.

For open applications, the menu will likely include at least one additional item—Quit, which does exactly as its name implies (that is, it quits the application). As discussed in the previous section, if the item is not a permanent member of the Dock, there will also be a Keep In Dock selection. Depending on the application, you may see additional items, intended to provide convenient access to specific features. When iTunes is open, for example, you can control playback from its Dock menu.

Figure 2.2

The Dock menu for iTunes.

For folders, the Dock menu also includes a list of every item contained within the folder. If the folder contains subfolders, you will get hierarchical submenus containing the contents of those subfolders. Drag the pointer to any item in the menu and release the mouse, and you will "open" that item (actually, you *open* a folder or document but *launch* an application), as appropriate. This works even if an item in a Dock menu is actually an alias for a folder.

SEE: • "Aliases and Symbolic Links," in Chapter 6, for more on this topic.

This means that if you drag the icon of your hard drive to the Dock, you will be able to access a hierarchical menu listing every item on your drive!

Finally, the menu for the Trash item offers the Empty Trash option: You use this command to delete the contents of the Trash. Before you empty the Trash, however, you can always click the Trash icon to open its window and drag any items out (should you decide you've placed them there in error).

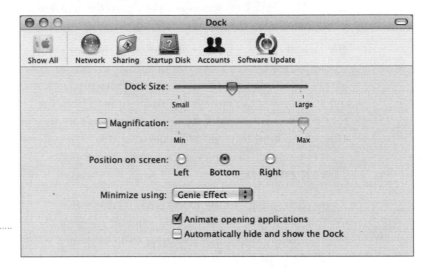

Figure 2.3

The Dock System Preferences pane.

Dock preferences: customizing the Dock

You can customize the Dock's appearance as well as the way several of its features work.

For example, if you move the pointer over the Dock's white separation line, the pointer changes to a bar with arrows on either side. If you move the pointer in the direction of either arrow, the entire Dock will get larger or smaller.

If you press and hold the Control key while the arrow pointer is visible, it brings up a special pop-up menu. From here, you have several options:

- **Turn Magnification On/Off.** With this option enabled, the Dock gets larger in the region where the pointer is located—convenient if the Dock is set very small by default, or if you have a large number of items in the Dock, causing it to shrink to fit everything.

- **Turn Hiding On/Off.** With this option enabled, the Dock vanishes from the screen until you move the pointer to the edge where the Dock resides—convenient if you need extra screen real estate.

- **Position on Screen.** This option lets you place the Dock on the left, right, or bottom edge of the screen.

- **Minimize Using.** This option lets you determine what type of animation effect is displayed when windows are minimized to the Dock.

- **Dock Preferences.** Choose this option to open the System Preferences pane for the Dock. (I discuss System Preferences in more detail later in this chapter.) For the Dock, this simply provides a way to access more or less the same options I just described—but from a single-window layout rather than a menu.

- **Dock System Preferences pane.** You can access the Dock Preferences pane directly (that is, without going through the Dock's pop-up menu) by choosing System Preferences (from the Apple menu or the Dock) and clicking the Dock item from the list of preference panes. The Dock pane contains some options that are not available in the Dock's pop-up menu, such as a slider for adjusting the magnification effect.

- **Dock command in Apple menu.** Apple wants to make sure you can find these Dock options, so it's also included a Dock command in the Apple menu. If you choose this command, you get a hierarchical menu with options similar to those in the Dock's pop-up menu.

Dock troubleshooting tips and hints

The Dock is quite reliable. Occasionally, however, problems may occur.

If you click an item in the Dock, and it either doesn't launch or doesn't function correctly, the first thing you should do is remove the item from the Dock and then re-add it by dragging the original item to the Dock. This should fix 90 percent of Dock-related problems. For the other 10 percent, here are some tips that should help you get out of any remaining trouble.

Question-mark icon in Dock. A Dock icon with a question mark superimposed over it means that the Dock is unable to locate the item the icon represents. In some cases, the item may have been deleted. If, however, the item is still on your drive, the solution is simple:

1. Place the pointer over the question-mark icon.

   The name of the missing file will appear; make a note of it.

2. Drag the question-mark icon off the Dock.

   The icon will disappear.

3. Locate the missing file in its Finder window and drag its icon to the Dock.

   Problem solved!

If you delete an item from your Mac that was previously added to the Dock, the question mark will not appear in the Dock until the Dock is relaunched (typically after a log-out or restart) or until you try to open the item. In other words, the Dock won't immediately reflect the fact that the item is no longer available.

Figure 2.4

A Dock icon with a question mark.

Dock fails to function as expected. Very rarely, the Dock may appear to stop functioning altogether—that is, clicking a Dock item has no effect.

To fix this problem, you need to quit and relaunch the Dock. However, because the Dock is a special application, there's no easily accessible Quit command. Even if you use Mac OS X's Force Quit window (by pressing Command-Option-Escape, as discussed in Chapter 5), the Dock will not be listed.

The solution is to launch Activity Monitor, a program included with Mac OS X and located in the Utilities folder. This utility shows all open processes (an application is a type of process), even ones that are not accessible directly from the Finder. From the Activity Monitor window that appears, do the following:

1. From the Show pop-up menu, choose My Processes (if it's not already selected).

2. Scroll the list of processes to locate the Dock item, then select it.

3. From the Process menu, choose Quit Process (Command-Option-Q).

4. When a dialog appears asking whether you really want to quit, click the Force Quit button.

    The Dock should quit, vanishing temporarily. It will then relaunch, and all should be normal again.

Poof does not evaporate. When you drag an item off the Dock, a poof of smoke appears; however, occasionally that poof may linger on your Desktop, refusing to disappear. Everything else works as normal, but you don't really want to stare at that poof. Logging out and logging back in will fix this problem, but it forces you to close all open applications. Don't despair—there's a better way! Simply quit the Dock (as described in the previous section), and the poof will disappear (with no ill effect).

Application fails to open or quit. Occasionally, you may click a Dock icon but its application refuses to open, leaving the Dock icon to bounce indefinitely. Alternatively, you may quit an application, but its Dock icon remains—even though it's not a permanent icon (and the application appears to have quit successfully). In either case, the problem is with the application itself, not the Dock. Thus, you usually can fix these problems by force-quitting the application.

In some cases you can force-quit directly from the Dock by holding down the Option key while accessing the application's menu. When you do this, the Quit command should change to Force Quit; choose it. If this command does not work (that is, you see the message, "Appliaction not responding," in the Dock menu), you can still try to force-quit by pressing Command-Option-Escape, as previously described.

SEE: • **Chapter 5 for more on the Force Quit option.**

TAKE NOTE ▶ Dock and Finder Shortcuts

Keyboard shortcuts provide an alternative method for accessing various commands and features. If you look at the menus of almost any application, such as the Finder, you will see shortcut equivalents for many of the commands. In the File menu, for example, you will see that Command-W is the equivalent of the Close Window command.

Some mouse-related shortcuts are less obvious, however, because they're not conveniently listed in menus. One example is the Control-click option for accessing the Dock menu from its separator line (which I described earlier in the chapter). I recommend that you experiment on your own by clicking your mouse button and/or holding down the Command, Option, Control, and Shift keys in various combinations and in various locations. See what happens.

To help you get started, here are some of the most common and useful shortcuts for the Dock and Finder (beyond those I've already covered in the main text or that are listed in Finder menus).

Dock shortcuts

Command-click. This is equivalent to choosing Show in Finder from an item's Dock menu. If you hold down the Command key and click an item in the Dock, a new Finder window opens, showing that item.

Command-Option-click. If you hold down Command-Option and click an application in the Dock, that application becomes the active application, and all open windows for other applications become hidden.

Clicking the Dock icon for any hidden item makes its windows visible again. To get everything back at the same time, from the Finder menu (or a similar menu for whatever application is active), choose Show All.

Finder window shortcuts

Option. If you hold down the Option key when you double-click a folder, the folder opens in a new window, and the previous window closes.

Command. When the toolbar is visible in a window, double-clicking a folder icon usually replaces the contents of the current window with those of the folder you just chose to view—that is, a new window does not open. If you hold down the Command key when clicking a folder, the folder opens in a new window. It will also open a new window automatically if the toolbar is not visible.

Shift. If you hold down the Shift key when opening a new window (such as opening a folder from the Desktop or in combination with the Option key), the folder opens in slow motion. This has no value other than for your own amusement.

continues on next page

TAKE NOTE ▶ **Dock and Finder Shortcuts** *continued*

Finder selections

Command. If you want to select several items from a list that are not contiguous, hold down the Command key while you make the selections—this is especially useful in List view.

Shift. To quickly select a contiguous group of items, click the first item in the list, hold down the Shift key, and then click the last item.

Finder copy and move shortcuts

Option-drag. Normally, when you drag an item's icon to a different folder on the same volume, it moves the item to that location rather than copying it. (That is, the item no longer exists at its original location; it exists only where you moved it.) If you hold down the Option key when doing this, however, you make a copy of the item rather than moving it.

Command-drag. Normally, when you drag an item's icon to a different volume from the one in which it resides, the Finder copies the item rather than moving it. If you hold down the Command key when doing this, however, you will move the item rather than copy it.

Note: These last two commands may not work as described if you do not have sufficient permissions to make the desired move or copy (see Chapters 4 and 6 for more information on permissions).

More shortcuts

Command-Tab. If you press and hold down the Command key, you will bring up a translucent window that contains icons of all of your currently running applications. If you continue to hold down the Command key while repeatedly pressing the Tab key, you can cycle through the highlighted applications. When you release the keys, the highlighted application becomes the active one. Command-Shift-Tab (or Command-~) cycles through the applications in the opposite direction.

Command-~ and Command-Shift-~. You can cycle forward and backward through open document windows in the current application by pressing Command-~ (tilde) for forward and Command- Shift-~ for reverse. In Cocoa applications, this feature is automatically enabled; however, you may need to update Carbon applications to use this feature (see Chapter 4 for definitions of Carbon and Cocoa).

See the following Apple Knowledge Base article for a long list of Mac OS X shortcuts, including ones that work at startup (most of which are covered in Chapter 5): http://docs.info.apple.com/article.html?artnum=75459.

The Finder

The Finder is the application in Mac OS X that you use to navigate to different locations on your mounted volumes. Whenever you click the Desktop background, you make the Finder the active application. Similarly, clicking any open Finder window or the Finder icon in the Dock makes the Finder active. In this section, I'm going to take you on a tour of the many things you can do in the Finder.

SEE: • "Take Note: Finder Folders vs. Unix Directories," in Chapter 4, for an explanation of the use of these two important terms.

TAKE NOTE ▶ Windows in Applications Other Than the Finder

Most applications use windows. An open document in a word processor, for example, is presented in a window.

Document windows vs. Finder windows. The options and actions available in document windows sometimes differ from those in Finder windows. Here are two examples:

- If you have unsaved changes in a document, a dot appears in the red jewel (close-window) button in the top-left corner of the document window, indicating that recent changes have not been saved. If you click the red button (in other words, attempt to close the window), a dialog will appear, warning that you have not yet saved your changes. Finder windows do not include this option.

- Document windows generally do not have the toolbar and sidebar features of Finder windows (though there are exceptions).

Applications with no open windows. If you close the last open window in an open application, in most cases the application remains open.

It does not work this way, however, for many Mac OS X utilities. For example, if you close the System Preferences window, the System Preferences application immediately quits. I guess this helps prevent the accumulation of open applications that you're no longer using. Still, it would be nice to have an option to toggle this behavior; there are times when I would prefer to close a utility's windows but still have it running.

Finder windows

To see a typical Finder window, click the Finder icon in the Dock. If no Finder windows are currently open, this action will open a new window. (Depending on how you've configured your Finder Preferences, the window will open to the area generically referred to as Computer, which lists all mounted volumes, or to your own Home directory.) Using your Home window as an example, I will now walk you through the major features of Finder windows. For the moment, I'm assuming you're viewing Finder windows in the Icon view.

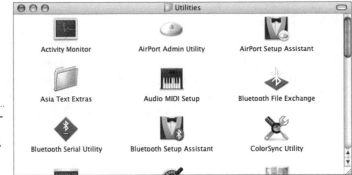

Figure 2.5

A typical Finder window, in Icon view, without the toolbar, sidebar, and status bar visible.

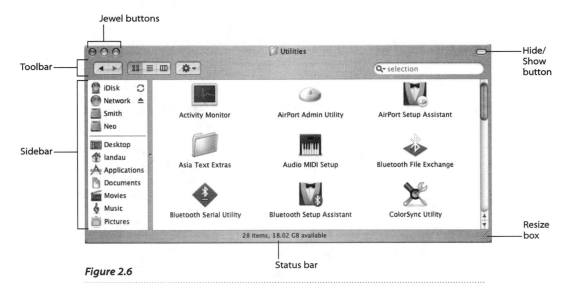

Figure 2.6

The same Finder window as in Figure 2.5, but with the toolbar, sidebar, and status bar now visible.

Jewel buttons. The top section of the Finder window is called the *title bar*. If the toolbar is visible, the title bar blends in with it because they share the same metallic background. In the top-left corner of the title bar are three jewel-like buttons. If you move the pointer over these buttons (from left to right), an *X*, a minus sign (–), and a plus sign (+) appear over each button in turn. If you click the left (red, *X*) button, you close the window. If you click the middle (yellow, –) button, the window is minimized to the Dock (see "The Dock," earlier in this chapter, for more on this feature). The right (green, +) button changes the size of the window, alternating between a larger and a smaller size. (This button is often called the *maximize* button, to complement the *minimize* button.)

Hide/show button. In the top-right corner of the window is an oval button. If you click it, you toggle between displaying and hiding the toolbar and the Places sidebar.

Window title. In the middle of the title bar is the title of the window. If you Command-click the title, a pop-up menu appears, showing all folders that are higher up in the directory hierarchy than the window itself (all the way back to the Computer level). Select any one, and go directly to that window.

If you click-hold the name/icon in the title bar, you can drag the name to another location in the Finder. This moves the contents of the folder to the new location. Option-click-hold copies, rather than moves, the contents to the new location. Command-option-click-hold creates an alias to the folder.

Tip: If you click a window in the background, and it does not become the active foreground window, try clicking the title portion of the window. This typically does the trick.

Toolbar. Below the title bar in a Finder window is the toolbar (assuming you set it to be visible). I discuss this in more detail in the following section.

Places sidebar. The Places sidebar, which borders the left side of each Finder window, is divided into two sections.

The upper section of the sidebar lists mounted volumes (according to your settings in Finder Preferences). Click an item to switch the window view to the root level of that volume. If any of the volumes are removable media, an Eject icon appears next to the item. Click it to eject the item.

This section of the Places sidebar can also contain icons for your iDisk and the local network. Click the iDisk icon to mount your iDisk. Click the Network icon to view all currently mounted network volumes as well as aliases to local volumes available for mounting.

SEE: • Chapter 8 for more on the iDisk and Network options in the Places sidebar.

The lower section of the Places sidebar lists various files, folders, and applications on your drive. Click any folder to view its contents. A selection of folders, including that for your Home directory (with the Home icon and your short name) and the Applications folder, are included here by default. You can also add or subtract items simply by dragging their icons into or out of the sidebar. (The first item I add to my toolbar is the Utilities folder!) You can similarly click-drag to rearrange the order of items.

If you Command-click a folder or volume in a sidebar, a new window will appear listing that item's contents.

If the window is too small to display all items in the sidebar, a vertical scroll bar appears. You can also adjust the width of the sidebar by click-holding the vertical divider along the right border of the sidebar and dragging it left or right. If you double-click the sidebar border, it will disappear completely.

Status bar. At the bottom of the window is the status bar. If it is not visible, from the Finder's View menu choose Show Status Bar. Note: This status bar will appear near the top of the window if you choose to hide the toolbar and sidebar by clicking the oval button in the title bar.

The text in the status bar shows how many items are in the displayed folder, as well as how much unused space is left on the volume that contains the folder.

If you select items in a Finder window, the status bar information shifts to list how many items you've selected (for example, "2 out of 25 items selected").

Depending on the window, you may also see symbols at the left end of the status bar. A Pencil icon with a line through it, for example, means that the current window's contents are read-only.

28 items, 18.02 GB available   1 of 28 selected, 18.02 GB available

Figure 2.7

The status bar in the Finder (left) without any item selected and (right) with an item selected.

Scroll bars and resize box. If you cannot see the full contents of the window at the window's current size, scroll bars on the right and bottom allow you to bring other items into view. You can also click-drag the mouse to the upper or lower borders of a Finder window to move the scroll bars.

In the bottom-right corner of the window is the resize box (several lines forming a triangle). Drag this box to resize and reshape the window as desired.

Window contents. Windows contain files (applications and documents) and folders. To select an item in a window, single-click it. The item's shading will change to indicate that it's selected, and its name will appear against a colored background (blue by default).

To open a file or launch an application, double-click its icon. To open a folder, double-click the folder icon. If you do this, the selected folder's contents will replace the contents of the open window (unless you've changed your Finder Preferences so that folders open in a new window, as discussed later in the chapter).

SEE: • "Take Note: Dock and Finder Shortcuts," earlier in this chapter, for variations on opening a folder.

You can edit the name of an item in a window (in Icon view) by clicking the name below the icon. After a second or so, a box should appear around the name and the text should be highlighted to indicate that you can edit it. (You can also press Return when an item is selected to enable editing of its name.) If the name is too long to fit on one line, it will wrap to a second or even a third line as needed.

If an item's name is still deemed too long to display when it's not the selected item, an abbreviated version of the name will appear. If you hold the pointer over the shortened name for a few seconds (or hold down the Option key and place the pointer over the icon to get an instant response), the full name will appear in an expanded text window.

Spring-loaded folders. To use this feature, click-drag an item to a folder's icon and hold it there. After a brief delay (which you can adjust via the Finder's Preferences dialog), the folder will spring open. You can then place the item in the folder (by releasing the mouse button), spring-open a sub-folder (by similarly dragging the item to the subfolder's icon), or simply move the pointer away from the folder (causing the folder to close with no other change). Note that if you press the spacebar while holding an item over a folder, it will instantly spring open—even if you've disabled spring-loaded folders in Finder Preferences.

THE JAGUAR WAY ▶ Finder Windows and the Toolbar

The major difference between Finder windows in Jaguar and Panther is that Jaguar windows don't have a Places sidebar. Instead, folder, application, and document icons are added directly to the toolbar. You can still do this with Panther's toolbar; however, you're more likely to use the lower part of Panther's Places sidebar instead.

Two other differences: 1) Jaguar does not include the Action button/menu (in the toolbar of Panther's Finder windows); 2) Jaguar windows do not have Panther's metallic background.

Toolbar and Finder views

Finally, in this tour of Finder windows, you return to the toolbar. In its default state, moving from left to right, here's what you'll find:

- **Back.** Click the Back arrow button to go back to the folder that was previously visible in this window. This works if you have replaced the original contents of a window by double-clicking a folder within it.

- **Forward.** Click the Forward arrow button to reverse the effect of clicking the Back button. Alternatively, to go forward in a different path, double-click any folder icon in the window being displayed.

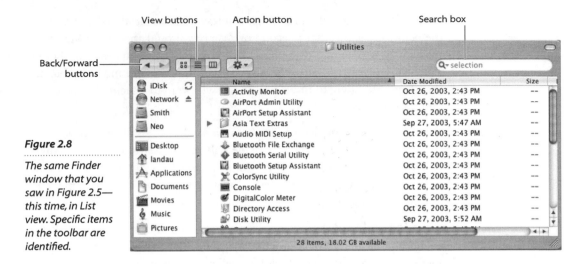

Figure 2.8

The same Finder window that you saw in Figure 2.5— this time, in List view. Specific items in the toolbar are identified.

- **View.** The View button is really three separate buttons, each of which affects how the contents of the window are displayed:

  Icon view. This is the traditional view, in which every file is represented by an icon with a name below it. You can move icons by dragging them.

  List view. In this view, all items are in a text list, with each item in its own row. The contents of a row are identified by the columns listed at the top. On the far left side is a column of icons and names for each file. This column typically is followed by columns for last modification date, file size, and kind (such as application, document, or folder). Clicking any column title sorts the window by that column. Clicking the same column again reverses the sort order.

  You can resize the width of a column by click-dragging the dividing line between two column headers. You can move a column by click-dragging the column header itself. (You can choose which columns are displayed for a selected window via the dialog that appears if you select Show View Options from the Finder's View menu.)

  To the left of each folder in the list is a disclosure triangle. Click the triangle to reveal a subdirectory list of the folder's contents within the current window (as opposed to opening the folder in its own window). If, instead, you double-click a folder, you open the window, replacing the current contents displayed.

  Column view. This view is new to Mac OS X; there is no counterpart in Mac OS 9. In this multicolumn view, the contents of a folder appear in the left-most column. If you click a folder in that column, its contents appear in the column to the right. This arrangement can continue until there are no more folders to open in the right-most window (at which point the selected item is previewed in the final column, as described below).

  You can use the horizontal scroll bar to slide back and forth among columns if they don't all fit within the current window.

If you click an item that is not a folder, the column to the right typically displays summary information about the file (such as its name, kind, size, version, and modification date). For documents, you may see a preview of the document's contents.

By clicking the small double vertical bars at the bottom of each column divider and holding down the mouse button, you can move the pointer to resize the column widths.

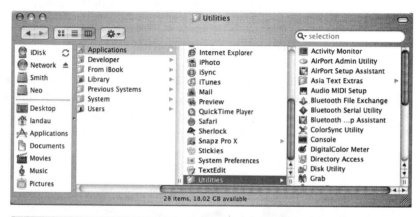

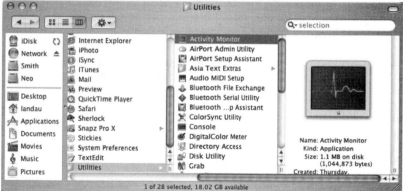

Figure 2.9

(Top) The Finder window in Column view; (bottom) a similar Column view, this one showing a file preview in the right-most column.

- **Action.** Click-holding this button reveals a menu from which you can select context-sensitive commands. If no item in the folder window is selected, the Action menu lists commands for the folder itself. If an item is selected, the Action menu's commands refer to the selected item.

  The contents of the Action menu are identical to or a subset of the list of items found in contextual menus.

  SEE: • "Take Note: Contextual Menus (and Folder Actions)," later in this chapter.

- **Search.** This is where you enter text to search the contents of your drive. You'll learn more about this in the "Find and Search" section, later in this chapter.

Customizing items in the toolbar. To add an item (such as a folder or application) to the toolbar, simply drag its icon to the bar. (In most cases, I recommend using the Places sidebar for this purpose.) To remove an item, Command-drag its icon off of the toolbar. You can rearrange the left-to-right order of items in the toolbar by Command-dragging them.

If you have more items in the toolbar than you can see in the window, an arrow will appear at the right end. Click it to access a pop-up menu of the remaining items.

To further customize the toolbar, from the Finder's View menu choose Customize Toolbar. (You can also Shift-click the Toolbar button in the upper right.) The Customize Toolbar dialog includes options only available via this dialog, such as a Get Info option (which opens the Get Info window for the selected item in the Finder's window) and an Eject option (as discussed in "Take Note: Eject Options," later in this chapter).

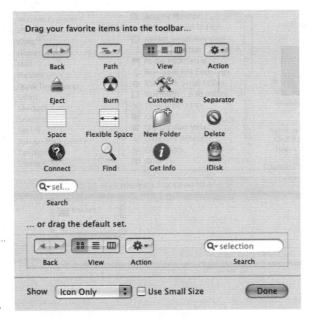

Figure 2.10

The dialog that appears when you select Customize Toolbar from the Finder's View menu.

Find and Search

When it comes to locating files and folders on your local or networked volumes, you have two options.

Find. From the Finder's File menu, choose Find (Command-F) to bring up the Find utility. To use it, follow these steps:

1. From the Search In menu, select a search location. Options include Local Disks, Everywhere (which includes local disks plus mounted network

volumes and removable volumes), Home (your Home directory), and Specific Places (you get to set up the criteria yourself).

With Specific Places selected, you can add volumes or folders via the Add button (or by simply dragging a volume or folder into the Specific Places area). For volumes that are already listed, you can enable or disable their check boxes to determine what will or won't be searched.

2. Enter the search criteria.

The default selection is Name. From the Name pop-up menu, you can choose among other criteria, such as Visibility, Content, Date Modified, Label, Type, and Creator.

For example, choose Visibility (and then select "invisible items") to search for invisible items. Choose Content to search based on the content indexes for a volume and/or folder. This option searches the text content of documents containing text.

SEE: • **The "Content Index" section of "Get Info," in Chapter 4, for more on the Content Search feature.**

If you want to add further criteria, click the plus (+) icon at the far right of any item. This adds another criterion line, which enables you to do a Boolean (and) search on the combined criteria. To delete a criterion, click the minus (–) icon next to its name.

Most criteria will include a second pop-up menu, where you define the parameters of the criterion. For example, for Name, the default selection is "contains." From the second pop-up menu, you can shift to other choices, such as "starts with," "ends with," or "is."

If you change the main criterion, the second pop-up menu choices change as well. For example, if you shift from Name to Visibility, the second pop-up menu choices change to "visible items," "invisible items," and "visible and invisible items."

3. Finally, add the specific text of your search in the text box.

For example, to search for all invisible items containing the word *global,* you would select the "Name contains" criterion and type in global. You would then add a second criterion line for "Visibility: invisible items."

4. Click the Search button, and a results list appears in a separate window. Single-click an item in the results, and the path to the item appears in the lower section of the window. Double-click any folder in the path or any file in the results, and you will either go to that folder in the Finder or open that file in the appropriate application.

To cancel a search in progress, click the X button in the upper-right corner of the window.

Prior to Mac OS X 10.2, this sort of search was included as part of the Sherlock 2 utility. I find this newer separate Find method to be significantly easier to use.

There are certain locations in which Find does not look by default. In particular, it will not look inside the contents of package files (such as application bundles, which end in .app), nor will it look inside folders owned by other users (such as folders in Users accounts other than your own). The Find feature will only search folders for which you have Read & Write access. This means, for example, that it will not search the contents of the root-level System folder, even if you're an administrator. For a standard user, it will not even search the contents of the root-level Library folder. To search in such folders, you may be able to use Find's Specific places option (selecting System, for example, as the place to search). Or you can go to the desired folder in the Finder and use the Finder window toolbar's Search feature (using the Selection option as described next). More generally, for a complete search of all files on your drive, you can use Terminal commands or a utility such as Locator.

Unless you select to include invisible items in your criteria, the results will not show items in the invisible Unix folders (such as var and etc) or any other invisible folders, even if the item within the folder is itself visible.

SEE: • **Chapter 3, for more on package files.**
   • **Chapter 4, for more on root access and permissions.**
   • **Chapter 6, for more on invisible files.**
   • **Chapter 10, for more on using Terminal and Locator.**

Note: Much of the software for Find indexing is located in the /System/Library/ Find directory. For example, there is a file here called SkipFolders that includes a list of all the folders that Find will never index.

Search. The Finder's Toolbar contains a Search text box (unless you removed it via the Customize Toolbar dialog). From any Finder window, enter criteria in this box, and Mac OS X does a "file name contains" search. How much of your drive it searches will depend on what you select from the magnifying-glass pop-up menu on the left side of the search box. You have four choices: Local Disks, Home, Everywhere, and Selection. These choices are the same as for the Find command, except that Selection replaces Specific Places. Selection refers to the current window, including files within folders in the window. (If you select a folder in the current window, the search will be constrained to the contents of that folder only.) Note: No similar pop-up menu exists in Jaguar. In that OS you can only do the equivalent of the Selection search.

A results list replaces the view of the window contents as soon as you enter the search term; there's no Go button to click. As with the Find command, if you click an item, the bottom part of the window displays the path to the item.

The Selection option provides a convenient way to do a quick search of a folder without having to invoke Find and set up this limited search. In addition, with Search, results appear instantly as you type. That is, if you decide to search for the word *Preview*, all you have to do is type pre, then pause, and all files containing *pre* will appear. Add a v, and the list will be parsed to show all files containing *prev*—and so on. The Finder's Find command is not capable of this type of interactive searching.

When you have completed your search, just click the Back button to return to the previous view of the window's contents. To halt a search, click the X button on the right side of the Search box. To redo a search, click the Recycle arrow button in the status bar of the Results window.

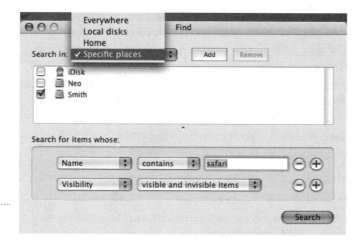

Figure 2.11

The Finder's Find window.

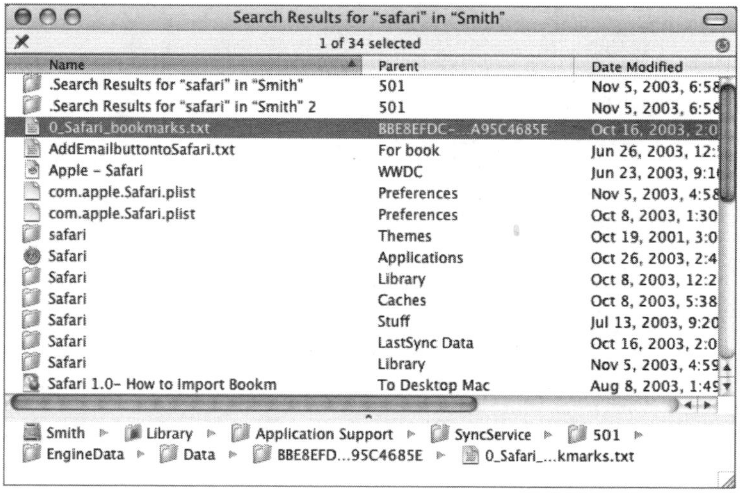

Figure 2.12

The Results window after typing an entry in the Search text box of a Finder window.

Finder menus

The following provides a tour of the key items in the menus you can access when the Finder is the active application.

Apple menu. This menu is common to all applications, not just the Finder. From here, you access a variety of universally available features. The About This Mac item provides info on your Mac (described in detail in "Take Note: About This Mac"). From the Apple menu, you can also select to access the System Preferences window, the Software Update System Preferences pane, the Dock System Preferences pane or Dock options directly via a submenu (as discussed earlier in the chapter), and Network Location options (covered in Chapter 8).

You can also access recently used applications via the Recent Items submenu, and when you're finished with your work, you can choose Sleep, Log Out, Restart, or Shut Down. Because of the stability of Mac OS X and the low power consumption of Sleep, most users will likely not need to restart or shut down very often. New in Panther, the Log Out command lists the name of the current user (for example, Log Out Ted Landau). This is because you can have multiple users logged in at the same time, via Fast User Switching (described later in this chapter).

You use the Force Quit command to quit applications that don't quit when requested to via the application's own Quit command.

SEE: • **Chapter 5 for more on the Sleep, Log Out, Restart, Shut Down, and Force Quit commands.**

Figure 2.13

The Apple menu.

TAKE NOTE ▶ About This Mac

The Apple menu's About This Mac command opens a window that tells you the amount of installed memory and the type of processor in your Mac. It also tells you the operating system version number (such as Mac OS X 10.3.0).

If you click the version number, you get something called the *build number*. A version of Mac OS X may have numerous builds, including prerelease builds and, occasionally, post-release builds. Shortly after Mac OS X 10.1 was released, for example, a security update was released that fixed a small but important bug that could allow a user to get root access without a password. After you installed the update, the About This Mac window still said you were at Mac OS X 10.1, but the build number went from 5G64 to 5L14.

The build number also changes whenever you update Mac OS X. For example, the build number of the initially released version of Mac OS X 10.2 was 6C115. After the upgrade to Mac OS X 10.2.1, it changed to 6D52.

Note: Shortly after Panther shipped, Apple released two security updates. Installing these updates, however, did not change the build number of Mac OS X. Thus, you could not use the build number as a means of checking whether the update had been installed. In such cases, the easiest way to check would be to run Software Update and see if the update is listed.

If you click the build number, you get the serial number for your computer.

Software Update. If you click the Software Update button, the Software Update application is launched directly, bypassing the need to access it via the Software Update System Preferences pane.

More Info. If you click the More Info button, System Profiler is launched to provide detailed information about your Mac, including installed hardware and software.

Figure 2.14

The About This Mac window.

Application (Finder) menu. The menu
immediately to the right of the Apple menu is
officially called the Application menu—because
its name is always the name of the active application, and it provides a way to access options
common to most applications, such as About,
Preferences, Services, Hide/Show, and Quit.

In the case of the Finder, this menu is called
Finder. Unlike most Application menus, it does
not include a Quit command. Since the Finder
normally runs constantly, the command is not
listed (though you can use various third-party
utilities, such as TinkerTool, to add one).

Figure 2.15

The Finder menu.

The Empty Trash command tells Mac OS X to delete anything in the Trash. As
mentioned earlier, anything you place in the Trash icon is not actually removed
until you empty it. Also note that each user maintains his or her own separate
Trash. Thus, any items left in your Trash when you log out cannot be deleted
by other users who may log in later. Such items will remain in the Trash until
you specifically empty it. If you click the Trash icon in the Dock, it opens a
window showing the current contents of the Trash. You can drag an item out of
the window before emptying the Trash if you decide it was placed there in error.

New in Panther is the Secure Empty Trash command, which enables you to
delete an item in such a way that it's virtually impossible for it to be recovered—
even by utilities that claim to be able to undelete files.

Note: Some undelete utilities, if installed on your drive prior to using Secure
Empty Trash, may preserve a separate copy of the file that survives a secure
delete. If this is of concern to you, check out how your undelete utility works
by using Secure Empty Trash and attempting to recover a file.

SEE: • **Chapter 6, for help in troubleshooting problems with deleting files.**

The Finder Preferences command brings up the Finder's Preferences window.
From the toolbar at the top, you can select among four panes: General, Labels,
Sidebar, and Advanced.

From the General pane, you can select among the following options:

- **"Show these items on the Desktop."** You select which types of volumes
  are shown as icons on the Desktop (for example, "Hard disks," "CDs,
  DVDs, and iPods," and "Connected servers"). If none of these options are
  selected, you would access these items primarily via the Computer window (from the Finder's Go menu select Computer) or via the sidebar.

- **"New Finder windows open."** You select from the pop-up menu
  whether a new Finder window shows by default the Computer window,
  your Home directory, or any other volume/folder of your choice.

- **"Always open folders in a new window."** You decide whether to open a new folder within the same window or a new window by default.

- **"Open new windows in column view."** This does precisely what its name implies.

- **"Spring-loaded folders and windows."** Use the slider here to adjust the delay time for spring-loaded folders from Finder Preferences. (Note that even if you disable this option, you can access spring-loaded folders on a case-by-case basis by pressing the space bar as you drag an item over a folder or volume.)

The Labels pane is used to assign names to the different label colors. (The Color Label command itself is in the Finder's File menu.) The Sidebar pane is used to enable or disable the default choices shown in the Places sidebars. Finally, from the Advanced pane, you can select the following options:

- **"Show all file extensions."** You decide whether to show file extensions of names displayed in the Finder (discussed more in Chapter 4).

- **"Show warning before emptying the Trash."** You choose whether you want to see a warning message when you choose Empty Trash.

- **"Languages for searching file contents."** You use this option in conjunction with Find's Content searches. Selecting fewer languages here makes for a smaller index file and a faster search. Because a number of languages are selected by default, I recommend deselecting all but the one (or more) you intend to use.

The Finder (as well as most other applications) also includes a Services command in this menu. I discuss this more under "Services," later in this chapter.

File menu. This menu contains many of the Finder's most commonly accessed features, including the following commands: New Finder Window, New Folder, Open (files and folders), Close Window, Make Alias, Show Original (of an alias), Add To Sidebar, Move To Trash (Command-Delete), Eject (removable media), and Burn Disc (to burn a CD). You will also find the Find (Command-F) and Get Info (Command-I) commands here.

Figure 2.16

The Finder's Application menu.

All of these items are discussed in more detail elsewhere in the book.

SEE: • **"Find and Search," earlier in this chapter, for more on the Find command.**

- **"Get Info," in Chapter 4, for more on the Get Info command.**

- **Chapter 6, for more on most of the other options, including opening files (and using the Open With command), deleting files, creating aliases, and ejecting media.**

New in Panther are the following:

- **Add To Sidebar.** This command adds the selected item to the Places sidebar. It replaces the Add to Favorites command in Jaguar.

- **Create Archive {of item}.** This command compresses the selected item, using the zip format. A new file with a .zip extension is created in the same location as the original file. The original file is not deleted. If you double-click one of these zip files, it is decompressed using a background process called BOM Archive Helper (located in /System/Library/CoreServices). These features eliminate the need for StuffIt Expander and DropStuff for basic archiving and expanding of files on your drive. However, you'll still find these Aladdin utilities useful for working with other compression formats, such as .bin and .sit, as found on the Internet.

- **Color Label.** This command allows you to assign a color (and text) label to individual items in the Finder. The Find command includes a Label criterion, allowing you to search for all items with a label of a selected color. Select *x* to have no label.

Edit menu. This is the menu where you select the Cut, Copy, Paste, and Undo commands. This menu also exists in all applications. In most applications, the commands here refer to content (text, graphics, and so on). However, in the Finder, these commands can also apply to files and folders. For example, you can select an item in the Finder, chose Copy {*name of item*} from the Edit menu, and then navigate to another location and choose Paste {*name of item*} to create a copy of the file at that location. This allows you to move an item from one window to another, for example, without having both windows open. The Undo command in the Finder lets you "undo" Finder actions (such as moving files to the Trash), and supports multiple levels of undo.

For a discussion of the Special Characters command, see "Fonts," in Chapter 4.

TAKE NOTE ▶ Contextual Menus (and Folder Actions)

If you Control-click an item in the Finder (or right-click if you have a multibutton mouse), you bring up a *contextual menu* for that item. This menu's contents will vary by item (such as file versus folder). Common selections include Open, Open With, Get Info, Move to Trash, Duplicate, Make Alias, and Copy {*name of item*}.

You can also install third-party contextual menus to extend those that are included with Mac OS X. If the software does not include an installer that handles the task, all you need to do is drag the {*CMname*}.plug-in file to one of the Contextual Menu Items folders, either in the Library folder of your Home directory or (allowed only if you are administrator) the Library folder at the root level of your drive.

continues on next page

TAKE NOTE ▶ **Contextual Menus (and Folder Actions)** *continued*

Starting in Panther, the Action menu (accessed from the button in Finder window toolbars) lists most of the same commands found in the contextual menu for a selected item. However, some commands only appear in contextual menus. The commands to Enable and Configure Folder Actions, for example, appear in an item's contextual menu but not in the Action menu. The same holds true for custom (third-party) contextual menu items you've added.

Folder Actions. Panther adds several new commands to contextual menus for folders, which are used for implementing folder actions. With Folder Actions, you can run an AppleScript every time some action is taken with that folder. For example, you can set it up so that every time a TIFF graphic file is dragged to a given folder, the file is converted to a JPEG file. This requires writing the relevant AppleScript (discussed briefly in "Take Note: AppleScript," in Chapter 4). Once you've done this, follow these steps:

1. From the folder's contextual menu, select Enable Folder Actions. This command toggles with Disable Folder Actions.

2. Again from the contextual menu, select Attach a Folder Action to select the desired script. This opens a Choose a File window, which typically defaults to /Library/Scripts/Folder Action Scripts. To check for more scripts, navigate to /Library/Scripts/Folder Actions and ~/Library/Scripts/Folder Action Scripts.

You can also add more than one script. To do so (as well as to remove or edit existing scripts), from the folder's contextual menu select Configure Folder Actions. This launches the Folder Actions Setup application, located in /Applications/AppleScript.

You can also access Folder Actions (and get a wider range of scripts) by enabling the Script menu (as described in "Enabling or disabling Menu Extras," later in this chapter).

Figure 2.17

A contextual menu (with a third-party item, XRay, added).

View menu. This menu's options in large part overlap with those in the toolbar, allowing you to switch among Icon, List, and Column views, for example. You can also select Customize Toolbar and Hide Toolbar from here. Selecting Hide Toolbar hides both the Toolbar and the Places sidebar—the same thing you would accomplish by clicking the oval button in the top-right portion of the window (as you will recall from our earlier discussion). To hide or show the status information at the bottom of the window, select the Hide/Show Status Bar command.

You can select the Clean Up command to line up and space all icons according to an invisible grid. Or you could select Arrange (plus an item from its hierarchical menu, such as By Name) to arrange all icons according to the selected criterion as well as push them to the top-left corner of the current Finder window.

If you select a subset of the items in a window, the Clean Up command changes to Clean Up Selection, allowing you to clean up just the selected items.

One caveat: Mac OS X still seems to have some problems with cleanup. More than occasionally, icons in a window you've "cleaned up" will return to their messy state on a subsequent visit. This is especially true for items on the Desktop.

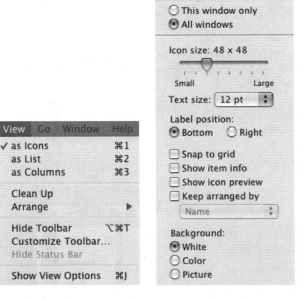

Figure 2.18

The Finder's View menu (left) and the options available (right) for Show View Options (for an Icon view).

The Show View Options command includes a number of options that vary according to whether the current window is in List, Icon, or Column view. For example, for an Icon view window, it lets you select options like the size of the icons and whether you want the icons to snap to a grid. For List view windows, it lets you select which columns you want to display. The following are some particularly interesting items available in View Options:

- **Text Size.** This adjusts the size of Finder text.

- **Show Icon Preview.** Accessible when Icon view is selected, this changes the icons of graphic files (such as JPEG or TIFF graphics) to thumbnails of the actual graphic image rather than the generic document icon of the application in which the document will open.

- **Label Position.** Accessible when Icon view is selected, this allows you to specify whether an item's name is listed at the bottom of or to the right of its icon.

- **Show Item Info.** Accessible when Icon view is selected, this adds various tidbits of information to items. For example, for folders, it adds a line of text that lists how many items are in the folder. For volumes, it lists the capacity of each volume and how much of that capacity is still free. For QuickTime movies, it shows the length of the movie in minutes and seconds.

Go menu. As its name implies, the Finder's Go menu is used to go to specific locations. At the top are Back and Forward commands (which work the same as the buttons in the toolbar). This menu also includes an Enclosing Folder command, which takes you to the parent folder of the currently displayed folder. This is convenient if the Back button would take you to some other location (as might happen if you use a command to open a folder other than one located within the currently open folder).

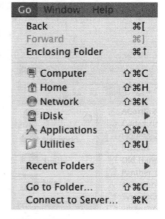

Figure 2.19

The Finder's Go menu.

The following provides an overview of the remaining items listed in this menu.

- **Computer.** Choosing this item takes you to a window that shows all mounted volumes, including hard drives, CD-ROMs, and iDisks.

  SEE: • "Take Note: Computer and Root-Level Windows," in Chapter 4, for more details on this window and its contents.

- **Home.** Choosing this item takes you to the top level of the Home directory of the logged-in user. Your Home directory is the one with your name on it, located within the Users folder.

  SEE: • Chapter 4 for more information on the Home directory concept.

- **Network.** This opens your Network folder, just as if you had selected Network in the Places sidebar.

- **iDisk.** This command has three subcommands:

  Select My iDisk to mount your own iDisk as a volume in the Finder (assuming you're connected to the Internet and have set up a .Mac account). Before you do so, however, go to the .Mac System Preferences pane and enter your name and password (or sign up for an account, if desired).

  Select Other User's iDisk or Other User's Public Folder, to access other iDisks.

  SEE: • ".Mac," later in this chapter and in Chapter 8, for more information on iDisk.

- **Applications.** Clicking this item takes you to the Applications folder, located at the root level of the Mac OS X volume. This folder houses all of the applications initially installed by Mac OS X, as well as any other applications that may have been installed there.

- **Utilities.** Clicking this item takes you to the Utilities folder, located within the Applications folder.

- **Recent Folders.** This simply lists folders that you have recently visited. Select one to go there directly. Note: To go to a recently used document or application, you would instead use the Recent Items submenu of the Apple menu.

- **Go to Folder.** This command lets you select a specific folder. If you know the exact path to a folder, you can use this option to access folders that would otherwise be invisible. I provide several examples of this feature, such as getting to the /private/tmp folder, in Chapter 3.

  SEE: • "Technically Speaking: Where Does Software Update Hide the Software It Installs?" in Chapter 3.

- **Connect to Server.** This command lets you connect to other volumes on a local network or over the Internet. To mount a local volume, click its name and then click Connect. You can access a remote volume by typing its URL in the Address field. For local networks (such as in a home or small office), despite the word *Server* in the name of the command, most listed volumes will simply be other locally connected computers. If you don't see the "server" you want in the Network window, use this command to access another computer via Personal File Sharing.

  SEE: • Chapter 8 for much more information on Sharing, Network, and Connect to Server.

Window menu. This menu lists all open windows and lets you choose which one you want to bring to the front. You can also use this menu to minimize the current window (that is, to move it to the Dock). Selecting a minimized window in the Dock restores it to the Finder.

Help menu. When in the Finder, you can choose Mac Help from this menu. This opens Mac OS X's Help Viewer application (located in /System/Library/CoreServices). Given the sparse documentation that comes with your Mac, this option is an important one. Exactly what you see when selecting a command from the Help menu depends on the application you're using and the command you've selected (the menu may include more than one command). After selecting Mac Help from the Finder, you can find the help you seek in one of three primary ways:

- Click any of the links from the first pane that appear to go directly to the information you desire (for example, What's New in Panther, Top Customer Issues, and so on).

- Click Browse Mac OS Help to get a scrollable list of help topics in a sidebar on the left. Select a topic you want to learn more about. (Note: When selecting Help in some other applications, this browse page is the first page that appears.)

- Type keywords in the Ask a Question search box in the toolbar. By accessing the magnifying-glass pop-up menu, you can choose to search just the current Help file (Mac OS X in this case) or all available Help files. Type format disks, for example, if you want to learn how to do that. Press Return to initiate a search. From the results list that appears, double-click the item(s) you want to see. More information will appear.

Click any links within a displayed page to go directly to the selected link. You can also navigate forward and back, using the arrow buttons in the toolbar, to return to any previously viewed page and back again. Click the Home icon to instantly return to the initial page. You can also navigate from Help Viewer's Go menu. Note: As with most Mac OS X software, you can customize Help Viewer's toolbar by selecting Customize Toolbar from the View menu.

Select the Library menu to see a list of all available Help files (AirPort, Sherlock, and so on). You can then select any of them to obtain further information about that software. Help for third-party software, such as Quicken, will also show up here if the developer included a Help file as part of the software installation.

When accessing help for a specific Mac OS X application, the initial pane will be different from the main one described here. Typically, you will get an overview description of what the application does and a link to more information.

Note: In some cases, Help pages are obtained via the Internet. In these instances, the Help page will not be displayed unless you're currently online.

Not all software supports Help Viewer. For this reason, the Help menu's contents may vary in applications other than the Finder. In some cases, the Help menu may include nothing more than a link to the vendor's Web site. In other cases, selecting the Help command for an application will open a different help system (provided by the application) or HTML-formatted help files in your preferred Web browser.

Beyond Help. In many applications in Mac OS X (including the Finder), if you pause the pointer over a command, button, item listing, icon, or just about any other application component, a yellow note box appears, providing additional details about the item beneath the pointer. This, of course, depends on whether the developer has provided this supplemental help—though it's quite common in software from Apple. Experiment to see what appears.

For further help, you have two primary options: You can either 1) go to a Web site (especially Apple's support site or a troubleshooting site such as MacFixIt.com); or 2) purchase a book on the Mac (such as the one you're now holding!).

Figure 2.20

Help Viewer: (top) the pane that appears when you select Mac Help from the Finder; (bottom) the results of a search for the term filevault.

TAKE NOTE ▶ Getting Help for Help

Most Mac OS X utilities are located, appropriately, in the Utilities folder. Help Viewer is an exception: It's located in /System/Library/CoreServices.

If Help Viewer is crashing on launch, the most likely cause is third-party Help aliases, primarily located in ~/Library/Documentation/Help. To prevent such crashes, delete these aliases. If this fails, try deleting the ~/Library/Caches/com.apple.helpui folder. A new folder, without the problem items, will be re-created as needed.

Note: Double-clicking an alias file (in the Finder) to a particular Help folder may do nothing—say, for example, if the original folder has been deleted. Similarly, choosing Show Original from the alias's contextual menu may not work, either. In this case, it could also be because the original Help file is located within an application package (the Finder will not locate an original that's inside a package).

If Help Viewer launches, but very slowly, its speed should pick up after several launches. Apple states that this slowness (especially if the stall occurs while the word *Retrieving* appears on the screen) is due to Help Viewer's downloading updated information from online sources.

Services

As noted in the previous section, the Application menu contains an item called Services. From its hierarchical menu, you can select an assortment of actions to be applied to the currently selected text, content, files, or folders. The options that appear (and whether they actually work within a given application) depend on the Services support of the currently active application. For example, although Services work by default in Cocoa-based applications, in Carbon applications the developer must manually code support for Services into the application. In addition, some Services only work in certain applications. (For example, an item that manipulates text might not be active in an application that does not permit any text editing.) An item that does not work for a given application will either be absent from the menu or dimmed.

The Finder's Services options include Make New Sticky Note, Open URL, Mail, and more. New in Panther is a Service called Search with Google. When you select this command, the Google Web site is launched in Safari, with your currently selected text as the search term. Other interesting options include Speech (to speak selected text) and Summarize (a fascinating feature that condenses the selected text to a brief summary, which it displays in a separate process called SummaryService, located in /System/LibraryServices).

Another service—available if you install the Developer software on the Developer (Xcode) Tools CD—is FileMerge, which allows you to compare the contents of two documents and report the differences (if any). This can be useful for comparing two versions of the same text document, for example. Third-party software may also add items to the Services menu (QuicKeys and Spell Catcher are two such examples).

To get an idea of using Services beyond the Finder, open a document in TextEdit, select a paragraph of text, and from the TextEdit menu select Services. Now select Make New Sticky Note. The Stickies application will launch, and the selected paragraph will appear in a new note.

Troubleshooting Services. Beginning with Mac OS X 10.2.6 (though possibly fixed in Panther), a bug has been reported in which having more than 70 Services (the number seems to vary depending on the installed software) causes the Services submenu to fail in some applications. Unfortunately, avoiding this bug can be tricky because it's not easy to figure out exactly how many Services you have. Mac OS X provides a number of Services by default; many applications provide Services; and you may have manually installed third-party Services packages. For example, one extremely useful set of third-party Services, WordService.service, provides more than 30 new text-related Services. Many users found that installing WordService.service "broke" their Services menu, while other users had no problems. In the end it was determined that the problem was not due to WordService.service itself but rather to the fact that for some users, these 30-plus new Services pushed them over the more-than-70 number, thus "breaking" their Services menus.

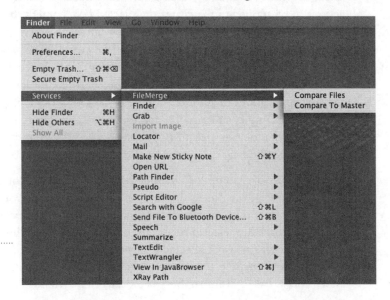

Figure 2.21

A list of Services with FileMerge selected.

Menu Extras

Menu Extras (sometimes called *menulets*) are the items that appear on the right side of the menu bar. They remain regardless of which application is currently active. The Extra itself is typically an icon: Simply click the icon to reveal its menu selections.

Common Menu Extras provided by Mac OS X or Apple software include the following: Volume (when clicked, it reveals a slider that allows you to adjust speaker volume), Displays (used to change your display resolution and color depth), and iChat (used to select your current iChat status). Other Extras indicate the current date and time, a laptop's battery status, an AirPort card's signal strength, whether your dial-up modem is currently connected, and more.

A few Menu Extras appear by default when you install Mac OS X. For the rest, you need to select an option to enable them. Some items are only relevant (and thus only enabled) if you have the appropriate hardware. For example, the Battery Extra will be available on notebooks but not on desktop Macs. The AirPort extra is available only if you have an AirPort card installed.

Enabling or disabling Menu Extras. In most cases, you add or remove Extras by selecting an option in the relevant System Preferences pane. (I discuss System Preferences a bit later in this chapter.)

To add the Displays Extra, for example, in the Displays System Preferences pane check the "Show displays in menu bar" option. To remove it, uncheck the option. Similarly, to install the Clock Extra, go to the Clock tab of the Date & Time System Preferences pane and check the box next to "Show the date and time." Then click the View in: Menu Bar button. New in Panther is a menu bar item for Classic, which you access by checking the "Show Classic status in menu bar" item in the Classic System Preferences pane.

You can also remove any Extra by holding down the Command key and dragging the Extra's icon off of the menu bar.

You can rearrange the left-to-right order of Extras by clicking an Extra icon with the Command key held down and dragging the icon to the desired location.

Most Menu Extras files are located in the /System/Library/CoreServices/Menu Extras folder. The items here all have a .menu extension. Thus, the Volumes Extra is called Volume.menu. If you cannot locate the check box for adding a specific Extra to the menu bar, go to this folder. Drag the desired .menu file from this folder to the menu bar (or simply double-click the Extra) and the Menu Extra will appear. The Eject Extra is one that needs to be enabled in this way (that is, it's not accessible via System Preferences).

This only works, however, if your Mac supports the feature referenced by the Extra. You cannot, for example, add the AirPort extra to a Mac that does not have an AirPort card installed.

Note: The .menu items may appear as folders in the Finder. Alternatively (especially in Panther), they may appear as documents identified as MenuExtra plug-ins. In either case, they are actually packages. Thus, even if they look like folders, you'll find that if you double-click them, they do not open a new window (as folders would); they launch instead. You can access their contents by using the Show Package Contents contextual menu item. In Panther, this is most easily selected by clicking the item and selecting the command from the Actions menu.

SEE: • **"Understanding Image, Installer Package, and Receipt Files," in Chapter 3, for more on packages.**

Figure 2.22

(Top) The contents of Panther's Menu Extras folder; (bottom) the Menu Extras selected to display in my menu bar. From left to right these are: Keychain, Bluetooth, AirPort, Battery, Volume, Input (from the International System Preferences pane), and Date & Time.

Some Menu Extras are stored in locations other than the Menu Extras folder. Here are two examples:

- **AppleScript menu.** In Jaguar, Script menu.menu is located in the /Applications/AppleScript folder. Double-click this item to add it to the menu bar. In Panther, there is instead an Install Script Menu and Remove Script Menu pair of applications in the same folder. Run Install Script Menu to install. Now check out the added menu, and you'll find a host of built-in scripts listed, including Folder Actions. See the following page for more details and links to a variety of scripts: www.apple.com/applescript/ macosx. These scripts are stored in the /Library/Scripts folder, or, for scripts only available to the current user, in ~/Library/Scripts.

- **Keychain.menu.** This menu is hidden within the Keychain Access application package. To view it, use the Show Package Contents command for Keychain Access and go to Contents/Resources. (See "Keychain Access," later in this chapter, for more on using this Extra.) You can also enable the menu from within the Keychain Access application.

SEE: • "Take Note: AppleScript," in Chapter 4, for more details on using AppleScript.

Check the following Apple Knowledge Base document for a complete list of all Mac OS X Menu Extras, their locations, and how to enable them: http://docs.info.apple.com/article.html?artnum=75466.

TAKE NOTE ▶ Eject Options

Mac OS X offers numerous choices for opening, ejecting, and unmounting devices (such as CDs, DVDs, and external hard drives).

Eject Menu Extra. You can install and use the Eject Menu Extra (located in /System/Library/CoreServices/Menu Extras). Select an optical drive listed here, and its tray will open (regardless of whether it's empty or contains media).

Eject key. You can also use the Eject key on the Apple Pro keyboard (F12 on other Apple keyboards) to eject the internal CD/DVD tray. If you have a desktop Mac that includes the option for two internal optical drives, press Option-Eject to select the second drive.

Note: When using F12, you need to hold down the key for a few seconds before it will eject the media. This is to prevent an accidental pressing of the key from resulting in an eject. You will know you've held it long enough when the translucent Eject symbol appears on the screen.

continues on next page

TAKE NOTE ▶ **Eject Options** *continued*

Finder's Eject command. Alternatively, you can add the new Eject item to the Finder's toolbar (via the Finder's Customize Toolbar command). This item works similarly to the Eject command in the Finder's File menu. Unlike the Menu Extra, the toolbar item ejects, opens the tray of, or unmounts virtually any device, including a hard drive. The simplest way to use this option is to open the Computer window, click the icon for the item you want to eject, and then click the Eject button. If the item cannot be ejected (for example, if it's the startup volume), the Eject button (and File menu command) will be dimmed.

Note: When you eject one partition of a drive, all other partitions also get unmounted (except for the startup partition, of course).

iTunes and DVD Player. iTunes and DVD Player both include an Eject button for CD/DVD drives.

Disk Utility. You can mount, unmount, or eject volumes from the Option menu in Disk Utility.

Third-party Menu Extras. Some items in the Extras region of the menu bar may come from third-party software. Typically, these are installed when you install the associated software, and they may only appear when the application is open and active. In some cases, there may just be a Menu Extra equivalent with no associated application. QuicKeys and StuffIt Deluxe are two examples of software that include Menu Extras. However, you will not find their Menu Extra files in Mac OS X's Menu Extras folder (it only contains Extras that are part of Mac OS X). Instead, you'll find them with the application software. For example, StuffIt Deluxe's MagicMenu.menu is located in the same folder that contains the StuffIt Deluxe application.

SEE: • **The following sidebar for related information.**

TECHNICALLY SPEAKING ▶ **Third-Party Menu Extras Not Welcome in Mac OS X**

Starting with Mac OS X 10.2, Apple has reserved menu-bar real estate for itself. Thus, if you upgrade from Mac OS X 10.1 to 10.2 or 10.3, you may find that non-Apple Menu Extras that previously functioned normally have now vanished. Apple's rationale for this move is that it wants Extras (even those from Apple) to be used only for "hardware devices or network adjustments." However, Apple then violates its own rules by creating Menu Extras such as iChat (for the iChat application) and Script Menu (for AppleScript).

The good news is that you can re-enable many of these banned Menu Extras via a utility called Menu Extra Enabler (www.unsanity.com/haxies), which is installed in the InputManagers folder of the ~/Library/Preferences folder. For the record, Apple warns against using this utility, stating, "Apple does not recommend, endorse, or provide technical support for use of such solutions or for complications arising from the use of such solutions."

continues on next page

TECHNICALLY SPEAKING ▶ **Third-Party Menu Extras Not Welcome in Mac OS X** *continued*

However, I believe Apple is blowing smoke here: There appears to be no harm in doing this, and should a problem occur, you can still change your mind and disable the utility.

Even with Menu Extra Enabler installed, a few third-party Menu Extras may still crash on launch. For these uncooperative items, an additional step is needed. The reason for the crash is that a framework folder in the System folder (called HIServices.framework) was relocated in Jaguar. The problematic Extras require this framework—which means that when they can't find it (because of its new location), they crash. The solution is to create a symbolic link to the framework and place it where the framework was located in Mac OS X 10.1.x. This will allow the Extras to track down the framework at its new location. To create this link, launch Terminal and type the following on one line (*{space}* indicates potentially nonobvious places where a space exists):

```
sudo ln -s {space} /System/Library/Frameworks/ApplicationServices.framework/
Versions/A/Frameworks/HIServices.framework {space} /System/Library/
PrivateFrameworks/HIServices.framework
```

Some developers have found their own way around Apple's prohibition. For example, the latest versions of StuffIt's Magic Menu work in Mac OS X 10.2 or later, even without Menu Extra Enabler installed. It uses a similar solution to Menu Extra Enabler, installing a MagicMenuEnabler in the /Library/InputManagers folder. Other software bypasses the Menu Extra method altogether, instead adding a menu via the application itself when launched. To get the menu to appear automatically at login, you must add the software to the Startup Items list.

The following are a few additional technical tidbits about Menu Extras—particularly relevant to how they affect third-party items:

- If you're using Menu Extra Enabler and you open the console.log file (via the Console utility), you're likely to see one or more lines that read as follows: "SystemUIServer[1695] Normally MMExtra would not have been loaded as a Menu Extra." This correctly indicates that the Extra has indeed loaded, despite the change in Mac OS X 10.2 designed to prevent it.

- Data in the SystemUIServer package determines which Menu Extras Mac OS X allows to load. To see this data, use an editor like BBEdit or TextWrangler to open /System/Library/ CoreServices/SystemUIServer.app/Contents/MacOS/SystemUIServer. Using the application's Find command, search for the name of any Menu Extra (such as a battery or AirPort), and you will arrive at a list of items that read, in part, like this: _ejectCanLoad_batteryCanLoad.

- You can use Property List Editor to open the com.apple.systemuiserver.plist file located in ~/Library/Preferences/. One of the listed properties will be menuExtras. Click its disclosure triangle, and you will get a list of all currently enabled Menu Extras, including third-party items (if you're using Menu Extra Enabler to enable them).

System Preferences

The System Preferences window provides a central location from which you can set up or customize a variety of Mac OS X features. In most cases, these features are not linked to a particular application and are not accessible by any other means. In some cases—especially with background applications and applications that don't otherwise include their own menus—this window is also where you'll likely find an application's Preferences settings.

You can access System Preferences from a variety of locations. The System Preferences Dock icon is probably the most common way. You can also choose System Preferences from the Apple menu or simply double-click the System Preferences application icon in the Applications folder. Whatever method you choose, you wind up in the same place.

Figure 2.23

The System Preferences window.

System Preferences overview

After launching System Preferences for the first time, check out the View menu. In addition to a list of all System Preferences, you'll find the following three commands (at the top of the menu): Show All Preferences (Command-L), Organize by Categories, and Organize Alphabetically. The Categories option is the default. Experiment to see which organization method you prefer.

At the top of the System Preferences window is the toolbar. As with all similar toolbars in Mac OS X, you can select to show or hide it by clicking the oval button in the upper-right corner. Note: Command-clicking this button cycles you through various toolbar views: large icon/text, small icon/text, large icon, small icon, large text, small text.

The first item on the left side of the toolbar is the Show All button. You can click this button at any time to return to the default display of all available preferences panes (listed either alphabetically or by category, as per your selection).

To the right of the Show All button is a collection of commonly accessed preferences. Several are placed there by default when you install Mac OS X; however, you can also customize this collection. To add an item, drag its icon from the bottom part of the window to the toolbar row; to remove an item, drag it off. Drag buttons to rearrange them from left to right.

The remaining portion of the window lists all of the preferences panes. If you selected to sort them by category, you would see the following: Personal, Hardware, Internet & Network, and System. There may also be a fifth category called Other, which is used for third-party panes not installed by Mac OS X. Click any icon, and the window shifts to show the options for that particular preference pane. To go to another preference pane, click its icon in the toolbar (if listed), choose its name from the View menu, or click the Show All button and select the desired preference from the full display.

Tip: To quickly open any System Preferences pane from its Show All screen, just type the initial letters of its name (for example, *cl* for Classic). This selects that pane. Then press the spacebar to open it.

All the panes installed by Mac OS X are located in the PreferencePanes folder of /System/Library. Third-party panes may be installed in the PreferencePanes folder of the Library folder at the root level of your drive and/or the one in your Home directory.

Some of the preferences can only be set by administrative users. If you're not an administrator, these options will either be dimmed or you will receive an explanatory message when attempting to access the feature.

System Preferences locked? Some System Preferences panes, such as Network and Accounts, have a padlock icon in their lower-left corner. If this icon is locked, you cannot make changes to the pane's settings. To unlock it, click the icon and enter your password when requested. To lock a pane that is unlocked, click the padlock icon.

If you unlock one pane, you unlock them all—unless you enabled the option in the Security pane that reads, "Require password to unlock each secure system preference."

Following are brief descriptions of all the standard System Preferences panes, by category. Some of these are covered in more detail in subsequent chapters (when I explore the topics for which they're used). For additional information, from the Help menu choose System Preferences Help.

THE JAGUAR WAY ▶ System Preferences

As has become Apple's habit when releasing a major Mac OS X update, the company has made significant changes to the organization of and options available from System preferences in Panther.

For starters, consistent with an overall design change, Panther has replaced with buttons the tabs that Jaguar System Preferences used to access different screens within a given preferences pane. They function the same; only their appearance has changed.

In Jaguar, if you closed the System Preferences window, the application remained open. In Panther, if you close the window, the application automatically quits.

In the main text of this volume, you can assume I'm referring to Panther versions of System Preferences, unless otherwise noted. For those of you who are still using Jaguar, the following provides a brief overview of the items that have been most significantly reorganized, added to, or changed in System Preferences:

- In Jaguar, Login Items is a separate preferences pane. In Panther, these options are included as part of the Accounts System Preferences pane, and are now called Startup Items.

- In Jaguar, the My Accounts preferences pane is used to edit the account of the currently logged-in user. In Panther, this capability is rolled into the Accounts preferences pane.

- The Accounts preferences pane itself has been redesigned in Panther.

- Jaguar's General preferences pane is called Appearance in Panther.

- Jaguar's Desktop and Screen Effects preferences panes have been combined in Panther to form a new preferences pane called Desktop & Screen Saver.

- The password-required-to-wake-up option has been moved from Screen Effects in Jaguar to the new Security preferences pane in Panther. Security is also where you now select to disable automatic login.

- Keyboard & Mouse in Panther includes a new Keyboard Shortcuts tab that replaces the Full Keyboard Access tab in Jaguar. It also adds Bluetooth support.

- Jaguar's Internet System Preferences pane is gone in Panther. In its place is a .Mac pane that just includes the .Mac and iDisk tabs from the Internet pane. The Email and Web panes are gone altogether. These tabs were used to set various defaults (such as the default Web browser, Web home page, and email application). Presumably, by eliminating these settings from this location, Apple is being more insistent that its own Mac OS X software (Safari and Mail) be the default choices. It will now be up to the third-party software (such as Microsoft Internet Explorer and Entourage, or utilities such as MisFox) to change the defaults. Or you can access them directly via the com.apple.internetconfig.plist file (as discussed more in Chapter 8).

Panther also includes some entirely new preferences (Security, Exposé, and Print & Fax), which are covered in the main text of this chapter.

Personal

System Preferences panes in the Personal category include the following:

Appearance. This is where you set a variety of basic preferences, such as the color of buttons and highlighted text. (Font-smoothing settings are discussed in more detail in Chapter 4, in "Font smoothing.")

New in Panther is a check box that allows you to "Minimize when double clicking a window title bar." This option is on by default, but you can turn it off.

Mac OS 9 includes a popular WindowShade effect for Finder windows: If you double-click the title bar of a window, all but the title bar itself disappears. Double-click the title bar again, and the full window reappears—as if the window were a shade you could raise and lower. Mac OS X does not support this feature. Instead, double-clicking a title bar either minimizes the window to the Dock or does nothing, depending upon whether the above Appearances option is enabled.

Note: In later versions of Jaguar (Mac OS X 10.2), you can get this WindowShade effect without using any third-party software: Simply Option-double-click the title bar. However, this is not a universal feature; it only works for Cocoa applications—such as Safari—and some Carbon ones. In addition, the feature is apparently missing entirely in some versions of Panther (Mac OS X 10.3.x). Finally, in any version of Jaguar or Panther, Option–double-clicking the title bar of any Finder window causes all currently open windows to be minimized.

For those of you who want the WindowShade feature back, there's a great alternative: the WindowShade X shareware System Preferences pane.

Desktop & Screen Saver. You use this pane to set the Desktop background and select a screensaver module. If you want to require a password to wake up from a screensaver, this option is located separately in the Security System Preferences pane.

Dock. I covered this pane previously in this chapter under "Dock preferences: Customizing the Dock."

Exposé. With this new Panther feature, you can use a function key (or other user-defined key combinations or even move the pointer to a corner of the screen) to temporarily view all of your open windows simultaneously (in reduced sizes so they don't overlap). When you're in this view, the name of each window appears as you move the pointer over the window. Click on any window, and it becomes the new active window, while all other windows return to their original positions (ending the Exposé display). As you can imagine, this can be a great convenience when you have many open overlapping windows.

You can also set Exposé to only show windows belonging to the current active application or only show the Desktop background (hiding all other windows). By default, the F9, F10, and F11 keys, respectively, are used for these three functions.

You can use the Exposé System Preferences pane to modify the keys used to invoke these functions. From here, you can also select Exposé to be activated when you move the pointer to a specified corner of the screen. The corner screen options can also be set to start or stop a screensaver.

Note: If you click-hold an item before invoking Exposé or in the middle of an Exposé session, the item remains in your view and can be dragged to any window in the Exposé display. Just release the mouse button when you've moved or copied the item to the new location.

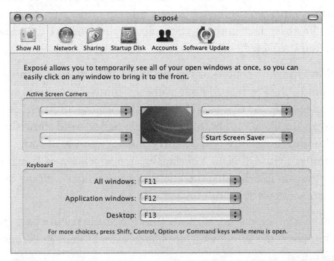

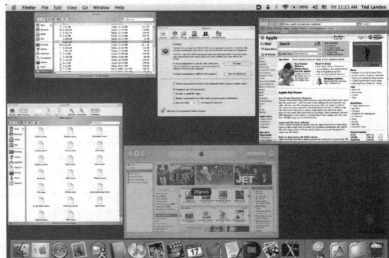

Figure 2.24

(Top) The Exposé System Preferences pane and (bottom) the Mac display with Exposé activated (and the pointer over the iTunes window).

International. This pane includes options for adjusting the characteristics of your Mac to match conventions used in different countries. It contains three main tabs:

- **Formats.** From this screen, you can change number, time, and date formats. A few options are relevant even if the only language you use is English. For example, this is where you can select whether to display the time in 12-hour or 24-hour format.

- **Language** and **Input Menu.** You use these screens when setting up a Mac to work with foreign languages. These options determine the language used for menus and dialogs. (Keep in mind, however, that to switch languages within third-party software, the developer will have to have built in the needed support.)

SEE: • "Working with Fonts," in Chapter 4, for more on the Language and Input Menu options of the International System Preferences pane.

Security. This new Panther System Preferences pane combines several options that were scattered among several different preferences in previous versions of Mac OS X—plus it adds some new ones.

- **FileVault.** In the top half of the Security pane are the controls for Panther's new FileVault feature.

  Enabling FileVault creates an encrypted version of your entire Home directory (using Advanced Encryption Standard with 128-bit keys [AES-128]). The purpose of FileVault is to protect the data in your Home directory in the event that your computer is lost or stolen. It will be virtually impossible for anyone to access the encrypted files (regardless of their file-recovery tools)—unless they have your login or Master Password.

  Before you enable FileVault for the first time, you must set a Master Password. To do this, simply click the Set a Master Password button. This password is intended as a safety net, in case you forget your own login password. With the Master Password, you can unlock any FileVault account on the computer. Thus, the security value of the FileVault protection is essentially eliminated if unauthorized people know the Master Password. Only administrators on the computer should be told this password. Once a Master Password is set, the button reads Change; you can then click it to change the password. However, you can only change the password if you know the old password. If you forget the old password, there is no method, even as an administrative user, to reset and start over.

  To enable FileVault, click the Turn On FileVault button. This logs you out, creates the encrypted version of your Home directory, and allows you to log back in. If you return to the Security System Preferences pane, the button will now read Turn Off FileVault; click it to reverse the process.

Note: To enable FileVault, you need an administrator's password as well as the user's login password. Nonadministrative users will be prompted to enter both passwords when clicking to turn on FileVault.

With FileVault enabled, the icon for your Home directory changes—from a house icon to a house icon with a combination lock inside. Your Home directory is now encrypted. In most cases, however, you won't notice any difference while you're logged in. All files appear in the Finder (just as if they weren't encrypted), and the Finder automatically decrypts them as needed—transparently and speedily behind the scenes. Ideally, you should not notice any delay due to these processes.

Note: The same FileVault options appear in the Security section of each user's account in the Accounts System Preferences pane.

SEE: • **"Technically Speaking: Inside FileVault," for more details about this feature, including recommendations about when you should and should not use it.**

Figure 2.25

The Security System Preferences pane.

• **...the rest.** The bottom half of the Security pane includes options for setting whether a password is required when waking your Mac (including from a screensaver set in Desktop & Screen Saver) and whether a password is needed to unlock secure System Preferences (ones that require administrative status).

Note: Requiring a password to "wake" from a screensaver is a relatively weak form of security. For example, any administrative user with an account on your Mac can use his or her name and password, rather than yours, to wake a screen effect activated by you. That user is then returned to *your* Desktop, just as if the screen effect had never been activated. Of course, administrative users can access your account in other ways as well; I just wanted to make it clear that this is a far-from-bulletproof form of a security.

The Security pane is also where you choose to "Disable automatic login." This option is enabled in the Login Options section of the Accounts System Preferences pane for a selected user. When that user starts or restarts his or her computer, he or she is automatically logged in (that is, without seeing the Login window or having to enter a password). When you disable this option here, it is similarly disabled in the Accounts window.

TECHNICALLY SPEAKING ▶ Inside FileVault

The following provides details about what happens when you turn FileVault on or off—including numerous caveats about its use.

FileVault on for your account. When you turn on FileVault for your account and log back in to your account, the following changes occur:

- An alias with the name of your home directory is created in the same Users folder where your unencrypted home directory would otherwise be. If you select Show Original from the contextual menu of the alias, you will be taken to the Computer window. You will not see an original directory there, however.

- Instead, if you go to the /Users directory, you will find an invisible folder named .{*username*} (that is, the name of your home directory but preceded by a period). One quick way to see this item is to launch Terminal and type 1s -a /Users (see Chapter 6 for more on how to view invisible items). If you double-click this folder, you will find a file inside called {*username*}.sparseimage. This is the encrypted version of your home directory. This file gets updated every time you change the contents of your home directory.

FileVault on for other accounts. What if FileVault was turned on for an account other than the one that is currently logged in? What do you see when you look at the other user's home folder (assuming the user is not logged in at the moment) from your account? You see a single file that represents the entire encrypted home directory of the user. If you go to the Users folder, you will find a folder with the name of the user, as expected. If you open that folder, however, you will find only one file inside: an image file with the name {*username*}.sparseimage. If you double-click this file, a dialog appears asking you to enter a password. If you enter the login password of the user, the home directory will mount as if it were an external volume. You will now have complete access to all of that user's files.

However, if the other user is also logged in (via Fast User Switching), you will see an alias for his or her home directory. You will not be permitted to access its contents.

FileVault off. When you turn off FileVault for your account, the encrypted disk image is mounted; its contents are moved back to a new user folder inside /Users; and it is then deleted—basically, your drive returns to its state prior to using FileVault.

continues on next page

TECHNICALLY SPEAKING ▶ Inside FileVault *continued*

Forget your password? If you forget your login password and have set a Master Password, you can use the Master Password to set a new login password (whether FileVault is on or off)—assuming you entered a password hint for your account. To do so, follow these steps:

1. Try to log in to your account repeatedly until the Password Hint option appears. At this point, click the Reset Password button.

2. Enter your Master Password at the prompt and click Continue. You will now be given the chance to create a new login password and hint.

Warning: If you forget both your own login password and the Master Password, your Home directory is gone forever (unless you created a backup somewhere else).

Prerelease Panther options. In prerelease versions of Panther, a separate unencrypted copy of your Home directory was created when you enabled FileVault. It was located in the Users folder and had the same name as your original Home directory but with an .old extension added. Similarly, a copy of your encrypted Home directory was created and located in the Users folder when you turned FileVault off. It had the name of your Home directory but with an fvCopy extension added. These copies served as backups, in case something went wrong with the encrypting/decrypting process. Once you were certain that all was well, you could and should have deleted these items. Apple may someday add these features back, perhaps as an option. For now, they're gone.

FileVault caveats. When deciding whether or not to enable FileVault, take note of the following caveats:

- Your files are protected only if you're not logged in. That is, if a person steals your computer while you're logged in (such as when your Mac is asleep, but your account is logged in), the person will have access to your Home directory even if FileVault is on. The solution is to make sure you are logged out whenever you leave your computer unattended.

- With FileVault on, various other processes may have trouble accessing your Home directory, especially when you're not logged in. These include accessing your files via file sharing, and backing up your data. There is no workaround for this other than to turn FileVault off.

- When backing up a volume, the Home directories of all users who have enabled FileVault (except the currently logged-in user) will be encrypted as a single .sparseimage file (as described above). The entire file will need to be backed up, even if only one unencrypted file has changed and even if you have your backup utility set to only back up changed files. This can make the backup take much longer than would otherwise occur (and makes for very inefficient backups!).

- At least until updated versions get released, backup utilities may have still other problems with FileVault. For example, for a logged-in user, it will likely back up both the unencrypted files and the encrypted image, in essence doubling the megabytes needed to back up your Home directory.

- More generally, to facilitate recovering data from a backup, I recommend turning FileVault off for all user accounts on your drive before backing up the entire drive.

continues on next page

TECHNICALLY SPEAKING ▶ **Inside FileVault** *continued*

- FileVault is not compatible with setups where you move your Home directory to another volume. As described more in Chapters 3 and 6, moving your Home directory is typically done to improve performance or to allow you to erase and reinstall your drive without losing your Home directory.

- If FileVault is enabled for your Home directory, operations such as copying files to your Desktop from another volume may take significantly longer—despite Apple's claim that this should not be the case. The work-around here is to turn off FileVault.

- Encrypting a Home directory requires creating a temporary file equal in size to the Home directory. Thus, make sure you have enough free space to do this.

- If you have Fast User Switching enabled, you will not be able to open the Home folder of a user who is also logged in and who has FileVault on. That user's Home folder icon will be an alias and will appear with a Network icon. If you double-click it, you will get a message that states you do not have "sufficient access privileges."

- A user cannot turn FileVault on or off when more than one user is currently logged in via Fast User Switching.

- You should not attempt to delete an encrypted account until you turn FileVault off for the account.

- When logging out of an account for which FileVault is on, you may receive a message stating that Mac OS X wants to "reclaim unused space." Accepting this request can result in the loss of files in your Home directory, including preferences files and even music files in your iTunes Library. Updating to Mac OS X 10.3.1 or later should fix this bug. In addition, with these later versions, the message now only appears when reclaiming space is needed instead of on every logout. However, a similar loss of data can still occur if you lose power or your Mac crashes during logout.

- Having FileVault enabled can reduce the performance of programs like iMovie and Final Cut. The solution is to either turn off FileVault (at least when using these multimedia applications) or move the document files for these programs to a location outside of your Home directory.

- Apple's documentation implies that an administrative user should be able to enable and disable FileVault for other users by selecting the Security tab for the user in the Accounts System Preferences pane and—after clicking the Turn On/Off FileVault button—entering the Master Password. However, I was unable to get this to work: Instead, the FileVault button remained dimmed and could not be clicked. In fact, even in other situations where a password option did appear (such as when trying to mount a .sparseimage of the Home directory), the Master Password did not work; instead, the user's login password was required. This may represent a bug in Panther that will be addressed in a future update. In any case, it makes turning FileVault on or off for multiple users a real pain.

I've discovered other FileVault quirks as well, which though not worth detailing here typically involve the way FileVault-encrypted accounts are viewed when logged in from other accounts. This new feature is obviously still rough around the edges.

Bottom line: Given all of these caveats, I recommend *against* using FileVault in most cases. If you're traveling with a laptop that includes sensitive data, FileVault makes sense. Otherwise, skip it.

Hardware

CDs & DVDs. This pane is where you select default actions that occur when you insert a CD or DVD. When you insert a blank CD-R disc, for example, you can specify whether the Mac will do the following:

- "Ask what to do." (This option causes a dialog to appear when you insert a CD, from which you make your choice.)
- "Open Finder."
- "Open iTunes."
- "Open another application" (for example, Toast).
- "Run script."
- "Ignore" (that is, do nothing).

If you select to have the blank CD-R disc open in the Finder, it directly mounts the disc with the name Untitled CD. If you decide you don't want to burn anything to the CD, you can choose Eject rather than Burn in the dialog that appears when you drag the CD icon to the Trash.

SEE: • "Take Note: Burning CDs (and DVDs)," in Chapter 6, for more details.

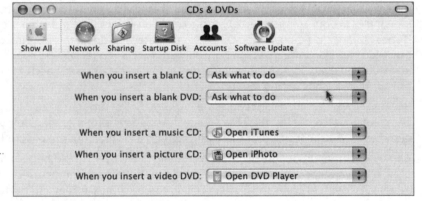

Figure 2.26

The CDs & DVDs System Preferences pane.

Displays. This pane is where you set the resolution and color depth of your monitor (via the Display tab) as well as select (or create) a ColorSync profile to match your display (via the Color tab).

If you have multiple displays, you also use this pane to select how the displays will work together. (For example, will one display mirror the other, or will the displays act as one large Desktop area that spans both?)

Energy Saver. This is where you set the options that determine when the Mac goes to sleep.

If you are using a notebook Mac, the default view will likely show just one pop-up menu called Optimize Energy Savings. The choices in this menu include Highest Performance, Longest Battery Life, DVD Playback, Presentations, and Custom (to make your own settings). The default choice is Automatic, which lets the Mac decide what it thinks is best to do at a given moment.

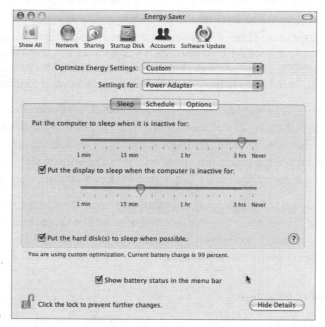

Figure 2.27

The Energy Saver System Preferences pane as selected from my PowerBook.

From this pane, if you are using a laptop, you can also enable "Show battery status in the menu bar" by clicking its checkbox. If you enable this option, you can then select the Show command in the Battery menu to determine whether the battery status is viewed in terms of Icon Only, Time, or Percentage (where 100% equals fully charged). Note: If you select Percentage and the number gets stuck shy of 100 percent when charging (for example, remaining at 94 percent indefinitely when the laptop is plugged into AC power), the solution is to let the battery drain (to below 50 percent). Then recharge; it should now go to 100 percent.

Finally, at the bottom of the pane will be a Show Details button. Select this to get access to the full set of Energy Saver options. The button will then toggle to read Hide Details.

None of the above options appear on desktop Macs. For these models, the Details mode is the only available mode.

On desktop Macs or after selecting Show Details on laptop Macs, you will find the following three tabs (selecting each one shifts Energy Saver to the corresponding screen):

- **Sleep.** From this screen, you can set customized times for display and computer sleep separately. You can also select whether the hard disk will sleep. If you're using a laptop, you can access the "Settings for" pop-up menu to create separate settings for Battery Power and Power Adapter.

- **Schedule.** From this screen, you can select times for the computer to automatically start up or shut down.

- **Options.** This screen presents you with several options, including whether to have your Mac automatically restart after a power failure. If you have a laptop, from the Processor Performance menu you can choose between Reduced and Highest. Choose Reduced if you want to maximize battery life.

Note: The Power Mac G5 as well as newer PowerBooks and iBooks include an additional setting in this menu: Automatic. If you select this setting, performance shifts between Reduced and Highest modes, as needed, via a process called *slewing*. This allows for maximum speed when you're actively using your Mac, and reduced power (and extra battery life on laptops) when the Mac is mostly idle.

Tip: To go as long as possible before you need to recharge your laptop battery, minimize activities that drain battery power. For example, dim the screen to the lowest acceptable level, minimize use of the CD/DVD drive, and turn off AirPort if you're not using it.

TAKE NOTE ▶ Sleep Problems

Computer Sleep (or "deep sleep") is the low-power mode in which the Mac appears to be off, except for the pulsing light on the Power button and/or on the monitor on desktop Macs—or similar locations on notebooks. If your Mac is not going to sleep as expected, the first thing to check is your Energy Saver settings: Make sure that automatic sleep is indeed enabled for the time period you want.

No deep sleep. In certain cases, the Mac may refuse to enter deep sleep. Typically in such cases, the Mac's fan and possibly the hard drive remain on—even after you've selected Sleep from the Finder or waited for automatic sleep to occur. This is a form of sleep, but it is not deep sleep.

A common cause of this problem is a peripheral device that does not support deep sleep— such as a SCSI PCI card or a USB scanner. In some cases, the problem can be fixed by software or hardware updates (such as a firmware and/or driver update for a SCSI card). To determine whether such a fix is available, check the Web site for the vendor of the SCSI card or other suspected hardware. You can determine the vendor via the Hardware section of the System Profiler window. If your SCSI card or other peripheral was part of the original equipment from Apple, check with Apple regardless of vendor.

continues on next page

TAKE NOTE ▶ Sleep Problems *continued*

Otherwise, as a work-around for a peripheral device such as a scanner, simply disconnect the device and then reconnect it. Sleep will now likely work until the next time you use the device.

For devices that you cannot easily disconnect, such as a SCSI card, you may be able to get around the problem by disabling the device's associated kext files (located in the /System/Extensions folder). For example, for a sleep problem caused by an Adaptec SCSI card, log in as a root user and disable all kext files with the word *Adaptec* in their names—either by moving them to a folder you create called *Extensions (disabled)* or by removing them from the System folder altogether. Alternatively, you can disable these files via a third-party utility such as MOX Optimize, eliminating the need to log in as the root user. The downside is that you will not be able to use the card (and thus any SCSI devices) once the extensions are disabled. However, if you only rarely need this capability, you can re-enable the extensions when you need them. After making a change here, restart your Mac to make sure the change takes effect.

In other cases, a sleep problem may be caused by a bug in Mac OS X itself and possibly also involve a conflict with third-party software. In earlier versions of Mac OS X 10.2.x, for example, enabling Personal File Sharing, Printer Sharing, or Internet Sharing (via the Sharing System Preferences pane) prevented automatic sleep as set by Energy Saver. Similarly, after you disconnect a FireWire or USB hard drive, the Mac may not go to sleep automatically after the idle period specified in Energy Saver.

To work around this, from the Apple menu choose Sleep, disable the feature that's causing the problem, or restart the Mac (which may restore the automatic feature).

Some causes of this symptom were fixed in later versions of Jaguar. However, if the problem remains, the ultimate solution is to wait for and then get the update to the Mac OS X or third-party software that fixes the problem.

Wake for administrators. The Options screen of Energy Saver includes an option to "Wake for Ethernet network administrator access." Note that this feature only works for computers connected to an Ethernet network; it does not work via AirPort. In addition, Apple states, "Applicable routers must be configured to allow directed broadcast of the wake-on-LAN (WOL) packet, also known as a *magic packet*. To remotely wake an eligible computer from sleep, use one of these applications: Apple Remote Desktop; Wake550, by Five Fifty Software; Wakeonlan."

Wake-from-sleep problems. There are a host of potential problems that can occur when waking from sleep—the most common of which is a crash, where the screen remains black, as described in Chapter 5.

SEE: • "Take Note: Miscellaneous Crashes," in Chapter 5, for advice on dealing with wake-from-sleep crashes and related problems.

TECHNICALLY SPEAKING ▶ **Hard-Drive Sleep**

You cannot set a specific time for hard-disk sleep from Energy Saver preferences in Mac OS X. Instead, your only option is to select "Put the hard disk(s) to sleep when possible." This uses a default setting of 10 minutes before spinning down the drive.

If you still want to regulate the timing for hard-drive sleep, however, you can do so via the pmset command, run as root in Terminal. To set a hard-drive sleep time to occur after 60 minutes of inactivity, for example, type sudo pmset —a spindown 60. You can use this command to spin down the hard drive before deep sleep is set to occur. The sudo command is needed because you must have root access to make this change. Spin-down settings changes work here even if you don't enable the "hard drive sleep" checkbox in Energy Saver.

For drives connected to your Mac after startup, spin-down may occur after 10 minutes even if the "hard disk to sleep" option is not checked. In this case, type sudo pmset —a spindown 0 to prevent any spin-down. Keep in mind, however, that this prevents spin-down for your startup drive as well. For more details on how this command works—including options for setting hard-drive sleep separately for battery (-b) and charger (-c) power on a laptop—type man pmset.

These settings are saved in a file called com.apple.PowerManagement.plist. In Panther, this file is located in /Library/Preferences/SystemConfiguration. As an administrator, you can make changes to this file by opening it in Property List Editor. For hard-drive sleep, change the value of Disk Sleep Time to the number of minutes you want until sleep occurs (to a maximum of 180).

For problems related to Energy Saver and sleep, a last resort is to delete this PowerManagement file entirely and restart. A new one with default settings will be created. In most cases, the problem will be fixed.

Note: In Jaguar, the file is called com.apple.PowerManagement.xml and is located in the /var/db/ directory. Because this directory is invisible in the Finder, you need to use the Finder's Go to Folder command to navigate to the directory, or you can navigate to it via Terminal. You also need root access to modify the file.

SEE: • **"Root Access" and "Preferences Files," in Chapter 4, for more on root access and using Property List Editor.**

• **"Using Unix to delete files," "Item cannot be placed in Trash or Trash cannot be emptied," and "Invisible Files: Working with Invisible Files," in Chapter 6, for related information.**

Keyboard & Mouse. This pane is used mainly for adjusting keyboard and mouse settings. It has five main tabs:

- **Keyboard.** You can use this screen to set the Key Repeat Rate and Delay Until Repeat intervals.

- **Mouse.** You can use this screen to set tracking and double-click speed for the device. If your mouse has a scroll wheel, you can also set the scrolling speed. Note: The Mouse tab will not appear on a PowerBook or iBook (unless you have a mouse attached).

- **Trackpad.** This screen is where you set tracking and double-click speed for your PowerBook or iBook trackpad. (This screen does not appear on desktop Macs.) In addition, you can choose whether to use the trackpad itself (rather than just the trackpad button) for clicking and dragging. You can also choose to ignore accidental trackpad input—basically, any trackpad activity that occurs while you're typing—and to ignore the trackpad completely if a mouse is connected to your laptop.

- **Bluetooth.** From here, you can set up and monitor the battery level of a Bluetooth mouse or keyboard. These options work in conjunction with several other Bluetooth components of Mac OS X, including the Bluetooth System Preferences pane, Bluetooth Setup Assistant, and Bluetooth File Exchange. I sort out all the details in Chapter 8.

- **Keyboard Shortcuts.** From this screen, you can reassign the shortcut keys for any of Mac OS X's shortcuts. For example, if you want to change the shortcut for a screen capture from Command-Shift-3 to something else, you can do so. You can even create your own shortcuts for menu commands. Finally, if you check the "Turn on full keyboard access" box, you can use the keyboard to perform much of the button and menu navigation that would otherwise require the mouse. This option may not work with some applications that are Carbonized from Mac OS 9.

Print & Fax. This is the System Preferences pane used for adjusting settings related to (surprise!) printing and faxing. For more on this pane, see Chapter 7.

Sound. This pane is where you select an alert sound and volume. It's also where you determine the audio input (microphone) and output (speakers) you're using.

Note: There is no option in this preferences pane to record sounds from a microphone. You will need additional third-party software to do this.

Ink and Bluetooth. Some Hardware System Preferences—notably, Bluetooth and Ink—appear only if the required hardware is attached or preinstalled. To see and use the Ink handwriting-recognition pane, for example, you need to have a graphics tablet attached. To use Ink, you also need to install drivers for the tablet that are new enough to recognize the Ink software. Otherwise, even if the Ink pane appears, you won't be able to use it.

SEE: • "Bluetooth," in Chapter 8, for more on Bluetooth.

Internet & Network

.Mac. This pane is where you adjust settings related to Apple's optional .iMac service. It includes two main tabs:

- **.Mac.** From this screen, you enter your .Mac name and password (assuming you've signed up for .Mac). If you haven't signed up for the service, there is a Sign Up button you can use to do so.

- **iDisk.** From this screen, you can check to see how much iDisk storage space you have left, determine the level of access allowed for your iDisk Public folder, and (new in Panther) create a separate local copy of your iDisk. With this last option, you can make changes to your iDisk content locally—with no Internet delays (or even being connected to the Internet)—and then have those changes updated to the actual iDisk later.

SEE: • "Setting Up System Preferences: .Mac," in Chapter 8, for more details.

Network. This System Preferences pane is essential if you plan to use the Internet or access another computer (even just another Mac connected via an Ethernet cable). Whether you have devices connected via Ethernet, AppleTalk, or AirPort—and whether you use a dial-up modem, cable modem, DSL modem, or Bluetooth—you will need to configure this System Preferences pane.

SEE: • "Setting Up System Preferences: Network," in Chapter 8, for more details.

QuickTime. This System Preferences pane is where you determine the settings for QuickTime Player (used to play multimedia files) and the QuickTime Plug-in that works with Web browsers (for example, to view movie trailers posted online). Apart from a brief mention in Chapter 6 ("Saving movie trailers that have the Save option disabled"), I don't spend much time discussing QuickTime in these pages. The following, however, are a few notes about features added to QuickTime 6.x for Mac OS X 10.2 or later:

- **MPEG-4 support.** MPEG-4 delivers DVD-quality (MPEG-2) video at lower data rates and smaller file sizes than MPEG-2; thus, it streams over the Internet much faster. See www.apple.com/mpeg4 for more details.

- **AAC support.** AAC (Advanced Audio Coding encoding, which is part of MPEG-4) compresses much more efficiently than formats such as MP3 while delivering "CD quality" audio. With QuickTime 6.2 or later, you can listen to AAC files in iTunes 4.

- **Instant-On.** From the QuickTime System Preferences pane, click the Connection tab. You will now see a button called Instant-On. To turn on this feature, click the button and check the Enable Instant-On box. Once you've done this, Internet streams, such as movie trailers, should play without delays and halts. Obviously, the faster your overall connection, the better this will work. You must have a broadband connection for starters. For Instant-On to work effectively, the Transport settings (which you select via the Transport Setup button), should be UDP and Port 554. If you selected to automatically determine the best port, this is likely what you will find selected.

Note: The QuickTime Player application itself is in the Applications folder. When you launch QuickTime Player, click the QuickTime (Q) button (on the right side of the window) to view a variety of QuickTime options available via an Internet connection.

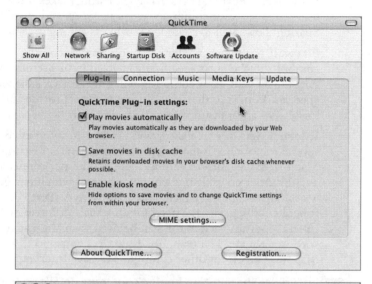

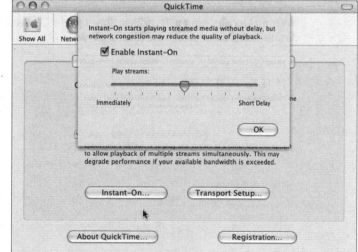

Figure 2.28

The QuickTime System Preferences pane: (top) the Plug-in screen (whose settings determine what happens when you access QuickTime from a Web browser) and (bottom) the Instant-On option in the Connection screen.

Sharing. This pane is where you set the options for sharing access to your computer with other machines. You also set your Computer Name here. This pane includes three main tabs:

- **Services.** Settings here are used to enable or disable various sharing services, such as Personal File Sharing, Personal Web Sharing, FTP Access, Remote Login, and Printer Sharing.

  For example, enabling Personal File Sharing makes it possible for other users to access your computer over a network, and enabling Printer Sharing allows you to share USB printers among several computers.

- **Firewall.** Settings here allow you to restrict incoming access to your computer to the ports specifically enabled in this screen. Thus, if you start the firewall, your computer will only be accessible via the ports with checkmarks next to them in this screen. This provides protection against unsolicited attempts to access your computer.

- **Internet.** Settings here allow you to share an Internet connection among several computers. You can select options here, for example, to set up a Mac that has an AirPort card to share its Internet connection (obtained over Ethernet via cable modem, for example) with other AirPort-equipped Macs. This is often referred to as a Software AirPort Base Station. This is because it bypasses the need for an actual AirPort Base Station. More generally, setups such as this can be used as an alternative to getting any hardware router. The main disadvantage, compared to a router, is that the Mac must be on for other computers to have Internet access.

SEE: • **"Printer Sharing," in Chapter 7, for more details on this feature.**

  • **"Setting Up System Preferences: Sharing," in Chapter 8, for more details on this System Preferences pane.**

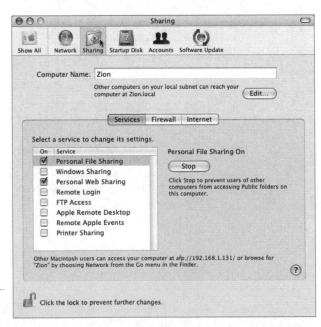

Figure 2.29

The Sharing System Preferences pane.

System

Accounts. This critical System Preferences pane has received a major redesign in Panther.

Direct access to Mac OS X on your computer requires a user account. When you install Mac OS X, the Setup Assistant software requires that you set up a User account for yourself. This first account is set up, by default, for an administrative user. If you want to modify the data you entered, or if you want to add, delete, or modify additional user accounts, you do so via the Accounts System Preferences pane.

Each account has its own folder in the Users folder. The logged-in user's folder becomes the Home folder (directory) for that session—an arrangement that allows each user to maintain customized preferences. This arrangement is also how Mac OS X determines each user's access privileges. If your computer has multiple users, you enter the name and password for your account when you log in (unless you assigned your account for automatic login).

In the left column of the Accounts pane is a list of all accounts currently on the system. The top account (labeled My Account) is for the currently logged-in user. In the examples discussed here, I will assume that this user is an administrator. You can always access certain options for your own account (such as changing your password). However, an administrator can access almost all options for any account. Simply click the name of the account, and the settings in the right side of the pane shift to represent those of the selected user.

Near the bottom of the left column you'll see a Login Options button. If you select this, the right side of the pane shifts to display a set of options that apply regardless of who logs in. In particular, you can select from among the following options:

- **"Display Login."** If you choose "Name and password" rather than "List of users," the names of users with accounts on your Mac will not be displayed. Instead, you're provided with a blank pair of boxes in which to enter a name and password. This offers a bit more privacy and security than showing the full list of users.

    One Mac OS X 10.1 option omitted from Mac OS X 10.2 and 10.3 is the Show Other Users check box. This option added Other as a choice when List of Users was selected as the Login option. This option is important if you want to log in as the root user. To get this option to appear, all you need to do is enable the root user in NetInfo Manager (as described more in Chapter 4). It then appears automatically.

If you select List of Users, you cannot enter a name for an unlisted user (especially if no Other option is available). Normally, this is not a problem (since all potential users should be listed); however, just in case the issue arises, here's what to do:

1. Press Option-Enter/Return.

2. Click the name of any listed user.

You should now get the Name and Password display, allowing you to enter any valid user name and password.

Figure 2.30

The Accounts System Preferences pane: (top) my account with Password selected, and (bottom) the Login Options screen.

TAKE NOTE ▶ Adding or Deleting a User

To add a new account, simply click the plus (+) button at the bottom of the Accounts pane. A folder with the short name of the new account will be added to the Users folder. This is the Home directory of the newly added user.

To delete an existing account, click the minus (–) button. A message will appear describing what will happen if you delete the account. If you click OK, the account is deleted and the entire folder for that user is automatically converted to a disk image file named {*deleted_user*}.img. The image is stored in a Deleted Users folder located in the Users folder at the root level of the drive. This Deleted Users folder is created automatically if you're deleting an account for the first time. At any point, as an administrative user, you can either open the disk image (to access files you may want to save) or delete the image file.

If you want to delete an account and not save this image file, click Delete Immediately.

Important: *Never* attempt to move any folders (for active accounts) from the Users folder to another location. If you do, those accounts will no longer be accessible. Similarly, do not relocate the Users folder itself.

Figure 2.31

The message that appears when you select to delete an account from the Accounts System Preferences pane.

Are you sure you want to delete the user account "Test Case"?

The contents of the user's home folder, "testcase," will be saved in a file in the Deleted Users folder, which is in the Users folder. To access the contents of the user's home folder, open the file. If you do not want to save the user's home folder, click Delete Immediately.

[Delete Immediately]   (OK)   (Cancel)

Figure 2.32

The User menu that appears when you enable Fast User Switching.

standarduser

Ted Landau

Test Case

Login Window...

- **"Automatically log in as** {*name selected from pop-up menu*}**."** Use this option to select the name of the user account to be used for automatically logging in. This setting determines the account that will be used if you want to bypass the Login window that would otherwise appear at startup. Obviously, you can only set this item for one user.

- **"Hide the Sleep, Restart and Shut Down buttons."** This item removes these buttons from the Login window. This is, in essence, a security measure, used to limit access to these options when the Mac is in a public location.

- **"Enable fast user switching."** This option, new in Panther, allows you to switch among logged-in users without having to first log out. This means, for example, that you and your spouse could both log in to the same Mac (from a menu, called the *User menu*, that appears in the upper-right corner of the menu bar when this option is enabled)—without either one of you having to log out.

  If a user does not have a password (as set up in the next Account's password screen), the switch occurs instantly. Otherwise, you will be requested to enter the user's password from the Login window whenever you attempt to make a switch.

  To log in a user not listed in the menu, select Login Window from the menu. This takes you back to the Login window without logging anyone out. You can use this to log in as the root user, for example.

  When at the Login window, the words "Currently logged in" will appear below the name of any currently logged-in window.

TAKE NOTE ▶ Problems with Fast User Switching

The ability to have more than one user logged in at a time is definitely cool. However, until Apple has worked the kinks out of this new feature, you can expect problems to occur that wouldn't with just a single user. These include the following:

- **Insufficient memory.** Multiple logged-in users mean additional memory is being used. If you plan to use this feature regularly (especially for more than two users at a time), make sure you've installed sufficient physical memory. If everything starts to slow down, it means you don't have enough memory to support multiple logins.

- **Denied access.** A crash in one account may prevent access to other logged-in accounts, forcing you to restart the computer.

- **One user's error affects *all* users.** Because multiple users are sharing processes that load prior to login, an error by one user (such as one that causes the loss of an Internet connection) may similarly affect other logged-in users.

- **Single-account processes.** Some processes cannot be open in more than one account. One example of this is Classic: If you try to start Classic in one account while it is already running in another, you will get a message stating that you cannot do this.

- **Restart/Shut Down.** If you select to Restart or Shut Down while multiple users are logged in, you will get a message asking you to enter an admin name and password (authorizing the logging out of all users and thus permitting the Restart or Shut Down). However, this does not appear to work. At least for me, I need to individually log out all additional users before I can restart the Mac.

- **Printing prohibition.** Similarly, you may find that only the first user to log in can print to a USB-connected printer.

SEE: • **"Logging in as root,"** in Chapter 4, for related information.

  • **"Restarting and shutting down with Fast User Switching enabled"** and **"Logging in as another user,"** in Chapter 5, for more on Fast User Switching.

  • **Chapter 9, for more on Fast User Switching and Classic.**

If you select an account from the account list on the left, the right side of the Accounts pane reveals several tabs, each of which brings up a different screen for the selected account:

- **Password.** Each user is assigned a name, short name, password, and (optionally) password hint. You can modify these settings from the Password screen.

  The short name is a nickname or shortened version of the full name. When you create a new user, a new folder is created in the /Users directory, with the user's short name appearing as the folder name. Technically, the short name can be as many as 255 characters; however, it must be 31 characters or less to work with the Macintosh Manager of Mac OS X Server. A short name is actually suggested *for you* by Mac OS X, and it's likely to be 8 characters long. You can accept this suggestion or replace it with your preferred short name. (Keep in mind that you'll likely have to enter this short name fairly often, especially as an administrator, so having a 255-character "short" name may be a bit of a hassle!)

  Note: An administrative password should not contain spaces or Option-keyed characters.

- **Picture.** From this screen, you select a picture to be associated with your account. You can choose from among Apple's included pictures or browse for one of your own. If you have chosen to show the list of users at login, these pictures will appear next to each user's name.

- **Security.** This screen offers the same FileVault options that the Security System Preferences pane does.

  This screen also includes an "Allow user to administer this computer" check box. Be cautious in giving other users administrative status. As an administrator, a user will have virtually the same access to the computer that you have, including the ability to access other users' data. The only exception is that the account of the original administrator (presumably you) cannot be modified by other administrators (though there may be bugs that allow you to circumvent even this exception).

  Note: Jaguar offers an additional option, called "Allow user to login from Windows." Panther does not provide this option, because all users can log in from Windows machines *by default* (assuming you've enabled Windows File Sharing).

- **Startup Items.** This screen is only available for the currently logged-in user. It provides a list of all processes and applications that automatically launch at login for that user. For example, if you have QuicKeys installed and want it to launch automatically at each startup, you would add it to this list. Some software automatically adds itself to the list when you install the software. Virex does this, for example, which is why the Virex application launches with each login.

  You can add or delete items from the list via the plus and minus buttons at the bottom of the screen.

In Jaguar, these items are called *login items*—a better name for them, in my view, since a separate set of *startup items* launches at each startup prior to login. However, Apple did not ask for my view. In these pages, I'll refer to them as *login items, login/startup items,* or *user-level startup items* to distinguish them from the "true" Startup Items (as described in Chapter 5).

Figure 2.33

The Accounts System Preferences pane: Startup Items screen.

SEE: • **"Disabling user-level startup (login) items" and "Take Note: Problems with User-Level Startup (Login) Items," in Chapter 5, for troubleshooting advice related to login items.**

• **Limitations.** This tab is only available when an administrative user accesses the account of a "normal" (nonadministrative) user. From here, you can limit the type of access such users may have. The default choice is No Limits. A second choice is Some Limits. From here, you can decide whether a user is allowed to change his or her password and access System Preferences, what applications they can use, and more. The third and final choice is Simple Finder. This provides a simplified Dock and allows access only to those applications contained in the My Applications folder in the Dock. You determine which applications are in this folder via this Simple Finder option.

TAKE NOTE ▶ Accounts Problems

The following describes a few problems that may crop up when using the Accounts System Preferences:

- **User short name.** You cannot change the short name of any user (including yourself) from the Accounts System Preferences pane. If you need to change a user's short name, you must do so via NetInfo Manager. To do this, launch NetInfo Manager and click the padlock icon (and then enter your password when requested): You now have permission to make changes. Once you've done this, you will need to change virtually *every instance* of the short name in the database to the new name.

  For starters, in the Directory Browser choose "users" and then click the name you want to change. (For the name *tedmac*, for example, you would go to users:tedmac.) In the fields that now appear in the bottom area of the window, change every instance of the old name to the new name. Then, change the name listed in all groups of which the user is a member (such as groups:admin and groups:wheel). Because it's easy to overlook something in this process—and thus fail to get the change to work (or even mess things up so that *nothing* works)—I recommend not changing a user's short name unless it's absolutely necessary. Overall, it's easier to create a new account with the name you want to use and then transfer the files to that account.

continues on next page

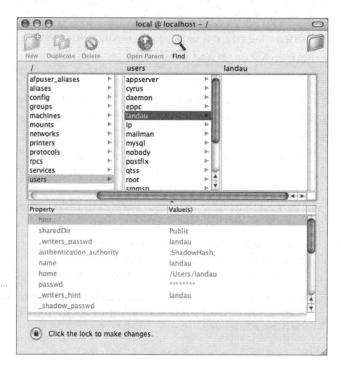

Figure 2.34

NetInfo Manager with the users:landau fields visible at the bottom of the window.

TAKE NOTE ▶ **Accounts Problems**   *continued*

Actually, the complete instructions for changing a short name are even more involved than I've suggested here. For a complete set of instructions, see the following Apple Knowledge Base document: http://docs.info.apple.com/article.html?artnum=106824. I also recommend that you check out the following alternative: www.macosxpowertools.com/content/shortusername.html.

  Whatever you do, *do not* try to change a short name by simply changing the name of the directory in the Users folder in the Finder. Assuming you have sufficient permissions to make the change, doing so can prevent subsequent login to the account!

• **Password Hint.** If you're using a volume upgraded from Mac OS X 10.1.x, you may not be able to edit the Password Hint box. If this is the case, to change the hint, you need to go to NetInfo Manager. From the navigation pane, go to /Users/{*your account*}. In the Property column at the bottom of the window, locate the line that says "hint" (it should be around the third or fourth line). To edit the hint, change the text in the Value(s) column and then save the change.

• **Editing as the root user.** In one situation, my account mysteriously lost its administrative user status. Because I was the only administrator on the system, no one else could log in and restore my status. Fortunately, I had previously enabled the root user account, which meant that I was able to log out of my account and then back in as a root user and access the Accounts System Preferences pane. From here, I was able to re-enable my administrative status.

SEE: • **"Root Access," in Chapter 4, for more on root access.**
  • **Chapter 5, for more on the Login window and startup issues in general.**
  • **Chapter 8 for more on Accounts and file sharing.**

Classic. This pane is used for settings related to running the Classic environment, which allows you to run Mac OS 9 from within Mac OS X. It includes three main tabs:

• **Start/Stop.** From this screen, you select the Mac OS 9 System Folder to be used for Classic. You also launch Classic from here or quit Classic if it is already running.

• **Advanced.** This screen provides useful troubleshooting features, such as the option to disable extensions at startup or rebuild the Desktop.

• **Memory/Versions.** This screen provides a graphical display of running Classic applications and their memory use, similar to what you would see in the About This Computer window if you were booted in Mac OS 9.

SEE: • **Chapter 9 for more details on these System Preferences, including the "Use Mac OS 9 preferences from your home" option (in the Advanced screen).**

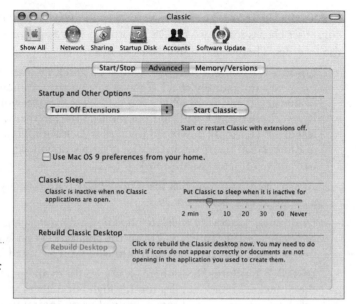

Figure 2.35

The Advanced screen of the Classic System Preferences pane.

Date & Time. This pane is where you set preferences for the date and time. It includes three primary tabs:

- **Date & Time.** From this screen, you can set the current date and time manually or elect to have it set automatically via a network time server. The automatic option only makes sense if you have an "always on" Internet connection (such as a cable or DSL modem).

- **Time Zone.** From here, you select your local time zone.

- **Clock.** This is where you set how the time is displayed. For example, you can select whether to display the time in the menu bar or in a window on the Desktop. (In Jaguar, the Desktop clock is available from a separate Clock application rather than this preferences pane.)

  The "Use a 24-hour clock" option here applies specifically to this clock. For more general date and time format settings (including 12-hour versus 24-hour clock), especially as they apply to settings used for different countries, use the Formats tab of the International System Preferences pane.

Software Update. The choices you make in this pane determine how your computer checks for new Mac OS X software that Apple makes available over the Internet. There are two main tabs in this pane:

- **Update Software.** From here, you set if and how often you want Mac OS X to automatically check for available updates. It then presents a list of updates, if any, from which you can select the ones you want to install. If you check the "Download important updates in the background" box, it will automatically download updates it deems important. (However, it does not *install* them automatically; it simply downloads them to your hard drive for later installation.)

  Alternatively, you can click the Check Now button at any time to manually check for possible updates.

  In all cases, to actually check for updates, a separate application called Software Update launches. This is the application that actually lists the new software and provides the options for you to install it.

- **Installed Updates.** From here, you get a list of all updates installed via the Software Update application (though not updates you've installed via other means, such as a direct download from Apple's Web site).

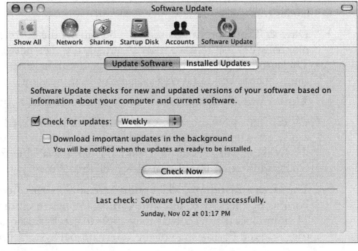

Figure 2.36

The Software Update System Preferences pane. Click the Check Now button to launch the Software Update application that actually lists the available updates.

SEE: • **Chapter 3 for more details on how Software Update works.**

Speech. This panes includes the settings that determine Mac OS X's ability to recognize speech input and provide spoken feedback (such as Talking Alerts). This pane is rarely relevant for troubleshooting issues; thus, I don't discuss it further in these pages.

Startup Disk. This is where you select the startup volume. If your Mac can still boot Mac OS 9, you can use this pane to switch between Mac OS 9 and Mac OS X. If you have more than one volume that can mount Mac OS X, this is where you would select the desired startup volume. (There are other ways to switch startup volumes as well, which I discuss in Chapter 5.)

This pane also includes a Network Startup option for NetBooting (assuming you're connected to a server that supports this option).

Figure 2.37

The Startup Disk System Preferences pane.

Universal Access. This pane contains tabs for four main screens: Seeing, Hearing, Keyboard, and Mouse. These options are designed primarily to assist people with physical disabilities; a few are of more general troubleshooting interest. Here are two examples:

- **Turn On Zoom.** You access this option from the Seeing screen. (Alternatively, you can press Command-Option-8 to toggle the option at any time.) With this enabled, press Command–Option–plus sign or Command–Option–minus sign to view the zoom effect on the display screen.

- **"Enable access for assistive devices."** This check box is at the bottom of the pane. It must be turned on for certain other applications to work correctly, especially ones that automate access to menus and buttons. For example, QuicKeys X requires this to be enabled for recording macros.

Other

Third-party software can also use the System Preferences interface. If you've installed any non-Apple System Preferences, these settings will appear in the Other section. TinkerTool, SharePoints, and WindowShade X (all discussed elsewhere in this book) are just three examples of the many popular System Preferences you may decide to install here.

Where System Preferences files are stored. The System Preferences files installed by Mac OS X are stored in /System/Library/PreferencePanes. There, you will see files with names like Classic.prefPane and Displays.prefPane.

In the Get Info window, these files are listed as Mac OS X Preference Pane. In most ways, however, they function just like ordinary applications, with the exception that launching them also launches the System Preferences shell.

Third-party System Preferences panes will be most likely stored in the ~/Library/PreferencePanes folder (in your Home directory). As a result, installed third-party preference panes will be available only for the user in whose account the file resides. If you have created more than one user account and want all users to have access to a specific preference, you will need to install it in each user's directory—or install it in the PreferencePanes folder in the Library folder at the root level of your drive (/Library/PreferencesPanes). Some installers for third-party panes automatically place the file in this latter location.

SEE: • **Chapter 4 for more on the /Users directory and its function.**
   • **"Technically Speaking: How Mac OS X Selects a Document or Application Match," in Chapter 6, for troubleshooting information regarding preference panes.**

If user-installed preferences panes do not appear in System Preferences. If user-installed third-party preference panes don't show up in the Other section of the System Preferences window, here is what to do:

1.   Quit System Preferences.

2.   Go to the Library/Caches folder of your Home directory and locate the file named com.apple.preferencepanes.cache.

3.   Delete the file.

4.   Relaunch System Preferences. A new version of the cache file will be created. Ideally, the previously missing panes should now appear.

This should also fix problems in which the same pane appears twice or when the icon for a preference pane is not correctly displayed in the System Preferences window.

Remove a user-installed preferences pane. To remove a pane listed in the Other section, Control-click its icon to access a contextual menu. Select Remove from the menu.

Figure 2.38

System Preferences panes not installed by Panther get listed in the Other section.

Applications

Mac OS X installs numerous programs in the Applications folder (as well as in the Utilities folder within the Applications folder). In this and the following sections, I provide a brief overview of those programs that are most relevant to troubleshooting. I also return to most of these programs again elsewhere in this book (when discussing troubleshooting problems for which they're used). In addition, I cover many of the applications *not* mentioned here later in the book. For example, Safari and Mail are covered in Chapter 8, and most of the i-software (iPhoto, iMovie, iCal, iSync, and so on.) is covered in Chapter 11.

I start here by describing five programs of general importance located in the Applications folder: Font Book, Preview, Sherlock, Stickies, and TextEdit. Then I move to the all-important Utilities folder.

Font Book

Although Font Book makes its first appearance in Panther, it's mostly a redesign of an existing interface; in both Jaguar and Panther, you can access an almost identical set of features from applications such as TextEdit (for example, select Format > Font > Show Fonts). Font Book makes these features accessible system-wide.

That said, there is one important new feature in Font Book: You can enable and disable Fonts and Collections. You can use this feature to restrict which font collections (as well as individual fonts within a collection) are listed in the Font panels of applications (such as TextEdit) that use this Mac OS X feature—without actually deleting the font and/or collection.

When you double-click a font from the Finder, it now launches Font Book.

SEE: • **Chapter 4 for more details on Font Book and related features.**

Preview

Preview opens graphics files of various formats. You can use it to view the GIF and JPEG files that are common on most Web pages, for example. You can also use Preview's Export command to convert a graphics file from one format to another: Choices include BMP, JP2, JPEG, MacPaint, PDF, Photoshop, PICT, PNG, QuickTime Image, SGI, TGA, and TIFF. (If you create a new graphic, the default choice is TIFF; if you choose Save As, the file will be saved in its current format using a different name.)

Preview also opens PDF documents. PDF, which stands for Portable Document Format, is the native format used by Acrobat Reader and is also Mac OS X's "native" file format for graphics.

Preview includes a thumbnails view, as well as the capability to zoom and rotate figures via buttons in its toolbar. The Panther version of Preview adds several new features, including a Tools menu (from which you can make a graphic selection of part of a page or select text to copy), a Find command, the ability to copy text and crop images, and active URL links. The Panther version is also much, much faster at loading and scrolling through pages.

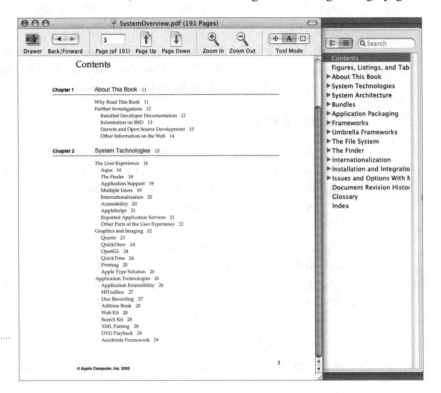

Figure 2.39

The Preview application with a document open.

Figure 2.40

The Preview button in a Print dialog.

Perhaps the best feature of Preview is its link to the Preview button in the Print dialog of almost any application that works with documents. If you click the Preview button, the Preview application launches and opens the selected document as a PDF file. The document should look virtually identical to how it looked in the application in which it was created. At this point, you have two choices:

- **You can print the document from Preview.** This option may be useful for occasions when you can't get the document to print from the application in which it was created.

- **You can save the file as a PDF file via the Save As PDF button.** Once you've done this, you can open the saved document in any application that can view PDF files, including Preview itself and Acrobat Reader. This option can be very useful for exporting documents to platforms (such as Windows) that would not otherwise open the original files. Because a Windows version of Acrobat Reader is available, Windows users will be able to open the PDF file.

Note: Acrobat Reader has some options that Preview does not—which means you shouldn't be in a hurry to throw out your copy of Acrobat Reader just because Preview is available.

Tip: If a document in Preview does not appear correctly (for example, the text looks blurry), your first step should be to uncheck the "Anti-alias text and line art option" in Preview's Preferences.

SEE: • "Technically Speaking: Type/Creator vs. Filename Extensions" and "Take Note: Filename Extensions," in Chapter 4, for related information.

• "Opening and Saving: Problems Opening and Saving Files," in Chapter 6, for a more extended discussion of opening and saving documents.

• Chapter 7 for more information on printing and additional PDF options.

Sherlock

Prior to Mac OS X 10.2, Sherlock was used to search both the contents of your mounted media and the Internet. Starting in Mac OS X 10.2, media searching has been shifted to the Finder's Find command (discussed earlier). Sherlock, called Sherlock 3 beginning in Jaguar, has been overhauled and is an Internet-only search tool.

To launch Sherlock, click its Dock icon or double-click its icon in the Applications folder or from the Dock.

The initial window contains a toolbar from which you can select a specific channel. You can also select a channel from the Channels menu. In Sherlock, a *channel* refers to a specific Web location with which Sherlock interacts to display its information.

The main window includes a Collections sidebar, which includes five items: Toolbar, Channels Menu, Apple Channels, Other Channels, and My Channels. Click an item to display its list of channels in the right side of the window. The first two items duplicate the lists in the Toolbar and Channels menu, respectively. You can drag items from other collections to these names in the sidebar to add a new channel to the Toolbar or Channels menu. Doing this does not remove the channel from its original location; it just adds it to the new location.

The Apple Channels collection lists all of the channels Apple officially supports. Other Channels is used for third-party channels. An initial collection of third-party channels (such as one for VersionTracker.com) is included with Panther. My Channels starts out empty; you drag channels to it to create your own customized list.

Channels. You can choose from an assortment of channels. Here are two examples:

- **AppleCare.** This channel is of special significance for troubleshooting because it's where you click to search Apple's Knowledge Base documents. Simply enter your search criteria, click the magnifying-glass icon to search, and then select an article from the results list. The bottom half of the window will now show the complete contents of the selected article just as if you were viewing it from a Web browser. This feature is generally more convenient than going to Apple's Web site (unless you need its additional features, such as the ability to limit searches by date).

  Note: Make sure that the Accept Cookies Always option is enabled in Sherlock's Preferences; otherwise, the contents of Knowledge Base documents will not appear.

- **Movies.** Another cool channel you should be sure to check out is Movies. Click the Movies icon, and you can search for what's playing in the theaters in your area, including showtimes.

Customizing Sherlock's toolbar. Sherlock's toolbar lists most or all of the available channels. Similar to how the Finder's toolbar works, you can customize Sherlock's toolbar via the Customize Toolbar command in Sherlock's View menu. (You can also customize it by dragging channels to and from the Toolbar collection on the left.)

Creating shortcuts. Using the Make a Shortcut command in Sherlock's Channel menu, you can save a channel as a file on the Desktop. Then, simply double-click the file to directly launch that channel.

The file is simply an XML document that contains the URL for the given channel. For example, the shortcut for the Movie channel contains the following URL: http://si.info.apple.com/sherlock3s/acno/channels/movies.xml.

Adding channels. To add a channel in Sherlock, go to the Web site that offers a channel and click the link provided to save the channel file to your drive. Then, from Sherlock's Channel menu select Add Channel. The Subscription options available in the Preferences window of Sherlock 3 in Jaguar are no longer included in the Panther version. Instead, these options are now determined by the Web site from which the channel originates. You're automatically subscribed to all Apple channels.

THE JAGUAR WAY ▶ Sherlock 3: Adding Channels

In Jaguar (but dropped from Panther), Sherlock's Preferences dialog includes several options, such as the Subscriptions tab, which allows you to subscribe to additional Sherlock channels. By default, you're subscribed to the Apple Channels service, which covers all the channels that Jaguar initially lists. Another Web site may start its own channel service, to which you could subscribe, and channels may appear and disappear from your Sherlock list without your doing anything because of changes made by the channel service itself.

If a Web site provides a Sherlock channel that is not included in Mac OS X, you can add it yourself by clicking the link for the channel on the Web page. This procedure is separate from subscribing to a channel service. More generally, Apple notes, "If you want to add channels from a Web site regularly, add the site to the Security pane in Sherlock Preferences so that you don't have to accept each channel individually."

TECHNICALLY SPEAKING ▶ Sherlock 3 vs. Sherlock 2

Because Sherlock 3 does not support the old Sherlock 2 plug-in architecture, Sherlock 2 plug-ins will not work in Sherlock 3. The Sherlock 2 plug-in files are located in the Internet Search Sites Site folder of each user's ~/Library folder. Although Sherlock 3 does not use this folder, it will still be present if you upgraded from Mac OS X 10.1.x. The Sherlock Prefs folder in the ~/Library/Preferences folder is no longer used, either; you can discard it.

Oddly, if you open the Sherlock 3 application package via the Show Package Contents contextual-menu command, you will find a folder in Contents/Resources called Channels. Inside this folder is a folder for each of the main channels in Sherlock 2, not Sherlock 3. These are no longer used, either.

In Panther, Sherlock 3 determines which channels to display via the information it finds in com.apple.Sherlock.plist in ~/Library/Preferences. This file exists in Jaguar as well; however, in Panther its function has been enhanced via the following new keys: SherlockChannelCache, SherlockChannelOrganization, and SherlockSubscriptions. These keys provide details of the names, URLs, and category organization of all of the channels Sherlock currently tracks. Channels for which subscriptions exist are automatically updated when Sherlock is launched. All Apple-supplied channels (including the initial list in Other Channels), for example, are subscription-based. Thus, when Apple updates its channels, this plist file is updated accordingly. The default list of subscriptions is found in the DefaultChannelSubscriptions property in the plist file.

continues on next page

TECHNICALLY SPEAKING ▶ **Sherlock 3 vs. Sherlock 2** *continued*

The ~/Library/Caches/Sherlock folder is where cache data for Sherlock is located. In particular, check the contents of the CheckPointCache.plist file, which also lists all currently tracked channels. In Jaguar, this folder includes a Channel Nibs folder, which contains a file for every channel in Sherlock. In Panther this folder no longer exists.

Note: Most of the actual Sherlock 3 software is located in /System/Library/PrivateFrameworks/ SherlockCore.framework.

If you want to know how to create a Sherlock 3 channel for your own Web site, check the following URL: http://developer.apple.com/macosx/sherlock. You can also check out the following documentation for more details: http://developer.apple.com/techpubs/macosx/ AdditionalTechnologies/Sherlock.

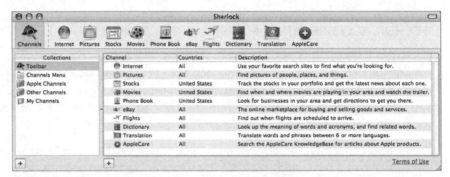

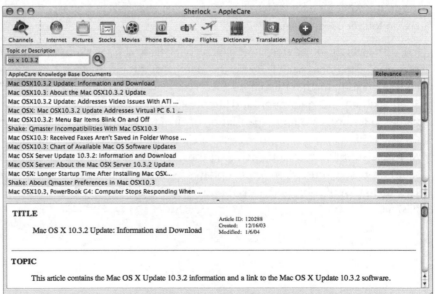

Figure 2.41

Sherlock 3: (top) main window and (bottom) AppleCare window.

Stickies

Stickies software allows you to save notes in colored windows that resemble Post-It Notes. One troubleshooting-related note about this program: The information you create and save in Stickies is stored in a file called StickiesDatabase, located at the root level of the Library folder in your Home directory. It's a good idea to back up this file as protection against accidentally losing all of your Stickies notes.

Prior to Mac OS X 10.2, this database file was in the same location but invisible in the Finder. Starting in Mac OS X 10.2, it's now in plain sight.

TextEdit

TextEdit is Apple's generic word processor. It can open plain-text files and Rich Text Format (.rtf) files. It can also display numerous types of graphics files and save them in a special type of Rich Text Format document. Starting in Panther, TextEdit can directly open and save Microsoft Word files. It can even save native TextEdit files in Word format.

SEE: • "Working with Fonts," in Chapter 4, and numerous sections in Chapter 6 for more on TextEdit.

THE JAGUAR WAY ▶ Utilities

Apple has made several significant changes to its utilities collection in Panther (as compared with Jaguar). The following summarizes the major changes:

- **Disk Copy no longer exists.** Most of the functions for creating, editing, and burning disk images have been rolled into the Disk Utility application.

- **The completely overhauled Disk Utility includes numerous new options.** Among these is a new Restore screen, which is used for backing up and restoring volumes, including bootable volumes.

- **Jaguar's Process Viewer has morphed into Panther's Activity Monitor.** It now includes the CPU Monitor options (this application no longer exists in Panther), as well as a host of new features not available from any previous Mac OS X utility.

- **Print Center is now called Printer Setup Utility.** The renamed utility includes several new features, including support for faxing and desktop printers.

- **Apple System Profiler is now called System Profiler.** The utility has undergone a major design overhaul in Panther.

You'll find more details about these changes throughout this chapter and the rest of the book.

SEE: • "Take Note: What Happened to Disk Copy?" in Chapter 3.

Utilities

The Utilities folder—which is contained within the Applications folder at the root level of your volume—contains a wealth of troubleshooting utilities. Starting in Mac OS X 10.2, most of these utilities employ a similar toolbar format, bringing a welcome consistency to their user interfaces. In this section, I provide an alphabetical overview of the most important of these utilities for general troubleshooting purposes. (I'll return to both these and other utilities throughout the book, as relevant.)

SEE: • **Chapter 4, for coverage of Directory Access, a Utilities folder utility not mentioned here.**

• **Chapter 8, for more on network-related utilities and related software such as Internet Connect, Mail, Safari, AirPort Admin Utility, Bluetooth File Exchange, and Network Utility.**

Activity Monitor

Activity Monitor is a critically important troubleshooting utility that can be used to view every open process. Although an application is, by definition, a process, many processes that Mac OS X can open are not traditional Mac applications. Activity Monitor's most important feature for troubleshooting purposes is that it can force-quit any process, even ones that aren't listed in the Force Quit window (which opens when you press Command-Option-Escape). It's also useful for monitoring performance-related statistics for open processes.

Activity Monitor is such a feature-rich utility that I'm only presenting an overview of it here. You'll find more details as well as discussions of additional features later in the book, as they relate to various troubleshooting topics.

Activity Monitor window: the process list. This list is able to display every open process. You can filter which processes are listed at any given time via the Show pop-up menu in the toolbar, which includes the following choices:

• **My Processes.** This shows all processes for which you are the User. These are generally either applications you launched or background processes launched at login. Applications with custom icons next to their names are listed in the Force Quit window.

• **Administrator Processes.** For these processes, the system is the User (that is, root is the name listed in the User column). In general, these processes monitor essential and maintenance activities of the OS, such as those initiated at startup prior to logging in, for networking, for printing, and so on.

- **Other User Processes.** If more than one user is logged in, via Fast User Switching, this window will show processes assigned to other logged-in users.

- **Active Processes and Inactive Processes.** These choices display processes currently in Active and Inactive Memory, respectively.

- **Windowed Processes.** These show all processes that can be launched from the Finder (and typically that can display windows in the Finder).

- **All Processes and All Processes Hierarchically.** These display every open process.

You can also filter any process list by entering text in the Filter text box in the toolbar. Only those processes that contain the text you type will be shown.

The process list provides information about each process (beyond its name), including its Process ID, its percentage of CPU usage, and the amount of real versus virtual memory it is using. This data is updated in real time (as determined by the selection you make in the Update Frequency command in the Monitor menu).

Quit Process. To (force) quit any listed process, click the name of the process and in the Activity Monitor window's toolbar click the Quit Process button (or from the Process menu select Quit). From the dialog that appears, choose Force Quit.

SEE: • "Force Quit," in Chapter 5, for more on Force Quit and Activity Monitor.

Performance monitors. In the bottom section of the Activity Monitor window are five tabs: CPU, System Memory, Disk Activity, Disk Usage, and Network. Click any of these to get data on the respective topic. (I'll show you how to interpret this data later in the book.)

SEE: • "Technically Speaking: Dividing Up Mac OS X's Memory," in Chapter 4, for more on System Memory.

     • "Utilities for monitoring and improving performance," in Chapter 6, for details about all of these options.

     • "Technically Speaking: Terminal Commands to Monitor and Improve Performance," in Chapter 10, for more details on Terminal commands and third-party utilities related to performance.

The Monitor menu. You will find several useful commands in this menu:

- Select Show Activity Monitor to get the window to return, should you ever close it.
- Select Dock Icon and then choose among the options in its hierarchical submenu to replace the Activity Monitor icon in the Dock with one that displays real-time performance data (such as CPU usage).

Note: If you select to show CPU usage in the Dock icon, you cannot select the Show CPU Usage command from the Monitor menu.

Most of the remaining commands in this window refer to separate windows that provide graphical displays of CPU usage and CPU (usage) history. These commands were part of a separate utility in Jaguar called CPU Monitor but are included as part of Activity Monitor in Panther. (CPU Monitor does not exist in Panther.)

SEE: • "Utilities for monitoring and improving performance," in Chapter 6, for related information.

Inspect button. If you select a process and click the Inspect button in the toolbar (or select Inspect from the Process menu), the Inspect window opens. From here, you can get details about each process (beyond what's shown in the process list). This window contains three tabs: Memory, Statistics, and Open Files.

Clicking the Memory or Statistics tab provides detailed performance data specific to the selected process. The Open Files tab displays a list of all shared files (primarily frameworks in the System folder) that the selected process may call to accomplish its tasks.

Clicking the Sample button at the bottom of the Inspect window brings up a snapshot of the functions the process is executing at a given moment. This (like most Activity Monitor features) is actually a graphical front end for a Unix function. Thus, if you launch Terminal and type man sample, you'll be provided with much more detail about what the Sample feature does.

In my view, however, the information provided by the Inspect options (especially the Sample feature) goes well beyond what most end-user troubleshooters need to know.

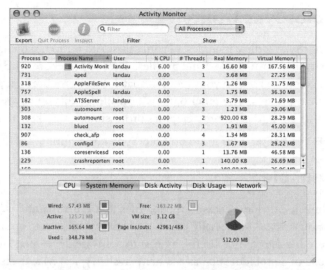

Figure 2.42

Activity Monitor:
(top) showing All
Processes and
System Memory;
(middle) showing
My Processes and
CPU; (bottom)
Activity Monitor's
Inspect window.

ColorSync Utility

ColorSync Utility includes a Profile First Aid button, which you can use to verify and repair ColorSync profiles. These profiles are used to make sure that the colors you see on your monitor match those produced on peripheral devices, such as printers. The other options available for this utility are beyond the scope of this book (that is, only graphics professionals are likely to need them).

SEE: • **Chapter 7 for more on ColorSync and printing.**

Console

Console provides access to the log files that Unix maintains. These files track various events—especially errors that occur while using your Mac. Viewing these log files can be useful, at least to software developers, in diagnosing the cause of a problem such as a system crash. Typical Mac users, however, won't find this text to be of much value. Occasionally, however, log output can be useful for diagnosing and solving problems. For example, my Console log file kept reporting a failure to delete a file, even though nothing was in the Trash at the time. It turned out that the file was in an invisible folder used by a third-party delete utility called Data Recycler X. Alerted by the log message, I located and deleted the problem file.

The log that appears by default when Console launches is called console.log and is stored in a folder that has the same name as the short name of your account, located in /Library/Logs/Console. (In Jaguar, this file is stored in /var/tmp.) This log focuses on events specific to your particular login session. Whenever you open or quit an application, for example, the log notes this. Various minor errors, most of which you can ignore, are also listed here.

A second important log is system.log, which is located in the Unix /var/log folder. This log focuses on system-wide events—that is, events that occur independently of any users who are logged in. However, many events are tracked by both the console and the system logs.

If you close either window, you can reopen them by selecting the appropriate Open command from Console's File menu.

Each log window displays a toolbar (by default) with four icon buttons and a filter text box:

- **Logs.** Clicking the Logs button opens a sidebar from which you can access any available log file. The first two items are used to directly access the console.log and system.log files. The remaining three items are folder locations for the three places where logs are stored: ~/Library/Logs, /Library/Logs, and /var/log. Click the disclosure triangle next to each name for a list of that location's logs and subfolders.

Of special importance are the two CrashReporter subfolders (one in each of the two Library/Logs folders). These contain log files created or updated each time an application crashes. Each one is named {*application name*}.crash.log. The information they contain can be critical for developers trying to debug the cause of a crash.

Note: To enable CrashReporter tracking in Jaguar, you need to select Preferences from the Console menu and then click the Crashes tab. Click the "Enable crash reporting" check box and, if you want Console to launch automatically after a crash, enable "Automatically display crash logs." In Panther, CrashReporter tracking is on by default, and there is no option to disable it. Console's Preferences in Panther are only for determining what to do when an open log is updated.

- **Clear.** This button clears the display of all log text. However, it *does not* erase the log file being viewed, even though it may appear to do so. Simply click the Reload button to view the log's contents.

- **Reload.** This button reloads the log from disk (entering any items that have been updated since you first loaded the file).

- **Mark.** This button time- and date-stamps the file.

- **Filter.** This feature works similarly to the Search text box in the toolbar of Finder windows.

    Note: You can add features to the toolbar, such as "Delete log file" and Mail Log, by selecting Customize Toolbar from the View menu.

SEE: • **"Technically Speaking: What and Where Are the Unix Files?" and "Take Note: Finder Folders vs. Unix Directories," in Chapter 4, for more on accessing Unix folders such as /var/log and understanding pathname notation.**

 • **"Application quits," in Chapter 5, for more information on Console, especially for using CrashReporter logs.**

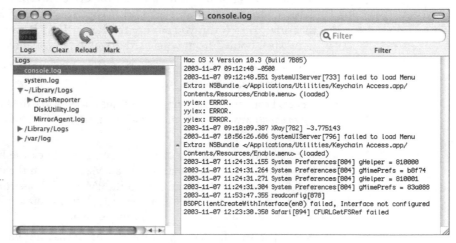

Figure 2.43

A Console window for console.log with the Log list shown on the left.

Disk Utility

Disk Utility combines what were four separate utilities in Mac OS 9: Disk First Aid, Drive Setup, Disk Copy, and Disc Burner. (Actually, Disk Copy was also a separate utility in Mac OS X prior to Panther; its features are now included in Disk Utility's Images menu.) The following provides a brief overview of Disk Utility's features.

Sidebar and main window. The sidebar on the left side of the Disk Utility window lists all currently accessible volumes. Typically, your first step, before doing anything else in Disk Utility, will be to select a volume, a partition of a volume, or a disk image from this list. Depending on what you select, different options will appear on the right side of the window. If the volume is unmounted, you will typically want to select Mount Volume from the File menu (or click the Mount button in the toolbar).

If you select a physical drive or volume (for example, a hard drive), you will be presented with five tabs from which to choose: First Aid, Erase, Partition, RAID, and Restore. If you select a partition of a volume, you will only be offered three of these choices: First Aid, Erase, and Restore. If you select an image file, the options vary according to image type; at minimum, First Aid and Restore should appear. The following provides a brief overview of these tabs' functions.

- **First Aid.** The First Aid screen is the main repair component of Disk Utility. From here, you can repair a volume and its disk permissions (for Mac OS X volumes).

  The ability to run First Aid from the Mac OS X Install CD (as described in Chapter 3) is important, because the Repair Disk component of the First Aid tab of Disk Utility cannot repair the drive currently running the OS. Thus, if you start up from a hard drive, you cannot use Disk Utility to repair that drive. (However, you *can* use the Repair Disk Permissions component when booted from your hard drive; in fact, it's preferable to do so.)

  SEE: • **"Performing repairs with Disk Utility (First Aid)," in Chapter 5, for more on this feature.**

- **Erase.** From the Erase screen, you can erase (also called *initializing* or *reformatting*) any writable media: a partition of a disk, an entire disk, or even a CD-RW.

  If you decide to erase the drive, remember to check the Install Mac OS 9 Drivers option if you intend to install Mac OS 9 on the drive or to access the drive from a computer booted into Mac OS 9 (assuming your computer can do this). You do not need to select this option if your only intended use of Mac OS 9 is running Classic.

  Note: The Install Mac OS 9 Drivers option may not be listed here when running Panther. It only appears on older Macs that can actually start up from Mac OS 9. This means you cannot format an external drive with

Mac OS 9 drivers from a new Mac running Panther, such as for use with an older Mac that can still boot Mac OS 9.

If you select an entire drive (not a partition of a drive), the Options button is enabled. Clicking the Options button brings down a dialog with the options "Zero all data" and "8 Way Random Write Format." These are more secure (but much more time-consuming) methods of erasing a drive. No data can be recovered after this type of erase, even by utilities that claim to be able to recover data from damaged or erased drives.

When erasing a drive, the options in the Volume Format pop-up menu include: Mac OS Extended; Mac OS X Extended (Journaled), and UNIX File System. If you select a drive (but not if you select a partition of a drive), an additional format option appears: MS-DOS File System. Use this option to format a drive to be compatible with Windows. Such drives will also mount on your Mac.

- **Partition.** The Partition screen is where you can partition the drive as well as determine the type of drive formatting you want to use (for example, Mac OS Extended). Note that partitioning a volume also erases it. If you're erasing an entire disk, you can use the Partition screen to divide it into separate partitions. Note: This option does not appear if you select a partition of an already formatted drive.

- **RAID.** The RAID (Redundant Array of Independent Disks) screen is only of use if you have multiple hard drives that you wish to set up as a RAID set. In brief, RAID coordinates the drives so that they act almost as if they were one larger drive. It can also provide automatic data backup. Since RAID sets are used primarily in institutional setups, I will not be covering them further here.

- **Restore.** From here you can create a backup version of a volume or restore a drive from a previous backup, especially a disk image. This is a new feature in Panther.

    SEE: • "Backing Up and Restoring Mac OS X Volumes," in Chapter 3, for more on this and related features.

Images menu. You use this menu primarily to open, create, and modify disk images. These are the files (typically with a .dmg extension) that, when opened, mount a virtual volume on your Mac that acts almost identically to a true external volume. You can also use the Burn command to burn images to a CD or DVD—especially useful for making an exact complete copy of a volume (which cannot be done by simply dragging files to a CD-R mounted in the Finder).

Toolbar. In large part, the buttons here duplicate commands accessible elsewhere—the toolbar simply makes them more convenient. Included are buttons for mounting, unmounting, and ejecting volumes as well as one for enabling journaling for a volume.

New in Panther is the Info feature. Select a volume and click this button to open a window that provides a detailed list of the characteristics of the volume. From here, you can learn, for example, whether a volume is bootable, whether you can repair permissions on the volume, whether journaling is on, and how many files and folders are on the volume.

SEE: • Chapter 3 (especially "Image (.dmg) files" and "Creating an Emergency Startup Volume") for more on using Disk Utility, including details on how to make a bootable copy of a startup CD.

• Chapter 5 for more on the First Aid component of Disk Utility and details about journaling.

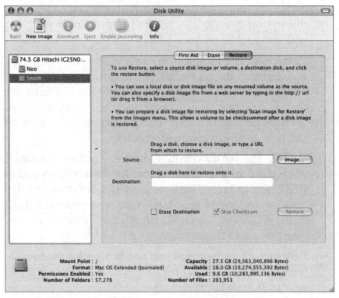

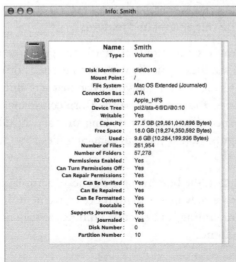

Figure 2.44

*Disk Utility: (top)
the Restore screen;
(bottom) an Info
window.*

Grab

Grab creates screen captures—that is, pictures of your screen just like those that illustrate this book. Personally, I find Grab to be a bit of a kludge; however, it has one saving grace: a Timed Screen capture, useful for those occasions when you can't access Grab the moment the screen is ready to be captured. This makes it easy to take a picture of a drop-down menu, for example. Beyond that, Grab is inconvenient to use and too often prevents you from getting the shot you want.

Fortunately, there are alternatives, as described in the following sidebar.

TAKE NOTE ▶ Screen Captures

In addition to the Grab utility, the main Mac OS X methods for taking screen snapshots (also called *captures* or *screen shots*) are via pressing Command-Shift-3 and Command-Shift-4 (both of which work similarly in Mac OS 9).

Command-Shift-3. This key combination allows you take a snapshot of the entire screen. It saves the file as a PDF document to the Desktop, named Picture 1. Subsequent saved captures are named Picture 2, and so on.

If you're in a Classic application, however, the files are saved as PICT documents at the root level of the volume containing the Classic application.

Command-Shift-4. Command-Shift-4 allows you to select a portion of the screen for capture. Simply drag the crosshair pointer to define the selection borders. Just as with Command-Shift-3, captured files are saved to the Desktop as PDF files.

However, if you press the spacebar before selecting a region, you get a special option: The pointer changes to a Camera icon. Now whatever window the pointer is over is selected automatically—and changes color to indicate this status. Click the mouse, and you get a snapshot of the selected window. You can also use this technique to take snapshots of icons on the Desktop. When you want to capture just a window, this method eliminates the need to try to line up the selection borders with the window border.

Note: You cannot use these commands to take pictures of anything that requires that you hold down a key or the mouse button to display. To take pictures of drop-down menus, for example, click the menu name in the menu bar, so that the menu remains visible even when you're not holding down the mouse button.

Canceling a capture. Pressing the Escape key (or Command-period) *before* you unclick the mouse to take a capture via Command-Shift-4 cancels the capture.

continues on next page

TAKE NOTE ▶ Screen Captures *continued*

Saving to the Clipboard. If you hold down the Control key while pressing Command-Shift-3 or Command-Shift-4, the screen capture will be saved to the Clipboard instead of as a file. You can then paste it into any graphics application or use Preview's File > New From Pasteboard command to open the screen shot in Preview; the advantage of this is that you can then export it to any supported graphics format.

Screen-capture format. You cannot use these commands to save screen captures in a format other than PDF (as you could in Mac OS X 10.1). When you open the PDF file in Preview, however, you can use Preview's Export command to change the file's format. The Grab utility also saves screen captures as TIFF documents.

Screen capture from Terminal. You can take screen captures from Terminal via the screencapture command. To learn more about its use, type screencapture and press Return.

Snapz Pro X. If you want more features than Grab or screen-capture shortcuts provide, try the shareware utility Snapz Pro X. Among other options, it allows you to select a default graphics format for saving captures and to create movies from your screen actions.

Installer

Installer is the utility that launches when you open an installer package file.

SEE: • Chapter 3 for complete details regarding this utility and installing software in Mac OS X.

Keychain Access

Keychain Access stores passwords for and regulates access to applications, email accounts, and Internet sites that use passwords.

Creating and setting up Keychain files. The first step in using Keychain Access is to create a Keychain file. Most likely, one was created automatically when you created your User account. The name of the Keychain file will be your short user name, and the file is opened by default when you launch Keychain Access. The actual file, called login.keychain, is located in your Home directory in ~/Library/Keychains. This file is used for your personal items. The name and password for this file will be the same as those for your account.

There is also a System Keychain file that's created by default. This file, named system.keychain, is located in the Keychain folder of the Library folder at the root level of your drive and is used to access items that are needed regardless of who's currently logged in. As an administrator, you can modify the contents of this file.

You can see a list of all Keychain files by clicking the Show Keychains button in the toolbar. To shift the display to a different Keychain file, just click its name. The Keychain List command, in the Window menu, brings up a separate window that lists all available Keychain files. From here, you can see that the System keychain will be accessed across all users because the "global" check box is checked.

You can create additional Keychain files by selecting New Keychain from the File menu. To add an existing keychain to the list, from the File menu select Add Keychain.

You can also lock and unlock Keychain files. If a file is locked, you will be asked to provide the Keychain file password before you can access any data within the file. You can lock and unlock a Keychain via the Lock/Unlock button in the toolbar or the command of the same name in the File menu.

To change a Keychain file's password, from the Edit menu select "Change password for Keychain." Keep in mind that the password for the login Keychain will also be changed if you change your login password in the Accounts System Preferences pane. (However, if an admin user changes another user's account password, this may *not* update that user's Keychain password; in such cases, users have to make the change themselves.)

Using Keychain files. One way you can use Keychain Access is as a database for storing sensitive information: You can manually store information in Keychain Access at any time. For example, to store a new password linked to an application or Web site, from the File menu select New Password Item (or simply click the Password icon in the toolbar). Similarly, you can store information unrelated to your Mac, such as a credit card number, by selecting to create a new Secure Note Item.

You can also use Keychain Access (with Keychain-aware software) to automatically enter your password when it's required—thus eliminating the need to remember multiple passwords. If an application is Keychain aware, it will typically include a check box to "remember" your password (the option will be available in the window where you enter the password). If you enable this option, the application will store the data in your login Keychain files and retrieve it when needed. Most Mac O S X applications that use passwords are Keychain aware; however, there are exceptions (Internet Explorer being one).

Attributes and Access Control. A Keychain file window lists all of its keys (password and note items) in the upper section. From the toolbar, you can delete a selected item or (if it's a URL) select to go to the Web site. The lower section of the window contains two buttons: Attributes and Access Control. The contents of the lower section depend on which of these buttons you click and which key is selected in the upper section.

- **The Attributes screen lists the basic information for each key.** For example, to see a particular password, select the key for the desired application, Web site, email account, or whatever from the list. Then, from the Attributes tab, check the Show Passphrase box. A window will appear that asks you to enter your Keychain file password. Do so and click the Allow Once or Allow Always button, and the requested password will appear. If you select Allow Always, you will not be asked for the Keychain file password on subsequent requests—obviously reducing your security protection.

- **The Access Control screen is where you select whether you want Keychain Access security to be in effect when you launch an application (or URL or other item) that's password protected.** If you select "Confirm before allowing access," you will be requested to enter the password each time you launch the application. If you select "Always Allow access," the request is bypassed (for the applications in the "Always allow access by these applications" list). The latter choice is essentially the same as selecting the Allow Always option when the password window appears within the given application.

  If you update Mac OS X to a new version, the Allow Always option is rescinded for all items; you will need to reselect it again. An update to a particular application can have the same effect for just that application.

Keychain First Aid. If you have problems getting Keychain Access to work as expected, select Keychain First Aid from Keychain Access' Window menu. It verifies and repairs (if necessary) a variety of potential problems. The following are some examples of the types of problems it addresses:

- Your .Mac password is not retained in the Internet System Preferences pane.

- Mail and iChat continue to prompt users for their passwords after saving them in the keychain.

- Applications are unable to retrieve items from a keychain file located on a network volume.

Keychain Access and changing passwords. If you change your account password, the password for login.keychain is automatically changed as well. This allows the keychain to continue to open automatically at login. However, if you (as an administrator) change another user's password in the Accounts System Preferences pane, the login.keychain password is not changed; the user must do this herself. However, to do so, the user must first enter the unchanged password—if he or she can't remember it, there's no backdoor to get into the Keychain file. The best the user can do in such situations is select Keychain First Aid and click the Options button. From here, the user can click the Reset My Keychain button to create a new Keychain file that uses the new password; however, the file itself will be empty. The old file is not deleted but rather saved in the Library/Keychains folder of the user's Home directory.

Note: In Jaguar, Keychain First Aid is a stand-alone free downloadable utility, available from Apple's Web site.

Show Status in Menu Bar. Finally, if you select Show Status in Menu Bar from the View menu, a Lock menu is added to the menu bar. You can use this menu to lock or unlock any Keychain file. One further surprise in this menu is the Lock Screen command: If you select it, your Mac will launch whatever effect you have selected in the Desktop & Screen Saver System Preferences. However, you will now need to enter your login password before you can get the screen effect to stop. This is an alternative to permanently requiring the use of a password via the option in the Security System Preferences pane.

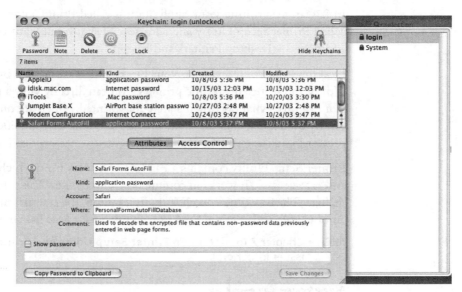

Figure 2.45

Keychain Access.

NetInfo Manager

The NetInfo Manager utility lets you access and modify the database that stores much of the critical information used by Mac OS X, including the details of each user's account (their passwords, short names, and so on). Several components of Mac OS X software, such as the Accounts System Preference, access this database. NetInfo Manager allows you to access it directly, though it provides little user-friendly help on how to use it.

SEE: • "NetInfo and NetInfo Manager" and "Root Access," in Chapter 4, for more on NetInfo Manager.

Network Utility

Network Utility tests and troubleshoots network connections. If you are having trouble with an Internet connection, this utility can help you diagnose the source of the problem.

SEE: • Chapter 8 for details on Network Utility and network issues in general.

Printer Setup Utility

Printer Setup Utility is what you use to select printers and manage print jobs. You need printer driver software for a given printer to be present before you can set up the printer via Printer Setup Utility. Mac OS X ships with a large number of printer drivers already installed; others may be available from the printer manufacturer or third parties. To actually print to a given printer, you must first add the printer to Printer Setup Utility's Printer List.

In Jaguar, the printing setup application is called Print Center. In Panther, it is called Printer Setup Utility and adds several significant features. The biggest additions are Desktop Printers and Faxing.

Desktop Printers are icons on your Desktop that are created by Printer Setup Utility and represent specific printers. You can directly view a printer's status (for example, what documents are being printed, which are on hold, and so on) by double-clicking the icon. You can also drag a document to a desktop printer to initiate printing of the document.

Printer Setup Utility contains a Fax List of devices from which you can send and receive faxes. It works in conjunction with the new Fax command in Print dialogs. The first time you click the Fax button, the internal modem will be automatically added to the Fax List (assuming your Mac has an internal modem).

SEE: • **Chapter 7 for details on Printer Setup Utility and printing and faxing issues in general.**

System Profiler

System Profiler provides details about the software and hardware currently in use. To open it, you can launch it from its icon in the Utilities folder or click the More Info button in the About This Mac window.

You can select what you want to do from the following four choices in the left sidebar:

• **Hardware.** Click the Hardware item, and you get a hardware overview in the pane to the right. The overview lists such basics as CPU type and speed, amount of memory, bus speed, and firmware (Boot ROM) version.

Clicking the Hardware disclosure triangle reveals a list of the following hardware subcategories: memory, PCI/AGP Cards, IDE (ATA), SCSI, USB, FireWire, AirPort Card, and Modems. When you click any item, the right-pane display shifts to reveal details regarding that item. For example, Memory displays the size, type, and speed of each memory card you have installed. There is no option to list devices connected via an Ethernet network (such as a printer).

If you're having problems with any external device, these items are a good place to check first. If the device is not listed, the Mac doesn't recognize it as being connected.

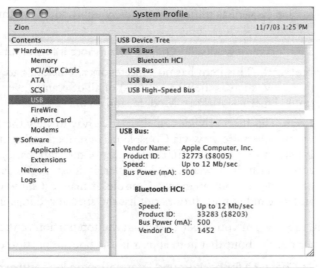

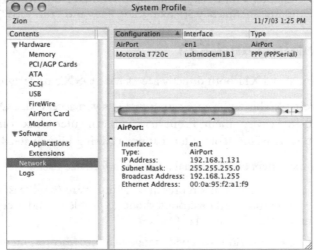

Figure 2.46

System Profiler: (top) USB list; (bottom) Network list.

- **Software.** Click the Software item, and you get a software overview in the pane to the right. This overview displays the System version (including build number), kernel (Darwin) version, and the names of the boot volume, computer, and current user.

  Clicking the Software disclosure triangle reveals a list of software sub-categories, including Applications and Extensions. Click either item, and the right-pane display shifts to reveal information regarding that item. Applications provides a list of all applications on your drive and their version numbers; Extensions provides a list of all kernel extensions (items located in /System/Library/Extensions, and described more in Chapter 5), their version numbers, and whether they loaded at startup.

  If you select Extended Report from System Profiler's View menu, an additional item is added to this list: Frameworks. This lists all the items in the /System/Library/Frameworks and /System/Library/PrivateFrameworks folders (as well as framework items possibly added by third parties in the /Library folder).

SEE: • **"Frameworks," in Chapter 4, for more information about this topic.**

- **Network.** This item has no subcategories. Click it, and you get an overview (such as the IP addresses) of all of your active network connections: Ethernet, AirPort, Modem, and so on.

- **Logs.** This item provides an alternative way to view the log files that you would otherwise view via Console (as described earlier in this chapter). It lists current log files (in the top part of the right pane) and shows their contents (in the lower part). However, it doesn't offer as complete a list of log files as you can get via Console. It may just show the console.log and system.log files. It does not list the specialized logs in /var/logs.

In all cases, when you select an item in the top portion of the right pane, further details about that item appear in the bottom portion of the pane.

SEE: • **Chapter 4 for background information on logs and extensions—particularly "Technically Speaking: Log Files and Cron Jobs," for more on logs.**

Terminal and X11

Terminal and X11 both directly access Mac OS X's underlying Unix software.

Terminal. This is the application that lets you access Mac OS X's Unix command-line environment. From here, you can enter Unix commands just as if you were using a computer that was running Unix instead of Mac OS X.

Terminal offers two potential advantages for Mac users:

- In some cases, Unix represents the only way (or at least the most reliable way) to solve certain troubleshooting problems and access otherwise hidden features in Mac OS X.

- It opens the door to a wide range of Unix features, including the Apache Web server; use of perl, php, and sendmail; and much more.

Although I provide many examples of using Terminal to troubleshoot problems, I've tried to emphasize *non-Terminal* solutions whenever possible because this book is targeted at users who want to become proficient at troubleshooting Mac OS X *without* having to become Unix experts as well. Still, with minimal effort, you can learn enough Unix basics to use Terminal as an effective troubleshooting tool. This book provides those basics. Using Unix for such matters as advanced Web server setups, FTP server setups, and using sendmail, however, is beyond the scope of this book.

X11. Unix is a text-only environment. Although this may not be a significant limitation for such tasks as troubleshooting and server administration, it makes Unix noncompetitive (in comparison with Mac OS and Windows) when it comes to dealing with such productivity tasks as word processing and spreadsheets—

and especially when dealing with anything for which graphics are a requirement (such as editing graphic image files). X11 was created to deal with this limitation, providing a graphical interface for Unix called the X Window System. There now exists a healthy collection of software written for X11—from productivity suites to games. Mac OS X's X11 allows you to run these programs on your Mac.

In some cases, software will need to be modified by the developer in order to port it to Mac OS X's X11. You will also need to know how to install it on your Mac so that it runs. Details about this process can be found on various X11 Web sites, such as www.xfree86.org/.

To run an X11 program, add it to the X11 list (using the Customize command in the Application menu). Once you've done this, simply select its name in the Application menu, and the program will now open in windows with a Mac interface; you may not even be able to distinguish it from "regular" Mac software.

In a sense, Mac OS X itself is a GUI for Unix—which would make X11 unnecessary on a Mac, and indeed I suspect most Mac OS X users will never employ X11. However, X11 software is often free or much cheaper than comparable software running in Mac OS X and thus offers a cost-saving alternative to standard Mac software.

X11 is not installed by default when installing or upgrading to Panther. To install it, you need to select a custom installation and then select the X11 item. Alternatively, you can install X11 separately via the software available from Apple at www.apple.com/macosx/x11/.

SEE: • **Chapters 1 and 4 for background on Unix.**

• **Chapter 10 for details on how to use Terminal for troubleshooting.**

TAKE NOTE ▶ **Developer Software**

Mac OS X comes with a collection of developer software. In Mac OS X 10.2 and earlier, this collection is called Developer Tools. In Mac OS X 10.3, it is called Xcode Tools.

If you purchase a retail copy of Mac OS X, this software comes on a separate CD, called Xcode (or Developer Tools). If you purchase a Mac, the installer package files for the developer software are located in the Installers folder inside the Applications folder at the root level of your drive. Should you need to reinstall the Installers folder, you can do so via the Restore Software option (as described in Chapter 3).

If none of these options apply to you, you can still get the software by going to Apple's Developer Connection Web site at http://developer.apple.com/tools/xcode/index.html. You need to be an ADC member to download the software; happily, the online membership category is free and includes permission to download the developer software. Even if you already have the software, you should check here occasionally to see if newer versions are available.

continues on next page

TAKE NOTE ▶ Developer Software *continued*

From the perspective of a nondeveloper troubleshooter, the software remains similar to the older Developer Tools. The main addition in Xcode Tools is the Xcode application itself, which is designed to facilitate creating and compiling programming code.

For troubleshooting purposes alone, I would not bother installing most of the software on this CD. Instead, I would select to do a Custom Install and just install the first item in the list: Developer Tools Software. Deselect any other items that are enabled by default.

After installation, the Xcode Tools software is located in a folder called Developer at the root level of your Mac OS X volume. This folder has two subfolders of particular interest to troubleshooters:

- **Applications.** This is where programs such as Property List Editor (inside the Utilities folder) and Interface Builder are located.

- **Tools.** This is where Unix commands such as CpMac and SetFile are located. Applications here are Unix executable files and work via the Terminal application.

You will find examples of using this software throughout the book.

Note: Should you later want to uninstall Xcode Tools, you can use the uninstall-devtools.pl command, located in the Tools folder.

SEE: • **Chapters 3 and 4 for several examples of using Property List Editor.**
- **"The Mac OS X Install CDs or DVD," in Chapter 3, for more background on installing software.**
- **"Take Note: Unix Executable Files and TerminalShellScript Files," in Chapter 10, for details on how and why to run the software in the Tools folder.**

Figure 2.47

The software in /Developer/ Applications/ Utilities. This is where Property List Editor is located.

Third-party utilities

As rich as the programs in the Utilities folder are, they do not come close to providing all the troubleshooting help you might want. Fortunately, third-party software developers have jumped in to fill the gaps, providing an array of useful utilities. These programs run the gamut from freeware to shareware to commercial. They include utilities such as XRay, BootCD, SharePoints, Pseudo, Locator, LaunchBar, Data Recycler X, and DiskWarrior. Rather than list and describe them all here, I cover them in my discussions of the topics for which they are intended.

3

Installing, Upgrading, Backing Up, and Restoring Mac OS X

Chances are, you were using Mac OS X even before you bought this book, since the operating system comes preinstalled (and is likely set as the default) on all Macs sold in the last few years. (In fact, if you bought a Mac in 2003 or later, Mac OS X may be the *only* bootable OS.) And even if you own an older Mac, the fact that you're reading this volume means you've probably already installed Mac OS X on it!

For that reason, I provided an overview of Mac OS X (in Chapter 2) *before* this description of how to install the operating system, believing that most of you are already up and running in Mac OS X. Even if that's the case, though, you may someday be called upon to install Mac OS X on an older Mac that's still running Mac OS 9. Or, even more important, you may need to *re*-install Mac OS X (to fix problems). Finally, as new versions of Mac OS X are released, you will need to upgrade your OS. For all of these occasions, this chapter explains what needs to be done (and why) and offers solutions to a variety of potential problems.

I start off by providing background information on installing Mac OS X for the first time, moving on to provide more general information about installing, reinstalling, and restoring Mac OS X software. You'll also learn about upgrading Mac OS X and find recommendations about how best to back up Mac OS X.

In This Chapter

What You Need to Install and Run Mac OS X

Well, for starters, you need the Mac OS X Install CDs or DVD. Beyond that, keep reading ...

Which Mac models can run Mac OS X?

Apple's official position is that only the following Macs can run Mac OS X 10.3.0 (older and newer versions of Mac OS X may have different requirements):

- Power Macintosh G3 (Blue and White)
- PowerBook G3 (with built-in USB)
- Any Power Mac G4 or G5
- Any PowerBook G4
- Any iMac or eMac
- Any iBook

Older versions of Mac OS X supported the original (beige) G3 Power Mac. Panther does not.

If you're uncertain of your own Mac processor, select About This Mac from the Apple menu and check the Processor line. (If you're currently running Mac OS 9, select Apple System Profiler from the Apple menu.)

Figure 3.1

The About This Mac window shows that this Mac is a PowerBook G4, which means it can run Mac OS X.

Does this mean that you absolutely cannot use Mac OS X on an older Mac—even one that's been upgraded to include a G4 processor (such as a Power Mac 7500 with a processor upgrade)? Apple's position remains firm: You cannot run Mac OS X on these Macs. However, some users (who won't take no for an answer!) *have* found ways to run Mac OS X on at least some of these older Macs. If you're willing to give it a shot, the utility XPostFacto provides a good starting point. Be aware, however, that if you have any problems running Mac OS X on these systems, Apple will not help you solve them.

For that reason, I strongly recommend that if you want to run Mac OS X, get a Mac that's sanctioned to run it.

That said, even some Macs that *are* on Apple's approved list have been known to have problems with Mac OS X. Here is one example:

PowerBook G3 (Lombard bronze keyboard model). There have been numerous reports that some of these PowerBooks cannot run Mac OS X if extra memory is installed in the top RAM slot. (The PowerBook typically shipped from Apple with this slot empty.) Freezes and system crashes (or *kernel panics*, as they're called in Mac OS X and as discussed in Chapter 5) are the primary symptoms. The consensus view is that the problem is caused by the processor used by some (but not all) of this model of PowerBook. The reason for this is that there appear to be two variations of the processor: copper-based and aluminum-based, the former of which appears to be the problem child. The best fix is to replace the logic board. As of this writing, however, Apple had not officially confirmed this information—which means you may or may not be able to get Apple to do a logic-board swap for free.

How much memory do you need?

If you know your Mac can run Mac OS X, your next step is to make sure it has enough memory (RAM) installed. Without sufficient RAM, Mac OS X may run, but performance may be unacceptably slow—to the point where the OS may seem to freeze at times.

Apple says you need at least 128 MB of memory to use Mac OS X. Consider this figure to be a bare minimum. To get the best performance from Mac OS X, I recommend at least 512 MB—more, ideally.

Every Mac can accommodate more memory than the minimum that ships from Apple. Typically, you add memory by purchasing a memory module and inserting it into the designated RAM slot(s) on your Mac. Each Mac model comes with instructions on how to do this, and Apple makes sure that process is relatively easy. On a desktop Power Mac, for example, you don't need any tools. Just open the door, insert the RAM into the location described in the manual, and you're finished.

How much hard-drive space do you need?

Apple says you should have a minimum of 2 GB of free space on your hard drive before attempting to install Mac OS X (3.5 GB if you intend to install the developer software). (The amount of "available" hard-drive space is typically listed at the top of each Finder window.) However, Mac OS X runs best when you have a good deal *more* unused space. Given the size and price of today's hard drives, I recommend that you make sure you have at least 5 GB of unused space on your Mac OS X volume *after* Mac OS X and any additional software have been installed.

We'll return to the issue of hard-drive space later in the chapter when I cover the pros and cons of partitioning a drive.

7 items, 40.07 GB available

Figure 3.2

The amount of disk space available, as viewed in Panther's status bar at the bottom of a Finder window.

Will you be installing Mac OS 9?

Mac OS 9 applications are able to run seamlessly within Mac OS X—a capability derived from Mac OS X's Classic-environment feature (which you'll learn more about in Chapter 9). To take advantage of this capability, however, Mac OS 9 must be installed somewhere on your drive. If you're running Mac OS X 10.2 or later, you need Mac OS 9.2.x installed.

If you don't know which version of Mac OS X is installed on your computer, just choose the About This Mac item from the top of the Apple menu. The window that opens provides this information. Similarly, to determine the version of Mac OS 9, select About This Computer from the Apple menu that appears when a Classic application is active in Mac OS 9 or when booted from Mac OS 9. Otherwise, you can check the version number by opening the Mac OS 9 System Folder, selecting Get Info (Command-I) for the System or Finder file, and checking the version information. If Classic is running, you can also get this information from the Memory/Versions tab of the Classic System Preferences.

Currently shipping Macs come with Mac OS X and Mac OS 9 preinstalled. If, for some reason (perhaps because you erased your drive and reinstalled just Mac OS X), Mac OS 9 is not installed, you can reinstall it by using a Mac OS 9 Install CD (if you have one) or the Software Restore disc(s) that came with your Mac.

SEE: • **"Using Software Restore" and "What About Mac OS 9?" later in this chapter.**

Other requirements

Check the Read Before You Install file for more information that may be relevant to your particular setup. This file is included as a text document on the Mac OS X Install CD (or DVD). The contents of the file are also presented when you run the Install utility.

SEE: • **"Cannot Select a Volume to Install," and "Software installs but fails to Work," later in this chapter, for related information.**

• **"Take Note: Startup Failure When Starting Up from an External Device," in Chapter 5, for more details.**

Installing or Reinstalling Mac OS X

There are three situations in which you will want to install or reinstall Mac OS X:

• Mac OS X has never been installed on your Mac. Presumably, you purchased a retail version of Mac OS X, and you now want to install it.

• You erased a drive on which Mac OS X was installed (perhaps because it contained corrupted data you could not fix), and you now want to reinstall Mac OS X.

• Mac OS X is installed on your drive, but you want to upgrade to a major new version (such as when going from Mac OS X 10.2 to Mac OS X 10.3), or you want to reinstall a version already installed (perhaps in hopes of eliminating suspected problems with the currently installed copy).

The primary way to install or reinstall Mac OS X is via the Mac OS X Install CDs (or DVD)—which either came with your computer or you purchased separately. In some cases, you may also want to use the Restore Software CDs/DVD that came with your computer. Finally, in those cases where you are installing an updated version of Mac OS X over an existing version, you may be using a Mac OS X Update CD instead of an Install CD. I discuss all of these variations in the sections that follow.

The Mac OS X Install CDs or DVD

The Mac OS X Install software is provided on either CD or DVD. The CD version contains three CDs: Install Disc 1, Install Disc 2, and Install Disc 3.

The main installation of Mac OS X software takes place from Disc 1.

Disc 2 includes numerous additional .pkg files in its Packages folder—including those that contain the software for iCal, iMovie, Microsoft Internet Explorer, iPhoto, iSync, iTunes, and StuffIt Expander—as well as files for additional printer drivers and for foreign language support. Disc 3 contains the X11 software, Additional Speech Voices, more printer drivers, and a few other components.

Figure 3.3

This is the window that appears when you launch the Install Mac OS X application from a Mac OS X Install CD.

Via the Installer's Custom Install option, you can bypass installing the Disc 2 and Disc 3 software by deselecting the software on those discs. Otherwise, after installing Mac OS X from Disc 1 and restarting your Mac, you're prompted to insert Disc 2 and Disc 3 to finish the installation. You needn't be concerned with what's actually on each CD; the Installer coordinates the entire installation.

On some Macs that come with DVD drives, Apple now ships the Install and Restore software on a single bootable DVD. The rules of use remain largely the same, except that you are working with a single DVD instead of multiple CDs, so you don't have any discs to swap. In the discussions that follow, I typically assume you're using the CDs.

Xcode Tools. The retail version of Mac OS X 10.3 (Panther) also includes an Xcode Tools CD, which installs software for developers. However, because some of the software is of more general value, I recommend installing it.

SEE: • "Take Note: Developer Software," in Chapter 2, for more details on obtaining and installing this software.

Startup from the Mac OS X Install CD/DVD

As you would expect, you start the installation process by using Mac OS X Install Disc 1 (or the single DVD). If you're currently running Mac OS 9 or Mac OS X from your hard drive, insert the CD and click the Install Mac OS X icon (it's in the Welcome to Mac OS X folder that opens by default when the CD mounts). From the window that appears, click the Restart button. Next, you will be prompted to give your administrator's password, if you are running Mac OS X. Do so, and you will restart from the CD.

Alternatively, select the CD or DVD as the startup volume via the Startup Disk control panel (in Mac OS 9, if your Mac is using Mac OS 9) or the Startup Disk System Preferences pane (in Mac OS X) and restart. You can also boot directly from the CD by inserting it at startup and holding down the C key.

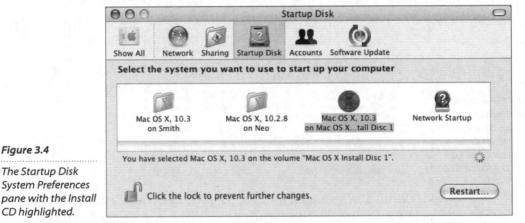

Figure 3.4

The Startup Disk System Preferences pane with the Install CD highlighted.

On restart, the gray Apple logo screen will appear, followed by the blue screen with the Mac OS X logo. Beneath the logo, you will see the words *Preparing installation*. This is quickly followed by the launch and appearance of the Installer utility.

Before you go any further, look at the menus available from the Installer utility. Two that are of special interest are Installer and File.

TAKE NOTE ▶ **Installing Mac OS X** *Without* **Starting Up from the Install CD?** *Maybe ...*

To install Mac OS X on a volume other than the current startup volume, you don't necessarily have to restart from the Mac OS X Install CD. Instead, mount the CD and go to the /System/ Installation/Packages folder (not found in the System folder on a hard drive running Mac OS X), which contains all the pkg files used by the Mac OS X Install CD. From within this folder, locate the OSInstall.mpkg file and then double-click it to launch the Installer utility. You should now be able to install the software.

Note, however, that you do this at your own risk: I've seen cases where it *hasn't* worked. The safest bet is to start up from the CD.

When installing Mac OS X Server on a Mac that already has the Mac OS X client installed, this method may be required. That is, you may need to start up from your hard drive (rather than the Server CD) and initiate the installation by double-clicking the MacOSXServerInstall.mpkg on the Mac OS X Server CD (rather than using the Install Mac OS X Server application). See the following Apple Knowledge Base document for details of one such example: http://docs.info. apple.com/article.html?artnum=107496.

The Installer menu

Included among the Installer menu commands are the following, which are of particular interest to troubleshooters:

Change Startup Disk. This comes in handy if you can't get your Mac to start up from a particular hard drive or get it to shift to an alternative bootable hard drive as its default choice. By selecting this command, you can specify any currently available bootable drive as the default. Once you've done this, click Restart to reboot the Mac using that drive.

Reset Password. If you've already installed Mac OS X, you can use this command to enter a new password for any Mac OS X user—an important back door of last resort in case you cannot recall your own password. Click Save to save your changes.

This arrangement also represents an obvious security weakness, since it means that anyone with a Mac OS X Install CD can change your password to gain access to your system (although you can set an Open Firmware password to prevent this, as described in Chapter 5). The security risk is the tradeoff for the ability to recover from a forgotten password. The user list displayed here includes all of the user accounts you've set up, plus the root user (if enabled) and an odd one called Application Server (appserver). Ignore this last one.

You can only access the Reset Password command if you're starting up from a CD. If you launch the Installer application from a hard drive, this option will not appear.

Actually, the CD Installer accesses a separate utility called Password Reset, which is also included on the CD. This utility works only if you start up from the CD, however. Should you copy the utility to a Mac OS X hard drive and try to run it from there, it will not work.

SEE: • "Logging in as root," in Chapter 4, for more on the Reset Password command.

Open Disk Utility. This command takes you to a window in which you can select First Aid (used to repair a disk) or a variety of other options to reformat or partition your drive. I cover Disk Utility in more detail elsewhere in this book (both later in this chapter and again in Chapter 5). For an overview of what is available via Disk Utility, see "Disk Utility" in Chapter 2.

In general, you will not need to use Disk Utility at this point—with one exception. The default setup for a drive, as shipped from Apple, is to have one partition. Should you want to have two or more partitions, you will need to use Disk Utility to set up the additional partitions.

SEE: • "Take Note: Why and How to Partition," below, for information on how and why you would want to partition a drive when using Mac OS X.
   • Chapter 5 for more on startup issues, including using passwords and Disk Utility.

TAKE NOTE ▶ Why and How to Partition

Partitioning a drive means dividing it into two or more separate volumes. Each volume in turn mounts separately when you launch your Mac. In most respects, the volumes behave just as if you had two (assuming you made two partitions) separate hard drives (rather than just one). The only times it will be apparent that just one hard drive is at work are when the hard drive fails or if you need to reformat it.

All drives ship from Apple with just one partition. Thus, if you want two or more partitions, you must create them yourself. Using Mac OS X software, changing the number of partitions on a drive requires erasing its contents. Thus, anything on your drive that you want to save, you will need to back up first—which is precisely why I recommend partitioning a drive the day you unpack your new Mac. There will be nothing to back up because you haven't used it yet—which means the process will be simplified considerably.

continues on next page

TAKE NOTE ▶ Why and How to Partition *continued*

Why Partition?

A primary benefit of partitioning is that if you make both volumes startup volumes, you have two ways of starting up your Mac from the same drive. If you're having trouble with Volume A, for example, and you need to restart from another volume to fix the problem, Volume B is ready to go. You don't necessarily need to seek out a CD or other external medium.

Even if you don't choose to make the second partition bootable, you can still use it to store backups of important personal files (such as documents and photos) that are stored on the first partition. Or (as I discuss more in Chapter 6), you can choose to store Mac OS X's virtual-memory swap files or even your entire Home directory on the second partition (to protect them from problems with the boot volume).

Note: The best and safest option is still to move or copy these items to another drive altogether, not just another partition of the same drive.

In any case, you can erase one partition (for example, via the Installer's Erase and Install option) without erasing any others. The day may come, for example, when Mac OS X files get so messed up that the only solution is to erase the volume and start over. With two partitions, you can erase the boot partition without losing whatever is on the second partition.

Mac OS 9 on the second partition. If you have a Mac that's still capable of booting from Mac OS 9, you can make the alternate volume a Mac OS 9 boot volume. In fact, the ideal arrangement is to maintain two Mac OS 9 System Folders: one on a separate partition from Mac OS X and a second on the same partition as Mac OS X. This technique allows you to use one version of Mac OS 9 (typically the one on its own partition) when you want to boot from Mac OS 9 and the other (the one on the Mac OS X partition) when you want to launch Classic. The benefit of this is that some files work in Mac OS 9 directly but not in Classic (for more on this, see Chapter 9). Thus, with only one copy of Mac OS 9 installed, you may have to choose between giving up on these programs (primarily extensions and control panels) so that you can use Classic or keeping them (so that you can boot from Mac OS 9) and giving up on Classic. With two Mac OS 9 Systems, you can have your cake and eat it, too!

A related benefit: If you hold down the Option key at startup (as discussed in Chapter 5), you can select a startup volume. If Mac OS X and Mac OS 9 reside on the same partition, however, only the most recently booted OS will appear. If you cannot start up from Mac OS X, for example, you will not be able to use this method to switch to starting up from Mac OS 9, because the Mac OS 9 System Folder will not be listed as an option. Your only option is to start up from a CD. With Mac OS 9 and Mac OS X on separate partitions, the Mac OS 9 choice would be available, and you could bypass the need for the CD—helpful if you need to boot in Mac OS 9 to back up files before erasing a troublesome Mac OS X volume.

continues on next page

TAKE NOTE ▶ Why and How to Partition *continued*

Mac OS X on the second partition. Alternatively, especially for Macs that cannot boot from Mac OS 9, you can have the second partition be a second Mac OS X boot volume. In this case, I would boot from the second partition only in emergencies, since regularly switching back and forth between two Mac OS X installations can lead to confusion and problems, such as permissions errors that prevent files from opening.

Bottom line: I recommend partitioning a drive, even if you don't have a Mac that can boot from Mac OS 9. The only exception would be if your hard drive was too small to adequately support separate partitions. In general, if your hard drive is at least 20 GB (and certainly if it's 40 GB or more), I strongly recommend dividing it into two partitions.

How to Partition?

The following are some general instructions for dividing a drive into two partitions. Remember: Doing so will erase all existing data on any and all current partitions for this drive.

1. After starting up from a Mac OS X Install CD (as described in the main text), from the Install menu select the Disk Utility command.

2. Select the drive you want to partition from the list in the left column of the Disk Utility window.

3. Click the Partition button.

4. From the Volume Scheme menu, select "2 partitions."

5. Click-hold the divider between the partitions to adjust their sizes as desired.

   Mac OS X works best when you have a healthy amount of unused hard-drive space on the boot volume. Thus, in choosing a partition size, make sure that you'll have at least several gigabytes of unused space *after* you've completed the installation. If this is not the case, I recommend getting a larger hard drive or not partitioning.

6. Click the first of the two partitions. In the Volume Information section, enter a name in the Name text box and select Mac OS Extended or Mac OS Extended (Journaled) in the Format pop-up menu.

   Now click the second partition and repeat the process.

   Note: If you intend to boot from Mac OS 9, make sure the Mac OS 9 Drivers Installed option is checked, if such an option is present. In Panther, if your Mac cannot boot from Mac OS 9 (as is the case for all currently shipping Macs), you will not get this option. Instead, you will see text that states, "No options available."

7. Click the Partition button.

8. Now that the partitions have been created, the next thing you'll likely want to do is install Mac OS X on one partition, including restoring all the additional software (including Mac OS 9) that was on your Mac when it first arrived. Refer to the sections on installing and restoring software, in the main text of this chapter, for details on how to do this.

continues on next page

TAKE NOTE ▶ Why and How to Partition *continued*

9. Finally, after restarting from your newly installed Mac OS X volume, if you want Mac OS 9 on the second partition, copy the Mac OS 9 System Folder—as well as the Applications (Mac OS 9) folder, if you want—to the second partition, via drag and drop, so that you have a separate copy of the System Folder there. You can delete the original Mac OS 9 software after you've copied it, should you want only one Mac OS 9 System on your drive.

   If you instead want Mac OS X on the second partition, don't drag and drop the Mac OS X System software from one partition to the other. This will not result in a bootable partition. To install Mac OS X on the second partition, use the Installer a second time.

Partitioning without erasing. There are now utilities that can partition your drive on the fly—without erasing its contents. With FWB's Partition Toolkit, for example, you can avoid most of the above steps. Simply partition the drive of your new Mac, creating a second empty one. Now drag the Mac OS 9 software to the second drive, and you're finished! Unfortunately, the current version of Partition Toolkit only works in Mac OS 9 and does not work in the Classic environment; thus, if you have a Mac that cannot boot into Mac OS 9, you will not be able to use this utility.

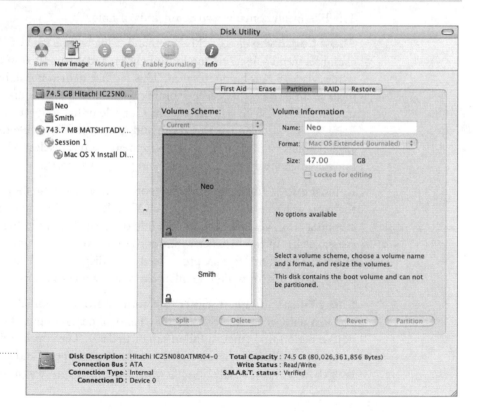

Figure 3.5

The partition options of Disk Utility.

TAKE NOTE ▶ Where Are the Utilities on the Install Disc?

The Choose Startup Disk, Reset Password, and Disk Utility applications are stored in the Utilities folder inside the Applications folder stored at the root level of the CD or DVD. When you select these applications from the Installer menu, it actually launches the copy of the utility found here. This /Applications/Utilities folder also contains the Open Firmware Password Utility (discussed in Chapter 5).

This folder is separate from the Utilities folder in the Welcome to Mac OS X folder.

Quit Installer. If you select this command before you install Mac OS X, a window appears asking if you are sure you want to quit the Installer. Your choices are Quit, Don't Quit, and Startup Disk. Choosing Startup Disk launches the same screen that appears when you select the Change Startup Disk command. If you choose Quit, your Mac simply restarts.

The File menu

The File menu contains two commands of note:

Show Log. If you choose this command, a log will be kept of all actions (for example, menu selections and button clicks) and errors (if any) that occur while Mac OS X is being installed. This log file, named install.log, is stored in the /var/log directory on the volume where Mac OS X is installed. After installing Mac OS X, you can use the Console utility to locate and view it. Prior to that, you can use this command to view the log while the Installer application is running. From a pop-up menu, you can select whether to limit log viewing to just errors, or errors and progress messages.

In most cases, you can ignore any reported errors, because they don't imply that you won't be able to install Mac OS X. If you really trip over a show-stopping error, you will almost certainly be warned about it directly, via a message alert in the Installer window. In other words, you won't need to check the log. The log may prove useful as a diagnostic aid, however, if a problem occurs for which no other explanatory message appears.

Show Files. You cannot select this command from the initial Installer display; you can only access it later—exactly when will depend upon the installation you're performing (that is, full install or update). The command will *likely* be active by the time the Select a Destination screen appears and certainly no later than after the installation has completed (and before you restart).

If you select this command, you will get a list of every file that gets installed by the current Installer setup and the exact folder locations in which each file will be placed. You can save this list as a text document. Although this information is not critical for the initial installation, it will become of more interest when you update the OS and want to see what files the updater installed.

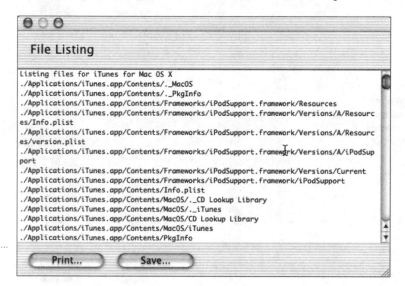

Figure 3.6

A Show Files listing in an Installer.

Introduction

Returning to the main Installer window, you begin with the Introduction screens. Your first job is to select a language from the Select Language screen. This determines the language used in the remaining windows as well as the main language used by Mac OS X after it is installed. Presumably, most readers of this book will select English. After you've selected a language, click the Continue button to reach the Welcome to Mac OS X Installer screen. Read the brief message and click Continue again. You have now completed the Introduction.

Read Me and Software License Agreement

Next up is the Read Me screen, which contains important information about the requirements for installing Mac OS X and what you need to do before actually installing it. For example, it will likely warn you about checking for firmware updates.

The Software License Agreement screen is up next: Simply agree to the terms and then move on.

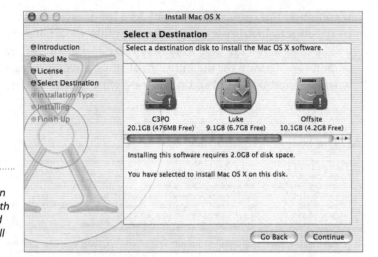

Figure 3.7

The Select a Destination screen of the Installer, with a volume selected on which to install Mac OS X.

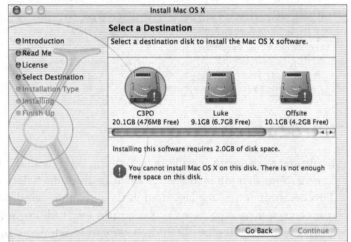

Figure 3.8

Installer refuses to install. The error message on the bottom appeared when trying to install Mac OS X on a volume with insufficient free space.

Select a Destination

Finally, we get to the first of the two critical screens for installing Mac OS X: Select a Destination.

In this screen, you will see an icon for every mounted volume (that is, each drive and partition of a drive). Some icons may include a symbol (such as a octagon with an exclamation point) indicating that you cannot currently install Mac OS X on that volume. If you do click on the volume, a message will appear at the bottom of the window, indicating what the problem is and what you can do about it. One problem, for example, might be insufficient free disk space.

Once you've selected a volume, click the Options button at the bottom of the screen. Select from among the following options and then close the window:

- **Upgrade Mac OS X or Install Mac OS X.** This option will read Upgrade OS X if your selected volume includes an updatable version of Mac OS X. If it does not, the option will read Install OS X and install a new copy of Mac OS X on the volume. Typically, the appropriate choice here is the default option—which means you actually could bypass this Options screen. However, in some cases, such as if there is insufficient disk space to upgrade, this option will be dimmed and you will have to select one of the remaining two. You may also decide to use one of the remaining options even if this one is available.

  With either option (but especially the Upgrade option), the Installer just installs or replaces the OS files that are new or updated. Thus, any documents you created or third-party software you added should be preserved.

- **Archive and Install.** This option, which made its first appearance in Mac OS X 10.2, is extremely welcome. For a volume that already contains Mac OS X, archiving will move the existing OS software (essentially the System, Library, and Applications folders, plus all Unix software) to a new folder named Previous Systems, located at the root level of your drive. The first time you do this, the software is placed in a folder named Previous System 1 inside the Previous Systems folder. If you repeat this process, a Previous System 2 will be created and used, and so on. A new copy of Mac OS X software is installed in place of the moved copy.

  This process also moves the Developer folder (if one is present) to Previous Systems. To replace this folder, you need to install the Developer Tools software separately.

  A sub-option here is Preserve Users and Network Settings. When you choose this option, both the contents of the Users folder (which contains your Home directory!) and your Network settings are preserved. In almost all cases, I recommend enabling this option; if you don't, you'll have to re-create your accounts from scratch. About the only reason you wouldn't choose to preserve would be if you thought files in your Home directory were causing a problem, which you didn't want to carry over to Jaguar.

  In addition to preserving the contents of your Users folder, this option also preserves your Network System Preferences settings. It may also preserve third-party software that would not get preserved via a standard Archive and Install (such as certain software in the Applications folder).

  Note: This option does not preserve *all* system settings, just *most* of them. For example, it does not preserve settings pertaining to whether a network time server is used; the list of configured printers (stored in /etc/printers.conf); the computer's time zone (stored in /etc/localtime); the resolution of your display(s), and other settings if more than one display is connected, such as arrangement (stored in the com.apple.windowserver.plist in /Library/Preferences, ~/Library/Preferences/ByHost/); and Sharing Preferences pane settings (stored in /etc/hostconfig). Most of this is minor stuff and can be easily reset if lost.

Note: If you proceed past the Select a Destination screen and then use the Back button to return, the Preserve Users and Network Setting option may be dimmed and unselectable. If so, select another volume (if possible) and then return to the original volume. Otherwise, you'll need to restart the Installer to re-enable the option.

SEE: • **"Take Note: Why and How to Use Archive and Install," for more details on this option.**

• **Erase and Install.** This option erases your drive and gives you the opportunity to reformat the volume as Mac OS X Extended (Journaled) or (the rarely used) Unix File System.

Obviously, you shouldn't choose this option if you're installing Mac OS X on a drive that includes software you don't want to erase.

Typically, you would only select the Erase and Install option if you suspected such severe drive problems that even a Mac OS X Archive and Install would be unable to fix them. In such cases, you would want to save any critical data on the drive before erasing it. To do this, start up from another hard drive or partition (assuming you can do so) and back up anything you want to save from the problem volume. Then relaunch the Install CD and select to Erase and Install.

Avoid using Unix File System (UFS) unless you know you need it—and you almost certainly won't! For starters, Mac OS X Extended is the same format that Mac OS 9 uses. If you select UFS, you will not be able to use that partition for Mac OS 9. UFS drives also prevent some Mac OS X applications from working correctly. About the only people who might prefer UFS formatting are the select few running Mac OS X Server and thus working primarily with the Unix software in Mac OS X, not the Aqua applications.

Note: Alternatively, you can use Disk Utility to erase any volume (other than the current startup volume) at any time. To do so, launch Disk Utility, select the desired partition or disk, and click the Erase button. From the screen that appears, select a name and format for the volume. Then click Erase.

SEE: • **"Disk Utility," in Chapter 2, for more details on using Erase, including additional format options available from here.**

• **"Performing Repairs with Disk Utility (First Aid)," in Chapter 5, for more on what "journaled" means.**

TECHNICALLY SPEAKING ▶ Case-Sensitive HFS Plus

If you're using Mac OS X Server, you will be presented with an additional Format option: Case-sensitive HFS Plus (+), which may also be listed as "Mac OS Extended (case-sensitive)."

This format is exactly like the ordinary Mac OS Extended format, except that all file and folder names are case sensitive. That is, a folder with the name My Memos is seen as distinct from one named "My memos."

continues on next page

TECHNICALLY SPEAKING ▶ **Case-Sensitive HFS Plus** *continued*

In contrast, both of these would be treated as the same folder in standard Mac OS Extended (in fact, you couldn't even create two folders with these names in the same parent folder; instead, you would get a message saying the name already exists).

Note: Although case is preserved in standard Mac OS X Extended—that is, the Finder remembers that the *M* in *Memos* is uppercase—the name is not treated differently in searches or file databases from one with a lowercase *m*.

The main rationale for this is that Unix is case sensitive. By setting up a server to be similarly case sensitive, it eliminates some potential problems and inconsistencies between Mac OS X's Unix base and the higher-level user interface.

However, although it may make sense for certain server setups to use this format, you should never use it in a client system. If you do, you risk seriously damaging your files and/or directory structure. For example, a repair utility (which is unaware of the case-sensitive format) may assume that My Memos and My memos, if in the same location, are the same folder and delete one of them. Actually, even for server setups, the case-sensitive option is intended only for data volumes, not startup volumes.

Note: If you run Jaguar's Disk Copy in Panther, you will see an option to format a new image as "Mac OS X Extended (Case-sensitive, Journaled)." I am not sure why this option pops up here, but I would not use it.

TAKE NOTE ▶ **Why and How to Use Archive and Install**

The Archive and Install feature in Mac OS X is similar to the old Clean Install feature of Mac OS 9. Rather than updating an existing installation, it in essence creates an entirely new installation of system software.

Why Archive? You would use the Archive option for either of the following reasons:

- **The Installer refuses to update or reinstall Mac OS X, and you don't want to reformat the drive.** This option is especially helpful when reinstalling Mac OS X from the CD would be a downgrade from the existing OS version (say, because you updated to Mac OS X 10.2.1 via Software Update after installing 10.2.0 from the CD). In Mac OS X 10.1.x, Apple strongly advised against doing any sort of downgrade installation, even if it seemed to be permitted by the Installer. At that time, Apple claimed that a downgrade could lead to the presence of files (especially Unix files and /System/Library files) from multiple OS versions in the same system—a potential source of conflicts. Apple's unwelcome solution was to erase your drive if you wanted or needed to do a downgrade installation. The Archive feature in Mac OS X solves this dilemma. Now you can downgrade without erasing by using Archive and Install to install the older version and then update to the newer version.

continues on next page

TAKE NOTE ▶ **Why and How to Use Archive and Install** *continued*

• **You want to preserve files from the previous OS version.** In some cases, you may worry that a simple upgrade will overwrite existing files that you may wish you had saved. The Installer may install a new version of an application that contains a new bug, for example. Going back to the old version may work around this bug until the inevitable bug-fix update is released. With the Archive function, the old application version is still in your Previous Systems folder and can be returned to active duty—assuming it works in Mac OS X. Similarly, you may want to replace some modified settings files—especially in the Unix software—with the new ones installed by Mac OS X, as detailed later in this sidebar.

For minor upgrades, such as from Mac OS X 10.2 to 10.2.1, the Options button is not available, meaning you cannot choose Archive and Install. Instead, your only option is Upgrade. However, if you're performing a major reference upgrade (that is where there is a change in the first number after the decimal, such as from Mac OS X 10.2.x to 10.3.x), you will be presented with a choice of options. In this case, I recommend using the Archive option and preserving the Users folders. There's pretty much no downside to this option, other than the additional disk space required to store the archived software. Some users recommend that you always select the Erase and Install option when you move to a major new OS version (such as from 10.2 to 10.3); however, I have not found this to be necessary.

Reinstalling software and resetting preferences after an Archive installation. After an Archive clean install, you may need to reinstall some third-party software to get it to work properly. You may also need to reset some serial-number registrations. For example, I needed to re-enter my QuickTime Pro 6 serial number, because updating via Archive and Install caused it to revert to my QuickTime Pro 5 number.

As noted in the main text, you may also need to re-create some Mac OS X Preferences settings. I needed to reset the time zone in Date & Time, for example, because it reverted to the Pacific time zone. I also had to re-enable the Network Time check.

Moving files after an Archive installation. After an Archive clean install, the archived OS software may contain a few files that you want to return to the now-current OS. As a general rule, I wouldn't move anything back until you discover that a setting or feature is missing and you can't re-create it easily by entering new settings. This way, you avoid the problems that can occur if you replace a needed newer file with an older one. Included among the items you may want to move back are the following:

• **Files and folders in the old /Library folder.** Files and folders that exist in your *archived* /Library folder but not in the updated /Library folder may contain additions and preferences files that you want to preserve. One example would be receipt files for third-party software in the Receipts folder. Also, if you're running a Web server from your Mac but are storing your files in the System's Web directory rather than your user-level Web directory, you should transfer any custom contents of /Library/WebServer/Documents. Third-party items in the Startup Items folder are also not moved.

continues on next page

TAKE NOTE ▶ Why and How to Use Archive and Install *continued*

- **Email addresses.** In some cases, especially prior to Panther, email addresses are not carried over after an Archive and Install. To fix this problem, do the following *before* launching Mail, Address Book, and iChat following the Archive and Install: Copy the Addresses folder from the Library folder of your previous Home directory to the Library folder of your current Home directory. Note that if you've already launched any of these applications, you will need to delete the AddressBook folder located in ~/Library/Application Support *before* you copy the Addresses folder.

- **Certain applications.** Some applications that need to have their password restored after an Archive and Install may not offer the option to re-enter the password. Instead, you may need to transfer an application's password/serial-number file from the Previous Systems folder. Otherwise, you may need to reinstall the application software.

If you do decide to transfer files back, you may be blocked from moving certain files due to insufficient permission access. In such cases, you will need to use techniques to modify permissions (such as those described in Chapter 6) so that you can bypass this blockade.

Deleting files after an Archive installation: Help files. You may want to delete some files that were carried over from the old Home directory to the new one. If you are having problems with Help Viewer, for example, check out "Take Note: Getting Help for Help" in Chapter 2.

Transferring Unix files. Finally, you may have reason to move back some directories and files in Unix's invisible /private directory. In particular, you may want to move the following files and folders:

- **/etc/hostconfig.** If you've set up sendmail on your Mac, this file is important and probably should be restored from Previous Systems to the current Mac OS X folder. (Note, however, that Panther uses postfix as its default Unix mail server, which means that this may be a good opportunity to switch, since postfix has a much better reputation than sendmail.)

- **/etc/httpd/httpd.conf.** If you edited your Apache configuration (used for Web server preferences beyond those you can set up via the Sharing System Preferences pane), move this file back.

- **/var/log.** This folder contains archives of system-level log files. If they're valuable to you, copy them over.

- **/var/root.** If you enabled the root user in Mac OS X, this folder is the root user's User folder: It contains the Desktop, Documents, and user-level Library directories, as well as any other files and folders that may have been created or saved to your Home directory when you were logged in as root or using an application as root. If this folder contains any files you want to save, transfer them back.

You may need to log in as a root user, launch a file utility as root, or boot from Mac OS 9 to make some of these changes.

continues on next page

TAKE NOTE ▶ **Why and How to Use Archive and Install** *continued*

Using the Previous Systems folder. One weakness of the Archive option is that the archived System is not bootable. In addition, the Installer does not offer a "switch back" option. Thus, if you decide that upgrading was a mistake (which is very unlikely!) and you want to return to Mac OS X 10.1.5, there's no easy way to do a reverse exchange. For that reason, make sure that your Mac OS X volume is backed up before doing the upgrade. Then if you decide to go back, you can restore the old Mac OS X version from your backup.

Note: The application software in the Previous Systems folder remains functional. Thus, if you double-click a document that uses one of these applications and a newer version is not available elsewhere, the document will attempt to launch via the application in the Previous Systems folder.

Preserve Users and Network Settings. As I stated in the main text, I generally recommend using the Preserve Users and Network Settings option when doing an Archive and Install. But what if you *did not* use it and later wish you had? Good news: You can still restore your Home directory; it will just be more work to do so. The directory is preserved in the /Previous Systems/Users folder. What you will need to do is create a new account for yourself, using the same short name as your old account. You can then copy files from the old account into the new one. You may need to reset permissions of some files, making yourself the owner, before you can use them. You can repeat this for any additional accounts you may have that you want to re-create.

Deleting Previous System (#) folder. After updating, you may eventually decide you no longer need any of the files stored in the Previous System 1 (or 2, and so on) folder and want to delete the folder to regain the disk space. To do so, you may need to change the ownership of the folder from System to your own name.

SEE: • **"Ownership & Permissions," in Chapter 4, for more on setting permissions.**

• **"Opening and Saving: Permissions Problems," and "Copying and Moving: Permissions Problems," in Chapter 6, for more on setting permissions.**

• **"Modifying invisible Unix files from Mac OS X applications," in Chapter 6, for related information.**

• **"Take Note: Deleting SystemConfiguration Folder Files," in Chapter 8, for more on where network settings are preserved.**

TECHNICALLY SPEAKING ▶ Custom Config Files After a Mac OS X Update

When you make custom changes to a config file, the changes may be wiped out when you update to a new version of Mac OS X. This is because the update replaces the customized config file with an updated default copy of the file. It will appear that all of your customized changes have been lost. In some cases, the Installer nicely preserves the customized file in the same directory, adding an extension to the name of the file, such as httpd.conf.applesaved or hostconfig.old. This allows you to recover your changes and add them back to the new file. Alternatively, you can swap the files so that the inactive file is returned to active duty. For example, for the httpd.conf files, give the active httpd.conf file a name such as httpd.conf.base and rename the applesaved file as httpd.conf. Doing this httpd.conf change requires root access and should be done with Personal Web Sharing turned off.

Starting in Mac OS X 10.2.5, Apple has reversed what happens when an update is installed, at least for the httpd.conf file. In describing this, Apple states, "Mac OS X 10.2.5 and later updates have a different installation method for the new httpd.conf file. The Installer checks to see if you have modified the existing httpd.conf file. If you have not, then it automatically replaces it with the new version. If you have modified it, then your modified file is left in place, and the new file is written as /etc/httpd/httpd.conf.default. At your leisure, you should add your modifications to the new file and retire the old one.

SEE: • "Modifying Invisible Unix Files from Mac OS X Applications," in Chapter 6, for related information.

TAKE NOTE ▶ Mac OS X Install CD vs. Upgrade CD

Any major Mac OS X update (typically defined as one in which the first digit after the decimal point changes, such as from 10.1 to 10.2) almost always requires a new full-installation Mac OS X CD—specifically, one that you must pay Apple to obtain. From this CD, you can fully install Mac OS X, even on an empty volume.

Between major updates, however, Apple releases minor updates. These free updates are available via Software Update or by downloading the update file from the Web. Such updates, however, can only be applied to already installed versions of Mac OS X (and sometimes only to just the immediately prior version). For example, a Mac OS X 10.2.3 Updater will only update a Mac OS X 10.2.2 installation. However, Apple might also release a "combined" updater (which Apple calls a Combo updater) that will update any version of Mac OS X 10.2 from 10.2.0 to 10.2.2.

continues on next page

TAKE NOTE ▶ Mac OS X Install CD vs. Upgrade CD *continued*

Falling somewhere between these extremes is the Update CD. For example, if you purchase the retail version of Mac OS X (Panther), the CDs are labeled Install Disc 1, Install Disc 2, and Install Disc 3. They function as described in the main text. If you instead obtain Panther from certain other sources, such as the Mac OS X Up to Date program (www.apple.com/macosx/uptodate/), the first CD of the pair may be labeled Upgrade Install Disc 1, or Install Disc 1 Upgrade Disc, instead of just Install Disc 1.

In the case of Jaguar upgrade discs, no Options button appears in the Installer's Select Destination window—meaning you don't have the Archive option. In fact, your only option is to update an existing version of Mac OS X 10.1. This limitation is significant, as it prevents you from using one of the key install features of Mac OS X: Archive and Install.

The Panther Upgrade CDs do include an Archive & Install option. However, it only works to upgrade a volume that is presently running Jaguar. You could not use this option, for example, to downgrade from Mac OS X 10.3.2 back to 10.3.0 (the version on the CD).

More generally, for any Jaguar or Panther Update CDs, you cannot install Mac OS X on a volume that does not already have an earlier version of Mac OS X installed. For such cases, you need the full Install CD software.

Installation type, installation, and finishing up

Finally, you'll reach the screen where you actually initiate the installation. By default, the Easy Install screen appears (unless your drive has insufficient disk space). This screen informs you of whether you need Disc 2 and/or Disc 3 for the installation. At this point, you can simply click the Install (or Upgrade) button and then sit back and relax. You have now reached the Installing stage. The installation may take 20 minutes or so to complete, during which time a variety of status messages appear, informing you of what is happening at each stage. Unless something goes wrong and the installation fails, you're finished with the installation process.

Custom Install. Rather than doing an Easy Install, you can click the Customize button to bring up the Custom Install screen. From here, you can enable or disable individual components of the installation—which means you can disable options you don't need in order to save drive space or simply reduce clutter.

Custom Install options include the following:

- **Essential System Software.** You cannot disable this option when installing Mac OS X; you can only do so when upgrading. And even then, I strongly advise against it—unless the only reason you're upgrading is to obtain a minor component of Mac OS X that you didn't install initially (such as a set of printer drivers).

- **BSD Subsystem.** The BSD Subsystem is made up of optional components of the otherwise essential Unix software at the core of Mac OS X (as discussed in Chapter 4). Although these components are technically optional, some applications may not run correctly without them. Again, other than for the reasons described above, I would never disable this option.

- **Additional Applications.** If you choose this option, you can omit the installation of specific applications such as Microsoft Internet Explorer.

- **Printer Drivers.** From here, you can elect to omit specific printer drivers (such as those for Epson or Lexmark printers). Panther also includes the Gimp-Print drivers, used for adding Mac OS X support to otherwise unsupported printers (as covered in Chapter 7).

- **Additional Speech Voices.** This option installs more voice choices for Mac OS X's text to-speech options.

- **Fonts and Language Translations.** These options provide the localized files and fonts that Mac OS X needs to support languages beyond English. If you're confident you don't need this support, disable these options. Doing so saves a significant amount of disk space. I always choose this option over an Easy Install when I install Mac OS X. If you want to just install files for one or two additional languages, you can do so. Click the disclosure triangle for Localized Files and enable the languages you want installed.

- **X11.** This installs the Unix X11 windowing system (see "Terminal and X11," in Chapter 2). This option is disabled by default, so you will need to do a Custom Install if you want to install it.

Restarting. When installation is complete (and you reach the Finish Up screen), you can choose to restart by quitting the Installer. If you don't, the Installer will restart automatically after a brief delay.

When you restart, the Mac should start up from the volume where you just installed or upgraded Mac OS X. If it instead boots from the CD, restart again and hold down the Eject key (or mouse button) until the CD ejects. If Disc 2 and/or Disc 3 are needed, you will be prompted to insert them at this point. The additional software on these discs is then installed. After you've completed this step (and if this is the first time you've installed Mac OS X), you will be prompted to set up an account for yourself, as well as Internet access, before you can log in. Otherwise, the Login window will appear or you will be automatically logged in, depending upon your preferences.

Checking for updates. Even if you've just installed Mac OS X, there may be minor updates that are newer than the installed version. For this reason, once you've successfully installed Mac OS X, you should run Software Update to check for and then install any updates. (If you're connected to the Internet on login, Software Update may launch automatically.)

Alternatively, if you previously downloaded the update files, you can install them directly from the .pkg files.

At this point, you can also install the Developer software from the Developer CD (if you have it). Updates to the Developer software are not listed in Software Update. Instead, you must check Apple's Developer Web site (http://developer.apple.com/tools) for updates to this software.

SEE: • **"Take Note: Developer Software," in Chapter 2, for more details.**

• **"Updating Mac OS X," later in this chapter, for more on updating.**

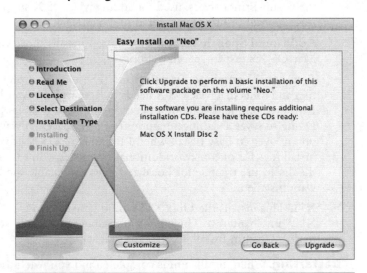

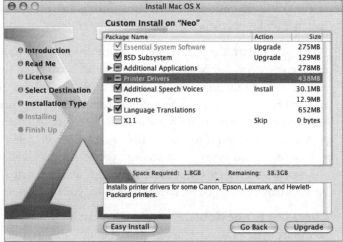

Figure 3.9

The Installer's Easy Install window (top) and Custom Install window (bottom).

Restoring Mac OS Software

The Mac OS X Installer installs the latest versions of the standard Mac OS X applications. However, your Mac may have come with a number of other applications, such as iDVD, games, and Mac OS 9. If you erased your drive prior to installing Mac OS X, or if one or more of these applications or Mac OS 9 has become damaged or corrupt, you'll probably want to get them back. Fortunately, most recent Macs (those that shipped with Jaguar or later preinstalled) come with Software Restore CDs (or a DVD). To restore the remaining software that may have come with your Mac, you need to use this Software Restore disc. (In fact, current versions of Software Restore discs are not bootable and no longer install Mac OS X–like older versions. They *require* that you install Mac OS X first.)

Note: The only thing that will not get restored by this method is the collection of music files included on most iMacs and iBooks. If you want to save these, you must back them up first. Software Restore also may not reinstall software that comes on its own CD, such as the World Book software.

Using Software Restore

To use Software Restore on recent Macs, follow these steps:

1. Insert the first Restore CD and double-click the Software Restore.pkg file. This installs and launches the Software Restore application in the Utilities folder (if it's not already installed); simply follow the instructions that appear.

    Note: On the Mac OS X Install and Restore DVD, double-click the Install Applications & Classic Support icon to begin this process.

    You can use this utility to restore software at any time—both immediately after you install Mac OS X and at some later point. Also note that Software Restore offers several Custom options, such as the ability to separately reinstall iMovie or iDVD. This is also how you would install (or reinstall) Mac OS 9.

    Note: If you want to do a "clean install" of Mac OS 9 (creating a new System Folder while preserving the old one), drag the Finder out of the existing Mac OS 9 System Folder (if you get a message saying you don't have permission to do this, give yourself permission, as described in Chapter 6). Once you've done this, change the name of the folder to Old System Folder and then proceed with installing Mac OS 9.

2. When you're finished using Software Restore, use Software Update to check for and install any more recent updates to the applications you just reinstalled. Alternatively, if you've already downloaded the updates to your drive, just launch the .pkg files directly and install them.

SEE: • "Updating Mac OS X," later in this chapter, for more details.

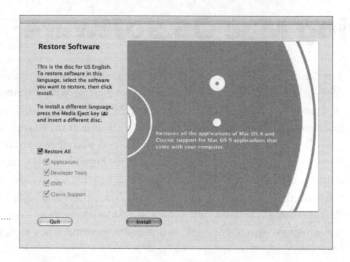

Figure 3.10

The Software
Restore window.

The core software used to run Software Restore is actually the Unix command asr (for *Apple Software Restore*), which you can access directly from Terminal. The cool thing about asr is that you can use it to restore anything, not just the files on the Software Restore CDs.

SEE: • **"Technically Speaking: More About Disk Utility's Image and Restore Features,"** later in this chapter.

If you have a pre-Jaguar Mac (that is, one that didn't come with Jaguar or Panther preinstalled), the Restore discs that came with your Mac may work differently than just described. In particular, note the following:

• **Pre-Jaguar Mac OS X Restore discs.** The pre-Jaguar Software Restore discs came in a set of four CDs. You booted from the first CD and followed the directions that appeared. It reinstalled *all* the software that shipped with your Mac, including Mac OS X and Mac OS 9. Thus, you did not need to install Mac OS X prior to using Software Restore. Software Restore was used instead of Mac OS X Install. The only caveat was that you needed to erase the drive before using Restore (the older Mac OS 9 Software Restore discs had options to restore without erasing).

• **Mac OS 9–only Software Restore discs.** If your Mac shipped with Mac OS 9 Software Restore discs (and thus came with only Mac OS 9 preinstalled), follow these steps to restore your software:

   1. Use the Mac OS 9 Restore disc to reinstall the original software.

   2. Restart with the Mac OS X Install disc to install Mac OS X.

   3. Restart and update the OS versions as needed. Remember: In order to work with Classic when running Jaguar, you need to update to Mac OS 9.2.2 (if you have an older version). Free updaters are available from Apple's Web site.

SEE: • **"Take Note: "Why and How to Partition," "What About Mac OS 9?" and "Technically Speaking: Don't Use Mac OS 9 Software Restore on a Mac OS X Volume!"** elsewhere in this chapter, for more details.

What About Mac OS 9?

From the moment Apple released Mac OS X, it began plotting the demise of Mac OS 9. First, it stopped all development of new versions of Mac OS 9. Beginning with Mac OS X 10.2, Apple initiated the next steps: No more Mac OS 9 CD included with the Mac OS X package and Mac models that could no longer boot Mac OS 9.

No more Mac OS 9 Install CD

The retail version of Mac OS X no longer includes a Mac OS 9 Install CD, nor is one included when you purchase a Mac. This can be a hassle if you want to retain access to Mac OS 9, either for using Classic or for booting—especially if you need to erase your drive. The following represent some solutions:

- Since Mac OS 9 still comes preinstalled on new Macs (for use with Classic), as long as you don't plan to erase your drive or move Mac OS 9 to another partition, you're already set to go.

- If Mac OS 9 and Mac OS X are on the same partition and you want to move Mac OS 9 to a separate partition or volume, you can simply copy the Mac OS 9 System Folder to the alternative volume.

- If you've deleted Mac OS 9 from your drive and want to restore it, you can use Software Restore to do so, even on a partition that already contains Mac OS X (as described in the previous section). Although this method only installs Mac OS 9 on the Mac OS X boot volume, you can easily drag the System Folder to another mounted volume after it has been installed. Note, however, that this only works with the Software Restore discs that are included with Jaguar or later versions of Mac OS X.

OS9General.dmg

Figure 3.11

The Mac OS9General.dmg file.

- Alternatively, while booted from your normal startup drive and after using a tool such as TinkerTool to make invisible files visible (a technique described in more detail in Chapter 6), check for an .images folder on the first Software Restore CD: It should include a file called OS9General.dmg. Copy this file to your hard drive and mount the image. The files contained within the image include a Mac OS 9 System Folder. To install Mac OS 9 on a volume, mount the image file and copy the files on the image to the volume. You can even create a bootable Mac OS 9 CD by copying the files to a blank image file and burning the image to a CD.

- If you own a Mac OS 9 Install CD, you can still use it with Mac OS X 10.2 or later (assuming your Mac supports booting from Mac OS 9). If necessary, any installation of Mac OS 9.0 to 9.2.1 can be updated to Mac OS 9.2.2 via the Software Update control panel when you're booted from Mac OS 9.

- Mac OS X owners can purchase a Mac OS 9.2.2 Install CD from Apple for $19.95. Check the following Web page for details: www.apple.com/macosx/upgrade.

For further details on installing (or reinstalling) Mac OS 9, see the documentation that came with your Mac or check out my previous book *Sad Macs, Bombs, and Other Disasters*.

TECHNICALLY SPEAKING ▶ **Don't Use Mac OS 9 Software Restore on a Mac OS X Volume!**

Imagine the following scenario: Your older Mac did not come with Mac OS X preinstalled, and your Software Restore CD (which only contains Mac OS 9) includes the following options for restoring the drive without erasing it: Restore in Place and Restore Saving Original Items. At some point, you installed Mac OS X on the same partition as Mac OS 9, and you now want to use Software Restore to restore the original Mac OS 9 software without erasing Mac OS X—don't!

Using Mac OS 9 Software Restore in such a situation may render Mac OS X unusable. In particular, when you attempt to start up in Mac OS X, a belted-folder icon may appear, indicating that startup has failed. Occasionally, less serious though still annoying symptoms occur instead.

If you used the Restore in Place option, you can generally solve the problem by reinstalling Mac OS X. If you used the Restore Saving Original Items option, however, things get much more complicated. In brief, after reinstalling Mac OS X, you also need to re-create the exact set of /Users directories that existed before. Then you need to type the following command in Terminal: sudo cp —R /Original\ Items/Users/* /Users. And you're still not finished! To find out exactly what to do next, consult the following Apple Knowledge Base document: http://docs.info.apple.com/article.html?artnum=106294.

Obviously, a far simpler solution is to prevent the problem in the first place by *never* performing a Mac OS 9 Software Restore on a volume with Mac OS X installed.

No more booting from Mac OS 9

Starting in January 2003, all new Mac models only boot into Mac OS X. (Note: This is limited to Mac models *introduced* after January 2003, not to all Macs sold as "new" after this time. This distinction is important because Apple continued to sell a few "older" models after January 2003, specifically because those models could still boot into Mac OS 9.)

Thus, if you bought a Mac model released in 2003 or later, you cannot boot from Mac OS 9, either via a Mac OS 9 System Folder installed on a hard drive or via a Mac OS 9 CD. Still, you should be able to run most Mac OS 9 software, as long as it works via Classic (which Apple still supports).

For most Mac OS X users, this is of little or no concern since there's almost no reason to boot into Mac OS 9 anymore. However, a few troubleshooting-related concerns remain:

- If you booted into Mac OS 9 to solve certain Mac OS X problems (such as to work around permissions restrictions), these workarounds no longer work.

- If you have a startup problem that prevents you from booting from your Mac OS X volume and you have Mac OS 9 installed on another partition, you can no longer use it to boot your Mac as a first step to solving the Mac OS X startup problem.

- When you're starting up from a Mac OS X CD, unless you used the third-party Boot CD software to create the CD, you do not have access to the Finder. This problem limits what you can do when starting up from a CD. In contrast, a Mac OS 9 startup CD gives you complete access to the Finder.

- Some programs, including some troubleshooting utilities and even some of Apple's firmware updates, work only when booted from Mac OS 9. Eventually, almost all of these will have Mac OS X equivalents, but for now the problem remains.

Selectively Installing Mac OS X Files

Suppose at some point after installing Mac OS X you accidentally delete an application (such as iPhoto or Disk Utility) from your drive. Or perhaps the application somehow gets corrupted and no longer launches. Even worse, you never made a backup copy of it. What can you do? You have several choices.

Reinstalling from a Web download

You can reinstall the desired Mac OS X software if a separate installer is available via a Web download or separate purchase—a viable approach for applications such as iPhoto and especially useful if the Web version is newer than the version on your Mac OS X Install CD.

Performing a Custom Install or a separate install from the Install CDs or DVD

If no downloadable update is available, you can obtain a fresh copy of an application like iPhoto by reinstalling all of Mac OS X. In doing so, however, you run the risk of overwriting a file you don't want to modify—not to mention the fact that you're reinstalling thousands of perfectly OK files to get the one file that's *not* OK. A better option is to perform a Custom Install.

If the software you want is selectable as a lone item from the Custom Install screen of the Mac OS X Install Disc software, this offers a reliable and relatively efficient way to reinstall the software. You can do this with iPhoto, for example, by selecting it from the Additional Applications list and deselecting everything else.

Note: When performing a Custom Install, the column to the right of each item will state Install (meaning the component is presently not installed) or Update.

Alternatively, you may be able to locate and launch the specific desired .pkg file from the Install CDs/DVD instead of restarting from the CD for a full install. In particular, check in /System/Library/Installation/Packages and in /Welcome to Mac OS X/Optional Installs on Install Disc 1. From Install Discs 2 and/or 3, check inside the Packages folders. You can locate and install iPhoto.pkg from Disc 2, for example. This is almost the same as selecting to install just this option from a Custom Install of the full Mac OS X Installer. The main difference is that you do not need to restart your Mac from the CD in order to install by launching iPhoto.pkg directly.

Note: In some cases, a .pkg file (especially an .mpkg file) may only serve to redirect the Installer to another .pkg file where the software is actually located.

If you have a Software and Restore DVD (which now comes with Macs that have a DVD drive), you need to try another variation on this theme. This is because many of the folders that are visible on the Install CDs are invisible on the DVD. On the DVD, you can still locate and run a specific .pkg file by using the Go to Folder command in the Finder and typing /Volumes/{*name of DVD*}/System/Installation/Packages. Thus, the *name of DVD* for an iMac would be iMac Software. From here, to reinstall the i-software included with Mac OS X (such as iMovie, iPhoto, and iTunes), you would double-click the AdditionalApplications.pkg and proceed with the installation.

Copying from the Mac OS X Install discs

If the latest version of the file you want is on the Mac OS X Install discs, as an accessible file, you can copy it directly from the disc.

On the Install Disc 1 CD, for example, check inside the System folder at the root level of the CD. Here you will find a Library folder that contains copies of most of the files that eventually get installed in /System/Library. Should you need to replace one of these files (perhaps because you tried a hack on one of the files, and it failed and you don't have a backup), you could use the copy here. One caution: Occasionally, a file used on a boot CD will differ from that used on a bootable hard drive. Overall I would be cautious about using this method and in general perform a Custom Install instead.

The /Applications/Utilities folder contains working copies of applications such as Disk Utility and Installer.

Figure 3.12

The /Applications/ Utilities folder on the Mac OS X Install CD or DVD.

Copying from the Software Restore discs

If the custom options available by running Software Restore are not sufficient, you can access specific software directly from the CDs. The software on the Software Restore discs (for Jaguar and later) are stored as image (.dmg) files in an invisible .images folder. To use it, locate the Restore CD that includes the specific image you want (if you have the Install and Restore DVD, it's all on the one DVD) and copy the .dmg file from the invisible folder to your drive. Next, mount the image file. In most cases, the files on the image can be used to directly replace existing files (see the discussion of the OS9General.dmg file in "What About Mac OS 9?" earlier in this chapter, for a specific example). If, instead, the software is a .pkg file, use one of the two methods described in the next sections.

SEE: • "Understanding Image, Installer Package, and Receipt Files," later in this chapter, for background information on these file types.

Extracting from an expanded .pax.gz file

If the file you want is contained within a .pkg file, such as a MacOSXUpdate10.3.2 .pkg, you will most likely need to extract the file from the larger update. Here's one way to do so:

1. Locate the .pax.gz file inside the Installer package file. (To view the contents of the package file, Control-click it and then select Show Package Contents from the menu that appears.)

2. Make a copy of the file outside the package.

   Although this step is not required, it serves as a good precaution against damaging the only copy.

3. Decompress the copied file.

   If the current version of StuffIt Expander does not decompress the file, use the shareware application OpenUp. For large update packages, expect this output to take up a healthy amount of disk space (since it contains every file in the update).

4. Locate the desired file and use it to replace the original.

You may need root access to do this. You can delete the remaining expanded files or save them in case you need to do this again someday.

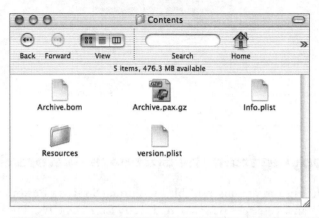

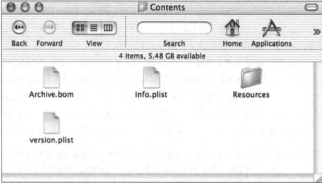

Figure 3.13

Inside the package file of a Keynote Updater (top) and the receipt file for the same updater (bottom). Note that the .pax.gz file is missing from the receipt file.

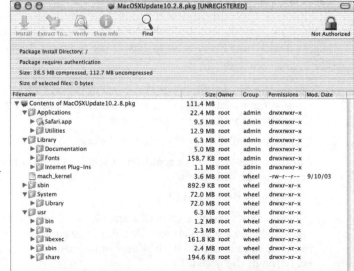

Figure 3.14

This Pacifist window displays the contents of a Jaguar Mac OS X update file. Clicking the disclosure triangles reveals subdirectory contents.

Use Pacifist

A simpler (and thus better) alternative to the previous procedure is to use a shareware utility called Pacifist. Simply open a package (.pkg) file from within Pacifist, and you will see a complete list of all files in the .pkg file. You can then choose to extract a single file (or more, if you wish)—either to its intended destination location or to any location you select.

Note: On the Mac OS X Install CD, most of the to-be-installed software is stored in .pkg files. For example, inside the System folder at the root level of the CD is a folder called Package, which contains several .pkg files (most notably Essentials.pkg) that include the bulk of the Mac OS X software. You can open these packages via Pacifist to extract individual files.

Of course, if you have a newer version of Mac OS X installed on your hard drive than the version on the Install CD, check any Update pkg file(s) you have to see if there is a newer version of the software than the version on the Install CD—unless you specifically intend to downgrade as part of some troubleshooting work-around (in which case you want the version on the Install CD).

SEE: • **"Understanding Image, Installer Package, and Receipt Files," later in this chapter, for more details.**

One caution about using Pacifist or otherwise extracting software from a pax.gz file: Sometimes the software you want to replace is part of a related set of files. For example, an application may require a file in an Application Support folder and/or an update to a Framework in order to function correctly. In such cases, if the additional files are not already present on your drive, just installing the application may not be sufficient. A complete reinstall of Mac OS X then becomes a better choice. You will know this is a possibility if the application does not work after the installation.

Upgrading Mac OS X

The terms *upgrade* and *update* are often used synonymously. In the context of Mac OS X, however, they carry important distinctions: An *upgrade* refers to moving from one major version of Mac OS X to another—such as *upgrading* from Mac OS X 10.2 (Jaguar) to Mac OS X 10.3 (Panther). An *update,* in contrast, refers to moving from one minor version to another—such as *updating* from Mac OS X 10.3.1 to Mac OS X 10.3.2. For upgrades, the number after the first period changes; for updates, the number after the second period changes. As you might expect, updates represent mostly minor changes (such as bug fixes), whereas upgrades typically introduce dozens of major new features.

Another important distinction is that upgrades are rarely free (unless you qualify for a free upgrade because you purchased your Mac a few weeks before the upgrade was released; check with Apple to see if this is the case). For example, the upgrade to Panther cost $129 even if you purchased Jaguar just a couple of months before.

Updates, on the other hand, *are* typically free.

Upgrading to a new version of Mac OS X always requires installing Mac OS X from a new set of Mac OS X Install CDs (or DVD). Thus, the procedure for doing so is exactly as described earlier in this chapter for installing Mac OS X the first time. Updates are usually handled via a single update .pkg file.

This section discusses upgrading; the next section covers updating.

Upgrade oddities. If you have an earlier version of Mac OS X installed, you may decide to use the Installer's Archive and Install feature; however, if you have not been too aggressive in customizing your Mac OS X environment and if you follow the procedures covered in the next section, the standard upgrade, as opposed to the Archive and Install, will likely work well.

There are, however, a few odd glitches that may occur when doing a standard upgrade—and even when doing an Archive and Install in some cases. This is because Panther changes the way a few settings work by default. For example, as discussed in other chapters, bash rather than tcsh is now the default shell in Terminal; the default group for files you create now has the same name as your owner name (instead of the name *staff,* as was the case in Jaguar); and your personal keychain file is named login.keychain in Panther (vs. {*your username*}.keychain in Jaguar). When you upgrade—or do an Archive and Install where users are preserved—these settings may retain their Jaguar status. New users that you create will follow the Panther rules instead. This can get confusing. If you want your account to use the new Panther settings, you can do an Archive and Install without enabling the Preserve User option (and then copy any needed files from the Previous Systems folder to your newly created account folder in the Users folder). Otherwise, you can do a standard upgrade and change the default settings in the relevant config/preferences files (seek additional advice from Web sites, books, or knowledgeable users, as to what files to change, if needed).

SEE: • **"Installing or Reinstalling Mac OS X" and "Take Note: Why and How to Use Archive and Install," earlier in this chapter, for more details.**

Before you upgrade

Before you insert the Mac OS X Install disc and begin the installation process, you should make sure you're prepared for any problems that may result. Here are the main things you should do before upgrading:

- **Back up.** In the event that something goes wrong, you can still return to your preupgrade state using your backup copy.

    SEE: • "Backing Up and Restoring Mac OS X Volumes," later in this chapter.

- **Remove or update software that's likely to be incompatible with the upgrade.** Once you've upgraded, you may find that software that worked perfectly previously no longer works. Although any third-party software on your drive could turn out to be the problem here, be especially wary of third-party System Preferences as well as items listed in your Startup Items list.

Ideally, you want to take care of these issues *before* you upgrade (rather than discover the problem afterwards). The best and most common fix for such problems is for the third-party developer to release an upgrade that addresses the conflict. If an update that fixes the problem is already available, install the update before upgrading the OS. Otherwise, you may have to disable, remove, and/or uninstall the problem software—until the update gets released.

How do you find out which software needs to be updated? To some extent, you can self-diagnose. That is, items that modify the system (such as WindowShade X, which changes how the Finder minimizes windows) are those that are most likely to need an update. Check with the developer's Web site for confirmation regarding these likely candidates. In most cases, the developer will have information about compatibility within a day or so of the OS's release.

Otherwise, check various Web sites (such as Apple's own Web site and MacFixIt) for news of compatibility problems.

The following are some examples of the types of conflicts that have occurred since Panther's release:

- Versions of Palm Desktop software and Norton Utilities available as of the Panther release date were incompatible with Panther. In the case of Norton Utilities, disks to be repaired or edited did not appear in the Norton Disk Doctor, UnErase, Volume Recover, or Speed Disk windows after upgrading to Panther; Norton Scheduler also failed to work. The solution to such problems is to wait for the vendor to update its software—which it usually does within days or weeks of the release of a Mac OS X upgrade. The quick release of compatibility updates is possible because vendors get prerelease copies of the Mac OS X upgrade and thus have months to work on such fixes before the Mac OS X upgrade ships.

On the other hand, sometimes updates come out much later, or not at all, in which case you'll have to find alternatives. Updated versions of Norton software, for example, were released about two months after Panther hit the shelves.

- A more frustrating problem is that some software you've set to automatically launch at login (by including it in your user-level Startup Items list) may no longer work after upgrading. This can thus cause problems immediately after you upgrade and log in. If you are unaware of the conflict, it may initially seem that the problem is with the Mac OS X upgrade itself rather than third-party software. For example, after installing Panther, older versions of Default Folder X (a utility that enhances the options available in Open and Save dialogs) no longer worked correctly. The symptom of the problem was that *every* application you tried to launch quit immediately. The work-around is to disable the conflicting version of the software and (if available) install the updated compatible version. A potential problem is that the symptom itself may prevent you from disabling the software. With the Default Folder problem, for example, you can't disable Default Folder from its System Preferences pane if the System Preferences application quits on launch. The solution is to log in with startup items disabled (as described in Chapter 5); you can now get to the Preferences pane and disable Default Folder.

- In a few cases, a conflict may result in hardware problems, such as an inability to mount an external drive. Again, an update is typically the solution, possibly involving a firmware update to the conflicting device.

Updating Mac OS X

Once you have installed and (if necessary) initially updated to the latest version of Mac OS X, you will want to keep it up to date. Apple regularly releases software updates (as opposed to *upgrades,* as covered in the previous section) and makes them available via both the Software Update System Preferences pane and its Web site. Because Software Update is the simplest and fastest way to stay current, I recommend using it. I provided a brief overview of how to use Software Update in Chapter 2; the following provides some additional details.

Apple releases two categories of updates, almost all of which are available via Software Update:

- **General updates to Mac OS X.** For certain OS updates—such as that for Mac OS X 10.2.6—two similarly named files are available: Mac OS X 10.2.6 Update and Mac OS X 10.2.6 Combo Update. The difference is that the Mac OS X 10.2.6 Update can only update a system currently running Mac OS X 10.2.5. The Combo update can update all prior versions of Mac OS X 10.2. As a result, the Combo update is a significantly larger file.

Note: In no case do these updates contain the complete set of software you need to run Mac OS X. For this, you need a Mac OS X Install CD.

- **Separate updates to specific components of Mac OS X as well as to software not included as part of Mac OS X.** For example, you may see a QuickTime update, an iPhoto update, or an AppleWorks update.

Although I generally recommend installing updates—Apple provides them to fix bugs and to add new features—I also recommend waiting a few days after an update has been released to do so. Use this time to check the Web (for example, the MacFixIt.com site) to make sure the software doesn't contain any significant bugs that weren't discovered until *after* its release. And always make backups of critical files before installing an update.

How and why things can go wrong. After installing software, you may start getting permissions errors when trying to launch various applications, including applications unrelated to the one you just installed. In extreme cases, the System may even become unusable. How can this happen simply as a result of running the Installer utility? The answer is two-pronged: When installing software, you're typically asked to enter your administrative password, which gives the Installer temporary root access. In addition, script files within an install .pkg that are run as part of the installation can contain instructions to modify permissions of files and folders—or even to delete certain files. These script files, typically located in the Resources folder inside the package file, have names such as *preflight*, *postflight*, and *postinstall*. If these scripts contain errors that cause permission changes or file deletions that should not occur, you can wind up with serious problems.

Basically, you just have to trust that the software developer has not made such an error—and usually your trust is well placed: Such mistakes are rare. Although the risk rises slightly with software that does not come from Apple even Apple can make a mistake here.

Here's one example: When Apple initially released iTunes 2.0 as a free upgrade on the Web, it was supposed to delete any older version of iTunes found on your drive before installing the new version. Unfortunately, the installer .pkg file contained a nasty quirk: Due to an error in how it was set up to work, the installation sometimes failed to install iTunes at all. Even worse, when attempting to remove an older version of iTunes, the installer sometimes also removed much of the data on your drive! This horrendous bug was fixed the same day via another iTunes update—but not before hundreds of users lost files.

In general, if an installer causes a serious mistake, you will need to reinstall Mac OS X to fix it—and then restore any lost files from your backups.

Updating from Software Update

The simplest way to check for and install updates is to select Software Update from the System Preferences window, the Apple menu, or the About This Mac window.

SEE: • **Chapter 2 for more on System Preferences.**

Software Update System Preferences pane. The Software Update System Preferences pane includes two tabs, each of which accesses a separate screen:

- **Update Software.** From this screen, you can enable the "Check for updates" option—at daily, weekly, or monthly intervals. With this option enabled, you can also select to "Download important updates in the background." With this selected, updates that Apple deems important will be downloaded without the System's first asking your permission (though you will still be asked for confirmation before the software is actually installed).

  Alternatively, you can manually check for updates at any time by clicking the Check Now button.

  If you click Check Now and there are no new updates, a message will appear telling you that you are currently up to date. Otherwise, you will have the option to install new uninstalled software, as described in "Software Update application," below.

- **Installed Updates.** This screen presents you with a list of everything you've installed via Software Update (though the contents may get wiped out each time you upgrade to a new version of Mac OS X). Alternatively, you can view this listing from a log file via the Open as Log File button.

SEE: • **"Installed Updates does not list previously installed updates," later in this chapter, for related information.**

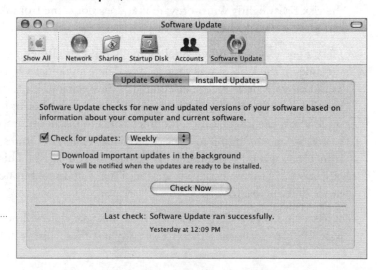

Figure 3.15

The Software Update System Preferences pane.

Software Update application. A separate application, also called Software Update (located in /System/Library/CoreServices), is launched after any of the following have occurred: You clicked Check Now from the Software Update System Preferences pane; an automatic check was initiated (assuming new software is available); or you clicked Software Update in the About This Mac window. The Software Update window displays a list of all available updates. Note, however, that it only lists Apple's Mac OS software and occasional third-party software (such as StuffIt Expander) that is included with Mac OS X.

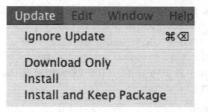

Figure 3.16

The Software Update application: The main window (top) shows a needed update—select it and click the Install 1 Item button to install it; (bottom) Software Update's Update menu.

To install the software listed in the Software Update application, you simply check the box(es) in the Install column for each item you want to install. Then click the Install Item(s) button. Alternatively, after selecting the items to install, you can go to the Update menu and select one of the following four commands:

- **Download Only.** This downloads the update file (typically a .pkg file, referred to as a *stand-alone update*) to a folder named Packages, located in the root-level Library folder. The folder is automatically opened in the Finder when the download is complete. You must then manually launch the .pkg file when you're ready to install it.

  This option is useful if you want to retain a copy of the .pkg file after installing the software. One reason to do this would be so that you can reinstall the update later (should you erase your drive, for example) without having to redownload it. Another reason would be to install the update on multiple machines without having to download the update from the Internet each time. Also, if the update provides any Custom Install options, running the Installer is the only way to access them.

If you use this option but do not install the software, Software Update will not "remember" that you downloaded the file. Instead, Software Update will continue to list the downloaded file as an uninstalled update until you actually install it. In fact, if you subsequently select the Install command, it will redownload the update, rather than using the copy you previously downloaded.

Note: In Jaguar, Software Update includes a Download Checked Items to Desktop command. This downloads the file to the Desktop but does not install it, similar to Panther's Download Only option. However, Jaguar keeps track of whether or not you have installed the software. For example, after using this option, Software Update lists the update status as "Not installed, downloaded"—as long as the file remains on the Desktop and is not installed. Software Update in Panther does not indicate that an update has been downloaded but not installed.

- **Install.** This is just like clicking the Install Item(s) button: It both downloads and installs the selected update(s). Onscreen messages inform you of Software Update's progress, from downloading to installing.

  The downloaded .pkg file(s) are kept hidden in the Finder. They are automatically deleted the next time you restart—making it difficult to save them for future use.

  The Install option is especially convenient for installing multiple items that require restarting the Mac. With the Download Only option, you would have to run each update separately (although you can have them all open in the Installer utility at one time). With Software Update, all updates are installed before any restart is requested. The Software Update option is also the simplest because it requires no further action on the part of the user.

  If you select this option and it stalls while installing the software (after having downloaded it), force-quit Software Update. Next time, select Download Only and manually install the software. This often works around the problem.

  SEE: • **"Technically Speaking: Where Does Software Update Hide the Software It Installs?" later in this chapter, for further details.**

- **Install and Keep Package.** This option combines the previous two options: It automatically installs the software, plus it saves a copy to the Packages folder. This is the option I typically choose.

- **Ignore Update.** If you select this option, the update is removed from the list. You will not be notified again of this update or of any subsequent updates for the same software. You may end up choosing this option for software you don't need (such as an iPod update if you don't own an iPod). Should you change your mind and want to get the update later, you can select Reset Ignored Updates from the Software Update menu.

If you don't choose to ignore an update but don't go ahead and install it either, this same software update will be listed again the next time you check for updates.

If an update requires administrator approval, you will be asked for your admin-level user name and password before the update will install.

If an update requires that you restart your Mac, a restart symbol will appear to the left of the update name.

Some updates only appear in Software Update if certain prior updates have been installed. For example, Apple at one point released an update to the Installer application itself. No newer updates would appear in Software Update until after the new Installer had been installed. For this reason, once you've installed an update, return to the Software Update System Preferences Pane and click Update Now again. Keep doing this until no new updates appear. Actually, you should no longer have to do this in Panther, because Software Update does this rechecking automatically—until no new updates appear.

After reinstalling Mac OS X via an Archive and Install, Software Update may not list the more recent updates because it erroneously believes that they are already installed. Thus, as a safeguard, check Apple's Web site for recent updates regardless of what Software Update says.

Note: In Jaguar or later, you can no longer update Mac OS 9 by running Software Update via Classic.

SEE: • "Ownership & Permissions," in Chapter 4, and "Opening and Saving: Permissions Problems," and "Copying and Moving: Permissions Problems," in Chapter 6, for details on checking and setting permissions

---

TECHNICALLY SPEAKING ▶ **Where Does Software Update Hide the Software It Installs?**

If you were wondering where Software Update hides the .pkg update file it downloads prior to installing if you don't select to save the update package, here's the answer:

When using Software Update to install files, the .pkg file is temporarily (until you restart) stored at /private/tmp/501/Temporary Items. This location is normally invisible from the Finder; however, you can access it via the Finder's Go to Folder command or via Terminal.

Note: The 501 number is your user ID (UID). It may be different from 501 if you're not the original administrative user for your Mac. You can check your user ID via NetInfo Manager: To do so, select Users and then the name of your account. Your UID will be one of the items listed in the bottom window. You can also find your UID by opening Terminal and typing id; the first item will be your UID.

Updating from the Installer package (.pkg) file

You can install a software update by first downloading the .pkg file from the Web (such as from Apple's Web site at www.info.apple.com/downloads). These stand-alone updates open in the Installer utility and proceed in a manner similar to how Mac OS X itself was installed from the Install CDs or DVD. The main difference is that you don't need to boot from a Mac OS X Install CD (or any other CD) to install these updates. You can do so while running Mac OS X, directly from your drive. You will be asked to enter your administrative password before you are allowed to perform the installation.

Recall that you can use the Show Files command, in the Installer, to view and save a list of all files that the update will install.

This method is essentially the same as using Software Update and selecting the Download Only option; however, there are three differences of note:

- Downloaded update files typically download as .dmg files. The actual .pkg file is on the mounted .dmg image.

  SEE: • **"Understanding Image, Installer Package, and Receipt Files," later in this chapter, for more on this matter.**

- Occasionally, updates (even those from Apple) are only available via Web download, with no Software Update option.

- A potential advantage of using Software Update to download the file is that it often lists the latest updates even sooner than Apple's Web site.

TAKE NOTE ▶ **Interrupted Downloads**

If you're using a dial-up (rather than broadband) connection to the Internet, downloading large updates can take a very long time. Even worse, you may occasionally get disconnected before the download is complete. If this happens, you may be able to resume the download from where you left off—avoiding the frustration of having to start completely over. This should automatically happen with Software Update, if you have not restarted your Mac in the interim.

Otherwise, your best bet is to download updates from Apple's Web site using an application that permits an auto-resume of a partial download, such as iGetter or Speed Download. In some cases, you may even have success with a standard Web browser, such as Internet Explorer. To try this with Internet Explorer, select Download Manager from the Window menu and double-click the name of the partially downloaded file. From the window that appears, click Reload.

TAKE NOTE ▶ **Updating or Adding QuickTime Components**

Although updates to Apple's QuickTime software are generally provided via Software Update, they are also available via a *separate* QuickTime Updater system accessed via the QuickTime pane of System Preferences. In addition, third-party QuickTime software (such as QuickTime Plug-ins) is also often available via the QuickTime Updater system.

To access this system, open the QuickTime Preferences pane and click the Update tab. By checking the "Check for updates automatically" box, you instruct the Updater system to check for new versions of the main QuickTime software each time you use it (by launching QuickTime Player, for example). You can also manually check for new QuickTime software by selecting either the "Update or install QuickTime software" radio button (for Apple updates) or the "Install new 3rd-party QuickTime software" radio button (for third-party updates), and then clicking Update Now. To check for both, you need to use the Update Now button twice—once for each option.

If you enable the "3rd-party QuickTime software" option and click the Update Now button, you will most likely be told that your software is up-to-date. However, if you click the Custom button in the resulting dialog, you'll see a list of available third-party QuickTime components, along with a note about whether each is installed and/or updated. Check the ones you want to install and/or update, and click the Update Now button to install them.

Skip the restart?

After you've completed your software installation, either via the Installer or Software Update, some installations will insist that your restart your Mac before continuing. You should follow this advice, especially if you intend to use the installed software immediately. However, on occasions in which it's not convenient to restart immediately (say, because you want to finish work or save documents in another application), you can simply switch to a different application and finish up. When you're ready, return to the Installer application and click Restart.

Alternatively, you may want to install a second or third program before restarting, so you don't have to restart each time. With Software Update, this is not an issue; it does all selected installations before requesting that you restart. If, instead, you are using the Installer application, you can accomplish the same goal by launching all desired Installer .pkg files without quitting the Installer application. This works because, starting in Panther, the Installer can have multiple packages open at the same time. You cannot actively install more than one at time, however; you must do each install sequentially. This still allows you to install multiple packages before restarting.

If you are using Jaguar or prefer not to use the above solutions, you can always force-quit the Installer or Software Update application. Alternatively, you can quit by selecting Quit (or, if needed, Option-Quit) from the Dock menu of these applications. Any of these options bypass the Restart request.

SEE: • **Chapter 5 for more on force-quitting.**

Downgrading and Reupgrading Mac OS X

Occasionally (though hopefully not often), you may decide that you need to downgrade to an older version of Mac OS X—perhaps due to a bug in the latest update.

Similarly, you may sometimes need to start over with a fresh installation of Mac OS X. Most likely, you will want to attempt this when you begin to have general problems running Mac OS X for which you can find no easier solution. In most cases, doing this means downgrading to an older version of Mac OS X and then reupgrading back to the current version.

Archive and Install; reupgrade

The best way to handle downgrades and reupgrades is to start with a complete reinstall of Mac OS X, using the Installer's Archive and Install feature, which you can access when starting up from a Mac OS X Install CD. If your Install CD doesn't include this feature, you should erase your entire volume and reinstall from whatever Install CD you do have.

Note: You cannot do a direct downgrade from Apple's Installer, even for a minor upgrade. For example, if you tried to install Mac OS X 10.2.5 on a volume running 10.2.6, the Installer would not allow it.

After doing an Archive and Install from the Install CD, you will likely be back at an older version of Mac OS X than the one you were previously running (for example, you may be back at 10.2.0, when you had been running 10.2.6).

To reupdate to the current version of Mac OS X, use Software Update; it automatically lists the needed update. Software Update should also list any updates beyond Mac OS X itself that you may need to reinstall as a result of the Archive and Install—and allow you to install them all in one step (while you leave to have lunch!).

Alternatively, assuming you want to reupdate to the latest version of the OS, download the most recent Combo Mac OS X updater (as described in "Updating

Mac OS X," earlier in this chapter) from Apple's Web site. Not only is the Combo Updater simpler and faster than downloading and installing multiple individual Mac OS X updates, but it's also more likely to remedy whatever symptom led to your decision to reinstall.

SEE: • **"Software installs but fails to work," later in this chapter.**

The main advantage of using a Web download rather than Software Update is that if you don't wish to return to your current version (perhaps you were running Mac OS X 10.2.6 but now want to downgrade to 10.2.5), you can do so by selecting the appropriate update file from the Web.

Of course, you cannot downgrade "lower" than the version installed by the Install CD. Thus, if you want to downgrade from Panther back to Jaguar, you would need to use a Jaguar Install CD.

SEE: • **"Select a Destination," earlier in this chapter, for more on Archive and Install.**

Edit SystemVersion.plist

The SystemVersion.plist file, located in /System/Library/CoreServices, contains the Mac OS X version and build number of the currently installed OS. If you change the information in this file, the version number and build number change in the About This Mac window.

This process does not really change any software on your drive. However, it may fool the Installer into letting you downgrade to an older version of Mac OS X that it would ordinarily prohibit. Although the procedure won't work in all cases, it may be worth a try.

In Jaguar and later versions of Mac OS X, you should no longer *need* to perform this trick if you can use Archive and Install instead (since Archive and Install is a safer alternative); however, you may still want to because it could be quicker than the less risky method. For example, you could use this trick to downgrade from Mac OS X 10.2.6 to 10.2.5, bypassing the need to reinstall 10.2.0 (assuming that is the version on your Mac OS X Install CD) and reupgrade.

To give this trick a try, follow these steps:

1. Log in as a root user and launch Property List Editor (part of the Developer software).

   or

   Drag the Property List Editor application to the Pseudo icon (Pseudo is third-party software) that opens applications with root access.

   SEE: • **Chapter 4 for more on root access and Pseudo.**

   • **Chapter 4 for more on preferences files and Property List Editor.**

2. Open the SystemVersion.plist file with Property List Editor, as located in CoreServices.

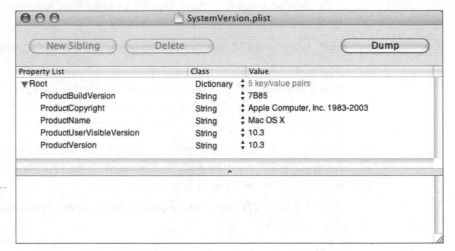

The contents of the SystemVersion.plist file as viewed in Property List Editor.

3. Click the build number in the Value column of the ProductBuildVersion row, and edit it as desired.

4. Click the version number in the Value column of the ProductVersion and ProductUserVisibleVersion rows, and edit it as desired. For example, if you want to fool the Mac into thinking you're running 10.2.3 when you're really running 10.2.6, type 10.2.3 here.

5. Quit Property List Editor, saving the modified file. If you logged in as root, log out and log back in as yourself.

You can now try running the Installer again with the "downgrade" package file. If it works, the SystemVersion.plist file should be updated and need no further changes. If the install still doesn't work, you will want to reverse the change you just made. Check the About This Mac window to determine what version is listed.

Warning: In some cases, this type of downgrade can result in installed software that's a mixture of two versions—which can cause more problems than the trick itself solves. Thus, employ this method at your own risk. In general, it's better to either erase the volume and start over or perform an Archive and Install.

SEE: • **"Select a Destination," earlier in this chapter, for more on Archive and Install.**

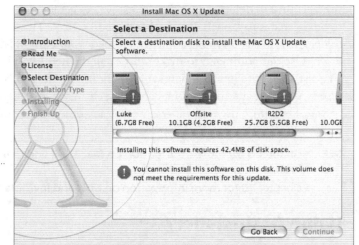

Figure 3.18

The message that
appears (in the
lower section of the
window) when you
attempt a prohib-
ited downgrade.

Uninstalling Mac OS X

Suppose you want to uninstall Mac OS X—because you no longer want to
use it, or you no longer want it on a particular volume, or you're having such
problems getting the OS to start up that an uninstall followed by a fresh
installation is the only possible solution. How do you go about it?

By far the most direct approach is to erase the entire volume. Of course, you'll
first want to back up any personal files (most of which will be located in your
Home directory) that you want to save.

Manual uninstall?

In some cases, you may be reluctant to erase the volume. Perhaps you also have
Mac OS 9 software installed on the volume and don't want to erase it. Or
perhaps you don't have a full backup of all the files you want to save (and
you're not prepared to back them up at the moment). In such cases, you
would prefer to just delete all files associated with Mac OS X and leave everything else intact. This is also likely to take less time than erasing the volume
and restoring saved files from your backup. Can this type of uninstall be done?

The answer is yes—but with difficulty. Apple offers no officially supported
uninstallation method. To do so requires starting up from another volume and
manually deleting all Mac OS X–specific folders. Many of the Unix software
folders (such as dev and var) remain invisible even when starting up from
another volume, so you will need either to make them visible in the Finder or

use Terminal to delete them. The fastest way to get an overview of what needs to be deleted is to launch Terminal and type 1s –a /. This lists all files and folders, invisible and visible, at the root level of your current Mac OS X startup drive. Use this command to make a list of all the items you intend to delete. The list should include .hidden, .vol, Applications, Library, Network, System, Users, Volumes, automount, bin, cores, dev, etc, mach, mach.sym, mach_kernel, private, sbin, tmp, usr, and var—as well as any other items you know you want to delete.

SEE: • **Chapter 6 for more information on Mac OS X and invisible files and folders.**

• **Chapter 10 for more information on Unix and invisible files and folders.**

Using DesInstaller?

DesInstaller is a shareware utility that can be used to uninstall any software that has a receipt file in the Receipts folder. It uses the information in a receipt file to remove all of the software that was originally installed—even if the software has been modified. It can even archive the removed files and create a reinstaller for future use. You can also create a reinstaller without removing the software—which can be useful for software for which you do not have the installer .pkg file.

DesInstaller is not really useful for a complete uninstall of all Mac OS X software, but it can be great for selective uninstalls of updates.

Keep in mind, however, that it's also a potentially dangerous tool. If it makes an error and uninstalls more or less than it should, you could wind up with an unstable system. For example, I would not use this utility to remove Mac OS X updates, as it might delete critically needed files. Ultimately, a complete reinstall of Mac OS X may be needed. So use at your own risk!

Understanding Image, Installer Package, and Receipt Files

The previous sections of this chapter made occasional reference to receipt, image, and package files, which I refer to elsewhere in this book as well. This section provides essential background on exactly what these files are and how they work.

TAKE NOTE ▶ What Happened to Disk Copy?

Disk Copy is a well-known Mac utility, a version of which has been around through many iterations of the Classic Mac OS as well as all previous versions of Mac OS X (including Jaguar). In Panther, however, it's conspicuously absent. What happened?

In Panther, Apple took most (but not all!) of the functionality of Disk Copy and split it up into two new locations.

To create new image files or edit existing ones, you now use the Images menu in Disk Utility.

To mount image files, you simply double-click the file to launch a background application called DiskImageMounter. This program is located in /System/Library/CoreServices. If you go there, you will see that it still retains the old Disk Copy icon!

Unlike Disk Copy, DiskImageMounter gives no sign that an application has launched (for example, no icon gets added to the Dock). This streamlines the process of mounting images a bit, which I suppose is the rationale behind the change.

If you use Terminal, Panther still includes the hdiutil command, which is the Terminal equivalent of the former Disk Copy application. This provides access to all of the old Disk Copy features, even the ones not included in Disk Utility's Images menu.

Using Disk Copy in Panther. If you're unsatisfied with Panther's eradication of Disk Copy, you might wonder if you can still use the old Jaguar version of Disk Copy when running Panther. The answer is a limited yes. It launches and works but is especially prone to unexpected quits. Thus, I would not count on it as a solution.

Disk Copy's Expert mode. If you're still using Jaguar's Disk Copy, try this: Using Property List Editor, open the com.apple.DiskCopy.plist file located in the /Library/Preferences folder of your Home directory. Add a new property and name it expert-mode; assign it a Class of Boolean and a Value of Yes. When you next launch Disk Copy, you will find two new features: (1) In the window that appears when you select to create a New Blank Image, there will be some new options, such as Image Layout and Image Format menus (which include the option to create a sparseimage); and (2) a Debug command appears in the Utilities menu.

SEE: • "Technically Speaking: More About Disk Utility's Image and Restore Features" and "The Jaguar Way: Creating a Bootable CD with Disk Copy," later in this chapter, for related information.

  • "Preferences Files," in Chapter 4, for more on editing preferences files.

Image (.dmg) files

Many files that you download from the Web (in fact, almost all Apple files and a healthy minority of non-Apple files) arrive in the form of image files. These files typically have names that end in .dmg (also called a *UDIF format*).

However, you may also see image files that end in .img: These are carryovers from an image format originally used in Mac OS 9. Over time, .img files will disappear from the Mac OS X scene; thus, I'm omitting further coverage of them from this book. Some image files may be self-mounting (with an .smi extension) and thus should work even if a mounting application is not available.

Note: For a more technical background on the history and nature of disk image formats, launch Terminal and type man hdiutil. Then press Return until you reach the sections on compatibility and history.

If you double-click an image file, the image file will *mount* (more technically referred to as *attach*). That is, a virtual volume appears, much as if you had mounted some sort of removable media, such as a CD. Some third-party software, such as StuffIt Deluxe, can also mount image files.

The name of the mounted image may differ from the .dmg file itself, though there's usually some similarity. Double-click the mounted image's icon, if necessary, to view its contents and access it from the Finder.

For Apple software updates, the contents of the mounted volume will typically be a package (.pkg) file. A Read Me file or other documentation may also be included. For third parties, the contents may similarly be a .pkg file or a separate third-party installer utility. A VISE Installer is currently the most popular alternative to .pkg files; it makes no use of Apple's Installer utility.

If the image contains an installer package file or some other form of install utility, the next step is to copy the file from the image to the user's hard drive. Technically, you can run the install directly from the image; however, it's safer to run it from a "permanent" copy on your drive—in case something goes wrong.

When you've finished doing what you need to do, you can unmount the virtual volume (by dragging the Volume icon to the Trash or by clicking the Eject icon next to the image's name in the Places sidebar of a Finder window). You can also delete any install software you dragged to your drive as well as the downloaded image file itself (if you don't want to save it as a backup).

Note: Some third-party image files may contain a fully functional newer version of the software in question rather than an installer. To update in this situation, you simply replace the previous version on your hard drive with the new version on the image.

Note: As I discuss later in this chapter, you can use Disk Utility to create image files—a convenient way to make exact copies of folders, discs, and other items you want to transfer over the Internet.

SEE: • **"Technically Speaking: Running Mac OS X Software from the Terminal," in Chapter 10, for more on the** hdiutil **command.**

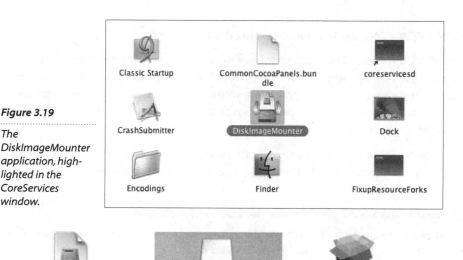

Figure 3.19

The DiskImageMounter application, highlighted in the CoreServices window.

Backup_2.0.dmg   Backup 2   Backup.pkg

Figure 3.20

From image file to package file in three steps: (Left) An image file downloaded from the Web; (middle) the virtual volume that appears when you mount the image; and (right) the package file contained in the volume.

Image files vs. compressed files

When you download software from the Internet, it often arrives in compressed and/or encoded format. Such files typically have a .sit, .sitx, or .bin suffix. In this case, the first step is to decompress and/or decode the file. Typically, this is done via Aladdin's StuffIt collection of software. The StuffIt component StuffIt Expander, which is included as part of Mac OS X, can be used for this purpose. In most cases, your Web browser is preset to automatically launch Expander (if needed) and "expand" the software.

In some cases, the expanded file will be an image (.dmg) file. If so, the image file will likely mount its virtual volume automatically. The resulting software (such as an Installer .pkg file) will now be accessible. You then proceed as described in the previous section.

In most cases, however, the decompressed file will be the "final" software itself, such as an installer or another application. You can use this directly.

TECHNICALLY SPEAKING ▶ Internet-Enabled Disk Images

Beginning with Mac OS X 10.2.3, Apple has simplified the procedure of working with downloaded disk images. For starters, .dmg files that are created as compressed (and read-only) are flat files that can be directly downloaded from the Internet. This eliminates the need to download a file as a .bin or .sit file and then expand it to a disk image—which in turn allows the user to skip the step that requires Expander.

To make things even simpler, the person who creates the disk image (.dmg) file can make it an *Internet-enabled* disk image. When you download an Internet-enabled disk image, the following occurs:

- The image is automatically mounted when the download is complete.
- The contents of the mounted image are copied to the user's drive—in the same location as the .dmg file itself or in a folder created at that location.
- If the mounted image contains a .pkg file, the Installer application may automatically launch and open the file, prompting you to install the software.
- The image is then unmounted, and the .dmg file is placed in the Trash.

The net result is that the user is left with the downloaded software ready to run or install—no additional steps required.

To save a .dmg file that has been moved to the Trash (in case you wish to do so for archival purposes), just drag it out of the Trash before you next choose Empty Trash.

Note that the Internet-enabled feature is cleared after the first time the image is mounted. This means that, after retrieving a .dmg file from the Trash, if you mount the image a second time, the automated actions will not occur.

Creating an Internet-enabled disk image. The Disk Utility application currently does not include an option to create an Internet-enabled disk image. If you want to create one yourself, you must use the `hdiutil` command in Terminal. In particular, type the following:

`hdiutil internet-enable –yes {path to disk image}/imagename.dmg`

In the above command, `imagename.dmg` is the name of an existing *read-only* disk image. If you now double-click the image file, it should behave as described above.

Substitute `no` for yes in the above command to remove an already-present flag.

Panther vs. Jaguar. The man file for `hdiutil` states, "If so enabled, upon first encounter with Disk Copy (on OS X 10.2.3+) or a browser using the feature for a download on Mac OS X 10.3, the image will have its visible contents copied into the directory containing the image.…" In other words, in Panther, this feature is dependent on your Web browser rather than the nonexistent Disk Copy. If the browser you're using in Panther is not upgraded to support Internet-enabled disk images, this feature will not work.

continues on next page

TECHNICALLY SPEAKING ▶ **Internet-Enabled Disk Images**   *continued*

My tests confirmed this difference. I could not get the feature to work in Internet Explorer or even in an older version of Safari when running Panther. That is, Internet-enabling a file succeeded in Terminal but had no effect on the file's behavior when I mounted it. However, the enabling did work as expected when I mounted the image in Jaguar instead, using Disk Copy. In fact, I'm still concerned that there may be a Panther bug that goes beyond Apple's stated explanation.

TAKE NOTE ▶ **Image Files That Won't Mount**

Occasionally, if you double-click a .dmg file, it may open as text in a text editor or otherwise fail to open. This may happen because the file is corrupted. If you downloaded it from the Web, the solution may be to simply download it again.

More likely, however, the problem is that the Finder doesn't know what application is needed to open the file. In this case, if instead of double-clicking the file you drag it to the DiskImageMounter icon (in /System/Library/CoreServices), it should mount just fine.

If you want to fix the file so that double-clicking works, you can use the Open With section of the Get Info window for the file. Basically, you just change the selected application from whatever it is to DiskImageMounter. Then click the Change All button to apply the change to all future image files.

SEE: • Chapter 4 for more details on using the Get Info window.

Installer Package (.pkg) files

A *package* (also referred to as a *bundle*) is really a folder in disguise. In this guise, it acts as though it were a single file rather than a folder containing a collection of files. These folders are disguised this way to simplify the user's experience of working with them.

The Installer utility uses one type of package file to install updates. These files typically have a .pkg extension at the end of their name (such as MacOSXUpdate10.3.2.pkg), though you may occasionally see one with an .mpkg extension. This latter type of extension represents a *meta-package*, which is the first file launched in an installation involving several .pkg files. Launching this file will not result in a successful installation unless all of the additional .pkg files are also in its folder.

One key advantage of this approach to OS updates is that the user sees what looks like a single file at the end of the process rather than the dozens of files scattered among several folders that Mac OS 9 updates typically require. When you double-click this item, it launches the Installer and you're on your way.

TECHNICALLY SPEAKING ▶ **Inside Packages**

Installer package files (as described in the main text) actually represent just one of several types of package files in Mac OS X. Receipt files (stored in /Library/Receipts) represent another type of package file and are very similar to Installer packages.

Most Mac OS X applications are also packages. Such files have an .app extension. The Finder hides the extension, however, so all you see is a single file called AppleWorks, as opposed to a file called AppleWorks.app—or, more properly, a folder called AppleWorks.app. The actual application file itself, as well as various accessory files used by the application (such as international language support), are stored within the package.

Inside the Mac OS X System folder, you will find .framework and .bundle files or folders. These are also considered packages and are covered in more detail in Chapter 4.

Viewing package contents. If you want to view the contents of a package from the Finder, simply Control-click (or right-click on a multibutton mouse) the package icon and choose Show Package Contents from the contextual menu. The same command is also accessible from the Action menu in Finder window toolbars. If that menu choice does not appear, the file is not a package.

continues on next page

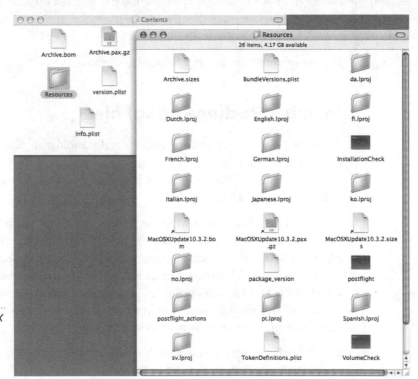

Figure 3.21

Inside the Mac OS X 10.3.2 update .pkg file: the Contents folder and the Resources folder.

TECHNICALLY SPEAKING ▶ Inside Packages *continued*

Although the Finder is designed to see a package as a single file, other applications may play by different rules. The Open or Save dialogs of some applications, for example, allow you to view a package as a folder and navigate within it. As a rule, you should not attempt to add new files to packages or delete or modify files within packages via this route unless you're confident of the consequences and specifically intend to do this (as in some hacks).

Search package contents. The Finder's Find command does not search the contents of package files. If you want to do a volume-wide search to locate an item inside any package, I recommend that you get the shareware utility Locator, which is a front end for the Unix locate command. To use it, first update the locate database (as Locator will request you to do on launch), then type (a) "/" (root) in the In text box and (b) your search term in the Locate text box. Click Start, and you should find what you seek. Just remember that search terms are case sensitive (unless you check the Case Insensitive box).

To search the contents of an individual package, you can use the Show Package Contents command to enter the package and then enter the desired text in the Search text box in the Finder window's toolbar (using the Selection option).

Another way to quickly navigate your volumes so that you can see inside packages, as well as all the normally invisible Unix directories and files, is to type file://local in your Web browser. In most browsers, this displays a list of the items at the root level of your startup volume. Each directory name is a hypertext link to the contents of that directory (assuming you have permission to view it). You can even display the contents of certain text documents via this method. In Safari, this command simply opens a Finder window for the root level of your startup volume; thus, in Safari the command offers no advantages over using the Finder directly.

What's inside a package? If you use the Show Package Contents contextual menu command to open a package file, the first thing you will typically see is yet another folder, called Contents. Inside most Contents folders are at least two files: PkgInfo and Info.plist.

The Info.plist file is a key file: It contains all of the critical information the Finder and other System software needs to understand what the package contains and how the package files should be treated. You can look at this .plist file (and similarly structured files) with any text editor (I recommend the discontinued freeware BBEdit Lite, which you can still download from VersionTracker.com, or its cousin TextWrangler). Even better, use the Apple Developer Tools utility called Property List Editor (covered more in Chapter 4).

PkgInfo contains a subset of the Info.plist data; the Finder uses it for quicker access.

If the package is an application, the top level (where the Contents folder resides) also sometimes contains an alias file to the actual executable code file, which is more deeply nested within the package.

continues on next page

TECHNICALLY SPEAKING ▶ Inside Packages *continued*

Depending on the type of package, the Contents folder may include MacOS and MacOS Classic folders (where the actual applications are stored) and a Resources folder, which contains graphics and other accessory items, as well as information for multiple-language support (in .lprog folders).

What's inside an installer package? Given that this chapter is about installing software, I want to note two files of particular interest that are included within installer packages:

- **Archive.bom.** The file extension .bom stands for *bill of materials.* This file contains the list of everything that the installer will install; it creates the list that appears when you choose Show Files from the installer's File menu. You may also see a matching file with the extension .bomout. This file contains essentially the same data, but in a form that can be read by any text editor, such as TextEdit, included in Mac OS X.

  Note: Receipt files left in the Receipts folder after an installation also contain an archive.bom file. This allows Mac OS X to check the .bom file for information as needed (such as when repairing permissions via Disk Utility).

  SEE: • "Technically Speaking: Repairing Disk Permissions and Receipts," in Chapter 5, for more details.

- **Archive.pax.gz.** The .gz and .pax extensions refer to separate compression schemes designed to reduce the size of this file, which contains all the files to be installed by the update.

  SEE: • "Extracting from an expanded .pax.gz file," earlier in this chapter, for more details.

Filename extensions and packages. In most cases, adding the appropriate extension to a folder's name is enough to convert the folder to a package. For example, if you take an ordinary folder and change its name from *foldername* to *foldername.pkg,* you will get a message that says, "Are you sure you want to add the extension 'pkg' to the end of the name? If you make this change, your folder may appear as a single file." If you click the Add button, the folder will now appear as a package file and launch the installer if you double-click it. Of course, the Installer will ultimately fail to open this pseudo-package, as the contents do not conform to what the installer expects to find.

You can make this same package conversion using the .app extension. In this case, the folder will adopt the generic application icon. If you double-click it, it will attempt to launch but ultimately fail to do so (as your folder is not really an application).

Can you reverse this process? Yes. You can take any file with a .pkg or .app extension and remove the extension. When you do this for an .app file, for example, you will get a message that says, "Are you sure you want to remove the extension '.app'? If you make this change, your application may appear as a folder." One glitch is that you cannot typically remove the extension from the Finder directly. Doing so simply prevents the extension from appearing in the Finder; it does not actually delete the extension. To truly delete it, select Get Info for the file and click the disclosure triangle for Name & Extension. Delete the extension from the name as it appears here. Then click the disclosure triangle again. At this point, the message described above will appear.

continues on next page

TECHNICALLY SPEAKING ▶ Inside Packages *continued*

Note: To be safe, I advise that you *not* try these tricks unless you're experimenting with files you've backed up elsewhere or don't care if they get ruined.

Bundle bits and packages. Another way the Finder determines whether a folder is treated as a package lies in something called *Finder attributes* (or *bits*). These bits determine whether a file is locked, for example. One of these bits is called the *bundle bit* (or *package bit*). Before the invention of packages (back in the Mac OS 8 days), this bit was only relevant to applications and had no effect on folders (whether on or off). Typically, the bundle bit was enabled for applications: It instructed the Finder to check the application for information about the type of documents the application creates. Starting in Mac OS 9, Apple decided to use the bundle bit with folders to indicate that a folder should really be treated as a package. Mac OS X similarly continues to use this bundle bit for folders.

Although bits are intended primarily for developer manipulation, numerous shareware utilities, such as XRay and FileXaminer, make it possible for anyone to manipulate them. Turn the bundle bit on to indicate a package; turn it off to indicate a normal folder. In this case, enabling the bit for an ordinary folder will typically result in the folder's adopting a document icon. However, if you double-click it, the item will still open as a folder. In most cases, assuming you have any need as a troubleshooter to make these conversions, I would recommend using the name extension method rather than fiddling with the bundle/package bit.

Creating a package. Creating a functional package (one that truly operates as an installer file or an application), as opposed to one that looks like a package but does nothing, requires more than just converting a folder to a package: You must set up the contents of the package according to specific guidelines described in Apple's Mac OS X documentation for developers. Apple's PackageMaker utility (available as part of Apple's Xcode Developer software) provides a convenient graphical interface for automating most of this process. You can only use it, however, to create new package files or to open an existing package template (.pmsp or .pmsm) file. You cannot, for example, download a package file from the Internet and open the file in PackageMaker with the intention of modifying the contents. Further details on using PackageMaker exceed what you need to know for typical troubleshooting.

Receipt files

Receipt files, as their name implies, are used by the OS to maintain a record of what the Installer application has installed. A receipt file is created each time you install new software via a package file. It's stored in a folder called Receipts, located in the root-level Library folder (/Library/Receipts).

When viewed from the Finder, a receipt file appears identical to the matching package file that was used to install the software. In fact, both files have identical names and share the same icon and description ("Installer package") in the Kind line of their Get Info windows. Indeed, if you use the Show Package

Contents contextual menu command to look inside a receipt package, you will see only minor differences between its contents and the contents of its matching installer package. The biggest difference is that the Archive.pax.gz file, which contains the actual updated software (as noted in "Technically Speaking: Inside Packages"), is missing from the receipt file. This is why the receipt file is so much smaller than its installer sibling—and why you can't use the receipt file to install an update.

If you double-click a receipt file, it will initially launch Installer (just as an installer file would). However, the launch is soon interrupted by an error message stating, "The Installer package {*name of file*} cannot be opened. The selected package is a receipt."

Figure 3.22

The contents of a Receipts folder for Panther.

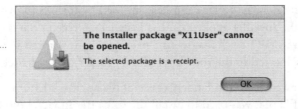

Figure 3.23

The error message that appears when you attempt to open a receipt.

What are receipt files used for? Receipt files are primarily used by Mac OS X to track the updates you've installed. This is relevant in several situations:

- Software Update may use receipt files to determine what software to list as uninstalled.

- The Installer application uses receipt files to determine whether a given installation should be listed as a new (full) installation or as an upgrade of an existing one. If it finds a receipt file, it considers the installation to be an upgrade.

- The Installer application may similarly use these files to check whether a given update can be installed on your computer (that is, it checks to see if the prerequired software is installed).

- The First Aid portion of Disk Utility uses the information stored in these receipt files to check the default permissions of installed updates so that they can be restored when using Repair Disk Permissions (as described in Chapters 5 and 6).

In actuality, when I tested the "rules" of how receipts are used, I found the process to be less than completely predictable.

- In no case did the presence or absence of a receipt file prevent a stand-alone installer from reinstalling an update.

- A receipt file did sometimes affect whether Software Update listed an update or not, but it did this mainly for non-OS updates (such as for iPod software). For updates of the OS itself, such as an update to Mac OS X 10.2.6, Software Update checks the OS version in a way that does not depend on receipt files. Mainly, it uses information stored in the SystemVersion.plist file, as described earlier in this chapter.

Removing receipt files. If you remove a receipt file in hopes of bypassing Mac OS X's refusal to list or install a given update, don't count on it working. In general, I recommend leaving these receipt files in place; ideally, you want Mac OS X to correctly track what you've installed.

You may, however, occasionally need to remove a receipt file to solve a problem with reinstalling a particular piece of software. For example, suppose you have software such as Apple's Keynote application on your drive. You decide to delete it and reinstall it via a Keynote.pkg file. If the Installer does not permit this reinstall, it's probably because you did not delete the receipt file of the same name from the Receipts folder. If this is the case, follow these steps:

1. Drag the receipt file for the problem software from its /Library/Receipts folder location to the Trash. (You need to be an administrator to do this.)

   Do not delete the file just yet: Deleting certain receipt files without successfully reinstalling the same software can cause problems (including failure to start up on restart).

2. Attempt the problem reinstallation again.

3. After the software has been successfully reinstalled, a new receipt file is created. You can now delete the old receipt file that you placed in the Trash.

If, after doing this, the install still fails, the receipt file is not the cause. Drag the receipt file back to its original location before restarting your Mac. Check for other causes, as described elsewhere in this chapter.

Note: Receipt files are only created by software installed via Apple's Installer utility.

SEE: • **"Technically Speaking: Repair Disk Permissions and Receipts," in Chapter 5, for related information.**

Backing Up and Restoring Mac OS X Volumes

Here's some advice you should already know: Back up the files on your drive(s)—and do so often! If a file on your drive gets corrupted or accidentally deleted and you don't have a backup, you may not be able to retrieve it. When this happens, you'll be glad you had a backup.

The danger posed by a lost or corrupted file my not seem serious if the file in question is a freeware program you downloaded from the Web. In this case, you can just download it again. Even here, though, if you destroyed a folder containing hundreds of such programs, it would be a real pain to remember everything you lost and then reacquire all of the software. More serious is the loss of irreplaceable files such as the near-final draft of a novel you spent the last two years writing.

To prevent such disasters, it's usually sufficient to back up just the files you've acquired, and, especially, the documents you've created. For these purposes, you don't need to back up your entire drive but instead can restrict your backup to your Home directory.

If you've installed applications in the Applications folder or added fonts to the /Library/Fonts folder, you may also want to back them up—especially if the software didn't come on a CD that could serve as a backup. Remember: Reinstalling applications from their installers is often better than just saving a backup of the application itself because an installer utility will install any accessory files (including invisible files), which you would not save by backing up just the application.

Note: If you've been using Classic, you may also want to back up your Mac OS 9 folders: System Folder, Applications (Mac OS 9), and (especially) Documents—to save any critical files and simplify a restore later.

There is, however, a good reason for maintaining a complete backup of your entire drive: If it becomes damaged in such a way that you need to either erase and reformat it or get a new drive, the simplest and fastest way to get up and running again is to restore the drive in its entirety from a current backup.

Restoring a Mac OS X startup volume presents some unique obstacles, the most critical of which is making sure your backup and restored volumes are bootable. If you're used to dealing with Mac OS 9, you will find that making a bootable volume is much trickier in Mac OS X.

For example, creating a bootable copy of a volume via drag and drop in the Mac OS X Finder does not work for the following reasons:

- File permissions are not preserved correctly.
- Invisible files, especially the critical Unix software, are not copied.
- Unix symbolic and hard links are broken.

TAKE NOTE ▶ Backing Up and Restoring a Home Directory

Even if you decide not to maintain a complete bootable backup of your Mac OS X volume (because it takes too long or requires costly additional hardware and software), you should at least maintain a backup of your Home directory. Since it should contain almost all of the files you've added and created since installing Mac OS X (except perhaps some programs in the Applications folder), creating a backup of it should at least prevent you from losing irreplaceable data. You can perform this type of backup in several ways, all of which I describe in the text that follows.

Using the Finder

Backing up. Here's one simple method that uses the Finder and thus does not require any third-party software (though it won't copy invisible files in the copied directories):

1. If there's something you want to save that's not yet in your Home directory, copy it there.

   (Most of what you want to save should already be there.)

2. Copy your entire Home directory to your backup location.

   Your Home directory (as well as those of other local users) is located in the Users directory at the root level of your drive.

   SEE: • Chapter 4 for more on the directory structure of Mac OS X.

   Ideally, your backup location should be a removable medium such as a CD-RW disc, DVD-R disc, or an iPod. Alternatively, you could use an online server such as Apple's iDisk, which Mac OS X fully supports (see Chapter 8).

continues on next page

TAKE NOTE ▶ **Backing Up and Restoring a Home Directory**   *continued*

The medium you select will depend on what types of drives you have available and how much space the backup requires. A small directory can fit entirely on a CD-R disc. Larger ones will require DVD-R discs, or an additional hard drive.

SEE: • **"Backing up Mac OS X: hardware strategies," later in this chapter, for more details.**

Do this often, so that your backup remains current. If you plan on erasing your Mac OS X volume, do it just before you erase the drive.

You are now set to restore individual files from your backup, as needed.

Restoring. Should you ever need to erase your entire drive and reinstall/restore Mac OS X, you will want to restore your entire Home directory (as well as any other user directories you backed up). To do this, you need to create new Home directories, ideally with the same names as the ones you backed up. As part of reinstalling Mac OS X, a fresh Home directory will be created for you, as the default administrative user. Use the Accounts System Preferences pane to create directories beyond the one automatically created for you.

continues on next page

Figure 3.24

.Mac's Backup
utility.

TAKE NOTE ▶ Backing Up and Restoring a Home Directory *continued*

To restore your Home directory:

• Copy the contents of each backed-up directory to the new folder of the same name. In some cases, such as the Desktop, you may need to copy directly from one subfolder to the other.

 To replace the contents for users other than yourself, you must be an administrator and use root access (as described in "Root Access," in Chapter 4).

 Warning! Do not copy a Home directory to the Users folder, and do not create a new folder in the Users directory via the Finder's New Folder command. These methods will not work because Mac OS X will not recognize the folder as a valid Users folder. You can set up a system so that your active Home directory is on a volume separate from your Mac OS X software, but that's a separate issue.

 SEE: • **"Technically Speaking: Moving Your Home Directory to a Separate Partition," below, for details.**

 If you're concerned that some preferences files, fonts, or other files in the Library folder of your old directory may be corrupt, you can bypass copying any or all files from the old Library folder.

 You can always copy these files later if you find that you need them and cannot re-create them.

Note: The following Apple Knowledge Base article includes information about how to back up and restore an entire Users directory (which contains all users' Home directories) using the Finder and Terminal: http://docs.info.apple.com/article.html?artnum=106941.

Note: If FileVault (which is described in Chapter 2) is enabled for a Home directory that is not the currently logged-in user, the directory will be encrypted. Ideally, you should unencrypt it before backing it up.

Using Backup Utilities

Synchronization utilities. You can use a variety of utilities, such as Duover, Synchronize Pro! X, and Synk X, to "synchronize" two folders. When you do this, the utility updates both folders so that they always contain the same data—useful when backing up your Home directory because just the new or modified files get backed up (as opposed to everything in the folders). Synchronizing is also useful for maintaining a backup of a folder whose contents change often (such as the contents of a Web site you maintain).

Some synchronize utilities can also serve as full volume-backup utilities. Check the utility's documentation for details.

Apple's Backup utility. If (and only if) you have a .Mac account, you can use Backup to back up selected files to your iDisk storage or to CD and DVD discs. Backup is preset to back up most of the critical files and folders in your Home directory. You can modify these settings.

continues on next page

TAKE NOTE ▶ Backing Up and Restoring a Home Directory *continued*

Although it may seem like you can set Backup to back up anything you want simply by adding the desired directory to the backup list via the plus (+) button, this is not exactly the case. Backup will not backup applications, for example. Although you can fool it into doing so by compressing or creating a disk image of an application before backing it up, if your goal is a complete backup, I recommend using another utility. In addition, you cannot use Backup to make a complete bootable copy of a Mac OS X volume; for that, you need a backup utility such as Dantz Retrospect or Prosoft's Data Backup. The final caveat? Using Backup can get expensive if your Home directory is large because you will need to pay for additional storage space (beyond the initial 100 MB that comes with your .Mac subscription).

Hint: To delete items stored in a backup on your iDisk, select Restore from iDisk in Backup's pop-up menu. When you do this, the plus button becomes a minus (-) button. Click an item followed by the minus button to delete the item. To delete files from within a folder item, click the folder and select Get Info (Command-I). From the Get Info listing that appears, select the item to be deleted and click the minus button.

Disk Utility. You can use the New Image from Folder command, in the Images menu of Disk Utility, to create a disk image of your Home directory. When you're finished, select Scan Image for Restore, from the Images menu, to verify that the image is OK to use for restoring. This can be a convenient and space-saving way to make a backup—especially if you've created a compressed image. You would later mount/attach the image to access the files for restoring. Alternatively, you could use the Restore feature of Disk Utility to restore an entire Home directory (obviously not for a user that is currently logged in).

SEE: • **"Backing up Mac OS X: Utilities for Volume Backups," later in this chapter, for related details.**

TECHNICALLY SPEAKING ▶ Moving Your Home Directory to a Separate Partition

As described in "Take Note: Backing Up and Restoring a Home Directory," you can easily copy your Home directory to a separate partition via the Finder, where it serves as a useful backup for your personal files (should you ever need to erase your Mac OS X volume and reinstall the OS from scratch).

However, if you want to *move* your Home directory to a separate partition and have it function from there as your active Home directory, you cannot do so simply by dragging the folder to the separate partition.

continues on next page

TECHNICALLY SPEAKING ▶ Moving Your Home Directory to a Separate Partition *continued*

Why would you even want to do this? Some users prefer this arrangement because it makes it even less of a hassle to erase their Mac OS X startup drives and reinstall Mac OS X since they don't have to worry about backing up and restoring items in their Home directories. This arrangement can also free up space on the Mac OS X startup volume, which can improve performance. That said, I doubt that many users will derive sufficient value from this to make it worth the bother.

If, despite my reservations, you still want to move your Home directory to a new location and use it as your active directory, there are several ways to do so. The following method requires Terminal. Note: Each command is one line in Terminal even if it appears as two lines in this text. Where a command is split into two lines here, enter a space before continuing to type the second line.

1. Launch Terminal and type the following:

   ```
   sudo ditto -rsrc "/Users/username" "/Volumes/volumename/Users/username"
   ```

   Volumename is the name of the partition/volume where the new Home directory is to go. *Username* is your user name and thus the name of your Home directory.

   This copies your Home directory, including all invisible files, to a Users folder on the separate volume; the -rsrc option ensures that all resource forks are copied.

2. Next, type the following:

   ```
   sudo niutil -createprop / "/Users/username" home "/Volumes/volumename/Users/username"
   ```

   This command reassigns your Home directory from the original location to the new location.

   Note: You can accomplish nearly the same thing as you do in the above steps via NetInfo Manager. To do so, launch the application and go to users/*username*. Then, in the lower portion of the window, scroll down until you see the Home line. Change its value from its current location (for example, /Users/*username*) to the new location (for example, /Volumes/*volumename*/Users/*username*). However, I have found that using Terminal instead is less likely to precipitate any problems.

3. Check that the newly created directory is working by logging out and logging back in. Repeat the previous step for any additional Home directories you want to move and save.

4. If all seems well, return to Terminal and type the following:

   ```
   sudo rm —dr "/Users/username"
   ```

   This command removes the old directory.

5. Now type the following:

   ```
   sudo ln -s "/Volumes/volumename/Users/username" "/Users/username"
   ```

continues on next page

TECHNICALLY SPEAKING ▶ Moving Your Home Directory to a Separate Partition *continued*

This command creates a symbolic link (similar to an alias) in the Users directory on the boot volume that points to the newly created Home directory on the new host volume. This creates the illusion that your Home directory is still in its expected location in the Users folder on the boot volume.

If you erase and reinstall your Mac OS X volume, you presumably can reconnect to this alternate directory via steps 2 through 5.

If the host volume is a removable volume or one that you sometimes unmount, you *must* either shut down or log in with a user not on the external volume before you can disconnect the external volume. Once it's disconnected, you can connect it to another similarly set up computer—both computers can thus share the same Home directory.

Note: If you intend to use Panther's FileVault security feature, you should not move your Home directory as described here.

SEE: • "Security," in Chapter 2, for more on FileVault.
   • "Aliases and Symbolic Links," in Chapter 6, for more on this subject.
   • Chapter 10 for more on using Unix commands.

Backing up Mac OS X: utilities for volume backups

Fortunately, the problems with backing up and restoring a Mac OS volume can be easily solved with a number of readily available utilities.

Third-party backup utilities. Although you can back up and restore volumes using just the software that came with your Mac, the best, most reliable methods employ third-party software. Thus, I'll begin my discussion with these.

- **Prosoft's Data Backup X** has an exceptionally clear interface that allows you to choose among the three primary types of backups:

  Mirror creates an exact duplicate of the drive—the best option if you want a complete, bootable copy of the drive.

  Incremental adds new files to the backup but does not delete old ones—best if you want to keep old versions of documents and applications as an archive.

  Synchronization ensures that two folders or volumes are "in sync," copying in both directions, always preserving the newer version of a file. Note that if you delete a file from your main drive, it will also be deleted from the "synchronized" volume. A variation of this approach, a *unidirectional synchronization,* is essentially the same as a mirror.

- **Dantz's Retrospect for Mac OS X** is the Mac OS X version of the gold standard of Mac OS 9 backup utilities. It includes numerous features that other backup utilities do not. One nice feature: It allows you to restore files while you're booted from the Mac OS X volume that's the intended destination.

- **Carbon Copy Cloner** is a shareware utility that uses Unix's ditto command to make backups. The author's Web page (www.bombich.com/mactips/image.html) provides many more details about backing up Mac OS X volumes via Unix.

Disk Utility. If you want to make a full backup of a volume using just Mac OS X utility software, use Disk Utility's Image and Restore features, which provide you with two options: You can back up and restore a volume directly, or you can create an image file for backup and restore.

To back up and restore a volume directly:

1. Launch Disk Utility, and from the window that appears click the Restore tab.

2. From the list in the left column, drag the volume you wish to back up to the Source text box. Although your currently active startup volume *can* be used as the source, I would advise against it (that is, you should start up from another volume instead). For example, the active startup volume may impose permissions restrictions that prevent a successful complete backup.

3. From the list in the left column, drag the volume you wish to contain the backup to the Destination text box.

   Note: Make sure the Ignore Ownership on This Volume option is disabled in the Finder's Get Info window in the Destination volume.

4. Check the Erase Destination box.

   If you do not select Erase Destination, the restore will add to the existing contents of the Destination volume rather than replace it—typically not what you would want.

5. Click the Restore button at the bottom of the window.

   If you have permissions problems when creating a backup (for example, you get a "Permission denied" error or other problems), log out and log in as the root user (or simply launch Disk Utility via root, using a utility such as Pseudo, as described in Chapter 4). Try the above again.

Assuming that both volumes you selected were hard-drive volumes, this should back up the source volume to the destination volume.

If the source volume was bootable (for example, it was a volume from which you could start up in Mac OS X), the backup should be bootable as well (see Chapter 5 if you're having problems booting).

To restore from the backup you created, reverse the above procedure—that is, start up from the backup copy you made and restore to your original volume location.

To back up to and restore from a disk image:

1. Launch Disk Utility, and from the list in the left column, select the volume you wish to back up.

2. From the Images menu, select New, and from the submenu, select Image from {*name of selected device*}. The name of your selected volume should appear as the device name.

3. From the Convert Image window that appears, do the following:

   Enter a name for the image.

   Select an Image Format. The default of "read-only" is the best choice overall; however, you should select "compressed" if you need to create a smaller image so that it will fit on the destination volume.

   Leave Encryption set to None (unless security of the image is a concern).

   Select a destination volume via the Where pop-up menu. This volume must be large enough to contain the image (which means it should have at least twice as much free space as the image itself will need).

4. Click Save and wait for the image to be saved.

   If you run into permissions problems when attempting to create the image (for example, you get a "Permission denied" error or other problems), log out and log in as the root user (or simply launch Disk Utility via root, using a utility such as Pseudo, as described in Chapter 4). Try the above again.

5. From the Images menu, select Scan Image for Restore. From the window that appears, select the image you just created and click Open. This verifies that an image can be used for restoring.

The image is now saved and ready to be restored.

If desired, you can burn the image contents to a CD or DVD (assuming they fit) by selecting the image and clicking the Burn command. This copies the mountable contents of the image to the CD or DVD, not the actual .dmg file itself. You can copy just the .dmg file without using Disk Utility: Just drag the .dmg file's icon to a mounted, unused CD-R or DVD-R in the Finder and burn the disc.

To restore from the image file:

1. Launch Disk Utility, and from the window that appears click the Restore tab.

2. If the image you created is in the left column, drag it to the Source text box. If not, click the Image button, then locate and select the image.

3. Drag the name of the volume to be restored from the left column to the Destination text box. Keep in mind that this cannot be the current startup volume because it will be erased.

4. Check the Erase Destination box.

5. Click the Restore button at the bottom of the window.

The volume should now be restored. Wait until restoration is complete, then restart from the restored volume.

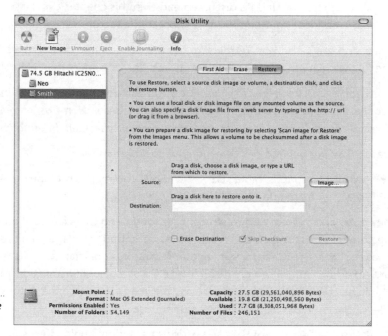

Figure 3.25

Disk Utility's Restore screen.

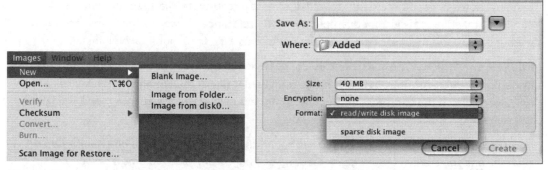

Figure 3.26

Disk Utility's Images menu (left) and New Blank Image dialog (right).

TECHNICALLY SPEAKING ▶ More About Disk Utility's Image and Restore Features

The Image and Restore features in Disk Utility are new in Panther. The following provides some background information to help you understand how they work.

The asr and hdiutil commands. Disk Utility's Restore features are actually a front end for the asr (Apple Software Restore) command in Terminal, and its image commands are similarly based on the hdiutil command. As discussed earlier in this chapter, asr is also the basis of the Software Restore application used to restore Macs to the factory-set configuration.

Type man asr and man hdiutil in Terminal to get the documentation (manuals) for these commands. The following are the opening comments from the documentation of for asr and hdiutil:

asr efficiently copies disk images onto volumes. asr can also accurately clone volumes. In its first form, asr copies source (usually a disk image) to target. In its second form, asr prepares a disk image to be restored efficiently, adding file by file and whole-volume checksum information.

hdiutil uses the DiskImages framework to manipulate disk image files.

As usual with Unix commands in Mac OS X, the above commands provide more options than are available via their front-end utility (Disk Utility, in this case).

Restore features and system administrators. Although end users can take advantage of Disk Utility's Restore features for their own backups (as described in the main text), Apple emphasizes the value of these features for system administrators—for example, in classrooms with computers. An administrator can create an image file of a default installation; place it on a CD, DVD, portable hard drive, or server; and then use the image to restore the status of the machines in the lab—after they've been modified by student use.

In the "How to use asr" section of the man asr documentation, Apple offers step-by-step instructions for using a combination of Disk Utility and Unix commands in Terminal to do this. In particular, it notes how you may want to initially create a read/write image so that you can eliminate machine-specific (for example, by host) preferences as well as the admin account used to set up the machine from the image before using it for a multimachine installation.

Image from Folder vs. Image from Device. To create a backup clone of a volume, the man asr documentation recommends using Image from Folder rather than Image from {Device} (as can be selected from the submenu of the New command in Disk Utility's Images menu). It states the following:

If you create an image from a device, you will not be able to block restore it to any volume larger than the one you created the image on. Creating an image from folder/volume is slower, but will give a better result (stretchable, defragmented). Beware that this operation requires two times as much free space on the volume to which you are saving the image as you have data on the source.

continues on next page

TECHNICALLY SPEAKING ▶ **More About Disk Utility's Image and Restore Features** *continued*

If some target volumes restore quickly and others slowly, the {slow} source image was probably created without stretch (i.e., "image from device" instead of the "image from folder/volume" recommended above). For example, if the source was a 60 GB volume, the image will block restore on 60 GB and smaller volumes, but file copy on an 80 GB target.

Despite all of Apple's advice, I've had problems using Image from Folder. In particular, I've received an "Operation not supported" error when using this option, whereas Image from Device succeeded. In addition, it's generally recommended (at least when making a copy of a bootable CD, as described in the main text) that you select Image from Device instead of Image from Folder—because the device image selection ensures that all of the mass-storage-device components (partition maps, drivers, and so on) that are required for the volume to be bootable are copied.

I go with what works for me and use Image from Device.

Segmented images. In Jaguar, the Disk Copy application includes an option to segment a large disk image, such as into 630 MB segments, allowing you to back up a large image to multiple CDs. (Note: If backing up to a hard drive or a DVD, you could pick a size as large as 2 GB.) This segmenting option is not included in Disk Utility's Images options. However, the segment options remains available via the hdiutil command in Terminal. Segmenting requires having enough free space on a single drive to hold the complete set of disk images you will need to create.

Mounted images. Disk image files will appear in the bottom of the left column of the Disk Utility window. If you mount an image, the attached volume appears as a subhead under the image file. These listings remain in the column as long as the files or volumes are available. If an image you want to use is not listed, drag its icon from the Finder to the column.

Blank image. When you create a new blank image via the New Blank Image command in the Images menu, you select the image size from the Size pop-up menu. You have numerous choices: For example, if you want to create a disk image that perfectly matches the size of a CD or DVD, there are specific options for these media sizes.

When creating a new blank image, the only options available in Format are "read/write disk image" and "sparse disk image." Not to worry: You can always change the format after you've create the image, using the Convert command from the Images menu. From here, you are presented with the same Format and Encryption options that you get when you select to create an Image from Folder or Device: read/write, read-only, compressed, and CD/DVD Master.

continues on next page

TECHNICALLY SPEAKING ▶ **More About Disk Utility's Image and Restore Features** *continued*

A blank image should start out as read/write or sparse because the whole point of it is to be able to add content to the image file after it has been created. To do this, mount the image and drag the desired files to the window of the mounted volume. If you create a blank read/write image of a given size, the size is fixed. Even as a blank image, the image is at the size you set. If you create a sparse image file, it starts out at a minimal size (usually around 10 to 14 MB) and grows to the maximum you specify in the Size option as you add files to the mounted volume. This allows you to create an image file that is never any larger than you need. In either case, you cannot add files that would exceed the maximum size you set.

To burn a CD from a blank image, add the content you want to the mounted volume, unmount the volume, select the image, and click the Burn button in the toolbar (or select Burn from the Images menu).

Checksum. The checksum is a calculation based on all the data on a volume. Thus, the checksums for a volume and an image created from that volume should be the same. The checksum thus provides a means of verifying the accuracy of an image you create. See the Disk Utility Help file for more details on checksum.

SEE: • "Take Note: Burning CDs (and DVDs)," in Chapter 6, for more on this topic.
  • "Technically Speaking: Running Mac OS X Software from the Terminal," in Chapter 10, for more details on using the asr and hdiutil Unix commands.

Using Terminal. If you're comfortable with using Terminal, you can back up a volume via Unix commands. The following provides an overview of what you need to know:

- **ditto.** The ditto -rsrc command copies directories (and their contents), correctly maintaining all permissions settings and copying any resource forks. As a result, ditto is a good choice for making a clone backup of an entire volume—one that will be bootable, if necessary. In fact, Carbon Copy Cloner is a front end for the ditto command, bypassing the need to use this command in Terminal.

  SEE: • "Unix: Copying, Moving, and Deleting," in Chapter 10, for more details on ditto and related copy commands.

- **rsync.** The rsync command acts as a directory-synchronization tool. Compared with ditto, rsync adds the option to copy *only* files that are new or that have changed from an existing backup, thereby reducing the time needed to complete the task. Its disadvantage is that, like cp, it does not preserve the resource fork. The solution here is a variation on rsync that copies resource forks: RsyncX. See the following Web page for more details: www.macosxlabs.org/rsyncx/rsyncx.html.

- **psync.** The psync command (see www.dan.co.jp/cases/macosx/backup-volume.html) is an excellent choice for doing backups. Like rysnc, psync can synchronize source and target directories. If you don't want to use Terminal, a front-end version of psync is available at http://sourceforge.net/projects/psyncx. Either variation can create full and bootable backups of Mac OS X. Note: Carbon Copy Cloner now includes psync software.

- **asr.** As noted in "Technically Speaking: More About Disk Utility's Image and Restore Features," the asr command may be used to "clone volumes" (that is, make full bootable backup copies). You can use it instead of Disk Utility's Restore feature.

   SEE: • "Technically Speaking: Type/Creator vs. Filename Extensions," in Chapter 4, for related information.

TAKE NOTE ▶ Backups of Bootable Volumes Don't Boot

If you back up a complete Mac OS X volume with the intention of using it as a bootable copy (such as by using Retrospect's Duplicate command), you may find that you can't boot from the backup volume once you're finished. In some cases, you may get an error during the backup attempt, which prevents the backup from completing.

The most likely cause of such an error is that the "Ignore ownership on this volume" option (located in the Ownership and Permissions section of the Get Info window for the volume) is enabled. If that's the case, *uncheck* this option and try the backup again. Then try to boot from the backup; it should work.

In addition, I've found that the most reliable way to boot from a newly created backup is to use the Startup Disk System Preferences to select the backup as the startup disk. Alternatives, such as holding down the Option key at startup (as described in Chapter 5), may not work until you've successfully started up via the System Preferences method.

Otherwise, depending on your Mac OS X version, Mac model, and external drive (SCSI, USB, or FireWire), you may have problems starting up due to issues with the drive itself, as noted later in this chapter (see "Troubleshooting Tips and Hints: Installing Software").

Backing up Mac OS X: hardware strategies

Over time, the preferred data-backup hardware has changed, just as the common backup media has shifted (for example, from floppy disks to DVD discs) and typical hard-drive capacity has increased (for example, from 20 MB to 100 GB and more). Backup hardware also varies as a function of the type of data you're backing up (a few files versus an entire disk).

Here are my current preferred backup choices. (You may find that using a combination of them provides the best option of all!)

- **CD-RW or DVD-RW drive.** You use a CD-RW or DVD-RW drive to back up data to CD-Rs or DVD-Rs—primarily for a limited subset of your data (in particular, data that doesn't change often or that you would not be able to replace). This method is perfect, for example, for backing up your MP3 music library, your collection of family digital photos, or the manuscript of that novel you're working on. It provides the most reliable way to store these files without risk of the backup itself becoming damaged or inaccessible. You can use this method (especially DVD-R) to back up an entire drive, though you won't want to do so often because it's likely to be very slow. You can also use RW discs in order to perform later backups with the same media; however, I recommend against this because writing to these discs is significantly slower than to the write-once media, and the discs are also more prone to becoming unreadable at some later point. In general, you can use the Finder to perform these types of backups.

If you're using CD-Rs (or similar media of limited size) and are unable to fit the entire contents of a directory onto one disc, you can split the contents across as many discs as needed. Your only problem would be if you had a single file too large to fit on one disc. In that case, you might want to use a utility like StuffIt Deluxe, which can create a segmented archive of the file; each segment can be stored on separate media. Apple's Backup application can also back up across multiple CDs. You can create a segmented set of .dmg files (as noted in "Technically Speaking: More About Disk Utility's Image and Restore Features," above). However, I recommend using a medium that can contain the entire volume (if possible): It's much faster and less tedious.

- **Tape drive.** A tape drive is a good choice for maintaining a regularly updated backup of an entire volume. I have a FireWire Ecrix tape drive, which I highly recommend. The maximum capacity of an Ecrix tape is 33 GB.

  With a tape drive, you're forced to back up using a utility such as Retrospect (tape drives don't mount on the Desktop, so the Finder does not "see" them). However, a tape drive is probably the most cost-efficient way to back up multiple drives and computers. For example, if you have a small network of four Macs plus some external drives, and you want to keep them all backed up, you can do it all with one tape drive and multiple tapes. The cost per GB of tape is probably cheaper here than with any other alternative. With this combination, you can even back up over a network (that is, you don't need to physically attach the drive to the computer you're backing up). Ecrix tape drives are also fast enough that you can back up even a multi-GB hard drive in a reasonable amount of time. On the other hand, you can't do an unattended backup (for example, at night while you're sleeping) if the backup will span more than one tape.

  With a tape drive and Retrospect, it's also easy to perform incremental backups. That is, you can instruct Retrospect to only back up files that are different from the last time you backed up (saving time over a complete backup), and you can have it so that Retrospect does not overwrite old versions of files when adding new ones. This latter option is especially useful for frequently changing files: If you discover that an old "deleted" version of a document contains a passage you want to retrieve, you may still be able to do so.

- **Hard drive.** Finally, you can do a full "mirrored" backup of a volume to another hard drive. This is especially useful if all you want to do is back up the internal drive in a single Mac. You can use Retrospect for this task (in exactly the same way I described for tape drives); however, Retrospect includes *another* option, called Duplicate, that I recommend instead. Here's what to do:

  1. Get an external FireWire drive equal to or larger in size than your internal drive.

  2. Format it with the same number and sizes of partitions as your internal drive.

  3. Use Retrospect's Duplicate option to create a duplicate of the drive. (You will have to do this separately for each partition.)

  With this method, instead of storing your data in a Retrospect archival file format, Retrospect creates a duplicate of each file, much as the Finder would do. Unlike the Finder, however, Retrospect copies all files (including invisible files) and maintains all permissions and links correctly. The result is an exact duplicate of your hard drive. You can even boot from it.

  Do this backup as often as you feel necessary.

  With Retrospect and a hard drive (or multiple hard drives), you can also do regularly scheduled incremental backups—great for users who need to back up an entire volume every day, or even every few hours.

  You can also use the previously mentioned utilities (such as Data Backup X and Carbon Copy Cloner) to do a mirrored backup of a hard drive.

- **Internet.** You can back up to a server on the Internet. Apple's .Mac, especially in combination with its Backup utility, is the best-known example of this for Mac users. Although it is slow (and potentially expensive for large backups), it has the advantage of being off-site. If disaster strikes (such as a theft or fire in your home), these Internet backups will still be available. Unless you maintain physical backups somewhere else (such as by placing backup CDs in a safety deposit box), this is the only protection you will have against such disasters.

  SEE: • "Take Note: Backing Up and Restoring a Home Directory," earlier in this chapter, for more on the Backup utility.

Finally, see the following Apple Knowledge Base article for more tips on backing up Mac OS X volumes: http://docs.info.apple.com/article.html? artnum=106941. See also the following Web pages for more background on the Unix backup commands: www.bombich.com/mactips/image.html and www.macdevcenter.com/pub/a/mac/2002/07/02/terminal_5.html.

Creating an Emergency Startup Volume

Troubleshooters often find it useful to have a startup disk other than the one that's normally used—typically, the Mac's internal drive. Alternative startup disks can be convenient when you're doing something that cannot be done to the current startup drive (such as disk repairs with some utilities). They become especially valuable if the data on your default drive gets corrupted in such a way that the disk cannot start up. At these times, an emergency bootable disk becomes an essential tool for repairing the problem drive, or at least recovering data from it.

Because the Mac OS Install disc is bootable and provides access to Disk Utility, you can use it as an emergency boot disc. Third-party repair utilities also typically come on their own bootable CDs. Still, these discs may prove less useful as updated versions of the software are released, for which you do not have a CD. In any case, it's convenient to be able to create your own custom bootable emergency disk—one that contains all the software of your choosing.

In past years, emergency bootable volumes took the form of floppy disks or (more recently) CD-Rs or Zip disks. More recently, that emergency volume could have been a portable FireWire hard drive. In this section, I discuss how to set up an emergency volume using several different media. Of special interest are the procedures for making a custom bootable CD.

Creating a bootable volume in Mac OS 9 was about as simple as it could possibly be: You just dragged a copy of a System Folder to the volume, and (assuming the software was recent enough to run on the Mac in question) you were able to start up your Mac from that drive. This method worked with hard drives as well as most removable media (such as Zip disks). CDs, however, presented a special problem: A CD needed some special boot code for the Mac to recognize the disc as a startup volume at a point in the startup process when it typically would not yet have loaded the code needed to recognize CDs in the first place! This problem was solved by utilities such as Roxio's Toast, which created a bootable CD with the needed special code from any original that contained a System Folder. Even Mac OS X's Disk Utility can burn a bootable CD if you first create a disk image of a bootable CD for it to copy.

Creating a custom bootable Mac OS X volume presents considerably more difficulties. The primary reason is that the essential System files are not all in the Mac OS X System directory. In addition, numerous invisible files, mostly related to the underlying Unix OS, need to be copied as well. And there is the potential issue of setting up a default user account.

Thus, you cannot simply copy a Mac OS X System folder to a Zip disk, for example, and expect it to function as a startup volume. In fact, given that Zip discs max out at 250 MB, and a typical Mac OS X system can require more than 600 MB, it's unlikely that you'll be able to use a Zip disk as a Mac OS X startup disc under any circumstances.

Bootable hard drive

If you've divided your internal hard drive into several partitions, the simplest thing to do would be to use a Mac OS X Install CD to install Mac OS X on more than one partition. You could then use the second Mac OS X installation as your emergency partition. One weakness of this approach is that if the entire hard drive fails, you will not be able to start up from any partition.

A better alternative is an external hard drive. Especially useful if you want to travel with an emergency startup drive are small, portable FireWire drives (such as LaCie's PocketDrives)—or even an iPod.

As an alternative to using the Mac OS X Install CD to install Mac OS X on an external drive, you can use a utility like Retrospect (as described in "Backing up Mac OS X: utilities for volume backups," earlier in this chapter) to make a bootable duplicate of your main drive. However, I would not use the same volume as both an emergency drive and a backup volume. Doing so puts your backup data at increased risk.

Bootable DVD

You should also be able to install Mac OS X onto a DVD-RAM (which has a capacity of at least 2.6 GB). To do so, however, you must have a DVD-RAM drive (which is different from a DVD-R drive), as well as a second CD drive. Apple provided DVD-RAM drives on some Power Mac G4s several years ago, but it's no longer an option. Of course, you can purchase an external DVD-RAM drive for any Mac, but this drive format has never achieved the critical mass needed for success. Thus, I doubt many Mac users have these drives. A drive that combines DVD-RAM and DVD-R formats may someday become a standard, but that day is not here yet.

If you do have the required DVD-RAM setup, you should be able to install Mac OS X on it just as if it were an external hard drive. Expect the process to take much longer, however.

A DVD-R (the type you use to burn movies with iDVD) functions more like a CD. It is likely that procedures similar to those I describe next for making a bootable CD would work for making a bootable DVD-R (Apple already makes a bootable DVD, so I know it can be done); however, I have not put this theory to the test. For now, unless you really need the extra capacity of a DVD, I recommend sticking with making bootable CDs.

Bootable CD

For troubleshooters, by far the most useful and commonly used bootable disc is a bootable CD. So, if you own a CD-RW drive, can you create one of these bootable CDs? Yes and no, for now. You can certainly create an exact copy of a bootable CD that will also be bootable, but making a useful customized bootable CD is not a user-friendly procedure.

Making a duplicate bootable CD. If all you want is to make an exact copy of a bootable CD (such as the Mac OS X Install CD for use as an emergency disk), it's relatively easy to do.

However, don't expect to use the Burn Disc feature in Mac OS 9's or Mac OS X's Finder to accomplish this feat. At least as of Mac OS X 10.3, you could not create a copy of a bootable CD using this feature.

Toast, a commercial disc-burning application, can make a bootable Mac OS X CD—and using it is as simple as clicking the Copy Disc button to copy the Install CD. This works especially well if you have two CD drives (only one needs to be RW)—one for the blank CD-R and another for the Mac OS X Install disc. If this doesn't work for some reason, first create a .dmg of the Install CD and then use Toast to copy the unmounted image file to the CD. You could do this by creating the image file via Disk Utility in Mac OS X. However, if you need to go this route, you might as well skip Toast altogether and just use Disk Utility.

To create a bootable copy of a Mac OS X Install CD with Disk Utility in Panther:

1. Booting from your hard drive, insert and mount the Mac OS X Install Disc 1 CD.

2. Launch Disk Utility.

3. In the left column, the Mac OS X Install Disc 1 CD will be listed in the following manner: At the top of the hierarchy will be the name of the drive itself (for example, Toshiba DVD-ROM SD-R002); the subheading under that name will be Session 1; the subheading under that name will be Mac OS X Install Disc 1.

4. Select Session 1.

   Note: For multisession CDs, each session would be listed separately here. To create a multisession CD, use the "Leave disc appendable" check box in Disk Utility's Burn window. These instructions assume you have a single-session CD.

5. From the Image menu, select "New." From the New hierarchical menu, select "Image from {*name of device*}." The name of the device should be something like *disk4s1*.

6. From the Convert Image dialog, name the image. Leave Image Format as "read-only" or change it to "DVD/CD master" (which is what I recommend)—or use "compressed" if you need to save space.

   The "read/write" format can be used if you intend to modify the contents of the image before burning it to a CD. In this format, you can mount the image and drag files to or from the mounted volume. Changes you make are saved to the image (.dmg) file. You need to unmount the image before burning the image to a CD. Ideally, you should also convert the image file to a read-only or compressed image (using the Convert command in the Images menu) before burning the CD.

7. Click Save.

8. Returning to the left column of the Disk Utility window, select the image you just created. Click the Burn button in the toolbar or select Burn from the Images menu.

9. Insert a CD-R at the prompt in the Burn Disc dialog that appears. At this point, the Burn button in the dialog will undim. Click it and wait for the burn to complete.

There are numerous combinations of selections you can make when selecting a CD to burn (for example, Session 1 versus Mac OS X Install Disc 1) and a format for burning (for example, read-only versus CD/DVD Master). I have not tried every combination, but I have tried several—and this was the only one that worked for me. Feel free to experiment with other combinations if you don't share my success.

SEE: • **"Take Note: Burning CDs (and DVDs)," in Chapter 6, for more on multisession CDs and related issues.**

Figure 3.27

Disk Utility's Burn Disc dialog in Panther.

THE JAGUAR WAY ▶ Creating a Bootable CD with Disk Copy

For those of you who are still using Jaguar—or are interested in how different the same task can be in the older OS version—here's how to create a bootable copy of a Mac OS X Install CD with Disk Copy (and only one CD drive):

1. Booting from your hard drive, insert and mount the Mac OS X Install Disc 1 CD.

2. Launch Disk Copy.

3. From the File menu, choose New and select Image from Device from the hierarchical menu.

Here, you see a series of listings: disk0, disk 1, and so on. Some items may have a disclosure triangle next to them. Click the disclosure triangles until you find CD_ROM_Mode_1 in the Description column. This is the Install CD. Starting in Jaguar, the name of the CD (Mac OS X Install Disc 1) should also appear in the Volume column.

4. Select the Install CD, and click the Image button.

5. In the window that appears, give the file a name in the Save As text box.

6. Choose an image format.

I chose DVD/CD Master. One or more of the other formats may have worked as well, but this one seemed best, given that what I wanted was a CD master. If you want to modify the contents of the image before burning the CD, and you have problems with the DVD/CD Master selection, try Read/Write as the format.

7. Leave encryption set to None.

The resulting image file will be named {*your selected name*}.cdr.dmg.

8. Eject the Mac OS X Install CD.

Do not try to mount the image.

9. From Disk Copy's File menu, choose Burn Image.

10. When you're asked to insert a blank CD, do so.

11. Click the Burn button to burn the CD.

When you're finished, you should have a bootable copy of the Mac OS X Install CD.

Making a modified copy of a bootable CD. The above procedure is all well and good. But what if you want to make a customized CD with your own utilities on it?

It may at first seem that the solution is to create a read/write image and add your own utilities to the image (deleting unneeded and nonessential files already on the image, if necessary). The problem is, a bootable CD created in this way does not load the Finder. In fact, the Finder is not even on the CD. Instead, the CD boots directly into the Installer utility, which is the only way the CD can start. Thus, although you may have other utilities on the drive, you would have no way to access them. Could you get the CD to boot into another utility instead of the Installer? It's possible to modify the rc.cdrom file (located in the etc directory of a bootable CD) to get it to boot another utility, but doing so is tricky enough that I wouldn't bother.

Actually, Apple has created software that developers can use to create custom bootable CDs. It is this software that the developers of programs such as DiskWarrior and TechTool Pro use to create the bootable CDs. However, Apple has not made this development tool available to the public. In fact, Apple even limits its availability to "qualified" developers who can demonstrate a need for making such CDs. Clearly, Apple does not want to encourage the creation of custom bootable CDs. And even in these cases, the CDs do not include a Finder and thus cannot access the Desktop (as Mac OS 9 bootable CDs could). The rationale here is that Apple does not want users to get a "free" version of Mac OS X by buying a utility that comes on a full-fledged bootable CD. Back in the days when the Mac OS was free, this was not an issue. Those days are over.

So what can you, as a typical user, do here? Get the shareware utility BootCD.

Making a custom bootable CD with Boot CD. BootCD (www.charlessoft.com) allows you to create a bootable CD that contains a Finder and a Dock. The Dock can be set up to contain any applications you choose. Here is an overview of how to use it:

1. Launch BootCD, type in the desired Volume Name, and click the "Create Bootable CD image" button.

2. Give a name to the .dmg file that BootCD will create, then click Save.

3. Next, choose which applications you would like to include on the CD and put in the CD's Dock. You do this via a file browser window that appears. Typically, you would add utilities that you might need for repair or recovery in an emergency. Click Open to add a utility. Click Cancel when finished. Disk Utility, Console, and Terminal are automatically included, so you don't need to select them.

4. Quit BootCD and launch Disk Copy (in Jaguar) or Disk Utility (in Panther) and select to burn a CD of the file you created.

To use your newly created bootable CD, insert it into your CD/DVD drive and then restart. Boot from the CD (by holding down the C key at startup). When startup is complete, you should be at the Finder. There will be a Dock that contains all the utilities you selected (plus Disk Utility, Console, and Terminal). Your startup drive volume/partitions will also be mounted. You have root user status at this point. (BootCD has the root password set to "BootCD.")

With the full contents of the hard drive now accessible, you can work with most applications on the drive (in addition to the emergency utilities on the CD). I could run the Chess game or create a document in TextEdit, for example.

The Restart, Shut Down, and Log Out commands in the Apple menu do not work on a CD created with BootCD. To reboot again from your hard drive, use the reboot command in Terminal. To make sure you don't reboot from the CD, hold down the Eject button on your keyboard until the CD ejects.

Note: The steps in this section are accurate for Jaguar. Although these same steps worked in Panther when I tried it, the author may update BootCD for Panther, and some details may change as a result.

See the following Web page for more technical information on creating a bootable CD: www.bombich.com/mactips/bootx.html.

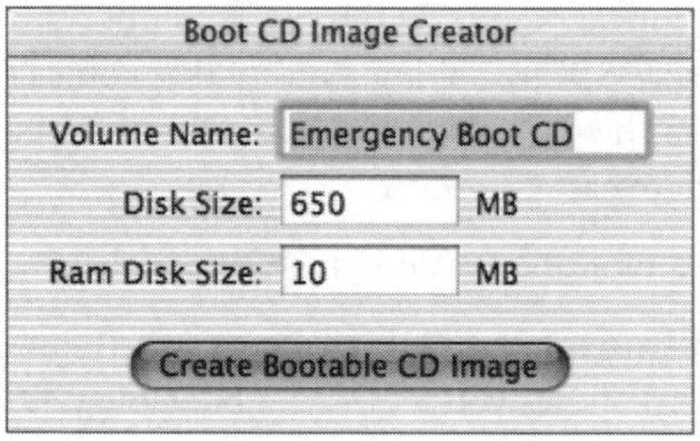

Figure 3.28

Making a bootable CD with BootCD.

```
              Boot CD Image Creator

Volume Name:  [ Emergency Boot CD ]

  Disk Size:  [ 650 ]     MB

Ram Disk Size: [ 10 ]     MB

       ( Create Bootable CD Image )
```

Troubleshooting Tips and Hints: Installing Software

Most Mac OS X installations go quite smoothly. As with any OS, however, problems can occur. The following covers most of the things that may go wrong, as well as what to do to get things right again.

Can't start up from Mac OS X Install CD

Some users are unable to get the Mac OS X Install CD to act as a startup disc for their Mac, getting the following error message instead: "Startup Disk was unable to select the install CD as the startup disk. (-2)." In other cases, the CD simply stalls at some point in the startup sequence, with or without displaying an error message. In the most extreme cases, the Mac drops into Open Firmware.

Problems like these are often caused by defective CDs. However, if the CD fails in some Macs but works in others, a defect is not the likely cause. In one case, the culprit was a third-party CD-ROM drive that replaced the internal drive that came with the Mac. The drive worked in general but not for the Mac OS X CD. In this case, if you were up to the task, you could reinstall the original CD drive and see if that worked. Or you could borrow or buy an external CD drive and try that.

SEE: • Chapter 5 for more information on Open Firmware and on startup problems in general.

By the way, if you installed an internal CD or DVD drive, you need to be careful about its settings. In particular, the drive, which is an ATA device, should be set for the master position, not the *slave mode* position. Users have reported that drives in the slave position do not work in Mac OS X. If you don't have a clue what I'm talking about here, don't worry—unless you decide to install an internal CD or DVD drive and start having problems. At that point, check my *Sad Macs* book, the documentation that came with the drive, or Apple's support Web site for more help.

In any case, because starting up from the disc is a requirement for installing Mac OS X, you cannot ignore symptoms like those described above. Apple advises that you follow these steps if you're unable to start up from a Mac OS X Install CD:

1. Inspect the Mac OS X CD.

   Verify that the shiny side of the CD is relatively clean (no particles, smudges, or other abnormalities).

2. Make sure that current firmware is installed.

   Your computer may require a firmware update for best Mac OS X compatibility. Check on Apple's Web site for possible upgrades.

3. Disconnect peripheral devices connected to your computer except for the Apple keyboard and mouse, including USB devices, SCSI devices, and PCMCIA cards.

4. Remove third-party hardware upgrades such as third-party memory (RAM) and third-party PCI cards.

SEE: • "Kernel panic," in Chapter 5, for a description of a problem with a third-party video card that may occur when trying to install Mac OS X.

After doing all of this, try starting up from the CD again. If it still fails, especially if the Mac drops into Open Firmware, you probably have a damaged CD/DVD. Contact Apple to replace the disc.

Cannot launch Installer successfully

If you're running Mac OS X from your hard drive rather than from a CD/DVD, you may find that the Installer application refuses to launch. Most likely, this will be a general issue that will occur no matter what software package file you attempt to use. In such cases, try the following until one works:

1. Quit all open applications. Make sure Classic is disabled as well. Try again. Do not attempt to perform any other actions on the Mac while the install is proceeding.

2. Restart the Mac and try again.

3. Disconnect all peripheral hardware devices, restart, and try the installation again.

4. Use Disk Utility's First Aid (or a similar third-party utility) to check whether disk repairs are needed.

   SEE: • **Chapter 5 for more information on disk and permission repairs.**

5. Use Disk Utility's First Aid tab to repair disk permissions on the volume.

6. Create a new administrative user (if the drive has only one local user), and install from the new user's account.

   If the installation succeeds, you can delete the newly created user account when you're finished.

   SEE: • **Chapters 3 and 8 for more information on creating and deleting additional users.**

7. Reinstall the Installer application itself, either by extracting it from the Mac OS X package (via Pacifist) or from a backup of a working copy, or by reinstalling Mac OS X altogether.

Cannot select a volume to install

When installing software via the Installer utility, the Installer may launch successfully, but when you get to the Installer's Select Destination screen, you may find one of the following problems:

- The volume that you intended to use to install your selected software is not displayed.

- The volume icon is displayed, but dimmed so that it cannot be selected.

- The volume icon is displayed, but a Stop Sign symbol with an exclamation point overlaps the volume icon, indicating that you cannot install the software on that volume.

Typically, a text message appears lower in the window, explaining the reason for the prohibition. The message, however, is not always very informative. One common explanation, for example, states, "You cannot install this software on this disk. This volume does not meet the requirements for this update." Another reads, "You cannot install this software on this machine."

The end result in all of these cases is that you cannot enable the Install button for the volume you wish to use. Here are some potential causes and solutions:

Make sure you meet the minimum requirements. The Read Me file that accompanies the software to be installed should supply the minimum requirements. For starters:

- Make sure you have at least the minimum installed RAM and free hard-drive space for the installation to proceed.

- You may need certain software installed for the current install to proceed. As an obvious example, you can't install any updates to Mac OS X 10.3 until 10.3 itself is installed. The solution here is to go back and install the needed software and then return to the problem installation. It should now work. Similarly, for update .pkg files, make sure that the required prior version of Mac OS X is on the destination volume. You can check your current version from the About This Mac window, which you access from the Apple menu.

Reinstall and downgrade problems. If you want to reinstall the same version of software that already exists on your drive (perhaps because you believe the software on your drive is corrupted), or downgrade to an older version of the software, the Installer will likely not allow it. If this happens (and the software to be installed is a single application), drag the application and its receipt file (in /Library/Receipts) to the Trash. Now try again.

To do this for an installation of or update to Mac OS X itself, you will need to do an Archive and Install back to the version that came on your Mac OS X CD, and then reupdate from there.

SEE: • Downgrading and Reupgrading Mac OS X," earlier in this chapter, for related information.

Eight GB partition limitation. If you have an older iMac or certain other older Mac models (the Read Before You Install file on the Mac OS X CD gives more precise details) and an over Eight GB hard drive that's partitioned, you must assign the first partition to be contained entirely within the first 8 GB. That is, the partition must be no larger than 8 GB, and you must install Mac OS X on that partition. Actually, some people have complained that this requirement applies even to some Macs that Apple says do not have this restriction.

If your first two partitions are both less than 8 GB total (such as 3 GB each), you should be able to install Mac OS X on either of them.

External drives. Mac OS X often will not install on an external SCSI drive. It also has problems installing or booting from some external FireWire and USB drives.

The problem is sometimes due to the specific external drive. In such cases, the solution may be to get a firmware update for the drive or to abandon the drive altogether. Other times, the problem may be with the Mac OS X software, requiring an update from Apple before the drive will work. Check with the drive vendor for exact recommendations. The drive vendor's name is available from the Apple System Profiler listing. Otherwise, check with Apple's support pages or MacFixIt.com for the latest details as to which drives work with Mac OS X.

Note: If you can't install Mac OS X on a drive and/or start up from a drive with Mac OS X installed, you can still use the drive as a nonstartup volume.

SEE: • **Chapter 5, for more on startup problems, especially issues regarding blessing of Mac OS X volumes.**

Secondary internal ATA drives. If you have a Power Mac G4, you can install more than one hard drive inside the case. If a secondary drive works just fine in general but does not show up in Apple's Installer, verify that the jumper settings on the drive are appropriate. For example, with Power Mac G4 (Mirrored Drive Doors) computers, additional ATA hard disks must be set for *cable select mode*, not the *master* or *slave mode*. In other cases, the reverse may be true: The drives need to be set as master and slave instead of cable select. Consult the documentation that came with your computer and your hard drive to learn how to determine the correct mode setting(s) for your drive(s).

SEE: • **"Can't Start Up from Mac OS X Install CD," earlier in this chapter, for related information on drive modes.**

Update CD. If the drive is listed but its icon is dimmed so that you cannot select it, make sure you're not using an Update CD and trying to install the OS on a volume that does not have a prerequired version of Mac OS X already installed.

If you have moved, deleted, or modified files in the /System/Library folder, it's possible that the Installer may not recognize the OS as the correct version, even if it is. In this case, unless you can move everything back correctly, you will likely need to start over with a reinstall from a full Mac OS X Install CD.

iPod. Apple's iPod is basically a FireWire hard drive. In principle, you can install Mac OS X on the drive and use the iPod as a portable emergency startup drive. To do so, you must enable iPod's Enable FireWire Disk Use option, which you access via the iPod options in iTunes.

However, you may not be able to install Mac OS X on an iPod via the Mac OS X Install CD. Exact symptoms may vary, but in my case, for the Jaguar Install CD, the Installer utility simply refused to display the iPod's icon in the Select Destination screen. When starting from the Panther Install CD, however, the iPod showed up just fine. If you do have problems here, you should still be able to work around the glitch by using a backup utility (such as Carbon Copy Cloner) to copy a preinstalled bootable copy of Mac OS X from another drive onto an iPod, though this is not as convenient as using the Install disc.

Note: After installing Mac OS X from an Install disc, installing further minor updates (for example, from 10.3 to 10.3.1) should work without any problems.

Note: After installing Mac OS X software on an iPod, you may not be able to update the iPod software.

SEE: • "Troubleshooting the iPod," in Chapter 11, for more details on these problems.

Checking console.log. If an update installation (not a full installation done when booting from a CD or DVD) fails, despite checking all of the above, launch the Console utility and check the Console log file that appears. The most recent entries will likely refer to what went wrong when the installation failed. The information *may* give you a clue as to how to solve the problem. For example, I've seen several reports where the problem made reference to a preferences file on the drive. Deleting the named preferences file and retrying the updater led to success.

Software Update does not list or install an update

If you believe a software update is available (perhaps you read about it on a Web site), but Software Update does not list it, you have several options:

- Make sure you have a working Internet connection.

- If you get a "server busy" error, or are otherwise unable to get Software Update to work as expected, there's probably a problem at Apple's end. Try again later (ideally in a day or so).

- If you get a message that says, "Your software is up to date," it may be that the desired software cannot be downloaded via Software Update. Apple sometimes provides certain updates only via its Web site.

- If multiple users are logged in via Fast User Switching, do not attempt to switch to another account while Software Update is running. Ideally, log out of all but one account prior to running Software Update.

- Make sure the file you want is really newer than the one you already have. For example, if you're trying to obtain Mac OS X 10.2.6, make sure you don't already have Mac OS X 10.2.7 installed. To check the current installed version, select About This Mac from the Apple menu.

- If the problem occurs because you reinstalled an older version of Mac OS X and now want to reinstall subsequent updates (that you had previously installed), check to see if the receipt files for those subsequent updates are still in the /Library/Receipts folder. If so, remove the receipt files and try again.

  SEE: • "Receipt files" and "Downgrading and Reupgrading Mac OS X," earlier in this chapter, for more details.

- If you recently downloaded and installed software via Software Update, try running Software Update again. The desired software may only appear after the initial software has been installed.

  As noted earlier in the chapter, Software Update in Panther automatically checks for newer updates after it completes an installation, assuming you chose to install the software rather than just download it.

- The software may not be needed for your computer: For example, a DVD Player update may not appear if you do not have a DVD drive.

- Needed hardware may not be accessible. For a PowerBook with a removable DVD drive, for example, installing a DVD Player update will not work if the DVD drive is not currently inserted in the expansion bay.

- If problems persist, your last resort is to completely reinstall Mac OS X.

If Software Update lists the update but will not successfully install it, download the update to the Desktop and run the stand-alone version using the Installer. This may work even if Software Update fails.

Installed Updates does not list previously installed updates

The Installed Updates list in the Software Update System Preferences pane may not list updates you previously selected and installed. You may encounter a similar problem in the log file maintained by Software Update. If this happens, try the following:

- **Make sure you really installed the update via Software Update.** If you installed an update by downloading it from Apple's Web site or by using Software Update's Download Only option, the Installed Updates screen will not list it. That screen only lists updates actually installed by Software Update.

- **Check the permissions settings for the relevant log file (Software Update.log in /Library/Logs).** In Panther, you (that is, your *username*) should be the Owner, and *admin* should be the Group. Owner should have Read & Write Access. Group and Others should have Read Only access. Note that in Jaguar, the owner is *System,* and both System and admin have Read & Write access. If your settings are different, edit them to match those described here.

  SEE: • "Ownership & Permissions," in Chapter 4, for details on how to make these changes.

- **If the problem began immediately after you upgraded to Panther, open the Software Update.log file in a text editor.** Delete all lines referring to updates installed *prior* to installing Panther, and then save the file.

Once you've done this, Installed Updates should list updates correctly.

SEE: • "Updating from Software Update," earlier in this chapter, for more on this feature.

Installation is interrupted

Whether you're attempting to install Mac OS X from the Install CDs or installing updates at some later point, Installer may bog down during the installation. Here are some common causes and cures:

- With Jaguar, there are two Mac OS X Install CDs; with Panther, there are three. Occasionally an installation will start successfully—and actually reach the point where you're asked to restart after the first CD has finished its work. However, the request for a second or third CD never comes. If software on these CDs is not needed (because you removed the relevant options via a Custom Install), this is expected, and no problems should occur. However, if the CD really is needed, the restart typically fails at this point, though it may sometimes proceed without asking for the second CD. In either case, the needed software is not installed.

  There appears to be more than one possible cause for this. In some cases, when trying to install Mac OS X on an external FireWire drive, there's a conflict between Mac OS X and the drive—in which case the solution is to hope that an upgrade to Mac OS X or the drive's firmware will fix the problem. If not, you won't be able to use the drive to install Mac OS X.

  On one occasion, the problem was with the Mac OS X Install CDs themselves. When another set of the CDs were tried, the problem did not occur.

- In general, when installing updates while running Mac OS X from your hard drive, turn off any settings in Energy Saver and Screen Saver System Preferences that automatically put the Mac to sleep or shift to a screen saver. Otherwise, the onset of sleep could halt the update process.

- If an installation of a Mac OS X update via Software Update gets interrupted, such as by a power failure, get the stand-alone version of the Installer—either via Software Update's Download Only command or Apple's Web site. Use the downloaded and saved installer file to try again to install the update. Note: If you try to use Software Update, it may report incorrectly that you no longer need the update. On the other hand, with a bit of luck, Software Update may recognize that an installation was partially completed and pick up the process from where it left off.

- When using Software Update, if you get an error message that say an update "could not be installed," choose Download Only to get the stand-alone updater and try again. If you're already using a stand-alone updater and it too "unexpectedly quits" or otherwise reports an "error while installing," run the installation yet again. There is a good chance it will now work. If not, the update file itself may be corrupted. In this case, download a new copy of the updater and run the install again. If this fails, log in as a different user; try the install again.

- If the update fails at the point where it says, "optimizing drive," don't worry too much—you've already completed the actual installation process. The only problem may be that you may have slower overall performance than you otherwise would get. To fix this, trying running the installer again, or run an `optimize/update_prebinding` command in Terminal.

SEE: • "Optimize Mac OS X volumes," in Chapter 5.
     • "Technically Speaking: Terminal Commands to Monitor and
       Improve Performance," in Chapter 10.

TECHNICALLY SPEAKING ▶ Checking Logs After an Installation Error

If an alert box appears with a message stating, "There was an error while installing," check the relevant log files for clues to a possible cause. There are three main log locations to check:

• **Installer log.** If you're using Apple's Installer utility, from the File menu select Show Log. If the information in the log window is not immediately helpful, check the Show More Detail box.

• **Software Update log.** If you're using Software Update, click the Installed Updates tab of the Software Update System Preferences. The same log information is also available as a log file, which you can access by clicking the Open as Log File button in the Installed Updates tab.

• **Console log.** Use the Console utility to check other potentially relevant logs used by Mac OS X, especially console.log and system.log. Look for messages containing the word *Install* or ones that appeared around the time of the installation.

With some luck, information in one or more of these locations will help you diagnose what went wrong with the installation and thus help you figure out how to fix it.

SEE: • **Chapters 2, 4, and 5 for more on Console and logs.**

Software installs but fails to work

In some cases, a Mac OS X update may install successfully (or at least appear to), but after you restart (if necessary) or attempt to use the new software, you discover problems that had not occurred previously. In the worst case, you may not be able to start up at all. The advice that follows focuses on installing Mac OS X updates, but much of it applies to installing any software update in Mac OS X (including third-party updates).

Bugs. Most often, problems with updates can be traced back to a bug in either the package file used for the installation or the software that was installed. If such a bug affects all Macs, it would almost certainly be discovered *before* the package file's release—which is exactly why most such problems affect only a small subset of users (ones that have a particular, often older, Mac model, for example). Unfortunately, sometimes the only fix is to go back to the previous version of Mac OS X and wait for Apple to release an update that corrects the problem. Otherwise, you may find some work-around posted to Web sites (such as MacFixIt.com) shortly after the update is released.

The unfortunate truth is that Mac OS X has become so complex that whenever Apple releases a new update, it seems to break (at least for some users) almost as many things as it fixes. Even though such updates are intended to fix bugs, they may inevitably introduce new ones. Common post-update problems include an inability to start up the Mac, date and time not being maintained correctly, external volumes not being recognized, an inability to maintain dial-up connections, an increase in kernel panics, an inability to add new printers or print to existing ones, wake-from-sleep crashes, and more.

Rather than wait for specific causes of and solutions to these bugs to be worked out (assuming that ever happens), your best bet is to try to avoid the problem in the first place. Here's some standard advice for avoiding and fixing these frustrations:

- **Use the combo updater.** If you're running the Mac OS X version immediately prior to the current update (for example, you're running Mac OS X 10.2.5 and updating to 10.2.6), the file you're updating with typically only works with that (immediately prior) version. The alternative, if you're running an even older version of Mac OS X, is to use a separate combo updater file (as discussed earlier in this chapter).

  However, you can use the combo update for 10.2.6 even if you're running 10.2.5, for example—though doing so may be of little benefit over running the 10.2.6 noncombo update. Some users, however, report better success with combo updaters, even in these situations.

  What's more likely to help avoid upgrade problems is to start over and reupgrade with the combo updater. For example, if your Mac OS X Install CD contains version 10.2.0, reinstall Mac OS X from the CD, using the Archive and Install feature, and then run the combo updater to get to 10.2.6. If this seems like a hassle, wait to see if you have problems after updating via the noncombo updater, and use this method only if problems occur.

  In such cases, it is also recommended that you download the updater and run it from your hard drive rather than let Software Update do the install.

- **Repair Disk Permissions.** Immediately after installing a Mac OS X update and restarting, access Disk Utility's First Aid and select Repair Disk Permissions. This is known to prevent a number of symptoms, including applications' failing to launch, that might otherwise occur.

- **Delete cache and preferences files.** If the problem is specific to a single application, delete any preferences or cache files associated with that application. You may also want to use a utility, such as Dragster or Jaguar Cache Cleaner, to more generally delete potentially corrupt preferences and cache files. If all of this fails, reinstall the update. Before reinstalling, do a search for files that include the name of the problem application, and delete any that show up.

If none of these suggestions help, check the sections that follow for more specific advice. Otherwise, your main option is to seek a solution elsewhere (such as a support Web site). If everything you try fails, you probably have a bug that was introduced in the new update or a conflict between the update and installed third-party software. If the problem is with third-party software, either remove it or upgrade to a compatible version (if one exists). For bugs in the OS itself, you'll have to learn to live with them (at least until Apple provides a fix) or downgrade back to the previous version of Mac OS X.

SEE: • **"Downgrading and Reupgrading Mac OS X," earlier in this chapter, for related information.**

• **Chapter 5, for details on Repair Disk Permissions, preferences, and cache issues.**

Startup problems. If your Mac crashes immediately after installing Mac OS X, consider the following:

• **SCSI.** The most common cause of these crashes is SCSI devices. SCSI refers to a technology for connecting peripheral devices, such as hard drives, to a Mac. No current Mac comes with a SCSI port as part of the logic board; instead, all new Macs use USB and/or FireWire as alternatives. The main places where you will still find SCSI included are older Macs and Power Macs that have a separate SCSI card installed in one of the PCI slots. In some cases, the SCSI PCI card itself is incompatible with Mac OS X and may lead to startup problems. Fixing this problem may require a firmware upgrade of the card or, at the very least, a software driver upgrade.

  In other cases, the problem may be with a device connected to the card or the way in which multiple devices are chained together, mainly involving what's called *SCSI termination*. This term refers to how SCSI devices are connected in a chain when you have more than one device. Mac OS X is much more sensitive to SCSI termination, so technically incorrect setups that did not cause a problem in Mac OS 9 may cause a problem in Mac OS X.

  Check with the vendor of the card (or Apple, if your Mac came with a SCSI card) for specific recommendations. Apple has an update for its Apple Ultra Wide SCSI PCI card (http://docs.info.apple.com/article.html?artnum=25176); you need this update if you intend to use the card with Mac OS X.

• **Memory.** In some cases, a Mac will not start up in Mac OS X due to a problem with a third-party memory (RAM) module, even though the same memory module works fine in Mac OS 9. If you get a black screen immediately at startup, I would suspect this problem. To check, remove the extra installed memory (especially memory not from Apple) and try again. If startup succeeds, contact your memory vendor about getting a replacement.

  If problems persist even after you remove the extra RAM, try running the Apple Hardware Test CD included with all recent Mac models. This CD diagnoses a variety of hardware problems and offers advice about how to solve them.

• **Firmware.** A firmware upgrade alters a special modifiable component of the hardware on the Mac's logic board. Before installing Mac OS X (especially if you have an older Mac), make sure your computer has the latest firmware installed. Failure to update firmware prior to installing Jaguar or Panther may lead to serious problems, including startup failures.

  If you plan on erasing your drive before installing Mac OS X, do the firmware update before erasing.

SEE: • "Take Note: Firmware Updates," in Chapter 5, for details on firmware updates.

• Chapter 5 for coverage of startup problems beyond those that immediately follow a Mac OS X installation.

Note: After Panther was released, a problem was discovered in which certain external FireWire drives could get hopelessly corrupted if they were mounted when restarting or shutting down from an internal startup volume running Panther. The primary solution is to upgrade the firmware for these drives. (You get the updates from the drive vendor, *not* Apple.)

SEE: • "Take Note: Startup Failure When Starting Up from an External Device," in Chapter 5, for related details.

• "Take Note: Problems Mounting and Unmounting/Ejecting Media," in Chapter 6, for more specific information on this Panther/FireWire issue.

Relocation problems. Sometimes an update installation only works correctly if the prior version of the software is in its correct default installed location—especially with older versions of Mac OS X. In these cases, the problem was that the Installer expected to find Mac OS X–installed applications (like Mail) in their default locations (such as inside the Applications folder). If, for example, you were to move Mail from the Applications folder and then install a Mac OS X update that updated the Mail application, Mail would not get updated properly. Instead, the Installer would place a nonfunctional (even nonlaunchable!) copy of Mail in the Applications folder. This copy would contain only the updated subset of files that make up Mail's .app package. Meanwhile, your relocated copy of Mail would remain unchanged. The result would be one copy of Mail (in Applications) that does not work and another copy (located elsewhere) that is not updated. You would not receive any warning message from the Installer that a problem had occurred.

If you're comfortable working inside packages, you could fix this problem by dragging the updated files in the .app package at the default location to their respective folders within the application package of the original version, replacing the older versions as needed. The process is a pain, but it should work. Otherwise, return the application to its default location and try reinstalling the update. Alternatively, you can use Pacifist to separately reinstall an individual application.

Apple states that, starting with Mac OS X 10.2.2, this problem no longer occurs. The Installer should locate the needed files wherever they may be (as long as they're on the boot volume) and update them correctly.

Still, I recommend playing it safe here by *not* moving Apple-installed files from their default locations.

With third-party installers, especially ones that allow you to choose the folder where the installed software should go, this should not be an issue.

External drives do not boot. If you have a bootable external drive (such as a FireWire hard drive), you may not be able to start up from the drive when it's attached to a Mac newer than the Mac OS X version installed on the drive. This may be because the new Mac requires an updated version of the operating system that includes the needed support files for an updated ROM in the new machines. For example, Apple's Power Mac G5s need to run Mac OS X 10.2.7 or later. In some cases, the version of Mac OS X on your external drive and on the new Mac may be the same—leading you to believe that there should be no problem. However, the build number may be different. In any case, the solution is to update (or do a complete new install, if the Installer refuses to do the update) the version of Mac OS X on your external drive to the version that came with the new Mac (or a newer version).

SEE: • "Take Note: Backups of Bootable Volumes Don't Boot," earlier in this chapter, for a related issue.

• "Take Note: Startup Failure When Starting Up from an External Device," in Chapter 5, for other reasons why you may have problems starting up from external devices.

Installer bug and reinstalling software

A bug in the initial version of the Installer utility is related to the use of pax as a compression format for files. Here's a quote from the Web site that first described the problem:

If during the installation of a package pax encounters a directory that already exists, it will set its permissions and ownership to the permissions of the version in the archive. This is especially annoying in the case of the /Library or /Applications directories, since many packages install into this location. However, it can have a much more serious impact, including preventing your system from booting, or applications from running.

A related second problem involving symbolic links (a type of alias used by Unix) also exists.

Without going into detail, I will just say that these problems appear more likely to occur when you're trying to install the same update a second time. Thus be cautious about doing so. If you do wind up with permissions problems, the likely symptom will be an inability to modify the contents of the /Library and/or Applications folders. I discuss how to fix this problem in Chapter 6. If problems occur, using Disk Utility's First Aid section to repair disk permissions (as described in Chapter 5) may help.

Apple has never officially confirmed that this bug has been fixed. However, I see fewer reports of it since the release of Jaguar, so perhaps it has been corrected.

Third-party software will not install

If you're trying to install third-party software that uses an installer utility (either Apple's or a competing one), and the install fails due to an unspecified error, this is almost always a permissions-related problem. The failure may occur during installation or on the initial launch of the application after installation. Specifically, the problem is that the installer attempted to install some file into a folder for which it did not have permission to do so.

The most common solution is to repair disk permissions with the First Aid component of Disk Utility (as described in Chapter 5), and then attempt the installation again.

You can also log in as the root user and perform the installation from there. As root user, you avoid any permissions hassles. In some cases, after completing the install and logging back in as yourself, you may need to adjust the permissions (including owner and group names) of the newly installed software (probably located in the Applications folder) to match that of other applications in the same folder. If the installer created a new folder, with several files and folders within it, you can use a utility like BatChmod to make the changes to all items in one step.

If you are using a VISE installer utility, make sure you disconnect from any remote networks before running the installer. Otherwise, the utility will search all computers and servers on the network prior to initiating an install. This could take sufficiently long that it will appear as if the utility has frozen.

If none of this works, check the vendor's Web site. It should either offer a specific work-around or indicate that the software has a conflict with the current version of Mac OS X (which the developer is presumably working to fix).

SEE: • Chapters 4 and 6 for more on root access and BatChmod.

Can't install a Classic application

If you're still using third-party Mac OS 9 software, you may occasionally need to upgrade this software to a newer version. In some cases, upgrading requires running an Installer utility that, of course, runs only in Mac OS 9. In general, this is not a problem. If you launch the Installer utility, it will load Classic, and the installation will proceed as if you had booted from Mac OS 9. However, there are a few installers that will only work correctly if you boot from Mac OS 9.

The solution here—if you have an older Mac that can still boot in Mac OS 9— is to reboot in the older OS and do the installation. Otherwise, you will have to get more creative. For example, you may need to find an older Mac, do the installation there, and then copy the updated installed files to your Mac.

Video issues warning

When Mac OS X 10.2.5 was released, Apple warned: "On certain computers, you should set the Displays preferences to the native resolution before installing the Mac OS X 10.2.5 Update. If you do not, temporary video issues may occur when the computer wakes from sleep." The affected computers were: PowerBook G4 (17-inch); iMac (17-inch 1 GHz); and Power Mac G4 with an nVidia GeForce 4MX or nVidia GeForce 4 Titanium display card connected to an LCD display.

Even if your Mac is not on that list, if you're using an LCD display, I would play it safe: Shift to the native resolution (via the Displays System Preferences) before installing an update. Typically, the native resolution is the highest one listed in Displays.

If you read this suggestion after the problem has already occurred, change the resolution to anything that works and restart. After restart, you can select the desired resolution successfully.

A collection of basic tips

In conclusion, I offer a summary of the most frequently needed advice for installation woes:

- Make sure you have enough disk space for the installation (and that you meet all other requirements listed in the Read Me file that accompanies the software).

- Make sure you have administrative status and know your password.

- Disable Screen Effects and Energy Saver sleep before performing an installation that may take long enough that these are invoked before it's complete.

- Turn off Classic (if it's running).

- Don't attempt other computer activities during an installation.

For further, more technical details on software installation, check out Apple's developer documentation at the following location: http://developer.apple.com/documentation/DeveloperTools/Conceptual/SoftwareDistribution/.

4

Mac OS X in Depth

There's more than one way to divide a pizza. There's the familiar method of cutting it into slices, of course, but you could also divide it into layers of topping, cheese, sauce, and crust, or—theoretically—distill it into its basic ingredients of flour, water, tomatoes, garlic, and milk. The way you think about dividing that pizza will depend on what you plan to do with it.

The same holds true for Mac OS X. You can look at it and take it apart any number of ways—each of which contributes to your understanding of the OS.

In This Chapter
. . . .

Aqua

Aqua is what most users think of when they think of Mac OS X: its user interface, the Finder, the Dock, the windows, the translucent buttons, the high-resolution icons, the menus, and all of the other things you *see* when you look at the screen. Many users never explore Mac OS X beyond its Aqua layer.

Users upgrading from Mac OS 9 will feel quite at home (at least initially), since much in the new interface works the same way as it did in Mac OS 9: You still double-click icons in the Finder to launch/open them; you still choose Save from an application's File menu to save a document; and you still open a folder icon to see its contents.

However, you will also instantly notice some significant differences—for example, the Finder window sidebars, a new column view, a very different Apple menu, and the Dock. For a basic discussion of all of these, see Chapter 2.

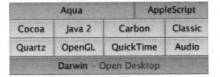

Figure 4.1

The layers of Mac OS X.

Application Environments

The main thing you do in Aqua is use applications. On the surface, most Mac OS X applications function similarly: You launch them; you use commands from their menus; you quit them. However, Mac OS X makes use of some fundamentally different types of applications. As a troubleshooter, you need to understand these categories.

Cocoa

The Cocoa environment is unique to Mac OS X. This means that software developed via Cocoa uses Mac OS X–only programming tools, and finished applications run only in Mac OS X. The advantage of Cocoa-based software is that it can take advantage of all of Mac OS X's built-in features. Take, for example, the TextEdit application that comes with Mac OS X: Its Font panel window, spelling checker, and ability to let users access Services from the TextEdit menu (by choosing Services) are all made possible—at least in part—by the fact that TextEdit is a Cocoa-based application. Only Cocoa applications can access Services by default; other applications need to be specially written to do so. Similarly, Cocoa applications are the only ones likely to use Font panel; others use the more traditional Font menu. Thus, non-Cocoa applications are unlikely to include these and other features.

Apple hopes that down the road most Mac OS X applications will be Cocoa-based. For now, however, there are many applications that don't use Cocoa, because writing a Cocoa-based application means pretty much starting from scratch. If you're a developer with a Mac OS 9 application that you want to work in Mac OS X, Cocoa isn't the fastest way to get there.

Carbon

Applications written for the Carbon environment run "natively" in Mac OS X. This means that in most cases, you will be hard-pressed to distinguish between Cocoa- and Carbon-based applications. Since Carbon-based (or *Carbonized*) applications can offer all the basic Aqua features (such as the look and feel of its windows), you can't quickly determine by looking in the Finder whether an application is Cocoa- or Carbon-based.

Developers can, however, determine how much of the Aqua interface they wish to support in their own Carbonized applications. As a result, some Carbon applications may look and feel more like Mac OS X applications than others.

The primary rationale for Carbon's existence is that it reduces the time it takes to rewrite existing Mac OS 9 applications to work in Mac OS X. That's why major Mac OS 9 applications such as AppleWorks and Microsoft Office are Carbonized applications rather than Cocoa ones. In addition, some developers find Carbon preferable even when creating applications from scratch. REALbasic, for example, is a programming language that creates Carbonized applications for Mac OS X.

There are two distinct subcategories of Carbon applications, and the differences between them depend on an OS feature called a *library manager.* This special program prepares other, more ordinary programs to be run. Library managers exist in both Mac OS 9 and Mac OS X. Carbon applications in Mac OS X can use two types of library managers:

- **CFM (code fragment manager)** is essentially the same as the CFM used in Mac OS 9. It works with an application's executable binary code, which is in a format called PEF (for *preferred executable format*). Unfortunately, this format is not preferred in Mac OS X.

- **Dyld (dynamic link editor)** is the library manager that only Mac OS X uses. It works with an executable binary-code format called Mach-O, which is what Mac OS X's kernel uses. Mach-O is derived from Unix.

Exactly what all of these managers and formats do, and how they differ, need not concern you. What does matter is the following:

- **CFM is not optimized for Mac OS X.** Mac OS X is a native dyld platform. This means that for CFM-based programs to work, they must bridge to the dyld platform via Carbon routines. This bridging step takes time, resulting in a performance penalty that does not occur with dyld-based software—that is, CFM-based software will not run as fast in Mac OS X as if the same program had been written to use dyld instead.

  The most visible sign of this bridging can be found in the LaunchCFMApp application (itself a Mach-O application), which is located in /System/Library/Frameworks/Carbon.framework/Versions/A/Support. This file (which is an updated version of the Mac OS 9 CFM) is used every time you launch a CFM-based application. In fact, prior to Mac OS X 10.2 (Jaguar), if you launched Process Viewer (now called Activity Monitor) and looked at the list of open applications in User Processes, you wouldn't see any CFM-based applications by name; instead, you would see multiple instances of LaunchCFMApp. Although Mac OS X 10.2 and later now display the CFM-based applications by name, the LaunchCFMApp process is still used to launch them, and this process is still what appears (instead of the name of the application) in the output of certain Unix commands.

  In addition, CFM applications (though they can be packages) may still use the single file format common in Mac OS 9. Thus, if you open the contextual menu for an application and no Show Package Contents command is listed, the application is almost certainly a CFM application. Dyld software will always use the preferred package format.

  SEE: • "Understanding Image, Installer Package, and Receipt Files," in Chapter 3.

- **Dyld (Mach-O) software cannot run in Mac OS 9.** So why bother with CFM at all? Two reasons: First, it may be easier to convert an existing Mac OS 9 application to its CFM-based cousin than to a dyld one. Second, CFM-based programs run equally well in Mac OS 9 and Mac OS X. Thus, you need only one application for both environments. Dyld-based software runs only in Mac OS X. By the way, Cocoa-based software also uses Mach-O.

  For those who want a dyld-based Carbon program to run in Mac OS 9 *and* Mac OS X, a solution is to create two versions of the application, a CFM version and a dyld version. You can then combine these versions into an application package that appears as a single file in the Finder. When the application is launched in Mac OS 9, the CFM version will be used; when it's launched in Mac OS X, the dyld version will run. This situation allows each OS to use the version optimized for it. (This type of division is more common when Classic and Carbon software versions are included in the same package, as you'll learn more about in this chapter.)

When a program is said to be Mac OS X–native, this generally means that it's either a Cocoa program or a dyld Carbon one (though some people consider any Carbon application to be native).

TAKE NOTE ▶ Faceless and Hidden Applications

Some applications run without an icon in the Dock or without being listed in the Force Quit window. Such applications are often called *faceless* applications because they run without a user interface. The loginwindow application, which you'll learn more about in Chapter 5, is one example.

Other applications have corresponding icons in the Dock but none of the other typical user-interface elements or windows. Default Folder X is an example of this. The only way you know it's running (besides its Dock icon) is by seeing its effect in the Open and Save dialogs.

You can also hide processes listed in the Startup Items list (located in Accounts System Preferences pane) by checking the Hide box adjacent to an item. If working as expected (and it sometimes does not), this is similar to hiding an application via other methods (such as the Hide command in a Dock menu). Once you've enabled the Hide option, an application's windows should not be visible at login even though the application launches.

Warning: Be careful about selecting the Hide option in the Startup Items list for background or faceless processes: Such items may lose their functionality if you do. When I chose to hide items that created menus in the menu bar, for example, the menus no longer appeared.

SEE: • "Take Note: Dock and Finder Shortcuts," in Chapter 2, for more details.

Figure 4.2

The Startup Items list with AppleWorks selected to be hidden.

TAKE NOTE ▶ **Identifying Application Formats**

Suppose you need to know whether a given application is Cocoa, Carbon-cfm, Carbon-dyld, or Classic: What's the fastest way to find out? A utility called Get Info for App works great—if it works (in the most recent versions of Mac OS X it kept crashing on me). Just drag the application in question to the Get Info for App icon, and a window opens, revealing the information you need.

For TextEdit, for example, you will see that the Framework is Cocoa and the Binary Kind is Mach-O. On the other hand, if you select Microsoft Internet Explorer, the window will say Carbon for the Framework and CFM for the Binary Kind.

As an alternative, you can use the ever-handy XRay. Although it doesn't distinguish between CFM and Mach-O, it does distinguish between Cocoa, Carbon, and Classic applications.

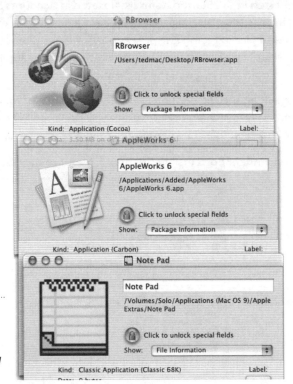

Figure 4.3

Three applications as listed in XRay. Note the Kind line distinction of Cocoa, Carbon, and Classic 68K.

Classic

Mac OS 9 programs that have not been Carbonized can still run in Mac OS X, but it requires a trick: Mac OS X needs to launch what is called the Classic environment. For a detailed discussion of this topic, see Chapter 9. For now, here's the short version of what happens when you launch Classic. A working version of Mac OS 9 (including extensions and control panels) is loaded when you launch Classic. The Mac OS 9 application then runs in this environment. In many ways, going back and forth between the two environments is almost seamless. You can cut and paste from a Classic program to a Mac OS X one, for example. Classic can even borrow your Mac OS X Internet and printer settings so that Classic applications can retain their access to the Web and your connected printers.

Still, running a program in Classic has a huge disadvantage: You aren't really using Mac OS X and thus get almost none of its advantages. Running an application in Classic is like running it in Mac OS 9—or perhaps not quite as good, since it will likely run slower and have more potential conflicts than if you had simply booted from Mac OS 9. The sole advantage of Classic is that it allows you to run Mac OS 9 programs that you could not otherwise run in Mac OS X. As time goes by, however, you will want to find Mac OS X alternatives to these applications (or hope that Mac OS X versions of them become available) so that you can eliminate your reliance on Classic.

SEE: • Chapter 9 for more information on the Classic environment.

Java

Mac OS X can also run programs written in Java. If you're like most users, you probably think of Java as something that certain Web sites use and your Web browser accesses. However, Java software can be created to run independently of a browser, and Mac OS X is able to run such applications. Apple has even provided a means for developers to incorporate Mac OS X's Aqua interface into Java code so that their Java applications look and feel like typical Mac OS X applications. For programmers, the main advantage of Java is that it's platform-independent—that is, the same Java software (with some minor modifications to accommodate the platform's user interface) can run on any computer that supports Java, including Windows PCs. At present, few Java applications are available for Mac OS X, so the jury is still out as to whether Java will play a significant role in Mac OS X.

Putting it together

All of these application environments are unified within the Aqua interface. There will be visible signs—some subtle, some obvious—when you shift from Classic to Carbon to Cocoa to Java; however, one of the great successes of Mac OS X is that you can switch among these environments almost effortlessly. And at least most of the time, it all works as Apple intended.

There is one other type of application that can run in Mac OS X: Unix software. For a detailed discussion of Unix, see "Darwin," later in this chapter.

Graphics Services

Running underneath the application layer is a set of core technologies that create the elements you see on the screen: fonts, graphics, movies, and so on. As a troubleshooter, you need not be concerned with the inner workings of this layer; however, you should be familiar with its terminology.

Quartz

Quartz—the Mac OS X technology used to create all two-dimensional images (including text)—is quite different from the QuickDraw technology used in Mac OS 9. Some of the most spectacular differences show up when you work with text. First, Quartz uses PDF (Portable Document Format) as a native format for documents. This format is the one employed by Adobe Reader, which means that almost anything you create—in any application—can be easily saved as a PDF document. This in turn makes it easy for anyone to view these documents, even on Windows PCs, with all their fonts, formatting, and graphics intact. Because PDF is a PostScript-aware format, it makes it easy to render any PDF document to a PostScript printer. Quartz is also responsible for the fact that virtually all text in Mac OS X has a smoothed (anti-aliased) look.

Also of relevance is Apple Type Services (ATS), a technology that unifies the display of fonts (regardless of format, be it TrueType, PostScript, or whatever) and provides the basis for multiple-language support.

Multimedia: OpenGL and QuickTime

Three-dimensional graphics use Mac OS X's OpenGL software, which comes into play mainly with 3D game software.

Mac OS X also supports QuickTime for multimedia. This software is used for playing QuickTime movies, such as the popular movie trailers available on Apple's QuickTime Web site.

On a related note, Mac OS X supports a variety of sound formats and includes DVD movie support.

Darwin

Now you're ready to delve into the deepest layer of Mac OS X—the core, if you will. The umbrella name for this layer is Darwin. Because Darwin uses open-source code (that is, code that's publicly available—in this case, at www.publicsource.apple.com), developers are able to study, modify, and improve it. Darwin is sometimes more generically referred to as the Mac OS X kernel environment.

In discussing the layers of Mac OS X, how do you determine whether something is considered to be at a higher or lower level? As a general rule, a component at a lower level is used by all higher-level layers. However, the converse is not necessarily true. Thus, an application, whether it's Carbon or Cocoa, uses the core Darwin technology; however, Darwin itself doesn't require any additional layers to run.

The Darwin kernel consists mainly of the FreeBSD 5 and Mach 3.0 technologies. Darwin also includes various core services, such as those involved in networking and device drivers, which we'll examine in detail in Chapter 5 (as I walk your through the startup sequence of events). Beyond that, as an end-user troubleshooter, you only need to be aware of the two key kernel components.

Mach

As a troubleshooter, you will rarely, if ever, work directly with Mach code. Nonetheless, it's important that you understand its basic concepts. Mach code not only handles the most fundamental aspects of Mac OS X (for example, the processes that enable the Mac to boot and recognize attached hardware), but it's also responsible for several of Mac OS X's most touted benefits:

Preemptive multitasking. This term describes Mac OS X's ability to schedule its processor activity among different open applications or processes. (Note: All applications are considered processes, but not all processes are user-accessible applications.) Mac OS 9 uses *cooperative multitasking*, which is not very intelligent. In Mac OS 9, unimportant but CPU-intensive background events can take up so much of a processor's time that more important foreground activities become sluggish and unresponsive. Neither you nor the OS can do anything about this situation. Mac OS X's Mach is much more flexible in the way it handles these matters. In essence, it can preempt any running process, giving another process more attention. It can intelligently note which activities are in the foreground and make sure that they get the lion's share of attention. Developers can also write hooks in their software to increase (or decrease) the priority that their software should get. As a result, operations that need the most processor activity at any moment should get it, enhancing overall performance. This is a good thing.

A related benefit of Mac OS X's multitasking capability is called *multithreading*. In Mac OS 9, when you launch an application, you typically must wait for it to finish launching before you can do anything else—a process that can take a minute or two. In this context, launching an application in Mac OS 9 is called a modal function. Mac OS X doesn't have these waiting games; it has far fewer modal functions. In Mac OS X, as soon as a program starts to launch, you can begin another activity—for example, checking your email while waiting for Classic to launch and Photoshop to open.

Protected memory. Metaphorically, protected memory means that the memory assigned to each open process is entirely separate *(protected)* from that of every other open process. The result is that system-wide crashes should almost vanish from the landscape. If and when an application does crash, the rest of the operating system should remain functional. In the event that a program freezes (such as when you get an endlessly spinning beach ball pointer), you will be able to switch to a different program (such as the Finder) and continue to work as normal, even while the problem application remains frozen. This would be impossible to do in Mac OS 9. Protected memory also means that you should almost never need to restart the Mac to recover from a crash.

Shared memory. The exception to the above-described Mac OS X "rule" that one crashed application will not affect other open applications comes in programs that use shared memory. As its name implies, *shared memory* refers to more than one process using the same memory—typically to share certain resources, such as graphics or sounds, that would otherwise consume large amounts of memory. The problem, as Apple describes it, is that "shared memory is fragile; thus, if one program corrupts a section of shared memory, all programs that reference that shared memory will also be corrupted."

Virtual memory. Virtual memory allows you to simulate memory (RAM) via special files on your hard drive. The main advantage of virtual memory is that if you don't have sufficient physical (built-in) RAM for your purposes, you may be able to get the RAM you need via virtual memory.

In Mac OS 9, you could choose to turn virtual memory on or off. Because virtual memory tended to slow performance, it was typically wise to turn it off if your physical RAM was more than adequate for your needs. In Mac OS X, virtual memory must always remain on. The good news is that until you really start pushing its limits (by having way too many applications open at the same time, for example), you should not notice a performance hit.

Still, you can't have too much physical RAM, and given the current low prices of memory, I recommend buying as much RAM as you think you will ever need—or more.

Dynamic memory. In Mac OS 9, the amount of memory assigned to an application is fixed (or *static*) when the program is launched. You assign this fixed amount via the Memory settings in the application's Get Info window. If, after an application has been launched, it needs more or less memory than was assigned to it, Mac OS 9 can't do much about the situation. You can add a limited amount of RAM to an application via an OS feature called *temporary memory,* but not all programs are able to use this feature, and even for those that can, it doesn't solve the problem completely.

As a result, you wind up getting "out of memory" error messages in Mac OS 9 when you technically have enough memory for the task at hand. Mac OS 9 simply can't shuttle the memory to where it's needed at the moment.

In Mac OS X, memory assignment is dynamic, which means that the amount of memory assigned to an application is increased or decreased as needed, automatically. Thus, if an application is idling in the background and hogging unused memory, the OS can grab some of this memory for another application that needs it more. Or it can reassign that memory to the pool of "free" memory so that it's available to applications that have yet to be launched.

Similarly, the total amount of memory available as virtual memory is adjusted on the fly in Mac OS X. In Mac OS 9, in contrast, if you wanted to change the total size of virtual memory, you would have to restart your Mac.

This combination of dynamic memory assignment and Mac OS X's virtual memory means that you should almost never see an "out of memory" error and encounter fewer memory-related system freezes and crashes.

Mac OS X manages all of these tasks and also allocates memory intelligently from physical and virtual memory so as to maximize the performance of each application. The result is that each application "feels" like it has almost infinite memory, no matter how little physical memory you've actually installed.

Still, as I implied earlier, memory availability in Mac OS X is *not* infinite. If you push your Mac to its memory limits, you will start noticing an overall decline in its performance. One reason for this is that Mac OS X attempts to keep a certain minimum amount of physical memory "free" at all times. If the free memory falls below a certain threshold value (which varies depending on how much physical memory you have installed), Mac OS X refills it from memory assigned to currently open applications that have not been accessed recently. The next time you go to access a previously "dormant" application, there will likely be an initial delay in its response. However, you will not receive an error message, just a slowdown in performance. This process is called *paging* (as covered in the following "Technically Speaking" sidebar). This problem lessens as you install more physical memory—which is why getting more physical RAM still makes sense.

Note: As described in more detail later in this chapter (in "Get Info"), Mac OS X's Get Info window still includes a Memory tab for Classic applications, needed because Classic applications do not take advantage of Mac OS X's dynamic-memory feature.

Figure 4.4

A graphical display of Mac OS X's memory divisions, as seen in Activity Monitor.

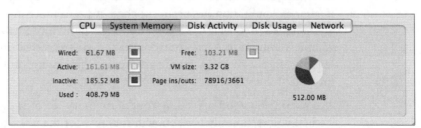

TECHNICALLY SPEAKING ▶ **Dividing Up Mac OS X's Memory**

In Panther (Mac OS X 10.3), you can view memory usage via the System Memory section of the main Activity Monitor window. Several third-party utilities, such as MemoryStick, also enable you to visually monitor memory.

If you use a utility to view your Mac's memory usage, it will typically reference different categories of memory use. These categories refer to the way in which the installed physical memory interacts with Mac OS X's virtual memory. In particular, they refer to the portion of the memory in use and whether the items in memory can be *paged out* to the swapfile(s) located in /var/vm on your hard drive (and used by virtual memory). Because it takes longer to access items that are paged out, the Mac tries to avoid paging out the most essential and actively used resources.

The following provides an overview of the different types of memory:

- **Wired memory.** This is memory that contains resources essential for the Mac to run. Items here are never "paged out" to the swapfile(s) on your hard drive—they must always be in physical RAM. User processes cannot assign wired memory; only administrative processes can do this.

- **Active memory.** Items in active memory are currently being used (or were used very recently) by open processes. As such, they will not be paged out.

- **Inactive memory.** Items here have been used less recently and are not immediately required for any open processes. As such, they may be paged out. For example, if you have several applications open, and one of them has not been the active application for quite some time, it would likely be placed in inactive memory. If you select a window from that application, the needed resources would be moved back to active memory. If the information had been paged to disk, it would be accessed first from there.

- **Free memory.** This is the memory not currently in use. Ideally, you want a healthy amount of free memory because this is what's used instead of paging items to disk. If free memory becomes too low, paging will occur.

When you quit an application, its resources may remain in inactive memory for a while—which means that the increase in free memory size will not match the resources you freed up by quitting the application. Thus, if free memory gets low occasionally and some page-outs occur, it may not be a source of concern. Wait a while to see whether the situation improves as inactive memory is returned to the free memory pool. However, if you frequently run low on free memory, and get numerous and frequent page-outs (especially if Mac OS X creates a second or third swapfile), this is a sign that you need to install more physical memory.

Occasionally, frequent paging out may be caused by a memory leak in an application or an unusually memory-intensive application. In such cases, even installing more memory may not alleviate the problem—you may just have to wait for the developers to fix the problem.

SEE: • "Maximizing Performance," in Chapter 6, and "Technically Speaking: Terminal Commands to Monitor and Improve Performance," in Chapter 10, for related information.

BSD (Unix)

BSD, which stands for Berkeley Software Distribution, used to be called the Berkeley version of Unix. For all practical purposes, the term means *Unix version*. BSD code is also used for a portion of the Mach code. In all cases, the code has been customized for Mac OS X.

Note: Part of the BSD installation is optional when you install Mac OS X. However, these optional components are installed by default *unless* you do a custom installation and choose not to install them. Overall, there is little cost (other than some disk space) in installing the optional files, and some Mac OS X features and third-party software will not work without them. For these reasons, I recommend that you stick with the default installation.

SEE: • "Mac OS X: The Down- *and* Upsides," in Chapter 1, for more on Unix's inclusion in Mac OS X.
  • Chapter 3 for more information on installing Mac OS X.

Mac OS X's Unix integration represents a significant change from Mac OS 9. In Mac OS 9, the System Folder *was* the OS. Except for a small number of invisible files (such as the Desktop files), all OS files were in the System Folder, where they were easily accessible. In Mac OS X, by contrast, the entire Unix layer remains largely invisible from the Aqua Finder. Thus, Mac OS X has a sort of secondary OS hidden beneath the visible OS.

Occasionally, troubleshooting will require that you access or modify these hidden Unix files. You access Unix commands and files in Mac OS X in three main ways:

- **Terminal.** In essence, the Terminal application (included with Mac OS X) provides a command-line environment where most Unix commands will work just as if they were being executed in a "pure" Unix environment rather than part of the Mac OS. Still, Terminal lets you know right away that you're in Apple's implementation of Unix, via its "Welcome to Darwin!" greeting. Any changes you make in Terminal, such as renaming or deleting files, will modify the Aqua environment as well, so you need to be careful.

- **Finder and text editors.** Tasks such as moving or deleting Unix files can often be done directly from the Finder. You can also modify some Unix files via text editors such as TextEdit and BBEdit. This will often require root user access and/or use of a utility that makes invisible files visible.

- **Aqua utilities.** Via Aqua-based interfaces, many third-party utilities let you do what would otherwise require you to use Terminal. In essence, such utilities simply run Terminal commands behind the scenes, providing a more user-friendly graphical user interface (GUI), or front end to the user.

SEE: • "Mac OS X: The Down- *and* Upsides," in Chapter 1, for more on why
          Unix is included in Mac OS X.

        • "Root Access," later in this chapter, for more information on this subject.

        • "Technically Speaking: Log Files and Cron Jobs," later in this chapter,
          for an example of accessing Unix files from the Finder and/or via
          GUI utilities.

        • Chapter 6, for other examples of how to access the invisible Unix files
          from the Finder.

        • Chapter 10, for more information on Unix and Terminal.

TECHNICALLY SPEAKING ▶ What and Where Are the Unix Files?

The Unix-based software at the core of Mac OS X is located at the root level of the Mac OS X
boot volume. You can see these invisible directories and files from the Finder by using a utility,
such as TinkerTool, to make invisible files visible (as described in greater detail in Chapter 6). In
addition, you can typically access files and folders within these directories (even when they're
invisible in the Finder) by using the Go to Folder command. (For example, entering /var/db/ in
the Go to Folder text box opens a Finder window that displays the contents of this folder.)

You can also use Terminal to view these files. To do so from Terminal, type the following: cd /.
Now type 1s. This will return a list of root-level contents.

The following is a sampler of the Unix directories and files found at the root level:

• **bin** is the directory where most of the main Unix commands (or *executables*) are stored.
  These are the equivalent of Mac OS X applications. **sbin** is a similar directory of executables.

• **dev** is where device drivers are stored. Your computer needs these files in order to interact
  with other hardware, such as external drives.

• **etc** contains a collection of administrative files. This is the location of the periodic directory
  (used by the cron software), the cups directory (used by the CUPS printing software), the
  master.passwd file, and various important configuration files, such as hostconfig and
  inetd.conf.

• **tmp,** as its name implies, contains files created by programs that are only needed temporarily. Unfortunately, some programs may forget to delete these tmp files, so you may
  find some files here permanently.

  The tmp item here is actually an alias (a symbolic link, as described in Chapter 6) to
  /private/tmp. This alias—which is needed by Mac OS X to work with Unix software—is not
  a standard Unix component.

• **usr** is another place where critical Unix OS commands are found. For example, the ditto
  and open commands are stored in usr/bin. In addition, the /usr/local directory is a common
  storage location for third-party software (that is, software installed after the initial installation of Mac OS X).

continues on next page

TECHNICALLY SPEAKING ▶ What and Where Are the Unix Files? *continued*

- **var** is yet another important location for essential files. For example, this is where the root directory (that is, the home directory of the root user) is located. The db directory, located within var, contains the netinfo database. The log directory, as implied by its name, contains the various system log files.

- **mach_kernel** is Unix's *kernel,* or the ncore code of the operating system. This is a file, not a directory. As noted in the main text, this kernel is the software equivalent of the Mac's CPU, the central processing location for all Unix commands. Without mach_kernel and mach.sym, nothing else would work.

Note: The etc, tmp, and var items at the root level are actually symbolic links to directories in /private.

Figure 4.5

A list of the Unix directories and files (for example, usr, bin) located in the root directory, as viewed from (left) Terminal and (right) the Finder (with normally invisible items made visible).

TECHNICALLY SPEAKING ▶ gdb: The Mac OS X Debugger

In Mac OS 9, developers and some users employed a program called MacsBug to debug software. In the event of a system crash, this program could occasionally be used to recover without restarting. For this and other uses, MacsBug was a valuable troubleshooting tool.

MacsBug, however, does not work in Mac OS X. The Mac OS X debugger is gdb, a Unix tool accessed via Terminal. I will not discuss its use in these pages.

TAKE NOTE ▶ Finder Folders vs. Unix Directories

In Finder windows, you will see many icons that resemble folders—and indeed this is the Desktop metaphor for what they are: containers that hold other items (documents, applications, or other folders).

Folders vs. directories. In the Unix world, folders are referred to as *directories*. Because Mac OS X has a Unix basis, I sometimes refer to its folders as directories—especially when I'm in a Unix environment like the Terminal application. Even in the Finder, I occasionally refer to folders as *directories*. For example, I typically refer to a user's Home *directory* rather than Home *folder* because of the Home directory's special significance in Unix. (This directory is the default location when you log in via Terminal, for example.)

Thus, an Aqua folder is best viewed as a graphical representation of a Unix directory. Moving an item into or out of a folder in the Finder changes the underlying directory in Unix. The terms *folder* and *directory* are sometimes used interchangeably when the distinction is not relevant.

Note that not all Unix directories are displayed in the Finder. In fact, most of them remain invisible to the Finder because typical Mac OS X users rarely, if ever, need to manipulate these files—and modifying them accidentally can lead to serious problems (including ones that can take down the system). Still, throughout this volume I will cover the essentials of how to access these files for troubleshooting purposes.

Pathnames. A *pathname* is what Unix uses to define the location of a file or directory. An *absolute pathname* starts at the top, or root, level of the hierarchy and works its way down. /System/Library/Fonts/Geneva.dfont, for example, is an absolute pathname. Slashes separate directory names; thus, an initial forward slash indicates that you are starting at the root level. This setup is important, for example, in distinguishing otherwise-identical fonts in multiple Fonts folders (such as /Library/Fonts versus /System/Library/Fonts).

A *relative pathname* is the path starting from your current location. Thus, if you were already in the System/Library directory, the relative path to the same font file would simply be Fonts/Geneva.dfont.

The ~ (tilde) symbol means to start at the top of the current user's Home directory. Thus, ~/Library/Fonts means to look in the Fonts folder inside the Library folder inside your Home directory.

Because the forward slash is used in all of these designations, you should not use this character in file or folder names in Mac OS X. The OS may treat the slash as a directory designator rather than as part of the file or folder name. In some cases (for example, when naming files in the Save dialog), Mac OS X will prohibit you from entering a forward slash (much as Mac OS 9 does not permit colons in file and folder names).

Mac OS X Domains

Having dissected Mac OS X's layers, we're now going to take the OS apart from a different perspective. In this section, you'll learn why Mac OS X has multiple Library folders and directories as well as the functions of each. You'll also get an overview of the files and folders they contain.

First, though, a bit of background: Mac OS X was born in 1997 when Apple acquired the NeXT OS (often referred to as OpenStep) at the time when Steve Jobs (founder of both Apple and NeXT) returned to Apple. As a result of this deal, much of the higher-level Mac OS X software was based on NeXT code. In fact, it's not unusual to peek inside a Mac OS X System software file and find a reference to NeXT or OpenStep.

At a practical level, this reliance on NeXT code means that the System Folder of Mac OS 9 is gone from Mac OS X, as are the control panels and extensions that populated the System Folder. Instead, in Mac OS X you have the Library folder—or, more precisely, a multitude of Library folders. This is because Mac OS X is inherently a multiple-user system, and different Library folders correspond to different domains or levels of the OS. At the top level (System), for example, changes affect all users of the Mac in question. At the bottom level (User), changes affect only the individual user who is logged in.

Levels of users. There are three main levels of users in Mac OS X. This, in turn, determines the nature of the domain and library structure of the OS.

- **Standard/Ordinary.** These users can only access files in their own Home directories (unless an administrator specifically grants them access to other files).

- **Administrative.** These users (often called *admin users* for short) are able to access sections of the OS designed to be shared among all users, such as the Applications folder. An ordinary user cannot add to or remove anything from the Applications folder; however, an administrative user can. By default, even administrative users are denied access to areas used by the System that are considered essential to running the OS. Administrators can, however, access these files via root access (if they have the root password).

- **Root/System**. This user is the only one who can modify and access the essential System software needed to keep the OS running, as well as anything else on the volume. This user is also sometimes referred to as the *system administrator*.

  SEE: • **"Take Note: Multiple Users: Mac OS X vs. Mac OS 9," "Ownership & Permissions," and "Root Access," later in this chapter, for related information.**
  - **Chapter 6 for solving troubleshooting problems that require modifying permissions settings.**
  - **Chapter 8 for more information on file sharing.**

TAKE NOTE ▶ **Multiple Users: Mac OS X vs. Mac OS 9**

For users familiar with Mac OS 9 but new to Mac OS X, all these domains, libraries, and permissions may seem a bit overwhelming. To help make sense of them, the following provides an overview of how Mac OS 9 works and why Mac OS X is different.

Mac OS 9 is an inherently single-user system—that is, it was designed with the idea that only one person (or perhaps one family) would be using a Mac. All users share the same resources in the single System Folder on the hard drive. In fact, the basic OS makes no attempt to distinguish among the various users of a single Mac. When you sit down to play a game on a Mac running Mac OS 9, you could be John Doe or Elton John; it doesn't make any difference to the operating system! This is the way most Mac users work with their Macs.

The idea of preventing certain users from accessing particular files was irrelevant to the original Mac OS. Although such security features were eventually added to the Mac OS (via file sharing and multiple-user options), they were never completely successful. The following describes a few of them:

- **The Users & Groups tab of the File Sharing control panel** allows you to restrict and customize access to your Mac—either over a local network or a remote connection—enabling you to make some folders accessible and others off-limits.

- **The Multiple Users control panel** allows you to set up your Mac so that different users have separate login passwords and—to some extent—maintain their own separate Preferences settings (stored outside the System Folder). This arrangement makes it possible for separate users to access the same Mac, each with his or her own customized settings and secure files. Unfortunately, the Multiple Users feature has never been a complete success. Too often, you wind up tripping over problems that arise from the fact that the OS was never designed to cope with such matters. A given application, for example, may not be aware of Multiple Users' "rules" and thus refuse to store its preferences settings anywhere other than the System Folder—a situation that prohibits individual users from maintaining their own customized preferences.

In contrast, Mac OS X was designed as multiple-user system. In fact, you can't turn off its Multiple Users feature! The software needed to sort everything out is set up by default when you install Mac OS X. You don't do anything to get it working. It just is.

When you install Mac OS X, you set up an initial account for yourself and are automatically assigned administrator status. The OS also, by default, turns off the requirement to log in at startup. (You can change this setting via the Login Options in the Accounts System Preferences pane.) Thus, when the OS starts up, you are not required to enter a password, making it appear that security is not being enforced—it is!

continues on next page

TAKE NOTE ▶ Multiple Users: Mac OS X vs. Mac OS 9 *continued*

In Mac OS 9, if you were the sole user of your computer (or the administrator for multiple users), you had read/write access to every file on the drive. No other "user" had higher access privileges. In Mac OS X, you're no longer on top: The user called System is higher than you. This means that if the System owns a file, you can't modify its permissions. Similarly, if you've set up users beside yourself, you can't access the files in their Users directories. There are ways around these restrictions if you're an administrative user with root access; more on that later.

Thus, even as an administrative user, you don't own the OS in the way you did as a Mac OS 9 user. In particular, the OS may tell you that you don't have permission to move or delete certain files, or to add files to certain folders. The truth is that you don't own Mac OS X; Mac OS X owns Mac OS X. You're just a privileged visitor.

This setup can be annoying if you're the only person using your Mac, forcing you to deal with overhead and complexity that you'll take advantage of yourself. The upside, though, is that if you do need a multiple-user setup, Mac OS X is far better equipped to handle it than Mac OS 9.

Bear in mind that Unix was created as an OS for large networked systems. As such, it needed to allow hundreds of people to log in to the same system. At the same time, it needed to maintain a level of security that prevented users from accessing other users' data. Just as important, it needed to restrict access to the main system software so that no user could deliberately or inadvertently bring down the entire system.

Mac OS X adopts the same Unix-based security features.

System domain

The first Library folder in our tour is found in the System folder at the root level of the Mac OS X volume. There are several ways to get to it:

One way is to select Computer from the Finder's Go menu (Command-Shift-C). A drive icon with the name of your current startup volume will appear in a window: Double-click it, and you're at the root level of the Mac OS X volume. Here you will find a folder called System (which should have an *X* on its folder icon). Double-click this folder to view its contents; you will now see a folder called Library—the first stop on our tour!

Another way to get to this folder is to Command-click the window name in the title bar of any Finder window, and from the pop-up menu that appears, choose the name of the startup volume (which should be the next-to-bottom item if it's listed). If your startup volume *is not* listed here, select the bottom name (your computer name) to bring up the same Computer window I just described. From here, you can similarly navigate to the /System/Library folder.

Finally, from the General section of the Finder's Preferences, you can select what you want to appear by default via the pop-up menu for the "New Finder windows open" option. If you select the name of your startup volume from the pop-up menu, you will be taken to the root level of your Mac OS X volume whenever you open a new window.

SEE: • Chapter 2, especially "Toolbar and Finder views," for more background on navigating Finder windows and using the toolbar.

TAKE NOTE ▶ Computer and Root-Level Windows

Computer window. To open this window, from the Finder's Go menu choose Computer. In this window you will find a list of all currently mounted volumes, including hard drives, CD-ROMs, and iDisks. It also includes the Network icon, as described elsewhere in this chapter.

A hard drive can be divided into multiple *partitions*, each of which functions almost as though it were a separate drive and has its own listing in this window. The term *volume* refers to a drive, a partition of a drive, or anything else that can be mounted in Mac OS X.

The name of the Computer window will not be *Computer* but rather the name you assigned to your computer when you first set up Mac OS X. You can access and edit this name from the Sharing System Preferences pane.

The icons at the Computer level are also represented by identically named icons on the right border of the Desktop (assuming you enabled the feature to show these icons on the Desktop via the Finder's Preferences). The Network icon is an exception; it does not appear on your Desktop.

Note: The Computer window is a bit odd. For example, if from the Finder's Go menu you select Go to Folder and type /, you will be taken to the Computer window, just as if you had selected Computer from the Go menu. However, if you instead type /Applications, you will be taken to the Applications folder at the root level of the startup volume (as described next)—not in the Computer window. Odd? Indeed. The Computer window is a special window created by the Finder that doesn't really exist as a folder anywhere on your drive. In almost all cases, the / symbol refers to the root level of your startup volume rather than the Computer window. The result of typing / in Go to Folder is the exception. To go to the root level of your startup volume from Go to Folder, type //.

Note: In Panther, the items in the Computer window may also be listed in Finder windows in the top section of the Places sidebar. Even the Computer window itself may be listed here. You determine what items are shown via settings in the Sidebar pane of the Finder's Preferences window.

continues on next page

TAKE NOTE ▶ Computer and Root-Level Windows *continued*

The root level of the startup volume. If you double-click the icon of the current Mac OS X startup volume in the Computer window, you are taken to the root level of that volume. The window that appears will contain at least four folders:

- **System.** This folder holds core Mac OS X software.
- **Library.** This folder contains "local domain" Mac OS X software.
- **Applications.** This folder houses all of the applications initially installed by Mac OS X, as well as any other applications that may have been installed there by you or by third-party installers. The Utilities folder is also within this folder.
- **Users.** This folder contains the Home directories for each user with an account on the volume. The Shared directory is also located here.

If Mac OS 9 is installed on this volume, there will also be a folder called System Folder, which may or may not have a *9* in its icon. This folder is *not* the Mac OS X System folder. There may also be a folder called Applications (Mac OS 9). This folder contains application software installed by Mac OS 9, such as SimpleText and QuickTime Player.

If you installed the software from the Developer Tools (Xtools) CD, a folder named Developer is also located at the root level.

Finally, the Unix directories (normally invisible in the Finder) are located here as well.

The root level of other volumes. Clicking any of the other volume icons in the Computer window will similarly take you to the root level of those volumes. The contents, of course, will depend on the nature of the volume. It could be another Mac OS X volume, a Mac OS 9 volume, or simply a volume that stores files (with no OS software at all).

In the structure of Mac OS X, the root level of the startup volume has a special status. For example, in Terminal (as covered in Chapter 10), *root level* refers only to the Mac OS X startup volume's root level. Other volumes are structured differently. If you select the Finder's Go to Folder command and type /Volumes, you will be taken to the Unix Volumes directory, located at the startup volume's root level. Here you will see a list of all the partitions on your drive as well as any other volumes that are currently mounted (or may have been mounted previously).

SEE: • **"Technically Speaking: What and Where Are the Unix Files?" earlier in this chapter.**
- **Chapters 2 and 8 for more on Sharing System Preferences and the Users folder.**
- **Chapter 3 for more information on partitioning a drive.**

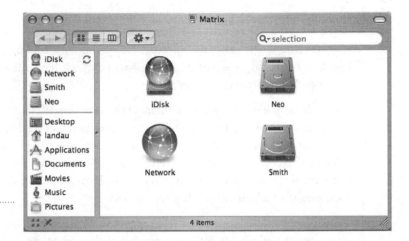

Figure 4.6

The Computer window.

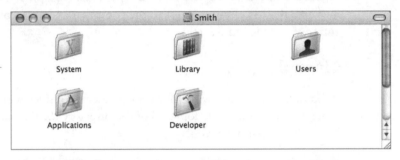

Figure 4.7

The root level of a Mac OS X startup volume (with invisible items invisible and without Mac OS 9 installed).

If the Mac OS X System folder strikes you as being the Mac OS X equivalent of the Mac OS 9 System Folder, you're more or less correct. The Library folder here contains the files that are essential to the operation of the OS. Nearly every file in this folder is installed by the Mac OS X Installer (or another Apple-supplied updater). The contents of this folder are rarely modified, other than by an update to the OS or, occasionally, a third-party kernel extension. In fact, Apple specifically warns against modifying the contents because doing so can result in failure to start up the computer. If you even attempt to make a change to this folder, you will typically be blocked—either by a message stating that the item can't be moved because "the Library cannot be modified" or by one asking you to "authenticate" (that is, enter your administrative name and password) before the OS will allow you to make the change.

SEE: • **"Take Note: Multiple Users: Mac OS X vs. Mac OS 9," earlier in this chapter, for background.**

• **"Using Panther's Finder Authenticate method," in Chapter 6, for related information.**

Occasionally, you will want to modify files in this folder—and, in fact, I provide some examples elsewhere in this book. However, by and large, I concur with Apple's assessment: Troubleshooting will rarely require that you modify the contents of this folder.

Local domain

If you return to the root level of the drive, you'll see a folder called Library. Inside it is an assortment of folders—some of which have the same names as the ones in the /System/Library folder.

This Library folder also gets its contents when you install Mac OS X. However, unlike in the /System/Library folder, most files here *can* be directly modified by any administrative user. Some files, such as those in the Preferences folder, offer read-only access even for administrators—meaning that administrators can view the contents but not modify them. However, even these can be modified if an administrator has root access.

This Library folder is intended as a repository for all the "modifiable" resources shared by the *local* users of a particular computer. A local user is anyone who has physical access to the computer and an account that enables him or her to log in directly.

User domain

Next, click the button with your short name in a Finder window's sidebar. This will take you to the top level of the directory for the person who is logged in (presumably you!).

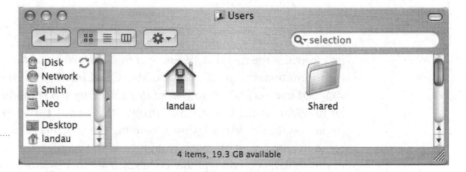

Figure 4.8

Inside my Users folder.

You can also get to your Home folder by opening the Users folder at the root level of Mac OS X. Inside, you will see at least two folders:

- **Shared.** The Shared folder houses files that any user can access and modify.
- *User name.* This folder will have the short user name you assigned when you set up the OS (in my case, landau). If you've created more than one user, you will find additional folders with those user names. Your folder (if you are the logged-in user) will have a house icon; the others will have a generic folder icon. If you open your own folder, you will be at the same place you would be if you had selected Home from the Go menu.

    SEE: • Chapters 6 and 8 for more information on the Shared folder and file sharing.

Inside your Home folder you'll find a third Library folder. Every user will have a comparable Library folder. These user-level Library folders contain resources specific to each user. Any personal preferences you set for an application will be stored here. That way, when you log in, those preferences will be in effect. When another user logs in, his or her preferences will be in effect instead.

Network domain

Your drive has a fourth level. To access it, return to the Computer window (via the Computer command in the Go menu) and double-click the globe icon called Network. (Alternatively, you can directly select Network in the Go menu or click the Network icon in the Places sidebar of a Finder window.) In the window that appears, you will see an alias icon called Servers.

This Servers item only comes into play if you're on a network that's connected to a central server—such as a computer running Mac OS X Server software—more generally referred to as a *network file system* (NFS). If you double-click this icon, you will see a list of servers to which you can connect or to which you are already connected. You can access these servers without using the Finder's Connect to Server command. You will most likely find this sort of setup in a university or large corporation, where the central server is accessible by all users and regulates what those users can do on the network.

Note: If you start up via Netbooting, you're actually using a central server as your startup volume. (See "Take Note: Netbooting," in Chapter 5, for more on this.)

Typically, even if you aren't on a server network, you'll still see an item in the Servers folder with the name of your own computer (it may also be called localhost). Double-clicking this icon takes you back to the root level of your Mac OS X volume.

If you can access a network server volume in the Servers folder, you may find a Library folder located on the server. This Library folder contains the shared resources (stored on the server itself) that can be used by all of the computers on the server's network.

I'm not going to tell you how to troubleshoot server networks in this book; that job is best left to server administrators! For that reason, I will not be discussing any possible Library folders that appear in this Network folder.

Finally, a few additional tidbits regarding networks, servers, and Library folders:

- The Network window will display icons for any computers that are on your local network node to which you can connect via file sharing. These are separate from the volumes contained in the Servers folder. If these local computers are running Mac OS X, they will contain Library folders just as your Mac does.

- If you have a .Mac account and you mount your iDisk, you will find a Library folder on your iDisk. (Note that iDisk is not listed in the Network window; instead, it's listed separately in the Computer window.)

- In Jaguar, the Network domain is structured differently. In particular, there is a Library folder at the level of the Network window itself. In Panther, I have seen this structure appear in a few instances when the Mac is not connected to any network. In general, however, it has been eliminated in Panther.

- The software largely responsible for the automatic mounting of items in the Computer and Network windows is the Unix automount command together with the items in the invisible automount folder at the root level of your startup volume. For more details, type man automount in Terminal.

    SEE: • Chapter 8, for more on file sharing, iDisk, and other networking issues.

TAKE NOTE ▶ Multiple Folders of the Same Name in Multiple Library Folders

As noted in the main text, several folders (such as Fonts and Sounds) appear in more than one Library folder. The reason for these multiple folders, including the multiple Library folders themselves, is the different levels of access that each folder provides. To make this arrangement as clear as possible, here is an overview that uses the different Fonts folders as an example.

- **User [~/Library/Fonts/].** The fonts here are only accessible to the user whose Home folder they reside in. That user can add fonts to or remove fonts from this folder as desired. This is the method by which nonadministrative users can install new fonts.

- **Local [/Library/Fonts/].** Any local user of the computer can use fonts installed in this folder. A set of these fonts is installed by the Mac OS X Installer; however, the OS does not require these additional fonts for system operation. An admin user can modify the contents of this folder, and this folder is the recommended location for installing fonts that are to be shared among users.

- **System [/System/Library/Fonts/].** This folder contains the essential fonts required for the OS to run (such as the ones needed for creating menus and dialog text). These fonts should not be altered or removed.

- **Classic [/System Folder/Fonts/].** This folder contains fonts used by the Classic environment. If more than one Mac OS 9.x System Folder is present, only fonts in the System Folder selected in the Classic pane of the System Preferences window are used. Mac OS X applications can use these fonts even when the Classic environment is not active. These fonts can be accessed even if they are in locations other than the Fonts folder.

Classic applications can only access fonts in the Classic System Folder, *not* those stored in Mac OS X Fonts folders. An exception: The third-party software Suitcase includes an extension called Suitcase (or Classic) Bridge. When installed in the Classic System Folder, this extension allows fonts activated in Mac OS X to be available to Classic applications.

continues on next page

TAKE NOTE ▶ Multiple Folders of the Same Name in Multiple Library Folders
continued

Fonts may also be stored in association with specific applications. Inside the Office folder of the Microsoft Office X folder, for example, is a folder called Fonts, which contains an assortment of fonts that are installed with Office. The fonts are copied to the Fonts folder of your Home directory the first time you launch Office. Similarly, Adobe applications may install fonts in ~/Library/Application Support/Adobe.

Note: Mac OS X may also use fonts found in the Fonts folders on mounted Mac OS X volumes that are not the current startup volume.

SEE: • **"Take Note: Problems with Duplicate Fonts in Fonts Folders," later in this chapter, for related information.**

Mac OS X: /System/Library

It's now time to take a close look at the contents of each of the main Library folders in Mac OS X, starting with /System/Library. There are far too many files and folders in any of these Library folders to cover even a bare majority here. Instead, I'm limiting the list to the ones that are most relevant to troubleshooting. Feel free to open these folders and browse around yourself: There's no fee for looking!

Figure 4.9

The /System/Library folder (partial view showing items beginning with A through I).

The /System/Library folder contains the essential OS software. Here's a sampling of the folders you'll find within.

CoreServices

CoreServices is the most critical folder in the /System/Library folder. Like the System folder itself, it has an *X* on it to denote its special status. It contains the BootX file, which is required for starting up from Mac OS X (as described in Chapter 5).

This folder also contains the Dock, Finder, Classic Startup, Help Viewer, and Software Update applications, as well as the loginwindow process (also covered in Chapter 5) and Menu Extras (covered in Chapter 3). There are also fake Mac OS 9 Finder and System files, created so that Carbon applications that expect to see these Mac OS 9–type files will "see" them. Yes, you will see the word *Fake* used in the Version description in the files' Get Info windows.

The SystemVersion.plist file determines what Mac OS X version is listed in the About This Mac window.

SEE: • **"Edit SystemVersion.plist," in Chapter 3, for more on this .plist file.**

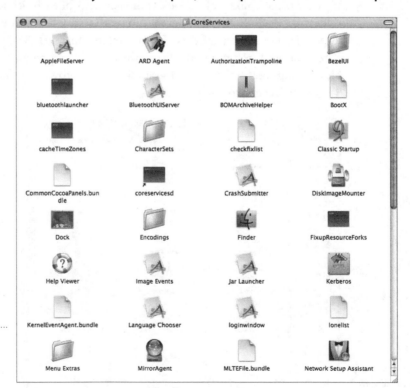

Figure 4.10

Some of the files and directories in the CoreServices folder.

CFMSupport

CFMSupport contains software used for running Carbon applications. The CarbonLib file is in this folder, for example.

Extensions

This folder contains the *kext* (short for *kernel extension*) files that load at startup, primarily acting as driver software for hardware peripherals. As their name implies, kext files are extensions of the basic kernel software that loads at startup (as covered in Chapter 5).

Fonts

This is one of several Fonts folders in Mac OS X. This one contains the fonts that are considered to be essential for Mac OS X.

SEE: • "Take Note: Multiple Folders of the Same Name in Multiple Library Folders," earlier in this chapter.

Frameworks

Frameworks are an important component of Mac OS X; however, you will have little reason to work with them directly in troubleshooting.

Briefly, frameworks are the Mac OS X equivalents of Mac OS 9's dynamic shared libraries, which means they are only executed when needed (dynamic) and contain code that can be used by more than one application simultaneously (shared). The code can be such things as Unix executable software or even a Mac OS X application. The basic idea is to eliminate the need to repeat code used by multiple applications.

Although they appear to be ordinary folders and can be opened without using the Show Package Contents contextual menu, frameworks are structured as package files. A framework package can contain multiple versions of the shared software; applications that require the newer version can access it, and those that are incompatible with the newer version will be able to access the older version.

Frameworks can occur in locations besides the /System/Library directory. The ones in this directory are simply the ones that are most essential for the OS.

Frameworks vs. private frameworks. Most frameworks are available for third-party developers to use. For example, if you wanted to write an application that could burn CDs, you would likely want to use Mac OS X's DiscRecording.framework. Among other things, a DevicePlugIns folder within this framework includes a separate device plug-in file for all supported CD-R drives.

However, some Mac OS X–installed frameworks are not available to third-party developers. These private frameworks are found in /System/Library/PrivateFrameworks. Only Apple is able to use these.

Frameworks and troubleshooting. As a troubleshooter, you usually won't need to bother with frameworks. However, there are a few exceptions.

In general, when Apple releases a Mac OS X update that alters Mac OS X applications such as the Dock, Preview, or the Finder, the improved code may not reside in the specified application itself. Instead, it may reside in a framework that the application accesses. For example, some improvements to the Finder may be contained in ApplicationServices.framework, which itself contains several subframeworks, including HIServices.framework (where *HI* stands for *human interface*) and LaunchServices.framework. A related framework is the HIToolbox.framework located within the Carbon.framework.

Framework and DVD Player. Here's one example of a troubleshooting problem resolved by accessing a framework: If an outdated version of the Developer Tools software is installed on your drive, an alert with error 1634955892 may appear when you open DVD Player. The solution here is to rename or remove the no-longer-needed HIServices framework installed by the Developer Tools package. To rename the framework, enter the following two commands in Terminal:

```
cd /System/Library/PrivateFrameworks/
sudo mv HIServices.framework HIServices-old.framework
```

SEE: • **"Menu Extras," in Chapter 2, for a related example of a framework fix.**

• **"Understanding Image, Installer Package, and Receipt Files," in Chapter 3, for more details on packages.**

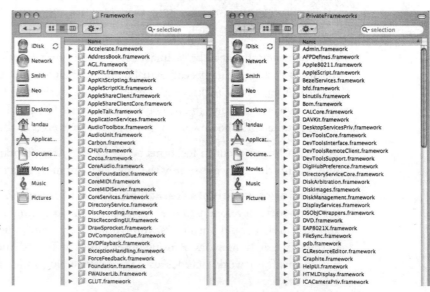

Figure 4.11

Partial contents of (left) the /System/Library/Frameworks and (right) /System/Library/PrivateFrameworks folders.

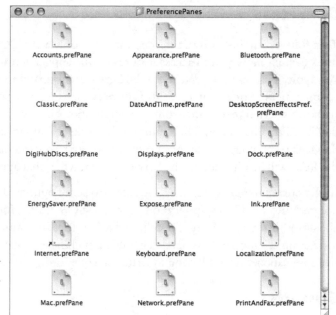

PreferencePanes

This folder contains the stock (Apple-provided) panes that you access via the System Preferences application.

SEE: • "System Preferences," in Chapter 2.

Printers

This folder contains the files needed for printers to work with Mac OS X. Among other things, it contains the PPD and PDE files required for LaserWriter printers in Mac OS X.

SEE: • Chapter 7, for more information on printing, including details on PPD and PDE files.

QuickTime

This folder contains QuickTime-related software, such as the QuickTime Updater application.

Screen Savers

This folder contains the basic screensaver options (Beach, Forest, and so on) that you can access from the Screen Saver System Preferences pane.

Services

This folder contains software needed for some of Mac OS X's Services features (which allow you to access features of one application while in another). You typically access this feature via the Services command in the active application's menu. For example, if this feature is working, you can open TextEdit with the selected text of the frontmost application already pasted into an untitled TextEdit document. This feature only works for applications that support Services technology. If a service is not supported by a particular application, the item will be dimmed in the Services menu when that application is active.

In the current context, Services also refers to some options that can be incorporated into any Cocoa application. As of Mac OS X 10.3, four such Services are stored here: AppleSpell, Speech, ImageCapture, and Summary. AppleSpell, for example, allows a developer to include a spelling-checker feature in his or her application without having to write the code for it.

Sounds

This folder contains the sound files (in AIFF format) that are listed on the Alerts tab of the Sound System Preferences pane.

Note: AIFF is one of several sound formats supported by Mac OS X. Others include the well-known MP3 format and the newer ACC format, commonly used for music files stored on your drive and used by iTunes and the iPod.

StartupItems

This important folder contains the various protocols that load at startup while you wait for the login window and/or Desktop to appear. These items include the Apache Web server, AppleShare, Networking, and Network Time.

SEE: • **Chapter 5 for more information on the startup sequence.**

Mac OS X: /Library

As I explained earlier in this chapter, this folder stores files that are available to all local users and can be modified by an administrative user. The following are some of the folders you'll find inside.

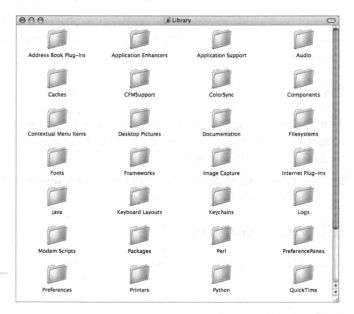

Application Support

This folder contains accessory software and support files for various applications. Support files will be in folders named for the base application or the application's software vendor. For example, if you've installed Adobe software, there will be an Adobe folder. Among other things, the folder contains a Fonts folder that holds fonts required for use with Adobe software.

ColorSync

The profiles you create via the Calibrate feature in the Displays Preferences pane are stored here.

Contextual Menu Items

This folder contains third-party software that adds items to Mac OS X's contextual-menu feature (accessed by Control-clicking an item).

Desktop Pictures

This folder contains the background pictures you can select via the Desktop System Preferences pane.

Documentation

Some programs that provide read-me files and other documentation (which you access via commands within the application, such as Help) store their documentation files here.

Fonts

This folder is similar in function to the Fonts folder in /System/Library; however, these fonts are not considered essential. As an administrator, you can add fonts to or remove fonts from this folder.

SEE: • **"Take Note: Multiple Folders of the Same Name in Multiple Library Folders," earlier in this chapter.**

Internet Plug-Ins

This folder stores plug-ins used with your browser, such as QuickTime and Shockwave.

Modem Scripts

This folder holds the modem scripts that you can choose from the Modem pop-up menu in the Modem settings of Network System Preferences.

SEE: • **"Take Note: Modem Scripts and Terminal Scripts," in Chapter 8, for more information.**

Preferences

A few system-wide preferences (.plist) files are stored here, such as those for loginwindow. In general, you'll have little reason to modify preferences files in this folder. However, the files inside the SystemConfiguration folder do appear on the troubleshooting radar from time to time—as does com.apple.AppleFileServer.plist.

SEE: • **"Preferences Files," later in this chapter, for more information on .plist files.**

• **Chapter 5 for more information on the loginwindow application.**

• **Chapter 8 for more on the SystemConfiguration and com.AppleFileServer.plist files.**

Printers

This folder is where you will find support software for printers (in addition to the LaserWriter support files located in /System/Library/Printers). In particular, drivers for Epson, Hewlett-Packard, and Lexmark printers are stored here.

SEE: • **Chapter 7 for more information on printing.**

Receipts

Every time you install a Mac OS X update, a receipt .pkg file for the update is stored in this folder. In certain situations, as discussed in Chapter 3, the OS (especially Software Update) uses these files to verify that a given update has been installed.

SEE: • **"Understanding Image, Installer Package, and Receipt Files," in Chapter 3, for more information.**

StartupItems

This folder is the equivalent of the StartupItems folder in /System/Library. The main difference is that this folder is used for third-party software, as opposed to the preinstalled Mac OS X items stored in the /System/Library folder. In fact, the folder may not even be present unless you have third-party items that need it. For example, if you install Timbuktu Pro, it will install a Startup Item in this folder called TimbuktuStartup. This item is needed for the Timbuktu software to be active at startup, no matter which user logs in. The actual Timbuktu application is located elsewhere, most likely in your Applications folder. Similarly, the Dantz Retrospect backup software also installs a folder, called RetroRun, in the StartupItems folder.

TECHNICALLY SPEAKING ▶ Log Files and Cron Jobs

Mac OS X maintains numerous log files that record events (mainly errors) that occur while running your Mac. Referring to these files can sometimes help in diagnosing a problem.

Log files and Library folders. The following is an overview of the main log files used by Mac OS X and their locations.

• **Console.log in /Library/Logs.** This log file opens when you launch Console; it's located in /Library/Logs/Console/{*username*}. This Console folder contains a separate folder for each user account. Each Console log maintains a record of recent activity (especially error messages) specific to the named account. Many of these errors are too minor to overtly affect your work—in fact, you probably wouldn't even know they had occurred if you hadn't checked the log. As such, you can often ignore these errors. However, if you do start to have problems, checking for errors here may point to the solution.

continues on next page

TECHNICALLY SPEAKING ▶ **Log Files and Cron Jobs** *continued*

- **System.log and other log files stored in /var/log.** The system.log file is similar to the console.log file except that it focuses on system-wide processes that are independent of a specific user. This file is stored in the invisible /var/log directory, along with numerous other log files.

- **CrashReporter log files in Library folders.** Both the /Library/Logs folder and the ~/Library/Logs folder contain a folder called CrashReporter. Contained within are log files, named for applications (or processes), that record what happens each time the named software crashes. The /Library/Logs folder also includes the panic.log file, which records information about kernel panics.

The easiest way to access any log file (visible or invisible) is via the Console utility. After launching Console, click the Logs button on the left side of the toolbar. From the list that appears in the sidebar, locate and open any desired log file.

SEE: • "Console," in Chapter 2, and "Crash.log files" and "Kernel Panic," in Chapter 5, for more details.

Doing log maintenance with cron jobs. The Unix system periodically compresses log files to save space, in the process deleting the oldest ones. This maintenance, along with other tasks (such as updating various Mac OS X databases), is performed by running special shell scripts, which are normally scheduled to be run by a utility called *cron*. Running scripts using cron is a Unix operation, and the cron schedules (called *crontabs*) are stored in Mac OS X's Unix directories.

If you're comfortable using Unix commands, you can run these maintenance scripts from Terminal via the `periodic` command (see Chapter 10 for more on this). For those who prefer to avoid Terminal, get a shareware utility called MacJanitor. This Aqua-based utility makes it easy to run the daily, weekly, and monthly maintenance scripts.

Why might you need to use MacJanitor? One problem with the default crontab schedule for maintenance scripts is that they're typically set to run at night—between 3 a.m. and 6 a.m., depending on the script. Thus, if you turn your Mac off each night, these tasks may never get run. In truth, this probably won't matter much; however, it can lead to very large log files (or a very large number of log files) that never get cleared.

A similar utility, called Macaroni, has the added benefit of being able to verify whether cron jobs have been run as scheduled and, if not, run them. This means that even if you turn off your Mac at night, the scripts will get run automatically via Macaroni.

If you're a bit more technically inclined, you can actually see the *system crontab*—the system-level schedule of cron events—without using Terminal. To do so, get a shareware utility called CronniX. Launch it, and choose Open System Crontab from the File menu to see daily, weekly, and monthly entries.

continues on next page

Mac OS X: /Users/Home/Library

The Home folder or directory is where you go when you click the Home button or enter ~ (a tilde) in the Finder's Go to Folder command. The path to your Home directory's Library folder can thus be written as ~/Library. This Library folder contains files that are only accessible to—and used by—the logged-in user. Each user account has a separate folder of this kind.

This Library folder is actually stored in /Users/*username*, where *username* refers to the name of the Home folder of the currently logged-in user. It is the user's short name. For example, the full pathname for my Home Library folder would be /Users/landau/Library.

The following list of this folder's contents is selective, emphasizing folders that do not have duplicates in the Library folders that I've already discussed. For those that *do* have duplicates, their purposes are the same as those located in /Library, except that they only apply to the user in whose Home directory they reside.

Figure 4.14

Partial contents of my /Users/landau/ Library folder.

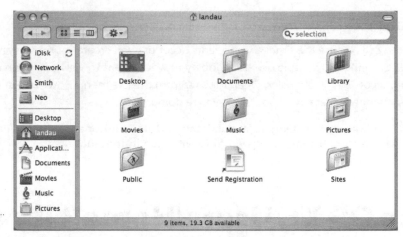

Figure 4.15

My Home directory.

TAKE NOTE ▶ Other Folders in the Home Directory

The Home folder/directory for each user contains standard folders (installed by Mac OS X) besides the Library folder. Of particular interest for troubleshooting are the following:

- **Public.** This folder is used for anything that you want to make publicly available. Any user who can access your computer, via a local network or even the Internet, will be able to access what's in the Public folder. Although these users won't be able to modify anything, they will be able to copy the files to their own folders (locally) or drives (remotely).

- **Documents.** This is where you will save most documents that you create in applications (since most applications select this folder as the default location for saving documents). Some applications also install important data for using the application in this folder (for example, AppleWorks installs an AppleWorks User Data folder here containing information about the list of starting points that appears when you launch the program).

- **Desktop.** This folder contains all the files and folders that are scattered about the Desktop. Because each user has his or her own Desktop folder, what appears on the Desktop will change depending on who is logged in.

SEE: • "Take Note: The Location of Desktop Folders," later in this chapter.

Application Support

This folder serves the same purpose as the Application Support folder in /Library, except that items in it are available only when the owner of the directory logs in and the directory becomes the current Home directory.

This folder has become popular with developers: I currently have support folders for about two dozen applications, including Adobe (for several Adobe software products), LaunchBar, Spell Catcher, and Jedi Knight II (it's where Jedi stores saved games!).

Caches

Cache files, such as the cache files created by Internet Explorer (selected in the Advanced tab of Internet Explorer's Preferences window), are located here. To see these Internet Explorer files, check the MS Internet Cache folder.

Contextual Menu Items

This folder is where third-party contextual-menu items are typically installed. There is a similar folder in /Library.

Favorites

This folder contains Internet Location files that are created via the Favorite Servers option in Connect to Server.

Other third-party software that includes a Favorites feature may store aliases here for favored locations (such as for the Documents folder in your Home directory); selecting an item from a Favorites list takes you to the original location of the selected alias item.

FontCollections

Open a Cocoa application (such as TextEdit), and from the Font submenu of the Format menu choose Show Fonts; the Font panel window appears. The names in the Collections column on the far-left side of the Font Panel are stored in this folder. You can edit Collections items in the Font Panel.

SEE: • "Font window," later in this chapter, for more information on the Font panel.

Fonts

This folder is the third item in the main trio of Fonts folders. This one is used for fonts that are only accessible when the owner of this particular ~/Library folder is logged in.

Note: I copy third-party fonts from my Classic System Folder and place them here if I intend to use them in Mac OS X. This method seems to result in fewer problems than if I access the font from the Classic Fonts folder. (Mac OS X uses a font in a Mac OS X folder before it uses the same font in the Classic folder.) Actually, if you know you won't need these fonts for Classic applications, it's best to delete them from the Classic System Folder.

SEE: • "Take Note: Multiple Folders of the Same Name in Multiple Library Folders," earlier in this chapter.

• "Viewing and Managing Fonts," later in this chapter.

Keychains

Your keychain file (which you access from the Keychain Access application in the Utilities folder) is stored here. A keychain file is a convenience feature that stores passwords for any number of applications and services (as long as they support Apple's Keychain technology). If it's working, when entering or creating a password, you may encounter a checkbox that says something like, "Add password to keychain." If you check the box, the password will be added to the keychain data. In the future, you will not need to re-enter the password.

SEE: • "Keychain Access," in Chapter 2.

PreferencePanes

System Preferences panes that appear in the Other section of the System Preferences window are installed here. Typically, if you download a third-party preferences pane, you install it simply by dragging it to this folder. The next time you launch System Preferences, this pane will be listed.

Preferences

This folder is the single most important folder in this Library folder and the one you will likely access most often. It contains the preferences files created by most applications you use—which means that it stores any customized changes you make via the Preferences command of these applications. Some OS-level preferences files are also stored here (such as the ones used by the Finder).

When something goes wrong with an application, a common early troubleshooting step is to delete its preferences file, since such files can get corrupted when modified. If this is the cause of the problem, deleting the corrupted preferences file will fix it. The application automatically creates a new default version of the file the next time it launches.

Note: Don't be too eager to delete preferences files: A few of them contain important information that you can't easily re-create after Mac OS X has created a new default version. The Favorites.html file (inside the Explorer folder in the Preferences folder), for example, contains all the URLs listed in Internet Explorer's Favorites menu. To be safe, make a backup copy of any file you intend to delete so that you can restore it if it turns out not to be the source of your problem.

Most of the preferences files you will work with have the .plist extension.

SEE: • "Preferences Files," later in this chapter, for more on preferences files.

• "Technically Speaking: Type/Creator vs. Filename Extensions," later in this chapter, and "Deleting or removing preferences," in Chapter 5, for related information.

Application-specific folders

Various applications, such as QuicKeys, may install their own folders in these Library folders.

TAKE NOTE ▶ Library Folders, Applications, and Accessory Files

One of the cited advantages of Mac OS X is that it ends the proliferation of application-related files, scattered in numerous locations, that often plagued Mac OS 9 users. This proliferation made it more difficult to troubleshoot problems (because you often couldn't find all of the relevant files!) and to copy applications to other locations (because if you failed to copy needed accessory files, an application might not work).

The Mac OS X solution is the application package (.app). The package concept allows developers to place the actual application together with its associated files in one location. The truth, however, is that there remain *many* locations in Mac OS X beyond the application package where an application's accessory files may get placed.

If an application you're using begins to develop odd symptoms—especially if simply replacing the .app file doesn't fix the problem—ferreting out these files and reinstalling or deleting them may help. This is because these files may have become modified in a way that prevents their expected use. Deleting often works because many of these files (such as .plist files) are self-regenerating: A new default copy is created the next time the application is launched. For non-regenerating files, reinstalling the entire application (from its installer) or getting a backup copy from your backup files are the most common ways to replace a suspected problem file. In some cases, however, modifying the ownership/permissions or editing the content of an accessory file may fix the problem. I cover specific examples of troubleshooting accessory files throughout this book, especially in Chapters 5 and 6.

Look for folders containing accessory files in both the /Library folder and the ~/Library folders. An application's installer utility will place a file in the /Library folder if it wants all local users to be able to access the file. It will place the item in your Home (~) Library folder if it expects that only you will be accessing the file(s). Sometimes an installer will give you a choice of which way to go. The majority of accessory files, however, will be in your Home directory.

Here is a short list of the most common Library folders that may contain application accessory files:

- Application Enhancers
- Application Support
- Caches
- Contextual Menu Items
- Documentation
- Fonts
- Individual iApp folders (iTunes, and so on)
- InputManagers
- Internet Plug-Ins
- Preferences
- PreferencePanes
- StartupItems (only found in /Library)

continues on next page

TAKE NOTE ▶ Library Folders, Applications, and Accessory Files *continued*

The /Library directory can also contain folders with application names. These, too, contain accessory files. For example, there is a Safari folder in ~/Library used by Apple's Safari Web browser. In some cases, the application-named folder may be within one of the above folders. For example, you'll find an Explorer folder inside the ~/Library/Preferences folder, and within this folder are several important files used by Internet Explorer, including the Favorites.html file that Internet Explorer uses to create the list of items in its Favorites menu.

Other Home-directory folders. Besides the /Library folder files, other folders in the Home directory may also contain accessory files. The most common example is the Documents folder, where you'll find the AppleWorks Users Data folder, the Microsoft User Data folder (used by Microsoft Office applications, especially Entourage), and the iTunes folder. Again, if these files are deleted or are not present, the application typically creates a new default version when the application is launched.

SEE: • **"Installer Package (pkg) files" and "Technically Speaking: Inside Packages," in Chapter 3, for more details on package files.**
  • **Chapter 5 for details about startup items.**

TAKE NOTE ▶ The Location of Desktop Folders

Desktop folders in Mac OS X. Anything you place on your Desktop in Mac OS X is actually stored in a folder in your Home directory called, appropriately enough, Desktop. To confirm this, simply open a Finder window, click the Home button in the toolbar, and open the Desktop folder in the window that appears. Inside you'll see every file and folder on your Desktop. Any changes you make in this folder will be reflected on the Desktop as well. That's because this folder *is* your Desktop (just as in Mac OS 9 an invisible folder called Desktop Folder contained the contents of your Desktop).

This setup means that when a different user logs in to your computer, he or she will neither see nor have access to the files on your Desktop. Instead, this user will see the contents of the Desktop folder in his or her own Home directory. There is no system-wide Desktop folder whose contents are visible to everyone. Thus, things that you want to make accessible to everyone need to be placed in shared locations, such as the Applications folder or the Shared folder in the /Users directory.

Mac OS 9 Desktop folders and Mac OS X. As mentioned above, in Mac OS 9, items placed on the Desktop are maintained in an invisible folder, located at the root level of the drive, called Desktop Folder.

In Mac OS X, especially if you have a Mac that no longer boots in Mac OS 9, there will likely be no items on a Mac OS 9 Desktop—in which case, the Mac OS 9 Desktop Folder might not even get created.

continues on next page

TAKE NOTE ▶ The Location of Desktop Folders *continued*

If the Desktop Folder does exist on a Mac OS X volume—and it contains items—it remains invisible even when running Mac OS X. Further, as implied in the previous section, none of the items in this invisible folder appear on your Mac OS X Desktop. Thus, there's no direct way to access the contents of this invisible Desktop Folder. Mac OS X solves this problem by creating a special alias file (actually a symbolic link) called Desktop (Mac OS 9). This folder contains the items that would be visible on the Desktop if and when you were to boot from Mac OS 9.

If a Desktop Folder with items exists, this folder will automatically appear at the root level of *any* volume with Mac OS X installed, *not* just the Mac OS X startup volume. There is one problem, however: If you double-click the alias icon, you're always taken to the Desktop Folder of the current startup volume, not the volume where the icon is located. This means you cannot use these aliases to access the contents of a Desktop Folder other than the one on the current startup volume.

For volumes that have a Desktop Folder but do not have Mac OS X installed, this problem is avoided. The Desktop Folder appears as a visible folder icon at the root level of the volume when running Mac OS X from another volume. No alias icon is used or needed.

For volumes that do have Mac OS X installed and also have this Desktop (Mac OS 9) alias, the easiest work-around (to access the contents of the Desktop Folder on the nonstartup volume) is to use the Finder's Go to Folder command. For example, to access the Desktop Folder contents on a secondary volume called R2D2, enter the following in the Go to Folder text box: `/Volumes/R2D2/Desktop Folder`.

If all items in a Mac OS 9 Desktop Folder are removed or deleted, the linked alias is removed automatically the next time the computer restarts. The alias has its permissions set so that it cannot be deleted in normal use. If the alias is deleted somehow, it will be re-created after the next restart.

The root user Desktop. If you log in as the root user, you also have a Desktop. Because there is no *root* folder in the Users folder, however, a question arises: Where is the Desktop folder for the root user?

This folder is located in an invisible location at /private/var/root/Desktop. You can view the folder icon by typing `/private/var/root` as the path in the window that opens when you choose the Finder's Go to Folder command. You will not be able to open the folder, however, because you do not have root access.

To see the contents of the folder, you can log in as root. Once you've done this, you can also move or delete the files located in the folder.

continues on next page

TAKE NOTE ▶ **The Location of Desktop Folders** *continued*

If you're an administrative user, you can also use Terminal to view the contents of this folder—even when you're not logged in as root. To do so, type the following commands:

`sudo -s` (then enter your admin password when requested)

`cd /private/var/root/Desktop` (to move to that directory location)

`ls` (to list the contents of the Desktop directory)

A third method of viewing these contents would be to boot from Mac OS 9 and go to the /private/var/root/Desktop folder. However, because this folder is invisible in Mac OS 9, you will need to use a utility that can access invisible files and folders (such as File Buddy).

In this case, logging in as a root user in Mac OS X is the simplest approach.

SEE: • "Desktop (Mac OS 9)" file is a symbolic link," in Chapter 6, for related information.
   • "Desktop folders in Mac OS 9/Classic vs. Mac OS X," in Chapter 9, for more information.

TAKE NOTE ▶ **The Location of Trash Folders**

As is the case with the Desktop folders, each user in Mac OS X maintains his or her own Trash (actually a folder, just like the Desktop). Thus, your unemptied trash will not be visible or accessible in another user's Trash if you log out and another user logs in. Likewise, other users can't delete items you've left in the Trash. (Mac OS X has no universal emptying of the Trash, as does Mac OS 9.)

.Trash. The files that you place in the Trash in Mac OS X are actually stored in an invisible folder in your Home directory called .Trash. Each user's directory (including the one for the root user, located at /private/var/root) has its own .Trash folder.

.Trashes. If you've mounted partitions or volumes in addition to the Mac OS X startup partition, anything you drag to the Trash from these volumes will still appear in the Trash window you access by clicking the Trash icon in the Dock. If you empty the Trash, those files will be deleted. The files are not stored in the .Trash folder in your Home directory, however; they remain stored in invisible .Trashes folders on each volume. These .Trashes folders have default write-only privileges; thus, you would need to change the privileges (as described in "Ownership & Permissions," later in the chapter) to view their contents, such as via a list (1s) command in Terminal.

There is also a .Trashes folder for the startup volume. However, it's unlikely to be used unless you reboot from another volume and mount the now former startup volume as a secondary volume.

continues on next page

TAKE NOTE ▶ The Location of Trash Folders *continued*

Network Trash Folder. There is also a Network Trash Folder, located at the root level of your startup volume, for trashing files over a network.

Mac OS 9 Trash. Items placed in the Trash while running Mac OS 9 (assuming you have a Mac that can still boot from Mac OS 9!) are stored in the invisible Trash folder used by Mac OS 9. There is one such folder at the root level of every volume that contains Mac OS 9.

Note: If you boot from Mac OS 9, files you left in the Trash while in Mac OS X will not appear in the Mac OS 9 Trash. To access their contents and try to delete them from Mac OS 9, you will need a utility that allows you to view and modify the contents of invisible folders (File Buddy, for example). Then you will need to navigate to the directory in the /Users folder containing the .Trash file that you want to empty.

Seeing invisible Trash folders. You can "see" invisible Trash folders via the Terminal utility. To see the .Trash folder for your home directory, for example, simply launch Terminal and type 1s –a. This command lists all files, including invisible ones, at the current directory.

If you prefer not to use Terminal, try TinkerTool (or a similar utility) to see normally invisible files in the Finder. To do so with TinkerTool, enable the Show Hidden and System Files option in the Finder section of TinkerTool. Then relaunch the Finder via TinkerTool's Relaunch Finder button. You can undo the change in TinkerTool to make invisible items invisible again.

SEE: • **"Problems Deleting Files" and "Invisible Files: What Files Are Invisible," and "Invisible Files: Working with Invisible Files," in Chapter 6, for more information on these subjects.**
• **Chapter 10 for more on using Terminal.**

Get Info

This and the remaining sections of this chapter form a category that I refer to as *advanced basics*. If this term sounds like an oxymoron, that's because it is. But here's what I mean by it: There are some topics in Mac OS X that the average user doesn't need to know much about but are so essential to understanding the way the OS works that you can't get far in troubleshooting without some basic knowledge of them. That's why I consider these topics *advanced basics*.

The starting point for any Mac OS X advanced-basics tour must be the Finder's Get Info windows. As you will remember from Chapter 2, you access a Get Info window by clicking an icon in the Finder and selecting Command-I (or selecting Get Info from the icon's contextual menu).

The window that appears will contain several sections, or panels. For a document icon, these sections include the following:

- General
- Name & Extension
- Open With
- Preview
- Ownership & Permissions
- Comments

The General section is visible by default. To view other sections, you need to click the triangle to the left of a section's name. Starting in Panther, any sections that you reveal this way remain revealed in subsequent Get Info windows (a real time-saver when comparing multiple windows).

Exactly which sections and options are listed will depend on whether you're viewing a document, application, folder, or volume. (You can even select Get Info for the Desktop by pressing Command-I when no item is selected!) In the sections that follow, I will list the full set of options.

Multiple Info windows. You can have multiple Get Info windows open at the same time. Just click Command-I for each.

Batch Info window. Alternatively, you can select multiple icons and then choose Get Info for all of them. This reveals one Get Info window representing all of the items you selected. Any change you make here will affect all of the items simultaneously. When you're working in "batch mode" like this, you're limited to the options that are available for *all* of the selected items. If, for example, a folder does not include an option that's available for a document, you won't be able to access any of the document options if your multiple-item selection includes a folder.

Old-style Inspector. The user interface of the Finder's Get Info window (called Show Info in Mac OS X 10.1.x) was overhauled in Mac OS X 10.2. To bring up the old Mac OS X 10.1.x Inspector-style window, press Command-Option-I. You can even have both the old-style and new-style windows open at the same time. This older version of the Get Info window accesses the different sections via a pop-up menu rather than the disclosure triangles. Also, if you click a different Finder icon while the old-style window is open, it shifts to display the information for that item. Thus, you cannot have two Inspector-style windows open at once—a convenience when you want to view information from several files in succession (you don't have to press Command-I for each and have several windows open) but inconvenient when you want to compare two Get Info windows side by side.

In almost all cases, you'll be working with the newer style of Get Info windows. Thus, that's the only style I'll be discussing here.

Get Info sections. Because the options available here are critical to so many troubleshooting tasks, I describe each in detail in the following sections (for the most part, following the order of appearance in the Get Info window).

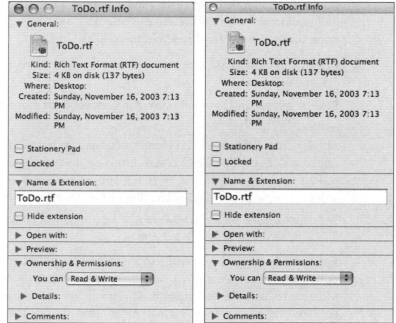

General

The General section of the Get Info window appears by default when you open the window. It provides basic information such as item type (application, document, folder, volume, or alias), item size, item location, version number (if the application provides one), and item creation and modification dates.

Note: A folder's modification date only changes when its contents change, not when items within it have been modified. Thus, if you were to modify and save a file within a folder, the folder's modification date would not change. However, if you were to add or delete a file to or from the folder, the folder's modification date would change.

If the file is a document, the Kind line typically identifies its type (that is, the application used to create it). For example a Microsoft Word document will say just that: "Microsoft Word document." However, the Kind line for an AppleWorks document will read, "com.apple.appleworks.document." Although this may seem an odd way to identify it, you still know that the document was created by AppleWorks.

If the item is a volume, such as a hard drive, the General section will list the capacity of the volume and how much of it is presently used versus unused (available).

If you have multiple drives, each subdivided into partitions, the Where line will not identify which is the drive of origin for a selected partition. To determine this, check the left-hand column in Disk Utility.

If the file is an alias, the General section will tell you where on your drive the original is located.

SEE: • "Aliases and Symbolic Links," in Chapter 6, for more information on aliases.

At the bottom of the General section, you may see one or more check boxes, one of which will be called Locked. If this option is enabled, you are prevented from deleting the file. In fact, if you try to place it in the Trash, you will get a message stating that you don't have sufficient privileges to do so.

SEE: • Chapter 6 for more information on problems with locked files and with deleting files in general.

For some documents, you will also have a Stationery Pad option. If this option is enabled, opening the document actually opens a *copy* of the document rather than the document itself. This allows you to make changes in the copy and still preserve the original. As its name implies, this option is useful for documents, such as stationery, in which you have some element (such as a name and address) that you want to preserve for use in future documents (such as letters you are writing).

There are some applications that you can open in either Classic (Mac OS 9) or Mac OS X—though by default these applications usually open in Mac OS X. If, for some reason, you want one of these applications to open in Mac OS 9, choose the Open in the Classic Environment option in the General section of the Get Info window. (If this option is not available, it probably means the application you're using is not a switch-hitter—that is, it can open in only one environment.)

As described in Chapter 9, there are cases (such as with AppleWorks 6) in which an application can open in either Classic or Mac OS X even though the Open in the Classic Environment check box does not appear.

If the application can open in Classic, there will be a Memory section that you can use to allocate the amount of memory assigned to the app when opened in Classic.

SEE: • Chapter 9 for more information on Classic.

Finally, the icon of a file or folder is visible in this window.

TAKE NOTE ▶ **Changing and Troubleshooting Finder Icons**

Changing the icon for a file or folder is usually done more for aesthetic reasons than true need.

Changing icons via Get Info. In most cases, if a Finder item has a custom icon, you can copy it from the item's Get Info window and paste it into the Get Info window of another item. The other item will then display that icon in the Finder. To do this, follow these steps:

1. First, determine whether the destination file already has a custom icon, and if it does, delete it: Select Get Info for the destination file, click the icon, and then from the Edit menu select Cut (Command-X).

   When you cut (Command-X) a custom icon, you're left with either a default icon (as assigned by the Finder, based on its creator or filename extension) or a blank icon.

2. If you did delete a custom icon, log out and log back in. This is really only necessary if the destination file is on the Desktop, but to be safe, you can do it in any case. If you don't, the icon you paste may not "stick."

   If you still have problems getting a custom icon to appear, make sure you're using Mac OS X 10.2.4 or later. The newer Mac OS X versions include a fix for a bug that caused this problem in older versions.

3. Select Get Info for the file with the desired icon.

4. Click the icon in the Get Info window, and from the Edit menu select Copy (Command-C).

5. Select the Get Info window for the destination file.

6. Click its icon, and from the Edit menu select Paste (Command-V).

   Pasting a custom icon works for most document files. It also works for applications, folders, and volumes.

If you're curious about where custom icons are stored, the answer is, it varies by file type:

- The icon for a volume is stored in an invisible file called .VolumeIcon.icns, located at the root level of that volume.

- A custom icon for a folder is stored in an invisible file called *icon* that's created within the folder when you add its custom icon.

- For .app application packages, the custom icon is stored in an invisible file called *icon*, located at the root level of the package.

Changing package-file icons. Although you can add a custom icon to an application package, the default icon obviously remains. That is, if you cut the custom icon, the default icon returns. Similarly, the information needed to assign the correct icons to documents created by the application remains. Where is all of this default information stored? And can you change it?

continues on next page

TAKE NOTE ▶ Changing and Troubleshooting Finder Icons *continued*

Here are the answers:

You need to have the desired icon in the form of an .icns file rather than a graphic on the clipboard. You can download .icns files from the Web, create them via icon-editing utilities, or "borrow" them from existing package files. For example, to place the .icns file from one package in another, you would do the following:

1. Select the application with the icon you want to copy and Control-click it to access its contextual menu. If a Show Package Contents item appears, the application is a package. (Note: Not all applications will be packages in Mac OS X.)

2. Select Show Package Contents. From the window that opens, navigate to the Contents/Resources folder, where you will find at least one .icns file. Look for the one named {*name of application*}.icns. (Note that the file may have a slightly different name. For example, NetworkConnect.icns is the name of the relevant .icns file for the Internet Connect application.) Whatever name it goes by, this is the file that's used to create the Finder icon for that application.

   The remaining .icns files, if any, are typically ones used for documents created by the application.

   Note: If you double-click an .icns file, it will open in Preview. This can help determine if you have the "correct" .icns file.

3. Option-drag this .icns file to the Desktop to create a copy of it there.

4. Select the application where you want the icon to go and, using the Show Package Contents contextual menu, go to the same Resources folder inside the package (as described in step 2).

5. Rename the .icns file on the Desktop to match the name of the one in the destination package's Resources folder.

6. Drag the renamed file to the Resources folder of the destination package, and click OK when asked if you wish to replace the file already there.

7. Close all opened folders.

8. Relaunch the Finder (for example, by holding down the Option key when accessing the Finder's Dock menu and selecting Relaunch). In some cases, for this or the alternate method described next, this may not be sufficient; if so, you will need to restart the Mac.

Another way to do this would be to try the following:

1. After obtaining the .icns file you wish to use (as described in steps 1 through 4 above), go to the Contents folder inside the destination package.

2. Using a text editor (such as TextEdit) or Property List Editor, open the Info.plist (or Info-macos.plist) file, as appropriate.

3. Change the value of the CFBundleIconFile key to the name of the new .icns file (do not included the .icns extension in the name). Save the change.

4. Move the new .icns file into the package's Resources folder. With this method, you don't overwrite the original .icns file or change the name of your newly added one.

continues on next page

TAKE NOTE ▶ Changing and Troubleshooting Finder Icons *continued*

Note: I recommend working with copies of the applications involved so that you don't have to worry about doing permanent harm if things don't go as planned. Be aware, however, that there's a bug in Mac OS X that affects this method: When you copy a package file, you may not be able to open the Contents folder within the package of the copy. This in turn means you won't be able to access the needed .icns file. The solution seems to be simply to log out and log back in again. Once you do this, you should be able to open the Contents folder.

Where to get icons. If you don't want to copy an icon from an existing item, you can create your own. One way to do so is with the IconComposer utility that comes with Developer Tools software. Third-party utilities like Iconographer X also work well and are more user-friendly. For folder icons, check out Folder Icon X. Another alternative would be to obtain icon files down-loaded from the Web and paste them as custom icons. You might even be able to paste graph-ics other than icons, such as images opened in the Preview application (though they won't look as good as a graphics specifically designed as icons).

Mac OS X System icons. Most of the icons used by Mac OS X itself—such as the ones for the Applications folder, your Home directory, and the Finder itself—cannot be changed simply by pasting a custom icon into the item's Get Info window: Mac OS X will not permit this. Still, with some extra effort, you can change these icons.

These icons are stored in /System/Library/CoreServices/SystemIcons.bundle. To access them, view this package's contents and navigate through Contents/Resources until you find a collection of system icons, such as ClippingText.icns, FinderIcon.icns, FullTrashIcon.icns, and iMac.icns. With root access, you can change these icons in the same way I described above for application icons.

For more icon-editing capabilities, you can use a third-party utility like CandyBar. And if you have Apple's Developer software installed, check out icns Browser and Icon Composer.

Note: In Jaguar, the most important file in SystemIcons.bundle is not an .icns file at all. It's called SystemIcons.rsrc, and you can't open it via a double-click. Instead, try opening it via the third-party utility Iconographer X. This utility reveals the mother lode of virtually every system icon you might want to modify. With Iconographer X, you can modify as well as view these icons. In Panther, this .rsrc file no longer exists. All the files it contained are now individual .icns files located in the Resources folder.

Troubleshooting: Icons that move. You may find that icons, especially ones on your Desktop, occasionally reposition themselves—often as a result of changing your monitor resolution via the Displays System Preferences. In addition, some games automatically change this resolution—in which case you might see this symptom even if you didn't change the resolution manually. Icons can reposition themselves at other times as well—for example, after waking from sleep.

The basic solution here is to simply move the icons back to their desired positions. In addition, some utilities, such as SwitchRes, may enable you to save and restore icon positions.

continues on next page

TAKE NOTE ▶ Changing and Troubleshooting Finder Icons *continued*

Note: Finder icon positions are stored in the invisible .DS_Store file in each folder. Other information about Finder windows, such as size and whether they're in icon or list view, can be found primarily in the .com.apple.finder.plist file (as set via the Show View Options command in the Finder's View menu). Suffice it to say that Finder window information settings are overly complex and not altogether bug-free. If you find that when you close and later reopen a window, it's not always the way you left it, you're not alone. One example: After copying a folder to a different volume, I found that the folder's settings had changed (for example, a list view had reverted to an icon view).

SEE: • "Preferences Files," elsewhere in this chapter, for more on using Property List Editor.

• "Take Note: Filename Extensions" and "Technically Speaking: Type/Creator vs. Filename Extensions," later in this chapter, for related information that can affect what icon an item displays.

• "Take Note: Launch Services Files and Beyond," in Chapter 6, for yet more related information.

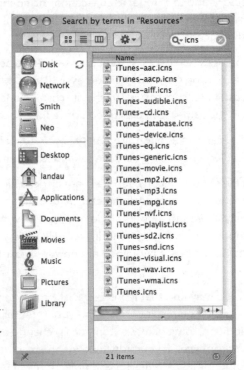

Figure 4.17

The .icns files inside the Resources folder of the iTunes.app package.

Name & Extension

This section of the Get Info window displays the name of the file and its extension (if any). All applications have the file extension .app. Other files, especially documents, may have extensions that identify their type (such as .gif to identify a file as a GIF graphic). Since Mac OS 9 does not use file extensions, converts from that OS may find it inconvenient or confusing to see these extensions listed in the Finder. This is why the .app extension is almost always hidden for applications. You can similarly choose to hide an extension for a given file by enabling the Hide Extension check box in the Name & Extension section of files that have extensions.

SEE: • **"Technically Speaking: Type/Creator vs. Filename Extensions," later in this chapter, for further details.**

• **"Technically Speaking: How Mac OS X Selects a Document or Application Match," in Chapter 6, for related information.**

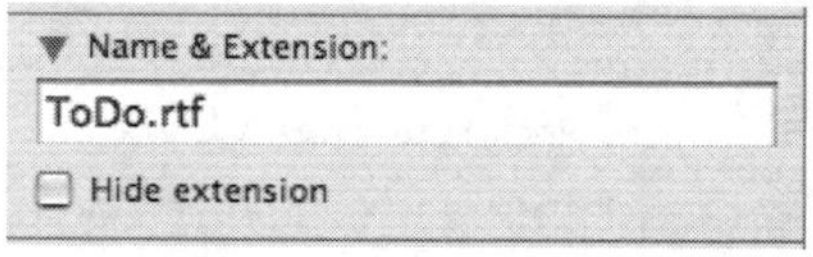

Figure 4.18

The Name & Extension section of a Get Info window.

Figure 4.19

An error message that may appear when you try to change an extension in the Finder.

TAKE NOTE ▶ Filename Extensions

Filename extensions have a wide range of effects and can be modified from a variety of locations. Here's what you need to know about them:

What is the function of filename extensions? File extensions are abbreviations stuck at the end of a file's name—for example, *.jpg* in picture.jpg. In this case, the .jpg extension indicates that the file is a JPEG document. Mac OS X uses filename extensions to determine file types. For documents, this type can determine what application opens the document if you double-click its icon in the Finder. The type can also determine which icon the document displays.

If an application can save files in more than one format, it may assign a different extension to each format. Thus, when Word saves a document in its own Word format, it uses the extension .doc; if it saves it in plain text, the extension will be .txt; if it saves it in Rich Text Format, the file will have an .rtf extension.

continues on next page

TAKE NOTE ▶ **Filename Extensions** *continued*

Showing vs. hiding extensions. In addition to the Hide Extension option in the Get Info window, most applications' Save dialogs include a Hide Extension option (though the exact wording may vary). This option pretty much duplicates the effect of toggling the Hide Extension setting in the Name & Extension section of the Get Info window. Another option that may appear in a Save dialog is Append File Extension. This is a bit different: Toggling it determines whether an extension is included in the filename, not merely whether it's visible in the Finder.

In addition, you can choose to hide or show virtually all file extensions in the Finder. To do this, open the Finder Preferences window and in the Advanced section deselect or select "Show all file extensions."

The following are some additional details about how these options work:

- If Hide Extension is enabled, a file's extension will not be shown in the Finder unless you enable "Show all file extensions" in the Finder Preferences window. That Preferences setting overrides the Get Info setting.

- If Hide Extension in the Get Info window is disabled, a file's extension is always shown, regardless of the setting in the Finder Preferences window.

- In general, if "Show all file extensions" is disabled, the option you choose in the Get Info window or the Save dialog will determine whether the file's extension is visible in the Finder.

   That is, even when the "Show all file extensions" option is disabled, you can display an individual file's extension in the Finder by unchecking the Hide Extension option in the Get Info window's Name & Extension section. This option is not always available, however. For example, the application extension .app is always hidden and typically never shown in the Finder. Still, you can at least see the .app extension listed in the Name & Extension section of the Get Info window for the application.

- In some cases (for example, with Microsoft Word), if you do not choose the Append File Extension option in the Save dialog, the Mac does not merely hide the extension; it doesn't add one at all. Thus, you create a file with no extension. In this case, the Hide Extension option in the Get Info window is checked, and the option is dimmed so that you cannot uncheck it (because there is no extension to show). Even in this case, you can choose to add your own extension in the Finder after you've saved the document. For the Word document, you could add .doc to the end of the document name. Now the Hide Extension option in the Get Info window will be unchecked, and you can enable it again if you want.

Problems with filename extensions. Whether you choose to hide or view filename extensions, the system has more than its share of problems. The following describes some of these problems as well as ways of dealing with them.

continues on next page

TAKE NOTE ▶ Filename Extensions *continued*

General advice: To confirm the true name of a file at any time, check its name in the Name & Extension section of the file's Get Info window. To be certain that the change you're making to a file's extension sticks, make that change from the Get Info window as well. When you close the Get Info window, a warning dialog will appear if Mac OS X considers your change ill-advised: You can click OK or Cancel. Don't expect changes you've made in a Save dialog to yield the results you anticipated.

More specifically:

- The fact that an extension can exist but remain invisible in the Finder is one source of confusion. For example, suppose a file's extension is hidden and you try to add one (for example, changing *sample* to *sample.txt*), either in the Finder or in a Save dialog: If a .txt extension exists but is hidden, you could end up changing the file's name to *sample.txt.txt* without even realizing it.

- Even if you choose to hide extensions, this setting will be overridden for files downloaded from the Internet. If a downloaded file was named fileone.rtf, it will remain that way. If you later change the name to myfile, however, the Finder will change the name and hide the .rtf extension (because you didn't type it). Thus, the .rtf extension will still be in the Name & Extension tab of the Get Info window; you just don't see it in the Finder. Similarly, you can wind up with a situation in which one .rtf file downloaded from the Web includes a visible extension but another that you created with TextEdit does not.

- Complications can occur when you save files using extensions. Mac OS X–compliant applications typically add the appropriate extension for their document type when you save a new document, even if you don't type the extension. Thus, when you save an AppleWorks word-processing document, AppleWorks will add .cwk to the name of the file. Although AppleWorks shows that it is adding this extension, other applications may do so without indicating it. Even if you delete the extension from the name in the Save As dialog, the extension still gets added.

  The application should also warn you against trying to assign an invalid extension (such as .jpg to an AppleWorks .cwk file). If you try to do this, you will have the option to end the name in both extensions (such as name.jpg.cwk), but the Finder will only look at the .cwk extension when it decides how to treat the file.

- When you save a document in an application, it should respect whether you've specified for extensions to be hidden in the Finder; however, sometimes applications do not. Extensions may be visible in a saved file's name even if you chose to keep extensions hidden, and vice versa.

continues on next page

TAKE NOTE ▶ Filename Extensions *continued*

- Another complication involves the interaction of filename extensions with the Open With section of the Get Info window. In particular, changing the application used to open a document and then choosing Change All will change the default application associated with that extension. Files with the extensions .txt and .rtf, for example, are opened by TextEdit by default. If you choose Change All for a .txt file, the Finder will open all .txt files in the new application you select. This system also respects type and creator codes. Thus, if the .txt file is specifically listed as having been created by AppleWorks, Mac OS X will change all .txt files created by AppleWorks. If no creator is listed, Mac OS X will change all .txt files that have no creator listed.

- The Finder's Find feature "sees" filename extensions even if they're not visible in the Finder. Thus, if you have a file called picture.jpg, but the .jpg extension is hidden, all you will see in the Finder is *picture*. However, if you search for a file that ends in *ture,* this file will not appear in the results, because Find sees *jpg* (not *ture*) as the end of the file's name.

It's hopeless to try to cover every possible extension-related permutation here. Extensions are not among Mac OS X's most logical features. To make matters worse, the filename extension is not necessarily the only method Mac OS X uses to determine what document goes with which application. The OS can also use the type and creator information used by Mac OS 9 (if that data is present in the file). In fact, if a creator is present, the Mac will use the creator setting in preference to the extension.

Editing file extensions and warning messages. You can edit a filename in the Name & Extension section of the Get Info window; in fact, you can even add or remove an extension. Similarly, you can do this directly from the Finder by clicking on the file's name field. There is, however, one twist: If you select to delete an extension visible from the Finder, you will only hide it, *not* delete it. This is why it's generally better to edit extensions from the Get Info window. In addition, to make sure you're actually removing (not just hiding) an extension, uncheck the Hide Extension option before you make the change.

Be careful, however: If you add, delete, or change an extension, you will typically get an alert box that asks whether you're sure you want to do this—and warning of the consequences of doing so when you should not.

For example, editing or deleting an .app file extension may change the application into a folder. Thus, if you confirm your change by clicking Yes at the alert, you will no longer be able to launch the application—that is, until you undo the change.

If changing a document's extension just alters which application the Finder uses to open it (and the new application is able to open the file), your change should be fine. But if changing an extension makes the Finder think you've changed the file's format (when you have not), problems are likely to occur.

continues on next page

TAKE NOTE ▶ File name Extensions *continued*

For example, if you change an extension from .doc to .txt, you haven't really changed the document's format from a Microsoft Word file to a plain-text document; however, the Finder may mistakenly think you have. Similarly, changing a file's extension from .jpg to .gif doesn't really alter the graphic format of the file; it just changes what the Finder *thinks* the file is—that is, the Finder will now be in error.

Troubleshooting tip: Sound files and extensions. Any sound file in the AIFF format that you place in your ~/Library/Sounds folder can be selected to serve as an alert sound from the Sound System Preferences pane. However, this will only work if the .aiff extension is included in the name of the file. It has to be exact. Even .aif will not work.

TECHNICALLY SPEAKING ▶ Type/Creator vs. Filename Extensions

Mac OS X identifies file types by either their filename extensions (introduced in Mac OS X) or their type and creator (a carryover from Mac OS 9). There's some controversy over which is the better approach.

Resource forks and data forks. In Mac OS 9, most files are made up of two components: a resource fork and a data fork. In the case of applications, most of a file's contents are stored in its resource fork. You can view (and even modify) this information (which includes application icons, dialogs, error messages, version info, and more) via Apple's ResEdit utility.

For documents, the data fork is more significant because it typically holds their essential data (for example, the words you type in a word-processing document). Most documents, such as text documents, only need a data fork. The resource fork does not usually contain actual user data.

Because Mac OS X has moved away from using resource forks (for reasons discussed later in this sidebar), Mac OS X–native applications store all this information in the data fork. In fact, these native files lack a resource fork altogether.

Type/creator. In Mac OS 9, every file is identified by a type and a creator. *Type* refers to the type of file (that is, application, system extension, AppleWorks document, and so on), and *creator* refers to the application that Finder views as the creator of a document. The information on the Kind line of a file's Get Info window is typically determined by the type and creator code for the file.

Type and creator information are essentially two separate four-letter codes. Each creator (vendor) has a unique code, and separate codes exist for different file types (for example, applications all have the type APPL). In Mac OS 9, this information was stored in an application's resource fork. In Mac OS X (with the exception of older software that still maintains the data in its resource fork), this data is stored in an application's Info.plist file (described next).

continues on next page

TECHNICALLY SPEAKING ▶ **Type/Creator vs. Filename Extensions** *continued*

Although Apple provides no utility for changing creator and type codes in a standard installation of either Mac OS 9 or Mac OS X, many third-party utilities fill this gap. In Mac OS X, for example, you can use utilities such as XRay or FileXaminer. You can also change these codes via the SetFile Developer Tools command in Terminal in Mac OS X.

The creator is especially important for documents that can be opened by several applications. When a plain-text document is double-clicked in the Finder, it opens in SimpleText (in Mac OS 9) if SimpleText is listed as the creator. The same file opens in AppleWorks if AppleWorks is listed as the creator.

The type can also affect how documents are treated. Read-only SimpleText documents (the ones with the newspaper icon) have a type of ttro, whereas read-write SimpleText documents have a file type of TEXT (case matters!). You can change a read-only file to an editable one simply by changing this type. In both cases, the creator for SimpleText should be ttxt.

By the way, in TextEdit (Mac OS X's equivalent of SimpleText), you can change an editable document to a read-only one via the Prevent Editing and Allow Editing toggle commands in the Format menu.

As a result of this system, no matter what you name a file, the Finder will always be able to figure out its type and (for documents) what application it should open in, simply from the type and creator information.

An application's Info.plist file. In Mac OS X, creator and type information for a native application are stored in its information property list (Info.plist) file, located inside the application package. This Info.plist file is where the Finder goes to determine what codes to assign to documents created by that application. This is consistent with Mac OS X's move away from storing this information in a resource fork. You can use Property List Editor (as covered later in this chapter in "Modifying a .plist file") to open the .plist file. Look for CFBundlePackageType and CFBundleSignature as the keys for the file type and creator. This information will be listed in the Value column of the row of that name. If the column says, "????," no type and/or creator has been assigned. You can also view and edit this information via third-party utilities such as XRay.

The Info.plist file also lists the filename extensions that the application recognizes as document types it can open—information that's stored in the CFBundleDocumentTypes property. If more than one application lists the same extension, the Finder uses predetermined rules of precedence to determine which to use with which application. For example, it will use a Cocoa application in preference to a Carbon one and a Carbon one in preference to a Classic one. At the top of the hierarchy are any preferences you have made via the Open With command in the Finder's File menu or in the Get Info window for the document. Selections made here are stored in the com.apple.LaunchServices.plist file in the ~/Library/Preferences folder.

continues on next page

TECHNICALLY SPEAKING ▶ Type/Creator vs. Filename Extensions *continued*

When a document is created and saved by an application, the relevant type and creator information (as taken from the application's Info.plist file) is stored in a special area of the document's data fork, along with its other attributes (such as creation and modification dates).

Note: Info.plist files include information beyond the focus of this sidebar. These are mainly of interest to developers. For example, the LSPrefersCarbon versus LSRequiresCarbon key determines whether certain applications must run in Carbon versus Classic, or let the user decide which environment to use (via an option in the Get Info window).

Metadata locations. Type/creator information is an example of a file's *metadata*. While type/creator information for an .app application is stored in the application's Info.plist file, you may wonder where this information is stored for the documents created by these applications. The answer is, it's stored in the volume directory (the same area that Disk Utility's First Aid checks for making repairs). As such, it is not nearly as accessible as the Info.plist data.

Other remaining metadata, such as anything you enter into the Comments field of a file (document or application), is stored in the invisible .DS_Store file located within every folder.

Problems with type/creator. Mac OS X can use the same type and creator information that Mac OS 9 does, but it does not require it. In fact, Apple prefers that developers no longer depend on it. Documents saved in Mac OS X's TextEdit, for example, include no type or creator code.

Why has Apple gone this route? First and foremost, no platform except Apple uses this type/creator system. Thus, when you send a file from the Mac to the Windows platform, its resource fork—and thus its type and creator data—is typically lost. Conversely, files created on Windows machines and sent to a Mac do not include this data. In addition, Unix does not support type and creator data—which means that a Mac OS X drive formatted with UFS (see Chapter 3) would not be able to use this data to identify files. Files on all of these other platforms consist only of data forks—a direction Mac OS X is moving in as well.

Extensions. Apple's "solution" to the type/creator problem has been to move to file extensions (as described in "Technically Speaking: Filename Extensions")—in essence the same solution used by other platforms, which is Apple's main rationale for the shift.

Advantages of type/creator (as compared to filename extensions). In addition to the basic problems with filename extensions noted earlier in this chapter, filename extensions are saddled with some disadvantages when compared with the type/creator alternative. For example:

- It's much easier to change the name of a file inadvertently than it is to change a file's type or creator. For example, if you were to assign a .jpg extension to a word-processing document, the Finder might mistakenly think you have a .jpg file, when in reality the file is *not* a JPEG and *will not* open in applications designed to work with .jpg files.

continues on next page

TECHNICALLY SPEAKING ▶ Type/Creator vs. Filename Extensions *continued*

- Eliminating an extension can make it very difficult to figure out a document's type and what application to use with it.

- By relying on just one bit of information (file extension) rather than two (type *and* creator), you lose significant flexibility. With type and creator, you can have two JPEG files with different creators. One may open in Preview; the other may open in AppleWorks. You can't do this with file extensions. All JPEG files open in the same application by default unless you override the setting in the file's Get Info window.

For all of the above reasons, there has been a considerable backlash against Apple's use of file extensions rather than type and creator. Many feel that Apple took something that worked very well and substituted something more likely to have problems. Regardless of your opinion, however, if you're a Mac OS X user, you're stuck with Apple's decision; you might as well get used to it!

SEE: • "Technically Speaking: How Mac OS X Selects a Document or Application Match," in Chapter 6, for related information.

Figure 4.20

Partial contents of the Info.plist file for TextEdit. Note the lines below the CFBundleType Extensions that indicate rtf (TextEdit documents) and doc (Microsoft Word documents), two of the extensions that TextEdit recognizes.

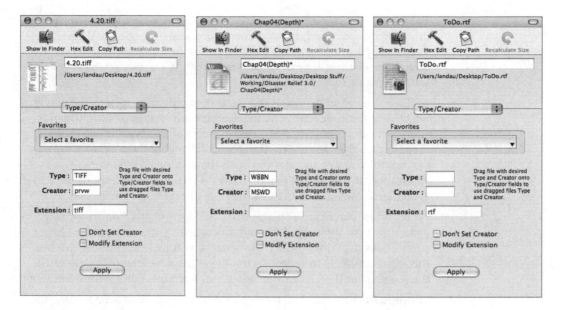

Figure 4.21

Type and Creator codes for three documents, as viewed in FileXaminer: (left) a Preview document in TIFF format (with Type and Creator codes plus a .tiff extension); (middle) a Microsoft Word document (with Type and Creator codes but no extension in this case); and (right) a TextEdit document (with no Type and Creator codes but an .rtf extension).

Open With

The Open With section only appears when you open the Get Info window for a document. The main reason you will use this section is if double-clicking a document's icon does not open it with the application you expected (or does not open the document at all). This section includes two options:

- **Pop-up menu.** The default selection here (visible in the menu before you click on it) is the application that will currently open the document. You know this because the word *default* appears in parentheses after the application name. You can change the choice by selecting another application from the pop-up menu. In most cases, the pop-up menu will list all applications that can potentially open the document; simply select the one you want, and you're finished.

  If an application you believe *should* work with the document is not listed, select Other from the pop-up menu. A Choose Other Application window opens, providing access to all applications on your drive(s). Initially, only a list of Recommended Applications will be selectable. However, you can change this (via the Show pop-up menu at the top of the window) to All Applications.

Below the file browser is a check box that says Always Open With. When this option is activated, the document should always open with the selected application (which I'll discuss more in a moment); however, I've seen cases where it appears to have no effect. When you've made your selection, click the Add button.

As a result of your changes, your document will now open in the newly selected application (until you make additional changes). This does not alter the default choice for other documents of this type; it just changes the effect for this document. Remember, changing these options doesn't ensure that you can successfully open the document with the selected application. It just means that it will try. Thus, if you attempt to open a QuickTime movie with the Calculator application, it won't work.

Note: When you make a change here, the document's icon may change to reflect the new application (though documents from some older Carbon applications may not do this). However, if you make additional changes, the icon is unlikely to reflect them. To get the new icon to appear, click the icon box in the Get Info window and from the Edit menu select Cut.

- **Change All button.** The lower part of the Open With section contains a Change All button, which is enabled when you make a change via the pop-up menu. Selecting Change All changes the default choice for similar documents to your changed selection—meaning that *all* documents of the type you just modified will open in the newly selected application. Before the change takes effect, you will get a warning message, asking if you're sure this is what you want to do and stating exactly which documents will be affected by the change. For example, when I did this for an Internet Explorer archive document, my message stated, "This change will apply to all Internet Explorer documents of the type 'WAFF.' " This information refers to the document's creator (Internet Explorer) and type (WAFF). Depending on the document's characteristics, the message may refer to files of a certain extension rather than type.

  SEE: • **"Technically Speaking: Type/Creator vs. Filename Extensions," earlier in this chapter, for further details.**

  One reason you might want to use Change All is if all files in a certain graphics format (say, JPEG files) open in Application A by default but you would rather they open in Application B. Or perhaps all documents of a certain type are opening in a Classic version of Application C, and you would prefer to use a Mac OS X version.

Open With (from Finder and contextual menus). The Get Info window is not the only place where you can select an Open With option. You can also do so via the Open With command in the Finder's File menu or via the Open With item in the contextual menu for the document (accessed when you Control-click the document icon). Both options work similarly to the Open With pop-up menu in the Get Info window—with one exception: If you select Open With from the Finder or a contextual menu, it only uses the selected application for that single launch. The next time you double-click the document, it will still launch the original default application. To make the change "permanent," hold down the Option key while selecting the Finder or contextual menu option. This changes Open With to Always Open With. However, this will not affect other similar documents. To apply your changes to all similar documents, you still need to use the Change All button in the Get Info window.

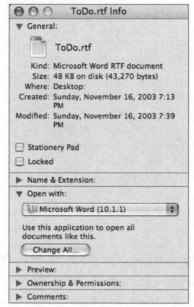

Figure 4.22

Get Info's Open With section, with the document changed from its TextEdit default to Microsoft Word. Note that the document's icon has changed to a Word icon.

Content Index

In the Get Info window for folders and volumes, a Content Index section appears. Click Index Now to create an index of the item's text contents that can be searched by the Content criterion of the Finder's Find command. Click Stop Indexing to stop an index in progress (useful if a long indexing process appears to be slowing your Mac), or click Delete Index if you want to delete the existing index for that item (useful if you want to free some disk space).

The index files used for these searches are invisible files that begin with .FBC (for *find by content*), especially .FBCIndex. Every volume or folder that's been indexed will have these invisible FBC files.

Mac OS X has no option for setting up an indexing schedule. However, indexing is initiated automatically for a folder or volume whenever you use the Finder's Find command to conduct a search that includes the Content criterion and is limited to that folder or volume. Thus, you are not required to use the Get Info window to create an index. However, using this command will ensure that the index gets updated to include any changes that may have been made since it was first created.

SEE: • "Find and Search," in Chapter 2, for more on the Find command.

Figure 4.23

A Get Info window's Content Index section for a folder.

TECHNICALLY SPEAKING ▶ **Index Formats in Mac OS X vs. Mac OS 9**

Index formats in Mac OS X and Mac OS 9 are different and stored separately. The Find by Content option in Mac OS 9's version of Sherlock does not see the indexes created by the Mac OS X version. Similarly, the Mac OS X version does not see indexes created in Mac OS 9.

In particular, Mac OS X uses an invisible .FBCIndex file and .FBCLockFolder folder within each indexed directory for storing indexing data, whereas Mac OS 9 uses an invisible TheFindByContentFolder folder containing a TheFindByContentIndex file at the root level of each indexed volume.

Languages

If the file you selected is a Mac OS X application, its Get Info window will likely include a Languages section. From here, you can turn on or off (via the check box by each language name) the ability to display the application's text in languages other than the default choice. You can also add or remove additional languages. The languages that appear here depend on what language support files are included within the application package. Whether you can use them or not depends on what languages (accessed from the International System Preferences pane) you installed with Mac OS X.

SEE: • "International language support: basics," and "International language support: troubleshooting," later in this chapter, for more details.

Plug-ins

Some applications may also include a Plug-ins section (iPhoto and Disk Utility are two examples), used to add modules (including ones from third-party developers) that provide additional features. As with languages, you can turn plug-ins on and off as well as add or remove plug-ins. Apple encourages developers to use this method instead of any other plug-in management method.

For an interesting example of how this works, select Get Info for Disk Utility. You will see modules (all with .dumodule extensions) for each of the main screens available from Disk Utility. If you uncheck a module (don't click to Remove it, just uncheck its check box) and then launch Disk Utility, the disabled module no longer appears. For example, if you uncheck RAID.dumodule, the Raid button no longer appears when you select a drive.

You can ignore the settings in this section of the Get Info window unless you have a module that you want to add (or remove for some reason). For third-party modules, the instructions that came with the software will provide further explanation.

Figure 4.24

The Plug-ins section of iPhoto's Get Info window.

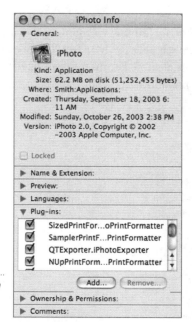

Preview

The Preview section of the Get Info window ranges from completely worthless to minimally useful. For applications, it's mainly worthless, as all it shows is the Finder icon of the file. For text documents, it displays the initial text. For graphics files, it provides a miniature version of the graphic content. For

QuickTime movies, you can actually run the movie from the Preview window. But why bother? If you want to see the movie, just open it in QuickTime Player and play it!

Memory (Classic applications only)

Memory allows you to set the amount of memory (RAM) used by Mac OS 9/Classic applications. This option appears only for applications that can run in Classic (and for those that can run either as Mac OS X or Classic applications, the settings here only apply when they are run in the Classic environment). It lists a suggested size and allows you to set a preferred size and a minimum size. The application will not open unless the amount of memory in the Minimum Size setting is available. Thus, you should almost never change this setting to be lower than the default. The Preferred Size setting is how much memory the application typically uses (assuming the amount is available). This setting is usually the same as the suggested size, though you can make it larger if you feel the program is not working well (running slowly, for example) due to the preferred size being insufficient.

Mac OS X programs are not assigned any preset level of memory because the OS itself allocates the appropriate amount of memory dynamically as needed. That's why this option doesn't appear for Mac OS X applications. The Mac OS X approach is much more flexible because it permits on-the-fly adjustments that Mac OS 9 does not allow.

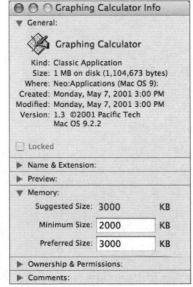

Figure 4.25

Get Info's Memory section (available for applications that run only in Classic).

SEE: • Chapter 9, for more on memory and Classic.

Ownership & Permissions

Ownership & Permissions is a section of the Get Info window where you can modify a file's permissions and ownership settings. If you ever get a message indicating that you cannot do something (such as move, open, or delete a file) because you don't have sufficient permission or privileges, this is the first place you should go to solve the problem. Beware, however: The permissions for Mac OS X's essential software are set so that you cannot easily move or delete the files. This is as it should be: Bypassing this restriction could result in a nonfunctioning OS. Still, there are many cases where modifying permissions is perfectly appropriate, such as for files in your Home directory.

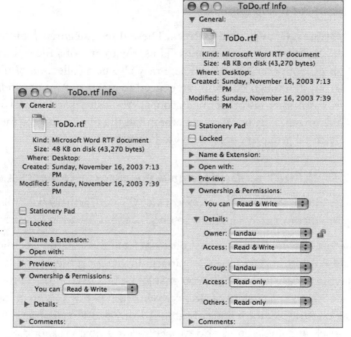

Figure 4.26

The Ownership & Permissions section of a Get Info window: (left) without details shown and (right) with details shown.

When you first access the Ownership & Permissions section, there will be two items:

- **You can.** This pop-up menu tells you what type of access you currently have to the file (for example, Read & Write, Read Only, or No Access). If you own the file, the access pop-up menu is active and you can modify the settings. Otherwise, the menu is dimmed.

    Note: Your personal access here is determined by your group membership as well as your ownership. For example, if you are a member of the admin group (which all administrators are) and the admin group has Read & Write access, you will have Read & Write access listed here, even though you may not own the file. If you are neither the owner nor a member of the listed group, your access is determined by the setting for Others (as described below).

- **Details.** Click this disclosure triangle to reveal the full set of options for Ownership & Permissions. The Details setup is new in Panther. In Jaguar, the full set of options appeared as soon as you clicked the initial disclosure triangle. This new arrangement appears to be a way to simplify the section's layout so that it's less intimidating to beginning users who rarely need to modify these options.

The Details subsection of the Ownership & Permissions section includes five pop-up menus: an Owner and Access pair, a Group and Access pair, and Others (which is an Access menu). Permissions settings appear for all types of items: documents, applications, folders, and volumes. Exactly what they imply, however, varies depending upon the type of item you've selected. In most cases, you will be working with permissions of document files—which is what I'll emphasize here.

Owner, Group, and Others. These three categories represent the different levels of permissions settings. Thus, the owner of a file can have different settings from everyone else. There may also be a collection of users that form a group (although you will rarely need to create groups yourself since Mac OS X has numerous predefined groups). You can separately assign permissions to the group. Finally, everyone other than the owner and the members of the selected group are considered to be Others.

TECHNICALLY SPEAKING ▶ Ownership & Permissions: Mac OS X vs. Unix

The Permissions settings in the Get Info window of Mac OS X are actually determined by—and are a subset of—the more complex Permissions settings of the underlying Unix base of Mac OS X.

In Unix, there are three attributes, somewhat different from those in the Get Info window: Read, Write, and Execute. Further, unlike in the Get Info window, choices are not mutually exclusive. To get read and write access, for example, you enable the first two of the permissions settings. To eliminate all access (the equivalent of No Access in Mac OS X), you turn off all permissions. Thus, there are six possible combinations of settings, from all off to all on. In addition, some special options—such as setuid, setgid, and sticky bit—have no corresponding options in the Get Info window. Also, the Execute (sometimes referred to as the *search*) permission does not apply directly to Aqua-based applications—that is, you can run an Aqua application even with this setting off. It does, however, apply to commands that run directly within Unix. It also has a special meaning when applied to folders.

When you make a change in the Get Info window, you're actually changing the corresponding Unix permissions settings. To make changes that do not fit into the subset of possibilities included in Get Info, you need a utility such as FileXaminer or XRay, both of which have options for editing owner and group names, privileges settings, and type/creator settings. They even include options for editing more obscure permissions settings (such as setuid and setguid).

SEE: • "Take Note: Multiple Users: Mac OS X vs. Mac OS 9," earlier in this chapter.
• Chapters 6 and 10 for more background on privileges and permissions.

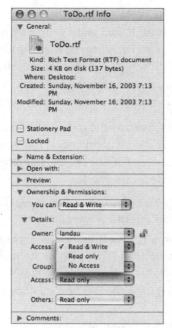

Figure 4.27

Permissions settings as viewed from (left) Get Info and (right) XRay. (See also Figure 4.5 for how permissions [rwx] are listed in Terminal.)

What determines the owner of a file? A file's owner is typically the user who created it. Thus, when you create and save a new document in AppleWorks, you are the owner of the file. You also own files that you copy to a drive—for example, files you download from the Web.

With a few exceptions, you own all of the files in your Home directory. One notable exception: If you move a file into your Home directory (such as from the Applications folder), it retains its original ownership. If you instead copy the same file (so that the original remains in its original location), the copy will inherit the properties of the folder where it now exists—that is, you will own the copy in your Home directory. Thus, copying a file can change the ownership of a file.

Modifying Ownership & Permissions settings. By default, the name of the Owner and Group are dimmed, signifying they can't be changed. However, if you are an administrative user, you *can* modify the Owner and/or Group. To do so, click the padlock icon to the right of the Owner name: The Owner and Group menus should now be enabled.

Even with the Owner and Group menus enabled, you still can't change Access menu settings unless you own the item. You can make yourself the owner by selecting your name from the Owner pop-up menu. Once you've done this, you can make Access menu changes. When you're finished, you can return Owner to its prior setting, if desired.

By changing both Owner and Access settings, you (as an administrative user) can give yourself access to any file on your drive. For example, if the owner of a file is *system* and you have no write access to the file, you can unlock the padlock, change the owner to yourself, and grant yourself Read & Write access. You can now do whatever you want to the file. If you're modifying the text of a Mac OS X system file, however, you'll probably want to change the settings back to the originals when you're finished. This avoids any possible problems with the system not being able to access the file later when needed.

Access permissions. If you're listed as the owner of a file, the short name of your account should appear as the owner name. If this is the case, you can easily change Access settings for yourself, the group, and others. These settings determine which type of file access you have:

- **Read & Write:** You can view and modify a document file's contents. If the file is an application, you can run the application.

- **Read only:** You can view but not modify the contents of a document file. If the file is an application, you can run the application. The Others category will typically be limited to Read Only permissions.

- **No Access:** You can neither view the file (if it's a document) nor run it (if it's an application).

- **Write only (Drop Box):** This option only appears for folders and volumes. It means that you can add files to the folder but not view the folder's contents.

You may find it surprising to learn that even if you have no access privileges to a file, you may still be able to delete it. This is because the ability to delete a file is a function of the Permissions settings of the *folder* that contains the file (rather than the file itself). If you have Read & Write access for the folder, you should be able to delete a file within it, regardless of the file's settings.

Typically, a file's owner has Read & Write access to the file—which makes sense. If you own the file, you should be able to modify it, and even delete it, if you want. In fact, the owner of the file is the only person who can change the Access settings.

One more example: The Group setting for the /Applications folder is *admin*; its access has been set to Read & Write. That same folder's Others setting has Read Only access. This is why administrative users can add or delete applications, while nonadministrative (standard) users can run applications in this folder but not add or delete files to or from it.

Owner and Group. When you click the Owner menu, you get a list of a file's potential owners—one of whom will be yourself, of course. The list will also include any other local users that have been set up, as well as a special user named *system* (which is the same as the root user). Additional owners listed here—conveniently set off by a separator line—are for various system processes and can typically be ignored.

When you click the Group menu, you get a similar list of potential group selections. Those that are of the most interest include the following:

- *{your short username}.* For each user created in Panther, Mac OS X creates a group with the same owner name—in both cases, the short name of the user account. In my case, for example, this group name is *landau*.

  The group with your name is assigned by default to files that you own. You are the sole member of this group.

  Note: In Jaguar, the default group for files that you own is *staff.* The same is true for all other local accounts on your Mac. Thus, all local users are members of this group. This group still exists in Panther; however, it no longer acts as the default assigned group, and no accounts are assigned to it by default. If you upgrade from Jaguar to Panther, however, existing accounts may still use staff as the default; newly created accounts will use the new user name group.

- **Admin.** All admin users are made members of this group automatically.

- **Wheel.** The only officially listed member of this group is the root user. However, all admin users are also indirect members of this group via their ability to gain temporary root access.

With all Group settings, the access level (for example, Read & Write versus Read Only) affects only members of the listed group. For any users other than the owner and the group members, access is determined by the Others setting.

SEE: • "Root Access," later in this chapter, for more details.

TECHNICALLY SPEAKING ▶ Group Settings Explained

If you take a look at the Get Info window for the Applications folder, you'll see that the folder is owned by the System. Does this mean that all applications are initially installed within it? And if so, how is it that you can work with these files almost as if you owned them? The reason is that the Group setting is Read & Write, and the group name is *admin.* If you're an administrative user (which you are if you set up Mac OS X initially), you're part of the admin group—and thus have read/write access to the files in the Applications folder. All administrators have admin group privileges to any file that is assigned to the group admin.

Typically, files included in the *wheel* group offer read-only access to members of the wheel group. Thus, a member of wheel can look at and use these files but not modify them. Most of the files in the /System/Library directory employ this setting.

If a wheel member wants to modify a file in /System/Library, he or she must change the file's ownership (for example, via the Get Info window), use root access (for example, by employing the sudo command in Terminal), or Authenticate in the Finder when attempting to move an item. This setup is designed to protect these files from being mistakenly moved or modified—an obvious safety precaution when you consider that these files are essential to the operation of the OS.

continues on next page

TECHNICALLY SPEAKING ▶ **Group Settings Explained** *continued*

Note: An admin user is not a member of the wheel group, so changes to the wheel group's access will directly affect an admin user's access. Instead, it's the Others setting that determines admin users' access to files owned by the System. Typically, Others access is also restricted to Read Only. You can test this by making changes to the access settings in the Get Info window and watching how the "You can" access shifts as a result.

Occasionally, you may find that a group is listed as "unknown." This is not necessarily an error; it simply means that the OS cannot determine the group—usually because one hasn't been assigned—which is typically the case with folders and files on a Mac OS 9 partition or on many forms of removable media. In some cases, however, a file is listed as part of an unknown group because an error has occurred—that is, its intended group name has been "lost." This can spell trouble—especially if such files are in the /System/Library or /Library folders—leaving you unable to access files you should be able to access. For more specific examples as well as instructions for how to fix them, see Chapter 6.

Who's in a group? To find out whether you're a member of wheel, admin, or any other group, you can use NetInfo Manager. Simply launch this utility and select the *groups* item in the first column in the window that appears. In the next column on the right, you will see a list of all groups (more than you might think, most of which are used by Unix and need not concern you). Scroll to find the group admin, for example. Click it. In the section at the bottom of the window, you will see a property called *users*. The names associated with this item, in the Values column, are the users who are part of the admin group.

Note: For all *user name* accounts as listed in NetInfo manager (for example, landau, in my case), no group members are listed. However, the group ID (GID) number is the same as your user ID (UID) number (for example, 501). In Mac OS X's version of Unix, this makes you a member of your self-named group. Thus, I am a member of the landau group even though I am not listed as such in NetInfo Manager.

Note: GIDs and UIDs are numerical representations of group and user names. The IDs can often be used interchangeably with names (for example, when entering commands in Terminal). To find out any user's UID via NetInfo Manager, select the *users* category in the leftmost column and then select the desired name from the middle column. The output at the bottom of the window will include a property called *uid*, the value of which will be the UID number. Similarly, to find out a GID for a group, select the *groups* category and then select the desired group name and look for the *gid* property in the output at the bottom of the window.

continues on next page

TECHNICALLY SPEAKING ▶ **Group Settings Explained** *continued*

As an administrator, you can use NetInfo Manager to create new groups or make changes to the membership of existing groups. These modifications are rarely necessary for Mac OS X client users. Instead, it is mostly of value to administrators of large networks (who will most likely be using Mac OS X Server). For example, if your were a network administrator at a university, you might want to create a separate group for each faculty department. If, as a Mac OS X client user, you do have a need to edit group settings, I recommend using SharePoints as a more user-friendly solution (as covered in "Take Note: Using SharePoints," in Chapter 8).

SEE: • "Root Access," later in this chapter, for related details.

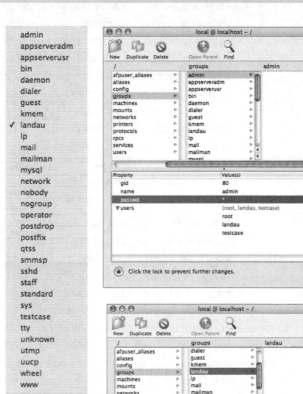

Figure 4.28

Groups: The list of groups selectable from the Get Info window (left); NetInfo Manager shows the members of the admin group (top right); NetInfo Manager shows the listing for my landau group (bottom right).

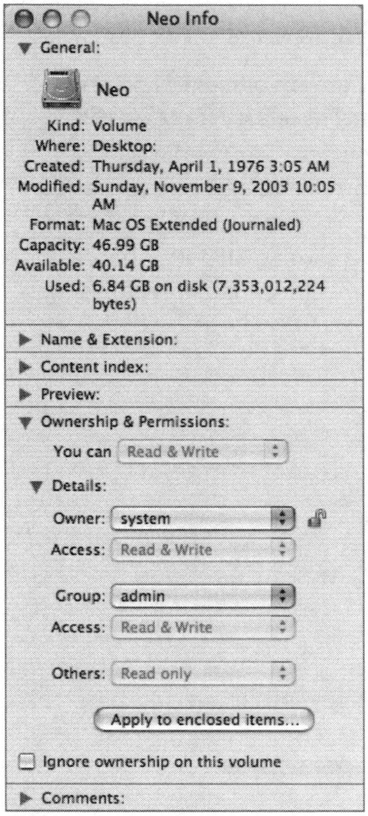

Figure 4.29

The "Apply to enclosed items" button and the "Ignore ownership on this volume" check box, as seen for the Neo volume.

Special options for folders and volumes. At the bottom of the Ownership & Permissions section for folders and volumes, you will see a button called "Apply to enclosed items." If you click this after making a change to the Access settings, it will apply the chosen Access settings to all items contained within the folder or volume. However, it will only apply changes to files that you have permission to modify (for example, files you own).

Finally, for nonstartup volumes, the Ownership & Permissions section contains a check box that reads "Ignore ownership on this volume." This option is primarily necessary for accessing external third-party storage devices, letting you bypass permission security that might otherwise prevent you from accessing the contents of the volume. Although this may seem like a security weakness, it's a necessary one. Basically, the OS assumes you did not steal the drive; therefore, if you can connect it to your Mac, the owner of the drive must have given you permission (or the drive actually belongs to you). As discussed in Chapter 3, you should disable this option when using the volume to create a bootable backup of a Mac OS X volume. In general, don't enable this option unless you need it to access files on the drive.

Bottom line. An understanding of Ownership & Permissions settings will help you solve all kinds of Mac OS X mysteries. If, for example, you try to move something from /System/Library, you'll typically find that you've copied rather than moved the item because (by default) you can't make changes within the System directory. Conversely, if you try to move something into the /System directory or drag something from the /System directory into the Trash, you may be prevented from doing so, instead getting an error message explaining that you can't do this because the item is owned by root. (You could also get a more general error message stating that you don't have sufficient privileges.) When you understand the implications of the Ownership & Permissions settings, this arrangement begins to make sense.

Note: In Panther, many (though not all) of these prohibitions are bypassed. Instead, you get a dialog asking you to *authenticate* (that is, enter your admin name and password). Once you've done this, you're permitted to carry out the action.

SEE: • Chapter 6, especially "Using Panther's Finder Authenticate method," for more on the Authenticate button as well as modifying Ownership & Permissions settings for troubleshooting.

• "Unix: Modifying Permissions," in Chapter 10, for using Terminal to modify permissions.

Comments

This final section of the Get Info window is where you input personal comments about the item. You can enter whatever information you wish—from the Web site where the file was obtained to the serial number of a product.

Note: Comments are stored locally on your computer as a property of the Finder (the same as icon positions). This means that a user accessing a file's Get Info window over a network will not see comments you add locally.

Root Access

Mac OS X can make you feel like a guest on your own computer—and in a sense, you are! But as an administrator, you can also give yourself *root access*. Doing so makes you the equivalent of the System user—meaning you can do pretty much anything you want (which is no doubt why root is sometimes referred to as the *superuser*).

To briefly review: Different levels of users have different levels of access. For example, an ordinary user can modify the files in the Library folder of his or her Home directory but not any *other* Library folders. An admin user can modify the files in the Library folder at the root level of the drive, but not the /System/Library folder. An admin user with root access can modify anything.

In Panther, many actions (such as deleting a system-owned file) that require root access are handled by the Finder's Authenticate option. For situations where this is not sufficient, you will need to separately obtain root access. There are several ways to do so—each with advantages and disadvantages. Three of them are covered here.

SEE: • "Using Panther's Finder Authenticate method," in Chapter 6.

Mac OS X utilities

The easiest and most user-friendly method of obtaining root access is via a third-party utility that offers temporary root access. In essence, you log in as you normally would and then launch the utility. Typically, whenever you attempt to make a change that requires root access, the utility will ask you for your password. If you give it (and you're an administrator), you'll be granted temporary root access and allowed to make the change. As soon as you quit the application, your root access will be denied. Several utilities use this method—including those used to change files' permissions settings (for example, FileXaminer and XRay), as well as many others (from Cocktail to Retrospect).

The main disadvantage of this approach is that it only allows you to do precisely what the application is designed to do. Want an option that's not included? You either need to find another utility or give up. Still, for the Unix-phobic user or anyone who values ease of use in a familiar GUI interface, this method is the way to go.

Pseudo. This shareware utility works a bit differently than those mentioned above: It lets you open just about any application as "root," even if that application doesn't directly support this. Simply drag an application to the Pseudo icon, and it launches with root access (though you'll still be prompted to enter your password). By letting you launch applications as root, Pseudo makes it possible for you to open and modify documents you couldn't otherwise—for example, allowing you to modify the contents of System Folder files (not something I recommend in most cases). BareBones' BBEdit or TextWrangler text editors are good applications to try with this technique; they include an Open Hidden command for accessing even the invisible Unix files in Mac OS X. Property List Editor (included as part of the Developer software) is another utility that works well for this purpose (since it's designed to work with the preferences, or .plist, files used by Mac OS X).

Log Out System Administrator. When an application opened via Pseudo is active, the Log Out command in the Apple menu will say Log Out System Administrator rather than Log Out {*your name*}, providing a quick way to determine whether an application is running with root access. *Do not,* however, select this Log Out System Administrator command: It won't work in this instance. Instead, either quit the application and then log out, or simply make another application active first.

SEE: • "Modifying invisible Unix files from Mac OS X applications," in Chapter 6, for related information.

Terminal

Anything you can do with Unix in Mac OS X, you can do via the Terminal application—the command-line interface utility that accesses the Unix OS. Likewise, any Unix action that requires root access can be performed in Terminal via the sudo command. To use it, type sudo followed by whatever command you want to use, all in the same line. This gives you root access for that one command. (Technically, you retain sudo status—and thus the ability to perform actions that require root access—until you have gone 5 minutes without using it. This makes it convenient to issue a number of commands as root in sequence without having to type sudo before each one.)

Note: You can duplicate Pseudo's effect, for many applications, by typing sudo followed by the path to the application that's in the .app package of the application. For example, to open TextEdit this way, type the following:

`sudo -b /Applications/TextEdit.app/Contents/MacOS/TextEdit`

SEE: • "Unix: The sudo and su Commands" and "Take Note: Opening Mac OS Applications from Terminal," in Chapter 10, for more details.

Logging in as root

If you want (or need) to ignore the preceding advice about keeping your root access to a minimum, you can actually log in as the root user. You remain in the familiar Aqua environment, except that you now have the power accorded to the root user. This means you can add or delete files to or from the System folder, for example, or access the Home directory folders of all of the users on the drive.

Before you can log in as a root user, however, you need to enable root user access. There are two main ways to do this.

Use Reset Password. This option is available when you start from the Mac OS X Install CD/DVD. Follow these steps:

1. Start your computer from the Mac OS X Install CD/DVD.

   To do so, hold down the C key at startup with the disc in the CD/DVD drive, or (if booted into Mac OS X or Mac OS 9) launch the Install Mac OS X application on the CD/DVD and restart.

2. From the Installer menu, choose Reset Password.

3. In the window that appears, select your Mac OS X startup drive's icon.

4. From the pop-up menu, choose "System Administrator (root)."

5. Enter the desired password in the text boxes.

6. Click Save.

Use NetInfo Manager. You'll find this application in the Utilities folder on your hard drive: Launch it and then follow these steps:

1. From the Security menu, choose Authenticate.

2. Enter your administrator password at the prompt.

3. From the Security menu, choose Enable Root User.

   If you're using this method for the first time, you will get a message stating that the password field for the root user is blank. You will be asked to set a password; do so. (Actually, if you're doing this for the first time, you can skip steps 1 and 2 and just start here.)

4. From this same menu, you will later be able to change the root password (via the Change Root Password command) or disable root access (via the Disable Root User command).

   Note: You can also change the root password via Terminal by using the passwd command, as described in "Take Note: Forgot Your Password?" in Chapter 5.

I use the same password for root as I do for my own admin account—even though this practice entails a slight security risk. This keeps things simple and, in my opinion, is all the protection most people need in home and small-office environments. If you expect more than one person to log in as root, however, you should use a unique password.

Note: Even if you never intend to log in as the root user, you should still create a password here. This will prevent another admin user from creating a root password and thus obtaining root access, possibly without your authorization to do so.

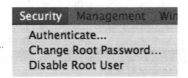

Figure 4.30

NetInfo Manager's Security menu.

SEE: • "Take Note: Securing Mac OS X," in Chapter 10, for related information

Logging in as root. After you've enabled the root account (using either of the previously outlined methods), you can log in as root. To do so, follow these steps:

1. From the Apple menu select Log Out and log out.

    Note: If Fast User Switching has been enabled, you can alternatively select Login Window from the Fast User Switching menu in the upper-right corner.

    Even after you've logged in as root, the System Administrator (root) user does not appear in this menu, This means that if you log in as System Administrator (root) and then switch to another user, you will have to return to the Login window to return to the System Administrator account.

    Note: I've had problems logging in as the root user via Fast User Switching. In particular, when I've tried to do so while another user is also logged in, the Desktop will typically appear but the Finder and the Dock never launch. The only thing to do at this point is restart the Mac. To avoid this problem, log out all other users before you attempt to log in as the root user.

2. What you see will depend upon whether you selected "Name and password" or "List of Users" from the "Display Login Window as" selection from Login Options in the Accounts System Preferences pane.

    If you selected "Name and password," simply enter *root* as the user name and the password you selected in the respective text fields.

    If you selected List of Users, an Others option should appear at the bottom of the list. Click it. Again, enter root and the selected password in the text fields that appear.

3. Click the Log In button.

Now you're logged in as the root user. Note that any customizations you've made to items on the Desktop or additions you've made to the Dock will not be visible: The Mac now considers you to be a different user.

As root user, you now have the keys to the kingdom. Use them wisely! Remember: You only want to log in as root as a last resort. Whenever possible, you should use a more temporary method of gaining root access so as to minimize the chance of making a change you end up regretting. As soon as you've completed the task at hand, log out as root user.

Note: If you expect to log in as root regularly, for whatever reason, you may wish to uncheck "Automatically log in as…" in the Login Options section. This will make it quicker to log in as the root user on initial startup because the Login window will appear by default.

Other does not appear in the Login window. As of this writing, there is a bug in Mac OS X that occasionally prevents the Other option from appearing in the List of Users Login window, even though you have enabled the root user. If this happens, do one or more of the following:

- Press Option-Return and click on a name. The blank Name and Password fields should now appear. Enter the root name and password as described above.

- To fix the problem permanently, go to NetInfo Manager. You will likely find that the Enable Root User command is active, even though you previously enabled the root user. Further, if you select the command, it will not work. That is, you cannot get it to toggle to Disable Root User. If this happens, quit NetInfo Manager and restart your Mac. Now return to NetInfo Manager. You should be prompted to create a new root user password, as if you had not done so before. After doing this, everything should work as expected; the Other option should appear in the Login window.

- Apple has stated that enabling NetInfo in the Directory Access application fixes this problem, although doing so can lead to a longer startup time. I have not found this to work on my Mac. But if nothing else has worked, give it a try.

    SEE: • Coverage of the Accounts System Preferences pane, in Chapter 2, for more details.

    • Chapter 5, especially "Login," "Alternative Mac OS X Startup Paths," and "Login Crashes," for more on logging in.

    • Chapter 10 for more information on Unix and Terminal.

NetInfo and NetInfo Manager

NetInfo Manager is a Mac OS X utility located in the Utilities folder. It provides access to the NetInfo database, allowing you to view and even modify the data it contains. The NetInfo database is the central database for network and administrative data in Mac OS X, keeping track of user accounts, printers, servers, and access.

Apple states: "NetInfo is the directory service database that is built into computers running Mac OS X and Mac OS X Server. NetInfo facilitates the management of administrative information used by Mac OS X computers. For example, NetInfo lets you centralize information about users, printers, servers, and other network devices so that all Mac OS X computers on your network, or only some of them, have access to it. It helps you set up and manage home directories for Mac OS X users on multiple, integrated Mac OS X Servers. And it simplifies the day-to-day management of administrative information by letting you update information that's used across the network in one central place. Every Mac OS X computer has a local directory domain called NetInfo. Only local applications and system software can access administrative data for this local domain. It is the first domain consulted when a user logs in or performs some other operation that requires data stored in a directory domain."

Every time you log in to your account or create a new user account, Mac OS X accesses the NetInfo database (for example, to confirm the login password or to store the new account information).

As discussed earlier in this chapter, NetInfo Manager is also where you go to enable root user access. In fact, apart from this, most Mac OS X users will rarely need to deal with the NetInfo database directly. However, there are occasions on which accessing and even modifying the data here can be of troubleshooting value. For example, you can easily check a user's ID number (UID) from here by selecting /users/{*name of user*} from the navigation columns and checking the value for the uid property that appears in the bottom part of the window.

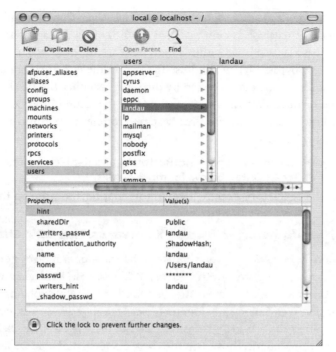

Figure 4.31

NetInfo Manager, with the listing shown for me (user = landau).

You're more likely to use the NetInfo database if you use Mac OS X Server—for example, creating new group categories here.

NetInfo and Unix. Mac OS X users can access and modify the NetInfo database via either NetInfo Manager or ni commands in Terminal. For example, the general-purpose utility nicl mimics many of NetInfo Manager's functions: The niload command loads information from standard input (such as a file) into a given NetInfo domain; the nidump command does the reverse. In Terminal, type man and the name of the command for more details.

NetInfo itself, however, stems from Mac OS X's NextStep heritage, *not* its Unix one. In a pure Unix system, much of what is handled by the NetInfo database would be handled by something called lookupd—which also exists in Mac OS X and works with NetInfo Manager. Actually, lookupd acts as a superset of NetInfo, getting information from other sources (such as a DNS server). It is beyond the scope of this book to go into much detail about this feature.

The NetInfo database is stored in the Unix directory /var/db/netinfo. The BSD Unix configuration (database) files accessed via lookupd are located in Unix's /etc directory.

Starting with Jaguar, Apple began to move away from NetInfo, relying instead on other database systems, such as the BSD files. In Jaguar and Panther, the database is used only within a local network. Even locally, it is sometimes possible to bypass NetInfo and use the files in the /etc directory instead. If you're on a server, the data accessed by the server is either the BSD configuration files or other databases as determined by the setup in the Directory Access utility. In fact, Apple has already started to refer to NetInfo as Mac OS X's "legacy" database.

SEE: • "Technically Speaking: Restoring and Replacing NetInfo and Directory Access Data," below, for more details.

• "Directory Access," later in this chapter, for more on this utility.

TAKE NOTE ▶ NetInfo Manager: Mac OS X Server vs. Mac OS X Client

As mentioned previously, Mac OS X Server is basically the same operating system as the Mac OS X you use on your own computer—with two major differences: First, the Server version of Mac OS X comes with server-specific administrative tools (such as NetBoot, Apple File Services, Macintosh Manager, and Web Objects) that aren't typically required in a desktop OS. Second, Mac OS X client can run both Carbon and Classic applications, whereas Mac OS X Server runs only Mac OS X–native applications. Thus, even the Desktop version of Mac OS X can function as an adequate server in many situations. In fact, the two versions of Mac OS X use many of the same administrative databases and tools. One of these tools is the NetInfo database.

Although most Mac OS X client users will rarely deal with the NetInfo database directly, administrators of the Mac OS X client system will find it helpful to understand what NetInfo is and how to use it to their advantage. For information beyond what I cover in the main text here, Apple offers a document titled "Understanding and Using NetInfo" (http://docs.info.apple.com/article.html?artnum=106416).

TECHNICALLY SPEAKING ▶ Restoring and Replacing NetInfo and Directory Access Data

The NetInfo database file is var/db/netinfo/local.nidb. A backup copy is maintained at /var/backups/local.nidump. You will need root access to enter these directories and access these files.

The backup copy is updated each time Mac OS X's maintenance jobs are run by cron (at 3:15 a.m., assuming your computer is turned on at that time). However, it's a good idea to maintain an additional current copy of the database on another volume. This way, you can restore it if your current database is corrupted or you mistakenly make changes to it (especially critical if the automatic backup has not been recently updated or it, too, has become corrupt).

continues on next page

TECHNICALLY SPEAKING ▶ Restoring and Replacing NetInfo and Directory Access Data *continued*

As a last resort, you can replace a corrupt version with the default version that came with Mac OS X; however, you will lose all the changes that were made to the database as a result. Even so, because a corrupt database can prevent Mac OS X from starting up, replacing one with a default version can be preferable to erasing your drive and reinstalling Mac OS X.

The details of how to back up and restore a NetInfo database are covered in Apple Knowledge Base document #107210. Similar advice is given on other Web sites, such as www.afp548.com/Articles/system/netinfobackup.html. The following provides an overview of what you need to do to restore a corrupt database from the automatic backup file:

1. Start in single-user mode (as described in Chapter 5). Type the following:
   ```
   mount —uw
   ```
   Note: If journaling is turned off (another topic described in Chapter 5), you should enter/run the following command prior to the mount command:
   ```
   fsck -y.
   ```

2. Rename the current local NetInfo database and replace it with the archived copy, using the following two commands:
   ```
   mv /var/db/netinfo/local.nidb /var/db/netinfo/local.nidb.bad
   /usr/libexec/create_nidb
   ```

3. Start the network and the NetInfo system, and load the local database with the backup data, using the following commands:
   ```
   /usr/libexec/kextd
   /usr/sbin/configd
   /sbin/SystemStarter
   /usr/bin/niload -d -r -t / localhost/local < /var/backups/local.nidump
   ```

4. Restart the computer by typing the following:
   ```
   reboot
   ```

If you don't have a good backup or if you just want to start over, you can restore from defaults. To do this, skip step 3 and instead remove the AppleSetupDone file by typing the following:
```
rm /var/db/.AppleSetupDone
```

This sets your computer back to a default NetInfo configuration (the way it was when you first installed Mac OS X). When the computer finishes starting up, Setup Assistant will appear.

continues on next page

TECHNICALLY SPEAKING ▶ **Restoring and Replacing NetInfo and Directory Access Data** *continued*

Setting Directory Access back to defaults. The Directory Service settings are stored in a folder called DirectoryService, located in /Library/Preferences. If files in this folder are corrupted, they may prevent your Mac from starting up, especially if Mac OS X is set to access an LDAP server at startup. The solution is to set the Directory Access configurations back to their default values:

1. After restarting in single-user mode, type:

/sbin/fsck —y

Followed by:

mount —uw

2. Then type:

mv /Library/Preferences/DirectoryService /Library/Preferences/DirectoryService.old

3. Finally, type:

reboot

On a related note, various Apple Knowledge Base documents provide solutions to other problems with starting up or logging in caused by incorrect Directory Service settings. For example, see http://docs.info.apple.com/article.html?artnum=107536 for coverage of an LDP issue.

Directory Access

Directory Access (called Directory Setup prior to Mac OS X 10.2), located in the Utilities folder, is not something you're likely to use if you're not part of a larger network maintained by a central server. Directory Services settings determine what services your computer checks at startup, as well as your ability to access them.

As Apple states: "When the user logs in to a Mac OS X computer, Open Directory (Apple's open-source, standards-based directory system) searches the computer's NetInfo database for the user's record. If NetInfo contains the user's record (and the user typed the correct password), the login process proceeds, giving the user access to the computer. This is the default behavior, but it can be changed by specifying an alternate search path in the Directory Access application."

If you are not connected to a central server, you can usually ignore this application altogether. If you are connected to a server, you will typically follow the specific instructions given to you by the network administrator. As such, I would not randomly experiment with the options here. For that reason, this section simply provides some general background. However, as noted in the previous section, Apple is moving away from its use of the NetInfo database. As this process proceeds, with each upgrade of the OS, the importance of the Directory Access application increases.

The Directory Access application includes three main tabs: Services, Authentication, and Contacts. Each brings up a different screen.

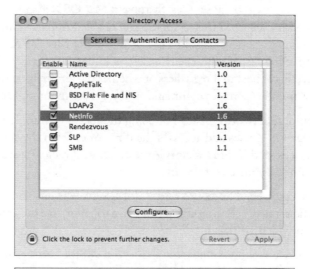

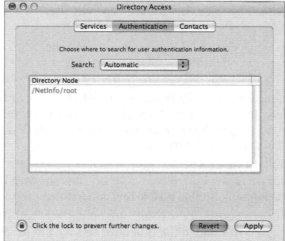

Figure 4.32

The Directory Access application: (top) Services and (bottom) Authentication.

Services. There are two categories of services listed here: 1) those that contain the database of user and administrative information that Mac OS X might use to check such things as passwords and group memberships; and 2) the types of services Mac OS X can discover on a network. This latter category accounts for the inclusion of AppleTalk and Rendezvous, for example. Check a service's check box to enable or disable access to the service.

SEE: • **Chapters 7 and 8 for more on file and print services such as Rendezvous, AppleTalk, and SMB.**

Note: In Jaguar, both AppleTalk and Rendezvous were enabled by default. In the initial versions of Panther, only Rendezvous was enabled by default. This represents a continuing shift away from the legacy AppleTalk service in favor of the newer Rendezvous or IP services. Starting in Mac OS X 10.3.3, however, responding to complaints from users, Apple again enabled AppleTalk by default. In any case, disabling a service only affects whether or not Mac OS X attempts to access it automatically, especially at startup. If you know the specific address of a server, you can still connect to it regardless of whether the service is on or off. For starters, you can use the Connect command in the Server menu of Directory Access.

For nonlocal networks, instead of using the local NetInfo database for storing data, Mac OS X uses and accesses the directories from the services listed in the Services section of Directory Access. These directories are located on the server, not on your client machine.

In some cases, the Configure button for a Service is enabled when you select a specific service. Clicking this allows you to enter specific settings for the server to which you want to connect.

Here are a few points of interest about some of the services listed:

- **NetInfo.** This is the local directory service used by Mac OS X. It's what you access when you open NetInfo Manager.

  If this box is checked, Directory Access will check for additional NetInfo databases on other Macs and servers in a larger network. You can uncheck this check box and still use the NetInfo database on your local Mac.

  From the Configure options, you can select how your Mac searches for a NetInfo database on a network. If no such databases exist on the network, don't enable any choices here: Doing so will only slow startup for your Mac (as it searches for databases it will never find).

- **BSD Flat File and NIS.** This refers to the files in the Unix directories (/etc) that Unix uses in place of NetInfo on non-Mac Unix systems. Again, you only need to enable this option to access nonlocal databases.

  However, if you click the Configure button, you will see the following message: "The node /BSD/local must be added to the Authentication and/or Contacts tabs for the information in /etc /to be used." This means that if you want your local system to check for password and contact information in the BSD files on your own drive (instead of NetInfo), you need to add the relevant information in Authentication and Contacts (as described in the next section).

- **LDAPv3.** Mac OS X Server now uses LDAP (Light Directory Access Protocol), an open standard that can be used by Macintosh, Windows, and Unix systems. If you logged in to a Mac running Mac OS X Server, you would likely be accessing its LDAP database instead of the NetInfo database on your drive.

Note: Some applications (such as Mail and Address Book) may connect directly to an LDAP directory. In this case, you make the selection in the Preferences window of the application (rather than through Directory Access).

- **SMB.** This is a protocol used by Windows machines for file sharing and printing. This is one place where a Mac user, even though not logged in to a server, might want to use Directory Access. You can use it to change the workgroup selected for SMB on a network. As stated by Apple: "A workgroup is to Windows File Sharing what an AppleTalk zone is to AppleTalk. It is a way network administrators can group related computers into smaller subgroups with meaningful names." The default workgroup for SMB is WORKGROUP. To change this:

  1. Select SMB from the Services tab in Directory Access and click the Configure button.

  2. Select a new Workgroup name from the dialog that drops down.

  3. Click the Apply button. Wait a few minutes for the change to take effect.

Authentication and Contacts. These sections of Directory Access designate where your Mac searches for password (authentication) and contact information. If the list contains more than one node, the Mac searches in the order in which the nodes are listed. You can rearrange their order; however, /NetInfo must remain on top.

The Search pop-up menu offers three choices: Automatic, Local Directory, and Custom Path.

All three choices start by checking the local directory, typically the local NetInfo database (/NetInfo/root). This means that even if you're connected to a server and a different database is accessed, your Mac is still set by default to check your local NetInfo database at login to see if your password is correct. Without this setup, you would not be able to log in to your Mac when not connected to the server.

Automatic (the default choice) additionally checks certain LDAP directories if available. If you choose Custom Path, you can create your own list of directories to check. For example, to add the /BSD/local option for authentication, as noted in the previous section, you would do the following:

1. Click the Authentication button.

2. From the Search pop-up menu, select Custom Path.

3. Click the Add button; /BSD/local should appear as an available directory.

4. Click the Add button.

5. If you want /BSD/local to be searched before /NetInfo local, drag that node to the top of the list.

6. Click the Apply button.

Note: Unless you're directly accessing the more advanced features of Unix, it's unlikely that you would want or need to make this change.

SEE: • **"Technically Speaking: Restoring and Replacing NetInfo and Directory Access Data," earlier in this chapter, for related information.**

• **Chapter 8, for more on file sharing.**

Preferences Files

Preferences files primarily refer to those files that store the customized changes you can make to an application, most commonly through an application's Preferences window. These preferences files are separate from the System Preferences panes accessed via the System Preferences application. Throughout this volume I refer to ways you can use these files for troubleshooting (see "Edit SystemVersion.plist," in Chapter 3, for one example). The following provides an overview of what these files are, where they're located, and how they work.

Format

The most common preferences files in Mac OS X are files that end in .plist (such as com.apple.finder.plist). The .plist extension stands for *property list*. All preferences files that end in .plist are thus also property list files. The term *preferences file* refers to the function of the file, whereas *property list file* refers to the format of the file. Thus, there are files that also end in .plist that are not preferences files (that is, they serve a function other than modifying preferences of an application). These files are also briefly noted in the following sections.

The .plist files are written in XML (Extensible Markup Language), which is essentially a superset of the HTML used for most Web pages. In fact, some property list files will have an .xml extension rather than .plist. In either case, the Kind description of the file (as viewed in the Get Info window) will be XML Property List File. For those familiar with XML, the document type declaration (.dtd) file for property lists is PropertyList.dtd and is located in /System/Library/DTDs.

Why the com notation? You'll notice that most .plist files begin with the abbreviation *com*. This is Apple's way of making sure that each application has a unique preferences file. Suppose two developers created applications called SuperText, and you had both of them on your drive. If both .plist files were named supertext.plist, how would the applications tell them apart? To deal with this problem, Apple has requested that developers prefix their files with their Web sites' domain-name information. Because no two domain names are identical, this setup ensures that each file will have a different name. Thus, Apple's Web site is http://www.apple.com, which converts for .plist purposes to com.apple. A .plist file for Apple's Finder is thus com.apple.finder.plist.

Locations

When it comes time to locate a preferences file, here's where to look:

- **~/Library/Preferences**. Most preferences files are located in the ~/Library/Preferences directory (in each user's Home directory). The files here are specific to each user. This is why when different users log in, they can have different preferences settings.

  Most files in this folder are standard Mac OS X preferences files ending in .plist. The loginwindow.plist file, for example, contains the list of items that you selected in your Startup Items list in the Account System Preferences pane. You may also find Mac OS 9–type preferences files and folders in this folder, however. And a few files don't fit into either category.

- **~/Library/Preferences/ByHost**. A few preferences files are likely tucked into the ByHost folder within the Preferences folder. In this folder, all filenames are structured as follows: {*com name*}.{*Ethernet address*}.plist. The Ethernet address is the Mac address (described more in Chapter 8) that you find listed at the bottom of the Network System Preferences pane. For example, a .plist file for Software Update may look like this: com.apple.SoftwareUpdate.00806466c832.plist. These ByHost files define preferences that are specific to a particular host machine (for example, the one with the listed Mac address).

  Files here could be used for those cases where your machine is part of a network and an application on your machine is run from another machine. In such cases, the preferences in this folder would be ignored.

  More generally, if you copy your Mac OS X software from one machine to another, preferences here with the Mac address of the source machine would be ignored on the destination machine. They should thus be deleted.

- **/Library/Preferences**. Several preferences files are stored in the Preferences folder of the /Library directory. Because these files will be accessed by all local users, they're typically ones that, if they can be changed at all, are restricted so that only administrators can change them (such as ones for those System Preferences panes that have the "Click the lock to prevent further changes" option).

  SEE: • Chapter 8 for details on the com.apple.AppleFileServer.plist and SystemConfiguration folder files located in /Library/Preferences.

- **/System/Library folder.** Occasionally, preferences files can be found in scattered locations throughout the /System/Library folder. The SystemVersion.plist file in the CoreServices subfolder, as noted in Chapter 3, is one example.

- **Unix directories.** There are files that use the property list format and are located in the invisible Unix directories on your drive. Go to the /etc/mach_init.d folder for several examples (such as DirectoryService.plist). You will rarely need to access these files.

  Note: Assorted other files are also included in these Unix folders, such as config files (especially in the /etc directory) that act like preferences files for Unix software. This is not the place to explore config files in any detail. I do cover some specific examples in "Modifying Invisible Unix Files from Mac OS X Applications," in Chapter 6.

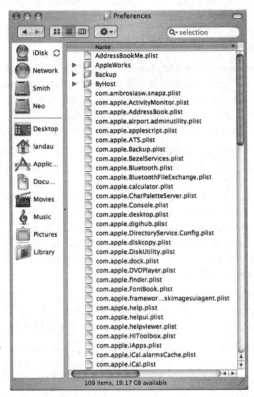

Figure 4.33

A partial view of the Preferences folder in my home directory.

Content

Preferences files contain "nonessential" information. By this, I mean the application should still be able to launch even if its preferences file is deleted; it simply creates a new default .plist file. Likewise, deleting a .plist file shouldn't delete important user data—other than a user's personal settings or perhaps a registration code. Initial default preferences are obtained from data stored within the application itself (most commonly in a file called defaults.plist, located in the Resources folder of the application package).

Each .plist file is primarily a list of items, called *keys* or *properties,* which can have different values. By changing the value of a key, you modify a given preference.

Viewing the content. Given that .plist stands for *property list,* it should come as no surprise that you can open and edit .plist files in an application called Property List Editor. This application is located in the /Developer/ Applications/Utilities folder (if you installed Developer Tools). Feel free to move it to a more convenient location.

Because .plist files are simply text files, you can also open them in any text editor (such as TextEdit). Property List Editor, however, provides a graphical interface for the file's contents that makes it easier to read and modify the file. There are also several third-party utilities, such as PrefEdit and Defaults Manager, that offer a similar graphical interface. In this volume, I use Property List Editor in almost all discussions of viewing and manipulating .plist files.

Finally, as covered below (in "Terminal's defaults command"), you can also view and edit the contents of a .plist file via the `defaults` command in Terminal.

Hidden properties. Applications sometimes include "hidden" preferences settings—by this I mean settings for which there's no user interface (such as an option in the application's preferences) to modify the setting. In most cases, such hidden properties are listed in the application's .plist file. Thus, the primary (and sometimes only) way to modify the setting is by changing the value in the .plist file—typically by using Property List Editor. Occasionally, a third-party developer will create a utility that allows you to make changes to specific "hidden" items; the utilities TinkerTool and Cocktail are examples. However, the value of the Property List Editor is that it allows you to make any changes, not just those the third-party utility permits.

In some cases, a property is so hidden that it doesn't even show up in the .plist file. Such a property simply remains set to its default value; the only way to modify its value would be to first add it to the .plist file. But how can you add a property when you don't even know it exists? Typically, you find out about such properties when the news gets spread via Macintosh Web sites (such as www.macosxhints.com)—or by reading a book like this one. In addition, Apple occasionally provides information about such properties in its Knowledge Base articles or in documents on its Developer Connection site.

SEE: • "Technically Speaking: Completely Hidden Properties: Changing the Finder," later in this chapter, for an example of a completely hidden property.

Properties that do not appear in .plist files until changed from their default values. In some cases, a preferences setting appears in an application's user interface but does not appear in its .plist file until the setting has been modified from its default value. In this case, when you open the .plist file prior to changing the default setting, the property will seem hidden because it is not there. However, it's not truly hidden because there's an option to modify the setting from the user interface (for example, via the application's Preferences command). Should you ever change the Preferences value from its default, the property will automatically be added to the .plist file. Should you later change the setting back to the default value, the added property typically remains in the .plist file.

Note: The other way to get such properties to appear in a .plist file is to add them to the file directly—typically via Property List Editor (as described later in the chapter).

Note: In some cases, the .plist file itself is not created until after you launch the application for the first time and change the default settings.

Troubleshooting: changes in application not saved to .plist file. Whenever you make a change to a preferences setting from an application's Preferences options, the corresponding .plist file should get updated. However, occasionally, problems occur. For example, several Microsoft applications store their Internet-related preferences in the same file—com.apple.internetconfig.plist—which can cause a glitch where changes you make don't get saved. For example, suppose you have Internet Explorer and Entourage open at the same time, and you make a change to Internet Explorer's preferences—say to its "auto-fill" settings. Now quit Internet Explorer and then Entourage, and then relaunch Internet Explorer: Your changes have vanished! What appears to have happened is that when you quit Entourage, it "updated" the preferences data and over-wrote the change you made in Internet Explorer. Thus, if you need to change settings that will get written to com.apple.internetconfig.plist, make sure to quit all applications other than the one in which you plan to make the change.

Modifying a .plist file

In most cases, you can modify the contents of a preferences (.plist) file without working with the .plist file directly. To do so, select the Preferences (or similar) command of the application that uses the file. Any changes to preferences settings you make in the application will modify the application's .plist file. However, you can also make the same change by editing the application's .plist file directly in Property List Editor. This conversely changes the setting as viewed from the application's Preferences command. If a property is hidden (as described above), you will need to use Property List Editor (or a third-party alternative) to make changes.

The following are two examples of how this all works.

Editing com.apple.Terminal.plist. This example shows how to use Property List Editor to edit a value that also could have been changed from the application's preferences settings.

1. In the ~/Library/Preferences folder double-click the com.apple.Terminal.plist file.

2. If you're asked what application you want to open this document with, choose Property List Editor. (If Property List Editor is installed, the document will most likely open in it directly.)

3. Click the disclosure triangle next to the word *Root* to display the list of items/keys.

   If you've only launched Terminal once and made no preferences changes, you will find a very limited list of properties in this .plist file. In my case, I found just two: FirstRun and StartupFile. If this is the case for you, close the .plist file and launch Terminal. From the File menu, select Show Info (Command-I) to open the Terminal Inspector. From the window that appears, click the Use Settings as Defaults button. This command adds all of the current settings as properties to the .plist file. Now reopen com.apple.Terminal.plist. You will find several dozen properties listed (I found 58). This is one example of how properties get added to the .plist file as a function of what you do in the application itself.

4. Scroll down to the TerminalOpaqueness item. Note its value. Its initial default value is 1.00000 (which means the Terminal window is completely opaque).

5. Close the .plist document.

6. Launch Terminal.

7. Open the Terminal Inspector (via Command-I). Select Color from the pop-up menu at the top of the window.

8. Move the Transparency slider all the way to the right. The Terminal window is now completely transparent.

9. Click the Use Settings as Defaults button.

10. Quit Terminal and reopen the com.apple.Terminal.plist file. Return to the TerminalOpaqueness item. Its value should now be changed, most likely to 0.050000.

As you can see, changing an application setting modified the value of a property in its .plist file. You could conversely change a setting by modifying its value in the .plist file itself. For example:

1. From the com.apple.Terminal.plist file, as opened in Property List Editor, type in a new value for TerminalOpaqueness, such as 0.600000. (You must first double-click the value to make it editable.)

2. Save the change and quit Property List Editor.

3. Launch Terminal and return to the Color item in the Terminal Inspector. The Transparency slider should now have moved to near the middle.

As you can see, you changed the transparency level without launching Terminal.

Editing com.apple.Finder.plist. The following demonstrates how to use Property List Editor to modify an application's hidden .plist item (that is, a setting not accessible from the application's preferences). In this case, you will change the Finder's Preferences so that normally invisible files are visible in the Finder.

1. Open the com.apple.finder.plist file, located in ~/Library/Preferences, in Property List Editor.

2. Click the disclosure triangle next to the word *Root* to reveal the list of keys.

3. Scroll down to find the item called AppleShowAllFiles.

   It will either have a Class of String and a Value of 0 or a Class of Boolean and a Value of No. The advantage of the Boolean class is that the Value choices appear in a pop-up menu and are thus easier to figure out.

4. If the item's value is No, click the pop-up menu and change the value to Yes. If the value is 0, double-click the value and change the 0 to a 1.

5. Save and close the .plist file.

6. If invisible files are not yet visible, choose Force Quit from the Apple menu, select Finder from the list of applications, and click Relaunch.

You could alternatively use a utility such as TinkerTool's "Show hidden and system files" command to make invisible files visible. All TinkerTool does is provide a user interface to make the same change you just made in Property List Editor.

Note: Other items in com.apple.finder.plist are directly linked to Finder Preferences settings. For example, the WarnOnEmptyTrash key is what gets changed via the setting in the Advanced section of the Finder's Preferences. Note, however, that this key may not be included the .plist file if you haven't changed the setting from its default selection.

Warning: bug in Property List Editor. Apple has acknowledged a bug in Property List Editor, still present as of this writing, that may prevent a property from appearing in an opened .plist file. If you suspect that a property is missing from a file, you can check for this bug by opening the file in TextEdit instead. The property, if present, should appear in TextEdit even if it does not appear in Property List Editor.

SEE: • "Take Note: The Location of Desktop Folders," and "Take Note: the Location of Trash Folders," earlier in this chapter, for more information on invisible files.

• "The Invisible Files" in Chapter 6.

• "Modifying or deleting the .GlobalPreferences.plist file," in Chapter 6.

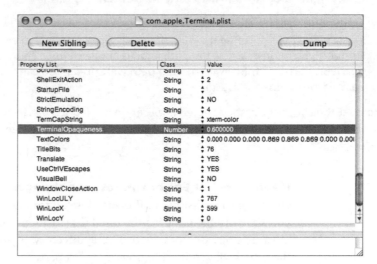

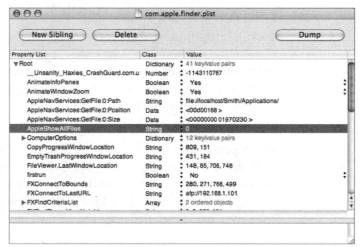

Figure 4.34

Property List Editor showing (top) the contents of the com.apple.Terminal.plist file and (bottom) the contents of the com.apple.Finder.plist file.

TECHNICALLY SPEAKING ▶ Completely Hidden Properties: Changing the Finder

The com.apple.loginwindow.plist contains settings that affect what happens when you log in. However, there is at least one property that does not appear in this file by default. This property is the one you use if you want to replace the Finder as the application that launches at login. To modify this property from its default setting, you will need to create a new key. Although most users will never have any reason to do this, you could use it to replace the Finder with a third-party Finder alternative (for example, PathFinder) or with Terminal (if you're a Unix geek).

1. In ~/Library/Preferences open the com.apple.loginwindow.plist file.

2. Click on the Root line and then click the New Child button.

3. In the Property List column, locate the newly created child and name it Finder.

4. In the Value column, enter the path of the application that you wish to substitute for the Finder. If you're unsure how the path should appear, launch Terminal and drag the application icon to the Terminal window; the path will appear. You can copy it from Terminal and paste it into Property List Editor.

The next time you log in, the selected application will launch instead of the Finder. Even though the Finder won't load at login now, you can still launch it manually by clicking its icon in the Dock.

If Property List Editor cannot save changes. In some cases, you may be able to open a .plist file in Property List Editor but not save changes because you have insufficient permissions. This situation is most likely to occur with .plist files that are not in your Home directory. If you want to modify one of these files, all you need to do is open Property List Editor with root access, using Pseudo (as explained in "Mac OS X utilities," earlier in this chapter).

As a rule, avoid making changes in such cases, especially if the file is somewhere in the System folder. Changing files in this folder is always risky: You may do more harm than good, perhaps even rendering your system unbootable. In any case, changes you make here will likely get wiped out the next time you update the OS (sometimes even the next time you restart).

Note: I once had a .plist file for which changes could not be saved, even though permissions were set correctly. Eventually, I made a copy of the file in the Finder and was able to make changes to the copy. However, I still couldn't discover any differences between the two files that would account for the inability to save the original, so I just dumped the original, made the changes to the copy, and substituted it for the original file.

Adding and deleting keys in Property List Editor. To add a new key to a .plist file, click the New Sibling button (it's called New Child if you select the Root item). You can now name the property and assign its value. To delete an existing property, select it and click the Delete button.

SEE: • "Technically Speaking: Completely Hidden Properties: Changing the Finder," above, for an example of adding a key.

Terminal's defaults command. You can use the `defaults` command, in Terminal, to access and modify the same data that Property List Editor does. This command also provides access to parameters that may not be listed in .plist files, such as the position of a window. Users comfortable with Unix may prefer this alternative. For details on how to use this command, type `man defaults` (or `defaults usage`).

For example, to read/view the value for AppleShowAllFiles in the Finder, you would type the following:

```
defaults read com.apple.Finder AppleShowAllFiles
```

As a second example, to launch Terminal at login rather than the Finder (as described in "Technically Speaking: Completely Hidden Properties: Changing the Finder"), type the following (on one line):

```
defaults write com.apple.loginwindow Finder
/Applications/Utilities/Terminal.app
```

Property list files: more locations

Files that have a .plist (or sometimes an .xml) extension show up in other standard locations beyond those already described. These files are typically not meant to be edited by the end user. Here are two examples:

Info.plist and other package .plist files. All application packages contain at least one essential .plist file: Info.plist. This file is located within the Contents folder inside the package, and it contains, at minimum, the following information:

- Name of application (displayed by the Finder)
- Type and creator codes (for example, APPL is the type for applications)
- Icon filename
- Version string
- Descriptive information (displayed by the Finder)
- Documents handled by this application, including their names, icons, role, types, and extensions
- URLs handled by this application, including names, icons, and schemes

If the Info.plist information is specific to Mac OS X or Classic, the OS name will be embedded in the filename—for example, Info-Macos.plist or Info-MacosClassic.plist. A related version.plist file contains summary information about the name and version number of the application. An InfoPlist.strings file (located in Contents/Resources/{*language*}.lproj) contains information used by Info.plist that has been localized for different languages. The Finder uses these files to determine how it interacts with the application, such as what documents go with what applications.

Installer package files also typically contain these .plist items.

StartupParameters.plist. Startup Items (which are described in more detail in Chapter 5) include a StartupParameters.plist file, which provides information about when, in the sequence of loading startup items, a given item should load.

Interface Builder

Interface Builder is an application that's included with Mac OS X's Developer Tools software. You'll find it, along with all of the other developer applications, in the /Developer/Applications folder. Because Interface Builder is designed to help developers build Aqua interfaces for their software, you'll have little use for it as a troubleshooter. There are, however, a few instances in which it might be helpful.

For example, if you don't like the brushed metal windows in Apple's Safari Web browser, you can change them in an instant with Interface Builder. To do so, follow these steps:

1. Select Show Package Contents for Safari.

2. Go to Contents/Resources/English.proj/ and double-click Browser.nib. It should open in Interface Builder (assuming you have installed the Developer Tools software).

3. From the Browser.nib window, click the Instances tab and single-click the Window item.

4. From the Tools menu, select Show Info.

5. From the pop-up menu, select Attributes, then go to the bottom section of the window and uncheck the Has Texture option (it's called Textured Window in Jaguar).

6. Save the change. Now when you open a new window in Safari, the brushed metal appearance is gone.

When you save the changed option, a new file called Browser~.nib is added to the English.proj folder. It contains the original settings—useful if you forget what you did and want to return to the default settings.

By the way, many shareware and freeware utilities that add features to or otherwise modify an application, such as Safari, take advantage of "tricks" like this. That is, the utility does not make its changes via some unique code written by the utility's programmer; rather, it takes advantage of functionality already built into Mac OS X. In essence, the utility does the grunt work for you: All you need to do is run it and make your selection.

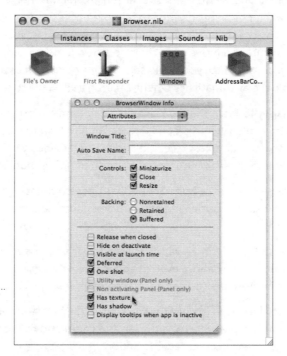

Figure 4.35

The contents of Safari's Browser.nib file, as viewed in Interface Builder.

Figure 4.36

AppleScript's Script Editor.

TAKE NOTE ▶ AppleScript

Although AppleScript is an incredibly useful tool in Mac OS X, it's not particularly helpful for troubleshooting—which is why I don't pay a lot of attention to it in this volume. Still, you should at least know the basics of its use—which is precisely what follows here!

AppleScript is akin to a programming language; however, it uses an English-like syntax that makes it much easier to learn than most programming languages. It's used primarily to automate repetitive actions (like a macro utility). Thus, if you wanted to convert dozens of JPEG files to TIFF files, give each a new name, and move all of them to a new folder, you could create an AppleScript to carry out these tasks. In fact, you could set up the AppleScript as a Folder Action, so that the conversion takes place automatically when you drag a JPEG file to the folder.

If you know Unix, you'll be happy to learn that you can even call Terminal commands from within an AppleScript. AppleScript also includes conditional commands so that scripts can adjust their decisions to the situation (for example, you could create the previously suggested script so that a JPEG file created more than a year ago would be trashed rather than converted).

Script Editor, the application used to create AppleScripts, has been completely rewritten and redesigned for Panther. New features include Find and Replace, contextual-menu support, and a Compile button in the toolbar.

AppleScript now also supports GUI scripting—which means you can access buttons and menu commands (via the System Events application) even in applications that don't directly support AppleScript. Check this page for more details: www.apple.com/applescript/GUI.

System Events—the file for which resides in /System/Library/CoreServices—drives much of AppleScript's functionality. For example, when a script sends a command to the Finder or when a Folder Action is called, System Events is spurred into action.

Creating a script. To create a new AppleScript, in the Applications folder locate the AppleScript folder and launch Script Editor. If you know AppleScript commands, you can begin writing a script immediately. If not, you can record a sequence of actions (just click Record and start performing!) and have your actions automatically converted into a script. Click Stop when you're finished. This isn't as powerful as actually writing a script (because it doesn't allow for conditional statements); however, it does provide a quick way of getting started. Unfortunately, many applications don't support auto-recording of AppleScripts (even though they otherwise support AppleScript). If nothing appears in Script Editor when you try to record a script, this is probably why.

To save a script, select Save As from the File menu and then choose a name and format for the file. In most cases, your selected format will be either Script (if the compiled script is to be an item in an application's script menu) or Application (for double-clickable AppleScript files that function much like ordinary applications). It's best to save a script as Text if you intend to edit it further in Script Editor. With the help of AppleScript Studio (which requires Developer Tools), you can make a script look and act just like a professional Mac OS X application—users wouldn't even be able to tell it had been created in AppleScript.

continues on next page

TAKE NOTE ▶ **AppleScript** *continued*

You can test a script before you save it by clicking the Run button in the toolbar. Click the Event Log tab in the bottom of the window, before clicking Run, to view a record of the script as it actually executed (that is, with actual values substituted for all variables).

Checking the dictionary. One limitation of AppleScript is that it works primarily with applications that have been specifically written to include AppleScript support. To determine what such applications are, select Open Dictionary from Script Editor's File menu. You can now scroll through the list of all supported applications. If you double-click the name of an application, it will reveal a list of all the actions in that application that can be scripted. Click an action and get the details of how to use it in a script.

Using existing scripts. Even if you don't ever intend to write a script yourself, AppleScript can still be a great bonus. This is because you can make use of scripts that other people have written. For starters, go to the following Web page: www.apple.com/applescript/apps. Here you will see a list of all applications included with Mac OS X that work with AppleScript. In many cases, clicking an application lead to a new page from which you can download a set of scripts that work in that application. In some cases (such as for iTunes), to use such scripts you need to correctly install them. Here's how:

1. Open the folder with the same name as the application, located in your Home Library folder (for example, ~/Library/iTunes).

2. If a folder called Scripts already exists, open it. if not, create a new folder with that name. Now drag the downloaded scripts to this Scripts folder.

3. Launch the application. On the right side of the application's menus (probably just to the left of the Help menu) will be an AppleScript icon. Click it to select the menu and see the list of scripts now available to you.

Third-party applications may also include a script menu option. For example, to add scripts that work with Microsoft's Entourage, add them to the Entourage Script Menu Items folder in the ~/Documents/Microsoft User Data folder. To find scripts that work with Entourage (or other applications), check Web sites such as Version Tracker.

You can also enable the Mac OS X Scripts menu with its collection of many useful basic scripts. To do so, double-click the Install Script Menu item that's in the same AppleScript folder as Script Editor. Note: If you want to open one of these scripts in Script Editor rather than execute it, hold down the Option button when selecting the script. Also note that the CDs & DVDs pane of System Preferences includes a Run Script option.

Folder Actions work via AppleScripts attached to a folder. To attach and enable an action script to a folder (in Panther), access the contextual menu for the target folder and select Attach a Folder Action. This opens a Choose A File window, from which you can select to attach a script. You can also select items from the /Library/Scripts/Folder Actions folder via the AppleScript menu, if installed (oddly, the similarly located Folder Action Scripts folder does not appear in this menu).

continues on next page

Font Formats

Given the complexity of the task, Apple has done a great job of implementing
fonts in Mac OS X. For the casual Mac OS X user, working with Mac OS X's
fonts is as simple as selecting and using them. In addition, it's easier to switch
among languages than it was in Mac OS 9. But for users who want to add and
delete their own fonts, who have problems getting certain fonts to work, or who
have troubleshooting symptoms that may be font-related, this section provides
the background information required to get to the heart of the problem.

You can use more than one type of font on a Macintosh. Because font formats
are not a Mac OS X–specific issue, I'm not going to provide detailed coverage
of them here. Instead, I'll simply present a brief overview—especially useful
for those new to the subject.

Figure 4.37

*My (left) /System/
Library/Fonts folder
and (right) /Library/
Fonts folder.*

TrueType fonts

TrueType fonts are Apple's preferred font for Mac OS X. Most or all of the fonts that ship with Mac OS X are TrueType fonts. With TrueType, the font displays and prints smoothly (with no irregular jagged edges), no matter what size (for example, 10 points versus 13 points) or style (for example, plain text versus bold) you select.

For this feature to work, you need only a single font file for a given TrueType font. However, individual font files will often include separate style variations (such as Times Italic and Times Bold). If such variations *aren't* present, you won't be able to select different styles for a given font in most Mac OS X applications.

Windows PCs can also use TrueType fonts; however, Windows TrueType font files employ a slightly different format than Mac TrueType fonts. Fortunately, Mac OS X recognizes the following Windows versions of TrueType fonts: TrueType fonts (with the extension .ttf) and TrueType collections (with the extension .ttc). Note: The .ttf extension may also be used for Macintosh TrueType fonts. Both Jaguar and Panther versions of Mac OS X are able to display both types correctly.

PostScript fonts

These font files contain the PostScript instructions needed to print to PostScript-supported printers. If your printer doesn't support PostScript, you should avoid PostScript fonts and stick with TrueType fonts (if possible). No PostScript fonts ship with Mac OS X, but you may have some in your Mac OS 9 System Folder, or you may have added them to your Mac OS X System folder.

PostScript fonts are printer font files that contain instructions only for printing the text to a PostScript printer. In Mac OS 9, you could not display PostScript fonts on the screen. A matching screen font version (either bitmap or TrueType) was needed to display them. This screen/printer font pairing didn't always work well. Often what you saw on the screen was different from what appeared on the printed page. This situation improved significantly, however, with the release of Adobe Type Manager (ATM). This utility uses the PostScript printer's font instructions to display the fonts on the screen.

ATM doesn't work in Mac OS X; however, it's not really needed. Whereas Mac OS 9 used a technology called QuickDraw to display fonts, Mac OS X uses Quartz. And the Quartz technology is able to display PostScript printer font information without the use of additional software (such as ATM). Note: ATM still works for displaying text in Classic applications.

You typically still need at least one matching TrueType or bitmap screen font (font suitcase) to get PostScript fonts (with a type of LWFN) to be listed in

Fonts menus. However, PostScript fonts of the SFNT type may work without separate matching screen fonts.

Multiple Master fonts. PostScript Multiple Master fonts (font files that end with MM) are supported in Mac OS X 10.2 and later. You cannot create them in Mac OS X, but you can correctly use existing ones. To create a new Multiple Master font, you need software from Adobe, which must be run under Classic.

OpenType fonts

Microsoft and Adobe jointly designed this relatively new font format, which boasts the advantage of allowing the same font file to work on both Mac and Windows platforms. Microsoft created OpenType to free itself from its dependence on Apple's TrueType—so in a sense the formats are competitors. At the time of this writing, most Mac users were still using TrueType fonts rather than OpenType fonts (which typically have an .otf extension).

Bitmap fonts

This, the oldest font type, is rarely used anymore. With this font type, each size requires a separate file (Times 10, Times 12, Times 14, and so on). If you select a size that doesn't have a separate file, the font will appear jagged.

Although you may get these fonts to work in Mac OS X, especially when you're working in Classic, they are not supported, so you should avoid them. Especially avoid older bitmapped versions of Chinese-, Japanese-, Korean-, and Vietnamese-language fonts: They will not work in Mac OS X. Also unsupported are older bitmapped fonts of the type FONT. Meanwhile, fonts of the type NFNT are supported for Classic/QuickDraw applications but ignored by applications based on Cocoa (such as TextEdit).

TAKE NOTE ▶ TrueType Fonts, Data Forks, and the .dfont File Extension

Mac OS X TrueType and .dfont. In Mac OS 9, a font file (like most Mac OS 9 files) has both a resource fork and a data fork. A file's main data (such as the text of a text document) resides in the data fork; the rest of its metadata (type and creator information, icon, and so on) would be stored as separate resources in its resource fork. Mac OS X prefers to avoid resource forks, instead keeping everything in the data fork. Apple claims this arrangement makes it possible for fonts to work in other operating systems, such as Windows, which do not recognize resource forks.

Data fork–only font files must have the file extension .dfont. They may also have the file type dfon.

continues on next page

TAKE NOTE ▶ TrueType Fonts, Data Forks, and the .dfont File Extension *continued*

Essentially, a .dfont file is a TrueType font with all the resource-fork info moved to the data fork so that only the data fork remains. Mac OS X can read both old-style TrueType fonts and the new .dfont type. Apple, however, clearly prefers the. dfont type, so that's primarily what gets installed by Mac OS X. Old-style TrueType fonts may still be installed by third parties.

Note: Mac OS X's dfonts will not work in Mac OS 9. Thus, if you need to print a document that uses these fonts via Mac OS 9, it may not print correctly. To work around the problem, in the Mac OS X Print dialog enable the Save As PDF option. This saves the file and prints the PDF from Mac OS 9.

OpenType and Windows TrueType. OpenType fonts and Windows TrueType fonts also store all of their data in the data fork and don't have the additional resource fork of Macintosh fonts. The data fork for Mac OS X TrueType format, however, is different from the data fork for TrueType font format used by Microsoft Windows. The difference is that data-fork Mac OS X files contain all of the resources associated with a Macintosh font, including FOND and NFNT resources, which are used with QuickDraw Text. OpenType and Windows TrueType fonts do not include this information. Windows TrueType fonts have the extension .ttf.

Want more info? If you're unfamiliar with terms like *FOND* and *NFNT resources,* you can check out my other book, *Sad Macs,* for more details. You can also experiment with Apple's ResEdit utility to see these resources in Mac OS 9. Or you can pick up any number of books that delve into the details of Mac typography, such as the latest edition of *The Macintosh Bible* (Peachpit Press), which has a chapter on fonts.

Identifying font formats

You open a Fonts folder and see an assortment of fonts: How do you tell which are TrueType, which are PostScript, and which are Open Type? There are several ways:

Font icon and Kind line in Get Info. Starting in Panther, almost all fonts have icons indicating that they are Font Book files. Font Book is Panther's new font-management application, and—with the exception of PostScript fonts—all font files open in Font Book when you double-click them.

In addition, if you look closely at each font icon, you will see that it includes either the four-character type code or extension name of the font's format. What's more, if you select Get Info for a font, the Kind line will fully describe its format. For example, a dfont will display *DFONT* on its icon, and the Kind line of its Get Info window will include the description, "Datafork TrueType font." Similarly, a PostScript font's icon will display the letters *LWFN,* and its Kind line in the Get Info window will say, "PostScript Type 1 outline font."

In Jaguar, in contrast, font icons vary according to font type. For example, a PostScript font has a different icon than a dfont. In addition, in Jaguar, the Get Info window identifies certain types of fonts correctly but simply says "Document" for some font types. Overall, Panther does a much better job of identifying font formats.

File extensions. As discussed earlier, if a font file's name includes an extension, this extension can indicate font type—for example, .otf is used for OpenType fonts.

Arial   Geneva.dfont

Figure 4.38

Font file icons: a DFONT and an FFIL font file.

Type/creator utilities. As you will learn more about in Chapter 6, numerous Mac OS X utilities are able to list a file's type and creator information. In Mac OS 9, every file needs to have these codes assigned; in Mac OS X, this information is optional. Most files (including most fonts), however, still include this information. In addition to the already noted font types like FONT, NFONT, SFNT, and LWFN, suitcase font files will have a type of FFIL and a creator of DMOV.

Utilities that can display type and creator data include XRay and FileXaminer.

Font utilities. If you open Font Book and from its Preview menu select Show Font Info (Command-I), you will see font information (including font type and format) for the selected font displayed beneath the font sample. Third-party font utilities, such as Suitcase, will also show font formats.

Figure 4.39

The Get Info window for the Geneva.dfont file.

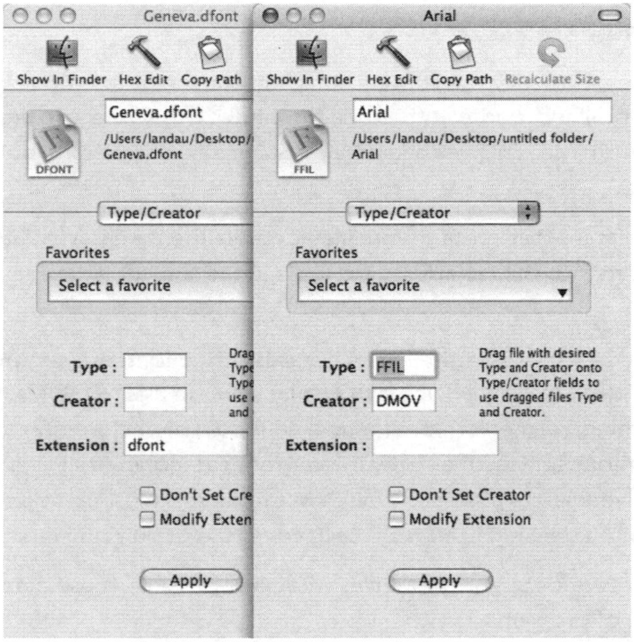

Figure 4.40

*The FileXaminer util-
ity, showing type,
creator, and exten-
sion data for the
two fonts shown in
Figure 4.38.*

SEE: • "Take Note: Font Book: An Overview," below.

• "Take Note: Type/Creator vs. Filename Extensions," earlier in this chapter, for more information on type and creator codes.

TAKE NOTE ▶ Font Suitcases

In Mac OS 9, a font could exist as an individual file or as one of several different font files combined into a font *suitcase*. TrueType and bitmap versions of the same font could be combined
in the same font suitcase. A single suitcase could even hold entirely different and unrelated
fonts (such as Helvetica and Times).

Mac OS X recognizes these suitcases (which have a file type of FFIL and a Kind line of Font
Suitcase when viewed in a Get Info window); however, it much prefers single font files or, at the
very least, no mixing of multiple font types in the same suitcase. Mac OS X finds mixed font
suitcases confusing because their names are unlikely to divulge clues about their contents.

In Mac OS 9, if you wanted to add or remove a font file from a font suitcase, you could double-
click the suitcase icon to open a window displaying its contents. Then you simply dragged a
font file from the suitcase to remove it or dragged a file into the suitcase to add it.

You cannot do this in Mac OS X. In Mac OS X, these suitcases are listed as a single file, and
double-clicking them does not reveal their full contents.

continues on next page

TAKE NOTE ▶ **Font Suitcases** *continued*

Thus, the simplest way to modify the contents of a font suitcase is to reboot in Mac OS 9 (if your Mac can still do so) and modify it there via the Finder. Otherwise, you may find utilities that let you do this from Mac OS X (either in Mac OS X itself or via Classic), but I haven't found any good ones so far.

If you open a font suitcase that contains multiple fonts via the third-party utility X Font Info, its Font pop-up menu lets you choose among the fonts in the suitcase. However, you cannot modify the contents.

As a result, although they may work well in most cases, mixed fonts are another potential source of trouble in Mac OS X. My advice is to restrict suitcase files to the Mac OS 9 Classic System Folder, assuming you need to use them at all. If possible, before upgrading to Mac OS X, convert all of your font suitcase files to individual font categories (that is, isolate each font, such as Times or Helvetica, into a separate file). You can do this most easily by duplicating the mixed font file and then deleting fonts from each copy so that only one type remains in each.

In general, it's wise to avoid Mac OS 9 font files whenever possible. These older fonts remain a too-common source of problems.

SEE: • **"Checking fonts," in Chapter 5, for more on troubleshooting font problems.**

Figure 4.41

TrueType font file icon and font suitcase icon as viewed when booted in Mac OS 9.

Arial Black suitcase   Arial Black

Viewing and Managing Fonts

Apple persists in overhauling the way Mac OS X works with fonts in each major upgrade. For that reason, the following sections are limited almost exclusively to coverage of Mac OS X 10.3 (Panther).

TAKE NOTE ▶ **Font Book: An Overview**

New in Panther, Font Book is Mac OS X's font-management utility. It allows you to do the following:

• **View fonts.** Font Book lets you preview each font as well as get more information about the font (such as its format).

continues on next page

TAKE NOTE ▶ Font Book: An Overview *continued*

- **Add and delete fonts and collections.** You can use Font Book to install new fonts. Once installed (by simply placing the font file in the appropriate Fonts folder within a Library folder), a font is immediately available for use in applications.

  Similarly, Font Book lets you group fonts in *collections*—subsets of the entire list of installed fonts. In applications that support collections (like TextEdit), you can select a collection from the Font window. This restricts the list of fonts to those in the collection. The idea here is that you can create different collections for different tasks (for example, preparing a newsletter versus working on a report).

  You can also disable and/or remove fonts and collections. Whether disabled or removed, the font and/or collection is removed from the applications list. The difference between disabling and removing is that a disabled collection or font remains listed in Font Book and can be re-enabled. A removed item, in contrast, is placed in the Trash.

  Note: At the top of the Collection column is an item called All Fonts, which you cannot disable or remove. As its name implies, it lists all of your fonts. Clicking the disclosure triangle next to its name reveals several subcategories: User (fonts in ~/Library/Fonts), Computer (fonts in /Library/Fonts and /System/Library/Fonts), and (if present) Classic Mac OS (fonts in the Classic System Folder).

- **Resolve duplicates.** An important troubleshooting feature in Font Book is the ability to resolve problems due to duplicate fonts installed on your Mac.

The sections on fonts in the main text of this chapter provide details regarding these features.

SEE: • "Font utilities," later in this chapter, for information about additional font utilities.

Figure 4.42

The main Font Book display, with the Show Font Info option enabled.

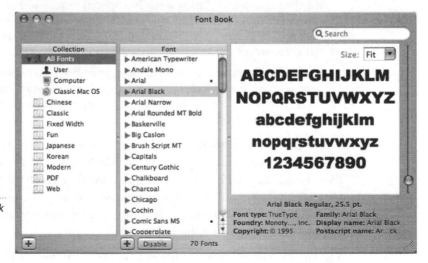

Viewing fonts

A font file in the Finder won't tell you anything about how the font looks. In Mac OS 9, double-clicking the font file helped out in this regard: It opened a window displaying the font. If the file was a font suitcase, it opened a window listing all fonts within the suitcase. In Jaguar, in contrast, double-clicking most types of font files resulted in an error message stating either "There is no application available to open document {*name of font*}" or "There is no default application specified to open the document {*name of font*}." If you happened to have the ancient Font/DA Mover utility on your drive, fonts *might* launch that utility in Classic; however, you couldn't expect it to work very well.

Font Book. Lucky for us, Panther provides significantly improved tools for viewing fonts. In particular, if you double-click a font file in the Finder, it opens Font Book in one of three ways:

- If the font is installed in any of your active Fonts folders, the main Font Book window opens with the double-clicked font selected and displayed.

  Note: Font Book even lists fonts in Fonts folders located on nonstartup volumes with Mac OS X installed.

  SEE: • "Take Note: Multiple Folders of the Same Name in Multiple Library Folders," earlier in this chapter.

- If the font is not installed in any of your active Fonts folders (such as one that you just downloaded from the Web and is now placed on your Desktop), a separate window opens with the name of the font and a sample of the font's text. (This is actually a special feature of Font Book, which is the active application when this window appears.) At the top of the window is a pop-up menu from which you can select different styles of the font (if there are any).

- If the file is a PostScript outline font, Font Book launches, but the file is not selected. Font Book cannot directly display PostScript font files; however, it does list the display font (for example, bitmap or TrueType) linked to the PostScript font files.

Third-party utilities. You can also view fonts in third-party utilities. In fact, if you have a third-party font utility (such as Suitcase) and want fonts to open there rather than in Font Book when you double-click them, you can use the Open With options in the Get Info window to change the default application from Font Book to your preferred choice. (Again, this method works more reliably in Panther than it did in Jaguar.)

You still can't open a suitcase file in Mac OS X and see a list of all its fonts (as described more in "Take Note: Font Suitcases," earlier in this chapter).

Figure 4.43

The Font Book display that appears when you double-click a noninstalled font file.

Installing fonts

To make a font available in your application's font menus, you need to install the font. In essence, this means placing it in one of the Library/Fonts folders that Mac OS X uses when checking for fonts. There are several ways to do this.

Double-clicking an uninstalled font to access Font Book. As described above, if you double-click an uninstalled font file in the Finder, it opens a special Font Book window for that font. At the bottom of this window is an Install Font button. Clicking this installs the font into your Home directory's Fonts folder (by default). The original copy of the font file is moved rather than copied (unless the original location is one from which you do not have permission to delete files).

You can change the default behavior of the Install Font button via Font Book's Preferences. From here, you can choose among the following options for where you want the font installed: "for me only" (the initial default choice), "for all users of this computer" (the font is installed in the /Library/Fonts folder), or "for Classic Mac OS" (the font is installed in the Mac OS 9 System Folder). From Preferences, you can also choose that installed fonts be copied, rather than moved, from their original locations.

Using Font Book directly. From Font Book's File menu, you can select Add Fonts (or click the plus [+] button at the bottom of the Font column). This opens a window from which you can select to install the font from among the same choices that are listed in Font Book's Preferences.

Note: If you install a font in your own Fonts folder (~/Library/Fonts) and later wish to make it available to all users (that is, by moving it to /Library

Fonts), you can do so from Font Book: Simply click the disclosure triangle next to the All Fonts collection to reveal (typically) three listings: User (you), Computer, and Classic Mac OS. Click User, and you should see the newly installed font listed in the Font column: Drag the font into the Computer user. (You can do the reverse as well.)

You can similarly create a new font collection by selecting New Collection from the File menu (or clicking the + button at the bottom of the Collection column). A new collection is empty by default. To add fonts to a collection, select All Fonts and then drag the font(s) you wish to add from the Font column to the collection name in the Collection column. This does not move the font's location in the Finder; it simply adds it to the list of fonts in that collection. Collection information is maintained by files with a .collection extension in the FontCollections folder of your /Library folder.

Performing a "manual" install. You can install a font "manually" from the Finder by dragging it to the desired Fonts folder (for example, ~/Library/Fonts). Of course, you can also drag a font out of one of these Fonts folders to uninstall it.

Note: For PostScript font files, you have no choice *but* to manually install them from the Finder (since you can't install them directly via Font Book). However, there is an exception: If you have both a font suitcase file (FFIL) for a PostScript font and the PostScript font files (LWFN) that work with it, you can select to install the suitcase file. When you do this, it will automatically install all the PostScript font files that are in the same location. When viewed in Font Book, the font will be correctly listed as a PostScript font (in the Font Info display). The available style variants will depend on the PostScript files you installed.

Using third-party utilities. With third-party font utilities, such as Suitcase, you can also activate and install fonts—including making fonts active that are not in any Library/Fonts folder.

Disabling and removing fonts

If you've installed fonts that you don't use or otherwise want to remove (possibly because you suspect they're corrupted), you can disable or remove them. The following describes how.

Using Font Book. To *disable* a font using Font Book, simply select the name of the font in the Font column of the Font Book window and click the Disable button at the bottom of the column. To disable an entire collection of fonts, in the Collection column select the name of the collection and then click the Disable button at the bottom of the Collection column. You can use the latter method, for example, to easily disable all Classic Mac OS fonts.

To completely *remove* a font or collection, from Font Book's File menu highlight the item and select Remove Font or Remove Collection. When fonts are removed, they're placed in the Trash.

Note: If you select to disable all the fonts in the Computer collection (the subcategory under All Fonts), essential system fonts such as Geneva and Lucida Grande remain enabled. You should almost never actually remove any fonts from this collection.

Performing a manual uninstall. Any user can manually remove a font from the Fonts folder in his or her ~/Library directory. As an administrator, you can also remove fonts from the /Library/Fonts folder and the Fonts folder in the Classic System Folder.

To remove fonts from the /System/Library/Fonts folder, you need (a) root access, (b) to Authenticate (if the dialog to do so appears), or (c) to change the ownership of the font to be removed from System to yourself (via the Get Info window). However, you will rarely want or need to remove a font from /System/Library/Fonts.

If you're using Font Book to manage fonts, I recommend not moving fonts in the Finder because doing so can cause problems within Font Book. For example, if you go to the Finder to remove a disabled font from its Fonts folder, it gets listed as enabled again in Font Book.

Using third-party utilities. With third-party font utilities, such as Suitcase, you can also deactivate and uninstall fonts.

Installing and removing fonts: troubleshooting

In most cases, you won't have problems installing or uninstalling fonts. However, for the occasional problems that crop up, note the following:

Fonts that *should not* be removed. In general, you should not move or otherwise deactivate system-critical fonts (that is, those in /System/Library/ Fonts). In fact, you shouldn't even rename fonts in the /System/Library/Fonts folder or Mac OS X–installed fonts in /Library/Fonts. If you do, Mac OS X may not be able to locate the fonts when it needs them.

An example of what can happen if don't heed this advice: If you were to remove the TrueType HelveticaNeue.dfont installed by Mac OS X in /Library/Fonts (as some users do to substitute a PostScript version), iCal will crash on launch. Apple says you can avoid this by immediately substituting the replacement font after removing the Mac OS X–installed one. However, many users have not found this to be the case.

Fonts that sometimes *should* be removed. The Times RO font is another one that can cause unexpected grief. While the font is not required by Mac OS X, it can cause Safari to unexpectedly quit. The workaround is to disable or remove the font.

Font changes and open applications. When installing or removing fonts, some currently open applications will not recognize the change until you quit the application and relaunch it. Others, in contrast, can "auto-update." If in doubt, quit all open applications before making changes to fonts.

Resolving duplicates. From the Collection column, select All Fonts. If you see an alert or bullet symbol next to the name of a font family (or an individual font), it means you have more than one copy of the font installed. To remedy this problem, use the Resolve Duplicates command from Font Book's Edit menu. There are two ways to use this command:

- Select the Font family that contains duplicates (that is, the one with a bullet next to its name) and then choose Resolve Duplicates to disable all duplicates within that family. If, for example, you had two sets of Verdana fonts (Regular, Italic, Bold, and Bold Italic), one complete set would be disabled (because all of the variants are contained within the single Verdana font suitcase file).

- Click the disclosure triangle next to the Font family name to reveal the full list of fonts. Assuming there are just two copies of each font, one of each pair will have a bullet next to its name. Click any font of the set you wish to remain enabled, then select Resolve Duplicates; the other set will be disabled.

Why would you ever need to use this second method? Here's why: When you use the first method, Font Book automatically selects which duplicate font (or font set) to disable. In most cases, it makes the "wise" choice—that is, if one set resides in your Home directory and the other is located in the System directory, it disables the one in your Home directory. This makes sense because fonts in the System directory are often required for certain applications to function properly. Disabling these system fonts could thus cause more problems than those you would solve by disabling the duplicate.

If, however, Font Book incorrectly disables a System font—or if you intentionally want to disable a System font—you can manually select which font to disable via the second method.

Note: The flip side of all this is a troubleshooting tip: If, after using Remove Duplicates, you start having unexpected problems in applications, check to see that you did not inadvertently remove the "wrong" duplicate.

How can you tell where each font is located, so you can decide which one you want to disable? Hold the pointer over the font name in the list; a yellow note box will appear that provides the font's complete pathname and version number. Alternatively, from Font Book's File menu, you can select Show Font File (Command-R). This will take you to the location of the font in the Finder.

Whichever method you use, after you choose Remove Duplicates, the disabled fonts will be dimmed in the list and the word *Off* will appear next to their names.

Finally, to re-enable a font disabled via Resolve Duplicates, simply select the font and click the Enable button at the bottom of the column. Conversely, you can use the Disable button, rather than Resolve Duplicates, to disable an active duplicate font; it has the same effect. Remember, though: Disabling a font does not remove it; it just prevents it from appearing in Font menus.

Note: One time when I launched Font Book, it listed fonts in Fonts folders on a second mounted partition with Mac OS X installed (in addition to correctly listing all fonts on the startup partition). As a result, numerous duplicates were listed. Oddly, when I tried to replicate this later, the external volume fonts were no longer listed. I'm not sure what went on here, but a word of warning: If this happens to you, avoid using the Resolve Duplicates command to disable fonts—especially if you could wind up disabling fonts on your current startup volume as a result.

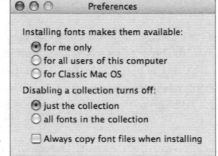

Figure 4.44

Font Book's Preferences.

Figure 4.45

Font Book: The bullet next to one of the Impact Regular fonts indicates that it's a duplicate. A similar conflict between two Monaco Regular fonts was addressed using the Resolve Duplicates command—which is why one of those fonts is listed as disabled (Off) here.

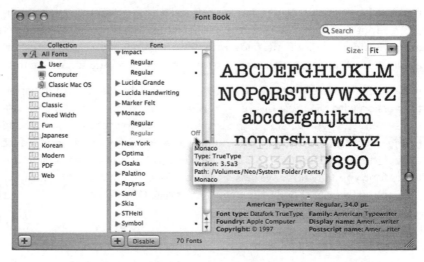

TAKE NOTE ▶ Problems with Duplicate Fonts in Fonts Folders

If you have two versions of the same font in different Fonts folders, how does Mac OS X decide which one to use? In general, it follows the typical Library hierarchy: first checking for and using the font found in the Fonts folder of your Home /Library directory, then (as needed) checking in the /Library directory, the Network Library (if one is present), the /System/Library, and finally Classic's Fonts folder.

Although it's usually OK to have two versions of the same font in different Fonts folders, *do not* place two versions of the same font in the same Mac OS X Fonts folder. This will almost certainly cause problems, especially within Carbon applications. The most likely symptom is that the application will crash when attempting to display the font or, sometimes, immediately upon launching. This has been known to affect Suitcase (a font-management utility), Microsoft Office applications, several Adobe applications, and more.

How or why would you wind up with two versions of the same font in a Fonts folder? It could happen by accident, such as if a Mac OS 9 font suitcase containing several different fonts were to be copied to a Mac OS X Fonts folder (most likely the Fonts folder in your Home directory, at ~/Library/Fonts). If one of the fonts in the suitcase had a name identical to one of the fonts already in the Fonts folder, you could trigger the problem.

Less often, problems occur if the same font is in two *different* Fonts folders—most commonly seen when there's a duplicate between a TrueType .dfont in the /System/Library/Fonts folder and a PostScript version of the same font that the user has installed in either /Library/Fonts or ~/Library/Fonts. (For example, the problem has been reported after installing an Adobe Helvetica PostScript font.) In this case, in addition to potential crashes, there may be oddities when displaying the font.

Problems occur here because an application must, of necessity, choose one or the other version when deciding how to display the font. If different versions of the same font appear in multiple Library/Fonts folders, the more "local" version generally takes priority. Thus, if you place a font in your Home directory's Fonts folder that is different from the same-named font in the /System/Library/Fonts folder, the version in your Home directory should be used in applications' Font menus. However, there is at least one situation where this does not occur.

In particular, if there are multiple font versions available, several Adobe applications will choose the version with the most glyphs (that is, visual displays of font characters)—which could be the system TrueType version in the System directory rather than the PostScript version in the Home directory. The result is that you may have fewer style variations available than you had expected by installing the PostScript font. That is, if the TrueType version does not include an italics font, you may not have italics available (because Mac OS X does not create an italics display on the fly from the plain-text version, as Mac OS 9 can do).

continues on next page

TAKE NOTE ▶ Problems with Duplicate Fonts in Fonts Folders *continued*

A solution to this problem, assuming you wanted access to the PostScript version of the font, would be to delete the corresponding TrueType font from the /System/Library/Fonts folder. In general, you can identify and disable duplicate fonts via Font Book's Resolve Duplicates command, as described in the main text.

This particular example aside, modifying or removing fonts from /System/Library/Fonts is generally considered a bad idea. Mac OS X system software reserves specifically assigned fonts in the /System/Library/Fonts folder for its own use, regardless of whether duplicates appear elsewhere. This applies, for example, to the fonts used for menu bar and dialog text. Thus, when using the Resolve Duplicates command, if one of the duplicate fonts is located in the /System/Library/Fonts folder, you generally should not choose that one to be disabled. If you do, crashes and display problems may occur.

The third-party utility Suitcase includes an option (in its preferences) to "Allow Suitcase to override system fonts." Be similarly cautious when using this option.

SEE: • **"Take Note: Multiple Folders of the Same Name in Multiple Library Folders," earlier in this chapter, for related information.**

Working with Fonts

This section covers issues regarding using fonts in applications.

Character Palette

In the Edit menu of all applications that ship with Panther (and other software that supports this feature) is an item called Special Characters. Certain older Carbonized applications, such as AppleWorks 6.x, will not have this command.

If you select this command, a window called Character Palette appears. The Unicode-based Character Palette window, which works in most Mac OS X applications (especially Cocoa ones), is used to locate and insert special nonalphanumeric characters into applications that accept text (word processors being an obvious example). The following provides an overview of how it works. The easiest way to follow along here is to open a TextEdit document and access the Character Palette.

1. The Character Palette contains two tabs: By Category and Favorites. If you select By Category, the left column will contain a scrollable list of character categories, such as Arrows, Currency Symbols, Crosses, and Greek. Make a selection, and you will see a graphic display of all characters in that category to the right.

2. Select the character you wish to insert and click the Insert button. With some luck, the character will appear wherever the insertion point is located in your document.

   The character will appear in whatever font is current at the insertion point. If the current font does not contain the character you selected, the character is shifted to one of the fonts that do contain the character.

3. To select a particular font for use with a character (especially helpful if the font in your document does not include the character), click the Font Variation disclosure triangle. From the Collections pop-up menu, select "Containing selected character." Scroll through the list of fonts and select the one you want. The Insert button will change to Insert with Font; click it, and the character will be inserted in the document in the selected font.

   Note: If a font supports glyph variants (such as a rotated version of the character), they will be listed at the bottom of the window after you've selected a character. You can further select the variant you want.

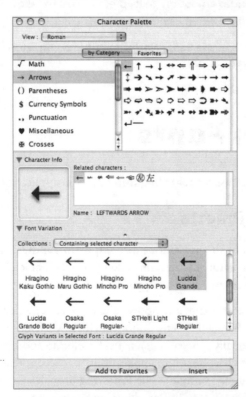

Figure 4.46

The Character Palette window.

4. For a list of related characters for a selected character, click the Character Info disclosure triangle. In some cases, when you click a related character, the top of the palette will shift. The tabs will now read Unicode Blocks, Unicode Tables, and Favorites. These provide even more character options; however, the details for these are well outside our troubleshooting focus.

Also in the Character Info section is an enlarged view of the selected character. You can drag this item to any text insertion point on your document as an alternative to using the Insert button.

5. Finally, if you click the Add to Favorites button, the selected item will be added to your personal Favorites list. You can view and edit the list by clicking the Favorites tab at the top of the window.

Font window

The Font window (sometimes called the Font panel) is where Mac OS X applications display font choices. In Mac OS X 10.1.x, only Cocoa applications could use this Font window. However, beginning with Mac OS X 10.2, Carbon applications are now able to access it as well (if they have been updated to do so).

Most Carbonized applications running in Mac OS X, including AppleWorks and Microsoft Office, continue to offer font choices in the same way they did in Mac OS 9—that is, via the same Font menus (which means there's no Mac OS X Font window).

TextEdit is an example of an application that does use the Font window. To access the Font window in TextEdit, from the Format menu choose Font > Show Fonts (Command-T). If you've already explored Font Book, you know that the Font window has a lot in common with the Font Book window. Font Book has columns for Collections and Fonts (with the typefaces for each font family accessible via disclosure triangles for the specific font). And the Font window has columns for Collections, Family, and Typefaces. Both windows have similar slider and text box options for adjusting font size. As you might suspect, changes in one window (such as enabling or disabling a font in Font Book) are reflected in the other window.

Note: Exactly what appears in the Font window depends on how you resize the window; some options get hidden as the window gets smaller. To see all of the options described here, enlarge the window as needed.

Here's a closer look at the Font window display:

Columns. The Font window contains four main columns:

- **Collections.** Use this column if you want to restrict your listed fonts to a subset of the total fonts installed. This method may be advisable when you're working on a project that will use only certain fonts and you don't want to be bothered with seeing the rest. Initially, you will see collections for All Fonts, Favorites, and Recently Used. There may also be additional preinstalled collections (such as Fun and Web). You can add or delete a collection by using the plus (+) and minus (–) buttons at the bottom of the window.

To add a font to a particular collection, select All Fonts. From the Family column, select the font you want to add and drag it to the name of the collection. To remove a font family from a collection, drag the family name to the Desktop, where it will vanish in a poof.

- **Family.** The fonts included in a selected collection appear in the Family column to the right of the Collections column. You can search for a specific family by entering text in the filter text box at the bottom of the window.

- **Typefaces.** If you select a font in the Family column, its available typefaces appear in the next column over. The typefaces that appear (italic, bold, and so on) will vary by font.

- **Size.** You can choose different sizes for a font via the Size column. If you choose the Edit Sizes command from the Action menu, you can modify which sizes appear in this column or switch to using a slider.

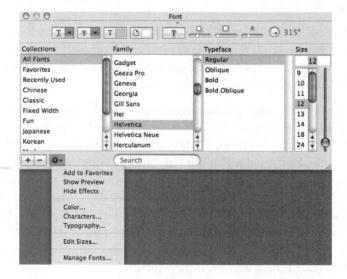

Figure 4.47

The Font window as accessed from TextEdit's Show Fonts command. The Action menu is shown at the bottom.

Dingbats, Symbols, and other graphic fonts. Whatever font you select in the Font window will be applied to the newly selected text in your TextEdit document. One exception: You cannot directly select the Symbol or Zapf Dingbats fonts (or other similar graphic fonts) from the Font window. If you try, the font selection reverts to another text font (such as Lucida Grande). To use the characters in these graphic fonts, select the Character Palette and enter them directly.

Why this difficulty in using graphic fonts? The answer lies in Mac OS X's use of Unicode in applications like TextEdit (see "Technically Speaking: ATSUI and Unicode," earlier in this chapter). More specifically, this is what Apple had to say on the matter: "In Mac OS 9, the Symbol and Zapf Dingbats fonts acted like other fonts, as if they worked with the usual alphabetic and numeric characters, when in fact they contained symbol characters. In a Unicode system, the special characters in the Symbol and Zapf Dingbats fonts have their own unique Unicode character codes. Typing a character like 'A' does not work when these fonts are used with Unicode, as the fonts don't contain an 'A' character."

Similarly, if you're using the .dfont version of these fonts (for example, /System/Library/Fonts/ZapfDingbats.dfont), the text document will likely not display these Unicode-based fonts correctly when viewed from Mac OS 9. To avoid this, use the PostScript version of these fonts instead of the .dfont version. Doing this may require a utility, such as Suitcase, that lets you select which version of a font to use.

Another similar problem may occur when importing a Word document from a Windows PC to the Mac. Certain Unicode symbols (such as fractions) that appear correctly on the PC will not appear in Word X for the Mac (because Word X is not yet Unicode-savvy). To see these characters correctly, you would need to open the document in TextEdit.

Font window's Action menu

At the bottom of the Font window is a pop-up menu with the same icon as the Action menu in Finder windows. The following provides an overview of the most troubleshooting-relevant items available from this menu:

- **Add to Favorites** adds the selected font to the Favorites collection.
- **Show Preview** opens a section at the top of the Font window where a sample of text in the selected font appears.
- **Show Effects** adds an Effects toolbar above the main part of the Font window. From here, you can select various text attributes, such as underline, strike-through, and color. To see what each item does, pause the pointer briefly over the item; a yellow tool tip should appear. For example, the controls at the end of the row are all for shadow effects (shadow opacity, shadow blur, and so on).
- **Color** opens a palette from which you get to choose a color for the text you have selected. The color palette accessible from here is the same one you get if you select Color in the Show Effects toolbar.
- **Characters** opens the same Character Palette accessible via the Special Characters command in the Edit menu of the application.
- **Typography** offers advanced typography options such as the ability to add spaces before or after characters via sliders.
- **Edit Sizes** allows you to select whether you want the Font window to show a fixed list of selectable font sizes, an adjustable slider that changes font sizes automatically as you move it up and down, or both.
- **Manage Fonts** opens Font Book.

Input menu

The Character Palette can be accessed more generally (in any application, even ones whose Edit menus do not include the Special Characters command) via an optional Input menu. To enable it, follow the steps outlined below:

1. Launch System Preferences and select the International pane. Click the Input Menu tab.

2. From the list that appears, enable the Character Palette item (it should be the top item) by clicking its On check box.

3. Optionally, you can also enable the Keyboard Viewer item a few items down.

   Note: The U.S. item should be enabled by default. Ignore this and the other items in the list for now; I'll return to them later in this chapter.

4. Click the "Show Input menu in menu bar" check box and close the pane.

The menu bar should now include a menu (on the right side) with a U.S. flag icon: This is the Input menu. If you select it, you will be presented with the following two choices (among others):

Show Character Palette. To open the same Character Palette already covered, select Show Character Palette from the Input menu.

Note: Although the Palette will work in applications (such as AppleWorks 6 or Microsoft Word) that do not offer full Unicode support, it will not work as well as it does in applications like TextEdit. When using a program such as AppleWorks, after clicking the Insert button in the Palette, an incorrect (non-Unicode) character may appear in the document. In some cases, you can fix this by selecting the character in the document, going to the application's Font menu, and selecting the font that contains the character (for example, Symbol or Zapf Dingbats). However, it's probably easier to select the font from the application's Fonts menu and bypass the Character Palette altogether. Overall, you should reserve use of the Palette for applications that support Unicode.

Show Keyboard Viewer. If you select this option, a small window opens containing a keyboard layout. The characters on the keys shift depending on what font you select from the pop-up menu and whether you're holding down modifier keys (such as Option). If you have a text document open, whichever character keys you press will also appear in the document. In case you were wondering, yes, this feature replaces the former Key Caps utility from Jaguar (and which dates back to Mac OS 9). The Key Caps feature does not exist in Panther.

Other inputs. Some third-party software may work via the Input menu. Spell Catcher, for example, is turned on or off from this menu. When you select Spell Catcher, an additional Spell Catcher menu appears in the menu bar.

This menu is also where you select to display keyboard layouts for different languages.

SEE: • " International language support: basics," later in this chapter, for information on keyboard layouts.

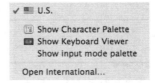

Figure 4.48

The International System Preferences pane's Input Menu screen (Left) and the menu that appears in the menu bar after you enable items from the list (right).

Figure 4.49

The Keyboard Viewer.

TAKE NOTE ▶ TextEdit: Format Options Beyond Show Fonts

Rich Text vs. Plain Text. The default format for files saved in TextEdit is Rich Text Format (RTF). Files saved in this format have inert extension. Rich Text Format allows you to include the specialized font, justification, stylized text, and other options that TextEdit is capable of producing. You can also open RTF files in applications such as Microsoft Word.

continues on next page

TAKE NOTE ▶ TextEdit: Format Options Beyond Show Fonts *continued*

Some applications (a number of email programs, for example) may not be able to understand Rich Text Format. In such cases, you may need to save the file in plain text format (which has the file extension .txt). To do so, from the Format menu choose Make Plain Text and then save the file. Once you've done this, virtually any application should be able to read the file.

You can make the text revert back to Rich Text Format by using the Make Rich Text command (which you access from the Format menu when viewing plain text files). Keep in mind, however, that any RTF formatting you applied will not return.

.rtfd. If you paste graphics into an .rtf document and then try to save it, you will likely get an alert box stating, "You cannot save this document with the extension 'rtf' at the end of the name. The required extension is 'rtfd.'"

An .rtfd file is actually a package that combines text and graphics (as TIFF images) data as separate elements. Should you decide to remove the .rtfd extension from the file's name in the Finder (such as via the Name & Extension section of the Get Info window), the file will revert to a folder. Adding back the .rtfd extension should get it to appear as a document file again.

Note: You can place more than graphics into an .rtfd document. Try dragging an application icon from the Finder to a TextEdit document; you'll see that this actually creates a copy of the application inside the .rtfd package. In the document itself, a small icon of the application appears. You can similarly copy QuickTime movies and sound files to a TextEdit document, and then play them from within the document. Try it!

Read-only. TextEdit's Format menu also includes an option to save a file as read only, via the Prevent Editing command. You may want to employ this option when creating the read-me files that accompany applications. Conversely, if you open a read-only file, the command in the Format menu will change to Allow Editing.

Saving SimpleText documents. You can use TextEdit to open and edit documents created in Mac OS 9's SimpleText application. However, when you select to save a modified SimpleText document, you will get an error message that states, "Please supply a new name. TextEdit does not save SimpleText format; document will be saved as rich text (RTF) instead, with a new name." If you click OK, you will be given the chance to save the document with a new name.

Wrap. The Format menu has a command that toggles between Wrap to Window and Wrap to Page. If text continues beyond the right border of a window (so that you cannot read it), choosing Wrap to Window will readjust the text so that you can read it all.

Font Styles. TextEdit supports styles—a broader use of the term *style* than merely changing the look of text to italics or bold. A style here refers to a full collection of type characteristics (font type, font size, font style, alignment, spacing, and so on). If you want to format text in a style you've used before in your document, simply go to text to which the style has been applied, and from the Font submenu select Copy Style. Now select the text you want to modify and select Paste Style from the same menu.

continues on next page

TAKE NOTE ▶ TextEdit: Format Options Beyond Show Fonts *continued*

Even better, the TextEdit toolbar at the top of each document now includes a Styles pop-up menu. Every time you make a change to a style element in your document, TextEdit remembers it. To see this, from the Styles menu select Other. A window appears where you can rotate through every style change in your document and then apply the one you want to use to selected text. If you expect to use this Style again, you can save it as a Favorite.

Working with Word documents. Finally, new in Panther, you can directly open and save Microsoft Word documents in TextEdit. If you've created a new TextEdit document, you can also select Word Format from the File Format pop-up menu in the Save As dialog, and save the document as a Word document. The conversion won't always be perfect (since Word supports features not found in TextEdit), but it's quite good.

Spelling. TextEdit supports Mac OS X's spelling-checker service. You can access it via the Spelling command in the Edit menu. If you Control-click a misspelled word, it will bring up a contextual menu with suggested alternatives.

SEE: • **"Technically Speaking: Type/Creator vs. Filename Extensions," earlier in this chapter, for more on SimpleText and TextEdit documents.**

• **"TextEdit can't save files in SimpleText format," in Chapter 6, for related information.**

Figure 4.50

The Save Warning message that appears when you attempt to save an RTF file after pasting a graphic into it.

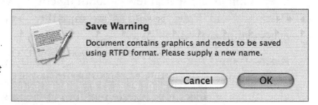

Figure 4.51

Inside the package of the .rtfd file (with graphic) that generated the warning in Figure 4.50.

> **TAKE NOTE ▶ Font Styles and Copy/Paste**
>
> In most Mac OS 9 (and Carbonized Mac OS X) text applications, a Style menu allows you to change the style of text from plain to italics to bold and so on. Although the situation gets a bit more complicated with PostScript fonts, these menu options generally allow you to change a font's style even if the font file itself has only the regular (plain) variant. In essence, the application uses built-in OS routines to create a good estimate of the style variation. Mac OS X Cocoa applications such as TextEdit, however, only support styles that exist in the font file itself. Thus, if a font file contains only regular and bold styles, only those styles will appear in TextEdit; you can't display that font in italics. As a result, even if you were to paste text of that font that had been italicized in another application, the italics would be lost when you pasted the text into TextEdit.
>
> Finally, if you add a version of a font to the Fonts folder in your Home directory, it will generally take precedence over versions of the same font in other Fonts folders (as covered more in "Take Note: Problems with Duplicate Fonts in Fonts Folders," earlier in this chapter). For applications such as TextEdit, adding a duplicate font could thus alter the available Style options.

Font smoothing

Even without any special font-smoothing effects, Mac OS X is able to display PostScript and TrueType fonts quite smoothly—at least as smoothly as text displayed in Mac OS 9.

Anti-aliased text. Mac OS X, via its Quartz layer, adds a font-smoothing option that was not built into Mac OS 9 (though special utilities could provide it): *anti-aliasing*. This feature modifies font edges to eliminate the inevitable "jagginess" of their display (which is due to the fact that an edge—especially an oblique edge—is a string of square pixels rather than a true line). Anti-aliasing fills in the gaps left by the pixels with various shades of gray pixels. The human eye views this display as a smooth line (unless the magnification level gets so high that you start seeing the gray shades).

Although anti-aliased text generally looks superior to non-anti-aliased text (which is why the technology exists!), it may not work as well for smaller fonts, which can end up looking more blurry than smooth (making them even harder to read).

For this reason, Mac OS X lets you turn off anti-aliasing for small font sizes. To do so, follow these steps:

1. Launch System Preferences and open the Appearance pane.

2. From the "Turn off text smoothing for font sizes {#} and smaller" option, choose your preferred font size limit from the pop-up menu that appears in the # location. Your choices are point sizes 4, 6, 8, 9, 10, and 12.

Thus, if small fonts are too blurry, choose a higher number to turn off smoothing for more font sizes. Conversely, if large fonts are too jagged, choose a lower number.

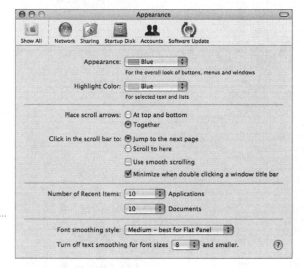

Figure 4.52

The Appearance System Preferences pane.

The Appearance pane does not allow you to disable font smoothing for sizes larger than 12 points. The third-party utility TinkerTool, however, does (that is, if you're using Mac OS X 10.1 or 10.2; it does not include this feature when running Mac OS X 10.3). Keep in mind, that TinkerTool doesn't implement any features of its own; instead, it simply unlocks features that Apple built into the Mac OS X software but did not make easily accessible (so-called hidden features). Thus, it's at the mercy of whatever changes Apple makes when it updates Mac OS X.

The Appearance pane also includes an option called "Font smoothing style." Typically, you should select Standard for CRT monitors and Medium for flat-panel displays. All but the Standard option use a technique called *subpixel rendering,* which employs colored pixels, rather than shades of gray, to achieve the smoothing effect. However, this technique only works well with flat-panel displays.

Carbon applications and Silk. In general, in Mac OS X 10.1.5 and later, font smoothing works in Carbon applications as well as Cocoa ones—without the need for third-party software. However, the application needs to be updated to hook into this feature. A work-around is to use a third-party program called Silk, which enables text smoothing for all Carbon applications.

However, Carbon support for text smoothing may cause problems (such as text that disappears) in some applications. Microsoft software, such as Internet Explorer and Office applications, appears to be especially prone to text-smoothing problems. In such cases, turning off the smoothing feature from within the application should solve the problem. In Internet Explorer, you would disable the "Enable Quartz text smoothing" option in the Interface Extras pane of Internet Explorer's Preferences window. Also disable the Silk utility, if you're using it.

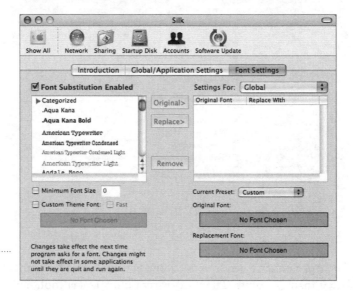

Figure 4.53

The Silk System Preferences pane.

Modifying default fonts

You can use TinkerTool to change the default font settings (such as name and size) that Mac OS X uses for its system font and applications. To do so, click the Fonts button in TinkerTool's toolbar and make changes to the list of fonts, as desired. You cannot access these modifications from any Mac OS X–supplied System Preferences pane. Not all applications will use these changes, however, and the changes will not affect the menu-bar font.

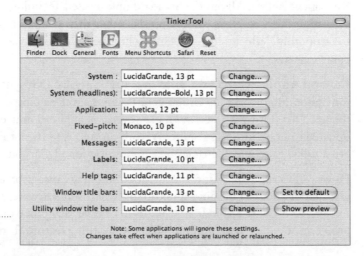

Figure 4.54

TinkerTool's Fonts dialog.

International language support: basics

Mac OS X lets you change the language used in its menus and dialogs. You can also use these international language characters in text you create in applications. For this book, I'm sticking primarily to troubleshooting in English (there's more than enough to cover!); however, it still pays to be aware of some basics of multiple-language support.

International System Preferences pane. To get your Mac to display its menus, dialogs, and most other standard elements in a language other than English, your first stop is the International System Preferences pane. Here's what to do:

- From the Languages screen, select the order of the languages listed by sliding them to their desired locations. Once you've done this and logged out and back in, a given application will display its menus and text in the first language in the list (if it's available and enabled for the application). If the application does not support the first language in the list (or that language has been disabled, as described below), it will display in the next language on the list. And so on.

  If a language you want is not listed, click the Edit button to enable it. If it is not listed here (or does not appear after being enabled), it probably means support for that language was not installed with Mac OS X (that is, you probably chose not to install the support via a Custom install) or you subsequently deleted the files (there are various third-party utilities that can do this).

- Click the Customize Sorting button. This only affects non-Unicode applications, but it's worth checking out. In essence, for a set of languages that share the same alphabet (for example, Spanish, French, Italian, and English), you can select which language behavior you want. This causes text (and related characteristics) to be sorted according to the specifics of the selected behavior.

- Having the language displayed correctly is all well and good. But what if you want to type in that language? Different languages are often matched with keyboards specific to that language. To type text in a given language, you may thus need to select a keyboard layout or input method specific to that language—especially important for Asian and Middle Eastern languages.

  To set up for this, go to the Input Menu tab and enable the keyboard layouts for all languages you may use. To enable a selection, click the check box next to its name. You can then switch among any of your selected languages via the Input menu in the menu bar—or by using Command-Option-Space (as enabled via the Options button in the Input Menu screen of the System Preferences pane). As you switch, the flag icon in the menu bar shifts to that of the selected country and the keyboard layout changes to match that of the keyboard for that country.

  Keyboards listed as Unicode in the Script column are available only in Unicode-compatible applications, such as Mail, TextEdit, and the Finder.

When you're typing within an application, the availability of these keyboards in the Input menu indicates whether that application works with Unicode.

Note: From the options dialog (which you access from the Options button in the Input Menu screen), you can select "Try to match keyboard with text." With this enabled, the Mac attempts to automatically shift to the correct layout for selected text.

SEE: • **"Input menu," earlier in this chapter, for more on setting up and using this menu.**

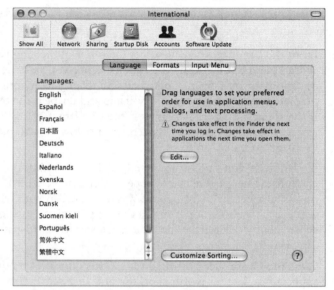

Figure 4.55

The Language tab of the International System Preferences pane.

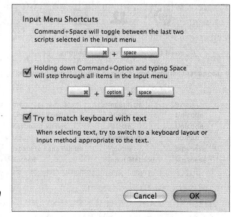

Figure 4.56

The options dialog that appears after clicking the Options button in the Input Menu tab of the International System Preferences pane.

Having done all of this, you still won't see use of languages other than English unless the specific applications you use support additional languages. Here are the details:

Multiple-language support files. Support for multiple languages in the OS itself (such as the Finder) or in any application that runs in Mac OS X is determined by whether the files needed for any additional language(s) are included with the application.

Using iTunes as an example (since it includes excellent multiple-language support), we're going to explore how all of this works:

1.   In the Finder, select the iTunes icon.
2.   Control-click the icon and from the contextual menu that appears, choose Show Package Contents.
3.   In the window that appears, open the Contents folder and then the Resources folder within the Contents folder.

Here, you'll find numerous folders that end with the extension .lproj (such as English.lproj and French.lproj). Each of these folders represents the required support for iTunes to run in the named language.

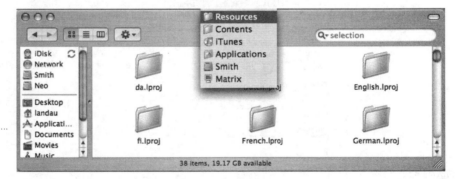

Figure 4.57

Some of the .lproj folders in iTunes' Resources folder.

Disabling or removing language support files. The language support files in iTunes take up most of the iTunes application (around 20 MB). Thus, eliminating these files (assuming you don't need additional languages in iTunes) can save a considerable amount of space.

To do this, you can simply remove the undesired .lproj folders from the iTunes package and drag them to the Trash (or anywhere else, should you want to save them). Or, if you don't care about space and want to save the files within iTunes but not have them accessible for display, drag them to the Resources Disabled folder in the Contents folder.

Alternatively, if you don't want to delve into package contents, you can do the same thing via iTunes' Get Info window. Follow these steps:

1. In the Finder select the iTunes icon.

2. Press Command-I to bring up its Get Info window.

3. From the pop-up menu choose Languages.

4. To *disable* a language, simply uncheck the appropriate check box; this action moves the language into the Resources Disabled folder.

   Or

   To delete the language resource (which is what you need to do to reduce the size of iTunes), select a language and click the Remove button. You cannot, however, remove a language that has been disabled. To remove a disabled language, you must first re-enable it. If the Remove button is still dimmed when you select an enabled language, Force Quit the Finder and try again.

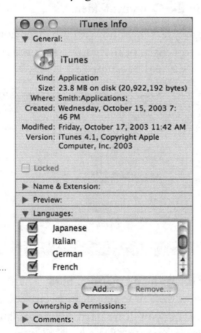

Figure 4.58

The Languages section of the Get Info window for iTunes.

Choosing to remove a language places its .lprog folder in the Trash. Until you actually empty the Trash, you could drag the language folder from the Trash and save it elsewhere. In this way, you could use the Add button to return it to the list later, should you want to. Note: You will have to close the Get Info window and reopen it before it will show that you have added a language.

Finally, you can use the third-party utility, Delocalizer, to remove unwanted language files.

Re-adding language support files. If you remove language support files (or if you never installed them when you initially installed Mac OS X), a time may come when you want to add some or all of the support files back. The easiest way to do so is to use the Mac OS X Install CDs for Panther. On the second CD, in the Packages folder, is a file called Languages.mpkg. Double-click this to launch it. When you get to the screen that includes a Customize button, click it. From here, select just the languages you want and click to install.

International language support: troubleshooting

The following describes a couple of problems (and their solutions) that can arise when using multiple languages in Mac OS X.

Additional software needed. Some languages may require additional software, such as a Mac OS 9 language kit or font. Apple writes: "For example, Mac OS X includes script bundles for Cyrillic and Central European languages. However, such a script bundle does not activate unless at least one font for that script is present. Installing a font that is compatible with the script bundle will activate it. Keyboard layouts associated with the activated bundle then appear in the International Preferences panel."

Localized OS needed. Some languages work only if you have a region-specific, or *localized,* version of the Mac OS installed. Thus, you may not be able to use these languages with a typical North American English Mac OS X system; you may instead need to install the version of Mac OS X specific to the language in question. Apple now releases each version of Mac OS X in a variety of localized versions. If you selected not to install provided language support when you originally installed Mac OS X, you can reinstall this support by selecting the desired .pkg file(s) from the Optional Installs folder on the Mac OS X Install Discs.

Font utilities

For many users, Panther's Font Book (covered earlier in the chapter) is the only font utility they'll ever need or use. However, a variety of other font-related utilities are available for tasks that go beyond Font Book capabilities. The following is a small selection of what you can find:

Extensis's **Suitcase,** which I've mentioned throughout this chapter, allows you to view, activate, and deactivate individual fonts separately for Cocoa, Carbon, and Classic applications. This utility can be especially useful when two fonts conflict or when a font causes a problem with a specific application. In such cases, you can use Suitcase to deactivate the problem font. There's a great deal of overlap between the features in utilities like Suitcase and those found in Font Book (with Suitcase offering more features). In general, you should use one or the other, but not both.

Insider Software's **FontAgent Pro** is another font-management utility similar in function to Suitcase.

FontDoctor (included with Suitcase) finds and repairs an assortment of font problems, including damaged and corrupted fonts, missing fonts, duplicate fonts, and font ID conflicts.

Pixit's **FontExampler** displays all of your installed fonts in WYSIWYG mode in a single window. You can also see how any selected font looks at different sizes.

Stone Design's **FontSight** adds a font menu to Cocoa applications such as TextEdit. This eliminates the need to access the Font panel just to change the font of selected text (which I find to be a much less convenient method than using a font menu).

Marcel Bresnik's **TinkerTool** allows you to change the default fonts used in many Mac OS X locations, such as window title bars (as described in "Modifying default fonts," earlier in this chapter).

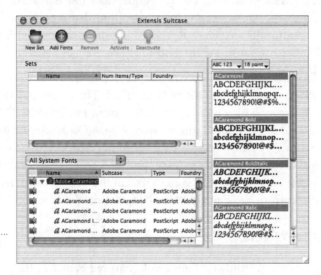

Figure 4.59

A view of Extensis's Suitcase.

Figure 4.60

The LastResort .dfont in the /System/Library/ Fonts folder.

Fonts: troubleshooting tips and hints

The following represents an assortment of troubleshooting tips and fixes for fonts:

Subfolders in Fonts folders work. In Mac OS X 10.2 and later, the OS can find fonts even if they're placed within a subfolder of a Fonts folder (such as /Library/Fonts).

Corrupt fonts. Mac OS X itself should not corrupt any fonts (since it doesn't modify them); however, fonts originally used in Mac OS 9 or modified by font utilities can become corrupted. Such fonts can cause an application to crash. Font utilities, as described above, can help isolate, and possibly repair, corrupt fonts. Otherwise, you will need to use trial and error to locate the problem font and remove it.

Corrupt font cache files. In Mac OS X 10.1.5 through 10.2.x, the Mac OS X System Font cache file can become corrupt, causing fonts to have a jagged rather than smooth appearance (among other font-related problems that may occur). A potential solution, in Jaguar, is to delete the font cache (Fcache) file, called com.FcacheSystemDomain, located in the /System/Library/Caches folder. (Panther does not use this file.)

If deleting the file in Jaguar doesn't work (or if you're using Panther), try deleting other font-related cache files in your Library folders, such as fontTablesAnnex files in /System/Library/Caches and (in Panther) the com.Apple.ATS folder in /Library/Caches. In particular, check in the com.Apple.ATS folder for subfolders that have your user ID (UID) number in their name. If you're the only or first user to have an account on the system, for example, your UID will be 501. Inside these folders are your font cache files. Deleting these files may, for example, fix a problem where Suitcase is not activating fonts correctly.

Applications, such as those from Adobe and Microsoft, may maintain their own font caches. For problems in these applications, try deleting their caches. For example, for Microsoft applications, you could delete the Office Font Cache (10) file in the Microsoft folder of your Home Library's Preferences folder.

File Name Encoding Repair utility. Mac OS X's Finder uses Unicode character sets to display filenames. Files or folders that were named when running Mac OS 9, however, may not display correctly when running from Mac OS X. This can happen if Mac OS 9 converts a name to the Unicode format incorrectly. It is only really likely to occur when dealing with multiple languages (such as a Japanese filename on an English-language system).

This problem should not occur in Mac OS X 10.3 or later; however, for earlier versions of the Mac OS, Apple's File Name Encoding Repair utility (available free from Apple's Web site) will likely be able to fix the display problem. Just drag the problem file or folder to the Repair utility icon. From the window that appears, choose the desired encoding from the "Correct text encoding" pop-up menu. If you're not sure which languages correspond to a particular encoding, continue to hold down the mouse button while the pointer is over the encoding name. A tip window will eventually appear, telling you which languages are supported by that encoding. After selecting the encoding, click Repair. See the following Apple Knowledge Base document for more details: http://docs.info.apple.com/article.html?artnum=86182.

LastResort.dfont. There is a font in /System/Library/Fonts called LastResort.dfont; however, it's not listed in any application's Fonts menus. This is because it's only used if a font is having problems displaying a particular Unicode character. The appropriate gylph from LastResort is then used instead. With luck, the clue from LastResort will allow you to determine what font you need in order to get the glyph to display as intended.

Word font error and preferences files. If you select a font in Microsoft Word and a different font is actually selected, quit Word and relaunch it. If this does not fix the error, delete the Office Font Cache (10) file—as well as the Word Font Substitutes and Word Settings (10) files—in ~/Library/Preferences/ Microsoft. Launch Word again and the problem should be fixed—at least temporarily.

More generally, to check for a potential problem with preferences and cache files, log in as another user. If the problem vanishes, you probably have a corrupted preferences or cache file.

SEE: • "Logging in as another user," in Chapter 5, for more details.

5

Crash Prevention and Recovery

Of all the things that can go wrong with a computer, the one users typically want to avoid most is a crash. Actually, the words *crash* and its first cousin *freeze* are generic terms that cover a wide range of symptoms and causes, some far more serious than others.

Relatively low on the seriousness scale is an application crash or freeze. In the simplest case, the application quits itself (often referred to as an *unexpected quit*). You may have trouble relaunching the application at this point, but your computer will likely run just fine otherwise. A bit more frustrating is the hang, or freeze. In this case, the application remains open and visible, but nothing works. In some cases, until you thaw things out, other programs may also be inaccessible.

More serious is a crash or freeze that's not limited to a single program but rather brings almost everything to a halt, forcing you to restart your Mac. For obvious reasons, the most serious of these situations is the crash that occurs during startup, thus preventing you from even beginning to use your Mac.

In this chapter, I'll cover all of these variations of crashes and freezes. I'll tell you how best to recover from them and offer some tips on how to prevent them.

One bit of good news: The more serious crashes, the ones that bring down your entire system, occur much less often in Mac OS X than they did in Classic Mac OS versions (Mac OS 9 and earlier). To learn why, see "Protected Memory," in Chapter 4.

In This Chapter

Uh-Oh!

What causes crashes and freezes?

Most crashes and freezes can be attributed to one of three things:

Software bug. Errors in programming code often cause application crashes. Sometimes, these errors are referred to as "pure" bugs—that is, they occur independently of other software or hardware. For example, an error in the code of a word-processing application that causes the program to crash every time you try to save a file with italicized text—regardless of what other software you're running—is a pure bug. However, bugs can also be caused by the way particular programs interact with one another. An application may crash on launch—but only if another particular program is open as well. The problem then is determining which program is the culprit. Ideally, at least one of the developers will agree to fix the code in order to resolve the conflict.

Corrupt file. Occasionally, a file on your drive will become modified to either include data from another file or lose vital data of its own. Say you saved a word-processing document just before a power failure occurred, resulting in a partial save of the file: Next time you open the file, you're likely to get a crash. Alternatively, in a critical OS file that gets updated periodically (such as one in the System folder), an error can occur when it's being written to disk, causing the file to stop working—another situation that can lead to a crash (which in this case may prevent you from starting your Mac). Corrupt preferences files are also common sources of system crashes. These files are usually updated quite frequently, increasing the odds of a copy error.

Hardware conflict. A problem with a hardware component, either external or internal, can also lead to a crash. A circuit can burn out on the logic board, or your memory may have been defective from the day it shipped. Conversely, your hardware might not be compatible with your particular Mac. For example, RAM comes in many speeds and sizes, but most Mac models work only with specific types. Although two RAM modules may look identical (and may even both fit in your Mac), one could be the wrong type—and that would lead to a startup crash.

Finally, hardware components that *should* work with your Mac may not, due to software problems. In particular, certain devices (such as hard drives, printers, scanners, and other peripherals) require that driver software be present on your startup drive in order to work. Some devices use drivers built into Mac OS X, while others require that you install driver software provided by the manufacturer. Bugs in the driver software can result in crashes, just as any other software bugs can. Hardware devices can also include firmware. Representing a sort of middle ground between software and hardware, firmware is software code that resides in a component of the hardware itself. Typically, you can upgrade firmware by running a special firmware-update program. Often, as new Macs and OS updates come out, hardware devices will require these firmware updates to remain compatible.

General strategies for fixing crashes

Most crashes are limited to specific applications—meaning you can continue to use your Mac despite the crash. You'll often even be able to relaunch the offending application. If the crash doesn't occur the next time you attempt the procedure (you may need to restart your Mac to stop the crash from recurring), you may well decide to ignore it—and hope that it's a one-time-only thing or that it happens so infrequently that it's not a problem. Otherwise, your goal will be to locate the cause of the crash and fix it. In general, the exact fix will depend on the type of crash.

For crashes caused by corrupt files, the solution may be as simple as deleting the file. If the problem is a preferences file, for example, you can simply delete the file and a new version is created automatically the next time the relevant application is launched. The default file should be free of whatever corruption caused the crash. You'll need to reinstate any changes you made to the preferences file, but at least the crash won't occur again.

Similarly, if you have a corrupt document (especially if you have a backup of the file), you can simply delete the corrupt version and start again with your backup. You can even delete and replace corrupt OS files, assuming you know where and how to get the replacements (for more on this, see Chapter 3). In some cases, you'll need a disk-repair utility, such as Apple's Disk Utility or Alsoft Software's DiskWarrior. And reinstalling the OS software can also provide a cure. (In the worst-case scenario, you may need to erase your drive before reinstalling the system software.)

For buggy software, you simply have to hope that the company provides a bug fix—and in the meantime find a work-around to prevent the crash.

Because so many problems occur as a result of something going wrong at startup (including a startup crash itself), we're going to take a look at the startup sequence of events before I go into detail about crash types and their solutions.

The Startup Sequence of Events

After you turn on your Mac, you must typically wait a few minutes before you can start using it: This is because your Mac is performing its "startup sequence." For you, this may simply represent an opportunity for a coffee break; for your Mac, however, it's a critical period during which a multitude of events occur that determine the success or failure of everything that follows.

An audiovisual overview of the startup sequence

When you turn on your Mac, you should hear the startup chime—typically even before your display screen lights up. Shortly thereafter, a gray screen appears with a gray Apple logo in the center (yes, the old Happy Mac icon has been retired!). At this point, you'll see a sundial cursor (which also looks like wheel spokes endlessly turning). Eventually, this screen is replaced by a blue screen with the Mac OS X logo in the center. During this time, various text messages will appear in the logo area indicating that several startup processes are loading. Next to appear will be either the Login window or (if you selected automatic login) the Finder's Desktop. If you get the Login window, you enter your name and password and then click to log in—at which point you'll be taken to the Finder's Desktop. You must now wait for items that load at login. Once this has occurred, the startup sequence is complete.

If a sequence other than the one described above occurs, you most likely have a problem. The following describes what happens behind the scenes during the startup sequence, what can go wrong, and what you can do to fix problems when they occur.

Boot ROM and Open Firmware

Boot ROM is software code stored within the circuitry of the Mac's logic board. Because the data does not reside on a hard drive, it can run even before a startup hard drive has been selected. Thus, this code is just about the first thing that gets checked when you turn on your Mac. This software is also independent of what OS version you're using. Thus, it gets checked whether you're booting Mac OS 9 or Mac OS X.

Boot ROM performs two main checks:

Power-on self-test (POST). This test checks the Mac's hardware and RAM (random-access memory). It resides in the Mac's ROM (read-only memory) and runs at startup (though only from a currently shut-down Mac; it won't run if you select the Restart command from a running Mac). If POST detects a problem, the startup sequence will likely halt almost instantly. In addition, you'll hear one of the following sounds:

- **One beep.** Indicates that no RAM is installed or detected.
- **Two beeps.** Indicates that an incompatible RAM type is installed.
- **Three beeps.** Indicates that no RAM banks passed memory testing.
- **Four beeps.** Indicates there's a bad checksum for the remainder of the Boot ROM. (*Checksum* refers to a method of determining whether data is corrupted.)
- **Five beeps.** This means there's a bad checksum for the ROM boot block.

Three beeps indicates a problem with RAM. If you've installed additional RAM on your Mac, it's time to check whether it's defective or otherwise incompatible with your system. The simplest way to do so is to remove the RAM and see whether the POST warning goes away. If so, contact your RAM vendor about getting a replacement.

Apple Hardware Test software. If the problem isn't with RAM and your Mac shipped with Hardware Test software, now's the time to use it. If you can't start up from the Hardware Test CD/DVD, you almost certainly have a hardware problem—which means it's probably time to take your Mac in for repair.

TECHNICALLY SPEAKING ▶ **The Apple Hardware Test Software**

Each Mac type (iBook, iMac, PowerBook, and so on) uses its own version of Hardware Test software—that is, don't try to use a Hardware Test disc with a Mac other than the model for which it was intended!

To start up from a Hardware Test CD, turn on your Mac, insert the CD, and hold down the C key.

If your Mac came with a single DVD, the Hardware Test software should be included on it. To start up from the Hardware Test component, restart while pressing down the Option key. From the list of bootable volumes that appears, select Hardware Test.

After your Mac has booted from the CD/DVD, Hardware Test will automatically load. Follow the instructions for the Quick and Extended tests, which examine components like AirPort, Mass Storage, and Memory. You can also use this software to diagnose hardware problems beyond startup ones, such as failures of USB and/or FireWire ports.

If the software detects an error, it displays an error code (for example, *ata1/6/3 HD:2,1*). You can then search Apple's Knowledge Base (http://kbase.info.apple.com) for documents that mention the error. You may find one that identifies the error and tells you how to fix it. If your search comes up empty, contact Apple directly.

Apple's Knowledge Base also includes information regarding bugs in Hardware Test. For example, one article notes that Hardware Test may state that the Bluetooth module is not present when it actually is. The solution in this case is to check for Bluetooth with System Profiler.

Other symptoms of hardware failure include the following:

- If you don't hear the hard drive spinning, but everything else appears normal, your hard drive may be damaged. In this case, you should still be able to start from a CD, but you will likely need to replace the hard drive.
- If you don't hear any noise (not even the fan) and the Mac is plugged in and has power, the power supply has probably failed. You will need to replace it.

None of this information is specific to Mac OS X, so I'm not going to delve into the topic further here; however, for more detailed help when it comes to hardware failure, check out my book *Sad Macs,* or go online to sites such as MacFixIt (www.macfixit.com).

Open Firmware. In essence, Open Firmware selects the operating system you use. It also makes first contact with (or *initializes*) hardware beyond the Mac itself, such as external drives. You access Open Firmware directly by pressing Command-Option-O-F immediately at startup. From its simple command-line interface, you can type Open Firmware commands to carry out actions beyond what Open Firmware does by default at startup. You'll normally have little need for this; however, you may occasionally want to run a specific Open Firmware command to solve a troubleshooting matter. Due to a bug, your Mac may briefly display the Open Firmware screen at startup, even if you *do not* press Command-Option-O-F. Even more rarely, startup may halt at the Open Firmware screen.

SEE: • "Take Note: Firmware Updates," "Technically Speaking: Open Firmware Commands," and "Technically Speaking: Open Firmware Password," below, for details on troubleshooting Open Firmware.

TAKE NOTE ▶ Firmware Updates

Apple periodically releases software called *firmware updates.* These updates are different for each Mac model. That is, an iMac firmware update is useless on a PowerBook. You can download the latest firmware updater for your particular Mac from Apple's Web site (www.info.apple.com/support/downloads.html). Once you have located and downloaded the updater, run it.

When you successfully run an update utility, it updates the Open Firmware software. Exact instructions on how to install these firmware updates vary from computer model to model but are included with each update. Don't worry if you're unsure whether you need a given update: If you already have the same or a newer version installed, the utility will alert you and refuse to install the update. If you need the update, simply follow the instructions that appear.

You can also tell which version you currently have installed by launching System Profiler and checking the Boot ROM Version line in the Hardware section.

continues on next page

TAKE NOTE ▶ Firmware Updates *continued*

As of this writing, most firmware-update utilities run exclusively in Mac OS 9—a problem since the newest Macs don't boot Mac OS 9. Similarly, the install procedure in many cases requires the Mac's Interrupt button. This button (typically paired with the Reset button) has been removed from recent Mac models. Most recently, at last addressing this dilemma, Apple has begun to release firmware updates that run in Mac OS X and with the most recent Mac models. The Power Mac G5 Firmware Update 5.1.4 is a good example. As you might expect, it's very simple to use.

In general, I recommend installing firmware updates as they're released: They fix bugs from the preceding version, and they may add new features. Occasionally, however, problems occur. A firmware update from a few years ago, for example, placed new restrictions on the type of memory the Mac found to be acceptable. As a result, the computer no longer recognized some previously installed RAM (primarily RAM from vendors other than Apple). In some such cases, the problem RAM needs to be replaced. In this case, however, an enterprising developer wrote DIMMFirstAid (www.mactcp.org.nz/DIMMFirstAid.sit), a Mac OS 9 utility that created a patch allowing the DIMM to be accessed. It's doubtful, however, that this utility fixes more recent examples of this symptom.

Be careful not to interrupt an in-progress firmware installation: Doing so could leave the firmware nonfunctional, and you might not be able to start up again—at which point there's no easy way to reinstall the firmware. A trip to an Apple Service Provider will likely be needed.

Even if you complete the update successfully, you can't downgrade to an older version. Thus, if you don't like something the update does, you're out of luck. On rare occasion, a firmware upgrade has even been known to *trigger* rather than solve problems. Thus, check a site like MacFixIt.com to see whether problems have been reported for a firmware update—and what the solutions are—before installing the update.

Finally, all of this information refers specifically to updating Apple's Open Firmware. Other peripheral devices, from Apple's AirPort Base Station to SCSI cards, may have their own firmware, which can also be updated. This firmware is separate from Open Firmware on the Mac itself.

SEE: • **Chapter 3 for coverage of firmware updates and installing and updating Mac OS X.**

TECHNICALLY SPEAKING ▶ Open Firmware Commands

If you press Command-Option-O-F immediately at startup, you get dumped into the Open Firmware environment, where you can run Open Firmware commands. To get a command to run, type the command and press Return. Open Firmware includes dozens of commands, which are summarized in the Apple Knowledge Base document located at http://docs.info.apple.com/article.html?artnum=60285. For most troubleshooting, however, you need to know only a small subset of these commands. The ones I've found to be most useful include the following:

eject cd and shut-down. Typically, to start up from a CD or DVD, you need to hold down the C key at startup with the CD inserted in the drive. Occasionally, the Mac may attempt to start up from the CD even if you aren't holding down the C key (for example, if you have selected the CD as the startup disk in System Preferences). Usually, holding down the mouse/trackpad button or the Eject key at startup will force the CD to eject before it's selected as the startup device. However, if even this method fails, you can boot into Open Firmware and type eject cd. This command will get the CD tray to open, at which point you can remove the CD.

Alternatively, you may want to start up from a CD that is not in the CD drive. If, due to a system crash, you cannot access the drive before restarting, you will need to get the CD tray to open (unless it's a slot-loading drive, as in iMacs), insert the CD, close the tray, and hold down the C key—all before the Mac selects the hard drive as the startup device. If this is too much to do in so short a time, use Open Firmware. Open the tray via the eject cd command, insert the CD, and close the tray. Then type shut-down. This command does what its name implies. Now you can restart as normal, holding down the C key, to use the CD as the startup disc.

reset-all. There's been some confusion among Mac users as to what the reset-all command does. Some people believed it resets the Open Firmware code to some default state—possibly all the way back to when your Mac first shipped, thus erasing any subsequent firmware updates. This is *not* the case. The command makes no changes in Open Firmware itself. Instead, it initiates the same sorts of changes that would occur if you pressed the Mac's Reset button or even simply restarted as normal. It rechecks the peripheral devices attached to your Mac, for example. Thus, if your Mac appears to not recognize a device such as a FireWire drive, using reset-all could help.

printenv, reset-nvram, and set-defaults. Though rarely necessarily, these commands can be lifesavers when you *do* need them. Typing printenv gets you a list of all of the configuration settings in the Mac's nonvolatile RAM (NVRAM). These settings are stored in a special type of RAM on the Mac's logic board. You can modify their contents, as you can with ordinary RAM, but the contents are preserved even after you shut down the Mac. Among other things, NVRAM maintains the setting for the default startup device, called *boot-device*.

continues on next page

TECHNICALLY SPEAKING ▶ Open Firmware Commands *continued*

You use the reset-nvram and/or set-defaults commands to return the NVRAM settings to their defaults (assuming you want to do so). These commands can come in handy if you can't get your Mac to attempt to start up from your internal hard drive, no matter what you do. The command combination of reset-nvram and set-defaults is similar to a well-known Macintosh troubleshooting technique called *zapping the PRAM* (parameter RAM). Among other things, using these commands may fix problems with a failure of a Mac to go to sleep or wake from sleep.

The reset-nvram command followed by reset-all (or just zapping the PRAM) should also eliminate the symptom where Open Firmware appears at startup even when you do not press the Command-Option-O-F keys.

bye or mac-boot. Whenever you want to exit Open Firmware and start up from the selected startup device, simply type bye, mac-boot, or reset-all to restart, or type shut-down to shut down.

TECHNICALLY SPEAKING ▶ Open Firmware Password

The latest versions of Open Firmware software (version 4.1.7 and later) allow you to add a password requirement. With this option enabled, you won't be able to start up from any device other than the default boot device, nor will you be able to start up in any way that bypasses the normal startup procedure (such as attempting to enter single-user mode). If you do try, you will be dumped into Open Firmware, or (in some cases) the bypass attempt will be ignored and the normal startup sequence will proceed. The only way to circumvent this is to enter the Open Firmware password in the Open Firmware window or (as a more permanent solution) disable the password. With certain settings, the protection prevents any startup at all without entering the password.

This is thus the ultimate password security protection and may be especially useful in public and semipublic environments where you're concerned about users' bypassing Mac OS X's other more vulnerable protections. For example, a user could bypass normal Mac OS X security by starting up with a bootable CD; Open Firmware protection would block this.

Enabling password checking. To create a password, enter Open Firmware and type password. You will not be asked to use this password at startup, however, until you enable the password-checking feature. To do this, type setenv security-mode {mode}. The {*mode*} is none, command, or full.

- The *none* mode (the default) means no password protection is enforced.

- The *command* mode allows you to start up (from the volume selected in Startup Disk only) without a password; however, you can't make any Open Firmware changes without entering the password. It also prevents starting up from devices other than the default boot device without the password. This is the most common and useful setting. If the password is needed, you typically get a screen at startup where you can enter it. You then click the arrow button and startup proceeds.

- The *full* mode prohibits you from starting up without entering the password.

continues on next page

TECHNICALLY SPEAKING ▶ **Open Firmware Password**   *continued*

Type reset-all after making a change to enable that change. Once you've done this, you cannot change password-enforced settings without first entering your Open Firmware password.

Note: Do not use the capital letter *U* in an Open Firmware password. If you do, certain Mac models (including any iBook, recent iMac models, and Power Mac G4s) will not recognize the password.

What password protection blocks. When you enable Open Firmware password protection in command mode, the following operations are blocked:

- Use of the C key to start up from a CD-ROM disc.
- Use of the N key to start up from a NetBoot server.
- Use of the T key to start up in Target Disk mode.
- Use of the Shift key to start up in Safe Boot mode or disable user-level login items.
- Use of Command-V to start up in Verbose mode.
- Use of Command-S to startup in Single-user mode.
- Use of Command-Option-P-R to reset the PRAM.
- Use of the Option key to access the Startup Manager and select a different startup device. (Actually, you can select a different startup device here, but only if you enter the Open Firmware password when asked.)

In full mode, all of the same actions are blocked, plus you cannot even start up from the default startup device (without entering the Open Firmware password).

Enabling password protection does not prevent access to Open Firmware itself (via Command-Option-O-F) but it requires entering the password before you can make any changes here.

To perform any of the above actions (or to perform them without providing a password), you need to disable the password requirement, as described in the following sections.

Disabling password protection. To disable the command or full password protection, simply re-enter Open Firmware and change the security mode back to none by typing setenv security-mode none (and entering your password when requested).

Apple's Open Firmware Password utility. There is an easier alternative to using the password commands in Open Firmware: You can enable and disable *command* mode (but not *full* mode) via Apple's Open Firmware Password utility. This utility is located on the Mac OS X Install CD, tucked away in the /Applications/Utilities folder located at the root level of the CD. If you run it and enter your administrative password, you will be able to create a password and enable its use.

continues on next page

TECHNICALLY SPEAKING ▶ **Open Firmware Password** *continued*

You can run this utility directly from the CD or copy it to your hard drive and run it from there.

Force-disabling password protection. The biggest risk of using Open Firmware password protection is that when *full* mode is enabled, if you forget your password (or the Mac refuses to accept it), you're locked out of your Mac. In such cases, you can remove Open Firmware password protection by following one of these procedures:

- Add a RAM module or (assuming you have more than one) remove one and restart in Open Firmware. Password protection may now be disabled.

  If the above doesn't work, restart again and reset (zap) the PRAM by pressing Command-Option-P-R on startup; do not release the keys until the Mac has chimed three times. Note: The ability to do this without a password is enabled when you change your RAM configuration.

  You should now be able to shut down your Mac, return your RAM configuration to its previous state, and restart again as normal. You can later reenable password protection, if you wish, selecting a new password as desired.

- Alternatively, you can use a Mac OS 9 utility called FW Sucker (www.msec.net), which will reveal the password (assuming you did not shut down your Mac before you realized you had forgotten the password).

Of course, the fact that the above two procedures exist also means that Open Firmware password protection isn't 100 percent safe. However, if you physically secure your Mac so that no one can open it and change the amount of RAM inside, you can prevent anyone from taking advantage of the first "back door." And if your Mac isn't booted into Mac OS 9, no one can take advantage of the second (FW Sucker doesn't work in the Classic Environment in Mac OS X).

Figure 5.1

The Open Firmware Password utility.

Figure 5.2

The screen that appears at startup if you must enter your Open Firmware password.

TAKE NOTE ▶ Zapping PRAM and Resetting the Power Manager

The following information is not specific to Mac OS X; however, it can still be helpful for solving various startup problems as described in the main text.

Zapping, or resetting, the PRAM. Zapping the PRAM resets your Mac's parameter RAM and NVRAM settings to their default values. PRAM holds such information as your time zone setting, startup-volume choice, speaker volume, recent kernel panic information, and more. To reset it, shut down your Mac and then turn it on again while holding down the Command, Option, P, and R keys. When the Mac has chimed three times, let go of the keys and let startup proceed. For additional details, see these Apple Knowledge Base documents: http://docs.info. apple.com/article.html?artnum=86194 and http://docs.info.apple.com/article.html?artnum= 2238. You can also check out the section on this topic in my book *Sad Macs*. In addition, you may be able to zap the PRAM via Open Firmware, as noted in "Technically Speaking: Open Firmware Commands," above.

Apple warns, "If you have a RAID setup, your computer may not start up if you reset parameter RAM (PRAM) when you restart. To fix this, restart your computer while holding down the Option key to select your startup system. If this doesn't work, restart your computer while holding down the Command-Option-Shift-Delete keys."

Resetting the Power Manager. On laptops, resetting the Power Manager accomplishes the same thing as zapping PRAM—with one additional bonus: It also resets the laptop circuitry responsible for power management (especially with regard to sleep and battery use). Exactly how to perform this reset varies with each Mac laptop model; the following Apple Knowledge Base document provides the details: http://docs.info.apple.com/article.html?artnum=14449. On most recent models, you reset the Power Manager by shutting down the Mac and then pressing Control-Option-Shift-Power for 10 seconds.

Recently, even some desktop Macs have started to include a Power Management Unit (PMU). Resetting this unit can eliminate certain system-level crash problems. Again, exactly how to do this will vary from model to model; see the following Apple Knowledge Base article for details on the technique for older Power Mac G4s: http://docs.info.apple.com/article.html?artnum=95037.

Startup Manager: Option key at startup

Holding down the Option key immediately on startup invokes Startup Manager. You can use this feature to select a startup volume different from the normal default (as selected in the Startup Disk System Preferences pane). Changes here don't modify the default selection: The next time you restart *without* holding down the Option key, your Mac will again start up from the default device.

Invoking Startup Manager brings up a screen with icons for the various volumes (drives, discs, and/or partitions) from which you can boot your Mac. The following details what you'll see in this screen and how to proceed once it appears:

- You will see one icon for each bootable volume. This means that if you have Mac OS 9 and Mac OS X installed on different partitions, you should see an icon for each OS. If a bootable CD or DVD is in the CD/DVD drive or a bootable external hard drive is attached, you should see icons for these as well.

- If you have Mac OS X and Mac OS 9 on the *same* partition, only one of them can be *blessed* (available as a bootable OS) at a time—which means that only one of them will ordinarily be shown in Startup Manager. Thus, when you hold down the Option key at startup, you will see either the Mac OS X icon or the Mac OS 9 icon, but not both. Which one you see will depend on which one was most recently selected as the bootable OS.

- If you have a newer Mac that does not boot in Mac OS 9, you will not see the Mac OS 9 options described above.

- If you do not see a volume that you expect to see, click the curved-arrow button (located below the icons), and the Mac will check again for potential startup volumes.

- Click the icon of the volume that you want to use as the startup volume. Then click the straight-arrow button, and startup will proceed.

- If you press Command-. (period) with this screen open, the Mac's CD/DVD drive tray should open, allowing you to mount a CD for use as the startup disc. This screen also allows you to eject a CD at this point—another option for accessing the CD tray at startup (as described in "Technically Speaking: Open Firmware Commands" earlier in this chapter).

Startup Disk System Preferences and control panel. Using Startup Manager to change a startup-disk selection does not change the default startup drive. That is, if you normally boot into Mac OS X but select a Mac OS 9 volume in Startup Manager, you will boot back into Mac OS X the next time you restart normally. In most cases, the way to change the default setting is to make a different selection in the Startup Disk System Preferences pane (Mac OS X) or the Startup Disk control panel (Mac OS 9). Simply select the volume (and the OS within the volume, if more than one is listed), and restart. That's it.

Unlike Startup Manager, the Startup Disk control panel in Mac OS 9 and the Startup Disk System Preferences pane in Mac OS X allow you to choose among multiple bootable operating systems (such as Mac OS 9 and Mac OS X) on the same volume.

I recommend using Startup Disk to change your startup-disk selection. Only use Startup Manager if the standard methods either don't work or aren't accessible (perhaps because you can't start up successfully).

In summary (assuming your Mac is an older model that can still boot in Mac OS 9):

- If you're currently in Mac OS X and want to restart in Mac OS 9, go to the Startup Disk System Preferences pane, select the desired Mac OS 9 volume, and click the Restart button. In the confirmation window that appears, click Save and Restart.

  Note: A gold *9* appears on the icon of a Mac OS 9 System Folder if that folder resides on the same volume as Mac OS X.

- If you're currently in Mac OS 9 and want to restart in Mac OS X, go to the Startup Disk control panel and select the desired Mac OS X volume. If a volume has more than one potential startup OS, a disclosure triangle will appear to the left of its name. In this case, click the disclosure triangle to reveal all OS options. Click the Mac OS X option to select it. Then click Restart.

TAKE NOTE ▶ Keyboard Startup Options

Various keys and key combinations (beyond the Option key used to invoke Startup Manager) can be used to modify the startup process. The following describes some of them:

C key at startup. You can hold down the C key at startup to start up from a bootable CD already in the drive.

X key at startup. By holding down the X key at startup, you can make a Mac that normally boots into Mac OS 9 boot into Mac OS X instead (assuming both systems are located on the same volume, and you last started from the Mac OS 9 System Folder on that volume). This technique allows you to work around the problem that the Option-key method does not list Mac OS 9 and Mac OS X at the same time if they are on the same volume. Also, unlike the Option-key method, holding down the X key saves the change—that is, the next time you start up normally, you will again start up in Mac OS X.

Command-Option-Shift-Delete. Holding down this combination of keys forces the Mac to bypass the typical default startup drive (your internal drive) in favor of an alternative bootable device, such as an external FireWire drive. This may succeed in cases where holding down the Option key does not access the drive you wish to use.

Command-D. Using this key combination, the Mac attempts to start from the internal drive or, if it is divided into partitions, the first partition on that drive. The first partition is the one at the top when viewed in Disk Utility's Partition tab.

Other options. Other keyboard startup options—Open Firmware, single-user mode, verbose mode, safe boot, and target disk mode—are covered elsewhere in this chapter.

SEE: • "Boot ROM and Open Firmware," "Single-user mode," "Verbose mode," and "Safe Booting," elsewhere in this chapter.
  • "Sharing via Target Disk Mode," in Chapter 8.

BootX

If you elected to start up in Mac OS X, have passed through the Boot ROM stage successfully, and are not starting up from a CD, the next file that the Mac looks for is called the BootX booter, which is located in /System/Library/ CoreServices. Its primary job is to load what is called the *kernel environment*. It is at this point that the gray screen should turn to blue.

Without a BootX file in your Mac OS X System folder—or, more precisely, somewhere on the volume—your Mac will not start up. This file is essential in the same way the System file is essential in Mac OS 9. Even though you can boot the volume if the file isn't in the System folder per se, I can think of no reason to move it. In fact, I've found that if you simply copy this BootX file onto any volume—even one with no other Mac OS X software—the Startup Disk System Preferences pane will be fooled into thinking you can start up in Mac OS X from that volume. (This attempt will fail, of course, if you do try.)

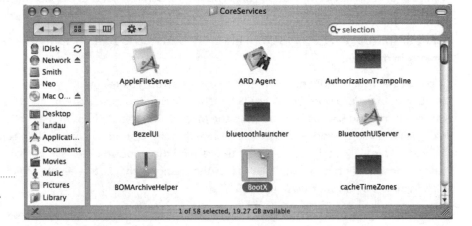

Figure 5.3

The CoreServices folder with BootX highlighted.

Kernel extensions. During this phase, the kernel extensions (*kext* items) are loaded. (Your Mac's screen will typically be gray at this point.) Kernel extensions are mainly device drivers for attached hardware, such as PCI cards, an AirPort Base Station, graphics cards, an iPod, or whatever. They are stored in /System/Library/Extensions.

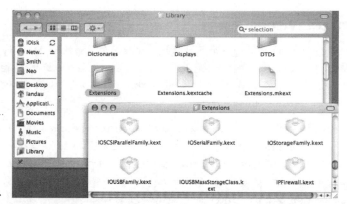

Figure 5.4

The /System/Library/Extensions folder (highlighted), with the Extensions.kextcache and Exrensions.mkext files to the right. Partial contents of the Extensions folder are also shown.

TECHNICALLY SPEAKING ▶ Understanding Kernel Extensions

One of BootX's jobs is to determine which kernel extensions should be loaded at startup and then load them. Two Unix utilities assist with this: *kextcache* (which creates the mkext cache file described in the next paragraph) and *kextd* (which loads and unloads specific kext items, as appropriate for the startup in progress).

Boot X first attempts to load a previously cached set of device drivers—an mkext cache file named Extensions.mkext that's located at the root level of the /System/Library folder. A related file, called Extensions.kextcache, is also located here. Each extension file/package contains information (in the OSBundleRequired key in its Info.plist file) describing its loading requirements.

If these two files are missing or corrupted, BootX will create new ones by rechecking the extensions set in /System/Library/Extensions for drivers and other kernel extensions set to be loaded at startup. In fact, deleting these files (which requires root access) occasionally fixes system crashes and/or kernel panics related to peripheral devices that use kext drivers.

Installing a new kext item. You typically install new kernel extensions indirectly via a Mac OS X update or third-party software installer. During the installation process, a script in the installer .pkg file should force the cache to be updated so that the Mac recognizes the presence of the new extension the next time it starts up.

Getting the Mac to recognize a newly installed extension is one reason you may need to restart your Mac immediately after installing a Mac OS X update. In fact, if you have problems with a hardware peripheral after installing new software (even if the software installer claims not to require a restart), it's a good idea to try restarting (or, even better, shutting down and restarting).

If even restarting doesn't get the extension to work, try deleting the Extensions.mkext item and restarting. You will need root access (explained in Chapter 4) to delete this file in Jaguar. In Panther, you can instead Command-drag the file to the Trash and then authenticate with your administrator's password when asked. Alternatively, you can force-update the mkext item by changing the modification date of the Extensions folder. To do so, launch Terminal and type `touch /System/Library/Extensions`.

continues on next page

TECHNICALLY SPEAKING ▶ **Understanding Kernel Extensions** *continued*

Another approach would be to type sudo kextload /System/Library/Extensions/{*name of kext item*} to load a single extension (presumably the newly installed one)—which doesn't require you to restart your Mac. Still, given that you don't install new kext items every day, I advise playing it safe and restarting.

Third-party kext files that do not load at startup. Due to Mac OS X's rules that determine when and if a kext file loads, it is possible that a third-party kext file for a peripheral hardware device may refuse to load at startup. As a result, the peripheral device does not work. In such cases, unplugging and replugging the device (hot-swapping) after startup is over will usually get the kext file to load—and thus the device to work. The ultimate fix for this is for the third-party developer to revise their kext file.

Working with kext items via Terminal. You can get information about, load, and unload specific kext items by entering any of the following commands in Terminal:

* kextstat provides information about currently active kext items.
* kextunload allows you to unload an active kext item.
* kextload loads a currently inactive kext item.

You can also type man {*name of command*} to get more details about each command.

System initialization

During the next phase of startup, an assortment of technical activities takes place. For troubleshooting purposes, the details are not important; the following provides a brief summary of what occurs:

* **The core software (kernel) of the Unix/BSD basis for Mac OS X loads.** This is initiated by a process called mach_init, which in turn initiates the BSD init process.

* **The system checks to determine whether the user is booting from a CD-ROM or via single-user mode.** If either is the case, a special loading procedure takes over. (I discuss single-user mode and starting from a CD later in this chapter.)

* **Special scripts (rc.boot and rc) in the normally invisible /etc folder are run.** These scripts handle the final initialization tasks, determining whether to run fsck at startup (as described in more detail later in the chapter), creating the swap file for virtual memory, and running the kextd process (which unloads kext items not needed for this startup).

   Final steps include running the register_mach_bootstrap_servers tool and SystemStarter software (as described in the next section, "Startup items and bootstrap daemons"). These processes in turn launch various system daemons—processes launched before a user logs in and that generally run in the background.

> **SEE:** • **"Technically Speaking: System Daemons," later in this chapter, for related information.**

Note: If you're starting up from a bootable CD, the critical information for booting is in a similar file in the /etc directory on the CD called rc.cdrom.

TECHNICALLY SPEAKING ▶ Hostconfig and Other Configuration Files

The rc scripts check the *hostconfig* file, located in the /etc directory. This file lists which system services should be started. To locate hostconfig in the Finder, select the Go to Folder command and enter /etc.

Hostconfig is a text file, which you can edit—for example, with TextWrangler (opened via root access) or in Terminal (by opening the pico text editor as root using sudo pico)—to modify what services (startup items) load at startup. For example, if the hostconfig file lists *DNSSERVER=-NO-,* and you want the DNS Server to load, simply change *NO* to *YES*. Typically, you modify this file indirectly by changing a setting in a System Preferences pane. However, in some cases, you may need to modify it directly.

You can also use third-party Aqua utilities, such as Infosoft's MOX Optimize, to modify which startup items are enabled or disabled at startup.

SEE: • **"Take Note: Why and How to Use Archive and Install" and "Technically Speaking: Custom Config Files After a Mac OS X Update," in Chapter 3, for related information.**
   • **"Modifying invisible Unix files from Mac OS X applications," in Chapter 6, for more information on editing config files.**

Startup items and bootstrap daemons

During the next phase of startup, bootstrap daemons and startup items are launched. This is typically when the Mac screen turns blue and the Mac OS X logo appears.

Startup items. Startup items installed by Mac OS X are located in /System/Library/StartupItems; startup items installed by third parties are located in /Library/StartupItems, where they're typically placed by the installers for the applications that use them (that is, you're not expected to manually place them in the correct folder).

While startup items are being loaded, the Mac OS X logo box (in the Startup window) displays text referring to the items being run. Thus, you may see messages like, "Starting {*name of item*}" or "Waiting for disks."

The Unix command SystemStarter (in the /sbin directory) handles the loading of these items at startup. You may also run this command from Terminal (at any time) to restart or stop individual startup items (as described in "Technically Speaking: SystemStarter").

The following are some examples of items in the /System/Library/StartupItems folder:

Figure 5.5

The StartupItems folder.

- **Apache.** Starts the Personal Web Sharing server (if enabled).

- **AppleShare.** Starts Apple File Service (needed for Personal File Sharing).

- **Cron.** Starts the cron utility, which runs automated events (updates, system-log cleanup, and so on).

- **LoginWindow.** Alerts SystemStarter that the OS is ready to display the Login window (that is, run the loginwindow process).

- **Network.** Configures the local network interfaces based on the data in the /etc/iftab file (setting IP info and so on).

- **Network Time.** Sets the OS to check for time and date.

Each startup item is itself a package or bundle folder that contains at least two items: the startup executable code and a .plist file.

SEE: • **"Technically Speaking: Creating Your Own Startup Items and BootStrap Daemons,"** later in this chapter, for more details.

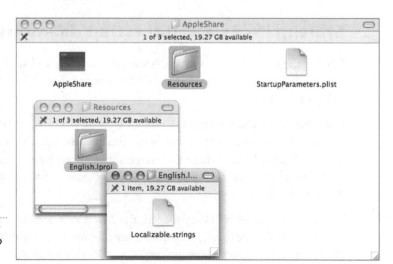

Figure 5.6

The contents of the AppleShare Startup Item.

TECHNICALLY SPEAKING ▶ SystemStarter

The Unix SystemStarter command—which you can run from Terminal after startup is complete—provides one potential way of resolving startup-item problems *without* truly restarting your Mac. In its basic form (that is, with no options enabled), this command restarts all startup items (as would normally occur when you restart your Mac).

To run SystemStarter, launch Terminal, type sudo SystemStarter, and enter your password when requested. By typing sudo SystemStarter -g, you also get a graphical Mac OS X logo display identical to what you see at startup.

For a list of additional features (such as starting or stopping individual startup items), type man SystemStarter. For example, if AppleShare stopped (due to some error), you could restart it by typing sudo SystemStarter AppleShare start. Be careful, however: Stopping an essential item could crash your Mac. In most cases, simply restarting your Mac is a simpler solution.

If there's a problem with a startup item, a diagnostic error message will appear in the Terminal window output when running SystemStarter. This can be especially useful for debugging a startup item you created yourself.

If you're using SystemStarter as a quick way to restart, be cautious: Using SystemStarter and regular restarting are not exactly the same. Unlike in a true restart, all open applications *remain* open and functional after using SystemStarter. Also, kernel extensions are not reloaded via SystemStarter (you use the kextload and kextunload commands for that). If problems occur, do a normal complete restart.

You can also use various third-party utilities, such as MOX Optimize, to individually turn on or off startup items and kernel extensions—a more user-friendly alternative to SystemStarter and kext Terminal commands.

Figure 5.7

Startup items as seen via (left) SystemStarter (with the graphic display option enabled) running in Terminal, and (right) the MOX Optimize utility.

TECHNICALLY SPEAKING ▶ Creating Your Own Startup Items and Bootstrap Daemons

As a troubleshooter, you won't have much reason to create your own startup items or bootstrap daemons. However, they're easy enough to create that it's worth knowing how. You could, for example, create one to run a function at startup that you wished to be in effect regardless of who was logged in to the machine. (Adding an item in the Startup Items tab of a given user in the Accounts System Preferences, in contrast, only affects *that* user.)

Startup items. Each startup item contains the following components:

- **Executable file/script.** First, create a folder with the name of your startup item (for example, MyStartupItem). Next, create a text file (using BBEdit or another editor that can maintain Unix line endings) with the same name. Store this file inside the folder. This is the executable file that actually contains the instructions performed by the startup item. Typically, this is a shell script file—in essence, a file containing commands like those you would normally run in Terminal. A simple shell script might look like the following:

```
#! /bin/sh
. /etc/rc.common
ConsoleMessage "Starting MyStartupItem"
touch /Users/tedmac/Desktop/testfile
```

  The first line tells the Mac to run the sh shell. The second line causes rc.common to run. (This is shell-script code that Apple recommends running prior to your own startup-item code; it contains routines that are useful for processing command-line arguments.) The third line causes the text "Starting MyStartupItem" to appear during the blue-screen phase of startup. The final line describes what the startup item actually does—in this case, the touch command simply creates a file called *testfile* on the Desktop of my own account (or updates the modification date of the file if it already exists). (In Chapter 10, I discuss some other simple shell scripts of more practical value.)

- **StartupParameters.plist file.** This file includes the data that determines if and when the startup item runs. The simplest way to create this file is to copy one from another startup item and then modify it by loading it in Property List Editor.

  For example, the OrderPreference attribute can have a value of First, Early, None (default), Late, or Last. These determine when in the load order the item will load.

  The Requires attribute tells Mac OS X that the startup item requires that *another* specific startup item be loaded first.

- **Resources folder.** Optionally, if you want to localize a startup item for different languages, add a Resources folder and include lproj folders (for example, English.lprog) for each desired language. The Resources folder will include a Localizable.strings file.

When done with all of the above, place the folder in the /Library/StartupItems folder.

continues on next page

TECHNICALLY SPEAKING ▶ **Creating Your Own Startup Items and Bootstrap Daemons** *continued*

You can optionally add a line to the /etc/hostconfig file (as noted in "System initialization" earlier in the main text) that determines whether the item loads at startup. To get this to work, you have to write code in the executable file that instructs the startup item to check this file. See the Apache file in the Apache startup item, in /System/Library/StartupItems, for an example.

Bootstrap daemons. Bootstrap daemon files are .plist files that can be opened in Property List Editor. They have three possible keys:

- **ServiceName.** The value of this key is the name of the bootstrap service. It typically takes .plist-style format (for example, the ServiceName value for the WindowServer.plist daemon is com.apple.windowserver), though technically it can be pretty much whatever you want.

- **Command.** The value of this key is the absolute pathway to the executable file that runs when the daemon loads. Most of the executables are either in Unix directories (for example, the configd and lookupd executables are in /usr/bin) or in /System/Library/Frameworks/ApplicationServices.framework (this is where windowserver is located).

- **OnDemand.** This is an optional key. By default, OnDemand is set to on. However, if this key is added and set to a Boolean value of False (or No), the on-demand feature is disabled.

You can easily create simple bootstrap daemons, such as one to launch an application from the /Applications folder (regardless of which user is logged in). For example, if you want Preview to always launch at login, you could create a bootstrap daemon file called LaunchPreview.plist and have the following as the value for the Command key: /Applications/Preview.app/Contents/MacOS/Preview. That's it (see **Figure 5.8**).

If you create your own custom bootstrap daemon for this purpose, place it in the /etc/mac_init_per_user.d folder. You will need to authenticate to get root access to place the file in this directory.

Note: You can also create a bootstrap daemon to run a shell script (as described above for startup items). The daemon then references the script, which is located elsewhere. There is no required location for this script. In my case, I created a folder called Bootstrap Daemons in the /Library folder and placed scripts there. However, I have had more success getting shell scripts to work as startup items than as bootstrap daemons.

Need more help? See the following Apple document for more details on how to create startup items: http://developer.apple.com/documentation/Darwin/Conceptual/howto/system_starter_howto/system_starter_howto.html.

For more background, see: http://developer.apple.com/documentation/MacOSX/Conceptual/BPSystemStartup.

SEE: • **"Preferences Files," in Chapter 4, for more on creating and editing .plist files.**
- **"Startup items," "Login," and "Take Note: Problems with User-Level Startup (Login) Items," elsewhere in this chapter, for related information.**
- **"Using a shell script," in Chapter 10, for related information.**

Bootstrap daemons. Now that you've learned all about startup items, here's the bad news: Apple is phasing them out! They still work in Panther (as just described), but I expect them to be gone by the next major revision to Mac OS X. In their place will be a new feature (first appearing in Panther) that uses the Unix command register_mach_bootstrap_servers (located in the /usr/libexec directory).

In Panther, bootstrap daemons have already assumed some of the functions handled by startup items in Jaguar. In a few cases, a startup item remains in place but no longer functions (that is, running it does not accomplish anything). In these cases, the item is retained for the sake of third-party startup items that may list it in their StartupParameters.plist files (as described in "Technically Speaking: Creating Your Own Startup Items and BootStrap Daemons"). One example of a nonfunctioning startup item is DirectoryServices: If you open the DirectoryServices executable file within the folder, you will see that it no longer contains any instructions beyond an exit line.

One major benefit of bootstrap daemons over startup items is that these daemons can launch on demand—that is, a loaded process can "sleep" when not needed, significantly reducing the system load.

Bootstrap daemons run twice during startup:

- **When the rc scripts are run.** This is comparable to when startup items are run. The rc script loads all of the files *(daemons)* found in the following directory: /etc/mach_init.d. These include system daemons such as configd and lookupd as well as a fix_prebinding daemon (which fixes out-of-date prebinding information for applications).

    SEE: • "Technically Speaking: System Daemons," later in this chapter, for more details.

    • "Optimize update_prebinding," later in this chapter.

- **When the loginwindow application is run.** These items are stored in /etc/mac_init_per_user.d. In a default Panther system, the only daemon in the mac_init_per_user.d directory is MirrorAgent.plist, which is used to manage the local copy of an iDisk (if present).

    SEE: • "Technically Speaking: Creating Your Own Startup Items and BootStrap Daemons," above, for more details.

The items in mach_init.d normally load only when you start or restart your computer. Thus, if you simply log out and then log back in (or another user logs in), these items won't be reloaded. The items in mach_init_per_user.d are loaded whenever a user logs in (as described next).

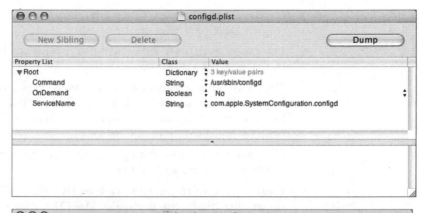

Figure 5.8

The contents of two bootstrap daemon files: (top) configd.plist and (bottom) launchpreview.plist (which I created).

Login

The last stage of the startup process begins with the appearance of the Login window. However, if you checked the "Automatically log in as" box in the Login Options of the Accounts System Preferences pane and named yourself as the person to be logged in (as described in Chapter 2), you will bypass this screen.

The Login window is, appropriately enough, handled by the loginwindow application, located in /System/Library/CoreServices. When loginwindow is launched during startup, the following things happen:

- **Your password is checked against information in Directory Services (typically obtained from the NetInfo database, unless modified via the Directory Access application).** The password-checking code here looks at only the first eight characters; anything beyond that length is ignored. The SecurityAgent application (located in /System/Library/CoreServices) handles this authentication.

  Note: Panther, by default, uses a more secure method for authenticating than was used in Jaguar. Called Shadow Hash, it's only used on accounts created in Panther, not ones upgraded from Jaguar. Older accounts still use the older method (called Basic). It's doubtful that any of this will affect your troubleshooting; however, if you need to know more, check out the document titled "Open Directory Overview," available from Apple's Developer Web site.

- **Daemons in the /etc/mac_init_per_user.d are loaded, as described in the previous section.**

- **Your customized environment (based on the preferences settings in your Home directory) is set up.** This includes launching items listed in the Startup Items portion of the Accounts System Preferences pane (as explained more in Chapter 2).

- **Files are set to show the appropriate permissions and privileges for your account and status.**

- **Unix-style environment variables (which are listed in the environment.plist file in the invisible .MacOSX directory in your Home directory) are checked and executed.** Note: This folder and document are only present if an environment value has been changed from its default state.

  SEE: • "Technically Speaking: What's a Shell?" in Chapter 10, for information on environment variables and the setenv command.

- **Other typical login tasks (such as displaying alerts) are completed.**

When you enter your correct user name and password, Mac OS X completes its startup sequence by launching the Finder, Dock, and applications in your Startup Items list.

The loginwindow program continues to run while you're logged in. It manages the Force Quit window and the logout process. It also relaunches the Dock and Finder automatically (as well as the SystemUIServer background process), should they quit. Note: If you should quit the loginwindow process, such as by force-quitting it from Activity Monitor, you're immediately logged out.

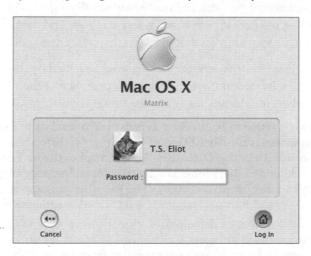

Figure 5.9

The Login window.

SEE: • The coverage of the Accounts System Preferences, in Chapter 2, for more details.

Replacing the Finder. The loginwindow process is what causes the Finder to always launch at login. You can assign a different application to replace the Finder, if you wish.

SEE: • "Technically Speaking: Completely Hidden Properties: Changing the Finder," in Chapter 4, for details.

U.S. Department of Defense Common Access Card at log in.

In Terminal, if you type sudo cac_setup, you will get a message that says, "Starting Smartcard Services." When you next go to the Login window, you will see an option that says, "Please insert a Common Access Card." This is to be used with a Department of Defense Smartcard viewer that is intended to protect against illegal access to the computer. Assuming you have no need for this setup, you will want to turn this off. To do so, log in (via the Other option in the Login window), return to Terminal, and type sudo cac_setup off.

TECHNICALLY SPEAKING ▶ System Daemons

If you launch Activity Monitor—especially if you select to view Administrator Processes or All Processes—you will see many running processes that are not end-user applications and are not listed anywhere else you would typically see running applications (such as the Force Quit window, described later in this chapter). In general, these are *background processes*—that is, processes that have no user interface and thus are not visible in the Finder. Many of these processes are launched automatically early in the startup process or when you log in—and are generally referred to as *system daemons*. Typically, you will have little need to interact with them. However, the following are some noteworthy items that should give you an idea what these processes are and do:

- **configd.** Automatically configures and maintains the network.

- **kextd.** Loads and unloads device drivers as needed.

- **lookupd.** A name resolver that expedites requests to NetInfo and DNS.

- **update.** Periodically flushes the system cache to help prevent data loss in the event of a crash. (For more on this, see "Technically Speaking: Connecting Remotely to a Frozen Mac: Killing Processes, Running Sync," later in this chapter.)

- **pbs.** Handles the Clipboard and clippings files.

Figure 5.10

Activity Monitor with All Processes selected: lookupd is highlighted, and its Info window is selected.

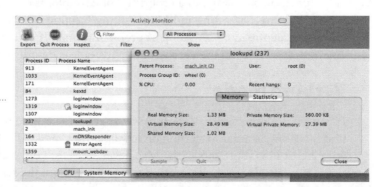

Alternative Mac OS X Startup Paths

I've already covered a couple of deviations from the normal startup procedure, such as starting up from a CD or booting into Open Firmware. Those methods function prior to the launch of Mac OS X itself. What follows are several more startup deviations that are specific to Mac OS X.

Single-user mode

If you press Command-S at startup, you start up in what is called *single-user mode*. In essence, this mode drops you directly into Mac OS X's command-line interface. The screen will turn black and begin to fill with a series of text lines in white (perhaps with some text in yellow). You can generally ignore this text. Eventually, the screen will stop at a command-line prompt, where you can enter text commands. If you've used Mac OS X's Terminal application, you should feel right at home.

For troubleshooting purposes, your main use for single-user mode will be to attempt disk repairs, especially when your Mac won't otherwise start up. From the single-user-mode screen, you can run a Unix utility called fsck (for *File System Check*), which is essentially the same as running the First Aid component of Disk Utility—which means it may be able to repair the startup (or other) problems.

Note: You will not want to run fsck if journaling is enabled, as explained later in this chapter in "Enabling and disabling journaling" and "Running fsck."

If you get the idea that starting up in single-user mode bypasses Mac OS X's admin password protections, you would be correct. A user in single-user mode has the same authority as a root user. If you want to block unauthorized users from single-user access, you need to enable Open Firmware password protection.

The text that appears prior to the command-line prompt will sometimes provide clues as to the nature of a problem. For example, as covered in "Take Note: Problems Mounting and Unmounting/Ejecting Media," in Chapter 6, doing this identified a FireWire port problem for me. If you only want to view text messages, you can use verbose mode instead, as described next.

Verbose mode

If you press Command-V at startup, you start up in verbose mode, which at first looks very similar to starting up in single-user mode. The main difference is that in verbose mode, the Mac never stops for you to enter commands. Verbose mode also provides continuing feedback about the startup sequence (for example, what processes are loading) that does not appear in single-user mode. After you see all the white (and sometimes yellow) text, a normal Mac OS X login process begins at the blue screen.

Thus, verbose mode is used mainly to check for error messages contained in the initial text. This information is usually of interest only to software developers. The white text, for example, provides information about the progress of the initialization process; the yellow text usually comprises an alert about a possible problem with a kext item. You could view most of this information from Console logs after logging in; however, verbose mode can be of use if the error in question is preventing a normal startup and thus preventing you from accessing the Console application. For everyday troubleshooting, however, you will almost never need verbose mode.

If you're familiar with Unix jargon, verbose mode may provide some clues about the source of a problem. One user, for example, was able to confirm that a problem with his Date & Time setting was due to a failure of the Network Time software loading at startup, as determined by a getGMTTimeOfDay error message in verbose mode. Shifting to a different server, as accessed from the Network Time tab of the Date & Time System Preferences pane, solved the problem.

Verbose mode may also indicate a problem with a startup or kext item. This would alert you to use a safe boot (described next) to bypass loading of kext items, allowing startup to proceed. At this point, you could replace or disable the problem file.

SEE: • **"Checking for extension (kext) problems,"** later in this chapter, for an example of a problem with the IOUSBFamily.kext file.

If you start up in verbose mode, your Mac should also return to verbose mode when you shut down—thus providing the same feedback for shutdown as it did for startup. Of course, once the Mac shuts down, the output is gone, so read it quickly!

Safe booting

If you're having problems starting your Mac, the first troubleshooting technique you should try is a *safe boot*. A safe boot accomplishes two things:

- **It forces the Mac to run the fsck disk-repair utility at startup.** This is thus an alternative to running it via single-user mode. Note: If journaling is enabled, fsck will not run (because it's generally not needed).

    SEE: • **"Enabling and disabling journaling"** and **"Running fsck,"** later in this chapter, for more details.

- **It prevents nonessential kext items (stored in /System/Library/ Extensions) and third-party startup items (located in /Library/ StartupItems) from loading.**

Invoking a safe boot. To invoke a safe boot, *immediately* after you hear the chimes at startup (but not before), hold down the Shift key until the Mac logo appears on the blue screen and the text "Safe Boot" appears in the logo box.

Figure 5.11

A safe boot at
startup.

Safe boot takes longer. When you do a safe boot (without journaling enabled), you'll notice that startup takes considerably longer than normal. This is mainly because fsck is being run. In addition, a safe boot ignores the cache of kernel extensions (/System/Library/Extensions.kextcache) used to speed startup.

Does fsck solve the problem? If journaling is off, simply running fsck may solve the problem. Thus, if a safe boot allows startup to proceed, immediately try restarting your Mac without a safe boot. If it works, your problem is solved.

To be extra cautious (or if journaling is enabled), you could also run Disk Utility's First Aid (by starting up from the Mac OS X Install CD) or manually run fsck via single-user mode at startup.

If, after all of this, you still encounter the startup problem, the culprit may be a startup item or kernel extension (as described next).

Deleting or disabling files to prevent a startup problem. Beyond running fsck, the main advantage of a safe boot is that it can circumvent a startup crash or kernel panic caused by one of the bypassed files. Once you've started up successfully, you can then locate the problem file (most likely a kext item or third-party startup item) and remove it from its folder.

If you have no idea which file is the culprit, you should begin by checking added and/or third-party files; starting up in verbose mode and checking for error messages may help identify the problem file.

You can use a utility like MOX Optimize to disable problem files. Once you've disabled the suspect item, you can restart normally. Contact the vendor of the problem file for further advice.

SEE: • **"Technically Speaking: Understanding Kernel Extensions," earlier in this chapter, for related information.**

• **"Check for extension (kext) problems," later in this chapter, for more troubleshooting advice.**

Disabling user-level startup (login) items

By holding down the Shift key later in the startup sequence, you can prevent user-level startup items (which you normally access from the Accounts System Preferences pane—and are called *login items* in Jaguar) from loading. As you might guess, this comes in handy when a startup item is causing a startup crash. (A user-level startup item is a likely culprit for crashes that don't occur until *after* you've logged in or until the Desktop background has appeared.) Reminder: User-level startup items are different from the system-wide startup items described earlier in this chapter.

SEE: • "Accounts," in Chapter 2, for more about this feature.

Safe boot vs. disabling user-level startup items. Despite its similarity to a safe boot, disabling user-level startup items is a completely separate procedure. You can choose to do both or either. Here's what you need to know:

- To accomplish a safe boot *only,* hold down the Shift key at startup (as described in the previous section) until the blue screen appears.

- To disable startup items *only,* hold down the Shift key any time *after* the Mac logo has appeared in the blue screen but *before* the logo disappears. Continue to hold the key until the Login window appears (it will appear even if you selected to automatically log in). Now enter your name and password, or (if you've selected to see a list of users) click your name and enter your password. Hold down the Shift key again and click the Log In button. Release the Shift key when the Desktop appears.

  Note: You will only need to employ the just-described method if you previously set your Mac to automatically log in (via Login Options in the Accounts System Preferences pane). If not, you can wait for the Login window to appear and enter your password (and name, if needed). Now hold down the Shift key and click the Log In button. There is no need to hold down the Shift key before the Login window appears.

- To combine these procedures, you need to combine the two methods. In particular, you must release the Shift key after the words "Safe Boot" appear and press it again later in the sequence.

  If the Mac is not set to automatically log in, once you let go of the Shift key at startup for the safe boot, you do not need to press it again until after the Login window appears. Holding down the Shift key again, when you click the Log In button, will be sufficient to disable user-level startup items.

  If your Mac is set to automatically log in, hold down the Shift key again almost immediately after you release it following the safe boot. The Login window will pop up even though you selected to automatically log in. At this point, enter your password and hold down the Shift key again, as just described.

  It's important to understand that if you hold down the Shift key to do a safe boot and just continue to hold it down until the Desktop appears (as would happen if you had selected to automatically log in), startup items will *not* be disabled. You need to register two separate presses of the Shift key to turn off the items. If you simply press the Shift key immediately at startup and continue to hold it, the Mac will not recognize it as a request to disable user-level startup items.

If you've already logged in and want to disable startup items, simply select Log Out from the Apple menu. This brings up a Login window. Once it appears, hold down the Shift key as you log back in again; you do not need to restart. You do, however, need to restart if you want to disable kext items via a safe boot.

SEE: • **Coverage of the Accounts System Preferences pane, in Chapter 2, for background on user-level startup items.**

• **"Take Note: Problems with User-Level Startup (Login) Items," later in this chapter, for more on troubleshooting user-level startup items.**

TAKE NOTE ▶ **Bypassing Automatic Login**

Suppose you selected to automatically log in at start up, but now you want to start up as another user (perhaps to troubleshoot as the root user or from a troubleshooting account). The typical way to do this would be to log in normally and then log out, bringing up the Login window, where you could then log in as the root user.

However, as noted earlier, holding down the Shift key during startup can also bring up the Login window—even if automatic login is active. If you time it right (holding down the Shift key after the Mac logo on the white background has appeared and releasing it after you click to log in), you can get the Login window to appear without doing a safe boot or disabling startup items. Not a big deal, perhaps, but it does provide a way to bypass automatic login for those times when you wish to do so.

Logging in as console

When you get to the Login window, you typically log in with your own user name. As covered in Chapter 4, however, you may also choose to occasionally log in as the root user, using *root* as the user name instead.

As it turns out, you can also use another name here: >*console*. (Note: This name is unrelated to the Console application in the Utilities folder.) Even though a password isn't required, you'll reach a screen that's very similar to Terminal—except that the text is white on black (as it is in single-user mode). You will need to log in at this screen, providing your name and password before you proceed.

When you're logged in via the >console option, it's just like being in Terminal. The only difference from single-user mode is that Mac OS X and all of its startup services are loaded and running normally. The primary reason to log in via this method would be if you want to use Terminal to solve a problem, but the problem itself prevents you from logging in via normal methods (thus prohibiting normal access to Terminal).

One example in which logging in as console could help is if a corrupt font or preferences file is causing an Aqua-related crash. In this case, logging in via console would allow you to remove the file because the Finder's Aqua environment does not load at this point and thus there will be no crash. The exact steps for logging in as console are as follows:

1. Type >console in the Name field at the login prompt (leave the Password field blank).

   If you selected "List of users" rather than "Name and password" in the Accounts System Preferences pane, you will not see a Name field. One solution would be to click the Other option; however, this option only appears if you've enabled the root user. If you haven't done so, you can press Option-Enter and then click any name in the list to get the Name and Password fields to appear.

   Note: You cannot log in as console if another user is currently logged in via Fast User Switching.

2. At the next prompt, log in with your normal name and password.

3. Using the rm or mv commands, remove, move, or rename the corrupt file so that it no longer loads at startup.

   SEE: • Chapter 10 for more on using these commands.

4. Type logout or exit to return to the normal Login window.

5. Log in as yourself, and hopefully all should be well.

TAKE NOTE ▶ Other Login User-Name Options

In addition to the >console command, a few other special commands work when you type them in the Login window's user-name text box. These commands include the following:

- >restart: Restarts the Mac.
- >power: Shuts down the Mac.
- >exit: Quits and relaunches the Login window.

TAKE NOTE ▶ Forgot Your Password?

What do you do if you've forgotten your login password? How do you find it so that you can log in again? Here's how:

- If you're not an administrative user, get an administrative user to log in; he or she can reset your password via the Password screen in the Accounts System Preferences pane.

- If you are an administrative user and there's more than one admin account, get the other administrative user to log in; he or she can reset your password via the Password screen in the Accounts System Preferences pane.

- If you entered a password hint for your account and created a Master password in the Security System Preferences pane, a Password Hint screen will appear once you've entered wrong password at login three times. From here, click the Reset Password button.

- If you're the only administrative user, use the Reset Password utility included on the Mac OS X Install CD. This is the only method that works if you've forgotten the root-user password.

- If you want to use Terminal, you can change forgotten passwords from here. For example, if you know your administrator password, you can reset any other passwords, including the password for root access. To reset the root password, for example, type sudo passwd root. Provide your administrator's password when asked. You will then be prompted to enter a new password for the root user.

  You can also use this command to enable root access, if you have not previously enabled it in NetInfo Manager.

SEE: • **"Technically Speaking: Inside FileVault," in Chapter 2, for more on using the Master password to reset your login password.**

• **"The Installer menu," in Chapter 3, and "Logging in as root," in Chapter 4, for details on using Reset Password.**

TAKE NOTE ▶ NetBooting

NetBooting refers to a process whereby a client computer running Mac OS X starts up from system software located on a central server. Thus, you need at least one computer running Mac OS X Server to use this feature.

Client computers typically use the BootP protocol set in the TCP/IP tab of the Network System Preferences pane.

continues on next page

TAKE NOTE ▶ **NetBooting**   *continued*

To start up via NetBooting:

*   Select Network Startup from the Startup Disk System Preferences pane, and restart.

    Or

*   Restart and hold down the N key.

NetBoot HD appears as a volume on the client's desktop if NetBoot has been successful.

Further details about NetBooting, such as how preferences and permissions are handled, are beyond the scope of this book. For more details, see Apple's Inside NetBooting document (available from the following Apple Knowledge Base article: http://docs.info.apple.com/article.html?artnum=50055).

Figure 5.12

The Network Startup option highlighted in the Startup Disk System Preferences pane. The question mark indicates that the Mac will search for a network volume at startup.

Startup Crashes

One of the hallmarks of Mac OS X is its stability. Once the operating system is up and running, you'll rarely experience a crash that requires you to restart the computer—small comfort, though, if you crash or freeze during startup. This section explores the various types of startup crashes and explains what you can do about them.

In addition to the advice contained in the following sections, check "Techniques for solving Mac OS X crashes," later in this chapter, for a laundry list of common fixes. Many of these fixes can be applied to startup problems, especially if you're able to start up from a safe boot. Finally, check the following Apple Knowledge Base document for another overview of startup problems and solutions: http://docs.info.apple.com/article.html?artnum=106464.

Gray-screen crashes

Figure 5.13

The prohibitory symbol indicates that a startup failure has occurred.

During the gray-screen phase of startup, instead of getting the expected Apple logo symbol, you may get no symbol (just a blank gray screen) or the *prohibitory symbol* (a circle with a line though it). On rare occasion you may get the Apple logo symbol just as startup stalls.

Causes. Gray-screen crashes can typically be attributed to one of three things: (1) hardware failure; (2) the intended startup drive is not recognized to be valid and bootable; or (3) essential Mac OS X software is missing or corrupted.

The following describes a few of the things that can precipitate a gray-screen crash:

- **SCSI cards.** Mac OS X won't start up if certain SCSI cards are installed in a desktop Mac's PCI card slots. Clearly, this problem should not extend to any PCI cards that ship from Apple; however, other cards may cause a problem. Similarly, if you have several SCSI devices attached to a SCSI card, a startup crash may occur in Mac OS X even though Mac OS 9 boots just fine. This problem is generally the result of improper termination of devices on the SCSI chain. See the Apple Knowledge Base article "Connecting SCSI Devices" (http://docs.info.apple.com/article.html? artnum=9387) or *Sad Macs* for more details on SCSI termination.

- **Memory.** If you've added memory (RAM) to your Mac, that RAM might not be compatible with your Mac model. Since there are subtle variations in the types of RAM available for Macs, your module could appear to be the correct type even when it's not. Or you could have a defective module—even if it is the correct type. Either situation can cause a crash.

  Note: If you're unable to get your machine to start up, incompatible or damaged RAM might not show up in Apple System Profiler. Instead, ASP will indicate that the RAM slot is empty.

  Sources such as Apple's own Specifications page (www.info.apple.com/ applespec/applespec.taf) offer details about the precise memory specifications for each Mac. In most cases, however, if you use a reputable vendor, you should get the correct memory simply by telling the vendor what Mac you have. If problems occur, the vendor should replace the memory free or for a nominal charge.

- **AirPort card.** An improperly installed AirPort card (for example, one that's not fully inserted in the slot) can cause a startup crash. Check the documentation that came with your AirPort card and/or your Mac for how to install it correctly.

- **External devices.** Any device added to the Mac's other ports (USB, FireWire, or PCMCIA) can precipitate a startup crash. Most such devices should work fine; however, those that have not been updated to work with Mac OS X may remain a problem.

- **Missing Mac OS X software.** If you delete a critical Mac OS X file (such as mach_kernel), you will get a startup failure, typically at the gray-screen stage. Similarly, do not delete the /etc or /var folders that may be visible on the Desktop when booting from Mac OS 9. (These items are invisible by default in Mac OS X, so as to make it more difficult to accidentally delete them.)

What to do. Consider the following suggestions when troubleshooting a gray-screen crash:

- Make sure you have the latest firmware update installed. If you need to update the firmware, you should reinstall Mac OS X afterward.

  SEE: • "Take Note: Firmware Updates," earlier in this chapter.

- Try a safe boot. If this succeeds, the problem is most likely related to a kernel extension for a peripheral device, such as a SCSI card. Deleting or disabling the extension may prevent the crash, but it will also disable the card. A better alternative is to get an updated version of the file that fixes the error. Alternatively, replacing the file from a backup may help if the file has become corrupt.

  More generally, deleting the Extensions.mkext and Extensions.kextcache files may be all you need to do to fix a crash that occurs on a normal boot.

  SEE: • "Safe booting" and "Technically Speaking: Understanding Kernel Extensions," earlier in this chapter, for more details.

- If the problem only occurs when you're trying to start up from an external volume, it may be caused by the way Mac OS X is installed on the drive.

  SEE: • "Take Note: Startup Failure When Starting Up from an External Device," later in this chapter.

- If your Mac can still start up in Mac OS 9 and you have a Mac OS 9 System Folder installed on your hard drive, try to boot from Mac OS 9. Alternatively, try to start up from a bootable Mac OS 9 or Mac OS X CD. If either of these succeeds, the problem is most likely due to the Mac OS X software on your drive (rather than a hardware problem).

  In such cases, make sure you're using the latest version of Mac OS X. Apple generally improves support for peripheral devices with each new release. If the OS was starting successfully with a particular device attached but no longer does, the existing software may have become corrupt. In this case, simply reinstalling the current version of the device-driver software (or Mac OS X) may be sufficient.

- If you believe the problem can be traced back to a deleted critical file, such as mach_kernel, boot from Mac OS 9 or another Mac OS X volume, and drag the mach_kernel file at the root level of a Mac OS X Install CD/DVD (or from a backup of the current Mac OS X volume) to the root level of the Mac OS X volume. Now restart in Mac OS X. Your only other alternative would be to reinstall Mac OS X.

  Note: This assumes that the CD/DVD contains the same version of Mac OS X (and thus the same version of the mach_kernel file) that's currently installed on the drive. If not, you can get the needed mach_kernel file from a previously made backup, or you can reinstall Mac OS X.

- To further check for problems with peripheral devices, such as SCSI cards or external drives, or even USB or FireWire devices, disconnect all peripheral devices and cards from your Mac and restart. If the Mac starts up successfully, one of these devices may have caused the crash. Start adding devices back, one at a time, restarting after each. When the crash reoccurs, the most recently added device is the likely culprit. The incompatibility could be in the firmware on the device or in the item's kext device-driver software. If so, updating the firmware or driver software of the device may fix the problem. Contact the vendor of the device or check sites such as MacFixIt to determine whether such fixes exist or whether you need to abandon using the device in Mac OS X altogether.

- If the problem is caused by a USB or FireWire device, you may be able to work around it by waiting to plug in the device until *after* startup is complete. In other cases, switching from connecting the device through a USB or FireWire hub and using the port directly on the Mac (or vice versa) may help.

- If you have incompatible or defective RAM, replace it. In some cases, updating the Mac's firmware, though generally recommended, may cause a startup failure due to a RAM incompatibility—even though the Mac worked prior to the upgrade.

- To check for other hardware problems, use the Hardware Test CD that came with your Mac. Problems turned up via this method will generally require taking your Mac in for a repair.

  SEE: • **"Technically Speaking: The Apple Hardware Test Software," earlier in this chapter.**

- If none of these fixes work, you may have a disk problem. If so, try to repair it.

  SEE: • **"Techniques for solving Mac OS X crashes," later in the chapter, for more on disk repairs and related fixes.**

TAKE NOTE ▶ Startup Failure When Starting Up from an External Device

CD/DVD drives. In some cases, a hardware conflict may prevent you from starting from a bootable CD (or DVD) even though you can start up normally from your hard drive. In such cases, the solution may be simple, if a bit inconvenient. If a USB device is the cause, remove the device, boot from the CD, and do what you need to do (such as install the software from the CD). Then shut down, reattach the device, and restart from your hard drive.

If your Mac refuses to start up from the CD, shifting instead to the hard drive, and the cause is not a connected device, the CD may not be a bootable CD—a situation that's especially likely to occur if you burned the CD yourself (since burning a bootable CD requires more than simply copying files from one CD to another). In this case, the solution is to reburn the CD correctly (as described in "Bootable CD" in Chapter 3).

continues on next page

TAKE NOTE ▶ Startup Failure When Starting Up from an External Device *continued*

In some cases, the latest Mac models will only start up via the Mac OS X software that came with that model (or newer versions). In other words, if the CD contains system software that predates your Mac model, it may not work. This is a particular problem for third-party developers who need to have their software on bootable CDs (such as Norton Utilities or DiskWarrior). Contact the vendor for advice if you get stuck in this situation.

External drives. Assuming the problem is not with the Mac itself or with the software installed on the drive, check with the drive vendor for possible firmware updates for the drive. In some cases, the fix may require that a hardware component of the drive be replaced. When you purchase a FireWire drive, make sure that it uses the Oxford 911 or newer chipset, which generally is needed for Mac OS X compatibility.

For FireWire or USB startup drives, if selecting the drive in the Startup Disk System Preferences pane does not result in starting up from the drive, restart and hold down the Option key at startup; then select the drive from the choices that appear in the Startup Manager screen.

In one case, not only was I unable to start up from an external FireWire drive, but attempting to do so prevented any startup at all—that is, a gray-screen crash occurred. Further, no startup volumes were listed if I held down the Option key at startup. The only solution was to disconnect the FireWire device from the Mac and restart.

Pressing Command-Option-Shift-D immediately at startup may force the Mac to attempt to boot from an external device that otherwise would not boot. You can also try turning off the power to the external drive briefly (especially if you're stuck at startup with no drive mounting) and then turning it back on. Based on my own experience, the probability of success here is low, but these tactics are worth a shot.

Occasionally you may find yourself unable to start up from an external drive because Mac OS X has been installed on it incorrectly—and thus the drive has not been "blessed" as bootable and/or permissions are not set correctly. There are several potential solutions to this situation, as described elsewhere in this book.

Finally, after updating to Panther, you may fall victim to a bug that renders your external drive unusable until you reformat it. Data on the drive will be difficult, if not impossible, to recover.

SEE: • "Take Note: Blessed Systems and Starting Up," later in this chapter, for more on blessing a drive.
   • "Troubleshooting Tips and Hints: Installing Software," "Bootable CD," and "Take Note: Backups of Bootable Volumes Don't Boot," in Chapter 3, for more information on potential causes of startup problems.
   • "Take Note: Problems Mounting and Unmounting/Ejecting Media," in Chapter 6, for related information, including more information on the Panther bug that can corrupt external FireWire drives.

Blinking question-mark icons

A variation on gray-screen startup problems is a gray screen containing a folder icon with a blinking question mark inside. Typically, this problem occurs when you're trying to start up in Mac OS 9 and the Mac can't find a valid Mac OS 9 System Folder. However, it can occasionally occur when you're trying to start up in Mac OS X as well.

In the benign variation of this problem, the question mark is soon replaced by the Mac OS X logo, and all proceeds normally. In the malignant variation, the blinking icon persists.

What to do. Consider the following suggestions when troubleshooting this symptom:

- The benign variation typically means that no default startup device is selected or that the default device is not connected to the Mac. In such cases, the Mac will search through the available startup devices and select one; it is this search that causes the delay.

  If this problem occurs each time you start up, you usually can fix it by opening the Startup Disk System Preferences pane and selecting a startup volume. The next time you restart, the blinking question-mark icon should no longer appear.

- For the malignant variation, you can try restarting in Mac OS 9 (assuming your Mac model can do this)—typically by holding down the Option key at startup and selecting an available Mac OS 9 volume. If no Mac OS 9 volume is listed or you can't start up in Mac OS 9, you can try to start up from a bootable Mac OS 9 CD. In either case, when you reach the Desktop, select the desired Max OS X volume in the Startup Disk control panel, making sure that the control panel version is 9.2.1 or later. Then restart. The Mac OS X volume should boot.

  If your Mac cannot start up in Mac OS 9, try starting up from a Mac OS X Install CD or another bootable external volume. Once your Mac is booted, go to the Startup Disk System Preferences pane and select the desired default startup disk.

- If the Startup Disk System Preferences pane does not allow you to select a Mac OS X installation as the startup OS, the OS software may be damaged or a critical file may be missing. You will likely need to reinstall Mac OS X at this point.

- You may be able to fix things by using the reset-nvram command in Open Firmware (as described in "Technically Speaking: Open Firmware Commands," earlier in this chapter).

- You may be able to start up normally by repairing permissions in single-user mode, as described in "Reinstalling Mac OS X," later in this chapter.

- If you can't start up from a hard drive under any circumstance, and if (after starting up from a CD) your hard-drive volume or volumes do not mount, your hard drive is probably in need of repair or replacement.

Blinking globe icon. If you get a blinking globe icon instead of a blinking folder icon, this means your Mac is trying to start up via NetBoot but cannot find a bootable OS on the network. Typically, within a few seconds the Mac should shift to booting from your default local startup drive. After startup is complete, you can change your startup disk selection, if desired, to prevent this symptom from occurring on future restarts. Of course, if you expect to return to NetBooting on your next restart, leave things as they are.

If you get a malignant variation, where the blinking globe remains indefinitely, follow the same advice as just described for the blinking folder icon.

SEE: • "Take Note: NetBooting," earlier in this chapter.

• "Take Note: Blessed Systems and Starting Up," below, for related information.

• "Techniques for solving Mac OS X crashes," later in this chapter, for advice on disk repairs.

TAKE NOTE ▶ Blessed Systems and Starting Up

A System folder that the Mac recognizes as one it can use for startup is referred to as a *blessed* folder.

BootX file. Located in /System/Library/CoreServices, the BootX file is an essential piece of software for booting from Mac OS X. In fact, if it's missing, you won't be able to start up Mac OS X from this volume—instead getting the blinking question-mark icon. Somewhat surprisingly, I found that the file doesn't need to be in the CoreServices folder to work: I was still able to start up even after I moved it to the root level of the drive. Only when I deleted it completely did startup fail.

In some cases, the Mac OS X System folder may become unblessed. You will know that this is the case if the *X* icon that appears on the CoreServices folder and Mac OS X System folder icons disappears. (This *X* is only visible when you boot in Mac OS X.) If this occurs, dragging the BootX file out of the System folder and returning it to its original location in CoreServices may help. However, to do this, you must somehow be able to boot your Mac and access files! Typically, you would boot from Mac OS 9 or from another drive that contains Mac OS X (for example, an external FireWire drive).

Note that a BootX file by itself is not sufficient to start up in Mac OS X. The rest of the Mac OS X software must also be present and in working order.

Blessing a volume via Terminal. You can use the bless command to bless a volume (typically an external drive)—which may just be the ticket for making the drive bootable. To do so, type the following (all in one line), where *volumename* is the name of the volume you want to boot:

```
sudo bless -folder /Volumes/{volumename}/System/Library/CoreServices
```

continues on next page

> **TAKE NOTE** ▶ **Blessed Systems and Starting Up** *continued*
>
> Apple has documented a variation of this problem in which newer Macs (the ones that can no longer boot from Mac OS 9) may be unable to start up from a (presumably external) hard drive that was previously used with an older (Mac OS 9–compatible) Mac or that was restored via an image file created on an older Mac. The solution (if the problem volume or drive is now connected to the newer computer) is to type the following (all in one line and with a space after –bootinfo):
>
> ```
> sudo bless -folder /Volumes/{volumename}/System/Library/CoreServices -bootinfo
> /usr/standalone/ppc/bootx.bootinfo
> ```
>
> See Apple Knowledge Base article No. 25506 for more details.
>
> **Blessed folder in Mac OS 9.** Just for the record, a similar situation exists in Mac OS 9. For the Mac to start up from Mac OS 9, it typically must locate a blessed System Folder. A blessed System Folder has a mini Mac-face icon (as you see when you boot in Mac OS 9). If Mac OS 9 and Mac OS X are on the same volume, however, and Mac OS X was the startup OS the last time you started up from that volume, you may not see this icon on the folder because the Mac OS 9 System Folder gets unblessed when Mac OS X is selected as the startup OS from that volume. You typically can rebless the System Folder by selecting it as the startup OS in the Startup Disk control panel. Otherwise, dragging the System file out of the System Folder and dragging it back in again should rebless the System Folder.
>
> I mention this to emphasize a point I alluded to in the main text: If the Mac cannot find *any* blessed Mac OS 9 or BootX Mac OS X System folder, you will get the persistent blinking question mark at startup.
>
> Complicating matters a bit, the Mac OS 9 System Folder that is currently selected to launch when you launch Classic will have a 9 icon in it when viewed in Mac OS X. This icon is separate from the blessed-folder icon described earlier in this chapter.

Figure 5.14

Icons on blessed System folders.

System   System Folder

Broken-folder and belted-folder icons

Another type of gray-screen startup crash occurs when you get a folder icon that appears to be ripped in two (the broken-folder icon) or a folder icon with a belt tightened around it.

I haven't seen these icons since updating to Mac OS X 10.2 and thus suspect that they no longer occur. Instead, the prohibitory symbol appears (as described in "Gray-screen crashes," earlier in this chapter). Regardless of which icon actually appears, here are some potential causes beyond those described in the section on gray-screen crashes:

Old version of Startup Disk control panel used. Selecting Mac OS X as the startup OS when you're booted in Mac OS 9 and using a pre-9.2.1 version of the Mac OS 9 Startup Disk control panel may cause one of the above-described icons to appear (as opposed to the related question mark–icon symptom).

TAKE NOTE ▶ Startup Disk Control Panel and "No Valid System Folder" Error

Note: The following is only relevant if you can and do boot from Mac OS 9.

If you use a pre-9.2.1 version of the Startup Disk control panel, you may get the following error message at startup:

The startup disk no longer has a valid System Folder. "System" and "Finder" must be in the System Folder. If you continue, you may not be able to restart the computer. Do you want to continue?

This message, which refers to Mac OS 9, may appear even if you've selected Mac OS X as the startup volume. If this situation occurs, follow these steps:

1. Click Cancel.

2. Obtain a copy of Startup Disk 9.2.1 or later and install it on your drive.

If you don't have this file on a Mac OS Install CD, you can get it from Apple's Software Downloads site (www.info.apple.com/support/downloads.html).

3. Use the updated control panel to select Mac OS X.

4. Restart.

Disk formatting and Mac OS X installation problems. Formatting a drive with software other than Apple's Disk Utility can cause this symptom if the formatting software is incompatible with Mac OS X. Check with the software vendor for Mac OS X compatibility information. The fix is to reformat the disk by booting from the Mac OS X Install CD and selecting the Disk Utility option (as described in Chapter 3). Then reinstall Mac OS X.

If you tried to install Mac OS X and the installation failed, further attempts may fail as well. When you try to start up in Mac OS X under this failed System, the broken-folder or belted-folder icon (or prohibitory symbol) may appear.

In this happens, your best bet is to try to reinstall Mac OS X—this time with the option to erase the drive selected (the Erase and Install option). This technique should bypass any problems with corrupted files that were the likely cause of the installation failure.

Before erasing the disk, reboot in Mac OS 9 or from another Mac OS X volume and save any files you haven't backed up.

SEE: • Chapter 3 for more information on installing and backing up Mac OS X.

Dumped into Unix

A rare startup problem can occur when you go from the gray screen directly to the command-line black screen that you normally see when booting via single-user mode.

In this case, you typically see the following line of text: "File system dirty, run fsck." You can run fsck directly at this point (that is, you don't need to restart and hold down Command-S to restart in single-user mode).

SEE: • "Running fsck," later in this chapter, for more details.

If running fsck doesn't correct the problem, it's likely that critical Unix files are missing or corrupted. Unix experts may be able to figure out exactly what went wrong and fix the problem from the command line; however, for most Mac users the solution at this point is to reinstall Mac OS X.

In some cases, the problem may be that one or more Unix files have incorrect permissions. You may be able to fix this by using the AppleJack utility to repair permissions (as described in "Running fsck," later in this chapter) or by modifying permissions well enough to start up successfully before reinstalling Mac OS X (as described in "Reinstalling Mac OS X," at the end of this chapter).

Blue-screen crashes and stalls

If Mac OS X successfully navigates the gray screen, the next thing that will occur is that the screen will turn blue, followed shortly by the appearance of the Mac OS X logo. Within the logo box, you will see a series of messages, stating that various Startup Item services (such as AppleTalk) have been initialized, configured, or started. When this process is complete, the Mac will either halt at the Login window or (if you've selected automatic login) proceed directly to launching the Finder and Dock.

If a crash (or freeze) occurs at the blue-screen stage, it's likely to be related to a service that failed to load—the symptom of which is generally a blank blue screen and the failure of the Login window or Desktop to appear. Here are some of the most common causes of such problems, along with advice for what to do about them.

Stalled Network Services. One of the most common causes of a blue-screen freeze is a problem with Network Services. If your network connections have changed from those you set in the Network System Preferences pane, you may get a long stall (most often at the Network or Network Time items). This could happen, for example, if the OS looks for an Ethernet network that no longer exists. Usually, the OS will eventually make it past this type of freeze—you just need the patience to outlast it (which can take several minutes). However, if it doesn't become unstuck, you may be able to modify your actual hardware network connections. In particular, if you have an Ethernet cable attached to your Mac, disconnect it. Conversely, if an Ethernet cable is normally connected to your Mac but for some reason is disconnected, reconnect it. If you use a cable modem and have disconnected it or turned it off, make sure the cable modem is active and connected. And so on.

If this technique works, the stall will end, and login will proceed immediately. In any case, when you finish starting up, if you intend to maintain whatever arrangement led to the stall, you may need to modify your settings in the Network System Preferences pane to prevent the stall from happening again.

In particular, make sure you have a valid DNS address in the Domain Name Servers field (see Chapter 8 for details). Next, disable any Ethernet or AirPort ports (in Network's Port Configurations list) that will not accessible at startup. For example, disable AirPort if your Mac won't be able to locate to any wireless network at startup.

If none of these measures help and you're still stalled at the blue screen, keep reading.

Other stalls and slowdowns. There are an assortment of other causes of stalls and slowdowns that may occur at this stage of startup. Here are a few examples:

- Selections in the Directory Access application can contribute to an unusually slow or stalled startup. In particular, if services (such as LDAP) are enabled when the service does not actually exist on your network, startup will be slowed while the Mac searches in vain for the non-existent service.

- Similarly, if your Mac is set to search for a specific server at startup, but that server is not currently available (for example, the network connection is down), startup will be slowed. However, this slowdown will only happen for the first startup after the server loss.

- A bug in Mac OS X 10.3.2 can cause a significant stall at startup—at least for some users. The cause is that a Unix executable file, called BootCacheControl, is missing from the /usr/bin directory. This file creates a cache that speeds up the startup process. Because the file is missing, the cache is not created and the speed-up does not occur. The solution is to place a symbolic link (a type of alias, as described in Chapter 6) in the /usr/bin directory that points to a copy of the missing file located in /System/Library/Extensions. To do this, launch Terminal and type (all in one line):

```
sudo ln -s /System/Library/Extensions/BootCache.kext/Contents/
Resources/BootCacheControl /usr/sbin
```

On your second restart after doing this, startup time should be reduced.

This bug was fixed in Mac OS X 10.3.3. However, it is still useful to be aware of the general cause and solution for this slowdown. Similar problems may occur in other situations.

- With Panther, I've occasionally encountered long stalls at the point where the message says, "Waiting for local disks." If I wait long enough (sometimes several minutes), startup completes successfully.

Corrupt files and permissions errors. An assortment of files (mainly Unix and /System/Library software) can become corrupt or acquire incorrect permissions—both of which cause blue-screen crashes. In such cases, performing a safe boot may allow startup to proceed. Alternatively, if you can start your Mac up in Mac OS 9, do so (for example, by holding down the Option key at startup). If not, you can start up in Mac OS X from a custom bootable CD (as described in Chapter 3) or an external drive. If none of these options are available, you may be able to solve the problem by starting up in single-user mode (as described in the auto-dial problem example that follows). In all cases, your next step is to locate and delete or replace the problem files or to fix permissions. Otherwise, you're looking at reinstalling your OS software. The following are some examples of problems that can be caused by corrupted files or permissions errors:

- **Disk corrupted; repairs needed.** A good general first step is to run Disk Utility and from the First Aid section select Repair Disk Permissions and Repair Disk.

  However, you will not be able to run Disk Utility from your hard drive if you're getting a crash at startup. The solution is to start up from an Install CD and run Disk Utility from there. You can also run fsck via single-user mode (or via a safe boot, if journaling is not enabled).

  If none of this works, you can try using a third-party repair utility.

  SEE: • "Performing repairs with Disk Utility (First Aid)," "Enabling and disabling journaling," "Running fsck," and "Using third-party disk-repair utilities," later in this chapter, for more details.

- **Auto-dial problems.** The PPP tab of the Internal Modem screen of the Network System Preferences pane includes a button called PPP Options. In the dialog that appears if you click this button is a check box for "Connect automatically when needed." Under certain conditions, if this auto-dial option is enabled, it may cause a blue-screen crash at login. Since you can't start up in Mac OS X to disable the option at this point, you must instead work in single-user mode. From here, you can delete the preferences file (preferences.plist) where these and all other Network System Preferences settings are stored. This causes a new default preferences.plist file to be created at startup. You lose any changes you made to Network System Preferences, but the problematic option is disabled. You can then go back and re-enter your customized settings when you finally log in. To perform this procedure, follow these steps:

  1. Hold down Command-S at startup to enter single-user mode.

  2. Type `mount -uw /` and press Return.

  3. Type `mv /Library/Preferences/SystemConfiguration/preferences.plist preferences.old` and press Return.

4. Type reboot and press Return.

This renames the existing preferences.plist file to preferences.old (in case you want to view it later), which forces a new default copy of preferences.plist to be created at the next startup.

Note: In Jaguar, preferences.plist was called preferences.xml and was stored in /var/db/SystemConfiguration. Thus, to make this change in Jaguar, substitute the following line in step 3:

`mv /var/db/SystemConfiguration/preferences.xml preferences.old`

- **Other preferences files problems.** In some instances, the com.apple .loginwindow.plist and com.apple.windowserver.plist files in /Library/ Preferences, or even .plist files in ~/Library/Preferences, can prevent a successful startup. To work-around this, you need to enter certain commands in single-user mode that will prevent these files from loading at startup. See this Apple Knowledge Base document for details: http:// docs.info.apple.com/article.html?artnum=106464.

- **Corrupt Mac OS 9 fonts.** To check for problematic Mac OS 9 fonts, remove the Fonts folder from the Mac OS 9 System Folder used by Classic, and drag it to the Desktop. Also consider removing any fonts in the Fonts folders of Mac O X that you may have added since installing Mac OS X— especially older fonts originally used in Mac OS 9. (See Chapter 4 for details on Fonts folders.) Restart again from the problem drive. If the crash no longer occurs, one of the fonts you removed is the likely cause. You can start replacing fonts and restarting to isolate the file. If removing fonts did not eliminate the crash, you can return all fonts to their respective locations.

  SEE: • "Checking Fonts," later in this chapter, for solutions to these problems.

- **Problem kext items or third-party startup items.** Crashes caused by these items may be prevented by a safe boot. After starting up successfully, you can remove or replace the problem item.

  SEE: • "Checking for extension (kext) problems," later in this chapter, for more details.

Hardware issues. If all else fails, the problem may be hardware-related. Refer to the preceding sections on gray-screen crashes for more advice.

SEE: • "Logout, restart, or shutdown stalls and crashes," later in this chapter.

• "Techniques for solving Mac OS X crashes," especially "Logging out, restarting, and resetting," and "Performing repairs with Disk Utility (First Aid)," later in this chapter.

Kernel panic

The most serious type of system crash you can get with Mac OS X is a kernel panic. Because kernel panics can occur at startup, I discuss them here. (If a kernel panic does occur at startup, it's most likely to happen during the gray-screen phase, since this is when the kernel extensions load.) However, they may also occur after startup is complete—most often when you launch an application or choose a command from one of its menus. The logic for finding a solution is the same in either case.

According to Apple, "A kernel panic is a type of error that occurs when the core (kernel) of an operating system receives an instruction in an unexpected format or that it fails to handle properly. A kernel panic may also follow when the operating system is not able to recover from a different type of error. A kernel panic can be caused by damaged or incompatible software or, more rarely, damaged or incompatible hardware."

Kernel panic message. If you get a kernel panic, a message box will appear on your screen that reads (in several languages), "You need to restart your computer. Hold down the Power button for several seconds or press the Restart button."

At this point, everything halts. The good news is that you're not responsible for the crash; the bad news is that you can't do anything to fix the problem except avoid the action that caused it and wait for a permanent fix from Apple (or the third-party developer that makes the offending software).

Kernel panic log. After a kernel panic has occurred, details of what happened are recorded in the panic.log file in /Library/Logs. How can this file record the data if a kernel panic has crashed the Mac? It works because kernel panic information is now temporarily saved in NVRAM and written to the log file at the next startup. If you can't find this log file, you probably didn't experience a kernel panic and have never had one previously.

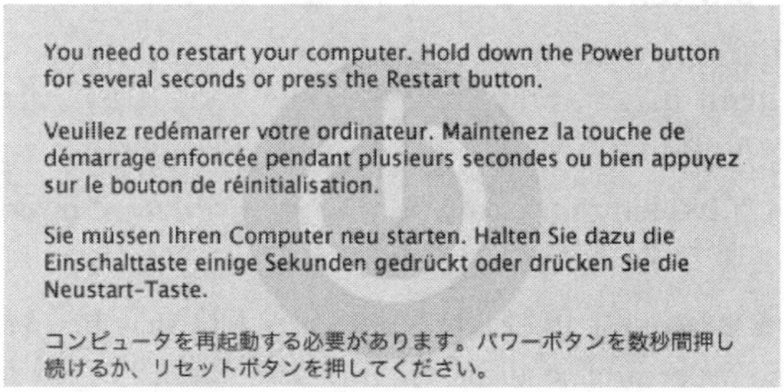

You need to restart your computer. Hold down the Power button for several seconds or press the Restart button.

Veuillez redémarrer votre ordinateur. Maintenez la touche de démarrage enfoncée pendant plusieurs secondes ou bien appuyez sur le bouton de réinitialisation.

Sie müssen Ihren Computer neu starten. Halten Sie dazu die Einschalttaste einige Sekunden gedrückt oder drücken Sie die Neustart-Taste.

コンピュータを再起動する必要があります。パワーボタンを数秒間押し続けるか、リセットボタンを押してください。

Figure 5.15

The kernel panic screen.

Because kernel panics are both serious and rare, Apple is always interested in getting user feedback about how and when such panics have occurred and what the error text said. Such information will help Apple figure out why the problem occurred and how to fix the bug that caused it. Check your panic.log and post relevant information and details at Apple's Discussion Boards (www.apple.com/support).

Hardware causes. Peripheral hardware devices (such as external USB or FireWire devices, PCI cards, or PC Cards) are by far the most common kernel panic culprits. Many of the causes and fixes described in the section on gray-screen crashes (such as doing a safe boot, updating firmware, and so on) apply here as well.

SEE: • "Gray-screen crashes" and "Verbose mode," earlier in this chapter, for related details.

• "Checking for extension (kext) problems," later in this chapter, for a specific example of a kernel panic problem.

Mac OS X software causes. The second major cause of kernel panic at startup is altered Mac OS X system software that prevents the OS from starting up properly. As you search for the culprit, you should be aware of the following:

• **Third-party kext items can cause kernel panic.** The solution is typically to contact the vendor and get an upgraded version of the kext item that works with the current version of the OS.

• **Apple reports that simply adding too many kext items to the /System/Library/Extensions folder can precipitate a startup crash.** The reason: insufficient memory to run BootX.

A safe boot can bypass this cause of a kernel panic; once you're up and running, you must determine the culprit file.

SEE: • "Safe booting," earlier in this chapter.

• "Checking for extension (.kext) problems," later in this chapter.

• **In general, you should avoid removing, deleting, or editing any files in the System directory.** Although you can make some changes inside this folder without causing harm (which you will occasionally need to do to fix certain problems), you must know what you can and can't do: any speculative troubleshooting in this area could easily lead to disaster.

• **Modifying (especially deleting) the contents of the normally invisible Unix folders (/bin, /var, and so on) can also lead to system crashes, kernel panics, other problems.** Again, it's *possible* to modify or delete files here without causing harm, but you need to know what you're doing. In other words, *avoid experimentation*.

• **Moving Applications, System, Library, or any other OS-installed folder outside its default location is strongly discouraged.**

• **Modifying permissions and ownership of critical Mac OS X files can cause similar problems.** Changing a file's access so that the OS cannot use it when needed is functionally equivalent to deleting it. Thus, don't even think about modifying the permissions settings for files in the /System/Library folder. If you want to limit or expand access to these files, there are other ways to do so (which are discussed in Chapter 6).

If you made any of the above-described modifications and can undo them (possibly via starting from another Mac OS X volume), do so. Then try to restart in Mac OS X from the problem volume. Ideally, the startup will work. If not, you're looking at reinstalling the OS.

SEE: • "Techniques for solving Mac OS X crashes," later in this chapter.

• "Checking for extension (kext) problems," later in this chapter, for related advice.

Third-party software causes. Occasionally, third-party software can be the cause of a kernel panic. When Mac OS X 10.1.5 was released, several third-party utilities that remapped the keyboard (that is, changed what happened when you pressed certain keys) resulted in kernel panics when they were loaded at startup (that is, during the loading of login items). This problem was fixed in Mac OS X 10.2.

The workaround solution here is to do a safe boot and/or disable user-level Startup Items at startup. Assuming this allows a successful startup, you can now disable the offending item.

SEE: • "Safe booting," earlier in this chapter, for more details.

Other examples. With each Mac OS X update, Apple fixes bugs that caused kernel panics in previous OS versions. Thus, whenever you describe specific causes of kernel panics, you must do so in reference to a particular version of Mac OS X. Here are two examples of kernel panics—and suggestions for fixing them:

- You may get a kernel panic when trying to boot from the Mac OS X Install CD or (especially) an Upgrade CD—or when you're trying to restart for the first time after installing Mac OS X 10.2 or 10.3. This may be caused by a problem with the user's hardware (for example, incompatible third-party RAM or video cards) that was ignored in earlier versions of Mac OS X.

  Apple warns, "If you have a third-party video card installed in your computer, you may need to remove it before you install Mac OS X." To do so, temporarily replace it with the card that came with your Mac.

  To check for these possibilities, disconnect all nonessential peripheral devices (including added PCI cards and third-party RAM) before booting from an Install or Upgrade CD. If removing these items doesn't solve the problem, the CD itself may be defective and need to be replaced.

- You may get a kernel panic as a result of optimizing a disk or after updating to a newer version of Mac OS X. In such cases, the panic.log file displays the following message: "Kernel loadable modules in backtrace com.apple.BootCache (with dependencies)." You can fix the problem by restarting while holding down the Shift key (to do a safe boot) and logging in as the root user. When startup is complete, use the Go to Folder command to go to /var/db. From here, delete the BootCache.playlist file. Restart as normal, and all should be well.

- Mac OS X 10.3.2 fixed a bug that caused a kernel panic when playing sound through an iSub speaker. The panic.log text typically includes references to "Apple02DBDMAAudio" and "IOAudioFamily."

For more in-depth technical details about kernel panics, get Apple's Developer Technical Note titled "Understanding and Debugging Kernel Panics" (http://developer.apple.com/technotes/tn2002/tn2063.html).

Kext warning

Beginning with Mac OS X 10.2 (Jaguar), some older third-party kext items no longer load due to a new permissions-checking procedure. Apple states: "Now, all kext bundles must have owner and group root:wheel with permissions 755 for folders and 644 for files in order to load. If a kext fails this check, the user is presented with a panel informing them that the kext could be a security hole."

The message panel the user is presented with states, "The program you are using needs to use a system file that may reduce the security of your computer." The panel includes Fix and Use, Use, and Don't Use buttons. Click Use if you're certain the file is correct as is (perhaps because you were so advised by the vendor). If you click Fix and Use, Mac OS X will change the file's permissions and attempt to use the file. If in doubt, click Don't Use, and contact the vendor for advice.

The versions of Symantec's Norton Utilities and SystemWorks that were current at the time of Jaguar's release are examples of software that trigger this error. In particular, the panel refers to one of the following four files: symfs.kext, SymOSXKernelUtilities.kext, SymEvent.kext, or npc.kext. Symantec advises that you select Don't Use in this case (even though this disables certain features); Symantec has updated its software to correct the problem.

Future updates to Mac OS X are likely to eliminate the options to use these noncompliant kext items. The current dialog is merely an interim measure until vendors have had time to update their software. I haven't encountered this message yet in Panther, so I'm not certain of its current status.

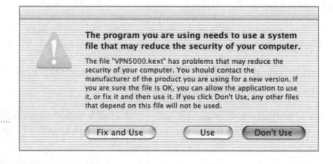

Figure 5.16

The kext warning message.

Login crashes

Log-in crashes are ones that occur after you've select to log in, typically after the Desktop background appears. These are almost always caused by one of two things:

- **A user-level startup item loads at login.** This is the most common cause. The initial work-around is to disable the loading of startup items.

    SEE: • "Disabling user-level startup (login) items," earlier in this chapter, for more details.

    • "Take Note: Problems with User-Level Startup (Login) Items," later in this chapter, for additional details.

- **A corrupt preferences file is accessed at login.** If your Mac crashes just as the Desktop appears and no user-level startup items appear to be the culprits, you may have a corrupt preferences file. (For example, the ~/Library/ Preferences/com.apple.scheduler.plist file, used by iCal, is a potential culprit.) The solution is to log in as the root user, locate the .plist file in your own User directory (not in the one for the root user), and delete the file.

    If you cannot easily diagnose the problem .plist file, the ultimate solution is to log in as the root user and remove the entire contents of your Preferences folder or even the entire Library folder from its current location and move it to another folder (such as your Desktop). You should now be able to log in using the former problem account. A default set of Library files will be created in the active Library folder. From here, you will need to do traditional trial-and-error troubleshooting to locate the problem file. If it isn't a preferences file, it's most likely a font.

    SEE: • "Logging in as another user," later in this chapter, for additional advice on this topic.

TAKE NOTE ▶ Miscellaneous Crashes

The following is a collection of causes and potential solutions for a variety of crashes not specifically described in the main text.

Display software–related crashes. Some Mac OS X crashes are directly related to the display software you're using and/or the display options you select. Here are two examples:

- **Older display software and newer Mac OS X.** Do not install Apple Display Software 2.1.1 or earlier on a Mac running Mac OS X 10.2 or later. Doing so will cause a blue- or gray-screen startup crash.

- **Blank display.** If, in the Displays System Preferences pane, you uncheck the Show Modes Recommended by Display box and then choose a nonrecommended resolution, the display may go blank. One solution is to boot in Mac OS 9 and delete the com.apple.windowserver.plist file in /Library/Preferences. If your Mac cannot start up in Mac OS 9, you can start up in single-user mode and use Unix's rm command to delete the file.

continues on next page

TAKE NOTE ▶ Miscellaneous Crashes *continued*

Sleep-related crashes and problems. A host of potential problems can occur when your Mac wakes from sleep. These include crashes, kernel panics, and simple failures to wake (that is, the screen remains black); no sound or no AppleTalk connection in Classic; and loss of a network connection.

The following are some things to be aware of (and do) when a crash or failure occurs when waking from sleep:

- If a peripheral cable (such as a USB, FireWire, or Ethernet cable) is connected to the Mac, disconnecting it may bring the Mac out of its coma.

  Disconnecting these devices *before* you put the Mac to sleep and keeping them discon-nected until you wake the Mac up may prevent the problem in the first place.

- If you have a PowerBook G3, Apple suggests pressing the brightness key on the keyboard to wake the Mac.

- A wake-from-sleep crash could be caused by a problem with a specific screensaver, espe-cially a third-party one (as selected from the Desktop & Screen Saver System Preferences pane). In this case, the obvious work-around is to shift to a different screensaver.

- More generally, enabling the "Wake for Ethernet network administrator access" option, in the Energy Saver pane's Options screen, can prevent some of these problems. Otherwise, if you get a wake-from-sleep crash, you will need to do a hard reset of your Mac to get it working again.

- Using the commands `reset-nvram` followed by `reset-all` in Open Firmware may fix the problem.

  SEE: • **"Technically Speaking: Open Firmware Commands," earlier in this chapter.**

- The ultimate solution is to wait for and/or get the Mac OS X update (or third-party software update) that fixes the problem.

Directory Services crashes. Incorrect settings in the Directory Access utility, or corrupted pref-erences used by this utility, can cause startup crashes and login failures.

SEE: • **"Take Note: Sleep Problems," in Chapter 2, for related information.**

- **"Technically Speaking: Restoring and Replacing NetInfo and Directory Access Data," in Chapter 4, for more on Directory Services–related problems.**

- **"Sleep problems," in Chapter 9, for more on sleep problems specific to Classic.**

Application Crashes

Most application crashes in Mac OS X will not bring down your entire system, nor will they require you to restart your Mac. Thus, in many cases, the cure for an application crash is to simply ignore it, relaunch the crashed application, and hope the crash does not occur again (or at least happens only rarely). If this is not sufficient, consider the solutions described in the following sections.

Freeze/hang

Applications occasionally stop functioning—often while attempting to perform some action, such as opening a document or receiving an email. In such cases, the spinning beach-ball cursor appears and just remains; the intended action is never completed. At the same time, attempts to otherwise interact with the program (such as selecting menu commands) also fail to work. This is your standard application freeze.

Occasionally, issuing a Cancel command (Command-period) will end the hung action and return control of the application to you; however, I've had only rare success with this in Mac OS X. Also occasionally, just waiting and doing nothing works—which means the application was just taking an unusually long time to complete its task. In such cases, if you come back a few minutes later, all will be well. (See Chapter 6 for some suggestions about how to improve application performance.) More likely, though, something has gone awry, and simply walking away from your Mac won't fix it.

The silver lining is that unlike freezes in Mac OS 9, those in Mac OS X are almost always limited to the affected application. That is, if you simply click the window of another application, the spinning cursor vanishes and your Mac is working normally again. Return to the problem application, and the symptom returns. Still, on the assumption that you would like to use the frozen application again, you'll want to fix the problem. To do so, try the following:

- Force-quit the application.

  SEE: • "Force quitting," later in this chapter.

- If force-quitting doesn't work, but you can still access the Apple menu, choose Log Out from there. When you log back in, things should work normally.

- If the Log Out command doesn't work, try choosing Restart. The logic is the same.

- Occasionally, an application will fail to launch, leaving its Dock icon to bounce endlessly. At this point, it's possible that no menu commands will work. If so, you can often force-quit the application; however, sometimes you may need to hard-restart/reset your Mac.

- Occasionally, a frozen application will cause the entire system to hang—that is, you get no response from any application, the Finder, or the Dock. In addition, the pointer itself may no longer respond to the mouse and the Force Quit command fails to bring up the Force Quit window. When this happens, there's typically been a freeze or crash of some critical process, such as loginwindow. In such cases, it's again time to hard-restart/reset your Mac.

   SEE: • "Logging out, restarting, and resetting," later in this chapter.

Diagnosing the hang. In many cases, a freeze is sporadic, meaning it may not occur again once you've applied one of the fixes described above. Even with consistently recurring hangs, however, you're unlikely to be able to diagnose the cause beyond saying, "It happens when I do this." Thus, the usual solution is to *not* do "this" and/or to wait for a bug-fixed upgrade of the relevant software to be released.

However, if you're determined to track down the precise cause of a freeze, you have a few other options—most of which won't be of much value to nonprogrammers. Even if you can identify the cause of your problem, it's unlikely that you'll be able to do anything about it. Then again, it can't hurt to check some of the following:

- **Sample feature in Activity Monitor.** To use this feature, launch Activity Monitor, select the frozen application, and press Command-I. From the Info window that opens, click the Sample button and then check the text output that appears.

   If you're lucky, you may find a term in the output that indicates a potential cause of the freeze. For example, if you see the word *CUPS* in the sample for a frozen application, it suggests that the CUPS printing software may have indirectly precipitated the freeze. Perhaps the CUPS software itself crashed. The quickest solution is a common one: Restart your Mac. Understanding the cause of a crash may provide clues about how to prevent it.

- **Spin Control.** The Spin Control application in the /Developer/Application/Performance Tools folder (assuming you installed the Developer software) also provides sample output. However, it focuses only on apparently hung applications.

- **The fs_usage command.** The Unix fs_usage command, entered in Terminal, may similarly help diagnose the cause of a frozen process (as described in "Technically Speaking: Terminal Commands to Monitor and Improve Performance," in Chapter 10).

Check the next section for related information, including further advice that can help diagnose a cause so that the freeze/hang does not happen again.

TAKE NOTE ▶ Problems with User-Level Startup (Login) Items

User-level startup (login) items (typically applications) load automatically when you log in—and are thus specific to each user, whose account maintains its own list of these items. As described in Chapter 2, users can add items here, and some software installers do so automatically.

In Jaguar, this list of items is found in the Login System Preferences pane. In Panther, the list is found in the Startup Items screen of the Accounts System Preferences pane. To find it, click the name for your account and select Startup Items from the row of tabs. (Yes, Apple called these *Login Items* in Jaguar.) To avoid confusing them with the startup items in the StartupItems folder (as described earlier in this chapter), I typically refer to them as *user-level startup items* (though I occasionally still refer to them as just *startup items* or even *login items*).

Too many items. If you have too many user-level startup items (the exact number will vary with different Mac OS X installations), some may not load successfully. To get around this problem, you can eliminate items from the list (by selecting them and clicking the remove [–] button) and launching items manually when needed.

If you have too many items in the list, you may find that in some cases when you try to open an application from the Dock—especially if login items are still loading—it will fail to open. In fact, it may even stall permanently, with an endlessly bouncing Dock icon. At this point, even a force-quit may not get the application to quit. Your only resort is to restart.

The order of login items can also sometimes cause conflicts. Check the Read Me files that come with third-party software. These should state whether the application needs to be placed in a particular order if it's added to the Login Items list.

Some items, if added to the user-level Startup Items list, may cause problems no matter where they fall in the list or how many other items the list includes. In such cases, the only solution is to remove the login item from the list or replace it with a bug-fixed update.

Disabling user-level startup items at startup. In worst-case scenarios, conflicts with user-level startup items can prevent the startup process from completing. If this happens, you will not be able to disable the item from the Accounts System Preferences pane because you cannot access System Preferences. The solution here is to disable all such startup items at startup by holding down the Shift key (as described earlier in this chapter).

A Login items manager. Mac OS X stores the Startup Items list in ~/Library/Preferences/loginwindow.plist. The list is contained in a subhead under the AutoLaunchedApplication-Dictionary property of this file. Assuming your problem doesn't prevent you from starting up, you can edit this list via Property List Editor as an alternative way to delete a login item.

continues on next page

TAKE NOTE ▶ Problems with User-Level Startup (Login) Items *continued*

On a related note, one of the weaknesses of the Startup Items screen in the Accounts System Preferences pane is that there's no way to undo remove (-). That is, if you delete a startup item and later want to add it back, there's no button to help you do so. Yes, there is an add (+) button, but because almost anything can be a startup item, it can be hard to know where to look to find the item you want to re-add. In particular, some programs add startup items when they're installed, and these items may be buried within the .app package for the application. If you remove the item and don't know where it's stored, locating it again will be difficult. Even the Finder's Find feature will not locate it, because it does not search within packages.

Note: If you pause the pointer over the item you plan to remove, a yellow tool tip will appear with its pathname. Save this as a record of where the item is located.

A more general solution would be to make a copy of ~/Library/Preferences/loginwindow.plist, which contains the paths to all of your current startup items. That way, if you want to locate an item that you've removed, you can find out its path from this backup copy. When you add new startup items (and you're sure you won't want to add back any previously deleted items), make a new backup copy.

Alternatively, when trying to determine which startup item is causing a problem, you can remove items one by one until you locate the culprit. Once you've done this, you can replace the loginwindow.plist file with the backup copy to restore your list as it was before you began removing items—this time removing just the culprit item (if you found one).

You can also install the third-party utility Panther Cache Cleaner, which includes an option to create a Log-In Items folder in the Library folder of your Home directory. (The feature itself is a user-level startup item.) If you enable this option, any item you place in the Log-In Items folder will launch at login, as if it had been added to the Startup Items list. Remove an item from the folder (via the Finder) and it no longer launches at login. This won't necessarily help for items that are automatically added to the list when installing software; however, it does provide a way to work around re-add hassles.

Items that require passwords. Apple states: "If you set up an application or file that requires a password as a Startup Item, it will not open, but will appear in the Dock. You must click its icon in the Dock and enter its password in order for it to finish opening. Examples of such items include certain email applications, encrypted files, and server administration applications."

Listed items not hiding? When you click the Hide check box for an application in the Startup Items list, the application should open as hidden at login (as if you had selected the Hide command for the application). Occasionally, however, this may not work. As far as I can tell, this is a bug in Mac OS X that will hopefully be fixed in a future update.

continues on next page

> **TAKE NOTE** ▶ **Problems with User-Level Startup (Login) Items** *continued*
>
> **Auto-loading Classic.** On a related note, to launch Classic automatically at startup, use the Classic System Preferences pane setting (no need to use the Startup Items list here!).
>
> **SEE:** • "Disabling user-level startup (login) items," earlier in this chapter, for how to use the Shift key at startup to disable login items.
>
> • "Logging out, restarting, and resetting," later in this chapter, for related information.
>
> • "Preferences Files," in Chapter 4, for more information on .plist files and Property List Editor.
>
> • Chapter 9 for more information on Classic.

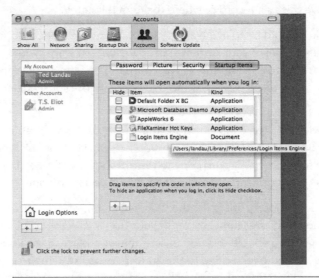

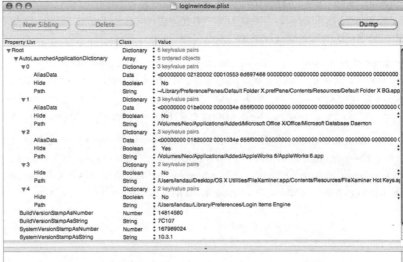

Figure 5.17

The user-level Startup Items list in the Accounts System Preferences pane (top), and the contents of the loginwindow.plist file with detailed listings for the five startup items (bottom).

TECHNICALLY SPEAKING ▶ Connecting Remotely to a Frozen Mac: Killing Processes, Running Sync

Remote access. Even when nothing appears to be working, your Mac may be running normally beneath the surface. What I mean is that the Aqua interface may have gone belly-up temporarily, but its Unix underbelly may still be working—if only you can get to it. This most often occurs when the loginwindow process freezes, often causing even a force-quit to fail. The only quick option is to restart.

You may, however, be able to access your Mac remotely via another Mac on your network—that is, if you enabled the Remote Login options in the Services tab of the Sharing System Preferences pane on the now-frozen Mac. If such is the case, you may be able to connect to the frozen Mac via an application that provides SSH (secure shell) access. If the connecting computer is also running Mac OS X, you can use Terminal (or a third-party utility like MacSSH) to initiate such a connection. You'll need to know the IP address of your Mac.

I discuss the details of how to connect remotely to a Mac (frozen or not) via SSH in "SSH and SFTP," in Chapter 8. Once you're connected, here's what you can do:

Kill a process. If a particular process is causing a freeze, killing it may provide the cure. Elsewhere in this chapter, we cover using Activity Monitor to kill processes; however, you can't use Activity Monitor if your Mac is frozen. The solution, in this case, is to issue a `kill` command remotely, via the Telnet connection. After doing so, you may be able to use your Mac again without having to restart—a valuable technique if you have unsaved files in other running applications that you would have lost via a restart (unless the process you kill results in the unsaved document being destroyed).

Run sync. Another command you could run is `sync`. In essence, this command takes all data in the RAM cache and makes sure that it is written to disk—a technique that's also known as *flushing the cache*. Normally, the Mac does this on its own when restarting or shutting down—as well as periodically when the Mac is idle. But when you perform a hard restart (such as by pressing the Reset button on the Mac), the Mac does not get a final chance to flush the cache. In such cases, data in the cache may not get written to disk, which can result in corrupted files that could cause new (and potentially more serious) problems when you try to restart. Although this scenario is not very common, it is more likely to occur in Mac OS X than in Mac OS 9, because Mac OS X flushes the cache on its own less often than Mac OS 9. Issuing a `sync` command remotely to a frozen Mac eliminates the potential danger.

If remote login is not possible and you're worried about sync problems, let the Mac sit idle for a minute or two before restarting. Assuming that the Unix subsystem is still running, it may sync on its own during that time. Alternatively, if you still have sufficient access to your Mac that you can run Terminal locally, try typing sync in the command line.

SEE: • "Killing Processes from Terminal," later in this chapter, for more on using the `kill` command.
   • Chapter 8 for more on remote access and other networking issues.

Application quits

The most common type of crash in Mac OS X occurs when an application "unexpectedly quits." When this occurs, you typically get a message in the Finder informing you of the "quit."

Unexpected quit and Submit Report. New in Panther, the "unexpected quit" error-message window includes a Submit Report button. Click it, and a Crash Report dialog opens up with two sections. In Problem Description, you can type in your own description of what led to the crash. In Crash Report is a copy of the crash.log for the application (as described in the next section). If you're connected to the Internet, you can click the Send to Apple button, and the entire bug report will be sent. Given how many of these reports Apple is likely to get each day, I'm not sure how much use Apple will make of your particular report; however, I suspect that if it sees a clear pattern (for example, thousands of people reporting the same bug), it could help speed up diagnosing and fixing the problem.

If you don't want to bother with any of this, simply click Cancel in the initial "unexpected quit" dialog.

Figure 5.18

The "unexpectedly quit" error message (top) and the Crash Report dialog that appears if you click the Submit Report button (bottom).

TECHNICALLY SPEAKING ▶ Modifying com.Apple.CrashReporter.plist

If you would prefer not to be bothered with the "unexpectedly quit" error message each time you get a crash, or you would rather bypass the initial screen and go right to the Crash Report window, you can do so. Here's how:

1. Use Property List Editor to open the com.apple.CrashReporter.plist file, located in ~/Library Preferences.

If this file does not exist, create one in Property List Editor. If you create a new file, immediately click the New Root button and then proceed.

2. Add a property (via the New Child button) called DialogType—with one of the following values:

prompt (default; the "unexpectedly quit" window appears after a crash)

crashreport (goes directly to the Crash Report window after a crash)

none (no windows, messages, or dialogs appear after a crash)

Alternatively, you can enter the following command in Terminal:
`defaults write com.apple.CrashReporter {value}`.

Crash.log files. You can potentially learn more about a crash, such as an unexpected quit, by checking the log created or updated when the crash occurred. You can view these logs via the Console utility. Mac OS X maintains several logs simultaneously; the one you're most interested in after a crash is the log specific to the application that crashed. For example, if Safari crashed, you would look for Safari.crash.log. These files contain detailed information about the cause of the crash and are updated with new information at each subsequent crash.

To locate these crash.log files, click the Logs button in Console's toolbar; a list of logs will be displayed in the left column. Go to either ~/Library/Logs or the /Library/Logs for a CrashReporter subfolder. Inside one of these folders will be a crash.log with the name of the crashed application. If an application is listed in both locations, start with the one in ~/Library/Logs. Click it to view it.

SEE: • "Console," in Chapter 2, for more on using this utility.

• **Chapter 4 for background information on logs, extensions, and framework (especially "Technically Speaking: Log Files and Cron Jobs," for more on logs).**

At this point, Mac OS 9 users may be asking, "How can Console show anything after a crash? Don't you have to restart the computer after a crash?" Well, no. Remember that most crashes bring the application down but not the OS itself. So everything but the crashed application will still be working, including Console.

Information about a crash, as viewed in a crash.log file, will usually begin with text such as the following:

```
Command: Microsoft Word
PID: 551
Exception: EXC_BAD_ACCESS (0x0001)
Codes: KERN_INVALID_ADDRESS (0x0001) at 0x25000000
```

This is typically followed by many lines of technical jargon, detailing the state of the Mac at the time of the crash.

Unless you're a software developer, this text will probably be of little use in figuring out what went wrong. And even if you are able to glean information from it, the likely fix will require updating the culprit software (which only the developer can do).

The information can, however, be of value on occasion—especially the first few lines of text and particularly when the crash is caused by something other than the crashed application itself. For example, it may reference a font or fonts in general, suggesting that a corrupt font is the cause. In this case, deleting the font should eliminate the crash. This information could also reference a background process—for example, something loaded as a user-level startup item. Similar to the above example, disabling the user-level startup item should allow you to work around the crash.

SEE: • **"Take Note: Problems with User-Level Start-Up (Login) Items," earlier in this chapter.**

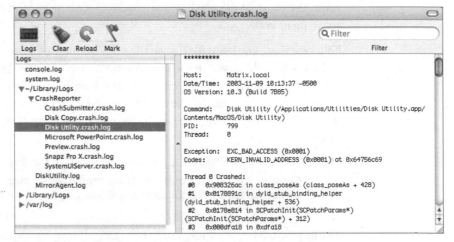

Figure 5.19

The Console utility with a crash.log file displayed.

Background-process crash. A background process (that is, a process with no icon in the Dock) can also crash—though you're unlikely to get an error message or any immediate indication of the crash. Console's console.log, system.log, or a CrashReporter log may indicate which process just crashed; otherwise, symptoms will occur when the crashed process is needed. For example, if background or Unix software essential for networking crashes, you may lose your Internet connection. In such cases, you may be able to restart the process (for example, by using SystemStarter, as described earlier in this chapter) assuming you can figure out exactly what crashed. More likely, your best solution is to restart the Mac.

Will a crash reoccur? After a crash has occurred (and you've decided whether to submit a report to Apple), the first thing you should do is determine whether it will happen again. In many cases, a specific crash will happen so rarely that it's not worth trying to determine the cause. To check for this, follow these steps:

1. Relaunch the application and try to replicate the action(s) you were performing when the crash occurred. Hopefully, the crash will not happen again.

2. If the crash does recur, log out and log back in. Again, the crash may not happen again after you do this.

3. If the crash persists, restart your Mac. Again, the crash may not happen again after you do this.

Diagnosing the crash. If the crash still returns, it's time to try to further diagnose its cause and search for a solution:

- **Pay particular attention to recent changes you've made to your system.** To cite one example, some users experienced an increase in system crashes (even kernel panics) after installing iTunes 2 (in Jaguar). The cause was the iTunesHelper file that was added to the Login Items list when iTunes was installed. Removing this item from the list eliminated the crash. In such cases, it remains for the developer (Apple, in this case) to fix the software so that you don't need to perform this type of work-around.

- **Check the state of the Mac at the time of the crash for possible clues.** A program may crash only if Classic is active, for example. In that case, quitting Classic before running the application could be a work-around.

- **If the crash.log file indicates the involvement of software other than the application itself (such as a font), disable or remove the other software.**

  SEE: • "Take Note: Problems with User-Level Startup (Login) Items," earlier in this chapter.

- **The crash may be caused by a preferences file used by the application.** If so, delete the preferences file.

  SEE: • "Deleting or removing preferences" and "Logging in as another user," later in this chapter.

- **Do you have multiple versions of the same application on your drive?** If so, when you double-click a document, the Mac may try to open a version of the creating application that's incompatible with the version of Mac OS X you are using—thus causing the application to crash. Here are two examples:

If you perform an Archive and Install, the Mac may attempt to launch an application from the resulting Previous Systems folder instead of from the active system software folders (for example, /Applications).

If you have two mounted volumes with different versions of Mac OS X installed (or otherwise have different versions of the same application available), the Mac may try to launch the "wrong" version. For example, I had a setup where both Jaguar and Panther were installed on separate partitions. When running Jaguar, if I double-clicked a document that required a Mac OS X application (such as TextEdit), the Panther version of the application opened instead of the Jaguar version. This happens because the Mac typically opens the newer version by default if it finds two versions of the same program. The result was a crashed application.

The immediate work-around for these problems is to (a) launch the correct application manually before double-clicking the document; or (b) drag the document icon onto the correct application icon. A more long-term solution is to change the default application via the Open With option in the document's Get Info window (as described in Chapter 4). The permanent surefire fix is to delete the duplicate software (assuming you only need one version).

SEE: • "Document opens in the "wrong" application," in Chapter 6, for more information.

• **Upgrade or downgrade the application software.** If the crash occurred after you upgraded to a new version of the software, a bug may have been introduced in the update. Reverting to the older version may eliminate it. Otherwise, check to see whether an even newer version fixes the problem.

• **Consider a hardware-related cause and work-around.** For example, a crash may occur only when the Mac is waking from sleep, which in turn may happen only when peripheral devices are attached to the Mac. If so, the work-around is to disconnect the devices before putting the Mac to sleep.

• **Occasionally, an application crash will result in a kernel panic.** If this happens, you will almost certainly need to restart. At this point, troubleshooting advice is virtually identical to what you do for a kernel panic at startup.

SEE: • "Kernel panic," earlier in this chapter.

• **Check sites (such as Apple's support site and MacFixIt.com) for possible solutions for specific problems.**

• **Consider other troubleshooting techniques, such as running repair utilities.**

SEE: • "Performing repairs with Disk Utility (First Aid),""Running fsck," and "Using third-party disk-repair utilities," later in this chapter.

• "Techniques for solving Mac OS X crashes," later in this chapter, for more advice.

If nothing works, you may have to give up on using the crashing software until an update is released that fixes the problem.

Bomb.app. The Developer software for Jaguar includes a small utility called Bomb.app that's located in the Developer/Applications/Extras folder. If you run it, it crashes itself, giving you a chance to check out the "unexpectedly quit" dialogs described above. Although the utility is not included with the Panther version of the Developer software, it still works in Panther. Thus, if you have this program from a Jaguar installation and you would like to see it in action, save a copy for use in Panther.

TAKE NOTE ▶ Classic Crashes and Freezes

Programs running in Classic may crash, just as they could if you were booted into Mac OS 9. When they do, what happens is similar to what happens if you were booted into Mac OS 9—that is, you may get a freeze, a Type 2 crash, or whatever. When such problems occur, there's a good chance that the entire Classic environment will crash (although Mac OS X and all applications open in Mac OS X will generally be fine). This means that you will lose all access to other applications open in Classic at the time. You will also need to restart Classic to use it again. The only good news is that you should not need to restart Mac OS X itself.

If you're trying to work with a Classic application and it freezes (or you otherwise can't use applications in Classic), try force-quitting the application. You will get a message warning that force-quitting a Classic application is likely to quit the entire Classic environment—and indeed this is almost always the case.

If Classic does not quit after an application freezes or crashes but it does not work, you will need to quit it manually. To do so, choose Quit or Force Quit in the Classic System Preferences pane. After Classic quits, you can restart it and hope that the problem does not recur.

I've found that problems with Classic are most likely to occur after I wake the OS up from sleep or when I wake Classic up from its sleep mode (as set in the Advanced tab of the Classic System Preferences). If you intend to work in Classic for an extended period of time, it's probably best to keep these options set to Never.

If you have problems with a crash or freeze when Classic launches, you probably have an old-fashioned extensions conflict with the extensions and control panels in the Mac OS 9 System Folder. Some files that work fine when you boot into Mac OS 9 do not work in Classic.

There is also a known issue where, if the Startup Items folder in the Mac OS 9 System Folder contains aliases to servers that are not currently available, a hang can occur when launching Classic.

SEE: • **Chapter 9 for information on troubleshooting Classic-related problems.**

Logout, Restart, and Shutdown Stalls and Crashes

When you select Log Out, Restart, or Shut Down from the Apple menu, a dialog appears asking if you're sure you want to do this. If you don't click Cancel, the operation will occur automatically after 2 minutes. Note: To bypass this window, hold down the Option key when you select the appropriate command from the Apple menu.

SEE: • **"Take Note: The Apple Menu and the Option Key," later in this chapter, for more details.**

When you select Log Out from the Apple menu, Mac OS X quits all user processes and returns you to the Login window. You can now log in again as yourself or as another user (assuming you know the needed password), or another user can log in.

When you select Restart or Shut Down, Mac OS X quits *all* open processes, including system-level processes that were opened at startup prior to logging in (such as loading of kernel extensions and startup items). With Restart, another startup is initiated immediately after everything has quit. With Shut Down, the Mac shuts down until you start it up again via the Mac's power button.

Quitting open user processes is handled primarily by the loginwindow process (as mentioned in the "Login" section, earlier in this chapter). It first quits foreground processes (such as user-opened applications), then background ones. If successful, logout (followed by restart or shutdown, if selected) occurs.

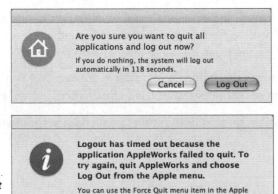

Figure 5.20

The standard logout message (top) and a "logout canceled" error message (bottom).

Logout stalls

If an application or process refuses to quit after you've selected Log Out (or Restart or Shut Down), logout (or restart or shutdown) stalls. If the stall lasts long enough, you will eventually get an error message stating that logout has canceled and indicating which process is responsible.

In rare cases, an application or the entire OS may crash during logout. In such cases, you won't get a cancel message. Instead, for example, you may get an empty blue screen without the spinning-disc cursor, and the Mac will not subsequently shut down or restart as expected.

What to do. If you get a logout stall or crash, here's what to do:

- A stall may occur if an application is waiting for you to save a modified document. In this case, simply save the document; logout should proceed automatically. (If, however, logout has been officially canceled, you'll need to reinitiate the logout.)

- You can usually get around a stall by quitting the application manually and then—if necessary—choosing Log Out, Restart, or Shut Down again.

- If the application or background process remains stuck, try to force-quit it via the Force Quit window, the application's Dock icon, or Activity Monitor.

    SEE: • "Force-quitting," later in this chapter.

- Force a logout, using methods such as quitting the loginwindow process, as described in "Logging Out, Restarting, and Resetting," later in the chapter.

- If problems persist, try pressing the power button on your Mac (if it has one). Although this will trigger sleep or shutdown in some Macs, in others it may initiate a logout.

- If all else fails, you can reset your Mac by pressing Control-Command-Power, pressing the Reset button, or pressing and holding the power button, depending on your Mac model.

    SEE: • "Logging out, restarting, and resetting," later in this chapter.

Restarting and shutting down with Fast User Switching enabled

In the Login Options section of the Accounts System Preferences pane, you'll find an "Enable fast user switching" option. If you enable this option (as explained in Chapter 2), more than one user can be logged in to your Mac at once. To switch from user to user, you access the fast user switching menu in the upper-right corner of the menu bar (which contains the names of all users).

When you select Log Out from the Apple menu, you will see that the name of the currently logged-in user has been added to the Log Out command. Thus, in my case, it would say Log Out Ted Landau. If I select this command, everything works as just described.

However, if you select to shut down or restart when more than one user is logged in, an extra step is required. For example, if you select Restart from the Apple menu and then click the Restart button from the dialog that appears, you will get a new message stating, "There are currently logged in users who may lose unsaved changes if you restart this computer." Before you're allowed to proceed, you must enter an administrator's name and password. After you've done this, the Mac will restart.

SEE: • **The description of the Accounts System Preferences pane in the "System Preferences" section of Chapter 2, for more on Fast User Switching.**

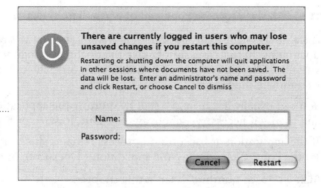

Figure 5.21

The message that appears when you try to restart with multiple users logged in.

Other logout, restart, and shutdown problems

The following are some less common problems that can occur when you select to log out, restart, or shut down.

Auto-logout crash. Occasionally, you may be logged out unexpectedly. That is, even though you did not select Log Out, you're effectively logged out and either sent to the Login window or (if you selected to automatically log in) returned to the Finder with all previous open processes now quit. This is caused by a loginwindow process crash (which in turn was likely caused by conflicting processes' running simultaneously). As noted previously, whenever loginwindow is quit, you log out.

SEE: • **"Login," earlier in this chapter.**

Typically, no fix is needed here. Just log in, if needed, and continue. This is a rare problem that should not likely recur any time soon.

Restart instead of shutdown. In rare cases, when you select Shut Down, the computer may restart instead. For example, Apple has stated: "A Power Mac G4 (Mirrored Drive Doors) computer may restart after the computer has been shut down when it is connected to certain third-party VGA and DVI displays using the DVI connector on the computer. These symptoms can be prevented by connecting the display to the video card's ADC port instead of the DVI port. It may be necessary to purchase an ADC to VGA or ADC to DVI adapter cable."

Software Installer bug and loginwindow. You may have a problem with loginwindow when you're running a third-party installer utility that insists on quitting all open applications before installing the software. In such cases, you may get the following message: "Warning! Quitting 'loginwindow' will log you out." The OS prevents loginwindow from quitting (so you're not logged out), or it does quit (and you are logged out). In either case, this situation prevents the software from installing.

If you're lucky, simply quitting loginwindow may allow the software to install. If you're having problems getting loginwindow to quit, launch Activity Monitor and then force-quit the process. Or, if you prefer to use Terminal, you can obtain the Process ID (PID) # from Activity Monitor and type `kill {PID}` to kill loginwindow and log out.

SEE: • "Killing Processes from Terminal," later in this chapter, for more details.

The real cause is a bug in the application's installer that will need to be fixed by the developer before you can get the installer to work.

Techniques for Solving Mac OS X Crashes

This section covers general techniques you can use to recover from and fix most common freeze and crash problems. The items are listed more or less in the order in which I recommend trying them, barring any specific information that would indicate which one to try first.

SEE: • Startup Crashes" and "Application Crashes," earlier in this chapter, for more specific advice.

Force-quitting

The Force Quit command accomplishes exactly what its name implies: It gets an application to quit when the normal Quit command fails. You can use this technique to quit applications in which the menu commands are inaccessible or do not respond.

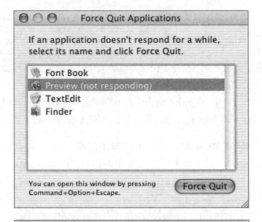

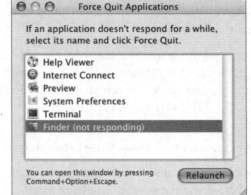

Figure 5.22

Force Quit windows when Preview is not responding (top) and the Finder is not responding (bottom).

Figure 5.23

You can also force-quit a frozen application from the Dock.

You can force-quit an application in several ways:

- **Force-quitting from the Force Quit window.** To do this, press Command-Option-Escape, or from the Apple menu select Force Quit. This brings up a window that lists all currently running applications. Select the one you want to quit; this can be any application in the list, not just the currently active one.

- **Immediately force-quitting the front-most application.** If you hold down the Shift key when selecting Force Quit, the Apple menu's Force Quit command changes to Force Quit {*name of active application*}. Select it and the named application is force-quit, bypassing the Force Quit window.

- **Force-quitting from the Dock.** Click the icon of an application in the Dock and hold down the mouse button to get the contextual menu. If you then press the Option key, the menu's Quit command becomes Force Quit.

  Note: For the Finder Dock icon, if you hold down the Option key prior to selecting its menu, a Relaunch command will appear (even if the Finder is not frozen). If the Finder is frozen, the Relaunch command should appear automatically.

  One advantage of selecting Force Quit from the Dock is that it bypasses the Force Quit window—allowing the action to succeed in situations where the Force Quit window itself is not responding properly.

TAKE NOTE ▶ Application Not Responding

If an application is frozen, Mac OS X typically identifies this as an application that is "not responding." More specifically, the phrase "Not responding" will appear next to the name of the application in the Force Quit window. (Note: In Jaguar, this is instead indicated by the name of the application appearing in red, rather than black, text.)

If you select the Dock menu for a frozen application, the Force Quit option will appear by default (that is, you don't need to hold down the Option key). Similarly, you will get a message stating, "Application not responding." Actually, this message typically appears in the Dock before it appears in the Force Quit window. As such, I would check the Dock menu first when seeking to confirm a freeze.

A word of caution: This message may also appear for a nonfrozen application if it's taking a very long time to complete a task, and other actions in the application cannot be accessed during this time. For example, if you were to select a modification in Adobe Photoshop that takes a few minutes to complete and other Photoshop commands don't work while the modification is in progress, Mac OS X may indicate that the application is not responding. If you assume that Photoshop is hopelessly frozen and force-quit it, you end up terminating a process that would have successfully completed if left alone. Bottom line: Exercise some patience before electing to force-quit.

TAKE NOTE ▶ Force-Quitting from the Dock to Cancel an Application Launch

Suppose you accidentally click an application's Dock icon so that it launches (or you otherwise unintentionally launch an application). You may want to cancel the launch immediately rather than wait for it to finish and then select to quit—especially if that program takes a long time to open (like Photoshop does on my Mac).

You can cancel the launch by force-quitting from the Dock. Just click and hold on the bouncing icon for the launching application. The command that normally reads Quit will now read Force Quit. Select it, and the launch will be instantly terminated.

- **Force-quitting from Activity Monitor.** This application lists all running processes—including background processes not listed in the Force Quit window. To force-quit a running process here, highlight it and from the Process menu select Quit (Command-Option-Q). This brings up a dialog that asks if you "really want to quit" the selected process. Click Quit or Force Quit to do so.

   In general, you should not need to quit processes that aren't listed in the Finder's Force Quit window. Specifically, you should be extremely cautious about quitting Administrator Processes in Activity Monitor, because these often carry out essential tasks that, if quit, could precipitate a crash. However, there are occasions when quitting from Activity Monitor can be useful. The Dock, for example, is listed in Activity Monitor but not in the Force Quit window. If you force-quit it from Activity Monitor, the Dock disappears briefly and then relaunches. Doing this can eliminate problems specific to the Dock.

   SEE: • **Chapter 2 for more information on Activity Monitor.**

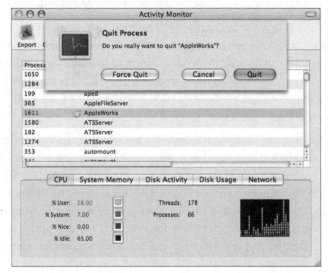

Figure 5.24

Click the Force Quit button to force-quit an application from Activity Monitor.

- **Killing processes from Terminal.** You can kill processes from Terminal—in essence the same thing as force-quitting from Activity Monitor, and a necessary alternative if Activity Monitor is not working. To do so, follow these steps:

   1. Launch Terminal, and type top. You will get a list of running processes that pretty much duplicates what Activity Monitor displays. The first column provides the Process ID (PID) of the processes listed in the second column.

   Note: If you don't see the process you want, you can try enlarging the window to view processes not visible in the smaller window. Otherwise, you can get a complete list of processes by typing ps –aux (or by using Mac OS X's Activity Monitor, if it's accessible).

2. Note the PID of the process you want to quit.

3. Type q to quit top.

4. Type kill {*PID*} to kill the process with the PID number you enter. (Note that if a process is owned by another user, such as the system or root users, you'll need to precede the kill command with sudo to run the command as root.)

Alternatively, you can use the killall command. This works similarly to kill except you enter the name of a process rather than its PID. This allows you to skip the step of locating the PID number. For example, you could type sudo killall lookupd to kill the lookupd process.

Type man kill and man killall for more details.

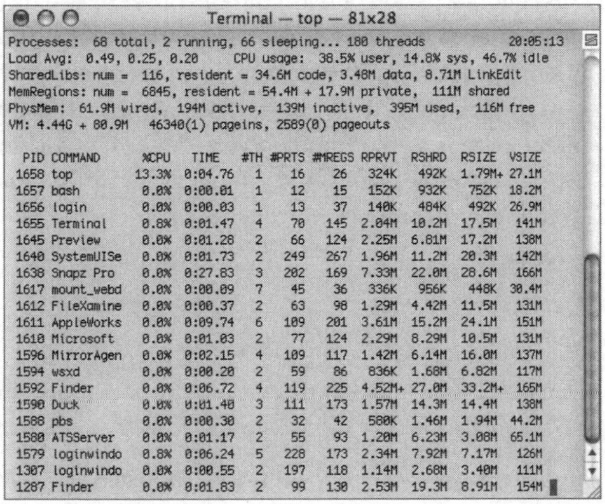

Figure 5.25

The top display in Terminal.

- **Using escapepod.** If none of Mac OS X's built-in Force Quit options work, and especially if a frozen process is preventing you from doing anything with your Mac, there's still hope—that is, if you previously launched the third-party application escapepod (www.AmbrosiaSW.com/utilities/freebies). With this utility installed, you can simply press Control-Option-Delete to instantly force-quit the front-most application. To kill the Dock, press Shift-Control-Option-Delete. Finally, as a last resort, to force-logout, press Command-Control-Option-Delete. In all cases, the action will occur without any prior warning message. To make sure that escapepod is ready when you need it, add it to your user-level Startup Items list.

TECHNICALLY SPEAKING ▶ Kill Signals

Although the term *kill* implies an all-or-nothing action, there are actually a number of degrees of "killing" when it comes to processes and applications. If the kill command (described in the main text) refuses to work in its default form, there are added kill options, called *signals,* you can try.

The default signal is *sigterm.* You do not need to specify this one when using kill. It causes an immediate and graceful termination (that is, temporary files get deleted prior to the kill).

For resistant processes, try the kill signal (for example, kill –KILL). For root-owned processes, you will also want to precede this with sudo. This is the "non-ignorable" kill (which implies that it should work even if the standard kill does not).

To mimic the kill that occurs routinely when you log out of your Mac, use the HUP (hang-up) signal. The process should automatically restart after the kill—desirable if you have a problem you believe you can fix by simply restarting the process. One case in which the kill HUP signal can be useful is when you're connected to the Internet via a broadband connection and almost all applications appear to be frozen or running very slowly. If possible, check your Console log: If it's filling up with error messages that reference "localhost lookupd," you need to kill the lookupd process. To do so, type the following:

sudo kill –HUP {*PID of lookupd*}

Or

sudo killall –HUP lookupd

Typically, the process will quit and automatically restart, hopefully without the Console log errors and with your Mac back to normal. Otherwise, you will need to restart the Mac.

You can also call these signals by their respective numbers. For example, the non-ignorable kill number is 9 and the hangup (HUP) kill number is 1. Thus, to issue a non-ignorable kill for a root process with a PID number of 513, you would type sudo kill –9 513. Then enter your administrative password when prompted.

SEE: • **"Technically Speaking: Editing the Completed Jobs List," in Chapter 7, for another example of using kill with HUP.**

TAKE NOTE ▶ Why Force-Quit (Relaunch) the Finder?

You can press Command-Option-Escape to bring up the Force Quit window and then select Finder to force-quit that application. Once you do this, the button in the window changes from Force Quit to Relaunch (since the Finder must be running for the OS to function normally). Similarly, as described in the main text, if you hold down the Option key prior to selecting the Dock menu for the Finder, a Relaunch command will appear. This relaunch technique can be useful in the following situations:

continues on next page

TAKE NOTE ▶ Why Force-Quit (Relaunch) the Finder? *continued*

- **When the Finder freezes.** If you get a never-ending spinning beach ball in the Finder, it's time to relaunch it.

- **To fix problems with the Finder itself (such as icons that don't display correctly).**

- **To make changes that would otherwise require logging out.** For example, if you select to make invisible files visible via the shareware utility TinkerTool, you need to relaunch the Finder before the change takes place. (TinkerTool includes its own option to relaunch the Finder, bypassing the need to use the Force Quit window.)

- **When the Finder crashes and does not relaunch automatically.** At this point, your Desktop will vanish, and the Finder will not be listed in the Force Quit window. You can typically relaunch the Finder from its Dock icon. However, if the Dock is also inaccessible, quit all other applications listed in the Force Quit window, and the Finder should reappear in the list. You can then select to relaunch it.

Finder Quit command. You can add a Quit command to the Finder menu. Numerous third-party utilities, such as TinkerTool, let you do this. And you can even do it yourself by adding to the com.apple.finder.plist file in ~/Library/Preferences a property called PutMenuItem with a value of True.

If the Finder is frozen, you won't be able to use this command. However, for situations in which you simply want to quit the Finder, it works as an alternative to Force Quit. To get the Finder back, simply click its Dock icon.

Figure 5.26

Three ways to relaunch the Finder: (top left) from the Force Quit window; (top right) from the Apple menu; (bottom) from the Dock.

Logging out, restarting, and resetting

As noted previously (in the "Application quits" section), a common way to solve a problem with a crash is to start over—by logging out, restarting, or (if necessary) doing a reset. Many problems only occur infrequently or under rare conditions. Logging out and/or restarting may clear those conditions, thereby eliminating the problem.

Start first by logging out via the Log Out command in the Apple menu. If that fails, select Restart instead.

Logout and Restart shortcuts. If you can't get the Apple menu commands to work, you can try a keyboard shortcut to access these options:

- **Command-Shift-Q.** This is the keyboard equivalent of the Log Out command. You can also try to log out by quitting the loginwindow process in Activity Monitor.

- **Command-Option-Shift-Q.** This key combination automatically logs you out without issuing the normal warning (asking whether you're sure you want to log out). It quits all open processes, including Classic if it is running (as long as a Classic application is not the current active application).

   Note: Except for the lack of warning, this is a normal logout. This means, for example, that if you have an unsaved document in an application, you will still be prompted to save the document before logout occurs.

- **Command-Control-Eject.** This should initiate a restart instantly (although it may give you a chance to save changes in open documents). (The Eject key is the one that has a triangle with a line underneath it.)

- **Command-Control-Option-Eject.** This works the same as the above key combo, except that it shuts down the Mac instead of restarting it.

- **Control-Eject.** This brings up a dialog that says, "Are you sure you want to shut down your computer now?" Click Cancel, Sleep, Restart, or Shut Down.

- **Control-Option-Eject.** This puts the Mac to sleep instantly. (Although it's not useful for solving a crash problem, I included it here to make the list complete!)

- **escapedpod.** If you have escapepod installed (described in the previous section on Force Quit), Command-Control-Option-Delete should initiate a logout. With this option, you log out without being given a chance to save unsaved documents.

- **Quit loginwindow.** Launch Activity Monitor, locate the loginwindow process, and select Quit from the Process menu. Quit the process to immediately log out, again without having a chance to save unsaved documents.

TAKE NOTE ▶ The Apple Menu and the Option Key

The Command-Option-Shift-Q command is actually a variant of the Log Out keyboard shortcut listed in the Apple menu. It is one of a trio of things that occur in this menu when you hold down the Option key. To see what I mean, pull down the Apple menu and then press the Option key. When the key is pressed, you will see that the ellipses disappear from the end of the Restart, Shut Down, and Log Out commands. In addition, the symbol for the Option key is added to the Command-Shift-Q shortcut for Log Out. This means that holding down the Option key when selecting any of these commands will bypass the normal warning messages that would otherwise occur.

Note: The third-party software FruitMenu can also eliminate the ellipses from the Restart and Shut Down commands.

Figure 5.27

The Apple menu (left) without and (right) with the Option key held down.

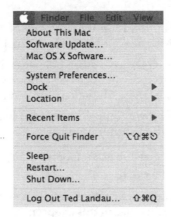 

Figure 5.28

The dialog that appears when you press Control-Eject.

Hard restart/reset. If you cannot get any of the above commands to work, you will need to do what's called a *hard restart*, or a *reset*. The way you do this varies a bit by model, but here are some things to try:

- **Press Command–Control–Power button.** On laptops and older Macs that don't use a USB keyboard, this should restart your Mac instantly. It doesn't work on current desktop Macs—primarily because their keyboards don't include Power buttons!

- **Hold down the power button for several seconds.** The power button has a circle with a vertical line coming out of its top. Its location varies: On flat-panel iMacs, it's located on the base unit, near the ports in the rear. On certain Mac models—notably iMacs, eMacs, and iBooks—holding down this button for 5 seconds or more shuts down the computer. Press the power button again to restart. See the following Apple Knowledge Base document for more details: http://docs.info.apple.com/article.html?artnum=88330.

- **Press the Reset button.** In general, you should use the power button rather than the Reset button. Use the Reset button (especially the internally located ones, described below) only if the prior methods fail. When you press the Reset button, the Mac should restart instantly. The exact location and appearance of the Reset button varies by Mac model. For example:

  On older desktop Power Mac G4s, the Reset button is a small button with a triangle on it on the front of the machine. It is next to yet another small button, the Interrupt button (which you can ignore in this situation).

  On newer Power Macs, the Reset button is internally located on the logic board.

  On most older iMacs, the button is on the right side of the machine by the ports. The flat-panel iMac does not have an external Reset button.

  On iBooks and PowerBook G4s, it is a small hole near the ports; you'll need an unbent paper clip to access it. The PowerBook G3 does not have a Reset button; on this model press Shift-Function-Control-Power.

  For more details, see the following Apple Knowledge Base document: http://docs.info.apple.com/article.html?artnum=86225.

Before doing any of these resets, give the Mac an opportunity to sync by letting it sit idle for a few minutes after a crash.

SEE: • **"Technically Speaking: Connecting Remotely to a Frozen Mac: Killing Processes, Running Sync," earlier in this chapter.**

• **"Technically Speaking: SystemStarter," earlier in this chapter, for a way to partially restart.**

Checking fonts

The selection of fonts accessible while you're running Mac OS X depends on the contents of the Fonts folders in the main Library folders on your drive (/System/Library, /Library, and ~/Library). In addition, Mac OS X accesses the fonts in the Mac OS 9 System Folder used for Classic.

Although the fonts in the /System/Library/Fonts folder should generally remain untouched, the ones in the /Library/Fonts folder—and especially those in the ~/Library/Fonts folder (in your Home directory)—may contain fonts added by applications installers or by you or other users. In some cases, these fonts can cause a crash at startup or when you're using certain applications. Even though a font may work in Mac OS 9, it may be incompatible with Mac OS X.

Bitmap fonts are especially likely to be a problem. These fonts should be needed only to display PostScript printer fonts, which are generally imported from Mac OS 9 systems. Mac OS X does not come with any bitmap or PostScript fonts, relying almost entirely on TrueType fonts instead.

More specifically, Mac OS X prefers to use fonts in a Mac OS X format called *.dfont*. These fonts have a .dfont file extension and are identified in the Get Info window as having a Kind of Data-Fork TrueType Font. The main difference between these fonts and the older TrueType fonts used in Mac OS 9 is that the older font format used both a resource fork and a data fork, whereas the new format uses only a data fork.

SEE: • "Technically Speaking: Type/Creator vs. Filename Extensions," in Chapter 4, for more information on resource forks and data forks.

Mac OS X can still read and use the older TrueType font formats, but they're more likely to be a source of trouble than the newer .dfont format, especially if the fonts are several years old. Fonts in Mac OS 9 font suitcases (especially when the suitcase includes more than one font type) are also a likely source of problems when imported to Mac OS X Fonts folders.

To check for problems, you can remove these font types from their folders and see whether the symptoms vanish. If so, one of the removed fonts is most likely the culprit. You can return the fonts one by one to determine which is the problem (assuming you need all the fonts).

Mac OS 9 (Classic) fonts. Since Mac OS X also reads the fonts in the Fonts folder of the Mac OS 9 System Folder used by the Classic environment, corrupted or outdated fonts here can cause a crash—even a startup crash—when the OS attempts to load them. To test for a startup problem here, reboot in Mac OS 9, if possible, or another Mac OS X bootable volume; drag the Fonts folder to the Desktop; and restart in Mac OS X.

If you *can* start up in Mac OS X, launch Font Book to disable Mac OS 9 fonts. Click the disclosure triangle next to the All Fonts item in the Collection column. Next, select the Classic Mac OS item and click the Disable button at the bottom of the column.

Once the fonts are disabled, relaunch the problem application and/or restart the Mac. If the problem vanishes, a font in the Fonts folder was the cause. If you want to use these Mac OS 9 fonts, you'll need to do some trial-and-error testing to determine the offending font. Otherwise, you can simply leave all these fonts disabled.

Duplicate fonts. Having more than one copy of the same font installed, especially in the same fonts folder, can also be a source of problems.

SEE: • "Viewing and Managing Fonts" and "Working with Fonts," in Chapter 4, for more information on adding and removing fonts, resolving problems with duplicate fonts, and using Font Book and other font utilities.

Deleting or removing preferences

Most applications maintain preferences files in the Preferences folder inside the Library folder of your Home directory. These files contain the settings that you modify via the application's Preferences command. They may contain additional settings as well. Because such files are frequently modified, they are at risk of becoming corrupted.

If preferences files associated with an application become corrupted, they can cause problems with the application, including a freeze or crash on launch. They can also cause other, less serious problems specific to certain features.

Diagnosing a preferences file problem. The quickest way to tell if your problem is due to a preferences file is to remove the entire Preferences folder from your home Library folder. To do so:

1. Quit the problem application.

2. Drag the Preferences folder from the ~/Library folder to a new location, such as the Desktop. Do not delete the folder.

3. Log out and log back in. A new Preferences folder will be created in the ~/Library folder, containing fresh copies of the preferences files needed at login.

    Note: An alternative to step 3 would be to maintain a separate user account with just default settings, and use this to test whether the application problem occurs in that account, indicating that files in your account are at fault. Using a test account simultaneously checks for potential problems with preferences, cache, and any other files in your Library folder.

    SEE: • "Logging in as another user," later in this chapter, for details.

4. Launch the problem application. A new default preferences file for the application will be created.

5. Check to see if the problem has vanished. If so, a corrupt preferences file in the original Preferences folder is almost certainly the cause of the problem. (If the problem still occurs, chances are good that it's not a problem with a file in your Preferences folder.)

If a preferences file does appear to be the culprit, the next step is to identify and delete it. To prepare for this, follow these steps:

1. Quit the problem application, if open.

2. Drag the newly created Preferences folder from the ~/Library folder to the Trash.

3. Drag the original Preferences folder back to the ~/Library folder.

4. Log out and log back in.

You are now ready to isolate and delete the problem file, as described in the next sections.

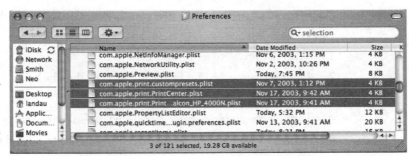

Figure 5.29

A peek into the contents of a Preferences folder, with com.apple.print files highlighted.

Determining the problem preferences file. If a problem is with a specific application, the most likely culprit is the preferences file that includes the name of the application. Many preferences files have names like com.{*developer name*}.{*name of application*}.plist.

To find all such files, open the Preferences folder and type the name of the application in the Search field of the window's toolbar. This will generate a results list of all files in the folder that include the name of the application.

Occasionally, an application may use a preferences file that does not include its name. For example:

• Mac OS X's Mail uses a file called MessageSorting.plist (in addition to com.apple.mail.plist).

• In Panther, Printer Setup Utility uses a file called com.apple.print.PrintingPrefs .plist (in addition to com.apple.print.PrinterSetupUtility.plist). In Jaguar, Print Center uses files such as com.apple.print.defaultpapersize.plist and com.apple .print.custompresets.plist (in addition to com.apple.printcenter.plist).

These atypically named files have been implicated in problems that are solved by deleting the files. How can you identify these atypically named files as the cause? If there's a preferences setting you can enable and disable to make the problem vanish and return, change the setting. Then sort the Preferences column by Date Modified (or use the Finder's Find command to search for items with a *date modified is today* criterion). Locate the most recently modified item, which is likely to be the culprit.

Check also in the ByHost folder inside the Preferences folder: It can contain the troublesome .plist file.

If you have little or no idea what the problem preferences file might be, launch the Console utility and select to view the system.log file (located in /var/log). From the Edit menu, select Find, and search for all instances of "parse failed." If a .plist file is mentioned in reference to this failure, it is the likely culprit. Delete the file from your Preferences folder.

SEE: • "Running Mac OS X software from the Terminal," in Chapter 10, for a related discussion of the plutil Terminal command and the Preferential Treatment utility.

Deleting the problem preferences file. Once you've identified the likely culprit(s), follow these steps to delete it:

1. Quit the problem application.

2. Drag the suspected preferences file(s) to the Trash.

3. Log out and log back in.

4. Launch the problem application. New default preferences file(s) are created.

5. If the problem is gone, empty the Trash to delete the old preferences file(s).

   The new preferences file(s) will contain default settings—which means you may need to make some changes in the application's preferences to get the application back to the state you desired.

6. If the problem remains, drag the original file from the Trash back to the ~/Library/Preferences folder. This saves you the hassle of re-creating preferences settings unnecessarily.

   A variation on this theme would be to rename the preferences file (such as to *name*.plist.old) rather than drag it to the Trash. A new default copy will still be created when needed. If it turns out that this fixes the problem, you can now delete the .old file. Otherwise, delete the newly created file and rename the old file back to its original name.

If your first attempt at deleting a preferences file does not lead to success, you'll have to get more creative. Consider preferences files that were last modified around the time the problem started. Or look for preferences for software that interacts with the problem application (such as a spelling checker or font utility that's active within a word processor that's crashing). Try moving these files to the Trash, following the same procedure as described above.

Tips for deleting preferences files. The following is a collection of tips for troubleshooting problem .plist files:

- **Log out.** In general, you should log out and back in before relaunching the problem application and forcing a new preferences file to be created. Otherwise, Mac OS X may re-create the corrupted .plist file from data cached in memory (rather than create a new default copy).

  In certain cases, you may need to log out and temporarily log in as the root user (or at least another user), deleting the preferences file from here in order to avoid this caching problem. This is important, for example, when deleting the com.apple.finder.plist file (to fix odd Finder-related symptoms): You need to log in as another user because you normally can't quit the Finder while logged in.

  Note: If you have Fast User Switching enabled, just switching to another user is not sufficient in these situations; you actually need to log out from your account and log back in.

  An alternative is to add a Quit command to the Finder, using a utility like TinkerTool. Once you've done this, drag the com.apple.finder.plist file to the Trash and immediately quit the Finder. Finally, empty the Trash via the Trash icon in the Dock and relaunch the Finder. Just to be safe, I'd also log out and back in again.

SEE: • **"Logging in as another user,"** later in this chapter, for related information.

- **Stay home.** In general, you should only delete preferences that are in the Preferences folder within the Library folder of your Home directory. Leave preferences files in /Library/Preferences alone unless you're specifically advised to modify or delete them (such as via a support document on Apple's Web site). You'll need administrator access to modify files in this folder, in any case.

- **Get permission.** Occasionally, you may be unable to replace a particular preferences file in your Home directory due to insufficient permissions. In most cases, although you cannot replace the preferences file with a copy, you can still delete the original file. In these instances, the solution is to drag the problem file to the Trash and *then* drag the replacement to the Preferences folder. Otherwise, use any of the other methods described in Chapter 6 for dealing with files that cannot be deleted.

SEE: • **"Deleting and moving instead of replacing,"** in Chapter 6, for more details.

- **Lock or unlock preferences.** Occasionally, preferences settings get reset to their default values when you log in—even if you don't delete the preferences file. You may be able to prevent this by locking the relevant .plist file after making the change. To do this, open the Get Info window for the file and check the Locked box.

    Note that you will be unable to modify the preferences file unless you unlock it again. And keep in mind that other unusual symptoms can result from a locked preferences file; if so, you will need to unlock it.

    In some cases, a preferences file may become locked even though you did not lock it. This situation can cause various symptoms, including an inability to install an update to the software. Sometimes, simply unlocking the file will cure the problem. Otherwise, unlock and delete the file.

SEE: • **"Preferences Files,"** in Chapter 4, for more details about these files.

    • **"Modifying or deleting the .GlobalPreferences.plist file,"** in Chapter 6, for related information.

TAKE NOTE ▶ Utilities to Delete .plist and Cache Files

For problems with .plist and cache files that are not obviously linked to a specific application, you may prefer to use a utility to delete these files rather than to manually diagnose the problem. Various shareware utilities, such as Kristofer Szymanski's Cocktail and Northern Softwork's Panther Cache Cleaner, automatically delete the most likely culprit cache files (and, in some cases, .plist files).

Especially if you have upgraded to Panther, make sure you're using a version of the utility that's compatible with your Mac OS X version.

SEE: • **"Take Note: Launch Services Files and Beyond,"** in Chapter 6, for related information.

Deleting cache files

Cache files (stored in the ~/Library/ Caches folder) are used by certain applications to store frequently accessed data. Items here typically have names that identify the application that uses them (such as iPhoto Cache). Through normal use, it's possible for these files to become corrupt. As with preferences files, deleting relevant cache files can solve application problems.

New cache files will be re-created as needed after old ones have been deleted. However, be cautious: In some cases, cache files contain information that cannot be easily re-created. Maintain a backup of cache files before deleting any (or remove the file

Figure 5.30

The contents of my ~/Library/Caches folder.

from the Library folder instead of deleting the file immediately). That way, if you discover that a cache file is not the culprit, you can restore the originals.

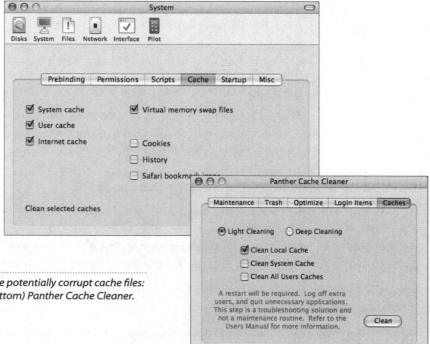

Figure 5.31

Utilities that can delete potentially corrupt cache files: (top) Cocktail and (bottom) Panther Cache Cleaner.

Figure 5.32

The contents of my ~/Library/ Application Support folder.

Checking for other corrupt files

Sometimes a program will crash on your computer when the same program seems to run fine on an almost identical machine. Why is this? Corrupted preferences or cache files, as just described, could be one cause. But there are other potential culprits as well. Consider the following:

- **The application itself could be damaged or corrupted.** Files within the application package may have been deleted or modified, accidentally or deliberately. The typical solution is to trash and reinstall the application. In the case of applications installed by the Mac OS itself, however, this can be tricky since you won't likely have easy access to individual files installed by the OS update.

  SEE: • "Selectively Installing Mac OS X Files," in Chapter 3, for details.

- **There could be problems with support files.** Sometimes, problems can occur with accessory files for an application that get stored in locations separate from the application itself, such as the Application Support folder or the InputManagers folder inside the ~/Library folder. These accessory files may not get updated properly when an update installer is run, for example. If you know that this has happened, you can usually correct the problem by deleting the out-of-date software and reinstalling the latest version.

  If you use the third-party Application Enhancer (APE) utility, items in the Application Enhancers folder, in your Library folder, are another potential source of problems. In some cases, the problem is with the APE software that's accessed by the APE modules: the APE Preferences pane and ApplicationEnhancer.framework (both located in the /Library folder). Reinstalling or updating this software may fix the problem.

- **Permissions and ownership of the file may have changed.** As discussed in Chapter 4, each file has a set of privileges/permissions, as well as an owner and a group name. If these settings change, a file may not open, or you may not be able to save documents in the file. Repairing permissions with First Aid may help (as described next). Otherwise, see Chapter 6 for solutions to this problem.

Logging in as another user

As indicated in the previous sections, rather than removing files from your Library folder to test for problem files, you can log in as another user. In fact, I advise creating a test user just for this purpose. Once you create this user account, don't add any third-party software or change the default settings. This way, the user's directory remains "clean." If changes you've made to your own directory are the source of a problem, the problem should not occur when you switch to this other user.

If the problem vanishes when you're logged in as another user.
If the problem does not occur when you're logged in to the test user's account, you can be almost certain that the cause of the problem is either a file in your Home directory (in the Library folder or in a folder in the Documents folder maintained by an application) or an item you've added to your user-level Startup (Login) Items list.

If a problem in your account is indicated, and you haven't already checked for problems with user-level startup (login) items, fonts, preferences, and cache files (as described in previous sections), these would be the most likely culprits. Otherwise, it's time to look elsewhere, starting with recently modified files in the Library folder.

SEE: • Chapter 2 for more details on how to use the Accounts System Preferences pane to create a new user.

If you identified the problem file, delete or replace it as appropriate. Otherwise, as a last resort, create yet another user account and transfer all of your critical files to it, deleting the original account when you're finished. As long as you're an administrator and owner of both accounts, you should have no problem doing this.

If the problem remains when you're logged in as another user. If the problem remains when you're logged in as a different user, the problem is at a more system-wide level, either in the Applications folder (if the problem is specific to a given application) or in one of the main Library folders (/System/ Library or /Library). If you have some idea about what the problematic file may be (and can work around any permissions hassles), you can try replacing it (assuming you have a good copy as a backup). Otherwise, you're probably looking at reinstalling the entire OS.

There could also be a problem with one of the files in the invisible Unix folders. Unless you're familiar with Unix or have specific advice from some other source (such as this book!), diagnosing and fixing problems here can be very difficult. In most cases, you will more likely wind up having to reinstall Mac OS X.

Logging in as another user and Fast User Switching. Prior to Panther, one hassle of logging in as another user to test for problems with your account was that you had to log out of your own account before you could log in to another one. This meant that all open files in your account were closed or quit on logout and needed to be relaunched when you logged back in.

With Panther, however, you can avoid this hassle by enabling Fast User Switching (via the check box in the Login Options section of the Accounts System Preferences pane). Now, just select the name of your test account from the menu in the upper-right corner and log in. This allows you to log in to the test account without logging out from your own account first.

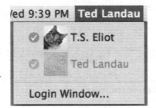

Figure 5.33

The menu for Fast User Switching.

Checking for extension (kext) problems

While kernel extension problems most often lead to startup crashes or kernel panics, these files can also be the root cause of a variety of other symptoms. Here are three examples:

- In the initial (Build 6R65) version of Mac OS X 10.2.8, a buggy kext file (AppleGMACEthernet.kext) caused many Mac users to lose their Ethernet connections.

- On some G3 Macs with more than 192 MB of RAM installed, the ATIDriver.bundle file (located in the AppleNDRV folder in the same Extensions folder that contains kext files) in Mac OS X 10.2.8 could cause the screen to go black when running certain applications (for example, Disk Utility and Microsoft Entourage).

  Removing the ATIDriver.bundle file was Apple's recommended solution for problems with this file that persisted even after updating to a later build (Build 6R73) of Mac OS X 10.2.8.

- The IOUSBFamily.kext file can cause startup problems in some versions of Mac OS X. In these cases, you need to find a way to start up successfully before you can solve the problem. If a safe boot doesn't work, start up from another volume. As a last resort (and if you feel up to the task), start up in single-user mode to delete or replace files as needed.

    In one specific case, kernel panics occurred a few minutes after startup as a result of certain USB hubs' being connected to a Mac running Mac OS X 10.2.5. The panic.log file for this crash referenced the IOUSBFamily.kext file. Abandoning use of the hub often solved the problem. Otherwise, the solution was either to downgrade to an older version of the IOUSBFamily.kext file or upgrade to Mac OS X 10.2.6 or later. Details regarding these types of fixes are described below.

Expect similar glitches to occasionally pop up in Panther, as updates get released. Checking for error messages in verbose mode may help identify a problem kext file. Figuring out the best solution for kext problems, however, can be a bit tricky. Consider these alternatives:

- **Updating the kext cache.** A general potential fix for problems here is to delete the Extensions.mkext and/or Extensions.kextcache items. Typically you would do this in Terminal by typing the following:

    ```
    sudo rm /System/Library/Extensions.kextcache
    ```

    or

    ```
    sudo rm /System/Library/Extensions.mkext
    ```

    Restart immediately after doing this by typing reboot in Terminal.

    SEE: • **"Technically Speaking: Understanding Kernel Extensions," earlier in this chapter, for more information.**

- **Removing or disabling the kext file.** Select the file in the /System/Library/Extensions folder, hold down the Command key, and drag the file to your Desktop (if you want to save the file) or to the Trash. (If you don't hold down the Command key, the file will be copied rather than moved.) A dialog will appear, asking you to enter an administrator's name and password. After you do this, the file is moved.

    Alternatively, you can use a utility such as Infosoft's MOX Optimize to disable (and later re-enable) kext files.

    Just be careful about what you remove or disable: Disabling an essential Panther-installed kext file can make startup failure a near certainty.

    To check the "essential" status of any kernel extension, use the Show Package Contents contextual menu for the extension, and locate its Info.plist file. Open the file with Property List Editor. One of the properties may read OSBundleRequired. It has several possible values. If its value is Safe Boot, the extension will load even if the Shift key is held down at startup. This means it is required. If it has another property, or there is no OSBundleRequired property at all, the item will not load during a safe boot; it is thus not an essential file. In the rare case that an essential kext item causes a crash, you will need to start up in single-user mode to fix it or (more likely) reinstall the entire OS.

If in doubt, contact Apple or the vendor of the problem software for advice.

A potential disadvantage of removing any kext file is that you lose whatever function the removed file provided. For example, if the file provided support for a PCI card that you have installed, you can no longer use the card.

- **Replacing the kext file.** It may be that a kext file has become corrupt and needs to be replaced. If you have a backup copy, just drag it to the Extensions folder. A dialog with an Authenticate button will appear. Click it, and you're on your way. Alternatively, you may be able to replace the file by rerunning the installer that first installed the kext file. If in doubt, check with the software vendor for advice.

- **Downgrading to an older version of the kext file.** When the Ethernet problem with the 10.2.8 update first appeared, users found they could solve the problem by replacing the buggy kext file with the version of the file used in 10.2.6. To do this downgrade, you need to either have the older file in your backups or be able to extract it from the previous version of the Mac OS X Update package using a utility such as Pacifist (as described in more detail in Chapter 3). Once you've done this, you can replace the newer file as just described. A similar solution worked for the IOUSBFamily.kext problem.

  There's always a risk when mixing kext files from different versions of Mac OS X. If they don't play together well, you may wind up with more problems than you solve. In particular, avoid replacing a Panther file with a Jaguar one. However, if no other solution presents itself, it's worth a shot.

  A safer alternative is to reinstall Mac OS X entirely (using the Archive and Install feature of the Installation disc), and then update back to the most recent symptom-free version as needed. However, this is a much bigger hassle than downgrading a single file.

- **Upgrading to a new version of the kext file.** This is the ideal solution. For example, Apple resolved the Ethernet problem with Mac OS X 10.2.8 by releasing a new version of 10.2.8 that included a bug-fixed version of the file.

  While you await a bug-fix upgrade, you may be able to work around a symptom by modifying your hardware setup rather than fiddling with kext files. For example, if a problem only occurs when using a USB hub, you can temporarily give up the hub and connect all USB devices directly to your Mac.

Whenever you make a change to the Extensions folder (other than via an Installer utility), you must delete the Extensions.mkext files (in the root level of the /System/Library folder) or change the modification date of the Extensions folder—and then restart.

SEE: • "Technically Speaking: Understanding Kernel Extensions," earlier in this chapter, for more background information.

Performing repairs with Disk Utility (First Aid)

Whenever you encounter otherwise inexplicable problems, a standard bit of troubleshooting advice is to run a disk-repair utility. These utilities check and, if need be, repair critical portions of a disk that can affect its ability to open and even locate files. In extreme cases, such problems can prevent a Mac from starting up, posing a risk that data on the drive may be irrecoverable.

It's a good idea to run a repair utility periodically, perhaps once a month, even if you aren't having problems: It may detect and fix subtle problems that, while not causing symptoms at the moment, may precipitate more obvious and serious problems as time passes.

Disk errors are especially likely to occur whenever data is copied to the disk improperly—for example, during an improper shutdown (such as turning off the Mac without using the Shutdown command, or after a kernel panic), a forced restart, or any power interruption. Installing new software or updates can also cause problems. If problems occur after such events, you should attempt to repair the disk. Apple includes one such repair utility as part of Mac OS X: Disk Utility. It's the first repair utility you should try. It may not always succeed, but it will almost never make the problem worse.

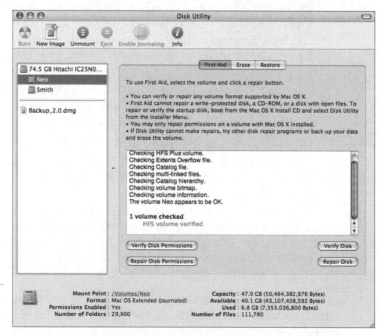

Figure 5.34

The First Aid screen of Disk Utility, after clicking Verify Disk.

Located in the Utilities folder, Disk Utility combines what in Mac OS 9 were two separate utilities: Drive Setup and Disk First Aid. In Panther, it also includes the functions formerly assigned to Disk Copy. It is the First Aid component that's the focus here.

SEE: • "Disk Utility," in Chapter 2, for an overview of Disk Utility.

• " Backing up Mac OS X: utilities for volume backups" and "Bootable CD," in Chapter 3, for additional details about Disk Utility features.

Accessing Disk Utility's First Aid. To access the First Aid component of Disk Utility, follow these steps:

1. Launch Disk Utility.

2. Click the First Aid tab at the top of the area to the right.

3. From the column on the left, select the drive, volume, or partition you wish to verify or repair.

Near the bottom of the right side of the window, you should see four buttons: Verify Disk Permissions, Repair Disk Permissions, Verify Disk, and Repair Disk.

Verify vs. repair. The Verify options check for and report problems but do not repair them. The Repair options check for and make any needed repairs.

The main reason to choose Verify is that occasionally there may be problems you don't want to fix (at least not right away) for fear that doing so may cause even more problems. For example, if Verify reports serious problems and you have files that are not backed up, you should back up these files before proceeding with repairs. This is because an attempt to repair the drive could potentially fail and result in an inability to restart the Mac at all.

For simplicity, in the examples that follow, I assume that you're ready to proceed with repairs and will thus omit further discussion of the Verify option.

Depending on the volume you select, one or both of the Repair buttons may be dimmed and unselectable. The following sections provide details about how to proceed.

Repair Disk. To repair a disk, click the Repair Disk button.

As the repair check proceeds, feedback will appear in the scrollable text area above the button. You will see lines such as Checking Catalog file and Checking volume bitmap. A progress bar will also appear in the window. When the work is complete, the progress bar will vanish.

If any errors were detected, they will be listed in the report text. In addition, the final lines of the text will indicate the overall result. If no problems were detected, it will say something like the following:

```
The volume {name of volume} appears to be OK.
Repair attempted on 1 volume
HFS volume repaired
```

If errors were detected, the final text will indicate that problems were found and that either repairs were made successfully or the volume could not be repaired. Here's what to do next:

- If First Aid reports problems and fixes them, run First Aid again. Keep doing this until First Aid no longer reports any problems. Sometimes a repair may uncover another problem that the next repair cycle will detect.

- If First Aid reports no problems or reports problems and fixes them, but your symptom persists, you could try another repair utility (just in case it can detect problems that First Aid cannot). Otherwise, disk repairs are not likely to be related to the cause of the problem.

- If First Aid reports problems but cannot fix them, definitely try another repair utility. Otherwise, erasing and reformatting your drive is the only likely way to repair the damage.

Finally, you may wonder what First Aid's sometimes-cryptic error messages mean. In general, they're concerned with problems with an invisible area of the drive called the Directory, which is the main component that First Aid checks and repairs. The Directory has nothing to do with Unix directories or folders; it mainly keeps track of where every file is located on the drive. In addition, because a file may be stored in several segments in different locations on the drive, the Directory contains the information needed to tie these segments together so that the application can run or the file can be opened. Obviously, if this information gets corrupted, it can prevent an application from working or a file from being usable. If the corrupted software is critical for startup, such damage can prevent the OS from starting up. If this sort of error cannot be repaired, your only choice is to reformat the drive.

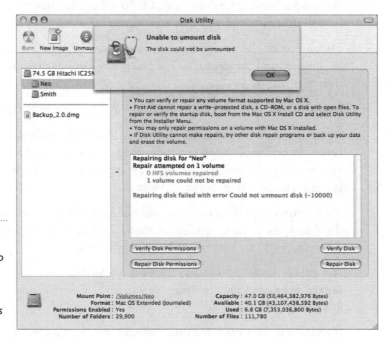

Figure 5.35

An error message that appears in First Aid if you try to check a volume that cannot be unmounted (perhaps because it has open files on it).

Verify/Repair Disk won't run. You cannot verify or repair the current startup volume—in which case the buttons will be dimmed and unselectable.

You also cannot repair any write-protected or read-only media, nor can you repair a volume that's in use (for example, one that contains open or launched files)—including the volume that contains Mac OS 9 (if Classic is active) or any partition that contains an open application or document (including Disk Utility itself). If you try to do so, you will get an error message after clicking the Verify or Repair buttons.

You can repair any other volume (assuming the volume's format is supported by Mac OS X)—even ones without Mac OS X installed on them.

The fact that you can't repair the startup volume is a significant obstacle to using First Aid, since the startup volume is by far the most likely volume you'll want to repair (in fact, for many Mac users, it's their *only* volume). There are several ways around this problem:

- **Boot from the Install CD/DVD.** The typical way to use First Aid to check the startup drive is to start up from the Mac OS X Install CD. When the Installer opens, from the File menu choose Disk Utility. As described above, go to the First Aid tab, select your normal startup volume, and click Repair Disk.

  A potential problem here occurs if Mac OS X has been updated since the version that's on your Install CD. Say you have Mac OS X 10.2.0 on your CD, but you're now running Mac OS X 10.3. If the updated version of Mac OS X includes an updated version of Disk Utility, the version you run when booted from the CD is no longer the latest version. Obviously, you want to use the latest version because it presumably includes bug fixes and checks for problems not present in the older version. If this is a relevant issue for you, consider one of the remaining alternatives.

  SEE: • "Take Note: Determining the Disk Utility Version," below, for related information.

- **Boot from a customized CD.** You can create a custom bootable CD and place the latest version of Disk Utility on it. The simplest way to do this is to make an editable disk image of the Mac OS X Install CD, replace the old copy of Disk Utility with the new copy, and burn the new CD.

  SEE: • "Bootable CD," in Chapter 3, for more details.

- **Boot from another volume that contains Mac OS X.** If you have an external drive with Mac OS X installed, boot from it. You can now check your normal startup drive. You can even use an iPod this way (if you've installed system software on it).

- **Boot from another Mac.** If you have two Macs, you can connect them via Target Disk Mode, and then start up from the Mac you do not intend to repair. This procedure makes the target computer mount as though it were an external drive—at which point you can run First Aid on it.

  SEE: • "Sharing via Target Disk Mode," in Chapter 8, for more information.

- **Run fsck automatically (at startup).** Starting up via a safe boot forces the fsck utility to run at startup (unless journaling is enabled). This is equivalent to running First Aid to repair a disk.

  Alternatively, if you restart the Mac without first selecting Restart or Shut Down (such as after a kernel panic, power failure, or any crash that requires a reset), the Mac should similarly run fsck at startup.

  Depending upon the nature of the restart, this fsck check occurs when the "Checking disks" text appears on your screen or during the gray-screen phase earlier in the startup process. Startup will take longer than usual because of this check.

  The main disadvantage here is that you get almost no feedback as to whether repairs were needed and made. However, if the problem disappears, you can assume fsck was successful.

  There is one potential feedback indicator: If repairs were made, the Mac should restart on its own. That is, before startup is completed, you will hear the startup chimes a second time, and the boot process will start over. This means repairs were made and were likely successful.

  Another alternative is to start up in single-user mode and run fsck. This has the advantage of providing feedback much as if you were running First Aid.

  Finally, the fsck_hfs command, run in Terminal, may be able to check the current startup volume, thus working around the First Aid restriction. However, as explained a bit later in the chapter, be cautious about using it.

SEE: • "Safe booting," earlier in the chapter, for related information.

• "Enabling and disabling journaling," later in this chapter, for an option that reduces the need to do First Aid repairs and prevents fsck from running at startup.

• "Running fsck," later in this chapter, for more information about fsck, especially about single-user mode and the fsck_hfs option.

TAKE NOTE ▶ Determining the Disk Utility Version

You can determine whether your Install CD contains an older version of Disk Utility than the one on your hard drive by comparing the version numbers listed in the About Disk Utility window (accessed from the Disk Utility menu) for each copy.

The version number will be something like 10.4 (v135); the higher the number(s), the newer the version.

On your hard drive, you'll find Disk Utility in the Utilities folder. On the Install CD, you can locate Disk Utility by double-clicking the CD icon after it has mounted. In the window that opens, open the Applications folder and the Utilities folder contained within it. Inside you'll find five applications: Disk Utility, Installer, Reset Password, Startup Disk, and Open Firmware Password.

To determine the versions of these two copies of Disk Utility, check the Version line in each application's Get Info window in the Finder—or launch each utility and check its About box.

Disk First Aid in Mac OS 9. Mac OS 9 has a Disk First Aid utility. You cannot run this application from Classic within Mac OS X, but you can run it when you're booted from Mac OS 9 (assuming your Mac can still run in Mac OS 9). Can you use this utility to attempt to repair a Mac OS X volume or a volume with both Mac OS 9 and Mac OS X on it? The answer is yes. Just make sure you're using a version that came with Mac OS 9.1 or later—ideally, the newest version available. However, I see no reason to do this anymore. Running the First Aid component of Mac OS X's Disk Utility is clearly preferred.

Repair Disk Permissions. Due to a variety of causes (most notably errors introduced during Mac OS X updates), some files and folders on your drive may acquire incorrect permissions. When this happens, you may be unable to access a needed file or folder because you lack sufficient permission—however, it may not be obvious that this is the cause of a problem. For example, an application may fail to launch but display no error message due to a permissions problem with an accessory file used by the application. This makes it especially difficult to fix the permissions problem directly (such as via the file's Get Info window): You won't know that a permissions problem is definitely the cause, and you certainly won't know with any certainty which file needs fixing.

Other "mysterious" permissions-related problems include -108 errors in Printer Setup Utility, -192 errors when trying to mount a disk image, and certain locked files that cannot be unlocked.

To repair these disk permissions, click the Repair Disk Permissions button. This forces all system-level Mac OS X files to revert to their default settings (ownership and access), eliminating any introduced errors. It should have no effect on files you created or added by any means other than a Mac OS X Installer or Apple-provided software updater. While the repairs are in progress, the scrollable text box will generate a list of errors as they're detected and fixed. When complete, you should see a message resembling the following:

The permissions have been verified or repaired on the selected volume. Permissions repairs complete.

The hoped-for result? All permissions-related problems have vanished!

Note: The Verify Disk Permissions and Repair Disk Permissions buttons are only enabled if you're attempting to check a volume that has Mac OS X installed. Unlike with Repair Disk, you can use these buttons with the current startup volume. In fact, it's preferable to do so, because Repair Disk Permissions uses the receipt files in the /Library/Receipts folder on the current boot volume to determine the correct permissions for system-level files. Thus, running Repair Permissions for your startup hard drive when booted from the Install

Mac OS X CD may not work as expected, because it would search (in vain) for a Receipts folder on the CD.

SEE: • **"Technically Speaking: Repair Disk Permissions and Receipts," below.**

Note: First Aid's Repair Disk Permissions function was added in Mac OS X 10.2. Apple previously released a similar but separate utility called Repair Privileges that works only in Mac OS X 10.1.5. (It does not work in Mac OS X 10.2 or later.)

Preventing problems by using Repair Disk Permissions. It's good preventive medicine to repair disk permissions before and (especially) immediately after installing any Mac OS X update—even if you haven't noticed problems. This can prevent update-related symptoms that might otherwise occur.

Occasionally, First Aid may "repair" a setting that was already correct, *causing* rather than fixing a problem. However, the risk of this is low. Thus, periodically repairing permissions remains a good idea.

Repair Disk Permissions error messages that are repeated. You may find that Repair Disk Permissions occasionally reports the same errors more than once, sometimes claiming to refix a problem it claimed to fix in a previous run. In most cases, you can ignore this repetition and assume the repairs were correctly made.

For example, with an early version of Mac OS X 10.2, Disk Utility would repeatedly report an error with /private/var/run/utmp. Apple said this could be safely ignored. Ditto for the error that refers to /private/var/db/netinfo/local.nidb/{*text*}.

Fix Mac OS 9 Permissions. Separate from the Repair Disk Permissions buttons, there is a command in Disk Utility's File menu called Fix OS 9 Permissions. If it's dimmed, you have not selected a System Folder to be the Classic System Folder. To do so, go to the Classic System Preferences pane and select a system folder. Once you've selected it, quit and relaunch Disk Utility. The button should now be selectable.

If you select Fix OS 9 Permissions, First Aid will check for and repair Classic System Folder permissions that might otherwise prevent Classic from launching.

SEE: • **"Permissions settings and running Classic," in Chapter 9, for related information.**

Figure 5.36

The message that appears after you've successfully run Fix OS 9 Permissions.

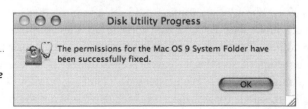

Disk Utility log. Disk Utility maintains a log of all your actions and their results. You can view this log by selecting Log from Disk Utility's File menu or via Console (the file is stored in /Library/Logs).

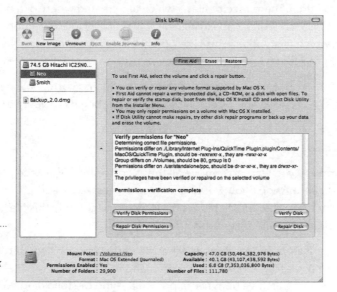

Figure 5.37

The First Aid screen of Disk Utility, after clicking Repair Disk Permissions.

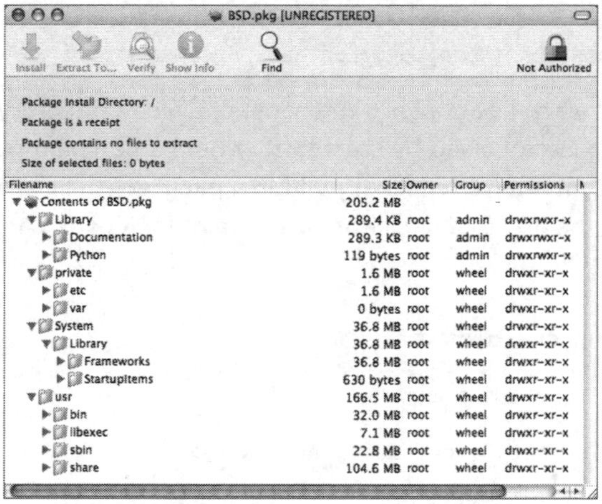

Figure 5.38

Pacifist opens a receipt file. Note that the right-hand column lists the permissions settings for each item (using the Unix format as described in Chapter 10).

TECHNICALLY SPEAKING ▶ **Repair Disk Permissions and Receipts**

Disk Utility obtains its information about permissions settings from the receipt files located in the /Library/Receipts folder. These receipt files—which are created when .pkg files are opened via Apple's Installer utility and software is installed—will typically include among their contents an archive.bom file, which First Aid uses to check permissions. Even third-party software may have receipt items in this folder if Apple's Installer was used to install the application.

The initial stage of the verify or repair process entails determining correct file permissions. It is at this stage that First Aid checks the receipt files. After this, it begins to verify or repair permissions, as needed.

Bottom line: *Do not move or delete the files in the Receipts folder.*

As an extreme example, if you were to remove all the .pkg files from the Receipts folder and then click Repair Disk Permissions, you would get an error message stating, "First Aid failed … No valid packages." Actually, the key file here is BaseSystem.pkg. If only this file is removed from the Receipts folder, you will still get this error message.

Viewing default permissions in Terminal. To view the default permissions settings of all files that were installed via a .pkg file, use the lsbom command in Terminal. It reads and displays the relevant contents of the archive.bom file. In particular, type the following command in Terminal:

```
lsbom -p FUGM /Library/Receipts/{name}.pkg/Contents/Archive.bom
```

This generates a list in which each line contains the name of a file or directory that was installed via the original .pkg file, followed by the item's owner name, its group name, and its permissions settings. It will separately list each file within a package (such as all the files in an .app package). For example, the first four lines from the receipt for iCal.pkg are as follows:

```
"." root admin drwxrwxr-t

"./Applications" root admin drwxrwxr-x

"./Applications/iCal.app" root admin drwxrwxr-x

"./Applications/iCal.app/Contents" root admin drwxrwxr-x
```

Alternatively, the third-party utility Pacifist also shows the default permissions for files included in a package.

SEE: • "Understanding Image, Installer Package, and Receipt Files," in Chapter 3, for more on receipt files.
   • "Ownership & Permissions," in Chapter 4, for more on these terms.
   • "Unix: Modifying Permissions," in Chapter 10, for more on Terminal commands and output regarding ownership and permissions.

Enabling and disabling journaling

Panther (Mac OS X 10.3) introduces a new file-system feature in Disk Utility called *journaling*. Actually, it was first introduced in Mac OS X Server 10.2.2, and it could also be accessed in Mac OS X client via a small hack, but Panther marks its official client debut.

Journaling is a method of quickly repairing a drive on restart after a system crash, power failure, or any other nonstandard restart (that is, any time fsck would normally run at restart). On such occasions, read and write processes get interrupted—which in turn can cause discrepancies between the file system directory and the actual location and structure of stored files. Journaling automatically fixes these inconsistencies via data tracked in its journal file— a faster and more reliable method than trying to repair a disk via First Aid's Repair Disk option or via fsck at startup (which is not recommended for journaled volumes). A bit more technically, Apple explains journaling as follows:

> *Journaling helps protect the file system against power outages or unforeseen failures in server components, reducing the need for repairs. It both prevents a disk from getting into an inconsistent state and expedites disk repair if the server fails. When you enable journaling on a disk, a continuous record of changes to files on the disk is maintained in the journal. If your server stops because of a power failure or some other issue, the journal is used to restore the disk to a known-good state when the server restarts.*

> *When journaling is turned on for a volume, the server automatically tracks file system operations and maintains a continuous record of these transactions in a separate file, called a journal. If the server fails in the middle of an operation, the file system can "replay" the information in its log and complete the operation when the server restarts. Although you may experience loss of user data that was buffered at the time of the failure, the file system is returned to a consistent state. In addition, restarting the computer is much faster.*

Keep in mind that journaling is *not* a substitute for backing up your data: You should still back up data to protect against damage that journaling cannot undo.

The main rationale for enabling journaling is vastly improved speed on restart. On a large multiterabyte RAID-array server with many files, journaling can reduce restart time after a crash from hours (needed to check the entire file system) to just seconds (because the OS only needs to replay recent transactions in the journal, bringing the system up to date and resuming operations that were interrupted during the failure).

The downside of journaling is the performance penalty after restart is complete. Because journaling is a continuous background operation, it can cause significant slowdowns when you're using your Mac.

For most individual Mac users, who have hard drives small enough that restart times after crashes are not unduly long, the performance balance tilts toward not using journaling. However, as journaling increases the probability of a successful recovery, it may be worth using for that reason alone.

On balance, at least if you have a newer, faster Mac, I would go with using journaling—and Apple agrees. That's why when you install Panther, journaling is automatically enabled by the Installer. In particular, if you select the Erase and Install option, you will see that the only Mac OS X format choice for the disk is Mac OS X Extended (Journaled). Actually, even if you select to Archive and Install or Upgrade/Install Panther, journaling gets enabled.

Note: There is no harm in enabling and/or later disabling journaling. The process only takes a few seconds. However, when you disable and re-enable journaling, you lose whatever journaling data was previously maintained, thus losing the prior protection offered by journaling as well. When you re-enable it, you start over with a blank slate.

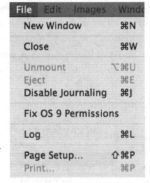

Figure 5.39

Disk Utility's File menu.

Enabling journaling. If you've installed Panther and want to use journaling, do nothing: Journaling is already enabled for your Panther startup volume. To enable journaling for other volumes (or to re-enable journaling on any volume on which it was disabled), do the following:

1. Launch Disk Utility.

2. In the list along the left side of the Disk Utility window, click the volume you want to modify.

   Keep in mind that you can select a volume other than the startup volume; however, doing so will have no effect unless (and until) you use the other volume as a startup volume.

3. In the toolbar, click the Enable Journaling button. Alternatively, from the File menu select Enable Journaling (Command-J).

Disabling journaling. If journaling has already been enabled for a given volume, the Enable Journaling button in the toolbar will be dimmed and unselectable. However, the command in the File menu will have toggled to read Disable Journaling.

Is it journaled? You can quickly tell if a volume has had journaling enabled by checking the Format line at the bottom of the Disk Utility window. The Format line for a selected volume will include *(Journaled)* if this feature is enabled.

THE JAGUAR WAY ▶ How to Enable Journaling

If you're still using Jaguar but want to enable journaling, there are numerous ways to do so, including the following:

- **Via a third-party utility.** This is certainly the easiest method. A variety of shareware utilities include the option to enable journaling. For example, I use Cocktail. To enable journaling, launch Cocktail, click its Disk tab, and in the Journaling section click the Enable button.

- **Via Terminal.** To enable journaling from Terminal, you use the `diskutil` command, a Unix version of Disk Utility. To turn on journaling for the current startup volume (called the root volume), for example, type the following:

`sudo diskutil enableJournal /`

To enable journaling for any other mounted volume, type this:

`sudo diskutil enableJournal /Volumes/{volume name}`

To disable journaling for any other mounted volume, use the same command lines but substitute `disableJournal` for `enableJournal`.

These commands should also work in Panther, though there's no reason to use them there; the Disk Utility option is simpler.

SEE: • "Take Note: Mac OS X vs. Mac OS X Server, in Chapter 2, for related information.

Journaling, fsck, and First Aid. With journaling enabled, you should not use fsck in single-user mode (a procedure described in the next section) to attempt to repair a drive. Journaling makes this procedure unnecessary and potentially harmful. In fact, if you select fsck in single-user mode, you will get the following message:

```
fsck_hfs: Volume is journaled. No checking performed.
fsck_hfs: use the -f option to force checking
```

If you insist on checking your drive in single-user mode with fsck, I recommend using both the -n and -f options (fsck -n -f), at least for a first run, so that it simply verifies the drive without actually making any changes. Also note that when journaling is enabled, fsck may report errors that can be ignored. These include "Volume bitmap needs minor repair," "Invalid volume free block count," and "Volume header needs minor repair."

However, there may be times when you need to repair even journaled volumes (for example, to fix a problem not automatically handled via journaling). To do so, you can run fsck in single-user mode (using just the –f option, as just described), use Disk Utility's First Aid (for a volume that is not the current startup volume), or use the `fsck_hfs` command (described in the next section) to repair the current startup volume when startup is over. In general, if problems persist after restarting when journaling is enabled (and verifying with fsck or First Aid reports problems), I would do the repairs. In such cases, repairing the drive will erase the existing journaling record. As long as journaling remains enabled, a new blank record will be created and tracking will proceed. This should not be a problem unless you get a crash very shortly after doing the repair, in which case you may not have the prior journaled data necessary to restore your Mac to the pre-crash state.

See the following Apple Knowledge Base document for additional information: http://docs.info.apple.com/article.html?artnum=107250.

Journaling tips and hints. If you decide to enable journaling, you need to be aware of the following:

- When using a third-party disk utility like Norton Utilities or DiskWarrior, make sure it's the latest, journaling-compatible version. If it has not been upgraded to recognize journaled volumes, it may disable journaling when repairing a volume. This doesn't cause any harm; you just need to remember to re-enable journaling after using the repair utility. The latest versions of all of these utilities have been upgraded to work with journaling. In fact, DiskWarrior actually uses the journaled data, if available, to help diagnose problems.

- After a journaled volume has been mounted on an older Mac OS X system that does not support journaling or on a system running Mac OS 9, the journal file may be invalid. To prevent problems here, once you're back on your journal-supported system, remove journaling and re-enable it.

For more details on journaling, see the following Apple Knowledge Base documents: http://docs.info.apple.com/article.html?artnum=107248 and http://docs.info.apple.com/article.html?artnum=107249.

Running fsck

The fsck (*file system check and interactive repair*) utility is a Unix program that checks for problems with Unix files and attempts to correct them. Apple has modified it so that it also includes the Mac-specific directory checks done by First Aid. Thus, in most cases, running fsck is a viable alternative to running First Aid. What makes this alternative especially attractive is the fact that you can use fsck to check your default startup drive without needing to start up from a separate volume (as described in the preceding section). This means you can do the check without getting out and booting from your Mac OS X Install CD.

If the problem you're having prevents you from starting up, the only solution is to run fsck from single-user mode. Otherwise, you can run fsck either via single-user mode or from Terminal. Note: As described in the previous section, if you've enabled journaling for the volume, do not run fsck from single-user mode.

Running fsck via single-user mode. Here's what to do:

1. To run fsck from single-user mode, restart your Mac and immediately press and hold Command-S until the single-user-mode screen appears.

   SEE: • "Single-user mode," earlier in this chapter.

2. When the initial text scrolling has stopped and you can enter text, type /sbin/fsck -y (or simply fsck -y), and press Return.

   The fsck utility will run. The -y flag tells fsck that you want to answer yes to all questions, ensuring that the process continues without further halts.

   As fsck is running, you will see text feedback that mimics what you would get from running First Aid from the Disk Utility application (for example, "Checking HFS Plus volume," "Checking Catalog file," and "Checking Volume bitmap").

   Note: If journaling is enabled (which it most likely is), fsck will not run as described here.

   SEE: • "Journaling, fsck, and First Aid," earlier in this chapter, for details.

3. If fsck makes any repairs, you will get a message that says, "**FILE SYSTEM WAS MODIFIED.**"

   If you get this message, run fsck again, because the first run may uncover additional errors that will require a further run to fix.

4. Repeat step 3 until the **"MODIFIED"** message no longer appears and you instead just get the one that says, **"The volume {*volumename*} appears to be OK."**

5. Type reboot, and press Return.

   Note: I've read that it may be better to type reboot -n -q than just reboot, if modifications were made. The additional-n option in particular prevents syncing from occurring (a process described in "Technically Speaking: Connecting Remotely to a Frozen Mac: Killing Processes, Running Sync," earlier in this chapter). Normally, running sync is recommended. However, in this case, that could cause changes that were just fixed to be undone by replacing the changed data with corrupted data that remains in RAM. Apple's instructions state that just typing reboot is sufficient. Thus, I'm more than a bit skeptical of the need for these -n -q options. However, I doubt it will cause problems if you do add them.

Ideally, the symptoms that led you to run fsck will be fixed by fsck. If fsck cannot repair the problems it finds, or if it finds no problems but the symptoms persist on restart, your best bet is to try other repair utilities, as described in the next section. Running First Aid will do no good since it's essentially the same utility as fsck.

The fsck utility does not have the options to repair permissions that Disk Utility includes. Thus, if you suspect or are concerned that this may be the cause of a symptom, your only option is to use First Aid's Repair Disk Permissions option.

Running fsck_hfs via Terminal. If you launch Terminal and try to run fsck, you will be unable to do so—for the same reason you cannot use First Aid's Repair Disk option on the startup volume. However, there is an alternative command, called fsck_hfs, that works around this restriction. The fsck_hfs command runs a consistency check specific to HFS and HFS+ volumes (the original fsck command is used only for UFS-formatted volumes), and may work even for the current startup volume. However, when running Panther, the command no longer appears to make repairs; it will only verify a disk, reporting that "**Cannot repair volume when it is mounted with write access**," if repairs are needed.

Assuming fsck_hfs will work on your Mac, here is how to use it:

1. Launch Terminal.

2. Type mount or df and press Return. Either command will generate a list of mounted devices. For example, the initial lines of output from the mount command on my system looks like this:

```
/dev/disk0s10 on / (local)
devfs on /dev (local)
fdesc on /dev (union)
<volfs> on /.vol
/dev/disk0s9 on /Volumes/Jedi (local, journaled)
```

The diskutil list command is yet another command that will provide the same device information.

The first term in the top item (/dev/disk0s10) is the device name for the current startup volume. The exact name can vary on different systems, which is why you need to check what it is. Copy this term to the Clipboard.

3. Type sudo fsck_hfs. Follow this with a space and then paste the device name. To have the best chance of getting errors repaired, especially if journaling is on, add the -f and -y options/flags. To verify (rather than attempt to repair) a disk, add the -f and -n options instead. Thus, the final result for a repair request will look something like this:

```
sudo fsck_hfs -f -y /dev/disk0s10
```

4. Press Return. Enter your password when asked and press Return again.

5. At this point, the check and repairs will be performed. You will get feedback output similar to what you would see in First Aid or when running fsck via single-user mode.

6a. When repairs are complete, the text will either read "**Repairing volume**" or something like "**The volume appears to be OK**." As is standard practice, if you get the "**Repairing volume**" message, run the utility again. The quickest way to do this is to press the up-arrow key. This will bring back the command you just typed. All you need to do is press Return, and the command will run again.

6b. In some cases, the "Repairing volume" line may be followed by two additional lines:

```
** Repairing volume.
***** FILE SYSTEM WAS MODIFIED *****
***** REBOOT NOW *****
```

In such cases, the repairs are deemed sufficiently serious to require an immediate reboot to prevent problems that might occur if you continued using your Mac. Reboot by selecting the Restart command from the Apple menu. At this point, you should strongly consider checking the disk again, either with fsck via single-user mode (on a nonjournaled system) or with First Aid via the Mac OS X Install CD. Do so until a run reports no more errors.

Using AppleJack: an alternative to fsck. The Apotek's AppleJack is a third-party utility designed to be accessible in single-user mode. After running its installer, you can access the utility from single-user mode simply by typing applejack. This utility allows you to repair disks (as fsck does). In addition, it can repair disk permissions (although a bug in the current version of Panther prevents this from working) as well as delete various cache and swap files. These latter functions can potentially fix startup problems that would otherwise require more specific knowledge of Unix commands to address.

Using third-party disk-repair utilities

When Mac OS X's built-in repair functions fail to do the job, it's time to consider third-party solutions. Before describing the specific utilities, here are a few general points to keep in mind:

- All of these utilities assume that you have formatted your Mac OS X volume with HFS Extended, not the rarely used UFS.

- Make sure you're using the latest versions of these utilities. Older Mac OS 9 versions in particular can damage your directory software rather than fix it. Do not use any version of Norton Utilities before 6.0, for example.

- None of these utilities are able to repair permissions or perform other similar Mac OS X–specific repairs.

- If the utility is on a CD, you may need to order a new CD when an updated version is released or if you purchase a new Mac that requires a newer version of Mac OS X than is on the CD. Alternatively, you may be able to create your own bootable CD.

 SEE: • "Select a destination," in Chapter 3, for more information on UFS.

 • "Creating an Emergency Startup Volume," in Chapter 3, for information related to using alternative drives to run repair utilities, including creating a bootable CD.

Among the popular choices for repair utilities are the following:

DiskWarrior. In 2003, Alsoft released a Mac OS X version of DiskWarrior. It now includes SMART technology to check for and monitor possible hardware problems with your drive(s).

DiskWarrior works by completely rebuilding the drive directory rather than attempting to repair an existing one. This is key to why it's often more successful than other repair utilities. You can even mount a preview version of the repaired volume at the same time that the original volume is mounted. This permits you to compare the two volumes, seeing what changes will be made. If repairing the volume appears to make matters worse (for example, deleting many files), this gives you the option of trying other solutions before doing the repair. In Mac OS X, using Preview mode requires a separate DiskWarrior Preview application when running DiskWarrior from the CD, because the special version of Mac OS X included on the CD does not allow you to access the Finder and thus cannot be used to see mounted volumes.

As with First Aid, DiskWarrior cannot repair the current startup volume. Thus, you will need to restart from a CD (or another bootable volume) to use DiskWarrior on your startup volume. However, this can present a problem when an updated version of DiskWarrior is released: You will have to purchase a new CD from Alsoft, run DiskWarrior from a second hard drive, or create a custom bootable CD to use the updated version. Actually, such solutions are required for all repair utilities when the problem is so severe you can't start up from the drive.

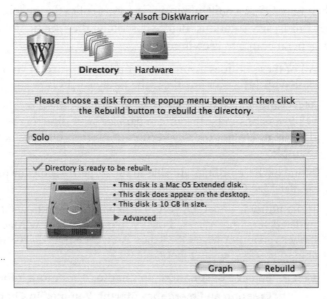

Figure 5.40

DiskWarrior's main window.

DiskWarrior has an excellent reputation for fixing problems that no other utility can repair. I used the Mac OS X version of DiskWarrior to fix a problem Disk Utility's First Aid could not handle—and it was a complete success. I had a minor glitch initially (in which DiskWarrior hung at the end of its run, as it attempted to make changes to the optimized directory); however, when I ran DiskWarrior a second time, all was fine. If First Aid alone is not sufficient, DiskWarrior remains my preferred alternative.

DiskWarrior was also a great repair utility in Mac OS 9. In fact, in its last Mac OS 9 versions, it could even fix Mac OS X volumes—and was one of the best utilities at doing so. On one occasion prior to DiskWarrior for Mac OS X's release, DiskWarrior for Mac OS 9 was the only utility that could fix an error on my Mac OS X volume.

One minor caveat regarding the Mac OS 9 version of DiskWarrior: If it's run from Classic, DiskWarrior will not repair Mac OS X problems on a volume that has both Mac OS 9 and Mac OS X installed; it must be a Mac OS X–only volume. However, if you boot from Mac OS 9 and run DiskWarrior, it *can* repair a volume with both Mac OS 9 and Mac OS X installed.

The versions of DiskWarrior released prior to Panther will not run in Panther. Make sure you get the Panther-compatible upgrade.

TechTool Pro 4 and Drive 10. When MicroMat released Drive 10, it was the first third-party repair utility for Mac OS X. It primarily checks for physical damage to a hard drive. These problems have nothing specifically to do with Mac OS X and, if present, will likely mean that your hard drive needs to be replaced. Drive 10's final test, however, is Volume Structure, which tests for software Directory problems, similar to what First Aid does. In its Services menu, Drive 10 also includes a Rebuild Volume Structures option. Rather than repairing the directory, this option deletes the directory and creates a new one, optimized for faster performance (similar, though not identical, to what DiskWarrior does).

TechTool Pro was MicroMat's more full-featured Mac OS 9 hardware and software repair utility. MicroMat has now released TechTool Pro 4, a Mac OS X–native version that combines all of the functionality of Drive 10 and TechTool as well as adding several new features. Among its new features is eDrive, which allows you to create an invisible partition on your drive that you can use as a startup volume in emergencies (just hold down the E key at startup). This can be done without having to erase your drive, and you won't need to run TechTool Pro from a CD to repair your normal startup volume. Actually, for most features, you can run TechTool Pro 4 or Drive 10 right from your normal startup drive. TechTool Pro 4 supports the same SMART tests included with DiskWarrior.

TAKE NOTE ▶ Get SMART

SMART—which stands for *Self-Monitoring Analysis and Reporting Technology*—is designed to monitor your hard drive for problems, alerting you if it detects one. The idea is to provide an alert *before* the problem becomes so serious that the drive "dies" and data recovery is either very difficult or impossible.

In order for it to work, you need two components: (1) A hard drive that has SMART support (most recent EIDE drives, which are the most common drives used with Macs, include it); and (2) software that can monitor the drive and report possible problems. DiskWarrior and TechTool Pro 4 both support SMART.

When using Disk Utility, if you click the Info button for a drive, it will tell you the "S.M.A.R.T status," typically either Verified or Not Supported.

Norton Disk Doctor. Norton Disk Doctor is one component of Symantec's Norton Utilities. Other components include SpeedDisk and UnErase. Today, Norton Utilities is most often sold as part of the suite of utilities called Norton SystemWorks (which includes Norton Utilities and Norton AntiVirus).

Norton Disk Doctor for Mac OS X remains a viable repair utility. I do not, however, particularly appreciate the fact that it installs so many visible and invisible files throughout your drive, in a variety of locations. Among other things, this means that uninstalling Norton software can be a significant hassle.

See the following Symantec document for advice on how to uninstall (and reinstall if desired) Norton Utilities 7.x: http://service1.symantec.com/ SUPPORT/num.nsf/docid/2002031315283411. An additional Symantec document describes how to uninstall Norton AntiVirus 8.x: http://service1 .symantec.com/SUPPORT/num.nsf/docid/2002020713322311. For Norton Utilities 8.x and Norton AntiVirus 9.x, life is simpler. You can obtain a Panther-compatible Uninstaller utility from the following Symantec Web page: www.symantec.com/techsupp/files/num/nu_mac_8_files.html.

Even the latest versions of Norton Utilities and Norton AntiVirus were not compatible with Panther when Panther was first released. Problems, including a kernel panic when using AntiVirus, could occur. These utilities have now been updated to address the conflicts. To avoid problems, always make sure you are using the latest versions of Norton software. Check the Symantec.com Web site for further details. Three additional cautions:

- Norton can check for and make some repairs even on the currently running startup volume. However, in such cases, Norton Disk Doctor may erroneously report that there are problems with a Mac OS X startup volume. According to Symantec, this is due to background processes (or even ordinary applications) accessing the volume at the same time that

Disk Doctor is performing its check. If the error is a false positive, Disk Doctor will likely not report it again if you run the check a second time. In general, for best results, quit all applications before running Norton Disk Doctor and don't do anything else on your Mac while a check is in progress.

- When checking a drive with Norton Disk Doctor, make sure the option to "check filenames beginning with a period" is disabled. Otherwise, you may inadvertently remove the period from the names of Unix files that need a period to work correctly.

- If no disks appear in the Norton Disk Doctor or UnErase window, this may be because the com.symantec.kext.symfs file (located in /System/Extensions) did not load into memory. One way to check this is via Terminal. Type kextstat. If the Symantec file is not in the list that appears, the file did not load. This usually means the file is corrupt or missing. To fix this, you need to uninstall and reinstall Norton Utilities.

Data Rescue X. Prosoft's Data Rescue X does not attempt to repair a drive. Rather, it attempts to recover files from a drive that is so damaged that nothing you try will fix it. It's especially useful for recovering important documents that you had not backed up. However, if you want to recover files that you deleted by mistake, Prosoft's Data Recycler X is a better choice (as I discuss in Chapter 6).

Optimizing Mac OS X volumes

Optimization is designed more to improve performance than to fix crash-related problems. Occasionally, however, it can solve or prevent a crash problem as well.

Optimizing with repair utilities. The Speed Disk component of Norton Utilities or SystemWorks is used to defragment and/or optimize a drive. The latest version of Speed Disk now runs natively in Mac OS X. (Previously, you had to run a Mac OS 9 version, though it could then optimize a Mac OS X volume). You must be booted from a CD (or a volume other than the one you wish to optimize) for it to work.

Drive 10 and TechTool Pro 4 can also optimize drives from Mac OS X.

What exactly are *defragmenting* and *optimizing*? In essence, a file on a drive may be stored in several locations on your drive. For example, a 10 MB file may have 5 MB stored in one location, 3 MB in a second, and 2 MB in yet a third. Mac OS X, using information stored in the drive directory, tracks these file segments (or fragments) so that when you view or access the file, it looks like and behaves as if it were a single file. Defragmenting a drive takes all of these fragments and combines them, so that the number of segments for each file is reduced to a minimum (ideally, one). The optimization process then relocates the segments so that all unused space is confined to a single large block. This may prevent problems that occasionally occur due to a file's otherwise being divided into a large number of fragments. It also may improve the speed with which files are accessed from the drive. You may be able to choose to defragment without optimizing. Normally, you would do both.

Before defragmenting, check your disk with First Aid. Defragmenting a drive that is usable but damaged can turn it into one that's no longer usable at all.

Exactly how much benefit you derive from defragmenting and optimizing continues to be a matter of hot debate. Personally, I've never noticed any significant effect. However, I expect that it can be useful for applications where unsegmented files and large amounts of contiguous free space are beneficial, such as working with digital video.

Note: DiskWarrior performs a form of defragmenting/optimizing, but only for the invisible Directory area of the drive, not for the entire drive. If you're using DiskWarrior, this occurs as part of the normal repair process.

Note: If you back up, erase, and restore your hard drive, it may get defragmented as well. Or it may not. It depends on the backup utility you use. Check the documentation for your backup utility to find out.

Panther's built-in defragmenting. Panther introduces a minimal form of "auto-defragmenting." When you open a small to moderately sized file (less than 20 MB), Panther checks to see how fragmented the file is. If it is broken into eight or more segments, Panther will defragment the file (unless the file is simultaneously in use by another process). Security note: If this defragmenting happens when opening a file as part of an attempt to delete it with Secure Empty Trash, the original fragments will not be securely deleted; only the newer ones are overwritten.

Optimize/update_prebinding. When you install software via Mac OS X's Installer utility, you will likely notice that the last step claims to be "optimizing" the newly installed software. Sometimes this is the most time-consuming step of the entire installation.

This optimization is different from the optimizing that Speed Disk or Drive 10 performs. This "optimizing" refers to a Unix-based process that can also help speed performance. Actually, you can perform optimizing at any time you choose. To do so, launch Terminal and run the Unix command update_prebinding. Several Aqua-based utilities, such as Cocktail, do the same thing without requiring Terminal. Cocktail includes an option to pick a specific folder to optimize, rather than the entire disk.

However, starting in Mac OS X 10.2, the need to separately run the update_prebinding command has largely been eliminated. The optimizing is done "on the fly," as needed, when an application is launched. In any case, prebinding affects only application launch times and works only for native Mac OS X applications, so there should not be much of an overall performance hit even in the worst cases. Still, I've seen a couple of reports indicating that update_prebinding fixed some odd symptoms (especially ones that occurred at application launch) that otherwise would not go away.

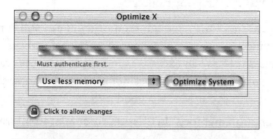

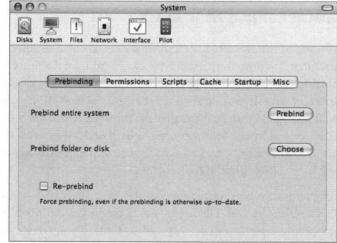

Figure 5.41

Utilities to optimize/ update_prebind an Mac OS X volume: (top) Xoptimize and (bottom) Cocktail.

SEE: • "Maximizing Performance," in Chapter 6, for related information.

• "Technically Speaking: Terminal Commands to Monitor and Improve Performance," in Chapter 10, for more on exactly what update_prebinding does.

The following sidebars, all earlier in this chapter, for related troubleshooting techniques:

• "Technically Speaking: Open Firmware Commands"

• "Take Note: Zapping PRAM and Resetting the Power Manager"

• "Technically Speaking: Understanding Kernel Extensions"

• "Technically Speaking: Connecting Remotely to a Frozen Mac: Killing Processes, Running Sync"

Adding memory

No matter what's wrong with your Mac, if you don't have an overabundance of physical memory (RAM), get more! Insufficient memory can cause numerous symptoms. Ideally, you should have at least 512 MB of RAM. Anything less than 256 MB is asking for trouble.

Even if you have more than enough memory, you can still run into trouble if you start opening too many applications at once or if a given application has a bug that causes it to use an excessive amount of memory (called a *memory leak*). Quitting open applications does not always solve these problems. In such cases, restarting your Mac is a good idea.

SEE: • "Not enough memory," in Chapter 6, for related information.

Reinstalling Mac OS X

If none of the previously described actions are able to solve your Mac OS X problem, it's time to reinstall Mac OS X. You can do this with or without erasing your drive. Erasing your drive improves your odds of success but is more of a hassle since it requires that you back up all files not included with Mac OS X and restore them after the reinstall. Reinstalling using the Installer's Archive and Install feature, on the other hand, allows you to maintain most of your customizations and added software while reinstalling the software that's the most likely cause of the problem.

Any reinstallation replaces most of the Mac OS X files—especially the files in /System/Library and /Library, as well as the invisible Unix files that work behind the scenes—with fresh default copies. Thus, if you were having a problem due to corruption of any of these files, a reinstallation would fix it. If only one file is corrupted, of course, this process can be like using a tank to shoot a fly. However, if you don't know which of hundreds of potentially corrupt files is the culprit, you may have little other choice.

When reinstalling Mac OS X, if your original Mac OS X Install CD is not the latest version of Mac OS X, you will need to reinstall the subsequent updates as well. In these cases, it is preferable to use a "combo updater" that combines several or all updates into one updater (such as an updater that goes from Mac OS X 10.2.0 to 10.2.6 in one step) rather than a series of single-step updaters.

SEE: • Chapter 3 for details on reinstalling Mac OS X.

Recover files before reinstalling. If you intend to reinstall Mac OS X because you cannot start up from your drive, and there are files on your drive that are not backed up, you can try a utility such as Prosoft Engineering's Data Rescue X to recover the files before reinstalling.

Otherwise, try the following:

1. Start up in single-user mode and run fsck, as described earlier in this section.

2. After fsck has made its repairs and while still in single-user mode, type `mount -uw /` and press Return.

3. Type `chmod 1775 /` and press Return.

4. Type reboot and press Return to restart.

If a permissions error was preventing startup, this technique changes the permissions settings on all files in such a way that startup should be successful. This technique does not necessarily restore permissions settings to what they were when Mac OS X was first installed, however, so a reinstallation is still advised—after you recover your un-backed-up files.

TAKE NOTE ▶ Mac OS X Maintenance

Throughout this chapter, I've suggested procedures that are useful not only to fix problems but also to *prevent* them. That is, they're useful for routine maintenance. Here's a quick summary:

- Restart your Mac periodically (at least once a week, even if you're not having obvious problems). This is especially good for remedying problems related to virtual memory.

- Run Disk Utility's Repair Disk and Repair Disk Permissions functions every month or so.

- Run Unix's maintenance scripts, just in case they were not automatically run recently. You can use a utility such as Brian R. Hill's MacJanitor to do this. This is covered in Chapter 4 ("Technically Speaking: Log Files and Cron Jobs").

- Consider deleting preferences files and cache files that are a known common source of problems. The easiest way to do this is via utilities such as Cocktail. Do this every few months, or any time you suspect a problem.

- Consider defragmenting and optimizing your drive.

- Consider checking log files, using the Console utility, to see if any error messages suggest a chronic problem that needs your attention.

6

Problems with Files: Opening, Copying, Deleting, and Beyond

This chapter covers the most common problems you're likely to face as a Mac OS X user: that is, those that occur when opening and saving files, copying and moving files, and deleting files. It also covers related issues regarding mounting and ejecting volumes. It concludes by examining various ways you can maximize your Mac's overall performance.

When Mac OS X is working as it should, all of the above-mentioned actions are easy to accomplish. However, things don't always go as planned. Sooner or later, problems will occur. When they do, this chapter is the place to turn to.

In This Chapter

Opening and Saving: Opening Files

This section covers the basics of opening files.

From the Finder

There are several ways in which you can open a file from the Finder:

Double-click the icon. To open any file (be it an application, folder, or document), simply locate its icon (or name, if you're in List view) in a Finder window and from the File menu select Open (or press Command-O). You can also simply double-click the file's icon or name in the Finder window. Whichever method you choose, the file will open.

- **Applications.** If you choose to open an application, it simply launches. Its icon appears in the Dock (if it's not already a permanent member of the Dock) and bounces until the application has finished opening. Thanks to Mac OS X's preemptive multitasking, if an application is taking a long time to launch, you needn't wait for it to finish before doing something else; you can still work with other applications.

- **Documents.** If you choose to open a document, the Mac will also open the application needed to work with the document (assuming the application is not already open). Thus, double-clicking an AppleWorks document, for example, will cause AppleWorks to launch and the document to open within it.

Note: To view all currently open applications and quickly shift among them to choose the active application, press Command-Tab.

SEE: • "Take Note: Dock and Finder Shortcuts," in Chapter 2.

Drag a document icon to an application icon. You can open a document by dragging its icon to an application's icon—especially helpful when you want to open a document in an application other than the one that would be selected if you double-clicked the document icon.

Select Open With. You can open a file by selecting Open With (rather than Open) from the Finder's File menu. If you choose this method, a submenu will appear listing all of the applications that the Finder *knows* can open the document. (The top item is the current default choice.) Select an application in which to open the document.

You will also see an Other item in the list, which allows you to select applications that the Finder *does not* include. From the dialog that appears, navigate to the application you want to use. If you want to select an application that's dimmed (and thus unselectable) when the default recommended application is in effect, from the Enable pop-up menu select All Applications. Be careful, however: The All option allows you to use applications that aren't necessarily compatible with your document—which means you may cause a launch failure or crash if you try.

If you hold down the Option key when you're in the Finder's File menu, Open With changes to *Always* Open With. You'll also find an Always Open With check box at the bottom of the Choose Application window. If you enable this option and then choose an application that's different from the current default one, the document will from that point on always open from the newly assigned application when you double-click it. Of course, if the selected application isn't capable of opening the document, this change won't work very well. In any case, the change *does not* affect other similar documents. If you want to change the default for *all* documents in a certain category (for example, to get all Preview documents to open in Adobe Reader), you need to use the Change All button in the document's Get Info window.

SEE: • "Open With," in Chapter 4, for more details on this option.

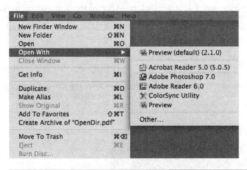

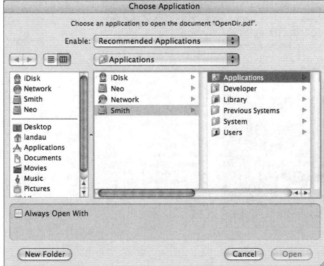

Figure 6.1

Using Open With: (top) the Open With menu when a .pdf file is selected; and (bottom) the window that appears when you select Other from the menu.

Figure 6.2

The applications in the Applications folder, as accessed from its Dock menu.

From the Finder's contextual and Action menus

You can access the same Open and Open With commands that are found in the Finder's File menu from contextual menus (which you access by Control-clicking an icon) and from the Action menu in the toolbar of Finder windows. The Open With command is only available for documents.

Select Open, and the item will open (as described above, documents will open in their default applications; applications will launch). Select Open With to open the document with a different application.

From the Dock

Single-click any application, document, or folder icon in the Dock, and the item will open. Similarly, for items listed in the Dock menu of an item (such as for a folder in the Dock), selecting the item will open it.

If an application has an icon in the Dock—either a permanent icon or one that's there because you launched its associated application—you should be able to open a document with that application by dragging the document icon to its icon in the Dock.

If a folder icon is in the Dock, you can access its Dock menu (by holding down the mouse button when selecting the folder) and open any item in the menu.

Figure 6.3

The Recent Items menu from the Apple menu.

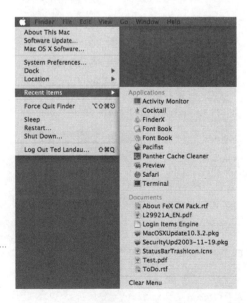

THE JAGUAR WAY ▶ Open and Save

In Mac OS X 10.3 (Panther), the Save and Open dialogs for applications have been significantly overhauled. For example, if you were to compare Open dialogs for TextEdit in Jaguar (**Figure 6.4a**) and Panther (**Figure 6.4b**), you would notice the following differences:

- The Panther dialog includes a Places sidebar, much like the basic windows in the Finder. This sidebar does not exist in Jaguar.

- The Add to Favorites button in Jaguar is gone in Panther; use the Places sidebar instead.

- Panther includes the option to switch from a List to a Column view. Jaguar's dialog only includes the Column view.

- Panther includes arrow buttons that you can use to move back and forth among previously navigated locations. These do not appear in Jaguar.

- Jaguar includes a "Go to" text box, where you can enter a file's Unix pathname. Typing ~/Documents, for example, takes you to the Documents folder in your Home directory. This feature is especially useful for navigating to folders that are invisible in the Finder and thus aren't listed in the Open dialog.

  A similar feature, "Go to the folder," exists in Panther Open dialogs; however, it is hidden by default. Press Command-Shift-G to access it. The main difference is that Jaguar's "Go to" box lets you type in an exact file path (ending in a document name, for example), whereas Panther's "Go to the folder" box only lets you go to a particular folder; you then need to select the desired document.

There are similar changes in the expanded view (accessed by clicking the disclosure triangle) in the Save dialog.

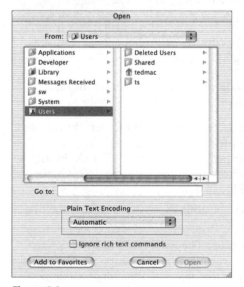
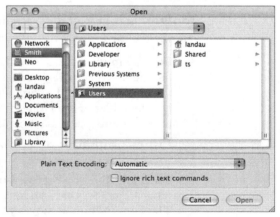

Figure 6.4

The TextEdit Open dialog in (a) Jaguar and (b) Panther.

From the Recent Items menu

You can choose applications or documents from the Apple menu's Recent Items submenu and launch (or open) them from there.

From third-party utilities

You can also use an assortment of third-party launcher utilities to launch (or open) items. These offer ways to sort and access the files that are, at least to some users, more convenient than using the Finder. Two of the most popular of these are James Thomson's DragThing and Sig Software's Drop Drawers. There's even a Path Finder utility (by CocoaTech) that acts as a complete replacement for the Finder, offering additional features such as the ability to create symbolic links or disk-image files.

If you have several applications open, you can also use third-party utilities to navigate among them (rather than the Dock). My favorite such utility is ASM: It brings back the Mac OS 9 Application menu, which lists each open application in a menu at the right end of the menu bar.

From within an application: the Open command

For documents, a final option is to open a document via the Open command in the File menu of an open application. You can only use this command to open documents that the application believes it is able to open. Other documents will either not be listed or will be dimmed and unselectable.

The exact style of, and options available from, the Open dialog vary by application, but all versions of the dialog have some basic elements in common. I'll use the Open dialog in TextEdit as an example.

Toolbar. At the top of the Open dialog is a toolbar. Moving from right to left, the toolbar includes the following:

- **Pop-up menu.** This shows the name of the current folder. By accessing the menu, you can also navigate back along the hierarchy from the folder's location to the computer name. For example, if I were in the Movies folder of my Home directory for a volume named Smith, the menu would appear as seen in **Figure 6.5.**

- **List vs. Column buttons**. These buttons allow you to switch the display from List to Column view.

- **Back and Forward arrow buttons**. The Back button allows you to retrace your steps to locations you've visited since opening the Open dialog. The Forward button moves you in the opposite direction. Exactly what locations appear when you click these buttons will depend on how you arrived at your current location (for example, from the pop-up menu, by clicking an item in the file list, or by clicking an item in the sidebar). I won't try to explain all the "rules" here. Suffice it to say that clicking the Back button immediately after making a change should always take you back to your prior location. It's like an Undo button. This is the most common use of these buttons.

Sidebar. Below the toolbar, on the left side of the window, is a Places sidebar that mimics what you see in all Finder windows in Panther (as described in Chapter 2). Click any item here and the file list shifts to display the contents of your selection.

File list. The file-list area is the main section of the Open dialog. This is where the files and folders in the currently selected location are displayed.

If you're using List view, you can click a disclosure icon for a folder (or double-click the folder) to reveal its contents.

If you're using Column view, click a folder and its contents appear in the column to the right. You can use the horizontal slider along the bottom to navigate to columns that are shifted out of view.

Click a file that the application can open, and the Open button at the bottom of the window is enabled. Click the Open button (or simply double-click the file name), and the file opens.

You can also open a document by dragging its icon from its Finder location to the Open window. When you do, the listing will shift to the location of the file, with the Open button enabled. Just click Open, and the document opens. Why do this instead of simply double-clicking the file in the Finder? Some documents can be opened in several applications. If you want the file to open in an application other than the one in which it normally opens when you double-click it in the Finder, this method is one way to do so.

Figure 6.5

The Open dialog in TextEdit, with the pop-up menu visible.

Command-key shortcuts (Desktop, Go to the Folder, and more).
Press Command-D in an Open dialog, and the file list instantly shifts to the Mac OS X Desktop.

Similarly, all of the Command-Shift-key navigational shortcuts in the Finder's Go menu work here as well. For example, pressing Command-Shift-C takes you to the Computer window.

Of special note, Command-Shift-G opens a "Go to the folder" dialog. From its text box, you can enter the path to any folder, including invisible ones, to instantly shift to that location (as described more in "The Jaguar Way: Open and Save," earlier in this chapter).

The bottom of the Open dialog. Along the bottom of the box are the Cancel and Open buttons. In addition, there may be application-specific options. For example, in TextEdit, there is a pop-up menu to select Plain Text Encoding (which in almost all cases you should leave in its default Automatic setting).

Other options. If the document you want to open is not visible in the window, or is dimmed and cannot be selected, you may be able to access and open it by changing a selection in various application-specific options that appear in Open dialog.

For example, in Microsoft Word, you would use the Enable pop-up menu at the top of the dialog. You could shift from All Office Documents to a more inclusive choice, such as All Documents. Just be aware that trying to open a document that is not intended for an application can have unpredictable results. The document window may be blank, for example, even though the file contains data. Or the file may be an almost nonsensical string of characters (as might happen if you tried to open graphics files as text in a word processor).

Some applications may have a separate Import command to open files in formats other than the one(s) native to the application.

Figure 6.6

The Open dialog in Microsoft Word, with the Enable pop-up menu visible.

Opening and Saving: Saving Files

When you're finished working with a document—or even *while* you're working with it—you will want to save it. Here's how.

From Save and Save As

To save an already-created document that you have edited, simply choose Save from the File menu. To save an already-saved document as a new file with a different name, choose Save As. For an untitled, not-yet-saved document, select either Save or Save As. In these cases, a dialog will drop down from the document's window below the title.

In this dialog's Save As text box, you can provide a name for the document. Typically, for a new untitled document, a default name with a default filename extension is provided.

From the Where pop-up menu, you select the location where you want to save the document. The default choice for a previously unsaved document is usually the Documents folder in your Home directory. For choices not listed in the Where menu, click the disclosure triangle to the right of the Save As text box. This reveals a display almost identical to the Open dialog. From here, you can navigate to any location, just as you could in the Open dialog.

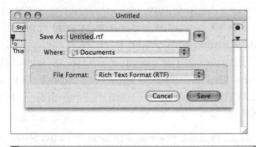

Figure 6.7

A TextEdit document with a Save dialog dropped down (top) before and (bottom) after the disclosure triangle is clicked.

If desired, click the New Folder button at the bottom of the window to create a new folder in the current location.

If the application lets you save documents in more than one format, you will also have the option to select a format. TextEdit, for example, has a File Format option at the bottom of the dialog from which you can select Rich Text Format (rtf) or Word Format. The latter option saves the document as a Microsoft Word–formatted file.

Note: To save a file as plain text, you need to use the Make Plain Text command in TextEdit's Format menu. There is no option to do this in the Save dialog.

When everything is the way you want it, click the Save button.

The Save dialog is attached to the document to be saved. In Mac OS 9, Save was a separate dialog. The arrangement in Mac OS X makes it easier to track what document you're saving if multiple documents are open within the application. A few applications that are Carbonized from Mac OS 9 versions may still use the old Mac OS 9–style Save dialog.

A document with unsaved changes will have a black dot in its close button. If you try to close the document without saving it, you will be prompted to save the document first.

From Export

If you want to save a document in a format other than the application's native format, but the format you want is not listed in the application's Save dialog (such as in a File Format pop-up menu), check if the application has an Export command in its File menu. For example, Preview's Save dialog has no options to convert formats. But if you select Preview's Export command, you'll be able to save a file in a variety of graphics formats, including TIFF, JPEG, PICT, and Photoshop.

SEE: • "Take Note: TextEdit: Format Options Beyond Show Fonts," in Chapter 4, for more on using TextEdit.

TAKE NOTE ▶ Filenames in Mac OS X

Related to the subject of saving files, here's an assortment of items regarding the limits of what you can and cannot do with filenames in Mac OS X:

Can't rename a file in the Finder. Normally, if you click the name of a file in the Finder (or simply click the file's icon and press Return), the name is shifted to an editable text box that allows you to change the file's name. If this text box does not appear, either you do not have the permissions required to make such a change, or the file is locked.

continues on next page

TAKE NOTE ▶ File Names in Mac OS X *continued*

Long file names. Mac OS 9 has a 31-character limit for filenames. In Mac OS X, a filename can be as long as 256 characters and span several lines.

Still, a couple of glitches are possible:

- In many applications (especially non-Cocoa ones), the Open and Save dialogs show only the first 31 characters of a filename. If you simply open and save a document that already has a longer name, the full name is preserved even though you don't see it in the Open and Save dialogs. If you use the Save As command to save a file under a new name, however, you will be limited to 31 characters (although you can add extra characters in the Finder later).

- Some applications may truncate a long name to 31 characters when saving a file. Some compression utilities may do this when compressing a file or folder.

Do not use a forward slash (/) in filenames. The forward slash (/) is used in Unix as a separator for directories. Thus, Library/Fonts means the Fonts folder inside the Library folder. Adding the forward slash character to the name of a file can confuse Unix into thinking that the slash refers to a subdirectory. It can also confuse the Finder. For example, if you use the Finder's "Go to the folder" command to go to a folder with a forward slash in its name, the command will not succeed. The solution is to avoid using the forward slash character in filenames.

Do not use a colon (:) in filenames. If you try to use a colon in a filename, the colon may be converted to a hyphen. More likely, you will get an error message stating, "The name cannot be used. Try another name with fewer characters or no punctuation marks." This is a carryover from a naming restriction in Mac OS 9, where the colon was the separator for directories (much as the forward slash is used in Mac OS X).

Do not use a period (.) at the start of a filename. As discussed in "Invisible Files: What Files are Invisible?," later in this chapter, a dot (.) at the start of a filename indicates that the file should be invisible, so the OS typically blocks you from naming a file in this way. Unless you are deliberately attempting to create an invisible file, do not attempt to work around this block.

Other issues. Including a space in a filename is normally fine. However, if the file may be used on another platform (such as Windows or Unix), a space in a name may be misinterpreted. Thus, try to avoid spaces in names if you intend to export the file to another platform.

Finally, nonalphanumeric characters in names may cause problems. Apple's Knowledge Base lists most of these instances. For example, one articles states, "Apple is unable to make prints of photos that have a question mark (?) in their filename."

SEE: • "Take Note: Filename Extensions," in Chapter 4, for related information.
- "Copying and Moving: Permissions Problems" and "Deleting: Problems Deleting Files," later in this chapter, for more details.

Opening and Saving: Problems Opening and Saving Files

The two most common problems that can occur when opening a file are: (1) The file opens in an application other than the one you wanted (or expected) when you attempt to open it from the Finder; and (2) a file fails to open entirely, yielding an error message instead.

Similarly, when saving a document, you may encounter an error stating that the file either cannot be saved at all or cannot be saved in the format you selected.

This section covers what you need to know if any of these problems occur.

SEE: • "Opening and Saving: Permissions Problems," later in this chapter, for coverage of problems related to ownership and permissions settings.

"Item {*name of item*} is used by Mac OS X and cannot be opened"

Many files, particularly ones in the /System/Library and /Library folders, are not intended to be opened, at least not by typical end users.

In general, when you're trying to open a file from the Finder, if you get a message that says, "Item {*name of item*} is used by Mac OS X and cannot be opened," leave the file alone. To see an example of this message, go to /System/Library/CFMSupport and try to open CarbonLib.

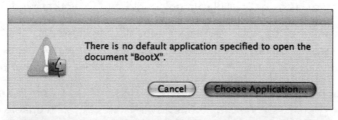

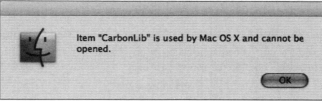

Figure 6.8

Two examples of error messages that may appear when you try to open a file from the Finder.

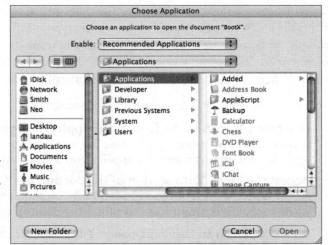

Figure 6.9

What appears if you click the Choose Application button in the first error message shown in Figure 6.8.

"There is no default application specified to open the document"

If, when you're trying to open a file from the Finder, you get a message stating, "There is no default application specified to open the document {*name of document*}," this typically means one of two things:

File should probably be left alone. Go into the /System/Library/Extensions folder, for example, and double-click any kext file there. Or go into almost any other folder in /System/Library and try to open any file with a blank icon. You will likely get this message. In most cases, unless you really need to see the contents of a selected file, simply click OK and go about your business.

If you really need to see the contents of the file, however, click the Choose Application button that appears in the error-message window, and select the desired application—assuming you know what application is needed to view the file.

Dragging the icon to the application you want to use may also work to open the document.

The Finder cannot find the needed application. It may be that the file is intended to be opened by an application that's not installed on your Mac— say if you've downloaded a document from the Internet (for example, a Microsoft PowerPoint slide show) but don't own the creating application (PowerPoint). In such cases, you would either:

- Acquire (purchase, if necessary) the needed application.

or

- Determine whether a free reader application (such as PowerPoint Viewer, in the PowerPoint example) can open the document. If so, obtain the reader application (from the Web, for example).

The remaining possibility is to open the file with some application you already own. This method may succeed because certain types of files can be opened by multiple applications. A TIFF document that appears as an Adobe Photoshop document, for example, can usually be opened in Mac OS X's Preview application. In fact, Preview can open most graphics applications.

More generally, your options include the following:

- **Drag the file icon to the icon of the application you want to open it with (such as Preview), or open the application and then try to open its document from the application's Open dialog.**

- **Access the Open With section of the document's Get Info window, select Open With from the Finder's File menu, or use the Open With contextual menu item to select the desired application.**

  SEE: • "Opening and Saving: Opening Files," earlier in this chapter, for details on Open With options.

- **Click the Choose Application button in the error-message window that appears when you double-click the document icon.** Select the desired application from the browser, navigating to it as needed. (You get the same file browser if you select the Other item from an Open With pop-up menu.)

  With Recommended Applications selected in the Enable pop-up menu (as it is by default), only applications that Mac OS X thinks should work with your document are selectable. If you're not content with the choices, select All Applications instead. Now you can select virtually any application from the browser list. As noted earlier in this chapter, be cautious with this option. If you try to open a document in an incompatible application, you can get unexpected results—from the document opening but displaying gibberish to the document not appearing at all or the application crashing.

- **Convert the document.** Some applications let you convert a document from one format to another when saving or opening it. For example, AppleWorks can open Microsoft Word documents as well as save documents in Word format so that Word can open these documents without having to convert them. You make these selections from the File Format pop-up menu in AppleWorks' Open and Save dialogs. Other applications may use special Import and Export commands to accomplish similar conversions. These may work even if Open does not. Finally, DataViz's MacLinkPlus is a standalone utility that specializes in these conversions. If your application does not have the needed conversion built in, MacLinkPlus may be the solution.

  SEE: • "From Export," earlier in this chapter.

If none of the preceding tips help and you have no idea what remaining applications on your drive might open a given document, how can you start narrowing down your choices? Here are some guidelines:

- For preferences files (files that end in .plist), it's typically best to open them with Property List Editor, which is installed with the Developer Tools software. If you have this application on your drive, double-clicking a .plist file should launch it automatically.

- For log files (files that end in .log), try Console. If double-clicking the file does not open Console automatically, drag the file's icon to the Console application.

- For font files (in the Fonts folder), try Font Book.

- For text files, including many of the files in the Library folders and the invisible Unix directories, try a text editor such as Apple's TextEdit or BareBones' TextWrangler.

It's a Unix application. Some "applications" on your hard drive are Unix programs that only run in the Unix environment (as accessed via Terminal). Most such applications are normally invisible; thus, there's little chance you'll attempt to open them accidentally. Occasionally, however, you may download a Unix program from the Web, thinking it's a normal Aqua-based Mac OS X application. In addition, Developer Tools contains a folder called Tools, located in the /Developer folder, that contains Unix programs.

In Jaguar, double-clicking such programs in the Finder results in the "There is no application ..." message. In such cases, you can't open the application directly in Mac OS X, but it will run from Terminal.

In Panther, such applications are most often listed as Unix Executable Files and will launch Terminal if double-clicked from the Finder.

SEE: • "Unix: Executing Commands," in Chapter 10, for details on how to run Unix software.

Document opens in the "wrong" application

In some cases, if you double-click a document in the Finder, it will launch and open an application, but the application may not be the one you want to use. A PDF document may launch in Preview rather than Acrobat Reader, for example.

A similar problem occurs if you have more than one version of an application on your drive. In such cases, when you double-click a document in the Finder, the document may open with a different version of the application than the one you intended. This can cause a variety of symptoms, including a crash of the application. For example:

- If you have both a Classic-only and a Mac OS X version of an application, when you try to open a document created by that application, it may launch the Classic version erroneously (rather than the Mac OS X version).

- After using the Archive & Install option in the Mac OS X Installer (as described in Chapter 3), a document is opened with an older version of an application, still residing in the Previous Systems folder, rather than the current version.

- If you have both a beta version and a release version of an application available, the beta version may launch instead of the current version.

- If you have Jaguar and Panther versions of the same application, the wrong version may open (for example, the Panther version may open in Jaguar).

- When you double-click a document icon, the Finder will generally prefer to launch a local copy of the associated application in preference to the same version located on a network volume. However, if the network copy is a newer version, it may be launched in preference to the local copy.

This section covers what to do in such situations. Some of the solutions are the same as those in the preceding section for documents that do not open.

SEE: • "Problems with applications," later in this chapter.

   • "Application quits," in Chapter 5.

   • "Problems launching applications" and especially "Take Note: Applications Packages Containing Two Application Versions ," in Chapter 9, for related information on Classic.

Delete unwanted additional and/or Classic copies of applications.
The simplest and permanent solution is to delete the additional versions, assuming you no longer need them and have access to delete them. Otherwise, proceed with the advice that follows.

In the most extreme cases, you may need to uninstall all traces of all versions and then reinstall the latest version. To do this, do a search for all files that include the name of the application and then drag all of them to the Trash. Restart your Mac and empty the Trash. Now reinstall the latest version. One reason for this is that some applications leave background processes running even after you delete the main application. This method ensures that they're turned off and deleted as well.

Compress the unwanted version of the application. Compress the unwanted version (using a utility such as StuffIt) so that the Mac no longer treats it as an application. If it is an .app file, removing the .app extension may be sufficient. With these options, you can still revert to the older version later, if desired.

Launch the application first. In some cases, if you simply launch the application before double-clicking the document, the document will open correctly. This works, for example, if the problem is that the document otherwise would launch with another (older or newer) version of the desired application.

Drag and drop. If you're unconcerned about *why* the wrong application was used and simply want to get the document to open in the desired application, drag and drop the document icon over the icon of the desired application— either in its enclosing Finder window or in the Dock.

One of these methods usually solves the problem. Occasionally, a document may still refuse to open, even if you're certain the application can access it. For example, I've seen Adobe GoLive refuse to open HTML files downloaded from the Internet when I tried to open them by dragging the document icon to GoLive's Dock icon. In such cases, continue exploring the following options until you find one that works.

Open from within the application. Launch the application and locate the desired document from the application's Open dialog. This method almost always works. If the Open dialog includes a pop-up menu of the types of documents it lists as available for opening, choose the one that matches what you're trying to open. If all else fails and you see an All Documents option, choose it.

Use the Open With options. We've been over this already.

SEE: • "Opening and Saving: Opening Files," earlier in this chapter, for details.

For even greater flexibility in assigning documents to open with specific applications, use a utility like Rainer Brockerhoff's XRay or Gideon Softworks' FileXaminer. These utilities not only allow you to make the same sorts of changes you can make in the Get Info window, but they also allow you to change type and creator settings.

SEE: • "Technically Speaking: How Mac OS X Selects a Document or Application Match," later in this chapter, for more information.
  • "Get Info," in Chapter 4, for much more background information.

Change the file's extension. Sometimes, changing a file extension for a document can change which application opens the file. Typically, I would avoid using this approach because it's not always successful. Instead, the document will open in the same application, but the application will consider it to be a different type of document.

SEE: • "Technically Speaking: How Mac OS X Selects a Document or Application Match," later in this chapter, for more details.

Solve problems that occur with the Test Drive version of Microsoft Office v. X. Your Mac may have come preinstalled with a Test Drive (demo) version of Microsoft Office v. X. Or you may have installed a copy yourself. If so, and if you later purchased the full version of Office v. X, you need to remove the Test Drive version before you install the full version. Otherwise, when you double-click Office documents in the Finder, they may open in the Test Drive version rather than the full version. To do so, you simply need to run the Remove Test Drive application included in the Microsoft Office X (Test Drive) folder. See the following Web page for more information: www.microsoft.com/mac/SUPPORT/OTD_support.asp.

If you've already installed the full version, the safest solution is to remove all Office software, then reinstall the full version. However, if you simply remove the Test Drive version and have no problems, that should be sufficient.

If you do not have the full version and are using the Test Drive version—and its applications quit on launch—the problem may be fixed by logging in via an administrator's account (assuming you weren't using such an account at the time). Then launch the Test Drive application. When you return to your original account, the application should launch correctly.

Delete Launch Services files. If you have two Mac OS X versions of the same application on your drive, you may find that double-clicking documents created by the newer application incorrectly launches the older version. If the icons are different in the two versions, the documents may also display the older version's icons. You may even be unable to get a document to open by dragging the document icon to the application's Dock icon.

The most likely culprits are one or more of Apple's Launch Services files. The solution is to close all open applications and delete these files.

SEE: • "Take Note: Launch Services Files and Beyond," for details.

TAKE NOTE ▶ Launch Services Files and Beyond

Mac OS X's Launch Services files maintain important data—such as which documents are linked to which applications. For example, if you change the default application for opening a document (via the Change All command in the Open With section of a document's Get Info window), this change is stored in these files.

Deleting these files is a possible solution if any of the following problems occur:

- Documents fail to launch or fail to launch with their matching applications.

- Package items (such as .app applications) appear and function as folders or otherwise fail to launch correctly.

- Files lose their custom icons.

- Other launch-related problems occur.

Unfortunately, Apple keeps shuffling the names, locations, and even the exact functions of these Launch Services files.

Mac OS X 10.0 and 10.1 include three Launch Services files—LSApplications , LSClaimedTypes, and LSSchemes—which are stored in the Preferences folder of your Home directory's Library folder (that is, ~/Library/Preferences). The operating systems also include invisible backup copies of these files (which have the same names as the originals but preceded by a period).

In Mac OS X 10.2 (Jaguar), the above three files have disappeared. In their place are two files: com.apple.LaunchServices.UserCache.csstore (in ~/Library/Caches) and com.apple.LaunchServices .LocalCache.csstore (in /Library/Caches). Also of potential relevance here is com.apple .LaunchServices.plist (in ~/Library/Preferences).

Finally, in Mac OS X 10.3 (Panther), the com.apple.LaunchServices.plist file remains, but the other two files are gone. The replacement for these files is a new file: /Library/Caches/com.apple .LaunchServices.6B.csstore.

continues on next page

TAKE NOTE ▶ Launch Services Files and Beyond *continued*

Note: If you're using Panther and still have the pre-Panther files on your drive, it's almost certainly because you upgraded from a previous version of Mac OS X. These files were not deleted when you upgraded, but they are no longer used and thus can be deleted.

You can fix the types of symptoms described above by deleting Panther's com.apple .LaunchServices.plist and com.apple.LaunchServices.6B.csstore files. To delete the .csstore file, however, you need to be an administrator. When you drag the file to the Trash, a dialog will appear, asking you to *authenticate* by entering your administrative password. Do so, and the file will be deleted. You don't need to authenticate to delete the .plist file (because it resides in your Home directory).

Alternatively, you may delete these files via the following sequence of commands in Terminal (the last command restarts the Mac):

```
rm ~/Library/Preferences/com.apple.LaunchServices.plist
```

```
sudo -s (and give password when asked)
rm /Library/Caches/com.apple.LaunchServices.6B.csstore
sync
reboot
```

Default versions of these files will be re-created automatically when you restart. In fact, you should restart immediately after deleting these files to prevent a cached copy of the data in memory from being used to re-create the file (and thus the problem).

As a final variation, you can use a "hidden" Terminal command called lsregister. To do so, enter the following command (all on one line) in Terminal:

```
/System/Library/Frameworks/ApplicationServices.framework/Versions/A/Frameworks/
LaunchServices.framework/Versions/A/Support/lsregister -kill -r -domain system -
domain local -domain user
```

Executing this command will delete the relevant "ls" cache files and rebuild new ones based on the applications on your drive. To learn more about the options available with this command (such as the dump option, used to view all data in the cache file), just type the path for the command itself, with no options.

The Terminal methods are especially recommended if it appears that the data in the file is being cached such that the deleted data is restored in the newly created files, rather than a default copy's being created.

More files to delete. If you're unable to drag and drop an item in the Finder and/or Dock, try deleting the com.apple.dock.plist and com.apple.finder.plist files in ~/Library/Preferences. Note that doing this will mean that you have to reset all your customized preferences for the Dock and Finder.

This was a known problem in Jaguar, which appears to have been corrected in Panther.

continues on next page

TAKE NOTE ▶ **Launch Services Files and Beyond** *continued*

Cache-cleaning utilities. Kristopher Szymanski's Cocktail, computer-supportech's Xupport, and Northern Softwork's Panther (formerly, Jaguar) Cache Cleaner are examples of utilities that can automate the deletion of the above-described cache files. These utilities often include other functions as well (which vary by utility), such as the ability to delete virtual-memory swap files, optimize network performance, or create a RAM disk.

Note: Make sure you update to the latest Panther-compatible versions of these utilities before using them in Panther.

SEE: • Take Note: Type/Creator vs. Filename Extensions," in Chapter 4, and "Deleting cache files," in Chapter 5, for related information.

TECHNICALLY SPEAKING ▶ **How Mac OS X Selects a Document or Application Match**

Here is what you need to know about how Mac OS X decides what application to use when trying to open a document:

Priorities

Mac OS X uses a technology called Launch Services to do what its name implies (launch files). It is responsible for launching applications and their associated documents. Launch Services uses the following rules to decide which application should be used to open a document:

1. The document is opened via the application specified by the user in the Get Info window, if the user has made a nondefault selection.

2. If the document has a creator assigned to it, the file will be opened with the application indicated by the creator.

3. If no creator is present and a file extension is included, the file will be opened with the default application for that type of document.

4. If neither a creator nor a file extension is present, Launch Services will check for a file type. If a file type is present, the default application for that type of file will be used to open it.

5. If no default application is set for the document type in step 3 or 4, and more than one application is found that can open that type of file, preference is given to Mac OS X applications, then to Classic ones; preference is also given to newer versions.

In brief, Mac OS X will use creator information over extensions if the creator information is present. This is why Mac OS X may appear to ignore extensions in some cases; it trusts the creator type instead. If you want Mac OS X to use the extension, you can use a utility to eliminate the file's creator code.

In fact, you can remove a document's type and/or creator codes altogether. After doing this, the Finder would have to rely on its extension to determine how to treat the file.

continues on next page

TECHNICALLY SPEAKING ▶ How Mac OS X Selects a Document or Application Match *continued*

Using Utilities Such As XRay and FileXaminer

XRay and FileXaminer are two of a number of utilities that allow you to change a file's settings in ways that exceed what you can do with Get Info. I use these utilities for two main functions:

- To extend the options accessible via the Get Info window's Open With section.

- To extend the options available via Get Info's Ownership & Permissions section.

Here, I focus on the first of these two functions. The second function is covered in "Opening and Saving: Permissions Problems" and "Copying and Moving: Permissions Problems," later in this chapter.

If you want to stick with just Mac OS X software, there are ways to make these changes, such as by using the Developer Tools' SetFile command in Terminal. But using these shareware utilities, as I show in the following examples, is easier. Maybe someday Apple will provide a similar utility or functionality with Mac OS X. But for now, I highly recommend getting the needed shareware.

XRay basics. To use XRay to change the Type and/or Creator for a document, follow these steps:

1. Drag the icon for the document you want to modify to the XRay icon (or, if XRay is open, drag the icon to the XRay window). Alternatively, if you've installed XRay's contextual-menu plug-in, you can access the contextual menu for the document and select the XRay item.

2. Choose Type, Creator & Extension from the Show pop-up menu.

3. From the window that appears, make whatever changes you want to these settings (as described in the following paragraphs).

4. Close the window.

5. Save your changes when prompted to do so.

continues on next page

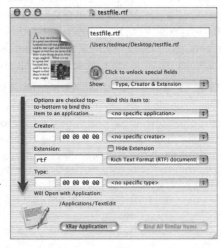 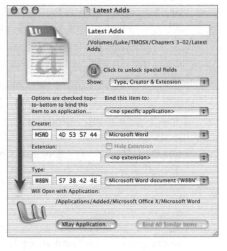

Figure 6.10

XRay's Type, Creator & Extension window for documents: two examples.

TECHNICALLY SPEAKING ▶ How Mac OS X Selects a Document or Application Match *continued*

Modifying Type, Creator, and Extension settings. The Type, Creator & Extension window includes four categories that you can modify, listed in the order in which Mac OS X checks them. That is, when deciding which application matches a given document, the Finder first checks the top item in the list. If it does not find a match there, the Finder moves to the second item in the list, and so on. If it finds no match anywhere, the Finder will likely tell you that it cannot identify an application to open the document. Following are the details on the four categories:

- **"Bind this item to."** This category is equivalent to the Get Info window's Open With option. XRay presents pop-up menus listing every native and Classic application on your drive and lets you pick the one you want.

  If you make a selection, the Bind All Similar Items button at the bottom of the window is enabled. This button works similarly to the Get Info window's Change All button. Any other documents that match the creator, extension, and type settings of this document will be "bound" to open with the selected application.

- **Creator.** The *creator* refers to the four-letter code that typically tells the Finder what application goes with what document. If you don't know what code to use, don't worry; XRay will help you out. Simply choose the desired application from the pop-up menu, and XRay will fill in the correct code. If you have not selected a specific application for the "Bind this item to" option, the Finder will use the creator code to decide what application goes with the document.

- **Extension.** This category refers to the file extension—typically, three or four letters that appear after a period (.) in the file's name. Changing the extension here changes the extension in the file's name (as you can also do in the Name & Extension tab of the Get Info window or in the Finder directly). In XRay, a pop-up menu lets you choose an extension that works with the application specified by the creator or binding option.

  Note: By removing a file's creator (such as choosing No Specific Creator from the Creator pop-up menu), you force the Finder to rely on the extension to determine a matching application (assuming that you didn't bind a specific application). This method can be useful if you do not want a given file to open with the application designated by the creator.

  Note: FileXaminer includes optional contextual-menu items in its FileXaminer CM Pack folder. One of them is a Clear Type & Creator contextual-menu item that makes this task especially easy.

  Note: XRay also includes the same Hide Extension option that is available in the Get Info window's Name & Extension section.

- **Type.** Type is another four-letter code, often forming a pair with the Creator code. Type identifies the format of the file; however, it does not necessarily specify an application to work with that format. Microsoft Word, for example, can open files of many formats and type: Word documents, plain-text documents, Rich Text Format documents, and so on. Thus, Type overlaps with File Extension, with which it should ideally match. That is, a document with an extension that specifies plain-text format should also have a plain-text type code. If a disparity occurs, the order of priority comes in: The extension takes precedence over the type. Again, XRay gives you a pop-up menu listing all the types associated with the creator or extension you selected.

continues on next page

TECHNICALLY SPEAKING ▶ How Mac OS X Selects a Document or Application Match *continued*

If you don't select a Binding or Creator option, the OS will search for any applications that claim the extension (if one is listed) or type (if one is listed and there is no match for the extension). If a match is found, that application will be listed at the bottom of the window. If more than one matching application is found, the OS will select native applications over Classic ones and newer versions over older ones.

Some document types are associated with a particular application. This is considered the default application for this type. If no creator or extension information is present, the document will open in this default application.

When even this fails to get a match, you will get an error message stating that the Finder cannot find a default application for the document.

To understand what *claimed types* and *claimed extensions* are, click the XRay Application button at the bottom of XRay's window. This opens the application listed to the left of the button. Go again to the Type, Creator & Extension window for the application, which will be quite different from what you see when you select it for a document. You will not be able to change much of anything; however, the two pop-up menus (Claimed Extensions and Claimed Types) show you what the application will accept as a document that it can and will open.

To learn more about what XRay can do, play around with it. As long as you work with a copy of the file you're modifying or don't save your changes, you can't do any harm.

SEE: • **"Take Note: Filename Extensions" and "Technically Speaking: Type/Creator vs. Filename Extensions," in Chapter 4, for more background information.**

Putting It Together: Print Preview Opens Acrobat in Error

When you click the Preview button in the Print dialog of most applications, Mac OS X should create a PDF version of the file and open the file in the Preview application (described earlier in this chapter). In some cases, however, the file may open in Adobe (Acrobat) Reader instead (perhaps even the Classic version of Acrobat, if you have that on your drive). To get the file to default to Preview instead:

1. Allow Adobe Reader to open the document after clicking Preview.

2. Save the document, using Adobe Reader's Save command.

3. Locate the saved file, and open it with a utility that can modify type and creator data. For this example, I dragged the document icon to the FileXaminer icon.

4. From the pop-up menu, select Type/Creator (Command-3).

5. From the Favorites pop-up menu, select Generic PDF Document.

6. Click the Apply button.

7. Quit FileXaminer.

continues on next page

TECHNICALLY SPEAKING ▶ **How Mac OS X Selects a Document or Application Match** *continued*

8. In the Finder, open the Get Info window for the same file, and open the Open With section.

9. From the pop-up menu, choose the Preview application.

10. Click the Change All button.

Now, when you click Preview in the Print dialog, the document should open in Preview rather than Acrobat. Also, the icon for the document should shift from the icon for Acrobat documents to that of Preview documents.

Putting It Together: System Preferences Window Does Not Open

Suppose you choose Dock > Dock Preferences from the Apple menu, and the Dock System Preferences pane does not open. In one such case, Mac OS X attempted to launch iDVD instead, as though System Preferences files were iDVD documents. The likely reason was that the link between the Dock System Preferences pane and the System Preferences application was broken. File corruption that occurred during the installation of Mac OS X update (or another software update) could have been the cause of this problem. To fix it, you would follow these steps:

1. Go to the /System/Library/PreferencePanes folder.

2. Click Dock.prefPane, and choose Get Info.

3. Go to the Open With section of the Get Info window.

4. If the pop-up menu reads anything other than System Preferences, choose the Other item from the menu.

5. In the window that appears, select the System Preferences application.

6. If it is dimmed, in the Enable pop-up menu change Recommended Applications to All Applications.

7. Click Add.

8. A dialog will appear, stating, "You don't have privileges to change the application for this document only. Do you want to change all your System Preferences documents to open with the application 'System Preferences'?" Click Continue.

At this point, the Dock and any other preferences windows with this symptom should open correctly.

Figure 6.11

An example of a message that may appear when making changes in the Open With section of the Get Info window for files in the /System/Library folder. Unless you know you want to make the change (such as to fix a problem), click Cancel.

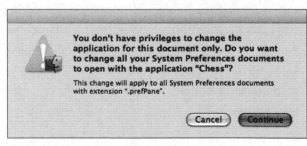

You don't have privileges to change the application for this document only. Do you want to change all your System Preferences documents to open with the application "Chess"?

This change will apply to all System Preferences documents with extension ".prefPane".

Cancel   Continue

An application takeover. Sometimes, after you install an application, you may find that the application is opening documents that previously opened with something else (or with nothing at all).

In Jaguar, for example, I found that after installing the shareware program Font Checker, almost all files in /System/Library with a type of BNDL were assigned to be opened by Font Checker. (You can determine the type by using a utility such as XRay.) Previously, these files had not been assigned to any application, and trying to open them would have resulted in the "There is no default application …" message. Getting things back to the initial "no application" state can be tricky, because the Get Info window offers no option for this. If resolving the situation is important, you can delete the application from your drive and restart. Otherwise, you may be able to use XRay to bind to no specific application.

Or you can choose to ignore the problem, which only has an effect on what happens when you double-click a document. In the case of Font Checker, you'd likely never double-click those documents, anyway. If you need to open an affected document in a different application, follow the general advice from the earlier section on documents that open in the "wrong" application.

SEE: • "Technically Speaking: How Mac OS X Selects a Document or Application Match," earlier in this chapter, for another example and solution for this problem, involving iDVD and System Preferences.

File is corrupt

Occasionally, a file will not open because it is corrupt. That is, the contents of the file have changed in such a way that the file no longer works. If this happens, the tactics are a bit different, depending upon whether the file is an application or a document.

Applications. Typically, this problem occurs with applications you've downloaded from the Internet—either because the file only partially downloaded or because an error occurred during the download process. In either case, missing or corrupt data prevents the file from opening.

For downloaded files, the most common solution is to simply re-download the file. In some cases, you may have greater success by holding down the Option key when you choose to download the file. Otherwise, try shifting to a different browser. If the URL begins with *ftp* (rather than *http*), you may also have better luck by shifting to an FTP client, such as Fetch Software's Fetch, rather than a Web browser. And if an FTP client fails to work initially, shift to passive FTP transfer and try again. You will find a Use Passive FTP Mode (PASV) option in the Proxies screen of Network System Preferences. In addition, your FTP client application may include a similar option.

SEE: • "Take Note: Troubleshooting Downloading Files," in Chapter 8, for more on this issue.

If the problem persists, there may be a problem with the server containing the file. If so, you might check MacFixIt for possible confirmation and a solution. Otherwise, check with the site's Webmaster for advice.

Sometimes an application you've been using for a while becomes corrupted during normal use. When this happens, the solution is either to download a fresh copy or to reinstall it from your install discs, depending on how you first obtained the application.

If the problem occurs when you're copying files from one volume to another, the drive itself may have a corrupted directory or a hardware problem. In this case, it's time to attempt disk repairs.

SEE: • **Chapter 5 for more information on repairing disks.**

• **Chapter 8 for more information on Internet-related problems.**

Documents. For a damaged document, the easiest solution is to use an undamaged backup copy. If you don't have such a backup, the solutions just described for applications may apply. Otherwise, there are several things to try before relegating the document to the Trash. I'll use a damaged Word document as an example here, but the principles are the same for other applications. Note that some options may not exist or may have different names in other applications. To recover text from a damaged Word document, try the following:

• If you can open the document, do so. Then convert the document to another format (such as an older version of Word or AppleWorks or whatever). The converted document may open undamaged.

• If you can open the document but not save it, copy and paste any undamaged text into a blank document. In the case of Word, first try this by copying all but the very last paragraph marker. (Microsoft claims it is this last marker that is often the source of the problem.) The paragraph marker is an invisible character at the end of each paragraph. If needed, you can show all these nonprinting characters by clicking the paragraph button (¶) in the standard toolbar.

• If the document cannot be opened, select File from Word's Insert menu. The text may still insert correctly into a new blank document.

• From the File menu, select Open. Then, from the Open pop-up menu (at the bottom-left side of the window) select Copy and try to open the document. If that fails, from the Enable pop-up menu select Recover Text from Any File and try again.

• If all else fails, try a third-party recovery utility like Symantec's Norton Utilities or Abbott CanOpener.

File is compressed or encoded

Files—especially those from the Internet—may download in a compressed or encoded format. Without the proper application to decompress or decode the file, you won't be able to open it.

The StuffIt Expander utility, which is included with Mac OS X, is able to expand many compressed file formats (for example, files with .sit, .hqx, and .bin extensions). If the file does not expand automatically on download, drag it to Expander, or launch Expander and select the file via the Open command.

There are, however, a few file-compression formats that Expander cannot open. In these cases, try the shareware utility OpenUp by Scott Anguish.

Files with .dmg or .img extensions are disk images, which you typically mount by double-clicking them in the Finder (which actually uses a background application called DiskImageMounter, as described in Chapter 3). This method opens a virtual volume that behaves as though it were a physical disk. The application or document you seek is actually on the image. Thus, you have to open the image window, locate the file, and either open it directly from the image or copy the file to your hard drive and then open that copy.

Figure 6.12

A .dmg file (left) and the mounted volume that opens when you double-click the image (right); you can open the mounted volume to access its contents, just as though it were an external drive.

Backup_2.0.dmg

Backup 2

Occasionally, a compressed or encoded file may be erroneously downloaded as a text file. Double-clicking it may open it in a text editor, such as TextEdit or BBEdit. You can work around this problem by dragging the file to the required application (such as DiskImageMounter or StuffIt Expander). If this problem happens with many files, you may want to make a change, via the Open With option in the Get Info window or a utility like XRay, so that similar files open correctly in the desired application.

Finally, sometimes when you click a download link on a Web page, you may get a message stating that your browser does not recognize the file type of the file you're attempting to download. It may offer to search for a needed plug-in or other helper file. If you just want the file to download, the best advice is to choose whatever option allows you to ignore the warning and download the file; then drag the downloaded file's icon to the desired decompression utility. The cause of these problems is either at the server end (someone mislabeled the file, for example, in which case you can do nothing to fix the problem) or, possibly, with your browser settings (especially the Helper settings). The latter problems can be fixed by changing a browser preference. I cover this a bit more in Chapter 8, but this topic quickly gets beyond the Mac OS X–specific scope of this book.

SEE: • "Image (.dmg) files" and, especially, "Technically Speaking: Internet-Enabled Disk Images," in Chapter 3, for related information.

• Chapter 8 for more information on Internet problems.

Problems with applications

You're generally less likely to have problems launching applications than launching documents. There are, however, a few instances in which things may go wrong.

Most Mac OS X applications are actually package files (also referred to as *bundles*). A package (covered in Chapter 3) is actually a folder. You can view the contents of the folder by choosing Show Package Contents from the contextual menu that appears when you Control-click the icon of the application. If Show Package Contents does not appear, the application is not a package.

Note: Most Open dialogs, as well as the Finder itself, will not allow you to navigate inside packages. This is consistent with maintaining the illusion that a package is really a single application file. The Show Package Contents option is the main way to access these files. Exceptions are BareBones' BBEdit and TextWrangler applications, which include an Open Hidden command that allows you to navigate to almost every location on your drive, including inside a package.

The .app extension. Package applications have an .app extension. The Finder keeps this extension invisible, however, even if you enable the Finder preference to show file extensions. The main way to confirm that the extension exists is via the Name & Extension tab of the Get Info window. If you do this for the Mail application, for example, you will see that its real name is Mail.app.

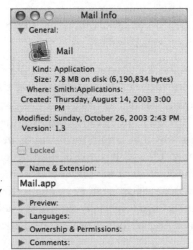

Figure 6.13

The Get Info window for the Mail application, showing that its true name is Mail.app.

If you were to eliminate the .app extension via the Get Info window, the Finder would change the application to a folder, which also means that the "application" would no longer launch. Clearly, you would not ordinarily want to do this. Fortunately, if you add the extension back, the folder reverts to an application, its icon returns, and it will launch properly when you double-click it.

Note: Turning a folder into a functioning .app package by adding the .app extension works only if the folder already contains the elements it needs to function as an application: the Contents folder with the .plist files, and so on. Thus, simply adding an .app extension to a folder with several Word documents in it will not turn the folder into a functioning application. I assume this is obvious, but you never know.

Applications as folders. Occasionally, applications may appear as folders rather than applications, even though you made no apparent change to cause this. If this problem occurs, you usually can fix it by deleting the relevant preferences and/or cache files. Another possible fix—if only a single application is affected—is to reinstall the offending application.

SEE: • "Take Note: Launch Services Files and Beyond," earlier in this chapter.

If that fails to work, you will likely need to create a new User account for yourself or completely reinstall Mac OS X.

The application is in the "application." The fact that the .app file is really a folder implies that the actual application that launches when you double-click an .app file is contained within the folder/package. This is true. In fact, sometimes more than one application is contained in the folder.

You may have two versions of the same application (such as Classic and Mac OS X versions, as is the case for AppleWorks). In such cases, you may want to occasionally launch an application directly from within the package, rather than by double-clicking the package file itself.

SEE: • "Take Note: Application Packages Containing Two Application Versions," in Chapter 9, for an example.
   • "Take Note: Opening Mac OS Applications from Terminal," in Chapter 10, for related information.

In other cases, there may be a secondary "helper" application inside the package with the main application. Should you ever want to directly launch such applications (which you should rarely need to do), you would have to delve inside the .app package to do so. Once inside, double-click the application to launch it.

For details of a rare case where helper-type applications may not launch, check out this Apple Knowledge Base article http://docs.info.apple.com/article.html?artnum=107672.

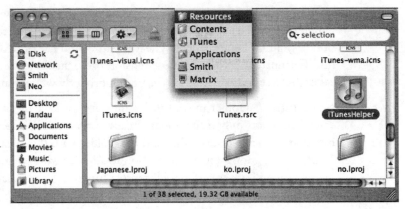

Figure 6.14

The hidden location of the iTunes Helper application inside the iTunes package.

.app files and installing Mac OS X updates. Suppose you decide to move the Mail application in the Applications folder to your Desktop. If a Mac OS X update comes out and you run the Updater, an updated version of Mail will be installed with the updated OS. Will the Installer locate the Mail application at its new location? Or will it have problems because the application is not in its default location, where the Installer expected it to be?

The answer is mixed. In older versions of Mac OS X, this was a significant problem. Starting in Mac OS X 10.2, however, Apple claims to have fixed it—that is, the Installer will search for the application wherever it may be on your drive. Despite Apple's assurances, though, I've seen instances where problems still occur (according to some reports, it's more prevalent in Panther than it was in Jaguar).

What happens if things go wrong? The application will likely not get updated properly. In particular, if only some of the files in the application package are being updated, and only those files are included in the Mac OS X update, those files—and only those files—will be placed in the Applications folder, where the Installer expected to find the old version of the application. The old version of the application, located wherever you moved it, remains untouched. Thus, you wind up with a nonupdated version of the application and a partially updated version that doesn't work. What are your options? You can choose among the following:

- You can delete the partially updated application, move the original Mail.app application back into the Applications folder, and attempt to reinstall the update. Occasionally, however, this method doesn't work: The updater refuses to run because it believes the update has already been installed. If this happens, you can try to work around it by fooling the Installer into running (as described in Chapter 3). Or you can downgrade to a version of Mac OS X that you can install, and then reupdate from there.

- You can open the packages of both the updated/partial and old/complete Mail.apps. Copy the new files from the updated application to the old one. Now you should have a complete application that will work.

- In some cases, the updater may contain a complete copy of the application, but the installation messed up something, anyway. In this case, you can simply extract the complete .app application from the update package file. The easiest way to do this is via the shareware utility Pacifist (by Charles Srstka), which lists all files contained in an update package file and lets you extract the one(s) you want.

    SEE: • **Chapter 3 for more information on fooling the Installer, selective reinstallations, and using Pacifist.**

- As a last resort, you can completely reinstall Mac OS X, with or without erasing your hard drive.

More generally, an application may fail to open or unexpectedly quit on launch if you have done a downgrade reinstall of Mac OS X using the Archive and Install option. This happens because when you double-click a document, Mac OS X typically tries to use the newest available version of the document's default application. In this case, it will use the newer version (still on your drive in the Previous Systems folder) instead of the version that was installed with the downgrade of Mac OS X (which is in your current /Applications folder). If the newer version of the application is incompatible with the older version of the OS, the crash occurs. The solution in this case is to reupdate to at least the version of Mac OS X you were using prior to the reinstall. Otherwise, drag the document you want to open to the compatible version of the application you want to use.

SEE: • **"Application quits," in Chapter 5, for related information.**

Application must be in required folder. Some applications will not launch unless they remain in the folder where they were first installed. In rare cases, the application will only work if installed in a specific folder, most often the /Applications folder. In such cases, the Read Me file for the software, or its Installer utility, should inform you of this. But it may not.

Multiple versions of applications. If you have more than one version of an application, the "wrong" one may open when you double-click a document for that application. Quirks like this have to do with the "rules" by which Max OS X decides which version to open (as well as some possible bugs in those rules).

Generally, you can avoid these problems by first launching the desired version of the application. Any documents you double-click should then open correctly.

SEE:
- **"Document opens in the 'wrong' application," earlier in this chapter, for specific advice.**
- **"Technically Speaking: How Mac OS X Selects a Document or Application Match," earlier in this chapter, for related information.**
- **"Application quits," in Chapter 5.**

Can't open a copy of an application. If you Option-drag an application package to another folder on the same volume or drag it to a new volume, the Finder creates a copy of the application. Similarly, pressing Command-D makes a duplicate of the file. Ideally, in all these cases, the resulting application should launch and run identically to the original. Problems occasionally occur, however.

SEE:
- **"SetUID attribute and the 'Items could not be copied' error," later in this chapter, for details on these problems.**
- **Chapter 5 for more information on what to do if a file crashes on launch.**

Applications that require a serial number. Some applications will not launch until you enter the serial number assigned when you purchase the application. In certain cases, the application may not be able to locate the serial number information, even after it has been correctly entered, for users other than the user who installed the software and/or administrative users. This is either because the serial number information is stored in the wrong location (for example, in a user's Home directory rather than in a location accessible by other users) or in a folder with restricted permissions (so that nonadministrative users cannot access it). Exactly what to do to fix this varies by incident: Check with the vendor of the software or Web sites like MacFixIt for advice about a given application.

Background applications. Some applications open in the background—which means their icons don't appear in the Dock (when they're opened), nor will they show up in most other application-switching utilities. You need a utility such as Activity Monitor to see that the application is open at all. Some Login/Startup Items work this way. If you come across one of these applications and double-click it, the application may not appear to launch. This is normal, but if you're concerned, check Activity Monitor to verify.

SEE:
- **"Technically Speaking: Type/Creator vs. Filename Extensions," in Chapter 4, for more on Info.plist files and background applications.**

Unstuffed file does not launch. After compressing an application with StuffIt and subsequently unstuffing it, you may find that the application no longer launches when you double-click it. Whether or not this problem occurs depends on the version of StuffIt in use, the application being compressed, and the compression format you use. Especially note that using StuffIt's newer .sitx format, instead of .sit, will avoid the problem.

The cause of the symptom is that the application's Unix executable bit is "turned off" by StuffIt when it compresses the file. This prevents the Finder from treating the file as launchable. For a simple fix that *doesn't* require Unix knowledge, get Aladdin's FixPermissionsOnPackages utility (available from the Aladdin Web site: www.aladdinsys.com/support/techsupport/qanda.php?id=534).

Application will not open in more than one account. If you enabled Fast User Switching (as first described in Chapter 2), you may not be able to open an application that's already been opened by another logged-in user. Of special note is the fact that you can only launch Classic for one user at a time.

The easiest solution here is to have the other user quit the needed application. However, if that's not possible and you're an admin user, you can quit the application yourself via Activity Monitor. To do so, from Activity Monitor's pop-up menu select Other User Processes and then select the application name from the list. Now, from the Process menu select Quit. If all else fails, you can quit the loginwindow process: This instantly logs out the other user—not a very friendly thing to do, though, since any unsaved changes will be lost.

Opening .app files from within Terminal. Sometimes, if you're having problems launching an application from the Finder, you may have success by using Terminal.

SEE: • "Take Note: Opening Mac OS Applications from Terminal," in
        Chapter 10, for details.

Delete preferences/repair/reinstall. For almost any other problems involving opening applications, it's a good idea to quit the application (if it's running) and then locate its .plist file (by entering the name of the application in the Search text box of the ~/Library/Preferences window) and delete the file.

Actually, it's safer to rename the preferences file (such as to *name*.plist.old) than to delete it immediately. A new default copy will still be created when you launch the application. If it turns out that this fixes the problem, you can go ahead and delete the old file. Otherwise, delete the newly created file and rename the .old file back to its original name.

If this doesn't work, try repairing disk permissions via Disk Utility's First Aid. Your next step should be to remove all traces of the application and its preference and support files, and then reinstall the application altogether. If even this fails, you will probably need to create a new User account for yourself and delete the old account (after transferring files you want to save).

Microsoft Word advice. If Microsoft Word crashes on launch, Microsoft advises that you do the following:

1. Move the file named Normal from the Templates folder in the Microsoft Office X folder to your Desktop.

2. Remove all files from the Microsoft Office X/Office/Startup/Word folder.

3. Restart Word.

4. If the problem persists, delete com.microsoft.Word.plist and the entire Microsoft folder from the ~/Library/Preferences folder in your Home directory.

   SEE: • **"Preferences Files," in Chapter 4, for related information.**

   • **"Techniques for solving Mac OS X crashes" and, "Deleting or removing preferences," in Chapter 5.**

   • **Chapter 8 for details on creating a replacement account for yourself.**

Losing track of saved files

When you're choosing Save (for a new file) or Save As, and you let the application select the location in which to save the file, be sure to note the name of the destination folder. The location will often be the Documents folder but can also be something else.

If the file was not saved in the location you expected, you may have trouble locating it later, should you want to move, delete, or reopen it. If this happens, use the Finder's Find command—or the Search text box—to track it down.

Note: If you have multiple partitions or volumes mounted, be careful when you save a file to the Desktop. If the application is located on a nonstartup volume, the document may be saved to the Desktop folder of that partition rather than to the Desktop folder in your Home directory. In this case, the file will not appear on your Desktop. The solution is to open the nonstartup volume's root window, locate the folder called Desktop Folder (or Desktop), and open it. The file will be in there.

SEE: • **"File does not appear after being moved," later in this chapter, for related information.**

TextEdit can't save files in SimpleText format

Some operations that you perform in Mac OS X may save text as a SimpleText document. If you select text in Microsoft Internet Explorer and drag the selection to the Desktop, for example, the selected text is saved as a SimpleText document. If you double-click this document, however, it opens in Mac OS X's TextEdit by default. If you make any changes in the document, the following message will appear when you try to save the modified document: "Please supply a new name. TextEdit does not save SimpleText format; document will be saved as rich text [RTF] instead, with a new name."

If you prefer to keep the document in SimpleText format, one work-around is to drag the file to a copy of the SimpleText application (included in the Applications [Mac OS 9] folder if you installed Classic; it only opens in Classic). The Mac OS X Developer software (that is, Xcode Tools) includes a Carbonized version of SimpleText that opens in Mac OS X; it's located in /Developer/ Applications/Utilities/Built Examples. Alternatively, using this application, you can open the Get Info window for the problem document, go to the Open With section, and select SimpleText as the application. Now double-clicking the file will launch SimpleText. If you want all SimpleText documents to open in SimpleText by default, click the Change All button.

Note: In a related problem, if a TextEdit document has been saved in RTF format, and you open it in SimpleText, it will display all the RTF code in addition to the text. To avoid this, from TextEdit's Format menu you can select the Make Plain Text command before saving the document. Now the document (assuming it was an all-text, unformatted document) will open correctly in SimpleText.

Figure 6.15

The message that appears when you're trying to save a SimpleText document in Text Edit.

SEE: • **"Open With," in Chapter 4, for more information on using this feature.**

• **"Take Note: TextEdit: Format Options Beyond Show Fonts," in Chapter 4, for related information.**

Copying and Moving: Copying vs. Moving vs. Duplicating Files

In this section, I cover the details on how to copy and move items in Mac OS X.

The basics

The primary ways to move a file from one location to another on your Mac include the following:

- **Copy via drag and drop.** The Copy command, as its name implies, places a copy of the original item in the new location while leaving the original item intact in its original location.

  If you want to make a copy of an item on a different volume or partition than the original, the simplest way is simply to drag its icon to the new location.

  If you want to copy an item to a new location on the same volume, Option-dragging the icon copies it to the new location. (If you don't hold down the Option key, you simply move the item instead.)

  When dragging an item to a folder, if you continue to click-hold, the folder will "spring" open. This allows you to continue to navigate to a folder within the folder, until you get to your desired destination.

  When dragging a file to be moved or copied, the pointer changes to reflect the status of the operation. If the copy/move can be completed successfully at the pointer location, a plus (+) symbol appears next to the pointer. If not, a prohibitory symbol appears.

- **Copy via Copy {*item*}.** If you highlight an item in the Finder and from the Finder's Edit menu select Copy {*name of item*}, you've "copied" the entire item (document, application, or folder) to the Clipboard. You can now go to any other location on any volume and select Paste. Actually, the command in the Edit menu will now read *Paste Item* rather than just *Paste*.

  Selecting Paste Item copies the item to the new location—more convenient than drag and drop if the destination location is nested within several folders.

  The Copy Item and Paste Item options are also available via contextual menus. Thus, if you Control-click an item, a Copy {*name of item*} command will appear. Then you can Control-click the destination location and choose Paste Item from the contextual menu.

Figure 6.16

The Copy {item} command.

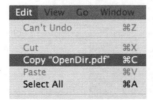

- **Duplicate.** This command is almost the same as Copy, except that the copy is created in the same location as the original and assigned a new name. To make a duplicate, from the Finder's File menu choose Duplicate (Command-D). The copy of the file will have the word *copy* appended to its name. If you otherwise drag a file icon to a different location within the same folder, you neither move nor copy the file; you just reposition the icon.

- **Move.** This command moves the item to the new location (without retaining a copy in its original location).

  To move an item to a different location on the same volume, drag the item to its intended location.

  To move an item to a different volume, you can Command-drag the item. A word of caution, though: If the move fails, the OS may delete the original without creating the copy, leaving you with no file. For this reason, if you get an error message when using Command-drag, choose Stop rather than Continue. Or, to be even safer, avoid this feature and just copy the file. Then delete the original after you know that the copy was made successfully.

TAKE NOTE ▶ Copying from Within a Document

In the main text, I cover copying and moving items in the Finder. Just for the record, I review here the basics of copying and pasting selections within a document:

Copy and paste. From within most documents (for example, those created in word-processing programs), you can highlight a portion of text or a graphic image, and select to copy it (by choosing Copy from the Edit menu or pressing Command-C). This places the text or image on the Clipboard (which you can view by selecting Show Clipboard from the Finder's Edit menu). If you now click elsewhere in the document, or in another document altogether, and select Paste from the Edit menu (or Command-V), the selected content will be pasted into the new location.

Using Cut instead of Copy is the equivalent of moving the content rather than copying it.

Clippings files. In many applications, you can drag and drop selected content from a document to the Finder (such as to the Desktop). What happens when you do this depends on the nature of the content. Here are three common examples:

- With general text, you create a text clipping. Double-click the clipping to directly view the text in a window, independent of any separate text application. For applications that support clippings, you can paste the content of a clipping by dragging it to a document window.

- If the item is a graphic, you will create a graphic clipping file that works similarly.

- If the text is a URL (such as from the Address bar of a Web browser), you create an Internet Location file. It will have a different icon than a text clipping. If you double-click this Location file, the URL will open in your preferred Web browser.

SEE: • "Take Note: Location Files and Browser Links," in Chapter 8, for related information.

Beyond the basics

Beyond the basics, you should know several additional variations on the theme:

Copy/Replace. When you attempt to move or copy a file to a location where a file of the same name already exists, you typically get an alert message warning you that the action will replace the existing file—in essence deleting it. Be careful about clicking OK. If the files have different content, you could erase something you wanted to save.

If you're replacing a single item, the message will tell you whether the file you are about to delete is older or newer than the file you are moving. This can help you decide whether you really want to make the replacement. For example, if you're trying to synchronize two locations so that both have the latest version of a file, you would not want to replace a newer version with an older one.

In some cases, such as when you're downloading files from the Internet, rather than offering to replace a file with the same name, the Internet software may instead append an extension to the duplicate file so that both files are saved. Thus, if you download the file CoolApp twice to the same location, the second download will likely have the name CoolApp.1.

Move results in a copy. If you attempt to move a file from a folder where you don't have sufficient permission to modify the folder contents, dragging the file typically results in a copy's being placed at the new location rather than the file's being moved. The original file remains intact, even if that was not your intention. Typically, no error message will appear. In some situations, the copy may fail completely, with an error message appearing.

SEE: • "Copying and Moving: Permissions Problems," later in this chapter, for more details.

Copy results in an alias. When you drag the icon of one volume to another or drag a mounted disk-image icon to a folder on a hard drive, an alias of the original volume is created rather than a copy. This is not an error. Mac OS X assumes that when you drag a disk image or a volume to a new location, you want to create an alias of it. You rarely would copy these typically large volumes except for backup purposes.

If you truly want to copy the actual volume contents, select the volume and choose the Copy Item command, followed by the Paste Item command, as explained in the preceding section; Option-drag the volume; or open the window for the originating volume, choose Select All, and then drag the selected files to the new location.

Actually, to make a true backup of a volume, you would be better off using a backup utility, as noted in the next section.

SEE: • "Aliases vs. symbolic links," later in this chapter, for more information.

Move to Trash. The other common variation of moving of a file is moving the file to the Trash. This special case deserves a section of its own, which you'll find later in chapter.

Copying to back up

Backing up your entire hard drive, or at least the most critical files on your drive, is a form of copying. If you're wise, you'll regularly do this. Backing up provides protection against software or hardware damage that could result in the loss of the contents of your drive. Backing up a drive in Mac OS X—especially if you want to make a backup that can restore a volume, including making it bootable—presents some challenges.

SEE: • "Backing Up and Restoring Mac OS X Volumes," in Chapter 3, for coverage of this issue.

Copying and Moving: Problems Copying and Moving Files

This section covers the problems that can occur when you attempt to copy, move, or duplicate an item.

SEE: • "Copying and Moving: Permissions Problems," for coverage of problems related to ownership and permissions settings.

Insufficient space

If you try to copy a large file to a volume that has less free space than the size of the file, you will be unable to do so. Not a surprise.

The solution is to delete unneeded files from the destination volume in order to free up space. Alternatively, you could move the unneeded files to a volume with more free space.

Occasionally, a volume may seem to have less space than you expected, based on the files you installed. This usually occurs because an OS-related file (sometimes an invisible one) is taking up more than the usual amount of space. Examples include the Console log files. If these files are not updated periodically, or if a recurring error is filling them rapidly, they can become very large. Internet Explorer cache files can also become quite large.

The simplest solution is to locate the files and delete them. You can use the Find command to search for files by size. This technique will help you spot unexpectedly large files. Because some large files may be invisible, select to search for both invisible and visible files.

Content Index files can also become quite large. You can delete them via the Delete Index button in the Get Info window of the relevant volume or folder.

The swapfiles used by virtual memory are yet another example of large files on your Mac. To delete swapfiles, restart your Mac.

SEE: • "Find and Search," in Chapter 2, for more on using Find.
  • "Technically Speaking: Dividing up Mac OS X's memory," in Chapter 4.
  • "Technically Speaking: Log Files and Cron Jobs," in Chapter 4, and "Application quits," in Chapter 5, for more information on Console.
  • "Technically Speaking: Swapfiles and RAM Disks," later in this chapter.

File is corrupt

Sometimes you will be unable to copy a file because the file is corrupted and the Finder is unable to read the file's contents. In general, your best bet is to delete the file and start over with a fresh download, backup copy, or new document.

If you absolutely need to recover the information in the file, you can try opening it in its creating application (such as Microsoft Word for a Word document), and then copying what you can to a new document and saving the new document. In other cases, a text editor such as BBEdit may allow you to at least view the text within the document, allowing you to save it even if nothing else can be saved.

Otherwise, attempting disk repairs (such as with Disk Utility) may recover the item, or you can restore a copy from a backup. Barring that, give up on the file and delete it.

SEE: • "Opening and Saving: Problems Opening and Saving Files," earlier in this chapter, for related advice.

File does not appear after being moved

Occasionally, when you're copying a file, especially to the Desktop, the file may not appear at the location once the copy is complete. This situation most often occurs when you're decompressing a file from an archive or downloading a file from the Internet, or when the file is being moved or created from an application other than the Finder itself.

In almost all cases, the file is there; the Finder just hasn't been updated to reveal it. You need to give the Finder a bit of a push. Locating the file with Find and double-clicking the filename in the Search Results window usually forces the Finder to update and show the file. Often, just typing the first letter of the name of the file, while you're on the Desktop, is sufficient to get the file to appear.

For files that don't appear after being downloaded from Internet Explorer, open Explorer's Download Manager; double-click the name of the missing file; and in the window that appears, click the Reveal in Finder button. The item should become visible. In Safari, use the magnifying glass button, next to the name of the file in the Downloads window, to accomplish the same thing.

More generally, you may be able to take advantage of the fact that your Desktop is simply a folder in your Home directory to reveal the new file. Open a new Finder window and navigate to ~/Desktop; when you open the Desktop folder, you'll most likely find the document inside, even if it isn't showing up "on" the Desktop.

As a last resort, choose Force Quit and reload the Finder. This procedure should always get the file to appear.

Figure 6.17

The magnifying glass button in Safari's Downloads window; click it to reveal the down-loaded item in the Finder.

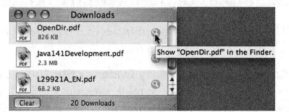

One other possibility, for files "saved to" or "copied to" the Desktop, is that the file was copied to a Desktop other than your Mac OS X Desktop. The file may have been copied to a Mac OS 9 Desktop that resides on the same volume as Mac OS X, for example. In this case, double-click the Desktop (Mac OS 9) icon that should be on your Mac OS X Desktop if Mac OS 9 and Mac OS X are on the same volume. When Mac OS 9 is on a separate volume, simply open the Desktop folder on the Mac OS 9 volume. You'll find the missing file there.

Opening and Saving: Permissions Problems

Some files will not open or will refuse to be saved (after being modified) because you do not have sufficient permissions to perform that action. If you try, you get an error message to that effect. Permissions settings here refer to the Ownership and Access settings as viewed and modified in the Ownership & Permissions section of the item's Get Info window. Similar (and more frequent) problems can occur when attempting to copy or move a file (which I cover in great detail in Copying and Moving: Permissions Problems," later in this chapter).

SEE: • "Ownership & Permissions," in Chapter 4, for background information.
• "Unix: Modifying Permissions," in Chapter 10, for background information.

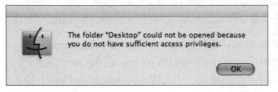
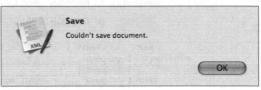

Figure 6.18

The permissions-related error message that appears when (left) trying to open another user's Desktop folder in the Finder and (right) trying to save a document owned by the root user.

Examples of permissions-related problems

The following are some examples of the permissions problems that can occur when opening and saving files.

Can't access secondary folder or file. If launching the application requires accessing files or folders beyond the application itself, such as a preferences file or a file elsewhere on your hard drive, you may not be able to launch the application if you do not have permission to access the required additional folder or file.

In one example of this, a user was unable to launch iTunes, getting an "insufficient permissions" error when she tried. There didn't seem to be a problem with the permissions settings for iTunes itself, so I looked elsewhere. I found the answer in the iTunes folder located in the Documents folder of the user's Home directory. Somehow, the owner of that folder was listed as the user's son (who also had an account on the system).

A similar situation may occur when you're trying to install an update to an application on your drive. I know of a case in which the owner of the Adobe folder located in /Library/Application Support was somehow changed to "unknown." This change prevented the successful update of an Adobe application that needed to access this folder but did not have permission to do so. The solution was to change the owner of the Adobe folder to System or to the administrator name.

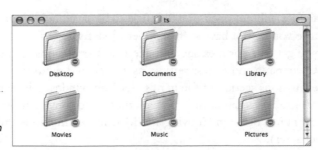

Figure 6.19

No-entry icons as seen on the folders for a user other than the logged-in user.

No-entry folders. More generally, certain folders on your drive will have a small no-entry (prohibitory) icon in the lower-right corner of their folder icon. These include most of the folders that reside in the Home directory of any user other than yourself. There are also folders in the Unix directories that include this icon. For example, use the Go to Folder command to go to the /var directory. There you will see at least three such folders: backups, cron, and root. If you try to open these folders, you will be told you do not have sufficient privileges/permissions to do so. If you select Get Info for these folders, you will see that you do not own them and that Group and Others access is set to No Access. If you know that one of these folders includes a document you want to open, you will not be able to do so directly.

SEE: • "Accessing other users' folders," later in this chapter, for details on solutions to this problem.

Document is owned by root. Most of the documents used by system software, including virtually all of the files in the /System/Library folder and all of the files in the invisible Unix folders (such as the /etc directory), are owned by the root (System) user. As an administrator, you typically have Read Only access to these files. This means you can open them and view their contents. But if you try to make any changes to them, you will get an error when you try to save those changes.

You would have a similar problem opening a file owned by any other user; however, the root-user problem is more common.

Item access set to No Access. Virtually all applications should have at least Read Only access assigned to Everyone (as set in the Ownership & Permissions section of the file's Get Info window). This access is the minimum level of access needed to launch the application. If the permissions setting for Others is No Access, and especially if you are not an administrator, you may not be able to launch the application. If you find this to be the case, you need to change the Others access to Read Only.

Problems for "standard" users. There are certain problems that can occur when opening files that only take place if you're a standard (nonadministrative) user. In one example I know of, an application kept asking if I wanted to register online every time it was opened. This happened even though it was supposed to show this message only on its initial launch. The cause was that the preferences file for this application, where the application kept track of whether or not this was an initial launch, was in the /Library/Preferences folder. Nonadministrative users cannot modify files in this folder. Thus, the file was never changed to indicate that an initial launch had occurred, when it was launched by a regular user.

In another example, a regular user could not launch an application at all because its permissions had been set so that only administrative users could access it.

Sometimes, the solution to this type of problem will require a fix from the application vendor (changing the application to use a preferences file in the ~/Library/Preferences folder, for example). In other cases, having an administrative user launch the application once will be sufficient. Otherwise, you will need to use solutions as described in the next sections.

Cannot open files in your Drop Box. In some cases, you may be unable to open or edit a file in your Drop Box. This can be avoided if the person dragging the file to your Drop Box holds down the Option key while dragging. Otherwise, you will need to modify permissions of the file, as described in the following sections.

Using Get Info: basics

To solve most of the above-described problems, you must modify the settings in the Ownership & Permissions section of the Get Info window for the relevant item. If, for example, the problem is a file or folder that you can't access, you need to (a) change the owner of the item to yourself, and/or (b) change Access settings (such as changing the Others access from No Access to Read Only). You need to be an administrative user to do all of this. Here are the steps you need to follow:

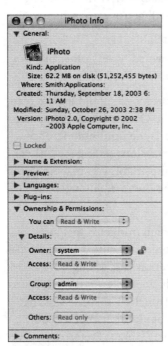

Figure 6.20

The Ownership & Permissions settings of iPhoto (located in the /Applications folder), as viewed from the Get Info window.

1. Select the file or folder and open its Get Info window (Command-I).

2. Go to the Ownership & Permissions section.

3. Click the padlock and enter your password when requested to unlock access to the settings. (It's possible that you may not be prompted for your password until after you attempt to make a change.)

4. Change the Owner from whomever it is (probably System) to your own account name.

5. If you also want to change the Group name or modify any Access settings, do so via the pop-up menus that are now accessible.

6. When you've finished making your changes, close the Get Info window.

Once you've changed its ownership, you can now open a prohibited folder by double-clicking it from the Finder—even if the no-entry icon is still present. You will similarly be able to open documents or launch applications that you could not open or launch before.

Using Get Info: concerns and caveats

There are caveats you should bear in mind when using, or considering using, Get Info:

When changes should be temporary. Unless you're correcting an erroneous permission setting, any changes you make to files or folders in the System or Unix directories should be temporary. To ensure that Mac OS X can access the software when needed, return the permissions setting to its original state when you are done.

Thus, if you change the owner of the aforementioned cron folder from System to yourself (in order to access a file in that folder), change it back to System when you're finished.

To avoid problems, a simpler solution may be to temporarily log in as the root user. You can now access the needed files without having to change their permissions—which means you don't need to worry about changing them back correctly.

When changes should be permanent. For most other cases, such as the iTunes folder example above, you probably want to make the change permanent. In some of these cases, you may also want to change the access permissions for Group and Others. For example, if the access for Group and Others is set to No Access, you may want to change it to Read Only or Read & Write, if you want other users beside yourself to have access to these files.

Batch changes. In some cases—the iTunes example above is again a good example—the problem may go beyond the permissions settings of the folder itself. The same permissions issue may exist for all files and folders *within* the initial folder. In this case, a potential solution is to click the "Apply to enclosed items" button at the bottom of the Ownership & Permissions section of the Get Info window for the folder. However, while this will change Access settings, it will not change the name of the owner or group. So this may still not solve your problem.

One solution here is to open the folder, select All (Command-A), and then open the Get Info window (Command-I). This opens a batch version of the Get Info window so that any changes you make will affect all of the selected items.

Even this may not work, however, if there are subfolders within the folder: Ownership of items in the subfolders will not be properly updated.

In the end, a simpler solution may be to use a shareware utility, such as Arbysoft's BatChmod or FileXaminer, that allows you to make changes, including nested ownership changes, in batch mode.

You can also make batch changes via the Unix chmod and chown commands in Terminal.

Alternatives to Get Info

To open, modify, and save documents owned by root, I recommend considering an application such as Bare Bone Software's TextWrangler (or its big brother BBEdit). It includes an option to open files that you would otherwise not have permission to access (assuming you're an administrator; you'll be prompted for your admin-level password to make changes).

Alternatively, you can use the Pseudo utility (from Brain R. Hill) to open any application with root access. To do so, drag the application icon to the Pseudo icon and provide your password when prompted. If you do this for a text editor, such as TextEdit or TextWrangler, you can then modify any document you open within the application.

Repair Disk Permissions

If you believe that at least some of the permissions settings for files and/or folders in the essential Mac OS X directories (such as System) are not correct, rather than try to fix this yourself (assuming you even know exactly what to fix), go to the First Aid tab of Disk Utility and select Repair Disk Permissions. Only if this does not fix the problem will you need to use Get Info.

SEE: • "Get Info" and "Root Access," in Chapter 4, for more background.

　　　　• "Performing Repairs with Disk Utility (First Aid)," in Chapter 5, for more on Repair Disk Permissions.

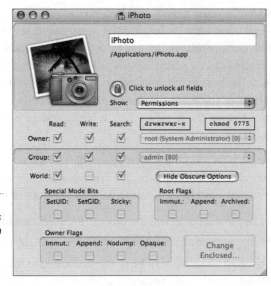

Figure 6.21

The Ownership & Permissions settings of iPhoto (located in the /Applications folder) as viewed from XRay.

TAKE NOTE ▶ A Primer on Ownership and Access

The following is an overview of how different ownership and access settings (as viewed in Get Info windows) affect your ability to copy, move, delete, and open items.

Default permissions settings. Files and folders in different locations have different default permissions. For example, items in the System folder have different permissions than items in the Applications folder, which in turn have different permissions than items in your Home directory. As one example, here are the default permissions for items initially installed in the Applications folder (as displayed in the Get Info window):

- Owner: system
- Owner access: Read & Write
- Group: admin
- Group access: Read & Write
- Other access: Read only

Because you (as an administrative user) are a member of the admin group, the access listed at the top of the section for "You can" is also Read & Write.

As displayed in XRay:

- Owner and Group: Read, Write, and Execute all enabled
- World: Read and Execute enabled
- Owner is "root (System Administrator)"
- Group is "admin"

Settings viewed in Terminal are essentially the same as those seen in XRay.

Item access. To view the contents of a file, you must have at least Read Only access to it. The access can be in any category (Owner, Group, or Others), as long as you belong to that category. (For example, if you are a member of the listed group and the group has Read Only access, you can view the contents of the file—even if Others has No Access and you do not own the file.)

To edit a file (such as to change the contents of a word-processing document), you must have Read & Write access for that file. If you have such access, you can modify the file even if you are limited to Read Only access to the folder that contains the file. This is because to Mac OS X, changing a file's contents does not modify the folder's contents.

Enclosing folder access. To move items from one folder to another, you need Read & Write access for each folder whose contents will be modified. This is because you must be able to both view the contents of the folder (Read) and modify the contents (Write). To move a file, you need access to both the originating and destination folders. If you want to copy a file to another folder, you need at least Read Only access to the original folder, and either Read & Write access or Write Only access to the destination folder. (With just Write access, you can add items to a folder but not view the contents.)

continues on next page

TAKE NOTE ▶ **A Primer on Ownership and Access** *continued*

Note that folder and file permissions are independent of one another. You can move an item to and from a folder even if you don't own the item and have only Read Only access to it (or even No Access), as long as you have Read & Write access to the folder that contains the item. This means, for example, that you could move a file that you do not own and for which you have no "access" to the Trash—as long as it's located in a folder for which you do have access.

Unix directories. If you found the previous section confusing, you may find it helpful to look at how Unix conceptualizes directories, because Mac OS X bases its own behavior on these Unix concepts.

In Unix, a directory is not really a folder in the way that a folder appears in the Finder—that is, a Unix directory is not a container but rather simply another file that lists the contents of what's considered to be in that directory. Thus, the permissions settings for a directory only determine the extent to which you can modify the listing, not your ability to modify the files themselves. The latter capability is determined by the permissions set for each file. In other words, a lack of read access for a directory means you can't read the directory listing. It does not mean you cannot read the contents of files within the directory. Nor does it mean that you cannot change the contents of the listing (a lack of Write access would mean this).

Administrator access. Administrators, because they are members of the Admin group, have more access to files and folders than nonadministrative users. This is the reason that nonadministrative users cannot move files into or out of the Applications folder, while administrative users can. The Applications folder is owned by System, with the Admin group having Read & Write access while Others have Read Only access.

The reason that you cannot similarly move things in and out of the System folder, even as an administrator, is that the group assignment is wheel (with Read Only access). Admin users are not members of the wheel group in Panther (and would have only read access even if they were members).

Of course, as an administrator, you can still change any of these access settings by unlocking the padlock in the Get Info window.

SEE: • "Technically Speaking: Group Settings Explained," in Chapter 4, for more background information.

Ownership of moved files vs. copied files. When an item is moved, it generally maintains its permissions. For example, an application in the Applications folder is owned by System. If you move it to your Desktop, it is still owned by System.

In contrast, when an item is copied, it generally adopts the default permissions of its destination location.

continues on next page

TAKE NOTE ▶ **A Primer on Ownership and Access** *continued*

For example, if you copy an application from the Applications folder to your Desktop, you now own the copy. Similarly, if you copy a file (owned by System and with Wheel as the Group) from the System folder to your Desktop, you become the owner of the copy, and all categories will have Read & Write access.

An important implication of this copy versus move principle is that if you *copy* a file from Applications, for example, and then delete the original (in the Applications folder) and *move* the copy back, the item now in the Applications folder will still be owned by you instead of by System (its original owner). If some later access to this application requires that it have its original owner (System), you will have problems. For example, you could wind up with an application in the Applications folder that has permissions that prevent nonadministrative users from launching it.

Conversely, if you *copy* a file you own from your Home directory to the Applications folder, its owner *may* change to System. You would thus no longer be the owner of the file you just copied. However, more likely, the file will be retained with yourself as owner.

Creating new files. When you create a new file (for example, via an application's Save command) or a new folder (such as via the Finder's Command-Shift-N command), you are assigned the owner of the item by default. The group assignment for the item is typically the same as that of the folder containing the item. Thus, items created in the Applications folder would belong to the Admin group.

Ignore ownership on this volume. On all mounted volumes except the Mac OS X startup volume, the Ownership & Permissions section of the Get Info window includes an "Ignore ownership on this volume" option. If you enable this option, it does what its name implies: You will be able to access files on this volume, even if you otherwise would not have the permissions to do so.

SEE: • "Ownership & Permissions," in Chapter 4, for more details, such as how and why you would use the "Ignore ownership" option.

Copying and Moving: Permissions Problems

Permissions issues can cause problems with copying and moving files. The problem can be with either the Access settings or the Ownership, as viewed and modified from Get Info windows.

Examples of permissions-related problems

The following are several examples of problems that can arise when copying and moving files.

Item is copied instead of moved. As mentioned earlier in the chapter, this is a permissions-related problem. The reason you can't move the file is that you don't have modify (write) access for the folder that contains it—meaning you can't change the folder's contents by moving a file out of it. If you attempt to move an item from that folder, Mac OS X does the best it can—which means creating a *copy* of it in the destination folder instead. In such cases, no error message appears. This assumes, of course, that you have sufficient access to the destination folder. If not, it will not even copy to the destination.

As one example of this, you can't move anything out of the Mac OS X System folder—in this instance, a good thing (meaning you typically *should not* try to work around the restriction). Removing items from the System folder is a bad idea—unless you know exactly what you're doing or want to see your Mac crash.

Occasionally, usually due to some bug in an installer package or utility, the ownership of a file or folder may be erroneously modified. In one example, the Applications folder permissions were modified such that even administrators no longer had write access to the folder.

SEE: • "Take Note: A Primer on Ownership and Access," earlier in this chapter, for an important implication of this copy versus move issue.

Item cannot be moved, copied, or replaced. When you try to move or copy certain items, you may get a message that says, "This operation cannot be completed because you do not have sufficient privileges for {*name of item to be moved*}". In this case, the problem is that you do not have sufficient permissions to access the item to be copied or moved. This may happen, for example, if you try to move a folder with a no-entry (prohibitory) icon on it.

When attempting to copy or move certain items, you may get a message that says, "The item {*name of item*} cannot be moved because {*destination location*} cannot be modified." In this case, the likely problem is that you don't have access permissions to modify the destination location. In Jaguar, this alert box offers no option to work around this problem.

Such messages were common in Jaguar. In Panther, however, most of them have been replaced by new authentication messages, as explained in the next section.

Using Panther's Finder Authenticate method

Prior to Panther, solving problems of the sort described in the previous section could be a bit of a hassle, since it often involved modifying an item's permissions settings and then restoring them after you had completed the copy or move.

In Panther, Apple has made dealing with such problems much simpler—perhaps too simple. It's now so easy to circumvent these restrictions that inexperienced users are more likely to move or delete files they shouldn't—which can lead to serious trouble. If you're confident you know what you're doing, though, Panther represents a big step forward in ease of use.

Exactly what messages you now get—or do not get—when trying to copy or move files in Panther varies, and it's not always immediately obvious what determines these minor variations. Happily, the overall theme remains the same. The following provides an overview of the types of messages you can expect to see.

Authenticate messages. In Panther, when you try to move or delete an item to a location for which you do not have permission, you will likely get the following message: "The item {*name of item*} cannot be moved because {*destination location*} cannot be modified." This message box includes two buttons: Authenticate and OK. If you click OK, no action is taken. If you click Authenticate, an Authenticate dialog appears. From here, you're prompted to enter an administrative name and password. If you do so, the selected action (for example, moving the item) takes place.

When you try to move an item for which you *do not* have permission to a destination for which you do have access, you typically get either the Authenticate dialog or a message warning that you may get the Authenticate dialog if you continue.

The above actions eliminate the need for changes to permissions settings, use of Terminal, or use of any third-party utility.

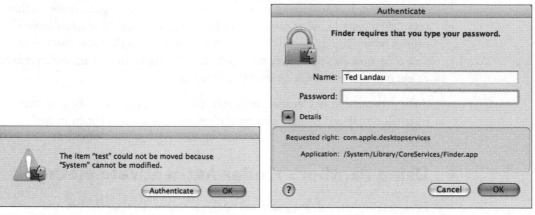

Figure 6.22

A message that appears when you select to move a file to a location that cannot be modified (left); and the window that appears (with Details exposed) after you click the message box's Authenticate button (right).

Figure 6.23

A message that appeared when I tried to drag a folder from another user's Home directory to my Desktop.

Command-drag to move; Authenticate. If you drag an item to move it from a folder for which you do not have write permission, the item may be copied instead (as previously explained). However, in Panther, if you Command-drag the item, this forces an attempt to move it—in this case, taking you directly to the Authenticate dialog. Again, enter the needed name and password, and the move will occur.

There are a variety of other messages you may get, depending on whether you're trying to move, copy, or replace a file and the specific permissions. In all cases, however, you will ultimately arrive at the Authenticate dialog. This is the key that unlocks all access for you. Only if the authenticate option does not appear or does not work, will you need the more tedious alternatives covered in subsequent sections.

The grace period. Starting in Mac OS X 10.3.3, you will get the Authenticate dialog and need to reenter your password each time you attempt an otherwise prohibited action. In Mac OS X 10.3.0 to 10.3.2, however, for a period of five minutes after first authenticating, you can do ordinarily prohibited actions, such a moving or deleting files for which you do not have permission, without needing to reenter a password (you will either get a mild warning message or no message at all).

This 5-minute grace period was convenient when trying to perform several moves in a short time (and is similar to the grace period when using the sudo command in Terminal). However, it also made it easier to mess things up by allowing you to delete something you thought you did not have permission to delete. It was also a security risk, as it meant that, during the grace period, any user with access to your computer had access to password-protected actions. Even worse, it turned out that almost any time you entered your password in the Aqua environment (such as when logging in or when accessing certain System Preferences panes), this also enabled the grace period in the Finder. Fortunately, Apple plugged this hole in Mac OS X 10.3.3; the grace period is gone.

SEE: • "Technically Speaking: Authorization Services," for more details.

TECHNICALLY SPEAKING ▶ Authorization Services

To be clear: When you authenticate in the Finder, as described in the main text, you are not invoking BSD's Unix su or sudo commands (as covered in Chapter 10), nor are you running as the root user (as covered in Chapter 4). Despite some similarities, this Authenticate window uses an entirely separate and independent Mac OS X feature. The details of how it all works are explained in a document available from Apple's Developer site (http://developer.apple.com/documentation/Security/) called "Performing Privileged Operations with Authorization Services." What follows are some key points regarding Authorization Services, especially as they apply to the Authenticate feature in Panther's Finder:

- To *authenticate* means to enter your name and password to verify your identity. *Authorization* refers to what Mac OS X allows you to do as a result of your authentication.

- Clicking the Details disclosure triangle in the Authenticate window (which appears in the Finder when you try to perform a prohibited action) reveals the following two lines:

```
Requested right: com.apple.desktopservices
Application: /System/Library/CoreServices/Finder.app
```

The Authenticate window also appears in other situations. Exactly what is shown in the Details section varies depending upon the situation. For example, if you select to make a change from the Finder's Get Info window, the Finder is once again listed as the application, but the requested right is com.apple.finder.ChangeGroup.

If you get an Authenticate window while in System Preferences, it will state

```
Requested right: system.preferences
Application: /Applications/System Preferences.app
```

In each case, what is listed is the name of the application requesting authorization (in the Application line) and the specific privilege (right) that is being requested.

continues on next page

TECHNICALLY SPEAKING ▶ Authorization Services *continued*

- The rights are maintained in a file called *authorization* (or authorization.orig, if *authorization* itself is an alias), located in the /etc directory. This is sometimes referred to as the *policy database*. You can open this file conveniently in Property List Editor.

  A comment line in the file offers advice on how the file is to be used. It states in part:

  The name of the requested right is matched against the keys. An exact match has priority, otherwise the longest match from the start is used. Note that the right will only match wildcard rules (ending in a '.') during this reduction.

  Thus, the exact right (and rule) invoked can vary as a function of what right an application requests, what rights are listed in the authorization file, and whether a wildcard match gets involved. If no match is made, rights and rules revert to their default selections (as I'll explain in more detail in a moment).

  Note: If you're using Property List Editor, you may need to copy the comment text and paste it into a text editor to read it.

- The authorization file contains two main categories: *rights* and *rules*.

  In the "rights" section, you will find the com.apple.desktopservices and system.preferences rights referred to above, for example. If you open the disclosure triangle for a right, it reveals a list of its properties. The two properties of most interest for this discussion are *shared* and *timeout*.

  The shared property can have a value or yes or no. If it is set to yes, it means that an authentication can be shared with certain other applications. That is, if applications A and B have the shared property enabled, and if you enter your password to authenticate in application A, you would also automatically be authenticated in application B.

  The timeout property has a numeric value that represents a number of seconds. If present, this property limits the authentication period to the time interval indicated. Thus, if timeout is set to zero, you will have to reauthenticate each time you attempt an action that requires authentication in the specified application. If timeout is set to 300, it means that you have a 5-minute grace period before you have to reauthenticate.

  The com.apple.desktopservices right has shared set to no and timeout set to 0. Thus, there is no sharing and no grace period. This is why you need to reauthenticate every time you attempt an otherwise-prohibited action in the Finder.

  As noted in the main text, in versions of Mac OS X prior to 10.3.3, the Finder behaved quite differently. There was a 5-minute grace period and sharing was enabled. The reason for this was that the com.apple.desktopservices right was somehow missing from the authorization file. As a result, the Finder instead used the settings in the *default* "rule" (found in the rules section of the authorization file). For the default rule, shared was enabled and timeout was 300.

continues on next page

TECHNICALLY SPEAKING ▶ **Authorization Services** *continued*

- You can edit the authorization file's rights and rules to suit your fancy. For example, if you are using Mac OS X 10.3.3 but would prefer for the Finder to revert to the 5 minute grace period it had in 10.3.2, do the following: Launch Property List Editor as the root user (via the Pseudo utility, as explained in Chapter 4). This allows you to save any changes. Open the authorization file and change the timeout value of the com.apple.desktopservices right from 0 to 300. Save the change and quit. Now relaunch the Finder (or log out and back in again) for the change to take effect.

Note: Before making changes to the authorization file, save a copy of the original, so that you can revert to it if anything goes wrong. In addition, because your modified file may be replaced by a subsequent update to Mac OS X, you should save a copy of it as well, so that you have a record of your changes.

Note: When third-party applications ask you to authenticate, they may actually be accessing the Unix sudo command instead of what's described here. Use of Mac OS X's Authentication Services is not yet supported in many applications.

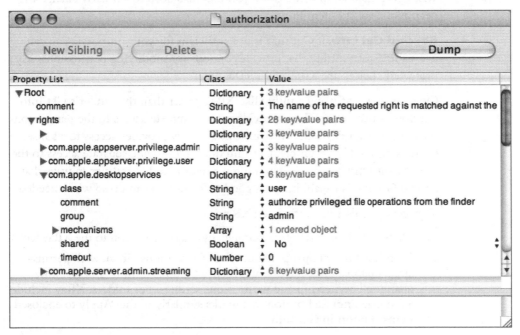

Figure 6.24

A peek at the /etc/authorization file, as viewed from Property List Editor, with the properties of the com.apple.desktopservices right visible.

Using Get Info and beyond

Assuming you're certain you want to override the Mac OS X restrictions for copying and moving files, a solution to these permissions issues is to temporarily or permanently change the permissions of the relevant files or folders.

Using Get Info. You can make most of the required changes via Get Info, as described in "Using Get Info: basics," earlier in this chapter.

For example, if you find an application in the Applications folder that *you* own and you want the system to own it instead, you can use Get Info to change the owner.

If you own a file (or make yourself its owner), you can change any of its other settings.

In general, to move an item that Mac OS X prohibits you from moving due to permissions restrictions, you will need to change the ownership and permissions of the original enclosing or destination folder so that you have Read & Write permissions. In some cases, you may also need to similarly change the permissions of the item itself.

Beyond Get Info. If Get Info is not sufficient for your purposes, you can use a third-party utility that provides options for modifying permissions. My preferred choices are XRay and FileXaminer.

One advantage of using a utility like XRay rather than the Finder's Get Info window is that such utilities provide more complete access to the permissions settings. The Finder's Get Info, in contrast, only provides access to a subset of the settings. (For example, Get Info does not provide separate access to the execute bit.) Although you won't often need to modify settings in ways that exceed Get Info's capabilities, it's good to know you can do so when needed.

To access permissions settings via XRay:

1. Open the file in XRay (for example, by dragging its icon to the XRay icon).

2. From the Show pop-up menu, select Permissions. To view all permissions options, click the Show Obscure Options button. You can now change all ownership and permissions settings. For folders, XRay includes a Change Enclosed button that works similarly to the "Apply to enclosed items" button in Get Info.

3. Save your changes.

Other options for changing permissions (beyond using Get Info) include (1) using the permissions-modifying commands in Terminal; (2) logging in as the root user (to bypass restrictions); and (3) using Disk Utility's First Aid to repair disk permissions (which may eliminate the need for any more-specific fixes). Details regarding these choices are covered in the following sections.

Figure 6.25

XRay's Permissions settings (with the pop-up menu for changing owners visible).

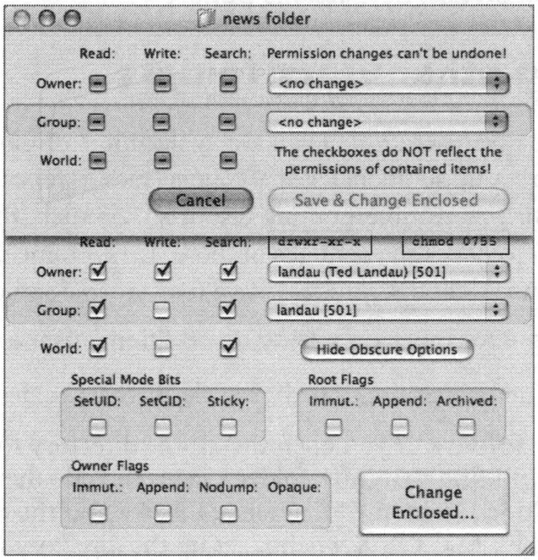

Figure 6.26

XRay's Permissions settings (with its Changed Enclosed window open) for a folder.

Deleting and moving instead of replacing

Occasionally, when you try to replace a file with a copy of the same name from a different location, an error message appears, stating, "There was an error reading this file from disk." Alternatively, you may get a message stating that you don't have sufficient permissions to perform the replacement. The usual cause is incorrectly set permissions (in essence, a lack of read and/or write access). This permissions error prevents the to-be-replaced file from being replaced. This can happen even for files in your own Home directory, which you should presumably have the needed access to replace.

The same error will appear if you try to replace an entire folder that contains one or more of these problem files with another folder of the same name. In this case, you will need to determine which files are the cause (by sequentially removing files from the folder and repeating the replace attempt each time) before you can fix the problem. The most likely cause is that the permissions were incorrectly set by the applications that created the .plist files.

A simple solution is to drag the problem files to the Trash. You can typically delete such files even if you can't get the Replace option to work. Once you've done this, you should be able to move or copy the items that you were previously unable to, since you're no longer attempting to replace anything.

The same settings errors may also prevent backing up these files, such as via Apple's Backup utility for .Mac accounts. In this case, the best solution is to modify the permissions settings of the problem files using Get Info, as described previously. Keep in mind that you may need to modify permissions of the files on the backup copy as well as the ones in your current Home directory.

SEE: • "Take Note: A Primer on Ownership and Access," earlier in this chapter, for more on how permissions work.

Accessing other users' folders

As an administrative user (which you are by default if you initially installed Mac OS X), you can set up additional user accounts (such as for other family members or colleagues, or as a troubleshooting resource). As such, there may be times when you want to check the contents of those users' Home directories. Can you do this? Of course—though you may have to overcome some obstacles to do so.

SEE: • Chapter 8 for more on setting up additional user accounts.

Obstacles. The above-mentioned obstacles vary by folder:

- **No-entry folders.** If you open the Home directory folder for another user, you will find that most folder's icons include the no-entry icon. These include Desktop, Documents, Library, and most of the other folders created by Mac OS X when it set up the directory (see **Figure 6.19**). The no-entry icon means just that—*no entry!* If you try to open folders with this icon, you will get the following message: "The folder {*name of folder*} could not be opened because you do not have sufficient access privileges" (see **Figure 6.18**).

  The reason this message appears is that these folders have permissions settings of No Access for Group and Others, as can be seen in the Ownership & Permissions section of the folders' Get Info windows. Thus, at least for the moment, only the owner of each User directory can access the contents of these folders.

  Note: This is one case where an Authenticate button does not appear as an override option.

- **Public and Sites folders.** Exceptions to this no-entry rule include the Sites folder (where you would store a Web site enabled by Web sharing, which needs to be available publicly) and the Public folder (which is where you store files that you want anyone to be able to access, such as other local users on your Mac or people who access your Mac with guest access via Personal File Sharing). These two folders have the Group and Everyone permissions set to Read Only (as opposed to No Access), so you can open and view the contents of the folder. However, what you can do with the viewable contents will depend on the permissions settings of each file and folder:

If a document has *Read & Write* permissions enabled for Everyone, you will be able to open and modify the file.

If the document's permissions are set to *No Access*, you won't be able to open the file, even though you can see its icon in the Finder.

If permissions are set to *Read Only*, you will be able to read but not modify the file. If you open the file, make a change, and try to save the file, you will get an error message. You will be able to copy the file to your drive, however, and modify the copy there. You will also be able to use Save As to save a copy to a folder for which you have Write access.

- **Drop Box.** Within each user's Public folder is an additional folder, named Drop Box. This folder is designed so that you can add to its contents but not view them—the opposite of the rest of the Public folder, which is designed to allow you to see but not modify the contents.

  The permissions settings for the Drop Box are *Write Only (Drop Box)* for Group and Others.

  The Drop Box allows you to leave files for the user who owns the Drop Box without being able to see or access what other people may have left. When you drag a file to the Drop Box, you get a message that states, "You do not have permission to see the results of this operation." Similarly, if you double-click the Drop Box, you will get the "You do not have sufficient access privileges…" error message.

  Note: To be safe, before dropping a file in a user's Drop Box, make sure you've assigned privileges to the file that will allow the user to view and modify it.

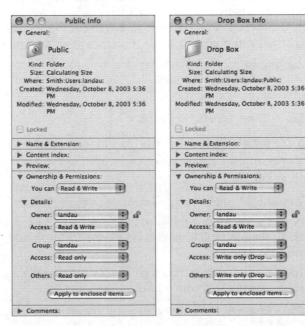

Figure 6.27

The Permissions settings of your (left) Public and (right) Drop Box folders, as viewed in their Get Info windows.

TAKE NOTE ▶ The Shared Folder

Inside the Users folder, in addition to the individual Home directory folders, is a folder called Shared. The permissions of this folder are set in such a way that everyone has Read & Write access. Thus, this folder is like a community folder: Any local user can view, modify, copy, or move items to or from the folder. Although this setup is not very secure, it's convenient for low-security items—for example to set up a common iTunes library, so that all users can share the same music.

Some applications also install items in this folder. Applications use it to store accessory files that need to be accessed by multiple users but that are not stored with the application itself. Font Reserve uses this folder for its Font Reserve database, for example, and America Online Instant Messenger (AIM) uses it for its icon and sound files. This can present a problem should you want to move the application. For starters, to copy the application to another volume, you would also need to remember to copy the files in the Shared folder. In some cases, however, simply moving the application from one location to another on the *same* volume can break the application's link to the files in the Shared folder, leading to problems with using the application. If this happens, use the application's installer to install the application in another folder rather than copy it.

Note: The contents of the Shared folder are not available to nonadministrative users when logged in remotely (a topic covered in more in Chapter 8).

Solutions. In the preceding examples, being an administrator did not directly give you access beyond what any other user would have. As an administrator, however, you can still acquire this access by doing any of the following:

- **Modifying permissions.** You can "unlock" a folder by modifying its permissions via its Get Info window so that you either make yourself the owner or otherwise give yourself Read & Write access. Once you're finished, however, you'll want to return the settings to their original values. Since this can become a hassle, I prefer one of the following solutions.

- **Logging in as root.** When you log in as root, you can access all no-entry folders and access-protected files. You can then not only view their contents but modify them as well.

  SEE: • "Root Access," in Chapter 4.

Using Terminal. You can also use the sudo command to accomplish your goals. For example, a simple way to view a list of the contents of a no-entry folder is as follows:

1. Type sudo ls followed by a space; don't press Return.

2. Locate the prohibited folder in the Finder and drag its icon to the Terminal window. The pathname for the folder should now appear in the command line.

3. Now press Return, and then enter your password when prompted. The list of contents will now appear.

   SEE: • Chapter 10 for more on using Terminal.

If you know the other user's password, you could also log in as that user. Alternatively, as an administrative user, you could go to the Accounts System Preferences pane and create a new password for the user, and use that password to log in. Of course, with the latter method, the original user would then be blocked from his or her account until you revealed the changed password.

Note: If a user has enabled FileVault, and you know his or her password, you can decrypt the FileVault folder to gain access to his or her Home directory. In this case, the folders will not have no-entry icons.

Sticky bits and the Drop Box

In this section, we'll take a closer look at Drop Box permission settings. Along the way, I'll also explain some generally relevant tidbits about the Unix permission setting called the *sticky bit*.

Drop Box permissions. As noted earlier in the chapter, the Get Info window's permissions for a Drop Box folder are set to Write Only for Group and Others. You might think that this setting means what it says—that is, that no one except the owner (or someone with root access) can read or modify the files in that folder. But you would be wrong.

As implied in "Take Note: A Primer on Ownership and Access," earlier in this chapter, you can modify the contents of a file in someone else's Drop Box (for example, deleting text within a word-processing document) if you have write access to the file, even though you can't view the folder's contents. And because you have write access to the folder, you can even delete a file in another user's Drop Box. Thus, files in a folder such as the Drop Box are less secure than they may seem (especially if you're accustomed to the different meaning of Write Only access in Mac OS 9).

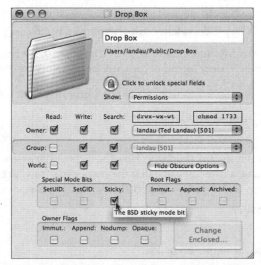

Figure 6.28

The permissions of the Drop Box, shown in XRay, with sticky bit enabled.

Typically, this situation is not much of a concern, because to modify or delete a file in a Drop Box that you do not own, you must at least know the name of the file. And since you can't view the Drop Box folder's contents, it's unlikely you'll have this information (unless it's a file you put there). Even the Find command won't help because it doesn't list results from folders for which you don't have read access. However, if you know the name of the file, you can probably read it and (depending on the file's permission settings) modify or delete it as well.

Of course, as an admin user, you can always gain access to another user's Drop Box by changing the ownership of the folder to yourself (using the folder's Get Info window). This would solve the problem of not knowing the name of a file in a Drop Box.

The sticky bit. So is there a way you can improve the security of the Drop Box? Yes. To further restrict access to the contents of this (or any other) folder, you can set the *sticky bit* for the folder. The sticky bit is a special Unix attribute setting that goes beyond the standard read, write, and search/execute ones.

If the sticky bit is set for a folder, anyone can add files to the folder, but only the owner of the folder can directly remove or rename items from it. (Actually, a file's owner should also be able to remove or rename that particular file.) This situation does not prevent someone from opening and reading a file in a Drop Box (assuming that person knows the name of the file and has read access to it), but it does prevent that person from renaming or removing the file. In some cases, the setting will also prevent modifications to the file. To guarantee that no intruders can read or modify a file in your Drop Box, you need to modify the permissions of the file itself (setting Group and Others to No Access), not the folder that contains it.

Setting the sticky bit. If you decide you want to set the sticky bit for your own Drop Box, you can do so in one of two ways: using Terminal or via a utility such as XRay. I'll explain both alternatives briefly.

SEE: • "Unix: Modifying Permissions," in Chapter 10, for background information on using Terminal for Unix permissions settings.

To use Terminal to add the sticky bit to the Drop Box folder, follow these steps:

1. Launch Terminal, and type cd Public.

2. Type ls -l.

   The permissions for the Drop Box should read drwx-wx-wx, which means that you have a directory (d); that the owner has "raw" (read, write, execute) permission; and that Group and Everyone have just -wx permission.

3. Type chmod 1733 "Drop Box."

   or

   Type chmod go=wxt "Drop Box."

For the initial chmod (change mode) command, a *0* as the first digit means that the sticky bit is off; a *1* means that it's on.

The latter chmod command has the same net effect as chmod 1733. Briefly, it sets the access for Group (g) and Other (o) to be equal to (=) write, execute, and sticky bit but provides no read access (-wxt).

4. Type ls -l again.

   The permissions should now read drwx-wx-wt. The last t indicates that the sticky bit is set.

To use XRay to add the sticky bit to the Drop Box folder, follow these steps:

1. Open the folder you want to modify in XRay (Drop Box, in this example). (Using XRay's contextual-menu command is probably the easiest way to do this.)

2. From the Show pop-up menu, open the Permissions tab.

3. Click the Show Obscure Options check box.

4. In the Special Mode Bits section, check the Sticky check box.

5. Save your changes.

Note: Examine the boxes just below the Show pop-up menu. You will see the same sort of attribute listing for the folder that you can see in Terminal when you list files by using ls -l. When you check the Sticky box, the last letter in the listing will change from *x* to *t*. For Drop Box, it will change from drwx-wx-wx to drwx-wx-wt. Again, this change indicates that the sticky bit has been set. The adjacent text box in XRay will similarly change from chmod 0733 to chmod 1733.

Sticky bit and the root volume. The sticky bit is enabled automatically for the root-level directory when you install Mac OS X. The root level is the level that has the name of the volume as its window name in the Finder (where you see System, Library, Users, Applications, and other folders). Thus, anything that is copied to that window cannot later be moved via a simple Finder drag by anyone other than the owner of the item or by someone who has root access. Thus, if another user on your Mac adds a file to that window when he or she is logged in, you will not be able to drag the item to the Trash, for example, even though you are an administrator.

The simplest way to get rid of the file is to do a Command-drag and use the Authenticate dialog when it appears. In some cases, this alone will be sufficient for the move to work.

Otherwise, use Get Info to make yourself the owner of the file or folder (as described in "Copying and Moving: Permissions Problems," earlier in this chapter). Then you can move or trash the file as desired.

More generally, for almost any problem that involves moving a file from a folder with the sticky bit enabled, you can turn off the sticky bit temporarily, complete your move, and then turn the sticky bit back on.

To do this via XRay for the root directory, drag the Mac OS X startup-volume icon to XRay and uncheck the Sticky check box. Alternatively, you use the following command in Terminal: sudo chmod 775 /.

After returning to the Finder and completing whatever you wanted to do, recheck the Sticky check box via XRay or return to Terminal and type sudo chmod 1775 /.

SetUID attribute and the "Items could not be copied" error

Occasionally, when you attempt to copy an application, you may get the following error message: "One or more items can't be copied. Do you want to skip them and copy the remaining items?" Or you may get a similar message that refers to "special permissions." If you click Continue, you will get what appears to be a copy of the application, but if you try to launch it, it won't work. Typically, you won't get an error message. Instead, the application will simply start to launch and then quit.

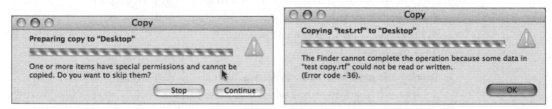

Figure 6.29

Two messages that may appear when attempting to copy a file for which the SetUID bit has been set.

If it seems odd that attempting to copy an application brings up a message referring to multiple items being copied, remember that most Mac OS X applications are actually packages, which contain multiple files and folders.

As to the reason for the error message, it usually occurs because at least one of the files within the .app package has its SetUID (set user ID) attribute enabled. The following sections provide more detail on this as well as instructions for working around the problem.

TECHNICALLY SPEAKING ▶ **SetUID and SetGID**

The SetUID command in Unix has little to do with copying .app packages in the Finder (as described in the main text). Instead, Unix users occasionally need it to access functions they would otherwise be prohibited from accessing. To change your password, for example, you need to access the function that changes passwords. However, such access is restricted to the root user (otherwise, any user could change someone's password). Unix works around this dilemma by providing an option that allows a user to access the password function just to change his or her own password—accomplished by enabling the SetUID bit for the function. This bit has a similar effect on any other command for which it is set.

When SetUID is enabled for a command, the command is run as though the person running it has the permissions of the owner of the file (root, in the password example) for the action attempted. As long as you have permission to access the other files needed to complete your request, the command should work. Thus, any user can change his or her own password.

The SetGID bit works similarly, except that the normal group permissions are shifted temporarily to those of the group that owns the command in question. This bit has a somewhat different effect when applied to a directory rather than a file. In any case, you will have no need for this command; I mention it only for the sake of completeness.

Finding the problem file. For simplicity, I'll assume that only one file in the .app package has this problem. How do you locate which file it is? By comparing the original application's package contents with the copy. You need to use the Show Package Contents contextual-menu command to open the .app packages so that you can examine their contents. The one item missing in the copy but found in the original is the culprit.

For example, I encountered this problem when attempting to copy Mail.app. (I have no idea how the sticky bit came to be set here, since it's normally not.) A search revealed that the file missing in the copy had the following pathname: Mail.app/Contents/MacOS/Mail. Since this file contains Mail's program code, it's no wonder the copy didn't work!

Disabling the SetUID bit. To confirm whether the Mail file (in our example) has its SetUID bit enabled, you can open the file via a utility like XRay or by using Terminal.

SEE: • Chapter 10 for more on using commands in Terminal.

If using XRay, use the Show Package Contents contextual menu command to access the contents of the Mail.app package; locate the Mail file; and open it in XRay. The SetUID bit is listed in the same Special Mode Bits section of the Permissions screen as the sticky bit. If it's checked, it's enabled.

If using Terminal, you would type the following:

```
ls -l /Applications/Mail.app/Contents/MacOS/
```

Or, more simply, type ls -l (followed by a space) and then drag the MacOS folder icon from within the Mail.app package to the Terminal window. Now press Return. If the SetUID bit is enabled, the Mail file listed in the output will have its attributes listed as -rwsrwxr-x. Note the s, instead of the more common x, at the end of the first trio of letters (rws instead of rwx). This s indicates that SetUID has been enabled for the owner.

If a file has its SetUID bit enabled, it cannot be copied in the Finder. In Unix, the file would be copied with the SetUID bit stripped off. In Mac OS X, the file apparently refuses to copy at all.

Thus, the solution to the problem is straightforward: Disable the SetUID bit for the file, and the file will copy successfully. The copy should also run successfully with SetUID still off, so you don't need to re-enable it (though if you have problems, you *can* re-enable the SetUID bit if necessary).

To disable (or re-enable) the SetUID bit, you can once again use a utility (such as XRay) or Terminal.

If you decide to use XRay, follow these steps:

1. From the contextual menu of the application that contains the SetUID-enabled file, select Show Package Contents.

2. Open the SetUID-enabled file with XRay.

3. Click the padlock icon, and enter your administrator's password when requested.

4. From the Show pop-up menu, select Permissions and click the Show Obscure Options button.

5. Uncheck the SetUID check box.

6. Save your change.

You can reverse the change later, if necessary.

If using Terminal, follow these steps:

1. Type sudo chmod u-s.

2. Press the spacebar and drag the Finder icon of the SetUID-enabled file (in the package of the application) to the Terminal window.

   This enters the pathname for the file.

3. Press Return.

4. Provide your administrator password when prompted.

   To verify that the change has been made (assuming you're still at the MacOS directory level), just type ls -l again. The permissions for the file should now read -rwxrwxr-x.

After using either method, if you attempt to copy the original application from the Finder, it should now copy successfully.

Unix commands such as ditto and CpMac may allow you to make the copy even with the SetUID bit enabled. However, if you want to copy the file from the Finder, the above-described steps are the way to go.

Note: Enabling SetUID can be an effective form of copy protection. If you enable the SetUID bit for a file located on a volume for which a user does not have administrative access, there's virtually no way that user can copy the file—launch it, yes, but not copy it.

Figure 6.30

The Chess application, with the SetUID option enabled, as seen in XRay.

Booting and copying from Mac OS 9. If your Mac can boot from Mac OS 9, another work-around to this SetUID issue is to boot in Mac OS 9. Permissions restrictions are not enforced in Mac OS 9, which means you can copy the application with no problem.

TAKE NOTE ▶ Package Contents Folder Won't Open

After making a copy of an .app application, if you try to access the contents of the package (by choosing the Show Package Contents command from the contextual menu), you may meet with resistance: Although the Show Package Contents command opens the package normally, the Contents folder inside is dimmed and cannot be opened.

Solution? Just log out and log back in. All should be well.

Deleting: Using the Trash

Deleting an item in Mac OS X is a two-step process. First, you put the item in the Trash; then you empty the Trash. I discussed the basics of this process in Chapter 2; the following provides an overview of Trash essentials:

Placing items in the Trash

To place an item in the Trash, do one of the following:

- Drag the file's icon to the Trash icon in the Dock.
- Click the item and from the Finder's File menu choose Move to Trash.
- Click the item and use the keyboard shortcut Command-Delete.

Until you empty the Trash, files placed there are not really deleted. You can view the contents of the Trash by double-clicking the Trash icon to open its window. Any item in the window can be dragged out again. You can also place an item in the Trash by dragging it to this open window.

Each user maintains his or her own Trash. Thus, you will not see items in other users' Trash when you log in. (The Trash contents will return for that user the next time he or she logs in.)

Mac OS X does not include a feature that allows you to create a Trash icon on the Desktop separate from the Dock. However, several shareware utilities, such as Norther Software's Trash X, provide a means to do this.

Emptying the Trash

To empty the Trash, do one of the following:

- From the Finder's Finder menu, choose Empty Trash.

  To overwrite the file data with meaningless information (so that there's no chance of the data being recovered), select Secure Empty Trash instead. Note: This security feature may be defeated if you're using a utility such as Prosoft Engineering's Data Recycler X to preserve deleted files.

- From the Trash's Dock menu, select Empty Trash.

- Press Command-Shift-Delete (a shortcut for the Finder's Empty Trash command). This is especially convenient (combined with Command-Delete to get the file to the Trash) as a quick way to delete a file. Just click the file's icon and press Command-Delete followed by Command-Shift-Delete. The file is gone.

Files that will not delete. Mac OS X will prevent you from deleting certain files, such as those critical to the running of the OS. This is a good thing. However, it sometimes prevents you from deleting items that are safe to delete. Later in this chapter, I explain how you to get around this prohibition.

Show warning

If you have the "Show warning before emptying the Trash" option enabled in the Advanced section of the Finder's Preferences window, every time you try to empty the Trash, you will get the following warning message: "Are you sure you want to remove the items in the Trash permanently?" This is useful because Empty Trash is one of the very few Finder commands that *cannot* be undone via the Finder's Undo command (Command-Z).

If you choose Empty Trash from the Trash's Dock menu, the Mac will empty the Trash without warning, even if the Finder warning option is enabled.

Changes in the Trash icon

Depending upon what you're dragging, the Trash icon in the Dock may change to indicate a change in its function or status. For starters, if there are items in the Trash, the icon changes to indicate this.

More generally, if you click-drag a volume or server icon, the Trash icon will change to an Eject icon. This indicates that placing the volume in the Trash will unmount, disconnect, or eject the volume—not delete its contents.

If you drag the icon of a CD-R—that has been set up for burning—to the Trash, the Trash icon will change to the Burn icon to indicate that placing the CD-R icon in the Trash will initiate the burn.

SEE: • **"Take Note: Problems Mounting and Unmounting/Ejecting Media,"**
    later in this chapter, for related information.

Figure 6.31

Talking Trash: The Trash's Empty Trash option (left); the Empty Trash warning (middle); the Trash icon when it's transformed to an Eject icon (right).

Deleting: Undeleting Files

After you delete an item in Mac OS X, there's no easy way to recover it. The Finder's Undo command will not bring it back.

However, if you're desperate to recover deleted files, there are third-party utilities that allow you to do so. To use them effectively, however, they should be installed and running *before* you need to use them to recover a file.

My preferred choice is Data Recycler X, which works by maintaining an invisible folder (called .DataRecycler Folder, located at the root level of your startup volume) where all deleted files are stored. When the number of files stored exceeds the capacity of the folder (which you set from Data Recycler's preferences), the oldest files are truly deleted to make room for newer "deleted" files. In the meantime, you can easily recover any deleted files. It even allows you to recover files deleted via Unix's rm command! To recover files, launch the Recycler application, locate the files you want to recover from the list, and click Undelete Files.

Norton Utilities for Mac OS X includes an UnErase feature that can similarly recover deleted files, though it's not as reliable as Data Recycler.

Deleting: Problems Deleting Files

This section explores the most common reasons (and a few uncommon ones) you might have trouble deleting a file and explains what you can do to fix the problem and delete the file.

Locked files

The most basic reason a file refuses to delete is that the file is locked, via the Locked check box in the file's Get Info window.

If a file is locked, a small padlock symbol is visible in the bottom-left corner of the file's icon.

In addition, if you attempt to move a locked file to the Trash (or even to another folder on your drive), you typically get an error message that states the following: "The operation could not be completed because the item is locked." In Mac OS X, holding down the Option key (a technique that works in Mac OS 9) has no effect on your ability to drag the item into the Trash.

Thus, to delete a file that's locked, you must open the Get Info window for the file and uncheck its Locked check box. Once you've done this, you can drag the item to the Trash and empty it. Unlocking a file also allows you to move it to a different folder location, other than the Trash, if you wish.

If a file is already in the Trash, you can still enable its Locked option, but doing so will have no effect. If you empty the Trash, the file will be deleted.

Occasionally, you may find that a locked item makes it into the Trash and refuses to be deleted. In such cases, you may not even be able to drag the item out of the Trash. Apple claims that pressing and holding down the Shift-Option keys while selecting Empty Trash (from the Finder) should work here. However, I've been unable to confirm this. If this method doesn't work, try unlocking the file and deleting it again.

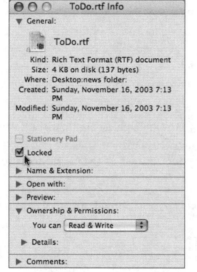

Figure 6.32

The Locked check box in a Get Info window (left), and the locked symbol in the file icon (right).

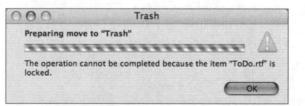

Figure 6.33

The "item is locked" error message that appears when you try to place a locked file in the Trash.

Batch-deleting locked files. If you select several files and then choose Get Info (Command-I) from the Finder's File menu, you will get one Get Info window for all the selected items. The top of the window will indicate the number of items selected. Any change you make (such as unlocking) will affect all selected files simultaneously. When they are unlocked, the files can be deleted.

SEE: • "Using Unix to delete files," later in this chapter, for related information.

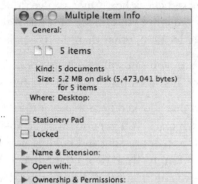

Figure 6.34

The Get Info window for a collection of items that have been "batch" selected.

TAKE NOTE ▶ How to Lock Folders

Mac OS X currently does not permit folders to be locked or unlocked via the Get Info window. Although the Locked check box appears, it is dimmed and cannot be selected. This means you can't lock Mac OS X applications that are packages, because a package is actually a special type of folder (as I explained in Chapter 3). Neither can you lock certain types of documents, including .pkg and .rtfd documents, which are also packages.

You can circumvent this restriction by using Terminal's chflag command. Alternatively, you can lock folders from Mac OS X by using (yet again!) a utility like XRay, which allows you to enable the Locked option for any item, including folders (as well as the invisible and package attributes, also not available in Get Info windows).

SEE: • "Take Note: TextEdit: Format Options Beyond Show Font," in Chapter 4, for more on .rtfd packages.
• "The chflags Command," in Chapter 10.

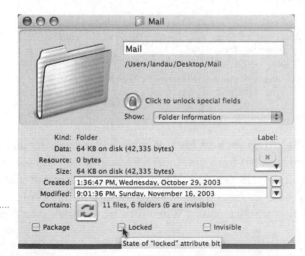

Figure 6.35

XRay window with the Locked option indicated.

"In use" files

A file cannot be deleted from the Finder if it is "in use" or "open." The following are some examples of documents that would be considered "open" or "in use."

- **The file is an open application.** In this case, you probably won't even be able to place it in the Trash.

- **The file is a document and is currently open in an application.** Most often, a document is only listed as "in use" if it has unsaved changes. The Mac is inconsistent here, however. For some documents open in some applications, you can delete the document at any time. For other documents and applications, however, you can't delete the document (even once you've closed it) until you've quit the application.

- **The file is an accessory file for an open application or process.** For example, a preferences file for an application may refuse to delete while the application is running.

- **The file is a disk-image file, and its image is mounted.**

- **An aborted partially downloaded file may be considered in use even after the downloading application has quit.**

The easiest way to delete an in-use file is to quit the application or process that's keeping the file in use. Thus, for a document, quit the opening application; for a disk image, unmount the image. If the problem involves a background process (that is, a process not shown in the Dock), you may need to use Activity Monitor to quit it. After quitting the process, the file should delete.

If this doesn't work, from the Finder's Finder menu select Secure Empty Trash. This should do the trick, bypassing any warning about the file being in use. However, avoid doing this if the file you want to delete is truly in use. For example, if you use this to delete a document that is currently open in an application, the application will likely crash (unexpectedly quit) when you next access it. Instead, first quit the application. Only if you cannot delete the document at this point should you try Secure Empty Trash.

If the file still does not delete, or if you're unsure which process is causing the problem, log out and log back in. If that fails, restart. At this point, it's almost 100 percent certain that you'll be able to delete the file. If not, proceed on to the next section!

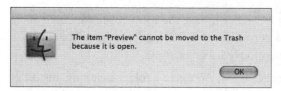 

Figure 6.36

The error messages that appear (left) when you drag an open application to the Trash and (right) when you try to delete a disk-image file while the image is mounted.

TECHNICALLY SPEAKING ▶ Finding Out Which Files Are in Use

If you prefer not to log out to solve an "in use" problem, and you're having a problem identifying the process that's keeping a file in the Trash "in use," you can try the `fstat` command in Terminal, which identifies the process that's keeping an application open.

For example, I had an AppleWorks document, test.cwk, in the Trash that would not delete because it was in use (because it was still open in AppleWorks). For the sake of argument, let's say I didn't know it was an AppleWorks document. In that case, I might use the `fstat` command as follows:

```
fstat ~/.Trash/*
```

This produces a list of all open files in the Trash. When I executed the command while the AppleWorks document was in the Trash, I got the following output (some of which I've deleted in order to fit the relevant output here):

```
USER   CMD       PID   MODE     NAME
tedmac LaunchCFMA 25183 -rw-r—r— /Users/tedmac/.Trash/test.cwk
```

Unfortunately, in this example, the output lists LaunchCFMA (the LaunchCFMApp process discussed in Chapter 4) as the parent process, *not* AppleWorks. The reason for this is that AppleWorks is a Carbon application that uses LaunchCFMApp to open. Although in this case the output was less than ideal, it could still help identify the application (at least you know it's a Carbon application now). In other cases, the `fstat` output will list the precise application/process. In such cases, if the process is not one shown in the Dock, you can use Activity Monitor to locate and quit the process.

Item cannot be placed in Trash or Trash cannot be emptied

You may get an error message when you try to place an item in the Trash, saying that you are prohibited from placing the item in the Trash for some reason. Or you may succeed in placing the item in the Trash but get an error message when you try to empty the Trash.

This can happen if the item is locked or in use (as just described); however, it can also occur with unlocked files that are not in use.

Causes. For files that are not locked or in use, the most common cause of these types of Trash errors is a permissions restriction—similar to the ones that can prevent files from being moved. For example:

- If you have Read Only access or No Access to a folder that contains the file you want to delete, you won't be able to move the file out of the folder (and into the Trash). Actually, with No Access, you won't even be able to open the folder to see the file.

Note: Having Read Only access for the file itself will not prevent you from deleting it. The settings for the containing folder are what matter. Further, you can probably delete the entire folder, even though you may not be able to drag an item out of it!

- If the sticky bit is set for a folder, and you're neither the folder's nor the item's owner, you likely will not be able to move items from the folder into the Trash.

In principle, if an item's permissions settings do not prevent you from moving it to the Trash, the settings should not prevent you from deleting the item once it's in the Trash. After all, you have Read & Write access to the Trash. In most cases, this is exactly how it works. There are, however, a few exceptions, which I describe in the following text.

Note: Regardless of what the permissions settings are, how they got that way, why they cause trouble, or even whether they're the root cause of the problem, your goal is the same: to delete the file. As such, it's often simpler to bypass the permissions settings altogether and focus on the task at hand—deleting the task directly, as described in the next section.

Solutions. Whether you cannot place the item in the Trash or cannot empty the Trash, try one of the following to see which solution works best for you:

- **Authenticate.** If an action (such as dragging an item to the Trash) is prohibited, an Authenticate dialog may appear. If so, enter your administrator's name and password when prompted. The item(s) should now move to the Trash and delete.

  Remember, though: If you've used this method (or entered your password for any other reason) within the last 5 minutes, you will be able to perform these actions without reauthenticating.

  Note: In Jaguar, you will not get an Authenticate option. Instead, trying to move an item from a restricted folder leads to the following error message: "The item cannot be moved to the Trash because it cannot be deleted."

  SEE: • **"Using Panther's Finder Authenticate method," earlier in this chapter, for more on the Authenticate dialog.**

- **Use a delete utility.** If an Authenticate option does not appear, there are numerous utilities that will "force-empty" the Trash. That is, they force a file in the Trash to be deleted even if the Finder's Empty Trash command fails. For example, Cocktail includes a Force Empty Trash option that works well (in the System>Misc screen) as well as an option to delete locked files (in the Files>Locked screen).

  There are a few utilities that can even delete files that aren't in the Trash—great for occasions when you can't move a file to the Trash. For example, with EHN and DIJ Oakley's DropObliter8, you just drop the problem file onto the DropObliter8 icon, and the problem should vanish. Another utility, Findley Designs' Delete It, offers a window with navigable access to anywhere on your drive. Simply select files from the list that you want to delete and then click the Delete button.

Similarly, if you've installed FileXaminer and its contextual-menu plug-ins, you can simply Control-click a problem file or folder and select Super Delete from the resulting contextual menu. After you've provided your admin user name and password, the file(s) will be deleted outright.

Once again, I advise caution: Some files, such as those in the System folder, may refuse to be moved to the Trash and deleted via this method—a good thing because they're critical to running the OS. *Do not* try to figure out how to delete these files: Leave them be!

- **Use Unix.** The just-cited utilities typically work as front ends for Unix commands; the commands actually do the dirty work. If you want, you can bypass these utilities and use the Unix commands directly via Terminal. Using Unix commands (primarily the rm command) to delete a file will almost always succeed, whether the problem is that the file is locked, is in use, has restrictive permissions, or whatever else you can imagine.

  SEE: • "Using Unix to delete files," below, for details.

- **Modify permissions.** Another workable solution is to modify the permissions of the item (and/or its enclosing folder) so that it can be deleted. To do so, you would assign yourself as the owner and give yourself Read & Write access. To make these changes, you can use the Finder's Get Info command, Terminal commands (such as chmod), and utilities like XRay, as appropriate.

  SEE: • "Opening and Saving: Permissions Problems" and "Copying and Moving: Permissions Problems," earlier in this chapter, for more details.

  • "Take Note: Adding or Deleting a User," in Chapter 2, for details on how to completely delete the Home directory of a user who will no longer be using your computer.

- **Log in as root user.** You should almost never need to do this, but it will work: Simply log in as the root user and delete the files from there.

  SEE: • "Root Access," in Chapter 4, for more details.

- **Empty the Trash before placing the item in the Trash.** If you try to drag a file to the Trash when a file of the same name already exists there, the Finder usually renames the file that's already in the Trash (for example, by adding a *1* to the name) so that the new file can be added. However, the Finder may balk at doing this and block you from adding a file with the same name. If so, empty the Trash and *then* drag the file to the Trash.

- **Rename the volume or folder.** If a file to be deleted contains a slash (/) in its name—or any other unusual character (such as a copyright symbol)—it may fail to delete. The solution is to change the name to remove the character(s). Further, if the volume that a file is on contains these characters, the file may also refuse to delete. The solution here is to change the name of the volume. If needed, you can change the name back after deleting the file.

- **Remove aliases from the Trash.** If you have too many alias files in the Trash, you may be unable to delete them. The solution is to drag the alias files from the Trash and return them in smaller groups (one at a time, if necessary). Then delete each group separately.

- **Create a new folder.** Create a new folder; place the uncooperative item in it; move the folder to the Trash; and select Empty Trash. This will usually work even if you weren't able to delete the file by dragging it to the Trash directly.

- **Use your Web browser to delete downloads.** If a file you've downloaded from the Web is interrupted before the download is finished, the partial file may refuse to delete. If this happens, try to delete the file via the browser application. For example, with Internet Explorer, open Download Manager, click the name of the problem file, and press the Delete or Command-Delete keys.

- **Boot from Mac OS 9 and delete from there.** If your Mac model is one that can still boot from Mac OS 9, doing this will almost always succeed in deleting the file.

  Note: Before switching to Mac OS 9, remove the problem file from the Trash and place it in a location that you can view easily when you're booted in Mac OS 9, such as the root level of your Home directory. The reason for this is that the contents of the Mac OS X Trash are invisible in Mac OS 9 (that is, they won't appear in the Mac OS 9 Trash folder because Mac OS X and Mac OS 9 Trash are not stored in the same location). Thus, if you do not remove the file from the Trash in Mac OS X, you will need to locate and move the file with a utility (such as SkyTag Software's File Buddy) that allows you to view and/or manipulate invisible files. (In the unlikely case that Mac OS X does not permit you to remove the item from the Trash, deleting the file in Mac OS 9 will require accessing the invisible Trash location.)

  SEE: • "Invisible Files," later in this chapter, for more information on working with invisible files.

  • "Take Note: The Location of Trash Folders," in Chapter 4, for related information.

- **Repair the disk.** Use Disk Utility's First Aid both to repair the disk and repair disk permissions. First Aid may repair a problem that is preventing a file from being deleted. If First Aid does not work, you can try other repair utilities, such as Alsoft Software's DiskWarrior.

  In my opinion, it's rare that these repairs will be needed to delete a file, but they are worth a shot.

  SEE: • "Performing repairs with Disk Utility (First Aid)," in Chapter 5 for details.

Using Unix to delete files

Although I prefer Aqua-based solutions, there are times when the only and/or quickest path to success is through Terminal. For problems with deleting files, there are two Unix commands you can try: chflags and rm. If one fails, try the other. I have never failed to have success with them.

SEE: • "Unix: The sudo and su Commands," "The chflags command," and "The rm command," all in Chapter 10, for more information.

Using chflags. The chflags (change-flags) command is used to turn file attributes on and off. In this case, you'll use it to turn off an attribute called the *immutable flag,* which is the Unix equivalent of a locked file. The file resists being deleted until the flag is turned off. In most cases, the status of this flag will match that of the Locked check box in a File's Get Info window. However, it may happen that this flag is on even if the Locked check box is unchecked. By turning this flag off in Terminal, you can then return to the Finder and delete the file. To do this, follow these steps:

1. From Terminal type chflags -R nouchg.

2. Press the spacebar.

3. Locate the files and/or folders you want to delete. In most cases they should already be in the Trash. Drag the icon of each file to the Terminal window. (You can drag multiple files at once.) The files' pathnames should be appended to the line following the space.

4. Press Return.

Alternatively, if all the files you want to delete are in one directory, such as your Home directory's Trash, you can type the following:

chflags -R nouchg {*name of directory*}

For example, for your Trash directory, the name would be ~/.Trash. The –R option (which stands for *recursive*) causes the flags of all files in the Trash directory to be changed, not just the directory itself. Again, you can drag a directory's icon to the Terminal window to add its pathname to the end of the command.

If the flag was on for any problem file, it should now be off. You can now return to the Finder and delete the files by selecting Empty Trash. If that doesn't work, try using the rm command, as described next.

Note: There is a special immutable flag called the *System Immutable flag.* If this is set for a file, none of the procedures described here are likely to work. The only way to get the file to delete is by using the chflags command while in single-user mode (see Chapter 5 for more on this mode). The XRay utility includes an option to set this flag, via an Immut check box in the Root Flags section of the Permissions screen. Before it turns the flag on, it warns you of the need to enter single-user mode to undo this. Basically, I see no reason to ever enable this flag—which means it's unlikely you'll confront this problem. For this reason, I'm skipping over single-user-mode details here.

Using rm. The rm (remove) command deletes files in Unix. In most cases, if the rm command would work, choosing the Empty Trash command in the Finder would have worked just as well—so there would be no point in bothering with rm. The need for the rm command arises when you want to delete an item for which you are not the owner, or in any other situation in which permissions restrictions prevent Empty Trash from working. In this case, using the remove command with root access (via the sudo command) will do the trick. To do this, follow these steps:

1. From Terminal, type sudo rm –R.

2. Press the spacebar.

3. Locate the files you want to delete. (In most cases they should already be in the Trash.) Drag the icon of each to the Terminal window. (You can drag multiple files at once.) The files' pathnames should be appended to the line following the space.

4. Press Return.

5. When prompted, enter your password and press Return again.

The files and folders should be deleted. You will not need to choose Empty Trash from the Finder. Even if the files you selected to remove were not in the Trash, they're now gone. And (with the exception of files protected by Data Recycler X), they're gone forever!

Be very cautious about using this command. If you make a mistake in typing, you could delete files you did not want to delete, possibly eradicating most of the contents of your drive!

SEE: • "Take Note: Using rm: Risk Management," in Chapter 10, for more details regarding the potential dangers of using the rm command.

Can't eject/unmount or burn media

Related to the coverage of deleting files is the issue of unmounting/ejecting media and burning CD or DVD media. Both deleting and unmounting share a common key step: dragging items to the Trash icon.

SEE: • "Take Note: Problems Mounting and Unmounting/Ejecting Media" and "Take Note: Burning CDs (and DVDs)," later in this chapter, for details.

TECHNICALLY SPEAKING ▶ More Trash Talk

If deleting files in the Trash individually via the rm command, as described in the main text, doesn't work, you can delete the entire Trash directory. Don't worry: A new one is created automatically the next time you drag an item to the Trash icon on the Dock.

Actually, there are several Trash directories you may want or need to delete. As covered in "Take Note: The Location of Trash Folders," in Chapter 4, there is a separate .Trashes directory at the root level of each volume, as well as a .Trash directory at the root level of each user's Home directory. There is also a Trash directory at the root level of every volume that contains Mac OS 9 (although these should not be affected by the problems described here, so I will not include them in the examples that follow).

continues on next page

TECHNICALLY SPEAKING ▶ More Trash Talk *continued*

To delete your own .Trash directory plus the .Trashes directory at the root level of the startup drive, type the following two commands in Terminal:

```
sudo rm -R ~/.Trash/
sudo rm -R /.Trashes/
```

For any .Trashes directories on volumes other than the startup volume, you need to enter the volume information in the pathname. For example, for a volume called Matrix, you would type the following:

```
sudo rm -R /Volumes/Matrix/.Trashes/
```

Repeat this as needed for as many volumes as you have.

Note: These directories actually maintain separate subdirectories for each user. The name of each subdirectory is the user ID for that user. The user ID of the initial administrator of the Mac is typically 501. In some cases, you may want or need to specify this ID in the rm command. For example, you could type the following:

```
sudo rm -R /Volumes/Matrix/.Trashes/501
```

This deletes any trash you put in the .Trashes directory while leaving items placed by other users untouched.

TAKE NOTE ▶ Problems Mounting and Unmounting/Ejecting Media

This sidebar outlines the ways you can mount and unmount a volume in Mac OS X, the problems that can occur when doing so, and the solutions to those problems.

Ejecting/unmounting disks. To eject removable media or unmount a server volume or disk image, try the following until one of the actions works:

- Drag the volume's icon to the Trash.

  Note that you *cannot* use Command-Delete as an alternative here.

- Select the volume icon and, from the Finder's File menu, choose Eject (Command-E).

- For external media, such as a drive connected to the FireWire port, click the Eject icon to the right of the volume's name in the sidebar of a Finder window.

- If your keyboard has an Eject key (or uses F12 as an Eject key), pressing that key should cause a mounted removable volume to eject or unmount from the internal drive. For a drive such as a CD drive, if there is no disc in the drive, the tray will simply open.

  If you have multiple removable devices mounted, select the one you want to eject before pressing the Eject key. Otherwise, you may eject/unmount multiple devices.

  SEE: • "Take Note: Eject Options," in Chapter 2, for still more ways to eject removable media.

continues on next page

TAKE NOTE ▶ Problems Mounting and Unmounting/Ejecting Media *continued*

Important: Do not disconnect a peripheral drive (such as a FireWire drive) before you unmount it from the Finder. Doing so can potentially damage data on the drive.

Eject/unmount problems: "in use" error. If you get a message that says a volume cannot be ejected (or put away) because the volume is "in use," this typically means that some document or application on the volume is still open. Thus, the fix is to close the open file. In the case of a document, you may need to quit its application entirely, not just close the file. If these methods don't work, consider the following:

- If you get this message when you've quit all files on the volume, try to unmount/eject the volume again. It will usually succeed. Otherwise, relaunch (force-quit) the Finder and try yet again.

- If you get an "in use" error when trying to eject a disk that contains files that were in use (but are apparently not in use anymore), choose the Clear Menu command from the hierarchical menu of the Recent Items command in the Apple menu.

- If you cannot unmount a network volume because of an "in use" error, the cause may be a process that remains open (the Office Notifications feature of Microsoft's Entourage is one example) even if the parent application (Entourage, in this example) is quit. If the application has been used to access data on the mounted network volume, the unmounting problem will occur. In such cases, quitting the process (by choosing Turn off Office Notifications from the Entourage menu, for example) should work.

  Note: You may also be able to use Activity Monitor to see if a process related to the application is still open (for example, checking the list of processes for a name that suggests it's the process you're seeking); if so, quitting it from within Activity Monitor may allow you to unmount the volume.

- When sending files via iChat, if you send a file located on a nonstartup volume, you will subsequently be unable to eject any removable media due to an "in use" error. The workaround is to log out and log back in.

SEE: • "'Inuse' files," earlier in this chapter, for related information.

continues on next page

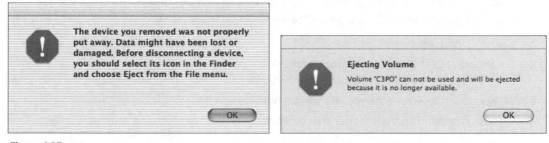

Figure 6.37

Unmounting errors: (a) The error message that appears if you disconnect an external device before unmounting it; (b) an error message that may appear in the Finder if a volume is unmounted by a means other than the Finder.

TAKE NOTE ▶ Problems Mounting and Unmounting/Ejecting Media *continued*

Eject/unmount problems: other errors. If the preceding methods do not work or do not apply, try the following until one works:

- Use Disk Utility to unmount and/or eject a volume.

  To unmount a volume, select the volume/partition from the list along the left side of the window. Then select Unmount from Disk Utility's File menu or toolbar.

  Sometimes, after you drag the icon of a removable-media volume (such as a CD or DVD) to the Trash, the volume's icon vanishes (that is, it unmounts), but the removable media does not eject. In such cases, select the Eject command in Disk Utility's File menu or toolbar. It may still work to eject the media.

  Alternatively, you can use the `diskutil` command in Terminal, which is the Unix equivalent of Disk Utility. Use `diskutil unmount {`*diskname*`}` or `diskutil eject {`*diskname*`}`. The disk name should be the full path (for example, /Volumes/DiskOne).

- Try the Eject buttons in iTunes or DVD Player, as appropriate. They may work even if the Finder fails.

- Log out and log back in. Now try to unmount/eject the media. This almost always gets the media to eject.

- For ejectable media, such as CDs and DVDs, restart and hold down the mouse button until the media ejects.

- Press the Eject button on the drive itself, if one exists. Normally, this will not work if media is in the drive. However, it's worth a try.

- If an ejectable disc is stuck in a drive, you may be able to eject it manually, typically by inserting an unbent paper clip into a hole located near the drive opening. Check with Apple or the vendor of the drive for specifics.

SEE: • "Technically Speaking: Open Firmware Commands," in Chapter 5, for more information on ejecting a CD or DVD at startup.

How to remount a volume. Occasionally, the opposite problem may arise: You unmount a volume that you did not intend to unmount. For removable media or remote volumes, the solution is simple: Reinsert the ejected media or reconnect to the server. But what if you have a hard drive (especially a multiple-partition one), and you unmount a partition by mistake? (Typically, if you unmount one partition, you unmount all of them, unless one is the startup partition.) To get the volume back on the Desktop, follow these steps:

1. Launch Disk Utility.
2. If needed, click the disclosure triangle to the left of the hard-drive icon to display the names of your hard-disk volumes and partitions.
3. Select a partition from the volume you want to remount.
4. Choose Mount from the File menu or toolbar.

continues on next page

TAKE NOTE ▶ Problems Mounting and Unmounting/Ejecting Media *continued*

In rarer cases, a connected but unmounted volume may not be listed in Disk Utility. This has happened to me with my iPod (which may unmount when my Mac goes to sleep). Disconnecting and reconnecting the iPod will get it to remount. But there is a faster way. Use the Finder's Go to Folder command to go to the /Volumes directory. An icon for the iPod (or other improperly unmounted volume) should be there. Double-click the icon and the volume should remount—assuming it is still connected to your Mac, of course.

Duplicate volumes in /Volumes. If your Mac goes to sleep while connected to an external volume, the volume may unmount when you wake the Mac up, and you may have problems remounting the volume. The main solution is to use the Disk Utility methods just described.

However, in some cases (due to the sleep issue as well as other problems), you may have multiple copies of the same volume (external or remote) listed in the /Volumes directory. These duplicate copies may persist even after the volume is disconnected from your Mac. These duplicates can lead to mounting and unmounting problems. To check for (and fix) this issue, use the Finder's Go to Folder command to go to the /Volumes directory. If you see several copies of the same volume (they will have similar names, such as iPod, iPod 1, and iPod 2), you can delete all duplicates that have a plain folder icon (the folder will be empty). Do not delete any items that have an alias server or drive volume icon! Doing so could delete the contents of an actively mounted volume. You will need root access to delete these folders (in Panther, you should be able to solve this by authenticating when asked).

Problem with data loss on a mounted external FireWire drive. A much more serious problem can occur in Panther if an external FireWire drive remains connected to the Mac when you select Restart or Shut Down. In such cases, the directory of the drive may become so corrupted (due to incorrect writing of data to the drive during the shut-down sequence) that all data on the drive is essentially lost! Using a repair utility such as Prosoft's Data Rescue, or sending the drive to a repair service such as DriveSavers (www.drivesavers.com), are about your only chances for recovering the data. The drive hardware itself remains fine, and you can still reformat the drive to use it again.

This problem is not universal; it affects some drives but not others (for reasons that are not entirely clear). FireWire 800 drives (with the Oxford 922 bridge) are especially vulnerable, though some FireWire 400 drives have also been bitten.

Note: The Oxford bridge chip is not part of the drive itself but rather sits between the drive and the external casing. It is needed to allow what is most likely an ATA drive to connect to the Mac via a FireWire port.

To be safe and to avoid this data-loss problem, unmount and disconnect all external FireWire drives before restarting or shutting down your Mac.

continues on next page

TAKE NOTE ▶ Problems Mounting and Unmounting/Ejecting Media *continued*

As to a permanent fix, Apple claims that updating to Mac OS X 10.3.1 or later eliminates at least some of the causes of the problem. However, it may also be necessary to upgrade the firmware for your drive. Contact the drive's vendor for information about such firmware updates.

Problem mounting certain MS-DOS or Windows-formatted media, such as Flash cards. The problem here is that an invisible file in the /Volumes directory on the media is preventing the volume or card from mounting in the Finder. The solution is to delete this file. See the following Apple Knowledge Base article for details: http://docs.info.apple.com/article.html?artnum=75509.

External ports lost. Occasionally, you may find that a given port appears dead. That is, no device connected to the port (USB or FireWire) mounts. Devices don't even get listed in System Profiler. In fact, the port itself (for example, USB or FireWire) may not be listed. Most often this is because the relevant port is not active and so the device is not recognized (assuming your hardware is working, the ultimate cause of this is usually a software bug in the OS itself, hopefully one that will be fixed in an update). More generally, try the following:

- Try the standard troubleshooting techniques and hope that one works: (a) Unplug and replug the device; (b) shut down the computer and disconnect all peripherals after the computer is shut down, wait several minutes, and then start it up again, reconnecting peripherals after startup is over; (c) bypass hubs if in use; (d) switch to an alternate port (if your Mac has more than one of the same port); and so on. Also note: Non-bus-powered FireWire drives need to be connected to AC power before connecting to a Mac or they may not mount.

- Try (a) repairing disk permissions with Disk Utility; (b) zapping the PRAM; and/or (c) resetting the Power Manager (as covered in Chapter 5). If none of these work, repeat the PRAM zap with all third-party RAM removed. Make sure that the needed kext files (for USB and FireWire) are installed (as also covered in Chapter 5). As a last resort, reinstall Mac OS X using the Archive and Install option (reupdating to more recent versions of Mac OS X if needed).

- If all of this fails, you're probably looking at a hardware repair. In fact, if you can determine that the port is not working even before Mac OS X begins to load, it's almost certain you have a hardware problem. For example, if you have an external bootable FireWire drive, connect it at startup and hold down the Option key. If the drive does not appear as a bootable drive (especially if it did before the problem appeared), it's likely time to take your Mac in for a repair.

  Checking the Mac with the Hardware Test software (as described in "Technically Speaking: The Apple Hardware Test Software," in Chapter 5) can also help diagnose hardware problems.

  Still another way to check for a hardware problem is to start up in single-user mode. If the first few lines of text reference a FireWire failure, for example, a hardware repair is needed. When this happened to me, I got a message that referred to a broken "FireWire PHY." To fix this, Apple told me I needed to replace the logic board. If you have a desktop Mac that's no longer under warranty, a cheaper alternative is to get a FireWire PCI card. Note: The most frequent cause of this FireWire problem is incorrectly inserting a FireWire cable and thereby damaging the port.

continues on next page

TAKE NOTE ▶ Problems Mounting and Unmounting/Ejecting Media *continued*

SEE: • "Technically Speaking: Hard-Drive Sleep," in Chapter 2.
 • "Take Note: Zapping PRAM and Resetting the Power Manager," in Chapter 5.
 • "Single-user mode" and "Verbose mode," in Chapter 5.

Problems with copy-protected audio CDs. Some audio CDs are now copy-protected. Such CDs usually have a sticker on them that reads, "Will not play on PC/Mac." And indeed, they won't. Even worse, the CD may get stuck in your drive, refusing to eject when you press the Eject button. In some cases, it can even result in a gray-screen crash at startup.

If any of these things occur, first make sure you've installed the Apple SuperDrive Update (if appropriate for your Mac). Check the following Web page for details: www.apple.com/hardware/superdrive.

Next, try the procedures outlined previously in this sidebar, especially the following ones: (a) holding down the mouse button at startup; (b) using the manual eject hole (if one exists for the drive); and (3) typing eject cd in Open Firmware at startup. If you can get the Mac to start up in Mac OS X (holding down the X key at startup may help), you can also try using the Eject command in iTunes or DVD Player. If none of these fixes work, you should probably bring the Mac to a service representative to get the CD removed. See the following Apple Knowledge Base document for further details: http://docs.info.apple.com/article.html?artnum=106882.

Problems mounting .dmg and .img files. If you attempt to mount a disk image, such as one downloaded over the Internet, you may get an error stating, "[*Filename*] failed to mount due to error -95. (no mountable file systems)." The most common cause is that the image was incompletely downloaded or otherwise damaged. The solution here is to redownload the file. If this fails to work, and you're confident the problem is not with the original file, try the following:

• Restart your Mac and try to mount the disk again.

• If StuffIt software is accessed at any point in the download-and-mount process, it could be the culprit. Check to see if an update is available that fixes the problem.

• Delete the com.apple.frameworks.diskimages.diskimagesuiagent.plist in the /Library/Preferences folder (assuming such a file has been created on your drive).

• As a last resort, reinstall Mac OS X.

Image keeps remounting. Mac OS X 10.2 and later will attempt to remount any disk-image files that were still mounted when you last logged out. However, an apparent bug in the OS can sometimes result in an inability to unmount the image. Instead, the image remounts within a minute or so of each attempt to unmount it. Even after unmounting the image and restarting the Mac, the image remounts. To fix this permanently, delete the image file from the drive (backing it up to another volume first, if desired) and restart. After doing this, you can return the file to the drive without the problem reoccurring.

Note: The software that regulates this automounting is the Unix program /sbin/autodiskmount.

TAKE NOTE ▶ Burning CDs (and DVDs)

One of the most common things people do with Macs is burn CDs. You may do this to back up data from your hard drive, to create your own bootable CD, or to make an audio CD from music in your iTunes Library. Most often, you will be burning to a CD-R. Once you burn to one of these discs, you cannot erase and reuse it. There are rewritable CD-RW; however, because they are more expensive and slower in speed than CD-R, it is often more convenient and economical to burn and discard a CD-R than to reuse a CD-RW. Also, some standard CD and DVD players, especially older models, cannot read CD-RW.

Note: You can erase a CD-RW via the Erase screen in Disk Utility.

Burning basics. When you insert a blank CD-R or CD-RW into a CD-RW drive, what transpires next depends on the options you've selected from the CDs & DVDs System Preferences pane. In particular, you can select what you want Mac OS X to do when you insert a blank disc—that is, ask what to do, or automatically open a selected application. Personally, I prefer the "Ask what to do" option because it gives me the flexibility to make a different decision each time I insert a CD. I will assume this option is in effect for the discussions in this sidebar.

Alternatively, you can launch any application that can burn CDs and insert a blank CD while the application is active. This bypasses the initial Finder dialog described here but otherwise works the same.

When you insert a blank CD with the "Ask what to do" option selected, a dialog appears that states, "You inserted a blank CD. Choose what to do from the pop-up menu." The Action pop-up menu presents several options:

- **Open Finder.** Select this option and a CD icon appears on your Desktop with the name selected in the Name text box ("untitled CD" by default).

  You can now drag files from your hard drive to the CD. Although you can drag audio files to the CD, you would not use this method to create an audio CD that you intended to play in a stand-alone CD player. Files copied in this way would be recognized as music files by computer software, such as iTunes, but not by a separate CD player.

  When you're finished adding files, select to burn the CD by either dragging the CD icon to the Trash (at which point the Trash icon changes to a Burn icon) or clicking the Burn icon next to the CD's name in a Finder window's sidebar. This causes another dialog to appear. This one reads, "Do you want to burn the disc?" You can select a Burn Speed here. Faster speeds mean the burn takes less time to complete; however, they also increase the risk that an error may occur during the burn. Still, in most cases, using the Maximum speed works fine.

  Select Burn, and a disc is burned in the HFS Plus/ISO 9660 hybrid disc format. You can mount the disc on PCs running Windows as well as Macs.

  Select Eject instead, and the disc is ejected without being burned. In this case, nothing you selected is copied to the CD. The CD remains unused and can be used later to burn something else.

continues on next page

TAKE NOTE ▶ Burning CDs (and DVDs) *continued*

- **Open iTunes.** Select this option, and a dialog may immediately appear, offering basic advice on how to burn a playlist via iTunes. Click OK to continue.

  To burn a CD, select a playlist. You cannot burn a CD simply by selecting songs from the Library. If necessary, create a playlist to burn by selecting New Playlist from the File menu. Add the desired songs to the playlist—either by dragging files already in the iTunes Library to the playlist or by adding new files from audio CDs via iTunes' Import option.

  With a playlist selected from the left column, the icon in the upper-right corner turns from Browse to Burn Disc. If the iris of the icon is closed, click the iris to open it. The yellow-and-black Burn icon will now be visible. Click this icon to initiate the burn. Note: If a CD is not already inserted, you can insert one at this point.

  This burns a disc in Audio CD (playable in a standard audio CD player), MP3 (ISO 9660, playable by most computers and many MP3-compatible CD players), or data CD (simply a disc with data files) format, as specified in iTunes Preferences.

- **Open other application.** If you select this option, you can choose any third-party software you may have that can burn CDs. Toast Titanium is a popular choice and is especially useful for copying CDs when you have two CD drives. With two drives, you can use it to directly copy an entire CD, mounted in one drive, to a CD-R or CD-RW mounted in the other drive.

  You can also select to use Mac OS X's Disk Utility. In Panther, this replaces Disk Copy as the utility to use for burning disk-image files.

  SEE: • **Chapter 3 (especially "Creating an Emergency Startup Volume") for more on using Disk Utility to burn CDs, including details on making a bootable copy of a startup CD.**

continues on next page

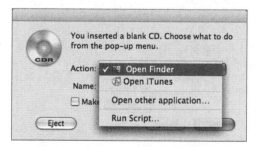
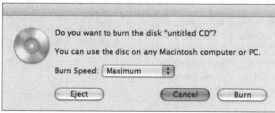

Figure 6.38

CD-related messages: A message that appears in the Finder when you insert a blank CD if you've set the CDs & DVDs System Preferences pane to "Ask what to do" (left); and a message that appears when you attempt to eject a CD-R that has not yet been burned (right).

TAKE NOTE ▶ Burning CDs (and DVDs) *continued*

- **Run script.** If you've created or downloaded an AppleScript file that automates a sequence of events for burning a CD, you would select this option.

Click the OK button to carry out your selected action. Or you can decide that inserting the media was a mistake and select the Eject button. Last, you can select Ignore; this leaves the media in the drive but does not mount it in the Finder. If you later launch iTunes, for example, you can still select to burn songs to the CD.

Troubleshooting CD burning. In most cases, burning a CD will work without hassles—especially when using an internal CD-RW or SuperDrive drive that ships with Macs. If problems do occur, consider the following:

- **CD drive not compatible.** After you insert a blank CD, Mac OS X may not recognize that a CD has been inserted. This may be because you have an external CD-RW drive that's not compatible with Mac OS X. Check with the vendor for details. Also make sure you have the latest firmware update for the drive.

  Another possible cause of this symptom is that you inserted a blank CD into a nonwritable drive (for example, you put a DVD-R in a drive that can only write CDs).

- **External drive not connected properly.** If drive compatibility doesn't appear to be an issue, but you still can't get an external CD-RW drive to work, launch System Profiler and select USB or FireWire (from the Hardware section in the left column) to see if the drive is listed.

  If the drive is not listed, no CDs will mount when inserted. To fix this, make sure that all cables to the drive are connected properly (including power cables). Also make sure the drive is turned on! If you're using a USB or FireWire hub, try bypassing the hub and connecting the drive directly to the Mac.

continues on next page

Figure 6.39

An example of a message that may appear if a burn fails. In this case, there's not enough space on the hard drive to store the temporary cache files needed when burning the CD.

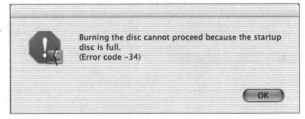

Figure 6.40

Burning CDs: (a) A Finder window with the Burn icon in the sidebar next to the Untitled CD; and (b) iTunes with the Burn Disc button (currently closed) in the upper right.

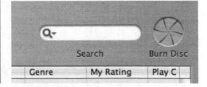

TAKE NOTE ▶ Burning CDs (and DVDs) *continued*

If the drive is listed in System Profiler, restart the Mac with the drive already on.

SEE: • **"Take Note: Problems Mounting and Unmounting/Ejecting Media," earlier in this chapter, for more advice.**

• **Interrupted burns.** Once a burn has started, the CD will be unusable if the burn is canceled or otherwise interrupted! So be careful: Once you start a burn, there's no going back.

Also, to recover disk space used by the temporary file created when burning a CD, restart your Mac.

• **Burn fails.** You may get to the point where you can click a Burn button and the burn is initiated, but the resulting CD-R does not mount or play as expected. Or you may get an error message during the burn, indicating that the burn has failed.

In such cases, retry using a new CD-R and making sure to keep other CPU activity to a minimum. (Do not try to play a QuickTime movie while burning a CD, for example.) Quit any unneeded open applications to make sure you have enough memory (add more physical RAM as a last resort here). These precautions are especially important on older Macs that don't have the "horsepower" of newer models.

Set Energy Saver to disable (set to Never) any sleep that might occur during a burn. If your Mac goes to sleep during a burn, the burn will likely fail.

If you're using software that allows you to adjust the burn speed, make sure you choose a speed that does not exceed the maximum needed to make a successful copy; lower the speed if you're unsure. Roxio's Toast Titanium has a feature that allows you to test the maximum allowable speed.

Burning requires a certain amount of space on your hard drive. If you do not have sufficient space, you will get an error message indicating that the "disc is full."

• **QuickTime needed.** QuickTime 6.2 or later is needed to work with the AAC (Advanced Audio Coding) format used by the iTunes Music Store.

• **Multisession CDs.** Although you cannot erase and reuse a burned CD-R, you can set it up so that only a portion of a CD-R is burned, leaving the remaining unused portion to be burned on a later occasion. This is called *creating a multi-session CD*. To do this, (1) create an image file of what you want to burn, using Disk Utility (as described in Chapter 3); (2) from the Images menu in Disk Utility select the Burn command and then select the image you want to burn; (3) from the window that appears, check the "Leave disc appendable" box from the choices in the Burn Options section (click the disclosure triangle on the right side of the window if Burn Options are not visible); and (4) click the Burn button.

When you later remount the CD, the multisession option remains selected and can be used to burn additional files to the CD. Each subsequent burn session will mount as a separate volume in the Finder.

• **Unwanted files and folders copied.** In older versions of Mac OS X, when burning a data CD, certain (usually invisible) files and folders used by Mac OS X bootable volumes (such as a Temporary Items folder, a Desktop folder, and Desktop DB files) might get copied to the CD. These files were not needed to use the CD and were a minor annoyance when the CD was mounted on a Windows system (where they would be visible). Starting in Mac OS X 10.2.3, these files should no longer get copied to a burned CD.

continues on next page

TAKE NOTE ▶ Burning CDs (and DVDs) *continued*

- **Disk Utility and images with MS-DOS–formatted volumes.** Disk Utility (and Disk Copy in Jaguar) will not burn disk images that contain MS-DOS–formatted volumes (such as FAT-12, FAT-16, and FAT-32). The only work-around for now is to save the image in a different format, one that Disk Utility can use.

- **Problems specific to iTunes.** If none of the above advice helped and you're trying to burn a CD using iTunes, check the following Apple Knowledge Base document: http://docs.info.apple.com/article.html?artnum=61102. Titled "iTunes: Unable to Burn a CD," it offers additional tips for solving problems that may occur.

DVD burning. Although specifics vary, the principles involved in burning a DVD (via the Finder or software like iDVD) are essentially the same as those for burning a CD. To burn DVD's you need a drive, such as Apple's SuperDrive, that can burn DVDs. A SuperDrive is essential if you intend to use iDVD.

Note: Writable DVDs come in several different formats, most notably DVD-R, DVD-RW, DVD+R, and DVD+RW. Prior to Panther, Mac OS X only supported the DVD-R(W) format. Panther adds support for DVD+R(W). To be safe, your best bet is still to get DVD-R discs when purchasing blank discs for an Apple SuperDrive.

SEE: • **"Running Mac OS X software from the Terminal," in Chapter 10, for more on the Terminal commands that handle disc burning: hdiutil and drutil.**

• **Chapter 11, for more on iTunes, iDVD, CDs, and DVDs.**

Aliases and Symbolic Links

An *alias* is a file that is a pointer to a real (original) file located somewhere else. Thus, when you double-click an alias, the other (original) file opens. No matter how big the original file is, its alias is never more than about 4K to 50K in size. By using aliases, you can list the same file in many locations without having to have real copies in each location. This provides flexibility in organizing files on your drive without wasting disk space by duplicating the full-size files.

For example, suppose you have a collection of applications at various locations on your drive, and you want to bring them together in the same folder for a specific task. However, you also want to retain them in their original locations. You can do both by creating aliases of the files and placing the aliases in the new folder. Now whenever you double-click an alias, it launches the original file, as though the file were in two locations at the same time.

The following are some other ways you can use aliases:

- Sometimes a program may look for a preferences file in the startup System Folder (in Classic). If you have different startup System Folders, the preferences may be different in each. You can prevent this problem by placing an alias of the original preferences file in each of the other System Folders. Now all of the folders will use the same preferences file, no matter what changes you make at what time.

- If you place an alias of a folder in a new location, when you open the alias folder, the original folder actually opens. By placing such an alias in a convenient location (such as on the Desktop), you get instant access to folder contents, even though the folder may be nested several folders deep in some other location.

- Making an invisible folder visible temporarily and making an alias of it is a useful trick for maintaining easy access to folders that are normally invisible. You can use this technique to maintain access to the invisible tmp folder, for example.

SEE: • **"Saving movie trailers that have the Save option disabled," later in this chapter, for an example of using this tmp folder.**

How to recognize an alias

The icon for an alias appears identical to that of the original file, except that a small arrow appears in the bottom-left corner of the icon.

If you access the Get Info window for an alias, you should find that the Kind setting for the file is Alias. I say *should* because in what appears to be a bug, an alias file may sometimes list the original file's kind as its own.

In addition, the Get Info window will list the location of the original file, in a field called Original. Right below that will be a button called Select New Original. Clicking this button allows you to change the file attached to the alias. You should not need to do this unless the original file has been deleted or the link to it has been broken.

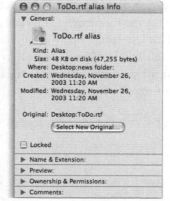

Figure 6.41

An alias file and its Get Info window.

How to locate an original via its alias

What if you want to locate the original file from its alias? To do so, first click the alias's icon, then select Show Original (Command-R) from the Finder's File menu or the alias's contextual menu. The Finder will go directly to the folder where the original is located and display it with the file selected.

Alternatively, after noting the path in the Original field of the alias's Get Info window, you can navigate there yourself.

How to create an alias

To create an alias, click the original file, and from the Finder's File menu or the file's contextual menu choose Make Alias (Command-L).

Whichever method you select, an alias will be created in the same location as the original file, with the word *alias* added to its name (before its extension, if the file has one). You can then rename or move the alias. The alias's relation to the original file will be preserved no matter where you move either file, at least as long as both stay within the same volume (there is one exception to this rule, as described in "Aliases vs. symbolic links," below).

Often more conveniently, you can hold down the Command and Option keys and drag the file's icon to a new folder location. This technique creates an alias at the new location with the same name as the original (the word *alias* is not added); the original file remains in its original location.

Fixing a broken alias link

If you delete the file to which an alias is linked, or if you move or modify the original file so that the alias can no longer locate it, you will get an error message when you double-click the alias file. This message will state the following: "The alias {*name of file*} could not be opened because the original item could not be found." This is called a *broken alias*.

At this point, the dialog provides you with three choices: (1) OK (thereby ignoring the issue for the moment); (2) Delete Alias (with the obvious result); or (3) Fix Alias. This last option opens a window similar to the one that appears when you click Select New Original in the Get Info window. From here, you can navigate via a file browser to the desired file and select it as the new destination for the alias.

Figure 6.42

The broken-alias error message.

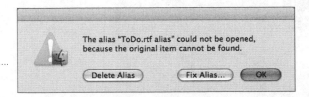

The alias "ToDo.rtf alias" could not be opened, because the original item cannot be found.

Delete Alias   Fix Alias...   OK

Note: One way to wind up with a broken alias is to copy an alias to a CD or other removable media, where the alias refers back to an item on your hard drive. If the disc is later mounted on another computer, the alias will not work.

Aliases vs. symbolic links

If you're familiar with Mac OS 9, much of this alias discussion probably has a familiar ring since aliases work in similar fashion in Mac OS 9. However, Mac OS X introduces a new wrinkle, compliments of Unix. That OS includes something similar to aliases: *symbolic links*. When you're in the Mac OS X Finder, a symbolic-link file looks and acts almost identically to an alias file, with the following exceptions:

- **Symbolic links refer to a specific path.** Thus, for example, a symbolic link to a file called Testing in your Documents folder will work only if Testing remains in the Documents folder. Move it anywhere else, and the link is broken. Symbolic links never link to a moved file.

  Just as important, if you move or delete the original file and create a new one with the same name in the original location, the symbolic link will point to that new file (because it has the same path).

- **Aliases, in contrast, are linked to the file or folder to which they originally point.** If you move the original file to a new location, the alias is able to keep track of this situation and maintain the link. When you double-click the alias, the moved original file still opens.

  Actually, starting in Mac OS X 10.2, this difference is no longer exactly true. Now, if you move an original file to a new location *and* create a new file with the same name at the original location, an existing alias will point to the newly created file, just as a symbolic link would. Only if that attempt fails (perhaps because you failed to create a file with the same name at the original location) will Mac OS X look to match the alias with the moved original file.

  The idea here is to provide greater consistency between how aliases and symbolic links work. To quote Apple: "If you replace a file with an identically named file, moving the old file to a new location, both aliases and symbolic links point to the new file. However, if you move a file without replacing it, symbolic links to the file break, while aliases do not."

When you install Mac OS X, the OS places symbolic link files in various locations, such as inside the Library folders, inside application packages, and in the invisible Unix directories. Because these locations are off the radar of most users, the typical Mac user rarely needs to work with symbolic links. Symbolic links may also appear in more commonly visited locations, where they will seem to be ordinary aliases. As I'll describe a bit later in this chapter, there may be one such symbolic link to your Mac OS 9 Desktop.

If you want to create a new alias, I recommend that you stick with the traditional Mac variety. Aliases are easier to create than symbolic links, and they generally work more like you would expect. About the only reason to use a symbolic link is if the link must be recognized as such by Unix software. (Unix does not recognize traditional Mac OS X aliases as links.) Still, an understanding of the distinction is useful for when links don't work as expected.

Finally, if you format a drive using UFS (which I *do not* recommend) rather than HFS, the Mac will *not* recognize aliases; it will recognize only symbolic links.

SEE: • "Select a Destination," in Chapter 3, for more information on UFS versus HFS.

Determining whether a file is a symbolic link or an alias

You can't tell from Finder icons whether a file is an alias or a symbolic link. Both file types have the same curved-arrow icon. Even the Get Info window for the two types of files does not offer an obvious solution, because both types may be identified with a Kind setting of Alias.

One way to determine whether a file is an alias or a symbolic link is to move the original file and then double-click the alias. If the original file still launches, you have a traditional alias. If you get a message that says the original could not be found, without the usual Delete Alias and Fix Alias options, you have a symbolic link.

Another, more tedious, way to figure this out is to reboot in Mac OS 9 (if your Mac can do so). In that OS, traditional aliases are identified in the Finder's Get Info window as having a Kind setting of Alias, whereas symbolic link files are identified as Mac OS X Alias. In Mac OS X, both types of files are identified simply as Alias.

As described in the next section of this chapter, symbolic links also differ from aliases in terms of how they're listed in Terminal.

Warning regarding deleting a symbolic link. In most cases, if you delete a symbolic link file, the item is removed. End of story. No change is made to the original item itself (just as is the case when you delete an alias). However, if you delete a symbolic link item from a folder for which you have Read Only permission, you will be asked to authenticate before the Finder permits you to trash the item. After entering your password to get permission, the original item (whatever folder or file the symbolic link references) is deleted instead of the link itself! This is almost certainly a bug, and a rather serious one, which I assume Apple will fix in a future version of Panther.

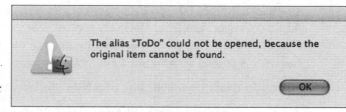

Figure 6.43

The message that appears when a symbolic link cannot find its original file.

How to create a symbolic link

Any alias that you create via the Finder's Make Alias command is a traditional alias. What do you do if you want to create a symbolic link instead? You have two choices: You can use Terminal, or you can use a third-party utility like XRay or Cocktail.

Terminal. To create a symbolic link in Terminal, follow these steps:

1. Launch Terminal.

2. Type the following:

    ln -s {original file path} {symbolic link path}

Note: Use an absolute pathway for the original file, not a relative one. As always, a shortcut for adding the absolute pathway is to drag the Finder icon of the original file to the Terminal window after typing ln -s.

SEE: • **"Take Note: Finder Folders vs. Unix Directories," in Chapter 4, for background on absolute versus relative pathnames.**

• **Chapter 10 for more information on pathnames and shortcuts in Unix.**

You can now use the cd command to navigate to the directory where you created the link and type ls –al. This displays a list of all items in the directory, including symbolic links. Notice two things in the list:

•   In the File Attributes column (where permissions are indicated), the first letter listed for a symbolic link file is l (rather than d for directory or a hyphen for files).

•   For symbolic link files, the path to the original file is listed to the right of the filename.

Traditional Mac aliases have neither of these attributes.

Now if you go to the Finder, the symbolic link file should appear in the same directory as listed in Terminal. If it does not, search for it via Find and then double-click its name in the Search Results output. This method forces it to show up. As a last resort, log out and log in again.

Cocktail. Probably the easiest way to create a symbolic link is with Cocktail. To do so, select Files from Cocktail's toolbar. Then click the Links button. From here, just drag an item to the indicated button area—a symbolic link to the item is created at the destination location you specify.

XRay. To create a symbolic link with XRay, follow these steps:

1. Open the original file with XRay, and from its File menu choose Make Alias.

2. In the window that appears, from the Alias Format pop-up menu choose either Absolute Symbolic Link or Relative Symbolic Link.

   With an absolute symbolic link, moving the original file to a new location will break the link. With a relative symbolic link (most commonly used for files inside Mac OS X packages), the link is maintained as long as the link file and the original file are in the same relative locations within a folder (even if that enclosing folder is moved). This arrangement allows you to move an .app package file—which is actually a folder and contains symbolic link files to other files within the package—without breaking the links.

Again, the link file should appear in the Finder at this point.

Note: The current version of XRay cannot show the permissions for an alias or symbolic link correctly; instead, it lists the permissions of the original file.

A word of warning: This alias/link confusion is rooted in Mac OS X itself and can affect functions in any utility. For example, some delete utilities, when you request to delete an alias or a symbolic link file, will delete the original instead of the alias/link file. Be sure to test how a utility works with aliases before using it to delete an alias to anything that you would not want deleted.

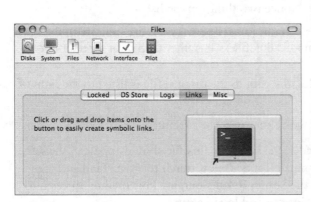 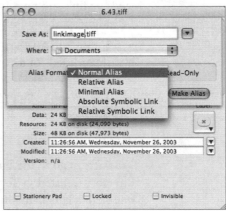

Figure 6.44

Create a symbolic link: (left) via Cocktail and (right) via XRay.

Fixing a broken symbolic link

What do you do if you click a symbolic link icon and find that it's broken (you get an error message stating that the original file cannot be found)? In most cases, to fix the link use you must create a new symbolic link file (for example, by using the ln command in Terminal, as just described.

A potentially more serious problem involves the multitude of symbolic links that exist in package files, Library folders, and invisible Unix directories. For example, the (normally invisible) tmp, var and etc folder icons at the root level of a Mac OS X volume are actually symbolic links to the identically named folders in the /private directory.

If any of these symbolic links get broken, you may have problems ranging from application failure to the inability to start up Mac OS X—serious problems that you will no doubt want to fix.

For example, if for any reason the symbolic link to /tmp is missing, you can expect symptoms such as an inability to print using Classic, as well as problems with file sharing, burning discs, updating software, connecting via PPP, repairing privileges, and more. To fix this problem, type the following:

```
sudo ln -s /private/tmp /tmp
```

In other cases, fixing such links is a far from trivial task: You may have trouble locating the problem files and reestablishing the links correctly, especially if the problem is preventing you from starting up your Mac.

To fix these problems, try the following methods:

- **Run disk-repair utilities.** You may get some help from disk-repair utilities such as Norton Utilities. If you have broken symbolic and/or hard links in the Unix directories, for example, run Norton Utilities (booting from its CD). The utility attempts to fix the problem.

   Using Repair Disk Permissions in Disk Utility's First Aid may also help, assuming you can still start up from your Mac OS X volume.

- **Add link in single-user mode.** If a missing symbolic link is preventing a normal startup of Mac OS X, you may be able to fix the problem by starting up in single-user mode and adding the link back. See this Apple Knowledge Base article for details: http://docs.info.apple.com/article .html?artnum=106908.

- **Reinstall.** If all else fails, you'll likely need to reinstall the problem applications or Mac OS X itself.

   SEE: • Chapter 3 for advice on reinstalling Mac OS X.

How, you may ask, do these links get broken in the first place (assuming you made no obvious change to cause the breakage)? There are several possibilities, including the following:

- If you back up and restore files via a backup utility, symbolic links may get broken unless the backup utility specifically knows how to restore them.

    SEE: • **Chapter 3 for advice on backing up Mac OS X. All utilities recommended there work correctly with symbolic links.**

- Archiving a folder or directory and later expanding it can cause problems unless the archiving utility knows how to handle the process. StuffIt Deluxe may still have some problems here.

- If designed incorrectly, an installer for an application can move files during the installation in such a way that symbolic links get broken.

    There's a relatively rare but significant problem with the .pax files contained in installer packages (see Chapter 3). If an installer .pkg file (likely one from a third party) writes to the invisible Unix files on your drive (such as the /etc directory), it may do so in such a way that it breaks existing symbolic links to these directories. In extreme cases, this situation can result in the failure of your drive to start up, ultimately requiring a reinstallation of Mac OS X (unless you're skilled enough to recognize and fix the broken symbolic links or have a third-party utility that can do the job for you).

There's no sure way to prevent these problems other than not using the software in question or checking online (such as at the software vendor's Web site) before using a backup/archiving/installation utility to determine whether it has any known problems with symbolic links.

"Desktop (Mac OS 9)" file is a symbolic link

As described in "Take Note: The Location of Desktop folders," in Chapter 4, an alias file called "Desktop (Mac OS 9)" is created automatically at startup, at the root level of the Mac OS X startup volume—but only if there are items on the Desktop for a Mac OS 9 System on the same volume as Mac OS X.

Note: If you add items to a currently empty Desktop folder, the alias will not appear until your next restart. Normally, items would only get added to this folder if you were booted in Mac OS 9 or via certain applications run in Classic.

This alias is of value because the Mac OS 9 and Mac OS X Desktops are entirely independent. That is, what you place on the Mac OS 9 Desktop (when you're booted in Mac OS 9, for example) and what you place on the Mac OS X Desktop are stored in different locations. Thus the items from one Desktop are not visible when you're viewing the other. Furthermore, accessing the contents of the Mac OS 9 Desktop when you're booted in Mac OS X is complicated by the fact that the Mac OS 9 Desktop Folder—located at the root level of the volume—is invisible in Mac OS X. The Desktop (Mac OS 9) alias allows you to work around this situation. When you open it, a window opens, showing the contents of the invisible Mac OS 9 Desktop. The contents are visible even though the folder itself is not.

If you have partitioned your drive into multiple volumes, you will not need a separate similar alias for the Desktop folders of the other volumes, because the Desktop folders for these volumes remain visible. These folders contain the files from these volumes that appear on the Desktop when you're booted in Mac OS 9. Thus, the Desktop (Mac OS 9) folder shows only the Desktop items that are stored on the Mac OS X boot volume.

Why am I mentioning all of this here? Because the Desktop (Mac OS 9) alias is actually a symbolic link. I'm not sure what Apple's rationale was in making it such (perhaps it didn't want it to continue to work if you moved the Desktop folder), but if you delete this alias/symbolic link accidentally, it should be re-created automatically the next time you restart. If this does not happen, you can still re-create the symbolic link yourself, by following a procedure similar to that described in "How to create a symbolic link," earlier in this chapter. For example, you would type the following in Terminal:

```
ln -s '/Desktop Folder' ~/'Desktop (Mac OS 9)'
```

The fact that the Desktop Folder is invisible presents no problems when using this command.

Cocktail. Once again, the third-party utility Cocktail provides a more user-friendly alternative. To use it, select the System icon from its toolbar and then click its Misc tab. From here, click the OK button next to the text that reads, "Recreate alias to Mac OS 9 desktop."

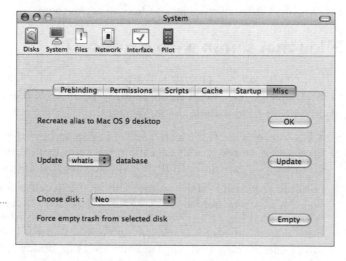

Figure 6.45

You can re-create the Desktop Folder alias via Cocktail.

> **TECHNICALLY SPEAKING ▶ Unix Hard Links**
>
> A hard link in Unix is a duplicate directory entry for a file. Even if you delete the original file, the hard link will still access the file's contents, because the original file and all its hard links point to the same data. Think of the data as being stored somewhere on your drive and the original file as being just a pointer to the data. Then a hard link is another pointer to the same data.
>
> I'm not aware of any case in which a hard link is used in the Finder, so hard links are relevant mainly for the workings of the invisible Unix files. About the only time they may become relevant for troubleshooting is when you're attempting to copy a Mac OS X volume to another drive. As is the case with symbolic links, the copy procedure will need to be able to maintain the hard links correctly.

Invisible Files: What Files Are Invisible?

Numerous files on a Mac OS X volume are deliberately set to be invisible. The general rationale for this is that invisibility minimizes the chance that users will meddle with them. Users should rarely need to modify, move, or delete these files. That said, however, there are occasions when you will need to do such things.

In this section, I explore what these invisible files are and why they are set to be invisible. I also explain why and how to access them.

Files that begin with a period (.)

If the first character of a filename is a period/dot (.), Mac OS X interprets that to mean that the file should be invisible. Some invisible files of interest that begin with a period include the following:

- **.DS_Store.** This file, which is likely to pop up in virtually every folder you access, stores various data about the items in a folder, such as the location of icons in the Icon view window for that folder.

  Should you want to delete some of these files (such as for a folder to be copied to a non–Mac OS X system where these files are not used), a utility called De_DDS (from Extraneous Software) makes it easy to do. Just drag a folder icon to the De_DDS icon, and the .DS_Store file inside the folder is eradicated. SkyTag Software's File Buddy X is another utility that is convenient for locating and deleting these files.

- **.FBC files** (such as .FBCIndex). These files are used in the Find by Content (FBC) Find searches. They occur in every folder for which a content index has been created (via the Index Now button in the Get Info window or via a Content search in the Find command).

- **.hidden.** This file is located at the root level of your Mac OS X volume and contains a list of files (with names that do not necessarily begin with a period) that are to be kept invisible. I discuss this file in the following section.

- **.Trash.** This directory contains items you place in the Trash and is located at the root level of your Home directory.

There are numerous other files that begin with a period. I mention some of them elsewhere in this book, as relevant. Most of these invisible items are text files.

TECHNICALLY SPEAKING ▶ Files That Begin with "._"

Built into Mac OS X is a mechanism called Apple Double that allows Mac OS X to work with disk formats that do not use resource forks, such as remote NFS, SMB, and WebDAV directories, or local UFS volumes. Apple Double does this by converting files with resource forks into two separate files. The first file keeps the original name and contains the data fork of the original file. The second file has the name of the original file prefixed by "._" and contains the resource fork of the original file. If you see both files on a non-Mac volume, the ._ file can be safely ignored. Sometimes, when deleting the data fork version of the file, the ._ component does not get deleted. If this occurs, you can safely delete the ._ file.

Files in the .hidden file list

The .hidden file list is a text file stored at the root level of the Mac OS X volume. The files and folders in this list are invisible in the Finder, regardless of the item's name or other attributes. This is because the Finder checks this list as one means of determining whether or not an item should be visible. All the items in this list are files or folders found at the root level of a Mac OS X volume. They include the Unix folders (such as bin, sbin, var, and etc) as well as the mach files (mach, mach_kernel, and mach.sym).

SEE: • "Technically Speaking: What and Where Are the Unix Files?" in
Chapter 4, for more details on these items.

This list also includes the Mac OS 9 Desktop database files (Desktop DB and Desktop DF) and the Mac OS 9 Desktop folder. These files appear both at the root level of your startup volume and at the root level of your Home directory. They are used only if you run Classic or boot from Mac OS 9.

Note: Some of the items in the .hidden list may be visible by default if booted from Mac OS 9. Also, some files that are invisible on this list that are on the Mac OS X startup volume may be visible if present on other volumes, even when you're booted in Mac OS X. The invisible Desktop and Temporary Items folders, for example, are visible in all partitions except the Mac OS X partition.

Viewing and/or modifying the .hidden file? Despite its invisible status, there are ways to open and view the contents of the .hidden file. You can also modify the contents of the .hidden file (though you need root access to do so) and thus change the invisibility of the listed files. However, I recommend not doing so. You can temporarily modify invisibility in other ways, if necessary, as described in "Invisible Files: Making Invisible Files Visible (and Vice Versa)," below.

SEE: • "Root Access," in Chapter 4, for how to open a file with root access.

Files with the Invisible (Hidden) bit set

The Invisible bit is left over from Mac OS 9. Turning on this bit (also called an *attribute* or *flag*) is the main way of making a file invisible in Mac OS 9, and it still works in Mac OS X. Some files may have the Invisible bit set and also have their names begin with a period. Perhaps this setup makes them doubly invisible?

Accessing and modifying the Invisible bit requires special utilities, described in the following section.

Invisible Files: Making Invisible Files Visible (and Vice Versa)

Should you ever need to locate, view, modify, or delete an invisible file, this is the section that explains how to do it.

Making all invisible files visible in the Finder

The simplest and most general way to work with invisible items is to make all invisible items visible in the Finder. To do this, you need to modify a setting in the com.apple.finder.plist file located in the Preferences folder of the Library folder in your Home directory. After doing this, invisible items will be visible regardless of what method was used to make them invisible (that is, whether their names begin with a period, their invisible bits are enabled, or they're listed in the .hidden file).

Note: I recommend making this change only on a temporary basis. Keeping all normally invisible files visible permanently may eventually cause problems. For starters, it makes it easier to inadvertently move or delete these files. Also, some applications may not work as expected when these files are visible.

Using PropertyList Editor. Although you can edit the com.apple.finder .plist file with any text editor, I recommend using Property List Editor. The specific property you need to modify is called AppleShowAllFiles. Changing its value (for example, from 0 to 1) toggles whether or not normally invisible files are visible in the Finder.

Relaunch the Finder for the change to take effect. Reverse the procedure to undo the change.

SEE: • "Modifying a .plist file," in Chapter 4, for step-by-step instructions on how to edit AppleShowAllFiles in com.apple.finder.plist.

Using Terminal. If you prefer to use Terminal, the `defaults` command can be used to make the same changes in a .plist file. For example, to make all invisible files visible, type the following:

```
defaults write com.apple.Finder AppleShowAllFiles 1
```

Relaunch the Finder for the change to take effect. To reverse the process, repeat the same command, using 0 instead of 1 as the value at the end of the command line.

Using a third-party utility. There are numerous third party utilities that automate this .plist file change. All you have to do is click a button or two. My favorite choices here are Marcel Bresnik's TinkerTool, Cocktail, and mac4ever.de's InVisibles.

With TinkerTool, check the Show Hidden and System Files box from its Finder options. Then click its Relaunch Finder button.

With Cocktail, check the "Show invisible items" box from the Interface > Finder screen.

With InVisibles, launch the utility and click its Visible button.

In all cases, after you have done what you want with the (normally) invisible file(s), reverse the procedure to make these now-visible files invisible again.

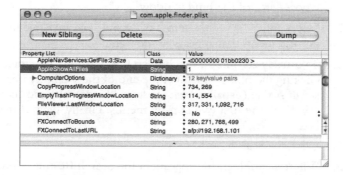

Figure 6.46

....

You can make invisible files visible by (top) modifying the AppleShowAllFiles property in the com.apple.finder.plist file (in ~/Library/Preferences) as viewed in Property List Editor or (bottom) running InVisibles.

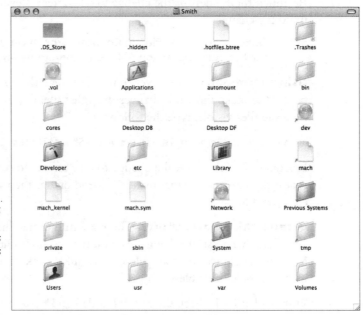

Figure 6.47

....

The root level of a Mac OS X volume, as seen in the Finder, with invisible items visible. Note that the icons for the normally invisible items are a shade lighter than the icons for the other items.

Using Finder's Find command

You can use the Finder's Find command to search for and (usually) open invisible items. The following describes how you can locate and open the .hidden file:

1. Select Visibility from the Name pop-up menu in the "Search for items whose" area of the Find window.

2. Select either "invisible items" or "visible and invisible items" from the pop-up menu that appears to the right.

3. To quickly zero in on the .hidden file, add a second criterion item by clicking the plus (+) icon at the end of the Visibility item row. Then select Name (usually already selected by default) and "contains" as the criteria in the first two pop-up menus. Finally, type `.hidden` in the text box.

4. Click the Search button.

5. When the .hidden file appears in the Search Results window, double-click it to open it. If it does not launch directly (probably via TextEdit), select the desired application from the dialog that appears.

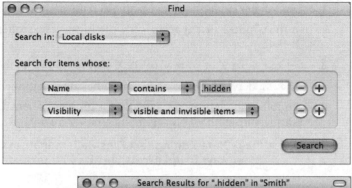

Figure 6.48

You can search for the .hidden file via the Finder's Find command (top); and you can double-click the high-lighted .hidden file in Search Results to open it in TextEdit (bottom).

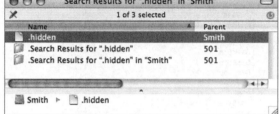

Using the Finder's Go to Folder command

In some cases, files within a folder are set to be visible, but the folder itself is invisible. Most of the files in Mac OS X's invisible Unix folders (located at the root level of the Mac OS X volume) work this way. For these folders, you can use the Finder's Go to Folder command to open a window showing the visible contents of the invisible folder. This bypasses the need to use the Find command to locate the item. However, it assumes you know the name and location of the invisible folder you wish to access.

To use this command, enter the folder's absolute pathname in the Go to Folder text box. For an example of how this works, see "Invisible Files: Working with Invisible Files," later in this chapter.

Using an application that lists and/or opens invisible files

Occasionally, you may want to edit the content of an invisible file. You can do this without making the file visible. TextEdit, for example, can be used to open invisible text files even when the file remains invisible in the Finder. However, third-party applications have features that allow you to do this with more ease than you can with TextEdit. My preferred choices here are BareBones' TextWrangler and BBEdit applications. For example, here's how you would use TextWrangler to view the contents of the .hidden file:

1. Launch the application, and from the File menu choose Open Hidden.

2. In the window that appears, slide the browser's scroller all the way to the left.

3. Select the name of your Mac OS X startup volume in the left-most column.

   The .hidden file should be listed in the column immediately to the right.

4. Double-click .hidden to open it. If you cannot select it, first select All Files from the Show pop-up menu (rather than All Readable Files).

   SEE: • **"Take Note: Editing Text Files via Terminal," in Chapter 10, for other ways to open invisible files with text editors.**

Figure 6.49

The contents of the .hidden file.

Toggling a file's Invisible bit

What if, rather than making all invisible files visible in the Finder or opening an invisible document in a text editor, you want to "permanently" change the visibility status of an individual file? You can do so.

If a file is invisible because its Invisible bit is enabled, you can disable the bit to get the file to appear in the Finder. Conversely, you can enable the bit to get any normally visible file to "disappear."

Unfortunately, Mac OS X's Get Info window does not include an option to enable or disable the Invisible bit for a file. However, several utilities (such as XRay, FileXaminer, and Bare Bones Software's Super Get Info) do include an Invisible bit option.

Making a visible item invisible. Open a visible item in FileXaminer (or a similar utility, such as XRay); locate the check box for the Invisible bit (it's in FileXaminer's Advanced section); and check it. Then click to Apply or Save the change. When you go back to the Finder, the item should vanish. As always, you may need to relaunch the Finder for this effect to take place.

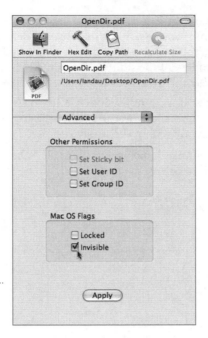

Figure 6.50

A file's Invisible bit option enabled via FileXaminer.

Making an invisible item visible. Changing the Invisible bit of an invisible file is trickier to do than changing it for a visible file. This is because the invisibility of the file makes it more difficult to access in the Finder. The problem is not insurmountable, however. Here's what to do:

1. **Access the invisible file.** There are several ways to do this:

   • You can make all invisible files visible in the Finder (as described above).

   • If you know the exact or approximate name of the file you're seeking, you can search for it via the Finder's Find command with the criteria set to search for invisible files (also as described above). With this method, you do not need to first make all invisible files visible.

   Note: The Find command will not list items in folders for which you do not have access (such as another user's Home directory). If you want such items listed in search results, you should use the third-party utility Locator (which is a front end to Unix's locate command), by Sebastian Krauss.

   • If you're unsure of the name of the file you want, you can instead use a utility such as File Buddy X or Path Finder. These list all invisible files on your drive. File Buddy even includes an option not to include the ubiquitous .DS_Store (Directory Store) files in such lists. Assuming you're not looking for a .DS_Store file (which is likely to be the case), this reduces the number of files you need to sift through to locate the desired file.

2. **Modify the invisible bit.** Once you've located the file, open it in a utility such as XRay or FileXaminer and disable the Invisible bit. For example, if using the Find command, when the file you want appears in

the Results window, select it and access its contextual menu. Select the XRay {*filename*} item if you're using XRay; select FileXamine if you're using FileXaminer. (You can also drag the file from the Results window onto the icon or window of the utility.) With the file now open in the utility, you can disable the Invisible bit to make the file visible.

Alternatively, if you're using a utility like File Buddy X or Path Finder instead of the Find command, you can modify the Invisible bit using options provided directly within the utility.

Note: The SetFile command (included with Apple's Developer Xcode Tools software) can be used to change the invisibility attribute of a file via Terminal.

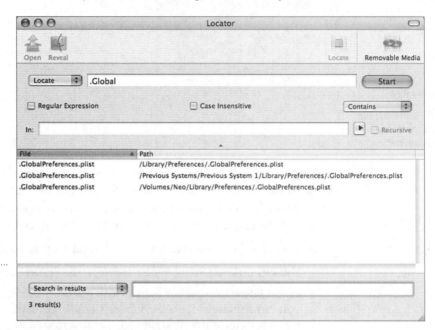

Figure 6.51

Locator finds all copies of an invisible file and their paths.

Figure 6.52

File Buddy's option to search for invisible files.

SEE: • **"Finding files: the find and locate commands,"** in Chapter 10, for related information.

• Chapter 10 for background information on how to use utilities such as SetFile.

Adding or removing a period at the start of a filename

You can make a visible file invisible by adding a period (.) to the start of its name. Conversely, for a file that's already invisible because its name starts with a period, you can make it visible by removing the period.

Although infrequent, there are occasions when you may want to do this. For example, I once downloaded a file from a remote Web server, via FTP, to my local Desktop. The filename began with a period. The result was that the file was invisible after the download was complete. To locate and work with the file, I wanted to eliminate the period (at least temporarily) so that I could more conveniently see the file in the Finder—without having to keep all invisible files visible.

Adding a period to the beginning of an item name from the Finder. Adding a period to the beginning of an item's name in the Finder is a bit trickier than it sounds. If you try to do this directly, you will get an error message that states the following: "You cannot use a name that begins with a dot '.', because these names are reserved for the System."

The solution is to first make all invisible files visible in the Finder (as described above). Now, when you try to add the period to the file's name, you will get a warning message but will be allowed to make the change. The warning message asks, "Are you sure you want to use a name that begins with a dot?" Click OK. When finished, make all invisible files invisible again. The file with the name change will become invisible.

Removing a period from the start of an item name from the Finder. To remove a period from the start of a filename, the simplest solution is to, once again, make all invisible files visible in the Finder (as described above). Once you've done this, locate the now-visible file and remove the period from its name. When finished, make all invisible files invisible again. The file with the name change will remain visible.

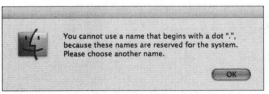

Figure 6.53

The error message that appears if you try to add a dot to the start of a filename in the Finder without first making invisible files visible.

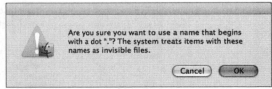

Figure 6.54

The warning message that appears when you add a period to the start of a filename while invisible files are visible in the Finder.

Adding or removing a period to or from the beginning of an item name using third-party utilities. Any utility that can list invisible files (such as File Buddy X and Path Finder) can be used to add or remove a period from the start of a file's name, without needing to first make all files visible in the Finder.

SEE: • "Toggling a file's Invisible bit," earlier in this chapter, for more details on how to access invisible files via these third-party utilities.

Adding or removing a period to or from the start of an item name using Terminal. You can use Terminal to add or remove a period from a file's name quickly. To do so, launch Terminal and type the following:

mv {*pathname*} {*.pathname*}

As I've said before, the easiest way to enter the pathname of a file is to drag the file icon from the Finder to the Terminal window. This technique gives you the full absolute pathname of the file. Once you've done this, enter a space and a period, and paste the same text a second time. This use of the move (mv) command creates a new file (with a period as the first character of the filename) to replace the original file in the same location. If you go to the Finder, the file icon will vanish.

You can later make the now-invisible file visible again by typing the opposite:

mv {*.pathname*} {*pathname*}

To make a visible copy of the file, instead of renaming it you could use the cp command.

Note: In Terminal, only items that begin with a period are considered invisible. Other items that are invisible in the Finder are listed as visible when using a command such as ls. To see a list of all files in the current directory, including invisible files, type ls –a. This lists the names of all files in the directory (including ones that start with a period).

SEE: • Chapter 10 for background information on using commands such as ls, cp, and mv.

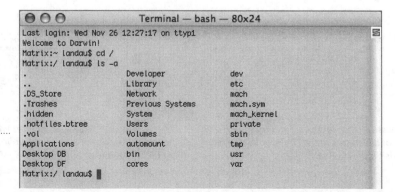

Figure 6.55

Viewing invisible files in Terminal via the ls –a *command.*

Invisible Files: Working with Invisible Files

Here are three examples of situations in which the ability to work with invisible files can help solve problems.

Saving movie trailers that have the Save option disabled

When viewing QuickTime movies on the Web, such as movie trailers, you can usually choose to save the movie to your hard drive (though you need to have upgraded to QuickTime Pro to do this). To do so, you use the Save options in the pop-up menu you access from the downward pointing triangle in the lower-right corner of the Movie window.

Sometimes, however, a Web site will disable this feature. Nonetheless, you usually can save the movie. Here's how to do this when using Internet Explorer:

1. Prior to moving the movies, enable the "Save movies in disk cache" option on the Plug-In tab of the QuickTime System Preferences pane. Also make sure that the "Enable kiosk mode" box is *not* checked.

2. Immediately after viewing the movie, go to ~/Library/Preferences/Explorer/Temporary Files.

   The QuickTime movie file may be stored there (though it will likely have a different name than that of the movie itself).

3. If you find the file, drag it out of that folder.

   You're finished!

If the preceding method doesn't work, access to invisible files comes into play. In most cases, the following step will work:

1. Make invisible files visible in the Finder (for example, by using InVisibles).

2. From the Finder's Go menu, choose Go to Folder and enter /tmp in the text box of the window that appears.

   The tmp folder window should now open in the Finder. You should find a normally invisible folder in the window with a number as its name (probably 501). This number is the same as the User ID number for the logged-in user.

   Note: If there's more than one numbered folder, you want the one with your ID. To find out what your ID is, launch NetInfo Manager, choose Users, and then select your user name. At the bottom of the window, search for the property that says uid. The number in the adjacent Value(s) column is your user ID. Alternatively, when you're in Terminal, type id. Your ID number will be presented in the Terminal window.

3. Open the folder for your ID number.

Inside, either at the root level of the folder or in a folder called TemporaryItems, there should be a file with a name that starts with QuickTimePlugIn.

4. Drag the file to the Desktop.

5. You can now make invisible files invisible again in the Finder by reversing step 1.

6. Use a utility such as FileXaminer or XRay to change the type and creator of the file to MooV and TVOD, respectively.

7. Open the Get Info window for the file and make QuickTime Player the Open with Application selection.

This change should also change the file's icon.

8. Rename the file however you want (ideally with a .mov extension).

9. Double-click the file and enjoy!

Modifying or deleting the .GlobalPreferences.plist files

The .GlobalPreferences.plist files contain various settings that are "global" to your account or to the system in general. There are three such files in Mac OS X 10.3. The first one is in ~/Library/Preferences (that is, your Home directory); the second one is in /Library/Preferences; and the third one (and the one least likely to need to be modified or deleted) is in ~/Library/Preferences/ByHost (this one has letters and numbers added to its name that are derived from your Mac's Ethernet/MAC address).

Each file contains different settings. The one in your Home directory Library folder contains your AppleID, your .Mac member name, your alert (beep) sound, and more. The one in the root-level Library folder contains your Energy Saver settings, time zone settings, and more.

If you wish, you can directly modify these settings from the .plist file, rather than from System Preferences, by using Property List Editor.

SEE: • "Modifying a .plist file," in Chapter 4.

Alternatively, if problems occur with items related to the file's settings (such as problems with your Mac's date and time), you can simply delete the relevant file and log out. A new default copy will be present when you log back in. Hopefully, this will fix the symptoms.

The main problem with doing any of these things is that the file is invisible, due to the period prefix in its name. To work around this, you can use almost any of the solutions described in the previous sections of this chapter.

More specifically, to modify the file, the simplest approach is to make invisible files visible in the Finder (such as via InVisibles). Then open the file in Property List Editor.

To delete the file, you can use the same technique to make the file visible—and then drag the file to the Trash. Or you can use the rm command in Terminal (because the file is accessible in Terminal even though it's invisible in the Finder).

Figure 6.56

The contents of the .GlobalPreferences.plist file in ~/Library/Preferences.

Modifying invisible Unix files from Mac OS X applications

Mac OS X keeps its essential Unix directories invisible in the Finder. These directories include /bin, /etc, /sbin, /tmp, /var, /usr, and /Volumes. In both Chapter 4 ("Take Note: What and Where Are the Unix Files?") and Chapter 10, I provide more details about the items in these directories and how to use Terminal to access their contents. For now, I want to focus on how and why to edit some of these Unix files using Mac OS X applications instead.

Unix uses configuration (config) files to determine the settings and preferences of a variety of features (such as network settings and Web server settings). In some cases, when you change a System Preferences setting in the Finder, you're modifying the contents of one of these Unix config files. These files are mainly text files in Unix's /etc directory. Occasionally, you may want to change a setting in one of these files that cannot be changed via System Preferences or any other Mac OS X feature. The solution is to edit the configuration file directly.

To do so, you open and edit these config files from Mac OS X text editors. In most cases, the permissions settings for the files will require that you have root access to modify the file.

You can edit these files in Terminal, using an editor such as pico in combination with the sudo command. Alternatively, you can edit these files directly in Mac OS X applications, such as TextEdit, by logging in as the root user. You can also modify these files directly in Mac OS X applications, even when logged in via your normal administrative account. This last method is the focus of the following sections.

SEE: • "Take Note: Opening Mac OS Applications from Terminal" and "Take Note: Editing Text Files via Terminal," in Chapter 10, for related information.

Using TextWrangler. A program that makes it easy to edit config files is Bare Bones' TextWrangler (BBEdit works similarly; the older BBEdit Lite does not include this option). To use it, follow these steps:

1. Access the desired file by choosing TextWrangler's Open Hidden command. From the Enable popup menu in the dialog that appears, select All Files. Navigate to the desired directory (for example, /private/etc) and select the desired file.

2. If the file requires root access, the initial Pencil icon in the toolbar at the top of the document will have a line through it. Click this icon.

   You will get a message stating, "The document is owned by root. Are you sure you want to unlock it?" Click Yes.

3. The line through the pencil icon is removed. You can now modify the document and save your changes.

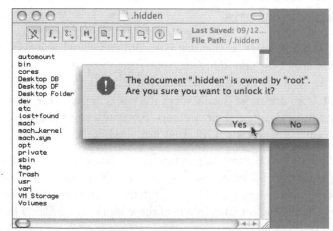

Figure 6.57

TextWrangler is about to grant root access to the .hidden file.

Using Pseudo and any text editor. If you don't have TextWrangler or BBEdit, you can alternatively open almost any application with root access. Having done this, you'll find that all documents you open from within that application are automatically modifiable, even if they would otherwise require root access to do so. The easiest way to do all of this is with the freeware utility Pseudo. To use it, follow these steps:

1. Launch Pseudo.

2. Drag the icon of the application you want to open to the Pseudo window, and enter your password when prompted. The application is now open with root access.

   Apple's TextEdit is a fine choice for an application to open in this way. The config files described here will be listed in TextEdit's Open dialog because the files are visible, even though the enclosing folder is invisible.

3. Open the desired file. To do so, select Open from the application's File menu and press Command-Shift-G to access the Go to Folder option. Enter the path to the folder you wish to access (for example, /private/etc or just /etc). You will now see a list of all files in the selected folder. Double-click the file you want to open.

4. Edit and save the file, as desired.

   SEE: • "Root Access," in Chapter 4, and "Take Note: Opening Mac OS Applications from Terminal," in Chapter 10, for ways to open Mac OS X applications with root access using Terminal instead of Pseudo.

   • "Using Shell Configuration Files," in Chapter 10, for a discussion of Unix line breaks and text editors.

Config files that may need editing. Following are two examples of Unix config files you might want or need to modify at some point.

• **inetd.conf.** Mac OS X uses SSH for making Telnet connections over a network. The SSH protocol provides greater security than the older Telnet. If you want or need to use the less secure Telnet, you need to change the /etc/inetd.conf file. To do so, open the file in BBEdit and then follow these steps:

   1. Locate the lines that read #telnet; #shell; and #login.

   2. Remove the # character from the start of each line.

   3. Save the file.

   4. Restart your Mac.

   SEE: • "Network Security," in Chapter 8, for more on SSH.

• **httpd.conf.** This is the Apache Web server configuration file. A problem in Mac OS X 10.1, where Web Sharing refused to start up, was solved by modifying the /etc/httpd/httpd.conf file. See the following Apple Knowledge Base article for details: http://docs.info.apple.com/article.html?artnum=106505. Other Web-related operations, more likely to be done with Mac OS X

Server than with the client, such as starting PHP, similarly require editing this file. See the following Knowledge Base document for an example: http://docs.info.apple.com/article.html?artnum=107292.

Note: Future updates to Mac OS X may provide more user-friendly ways of making these changes, eliminating the need to directly access these config files. Still, it's likely that there will always be some actions that require this direct access to the files.

SEE: • **"Take Note: Why and How to Use Archive and Install" and "Technically Speaking: Custom Config Files After a Mac OS X Update," in Chapter 3, for related information.**

• **"Technically Speaking: Hostconfig and Other Configuration Files," in Chapter 5, for related information.**

Maximizing Performance

Most computer users are never completely satisfied with how fast their computers run. They always want their Macs to run just a little bit faster. Although hardware and software place certain limits on a computer's speed, computers often run slower than they're capable. In this section, I describe some ways you can make sure you're getting the best performance from your Mac.

A Mac OS 9 program Carbonized to run in Mac OS X should run about as fast as the original Mac OS 9 version would run in Mac OS 9. Sometimes it may run faster, and occasionally it may run a bit slower. A Mac OS 9 program running in Classic, while booted from Mac OS X, will generally run slower than the same program running in Mac OS 9. A program written specifically for Mac OS X, especially a Cocoa program, is capable of running significantly faster than it would had it been written to run in Mac OS 9. Of course, when comparing running applications in Mac OS 9 on an older Mac versus in Classic on a much newer and faster Mac, the newer Mac will likely show more favorable results.

In general, if your Mac appears to be running significantly slower than usual or simply runs too slowly in general, consider the following causes and solutions.

SEE: • **"Technically Speaking: Terminal Commands to Monitor and Improve Performance," in Chapter 10, for related information.**

Not enough memory

Due to Mac OS X's dynamic memory, you will rarely, if ever, get "out of memory" messages, no matter how many applications you have open. This is because Mac OS X assigns an increasing amount of the memory load to virtual memory, as needed—which can make it appear that your Mac has unlimited memory. This is not the case. At some point, as you open more and more applications, the overall performance of every aspect of your Mac will slow. Keep pushing the memory envelope, and you will likely precipitate a crash. Otherwise, you might eventually get a memory-related error message, advising you to close windows and quit applications to free up more memory.

Following are the three surest solutions:

- **Quit unneeded applications.** The quickest solution, although often the least effective, is to quit any open applications you don't need (as the potential error message advises). Quitting Classic, if you don't need to use it, is always a good idea.

  Different programs use different amounts of memory. Thus, quitting Application A may have little effect, whereas quitting Application B may have a tremendous effect.

- **Run System Profiler.** I've found that running System Profiler and clicking to check any hardware component (or clicking the Devices and Volumes tab in the Jaguar version of the utility) will reduce the amount of inactive memory, adding it back to free memory. This can help eliminate memory-related problems. It's definitely helped me in Jaguar, though it may be less effective in Panther.

- **Log out or restart.** If a problem has become severe, you may need to log out and log back in before performance improves. Even better, restart your Mac. This is the surest way to free up memory that may have been causing a problem. It also resets the swapfiles(s) back to a default state (as discussed more in "Technically Speaking: Swapfiles and RAM Disks," below).

- **Add more memory.** The best solution to memory problems, especially if they happen frequently, is to purchase more memory. How much? As much as you can afford and/or your Mac can hold. You can't have too much. Mac OS X devours whatever RAM you give it. And the less RAM you have, the more performance slowdowns you'll have.

About This Mac. How do you know how much memory you have and how much you're using? The About This Mac window, which you open from the Apple menu, tells you how much physical memory (RAM) you have installed.

SEE: • "Technically Speaking: Dividing Up Mac OS X's Memory," in Chapter 4, for more on virtual versus physical memory, and related issues.

• "Utilities for monitoring and improving performance," later in this chapter, for more on memory issues, including memory leaks.

TECHNICALLY SPEAKING ▶ Swapfiles and RAM Disks

What and where is a swap file? When Mac OS X doesn't have enough physical memory (RAM) for what it needs to accomplish, it pages out some of the least-used contents of RAM to your hard drive as virtual memory. These page-outs are stored in swap files, located in /var/vm on your hard drive. Initially, there is one swapfile, named swapfile0, which is 80 MB. If additional space is needed, additional 80 MB swapfiles are created, named swapfile1, swapfile2, and so on. MemoryStick (from mattneub) is a useful utility that displays the current number of swapfiles, updated every few seconds. (Actually, these additional swapfiles files are really part of one overall swapfile. For convenience, the Finder creates separate icons as the swapfile is incrementally increased.)

If you find that you frequently have more than one swapfile, this is a sure sign that you're pushing the memory limits of your Mac.

Once additional swapfiles have been created, they aren't automatically deleted when no longer needed, nor should you attempt to delete them manually. The simplest and surest way to reset back to a lone swapfile is to restart your Mac. A utility such as NoName Scriptware's Cache Out X or Cocktail can delete all swapfiles without forcing a restart, but I recommend against this. I would only use this function if (as occasionally happens due to some bug) restarting the Mac fails to delete additionally created swapfiles. Even so, after deleting all swapfiles, I would restart as soon as possible.

Moving swapfiles to a separate partition. Fragmentation of a hard drive occurs when a file is stored in several segments in different locations on the drive, typically because no single free section of the drive is large enough to hold the entire file as one segment. As more files become fragmented, the overall level of disk fragmentation increases. If the fragmentation level gets high enough, drive performance can start to decline. Disk optimizers such as Norton Utilities' Speed Disk are designed to reduce this fragmentation.

Larger files are more subject to fragmentation than smaller ones. Thus, because swapfiles are large, they're especially vulnerable to fragmentation. Moving swapfiles to a separate volume (presumably one with lots of free space) from the one that contains Mac OS X can help reduce fragmentation. This change may in turn improve virtual-memory performance and, especially. disk performance.

However, I'm still not convinced that the benefit is worth the effort. If you want to give it a try, there are utilities that can assist you. A utility called Swap Cop (from J. Schrier) automates the procedure for you, and MemoryStick (mentioned above) similarly lets you move your swap files. Otherwise, the procedure—which requires considerable work in Terminal and/or with Unix files—is beyond the scope of this book. If you want the details, see ResExcellence (www.ResExcellence.com/hack_html_01/06-01-01.shtml) or the following Web page: www.bombich.com/mactips/swap.html.

continues on next page

TECHNICALLY SPEAKING ▶ Swapfiles and RAM Disks *continued*

RAM disks. RAM disks mimic the behavior of a mounted disk, except there's no physical media; it's all in memory. A mounted image (.dmg) file is a bit like a RAM disk. RAM disks were a supported feature in Mac OS 9; however, Mac OS X offers no equivalent feature. Indeed, developers report that writing a program that creates RAM disks in Mac OS X is a much more difficult task than it was in Mac OS 9. In addition, Mac OS X's virtual memory works so well that the speed benefits associated with a RAM disk in Mac OS 9 are not nearly as great as in Mac OS X. As a result, you won't see much use of RAM disks in Mac OS X.

Still, if it's a RAM disk you want, you can get one via third-party utilities like Clarkwood Software's ramBunctious. Because Apple does not directly support RAM Disks (unlike disk images), they're more prone to problems—especially after an update to the OS. Be cautious in using them.

SEE: • "Technically Speaking: Dividing Up Mac OS X's Memory," in Chapter 4, for related
information.
  • "Optimizing Mac OS X volumes," in Chapter 5, for more on fragmentation.
  • "Technically Speaking: Technical Commands to Monitor and Improve Performance,"
in Chapter 10, for still more information on memory and swapfiles.

Processor or graphics card is too slow

If your Mac is more than two years old, getting a new Mac will likely give you significantly better performance; however, upgrading the processor or graphics card on your existing Mac may be a more cost-effective solution. Keep in mind, though, that with the rapid rate at which computers advance, it's often a better deal to get a new computer than it is to spend hundreds of dollars upgrading an old one—even if it costs a bit more to do so.

A Mac with a G4 or G5 processor, for example, will be noticeably snappier than one that uses a G3. The difference in processor speed is usually more noticeable when you're running Mac OS X than it is in Mac OS 9, because Mac OS X places more demands on the processor. Mac OS X also includes dual-processor support for OS functions; Mac OS 9 did not. Thus, if you have a dual-processor Mac, it should seem faster in Mac OS X than it does in Mac OS 9.

A faster graphics card (ATI and nVidia are always coming out with new and improved models) can also enhance speed in specific situations, such as when you're using multimedia or playing games. They do not, however, increase the overall speed of your Mac.

Note: Quartz Extreme is a hardware-accelerated update to Mac OS X's Quartz graphics engine, included in Mac OS X 10.2 and later. The good news is that it's faster at drawing graphics onscreen. The bad news is that some of its acceleration features work only with newer graphics cards from nVidia (such as GeForce2MX, GeForce3, GeForce4 Ti, GeForce4, or GeForce4MX) and ATI (any AGP Radeon card).

Drive is too small

As a rough estimate, you should always keep at least 10 percent of your drive free. Thus, for a 60 GB drive, try to keep at least 6 GB unused. Even on smaller drives, I don't recommend going below 3 GB of "free" space. If you do, you're likely to see performance declines. At some point, as free space continue to decline, you will get error messages stating that you're almost out of disk space and advising you to delete files from the drive. You may even be prohibited from performing some action, getting a message that claims you don't have sufficient free space to perform it. This can occur even if it seems as if you have enough free space. In such cases, this is usually because the operation requires more space than it will ultimately use. Some software updates work this way, for example, by maintaining a copy of the old software until after the new software has been completely installed. Thus, unless you have enough free space to hold both the old and new software simultaneously, the operation is prevented.

An increase in the number and size of certain files maintained by the OS itself (such as swapfiles and cache files) may cut into the amount of free space that was available when you first booted, even though you aren't saving any new files to the drive. In this case, simply restarting and/or deleting the cache files could free up enough space to solve an immediate crisis.

Figure 6.58

The error message that appears when your startup disk is almost full.

Too little free space can also prevent additional virtual-memory swapfiles from being created when needed. Actually, even with a minimally sufficient amount of space, fragmentation of swapfiles (which increases as free space declines) can lead to a performance decrease.

To solve problems associated with too little disk space, try the following:

- Delete large and unneeded files from your hard drive.
- Defragment your hard drive to make more contiguous free space.
- Purchase a larger hard drive to replace your existing one or as an additional drive to offload rarely used files. Newer hard drives also tend to be faster than their older predecessors.

- Reduce the need to access virtual memory by (a) decreasing the number of processes and applications running and/or (b) adding more physical memory.

SEE: • "Technically Speaking: Swapfiles and RAM Disks," earlier in this chapter, for related information.

• "Insufficient space," earlier in this chapter, for related information.

• "Optimizing Mac OS X volumes," in Chapter 5, for more on fragmentation.

Internet connection is too slow

If your speed problems are primarily restricted to surfing the Internet (for example, Web pages are slow to load) and you have a dial-up modem connection, it's time to think about moving to a broadband connection (cable or DSL). Not only will speeds be much increased, but you'll also have a 24/7 connection with no need to log on and no dropped connections.

If you already have a broadband connection, there are still ways you can improve performance. The utility MOX Optimize (by Infosoft), for example, includes an option to speed Ethernet networking by optimizing buffers—in essence a front end for an operation you could otherwise perform in Terminal. Utilities like Cocktail and Northern Software's Panther Cache Cleaner have similar Network Optimization features.

If you're plagued by slow launch times for your Web browser, check the /Library/Internet Plug-Ins folder and make sure there are no unneeded or out-of-date plug-in files. If you find any, delete or update them. If you're not sure whether you want a certain plug-in, remove it from the folder but don't delete it. You can always return it later if you want.

SEE: • Chapter 8 for more information on network and Internet issues.

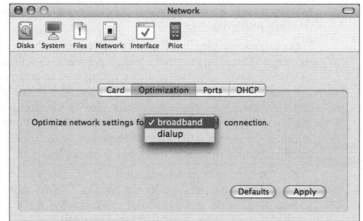

Figure 6.59

Cocktail's Network > Optimization screen.

Utilities for monitoring and improving performance

With so many possible causes of suboptimal performance, how can you best diagnose whether your Mac is performing up to par? And if it's not, what's the quickest way to determine the primary cause? The answers to both of these questions reside in a host of utility software.

For starters, Mac OS X comes with several performance-related utilities. For example:

Activity Monitor. Activity Monitor is located in the Utilities folder. I first mentioned this utility in Chapter 2, where I explained its basic features. In Chapter 5, I discussed this utility again, primarily as a means to force-quit processes. Here, I focus on several features specifically related to monitoring performance.

The values described here are updated at an interval you select via the Update Frequency command in the Monitor menu. The default is every 2 seconds.

- **Real Memory and Virtual Memory.** These two columns in the main Activity Monitor window list how much real (physical) memory and how much virtual memory are used by every listed process.

  You can sort the list by the values in any column by clicking the column name. Thus, to see which applications are using the most memory, click the Real Memory or Virtual Memory titles at the top of the column. Processes that move to the top of the list are the ones that are the most likely culprits in any memory-related performance problems. (If the list shows smaller numbers first, click the column head again to reverse the sort.) Quitting one or more of these processes is likely to have the biggest effect. However, regardless of what the results may be, do not quit any processes that you do not recognize, especially administrator processes (which you can view by changing the selection from My Processes in the pop-up menu). Quitting certain processes can cause you to be logged out or crash your Mac.

  You can also use memory listings to determine whether a process has a *memory leak* bug. In a memory leak, a process uses an increasing amount of memory over time—even if it's sitting idle. In extreme cases, memory use may get so enormous that it bogs down the entire Mac. By watching changes to the Memory columns in Activity Monitor, you can determine if a leak is likely and which process is the culprit. About the only solution at this point is to restart. The ultimate long-term solution is to get a bug-fixed version of the application that does not leak.

  Note: Classic applications are not listed separately in Application Monitor but are instead included under the "(null)" process. For a list of each open Classic application and its memory use, check out the Memory/Versions section of the Classic System Preferences pane.

- **% CPU.** The percentages in the % CPU column list how much of the processor's activity is used by each listed process. If overall CPU demand gets too high, the Mac's speed may slow significantly. Use this column to determine which processes are placing the most demand on the CPU.

- **Performance monitors.** As noted in Chapter 2, the bottom section of the Activity Monitor window contains five tabs: CPU, System Memory, Disk Activity, Disk Usage, and Network. Click each one to get data regarding these matters.

  CPU. CPU provides information about CPU usage that in Jaguar was provided by a separate utility called CPU Monitor. You can still get the floating windows used by the former CPU Monitor via the Show CPU commands in Panther's Activity Monitor's Monitor menu. The graphs, in one manner or another, show the ever-changing rise and fall of CPU usage. Don't be alarmed if the level occasionally gets to 100 percent; that's OK as long as it doesn't stay there for a sustained period. If the level remains at its peak for an extended time, you are likely trying to do too many processor-intensive activities at the same time. Quitting some applications (especially ones showing a high CPU percentage) or reducing how many tasks you have going simultaneously will likely help.

  If you click the CPU tab at the bottom of the main window, you will see that CPU usage is broken into four categories: % User, % System, % Nice, and % Idle. The distinction between User and System is essentially the same as between User and Administrator processes, as described in the Activity Monitor section in Chapter 2. A *niced* process is one whose CPU priority has been modified from its default value, so as to take up more (or less) CPU time than it otherwise would (as explained more in "Technically Speaking: Terminal Commands to Monitor and Improve Performance," in Chapter 10).

  System Memory. System Memory shows how memory is divided up into its four main categories: Wired, Active, Inactive, and Free. It also shows Page Ins/Outs. All of this is covered more in "Technically Speaking: Dividing Up Mac OS X's Memory," in Chapter 4.

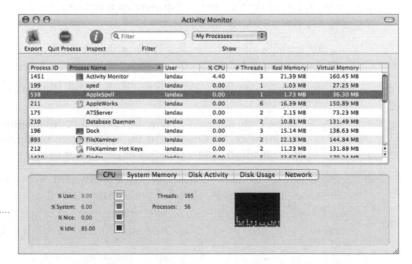

Figure 6.60

Activity Monitor's main window with CPU display.

Disk Activity. Disk Activity provides data regarding hard-disk access, including transfer speed (Data in/sec and Data out/sec).

Disk Usage. Disk Usage provides information about the amount of space on each volume that's utilized versus free.

Network. Network provides basic information that indicates when data is being transferred over your network and the speed of the transfer.

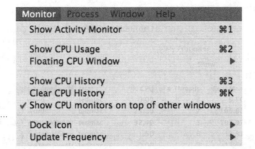

Figure 6.61

Activity Monitor's Monitor menu.

Network Utility. Network Utility, particularly in its Info and Netstat tabs, provides additional statistics about network performance.

SEE: • "Diagnosing Internet problems with Network Utility," in Chapter 8, for more on this utility.

• "Technically Speaking: Terminal Commands to Monitor and Improve Performance," in Chapter 10, for coverage of the `netstat` command accessed from Terminal.

Terminal commands and third-party utilities. The information provided by utilities such as Activity Monitor is also available via Unix commands entered in Terminal. For example, much of the information listed in Activity Monitor overlaps with what you get via the Unix top command.

Other utilities, primarily from third parties, are front ends for Unix commands, providing a graphical Aqua-based interface for what would otherwise require the use of Terminal.

As one example of this, Pepsan's Perfboard provides a quick view of a variety of performance-related data. In its default view, you get a constantly updated look at CPU percentage, system load, memory use (including page-outs), network ins and outs, and disk reads and writes.

SEE: • "Technically Speaking: Terminal Commands to Monitor and Improve Performance," in Chapter 10, for more details on Terminal commands and front-end utilities related to performance.

Also check out utilities such as Cocktail and Xupport. For example, Cocktail (mentioned several times already in this chapter and illustrated in **Figures 6.44, 6.45,** and **6.59**) allows you to perform a variety of actions that would otherwise require several Mac OS X and third-party utilities. Here is a partial list of what Cocktail can do:

- Show invisible files in the Finder
- Add a Quit command to the Finder
- Enable the debug menu in programs such as Safari
- Renew a DHCP lease
- Optimize network settings for broadband versus dial-up
- Set Ethernet speed, duplex, and MTU values
- Delete locked or otherwise undeletable items
- Delete DS_Store files
- Delete archived log files
- Delete cache files
- Perform the Unix optimizing/prebinding function
- Run cron scripts
- Create symbolic links
- Re-create the "Desktop (Mac OS 9)" symbolic link file
- Enable disk journaling
- Set hard-drive spin-down times

SEE: • "Take Note: Launch Services Files and Beyond," earlier in this chapter, for more on Cocktail and related utilities.

Other miscellaneous performance tips

Finally, you can do a host of other minor tweaks to bring about an incremental effect on performance.

Turn off unneeded Finder and Dock features. Turning off certain Finder and/or Dock features can reduce overall CPU usage and thus improve performance. It's up to you to decide whether the trade-off is worthwhile. Any one feature is not likely to have a big effect, but turning off a combination of items may be significant. Such actions are likely to have the greatest effect on older hardware. Features to consider turning off include the following:

- Genie effect for minimizing folders to the Dock (use Scale instead)
- Dock magnification (keep to a minimum)
- Bouncing icons in the Dock
- Languages for searching file contents (turn off all but the language you use)
- Content indexing (if in progress)
- Text smoothing (set it to be off for the largest font size available)
- Zoom rectangles
- Window shadows

The on/off switches for these features can be found in the Finder's Preferences, the Dock and Appearance System Preference panes, Get Info windows, and various third-party utilities that provide access to some settings not available via Apple's Mac OS X software. MOX Optimize has an especially rich selection of options, including the capability to increase the Finder's Unix nice priority (see "Technically Speaking: Terminal Commands to Monitor and Improve Performance" in Chapter 10). Other potentially useful utilities include TinkerTool, Cocktail, and Unsanity's ShadowKiller and Dock Detox.

Remove unneeded login and startup items. Check the applications/processes listed in the Startup Items list in the Accounts System Preferences pane. You may have some items for software that you no longer want to use. In such cases, remove the item. Otherwise, the item continues to launch at login and may contribute to a decrease in performance.

Don't put hard drives to sleep. Uncheck Energy Saver's "Put the hard drive to sleep when possible" option. This can significantly improve performance related to hard-drive access, especially for external FireWire drives.

Disable journaling. If journaling is enabled (as described in "Enabling and disabling journaling," in Chapter 5), turning this feature off can improve overall performance. However, in newer Macs, the performance gain is probably not worth the loss of this feature. Note: Journaling is enabled by default in Panther.

Speed up application launches. To improve application launch times, Mac OS X maintains certain information about each application in /var/vm/app_profile. The files here are typically re-created on restart. If application launch times become unusually slow, and especially if the app_profile directory is very large, deleting the directory may return speeds to normal. You need root access to do this. To do so via Terminal, type the following:

```
sudo rm -R /private/var/vm/app_profile
```

Then restart your Mac. To do so, type reboot.

Delete unmounted volumes in /var/automount. After you disconnect from any local or remote volume on a network, a folder with the name of the volume may remain in the /var/automount/Network folder. The presence of these volume folders may slow down the Finder's performance (in cases where it attempts to scan the disconnected volume). The solution is to delete these folders. To do so, use the Finder's Go to Folder command to navigate to the Network folder; then drag the volume folder icons to the Trash (authenticating as needed).

Disconnect from remote servers before installing software. This is especially recommended if you're using the VISE installer software. Being connected to a server (even your iDisk) while installing can significantly slow the computer's response.

Defragment/optimize your drive. Use a utility such as Norton Utilities Speed Disk to do this.

SEE: • "Optimizing Mac OS X volumes," in Chapter 5.

Check the Web. Various Mac Web sites post frequently updated tips for enhancing Mac OS X performance. One good site is "Mac OS X speed FAQ" (www.index-site.com/Macosxspeed.html).

7

Troubleshooting Printing

Given the Mac OS's historically strong position in the graphics and publishing industries, you might assume that Mac OS X would include advanced printing features—and you would be right! Mac OS X provides Mac users with a brand-new, high-tech printing engine, which includes built-in support for many printers and tools for managing your print jobs. It also does some things differently from previous versions of the Mac OS, however, and requires different solutions when things go wrong. In this chapter, I'll show you how printing works in Mac OS X and what to do when it doesn't.

In This Chapter

TAKE NOTE ▶ Printing: A Behind-the-Scenes Intro

As with Fonts folders (described in Chapter 4), there are multiple Printers folders in the various Library folders on your drive. Each folder serves a different function.

/System/Library/Printers. This folder is the main location for the non-Unix printer software installed by Mac OS X. Within this folder is a collection of other folders. In general, you should not modify any of the files here. The folders of most interest include the following:

- **PPDs.** This folder contains (buried in /PPDs/Contents/Resources) the lproj (language-specific) folders, which hold the PostScript Printer Description files for Apple's LaserWriter printers. The en.lproj (English-language) folder must be there in order for the system to work; the rest of the folders are optional, based on the language support you've installed with Mac OS X.

  The PPDs are archived as gzip files. If you double-click one, it launches StuffIt Expander. From here, you can save the expanded copy to your Desktop for viewing. The PPD is a Unix Executable File (see Chapter 10 for more on this term) and can be opened in a text editor.

  Note: The active PPD files for the printers added to your Printer List in Printer Setup Utility are actually stored (uncompressed) in the Unix directory /etc/cups/ppd.

- **PBMs.** This folder contains Printer Browser Modules files, which determine the basic options available in the pop-up menu of Printer Setup Utility's Add Printer dialog. The names of the files mirror the options they provide: PB_AppleTalk.plugin, PB_LPR.plugin (IP Printing), PB_USB.plugin, PB_NetInfo.plugin (Open Directory), PB_Rendezvous.plugin, and PB_Advanced.plugin.

/Library/Printers. This folder is primarily for third-party printer software (Hewlett-Packard, Epson, Canon, and so on) installed by Mac OS X or the user. It includes PPDs for PostScript laser printers, as well as separate vendor-specific folders for inkjet printers.

~/Library/Printers. This folder, located in each user's Home directory, can contain the same sorts of folders and files as /Library/Printers. The main difference is that files in this folder are accessible only when the user of that name is logged in, whereas files in /Library/Printers are accessible to all local users. In Panther, this folder is also where printer proxy applications are stored (as described later in this chapter in "Take Note: Printer Queue (Proxy) Applications.")

If matching files that correspond to the same printer appear in more than one of these folders, Mac OS X will use the one in your Home directory over the one in the /Library directory, which in turn overrides the one in the /System/Library folder.

Classic. Mac OS X also looks in the Printer Descriptions folder (inside the Extensions folder) of your Classic Mac OS 9 System Folder for additional PPD files, but only if it has not already found a match in the Mac OS X Library folders.

continues on next page

TAKE NOTE ▶ Printing: A Behind-the-Scenes Intro   *continued*

When you're printing from Classic (or booted from Mac OS 9), however, none of the Mac OS X folders described here are directly checked. When you print in Classic, the OS checks for PPDs only in the Mac OS 9 System Folder and uses the Chooser (rather than Printer Setup Utility) to select a printer. However, in Panther, Classic does at least check for the presence of PPD files in Mac OS X and will install them into the Mac OS 9 System Folder, as needed, so they are accessible from there.

SEE: • Chapter 9 for more information on printing in Classic.

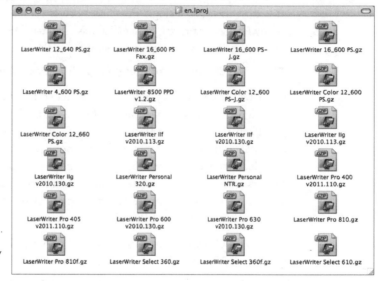

Figure 7.1

....

The PPD files (compressed) in /System/Library/Printers/PPDs/ Contents/Resources/en.lproj.

Printer Support in Mac OS X

Before I begin talking about setting up printing in Mac OS X, I'm going to go over the types of printers and connections that are supported, as well as the differences between these printer types.

One of the initial problems with Mac OS X was that it didn't support many of the most common printers—especially inkjet printers. In addition, it provided little, if any, support for connecting to printers over an AppleTalk network. These limitations have largely been addressed via the latest versions of Mac OS X and the various printer updates released by Apple and printer vendors. Thus, if you're having printer problems, the first thing you should do is make sure you're using the latest software available for your printer.

What types of printers does Mac OS X support?

Mac OS X supports both PostScript (Level 2 and Level 3) and non-PostScript printers. The nature of that support, however, differs.

PostScript printers. PostScript is an Adobe-developed programming language that allows the operating system to describe the appearance of a printed page precisely to the printer. PostScript has long been the standard for professional publishing and printing, but as technology has advanced, PostScript support has also become fairly common among home and small-office printers. Because PostScript is a standard language, all PostScript-compatible printers receive the same basic instructions from the operating system on how to print the same document, so a single PostScript driver can provide basic printing support for *any* PostScript printer. Mac OS X has a built-in PostScript driver, so it supports any PostScript 2 or 3 printer on a supported connection right out of the box.

SEE: • "What types of printer connections does Mac OS X support?" below.

If a particular PostScript printer provides added features or functionality (multiple paper trays, various resolutions, different paper sizes, and so on), the printer manufacturer provides a PostScript Printer Description (PPD) file. A PPD tells the PostScript driver what is different about (or what additional features are provided by) that printer. Mac OS X includes PPD files for many PostScript printers from Apple, Hewlett-Packard, Lexmark, Tektronix, and Xerox. Even better, Mac OS X's Software Update may provide updates for these PPDs automatically, as well as PPD files for additional printers as support is added.

Note: Mac OS X cannot print to older PostScript Level 1 printers, such as the Apple LaserWriter NT or LaserWriter Pro 400 or 405.

SEE: • "Take Note: Why and How to Create PDF Files," later in this chapter.

Non-PostScript (raster) printers. Other recent printers (such as most inkjet printers) commonly use Printer Control Language (PCL) rather than PostScript. Because such printers don't support a universal printing system, each printer requires its own model-specific driver. On the other hand, because these drivers are printer-specific, PPD files aren't necessary; the print driver itself usually includes all of the information the OS needs for full feature support. Mac OS X comes with drivers installed for many inkjet printers, such as Apple, Canon, Epson, and Hewlett-Packard models. Again, Software Update may update these drivers or install new ones for printers from these and other manufacturers.

QuickDraw printers. In what may be disappointing news for some users, Mac OS X does *not* support older QuickDraw printers. Some older Apple printers (such as the ImageWriter series, StyleWriter series, and a few LaserWriter models) use Apple's own QuickDraw printing technology to communicate between the OS and the printer. Unfortunately, these printers are currently unsupported, and there's no indication that Apple will support them in future versions of Mac OS X.

If your printer is advertised as being Mac OS X–compatible, but Mac OS X does not come with a driver or PPD for it, you'll probably need to install the appropriate support files manually.

SEE: • "Installing Printer Drivers," below.

What types of printer connections does Mac OS X support?

Mac OS X supports several connection types for printing. You can connect a non-AppleTalk printer directly to your Mac, using USB (Universal Serial Bus), Ethernet, FireWire, or (on older Macs) serial/printer/modem ports. You can also connect non-AppleTalk serial-port printers to newer Macs by using third-party serial-port adapters.

If you have an AppleTalk printer, your options for direct connections are a bit more limited. Because Mac OS X does not support LocalTalk (AppleTalk via serial/printer/modem ports), and because AppleTalk is generally not supported over USB or FireWire, your only real option is Ethernet. If you have a LocalTalk printer, you would need to purchase a third-party LocalTalk-to-Ethernet adapter. Unfortunately, these adapters cost approximately $100, so unless your LocalTalk printer is worth a lot of money, your best bet may simply be to get a newer printer that has a supported connection type.

In addition to the direct connections described in the preceding paragraphs, Mac OS X fully supports network printing to both AppleTalk and non-AppleTalk printers. If your Mac can "see" a printer, it can print to it. You can use any printer on a local or AirPort (wireless) network, as well as any printer anywhere on the Internet that has its own IP address (by using LPR, described later in this chapter).

The type of connection you use is largely determined by the printer itself. If it requires a USB connection (as most current inkjet printers do), that connection is how you connect the printer to the Mac. Some printers have multiple connection options. An inkjet printer, for example, may include a USB port and—via a network card—an Ethernet network connection. This card may come with the printer, or you can purchase it as an add-on.

Unfortunately, Mac OS X does not support IrDA printing to printers with infrared ports. On the plus side, if your Mac has a Bluetooth module, after installing Bluetooth Firmware Updater 1.0.2 or later as well as Bluetooth Update 1.5 (included as part of Mac OS X 10.3.3), you will be able to print-wirelessly to Bluetooth-supported printers. A Bluetooth Printers item wil be added to the Printers pop-up menu in the Print dialog.

SEE: • "Bluetooth," in Chapter 8, for more details.

Installing Printer Drivers

As mentioned earlier in the chapter, Mac OS X comes with drivers and/or PPD files installed for many Apple and third-party printers. If you have a recent printer model, you should be able to configure Mac OS X to use your printer right out of the box. If support is not included, you'll need to install the appropriate software first.

If your printer is Mac OS X–compatible but a driver is not already installed, you'll need to install it.

How do I tell if my printer is already supported?

There are several ways you can determine whether Mac OS X already supports your printer. For newer USB printers (both PostScript and non-PostScript), the easiest way is to connect the printer to the Mac via the USB ports on both devices. Mac OS X can recognize a supported USB printer automatically, select the appropriate PPD file (for PostScript printers) or driver (for non-PostScript printers), and set up a print queue for it in Mac OS X's Printer Setup Utility, which is where all printer and print-queue management is coordinated (as described in detail later in the chapter). Mac OS X should similarly auto-discover and set up printers on your local network that use Rendezvous.

For other printers, you can see whether support is included by checking the printer support files on your hard drive.

For non-PostScript printers, check /Library/Printers/{*name of printer vendor*}. Within these directories, you'll find support files listed by model number. Drivers for Canon printers, for example, are in /Library/Printers/Canon/BJPrinter/PMs. Drivers for Epson inkjet printers are in /Library/Printers/EPSON.

You may also find manufacturer-specific printer utilities in these directories. Inside /Library/Printers/EPSON/Utilities is the EPSON Printer Utility, for example. Launch this application (and select the desired Epson printer from the list that appears) to access the ink-level, nozzle-check, head-cleaning, and head-alignment features of the printer software.

PPD files for third-party PostScript printers are located in the /Library/Printers/ PPDs/Contents/Resources/*name*.lproj folders. English-language PPD files, for example, are in the directory en.lproj—listed by printer manufacturer (for example, HP LaserJet and Lexmark Optra) and model number.

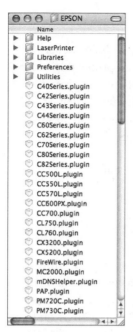

Figure 7.2

*Partial contents of the
/Library/Printers/EPSON folder.*

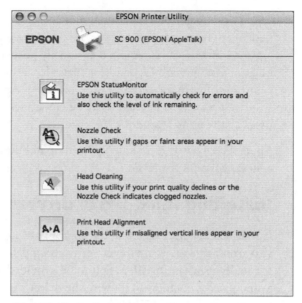

Figure 7.3

The EPSON Printer Utility.

Note: You can also copy PPD files from the Mac OS 9 System Folder to the appropriate language folder in Mac OS X. The files will work in Mac OS X. In addition, if Mac OS X cannot find a PPD file for your printer in the preceding directories, it will search for PPD files in the Mac OS 9 System Folder.

SEE: • **"Take Note: Printer Models with Drivers Built into Mac OS X," below.**

TAKE NOTE ▶ Printer Models with Drivers Built into Mac OS X

Mac OS X includes printer drivers and PPD files for many popular printers. Although the list of printers that Mac OS X supports out of the box is too long to print here, you can view this list on Apple's Web site at www.apple.com/macosx/upgrade/printers.html.

In addition, a third-party Web site (www.index-site.com/printersx.html) has compiled a list of printers supported by Mac OS X, which includes drivers not provided by Apple and assorted troubleshooting information.

SEE: • **"Take Note: Using Gimp-Print," later in this chapter.**

Updating via Software Update?

When you update to a new version of Mac OS X, it may include support for new printers and/or fixes to software for already supported printers. In older versions of Mac OS X, Apple occasionally posted vendor-specific printer updates via Software Update (for example, an update that just contained printing software for certain Epson printers). Apple no longer does this. Instead, for support beyond what's included with Mac OS X, Apple refers users to the printer vendor's Web site.

Apple may, however, include updated or additional printer support files in a general Mac OS X update.

Installing third-party drivers

If Mac OS X doesn't include the appropriate support files for your printer and you aren't able to get them via Software Update, you'll have to install them manually using an installer application provided by the printer manufacturer. Some printers include a CD with the driver installer; others will tell you to go to the manufacturer's Web site to download the installer. (Going to the Web site is probably a good idea either way, because the drivers available from the Web site are often newer than those that come with the printer.) After you've obtained the appropriate installer, installation usually involves simply double-clicking the installer application and following its instructions.

SEE: • "Troubleshooting Printing: Checking Printer Drivers," later in this chapter, for more details.

Using CUPS software

As explained later in this chapter, Apple completely overhauled its printing architecture in Mac OS X 10.2, shifting to using CUPS. One advantage of this is that users familiar with Unix can configure the CUPS software to support printers that are otherwise unsupported by Mac OS X. For those unfamiliar with Unix, Gimp-Print software (which is mainly a collection of printer drivers) does most of the work for you. Gimp-Print is included as part of Panther and is installed by default.

SEE: • "CUPS" and "Take Note: Using Gimp-Print," later in this chapter, for details.

Deleting unused printer drivers

If you use a single printer and don't plan on getting a newer one for a while, you can regain quite a bit of hard-drive space (well over 100 MB) by deleting unused printer drivers and PPDs in the /Library/Printers folder. The easiest (and safest) way to do so is to simply delete the folders belonging to other manufacturers' support files. (If you have an Epson printer, for example, delete the Canon and HP folders.) If you're using only the U.S. English version of the Mac OS, you can also delete all of the folders except en.lproj within the /PPDs/Contents/Resources folder (since the other folders provide support for non-English languages). To make these deletions, you'll need to be an administrative user.

As a side note, even if you *don't* use the U.S. English version, the en.lproj folder must be present; if it's not, Mac OS X won't be able to find the non-English versions of your printing software automatically. You will still be able to use non-English versions, but you will have to select them manually in Printer Setup Utility.

The downside to removing these files is that if you ever need to support other printers or languages, you'll need to reinstall the support files.

Note: If you're a laptop user, it might be worth leaving drivers for all printers installed—you never know where you'll be and what printers will be available when you need to print on the road.

Note: If you plan ahead, you can mostly avoid the need to delete unused printers: When first installing Mac OS X, if you elect to do a Custom Install, you will have the opportunity *not* to install selected brands of printers (for example, Epson). Since they never get installed, you don't need to worry about deleting them later.

SEE: • "Take Note: How to Reinstall the Mac OS X Printer Drivers," below.

TAKE NOTE ▶ How to Reinstall the Mac OS X Printer Drivers

If you've deleted any of the printer drivers or printing support files that come installed in Mac OS X (perhaps to save hard-drive space) and later need one or more of them, there is an easier way to get them back than reinstalling Mac OS X.

The solution is to mount Mac OS X Install Discs 2 and 3. From here, you will see several .pkg files (inside the Packages folders on the CDs) with names that refer to printers: CanonPrinterDrivers.pkg, EpsonPrinterDrivers.pkg, HewlettPackardPrinterDrivers.pkg, LexmarkPrinterDrivers.pkg, and Gimp-PrintDrivers.pkg. Double-click the file with the brand name that you want.

Note: On Disc1, there is an AdditionalPrinterDrivers.mpkg file (in /System/Installation/Packages) that you can use to reinstall all printer drivers at once.

Once the Installer has launched, enter your password when asked and select the desired Mac OS X volume as your destination volume. Then click to Upgrade or Install, as indicated. You do not need to restart from a CD to do this.

Note: On the Install DVD, the needed files are invisible. You can locate them by using the Finder's Go to Folder command and going to /Volumes/{*name of DVD*}/System/Installation/Packages.

Print & Fax System Preferences Pane

To access the Print & Fax System Preferences pane, either (a) open Printer Setup Utility and from the Printer Setup Utility menu select Preferences; or (b) open System Preferences and select Print & Fax.

The Print & Fax pane includes two main buttons, named (appropriately enough) Printing and Faxing. Click a button and the pane shifts to display the matching options. The explanations that follow reference aspects of printing and faxing that are covered in more detail later in the chapter. Check the relevant sections if you need more background information.

Printing screen

The Printing screen includes four options:

- **Set Up Printers.** If you click this button, Printer Setup Utility launches.
- **"Selected printer in Print Dialog."** From the pop-up menu here, you can select which printer should appear as the default printer in Print dialogs. If you select "Last printer used" (the initial choice), the default printer will always be whatever printer you last selected. However, suppose you want to occasionally use an alternative printer (say a color printer) but want the Print dialog to revert back to your standard printer automatically the next time you select to print. In this case, select the name of the printer from the menu. If the name is not present, select Edit Printer List and you will again be taken to Printer Setup Utility.

  Note: This option is not present in Jaguar. In Jaguar, the default printer always switches to the last printer used.

- **"Default paper size in Page Setup."** The default paper-size choice in Page Setup dialogs is typically US Letter. To change the default selection, choose your desired size here. To make a selection other than the default, use the Page Setup dialog.
- **"Share my printers with other computers."** Checking this box does the same thing as enabling Printer Sharing in the Services section of the Sharing System Preferences pane. If you do this, all printers in your Printer List (in Printer Setup Utility) are shared, whether they're directly connected to your computer (for example, via a USB port) or connected over a network. In most cases, however, you would use this option to share a USB- or FireWire-connected printer. For printers on an Ethernet network, other users would likely already have access because they are on the network as well.

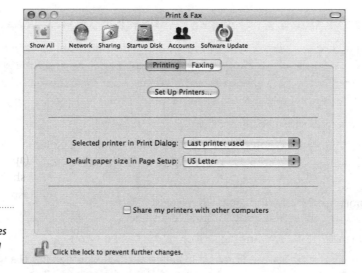

Figure 7.4

The Print & Fax System Preferences pane: the printing screen.

Faxing screen

You can use the options available from the Faxing screen to set up to receive faxes. The main options include the following:

- **"Receive faxes on this computer."** Enable this option if you want to be able to receive faxes.

- **When a Fax Arrives.** Select options here to tell the Mac what to do with an incoming fax.

SEE: • "Faxing," later in this chapter, for details.

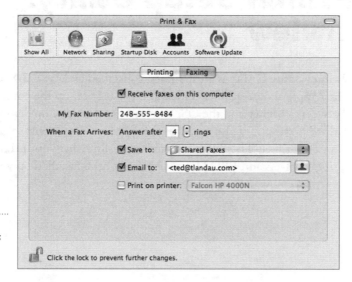

Figure 7.5

The Print & Fax System Preferences pane: the Faxing screen.

TECHNICALLY SPEAKING ▶ Changing the Default Paper Size for Epson Printers

Epson printers may not use Apple's system-wide printing defaults. Instead, each model may use its own default settings. In this case, selecting a default paper size from the Print & Fax pane may have no effect. If so, to change the default paper size for an Epson printer (from na-letter to iso-a4, for example), follow these steps (assuming you are using U.S. English):

1. Open the /Library/Printers/EPSON/ folder.

2. Find the plug-in for your Epson printer (for example, mine is SC900.plugin).

3. Control-click the plug-in's icon, and from the contextual menu choose Show Package Contents.

4. In the package contents, find the following file: /Contents/Resources/English.lproj/Localizable.strings.

5. Open the file in TextEdit by dragging its icon to the TextEdit icon.

Note: If you have the Developer Software installed and you double-click the file, it will likely open in the Xcode application. You can make the change here as well as in TextEdit.

6. In the line that says "DefaultPaperSize = na-letter," change na-letter to iso-a4.

7. Save the file.

8. Log out and then log back in.

You can use a similar procedure for other paper sizes. Note: You may also need to change the file of the same name in en_US.lproj.

Using Printer Setup Utility: An Overview

Printer Setup Utility is an application installed by Mac OS X and located in the /Applications/Utilities folder. You use it to set up the communication between a printer and the OS. You also use it to set a modem for faxing. For printing, the utility also manages the queue of documents selected for printing on each printer. The following sections assume that your printer's required printer drivers and PPD files have already been installed on your drive (as described previously).

THE JAGUAR WAY ▶ Print Center vs. Printer Setup Utility

In Jaguar, the main printing utility is called Print Center; in Panther, it's called Printer Setup Utility. As you might guess, the differences between these two utilities go far beyond the name change. Here's an overview of what's new and different:

- Printer Setup Utility supports the creation of separate Desktop Printer files. Print Center does not.

- Print Center has a Jobs menu. This menu no longer exists in Printer Setup Utility. Jaguar's Jobs commands have mostly been moved to the Printers menu in Printer Setup Utility.

- Printer Setup Utility's Printers menu has commands, such as Print Test Page and Pool Printers, that Print Center does not include.

- Printer Setup Utility can set up fax transmissions (that is, sending and receiving). To get started, from the View menu select Show Fax List. Jaguar, in contrast, does not include faxing capability.

- From Printer Setup Utility's Printer Setup Utility menu, select Preferences, and you get taken to the Print & Fax System Preferences pane. In Jaguar, Print Center has its own Preferences window separate from System Preferences. There is no Print & Fax pane in Jaguar.

- The Default Paper Size option (as well as a few other options, which are discussed in the main text) in Print Center's Preferences has been moved to the Print & Fax pane in Panther.

- Printer Setup Utility supports Windows printing; Print Center does not.

- Printer Setup Utility also includes improved support for Rendezvous-enabled printers.

- Print Center's Configure item in the toolbar is called Utility in Printer Setup Utility. Printer Setup Utility also has a new toolbar item for launching ColorSync Utility.

- Print Center's "Show printers connected to other computers" preference does not exist in Printer Setup Utility.

Print Center alias in Panther. Mac OS X 10.3 (Panther) contains an invisible alias file named Print Center. The alias points to Printer Setup Utility as the original and is located in the same folder (/Applications/Utilities) as Printer Setup Utility. The alias file's function is to prevent problems that may occur with third-party software, not specifically updated for Panther, that may check for Print Center and fail to work if it does not find a file with this name.

Printer Setup Utility menus

The following provides an overview of the most important commands in Printer Setup Utility's menus:

Printer Setup Utility menu Preferences command. This opens the Print & Fax System Preferences pane.

SEE: • "Print & Fax System Preferences Pane," earlier in this chapter, for more details.

TAKE NOTE ▶ Showing and Hiding Printers

In Jaguar, Print Center's Preferences window includes an option to "Show printers connected to other computers." You need to check this box if you're on a network and want to see shared printers that are connected to other computers. If this option is selected, these printers are automatically displayed even though you did not specifically add them.

In Panther, these printers are displayed by default; there is no option *not* to display them in Printer Setup Utility's Printer List. Even selecting to Delete Selected Printer will not work. However, if you don't want a printer to appear in Print and Page Setup dialogs, you can uncheck the box next to its name in the In Menu column.

The Favorites column in Jaguar's Print Center has the same function as the In Menu column in Printer Setup Utility. If the Favorites column is not present by default, you can add it by selecting it from the hierarchical menu of the Columns command in Print Center's View menu.

View menu. There are two pairs of commands of interest here:

- **Show Printer List and Show Fax List.** These commands open the two main windows of Printer Setup Utility. The former displays a list of all printers that are available to your computer. The latter shows a list of all available fax modems.

- **Hide Toolbar and Customize Toolbar.** As in most Mac OS X applications that include toolbars, you can select to hide or modify the toolbar by choosing between these options. By default, the Printer List toolbar includes Make Default, Add, Delete, Utility, ColorSync, and Show Info icons. The Fax List toolbar includes Delete, Show Info, and Stop Jobs.

Figure 7.6

Printer Setup Utility's (left) View and (right) Printers menus.

Printers menu. If no printers have been added, or if you haven't selected a printer from the list, the only choice that will be enabled is Add Printer. Otherwise, the available options depend upon what printer(s) you have selected. The following provides a brief overview of the available commands:

- **Make Default.** You can use this command to change the default printer (that is, the one that appears as the initial choice in Print and Page Setup dialogs).

- **Add Printer.** You can use this command to add a new printer to the Printer List. (The details of how to do this are the focus of the next few sections of this chapter.)

- **Delete Selected Printers.** You can use this command to delete printers from the list. However, because the driver software is not deleted when you select this command, you can still re-add the printer later, if you wish.

- **Pool Printers.** To use this command, first select more than one printer; then select the command. From the window that appears, drag the printer names in the order in which you prefer each printer to be selected. Give the pool a name and select Create. The pool you just created will appear in the Printer List just as if it were another printer. If you select this printer from a Print dialog, the document will print to the first printer on the list (if it's available). If that printer is busy, it will try the next printer—and so on until it finds an available printer.

  If all printers are busy, the document should be queued for printing in the first printer on the list. The Printer Pool item in the Printer List will display the icon for this first listed printer. This printer is also the one that will determine which printing options are available in Print and Page Setup dialogs when the pool is selected.

  You cannot rearrange the order of printers in a pool after you create it. To do so, delete the pool and re-create a new one with the desired order. Note: You can view and possibly edit the order of printers in a pool via the Classes page of the CUPS interface.

  SEE: • **"Accessing CUPS from a Web browser," later in this chapter.**

- **"Configure printer."** This command accesses the same software that the Utility icon in the toolbar accesses. This option is dimmed unless the currently selected printer has a separate configuration utility available. This option is available, for example, for my Epson Stylus 900N printer. When I select Configure Printer, it launches the EPSON Printer Utility mentioned earlier in this chapter. Actually, it first opens a List window from which I select the utility. The utility then appears, providing options such as to do a nozzle check, do a print-head alignment, or clean the head.

  To configure options for printers that do not have a separate utility, or for options not available from the separate utility, select instead the Show Info command.

- **Print Test Page.** This command does exactly what its name implies. It provides a useful way of determining whether a printer is correctly connected and working. If the test page prints and you're otherwise having problems getting a document to print from an application, this suggests that the problem is with the document, the application, or some other Mac software rather than with the printer itself.

- **Show Info.** This command is used to configure a selected printer's options.

  SEE: • **" Changing printer configurations (Show Info)," later in this chapter, for details.**

- **Show Jobs.** This command opens the queue for the selected printer. The same thing happens if you double-click the name of the printer in the Printer List.

  SEE: • **"Take Note: Printer Queue (Proxy) Applications," below for related information.**

- **Stop Jobs.** This command stops any jobs that are currently in the queue of the selected printer. You can also do this via the Stop Jobs item in the Toolbar of the printer queue (if the queue is open).

- **Create Desktop Printer.** This creates an alias of the selected printer on the Finder's Desktop. If you double-click this icon, it opens the queue window/application, just as if you had selected Show Jobs from Printer Setup Utility's Printers menu. Even more useful, if you drag a document icon to a desktop printer, it immediately prints the selected document in its default application, bypassing the need to open the application and select the Print dialog!

  SEE: • **"Using Printer Setup Utility: Managing Print Jobs" and "Printing," later in this chapter, for more on these menus and on desktop printers.**

TAKE NOTE ▶ Printer Queue (Proxy) Applications

If you select Show Jobs for a selected printer or double-click the name of a printer in Printer Setup Utility's Printer List, a queue window for the printer opens. Each queue window is actually a separate application, often referred to as a *printer proxy application.*

You can tell that the window represents a separate application because when it launches, a separate icon opens in the Dock with the name of the printer. In addition, the menus in the printer application's menu bar shift from those accessed in Printer Setup Utility. For example, there is now a Jobs menu, from which you can select to delete, hold, or resume a job.

These printer proxy applications are stored in your ~/Library/Printers folder.

Creating a desktop printer. If you create a desktop printer for a printer, all you're really doing is creating an alias to the proxy application. You can delete these aliases from the Finder and re-create a new one any time you wish.

Deleting proxy applications. When you select to delete a printer from Printer Setup Utility's Printer List, its proxy application in ~/Library/Printers should also get deleted. If you created a desktop printer for this printer, however, that icon *does not* get deleted. If you double-click it, you'll get an error message stating that the original for the alias can no longer be found. The obvious solution is to delete the desktop printer.

continues on next page

TAKE NOTE ▶ Printer Queue (Proxy) Applications *continued*

Occasionally, you may find that a proxy application remains even after you've deleted the printer in Printer Setup Utility. This can cause immediate glitches because some Mac OS X features continue to access the proxy application, not realizing that the printer has been deleted from Printer Setup Utility. Similarly, if you later re-add a printer with an identical name, this can cause confusion as well. Thus, I recommend making sure that the printer proxy application in the ~/Library/Printers folder has been deleted after you delete a printer from Printer Setup Utility.

If you accidentally delete the proxy application for a printer that is still listed in the Printer List, delete the printer from the list and re-add it. Otherwise, it will no longer work.

Shared printers. When you select to access the queue of a shared printer, a proxy application is created for that printer. You can even create a desktop printer for the shared printer. Obviously, if the host computer later turns off Printer Sharing, you will no longer be able to print from the desktop printer. Instead, you will get an error stating the network host is busy (as shown in **Figure 7.40**).

SEE: • "Printer Sharing" and "Printer Queue window," later in this chapter, for related information.

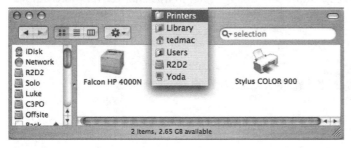

Figure 7.7
....
Printer proxy applications (Falcon HP and Stylus_COLOR) in ~/Library/Printers (left); a desktop printer icon on the Desktop (right).

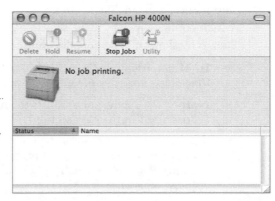

Figure 7.8
....

An example of a Printer Queue window that appears if you open a printer proxy application— by double-clicking the proxy application file itself, double-clicking a desktop printer file you created, or double-clicking the name of the printer (or selecting Show Jobs) in Printer Setup Utility.

Printer Setup Utility toolbar

Printer Setup Utility includes two toolbars, one for Printer List and the other for Fax List.

Printer List. The Printer List toolbar includes icons that mainly duplicate options that are also available from the Printer Setup Utility's menus. For example, you can select Show Info from the toolbar or from the Printers menu.

The only exception is ColorSync, for which there's no equivalent command. If you click this icon while a printer is selected, the ColorSync Utility (which is briefly described in Chapter 2) launches. From here, you can select a specific ColorSync profile for your printer. This can help improve the accuracy of which color documents get printed. Details of how this works, however, are beyond the scope of this book.

SEE: • "Printing," later in this chapter, for related information on selecting ColorSync settings from the Print dialog.

Fax List. From the Fax List toolbar, you can select Delete, Show Info, or Stop Jobs. These commands are specific to faxing and are separate from the same commands for the Printer List.

SEE: • "Printer Setup Utility and faxing," later in this chapter, for more details.

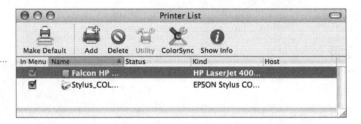

Figure 7.9

Printer Setup Utility's Printer List window, with its toolbar displayed.

Printer Setup Utility's Printer List window

The Printer List window lists every printer that you've added or that's been automatically added. There are several columns in the list. You can determine which columns appear by the selections you make in the View > Columns hierarchical menu. The default columns include the following:

*   **In Menu.** If you uncheck the In Menu box for a printer, its name no longer appears in Print and Page Setup dialogs.

*   **Name.** The Name column lists the name you assigned to the printer (as described in the next section).

*   **Status.** The Status column typically remains empty unless a print job is in progress (in which case it reports the current status of the job; for example, *Printing*) or you have selected to Stop Jobs (in which case it will say *Stopped*).

- **Kind.** The Kind column lists the model name as selected via the Printer Model option (as described in the next section). For PostScript printers, this is determined by the PPD file.

- **Host.** The Host column provides information about the Host computer to which the printer is connected.

SEE: • "Printer Sharing," later in this chapter.

Using Printer Setup Utility: Adding and Configuring Printers

Even though your printer's required software is installed on your drive, you can't print until you've added your printer to Printer Setup Utility's Printer List. Exactly how you do this depends on what type of printer you have. The following sections provide the details.

Note: Mac OS X locates and adds many printers automatically, thus bypassing the steps outlined in this section. However, you still may need to follow these steps to manually *reinstall* a printer (for troubleshooting reasons, as described throughout the chapter).

The first thing you do to add a printer is launch Printer Setup Utility. If no printers have been added yet, a dialog will appear asking if you want to add a printer. If you're ready to do so, click Add. Otherwise, click Cancel. This will leave an empty Printer List window. You can then add a printer at any later time by clicking the Add icon in window's toolbar.

Once you've added printers, those printers are listed in the Printer List window. From here, you can further configure them.

Adding a printer: an overview

To add a printer to the printer list, click the Add button in the toolbar. This brings up a dialog with a pop-up menu (at the top), where you can choose among different types of printer connections. At top of the menu you will see six options: AppleTalk, IP Printing, Open Directory, Rendezvous, USB, and Windows Printing. The bottom part of the dialog includes choices for specific printer brands, such as Epson AppleTalk, hp IP Printing, and Lexmark Inkjet Networking. The printer brands listed here vary according to whether you installed all the printer software when Mac OS X was installed. If your printer fits one of the categories included among the bottom choices, select it over a preference in the top section. (For example, I used the Epson AppleTalk option to add my Ethernet-connected Epson 900N printer.) Otherwise, pick from the top choices.

How do you know which choice to pick? In most cases, if you have a USB printer, pick USB. If your printer is on a network, USB or not, you will most likely select AppleTalk or IP Printing. If your printer supports Rendezvous, try that choice. You should only need Open Directory if you're connected to a network with printers accessed via a server. In any case, if no printers appear in the text area when you make a selection, try another choice. The main exception to this "try and see" rule is IP Printing, which does not list available printers but requires that you enter IP information.

In the following sections you will be instructed to select the printer model you're using. If your printer is not listed, it probably means that the needed printer driver software was not installed by Mac OS X. If this is because you did a custom install of Mac OS X and chose not to install the specific printer software, you should go back and install it (as described in Chapter 3). If the problem is that Mac OS X does not include the driver software, contact the printer vendor for the needed software or for other assistance.

For PostScript printers, if the printer model is an AppleTalk- or USB-connected printer, the PPD file for the correct model should be automatically selected via the Auto Select option, including the appropriate installable options. For a Rendezvous- or Open Directory–connected printer, the correct PPD file should also be automatically selected. IP-connected printers are the main exception here: For these printers, you almost always need to select a specific printer model.

Option key. If you hold down the Option key while choosing Add Printer, an Advanced option appears at the bottom of the pop-up menu. If you're knowledgeable about printer settings or have found the required information (such as from tips posted to Mac Web sites), you can use this option to configure a printer that might not otherwise work. Together with Gimp-Print, for example, the Advanced option can be used to enable an otherwise unsupported AppleTalk printer. However, in Panther, you may be able to access the Gimp-Print driver directly from the main choices (for example, USB).

SEE: • **"Take Note: Using Gimp-Print," elsewhere in this chapter, for details.**

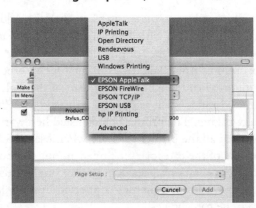

Figure 7.10

The Add Printer dialog that drops down after selecting the Add (printer) button from Printer Setup Utility's toolbar. The Add dialog's pop-up menu is shown: In this case, the Option key was held down to make the Advanced option appear.

Adding a USB printer

As described earlier in this chapter, after you plug a newer USB printer into a USB port on your Mac, Mac OS X should recognize the manufacturer and model automatically, select the appropriate PPD file (for PostScript printers) or driver (for non-PostScript printers), and set up a print queue for it in Printer Setup Utility. If you open Printer Setup Utility, your printer should already be listed by name/model.

If you have an older USB printer or Mac OS X did not recognize your printer automatically, you will need to add your printer manually. To do this, follow these steps:

1. Make sure the printer is on and connected. Launch Printer Setup Utility.

2. Click the Add button in the dialog that may appear; otherwise, click the Add button in the toolbar.

3. In the Add window that appears, from the pop-up menu choose USB. Your printer should appear in the list.

    Note: If there is a choice such as EPSON USB, and you have a printer by the named vendor (that is, Epson in this case), select this option in preference to the general USB choice.

    Note: If you're adding a printer accessed via an AirPort Extreme network, select Rendezvous instead of USB.

    SEE: • **"Adding a Printer via Rendezvous" and "Take Note: AirPort Extreme and Printer Sharing," later in this chapter, for more details.**

4. If the appropriate driver or PPD file is not auto-selected via the default Auto Select option, choose it from the Printer Model pop-up menu. To do so, select the printer brand (if it appears in the general USB window) and then select the model from the list that appears.

    If your printer model isn't listed, choose Other from the Printer Model pop-up menu and navigate to the appropriate driver/PPD for your printer (in the /Library/Printers folder). As a last resort, you can select Generic.

5. Select the printer name, and click the Add button.

    This returns you to the Printer List window, where the printer should be listed.

Note that some USB printers don't work properly when attached to a USB hub (including the hub built into Apple USB keyboards). If your supported USB printer does not show up in the Add dialog, make sure that it's attached directly to one of the USB ports on your Mac. Also make sure that the printer is attached and powered on before you start up the Mac.

Adding an AppleTalk printer

If you have an AppleTalk printer, here's what you need to do to get it to work with Mac OS X:

Enable AppleTalk. The first thing you need to do is make sure that AppleTalk is enabled for the appropriate network type. To do this, go to the Network System Preferences pane, and from the Show pop-up menu, choose the network port configuration by which your printer is connected (for example, Ethernet or AirPort). Check the AppleTalk tab and make sure that the Make AppleTalk Active checkbox is checked. AppleTalk can only be enabled for one configuration at a time. Thus, you cannot enable AppleTalk for both Ethernet and AirPort simultaneously.

In Panther, you may also need to enable AppleTalk in the Directory Access utility (in /Applications/Utilities). After you launch Directory Access, click the padlock icon at the bottom of the window to unlock it (if necessary), and then provide your admin-level user name and password when prompted. Make sure that AppleTalk is checked, and click the Apply button.

SEE: • Chapter 8 for much more on Network settings.

Use Printer Setup Utility. Once you've enabled AppleTalk, follow these steps:

1. Make sure the printer is on and connected, then launch Printer Setup Utility.

2. Click the Add button in the dialog that may appear; otherwise, click the Add button in the toolbar.

3. In the Add window that appears, from the pop-up menu choose AppleTalk. (If you're on a large, multizone AppleTalk network, you'll also need to select the appropriate zone from the second pop-up menu.) Your printer should appear in the list.

4. If the appropriate driver or PPD file is not auto-selected via the default Auto Select option, choose it from the Printer Model pop-up menu. To do so, select the brand of the printer and then select the model from the list that appears.

   If your printer model isn't listed, from the Printer Model pop-up menu choose Other, and navigate to the appropriate driver/PPD for your printer (in the /Library/Printers folder). As a last resort, you can select Generic.

5. From the Character Set pop-up menu at the bottom of the box listing available printers, make sure Western (Mac) is selected, assuming you're using English. Otherwise, the printer's name may be garbled in the Printer List window.

6. Select the printer name, and click the Add button.

   This takes you back to the Printer List dialog, where the printer should be listed.

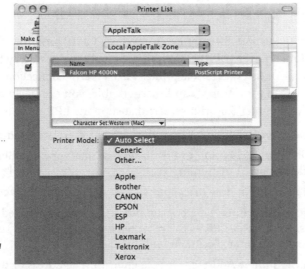

Figure 7.11

The AppleTalk option in Printer Setup Utility's Add dialog. In most cases, you can use the Auto Select option from the Printer Model menu as shown.

TAKE NOTE ▶ Using the Print Command to Get Summary Information

For many USB and AppleTalk printers, Printer Setup Utility selects a PPD or printer driver automatically, though it won't necessarily tell you what PPD or driver file it selected, and it may select a PPD that has a different name than the printer. Printer Setup Utility does not display this information; instead, the Printer Model pop-up menu simply states Auto-Select.

To find out what PPD file was selected, choose the Print command in any Mac OS X application, and then from the Printer pop-up menu choose the appropriate printer, and from the main options menu choose Summary. The PPD or printer driver selected by the OS will be displayed in the summary info for the printer.

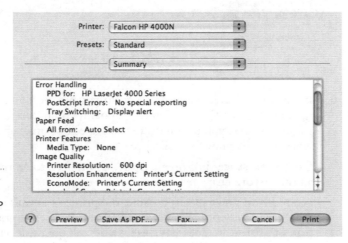

Figure 7.12

The summary information in the Print dialog shows the HP LaserJet 4000 Series as the PPD.

Adding a printer via IP Printing

Mac OS X supports IP printing via various TCP/IP protocols, the most common being Line Printer (LPR). The LPR protocol provides a way to print to a networked or Internet-accessible printer via a TCP/IP connection. If your printer is connected to your Mac via an Ethernet cable, you can likely use this option. If you have a printer (or print server) that supports LPR, here is how to set it up:

1. Make sure the printer is on and connected, then launch Printer Setup Utility.

2. Click the Add button in the dialog that may appear; otherwise, click the Add button in the toolbar.

3. In the Add window that appears, from the pop-up menu choose IP Printing.

4. From the Printer Type pop-up menu, select your desired printer type. I'm assuming LPD/LPR as the most likely choice; however, if this does not work, you can experiment with other choices.

5. In the Printer Address text box, enter the IP address or domain name of the printer or printer queue (see "Take Note: How Do You Determine the Printer's IP Address?" below).

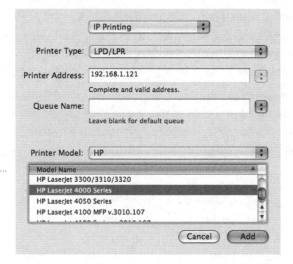

Figure 7.13

The IP Printing option in Printer Setup Utility's Add listings. Use this to set up an LPR printer.

6. If you want to give the printer a custom name, or if your printer requires it, enter it in the Queue Name text box. If you're accessing a printer on a larger network, you may need to use a specific name; check with the network administrator for assistance.

   Do not use spaces in a queue name; if you need to represent a space, use an underscore character instead.

   Note: If you don't specify a name, the printer's default queue is used—which is usually fine. However, on certain PostScript printers, if your printer's firmware does not specify a default queue, leaving this blank can cause print jobs to fail. In this case, the solution is to delete the printer from Printer Setup Utility and re-add it. When entering the settings for

IP Printing, enter a known queue name for the printer. Refer to your printer's manual for a list of proper IP or LPR queue names.

7. To select a PPD for the printer other than the default Generic setting (which may enable you to access specialized printer features not available via the generic PPD), from the Printer Model pop-up menu choose a PPD (typically one with the same name as your printer model).

8. Click the Add button.

This brings you back to the Printer List window, where the printer should be listed.

In many cases, a printer connected to an Ethernet network may work via either AppleTalk or IP printing. In this case, choose which method you wish to use when you set up the printer. Keep in mind, however, that using IP printing is generally faster and more reliable than using AppleTalk, which is a legacy technology that may eventually be phased out of Mac OS X.

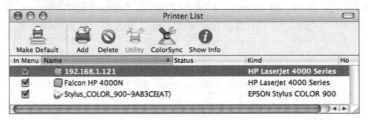

Figure 7.14

The LPR host printer, as set up in Figure 7.13, has been added to the Printer List window. It's the same HP 4000 printer listed in the second line in the Printer List; the second listing is for connecting to the printer via AppleTalk.

TAKE NOTE ▶ How Do You Determine the Printer's IP Address?

If your printer supports IP printing, you will need to enter its IP address (or domain name, if it has one) in the Printer Address text box within Printer Setup Utility's IP Printing settings. How do you find out what your printer's IP address is? The procedure varies, depending on your printer and network setup. Here's how I did it for my HP LaserJet 4000N printer:

1. Locate and launch the HP LaserJet utility that comes with the printer (and which currently runs only in Classic).

2. From the window that appears, choose the Settings tab from the column on the left and then choose the TCP/IP option from the "Please select a setting" list.

3. In the TCP/IP dialog that next appears, choose the option to manually specify a TCP/IP configuration.

4. Enter the information necessary to set up the printer as a device connected to your router, just as you would do for the Mac itself in the Network System Preferences pane (as described in Chapter 8). See **Figure 7.15** as an example.

continues on next page

TAKE NOTE ▶ **How Do You Determine the Printer's IP Address?**   *continued*

5. Launch Printer Setup Utility, click the Add button, and from the pop-up menu select IP Printing. Configure the printer as described in the main text, using the IP address you set up as the one you enter in the Printer Address text box.

Note: If you enter an incorrect IP address in Printer Setup Utility, the printer will still be added to the Printer List; you just won't be able to print to it.

"hp IP Printing" option. If you select "hp IP Printing" from the Add pop-up menu instead, you get a window with two main buttons: Auto and Manual. From the Add dialog, if you click the Discover button, it should find any auto-discoverable (Rendezvous-enabled) IP printers on the network. If it does not find the one you want, and you know its IP address, you can select Manual instead. From this screen, enter the IP address and select Connect. If it locates the printer, it should appear in the list below. In either case, you can now click the Add button.

Or at least that's the theory: I was unable to get this to work. I could add my HP printer via the standard IP Printing selection but not via "hp IP Printing." With "hp IP Printing," the printer was neither discovered in Auto nor listed in Manual (after I entered its IP address).

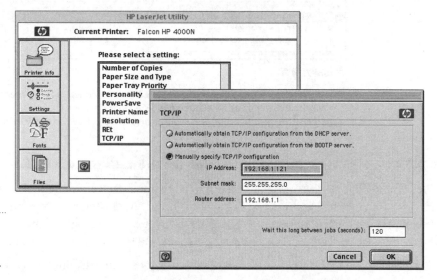

Figure 7.15
....
*Setting up an IP
address via the
HP LaserJet utility
(running in Classic).*

Adding a Printer via Rendezvous

Rendezvous is Apple's zero-configuration networking protocol. It eliminates the need to enter the IP address of an IP-connected printer, as described in the previous section. Instead, the Mac discovers the printer on its own and lists it. All the work is done for you. However, for this magic to occur, the printer must be "Rendezvous enabled." All major printer vendors have announced their support for this technology, and a few such printers are already available. Expect this to be a common feature of Mac-compatible printers in the years ahead.

In most cases, a Rendezvous-enabled printer will be automatically detected and set up—that is, you won't need to select to add a printer. Remember, however, that this only works for printers on the same *subnet* of the same local network as your Mac. Printers on another subnet of your network cannot be connected via Rendezvous, even if they're Rendezvous-enabled.

If for some reason a printer you expected to see via Rendezvous does not appear, you can attempt to add it manually. To do so, select to add a printer and from the pop-up menu select Rendezvous. Any Rendezvous-enabled printers should appear. After that, follow the instructions for adding a USB printer.

For printers on a TCP/IP network, if the above does not work, from the same pop-up menu where you selected Rendezvous, select IP Printing instead. Then, from the Printer Type pop-up menu select Rendezvous. You don't need to enter an IP address at this point; the Printer Address field is thus disabled. Otherwise, follow the instructions from the preceding "Adding a Printer via IP Printing" section.

SEE: • **"Adding a USB printer," earlier in this chapter.**

• **Chapter 8, for more on Rendezvous.**

Adding a printer via Open Directory

Mac OS X supports several types of network services, such as NetInfo (which is part of Mac OS X) and LDAP. Used mostly in large networked environments, Open Directory provides a way for users to print to shared printers on these networks. To add a printer by using Open Directory, follow these steps:

1. Launch Printer Setup Utility.
2. Click the Add button in the dialog that may appear; otherwise, click the Add button on the toolbar.
3. In the Add dialog that appears, from the pop-up menu choose Open Directory.
4. Select a printer from any that appear in the list.
5. Click the Add button.

    This brings you back to the Printer List window, where the printer should be listed.

Note that with Directory Services, you don't have the option of selecting a PPD or printer model because the printing queue has already been set up by a network administrator somewhere else on the network.

Note: For this to work, the printer must be registered in a directory service accessed by your computer. To check which services you've enabled for access, use the Directory Access utility (which is described in more detail in Chapter 4).

Adding a Windows printer

With Mac OS X, you can print to a printer shared by a Windows computer via SMB, by doing the following:

1. Launch Printer Setup Utility.

2. Click the Add button in the dialog that may appear; otherwise, click the Add button in the toolbar.

3. In the Add window that appears, from the pop-up menu choose Windows Printing.

4. From the WORKGROUP pop-up menu select the desired network workgroup, or select Network Neighborhood to find a local workgroup and then select it from the list that appears. Click the Choose button.

   Any Windows printers in your selected network should now appear in the Printer List.

SEE: • **Chapter 8 for more on SMB sharing and workgroup selections.**

Adding and using unsupported printers

If the default drivers that come with Mac OS X don't support your printer, you may simply need to install additional software from your printer's vendor: Check for software that came with the printer or go to the vendor's Web site.

Some printer models that have no specific driver software will still work in Mac OS X if you choose a similar printer driver from the Printer Model pop-up menu or (for PostScript printers) if you choose the generic PPD file. Some Epson inkjet printers that don't have Mac OS X drivers, for example, work fairly well with the drivers for similar Epson printers. Keep in mind, though, that if you try this method, you may not get your printer's full functionality and you might experience problems printing. If this is the only way you can use your unsupported printer, however, it's worth a try.

In some cases, advanced users have hacked a driver designed to work with one printer so that it works with similar printers. Such hacks are available on the Web. Again, use such methods with caution: They may cause problems due to the unintended way in which they are used.

Finally, you can use Gimp-Print to get an unsupported printer to work.

SEE: • **"Take Note: Using Gimp-Print," later in this chapter, for information on using this driver.**

TECHNICALLY SPEAKING ▶ Creating a PostScript File for Printing

Although most people choose to print directly to a printer, it's sometimes useful to save a file in PostScript format. This way, the file is saved in the language of PostScript printers, which means you can later send it to a printer without opening any application.

You can save a Microsoft Word file as PostScript, for example, and later send the file to an LPR printer via Terminal without opening Word. Similarly, you can save a document from within a Mac OS X application and then boot in Mac OS 9 (or, in some cases, use Classic) to print the document on a printer that does not support Mac OS X. In the latter case, however, it's probably simpler to save the file as a PDF document, as described in "Take Note: Why and How to Create PDF Files," later in this chapter.

Creating a PostScript file. To create a PostScript file, open the document you want to convert, then follow these steps:

1. From the File menu of a Mac OS X application, choose Print.
2. In the Print dialog that appears, from the Printer menu choose your desired PostScript printer.
3. From the pop-up menu showing Copies & Pages, choose Output Options. The dialog changes to display the options available.
4. Check the Save as File box that now appears in the dialog.
5. From the Format menu Choose PostScript.
   The Print button will change to Save.
6. Save the file, in PostScript format, in your desired location.

PostScript files saved in this manner will automatically launch in Preview when double-clicked from the Finder; Preview then converts the files to PDF documents.

Creating a virtual printer. When you save to PostScript, you're really "printing" to a PostScript printing queue on your own computer. If you don't have a PostScript printer set up in Printer Setup Utility, and no such printer is connected to your Mac, the option to save as a PostScript file does not appear. You can work around this by creating a virtual printing queue. To do this, follow these steps:

1. Launch Printer Setup Utility and click the Add button.
2. From the pop-up menu in the dialog that appears, choose IP Printing.
3. For Printer Type, select LPD/LPR.
4. In the Printer's Address text box, type localhost.
5. Choose Generic PPD or a particular PPD file (if you know what printer you'll be printing to).
6. Optionally, add your own queue name (for example, Virtual-Printer).
7. Click the Add button. Your PostScript "printer" is now ready.

To create a PostScript file using this printer, select the name of the virtual printer from the Printer pop-up menu in the Print dialog, then follow the instructions above.

continues on next page

TECHNICALLY SPEAKING ▶ **Creating a PostScript File for Printing** *continued*

Printing PostScript files from Terminal. You can send a PostScript file directly to an LPR printer for printing. If you have an LPR printer set up, launch Terminal and type the following:

```
lpr -P printername filepathname.ps
```

You can also print a PostScript file to an AppleTalk printer. However, to do this you must enable the at command via the crontab file (as described in "Technically Speaking: Terminal Commands to Monitor and Improve Performance," in Chapter 10). The need to do all of this, however, is sufficiently rare that I'm omitting the details.

Changing printer configurations (Show Info)

After you've added a printer, you may later want to change the settings you created. To do so, you can use the Show Info command.

Show Info also gives you access to some options not available when you first set up the printer. And if you want to make changes that even Show Info does not allow, you may be able to do so via the CUPS Web interface, described later in this chapter. In some cases, you may be able to make changes via a separate utility accessed by the Configure Printer command, as described earlier in this chapter. Otherwise, your last resort is to delete the printer, making the desired changes when you re-add it.

Using Show Info. To use Show Info, follow these steps:

1. Select the printer you want to modify.

2. From the Printers menu choose Show Info, or click the Show Info icon in the toolbar. The Printer Info window opens.

3. From the pop-up menu at the top of the window, choose among the following options:

    Name & Location. You can rename a printer from here or give it a location. Assigning a location (such as a room number) can be useful if people using the printer may not know where to collect their output.

    This window also lists the driver version—useful if you need to determine whether you're using the latest version.

    Printer Model. This allows you to change the printer model (for example, PPD file for PostScript printers) from what you initially selected when you added the printer. To make a change, select a vendor from the pop-up menu and then select a model from the list that appears.

    Installable Options. The options available here depend on the printer model selected. If your printer supports optional features, such as Duplex Printing or an Envelope Feeder (and you have those features installed), this is where you enable or modify them.

You may also find some software options in this window, such as what the printer should do if a document is too big to fit on a page (for example, prompt user for a choice versus automatically shrink to fit versus automatically crop).

If you don't see the options you expected to find, you may not have selected the correct vendor and model when you first added the printer. To fix this, select the Printer Model option noted above.

4. Click the Apply Changes button.

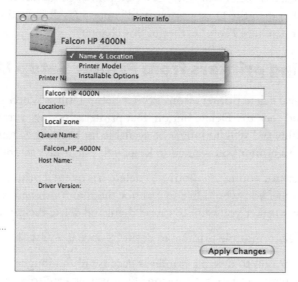

Figure 7.16

Printer Setup Utility's Printer Info window.

Limitations of Show Info. You will not be able to use Show Info to change settings for printers that are shared by other Macs on your network. To change settings for such printers, you must access Printer Setup Utility from the computer to which the printer is connected directly.

You also cannot use Show Info to configure a USB printer connected to your computer using AirPort Extreme. You must connect the printer directly to your computer to make changes (after which you can reconnect it to the AirPort Extreme Base Station).

Setting and changing the default printer

If you've added more than one printer, you'll notice that one printer's name is in bold in Printer Setup Utility's Printer List window, while the rest are in plain text. The bold text indicates the default printer.

If you have multiple printers set up in Printer Setup Utility, the default printer is the one that's used when you select to print unless you switch to another printer by choosing it from the pop-up menu in the Print dialog (as described in "Printing," later in the chapter).

If you want to change the current default printer, click its name in Printer Setup Utility and then click the Make Default button in the toolbar, or from the Printers menu select Make Default (Command-D).

Note: If you switch to a different printer in the Print dialog, the selected printer may become the new default printer. To prevent this switch, you need to go to the Print & Fax System Preferences pane and select the name of the desired default printer from the "Selected printer in the Print dialog" pop-up menu rather than the "Last printer used" option (as described in "Print & Fax System Preferences Pane," earlier in this chapter).

Deleting printers from Printer Setup Utility

You can also delete printers from Printer Setup Utility. When you select a printer and click the Delete button, that printer is removed from Printer Setup Utility and will no longer be available for printing. (Don't worry: If you delete a printer you wanted to keep, you can always re-add it.)

If a printer that you're attempting to delete has queued print jobs, you will be asked whether you would like to wait for them to finish before deleting the printer, or whether you want to cancel them and delete the printer immediately.

You can select multiple printers to delete at once if you wish.

The main reason to delete a printer is because it's no longer connected or you no longer intend to use it. Occasionally, you may want to delete a printer (and re-add it) even when you do intend to use it. One reason to do this is if you change languages for Mac OS X (via the International System Preferences pane). Deleting and re-adding the printer ensures that dialogs related to the printer appear in the newly selected language. Another reason to delete and re-add a printer is to fix problems with the printer, as described in "Deleting and re-adding a printer," later in this chapter.

SEE: • **"Take Note: Printer Queue (Proxy) Applications" and "Take Note: Showing and Hiding Printers," earlier in this chapter, for important related information about deleting printers from Printer Setup Utility.**

TAKE NOTE ▶ Updating PPD Files

Printer manufacturers often provide updated or improved printer drivers and PPD files (often via a software download). If you have already installed and are using a PostScript printer in Mac OS X and later install an updated PPD file, you probably won't be able to simply select the new PPD file. You need to delete the printer in Printer Setup Utility.

SEE: • **"Deleting corrupt print jobs," later in this chapter, for related information.**

Printer Sharing

Starting in Mac OS X 10.2, you can share printers that are connected to your computer. Mac OS 9 includes a similar feature; however, it's limited to USB printers. In Mac OS X, it works with any type of printer connection—USB, IP, whatever.

Enabling Printer Sharing

To allow other computers on your local network to share your printers, open System Preferences and select the Sharing pane. From the Services screen either (a) check the box next to Printer Sharing, or (b) select Printer Sharing and click the Start button. As a third alternative, you can select the "Share my printers with other computers" option in the Print & Fax System Preferences pane. Your sharable printers will now appear in the Printer List of the Printer Setup Utility of other Macs on your network. Conversely, you will see printers that other users have shared in your own Printer Setup Utility.

When someone selects to print a document to your shared printer, your hard drive holds the queue information for the document. Thus, you obviously cannot print to a shared printer unless the computer to which it is connected is on. This also means that if problems occur with printing the document, they must be diagnosed from the Printer Setup Utility application on the computer to which the printer is connected.

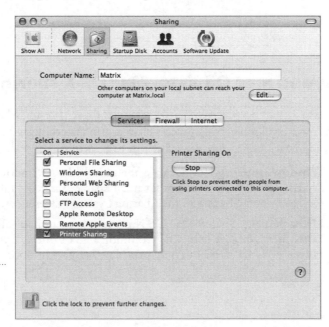

Figure 7.17

The Printer Sharing option selected in the Sharing System Preferences pane.

To access shared printers from your Mac

If Printer Sharing has been enabled on another Mac OS X computer on your network, any sharable printers connected to that computer should appear automatically in your Mac OS X Printer List, without any further action needed.

If you click the disclosure triangle next to the Shared Printers heading in the Printer List, a complete list of shared printers will be displayed. Likewise, if you select the Printer pop-up menu in Print dialogs, a Shared Printers sub-menu will list the printers shared by other Macs on your local network.

If you select to Show Jobs for a shared printer, a queue window will open for the printer. You can monitor the progress of print jobs from here. You can also select to delete a job waiting to be printed. However, you cannot select the Hold Job or Stop Jobs commands; you can only choose these from the computer to which the printer is directly connected.

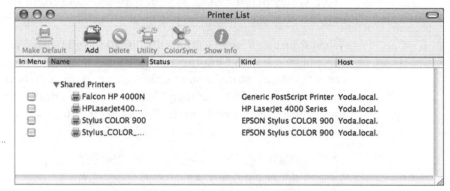

Figure 7.18

Shared printers listed in the Printer List window.

Beyond Mac OS X–to–Mac OS X sharing

Users not running Mac OS X (for example, those running Mac OS 9, Windows, or Unix) can also access shared printers connected to a computer running Mac OS X. Here are a few tips to bear in mind:

- **Windows sharing.** To make a printer available to Windows users (via SMB), the Mac OS X computer must enable Windows File Sharing as well as Printer Sharing in the Sharing System Preferences pane.

- **Unix sharing.** Shared Mac OS X printers are automatically available to Unix users who are using the Common Unix Printing System (CUPS). However, Unix users can only print PostScript print jobs.

- **Mac OS 9 sharing.** If you want Mac OS 9 users to be able to access a USB printer on your Mac OS X Mac, you need to make sure Classic is running, and then separately enable this feature via Mac OS 9's USB Printer Sharing control panel in Classic. Turning on Printer Sharing in Mac OS X has no effect on Mac OS 9 sharing. The Mac OS 9 user will need to access your printer via the Desktop Printer Utility.

  Unfortunately, you can't easily enable both Mac OS X and Mac OS 9 printer sharing. If you need such functionality, you'll need to do a bit of extra homework. See the following Apple Knowledge Base document for details: http://docs.info.apple.com/article.html?artnum=107060.

For more details on these sharing variations, check Mac OS X's Help files and enter *printer sharing* as the search term.

SEE: • "Take Note: Troubleshooting Shared Printers," later in this chapter.

TAKE NOTE ▶ AirPort Extreme and Printer Sharing

Apple's latest version of its AirPort Base Station is called AirPort Extreme. It includes a USB port to which you can connect a USB printer. This printer can then be accessed by all users on the wireless network. Although this setup works similarly to the Printer Sharing feature described in the main text, it has the advantage that the printer is available to any user on the network without having to go through another computer (and thus without having to worry whether or not that computer is currently on).

When first set up, the printer can be shared by all users on your local network. It should appear in Printer Setup Utility automatically as a Rendezvous-connected printer. If not, you can add it as a Rendezvous printer (select Rendezvous from the Add Printer window). If even this fails, you may have an AirPort-incompatible printer. See the following page for a list of AirPort Extreme–compatible printers and some basic advice on setting up the printer: www.apple .com/airport/printcompatibility.html.

In any case, some printer features, such as error messages and access to printer utilities, may not function when connected via AirPort Extreme. To access these features, you will need to connect the printer directly to your Mac.

Computers connected via the Base Station's WAN port cannot access the shared printer. However, using the AirPort Admin Utility, you can configure the Base Station so that the printer can be accessed in Printer Setup Utility via Rendezvous. The simplest method is to turn on WAN-LAN bridging: To do so, simply uncheck the Distribute IP Addresses box in the Show All Settings > Network screen of the AirPort Admin Utility. For more details, see the following Apple Knowledge Base article: http://docs.info.apple.com/article.html?artnum=107511.

SEE: • "Setting Up System Preferences: Sharing," in Chapter 8, for more on Printer Sharing and sharing in general.

 • Chapter 8 for more on AirPort and wireless connections.

Determining the host name and location (unshared and shared)

To find out which computer is connected to a given printer, you can hold the pointer over the printer's name in the Printer pop-up menu of the Print dialog. A tool tip with the information will appear. You need to click-hold to bring up the menu for these notes to appear.

For printers connected to your computer or connected on your local network but not shared by another Mac, the Host should say Local. For shared printers, the Host name indicates the shared host to which the printer is connected. For example, if you're sharing a printer connected to a computer named Yoda on your local network, the Host name will read Yoda.local.

If a location was assigned to a printer (via the Show Info window in Printer Setup Utility), it will appear in the yellow note as well. This is a quick way to determine a printer's physical location.

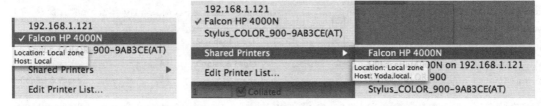

Figure 7.19

The Printer pop-up menu in the Print dialog with host information in the yellow note box for (left) an unshared printer and (right) a shared printer.

SEE: • **"Changing printer configurations (Show Info)," earlier in this chapter.**

Alternatively, you can access this same host information from the Host column of the Printer List in Printer Setup Utility. For printers directly connected to your computer, the Host column will either be blank or read Local (as in the yellow notes described above). Otherwise, the Host name will again indicate the host to which the printer is connected.

If you do not see a Host column, you can enable it by selecting Host from the View > Columns submenu in Printer Setup Utility.

You cannot delete a shared printer from the Printer List. If you try, it will momentarily vanish and then return. However, via the In Menu column, you can prevent a given printer from showing up in Print and Page Setup dialogs.

SEE: • **"Printer Setup Utility's Printer List window," earlier in this chapter.**

Printing

After you've set up your printer(s) in Printer Setup Utility, you're ready to print. You have two main options:

You can print a document from an application. In most cases (assuming you don't want to modify default settings and no problems occur), printing is as simple as choosing Print from the File menu of an application that can open the desired document. In the standard Print dialog that appears, select the number of copies you want and (optionally) the desired page range. Then click the Print button. That's it. If desired, you can select additional options in the Print and Page Setup dialogs (which I describe in following sections).

Once you've selected Print, the Printer Queue application for the default printer launches, and its icon appears in the Dock. Your document is then printed. When it's no longer needed for the selected job(s), the Printer Queue application closes automatically and its icon disappears from the Dock (unless you manually placed it in the Dock, in which case it will remain there).

You can print a document from the Finder or Printer Setup Utility. You can print a document directly from the Finder if you previously created a Desktop Printer for the desired printer. To do so, simply drag the document icon to the Desktop Printer icon.

If, instead, you drag the document icon to the Printer Setup Utility icon, it also prints—using the default printer. Similarly, if you launch Printer Setup Utility, open the Printer Queue window for any listed printer and drag a document to the Queue window—the document will print to the selected printer.

If you have two or more printers, you can even drag a pending print job from the queue list of one printer to that of another printer. This works in most cases, although it may fail if the printers are of different types (from example, non-PostScript versus PostScript).

In all of these cases, the creating application opens, but the document itself does not and the Print dialog is bypassed. One exception: If the document is a PDF or PostScript file, it will print without a creating application opening.

Note: There is no Print command in the Finder's File menu in the release version of Panther. However, this command appeared and disappeared over various beta builds of Panther. If Apple should add it back in a future update to Mac OS X, you could also print a document by using this command.

SEE: • **"Take Note: Printer Queue (Proxy) Applications," earlier in this chapter.**

   • **"Printer Queue Window," later in this chapter.**

TAKE NOTE ▶ Printing Finder Windows

Because the Finder doesn't include a Print command, there's no automatic way to print a list of the contents of a Finder window. There are, however, work-arounds; try these:

- Drag a folder icon to the Printer Setup Utility icon. If a Printer Setup Utility icon is in the Dock, you can just drag the folder to the Dock icon.

- If you've created a desktop printer for the desired printer, you can alternatively drag the folder icon to the Desktop Printer icon.

A Print dialog will appear. Select to print, and you should get a text listing of all items in the folder, including their names, sizes, and date last modified. Note: Occasionally, this has failed to work for me (for example, I once got an error stating that the desktop printer could not be opened); however, updating to Mac OS X 10.3.1 improved the reliability.

SEE: • **"The Jaguar Way: Print Center on the Dock," elsewhere in this chapter, for related information.**

THE JAGUAR WAY ▶ Print Center on the Dock

If you're still using Jaguar, I recommend that you make Print Center a permanent icon on your Dock (by dragging its icon from the Utilities folder to the Dock) or that you make an alias of Print Center on your Desktop. This serves two purposes.

- It makes it easier to launch Print Center when needed for troubleshooting.

- If you drag a document to the Print Center icon, Print Center will print it via the selected default printer—even if the needed application is not open. Depending on the application called, it may do this without displaying a Print or confirming dialog. Or it may halt at the Print dialog, giving you the option to modify settings before printing. In either case, it's very convenient.

With Panther, Printer Setup Utility can be set up in the Dock as well. However, it's far less critical to create a permanent Dock icon or an alias, because Printer Setup Utility's desktop printers (as described in the main text) substitute for these items. You can also place the Print Queue application for one or more printers in the Dock, and then print to a printer by simply dragging a document icon onto a printer in the Dock.

Page Setup

You can access the Page Setup dialog from the File menu of any application that can print. Usually, you'll only require the Page Setup dialog if you want to modify the default layout settings—not a common requirement.

Basic options. The first item in this dialog is the Settings pop-up menu. Three of its options are available in all applications:

- **Page Attributes.** With the Page Attributes item selected (which is what you see when the Page Setup dialog first opens), you can choose from several options in the remainder of the window:

    Paper Size—for choosing a size other than the default.

    Orientation—for selecting among portrait, landscape, and reverse landscape.

    Scale—for reducing or enlarging the copy by a given percentage.

    Format for—the default selection here is Any Printer. Some printers have special formatting requirements for a page to print correctly. If you're having problems with the Any Printer option, select the printer name from the pop-up menu that matches the printer you will be using.

    SEE: • "Tke Note: Why and How to Create PDF Files," elsewhere in this chapter, for related information.

    The changes you make to these attributes will be applied to all documents that are currently open in the application containing the selected document, as well as any new documents that you create in the application (while it's still open).

- **Custom Paper Size.** You can use this option to design a paper size other than those listed in Paper Size.

- **Summary.** This option simply provides a table that summarizes your settings, along with a bit more detail about what those settings mean (such as the current margin settings in the application).

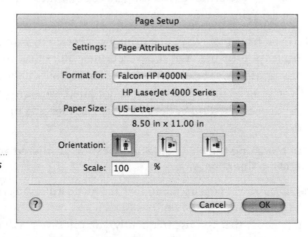

Figure 7.20

The Page Attributes option of the Page Setup dialog, formatted for an HP printer.

Application-specific options. Applications may provide additional options. For example, Microsoft Word adds its own Settings screen, which provides its own options for custom page sizes and paper-feed method, and allows you to apply the Page Setup settings to only part of the document, if desired.

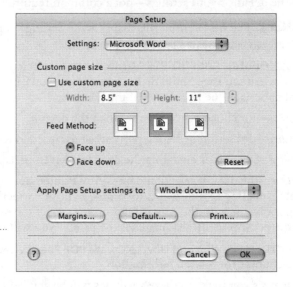

Figure 7.21

Microsoft Word's additional Page Setup options.

Print

As already mentioned, when you're ready to print a document, you can simply choose Print from the application's File menu. In the Print dialog that appears, you can select from a variety of options before printing the document. Note that unlike settings in the Page Setup dialog, changes in the Print dialog only apply to the document about to be printed. The following paragraphs describe the options. For basic printing, you can ignore all of these options and immediately click the Print button.

Printer. If you have more than one printer connected to your Mac, you can use the Printer pop-up menu to choose a printer other than the default printer. Any printer you set up in Printer Setup Utility will be available in this menu. If you want to use a printer that is not listed, you can choose Edit Printer List to open the Printer Setup Utility and then add or delete printers as needed.

SEE: • "Determining the host name and location (unshared and shared)," earlier in this chapter.

Presets. The Presets pop-up menu lists the Standard settings by default. If you have a particular group of settings (which you created by modifying the following options) that you use frequently, you can save it as a custom preset and choose it at any later time from this menu.

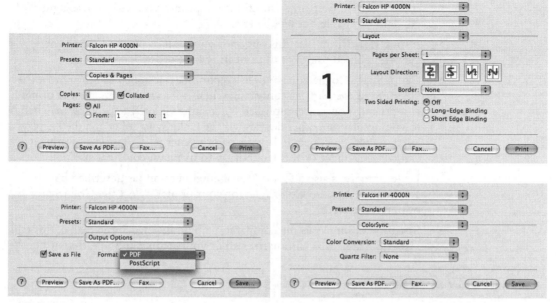

Figure 7.22

Several of the option screens in the Print dialog (as accessed from TextEdit): (top left) Copies & Pages; (top right) Layout; (bottom left) Output Options; and (bottom right) Color Sync.

Printing options. Just below the Presets pop-up menu is an unnamed pop-up menu, commonly called either Printing Options or Copies & Pages (because that's the default item in the menu). The options in this menu vary by application and printer. The following options are almost always listed:

- **Copies & Pages.** These options allow you to select the number of copies to print (and, if you print multiple copies, whether they should be collated or printed by page), as well as whether to print the entire document or a subset of pages.

- **Layout.** These options allow you to print multiple document pages on each piece of printer paper, as well as to arrange the pages. You can also choose to include a thin border around each page. On the left is a sample printer sheet that shows you how document pages will be printed.

- **Output Options.** These options allow you to save the current document as a PostScript file or PDF file. To do so, check the Save as File box, and choose PDF or PostScript as the format. If you choose this option, the Print button at the bottom of the window will change to Save; click it to save the file. Next, give the document a name, specify where to save it, and then click Save.

    SEE: • "Technically Speaking: Creating a PostScript File for Printing," earlier in this chapter, and "Take Note: Why and How to Create PDF Files," later in this chapter.

- **Scheduler.** This is where you can set a print document to be printed at some specified later time—useful if the printer you wish to use is not currently available but will be later.

- **Paper Handling.** Use this option if you want to print only odd- or even-numbered pages, or to print in reverse order.

- **ColorSync.** ColorSync is Apple's technology designed to ensure that the color of a image remains consistent, whether it's viewed onscreen or printed to a printer. This is accomplished by creating ColorSync profiles, matched to your display and other devices, via the ColorSync utility and the Displays System Preferences pane. If your color printer is "ColorSync aware," it can take advantage of this technology to maintain color consistency.

  Note: If there is also a Color Management option (as described below) and you want to use ColorSync for your printer, select the ColorSync option from there.

- **Summary.** Similar to the companion tab in the Page Setup dialog, this tab presents a table that summarizes all of your settings in the different tabs.

TECHNICALLY SPEAKING ▶ Using ColorSync

The details of how to use the ColorSync printing options are not only largely beyond the scope of this book, but they're also beyond the needs of most Mac users. However, if you do need these features, check the Help files for ColorSync Utility for assistance.

For starters, here are two tips regarding the ColorSync option in the Print dialog:

- From the Color Conversion pop-up menu, select Standard if you want the application you're using to control the color management of the printed output, or select In Printer if you want the printer you're using to control the color management of the printed output.

- From the Quartz Filter pop-up menu, select a filter to vary the appearance of a specific document (for example, adding a sepia tone). The filters are stored in /System/Library/Filters. You can modify a filter, create a new one, or view how a file will look with a filter selected via the Filters option in ColorSync. Select Add Filters from the Quartz Filter pop-up menu to directly open a PDF preview of your document in ColorSync; you can select different filters from here.

Other common options available in this pop-up menu, depending on the selected printer, include the following:

- **Error Handling.** For PostScript printers, you can choose to ignore the reporting of PostScript errors or to have your printer create a detailed report. This screen also provides printer-specific options such as Tray Switching, which specifies what to do when a tray runs out of paper on a multiple-tray printer.

- **Paper Feed.** If your printer has multiple paper trays or feeds (an envelope feed, a manual feed slot, and so on), you can specify which tray you want to use. You can even have the first page come from one source and the rest of the document come from another source. (This option is frequently used for letterhead for the first page of multipage correspondence.) The options here may vary because they're typically provided by the printer driver or PPD for the printer chosen in the Printer pop-up menu.

- **Image Quality.** This is another option where you may find menus for selecting a printer's resolution or levels of gray.

- **Printer Features.** This screen, which is common for laser printers, allows you to modify other printer-specific features, such as the type of paper used and printing resolution.

- **Print Settings** (may also be called Print Mode or Print Quality). Common for inkjet printers, this screen allows you to specify the paper, ink (black or color), and/or print quality you desire.

- **Color Management.** This includes printer-specific options for adjusting how screen colors are translated to printed colors.

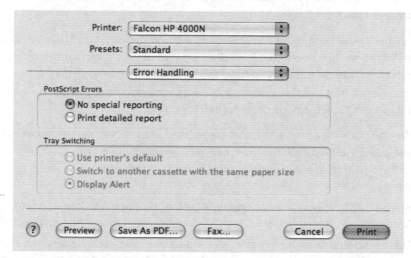

Figure 7.23

The Error Handling screen in the Print dialog (as accessed from TextEdit).

Applications may also provide a menu choice, usually named after the application, that provides extra options specific to the application. Most of these application- and printer-specific options are determined by the PPD and/or PDE files that are installed.

Note that a few applications, such as iPhoto, may initially display a completely customized Print dialog. In the case of iPhoto, you can still get to the standard options by clicking the Advanced Options button.

SEE: • **"Take Note: PDE Files," later in this chapter, for details on PDE files.**

• **"What types of printer connections does Mac OS X support?" and "How do I tell if my printer is already supported?" earlier in this chapter, for more information on PPD files.**

TAKE NOTE ▶ PDE Files

PDE (Printer Dialog Extension) files allow an application or printer (PostScript or non-PostScript) to add application- or printer-specific options in the Print dialog. (Note: These files differ from the PPD files described earlier in this chapter. PPD files allow Mac OS X's built-in PostScript driver to support features specific to a particular PostScript printer.)

PDE files determine what options are available in the Printing Options pop-up menu—such as the Output Options and Error Handling options noted in the main text. A standard suite of these files is installed with Mac OS X. Additional ones may be installed by other software.

In Panther, the Mac OS X–installed PDE files are buried in a framework within the System folder. A separate set of these files exists for each language installed. For example, the English language PDEs are stored in the following location:

/System/Library/Frameworks/Carbon.framework/Versions/A/Frameworks/Print.framework/Versions/A/Resources/ English.lproj/

The files here have names like ErrorHandling.nib and PaperHandling.nib, which correspond to options of the same name in the Print dialog. If you double-click one of these files, it opens up in Interface Builder (assuming you have the Developer software installed). From here, you see the same layout that's visible in the Print dialog. For example, if you open PaperHandling.nib, you will see the "Reverse page order" option and so on.

Note: In Mac OS X 10.1, these PDE files are located in a PDEs folder in /System/Library/Printers. They include a .pde extension rather than .nib. Personally, I find this location and name extension more logical than the current arrangement, but Apple must have had its reasons for the change.

Printer-specific PDE files. Printer-specific PDE files for most non-Apple printers (PostScript and non-PostScript) are stored in various subdirectories of the /Library/Printers directory. For example:

- PDEs for several brands of PostScript printers (for example, Lexmark and Hewlett-Packard) are stored in the /Library/Printers/PPD Plugins folder in this directory. These plug-in files are packages, so you can use the Show Package Contents command to examine their contents.

- For non-PostScript Hewlett-Packard DeskJet printers, there is a PDE file called hpdjPDE.plugin, located in the /Library/Printers/hp/deskjet/directory. There is also a separate /Library/Printers/hp/PDEs directory that contains several separate .plugin files representing different PDEs.

- For Epson printers, inside /Library/Printers/EPSON is a .plugin file for each supported printer. Select a file (SC900.plugin for example) and use Show Package Contents to navigate to Contents/Resources/PDEs. Inside this folder you will find the PDE .plugins for the named printer.

Application-specific PDE files. Some applications add their own PDE-file-based options to the Print dialog. These application-specific PDEs are typically located inside the application package. Microsoft Word v. X is one exception: Its PDE file, WordPDE.plugin, is located in the Office folder inside the Microsoft Office X folder.

Bottom buttons. The bottom of the Print dialog contains five buttons: Preview, Save As PDF, Fax, Cancel, and Print/Save.

- **Preview.** This option creates a temporary PDF file of the current document and opens it in Mac OS X's Preview application.

- **Save As PDF.** The Save as PDF button is the most convenient way to save a document as a PDF file, eliminating the need for the Preview button and the Output Options selection.

     SEE: • "Why and How to Create PDF Files," below, for more details on the Preview and Save As PDF options.

- **Fax.** I discuss this option later in this chapter in "Faxing."

- **Cancel.** Click this button to exit the Print dialog without printing.

- **Print/Save.** This is the most important button in the entire window: You click it to print your document. If you've chosen to save the document as a PDF or PostScript file (via Output Options), the button name will change to Save.

Figure 7.24

The bottom row of buttons in the Print dialog (top) before and (bottom) after enabling PDF Services. The PDF Workflow buttons are displayed in the latter case.

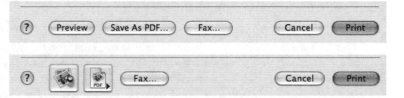

TAKE NOTE ▶ **Why and How to Create PDF Files**

PDF stands for *Portable Document Format*. Adobe created the format.

Why to create PDF files. Saving a document as a PDF file can be useful for two related reasons:

- PDF files can be viewed on almost any platform via the free Adobe Reader (formerly called Acrobat Reader) application or any other PDF-compatible application (such as Preview in Mac OS X)—great if you need to send a document to someone who does not have the application you used to create it. Even Windows users can open a PDF file created on a Mac without any need for file conversion.

- A PDF file can be created from any document. All text, graphics, and formatting are embedded within the PDF file. This means that the PDF file of the document can be viewed just as it looked in the original application. You don't even have to worry whether the recipient of the file has the appropriate fonts or styles installed.

continues on next page

TAKE NOTE ▶ **Why and How to Create PDF Files** *continued*

The one (admittedly small) drawback is that PDF files are formatted for the specific printer you choose when you "print" them. If the recipient prints a PDF file on a printer that is drastically different from yours, he or she may experience minor margin or spacing issues. Note: The "Format for" option in the Page Setup dialog may help prevent problems here. For example, if you know what printer the recipient has installed, and you have the same printer, select it here before creating the PDF file. Otherwise, use Any Printer.

How to create PDF files. In Mac OS 9, creating PDF files required separate applications, such as Adobe Acrobat. You can still use Acrobat in Mac OS X—and, in fact, you may need to if you intend to use advanced PDF features (such as a table of contents) or if you wish to edit an existing PDF document. However, because PDF support is built into Mac OS X, you can create a basic PDF file of any printable document. No additional software is needed.

As briefly covered in the main text, there are several ways to create PDF files in Mac OS X:

- From the Print dialog, click the Save As PDF button. This is the most direct route and the one you're likely to use most often.

- From the Print dialog, click the Preview button, then from Preview's File menu choose Save As.

   This feature is especially useful for applications that don't provide their own Preview command. It allows you to see exactly how the document will look when printed. If you like what you see, you can close the preview and return to the Print dialog to print the document.

   You can also print directly from Preview, but your document will be printed with the preferences you set there rather than in the Print dialog of the original application. You can also save the previewed document as a PDF file in Preview, which is an alternative to saving a document as a PDF file from the Print dialog of the original application.

   Note: To get the best-quality printed output, print the original document in its creating application. If you select Preview and then print the PDF file in the Preview application, print quality may be decreased. If your initial application is Preview (used to open an existing PDF file, for example), don't use the Preview button from its Print dialog. This creates a PDF of a PDF, which, again, is likely to decrease the quality of the output.

- From the Print dialog, choose Output Options and then check Save as File and select PDF as the format. The only advantage this method offers over either of the other methods is that you can save the setting via the Presets option—helpful if you have to save to PDF often or if you use the PDF option within AppleScript solutions.

Finally, via any of these methods, in the Save dialog that appears, give the document a name, specify where to save it, and click Save. Now you have a cross-platform PDF file of your document.

continues on next page

TAKE NOTE ▶ Why and How to Create PDF Files *continued*

PDF Workflow. In Mac OS X 10.2.4, Apple added a hidden PDF feature called PDF Workflow. To enable it, you must create a folder named PDF Services, in the /Library folder or your ~/Library folder. After doing this, if you select Print, you will note that the Preview and Save As PDF buttons have been changed. In particular:

- Instead of a button that says Preview, there's a button with the icon of the Preview application. The effect of clicking the button remains the same.

- Instead of a button that says Save as PDF, there's a button with the icon of a PDF document. If you click this button, a hierarchical menu appears with Save as PDF as the only choice. Selecting this is the same as clicking the Save as PDF button in the standard dialog.

So what's the point? Other than the shift to icons rather than text, there's nothing new here. The point is this: By adding items to the PDF Services folder, you create additions to the pop-up menu that appears when you click the PDF document button. Here is what you can add to the folder:

- **A folder or alias to a folder.** When you select the folder, a PDF version of the document is automatically saved to that folder; no Save dialog appears.

- **An application or an alias to an application.** If you select the application, a PDF file is created and opened in the selected application. You can use this, for example, to open the PDF in Acrobat or Adobe Reader rather than Preview.

- **A Unix tool or an AppleScript file (or an alias to either).** If selected, the actions specified by the Unix tool or AppleScript file will be performed on the PDF file. This is the most powerful option; however, it requires more advanced skill to create the tool or script needed. You can use this option to automate a series of actions, such as opening your email application, creating a new message, and automatically adding the created PDF document as an attachment. See the following Apple Web page for more details on this feature: www.apple.com/applescript/print. Check the Web for free or shareware "canned" scripts to use here.

Using Printer Setup Utility: Managing Print Jobs

Each printer you set up in Printer Setup Utility has a corresponding printer queue.

SEE: • "Take Note: Printer Queue (Proxy) Applications," earlier in this chapter.

After you click the Print button in an application, your document (now known as a *print job*) is sent to the print queue for the appropriate printer, where it's spooled to the printer or (if other documents are already waiting to be printed) waits in line for its turn (is *queued*). From the printer queue for a printer, you can view and manage print jobs.

Printer List and Status

The Status column of Printer Setup Utility's Printer List window indicates the current printing status of each listed printer.

SEE: • "Printer Setup Utility's Printer List window," earlier in this chapter.

Figure 7.25

Printer Setup Utility's Printer List window. The Status column indicates that the Falcon printer has stopped jobs.

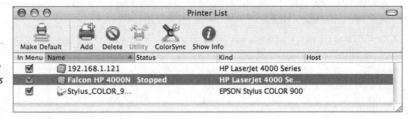

Printer Queue window

To get a more complete picture of the status of a given printer's print jobs—not to mention more control over their progress—double-click the name of the printer in Printer Setup Utility's Printer List window. This opens the Printer Queue application for that printer. Alternatively, you can do the same thing by (a) clicking the name and then from the Printers pop-up menu choosing Show Jobs (Command-O) or (b) double-clicking the desktop printer for the printer (assuming you've created one).

SEE: • "Take Note: Printer Queue (Proxy) Applications," earlier in this chapter.

The window that appears goes by various names: Queue window, Desktop Printer Jobs window, Show Jobs Window, or even the name of the printer itself. Whatever you call it, this window displays a list of all documents currently printing or waiting to be printed. If there are no such documents, it simply states, "No job printing." By default, documents are listed in the order in which they will be printed. The document that is being printed will be listed by name at the top of the scrollable text area, and the entry in the Status column will read Printing.

The Printer Queue window has its own toolbar with Delete, Hold, Resume, Stop Jobs, and Utility buttons. The Utility button functions identically to the Utility button in the Printer Setup Utility toolbar. The other buttons function as follows:

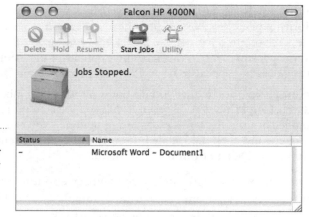

Figure 7.26

The printer proxy application (Printer Queue) window for an HP LaserJet printer, showing Jobs Stopped.

Figure 7.27

A printer proxy application's (left) Printer and (right) Jobs menus.

- **Stop Jobs/Start Jobs.** You can halt the entire queue for a printer by clicking the Stop Jobs button in the toolbar of the Printer Queue window or by selecting Stop Jobs from the application's Printer menu.

  Alternatively, you can select Stop Jobs from Printer Setup Utility's Printers menu while the desired printer is selected in the Printer List window.

  When you want the queue to resume, choose the toggled Start Jobs option.

  Note: When a printer is stopped, an exclamation point appears next to its name in the Printer pop-up menu of the Print dialog. The exclamation point also appears in the printer's icon in the Dock.

  Stopping jobs can be useful, for example, if you notice that your printer is about to run out of paper: You can stop all jobs until you've added more paper. It can also be helpful to stop jobs if you're not connected to your printer continually. When you're using a laptop, for example, you could stop the print queue while you're on the go; any documents that you "print" will be sent to the queue and held there. When you connect to your printer later, you can start the queue, and the documents will print.

- **Hold Job/Resume Job.** If there's more than one job in the queue, you can stop a particular job from printing while allowing the remaining items to continue. To do this, simply select the item you want to halt and then click the Hold button in the toolbar of the Printer Queue window or select Hold Job from the application's Jobs menu.

  When you want to resume printing, select the held item and then click the Resume button in the Toolbar, or select Resume Job from the Jobs menu.

  Unfortunately, Mac OS X does not yet allow you to set or change the priority of print jobs here. Using the Hold button to delay the printing of less important documents is the closest you can get for now. There is a Priority pop-up menu in the Scheduler options of the Print dialog, but this setting does not appear to be available from the Printer Queue window.

- **Delete.** If you decide that you do not want to print a job at all (perhaps after clicking Print, you discovered that you selected more pages than you intended or used the wrong formatting options), you can select the job in the queue and click the Delete button in the toolbar or choose Delete Job (Command-Delete) from the Jobs menu.

All of these options come in handy when you get a printing error. A printing error may prevent a job from being printed, automatically holding or stopping the queue. If the problem is something you can fix, you can make the necessary adjustment and then click Resume or Start. Otherwise, you can delete the problem job and at least allow other documents to print.

Transferring print jobs. If you have a print job in a queue, you can open up another printer's queue window and drag the job from one window to the other. This transfers the job to the new queue (and thus a different printer).

SEE: • "Nothing Prints," later in this chapter, for related information.

TAKE NOTE ▶ When You Need to Delay a Print Job

Suppose you want to print a document but either you don't want it to print immediately or you can't get it to print immediately. In such cases, you can do any of the following:

Use Scheduler. From the Printing Options menu in a Print dialog, select Scheduler. From the options that appear, select the desired print time The print job is added to the queue and will print at the designated time.

If desired, you can simply select the On Hold option to place the document on hold. You can then select to resume the job whenever you wish via the Print Queue window.

Finally, you can assign a Priority level here. If multiple jobs are scheduled to print at the same time, the higher-priority jobs will print first.

continues on next page

TAKE NOTE ▶ When You Need to Delay a Print Job *continued*

From the Queue window, select Hold Job. This works the same way as selecting On Hold from the Scheduler options. The advantage of the Scheduler route is that for a quick-to-print document, the document may print before you can even get the Queue window to appear.

From Printer Setup Utility or from the Queue window, select Stop Jobs. This halts all print jobs—useful if you're not currently connected to the desired printer (such as while working with a notebook computer while traveling). If you select to Stop Jobs, any documents you select to print will be queued and waiting next time you select Start Jobs (assuming the printer is connected).

When jobs are stopped, after you click the Print button, an alert box appears informing you that you cannot print at the moment. Click the Add to Queue button to add the document to the queue for later printing.

Create a PDF or PostScript file. As a last resort, you can save the document as a PDF or PostScript file (as described elsewhere in this chapter) and then print the PDF or PostScript file at some later point.

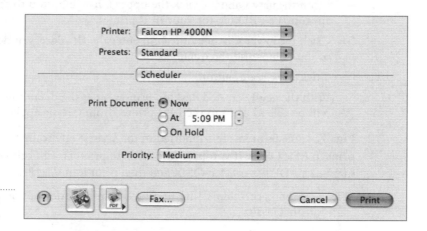

Figure 7.28

The Print dialog's Scheduler screen.

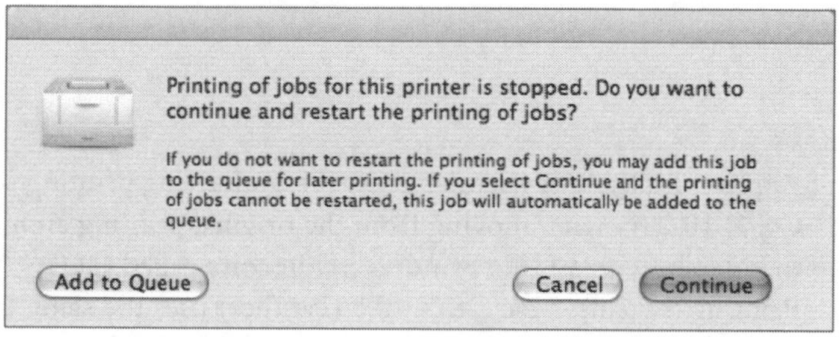

Figure 7.29

The message that appears when you select to print a document when jobs have been stopped for the printer.

Printing from Classic

As long as you have a printer supported by Classic, you can print directly from Classic applications. To do so, however, you need to set up your printers within Classic, even if you've already set them up in Mac OS 9.

Selecting USB and AppleTalk network printers in Classic is pretty much identical to how you select them in Mac OS 9. In essence, you use the Mac OS 9 Chooser just as you would do if booted from Mac OS 9.

If you use an LPR printer in Mac OS X and want to use it in the Classic environment as well, use Desktop Printer Utility (installed by Mac OS 9) and follow these steps:

1. Launch the Mac OS 9 Desktop Printer Utility. This will launch Classic if Classic is not already running.

2. A New Desktop Printer window should appear by default. If not, from the File menu choose New.

3. From the list in the window, Choose Printer (LPR) and click OK. A new window, named Untitled 1, opens.

4. From the new window, click the upper Change button to select the appropriate PPD file for your LPR printer.

5. Click the lower Change button to enter the IP address or domain name of the printer and the queue name.

6. Click the Create button.

   With the newly created desktop printer set as the default in Classic, you will be able to print to the LPR printer from Classic applications.

Finally, some printers are supported in the Classic environment but will not print in Mac OS X. If you have one of these printers, you can save a document as a PDF file in Mac OS X and then print it in Classic.

SEE: • **"Printing problems," in Chapter 9, for more information on printing from Classic.**

CUPS

Apple completely revised Mac OS X's underlying printing software in Mac OS X 10.2 (Jaguar), moving from the original printing architecture to one that depends on a Unix printing architecture called CUPS (Common Unix Printing System). Mac OS X 10.3 (Panther) uses the same CUPS software. You can obtain more background on CUPS at the following Web site: www.cups.org.

Mac OS X's Aqua-interface printing software, notably Printer Setup Utility, uses the CUPS software for printing. This section gives you an overview of how CUPS works with Mac OS X and how to use it to solve problems.

Where CUPS software is stored

The CUPS software for Mac OS X is located in the invisible Unix directories. The software consists of numerous files stored in several different locations. The following provides an overview of the CUPS software locations of most interest:

/private/etc/cups. This is where you'll find the CUPS software you're most likely to access for troubleshooting.

Open the ppd subdirectory located here, for example, and you will see a ppd file for each printer listed in Printer Setup Utility's Printer List.

Also important is the cupsd.conf file, which contains configuration data, such as where the CUPS log files are stored.

SEE: • "Accessing CUPS from a Web browser" and, especially, "Technically Speaking: Editing the Completed Jobs List," later in this chapter, for related information.

/private/var/spool/cups. The spool directory contains various subdirectories for holding spooled printing files. One subdirectory is named cups.

You cannot open the /cups subdirectory without root access. To view a list of its contents via Terminal, use the sudo command (that is, sudo ls /private/var/spool/cups). Alternatively, from the Finder, open Get Info for the cups folder and change the owner from *system* to yourself. Then change the access for Others from No Access to Read & Write. Finally, change the owner back to *system*. You can now enter the folder whenever you wish (although it's unlikely you'll have much need to do so). Note: If you're concerned about the security risk involved in making this change, you can instead enter the folder after you've changed the owner to yourself and then change the owner back to *system* when you're finished.

SEE: • "Ownership & Permissions" and " Root Access," in Chapter 4, for related information.
      • Chapter 6, for more on problems opening and saving files due to permissions restrictions.

/private/var/log/cups. This directory holds the log files created by CUPS.

/usr/libexec/cups and /usr/share/cups. These directories contain various CUPS interface software, including the user-interface files for when you access CUPS from your Web browser (as described in the next section).

The /usr/share/docs/cups directory holds CUPS documentation. Gimp-Print software is located in /usr/share/cups/model.

/usr/sbin and /usr/bin. These locations contain the printing commands used when printing from Terminal. These include cupsd and lpadmin (in /sbin) and the more general printing software, lp and lpr (in /bin). See the CUPS documentation, described in the next section, for details on using these commands.

The non-CUPS printing software, as described in the previous sections of this chapter (for example, the software in /System/Library/Printers and /Library/Printers), work in coordination with the CUPS software described here. Both are needed for Mac OS X printing to function.

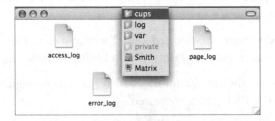

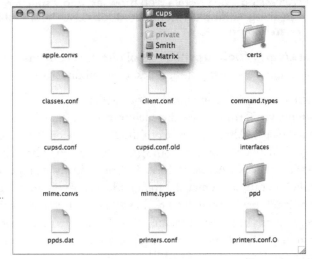

Figure 7.30

Two examples of Unix directories that contain CUPS software.

Accessing CUPS from a Web browser

Many of the options accessed from Printer Setup Utility and from Print dialogs actually call up CUPS routines. Although I won't discuss this much, you can also access CUPS via commands in Terminal (not surprisingly, since CUPS is Unix software). However, you can directly access the CUPS software more conveniently via a Web interface built into CUPS. From here, you can even access CUPS options that are not available from Printer Setup Utility or Print dialogs.

To load this Web interface, enter the following local address in your browser: http://127.0.0.1:631/. This will load the CUPS main page, with links to several other locations. You can also access these links from the buttons at the top of the window. The following provides an overview of the various links:

Do Administration Tasks. This takes you to the Administration page. From here, you can select to Add Class or Add Printer. You can also select to go to the same Manage pages more directly accessed via the Manage links listed below.

Note: A *class* is a group of pooled printers (as described in "Printer Setup Utility menus," earlier in this chapter).

Manage Printer Classes. This takes you to the Classes page. If you've created classes (for example, via Printer Setup Utility's Pool Printers command), you will be able to perform such tasks as modifying or deleting the class. The Modify Class command is of particular interest because it allows you to change the printers included in the class. You cannot do this from Printer Setup Utility. In fact, Printer Setup Utility does not even tell you what printers are in the class.

On-Line Help. This takes you to the Help page. From here, you can access CUPS documentation and learn just about everything there is to know about CUPS—including how to access printing via Terminal commands (such as 1p, 1pr, and 1pstat).

Manage Jobs. This takes you to the Jobs page. From here, you can release or cancel a currently active print job, as you can also do from the Printer Queue windows. Click Show Completed Jobs to get a list of all recently completed print jobs (an option not available from Printer Setup Utility or Printer Queue windows).

Manage Printers. This takes you to the Printers page, where you will see a list of all added printers (similar to what you would see in Printer Setup Utility's Printer List window). In each case, you have several options, including Print Test Page, Modify Printer, and Configure Printer. Most of what you can do here can also be done via Printer Setup Utility.

Download the Current CUPS Software. This takes you to the CUPS Web site (www.cups.org), where you can check for a newer version of the CUPS software. In general, however, I recommend ignoring this option. Let Apple update the CUPS software, as needed, via Mac OS X updates.

There's a good deal of redundancy built into these pages. For example, if you click the link for a printer's name from any page where it's listed, you go to a page that contains both the Manage Jobs and Manage Printers information just for that printer.

Troubleshooting printing from CUPS Web pages. The CUPS Web interface provides an opportunity to do some troubleshooting you could not otherwise attempt. Here are two examples:

- **Enabling options.** Suppose you try to add an option such as an additional paper tray via the Installable Options selection in Show Info from Printer Setup Utility and it doesn't work: You can try to accomplish the same thing from the CUPS software instead. To do so, on the Manage Printers page click the Configure Printer button. This may succeed even when an attempt from Printer Setup Utility does not. You may also find options, such as for Starting and Ending Banners, not listed in Printer Setup Utility.

- **Canceling jobs.** You cannot stop jobs from a shared printer via Printer Setup Utility or a Printer Queue window on the client computer (you can only do this from the computer to which the printer is physically connected). If you want to try to stop a job from the client computer, go to the CUPS Jobs page, select the problem job, and click the Cancel Job button. This may get the job to delete.

Note: Not all Web-browser CUPS options will work from the browser, at least not by default. For example, whenever I selected the Restart Job button (on the Show Completed Jobs page), I got the following error: "client-error-not-possible." To get this feature to work, you would need to set PreserveJobFiles to Yes in the cupsd.conf file.

SEE: • "Technically Speaking: Editing the Completed Jobs List," below, for general guidelines on doing this.

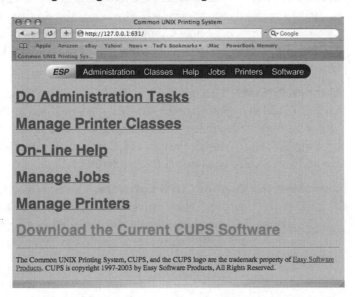

Figure 7.31

The main page of the CUPS software as accessed via its Web-browser interface.

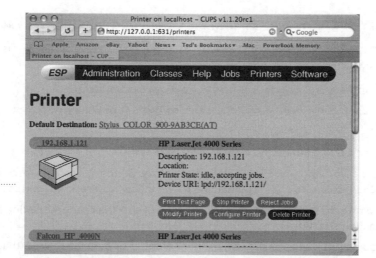

Figure 7.32

The page that appears after clicking Manage Printers from the CUPS main page.

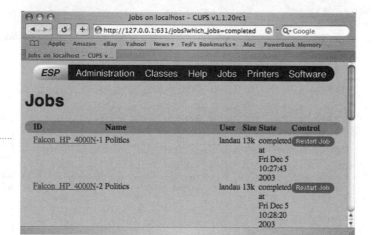

Figure 7.33

The page that appears after clicking the Show Completed Jobs button from the CUPS Manage Jobs page.

TECHNICALLY SPEAKING ▶ Editing the Completed Jobs List

As stated in the main text, if you click the Show Completed Jobs button on the Manage Jobs page of the CUPS Web interface, you get a list of all recently printed documents. This Web page can be easily accessed by any local user. In fact, if your Mac is on the Internet and other users know your computer IP address, they can access any part of the CUPS Web interface for your Mac by typing http://{*your_IP_address*}:631/. They can do this remotely, even if Web Sharing is not enabled (assuming that you have not blocked the 631 port via a firewall). You may well consider this a security risk or a privacy invasion (for example, you may not want others to know what you've been printing).

continues on next page

TECHNICALLY SPEAKING ▶ Editing the Completed Jobs List *continued*

To avoid this risk, you need to delete the items listed there and prevent new items from being added. Here's a way to do so that bypasses using Terminal to edit files:

1. Using the Finder's Go to Folder command, go to /private/etc/cups.

2. Open the cupsd.conf file in a text editor, such as TextEdit or BBEdit, with root access, using Pseudo.

   SEE: • "Mac OS X utilities," in Chapter 4, for details.

3. Use the Find command to locate PreserveJobHistory. Go to the line that reads as follows: **#PreserveJobHistory Yes**. Change that line to the following: **PreserveJobHistory No**.

   Note: Removing the pound (#) symbol at the start of the line changes the line from a comment to an active setting.

   There is also an option to adjust the maximum number of print jobs saved (that is, MaxJobs; the default limit is set at 500). However, changing this to zero means there is no limit, rather than that none are saved.

continues on next page

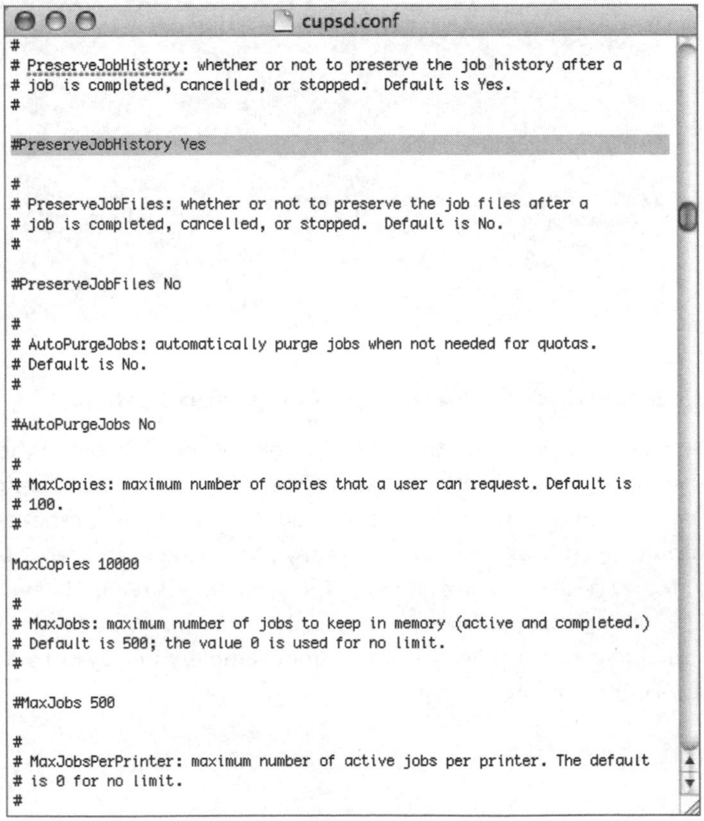

Figure 7.34

A partial view of the cupsd.conf file; the PreserveJobHistory line is highlighted.

TECHNICALLY SPEAKING ▶ Editing the Completed Jobs List *continued*

4. Save the modified file. Now, subsequent print jobs will not be saved in the Completed Jobs listing of the browser display. However, this does not get rid of any completed jobs already listed. To do that, proceed to the next step.

5. Launch Terminal and type the following:

`cancel -a {name of printer}`

For the name of the printer, use the name as listed in the CUPS Web pages (for example, my HP LaserJet was listed as Falcon_HP_4000N). Press Return.

Repeat this for any other printers that still show completed jobs listed.

Note: /var/log/cups/page_log retains a record of completed print jobs but not the name of each document. The data that's actually used to generate the Completed Jobs Web page is located in /private/var/spool/cups. There is a separate file (beginning with the letter *c* and followed by a series of numbers) for each job listed on the Web page. The only problem here is that the cups folder is owned by root. Thus, even as an administrator, you cannot directly open this folder from the Finder. You can work around this by changing the owner in the Get Info window of the folder (as described in "Where CUPS software is stored," in the main text). However, it is probably simpler to use the `cancel` command, as described above.

6. Restart your Mac. Now all existing completed jobs for that printer are no longer listed when you select Show Completed Jobs.

The purpose of the restart is to relaunch the CUPS software so that the change to the conf file takes effect. To save yourself the hassle of restarting the Mac, you could instead launch Terminal and type `sudo killall -1 cupsd`.

You have now wiped the Completed Jobs record clean and turned off the option to add new jobs to the list.

Restart jobs. If you change the **#PreserveJobFiles No** line in cupsd.conf to **PreserveJobFiles Yes**, you will now be able to use the Restart Job button in the Completed Jobs screen to reprint a previously printed document. However, it will only work for jobs saved after you enable this option. And, of course, you also have to make sure that you don't disable the Completed Jobs feature, as just described.

TAKE NOTE ▶ Using Gimp-Print

One plus to having CUPS in Mac OS X is that it's relatively easy for Unix-savvy developers to write driver software for printers. These drivers can support printers whose manufacturers have not updated their drivers to work in Mac OS X 10.2 or 10.3.

However, you don't have to know any Unix to take advantage of these drivers. With Gimp-Print, any Mac user can benefit from this approach. Gimp-Print is a collection of drivers that provide support for, or a way to work around problems with, a variety of printers and printer drivers.

continues on next page

TAKE NOTE ▶ Using Gimp-Print *continued*

With Panther, Gimp-Print is installed automatically as part of the standard printing software when you first install Panther. The drivers (ppd files) can be found in the following location: /usr/share/cups/model (look especially in the C folder).

With Jaguar (or if you want a newer version of the drivers than the one that came with your copy of Panther), you need to download Gimp-Print (http://gimp-print.sourceforge.net) and install it. Checking for a newer version is useful if you're having any problems printing via the current version of Gimp-Print drivers. A newer version may have fixed bugs or added support for a previously unsupported printer.

Note: Gimp-Print may be unable to print files that contain PostScript code opened in Carbon applications (such as most Adobe applications and AppleWorks). You can work around the problem by saving the file as a PDF document and printing the PDF file. Otherwise, you can use a program called ESP GhostScript, which allows Gimp-Print to work with these otherwise Gimp-Print–resistant applications.

Using Gimp-Print with a USB printer. Here's how you set up Gimp-Print to work with an unsupported USB printer (and with most printer setups except those for IP-connected printers):

1. Launch Printer Setup Utility.

2. Hold down the Option key and click the Add button.

3. From the pop-up menu select Advanced.

4. Access the Device pop-up menu that appears. Assuming Gimp-Print supports the printer, its name should be at the bottom of the list. Select it.

5. From the Printer Model pop-up menu and scrollable text list, select the printer vendor and model. In Panther, models that use Gimp-Print will be listed as such. For example, if you select Epson as the vendor, you will see models such as Epson CL-700+Gimp-Print v.4.2.5. If you have an Epson CL-700, select this item. If your laser printer model isn't listed, select Other and search directly for the relevant PPD file.

6. You can change the Device Name if you wish, but leave the Device URI unchanged.

7. Click Add.

Note: A USB printer may automatically appear in the Printer List with the words *Gimp-Print* in the Kind column. In this case, the printer may work directly. If not, you will need to add the printer driver, as just described.

If none of this works, it may be that even Gimp-Print does not support your unsupported printer.

Using Gimp-Print with an IP-connected printer. If your printer is on an Ethernet network, to get it to work you should follow the instructions in Adding a printer via IP Printing in the main text. The only difference is that with Gimp-Print installed, the desired Printer Model should be listed—whereas it may not have been listed before.

More info. In addition to the Gimp-Print Web site itself, see the following Web page for more details on how to install and use Gimp-Print: www.allosx.com/1030154694/index_html.

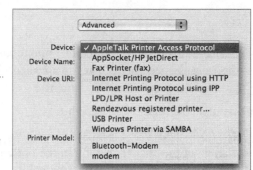

Figure 7.35

The options that appear after selecting Advanced from the Add dialog in Printer Setup Utility; the Device pop-up menu is shown.

Faxing

New in Mac OS X 10.3 (Panther) is the ability to fax documents. Previously, you needed third-party software to do this. To get you started, here's some general information:

- To receive a fax, you must be connected—via the Modem port on your Mac—to the phone line (that is, the phone number) that people will be using when sending you a fax. To send a fax, you can be connected to any phone line.

- You can't be connected to the Internet via your modem and send and receive faxes at the same time.

- You can receive a fax even if you're not logged in to your account at the time it arrives. However, you cannot receive faxes when the computer is asleep.

The following sections cover the remaining essential information on faxing.

Setting up Print & Fax to receive a fax

Before you can receive a fax, you must first set up the preferences in the Print & Fax System Preferences pane (see **Figure 7.5**). To do so, follow these steps:

1. Launch System Preferences and select Print & Fax. Click the Faxing tab.

2. Check the "Receive faxes on this computer" box.

3. Select an option for what to do When a Fax Arrives: Save it as file to a specified folder; immediately print it to the selected printer; or email it to a specified address. For the email function, you should ideally be connected to the Internet via a separate line from the phone (for example, via a cable modem).

    Also specify the number of rings before the fax feature "answers."

4. Enter your fax number in the My Fax Number text box. This is only used for identification purposes when sending and receiving faxes.

This is all you need to do to receive a fax. To send a fax, read on.

Sending a fax

If you have a modem that's currently connected to a phone line, you're ready to send a fax. No other settings need be adjusted in advance. To send a fax (such as an AppleWorks or Microsoft Word document):

1. From the application's File menu, choose Print.

2. From the Print dialog that appears, click the Fax button.

3. From the new dialog options that appear, fill in the options as indicated. The most important of these options are the following:

   To. Enter the phone number (and name if desired) where the fax is to be sent. You can alternatively select a fax number from your Address Book by clicking the icon to the right of the text box. If there is a required dialing prefix that is not part of the phone number, enter it in the Dialing Prefix field.

   Modem. If you have more than one available phone line/modem (such as your own internal modem and a mobile phone paired with your Mac), select the one you want to use.

   "Cover page." If desired, click the "Cover page" checkbox and enter the text you want to appear on the cover page.

   Modem Settings. From the pop-up menu showing Fax Cover Page, select Modem. Select the desired dialing settings.

   Scheduler. From the pop-up menu showing Fax Cover Page, select Scheduler. Use this if you want to send the modem at some later time (useful if you are currently on the Internet for example).

4. Click the Fax button. If your phone line is currently in use, the fax will be sent as soon as the phone line is free.

Managing fax jobs. If all goes well when you select to send a fax, a modem icon (which looks like a fax machine) will appear in the Dock. This is similar to the Printer icon that appears when you print a document. If you double-click it, it opens a Queue window that is again similar to what appears if you double-click a printer icon. From here you can monitor the status of a fax. If a problem occurs, a message will appear here. It will also indicate when the fax is complete. If desired, you can stop or delete a queued fax job from here. Otherwise, when the modem icon vanishes from the Dock, you can assume that the fax has been sent.

Fax sharing. Enabling Printer Sharing in the Sharing System Preferences pane also enables fax sharing. Your modem will automatically appear (to other computers on your local network) in Printer Setup Utility's Fax List window and any dialogs that list fax modems. Similarly, if a user on your local network enables Printer Sharing on his or her computer, that user's modem will appear on your Fax List and dialogs.

Note: If a document needs to be temporarily stored on a hard drive while waiting to be faxed, it is stored on the shared drive (not the drive of the user sending the fax).

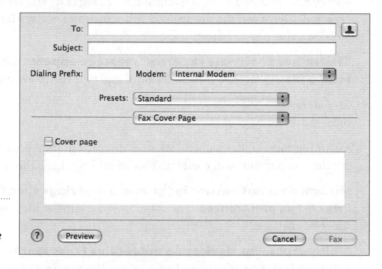

Figure 7.36

The options that appear when you select Fax from the Print dialog.

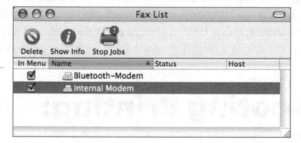

Figure 7.37

The window that appears when you select Show Fax List from Printer Setup Utility's View menu.

Printer Setup Utility and faxing

After the first time you select to send a fax from a Print dialog, the modem you used will be listed in the Fax List window of Printer Setup Utility. Shared modems are listed automatically in any case.

Via the Fax List window's toolbar, you can click buttons to delete a selected modem, stop jobs for a modem, or choose Show Info (which I just about never use for a fax modem; it's really designed for printers). There is no Add button here. Modems are added as just described in "Sending a Fax."

Double-clicking a modem name in the list opens up its Queue window.

When the Fax List is the active window, the commands in Printer Setup Utility's menus shift, as appropriate, to access Fax List options instead of Printer List options. For example, if you select Customize Toolbar, the settings will apply to the Fax List toolbar rather than the Printer List toolbar.

Troubleshooting faxing

Assuming you have a telephone connected to your Mac and have set up the software as described here, sending and receiving faxes should work as expected. Of course, the unexpected will sometimes occur. Here are three problems that you may have:

"There was a software fax error" message appears when trying to send a fax. To fix this, launch Terminal and type the following two lines:

```
cd /var/spool
sudo mkdir lock
```

Assuming that a folder named lock does not exist in the /spool folder, executing these commands will create it. This should eliminate the error.

Modem does not answer in the number of rings specified in the Print & Fax preferences. The solution is the same as just described for the fax error message.

Multipurpose fax devices do not receive faxes sent from a Mac running Panther. If you send a fax to a multipurpose device (such as one that acts both as a telephone and a fax machine), the fax may not be received. As a work-around, either have the recipient set the device to receive a fax manually, or set the device's receiving mode from auto-recognition to fax-only.

Troubleshooting Printing: Overview

This section covers a variety of printing problems as well as the solutions required to get things working again.

Nothing prints

Perhaps the most common and frustrating printing problem is when a printer refuses to print—regardless of what document or application you're using. There are at least three variations of this problem:

- The printer responds and attempts to print the document, but the output never appears.

  This symptom usually means there's a problem with the printer itself. For help, start with the section below titled, "Troubleshooting Printing: Checking Printer and Connections."

- Nothing prints, no error message appears, and the printer does not respond. In other words, the Mac and printer behave as if you had never selected to print.

  Too often this means a problem with the printer. However, it can also mean a problem at the Mac end. For help, start with the section below titled, "Troubleshooting Printing: Checking Printer and Connections." Then proceed to "Troubleshooting Printing: Checking Printer Setup Utility and Desktop Printers."

- An error message appears when you try to print.

  In this case, the message text should help you identify the problem and determine what to do. For more help, check the following sections for the particular error message or a similar one. Otherwise, look for any section that best describes your specific symptom.

Other printing problems

A common printing problem is an inability to add a new printer to Printer Setup Utility's Printer List.

Finally, there is an assortment of problems where some documents print but others don't, or you get printed output but there's something wrong with it (garbled text, incorrect format, and so on).

These issues are all addressed in the sections that follow.

Troubleshooting Printing: Checking Printer and Connections

There are numerous hardware-related reasons why things may go wrong with printing. Although these are not necessarily Mac OS X–specific issues, this is a good place to start your troubleshooting.

In general, there are two types of solutions to hardware-related printing problems: Either you can fix the problem yourself (for example, by replacing a cable or turning on the printer), or you will need to repair or replace the printer.

In all cases in this section, I am assuming that you previously added the printer in Printer Setup Utility successfully.

Checking the printer

To check for printer-related problems, consider the following:

- Turn your printer off and back on again. This alone may be enough to fix the problem.

- Make sure the printer is turned on, with paper and ink/toner in place. For some printers, such as Epson inkjet printers, you can check ink levels via a utility accessed from the Utilities button in Printer Setup Utility.

  Note: In some cases, a lack of ink prevents the printer from even attempting to print. In such cases, you may get an error message indicating a printing problem but not specifically describing this as the cause.

- Make sure any optional hardware additions you made to your printer are correctly installed.

- If you have more than one printer, check to see if a document will print to other printers. If so, this isolates the original printer or its connection to the Mac as the cause. Check with the documentation that came with your printer for troubleshooting advice, and proceed to the sections below.

- Make sure the problem is not specific to a particular document or application, rather than a general problem with the printer itself. Try printing other documents and printing from other applications.

  SEE: • **"Document or application problems," later in this chapter, for more specific advice.**

Printing a test page

Try printing a test page directly to your printer. The best way to do this will vary according to printer. Try one or more of the following, as appropriate:

- Select the printer in Printer Setup Utility's Printer List and from the Printer menu choose Print Test Page. The CUPS Web interface described previously in this chapter includes the same test-page option.

- Select the printer in Printer Setup Utility's Printer List and click the Utility button in the toolbar (if available). Check to see if the utility includes a test-page option. If so, try it.

- There may be a test-page button on the printer itself. To determine if this is the case, check the documentation that came with your printer.

If you can successfully print a test page, it indicates that the problem is a Mac OS X software problem. If you can't print a test page, it indicates a hardware problem. In either case, continue with the sections below for more specific advice. Note: Successfully printing a test page from a button on the printer itself does not rule out a problem with the connection from the printer to the Mac; it just rules out a problem with the printer.

Checking USB and FireWire hardware connections

For USB- or FireWire-connected printers, launch System Profiler to see if the printer is listed as connected to the relevant port. If not, you have a problem with the printer itself or the connection to the Mac.

In any case, make sure your printer is connected to the proper port (USB or FireWire) with the correct cable and that the cable is not faulty. Make sure the printer's status lights or other indicators indicate a normal status.

Note: Apple has confirmed that there are potential printing failures when using a USB-to-parallel cable or adapter. You should use a USB cable whenever possible.

If your computer is connected via a USB or FireWire hub, connect the printer directly to the Mac instead. If it still does not work, leave the printer connected and restart, and see if it prints properly now.

Checking Bluetooth connections

If your printer is connected to the Mac via Bluetooth, make sure that Bluetooth is working correctly and that your printer is recognized.

SEE: • "Bluetooth," in Chapter 8, for more details.

Checking Ethernet network connections

If your printer is connected to an Ethernet network, make sure it is a networkable printer and is connected to the network with the correct cable. In addition, consider the following:

- Use Network Utility to "ping" the printer to determine whether the printer is available after being connected. You need the DNS name or IP address of the printer to do this. Check Printer Setup Utility to get this information. If there's a problem with the printer connection, you may see a message such as "Host is down" when you ping the printer.

- Make sure that all settings in the Network and Sharing System Preferences panes are correct. If you're using AirPort and/or Printer Sharing, check these settings. Details on these issues are covered in other sections of this chapter and in Chapter 8.

- For shared printers, make sure the user who owns the computer to which the printer is connected still has the printer and computer turned on, and has Printer Sharing enabled.

- For a Rendezvous-connected printer, make sure it is still on your local network.

- If you're using AppleTalk, make sure AppleTalk is enabled in the Network System Preferences pane and, if necessary, in the Directory Access utility.

    If you're using AppleTalk and you get an error that says, "No AppleTalk printers are available because AppleTalk is currently disabled," in an error message or in Printer Setup Utility, it probably means that you did not enable AppleTalk for the appropriate network (the one on which your printer is located). The solution is to select the appropriate network (Ethernet or AirPort) in the Network System Preferences pane, click the

AppleTalk button, and then check the Make AppleTalk Active box in the AppleTalk screen.

Note: Prior to Mac OS X 10.2, you could have AppleTalk enabled on multiple network configurations (for example, both Ethernet and AirPort). This could also cause a problem. However, this option no longer exists in Mac OS X 10.2 or later.

Note: AppleTalk is turned off by default and is normally not needed for USB printers.

Sometimes, you may not be able to add an AppleTalk printer in Printer Setup Utility, even if you have correctly enabled AppleTalk in the Network System Preferences pane. In this case, open Network System Preferences and from the Location pop-up menu choose New Location. Type a name for the location, and click OK. Click Apply, and then change the location back to your original location (Automatic, if you're using the default choice) and click Apply again.

In addition, from the Show pop-up menu select Network Port Configurations and make sure that the port with AppleTalk enabled is the top choice. I once had a problem where I could not connect to an AppleTalk printer until I had made this change.

Doing all of this often fixes the glitch, and you should be able to add and print to the AppleTalk printer.

Check out the following Apple Knowledge Base document for more advice on AppleTalk and printing problems: http://docs.info.apple.com/article.html?artnum=106613.

If nothing you try succeeds, you may be able to get the printer to work by adding the printer via IP Printing rather than via AppleTalk.

SEE: • **Chapter 8 for more on Network Utility as well as the Network and Sharing System Preferences settings.**

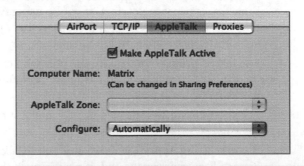

Figure 7.38

The AppleTalk options in (top) the Network System Preferences pane and (bottom) the Directory Access application.

Troubleshooting Printing: Checking Printer Drivers

The first step in using a printer in Mac OS X is to add the printer to the Printer List in Printer Setup Utility. I covered the basics of doing this earlier in this chapter.

SEE: • "Using Printer Setup Utility: Adding and Configuring Printers" and "Using Printer Setup Utility: Managing Print Jobs," earlier in this chapter.

Even if you previously added a printer successfully, many problems can be resolved by updating, reinstalling, or deleting printer-driver software. You need to be an administrative user to do this; in some cases, you may need root access as well.

"Driver not installed" message

If you see your printer listed in Printer Setup Utility but a "Driver not installed" message is next to its name in the Printer List, or the message appears when you try to add the printer, it generally means that the needed printer-driver software is not installed. This is probably because it was not installed as part of Mac OS X. Assuming that you did not prevent installation of the needed software via unchecking options in a Custom Install of Mac OS X, you will need to obtain the driver software and install it.

Start by checking for software that may have come with the printer. Otherwise, check the printer manufacturer's Web site. Once you locate the software, install it and return to Printer Setup Utility.

If you get this message even though you believe you have the software installed, it typically means that you have to specifically select your model from the Printer Model pop-up menu in the Add Printer dialog.

If neither of these fixes works, you probably have an unsupported printer. Using the Gimp-Print driver may help. Otherwise, you may not be able to use the printer with Mac OS X.

Getting updated or third-party printer software

If you upgrade to a new version of Mac OS X and your printer software is not among the software that gets updated automatically as part of the Mac OS X upgrade, you may have printing problems if your current driver is incompatible with the new Mac OS X update. In this case, contact the vendor about getting a new version of the driver software, and then install it. In particular, you should note the following:

Install updated PPD. For PostScript printers, an update usually consists of a PPD file that you're instructed to manually install. Here is a typical set of instructions for updating the PPD file of a printer already listed in Printer Setup Utility:

1. After obtaining the updated PPD file (typically from the vendor's Web site), install it in the /Library/Printers/PPDs/Contents/Resources/ en.lproj folder.

2. Launch Printer Setup Utility, select the printer from the Printer List, and click the Show Info button in the toolbar.

3. From the pop-up menu, select Printer Model.

4. Select Other as the model.

5. Navigate to the en.lproj folder where you just installed the PPD file and select the file.

6. Click the Apply Changes button.

If the driver still appears not to be recognized by Printer Setup Utility or other applications, it may be that the PPD file has incorrect permissions. For example, you may be incorrectly listed as the owner of the file rather than *system*. Selecting to Repair Disk Permissions with Disk Utility is not likely to help here. Instead, you should check the permissions of another file in the same folder and change the permissions of the newly installed file to match it.

Otherwise, use the Printer Setup Repair utility to install the PPD files. This utility makes sure they are installed with the correct permissions.

SEE: • "Using Printer Setup Repair," later in this chapter.

If the software comes with its own installer utility, it will likely take care of these permissions issues automatically.

Use third-party drivers. For PostScript printers, you can resolve some problems by replacing the printer's "official" PPD file with a modified one created by a third party, as obtained from the Web. To do so:

1. Manually install the PPD file (in the relevant en.lproj folder, as described in the previous section).

2. Launch Printer Setup Utility. Select the problem printer and click Delete from the toolbar.

3. Click Add from the toolbar. Locate the printer you want to add. From the Printer Model menu in the add sheet, select Other rather than Auto Select. Then select the modified PPD file.

Reinstalling corrupted printer software

Occasionally, a printer driver or PPD file becomes corrupt and needs to be replaced. This is especially likely to be the case if you're unable to print to a printer that previously worked fine.

Deleting and re-adding the printer won't solve the problem because you'll just be re-adding the corrupted software.

In most cases, it will be enough to just reinstall the software. Thus, to reinstall printer-driver software that came with Mac OS X, use the AdditionalPrinterDrivers.mpkg on the Mac OS X Install CD/DVD.

SEE: • **"How do I tell if my printer is already supported?" and "Take Note: How to Reinstall the Mac OS X Printer Drivers," earlier in this chapter, for more details.**

For other drivers, check the software that came with your printer or the vendor's Web site. In some cases, you may need to manually remove the problem software (typically from /Library/Printers) before you can reinstall it. The instructions that come with the software should indicate whether this is required.

Note: Unless you believe this is the likely cause of your problem, I recommend first trying some of the less "invasive" fixes in the next section, "Troubleshooting Printing: Checking Printer Setup Utility and Desktop Printers."

Removing incompatible printer support files

The software for one printer may prevent printing on another brand of printer—possibly because of corrupt printer software, improperly installed software, or software that otherwise causes a conflict with the printer in use. In some cases, printing to an Epson printer does not work if Canon printer software was installed, and vice versa.

If the problematic software is for a printer you don't own (for example, it was included in a standard Mac OS X installation), an obvious solution is to delete the unneeded software. To do so, go to /Library/Printers and delete the folders for the printers you don't own.

SEE: • **"Installing Printer Drivers," "Using Printer Setup Utility: Adding and Configuring Printers," and "Take Note: Using Gimp-Print," earlier in this chapter, for related advice.**

Troubleshooting Printing: Checking Printer Setup Utility and Desktop Printers

This section explores Printer Setup Utility problems and the diagnostic techniques and fixes that require Printer Setup Utility. It assumes you have ruled out a general problem with the printer, its connections, or its driver software, as described in the previous sections.

Note: For shared printers, you will probably need to work with the computer to which the printer is attached, not your own Mac.

Checking for printer queue window (Desktop Printer) error messages

Whenever you have a problem printing that you cannot otherwise diagnose, go to the printer queue window to check for error messages. You can do this by (a) launching Printer Setup Utility and double-clicking the printer's name in the Printer List; (b) clicking the printer's icon in the Dock (if included); or (c) double-clicking the printer's Desktop Printer icon (if you created one).

In the middle area of the window (to the right of the printer icon), you will likely see an error message describing the problem. For example, it might say, "Printer not responding" (which would suggest that you make sure the printer is on) or "Unable to make connection" (which would suggest a problem with the network connection).

Sometimes a separate error message box will appear when you access this window. For example, you may get one that says, "Communication error with printer"—with options to delete or stop the job.

The Status column of Printer Setup Utility may sometimes include a similar error message. However, even if the Status column says Printing, you should still check out the queue window. If the message suggests a likely solution, try it. Otherwise, try the suggestions that follow.

TAKE NOTE ▶ Printing Error Messages

Prior to Mac OS X 10.2, when you selected to print a document and it failed, you would typically get an error message briefly describing the problem. Often, the message would include a Show Queue or Retry button. Clicking the button would take you to Printer Setup Utility, where you would be greeted by yet another error message, with more details of the error and the opportunity to perform some of the same actions (such as stopping a job) that you can do from the Show Jobs window.

In Mac OS X 10.2 or later, probably due to the shift to CUPS, most of these error messages have vanished. For some issues (such as if a printer's queue has been stopped), a message will appear when you select to print. More often, you will get no error at all. The main sign of trouble will be the Printer Setup Utility icon or desktop printer icon in the Dock. For example, it may shift to an icon with an exclamation mark over it, indicating a printing problem and that the print queue has stopped as a result. Beyond that, the main way you'll know you have a problem is simply that nothing happens, and nothing is printed.

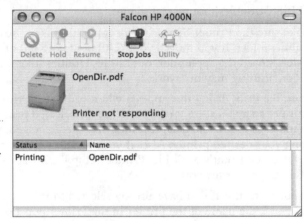

Figure 7.39

The "Printer not responding" message that appears if you try to print to a printer that is currently turned off or disconnected.

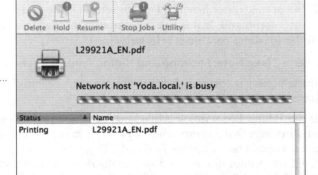

Figure 7.40

The error that appears when trying to print to a shared printer that cannot be located (perhaps because Printer Sharing has been turned off).

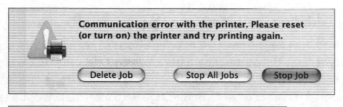

Figure 7.41

Two examples of printer error messages that may appear in the Finder after you select to print a document.

Checking the basics

If you're having a general problem with printing, start with these basic Printer Setup Utility troubleshooting techniques:

- Make sure the Printer Setup Utility application is in the /Applications/ Utilities folder. If you moved your /Utilities folder out of the /Applications folder, moved the application out of the /Utilities folder, or renamed either folder, printing may not work.

- From the Print dialog that appears when you select Print from the File menu of an application, make sure that the selected printer is the one you intended to use. If the default printer has been changed, you may not be using your desired printer. Also, if your default printer is a shared printer and it isn't currently available, Printer Setup Utility automatically selects a different printer for you.

  To check for this if you have already selected to Print, choose Print again and check the name of the printer in the Printer pop-up menu.

- If the printer you want is not in the list in the Print dialog, from the pop-up menu select Edit Printer List. This takes you to Printer Setup Utility.

  If the printer is not listed in Printer Setup Utility, add it via the Add Printer command. If it is listed, make sure the checkbox next to its name in the In Menu column is selected.

  SEE: • **"Take Note: Showing and Hiding Printers," earlier in this chapter.**

- If the printer is correctly listed in the Printer List, check whether jobs have been stopped for the printer.

  If the Printer List window's Status column, the printer queue window, or a message that appears when you select to print indicates that jobs have been stopped (see **Figures 7.26** and **7.29**), select Start Jobs (for example, from the printer queue window's toolbar). Actually, it's worth toggling Stop Jobs and Start Jobs even if jobs are not stopped; it may still get things working.

If jobs are automatically stopped again after selecting Start Jobs, it indicates a problem with the document. Whenever printing fails, jobs are stopped even though you did not select the command to do so. In this case, select to delete the current job (as described next) and start over.

- If a specific document is listed as on Hold, from the printer queue window's toolbar select Resume to get the document to print.

- For related problems specific to shared printers, see "Take Note: Troubleshooting Shared Printers," below.

TAKE NOTE ▶ Troubleshooting Shared Printers

If you're having problems accessing or using a printer made available to your Mac via Printer Sharing, note the following:

- To manage print jobs with Printer Setup Utility, you need to use Printer Setup Utility on the computer to which the printer is connected.

- A shared printer will vanish from your Printer List if any of the following occurs: The computer that is hosting the printer is turned off; the printer is turned off; or Printer Sharing is turned off.

- If the owner of a computer hosting a shared printer changes the name of the computer, print jobs sent from a client computer to the shared printer will fail until the sharing computer is restarted. After the host computer has been restarted, clients should then delete and re-add the printer in Printer Setup Utility.

- In a more specific case, if you change your Rendezvous name in Sharing, any users connected to a printer via Printer Sharing may have certain printing preferences corrupted. To fix this problem in Jaguar, delete the following three .plist files from the ~/Library/Preferences folder, and set up the printer again:

  com.apple.print.PrintCenter.plist
  com.apple.print.defaultpapersize.plist
  com.apple.print.custompresets.plist

  If this occurs in Panther, delete the following files from the same folder:

  com.apple.print.PrintSetupUtility.plist
  com.apple.print.custompresets.plist
  com,apple.print.PrintingPrefs.plist

  To avoid this problem completely, turn off Printer Sharing before changing your Rendezvous name.

  Note: If you are using an account that was created in Jaguar and upgraded to Panther, one or more of the Jaguar files may still be present and active. For example, com.apple .print.PrintCenter.plist is likely to be in use instead of com.apple.print.PrintSetupUtility.plist.

- If applications crash (unexpectedly quit) when attempting to print to a shared raster printer, the problem may be a conflict between the printer-driver software on your computer and on the host computer. To fix this, make sure that both computers have the latest software available (or at least the same version). Check the printer vendor's Web site for the latest updates.

Deleting corrupt print jobs

If a document has become corrupt, Printer Setup Utility may stall indefinitely as it tries and fails to print the document. The solution is to delete the print job causing the block.

To delete a print job, select Show Jobs for the printer or otherwise access the printer's queue window. From the window that appears, if the Status column and/or error message area indicate a problem with a document, select the document and click the Delete button.

Remember that deleting a print job does not delete the document itself; it deletes the temporary spool file created to print the document.

If you have more than one item in the queue and more printing problems occur, it's a good idea to delete all queued jobs. After all jobs have been deleted, make sure that the queue is started and try to print the document(s) again.

Checking for Printer Setup Utility memory problems

Sometimes, Printer Setup Utility claims to be printing a particular document, yet the document isn't printing. Other documents may print without problems. If you can print simple documents but not larger or more complex documents, the problem may be memory-related. Despite Mac OS X's superior memory-management skills, Printer Setup Utility may have insufficient memory to print. Unfortunately, no error message appears to indicate that this is the case.

If you suspect this problem, cancel the print job, quit all open applications that you don't need at the moment, and try to print again.

Deleting and re-adding a printer

If problems remain, delete a printer from the Printer List altogether and then re-add it.

When re-adding the printer, make sure that all settings are correct. For example, for IP Printing, make sure you have the correct IP address.

If you have certain brands of printers, make sure you made the correct selection in the Add Printer dialog. For example, to add an Epson USB printer, select EPSON USB, not USB. Otherwise, you may have problems such as the printer names not appearing in the Printer List or appearing with a question mark on the printer icon.

SEE: • "Using Printer Setup Utility: Adding and Configuring Printers" and "Deleting printers from Printer Setup Utility," earlier in this chapter, for details.

• "Troubleshooting Printing: Checking Printer Drivers," earlier in this chapter.

Deleting Printer Setup Utility's preferences

Some printing problems can be attributed to corrupt Printer Setup Utility preferences (.plist) files. To fix such problems, delete the Preferences file by following these steps:

1. From Printer Setup Utility, select to Stop Jobs for the problem printer.
2. Make sure all jobs currently in its printer queue are deleted.
3. Go to the ~/Library/Preferences folder and delete the file named com.apple.print.PrintCenter.plist (yes, it still says Print Center, not Printer Setup Utility).
4. Select Log Out and then log back in.
5. From Printer Setup Utility, select to Start Jobs for the printer. Try again.

Other printing preferences. If deleting the PrintCenter.plist file doesn't solve your problem, try deleting all files in ~/Library/Preferences that begin with com.apple.print. This may include com.apple.print.custompresets.plist, com.apple.print.favorites.plist, com.apple.print.PrintingPrefs.plist, com.apple .print.PrinterSetupUtility.plist, and a separate .plist file for every named printer and fax in your printer and fax lists. Also delete the printing-related .plist files in the ~/Library/Preferences/ByHost folder.

SEE: • "Take Note: Troubleshooting Shared Printers," above, for related information.

• "Deleting or removing preferences," in Chapter 5, for more general advice.

TAKE NOTE ▶ Print-Related Crashes

If Printer Setup Utility crashes when you try to add a printer, launch Disk Utility's First Aid and select to Repair Disk Permissions. If this fails, there may be a conflict with software running in the background, launched as a Login Item (called Startup Items in Panther, as described in Chapter 5). To test for this, start up with these items disabled.

If a crash of Printer Setup Utility occurs whenever you try to print to a particular printer, try deleting and reading the printer software in Printer Setup Utility. If most of your applications quit whenever you select to print: (a) make sure you are using the latest version of the printer driver(s) and (b) update to Mac OS X 10.3.3 or later. If the crashes continue, delete the com.apple.print.custompresets.plist file in ~/Library/Preferences (you'll have to recreate any custom presets after doing this).

One more specific example: When you try to print to a PostScript printer, the application you're printing from may crash if the PPD for that print queue incorrectly identifies the default paper tray. You may be able to print to the printer by deleting it from Printer Setup Utility and re-adding the printer but selecting Generic PPD as the Printer Model. This is supposedly fixed in Mac OS X 10.2.3 and later.

SEE: • **"Getting updated or third-party printer software," earlier in this chapter, for a related issue involving HP LaserJet 4V and LaserJet 4MV printers.**

Question mark icon in Printer Setup Utility

If a question mark icon appears next to a printer's name in Printer Setup Utility, you need to install or reinstall the printer's software. The problem is that (a) the needed software is not included as part of Mac OS X; (b) you did not make the correct connection selection (for example, USB or AppleTalk) when you added the printer to the list; or (c) you deleted the needed driver software after adding the printer.

SEE: • **"Take Note: How to Reinstall the Mac OS X Printer Drivers," "Adding and using unsupported printers," and "Troubleshooting Printing: Checking Printer Drivers," earlier in this chapter, for more information.**

Using Printer Setup Repair

A third-party utility called Printer Setup Repair (or Print Center Repair in Jaguar), by Fixmac Software includes a variety of options for fixing problems that may occur when using Printer Setup Utility (for example, the applica-tion will not launch or printers cannot be added), as well as when printing any documents.

If you use this utility, first make sure you're using the latest version; in partic-ular, note that the older Print Center Repair will not work in Panther.

Everything that Printer Setup Repair does can be done "manually" with just Mac OS X software. The utility simply automates and simplifies the process. The documentation that comes with Printer Setup Repair details the symptoms it can fix and exactly what it does to fix them. Because Panther fixed some of the bugs that necessitated the use of this utility, the utility does not do as much in Panther as it did in Jaguar. However, it's still useful.

The utility can repair the spool directory, repair the CUPS directory, delete temporary files, fix printing-related permissions, delete printing-related preferences, and install PPD files.

SEE: • **"Getting updated or third party printer software,"** earlier in this chapter, for related information.

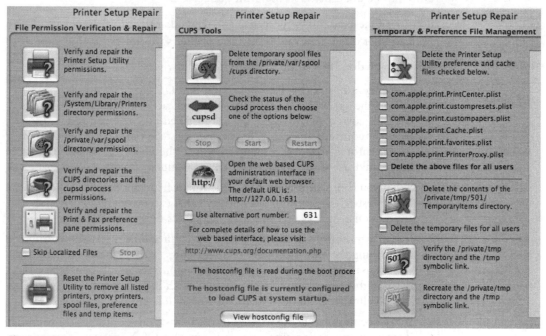

Figure 7.42

A peek at just some of the things you can do with Printer Setup Repair: (left) File Permission Verification & Repair; (middle) CUPS Tools; and (right) Temporary & Preference File Management.

Printing Quick Fixes

This section covers a variety of fixes that did not fit into the preceding sections.

Document or application problems

If a document in a given application does not print (or prints incorrectly), try printing another document from within the same application. Ideally, create a new test document and type just a few characters, then select to print it.

If this fails, try printing a document from a different application, one that currently has no documents in the print queue.

If either of these attempts succeeds, it suggests that the problem is with the application or document rather than the printer software or OS.

What do you do if this is the case? Try the following:

- If testing indicates that the application is at fault, try deleting and reinstalling the application. Make sure the application and its accessory files have the correct permissions and are installed in their required locations (if such requirements exist). In general, the read me file for the software should inform you of any requirements. Otherwise, follow the guidelines you would use if the application failed to launch, as covered in Chapter 6.

- See if you can print the problem document from another application. This is especially useful for documents that can be opened in several applications, such as plain-text files, graphics files, and PDF files.

- If testing indicates that the document is at fault and thus possibly corrupted, try copying the text from the document into a new blank document. If you were using any unusual page layouts, fonts, or graphic inserts, avoid them in the new document, if possible. With luck, this work-around should eliminate the need to start from scratch and retype the text.

- If the document is being printed in the Classic environment, try printing it from an application that runs native in Mac OS X instead. This works around the possibility that the problem is specific to the Classic environment.

- Apple notes, "When you print a document, Mac OS X sends a 'Digital Master' PDF file of your document to the printer to ensure good quality. This file is larger than a typical PDF file because the resolution of images in the file is not scaled down."

  Because of the large size of this file, printing may slow. This is especially likely if your print job contains numerous, large, and/or high-resolution graphic images. Solutions include (a) lowering the resolution of the images (if this is acceptable to you); (b) splitting images into separate documents (if feasible); or (c) selecting the Black & White Quartz filter from the ColorSync options in the Print dialog (if printing a color document to a black-and-white-printer).

- As of this writing, Adobe Reader 6.0 was known to have several printing-related problems. For example, it does not print multiple copies as requested. Until Adobe fixes these issues, you can work around the problems by using Acrobat Reader 5 instead.

  More generally, for problems printing from Reader, Adobe suggests clicking the Advanced button in the Print dialog and checking the Print as Image box. See the following support document for more advice: www.adobe.com/support/techdocs/a9da.htm.

- If none of this works, check the remaining sections of this chapter for more printer-related advice.

Page Setup issues

If a document prints but formatting is incorrect, recheck your Page Setup and Print dialog settings to make sure they're as you intended.

In particular, from Page Setup's "Format for" pop-up menu, select the printer you're using rather than the default Any Printer option.

In some cases, selecting a paper size is also important. For example, to get duplex printing to work in a DeskJet 970C printer, you need to select the printer in the "Format for" menu and select A4 in the Paper Size pop-up menu; selecting A4 as the size in the Print & Fax System Preferences pane is not sufficient.

SEE: • "Margin errors," later in this chapter.

Font problems

Occasionally, a printing problem may have nothing to do with the document itself, the application being used, or the printer software. Instead, the culprit may be a font selected for use in the document. The font file may be corrupt or otherwise incompatible with Mac OS X—with the result being that printing fails when you select the problem font in your document.

The work-around is to select a different font. Be especially suspicious of older fonts located in the Classic System Folder or transferred from a Mac OS 9 System Folder to a Mac OS X /Library/Fonts folder (most likely, the one in your Home directory). To prevent a repeat of the problem, delete the font after you've identified it as the cause. If you need the font, check with the font vendor to see whether a newer version of the font may prevent the problem.

Older versions of Times New Roman and Arial cause problems.
These two fonts ship with Mac OS X but are also provided by Microsoft. Some versions have been reported to cause printing problems in several applications, usually manifested in PostScript or general printing errors (in both Mac OS X and Mac OS 9). Microsoft has updated the fonts, but some people have found that the updated versions were not installed by Mac OS X or by

any Microsoft products (Office or Internet Explorer, for example). The solution is to download the current version of these fonts from www.Microsoft.com/mac/download/office2001/fontsupdate.asp.

SEE: • The sections on fonts in Chapter 4, for other font-related information.

Preview problems

The following are two problems that can occur when using the Preview feature in the Print dialog:

Bugs in Preview. A bug in the Preview application may prevent certain PDF files from opening or printing from Preview. There were several documented cases of this occurring in Jaguar (such as one that led to the following error message: "ERROR NAME: limitcheck ... COMMAND: Type42BuildGlyph ... OPERAND STACK). These bugs are presumably fixed in Panther, but other similar bugs may yet crop up.

The immediate work-around for this problem is to open and print the offending PDF file(s) in Adobe Reader. If you want, you can choose to make Reader the default appli-cation for opening PDF files (via the Open With option in the Get Info window of a PDF document).

Preview launches Classic Acrobat Reader. If you click the Preview button in a Mac OS X Print dialog, the Classic version of Acrobat Reader (the old name for what is now called Adobe Reader) may launch instead of Mac OS X's Preview application. The solution, once again, is to access the Open With section of the Get Info window of any PDF file. From here, select Preview as the application in the pop-up menu and click the Change All button. Preview is now the default PDF application. It should launch the next time you click the Preview button in a Print dialog.

SEE: • "Technically Speaking: Type/Creator vs. Filename Extensions," in Chapter 4, for more details on how to make these changes.

Checking for PostScript errors

If you're using a PostScript printer, you may have printing problems that are specific to PostScript. In such cases, knowing the exact nature of the error may assist in finding a solution.

To get a printout of PostScript errors that may have occurred when trying to print, go to the Print dialog and from the print options pop-up menu select Error Handling. Then click the "Print detailed report" option. If a PostScript error occurs the next time you try to print, you should get a printed report of the problem. If the report does not suggest a solution, contact the printer vendor for advice.

Classic problems

Some printers will not print in Mac OS X when Classic is running. In this case, the usual solution is to quit Classic before attempting to print.

SEE: • " Printing problems," in Chapter 9, for additional information.

Checking Console

You may be able to track down the cause of a printing failure by using the Console application. Launch Console before printing. The error text that is generated when the print job fails may provide a clue to the source of the problem. If the error message refers to fonts, for example, a font selection in the document may be the cause of the problem.

SEE: • Chapters 2 and 5 for coverage of the Console application, especially the Crash Reporter feature.

Margin errors

If text along the right margin of a document appears to be cut off when printed, determine whether your application has a preference to enable fractional (character) widths. If so, enable it. This should fix the problem. For example, in AppleWorks, go to General Preferences and select the Text topic. A Fractional Character Widths check box option will appear.

More generally, if you get a printing-related error message that says something like, "Some margins are smaller than the minimum allowed by the printer. Your document may be clipped," make sure the margins are big enough. In AppleWorks, these settings are in Format > Document. Margin limits vary from printer to printer; however, they usually cannot be smaller than one-half inch.

If the error message persists even though it appears that margins are set correctly, ignore the message and try printing. It may succeed. If not, check the paper size (as listed in Page Setup) and the default paper size (as selected in the Print & Fax System Preferences pane). Make sure they are set as you intended. If so, delete the com.apple.print.custompresets.plist in ~/Library/Preferences. Try printing again.

Permissions error

The initial version of Mac OS X 10.3 contains a bug in which certain system users (lp and postfix) needed to print and (especially) to fax are not properly created. This only happens if you select the Upgrade option when running the Installer from the Mac OS X Install CD. You may not have any symptoms until after you select to Repair Disk Permissions from Disk Utility's First Aid. At this point, Disk Utility "fixes" the permissions by assigning ownership to these users who do not exist. Receiving a fax may also trigger this problem. The result is printing and faxing failures (a typical error message states "Can't open /private/var/spool/cups/{*spool file name*}").

The simplest solution is to upgrade to Mac OS X 10.3.1 or later, which fixes the problem. Alternative solutions exist, though I don't see why anyone would prefer them to installing the Mac OS X update. For the record, these solutions include running a patch program called Print Aid (www.allosx.com/1067395661) or using the File Permission Verification and Repair functions in the Printer Setup Repair utility.

Printer software and CPU slowdowns

When Mac OS X 10.2.2 was released, users of certain Hewlett-Packard printing and scanning devices (for example, All-in-One and ScanJet models) experienced an overall slowdown in the performance of their Macs. The precise cause was an increased processor (CPU) usage attributable to the HP Communications item included with the ScanJet Manager software (which is installed in the /Printers/Library/HP folder). HP confirmed this, noting, "When the ScanJet Manager software conflicts with another piece of software which also manages the USB ports, increased processor usage will result as the ScanJet Manager is forced to increase polling to detect button presses. HP Communications (version 4.6.3) is the cause of the slowdown. Killing the process can help."

The problem with killing the process is that you have to do so each time you restart the Mac. A more general solution is to try any one of the following:

- Downgrade to the prior version of Mac OS X (for example, 10.2.1).
- Revert to the prior version of the Mac OS X IOUSBFamily.kext file (located in /System/Extensions).
- Delete the HP software and use an alternative driver.
- Upgrade to a version of the Mac OS X and/or HP software that fixes the problem (assuming such an upgrade exists).

While the above-cited issue has largely been fixed by more recent updates to Mac OS X and HP software, related problems still occur. For example, HP recently confirmed that "the HP Communication application used by the Photosmart printer may interfere with printing to the LaserJet 1200 printer." The solution in this case is to kill the process when using the LaserJet and relaunch the application when using the Photosmart printer. Similar solutions continue to be cited for a variety of other USB problems, including those with devices such as Palm PDAs.

SEE: • "Force quitting," in Chapter 5, for more on killing processes.

• "Checking for extension (.kext) problems," in Chapter 5, for more information on the IOUSBFamily.kext file.

• "Maximizing Performance," in Chapter 6, for related information.

TAKE NOTE ▶ Scanners and Mac OS X

During the first year after Mac OS X was released, there was very little Mac OS X support for scanners. The primary reason for this drought was that until Mac OS X versions of photo editing software such as Adobe Photoshop were released, there wasn't much incentive to write scanner software for Mac OS X.

However, once Photoshop for Mac OS X was released, scanner software for Mac OS X began to take off. There are now Mac OS X drivers for almost all Epson and Canon scanners. There are also shareware drivers, such as Hamrick Software's VueScan, that work with a variety of scanner models for which the vendors do not offer Mac OS X support.

Scanner drivers work via either a plug-in for Photoshop (most commonly) or a separate scanner utility.

Note: Your scanner software may need to be updated to work in Panther. There have been numerous reports of scanners failing to scan after upgrading to Panther. As always, check with your scanner vendor for specific advice.

Even if a Mac OS X driver does not yet exist for your scanner, you can probably still use the scanner in Mac OS X. You just have to use it via Mac OS 9 software, which you access from the Classic environment.

Checking for other Mac OS X software problems

If none of the preceding suggestions had a positive effect, try the following general software fixes:

- Is Fast User Switching enabled (as described in Chapter 2)? Are two or more users currently logged in? If so, you may find that only the first user to log in can print to a USB printer. If you are not the first logged-in user, the solution is to get the user who *was* first to log out, so that you can print.

- Restart your Mac. This is a potential panacea for a variety of ills, including printing problems.

- Launch Disk Utility and select to Repair Disk Permissions. Some general printing problems (primarily associated with Printer Setup Utility) are permissions-related and are fixed by repairing them. For example, doing this fixed a problem with a –108 error that was known to occur when trying to print in earlier versions of Mac OS X.

- As a last resort, reinstall Mac OS X. If you still can't print, it's time to seek out a witch doctor to remove the spell from your Mac.

8

Troubleshooting Networking: File Sharing and the Internet

You can merrily run Mac OS X independent of the rest of the computing universe, creating documents in your word processor, listening to music with iTunes, and much more. In fact, flying solo was the norm for Mac users until the Internet explosion of the early 1990s. Now it's the exception. These days, almost all Mac users are on some type of network.

For most Mac users, there are two primary reasons to network their Macs:

- **To access the Internet.** This is what you need to do to use email, browse the Web, or connect to remote servers. In networking terms, the Internet is a form of *wide area network* (WAN).

- **To access and share data over a local network.** Computers that are in the same general physical location (for example, a room, an office, or a building) and are linked to one another via a network make up a *local area network* (LAN). Computers on the same LAN can be set up so that files and devices (such as printers) can be shared among them. To accomplish this, you must know (1) how to access the other computers on the LAN, and (2) how to set up your computer so that other users can access it.

These interrelated topics are the subject of this chapter.

In This Chapter
. . . .

Network and Connection/Port Types

When techies talk about *networks*, they're generally referring to a type of system in which multiple computers or computing devices are interconnected. A network may be two computers and a printer in an office, a classroom of computers connected to a central server, a corporate network that extends to several locations across the country, or the Internet itself (which is essentially a global network). Regardless of the arrangement, the purpose of a network is to allow computers to communicate with each other and/or peripheral devices.

Network *connection types*, on the other hand, refer to the ways in which computers connect to each other or to a larger network. Mac OS X calls these different connection types *ports* or *network ports*, and supports a good number of them: Ethernet, modem, AirPort, Bluetooth, and, most recently, FireWire. If you think of a highway system as a network between cities, consider a network port in Mac OS X the vehicle you choose to travel the roads.

I make this distinction between *networks* and *network ports* because it's important to understand that *connection type* and *network type* are not intimately linked. That is, the same connection type can be used for more than one network and, conversely, multiple computers can connect to the same network using different types of connections. As a common example, an Ethernet connection can be used for both a local network and a connection to the Internet.

Although this situation can be a bit confusing, it means that Mac OS X is incredibly flexible in its networking capabilities. You can use Ethernet to communicate with other computers in your home or office while at the same time using a modem to connect to the Internet. Or you can use an AirPort Base Station for both local networking and Internet access. In addition, if your connection and network types change frequently (for example, if you travel with a PowerBook and connect in different ways at different locations), Mac OS X allows you to set up *Locations* that store groups of network settings; you can switch between Locations when necessary.

In the sections that follow, I'll explain each type of network connection and how to set it up for local and Internet connectivity.

Setup Assistants. The first time you start up Mac OS X after installing it, the (Mac OS X) Setup Assistant and/or Network Setup Assistant software (located in /System/Library/CoreServices) automatically launches and offers to walk you through setting up your network and Internet connection. In answering its questions, you're actually editing your Mac's Network preferences, just as if you had entered data in the Network pane of System Preferences. This arrangement simplifies the setup process—especially welcome for novice users. However, if you ever want to alter these settings, or if you opted out of using the Setup Assistants, you will need to know how to interact directly with Mac OS X's networking software, as described in this chapter.

Setting Up System Preferences: Network

The Network pane in System Preferences is where you manage network settings—a task that can seem overwhelming at first because of the myriad combinations of screens and settings. To simplify things, consider first that this preferences pane includes just three basic categories of network settings:

- **Network port configurations.** These settings show which connection types (*ports*) are enabled by you for use (*active* versus *inactive*) and the order (*priority*) in which Mac OS X tries to use them.

- **Connection-specific settings.** These are your network settings for each type of connection. Exactly which options appear will depend on your connection type.

- **Locations.** You can create different combinations of network ports and port-specific settings for different network environments. For example, if you use a laptop, you can have one set for home, a second set for work, and a third set for when you travel. Creating different Locations facilitates these switches.

On the bottom-right side of the Network Preferences pane you will find two buttons:

- **"Assist me."** Click this and the Network Setup Assistant application launches. It walks you through the steps needed to set up Network preferences, just as occurs automatically when you first start up into a new installation of Mac OS X.

- **Apply Now.** Anytime you make a change to a setting in Network preferences, clicking this button saves the change (modifying the file where the settings are stored, as I discuss later in this chapter). This is an essential final step before closing the pane, assuming you made changes you want to save.

At the top of the pane you will find two pop-up menus:

- **Location.** I discuss this in detail in the "Locations" section later in the chapter. Its initial selection is Automatic. Unless you create a new location, this will be the only selection you ever use.

- **Show.** Your selection from this menu determines what the main part of the preferences pane displays. You can select either a particular network port, an option called Network Port Configurations, or an option called Network Status. The Status option is typically the default option when you first access the pane. All of these choices are explained in the following sections.

Figure 8.1

The Network System Preferences pane with Network Status selected.

Network Status

The Network Status screen (which you access by choosing Network Status from the Show pop-up menu) is new in Panther, and a welcome addition. It lists all currently active ports (as set from the Network Port Configurations screen—such as AirPort, Ethernet, and Internal Modem) and the current status of each. For example, if you were connected to the Internet via AirPort, the summary next to AirPort would say something like this: "AirPort is connected to the network {*name of network*}. You are connected to the Internet via AirPort." Similarly, if you had the FireWire port enabled but no cable plugged into it, the FireWire port item would state, "The cable for Built-in FireWire is not plugged in."

In some cases, even if a port is enabled in the Network Port Configurations screen, it may not appear in the Network Status screen. For example, this happens if Built-In Ethernet is enabled but there is no cable plugged into the Ethernet port.

To modify the settings for any listed port, you have three choices: (a) Double-click the name of the port in the Network Status screen; (b) single-click the name of the port in the Network Status screen and click the Configure button near the bottom of the window; or (c) access the Show pop-up menu and select the desired port.

To return to the Network Status screen at any time, select it from the Show pop-up menu.

Finally, next to the Configure button is a Connect/Disconnect button. This button is only "live" if the currently selected item can actively connect or disconnect (for example, a modem, an Ethernet connection using PPPoE, or an AirPort connection). If the selected item is currently connected to the Internet, the button will read Disconnect. If the currently selected item is not connected to the Internet but is set up so that you can attempt to connect via the port, the button will read Connect. What happens *after* you click this button depends on the type of port: Often, the Internet Connect application is launched; from here you can select to disconnect from an AirPort or modem connection.

Network Port Configurations settings and port priority

I have a PowerBook that's connected wirelessly to my cable modem via an AirPort Base Station. At times, however, I would prefer to connect the PowerBook via an Ethernet cable as part of my wired local network. Alternatively, if my cable modem goes down, I am also set up to access the Internet via the PowerBook's internal dial-up modem. With Mac OS X, I can set up all three of these connection types, and have them active simultaneously, via the Network Port Configurations settings. Technically, this process is called *multihoming*. Mac OS X users just call it *great!*

Although you could achieve similar setups in Mac OS 9, Mac OS X offers a unique advantage: You can prioritize connection ports in Mac OS X, and the OS will try each port automatically, in the order you specify, until it obtains a working connection. If the AirPort software is disabled, for example, the PowerBook automatically skips the attempt to connect via AirPort and tries Ethernet instead. Unlike Mac OS 9, Mac OS X requires no modification of settings for this switching to work. You can have multiple ports active at the same time, even for the same network type. (In truth, the switching doesn't *always* work as well as intended. I cover what to do in those situations in "Troubleshooting Applications" and "Troubleshooting Sharing," later in this chapter.)

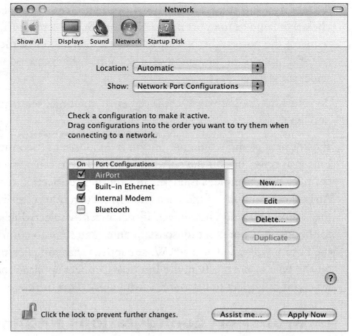

Figure 8.2

The Network System
Preferences pane
with Network Port
Configurations
selected.

To set up your Network Port Configurations, follow these steps:

1. Launch System Preferences; select the Network pane; and from the Show pop-up menu choose Network Port Configurations. The window will change to show a list of all available ports, with a check box next to each.

   Note: If you add the capability for a new port (such as by adding a Bluetooth adapter to your Mac), you will typically get a New Port Detected message when you next launch Network. It is automatically added to the Network Port Configuration list.

2. Turn on each port you plan to use. Similarly, turn off ports you won't be using.

   To turn on a port, also called making it *active,* check the box next to its name.

   To turn off a port (that is, make it *inactive*), uncheck the box by its name. If you will be using your modem and AirPort card, for example, but not your Ethernet port, you can uncheck the Built-In Ethernet box.

   Actually, if you're sure you'll *never* want to use a certain port, you can delete the listing by clicking the Delete button on the right side. Although a warning appears saying that this cannot be undone, you can always re-add the port via the New button, as described next. However, you will need to reenter the settings for the port. Thus, I recommend making a port inactive rather than deleting it—unless you're 100 percent certain you'll never want to access it again.

   Items that are active are listed in the Show pop-up menu. From here, you can select each item to configure its settings (more on that in a bit).

3. If a port type that you know you have isn't listed, add it by clicking the New button.

   If you have an internal modem, for example, but there's no listed port configuration for Internal Modem, click New and then choose Internal Modem from the Port pop-up menu in the dialog that drops down. You can name the connection type anything you want, but for clarity, I recommend something obvious (such as Internal Modem).

   The ports that are available in the Port menu will vary depending on what hardware is connected to or built into your Mac. For example, unless you have a Mac with built-in Bluetooth support or have added a USB Bluetooth adapter, Bluetooth will not be listed as an option. Similarly, if your Mac did not come with an internal modem, and you have not added one, Internal Modem will not be an option.

   SEE: • "Take Note: Ports Created by Other Applications and Devices," below, for related information.

   Note: AirPort is a bit of an oddity—it's not listed in the Port menu even if you have an AirPort card installed in your Mac. Nonetheless, for AirPort-equipped Macs, an AirPort item is listed in the Network Port Configurations list. If you select to delete the item, however, it automatically returns. Presumably, this is designed to prevent more than one AirPort configuration (which is also why the Duplicate button is dimmed when AirPort is selected).

   Note: The 6 to 4 port, listed in the Port menu, is a special port used to connect to an IPv6 address from your Mac (assuming your Mac is using an IPv4 address).

   SEE: • "Technically Speaking: IPv4 vs. IPv6," later in this chapter, for details.

4. If necessary, for some ports, you can create additional ports for the same type of connection.

   Suppose, for example, that you have more than one dial-up Internet service provider (ISP). You can create a separate Internal Modem port for each ISP. To do this, click the New button and create a new Internal Modem port (in addition to the one that's presumably already present). To distinguish between them, give each a different name.

   Alternatively, if you want to create a new port configuration that uses the existing Internal Modem settings as a starting point, select Internal Modem from the list and click the Duplicate button. You can then change the name of the duplicated port by selecting it and clicking the Edit button.

   You are now set to modify the settings of each Internal Modem port, as needed, by selecting each port from the Show pop-up menu.

5. Drag the ports to rearrange their order in the list, as desired.

   The order in which ports are listed in this dialog is important. If you try to initiate a network connection (local or Internet), Mac OS X first tries to connect via the port listed first. If it connects, it stops there. If the connection is unsuccessful, Mac OS X tries the next port. This process continues down the list until a successful connection is made, or until all ports have been tried to no avail (at which point you generally get an error message). What this means for you is that if you have both DSL and dial-up Internet access and want your computer to try to use the DSL connection first, using the modem only if DSL is not available, you should click Built-In Ethernet and drag it *above* Internal Modem. Likewise, if you want your laptop to attempt to dial up your ISP only if it cannot find your AirPort network, make sure that AirPort is listed above Internal Modem.

Once you have created and enabled the ports you wish to be active, your next step is to enter the settings for each port type.

TAKE NOTE ▶ Ports Created by Other Applications and Devices

A few ports may show up in your Network Port Configurations list that are not listed in the Port menu (that is, the menu you access from the dialog that drops down when you click New). How did these items get added? Typically, in one of two ways:

- Certain devices, when connected to the Mac, cause a new port to be created. For example, certain mobile phones (primarily those from Motorola) connect to a Mac via a special USB cable (which you purchase from a mobile-phone vendor). When you open the Network System Preferences pane with such a phone connected, it creates a new modem port and names it using the model name of the phone (for example, *Motorola T720c*). The port name is dimmed and unselectable unless the phone is attached.

   Note: Setting up a Motorola phone port, such as just described, is necessary to sync the data on the phone with your Mac via iSync (as covered in Chapter 11). Theoretically, you could also set up the phone to act as a modem, and thus use it to connect to the Internet. However, this would require having a modem script for the phone that works with the Mac.

   I am aware of one such script, offered by Verizon (called Verizon_Wireless_STD_driver), designed to work specifically with Verizon's CDMA-2000-1XRTT service (also known as its Express Network). However, as of this writing, I have been unable to get my Motorola phone, using this or any other script, to act as a modem for any other dial-up ISP. This will often be the case (that is, a mobile phone will only connect to the Internet via its own pro-prietary method).

- Certain selections in Internet Connect result in the creation a new port. For example, if you select New VPN Connection and then click the radio button for PPTP, a new port called PPTP or VPN (PPTP) will be created in the Network System Preferences pane. When this happens, a message will appear that says, "Your network settings have been changed by another application."

- Devices connected to "serial ports" set up in Bluetooth Serial Utility may optionally be selected to appear in the Network System Preferences list.

SEE: • "Modem" and "Internet Connect," later in this chapter, for more details on Internet Connect, VPN, and modem scripts.
   • "Bluetooth Serial Utility," later in this chapter, for more on this utility.

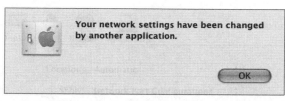

Figure 8.3

The messages that appear in the Network System Preferences pane (top) after a VPN (PPTP) connection is set up in Internet Connect; and (bottom) after a Motorola T720c mobile phone has been attached to the Mac via the USB port.

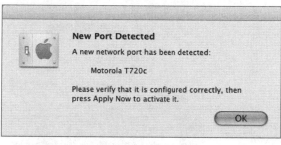

Figure 8.4

The Network Port Configuration list showing VPN (PPTP) and Motorola T720c added.

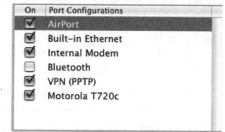

Ethernet (including cable and DSL Internet)

The Ethernet port is the one you use if you're connected to any type of network (including the Internet) via an Ethernet cable. The most basic Ethernet connection is one that goes from the Ethernet port on the back of your Mac to a cable or DSL modem. More complex setups involve the use of an Ethernet hub or router to join multiple devices on the same local network.

To configure the Ethernet port settings, go to the Network System Preferences pane, and from the Show pop-up menu choose Built-in Ethernet. From here, you will be able to configure the various types of connections you'll be using over your Ethernet port.

Note: If you've added extra Ethernet ports via third-party Ethernet PCI cards, the configuration for them will be the same, and you will be able to choose each port's configuration panel from the same Show pop-up menu (they will have something other than "Built-in" in their name).

The Ethernet port settings include five main tabs: TCP/IP, PPPoE, AppleTalk, Proxies, and Ethernet. Each tab brings up a separate screen.

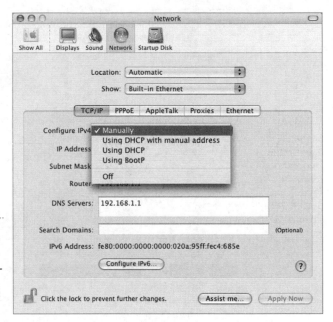

Figure 8.5

....

The Network System Preferences pane with the TCP/IP screen of the Ethernet port selected— and Manually selected from the Configure IPv4 pop-up menu.

TCP/IP. If you access the Internet via a DSL or cable modem or through a company network, you typically enter the required settings in the TCP/IP screen. There are too many settings to cover all the possibilities here: Either you know what you're doing (and thus don't need this book to advise you), or you don't (in which case you'll simply enter what your network provider tells you to, or the settings will be entered automatically as explained below). Still, it's worthwhile to provide a broad overview of these settings.

From the Configure IPv4 pop-up menu, you determine whether you will be entering IP addresses and related information manually or whether a server will provide the information. There are five options:

- **Manually.** If you have a *static IP address* (that is, one that always remains the same), you would generally select Manually. You would then enter the IP address and other ISP information (subnet mask, router, and DNS servers) in the text boxes below the pop-up menu.

- **Using DHCP.** This is the most common option used by cable/DSL providers as well as many large networks. Typically, after making this selection, you're finished! All remaining settings in the TCP/IP pane, including the IP address, are automatically assigned via your ISP or office network's DHCP server. (In some cases you may be asked to provide a DHCP Client ID or domain name server.)

  This setting typically uses a *dynamic IP address* (that is, one that can change over time due to reassignment by the DHCP server).

  With this option selected, an additional button appears in the window: Renew DHCP Lease. Your DHCP address is set to renew after a certain period of time. Renewing a lease typically results in getting a new IP address; however, sometimes your current address is retained after a renewal. In either case, your ISP has rechecked your connection as part of the renewal process. If you click this button, you force an immediate renewal of the lease. If you're having problems with your DHCP connection, clicking this button may help you reconnect successfully.

- **"Using DHCP with manual IP address."** This option is a less common variation of DHCP in which you need to enter a static IP address but the DHCP server provides the rest of the settings.

- **Using BootP.** BootP works much like DHCP; however, it uses a BootP server (common mostly in large office environments) to assign IP addresses and other settings. (If your network administrator asks you to enter DNS information, you enter it here.)

- **Off.** Select this option if you will not be using an IPv4 address at all, but will instead be using an IPv6 address exclusively.

Speaking of IPv6, at the bottom of the window, no matter which Configure IPv4 option you select, you'll find a button labeled Configure IPv6. You may need to click this if you're using an IPv6 address.

SEE: • **"Technically Speaking: IPv4 vs. IPv6" and "Take Note: What Are the TCP/IP settings?," below, for more details on IPv6 and on the other settings shown in the TCP/IP screen.**

Note: If you have cable/DSL Internet access but are using an AirPort card with an AirPort Base Station or third-party wireless router/access point, you should enter your TCP/IP settings in the AirPort screen, rather than the Ethernet one.

SEE: • **"AirPort," later in this chapter.**

TAKE NOTE ▶ What Are the TCP/IP Settings?

The entries in the TCP/IP screen of the Network System Preferences pane are vital to a successful Internet connection. Unfortunately, most users have no idea what they mean. If you're curious, here's a quick primer.

IP Address. If you want a friend to be able to write you a letter, you give him or her your street address. Likewise, if you write a letter to a company, you generally include a return address so that the company can reply to you. The Internet works in much the same way. For someone to contact you, that person needs to know your address, and if you contact someone else, you must provide your address so that he or she can send data back to you.

Your IP (Internet Protocol) address is that address. An IPv4 address is a unique string of numbers (in the format xxx.xxx.xxx.xxx, in which each *xxx* is a number from 0 to 255) that identifies your computer to the rest of the Internet. If you request a Web page, your Web browser provides your IP address to the Web server; the Web server sends the content of that Web page back to your IP address.

continues on next page

TAKE NOTE ▶ **What Are the TCP/IP Settings?**   *continued*

If you have a *static* IP address (generally entered manually in Network preferences), your IP address is always the same. In most other cases, as with most DHCP connections, your ISP (Internet service provider) assigns a temporary IP address when you connect; it lasts until you disconnect or for a certain amount of time set by the ISP or your network administrator (generally days or weeks). This type of address is called a *dynamic* IP address.

Subnet Mask. As just mentioned, an IP address is a string of numbers in the format xxx.xxx.xxx.xxx. The address actually has two parts. The first part identifies the specific local network on which the IP address resides; the second is the particular node (location) of the computer in question on that network. A *subnet mask* delineates which part of your complete IP address refers to the local network and which refers to the node. For a hypothetical IP address of 148.152.168.02, a subnet mask of 255.255.255.0 indicates that the 148.152.168 part of the address refers to the local network, and the .02 refers to the node. A subnet mask of 255.255.0.0 means that the local network is described by 148.152, and .168.02 refers to the node. These delineations are also referred to as *subnet classes*.

Router. An Internet router generally provides a gateway between your computer and the Internet. You send data to the router, which then forwards it on the appropriate path to its destination; data sent to your computer first hits your router and is then directed to you. Unless you have selected Manually from the Configure menu, the router address (if needed) as well as the IP address and subnet mask are typically assigned for you by your ISP or network administrator.

If you're using a locally connected Internet router, you generally enter a specific, local-only "private" router address, as described in "Using a Router," later in this chapter. An address of this type is used for LAN connections because it has been arbitrarily assigned for this purpose. These addresses will never be assigned to any device on a WAN, so there is no chance for confusion between a LAN and a WAN IP address.

Domain Name Servers. The DNS Servers section of the Network System Preferences pane is where you enter the numeric address for any DNS servers you use. You obtain these addresses from your ISP, just as you do for the previously covered settings. Entering one or more addresses here is usually optional because for most types of connections, the ISP connection (for example, DHCP) provides them automatically. Some setups (notably Manually), however, require that an address be entered.

Troubleshooting tip: Entering the wrong DNS Server address can prevent a successful Internet connection. For example, when I switched from @home to Comcast for my cable connection, the DNS address that I had been using (which was still entered in the DNS Servers tex tbox) was no longer valid. Until I realized this fact and deleted the previous address, I was unable to connect to the Internet!

continues on next page

TAKE NOTE ▶ **What Are the TCP/IP Settings?** *continued*

If you're using an Internet router (especially if you selected Manually as the Configure option in the TCP/IP screen of Network System Preferences), you may circumvent certain connection problems by entering your router's IP address (that is, the same address listed in the Router text field) in the DNS Servers field rather than entering your ISP's DNS Server address or leaving the field blank.

Note: Your ISP's DNS address(es) will still be listed in the router's settings (as covered in "Configuring a Router," later in this chapter).

Here's what a DNS Server does and why you need one:

When you enter a Web address, such as www.apple.com, you're entering a "readable" substitute for the true numeric IP address of the site. Special software on the Internet, called *domain name system* (DNS) servers, converts this domain name to the appropriate IP number. More specifically, domain name servers host databases that translate the readable text domain name to the specific IP address to which it corresponds. Thus, when you enter `www.apple.com`, your computer contacts the DNS server(s) listed in this field and retrieves the actual IP address of that domain name; then it contacts the IP address directly.

This is all necessary because the connection requires the true IP address, not the domain name. The domain name system allows you to use an easy-to-remember URL without having to know the IP address. It similarly means that a Web site can change its IP address without your needing to relearn it. If the DNS server is not working correctly, however, you may find that you cannot access a Web page via its domain name (though you can still access it via its IP address).

What if you don't know the IP address of a Web site? You can find it in several ways. One method is to use the ping function of the Network Utility included with Mac OS X (though you need to do this before a DNS problem appears for the function to work). Enter `www.apple.com` as the address to ping, and the results window will show you the IP address (17.254.0.91 or 17.254.3.183, at the time of this writing). You can test it yourself by entering `http://17.254.0.91` in your Web browser. This action should take you to the Apple site (unless Apple's IP address has changed since I wrote this, which is always a possibility).

Search Domains. If you frequently access servers or Web sites that reside within a single larger domain (*sales*.domain.com, *finance*.domain.com, and so on), you can place the local network name (*domain*.com) in this field. The contents of this field will be added to the end of any incomplete domain names (*sales*, *finance*). Most users will not need to use this option.

SEE: • **"Technically Speaking: IPv4 vs. IPv6," below, for more on the new-in-Panther IPv6 feature.**

TECHNICALLY SPEAKING ▶ IPv4 vs. IPv6

There' a problem with IPv4 addresses that no one could have anticipated back when the system was created and before anyone knew how popular the Internet would become: We're rapidly running out of IP addresses! The IPv6 configuration solves this by increasing the address size from IPv4's 32 bits to 128 bits. The longer addresses also allow for simpler auto-configuration—which means you rarely need to enter your own settings with this protocol.

IPv6's use is currently limited, primarily to large research and educational institutions. Thus, it's unlikely you'll be using it. In addition, in most cases, your ISP will automatically assign your IPv6 addresses—which means you don't need to do anything extra even if you are using IPv6. Thus, most Mac users can ignore the entire IPv6 issue for now.

For those rare cases in which you need to manually set up an IPv6 address, click the Configure IPv6 button at the bottom of the TCP/IP screen, and from the Configure IPv6 pop-up menu select Manually. Then enter the Address, Router, and Prefix Length data supplied by your network administrator.

The default IPv6 setting is Automatic. This is why you do not even need to click the Configure IPv6 button if your address is automatically assigned.

Note: To completely disable IPv6, select Off from the pop-up menu.

Note: The current IPv6 address is listed in the IPv6 Address line (below the Search Domains setting in the TCP/IP screen)—assuming an Ethernet cable is currently plugged into the Ethernet port. The automatically calculated IPv6 address adds your Ethernet MAC (Media Access Control) address to the tail end of the IPv6 address. (Compare the similarity of the MAC address, as listed in the Ethernet screen, with the IPv6 address.)

"6 to 4" network port configuration. If you need to connect to an IPv6 address and your Mac is using IPv4, you can still do so; simply follow these steps:

1. From the Show menu for the Network System Preferences pane, select Network Port Configurations.

2. Click the New button.

3. From the Port pop-up menu, select "6 to 4."

4. Assign a name to the selection (for example, *6 to 4*) and click OK.

5. Turn on the "6 to 4" port in the Configuration list, if not already on, by clicking its On check box.

6. If you need to manually set up a relay address, select the "6 to 4" port from the Show pop-up menu, and from the Configure pop-up menu select Manually.

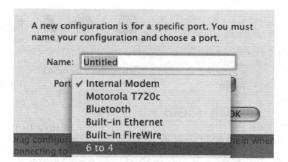

Figure 8.6

The "6 to 4" port, as listed in the Port pop-up menu in the dialog that appears after you click New in the Network Port Configurations screen of the Network System Preferences pane.

TAKE NOTE ▶ Ethernet Hubs, Switches, Routers, and Cables

Before you take even the first steps in setting up your Ethernet network, you should be familiar with some basic terminology.

Hubs, switches, and routers. If you have only two Ethernet devices, your network is very simple: a single cable connecting the two. If you have more than two devices with Ethernet ports (multiple computers, printers, and so on), you need a way to connect them. Hubs, switches, and routers provide such functionality in different ways. By far, the most common device in use today is the router. As such, it will be the focus of the coverage in this chapter. The following, however, provides a brief description of each type:

- **Hub.** A hub takes incoming data from one Ethernet port and broadcasts it to every other Ethernet port on the hub. This setup is fine for small networks, but when it's used in larger networks with many devices, performance can degrade, because every device attached to the hub has to filter through the data being sent by every other device.

- **Switch.** Switches are similar to hubs, but instead of sending incoming data back out to every connected device, a switch checks the destination address contained in the data (usually the MAC address of the appropriate Ethernet port) and forwards the data only to the appropriate machine. In addition, if the destination address is not valid (doesn't exist on any devices connected to the switch), the data basically dies at the switch. Switches learn the MAC address of connected devices by examining the data that passes through the switch.

- **Router.** Routers are similar to switches, but instead of directing traffic based on hardware (MAC) addresses, routers rely on network addresses (IP addresses). Unlike a switch, which generally configures itself, routers need to be configured by the user. Because routers can isolate parts of your network on different subnets, they allow you to share a single IP address among several network devices.

  An Internet router, used for sharing a broadband or modem connection to the Internet (discussed elsewhere in this chapter), is a specific type of router.

  A wireless router is a combination of a traditional router (which uses Ethernet cables to connect devices) and a *wireless bridge* (which *bridges* a wired network with a wireless one). An AirPort Base Station is an example of a wireless router (albeit one with fewer Ethernet ports than a traditional router).

continues on next page

TAKE NOTE ▶ Ethernet Hubs, Switches, Routers, and Cables *continued*

Note: These devices, as well as the Macs to which they connect, may operate at different speeds, such as 100 Mbps or 1 gigabit. In general, the slowest device in the chain determines overall speed. Thus, data traveling between two Gigabit Ethernet Macs connected via a router with a maximum speed of 100 Mbps will travel at 100 Mbps.

Ethernet cables. Devices on an Ethernet network are connected by Ethernet cables. Two kinds of Ethernet cables are available: standard and crossover. The difference between the two has to do with how the strands of wire in the cable are arranged.

- **Standard.** This type of cable has the strands of cable used for sending and receiving data in the same location on both ends. You generally use this type of cable to hook devices to a hub, switch, or router in a multiple-device network: computers to hubs, printers to hubs, hubs to routers, and so on. The data is transferred from the send wires of the incoming cable to the receive wires of the outgoing cable as data passes through the hub, switch, or router. Most printers with Ethernet ports also use a standard cable to connect to a computer.

- **Crossover.** This type of cable has its send and receive wires switched (so that the signal "crosses over"), and is often used to network two computers directly (without any kind of hub, switch, or router).

Because most users can't easily visually distinguish between the two cable types, cables are a frequent source of trouble when connecting computers. Using a crossover cable where a standard cable is needed (or vice versa) will result in a failed connection. Note that many hubs, switches, and routers have an Ethernet port marked Uplink. This port is designed to accept a crossover cable rather than a standard cable. The port for an Internet connection may also use a crossover cable.

The latest Macs use Ethernet ports that sense the type of cable and automatically adjust to work with either type. If your Mac has this capability, it will be listed as such in the technical specifications section of the documentation that came with the computer. Alternatively, check the following Apple Knowledge Base article for which Macs still require a crossover cable: http://docs.info.apple.com/article.html?artnum=42717.

SEE: • "Using a Router," later in this chapter, for more information on routers.
  • "Take Note: What Are the TCP/IP Settings?" earlier in this chapter, for related information.

PPPoE. Some ISPs that provide DSL or cable Internet access use a protocol called *PPPoE* (short for Point-to-Point Protocol over Ethernet). This protocol is a variation of the older modem-style Point-to-Point Protocol (PPP) that has been adapted for use for broadband connections. If your ISP uses this protocol, PPPoE verifies your user name and password when you connect to its servers.

Enabling "Connect using PPPoE" in the PPPoE screen allows you to connect via PPPoE. It also changes your settings in the TCP/IP screen: The only options now available from the Configure pop-up menu will be Manually and a new option, PPP. Generally, you will want to use PPP, which generates the rest of the needed settings being entered by the PPPoE server.

Back in the PPPoE screen, you need to enter an account name and password for your ISP account. These are used to determine your status when you attempt to connect, in what amounts to a login procedure. Thus, until you connect and log in, you will not have an active Internet connection (even though your Network settings are correct). (Typically, you connect via a menu bar item or the Internet Connect application, as described two paragraphs down.)

If you click the PPPoE Options button, a dialog drops down, from which you can select different Session options. These options determine whether Mac OS X automatically attempts to connect when needed (for example, when an Internet application such as a Web browser is launched), and whether the OS should disconnect automatically (for example, after a designated period of idle activity). A few advanced logging and connection options are also presented.

If you select "Show PPPoE status in menu bar," a PPPoE item is added to your menu bar. From here, you can connect or disconnect from the PPPoE server. The menu will also indicate the current status of your connection (for example, idle, connected, or disconnected). The Internet Connect application similarly lets you initiate a PPPoE connection and monitor its status, as long as you have selected PPPoE and enabled Ethernet as an active network port.

SEE: • "Internet Connect," later in this chapter.

AppleTalk. This "legacy" Mac OS protocol is used primarily to connect multiple local devices, such as a few Macs and a printer. However, a TCP/IP connection can accomplish the same task (without using AppleTalk), and in general, Mac OS X prefers it. In fact, future versions of Mac OS X may not even support AppleTalk. Still, if you prefer to use it, or if you have devices that can *only* connect via AppleTalk (such as a Mac running an older version of the Mac OS that does not support TCP/IP sharing or an Ethernet printer that is AppleTalk-only), you will need to enable AppleTalk over the Ethernet port.

To enable AppleTalk, check the Make AppleTalk Active box in the AppleTalk screen.

The other AppleTalk settings are generally only applicable if you're on a large network, such as at a university. If your network has multiple AppleTalk zones, you can select the zone in which you want your computer to appear. In addition, if you need to change your AppleTalk node or network IDs (which you should only do if you've been told to by a network administrator), you make the change by choosing Manually from the Configure pop-up menu. Note that the Computer Name option in this screen is set in the Sharing pane of System Preferences.

Starting with Mac OS X 10.2, you can only enable AppleTalk for one network port at a time. Thus, if you have AppleTalk enabled for Ethernet, you cannot also enable it for AirPort. If you try to enable AppleTalk on a second port, you will get an error message stating that AppleTalk can be active on only one port and that if you continue, AppleTalk will be disabled on its currently enabled port.

In addition, if you use PPPoE on an existing Ethernet port, you cannot enable AppleTalk on that port. If you try, you'll get the following error message: "AppleTalk cannot be used with PPPoE. To use AppleTalk, select the Advanced pane and create a new Ethernet configuration." You can create multiple configurations of the same Ethernet port to allow access to AppleTalk.

SEE: • "Setting Up System Preferences: Sharing," later in this chapter.

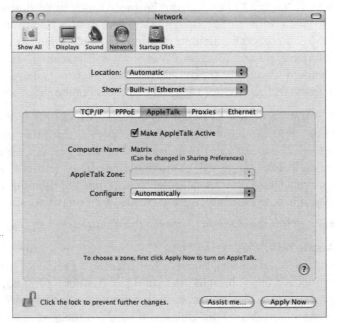

Figure 8.7

The Network System Preferences pane with the AppleTalk screen of the Ethernet port selected.

Proxies. A proxy is generally a server that sits on a network (or is implemented by an ISP) and intercepts requests from individual computers before they go out to the Internet at large. There are separate proxy server settings for different Internet services (for example, FTP and Web).

Acting as an intermediary between these computers and the Internet, the proxy server performs a few different functions. First, a proxy often works with a firewall to provide protection for computers on the local network. Second, proxy servers often implement content filters that allow or restrict access to particular data or Web sites. Finally, most proxy servers cache data so that multiple or repeated requests for the same Web page from within the network require only a single external request (the proxy requests the remote page and then stores it and "serves" it to everyone on the local network).

Most users will not need to deal with proxies. If your network is served by a proxy, your network administrator will supply the information you need to fill in the fields in the Proxies screen.

If you do need to enable proxies, you may have difficulties accessing some network features. For example, accessing the iTunes Music Store was blocked by certain proxy settings when using iTunes version 4.0 (this problem was fixed with iTunes 4.0.1).

SEE: • **"Take Note: Troubleshooting Downloading Files,"** later in this chapter, for one example of using this Proxies screen.

Ethernet. The Ethernet tab is new in Panther. If you click it, you will see two items:

- **Ethernet ID.** An IP address is assigned in software and can be changed at any time. By contrast, an Ethernet ID (also called a MAC address) is a hardware address that identifies your computer uniquely and is hard-coded into your computer before it ships. ISPs and network administrators may use your Ethernet address for verification purposes (such as to make sure that it really is you trying to connect via your DSL connection). If your ISP uses such verification, this can be a problem if, for example, you purchase a new computer; the result can be no Internet connection until you contact your ISP and get it to update its records to include the ID for your new hardware.

  The Ethernet ID is also used in IPv6 addresses, as well as for machine-specific preferences (for example, the ones located in the ByHost folder of the Preferences folder in your Library folder).

  SEE: • **"Preferences Files,"** in Chapter 4, for more on ByHost preferences.

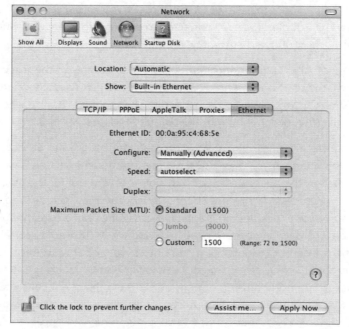

Figure 8.8

The Network System Preferences pane with the Ethernet screen of the Ethernet port selected—and Manually selected from the Configure pop-up menu.

- **Configure pop-up menu.** The default setting from the Configure pop-up menu is Automatically. If, like most users, this is your setting, you'll need never access this screen. If, however, you select Manually (Advanced) from the Configure menu, a set of modifiable options appears. These include

Speed, Duplex, and Maximum Packet Size (MTU). The only time you will need to change these settings is to solve certain troubleshooting problems.

SEE: • "Technically Speaking: Ethernet Speed, Duplex, and MTU Problems," below, for more details.

TECHNICALLY SPEAKING ▶ Ethernet Speed, Duplex, and MTU Problems

The options that appear when you select "Manually (Advanced)" in the Ethernet screen of Network's Ethernet port settings allow you to modify the speed, duplex, and MTU of your Ethernet connection. Although it's unlikely that you'll need to make changes in this screen, the following explains what the settings mean and when you might need to alter them.

Speed. Changing this setting from its default of autoselect forces your Ethernet port to use a particular supported speed (10base or 100base or 1000base) for sending and receiving data. You should only change this setting if your Mac does not seem to be selecting the correct speed automatically.

SEE: • "Take Note: Ethernet Hubs, Switches, Routers, and Cables," earlier in this chapter, for more background.

Duplex. This setting can only be changed from its default of auto if you select a specific speed option in the setting above. You have two choices: full-duplex and half-duplex. Full duplex means that data can travel both to and from a computer at the same time. Half duplex allows only one direction at a time and is thus slower. In most cases, you would select full-duplex. You're only likely to need half-duplex if you're connected to certain large networks where a full-duplex connection cannot be configured automatically.

MTU. This setting, which stands for *maximum transition unit*, controls the size of the largest packets of data that your Mac will send over a network. You can select Standard (the default), Jumbo, or your own Custom value. You may need to change the MTU rate when connecting to certain ISPs that don't work correctly with the default MTU rate—as in the following example:

If you're using Internet Sharing to share your Internet connection with other computers (as covered later in this chapter), you may find that your Internet connection is working fine with the primary computer (the one connected to the Internet) but not for the machines that are getting their Internet access via Internet Sharing. Symptoms may include Web pages' not loading, an inability to use Sherlock, and an inability to use iTunes' radio (streaming audio) feature. The cause may be a somewhat obscure issue involving the MTU used by certain ISPs. When the problem occurs, the Internet Sharing client computers are probably attempting to use an MTU of 1500, whereas your ISP may be maxing out at a lower number, such as 1454 or 1492. The result is that packets are not received correctly. Fortunately, the major cause of this problem was a bug with Mac OS X 10.2 through 10.2.4; thus, you can avoid it by upgrading to Mac OS X 10.2.5 or later (including 10.3, of course). If you continue to have this problem in Mac OS X 10.3, you can modify the MTU rate (so the Mac's value matches that of your ISP) by clicking the Custom radio button and entering the desired MTU value.

continues on next page

> **TECHNICALLY SPEAKING ▶ Ethernet Speed, Duplex, and MTU Problems**
> *continued*
>
> Note: In Mac OS X 10.2 (Jaguar), these changes required a rather complex procedure that involved using the ifconfig command in Terminal. Mac OS X 10.3 (Panther) makes things a lot easier!
>
> Note: If you use a router, the router software may include an option to vary the MTU value, especially when using a PPPoE connection (which is when this issue is most likely to be relevant). You can use this option instead of the MTU option in the Network System Preferences pane, if you prefer.

AirPort

If you have an AirPort card installed in your Mac and you want to use it to connect to a wireless network, you will need to set up the Network System Preferences pane for AirPort. (For the purposes of this discussion, *AirPort* refers to both the original AirPort and the newer AirPort Extreme, unless specifically stated otherwise.)

If you're connecting to a wireless network that has already been set up, the Network System Preferences pane is your starting point: From the Show pop-up menu select AirPort. Setting up the TCP/IP, AppleTalk, and Proxies data for AirPort is very similar to the procedure just described for Ethernet. The one tab that's not found in the Ethernet settings is called, appropriately enough, AirPort.

Note: If you intend to connect to your own wireless network and have not yet set it up, your initial step is to set up your AirPort Base Station, compatible wireless router, or software router connection.

SEE: • "Take Note: Setting Up an AirPort Base Station and Network," "Using a Router," and "Internet," later in this chapter, for information on setting up a router prior to using the AirPort settings in the Network System Preferences.

• "Internet Connect," later in this chapter, for related information.

AirPort. The AirPort tab is the first one in the row of four tabs. The settings here determine how your Mac connects to a wireless network.

There are four items of note in the AirPort screen:

• **AirPort ID.** This sequence of letters and numbers uniquely identifies your AirPort card. In essence, it's the MAC address of the card.

Note: An AirPort Base Station also has an AirPort ID, which you may need on occasion (such as when setting up a wireless distribution system). You can find it on the bottom of the Base Station next to the AirPort symbol. For AirPort Extreme Base Stations, it is also listed in (a) the initial screen of the AirPort Admin Utility (in the pane on the right after you select the

Base Station from the list on the left); and (b) the AirPort screen of the Internet Connect utility.

- **"By default, join" pop-up menu.** This menu offers two choices: Automatic and "A specific network." If the desired network is the only one within range, or if you want to connect to the strongest signal, leave the selection as Automatic—the Mac locates the network with the strongest signal (which may or may not be the nearest base station) and tries to join it. If a password is required to join the network, you will be prompted to enter it.

  If you want to connect to a specific network, even if it is not the nearest or strongest one, select the "A specific network" option and enter the Network and Password information. You can access the names of currently available networks from the pop-up menu at the end of the Network text box. Note, however, that you can only set up one network in this way. If you have several AirPort networks that you want to set up in this way, you will need to create a separate Location for each.

  Note: You can also use the "A specific network" option to join a closed network.

  Note: If you're setting up your own AirPort network, you can create passwords via the AirPort Setup Assistant application.

  SEE: • **"Locations,"** later in this chapter, for details on setting up multiple locations.
  - **"Take Note: Setting Up an AirPort Base Station and Network,"** later in this chapter, for more on closed networks.
  - **"Take Note: Passwords and Joining a Wireless Network,"** later in this chapter, for more information regarding passwords.

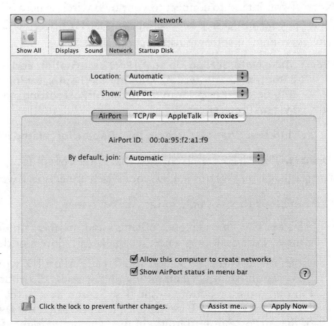

Figure 8.9

The Network System Preferences pane with the AirPort screen of the AirPort port selected.

- **"Allow this computer to create networks."** If you enable this option, your Mac will be able to set up a computer-to-computer wireless network. This allows two Macs with AirPort cards to connect to each other via a temporary network without needing an AirPort Base Station as an intermediary. You create the actual network via the Create Network command in the AirPort menu bar. Cool.

  SEE: • The "AirPort" section of "Internet Connect," later in this chapter, for details.

- **"Show AirPort status in menu bar."** If you check this box, an AirPort Signal Strength icon is placed in the menu bar. The icon provides a graphical representation of both your active AirPort connection (gray when not connected, black for an active connection) and the strength of your signal. If you click the icon, you access a menu that includes options to (a) turn AirPort on or off (turning AirPort off prevents AirPort connections until you turn it back on, as well as conserving battery power on laptops); (b) join an existing AirPort network, either to a Base Station (or other wireless router) or via a computer-to-computer network (done by selecting one of the networks listed or by choosing Other to connect to a closed network that's not listed); (c) create your own computer-to-computer network (via the Create Network command); (d) open Internet Connect; or (e) enable Use Interference Robustness (which you may want to do if you have an AirPort Extreme card and suspect that interference from a nearby wireless device, such as a cordless phone, may be causing problems with your AirPort connection). You may sometimes need to turn on AirPort and select a network from this menu even if you selected to automatically connect to a network in the Network System Preferences pane.

  Note: Connecting to a network is a separate issue from connecting to the Internet. Thus, you may successfully connect to an AirPort network, but unless the network to which you're connecting is itself successfully connected to the Internet, you still won't be able to access Internet services such as email or Web browsing.

  Note: If you purchased an AirPort Extreme Base Station that contains a modem, and set up the Base Station to connect via that modem, you should see a hierarchical menu off of the network name in the AirPort menu. This submenu includes options to connect to or disconnect from the Internet via the modem.

Figure 8.10

The AirPort menu in the menu bar.

SEE: • **"Take Note: Setting Up an AirPort Base Station and Network,"**
later in this chapter, for more details.

• **"Internet Connect," later in this chapter, for more details.**

• **"Troubleshooting wireless connections," later in this chapter,**
for more on Use Interference Robustness and other options for
improving the quality of an AirPort connection.

Note: The AirPort screen options in Panther have been considerably reorganized from what they were in Jaguar. For example, Jaguar includes options to
automatically join the network with the best signal versus the most recently
used available network. These options have been eliminated in Panther.

TCP/IP. When using AirPort or another type of wireless router to access the
Internet, you will enter your TCP/IP settings here. (These settings work just
like the corresponding ones on the TCP/IP screen for Ethernet port configurations, described earlier in the chapter.) If your wireless router is set up to
use DHCP or BootP, you can simply choose the appropriate setting from the
Configure pop-up menu, and the router will take care of the rest. If your
router is set up for static IP addresses, you will need to enter each setting
manually. (Your IP address will usually be something like 192.168.1.x or
10.0.0.x, and the router address will generally be 192.168.1.1 or 10.0.0.1.)

SEE: • **"Take Note: Setting Up an AirPort Base Station and Network," later in**
this chapter, for how to set up an AirPort Base Station.

If your ISP requires that you use certain domain name servers, you may need
to enter their addresses as well (see "Take Note: What Are the TCP/IP
Settings?" earlier in the chapter, for more details).

AppleTalk. If you plan to use AppleTalk over an AirPort network, this
screen is where you enable it (by checking the Make AppleTalk Active box).
An AirPort AppleTalk network does not require an AirPort Base Station; you
can create a network between two AirPort-equipped computers directly. You
can also choose an AppleTalk zone (if applicable) and manually configure your
AppleTalk node ID and network ID.

Note that some third-party wireless routers do not support AppleTalk over
AirPort and wireless connections. If your wireless router is one of those,
you'll need to create a computer-to-computer network to communicate with
another computer via wireless AppleTalk.

SEE: • **"Internet Connect," later in this chapter, for more details.**

Proxies. If your ISP or network requires proxies, you enter proxy information in this screen.

TAKE NOTE ▶ Setting Up an AirPort Base Station and Network

An AirPort Base Station is not the only hardware device for creating a wireless network to use with Macs. You can use AirPort cards with third-party wireless routers instead of an AirPort Base Station. In fact, you can even use wireless PC cards instead of AirPort cards in PowerBooks with PC Card slots. However, the AirPort Base Station is the only such device made by Apple—and the only to have software support built into Mac OS X. Therefore, this sidebar focuses on how to setup an AirPort Base Station.

Base Station models. Apple has released three AirPort Base Station models:

- **Graphite.** The original model was called the Graphite version (because of its color).

- **Dual Ethernet.** The next model (white instead of Graphite) was called the Dual Ethernet model because it added a second Ethernet port, providing one for WAN and one for LAN connections. In general, you connect to your cable or DSL modem via the WAN port, and you connect to other Macs on your local network via the LAN port. This is especially helpful for troubleshooting a Base Station when the wireless connection is not working; you can still connect to the Base Station via the LAN Ethernet port while your broadband modem remains connected to the WAN port.

- **Extreme.** The most recent Base Station is AirPort Extreme. This model uses a newer version of the wireless transmission protocol (802.11g, as opposed to the 802.11b) that can transmit data five times faster (54 Mbps). To get this speed bump, you must use new AirPort Extreme cards (which only fit in the AirPort Extreme slots on newer Macs). However, the Extreme Base Station is backward-compatible, so it can still connect to the original 802.11b cards. The Extreme Base Station also includes a USB port that allows you to connect a printer and share it with computers connected to the wireless network. AirPort Extreme also supports Rendezvous, for quickly finding and making connections to compatible devices.

  Finally, if your AirPort Extreme Base Station has a built-in modem (optional on the Extreme), you can call in to the modem while on the road and gain access to your entire wireless network. As with previous models that included a modem, the Base Station automatically attempts to make a connection to your dial-up ISP whenever you launch an Internet application.

  This model also has separate ports for LAN (with the double-arrow Ethernet icon) and WAN (with the circle-of-dots icon), as introduced in the Dual Ethernet model.

Because the newer models offer options not available in the older ones, the options accessible in the AirPort software may vary depending upon which Base Station you're using. For the remainder of this sidebar, I will be referring to AirPort Extreme options unless otherwise noted.

continues on next page

TAKE NOTE ▶ **Setting Up an AirPort Base Station and Network** *continued*

Internet Connection Warning message. If you connect to the Internet via a wired router, you may decide to attach an AirPort Base Station to the network, so that AirPort-connected Macs can access the Internet. In this case, the Base Station's LAN Connector (port) connects to the router, which in turn connects to the Internet. The WAN Connector remains unused. This is called a *bridge* connection. In such cases, you may get an Internet Connection Warning message when you first connect to the Base Station. The warning states that you should be connected via the WAN port instead of the LAN port. In this setup, you can typically ignore this warning. Actually, in this setup, I have found that connecting via either port usually works. For other setups, if you get this message, follow its advice. In general, use the WAN port to connect to whatever device connects to the Internet; use the LAN port to connect to wired clients.

Base Station software. This software contains two primary components:

- **AirPort Admin Utility.** This utility, located in the Utilities folder in Mac OS X, allows you to connect to a Base Station and input the settings needed for connecting the Base Station to the Internet—or otherwise modify your AirPort network settings.

- **Base Station firmware.** The Base Station itself has firmware code built into it. Occasionally, Apple will release an update to the firmware, usually as part of a general update to the Admin Utility. If installing the new Admin Utility doesn't automatically update the firmware, you can manually update it via the Upload command in the Base Station menu of the Admin Utility. (You first have to access the Base Station, as described below.)

AirPort Setup Assistant. In addition to the Base Station software, there's one more piece of AirPort-related software: the AirPort Setup Assistant (located in the Utilities folder). It provides the simplest and most user-friendly way to set up an AirPort network. After launching Setup Assistant, you can choose to either (a) set up your computer to join an existing AirPort network, or (b) set up an AirPort Base Station.

- **"Set up your computer to join an existing AirPort network."** In most cases, this option accomplishes the same connection goal that you can accomplish via the methods described in the main text (selecting an existing network in Internet Connect or via the AirPort menu in the menu bar).

- **"Set up an AirPort Base Station."** Choose this option if you're using AirPort for the first time—that is, no existing network has been set up—and you need to set up your Base Station. If this is the case, you probably don't have an active wireless connection. If so, you'll need to connect the Base Station to your Mac via an Ethernet cable in order to set it up. The Assistant walks you through the steps, including setting up the initial network. When you're finished, the Assistant uploads the information to the Base Station. You're now ready to set up and join a network.

  You will also use this option in AirPort Setup Assistant any time you want to communicate with a Base Station but can't get the AirPort connection to work. The steps differ a bit in this case, but the Assistant again walks you through the process, allowing you to modify or troubleshoot the network.

continues on next page

TAKE NOTE ▶ Setting Up an AirPort Base Station and Network *continued*

If you use AirPort Setup Assistant, your Base Station will only be able to use DHCP (as set in the Internet screen of the Base Station and in the TCP/IP for AirPort screen of the Network System Preferences for the client computer) to communicate with other devices on the network. If you want to assign IP addresses manually, you must use the AirPort Admin Utility to set up the Base Station. In fact, if you used the Admin Utility to set your Base Station *not* to use DHCP but then connect to the Base Station using Setup Assistant, you will receive an error message warning that Setup Assistant cannot configure the Base Station until DHCP is turned on. Depending on the version of the software you're using, the Assistant will either offer to change your settings (turning on DHCP) or instruct you to use the AirPort Admin Utility instead. Thus, if you want to make changes beyond what the Setup Assistant can handle, you will need to use the Admin Utility.

continues on next page

Figure 8.11

The AirPort Internet Connection Warning message.

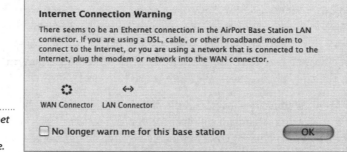

Figure 8.12

The AirPort Setup Assistant utility: the screen that appears upon launch.

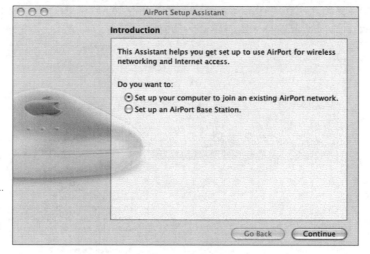

TAKE NOTE ▶ Setting Up an AirPort Base Station and Network *continued*

Finally, the Setup Assistant utility only works if you have an AirPort card installed. If you want to configure a base station from a Mac that does not have an AirPort card installed (using a wired Ethernet connection, for example), you will (again) need to use the more full-featured but somewhat less user-friendly AirPort Admin Utility. Personally, I use the Admin Utility exclusively, at least after the initial setup is complete.

AirPort Admin Utility. The first time you launch this utility on an AirPort network, you'll get a list of all base stations within range. If the one you're looking for is not listed, click the Rescan button to try again. If that technique fails, and you know the IP address of the Base Station, click the Other button and enter the IP address and password. If neither of these approaches works, you need to check your basic network connections (as described in the main text for the Network System Preferences) to make sure that the Base Station is correctly connected to the network.

Note: As mentioned earlier, if you're using a Base Station for the first time and thus have no AirPort network setup, the Base Station must be connected to the computer running the Admin utility via an Ethernet connection. You may also access a Base Station from a Mac that does not have an AirPort card—at any time—by connecting the Base Station to the Mac over an Ethernet connection. In such cases, only the Base Station(s) connected via Ethernet will be listed in the AirPort Admin Utility window. Recall that if your AirPort Base Station has both WAN and LAN ports, you typically connect it to the Mac via the LAN port.

When the appropriate Base Station is listed, double-click it (or select it and then click the Configure button) to access its settings. If the Base Station has already been configured, you will have to enter its password. (Even if it has not been configured before, you may need to enter a default password: *public*.)

Note: If you select to add the password to your Keychain (via the option in the Password dialog), you won't be prompted to enter it in the future.

continues on next page

Figure 8.13

The AirPort Admin Utility: the Select Base Station dialog that appears upon launch.

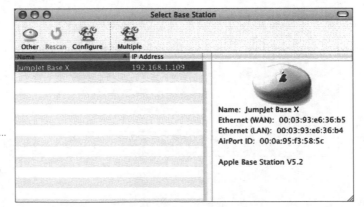

TAKE NOTE ▶ Setting Up an AirPort Base Station and Network   *continued*

Note: If you enter the wrong password, you will get an error message that states rather ambiguously, "An error occurred while reading the configuration." Note also that the Base Station password is separate from the password you use to join a network. Each network can have its own unique password, separate from other networks as well as from the Base Station.

After you connect to a Base Station using the Admin Utility, you will be presented with buttons for four options. In addition, there will likely be a toolbar with four icons.

Toolbar icons. Listed across the top of the window are the following four icons:

- **Restart.** Restart (also called a *soft reset*) is the AirPort equivalent of restarting your Mac; it may fix temporary connection problems.

- **Upload.** If you want to upload a newer firmware version to the Base Station (such as an update released by Apple), click the Upload button and then select the update file in the dialog that appears. (Note: In most cases, after you install an update of the AirPort software on your Mac, the Admin Utility will prompt you to update the Base Station immediately after you click the Configure button.)

- **Default.** Default loads the default version of the AirPort Base Station firmware to the Base Station. If you place the pointer over this button but do not click it, some pop-up text will appear, telling you the version number of the default software.

- **Password.** Clicking the Password icon reveals the form of the WEP or WPA password (if enabled) that computers using wireless software other than AirPort need to use. For example, you'll need to know this password information if you're connecting to a base station using a third-party wireless card (rather than an Apple AirPort card).

Buttons. Each button brings up a different screen:

- **Show Summary.** This screen provides summary statistics regarding the Base Station, such as its name, firmware version, WAN address, and so on. This is the default screen that you typically see when you first arrive.

- **Name and Password.** From here, you can enter and/or change (a) the Base Station name as well as the password used to access the Base Station; and (b) the network name as well as the password used to connect to the wireless network provided by the Base Station.

  To modify the Base Station password, simply click the "Change password" button in the top half of the screen.

  To set or modify the network password, click the Change Wireless Security button in the lower section of the screen. From the dialog that opens, select the desired type of password from the Wireless Security pop-up menu. If you don't want any password, select Not Enabled. If you want to use WEP, you can select either "40 bit WEP" or "128 bit WEP" (this affects the length of the encrypted password). Note: You cannot join a 128-bit encrypted network from a wireless card that only has 40-bit support.

continues on next page

> **TAKE NOTE ▶ Setting Up an AirPort Base Station and Network** *continued*
>
> For WPA security, which requires Panther and AirPort Extreme, you will almost certainly want to select WPA Personal (the WPA Enterprise option is only needed by systems that use a RADIUS server). For WPA, you can also choose between a Password (your most likely choice) and a Pre-Shared Key. A Pre-Shared Key must be 64 hexadecimal characters; this is more protection than most users will care to bother with.
>
> With any password option enabled, users seeking to join the network will be required to enter the password.
>
> SEE: • "Take Note: Passwords and Joining a Wireless Network," later in this chapter, for additional information on WEP and WPA.
>
> *continues on next page*

Figure 8.14a

The AirPort Admin Utility: the Show Summary screen.

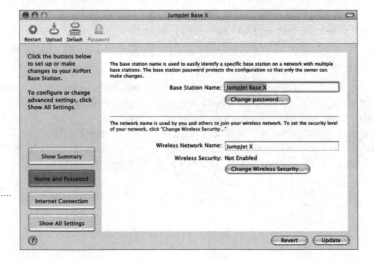

Figure 8.14b

The AirPort Admin Utility: the Name and Password screen.

TAKE NOTE ▶ Setting Up an AirPort Base Station and Network *continued*

- **Internet Connection.** This is where you set up the Base Station for connecting to the Internet. In general, you enter the settings you would have entered in the TCP/IP screen of the Network System Preferences pane if you were connecting to the Internet directly from your computer. If you're using a router (rather than the Base Station) to connect to the Internet, you will likely enter the TCP/IP settings to connect to your router here.

  Note: From the "Connect using" pop-up menu, you can select a few options that are unique to AirPort setups. In particular, AirPort (WDS) is used when setting up a wireless distribution system (WDS) consisting of two or more AirPort Extreme Base Stations. You would use this setting to connect the currently accessed Base Station to a main Base Station that is, in turn, connected to the Internet (as described more later in this sidebar).

- **Show All Settings.** Click this button, and the display shifts dramatically. You can now choose among seven screens: AirPort, Internet, Network, Port Mapping, Access Control, and WDS. These settings allow you to do everything you could via the other three screens, plus much more. It's beyond the scope of this book to detail all of the options available here; however, the following are some highlights:

  AirPort. This screen overlaps with the Name and Password screen but provides additional options for both Base Station and AirPort Network. For example:

  From the Base Station settings, you can select the WAN Privacy button. From here, you can uncheck the default-selected options to Enable SNMP Access and Enable Remote Configuration. Doing so makes it more difficult for others to "see" your AirPort; however, it also provides greater security—particularly in protecting against denial-of-service (DoS) attacks (a hacker's attempt to bring down your network by flooding it with data).

continues on next page

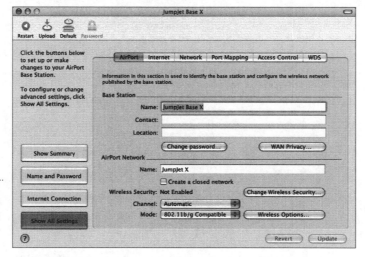

Figure 8.14c

The AirPort Admin Utility: The Show All Settings screen with the AirPort tab selected.

TAKE NOTE ▶ Setting Up an AirPort Base Station and Network *continued*

From the AirPort Network settings, you can select to "Create a closed network." When this option is enabled, your network will not automatically be listed in the AirPort menus of computers within range. To access the network, users have to enter its exact name and password (via the dialog appears after selecting the Other command in the AirPort menu or in Internet Connect). This option makes it harder for unauthorized users to find your network.

You can also select a specific channel from this screen: This allows you to improve your signal strength if your current channel isn't responding well.

You use the Mode menu offered here to determine whether the Base Station can connect to AirPort cards that use the older (slower) 802.11b protocol, the newer (faster) 802.11g protocol, or both.

Click the Wireless Options button to access still other options, including the one to "Enable interference robustness" (as covered in the main text).

There is also the same Change Wireless Security button described earlier in the sidebar, as accessed via the Name and Password screen.

Internet. This screen essentially duplicates the settings in the Internet Connection pane.

Network. This critical screen determines how the Base Station works with the other computers on your local network. The most common choice is to enable "Distribute IP addresses" together with "Share a single IP address (using DHCP and NAT)." From the pop-up menu, you can also select the range of local addresses to be used by NAT. This setup allows you to share an Internet connection among several computers and provides IP addresses to connected computers. (Users on those computers will be able to select the DHCP setting in Network System Preferences and have the settings provided automatically.)

continues on next page

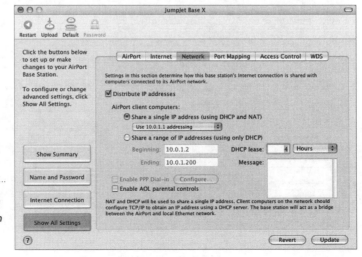

Figure 8.14d

The AirPort Admin Utility: the Show All Settings screen with the Network tab selected.

TAKE NOTE ▶ **Setting Up an AirPort Base Station and Network**   *continued*

Alternatively, if you have a separate Internet router that is assigning IP addresses manually or via DHCP, you may choose to disable the "Distribute IP addresses" option. (With non-Extreme Base Stations, you'll also probably select the "Enable AirPort to Ethernet bridging option"; the Extreme Base Station doesn't offer an option to do this—it's automatically enabled.) This setup lets the router handle the address sharing that would otherwise be performed by the Base Station.

Whatever choices you make, the text at the bottom of the window provides a summary of what you've done and how other computers must be configured as a result. This information can help you decide whether or not you have made the correct decision.

Admittedly, making the correct decisions here can be difficult if you're not familiar with how computer networks work. To help you, Apple has created PDF documents describing how to design AirPort networks. The most recent PDF for AirPort Extreme is available from Apple's AirPort Web site: www.apple.com/airport. PDFs for older models and older Mac OS X versions can be found by searching Apple's Knowledge Base: http://search.info.apple.com/ (search for the exact phrase *designing airport*).

WDS. This option is only included with AirPort Extreme. You will need to configure options here if you're setting up two or more base stations to form a wireless distribution system (WDS). This allows you to extend the range of an AirPort network beyond the limits of a single base station. In particular, you will have to enable the Base Station as a WDS *main, remote,* or *relay* station. See the information text provided in the WDS screen, as well as the additional documentation in AirPort Help, for assistance in doing this.

Port Mapping, Access, and *Authentication.* Most users will never use these options. Access and Authentication are used to restrict access to your Base Station to specific authorized users. I cover Port Mapping in "Internet routers and port mapping," elsewhere in this chapter.

When you've finished making changes to your Base Station settings, remember to click the Update button at the bottom of the window. This action saves the changes, uploading them to the Base Station and restarting it.

Finishing up. After you finish setting up a Base Station and wireless network, your next step (if you have not already done so) is to input the AirPort settings in the Network System Preferences pane, as described in the main text. Remember that what you enter here will vary depending on how you set up the Base Station's Network screen and what type of network you have. Fortunately, once you've established these settings, you won't need to refer to them again unless problems occur.

Finally, you need to turn on your AirPort card and choose the desired network (usually via the AirPort menu bar item or Internet Connect). Congratulations—you're now on a wireless network!

continues on next page

TAKE NOTE ▶ Setting Up an AirPort Base Station and Network *continued*

Performing a hard reset of the Base Station (for Base Station problems). If you're having problems with your Base Station, perhaps congratulations *weren't* in order! Perhaps you're unable to access your Base Station, or maybe things worked for a few days but don't any longer. Or perhaps the flashing lights on the Base Station are showing a color or a pattern other than what's "normal." Whatever the case, it's time to do a hard reset of the Base Station.

The way you do this will vary depending on which AirPort Base Station model you have. The AirPort Extreme Base Station provides the simplest procedure: Just push and hold the Reset button, located on the Base Station itself, for 5 seconds. For other models, check with the manual that came with the Base Station or the relevant Apple Knowledge Base document. For the dual Ethernet model, check the following address: http://docs.info.apple.com/article.html?artnum=106602. For the Graphite model, check this address: http://docs.info.apple.com/article.html?artnum=58613. For more details on the AirPort Extreme model, check this address: http://docs.info.apple.com/article.html?artnum=107451.

After performing a hard reset, the initial password will be *public*. You will need to reenter all settings, just as you did the first time you set up the Base Station.

Performing a soft reset of the Base Station (for forgotten password). If the problem is only that you forgot your Base Station password, the solution is to do a soft reset.

Again, details vary according to Base Station models, but similar to a hard reset, performing a soft reset involves pressing the Reset button on the Base Station. See the documentation that came with your Base Station or the documents cited in the hard reset section of this sidebar for complete instructions.

After doing this, depending on your Base Station model, you either will be prompted to create a new password, or the password will be reset to *public* as with a hard reset. In the latter case, you can create a new password from the Admin Utility. (You can only use *public* for 5 minutes.)

Modem

You may not think of a dial-up connection to your ISP (AOL, EarthLink, and so on) as being a network connection, but it is. Just as with an Ethernet- or AirPort-based Internet connection, the modem is linking your computer to other computers on the Internet. As a result, the settings for modem connections are located in the Network pane of System Preferences. To set up your Mac's built-in modem, from the Show pop-up menu select Internal Modem. (If you have a USB or Bluetooth modem attached, the port configuration will have the name you assigned when you created a new port configuration for that modem.)

Note: The Internet Connect utility and the Internet Connect menu both let you *initiate* dial-up connections. Before you can do so, however, you must go to the Network System Prefernces pane and *set up* a modem port configuration, enable Internal Modem (or whatever the name of that modem configuration might be), and then enter the appropriate settings in the Modem configuration screens.

SEE: • "Internet Connect," later in this chapter.

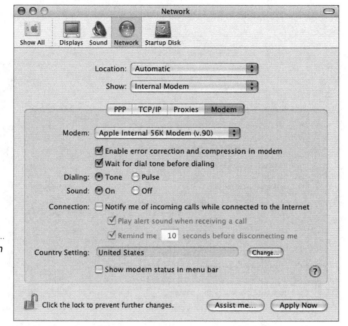

Figure 8.15

The Network System Preferences pane with the Modem screen of the Internal Modem port selected.

PPP. This screen is where you enter the information required to connect to your dial-up ISP. To do so, follow these steps:

1. In the Service Provider field enter your ISP's name. Although this step is optional, the name you input here shows up in Internet Connect—helpful in determining the current default if you have multiple dial-up ISPs.

2. In the Account Name field, enter your account name. This is your ISP account name, not your Mac OS X login name. For some ISPs, your account name is simply your user name; other ISPs require your entire email address. Check with your ISP to determine which it requires.

3. In the Password field enter your ISP account password.

4. In the Telephone Number field, enter the phone number you dial up to connect to your ISP.

5. If you have a second number, enter it in the Alternate Number field. (If the first number is busy or not responding, Mac OS X will try the second number.)

6. If you want Mac OS X to remember your password so that you don't have to type it each time you connect, click the "Save password" check box.

7. You can now click the Dial Now button to immediately connect, or use the Internet Connect application and/or menu as a more convenient way to connect at any later time.

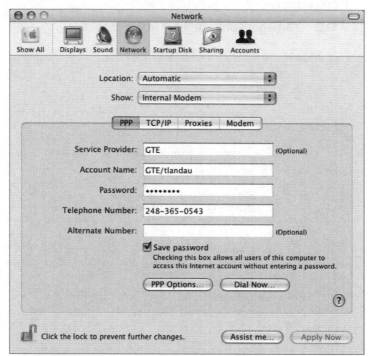

Figure 8.16a

The Network System Preferences pane with the PPP screen of the Internal Modem port selected.

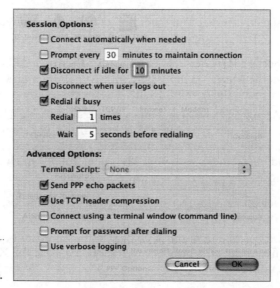

Figure 8.16b

The PPP Options dialog, as accessed from the PPP screen.

8. (Optional) If you click the PPP Options button, you can enable or disable a variety of PPP settings. Most users will be content to leave these options at their default settings. However, two choices in this screen are worth special mention:

"Connect automatically when needed." With this option enabled, Mac OS X will automatically initiate a connection—if you aren't already connected—when you launch an application (such as a Web browser) that requires Internet access.

"Disconnect if idle for *??* minutes." You can set this option to automatically disconnect you from your ISP if you have not used the connection for the specified period of time. This option can be useful if you leave your computer with your connection still active, especially if your ISP charges you according to the time you're connected. However, it can be annoying if you want to maintain the connection despite an idle period. Note that some dial-up ISPs may disconnect you after a period of idleness regardless of how you set this option.

TCP/IP. As with AirPort and Ethernet, this screen is where you enter your ISP's TCP/IP settings. The Configure pop-up menu offers three options: Manually, Using PPP, and AOL Dialup. If you're one of the few people who have a dial-up connection with a static IP address, choose Manually. However, if you're like most users, you'll choose Using PPP. The only additional data you may have to enter is the address of your ISP's domain name server.

AOL users may select AOL Dialup. This disables almost all other options for the Internal Modem settings. This is designed to allow you to dial up via AOL's own custom software—you then enter your dial-up settings in that software instead. If you try to connect via Internet Connect with AOL Dialup selected here, you will get a PPP error message. See the following Apple Knowledge Base article for more on connecting to AOL in Mac OS X: http://docs.info.apple.com/article.html?artnum=106686.

TAKE NOTE ▶ When Connecting Automatically Is Not a Good Idea

Although enabling "Connect automatically when needed" can be convenient, it can also mean that a connection will be attempted when you do not want it to be. For example, if you're not connected to a phone line and you launch your Web browser (perhaps to view a page offline), the Mac will attempt to make a connection and fail to do so.

continues on next page

TAKE NOTE ▶ When Connecting Automatically Is Not a Good Idea *continued*

To avoid this situation, you can simply not enable this option. The other alternative is to create a separate network Location for those times when you are not connected to any network or phone line. You would disable all ports for this Location and then switch to this Location at times when you are not connected.

A slightly different variation: If you have File Sharing or Web Sharing enabled, and you have the "Connect automatically" option enabled, your Mac may try to initiate a dial-up connection at startup. To prevent this situation, follow the same suggestions I just described or turn off the sharing options (via the Sharing pane of System Preferences). If you need to use Sharing Services, simply turn them off before shutting down or restarting, and reenable them after startup.

SEE : • **"Blue-screen crashes and stalls," in Chapter 5, for coverage of a problem with the "Connect automatically" option that can cause a crash at startup.**

• **"Locations," later in this chapter, for more information on network Locations.**

Proxies. If your ISP requires proxies, you enter proxy information in this screen.

Modem. This screen is where you configure your modem itself for PPP connections. The Modem pop-up menu is where you choose the modem mode. (Note that for most recent Apple computers, the model is chosen for you: Apple Internal 56K Modem—typically v.90 or V.92.) If you have an older Mac or are using a third-party modem, choose the appropriate model. Other check box options available in this screen include "Enable error correction and compression in modem," "Wait for dial tone before dialing," and "Show modem status in menu bar." (The menu bar item is a useful way to connect, as well as to tell whether your dial-up connection is active; this is the same menu you can enable from Internet Connect.) Other options include Sound (determines whether you can hear the modem dialing and connecting through your speakers), Dialing (for selecting tone versus pulse dialing), and Country Setting (useful for international dial-up connections). Some systems may also include the option "Notify me of incoming calls while connected to the Internet."

Once again, after making any changes to your Network settings, click the Apply Now button to save your changes.

TAKE NOTE ▶ Modem Scripts and Terminal Scripts

When setting up a modem, you may see references to two types of scripts: *modem scripts* and *terminal scripts*. Here's what you need to know about them:

Modem scripts. When you select a modem model/type in the Modem screen of Network System Preferences, you're actually telling Mac OS X which modem *script* to use when initiating a dial-up connection. Because every modem is slightly different, these scripts (located in /Library/ Modem Scripts) tell Mac OS X how to interact with each modem. A modem script generally describes the modem's initialization string, maximum data speed, buffer size, data-compression settings, error-correction settings, and any other special features the modem supports. You can open and view any of these modem scripts in a text editor such as Bare Bones Software's BBEdit. (You can even edit them, though I advise against it unless you really know what you're doing.)

Generally, all you need to do is choose your modem's name from the Modem pop-up menu and connect. At times, however, the "right" script for your modem may not work as well as it should. Your modem may try to connect at a speed your phone line can't sustain, for example, resulting in frequent disconnects. Or maybe you have a v.90 modem, but your ISP supports only the slower v.34 standard. Choosing a different modem script from the Modem pop-up menu may help. In particular, for the Apple Internal Modem, shifting from Apple Internal 56K Modem (v.90) to Apple Internal 56K Modem (v.34) may help.

In addition, modem manufacturers sometimes release updated scripts for their modems. In this case, you simply place the updated script in the Modem Scripts folder (/Library/Modem Scripts) and then choose it from the Modem pop-up menu in the Modem screen.

Terminal scripts. Sometimes called *connection scripts,* these have nothing to do with the Terminal application. (They are so called because, years ago, all dial-up connections were initiated via a terminal connection between your computer/modem and the ISP's servers/modems.) These scripts contain a series of commands needed to log in to your ISP. It's rare for such scripts to be needed nowadays, but some dial-up ISPs still require them. If your ISP supplies such a script file, here's how you install and use it:

1. Create a folder called Terminal Scripts in the root-level Library folder (/Library), if one does not exist. Place the script file in this folder.

2. Go to the Network System Preferences pane, and from the Show pop-up menu select Internal Modem.

3. Click the PPP tab and check the PPP Options button.

4. From the Terminal Script pop-up menu that appears in the dialog that drops down, select the name of the script you installed.

5. Click OK, and then click Apply Now.

Bluetooth modem

If your Mac came with internal support for Bluetooth, or if you connected a third-party USB Bluetooth adapter, you can use a Bluetooth-enabled mobile phone to connect to the Internet via a dial-up connection (assuming your mobile-phone provider offers data connection and Internet support). Because Bluetooth is wireless technology, you're actually getting a "double wireless" connection—one wireless connection between your Mac and your mobile phone, and another between your mobile phone and your ISP.

SEE: • "Bluetooth," later in this chapter, for more details on Bluetooth and its software.

If you've never used Bluetooth and you attach a USB Bluetooth adapter to your Mac, the first time you open the Network System Preferences pane, you'll get a message saying that a new port has been detected and added. If your Mac has Apple's Bluetooth internal hardware installed, the port should already exist.

Using a Bluetooth-enabled mobile phone as a modem requires two steps: (1) "pairing" your phone with your Mac, and (2) configuring the Network System Preferences pane to connect to your Bluetooth modem.

To pair your phone and your Mac, follow these steps:

1. Open the Bluetooth System Preferences pane.

2. From the Settings screen, check the box next to Discoverable; this makes your Mac available for pairing with other Bluetooth devices. This is probably not a required step in this case, but it can't hurt.

3. Using the documentation that came with your phone, make your phone discoverable as well.

4. In the Bluetooth System Preferences pane click the Devices tab.

5. Click the Pair New Device button. A new window will open, and Mac OS X will scan for Bluetooth devices within range.

6. When the scan is complete, select your phone from the list of Bluetooth devices and click the Pair button.

   Note: If you have a long list of devices, you can limit what's displayed in the list by using the "Show only" and Device Category pop-up menus.

7. When prompted by Mac OS X, enter a four-number passkey.

8. When prompted by your phone, enter the same four-number passkey.

9. A dialog will appear, asking you how you want to use the phone with Mac OS X: Choose the option for using the phone as a modem.

   Your Bluetooth-enabled mobile phone is now available as a modem. Alternatively, you could click the Set Up New Device button at the bottom of the window to launch Bluetooth Setup Assistant, which walks you through the steps in setting up a Bluetooth device.

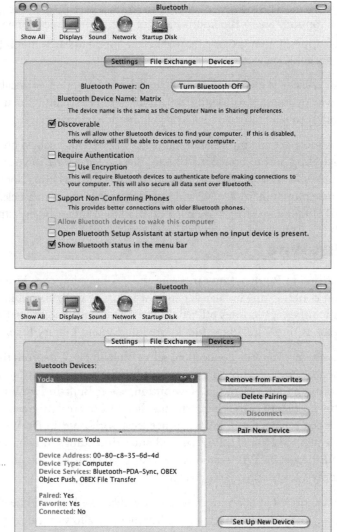

Figure 8.17

The Bluetooth System Preferences pane: (top) the Settings screen and (bottom) the Devices screen.

To configure the phone to connect to the Internet, follow these steps:

1. From the Network System Preferences pane, choose Network Port Configurations from the Show menu and make sure that Bluetooth is enabled (that is, the On check box for the Bluetooth port is checked). (Note: If this port is not in the menu, select Network Port Configurations; click the New button; from the Port pop-up menu select Bluetooth; name the port; and click OK to create the port.)

2. From the Show pop-up menu select Bluetooth.

3. Configure the TCP/IP and PPP screens as you would for any modem. From the Modem screen, select the name of your Bluetooth-enabled phone from the Modem menu (rather than the Mac's internal modem).

Note: The "Show modem status in menu bar" option is joined by the option "Show Bluetooth status in menu bar." I recommend enabling both.

4. Open Internet Connect (or use the modem-status menu bar item) and click Connect.

For assistance in setting up a Bluetooth modem or any other Bluetooth device, you can also use the Bluetooth Setup Assistant, which includes an option to search for and list available mobile phones.

For more specific information on using a Bluetooth-enabled phone as a modem, including how to connect a Bluetooth-enabled phone to your computer, see Apple's Knowledge Base articles on the topic, such as http://docs.info.apple.com/article.html?artnum=34745 and http://docs.info.apple.com/article2.html?artnum=86151 (assuming they have been updated for Panther by the time you read this).

FireWire

Starting in Panther, you can make an IP connection over FireWire. Actually, you could do this in later versions of Jaguar as well, via public beta software; in Panther, it becomes official. Note: The essential software that allows this is the IOFireWireIP.kext file, located in /System/Library/Extensions.

To set up a FireWire connection, select Built-In FireWire from the Show pop-up menu. (Note: If this port is not listed in the menu, select Network Port Configurations; click the New button; select Built-in FireWire from the Port pop-up menu; name the port; and click OK to create the port. Then check the box for Built-in FireWire, if needed.) With Built-in FireWire enabled and selected, click the TCP/IP tab and enter the settings, much as you would for an Ethernet TCP/IP screen (as described previously in this chapter). Click Apply Now to save your changes.

To get an Internet connection directly over FireWire, you need a device (such as a router) that connects to the Internet and allows connections from a Mac via a FireWire cable. Currently, such devices are rare. However, you can easily connect two Macs to each other via a FireWire cable, which allows you to do the following:

- **Exchange data between Macs connected via a FireWire cable.** To do this, you must enable Personal File Sharing from the Services screen in the Sharing System Preferences pane of the Mac that is to be shared. You must also enable Personal File Sharing in the FireWire configuration setup in the Network System Preferences pane of the Mac that will be accessing the shared Mac.

- **Share an Internet connection among FireWire-connected Macs.** To do this, you need to set up Internet Sharing from the Sharing System Preferences pane of the Mac that is to be shared, as well as the set up FireWire configuration in the Network System Preferences pane of the Mac that will be accessing the shared Mac.

Note: In Jaguar, Internet Sharing via FireWire involved a complex setup procedure that happily is no longer required in Panther. Internet Sharing via FireWire in Panther is as easy to set up as any other category of Internet Sharing (for example Ethernet and AirPort).

SEE: • **"Take Note: Setting Up and Using Internet Sharing and File Sharing,"
later in this chapter, for more details.**

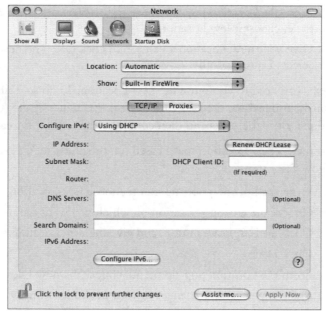

Figure 8.18

The Network System Preferences pane after adding the Built-in FireWire port: the TCP/IP screen of the Built-in FireWire port.

Locations

The discussion up to this point has assumed that for the most part, you use your Mac or PowerBook in an environment where your network settings are static. In many situations, however, you may have multiple groups of network settings. Perhaps you use your PowerBook at work and at home, and each location requires different network settings.

Mac OS X addresses these situations through network Locations—groups of network settings that you set up based on the environments in which you'll be using your computer. You can create any number of Locations.

Mac OS X's Locations are similar to the Location Manager in Mac OS 9 in that you can create groups of settings and switch among them easily. However, whereas Location Manager allowed you to switch network settings, printers, time zones, startup files, QuickTime settings, sound volume, and many other things, Mac OS X's Locations control only network settings.

The flip side of this is that while Location Manager was one of the more confusing utilities to confront a Mac user, Locations are very simple to set up in

Mac OS X. In fact, if you used the preceding instructions to configure your network settings, you've already been working with Locations. This is because all of your initial network settings are part of a default location called Automatic, which is really no more or less "automatic" than any other Location you may set up. Apple simply calls the first Location by this name.

To create a new Location, follow these steps:

1. From the Location pop-up menu in the Network System Preferences pane, choose New Location.

2. Give your new Location a name, and click OK. The new location is selected automatically.

Next, you need to configure the new Location. To do so, follow the steps previously outlined for the Network System Preferences pane (that is, configure and prioritize the ports and then configure the settings for each port).

To create a new Location that's based on, or similar to, an existing Location, follow these steps:

1. From the Location pop-up menu choose Edit Locations.

2. Choose the existing Location on which you want the new Location based.

3. Click the Duplicate button, and give the new Location a name.

4. Click Done.

5. From the Location pop-up menu, choose the new Location.

6. Make any necessary changes in your network settings.

When you've created multiple Locations, you can switch among them easily. To do so, do either of the following:

- Open the Network pane of System Preferences and choose a location from the Location pop-up menu; click the Apply Now button.

- Choose Location from Mac OS X's Apple menu and select the desired Location from the hierarchical menu.

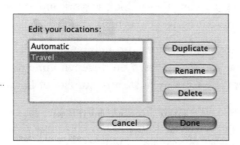

Figure 8.19

The Network System Preferences pane's Edit Locations dialog.

Internet Connect

If your Mac is not automatically connected to the Internet when it starts up or when you use an Internet application (Web browser, email client, and so on), you will need to manually connect to the Internet (or perhaps to an AirPort network that provides access to the Internet).

For such occasions, it's convenient to use Mac OS X's Internet Connect utility (located in the Applications folder). Internet Connect allows you to manually initiate a modem, AirPort, or PPPoE connection. It gets its default settings from the Network System Preferences pane, but you can also manually enter ISP telephone numbers as well as your ISP account password (assuming you've chosen not to have it remembered by the OS).

After you launch Internet Connect, select the screen for the connection type you want to use by selecting the desired button in its toolbar. The options that appear in the toolbar are generally determined by which ports are active in the Network System Preferences pane. The following sections summarize the main options.

Summary

This pane summarizes the status of the different devices that you can currently access from Internet Connect. For example, it will tell you whether you're connected to an AirPort network, as well as list the status of a modem and include a toggled Connect/Disconnect button for the modem.

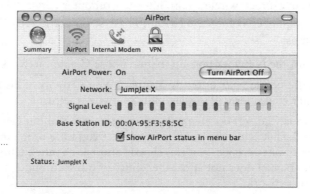

Figure 8.20

The Internet Connect utility: the AirPort screen.

AirPort

If you have an AirPort card in your Mac and have set up AirPort in the Network System Preferences pane, you can select the AirPort button from the toolbar to initiate a connection.

The first option you're presented with is AirPort Power, which states whether AirPort is currently on or off. If it's on, you can click the Turn AirPort Off button to shut down your AirPort card; if it's off, you can click the Turn AirPort On button to turn it on. You can conserve a good deal of battery power on a laptop by turning your AirPort card off when you're not using it.

This screen also includes (a) a graph showing the signal level of the AirPort connection; (b) the Base Station ID; and (c) a Connect button, present if your AirPort Base Station includes a dial-up modem and you have set it up to do so. (Note: To temporarily use a different number than the one set in the AirPort Admin Utility, hold down Option when clicking Connect.)

From the Network pop-up menu, you select an AirPort network. If a network is within range and is not a closed network, its name should appear automatically. If you're in the vicinity of multiple networks, you can choose which one you want to join. If a network is not listed (that is, it's closed), choose Other and enter the appropriate network name and (if needed) password.

If a network is password-protected, open or closed, you will be asked to enter the appropriate password when you attempt to join it. Before entering a password, you may need to select the correct type of password from the Wireless Security pop-up menu.

SEE: • **"Take Note: Passwords and Joining a Wireless Network," below, for more details.**

Also in the Network pop-up menu is an almost-hidden gem (assuming you enabled this option in the AirPort pane of the Network System Preferences pane, as described earlier in this chapter): Create Network. This option lets you create a direct, wireless computer-to-computer network between two AirPort-equipped computers (with no base station required). To do so, follow these steps:

1. From the Network pop-up menu choose Create Network.

2. In the Name field, enter the name of your network. This is the name the other computer will display in its Network menu.

3. Choose the AirPort channel you want to use. You can generally stick with the default selection (Automatic), but if you have problems connecting due to interference, you can choose another channel. Choosing a different channel does not affect the ability of other computers to connect to your network.

4. If desired, click the Show Options button. This expands the window to display additional options for adding a password. If you want the network to be private, select "Enable encryption (using WEP)" and enter a password.

SEE: • **"Take Note: Passwords and Joining a Wireless Network," below, for information about WEP keys and passwords.**

5. Click OK.

The other computer can now use its own Internet Connect utility to connect to your newly created network.

Airport menu bar item. The AirPort window of Internet Connect includes the same "Show AirPort status in menu bar" option as was available in the Network System Preferences pane. This menu provides all of the same options as the AirPort screen of Internet Connect. You can use the menu bar access as a shortcut to many of the options otherwise available via Internet Connect.

SEE: • "Show AirPort status in menu bar," earlier in this chapter, for related information.

TAKE NOTE ▶ Passwords and Joining a Wireless Network

A wireless network, AirPort or not, may require a password in order for you to join it. Here are some guidelines for entering a password correctly:

AirPort card to AirPort Base Station. For Mac users, this is the most common situation: You're connecting from a Mac with an AirPort card to an AirPort Base Station. A network password may have been set up in the Base Station via the AirPort Admin Utility, using either *wired equivalency privacy* (WEP) or (starting in Panther and with an AirPort Extreme Base Station) *Wi-Fi Protected Access* (WPA). WPA provides greater data protection than WEP.

If the Base Station has been set up to require a password, you will need to enter it when you first attempt to join the network (for example, from the AirPort menu or from Internet Connect, as described later in this chapter). Before typing the password in the Enter Password dialog that appears, you must first select the type of password from the Wireless Security pop-up menu.

Note: If you select a listed network name, the Wireless Security menu will only list options relevant to that network (for example, WEP or WPA). If you select Other, the pop-up menu in the resulting window will always show the full range of choices (for example, WEP and WPA).

For a WEP password, for example, you will have three options: WEP Password, WEP 40/128-bit hex, and WEP 40/128-bit ASCII. Your best bet in this case is usually WEP Password. You can only take advantage of the latter options if the password meets the 40- or 128-bit restrictions in password length. Thus, a 40-bit password must be exactly 5 ASCII characters or 10 hexadecimal digits. For 128 bit, the password must be 13 ASCII characters or 26 hexadecimal digits. If the password, as entered in Admin Utility, is shorter or longer than this number of characters, you cannot use the ASCII option when attempting to connect. However, you can still use the hex option if you have the hexadecimal equivalent password (which you obtain by clicking the Password icon in the AirPort Admin Utility's toolbar). With the plain WEP Password, you just enter whatever ASCII text was entered in the Admin Utility: Length does not matter.

continues on next page

TAKE NOTE ▶ Passwords and Joining a Wireless Network *continued*

For WPA Personal, on the other hand, you will only be presented with one choice: WPA Personal. Much simpler! However, WPA is only available with AirPort Extreme (and Mac OS X 10.3 or later). You cannot join a WPA-protected network from a Mac with a non-Extreme AirPort card.

Note: ASCII characters are the plain text you're familiar with using in creating passwords and typing in general (that is, the full alphabet and the numerals 0 to 9). Hexadecimal characters are restricted to the following: abcdef0123456789.

Note: If from the Enter Password window you select the Add to Keychain option, you shouldn't get asked to enter the password again.

Mac with AirPort card to non–AirPort network. If you have an AirPort card installed in your Mac, you can use it to connect to almost any wireless network, not just ones that use an AirPort Base Station. (*AirPort* is simply Apple's name for the 802.11b wireless protocol; *AirPort Extreme* is similarly Apple's name for 802.11g.) It is becoming increasingly common to connect to publicly accessible "hot spots" in coffee shops and airports, for example. If you want to join a wireless network that does not use AirPort and requires a password, you can typically use the same method as just described: Select the type of password from the Wireless Security menu and enter the password.

Note: You may need to ask the administrator of the network to find out what type of password is being used. The AirPort software does not automatically detect this.

Note: Prior to Panther, when entering passwords for third-party networks, you typically needed to employ some special tricks. In particular, you had to precede a hexadecimal password with a dollar sign ($)—referred to as the *Hex Escape*—and you had to enclose ASCII passwords in quotation marks (for example, *"password"*). Although you shouldn't need to employ such tricks in Panther, if you're having trouble getting a password accepted, it may be worth a try.

Check out various Apple Knowledge Base documents (such as http://docs.info.apple.com/article.html?artnum=106424) and AirPort Help (on your Mac) for additional advice.

Non–AirPort computer to an AirPort Base Station. If you have an AirPort Base Station network that requires a password, a person using a computer with wireless software other than AirPort may not be able to use the password in its plain text version to access the network. Instead, that person may need to use an encrypted form of the password, especially if using WEP.

You can always obtain the form of the password needed for non-AirPort computers by clicking the Password icon in the toolbar of the AirPort Admin Utility.

SEE: • **"Take Note: Setting Up an AirPort Base Station and Network," earlier in this chapter, for additional information on WEP and WPA.**

Figure 8.21

The Enter Password screen for (above) a network that uses WEP; (above-right) a network that uses WPA; and (right) a closed network (accessed via the Other command in the AirPort menu).

Built-in Ethernet (PPPoE)

If you have a DSL or cable-modem connection using PPPoE, and you have set up Network System Preferences for PPPoE, click the Built-in Ethernet button in the Internet Connect toolbar. You can use the options that appear to manually connect and disconnect from the network.

Your PPPoE Service Provider and Account Name are entered automatically, using the values you supplied in the Network System Preferences pane (as is your password, if you told Mac OS X to save it). If you didn't choose to save your password, you can enter it here each time you connect. Click the Connect button to connect.

The Status section provides your IP address, the time you have been connected, and a graphical representation of data being sent and received over your connection.

PPPoE menu bar item. You can choose to show your PPPoE status in the menu bar. If so, a PPPoE menu item appears, from which you can select to connect or disconnect to your PPPoE connection.

Internal Modem

To connect via your Mac's internal modem, click the Internal Modem button in the toolbar.

From the Configuration pop-up menu, you can select the dial-up settings you created in the PPP screen of the Internal Modem section of the Network System Preferences pane. You can create still other dial-up settings by selecting the Other item in the menu and entering the telephone number, account name, and password in the fields below the menu (you will be prompted to name and save this configuration before closing Internet Connect). Each new configuration you create is added to the pop-up menu.

Finally, if you select Edit Configurations from the pop-up menu, a dialog opens from which you can (a) edit existing configurations (including a few options not available from the main Internet Connect window, such as selecting a specific modem script), and (b) add a new or delete an existing configuration (via the plus and minus buttons in the lower left).

Note: You cannot edit the configuration set up in Network System Preferences via Internet Connect; edit that one directly from Network.

Note: The first time you select Edit Configurations, if you have not already created additional configurations via the Other command, a default configuration called Modem Configuration is created.

Note: The password for the configuration set up in the Network System Preferences pane will only appear for this configuration if you checked the "Save password" box in the Network System Preferences pane. Otherwise, you need to enter it manually each time you connect via Internet Connect.

Via all of these options, you can maintain a set of phone numbers to use for dial-up (which you may need if you travel and dial up using different local numbers in different locations). Simply choose the preferred configuration from the pop-up menu and then click Connect.

In the Status section at the bottom of the window, you can see your connection speed (or at least the speed you had when you first connected), the length of time you've been connected, your IP address, and a graphical representation of data being sent and received. Note: If these graphs indicate no activity, you probably no longer have a connection, even if other settings indicate you are still connected.

Figure 8.22

The Internet Connect utility: the Internal Modem screen, after a successful dial-up connection has been made.

Modem menu bar item. You have the same "Show modem status in the menu bar" option as is available in the Network System Preferences pane. The menu bar icon includes a menu from which you can choose Connect (or Disconnect, if connected), which eliminates the need to open Internet Connect at all (assuming you intend to use its current default settings). You can also switch between modem configurations (including Internal Modem and Bluetooth) from the Modem Status menu.

The "Show time connected" and "Show status while connecting" options can be enabled to provide feedback directly in the menu bar.

Bluetooth Modem

If have a Bluetooth-enabled mobile phone, and you've set up the Network System Preferences pane to use it as a modem (as explained earlier in the chapter), you can connect to the Internet via this phone.

The settings in this screen are virtually identical to those just described for internal modem.

SEE: • **"Bluetooth modem," earlier in this chapter, and "Bluetooth," later in this chapter, for more details on Bluetooth and its software.**

VPN connections

A *virtual private network*, or VPN, allows a remote user to connect to a private network (such as the internal network at a large company or even a small home-office network) via the Internet. It does this by creating a secure tunnel between the two: Data is encrypted as it travels through the tunnel so that anyone who might intercept it as it travels over the Internet will not be able to access it. A VPN thus ensures that all communication between the remote computer and the network remains private.

To connect to a VPN:

1. From Internet Connect's File menu select New VPN Connection. From the window that appears, you have two choices: "L2TP over IPSec" and PPTP. The one you select will depend on the network to which you're connecting; check with your network administrator for this information.

   After making this selection, click Continue. A new port called VPN (PPTP) or VPN (L2TP) will be added to your Network Port Configurations in the Network System Preferences pane (the System Preferences icon in the Dock will likely start bouncing to indicate that this change has occurred). In most cases, you will not need to configure this port; you simply make sure it is enabled.

   Note: *PPTP* refers to Microsoft's popular Point-to-Point Tunneling Protocol. The IPSec protocol is common on many Unix systems. Some networks use proprietary Cisco VPNs. Cisco provides its own Mac OS X

VPN client for use on these networks. Your system administrator should provide you with this client; use it instead of Internet Connect.

SEE: • **"Take Note: Ports Created by Other Applications and Devices,"
earlier in this chapter.**

2. Select the newly added VPN button in Internet Connect's toolbar.

The options that appear are almost the same as those for the Internal Modem settings described above. The main difference is that there is a Server Address field (instead of a Telephone Number field). In this field, enter the VPN server's IP address or domain. Note: Some VPN servers require that you enter your account name as *domain/username*, where *domain* is the network domain of the part of the remote network to which you are connecting.

3. Click Connect. After connecting via VPN, you should be able to browse Mac or Windows shares as if your Mac were actually on the network.

Note: Some VPN servers do not allow connections from users behind Internet routers. If you're having problems connecting to a supported VPN from behind an Internet router, you have two choices: The first is to connect directly to the Internet when you need to connect to the VPN (in other words, disconnect the router temporarily and connect to the Internet directly from your Mac). The second is that some routers include their own PPTP clients—you can set up your router to connect to the VPN and then access the VPN through your router. Check with your Internet router's manual to see if it supports PPTP connections.

Also see the following Apple Knowledge Base document for a work-around that solves some problems logging in to a PPTP network: http://docs.info.apple.com/article.html?artnum=107706. It explains how to edit the preferences.plist file (in /Library/Preferences/SystemConfiguration) to match the requirements of your ISP.

VPN menu bar item. Select "Show VPN status in menu bar" to add a VPN menu. It functions in a manner similar to how the modem menu functions for modems (as described above).

Additional toolbar icons

If you have an external USB modem attached to your Mac and set up in Network System Preferences, a separate button for this modem should appear in the Internet Connect toolbar. Similarly, you can create more than one VPN connection button.

If your Mac is equipped with infrared technology, there will be an IrDA button in the toolbar. Click it to connect to another IrDA device or computer.

Menu bar items

Most of Internet Connect's connection choices include the option "Show {*name of connection method*} status in the menu bar." These items are noted separately in the preceding sections for each choice. More information on these (and related) menu bar items is also located in other parts of this chapter (for example, "Setting Up System Preferences: Network," earlier in this chapter, and "Bluetooth System Preferences," later in this chapter).

Figure 8.23

Menu bar items for (left) Modem and (right) Bluetooth. See Figure 8.10 for the AirPort menu.

Internet Connect's menus

Internet Connect's menus offer a few useful options not accessible from its main window. I discussed one already: New VPN Connection. Here are some others:

- **New 802.1X Connection (in the File menu).** This protocol is designed to provide increased security for local networks. It can be used to connect to an existing Ethernet or AirPort network. When you select New 802.1X Connection, an 802.X button is added to the Toolbar. Select it to configure the connection and connect. Your network administrator should provide the data you need to fill in the configuration fields.

- **Import and Export Configurations (in the File menu).** Select these items to export a set of configurations as a separate file or to import a previously saved set. This could be useful, for example, for transferring a set of configurations from one computer to another.

- **Connection Log (in the Window menu).** The Connection Log tracks the details of every modem connection you make. As such, it can be helpful in troubleshooting a problematic dial-up connection. You can view your Connection Log by choosing Connection Log.

Bluetooth

Bluetooth is the odd name given to a wireless technology that facilitates short-range, direct connections between a variety of digital devices, including mobile phones, mice, keyboards, other computers, personal digital assistants, printers, scanners, and digital cameras.

Think of Bluetooth as the offspring of a union between infrared and AirPort wireless technology. With Bluetooth, similar to AirPort, you can connect to any device within a given range (10 to 100 feet with Bluetooth, which is generally smaller than the 50- to 150-foot range for AirPort), and the connection is omnidirectional (that is, you don't have to point two devices directly at each other). However, unlike AirPort and more similar to Infrared, Bluetooth doesn't require you to set up a TCP/IP network to use it. Any two Bluetooth-compatible devices can almost instantly talk to each other.

I said above that Bluetooth is designed for *direct* connections. Unlike AirPort, which allows multiple devices to form a common wireless network, Bluetooth works by "pairing" devices: a computer and a printer, a cellular phone and a laptop, two computers. With Bluetooth software 1.5 or later, you can even connect a Mac to Bluetooth headphones. Devices must be paired before they can communicate, and once paired, they can remember each other indefinitely to facilitate easy pairing in the future. (Note: In some cases, a device can be paired with more than one other device at a time.) Thus, if AirPort is the wireless equivalent of Ethernet (a full-featured networking protocol), then Bluetooth is the wireless equivalent of USB (intended for direct device-to-device "paired" connections).

Newer Macs models (for example, PowerBooks and G5s) have a Bluetooth module hardware built in (though in some cases it's an optional feature). For other Macs, you can add Bluetooth compatibility via a third-party Bluetooth adapter that attaches to any available USB port.

Note: For Macs without built-in Bluetooth, Apple's Bluetooth mouse and keyboard require a D-Link DBT-120 USB Bluetooth Adapter (hardware version B2 or later). Older D-Link DWB-120M adapters are not supported.

Note: Bluetooth and AirPort both use the 2.4 GHz frequency band. In some Mac models with built-in Bluetooth, Bluetooth and AirPort also share the same antenna. Thus, they may interfere with each other's reception. If you're using either AirPort or Bluetooth, but not both, turn off the one you are not using.

See the following Web page for more background information on Bluetooth: www.apple.com/bluetooth.

Bluetooth System Preferences

Assuming your Mac has Bluetooth hardware installed (built in or via an adapter), typically the first thing you need to do to connect to another Bluetooth device (or to allow a device to connect to your Mac) is to open the Bluetooth System Preferences pane and configure it as desired. (This pane won't appear in System Preferences unless your Mac has the requisite Bluetooth hardware installed or connected.) The pane has three main buttons: Settings, File Exchange, and Devices.

Settings. The Settings screen provides general Bluetooth preferences. The troubleshooting-relevant options here include the following:

- **Turn Bluetooth On/Off.** Use this button to do what it says.

- **Discoverable.** If you check this box, the Mac broadcasts a signal over Bluetooth frequencies so that other Bluetooth devices within range can see it. If you don't enable the Discoverable option, other Bluetooth devices will only be able to initiate a connection to your Mac if they have previously been paired with it. Note that although you may want your Mac to be discoverable at a specific moment (to allow another device to connect to it), you do not have to keep it discoverable all the time. In fact, you can use the Bluetooth menu item (discussed below) to enable Discoverable mode, and then disable it immediately after the pairing is complete.

- **Require Authentication.** If you check this box, other devices will be required to provide a password before they can connect to your Mac.

  The Use Encryption suboption encrypts all data transferred via Bluetooth; only devices that have authenticated via the password will be able to decrypt the data. This prevents other Bluetooth-enabled devices that "snoop" for Bluetooth broadcasts from accessing your data.

- **Support Non-Conforming Phones.** If you have an older Bluetooth-enabled mobile phone and find that you have problems connecting to your Mac, check this box. However, you shouldn't use this option unless you need to, because it reduces performance with newer phones.

- **"Show Bluetooth status in the menu bar."** If you use Bluetooth devices, you will almost certainly find it convenient to enable this option.

  From this Bluetooth menu, you can (a) turn Bluetooth on or off; (b) enable and disable Discoverable mode; (c) launch Bluetooth Setup Assistant; (d) launch the Bluetooth System Preferences pane; and (e) use the Send File and Browse Device items to access the Bluetooth File Exchange utility (this utility is described more in the next section).

  Note: The icon for the Bluetooth menu will change depending on the current status of the connection. For example, if the icon is gray, it means that a Bluetooth adapter is connected but Bluetooth is turned off. If you turn Bluetooth on, the icon turns black. See the following Apple Knowledge Base article for details of other icon variations: http://docs.info.apple.com/article.html?artnum=107679.

File Exchange. This screen has two sections: Bluetooth File Exchange and Bluetooth File Transfer.

The Bluetooth File Exchange section is where you decide how files sent to your Mac from other Bluetooth devices are treated:

- **"When receiving items."** This pop-up menu lets you decide whether you want to automatically accept items sent to your Mac, automatically refuse all items, or be prompted to accept or refuse each item.

- **"When PIM items are accepted"** and **"When other items are accepted."** Once an item is accepted, the settings available from these two pop-up menus determine what happens to it: You can choose to have items automatically saved to your hard drive or automatically opened with the appropriate helper application, or you can be asked for each item. Note: PIM stands for personal information manager (such as Address Book).

- **"Folder for accepted items."** Items that are saved to the hard drive are automatically saved to the directory you choose via the Choose Folder button.

The Bluetooth File Transfer section lets you decide whether you want to "Allow other devices to browse files on your Mac" (a form of file sharing). If you enable this feature and select a folder for browsing via the Choose Folder button, other computers can actually browse the selected folder over a Bluetooth connection (and download or upload files). The default selected folder is the Shared folder in the /Users directory. I describe how to connect in this manner in the section on the Bluetooth File Exchange utility below.

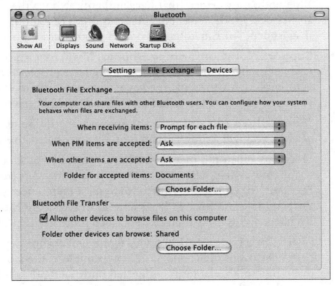

Figure 8.24

The Bluetooth System Preferences pane: the File Exchange screen. See also Figure 8.17.

Devices. This is the key screen from which you pair Bluetooth devices so that they can work with each other. The Devices screen also lists all paired devices, including ones that are currently connected to your Mac.

Click the Pair New Device button to initiate a new connection with a device (or to reestablish one that you deleted). This brings up a new window from which you can search for discoverable devices that are within range. Once you have found the desired device, click the Pair button. The device is then added to the list on the left side of the Devices screen. You should now be able to use and contact the Bluetooth-connected device.

SEE: • "Bluetooth modem," earlier in this chapter, for a more detailed example of using the Pair New Device option.

• "Take Note: Problems Pairing Bluetooth Devices," below, for related information.

TAKE NOTE ▶ Problems Pairing Bluetooth Devices

The following describes a few common problems with pairing devices—as typically performed via the Pair New Device option in Bluetooth System Preferences—and their solutions:

• **Device not found.** If a search does not list a device you expected to find, make sure that the device is on, that Bluetooth is on, and that the device is discoverable. Thus, for connecting to another Mac via Bluetooth, go to the Bluetooth System Preferences pane of the other Mac and check the just-cited settings.

• **Passkey problem.** If you click to pair with certain devices, such as another Mac, you may be prompted to enter a passkey. For two Macs, this can be almost any short string of letters and numbers. The important thing is that after entering it, you will be prompted to enter the same passkey on the other Mac. This is a security protection against unwanted pairings. If the passkey is not entered on the second Mac, the pairing will fail.

My understanding is that these passkeys should only be requested if you have selected Require Authentication from Bluetooth's Settings screen. However, on my Macs, the passkey was requested whether this option was on or off.

• **Validation fails.** The Mac may successfully locate a device for pairing but then claim that validation failed after you click the Pair button. If this happens, check all of your Bluetooth-related settings on both devices, to make sure everything is as it should be. Try again. If that fails, restart your Mac and try yet again. On one mysterious occasion, I couldn't make this error go away regardless of the changes I made. Later that day, I tried again, and it worked immediately. Go figure.

Clicking a device from the list in the top box on the left displays information on that device in the bottom box. Note: If a key icon appears next to a device name, this means that data will be encrypted when transferred from one device to the other, if possible.

When a device is selected, you can click the Add to Favorites button to add that device to your Favorites list. Making a device a Favorite means that if you temporarily lose your connection to the device (for example, due to low battery power or moving the device out of range), the Mac will automatically seek to connect to it again when it becomes available (for example, when the batteries are replaced or the device is moved back in range). Items that are Favorites have a heart icon next to their name. For such items, the Add to Favorites button will toggle to Remove from Favorites.

To connect to a paired device, click the Connect button. Conversely, you can select to Disconnect from an already-paired device. A device that is disconnected will no longer work with the Mac. However, you can simply click the Connect button to get it working again; you don't need to repair the device. If you want a paired device to be removed from the list, select Delete Pairing.

Click the Set Up New Device button to launch the Bluetooth Setup Assistant utility. This is an alternative to using the Pair New Device option; it walks you through the steps needed to set up the device in a more user-friendly manner.

SEE: • "Bluetooth Setup Assistant," later in this chapter, for more on this utility.

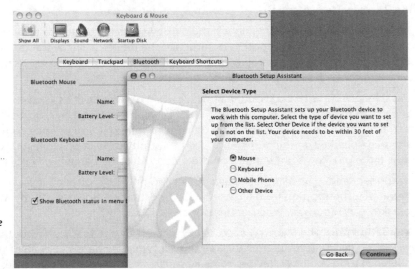

Figure 8.25

The Bluetooth screen of the Keyboard & Mouse System Preferences pane (back) and the initial screen of the Bluetooth Setup Assistant (front).

TAKE NOTE ▶ Setting Up and Using a Bluetooth Mouse and/or Keyboard

Apple now sells a Bluetooth wireless keyboard and mouse. Third-party vendors offer similar devices. For connecting (pairing) these two pieces of hardware to a Mac, Mac OS X offers a procedure different from the Bluetooth options described in the main text. In particular, you will need to follow these steps:

1. Select the Keyboard & Mouse System Preferences pane (not Bluetooth!).

2. From this pane, click the Bluetooth button.

3. From the screen that appears, click the Set Up New Device button. This launches Bluetooth Setup Assistant. Click the Continue button, and select Mouse or Keyboard from the next screen (as appropriate). The assistant should now guide you through the process of finding and pairing the device with your Mac.

4. When you're finished, the name of the device will appear in the Bluetooth screen of the Keyboard & Mouse pane. In addition, the battery level of the device will be indicated (to help you know when it's time to replace the batteries).

If you enabled the Bluetooth menu, the device name will also be listed there; select the name to return to the Keyboard & Mouse System Preferences pane.

continues on next page

TAKE NOTE ▶ Setting Up and Using a Bluetooth Mouse and/or Keyboard
continued

The following are some tips regarding using a Bluetooth mouse and/or keyboard.

Battery issues. Bluetooth mice and keyboards run on battery power. Apple's Bluetooth mouse, for example, runs on two AA batteries. The mouse also has a slide switch to turn the mouse power off; this conserves battery power but breaks the connection of the mouse to the Mac. Turning the mouse back on automatically re-establishes the connection (assuming it is a Favorite). Some devices may also have their own power-saving modes that kick in when they're idle for a period.

Discoverable issues. A Bluetooth mouse or keyboard can only be paired with one Mac at a time. This makes sense since it's unlikely you'd want to move the pointer on two Macs at the same time. However, this means that if you want to transfer the use of a Bluetooth mouse from your desktop Mac to your laptop, for example, you must first delete the pairing to your desktop Mac (via the Bluetooth System Preferences pane's Delete Pairing button) and then pair it with the laptop.

Pairing and connect issues. To re-pair an unpaired Bluetooth mouse or keyboard, you must temporarily use a wired mouse and/or keyboard (to open the needed software and click the relevant buttons and so on). Thus, you should retain your wired devices even if you shift to using a Bluetooth device all the time.

Startup issues. As described primarily in Chapter 5, your Mac (and Mac OS X) supports numerous special startup modes that require holding down keys at startup (for example, holding down the Shift key at startup to perform a safe boot). A potential problem here is that these startup modes cannot be initiated via keyboard commands from a Bluetooth keyboard if the Bluetooth connection to the keyboard is not established until after the time to enter the keyboard commands at startup has passed. Apple has solved this problem via an update to the Bluetooth firmware (version 1.0.2). This update is included on the CD that comes with these devices, and it's also available on Apple's Web site. (Newer Macs will have this initial firmware update already installed; Apple may release subsequent firmware updates, however, so check Apple's Web site for the latest version).

Once you've installed this firmware update, most startup functions are supported with Bluetooth devices. For example, holding down the mouse button at startup ejects a CD from the internal drive. And from the keyboard, Command-Shift (for safe boot), Command-S (for single-user mode), C (to start up from a CD), Option (to access the Startup Manager screen), T (for Target Disk Mode), and Command-Option-O-F (to access the Open Firmware screen) all work.

In some cases, however, your success with these startup modes may be short-lived. For example, after starting up in single-user mode or via a safe boot, the Bluetooth keyboard and mouse will not function. Similarly, after starting up from a bootable CD, a Bluetooth mouse or keyboard may not function—because the pairing information (set in Bluetooth System Preferences) is not present on the CD. The solution, in such cases, is to switch to a wired keyboard and mouse.

Bluetooth utilities

In the Utilities folder, you will find three Bluetooth utilities: Bluetooth Setup Assistant, Bluetooth File Exchange, and Bluetooth Serial Utility.

Bluetooth Setup Assistant. This utility walks you through the steps entailed in setting up new Bluetooth devices for use with your Mac. You can launch it in one of three ways: by clicking the Set Up New Device button in the Devices screen of the Bluetooth System Preferences pane, by selecting Set up New Device from the Bluetooth screen of the Keyboard and Mouse System Preferences pane, or by selecting Set up Bluetooth Device from the Bluetooth menu bar.

Once Setup Assistant has launched and you've selected Continue to move past the first screen, you will be asked to select which type of device you're setting up (Mouse, Keyboard, Mobile Phone, or Other Device). The assistant then searches for and lists discoverable Bluetooth devices in range. You select the device from the list and click Continue, and a connection is initiated. For some devices, you'll be asked to provide a passkey (for authentication); in such cases, you'll need to enter the same passkey on the Bluetooth device. After going through the requisite steps, the device is set up for use with your Mac.

Bluetooth File Exchange. This utility provides a way to exchange files with other users of other Bluetooth-equipped Macs. You can launch it manually, or by selecting either Send File or Browse Device from the Bluetooth menu. If you launch it manually, these same two commands are accessible from Bluetooth File Exchange's File menu.

- **Send File.** If you select Send File, you will be asked to select a file from your mounted volumes (via a standard file dialog) to send to the connected Bluetooth device.

  Note: The Send File option is opened by default when you launch Bluetooth File Exchange. You can change this behavior via the preferences settings.

  After you've selected to send a file, you will be prompted to select a Bluetooth device to which the file should be sent. This is essentially the same window that appears when you select Pair New Device from the Devices screen of the Bluetooth System Preferences pane.

  Note: The Select Bluetooth Device window lets you view devices by Device Type (Phones, PDAs, Computers, and so on) or by Device Category (Discovered, Favorites, Recent), which can be useful if you've set up a number of Bluetooth devices.

  Note: You can also drag a file onto the Bluetooth File Exchange icon in the Finder or the Dock to send the file; you'll be asked immediately to select a device as the recipient.

  After selecting a device, click Send to send the file. A dialog will display the status of the sent file. The way in which the transfer is initiated will depend on how the receiving device is configured to receive files (as set in the Exchange screen of the Bluetooth System Preferences pane, where you can choose among options like "Accept files without warning" and "Prompt for each file").

- **Browse Device.** If you select Browse Device, you again get the Select Bluetooth Device window, used to select a Bluetooth device. After selecting a device from the list and clicking the Select button—assuming the device allows browsing—a window appears, displaying the list of contents in the folder (on the other computer) that was selected (on the other computer) in the Bluetooth File Transfer section of the Exchange screen of the Bluetooth System Preferences pane (as described earlier in this chapter).

  You can now get a file from this folder or send a file to this folder via the Get and Send buttons at the bottom of the window. Selecting a file in the browser and clicking the Get button brings up a dialog that lets you save that file to any location on your own computer. Clicking the Send button lets you choose a file from your own computer to be saved to the current selected folder on the Bluetooth device.

  There are three additional buttons to the left of the Get and Send buttons: The back arrow takes you to the previous folder; the home button switches from the current directory to the default folder (assuming you've navigated to another subfolder from the list above); and the folder button lets you create a new folder in the current directory.

Bluetooth Serial Utility. This utility is used to add emulated serial ports to your Mac. You would use this functionality to enable connections with devices such as Bluetooth-equipped personal digital assistants (such as a Palm handheld organizer). An item called Bluetooth-PDA-Sync should be present by default. The utility's main options include the following:

- **New.** To add Bluetooth serial ports, click the New button. From the dialog that drops down, provide a name for the port (for example, Palm Tungsten if you're going to be connecting to a Palm Tungsten PDA). You have the option to select Incoming or Outgoing as the Port Direction. However, it's easier to instead click the Select Device button and then choose the actual Bluetooth device; this automatically selects the right setting for you.

  Note: After clicking Select Device, in the window that appears click the desired device in the list. At this point, you may be given a list of services for that device (to the right of the device name list). If so, select the service that most closely resembles that which you intend to use the device for (for example, Fax for a Bluetooth-enabled mobile phone that you intend to use as a fax line).

  From the New dialog, you can also select to Require Authentication and Require Encryption, as well as to have the device Show in Network Preferences. Finally, choose the Port Type. If you'll be using this new port with other software or hardware (such as a PDA), be sure to read the documentation to see which options you should choose.

  Finally, click OK to add the new port.

- **On/Off.** You can temporarily disable a port by unchecking the On/Off box next to its name.

- **Edit/Delete.** To edit or delete a serial port, select the port in the list and then click the Edit or Delete button, respectively. Unfortunately, the Edit dialog doesn't provide you with all of the same options you had when you first added a serial port. Specifically, you cannot change the incoming/outgoing status of a port, nor can you switch between different services for a device (the additional options that appear when first selecting a device, described above). If you need to change one of these settings, you'll need to delete the port and re-create it.

Note: If you delete a device that was added to the Network Preferences list, you will also need to separately delete it from the Network pane of System Preferences.

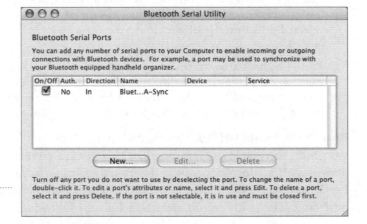

Figure 8.26

Bluetooth Serial Utility.

TAKE NOTE ▶ Rendezvous

Rendezvous (Apple's catchy name for the zeroconf standard) is a new industry standard for automatic discovery (zero configuration) of computers, devices, and other services on *local* IP networks. With Rendezvous, you can browse a network, find other Rendezvous-enabled devices, and connect to those devices without having to fiddle with TCP/IP settings. I emphasize *local* because Rendezvous's magic is limited to devices on the same subnet of your local network.

Rendezvous is actually used in a number of places in Mac OS X. Printer Sharing, discussed in detail in Chapter 7, uses Rendezvous to make shared printers available to other Mac OS X computers on the local network. Even Personal File Sharing, discussed later in this chapter, supports Rendezvous: If you have Personal File Sharing enabled, other Mac OS X Macs will be able to connect to your computer without needing to worry about your IP address. You can also use Rendezvous in iChat to connect to other users on your local network (as an alternative to the Buddy List method). Selecting Log Into Rendezvous from the iChat menu makes you available to chat with other local users and displays other users in your iChat Rendezvous window.

continues on next page

TAKE NOTE ▶ Rendezvous *continued*

Rendezvous is also used in iTunes 4.x: If from the Sharing screen of iTunes' Preferences you enable "Share my music," any Rendezvous-capable computers on your local network will automatically discover your iTunes music when they launch iTunes. Your music files will be listed in their iTunes Playlist listing, under the name you provided in your iTunes Preferences. No special network configuration settings or IP addresses need be entered for this to work.

Finally, Rendezvous is also supported in many newer printers, allowing them to be discovered on a network without users' entering any configuration settings. When you open Printer Setup Utility and select Add Printer, these printers automatically show up when you choose Rendezvous from the pop-up menu. Select a printer and click the Add button, and you're ready to print.

The beauty of Rendezvous is that it requires very little setup, and it works over your existing network (AirPort, Ethernet, FireWire, and so on). The only prerequisite is that a network port configuration is active in the Network System Preferences pane for the type of network (Ethernet, for example) to which you're connected and intend to use for Rendezvous. You don't even need to fill in any of the settings for that port if all you're doing is using Rendezvous! To enable Rendezvous for sharing services, for example, next open the Sharing System Preferences pane and enable the desired Sharing service(s).

How does it work? When your Mac connects to a network, Mac OS X selects an IP address from a specific subset of available addresses that have been set aside for Rendezvous/zeroconf networking. (This IP address is *separate* from any IP address you may have already given your Mac, or that has been given to your Mac by your ISP, for Internet access. It is also a local-only address, meaning it cannot be used to connect to your computer from outside of your own subnet on your local network.) After choosing this local IP address, your Mac uses the Address Resolution Protocol (ARP) to query the rest of the subnet and see if any other device is already using that IP address. If not, Mac OS X claims that address as its own. If the address is already taken, another address is chosen, and then another query is sent out, and so on, until an unused address is found.

Once your Mac has claimed one of these local IP addresses, it uses a technology called *Multicast DNS* (a variant of the DNS protocol used on the Internet at large) to equate that IP address with its own Rendezvous (.local) name. However, instead of connecting to an actual DNS server to resolve a Rendezvous name into an actual IP address, each Mac knows its own Rendezvous name and responds to requests directly via IP multicast (basically a kind of "broadcast" over the entire local network).

continues on next page

TAKE NOTE ▶ **Rendezvous** *continued*

If you look at the Sharing pane of System Preferences, beneath the Computer Name field, you will see the following sentence: "Other computers on your local subnet can reach your computer at {*ComputerName*}.local." You can modify the name by clicking the Edit button. Technically, this local hostname name is not the same thing as the Rendezvous name. Instead, it is a DNS name (which is why the name cannot contain spaces, as DNS naming conventions do not allow it). However, at a practical level, it is useful to think of it as the Rendezvous name, and I will often refer to it that way in the discussions that follow.

A local hostname is needed because the DNS protocol requires that domain names include an identifiable top-level domain, such as .com, .net, or .edu. The .local domain has been assigned to Rendezvous, so all local Rendezvous-enabled devices will have domain names that take the following form: *RendezvousName*.local. Services provided by that device will have an address of *Service@RendezvousName*.local. For example, when you connect to a printer that is being shared by another Mac, if you use Printer Setup Utility to get information about the printer, you'll see that the Host name of a shared printer is *OtherComputerName*.local. If you select Show Info for this printer, you will see that its Queue Name is listed as *PrinterName@ OtherComputerName*.local. In another example, if you have Personal Web Sharing enabled, other local users will be able to connect to your Mac's built-in Web server by pointing their Web browser to http://*RendezvousName*.local.

Because all Rendezvous-enabled devices will end in .local, if you enter .local in the Search Domains field of the TCP/IP screen of the Network System Preferences pane (for the port configuration used for your local network, of course), you can then avoid having to type .local as part of a server name. This would apply, for example, when connecting to a Rendezvous-enabled Web server or file server.

Missed Rendezvous devices. Rendezvous includes a security measure to prevent a specific type of network attack. Unfortunately, this security measure may also prevent some local devices—mainly those that do not carefully follow the Rendezvous specification—from being seen. If certain Rendezvous devices aren't available when they should be, you can temporarily turn off this security measure to see if doing so reveals the device. To do so, open Terminal and type the following:

```
sudo sysctl -w net.inet.ip.linklocal.in.allowbadttl = 1.
```

If you find that the device now works, you know that the problem is that the device isn't fully Rendezvous-compliant. Unfortunately, the above command only remains in effect until the system is shut down or restarted; thus, if you need to employ it, you must reenter it after each startup.

SEE: • Chapter 11, for more on iChat and iTunes.

Using a Router

As home networks proliferate, routers have become increasingly common. Many users, otherwise unfamiliar with the details of networking, purchase routers to manage their local networks and share Internet connections.

Internet routers—the most common router type (and the only one I cover here)—typically allow you to (a) interconnect multiple local devices on a common network; (b) connect to the Internet (via a broadband device such as a cable or DSL modem connected to the router); (c) provide firewall protection (preventing unauthorized access to your computer from outside the network); and (d) allow you to share a single Internet connection between multiple computers.

Some routers require Ethernet cables for all connected devices, whereas others support both wired and wireless connections (an AirPort Base Station is actually a router in this sense).

I covered issues specific to wireless routers in the section on AirPort, earlier in this chapter. Here I cover general router issues, especially those relevant to wired routers. It is beyond the scope of this book to provide extended coverage of router and networking issues (which could easily fill a book of their own). Instead, I focus on issues relevant to Mac OS X troubleshooting.

Connecting to the Internet via a router

Most Internet routers are broadband-based devices, meaning they're designed to work with cable or DSL Internet connections. LinkSys, for example, makes routers that are quite popular for use with Macs. Instead of hooking up your DSL or cable modem to your computer, you hook it up to a special WAN port on the router. Then you connect multiple computers to the additional Ethernet ports on the router. In the case of wireless routers (including Apple's AirPort Base Station), additional devices may be connected via a wireless connection (see "Take Note: Setting Up an AirPort Base Station and Network," earlier in this chapter). Then the Internet router directs Internet traffic between your ISP and each computer on the network, typically using Network Address Translation (NAT) to share one address among multiple machines. All of your computers get Internet access, but it appears to the outside world that only a single computer is accessing the Internet.

Some Internet routers may also include dial-up modems; Apple's AirPort Base Station is one. These routers are useful to people who have only modem-based (dial-up) Internet access. Internet routers using a modem work the same way as those using a broadband connection, except that when someone on the network tries to access the Internet, the router dials up the ISP just as you would when you use a modem on your own computer. When the router dials up, everyone on the network can access the Internet (although at much slower speeds, because multiple users are sharing a single modem line).

Note: Although almost any router will work with a Mac, some routers are not entirely Mac-compliant. In particular, some will not work with devices connected via AppleTalk and/or Rendezvous. Check with the vendor before purchasing a router if this is of concern to you.

TAKE NOTE ▶ Software Routers: Software AirPort Base Station and More

In addition to the hardware-based Internet routers described in the main text, several software-based Internet routers are also available. This type of software is installed on the computer that is connected directly to the Internet, and you then connect other computers to the base computer via an Ethernet hub or switch, or an AirPort/wireless connection. The base computer routes Internet traffic to and from the client computers so that all of the computers on the network have Internet access.

Mac OS X includes a software Internet router, called Internet Sharing, which you can access via the Internet screen of the Sharing pane of System Preferences. You can set up Internet Sharing with almost any type of network.

Software routers are commonly used to allow multiple devices with AirPort cards to connect to the Internet via the base computer without a hardware base station. The advantage of this capability—called a Software Base Station in Mac OS 9 but now simply a feature of Internet Sharing—is that you eliminate the expense of a separate hardware device (that is, you only need to purchase an AirPort card for each connected device). The main disadvantage is that the computer sharing its Internet connection must always be up and running (and connected to the Internet) for the AirPort network to be active. Internet Sharing also uses the sharing computer's CPU, possibly reducing performance of other processes on the computer.

Sustainable Softworks' IPNetRouter is a third-party example of a software Internet router, which could be used instead of Mac OS X's built-in Internet Sharing feature.

SEE: • "Take Note: Setting Up an AirPort Base Station and Network," earlier in this chapter, for more on using AirPort.
• "Take Note: Setting Up and Using Internet Sharing and File Sharing," later in this chapter, for more on Software Base Station setups.

Network Address Translation

When you have a dial-up or broadband connection, you generally have only a single IP address assigned to your household or connection. If you were connecting a single computer to the Internet, that IP address would be assigned to that computer. However, many Internet routers allow you to share a single IP address among multiple computers using a feature called Network Address Translation (NAT). An Internet router using NAT masquerades as that single IP address and then manages all traffic between the various computers on your network and the Internet. It does this by assigning each computer on the network an internal address (such as 192.168.1.x) and then translating that address to the single IP address that is supposed to represent your Internet connection. For example, when you request a Web site, your co-worker or family member checks an email account, and the computer down the hall requests a file to download, the router uses Network Address Translation to keep track of which computer requested what, and then to send these requests out to the Internet. Conversely, when the Web page, the email, and the file are sent back to your IP address, the router knows which computers on your network to send them to.

As explained earlier in the chapter, Mac OS X's Internet Sharing feature is simply a software implementation of an Internet router. Therefore, it uses Network Address Translation to share your Internet connection, just like a hardware router.

SEE: • "Internet" in "Setting Up System Preferences: Sharing," later in this chapter, for more details.

• "Network Security," later in this chapter, for more information on NAT.

Configuring a router

The following provides a brief overview of what to expect when you set up a router. For more details, see the instructions that came with your router.

Routers include built-in settings that you access via either a special utility designed to work with the router or a Web-based interface (also built into the router) that you access from your Mac's Web browser.

For example, to access most LinkSys routers, which use a Web-based interface, you would type http://192.168.1.1 in any Web browser. This brings up a dialog asking for the router's administrative password (if this is the first time you're accessing it, the router expects a default password; you need to check the router's documentation to get it). After entering the correct password, you get a Web page that provides access to all of the router's settings.

What settings do you enter here? For starters, you will want to provide the information necessary for making a WAN connection to the Internet. This includes telling the router whether you're using a static IP address (and if so, what it is), a DHCP dynamically generated IP address, or a PPPoE address (which requires entering a name and password). Your ISP should tell you which option to select and what data (if any) to enter.

You will also instruct the router whether and how you want IP addresses to be distributed to other computers on your local network (in other words, if you want to manually assign IP addresses in each computer's TCP/IP preferences, or if you want the router to automatically assign IP addresses). Typically, you will have the router assign IP addresses to computers dynamically, via DHCP. To use DHCP with a LinkSys router, you would click the DHCP screen in the router's browser display and enable the DHCP server. Otherwise, you can leave DHCP disabled and have each computer use a local IP address (such as 192.168.1.101, 192.168.1.102, and so on), entered for each client computer at its TCP/IP settings.

If you connect to the Internet via a dynamic IP address (such as via a cable modem using DHCP), the router settings are also where you go to determine your current IP address. For example, with a LinkSys router that has been set up to "Obtain an IP automatically" in the Setup screen, click the Status button to view your WAN IP address and DNS Server addresses. From the Status screen, you can also renew or release your DHCP IP address. With an AirPort Base Station, this same information is accessed via the Internet screen of AirPort Admin Utility.

Finally, the LinkSys router interface allows you to perform more advanced actions, such as port forwarding and mapping, enabling a DMZ host, and MAC address cloning.

SEE: • "Take Note: What Are the TCP/IP Settings?" and "Take Note: Ethernet Hubs, Switches, Routers, and Cables," earlier in this chapter, for related information.

• "Internet routers and port mapping," below, for information on port mapping.

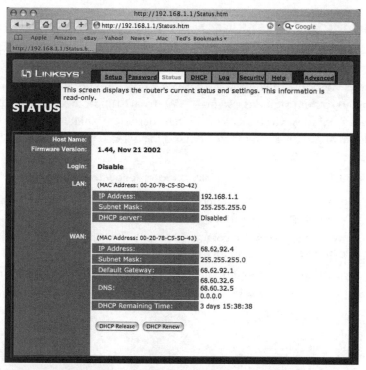

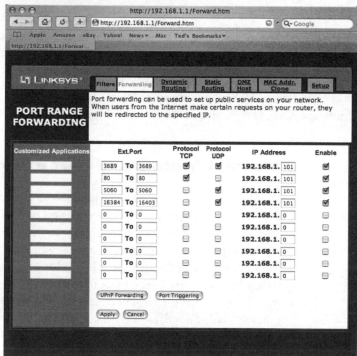

Figure 8.27

Two screens from a LinkSys router's software: (top) the Status screen, showing the current LAN and WAN settings, and (bottom) the Port Forwarding screen, showing various ports opened for the Mac with an IP address of 192.168.1.101.

TECHNICALLY SPEAKING ▶ Upgrading the Firmware on a LinkSys Router

The vendor for your router may occasionally release firmware upgrades, usually available from the Web. These upgrades add features and bug fixes to the existing firmware. Unfortunately, not all vendors provide a Mac interface for performing these firmware upgrades. For example, LinkSys router upgrades use the TFTP (Trivial FTP) protocol. In Mac OS 9, the main way to install these upgrades was typically via a third-party TFTP utility. In Mac OS X, however, you have a built-in alternative: the `tftp` command, included as part of Mac OS X's Unix software and accessible via Terminal.

To update the firmware of a LinkSys router, follow these steps:

1. Go to the router's Web interface (that is, 192.168.1.1). From the Password screen, remove the router password. Apply the change.

2. In Terminal, use the `cd` command to go to the directory where the firmware upgrade file is located. You're looking for a file called code.bin.

3. Type `tftp` and press Return. This should change the prompt to `tftp>`.

4. At the prompt, type the following four lines, pressing Return after each:

   ```
   connect 192.168.1.1
   binary
   put code.bin
   quit
   ```

5. Quit Terminal, return to the router's Web interface, and reenter your password.

Your firmware has now been updated. The firmware version in the Status screen should indicate the new version number.

Note: Recent versions of the LinkSys firmware include an Upgrade Firmware option, available from the Help screen of the Web interface. If this works (and I have found that it sometimes does not), you can use it instead of the above method.

Internet routers and port mapping

Using a router to allow multiple computers to share an Internet connection generally works very well. However, if you plan to enable any type of file sharing, and want to share files with users who are not on your local network (for example, users connecting from elsewhere on the Internet), an Internet router complicates things a bit. The problem is that whereas your Internet router knows where to send incoming Internet data that has been requested by a computer on the local network, it doesn't know what to do with "unrequested" incoming data—data that is not in response to a specific request the router previously sent out. To put it another way, a request by a remote computer to access files shared by your computer has not been specifically requested by your computer. Rather, someone outside your home or office is trying to initiate contact via your external IP address—which basically is your router. Your router has to decide which computer should receive the incoming data, but it doesn't know where to send it.

Although this may sound serious, the good news is that most modern Internet routers have addressed such scenarios by adding support for what's known as *port mapping* (or port *forwarding*). In addition to its IP address, every server has *ports* that are reserved for different types of connections. When you point your Web browser to www.servername.com, for example, you're actually connecting to www.servername.com:80. Port 80 is the network port that generally receives requests for Web pages on a Web server.

Because each sharing service uses specific ports, you can use port mapping to tell the router that any incoming requests for a particular port should always be directed to a specific computer on the internal network. For example, AFP (Apple Filing Protocol, used for Personal File Sharing in Mac OS X) uses Port 548. If you "map" Port 548 to one of the computers connected to your router, all File Sharing requests from the Internet will be directed to that computer.

Note that port mapping requires that the computers on your network have manually assigned IP addresses; you cannot assign addresses via DHCP. Also, each port can only be "mapped" to a single computer (meaning that, for example, remote users can only access Personal File Sharing on a single computer on your local network).

A list of ports used by various Mac OS sharing services is available via the following Apple Knowledge Base document: http://docs.info.apple.com/article.html?artnum=106439.

The specifics of enabling port mapping and forwarding vary a bit from router to router. In general, there will be a location in which you can specify the port(s) you wish to forward as well as a location (in the same row) for specifying the IP address of the computer to be mapped to that port. Thus, to map Port 80 (used for Web sharing) to a specific computer, you would enter 80 as the port to be mapped and the IP address of the computer you wish to share (listed in that computer's TCP/IP screen of Network System Preferences) as the target.

Note: These ports are the same ones that are opened and closed via firewall software, such as Mac OS X's firewall (accessed via the Firewall screen of Sharing System Preferences). Mac OS X's firewall is discussed later in this chapter.

TCP vs. UDP. Your router's Port Sharing or Port Forwarding window will likely include separate options for TCP and UDP, for each port listing. TCP is used for services that require a persistent connection, such as for an FTP transfer. UDP is a "connection-less" method that is used when only a brief connection is needed, such as to check a domain name. When in doubt, when you open a port, open it for both TCP and UDP.

DMZ host. Some routers offer an additional solution: You can specify one computer to be the DMZ host, which is akin to enabling port mapping for *every* port, all forwarded to that one computer. The computer will then receive all incoming data requests of any type. This feature has two significant draw-backs: First, if the DMZ Host option is enabled for a particular computer, you cannot enable port mapping for any other computer on the local network—all unrequested data is "mapped" directly to the computer specified as the DMZ host. More important from a security point of view, designating a computer as a DMZ host allows *all* external requests, on *all* ports, to be passed on to that particular computer, thus negating the firewall value of the Internet router itself. The only reason you should use the DMZ Host option is if you need to use port mapping on many different ports and your Internet router's port-mapping settings do not accommodate them all (for example, some routers only allow you to specify ten ports for port mapping).

Network System Preferences settings vs. router settings

After setting up your Internet router, you'll need to enter the appropriate settings in Network System Preferences on each computer. Your settings will differ from what they would be for a direct connection to the Internet, especially if you're using a manually assigned IP address. In particular, note the following when entering data in Network System Preferences:

- **Ethernet router.** For a manually entered IP address, in the TCP/IP screen of the Built-In Ethernet section, enter a local IP address (usually 192.168.1.x or 10.0.0.x, where x varies for each computer on the network). The IP address entered in the Router field typically will be 192.168.1.1 or 10.0.0.1. The Subnet Mask typically is something like 255.255.255.0. Again, the router instructions will provide specifics.

   For a DHCP address, just choose Using DHCP.

- **Wireless router.** The logic is the same, except that you enter the information after choosing AirPort from the Show pop-up menu. You will be accessing the Internet via an AirPort card through the router.

The important general principle here is that the settings entered into your router are typically the settings you would enter in the TCP/IP screen of the Network System Preferences pane if you were not using a router. Having entered these settings in the router, the TCP/IP screen settings on each computer on the local network refer to the router, rather than a direct connection to your ISP.

SEE: • "Firewall" and "Firewalls," later in this chapter.

THE JAGUAR WAY ▶ Internet System Preferences Pane

Jaguar includes an Internet System Preferences pane. Any Mac OS X application that can access Internet System Preferences settings can use these settings rather than require you to enter them separately in the Preferences dialog of the application itself—thereby reducing the need to enter the same data in multiple applications.

The Internet pane consists of four tabs: .Mac, iDisk, Email, and Web.

In Panther, the .Mac and iDisk tabs have been moved to the new .Mac System Preferences pane.

What happened to the Email and Web features? They're gone—well, sort of. The main function of these tabs was to set up default email and Web browser applications, respectively. In an effort to encourage you to maintain Mac OS X's Mail and Safari applications as defaults, Apple removed these options in Panther. However, if you have other email or Web browser applications (such as Microsoft Entourage and Internet Explorer), you can still set these up as defaults via options that appear when launching them. Additional email and browser settings (such as the default browser home page) are similarly set up in the default application (whatever it may be).

In general, all of these settings are maintained in a common preferences file called com.apple.internetconfig.plist. You can access and modify these settings directly, if you wish, from the .plist file.

SEE: • "Technically Speaking: Internetconfig Preferences," below.

TECHNICALLY SPEAKING ▶ Internetconfig Preferences

Although applications like Safari and Mail have their own preferences files (for example, com.apple.safari.plist and com.apple.mail.plist), many preferences settings for these applications (especially ones that would be common to any email or Web browser application) are stored in a special preferences file called com.apple.internetconfig.plist, located in ~/Library/Preferences.

This .plist file thus also holds some of the data that you access via the Preferences command in Internet Explorer and Entourage—including the settings for Internet Explorer's File Helpers and Protocol Helpers. (These settings determine the applications used to open certain types of files, such as StuffIt compressed files.)

Preventing preferences changes from being overwritten. When you change com.apple .internetconfig.plist via an application's preferences, be cautious if you have two applications that use this file (such as Entourage and Internet Explorer) open at the same time. In such cases, any changes you make via Application 1 may get eliminated when you quit Application 2—especially if you quit Application 2 before quitting Application 1. What appears to happen is that when Application 2 quits, it overwrites the changes you made via Application 1. The work-around is to quit all applications that could affect the .plist file *except* the one in which you intend to make changes. Then quit that application before opening any other relevant applications. After that, all should go well.

continues on next page

TECHNICALLY SPEAKING ▶ **Internetconfig Preferences** *continued*

The com.apple.internetconfig.plist file and Internet settings. This file stores the default home page selection made in Safari (it's listed in the WWWHomePage key, as most easily viewed in Property List Editor). It also stores the default home page selection for Internet Explorer. However, it's stored in a separate key called 4d534945·WWWHomePage (which stands for MSIE·WWWHomePage, because *4d 53 49 45* are the hex codes for the ASCII characters *MSIE*). Thus, even though both applications use the same file to store this preference, the default preference need not be the same for each application. Other applications have the option to do this as well.

The com.apple.internetconfig.plist file and crashes (unexpected quits). If applications that obtain some of their settings from com.apple.internetconfig.plist are crashing, try removing the file from the Preferences folder. A new version with default settings will be created the next time you launch any application that uses this file. You will have to re-create some of your preferences, but the crashes will likely disappear. Still, just in case this technique doesn't fix the crashes, save the .plist file in a different location (rather than delete it right away). You can move it back if you conclude that removing it didn't fix the problem.

Another suggested fix for Internet Explorer crashes is to delete Explorer's cache files—notably, those that may not get deleted via Explorer's Preferences dialog. These files are the files that end in .waf in the ~/Library/Caches/MS Internet Cache/ folder and the Download Cache file in ~/Library/Preferences/Explorer/. You may have to log out and log back in before you can delete these files. There are several third-party utilities, such as Northern Softworks' Panther Cache Cleaner, that will also delete these (and other) cache files.

File Mappings and Protocol Helpers. Internet Explorer's Preferences allow you to view and modify the File Mappings and Protocol Helpers lists. These lists, if changed in Explorer, will affect Safari as well—because they share the common internetconfig.plist file. However, Safari includes no options to edit these lists directly. If you use Safari and don't want to bother with Explorer to edit these settings, you can use a third-party System Preferences pane called More Internet (from Monkeyfood) or an application called MisFox (from iCab Company).

Note: File Mappings interpret a file's "content-type" or name extension so that the Mac knows what to do with the file (post-process) after it is downloaded (for example, unstuff a .sit file or open an AAC file in iTunes). Protocol Helpers are used to match a specific Internet protocol to its appropriate application (for example, specifying which application should be used for FTP access, mailto URLs, and so on).

Among the things you can do when editing a File Mapping, for example, is change what post-processing does (for example, from opening a file in iTunes to just saving the file to disk without opening any application).

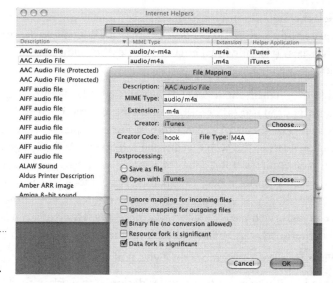

Figure 8.28

Editing the post-processing of a file mapping in MisFox.

Setting Up System Preferences: .Mac

Mac OS X's .Mac System Preference panes is where you set up preferences related to your .Mac account. It consists of two screens: .Mac and iDisk.

What is .Mac? Provided by Apple, .Mac provides a wide range of services—including, for example, a mac.com email address and access to an Internet-based server (called iDisk) on which you can store files for backup or for others to access. You can use .Mac's HomePage feature to create sophisticated-looking Web pages with next to no effort. You can send email greeting cards (called iCards) to your friends and relatives. Additional features are described in the sections that follow. For more details on .Mac and access to other .Mac features, such as HomePage and iCards, go to www.mac.com or click the .Mac button on Apple's home page.

.Mac

If you have a .Mac account, the .Mac screen is where you enter your .Mac member name and password—information that can be used when you access .Mac features from any application. For example, Mail can use this information to receive email from your .Mac account.

Click the Sign Up button to open an account if you're not already a member. Membership costs $100 per year. A small additional charge provides email-only access (via individual email addresses) for individuals other than the primary member.

Aside from email, the most commonly used .Mac feature is the ability to mount your .iDisk (as described in the next section). In addition, .Mac works with several other Mac OS X utilities. For example, iCal works with .Mac to post calendars to the Web that anyone can access. With iSync, you can synchronize your Address Book contacts, iCal calendar data, and Safari bookmarks to your .Mac account. These can then be synced to any other computer that accesses your .Mac account. You can post photos in your iPhoto Library directly to a Web page via your .Mac account. The Backup utility, available to .Mac members, can be used to back up files on your drive to your iDisk.

SEE: • Chapter 11 for more on iSync, iCal, and iPhoto.

Apple has also released free utilities designed to work with .Mac: Mac Slides Publisher, for example, can post a collection of photos as a slide show to your iDisk (which you can then share over the Web). And iDisk Utility—which is available to nonmembers (there's even a Windows version)—can be used to locate and mount the Public folder or (if you have authorization) the entire contents of any iDisk. (In Panther, iDisk Utility's features are built into the Finder. as described in the next section.)

iDisk

iDisk is an online storage space that allows you to store documents, music, pictures, Web sites, and movies—basically, any kind of file you desire. In addition, Apple stocks each iDisk with software updates and a selection of third-party software (applications, music files, and even drivers for third-party peripherals).

iDisk storage. The iDisk screen of the .Mac System Preferences pane features a bar graph showing how many megabytes of your iDisk are currently being used. You have 100 MB by default. If you need more, click the Buy More button; it takes you to a Web site where you can make a purchase.

Your Public folder. One of the folders on your iDisk is called Public. By default, anything you place in this folder can be accessed by anyone with an Internet connection. You can set it so that this folder has "Read only" or Read & Write access. If you don't want the folder to be completely public, you can also select to require that a password be used to access your Public folder.

"Create a local copy of your iDisk." If you check this box, a local copy of your iDisk is created on your hard drive (which may take a while, depending on the amount of data on your iDisk and the speed of your Internet connection). This local copy will appear as a volume in the Places sidebar of Finder windows as well as all other locations where volumes are listed. Open the volume window to access the iDisk's contents.

The advantage of this arrangement is that once the local copy is created, you can copy items to or from your iDisk at the speed of your hard drive rather than the slower speed of your Internet connection. You can also access your iDisk's content even when you aren't connected to the Internet. Of course, when you make changes to the local copy, those changes aren't immediately reflected in the "real" copy on the server. For this to happen, you must synchronize the local copy with the server copy. The iDisk screen offer two options for doing this: Automatically and Manually. Apple recommends Automatically. With this set, syncing is done in the background at set intervals as long as you are connected to the Internet. Alternatively, a manual sync is only performed when you specifically request it.

To sync an iDisk at any time (even if you selected Automatically), click the Sync button (which looks like two arrows chasing each other in a circle) located next to the iDisk listing in the sidebar of any Finder window. When you do this, the phrase *Synching iDisk* will appear in the status bar at the bottom of the Finder window. A progress bar indicates how much syncing is left to be done. When finished, the status bar will indicate the time of the last sync.

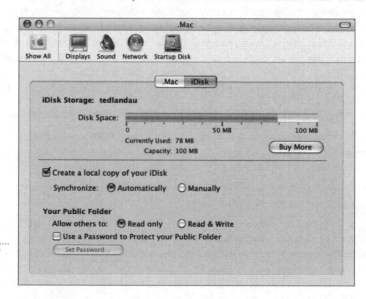

Figure 8.29

The iDisk screen of the .Mac System Preferences pane.

TAKE NOTE ▶ Mounting and Working with iDisks

This sidebar provides details about mounting and working with an iDisk (especially a local copy).

Mounting and unmounting an iDisk. If your iDisk isn't currently mounted on your drive, you can use one of two primary methods to mount it:

- **Go > iDisk.** In the Finder's Go menu, select iDisk, and from the hierarchical menu that appears, choose My iDisk (or press Command-Shift-I). If your member name and password aren't already entered in the .Mac System Preferences pane, you will be prompted to enter them now.

  This mounts the actual server copy, which will include your member name as the name of the volume and appear in your Computer window as well as on your Desktop (if the preference to mount volumes on your Desktop was selected)—as if it were an external drive.

  To unmount (disconnect from) the iDisk, drag the iDisk icon to the Trash.

  Note: From this iDisk item in the Go menu, you can mount anyone else's iDisk by selecting either Other User's iDisk (used if you know the member name and password for the iDisk; this gives you full access to the iDisk as if it were your own) or Other User's Public Folder (you typically only need the user's member name for this).

- **From the .Mac System Preferences pane, select "Create a local copy of your iDisk."** This mounts a local copy of your iDisk. After you select the option, you will likely need to leave the .Mac System Preferences pane to initiate this process. When you do, a dialog will appear, stating, "A copy of your iDisk is being created on your computer." The dialog will include a bar that displays the progress of the process.

  You cannot unmount this local copy by typical means (such as dragging the icon to the Trash). To do so, you must uncheck the "Create a local copy of your iDisk" option. When you do so, you will be asked if you're sure you want to do this; click "Turn off local iDisk" to confirm. Doing this removes the active local copy but leaves behind a disk image file called Previous local iDisk for {*membername*}.dmg. You can double-click this image file to mount it. You can now copy files from the mounted image to your hard drive. However, the mounted image will no longer sync with the server copy. To re-create a new synched copy, you must reselect the "Create a local copy…" option. Thus, once you have decided there is nothing in the "previous" disk image that you want to copy to your drive, you can and should delete the image file.

Using the local copy of your iDisk. Here are some tips for using a local copy of your iDisk:

- In addition to syncing by clicking the sync icon in the Finder's sidebar (as noted in the main text), you can select Sync Now from the iDisk's contextual menu (for example, when the iDisk icon is highlighted on your Desktop).

- To temporarily toggle automatic syncing on and off, select the Automatic Syncing command from the iDisk's contextual menu.

- The local copy of your iDisk does not include *all* files on the server. In particular, software maintained on the iDisk by Apple, for which you have no access, is not copied. Neither are the Library, Software, and (if you used the Backup utility) Backup folders and their contents. These folders are represented on your iDisk as aliases. If you double-click them, you are taken to the content on the server (assuming you have an active Internet connection at the time, so that the server copy is accessible).

continues on next page

TAKE NOTE ▶ **Mounting and Working with iDisks** *continued*

- When a local copy is mounted, there is no command or button that can be used to access the server copy directly. For example, if you select My iDisk from the Finder's Go menu, it will open the local copy, not the server copy.

  However, you can access the server copy indirectly via the folder aliases just described. To do so, select Show Original from the contextual menu for the alias. This opens up a new folder window (with your member name as the name of the window). This is the actual server copy of your iDisk. Changes made to this folder immediately modify the folder (no syncing required).

  Actually, the server copy is mounted even before you do this; it just remains invisible in the Finder. For example, you can see the server copy by launching Terminal and typing `ls /Volumes`. Thus, you could also access this copy by selecting Go to Folder from the Finder's Go menu and entering `/Volumes/{membername}`.

- Where is the actual local copy of your iDisk stored? That is, where on your hard drive are the files that are contained in the local copy? They are maintained in an image file named *{membername}*.dmg, located in ~/Library/Mirrors/*{hexcode}*.

- If you make different changes to the same file on your iDisk using more than one computer, you have a synchronization conflict. To address this, the Mac will ask which version of the file you want to save. Select either the version on the computer or the version on the iDisk, and click Keep Selected. To save both versions to your iDisk, click Keep Both.

- The process used to create and perform syncing of your local copy of iDisk is called MirrorAgent. It is located in /System/Library/CoreServices. If MirrorAgent detects any problem with syncing, it will send an alert message. Examples of such messages include the following: "Creating the iDisk on your computer failed (Not enough free space)" and "There is a problem deleting the file."

  Note: If you get persistent unexpected error messages from MirrorAgent, try quitting MirrorAgent (from Activity Monitor) and relaunching it (by double-clicking the file in CoreServices).

.HSicon files. When you connect to an iDisk from a computer other than a Mac (say a Unix or Windows system), you may see .HSicon files (normally invisible on a Mac). Do not delete these. The .HSicon files display the images of an iDisk or an iDisk Public folder when connected using AFP (Apple Filing Protocol) in Mac OS 9.

Alternative ways of mounting an iDisk. If, for some reason, you don't want to use the main methods of mounting an iDisk (as described above), or you're not using Panther, there are alternatives:

- **Connect to Server.** In the Finder's Go menu, select Connect to Server. In the Address field enter `idisk.mac.com`. When you click the Connect button, enter the user name and password of the .Mac account you want to access.

  Alternatively, you can type `http://idisk.mac.com/{membername}` in Connect to Server. Clicking Connect brings up a WebDAV dialog, in which you can once again enter the name and password of the selected account.

  In either case, the selected iDisk will mount as a remote volume.

continues on next page

TAKE NOTE ▶ **Mounting and Working with iDisks** *continued*

- **iDisk Utility.** Apple's iDisk Utility allows you to mount your own iDisk using the Open iDisk button. You can also mount the Public folder of another user's iDisk via the Public Folder Access button. You would only likely need this on a Mac not running Panther or on a Windows PC.

- **Alias files or Dock icons.** Once an iDisk is mounted, you can create an alias to the volume that you can use when you later want to remount an iDisk (just as you can with any shared volume).

  Similarly, if you drag the icon of a shared computer or server to the Dock, it creates a permanent Dock icon for the server. Click it to later remount the server.

- **Internet Location files.** You can create Internet Location files (which are described later in the chapter) that allow you to quickly mount an iDisk or iDisk Public Folder.

- **WebDAV utilities.** Finally, because iDisk uses WebDAV technology for its access, you can mount an iDisk via any WebDAV-capable utility. For example, the third-party utility Goliath (by WebDAV) includes an Open iDisk Connection command in its File menu. Select it, enter the name and password of the account, and you're in! Rather than having the iDisk mount as a volume on your Desktop, however, Goliath opens its own directory window that lists all of the files and folders on your volume. With Goliath, performance is typically faster than with Mac OS X's native iDisk access.

- **HomePage.** You can use .Mac's HomePage option to create a Web page that gives anyone access to the Public folder on your iDisk. To access this Web page, use the following URL format: http://homepage.mac.com/{*yourname*}.

As is always the case, these methods won't work if the desired server is not on the network at the time, or if you don't have access permissions for the server.

If you can no longer access your iDisk at all, the iDisk may have "crashed." To check for this, launch Activity Monitor and search for a process named *mount_webdev*. If you cannot find it, the iDisk has crashed. To get it going again, you need to restart your Mac.

SEE: • **"Using Network and Connect to Server," later in this chapter, for related information.**

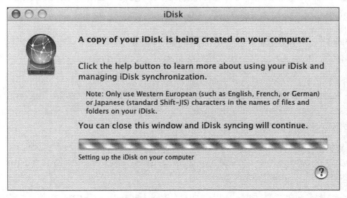
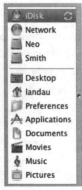

Figure 8.30

The message that appears when you select to create a local copy of your iDisk (left); after the copy is created, the iDisk appears in the Finder's sidebar with a sync icon next to its name (right).

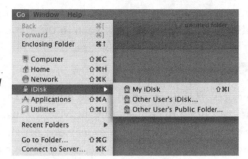

Figure 8.31

You can use the iDisk command in the Go menu to mount your own iDisk as well as the iDisk or Public folders of others (left); the Public folder of my iDisk mounted on a Desktop (right).

Setting Up System Preferences: Sharing

The Sharing pane of System Preferences is your one-stop shop for almost any sort of sharing that you intend to do. It is where you control whether (and how) users on other computers can access your computer and its contents. After the Network System Preferences pane, it is the most critical pane to configure if you're on the Internet.

For starters, you enter your computer name at the top of the window. A matching local hostname (.local) name is automatically created (though you can change the name by clicking the Edit button). These names identify your computer when users attempt to connect to it. Note: The computer name can have spaces in it; the local hostname cannot. The local hostname, as described earlier in the chapter, is used when attempting to locate computers via the Rendezvous protocol.

SEE: • "Take Note: Rendezvous," earlier in this chapter, for more details.

TAKE NOTE ▶ Sharing and the Accounts System Preferences Pane

Creating users in the Accounts System Preferences pane, though not covered in this chapter, is an important prerequisite for using certain Sharing services, such as Personal File Sharing. In addition to creating a list of users who can locally log in to a Mac, the Accounts settings determine who can access your Mac remotely via Sharing. If you want someone to be able to access files on your computer over the Internet or a local network, other than as a Guest, that user must have an account on your computer—even if he or she will never use the computer in person.

SEE: • "System Preferences," in Chapter 2, for details on setting up and using the Accounts System Preferences pane.

• "Take Note: Using SharePoints," later in this chapter for an exception to this restriction: File Sharing Only users.

The Sharing System Preferences pane consists of three screens: Services, Firewall, and Internet. I describe each in the sections that follow.

Services

The Services screen is used to enable or disable the various methods by which users are permitted to connect to your Mac. To enable a desired Sharing service, simply click the check box next to its name or select its name and click the Start button. To turn off the service, uncheck the box or select the service and click the Stop button.

SEE: • "Sharing Services: A Closer Look," later in this chapter, for more details.

The services available from the Services screen include the following:

- **Personal File Sharing.** This service provides a way for users (specifically, those with accounts and, in a more limited capacity, those who are guests) to access files on your Mac from another Mac.

  Mac OS X users connect to your Mac via the Finder's Connect to Server command or the Network (Browser) window. Most Macs running Mac OS 9 or older can connect via AppleShare (which they access in the Chooser) or the Network Browser application.

  A maximum of ten users can be connected via Sharing. If you need more than that, you need Mac OS X Server.

  SEE: • "Personal File Sharing" and "Using Network and Connect to Server," later in this chapter, for more details.

- **Windows Sharing.** This service makes it easy for Windows users to access files stored on your Mac using the SMB/CIFS protocol (a standard Windows/Unix file-sharing standard). After enabling this feature, you will also need to create accounts for the Windows users in the Accounts System Preferences pane. Note that because SMB/CIFS is also a Unix standard, enabling Windows File Sharing also allows Unix users to connect to your Mac.

  SEE: • "Windows File Sharing" and "Using Network and Connect to Server," later in this chapter, for more details.

- **Personal Web Sharing.** This service allows users to have Web browser access to the files (such as HTML files) in the Sites folder of your home directory.

  SEE: • "Personal Web Sharing," later in this chapter, for more details.

- **Remote Login.** This option allows access to your computer via the encrypted SSH protocol. SSH can be used via Terminal or specialized third-party SSH applications. It also allows SFTP (Secure FTP) access to your Mac.

  Allowing remote login can be useful in some troubleshooting situations—that is, you may be able to access an apparently frozen Mac remotely via SSH from another Mac. In this case, despite the freeze, you could access the computer via Terminal from another Mac on the network—which in turn might allow you to modify or delete files that are preventing the Mac from starting up without freezing.

SEE: • **"Network Security," later in this chapter.**

• **"Technically Speaking: Connecting Remotely to a Frozen Mac: Killing Processes, Running Sync," in Chapter 5.**

- **FTP Access.** This service enables users with local accounts to connect to your Mac via any FTP client software, including a Web browser. These users just need to know the IP address for your Mac (which would be entered in the format ftp://192.168.1.878, for example, followed by a user name and password when asked).

  SEE: • **"FTP access," later in this chapter, for more details.**

- **Apple Remote Desktop.** This service makes it possible for other users to access your Mac via the Apple Remote Desktop application (see www.apple.com/remotedesktop for details).

- **Remote Apple Events.** Enabling this option allows applications (including AppleScripts) running on remote computers to interact with your computer. Unless you have a specific reason to allow such scripts and applications from a trusted user, you should keep this option turned off: People can do some very malicious things to your computer by using Apple Events and AppleScripts.

- **Printer Sharing.** This option resurrects the USB Printer Sharing feature from Mac OS 9, letting users on your local network print to printers connected directly to your Mac. However, whereas Mac OS 9's USB Printer Sharing was limited to USB printers, Mac OS X can share any printer that is listed in Printer Setup Utility (whether connected via USB, Ethernet, FireWire, or AirPort).

  SEE: • **"Printer Sharing," in Chapter 7, for more details.**

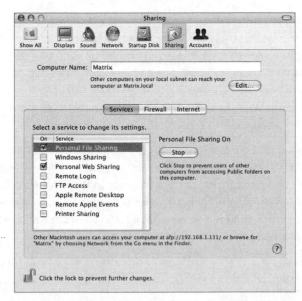

Figure 8.32

The Services screen of the Sharing System Preferences pane.

TAKE NOTE ▶ When Services Addresses Are Not Correct

When you click a Service name, a brief description of its function appears below the Start/Stop button in the Services screen. If you enable the service, the address information needed to access your computer via that service is summarized at the bottom of the pane. For example, after enabling Personal File Sharing, that description will read something like the following: "Other Macintosh users can access your computer at afp://68.60.48.4 or browse for 'Ted's Mac' by choosing Network from the Go menu in the Finder." A similarly appropriate message appears, citing the URLs needed for Web access, if you enable Personal Web Sharing. And so on.

If you attempt to use an address listed in the Services pane, and it does not work, there are two likely explanations:

Addresses and routers. If your Mac is connected to a hardware router (including an AirPort Base Station) using NAT, the URL will be incorrect. The address shown in Services will be the local IP address, which will work for users connecting from elsewhere on your local network, but not from remote locations. For example, if the address is something that begins with 192 or 10, it's only good for local machines connected to the same router.

To access your Mac from remote locations, you need to use the WAN IP address of the router itself. For an AirPort Base Station, for example, you can access the WAN IP address by launching AirPort Admin Utility, choosing the option to configure the Base Station, and then clicking the Internet screen. If you don't want to bother checking the router directly to find out your true current IP address, there are various shareware utilities and even Web sites that provide this information. For example, try www.whatismyipaddress.com.

You will also likely need to use your router's port-mapping functionality to map the relevant port used for the service to your computer. For example, to get Web Sharing to work, you would need to map Port 80 from your router to your computer.

Dynamic IP addresses. An IP address may be correct when you check it (either via the Sharing System Prefernces pane or via your router software, as appropriate). However, unless it is a static IP address (which is unlikely for users with a dial-up or DHCP connection), the IP address will change periodically. Thus, if you later try to use the address from a remote location, it may not work (if it has changed since you last checked). This means you can't use these dynamic IP addresses as permanent addresses—frustrating if you want to give a "permanent" URL for accessing your Web site, for example.

One solution is to get a static IP address—if your ISP provides this option. Otherwise, you may be able to use a *dynamic DNS service*. These services assign your machine a permanent domain name that remains linked to your machine despite changes in the IP address. One site that offers this service is www.dyndns.org. A final option for getting a static IP address, desirable if you expect frequent access to your Web site, is to get a static IP address and register a domain name (such as www.*yourname*.com) via www.networksolutions.com.

SEE: • "Take Note: What Are the TCP/IP Settings?" and "Internet routers and port mapping," earlier in this chapter, for more details.

Firewall

In brief, a firewall is software (which can run on your own computer, a router, or dedicated firewall hardware) that prevents incoming data that has not been specifically requested from reaching your computer. Firewalls exist primarily to prevent hackers from accessing your computer without permission. However, there may be times when you *want* unrequested data to get through a firewall. Why? As described earlier in the chapter (in discussions about port mapping), Sharing services count on remote users' being able to connect to your Mac without your first contacting them. If you enable Personal File Sharing, for example, it means you want incoming data from remote sharing users passed to your computer. Thus, if you turn the firewall on in general, you would still want to selectively disable it for Personal File Sharing.

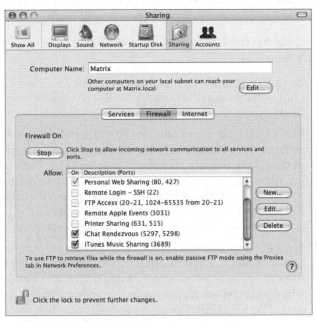

Figure 8.33

The Firewall screen of the Sharing System Preferences pane (top) and the dialog that drops down if you click the New button in the Firewall screen (bottom).

To understand how you can "open up" a firewall for certain services, think back to the earlier discussion of ports. I explained that each service on a server (for example, Web Sharing, Personal File Sharing, and FTP in Mac OS X) uses a specific port. File Sharing, for example, uses Ports 427 and 548. Thus, by allowing incoming traffic destined for Ports 427 or 548, your firewall would remain largely effective, but remote users would be able to access Personal File Sharing.

Mac OS X has always included a built-in firewall (specifically, the Unix firewall ipfw). However, in Mac OS X 10.1.x and earlier, you needed to use Terminal or third-party software (such as Brian R. Hill's BrickHouse) to activate it. No more. Mac OS X 10.2 and later include their own graphical front ends for the firewall, found in the Firewall screen of Sharing System Preferences. Although the features here aren't as complete as those available through a utility like BrickHouse, they're all that most people will need.

To enable and modify the firewall in the Sharing System Preferences pane, here's what to do:

- To turn on the firewall, click the Start button. Once the firewall is running, you can selectively enable or disable specific ports and services. Well... almost.

  Mac OS X includes a collection of preinstalled firewall rules. (A *rule* instructs the firewall to allow or deny specific kinds of traffic.) The names of the rules (together with their respective port numbers) are provided in the Allow list in the Firewall screen. All of these rules *allow* the named service. Thus, if the Personal File Sharing rule is enabled, the ports for Personal File Sharing are open even when the Firewall is running. A rule is enabled (or active) when the On check box next to its name is checked.

  Most of the preinstalled rules pertain to the services listed in the Services screen of Sharing System Preferences. You do not enable or disable these rules from the Firewall screen. Instead, they are automatically enabled when you turn the service on in the Services screen. For example, if you enable Personal File Sharing in Services and then switch to the Firewall screen, you'll see that the Personal File Sharing rule has been activated. In other words, Mac OS X's firewall is smart enough to automatically open those ports needed for the services you've activated.

  Panther's preinstalled list contains two rules that don't correspond to services from the Sharing list: iChat Rendezvous (5297, 5298) and iTunes Music Sharing (3689). You will likely need to enable these rules to use the services for which they are named.

  Note: To turn off the firewall at any point, click the Stop button (which was the Start button before you turned the firewall on).

  When making any changes to rules (as described next), turn the firewall off. Turn it back on when you are done with your changes. Otherwise, the change will not take effect.

- To create a new rule (that is, one that's not preinstalled), click the New button. A dialog drops down that includes a Port Name pop-up menu and a Port Number, Range or Series text box. The pop-up menu includes some services that Panther already knows about (MSN Messenger, Retrospect, and Timbuktu, for example). If you select one of them, the Port Number, Range or Series box is filled in automatically. Click OK, and the new rule is created. It is automatically added to the list of rules in the Allow list; it is also enabled (that is, its On check box is checked). This means that the port for the service is open even when the firewall is running.

  If you want to create a firewall rule for a service that is not listed in the Port Name pop-up menu, choose Other from that same menu. This allows you to manually provide the port (or range of ports) that need to be "open" for the service to work. Give the new rule a descriptive name and then click OK to create it. I provide more details on how to do this just below.

- To edit an existing rule, select the rule and click the Edit button. This drops down the same dialog that appeared when you selected New—except that the settings for the selected Port are already present and accessible for editing. Similarly, to delete an existing rule, select the rule and click the Delete button.

  One exception: You cannot edit or delete a rule that's linked to services from the Services list (such as Personal File Sharing). If you try, you will get the following error message: "You cannot change the firewall settings for this service." This means that the only preinstalled rules that you can edit or delete are the ones for iChat Rendezvous and iTunes Music Sharing.

Opening specific ports. When you're unable to connect to another computer or a user is unable to connect to your computer, and the connection settings appear correct, the cause may be the firewall. The quickest solution is to turn the firewall off temporarily. Alternatively, and more securely, you can create and/or open the port that's needed for the sharing to work. Here are a few suggestions about ports you might want to create or enable:

- **iChat AV Rendezvous text messaging.** If you're having trouble receiving iChat messages over Rendezvous and Sharing's firewall is on, make sure you've enabled the iChat Rendezvous rule to open Ports 5297 and 5298.

Figure 8.34

The message that appears when you launch iChat AV—if Sharing's firewall is on, the iChat Rendezvous rule is not enabled, and Rendezvous is enabled in iChat AV.

- **iChat AV file transfers.** If you're having trouble sending or receiving files via the AIM component of iChat when the firewall is enabled, the solution is to create a new rule that opens Port 5190. To do so, follow these steps:

    1. Open the Sharing System Preferences pane and select the Firewall screen.
    2. If the firewall is running (which it presumably is), click the Stop button.
    3. Now click the New button.
    4. From the Port Name pop-up menu, choose Other.
    5. In the Port Number field, type 5190.
    6. In the Description field, type something descriptive, such as iChat AV.
    7. Click OK to create the new rule.
    8. Click the Start button to restart the firewall.

    Note: In Jaguar, the Port Name pop-up menu contains an item called AOL IM (for America Online Instant Messenger). This rule opens the 5190 port. You could select this item in lieu of using the Other command. As its name implies, enabling AOL IM also potentially solved firewall-related problems using the AIM-based Buddy List chat. Panther no longer includes the AOL IM item—which is why (if needed) you must create the rule.

- **iChat AV invitations.** Port 5060 is used for the signaling and initiating of AV iChat invitations. If you're having trouble getting this feature to work, open this port. To do so, you could include Port 5060 in step 5 above. That is, type 5060, 5190.

    Combining this advice with the first item above, you should open a total of four ports to ensure access to all services in iChat AV when Sharing's firewall is on: 5060, 5190, 5297, and 5298. The other alternative, of course, is to turn the firewall off while using iChat AV.

- **iChat AV and UDP ports.** The firewall component of the Sharing System Preferences pane only blocks TCP ports. Thus, it is generally not necessary to use Sharing's firewall to create rules to open access to UDP ports; such ports are open by default. Apple states that all iChat AV traffic is UDP-only except for Ports 5190 and 5298, which need to be open for both TCP and UDP. This seems to imply that opening ports 5060 and 5297 (as described above) should not be necessary with Sharing's firewall. However, Apple recommends opening these ports anyway. You can experiment to see exactly what's needed for your setup.

    More generally, if you use firewall software other than Sharing's firewall, it will likely block both TCP and UDP traffic. Thus, you may need to open additional ports for iChat AV to work. For example, iChat AV uses Ports 16384 to 16403 to send, receive, and optimize AV streams. I had to open this range of ports (for UDP) in my LinkSys router's Port Forwarding settings before I could get iChat AV to work. See the following Apple Knowledge Base document for more details: http://docs.info.apple.com/article.html?artnum=93208.

Note: If you use a router you may have to open the same ports (TCP and UDP) on your router as you do in Sharing's firewall.

SEE: • **"Internet routers and port mapping," earlier in this chapter, for more on TCP versus UDP.**

- **iTunes.** To enable locally connected users to share your iTunes 4.x music library and to access other users' music, enable the "Look for shared music" and "Share my music" options in the Sharing section of iTunes' Preferences. If, after doing this, you still cannot get this feature to work, the problem may be caused by the firewall running on one or both of the interacting computers. To fix this, enable the iTunes Music Sharing (3689) rule.

  Note: In Jaguar, the iChat Rendezvous and iTunes Music Sharing rules are not preinstalled. Instead, you need to add them yourself, following the steps described above.

- **iSync.** iSync may not be able to establish a connection with some Nokia or Sony Ericsson phone models if the firewall is on. To fix this, you need to open Port 3004. To do so, follow the same general steps described above (in "iChat AV file transfers"), except enter 3004 in the Port Number field and type something like Bluetooth in the Description field.

SEE: • **"Network Security," later in this chapter, for more on firewalls and related topics.**

• **"Internet routers and port mapping," earlier in this chapter, for more on ports.**

• **"Technically Speaking: Using ipfw," later in this chapter, for the solution to a problem where you get a message that says, "Other firewall software is running on your computer."**

• **"Take Note: File Sharing: It's Your Choice," later in this chapter, for related information.**

• **Chapter 11, for more on iChat, iTunes, and iSync, including other firewall-related issues.**

Internet

Earlier in the chapter I talked about using software Internet routers to share a single Internet connection with multiple computers. Mac OS X includes such a router, which you can access via the Internet screen of Sharing preferences. With Internet Sharing, you can share your primary Internet connection (such as a cable modem connected to your desktop Mac) with other computers on your Mac's network. Note that if you already have a router or an AirPort Base Station, you need not bother with this feature. Indeed, trying to do so may even cause a conflict that interrupts Internet access.

SEE: • **"Using a Router," earlier in this chapter, for related information.**

If you don't have an Internet router or AirPort Base Station, and you have more than one computer on your local network, you will almost certainly want to use this feature. For users who have AirPort cards but no base station, the most exciting thing about the Internet screen is that it brings Mac OS 9's Software Base Station feature to Mac OS X. That is, you can share an Internet connection among all computers that have AirPort cards, even if you don't have a hardware base station.

SEE: • **"AirPort" and "Take Note: Software Routers: Software AirPort Base Station and More,"** earlier in this chapter, for related information.

One caveat to using Internet Sharing is that, with the exception of the Ethernet port, you cannot share connections via the same port that's used for your Internet connection. Thus, if you get your Internet connection via AirPort, you cannot simultaneously share that connection via AirPort. Neither can you create two active AirPort ports in the Network System Preferences pane. And if AirPort is your only active port in Network and is used for your Internet connection, no options will be listed for sharing in Sharing System Preferences' Internet screen. Thus, to share an Internet connection among computers via AirPort, the Internet connection itself would need to come from another port, such as Built-In Ethernet, using a set-up as shown in **Figure 8.35**. In general, the recommended setup in the Network System Preferences pane is to move the port for the Internet connection to the top of the Network Port Configurations list, with the sharing port enabled and second in the list.

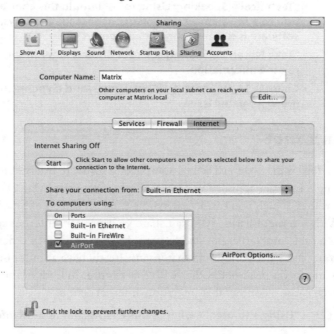

Figure 8.35

....

The Internet screen of the Sharing System Preferences pane.

The first time you open the Internet screen of Sharing preferences, it will say Internet Sharing Off. To get Internet sharing running, follow these steps:

1. From the "Share your connection from" pop-up menu, select the port to which you will be connected to the Internet when Internet Sharing is on.

2. The "To computers using" list will include all ports that can be used to share your Internet connection with other computers. For a port to be used, it must be enabled in the Network System Preferences pane, the needed cables or other hardware must be connected, and it must not conflict with your Internet connection port (as just described). If your desired port meets these requirements, check its On box. Note: You can enable more than one port from this list, if you wish.

3. The Start button should now be enabled. Click it to turn Internet Sharing on.

   Note: You cannot make further changes to these settings until you click the Stop button to turn Internet Sharing off again.

After turning Internet Sharing on, you will see a warning to turn Energy Saver's Automatic Sleep off. If your Mac goes to sleep while Internet Sharing is running, you will have to restart Internet Sharing.

SEE: • **"Take Note: Setting Up and Using Internet Sharing and File Sharing," below, for a more detailed example, using Internet Sharing over a FireWire connection.**

TAKE NOTE ▶ Setting Up and Using Internet Sharing and File Sharing

As an example of how to set up and use various sharing options, this sidebar explains how to set up and use File Sharing and Internet Sharing over a FireWire connection. This example assumes you have an iMac connected to the Internet via Ethernet, as well as an iBook with which you want to share your Internet connection via a FireWire cable.

Internet Sharing. To set up Internet Sharing for FireWire, follow these steps:

1. Connect a FireWire cable between the two Macs.

2. In the Network System Preferences pane on the iMac, make sure that the FireWire port configuration is enabled.

   Note: It doesn't appear to matter what's selected from the Configure menu in FireWire's TCP/IP screen—it can even be Off. The important thing is for the port be enabled in the Network Port Configurations list.

3. From the Sharing System Preferences pane of the iMac, click the Internet button. Assuming the iMac is connected to the Internet via Ethernet, the "Share your connection from" pop-up menu should say Built-in Ethernet. If not, select it.

4. From the "To computers using list," select the desired port (if more than one is listed). To do this, click the On check box. In this example, select the Built-in FireWire option (or whatever you named the FireWire port).

continues on next page

TAKE NOTE ▶ **Setting Up and Using Internet Sharing and File Sharing** *continued*

5. Click the Start button above to turn on Internet Sharing. Internet Sharing is now active. You are now set to share the iMac's Internet connection with the iBook.

Note: A warning message may appear, informing you that this could disrupt other Network connections. Click the Start button here as well.

Note: Once you've done this, the Start button will shift to a Stop button; I'm sure you can figure out what this button does.

6. Over at the iBook, go to the Network System Preferences pane. Enable the FireWire port in Network Port Configurations (if it's not already enabled).

Note: Also move the FireWire port to the top of the list (if more than one port is active). This is necessary if you will be selecting Using DHCP in the next step (as would be most common). Otherwise, you will need to select Manually from the Configure pop-up menu in the next step.

7. Select the FireWire port from the Show pop-up menu. From the TCP/IP screen that appears, select Using DHCP from the Configure pop-up menu.

8. The shared Internet connection should now be established. To confirm this, from the Show pop-up menu on the iBook select Network Status. The listing for the FireWire port should now read, "You are connected to the Internet via Built-in FireWire." If so, all is well!

You should now be able to use the shared connection, such as to browse the Web in Safari.

Some additional notes regarding setting up Internet Sharing:

• You can follow the same general rules to set up other variations. For example, if you want to connect to computers using AirPort, you are in effect creating an AirPort Software Base Station (as it was called in Mac OS 9). In this case, you obviously would not need to connect the Macs via a FireWire cable. Instead, both Macs would need AirPort cards. You may also need to select to connect to the AirPort network before Sharing will work.

• If you select to share an Ethernet connection with other computers using Built-In Ethernet, you will get a warning that doing so may violate the terms of your agreement with your Internet service provider and that this might disrupt a cable network. This is very unlikely to happen. In general, you can ignore this warning. Click OK to the caution message.

• If you select to share a connection with other computers using AirPort, click the AirPort Options button if you wish to set up password and encryption options.

continues on next page

Figure 8.36

The message that appears when you select to share an Internet connection to computers using Ethernet. You can usually ignore this warning.

If you turn on this port, your Internet Service provider might terminate your service to prevent you from disrupting its network.

In some cases (if you use a cable modem, for example) you might unintentionally affect the network settings of your ISP and violate the terms of your service agreement.

OK   Cancel

TAKE NOTE ▶ **Setting Up and Using Internet Sharing and File Sharing** *continued*

File Sharing. To set up File Sharing for FireWire, follow these steps:

1. On the host Mac (for example, the iMac), in the Services screen of the Sharing System Preferences pane turn on Personal File Sharing.

2. Both computers (for example, the iMac and the iBook) must be actively connected to the shared port. For connecting via FireWire, for example, a FireWire cable must be connected between the two computers. Similarly, for Ethernet sharing, both computers must be on the Ethernet network (via Ethernet cables) and Ethernet must be enabled and configured in the Network System Preferences pane.

Note: In theory, Internet Sharing *does not* need to be enabled for file sharing to work. In my testing, I found this to be true—except with FireWire. For file sharing over FireWire, I did need to enable Internet Sharing over FireWire, as described above. In general, I've found that sharing via FireWire is less reliable and more unpredictable than with other ports. On numerous occasions, I've found that the exact same FireWire connection setup that succeeded one day fails on another.

3. From the Finder's Go menu of one of the computers select Network. An icon for the other computer should be present. Double-click it to mount the computer (you will need an account name and password to mount the computer other than via Guest access).

Note: If the computer icon does not appear in the Network window, select Connect to Server from the Go menu instead. From here, for the Server Address, enter the local hostname name of your computer (for example, {*ComputerName*}.local) or its IP address (as listed in the Services screen of the Sharing System Preferences pane). Click Connect. I have found that this often works even if the Network window method does not.

4. The computer should now be mounted on your drive. You can now transfer files back and forth, as desired.

SEE: • **Numerous other sections of this chapter for more general information regarding the Sharing and Network System Preferences panes and the Network and Connect to Server items in the Finder's Go menu.**

Sharing Services: A Closer Look

In this section, I explore further details of some of the services you can enable via the Services screen of the Sharing System Preferences pane.

SEE: • "Services," earlier in this chapter, for a complete list and short description of available services.

Personal File Sharing

Other than via Guest access, only those users who have accounts set up on your Mac can access it via Personal File Sharing. Further, access limitations are determined largely by user level (admin versus nonadmin).

SEE: • "Using Network and Connect to Server," later in this chapter, for details on how to connect to a computer via File Sharing.

Nonadministrative users. What a standard (nonadministrative) user can access on a Mac depends on whether he is physically logged in to the Mac (that is, using the Login window on the Mac itself) or connected over a network from another Mac (via Personal File Sharing).

A logged-in nonadministrative user can access files in her Home directory and the Shared directory, and has at least Read Only access to files in other users' Public and Sites folders. This nonadministrative user can also run applications in the Applications folder, and open and read many other system files; however, she cannot edit or move those files.

SEE: • "Accessing other users' folders," "Take Note: The Shared Folder," and "Sticky bits and the Drop Box," in Chapter 6, for more on access to shared and other users' folders.

This same user, connected via Personal File Sharing, however, has much more restricted access. She will only be able to access her own user directory (Home folder) and the Public folders of other users. She will not be able to access other directories outside her Home folder (not even the Shared user folder), nor will she be able to access other mounted volumes. This means that if you want to make a file available to a remote File Sharing user, you should place it in your or their Public folder.

Administrative users. Administrative users have virtually the same access whether they're logged in to their accounts locally or connected via Personal File Sharing. In fact, in some cases they have even more access when connected via Personal File Sharing.

More specifically, when connecting to the Mac via Personal File Sharing, an administrative user will see all mounted volumes (included CDs and DVDs, iDisks, and external drives) just as he would if logged in locally. In addition, there will be a separate share for the user's own Home directory. To access files from your own Home directory, use this icon. If you (as an administrative user) try to navigate to your Home directory via the /Users folder on the startup volume instead, you will see that access is prohibited.

You can, however, navigate to the /Users folder to access the Home directories of other users (as well as the Shared directory). As when logged in locally, you are prohibited from opening all but the publicly accessible folders within another user's Home directory.

Note that as an administrative user, you can bypass this restriction and access another user's files when connecting remotely. To do so, when prompted for a name and password, enter the user's name but your *own* administrative-level password. Mac OS X will log you in as if you actually were that other user—which means you'll have the same level of access as that user would have. In other words, you will have complete access to the user's Home folder and the same limitations on accessing any other files and folders.

This "feature" is really a remnant of traditional Unix administration, in which the administrator always has access to other accounts on the system so that he or she can verify operations and fix problems. By logging in as another user, the administrator can see and do exactly what that user can, making it a good way to test accounts. This may seem like a security hole, but since an administrative user can technically access any "private" files (by changing permissions to the prohibited folders) or even log in as root, it's not a unique risk. However, it does underscore the risk of giving too many people admin-level access to your Mac.

Another way to access other users' accounts is to log in as the root user. This gives you complete access to all accounts in a single login.

SEE: • **"Using Network and Connect to Server," later in this chapter, for details on how an administrative user can connect to a Mac remotely.**

   • **"Root Access," in Chapter 4, for details on logging in as the root user.**

Guests. When accessing a Mac via Personal File Sharing, there is a Guest button in the dialog that requests your name and password. If you click this button, you are immediately connected to the Mac. However, access is limited to the Public folders of all users on the Mac.

Note: Although Mac OS X has Guest access enabled by default, other operating systems (Mac OS 9, Windows) may not permit guest access or may have it turned off. In such cases, the Guest button, even if enabled, will not work.

Note: For logging in locally (not using Sharing), Mac OS X doesn't provide a Guest account. If you want one, however, you can create it yourself. To do so, create a nonadministrative account (via the Accounts System Preferences pane) and name it Guest (or something like that), and do not assign a password for the account. Now anyone can log in to your Mac using that account, without having to know a password. Once logged in, users would have the same status as any nonadministrative user. If you wanted to further limit this guest access, you could use the Limitations options in the Accounts System Preferences pane to enable Simple Finder and so on. Users can also access this account remotely, as an alternative to the "built-in" Guest access.

TECHNICALLY SPEAKING ▶ Modifying Apple File Server Preferences

Suppose you wanted to enable Personal File Sharing but prevent anyone from having Guest access to your computer—that is, you would prefer that the Guest button be removed from or dimmed in the dialog where it normally appears.

Or suppose you wanted to turn off the feature that allows administrative users to log in to other users' accounts with their administrative password (as described in the main text).

Or suppose you wanted to enable AppleShare logging and determine who's currently connected to your Mac.

Can you do these things? Yes. The solution is to edit the com.AppleFileServer.plist file in /Library/Preferences. Ideally, use Property List Editor to do this. With this file open, do the following:

Disable Guest access. To disable Guest access, follow these steps:

1. Turn Personal File Sharing off.
2. From the Property List column of the com.AppleFileServer.plist file, locate the property named guest_access.
3. From the Value item for this property, change Yes to No.
4. Save the change and turn Personal File Sharing back on.

The next time you attempt to access an account, the Guest option will be dimmed and unselectable.

With Guest access disabled, if you want specific users to be able to have Guest access to your computer, one solution mentioned in the main text is to create a separate account named *guest*. Alternatively, you can create a File Sharing Only account via SharePoints (as described in "Take Note: Using SharePoints," later in this chapter). Actually, you can also use SharePoints to disable guest access.

Enable AppleShare logging. In Mac OS 9 and earlier, File Sharing kept a log of all File Sharing activity that you, as the owner of your computer, could view. Mac OS X also has this capability, but it is turned off by default. To enable File Sharing logging, follow these steps:

1. Turn Personal File Sharing off.
2. From the Property List column of the com.AppleFileServer.plist file locate the property named activity_log.

continues on next page

TECHNICALLY SPEAKING ▶ Modifying Apple File Server Preferences *continued*

3. From the Value item for this property, change No to Yes.

4. Save the change and turn Personal File Sharing back on.

The next time someone logs in to your Mac remotely via File Sharing, a log file named AppleFileServiceAccess.log will be created in the /Library/Logs/AppleFileService directory. The log's contents will be updated as it logs all future File Sharing activity. You can best view the contents by opening the log file in the Console application or any text editor. (You can also enable AppleShare logging by using the third-party utility SharePoints, from HornWare.)

This log provides a useful way of determining who's currently connected to your computer via File Sharing. This was much easier to check in Mac OS 9 (you viewed the Activity Monitor in the File Sharing control panel). Maybe in the next Mac OS X upgrade Apple will make it a more accessible feature.

Disable admin logins to other accounts. To prevent administrative users from using their password to log in to other accounts via Personal File Sharing (as described in the main text), follow these steps:

1. Turn Personal File Sharing off.

2. From the Property List column of the com.AppleFileServer.plist file locate the property named attempt_admin_auth.

3. From the Value item for this property, change Yes to No.

4. Save the change and turn Personal File Sharing back on.

Notes. Here are a couple of related notes regarding this .plist file and its settings:

• If you delete this .plist file, a new default copy is created. Where do the default settings come from? They're stored in the AppleFileServer application in /System/Library/CoreServices. Select Show Package Contents for the application and navigate to the Resources folder. In here are two defaults files: Defaults.plist and PFSDefaults.plist.

• In Jaguar, you access these settings via NetInfo Manager: Select the config item, and from the sublist that appears, select AppleFileServer.

Figure 8.37

You can disable guest access via the setting in the com.AppleFileServer .plist file.

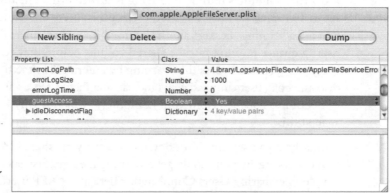

Sharing and FileVault. If you connect to a computer when your account is not currently logged in locally, and FileVault is enabled for your account, all you will see in your Home directory is the FileVault sparseimage file. To access your files, double-click the sparseimage file and enter your password when requested. The sparseimage will mount on your Desktop. You can now read and write to the mounted volume.

Other users who connect via File Sharing will not be able to access your account (not even the Public folders) if FileVault is enabled and you're not logged in locally. At most, they will see the sparseimage file. In principle, if you're an administrative user and know the FileVault master password, you should be able to use it to mount sparseimage files of other users. However, this does not work—or at least not as of this writing.

SEE: • "FileVault," in Chapter 2, for more on this feature.

Sharing individual folders. In Mac OS 9, you could select a folder in the Finder and then set up File Sharing access to that folder, including which users had access. A significant limitation of Personal File Sharing in Mac OS X is that you cannot easily share individual folders (or *share points,* as they're technically called)—useful, for example, if you wanted to make your Pictures folder accessible to other users. Mac OS X actually includes the ability to modify the default Sharing settings and access share points directly. However, the Sharing System Preferences pane does not provide access to this capability. If you want to separately assign sharing for individual folders, you need to do so either via NetInfo Manager (or Terminal commands that access NetInfo) or third-party software such as SharePoints.

SEE: • "Take Note: Using SharePoints," later in this chapter.

Stopping File Sharing with users connected. To turn off Personal File Sharing, select its name in the Services screen and click the Stop button.

If you select to stop Sharing when other users are connected to your Mac, a dialog drops down, stating, "There may be users connected to this machine. How many minutes until File Sharing is turned off?" The turn-off time is set to 10 minutes by default. If you select this, users on connected computers will get a warning message about the impending disconnect. This gives those users a chance to unmount the shared volume before they're disconnected. However, you can bypass this warning by entering 0 as the time delay, thus disconnecting users immediately (and causing them to lose any unsaved changes in documents opened from your computer—which is why I recommend against this).

Similarly, if you select to shut down or restart your shared Mac, a disconnection occurs. Again, you should get a warning message first, such as the following: "Apple File Sharing Users Connected. There are # AFP user(s) still connected. Are you sure you want to restart?"

SEE: • "Host (or client) unexpectedly disconnects" in "Troubleshooting Network Browser and Connect to Server," later in this chapter, for related information and figures.

TAKE NOTE ▶ Using SharePoints

By default, Personal File Sharing in Mac OS X shares only the Public and Sites folders of each user's Home directory. However, you can share other folders by creating other *share points*—Mac OS X's term for a shared directory. The "official" way to create and modify share points is by using NetInfo Manager. An easier (and safer) way, however, is to use one of several third-party utilities that simplify this process. My favorite is HornWare's SharePoints.

SharePoints is available as a stand-alone application or as a System Preferences pane. Although both versions operate identically and provide the same functionality, the pane version is a bit more accessible (because you generally have the System Preferences window open when you're working with Sharing, anyway).

Before making any changes, click the padlock icon to unlock the settings (to do so, you must provide your administrator user name and password when prompted).

Adding share points. To add a share point, follow these steps:

1. Click the lock icon to authenticate your user name.

2. Click the "Normal" Shares screen.

3. Enter a name for your share point in the Share Name field.

4. In the Directory field, enter the path to the folder you want to share (or click the Browse button to navigate to the folder).

5. Click the Show File System Properties button. From the drawer that slides open, select the Owner, Group, and Permissions for the folder using the pop-up menus. If you set permissions for Everyone to Read or Read/Write, any remote user will be able to view the new share point.

   Note that the permissions you set here apply only to the top-level folder; enclosed files and folders will keep their original permissions for security reasons. If you want enclosed files and folders to reflect the new permissions, you'll need to set them separately, using the Finder's Get Info window or a utility such as XRay. However, if you check the "Inherit permissions from parent" box, items later added to the share point folder will acquire the permissions of the share point (parent) folder.

6. From the AppleFileServer (AFS) Sharing pop-up menu, select Shared (+).

7. Click the Create New Share button to create the new share point.

If you want to add another share point, repeat these steps.

continues on next page

TAKE NOTE ▶ Using SharePoints *continued*

To remove a share point from the list, click it and then click the Delete Selected Share button. This will not undo changes made to Owner, Group, and Permissions settings, nor will it actually *delete* the folder in the Finder; however, it will prevent the folder from being accessed via File Sharing.

To edit an existing share point, make the desired changes and click the Update Share button.

Unsharing a Public share point. SharePoints also allows you to *prevent* a user's Public folder from being shared. If you want to disable Public-folder sharing, follow these steps:

1. Click the Users & "Public" Shares tab.

2. In the User column on the left, select the user whose Public folder you *do not* want to share.

3. In the "Public" Directory Shares box, click the Disable Selected button. (You can also choose No from the Public Directory Shared? menu in the Individual Users box, and then click the Update User button.)

Note that if you wanted to disable *all* sharing of Public folders, you would click the Disable All button in the "Public" Directory Shares box.

File Sharing Only users. A handy SharePoints feature allows you to create File Sharing Only users—that is, users who can *only* log in via File Sharing (that is, they can't log in locally, nor can they log in via a Terminal connection, FTP, or any other service). The advantage of File Sharing Only users is that you don't have to clutter up your Mac with accounts for users who will never use it locally. To create a File Sharing Only user, follow these steps:

1. Click the Users & "Public" Shares tab but *do not* click an existing user. (If a user is already selected, click in the empty space in the Users box to unselect it.)

2. Fill in the information for the user in the Full Name, Short Name, Group, and UID fields. (You should click Get Next UID if you're unsure what number to assign.)

3. Click the Add New User button. You will be asked whether you're sure that you want to add a File Sharing Only user; then you will be asked to enter a password for the new user.

Creating new groups. As discussed in Chapters 4 and 6, each file and folder in Mac OS X is assigned to a group. You can view an item's group by opening the Get Info window for the item and viewing the Ownership & Permissions section. You can change the group assignment for an item from here, but you cannot create or delete groups. You *can* do this via SharePoints—something you can otherwise accomplish only via NetInfo Manager. To do so, follow these steps:

1. Click the Groups tab.

2. In the Group field, type a name for the new group.

3. Click the Get Next GID button to have SharePoints find the next available group ID number.

4. Click the Add New Group button.

continues on next page

TAKE NOTE ▶ Using SharePoints *continued*

5. To add users to the group, select the group in the Group window on the left; then add users by selecting user names in the Users window on the right and clicking the Add (+) button.

6. Click the Update Group button.

SEE: • "Technically Speaking: Windows File Sharing: Custom Options and SharePoints," later in this chapter, for related information.

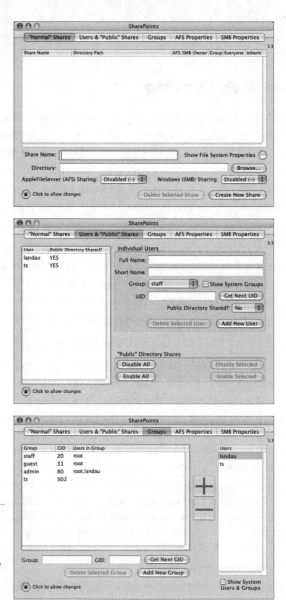

Figure 8.38

The SharePoints utility: (top) "Normal" Shares; (middle) Users & "Public" Shares; and (bottom) Groups screens.

> **TAKE NOTE ▶ Sharing via Timbuktu and Apple Remote Desktop**
>
> Timbuktu Pro is an application from Netopia (www.netopia.com) that offers an alternative way to share files between two computers (even Mac OS and Windows computers). With Timbuktu Pro, you can go beyond simply sharing files: You can control a remote computer just as though you were sitting in front of it. The Desktop of the remote computer opens in a window on your computer. You can observe the remote computer for collaborative work or for helping another user troubleshoot; you can even send instant messages and voice messages to the remote computer. Timbuktu Pro supports Mac OS X's Users and Privileges settings.
>
> Apple's Apple Remote Desktop provides a similar alternative. It is designed primarily for classroom environments, so that an instructor can have access to the computers of all students.

Personal Web Sharing

With Personal Web Sharing enabled, anyone—regardless of whether or not they have an account on your Mac—can use a Web browser from any computer connected to the Internet to access Web pages stored in the special Web site folders located on your computer. Each user on your computer has his or her own Web directory, called Sites, located in his or her Home folder. In addition, your computer has a general Web directory located at /Library/WebServer/Documents.

To access the contents of the pages in a specific Sites folder, type `http://` followed by the IP address of the computer, a forward slash, a tilde, and the user's short name. For example, to access the Sites folder contents for a user named *naomi* on a computer with an IP address of 68.62.15.134, you would type `http://68.62.15.134/~naomi/`. (If you have not placed anything in the Sites folder yourself, a default index.html page supplied by Apple will appear.)

When using Personal Web Sharing, you should be aware of the following:

- You can find the IP address for your computer (needed for the URL to access your site) in the bottom of the Services screen of Sharing System Preferences when Personal Web Sharing is selected.

  However, if you use a router, this is probably not the address you need. Instead, you need the WAN IP address as listed by your router. Note: Unless you have a static IP address, the WAN IP cannot be counted on as a permanent IP.

  If you want to check out how your own Web pages look in a browser via Web Sharing, you can do so most easily by using your Rendezvous address. For example, typing `http://yoda.local/~naomi/` will load the Web site in the Sites folder of the naomi account on my system (named yoda). This will work from any computer connected to your local network (LAN).

  Alternatively, you can use the word *localhost* instead of the IP address. Thus, Naomi could check out her site from her computer by typing `http://localhost/~naomi/`. She could also substitute 127.0.0.1 (the default IP address for accessing your own computer) for localhost, or even omit initial text, just typing http://~naomi/ (notice the third slash).

Finally, the IP address listed in Sharing System Preferences, even if it is a local address generated by a router, can also be used for access via a local connection.

SEE: • **"Take Note: When Services Addresses Are Not Correct," earlier in this chapter, for more details.**

• If you type just http:// followed by the WAN IP address for your machine (http://68.62.15.134, for example), you will get whatever Web pages are stored in /Library/WebServer/Documents. Mac OS X places a default index.html page in that folder, but you can replace it with your own custom page(s). This folder can be used for a site that you do not want linked to a particular user on your Mac.

Again, to access this site locally, you can instead type http://{Computer_Name} .local. In my case, for example, I would type http://matrix.local. You can also type http:///.

Figure 8.39

Default (index.html) screens for Personal Web Sharing.

• If a Web-site folder has a document named *index.html* at the root level of the folder used for Web Sharing, that document will be used as the home page of the Web site. If such a document does not exist in a Sites or WebServer/Documents folder, anyone trying to view the default page will receive an error message. The default setting for Mac OS X's Web Server is to *not* display directory contents when a default page is not present.

• If you're using a router, accessing a user's Sites folder will likely require that you open Port 80 for the computer. This is done via the router's port-mapping/forwarding feature. In such setups, only one of your local computers can be set as a Web server at any one time.

SEE: • **"Internet routers and port mapping," earlier in this chapter.**

- When accessing a user's Web page, you should ideally place a slash after the name in the URL. That is, for example, type /~naomi/, not just /~naomi. If you leave off the last slash, you may get a localhost error (it may attempt to connect to 127.0.0.1 and fail), though this appears to be fixed in the latest versions of Mac OS X.

- Unlike with File Sharing, a remote user connecting to Personal Web Sharing cannot access *any* files outside the Sites folder or the computer's WebServer Documents folder, which makes Web Sharing a more secure way to share files with the public. In addition, users can access only files linked from a Web page accessible from the home page, or via a specific URL you have given them. Thus, if Naomi placed a compressed file called *myapp.sit* in her Sites folder, a user could download it via a URL to access that file, such as: http://68.62.15.134/~naomi/myapp.sit.

- When you enable Web Sharing, you're actually activating a full installation of the widely used (and feature-rich) Apache Web server for Unix, which is included in Mac OS X. If you are familiar with Unix, you can access many more advanced Web Sharing features (such as working with Perl scripts and CGI commands) via Apache commands entered in Terminal.

.Mac HomePage. A simpler but more limited way to create a Web site is to set it up on your iDisk via Apple's .Mac HomePage feature. This method has the advantage of providing a permanent URL, and access does not require that your computer be on and connected to the Internet. You must be a .Mac subscriber to use this feature.

FTP access

If you check the FTP Access box on the Services screen of the Sharing System Preferences pane, Mac OS X's built-in FTP server starts up. Anyone with an account on your computer and an FTP client (such as Fetch Softworks' Fetch, JomoSoft's osXigen, or RBrowser) will be able to connect and browse files by entering the IP or domain name of your computer, along with a user name and password. Users can also connect via FTP from another Mac OS X computer by using the Connect to Server command and entering ftp:// as the address prefix (as opposed to the default afp:// used for Personal File Sharing). This creates a volume on the Mac, similar to what would happen if you mounted a network file via file sharing. However, as of this writing, using Connect to Server (instead of a dedicated FTP client) means you'll only be able to download files; you will not be able to upload files or perform any other file-related actions.

Because most Web browsers support the FTP protocol, you can also connect via a Web browser. For example, typing ftp://{*IPaddress*} in Internet Explorer brings up a dialog asking for a name and password. If you have an account on the specified computer, enter your name and password, and you will get a directory listing of your Home directory. Each directory item will be a link;

click a link to view the contents of the directory. If you click a file, it is downloaded to your computer.

Note that if the FTP Access box is checked, FTP access will be enabled even if you have File Sharing and Web Sharing disabled.

FTP Access limits users to the same access they would have if they were physically sitting at the computer, logged in to their account. They will have full read/write access to their own User folders, as well as read access to other users' Public folders, but they will also have read access to most other system-level files. Because read access via FTP means the ability to view and download, FTP users will be able to download system, application, and settings files located outside private Users folders. They won't be able to alter or delete these files, but you should stop to consider whether you have sensitive files or information in nonprivate areas of your computer.

One other (serious) caveat to FTP Access is that FTP is not a secure protocol: When you connect to an FTP server, your user name and password are sent over the Internet in plain text, so anyone who might be able to intercept your connection attempt will be able to see your user name and password (and may be able to use them to gain access to your Mac via FTP Access or even another service). A secure alternative to FTP is Secure FTP (SFTP), discussed later in the chapter, in "SSH and SFTP."

Windows File Sharing

Whereas Personal File Sharing allows you to share files with other Macs, Windows File Sharing uses the SMB/CIFS (Server Message Block/Common Internet Filesystem) protocol, a standard on Windows and Unix computers. (The actual server software is called Samba.) If you enable Windows File Sharing in the Sharing System Preferences pane, anyone with a user account on your Mac will be able to connect from a Windows (or Unix) computer and access his or her Home directory. (By default, there is no guest access via Windows File Sharing.)

To let Windows users access your Mac, all you need to do is enable Windows Sharing in the Services screen of the Sharing System Preferences pane. As with Personal File Sharing, a user must have an account on your Mac to access the Mac (unless you enable Guest access, as described later).

By default, Windows File Sharing allows remote users to access their own Home directories; however, unlike with Personal File Sharing, these users won't be able to access other users' Public folders. This means that to share a file with a remote Windows user, you'll need to place it in *that user's* Public folder (which means you must place it in his or her Drop Box).

Note: In Jaguar, providing Windows users with access to your Mac entails an additional step: In the Accounts System Preferences pane, select a user and click the Edit User button. In the resulting dialog, check the box next to "Allow user to log in from Windows." This procedure must be performed for *each* user who needs access from a Windows computer. Happily, this procedure is no longer needed in Panther (and the option is gone).

Note: Although it sounds odd, you can also connect two *Macs* via Windows Sharing, just as you can via Personal File Sharing. In fact, if a Mac on your local network has both Windows File Sharing and Personal File Sharing enabled, it may get listed twice in the Network Browser. If so, choose only one server icon to access the Mac. If you want to connect to another Mac via Windows File Sharing using Connect to Server, you would precede the address of the Mac with smb:// (as described more in "Connect to Server," later in this chapter).

SEE: • "Network Browser," later in this chapter, for more on this feature.

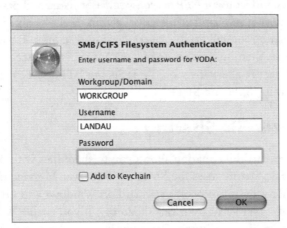

Figure 8.40

The login screen that appears after accessing a computer (either a Windows machine or a Mac with Windows File Sharing enabled) via an smb:// URL in Connect to Server.

Connecting from a Windows machine to a Mac. The procedure Windows users employ to connect varies depending on whether they're connecting from a local network or over the Internet, and on which version of Windows they're using.

For a user on the same local network, follow these steps:

1. From the Start menu open Network Neighborhood (called My Network Places in Windows XP).

2a. Provided that your Workgroup name is the same as the one for the Windows user, your Mac will be visible from the Network Neighborhood window. On XP, the user should click View Workgroup Computers in the Explorer bar.

2b. If your Workgroup name differs, the user should open Entire Network and find your Workgroup. In XP, the user should click Microsoft Windows Network in the Explorer bar. If the user still does not see your Mac, he or she should click "Add a network place" in the Explorer bar and follow the onscreen instructions to add the Mac to My Network Places (when asked for a server address, enter your Mac's network address).

Note: If Workgroup names are not the same, an easier solution may be to change the Workgroup name on your Mac, via the Directory Access utility, so that they match.

3. Double-click the desired computer/share. Enter the user short name and password when requested.

Users connecting over the Internet need to use a slightly different procedure (which also differs depending on the version of Windows being used):

1. Do one of the following: Open My Computer and choose Tools > Map Network Drive (Windows XP); open My Computer and choose Tools > Map Network Drive, and then click "Web folder or FTP site" (Windows 2000); or open the Web Folders icon and then double-click the Add Web Folder icon (Windows 98).

2. Enter *IPaddress**sharename*, where *IP address* is the IP address of your Mac, and *sharename* is the name of the share they want to access (by default their short user name, since they can only access their Home directory).

SEE: • **"Using Network and Connect to Server,"** later in this chapter, for details on how to connect to a Windows machine from a Mac.

• **"Technically Speaking: Windows File Sharing: Custom Options and SharePoints,"** below, for related information.

• **"Directory Access,"** in Chapter 4, for more on changing a workgroup name.

TECHNICALLY SPEAKING ▶ Windows File Sharing: Custom Options and SharePoints

By default, the Windows File Sharing option in the Sharing System Preferences pane only shares each user's Home directory, and only with that user. However, you can customize the Samba server settings to share other directories as well as to make a few other useful changes. Although you can edit the Samba Preferences file (/etc/smb.conf) directly, an easier method is to use the SharePoints utility.

Using SharePoints to share additional folders with Windows users is almost identical to the procedure for sharing additional folders with other Mac users. Simply follow the instructions in the "Take Note: Using SharePoints" sidebar earlier in this chapter, but instead of choosing "Shared (+)" from the AppleFileServer(AFS) Sharing menu, choose the same option from the Windows (SMB) Sharing menu. In fact, if you already have additional Personal File Sharing share points that you want to also share with Windows users, simply open the "Normal" Shares screen of SharePoints, select an existing share, and then select "Shared (+)" from the Windows (SMB) Sharing menu to add Windows sharing for that folder. You would then click the Update Share button to begin sharing it. Note: To allow Windows guests (users without a password), click the Show File System Properties button and enable the Allow Windows Guests option.

continues on next page

TECHNICALLY SPEAKING ▶ Windows File Sharing: Custom Options and SharePoints *continued*

SharePoints' SMB Properties screen allows you to customize various properties of the Samba server:

- From the General Properties pop-up menu item, you change your Mac's NetBios name, which is the name Windows computers see when connected to your Mac. More important, you can also change the Workgroup name; if you're on a local network, it makes it easier for everyone if your Workgroup name is the same as the computer that will be connecting to your Mac. (If you're on a Windows NT network, your Workgroup name *must* be the same.)

- From the File Visibility pop-up menu item, you hide or prevent access to certain files. By placing names of files in the Hide Files field (separating multiple filenames with forward slashes), you ensure that these files will not be visible to connected Windows users. The Hide Files Starting with a Period option hides files that have names beginning with a period (files that are usually invisible in Mac OS X). However, these two options only *hide* files—they don't prevent access. A Windows user who has chosen to view hidden files can still get to these files. You can prevent files from being accessed at all by placing their names in the Veto Files field (again, separating multiple filenames with forward slashes; some files are already listed). Note that this field supports the wildcard (*) character; to prevent Windows users from accessing normally invisible files, include the following: ".*". You could also prevent Windows users from accessing Microsoft Word files by including "*.doc".

- From the Home Directories pop-up menu item, you determine how users can interact with Home directories. The Shared option, when unchecked, lets you disable Home directory sharing altogether; Windows users will only be able to connect to shares that you've specifically created in the "Normal" Shares screen. The "Browseable" option, when disabled, prevents local Windows users from seeing Home directories in My Network Places or Network Neighborhood; to connect, they'll instead need to use the procedure listed in the main text for connecting over the Internet. The Read Only option, when enabled, only allows users to copy files from their Home directory when connected from a Windows computer; they won't be able to save files to the directory or edit files in it.

SEE: • "Take Note: Using SharePoints," earlier in this chapter, for the basics of using this utility.

Sharing access from non-Mac computers: beyond Windows File Sharing. If you want to share files with users on non-Mac computers, you can also use Personal Web Sharing, FTP Access, or SFTP. Because each of these protocols is platform-independent, any user on a Windows, Unix, or other computer can connect by using a Web browser, FTP client, or Telnet/SSH client, respectively. Accessing a Mac via Personal Web Sharing (as with guest access via Personal File Sharing) doesn't even require the user to have an account on the Mac. Conversely, since Mac OS X 10.2 and later support connecting to SMB/CIFS volumes via the Connect to Server dialog, you can enable Windows File Sharing to allow access to Windows users, Unix users, and Mac users running Mac OS X 10.2 or later, all via a single service.

Using Network and Connect to Server

I've talked at length about the various ways you can set up to allow other users to share files on your computer. But what about your access to shared files on *other* computers? And, related to this, how do other Mac OS X users connect to your computer?

Panther offers two means of connecting to these servers: the Network Browser, which is primarily for accessing devices on your local network, and the Connect to Server command, which you can use to locate and connect to any device, local or otherwise.

This section covers both methods.

Note: A server in this context typically refers to any other computer to which you can connect via file sharing. It does not have to be a "true" server, such as one running Mac OS X Server software. Any Mac, Windows, or Unix computer that is sharing files is technically a "server." Even an iDisk is considered a server in this context.

Network Browser

The easiest way to access the Network Browser is to either select the Network command in the Go menu or select the Network icon in the sidebar or toolbar of any Finder window. You can also access the Network Browser by going to the Computer window (from the Go menu select Computer, or press Command-Shift-C) and clicking or double-clicking (depending on your view mode) the Network icon that appears.

If you do any of these things, a window named Network will open. This is called the Network Browser.

At minimum, and assuming you are now or have previously been connected to a network, the Network window will contain an item called Servers, which is an alias file. If you open this, an alias to your computer appears: {*Computer_Name*}.*local*. Open this alias, and you arrive at the root level of your startup volume. If you're on a large network that uses a server (such as Mac OS X Server), the server volume may also be listed here. My focus in this chapter, however, is in connecting to shared computers, not actual servers. For this, I return to the root level of the Network folder.

If you have a local network (such as one that includes several computers connected via an AirPort Base Station or an Internet router), all other Macs on the network that currently have Personal File Sharing enabled should have alias items in the Network window on your Mac.

This ability to browse local servers and shares is not limited to Macs with Personal File Sharing enabled. Mac OS X 10.2 and later include support for SMB browsing, so if there are Windows file sharing servers on your local network, the Network window should also show Windows workgroups and computers in those workgroup. You can connect to them just as you can connect to other Macs.

Note: Icons in the Network window may show up as either server icons or folders. Don't worry about this. Both are OK. The difference depends on how your Mac and the server to which you want to connect are set up. For example, Windows file-sharing servers (SMB) will likely be contained within a WORKGROUP folder.

Mac OS X 10.3.0 to 10.3.2 alert. Apple made significant changes to how the Network Browser works in Mac OS X 10.3.3. The following assumes you are using Mac OS X 10.3.3 or later. If you are using an earlier version of Panther, some of the specifics described here will not apply.

SEE: • "Take Note: Connect to Server vs. Network: What's the Difference?" later in this chapter, for more details.

Connecting. There are two basic ways to connect to any of the shared computers in the Network window.

- If you're using the Finder's Column view, click the icon for the shared computer in the Network window. In the column to the right, a Connect button will appear. Click it, and you will be presented with a Login window. Enter your name and password. Or, if you don't have an account, click the Guest button.

- If you're using Icon or List views, simply double-click the desired icon in the Network window: You will be presented with the same Login window as cited above.

In either case, you will next be presented with a Volumes window that lists every volume and user account that you can select to mount. Exactly what shared volumes wind up appearing depends on the account accessed as well as your privileges on the shared computer (for example, whether you're an administrative user). As an administrative user, the list will typically include every mounted volume/partition on the shared computer as well as an additional item for your Home directory on that machine.

When you select the desired volumes/accounts and click OK, the items will mount. If you selected the relevant Finder Preferences' options to show servers, icons for the items will appear in your Finder's sidebar and on your Desktop. In any case, the items will also show up in your Computer window (accessed via Command-Shift-C).

Once connected, you can browse the contents of these items in the Finder, just as you would a volume physically connected to your Mac.

If you double-click a server icon in the Network Browser window after already mounting one or more volumes from the server, the server's volume list will reappear (allowing you to mount additional servers if desired).

Disconnecting. To disconnect from the volume: (a) drag the server icon on the Desktop to the Trash; (b) click the Eject icon next to the name of the server in a Finder window's sidebar; or (c) select the server icon and then select the Eject command either from the Finder's File menu (Command-E) or from the server icon's contextual menu.

Do not attempt to disconnect by dragging the server icon in the Network Browser window to the Trash. This worked in Mac OS X versions prior to 10.3.3 but does not do so anymore.

SEE: • "Personal File Sharing" in "Sharing Services: A Closer Look," earlier in this chapter, for details on administrative versus standard access, and so on.

• "Connect to Server: The Connect/Login window," "Connect to Server: The Volumes window," and "Connect to Server: Connection Completed," later in this chapter, for more details on those features of Network Browser that are the same in Connect to Server.

• "Troubleshooting Network Browser and Connect to Server," at the end of this chapter, for advice on what to do if you cannot connect or disconnect successfully.

Figure 8.41

The Network Browser window. The volume Luke from the server Yoda is seen in the window's sidebar.

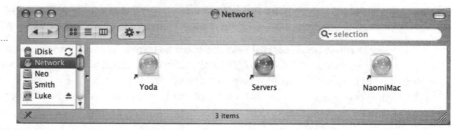

TAKE NOTE ▶ Connect to Server vs. Network: What's the Difference?

How do you decide whether to attempt to connect to a shared computer or server via the Network Browser or the Connect to Server command? What are the key differences, advantages, and disadvantages of each method? This sidebar provides the answers.

A quick comparison. Here are the two key differences between the two methods:

• With the Network Browser, you can only connect to servers that are shown in the Network window.

  With Connect to Server, you can connect to any server accessible over your network.

continues on next page

TAKE NOTE ▶ **Connect to Server vs. Network: What's the Difference?** *continued*

- With Network Browser, you can connect to a server without knowing the address (URL) for the machine.

  With Connect to Server, you must enter a server address (unless you're returning to a previously entered address, in which case you may find it in the Recent Servers or Favorites listings).

Which method should you use, and why? In general, the Network Browser method is quicker and easier to use, assuming the server you want is listed. It's also desirable when you don't know what's available and literally wish to "browse." The Connect to Server method is essential only when you need to connect to a server not listed in the Network Browser—typically only for servers outside your local network.

If a server is listed in the Network Browser window, you can choose to connect to it via either method. Most often, you will choose the Network Browser because of its simplicity. You may occasionally find, however, that a connection error occurs when you try to use the Network Browser, whereas using Connect to Server succeeds (although this should be less common when using Mac OS X 10.3.3 or later).

The Network Browser method, being newer (it was introduced in Panther), has more bugs. I've had numerous problems copying files (for example, a file will copy from Mac A to B but not the reverse) and having connections freeze the Mac, when using the Network Browser. If such problems persist, give the Connect to Server method a try. Again, these problems should be largely gone in Mac OS X 10.3.3 or later, as both methods now work in essentially the same way.

What items appear in the Network Browser? The following explains what determines whether a server or shared computer on your network appears in the Network Browser window. In brief:

- **The server must be accessible on the local network.** The volume must be accessible via your connection to the network. Thus, if you're connected via Ethernet to a specific network, only computers on that network are accessible. Typically, if you're on a large network, browsing is restricted to a local *subnet* of the larger network. The nature of your subnet is determined by a network administrator.

  Note: It is possible that a server accessible via Ethernet cannot be seen when using AirPort (or vice versa), because they are set in Network System Preferences to access different networks.

- **The server must be discoverable.** Thus, for a Mac, Personal File Sharing must be enabled. In addition, it must broadcast a signal announcing its availability. Mac OS X does this via the Rendezvous technology. Directory Services is another form of discovery technology (as described next).

continues on next page

TAKE NOTE ▶ Connect to Server vs. Network: What's the Difference? *continued*

- **Your computer must have the needed service enabled.** You will not see a particular server in the Network Browser window if the needed service is not enabled via the Directory Access application on your computer (located in the Utilities folder, as covered more in Chapter 4). In most cases, you needn't worry about this, because the default settings should suffice. However, in Mac OS X 10.3.30 to 10.3.2, AppleTalk was disabled by default. Thus, for these versions of Panther, to see an AppleTalk-connected server in the Network Browser, you would need to enable this service. To do so, launch Directory Access and click the Enable checkbox next to AppleTalk. Simply enabling AppleTalk in the Network System Preferences pane for the port in use (which you also need to do) is not sufficient.

See the following Apple Knowledge Base article for more details on Network Browser and Connect to Server: http://docs.info.apple.com/article.html?artnum=107804.

Network Browser aliases. The Network Browser window employs aliases in an atypical way. In particular:

- All of the server icons in the Network window are alias files. Starting in Mac OS X 10.3.3, if you select to Show Original from the contextual menu for one of these items, you are not taken to an "original" file elsewhere on the drive. Instead, you are taken to the Login or (if the server already has a mounted volume) the Volume list dialog. The alias itself will likely also disappear briefly and return in a new location of the Network window after you access the contextual menu.

- The Servers item in the Network window behaves a bit differently: If you select the Show Original command for *this* alias, you're taken to the Computer window. Similarly, if you select Go to Folder from the Finder's Go menu and enter /automount, you will see another alias called Servers. This alias behaves the same as the one in the Network window.

Note: If you drag any of these alias files to the Trash, you may succeed in deleting them. However, I don't recommend doing so because problems connecting to servers may result. Still, I've never found any permanent harm caused by doing this. In the worst case, restarting the Mac restores things back to normal.

Network Browser in Mac OS X 10.3.0 to 10.3.2. In versions of Panther prior to Mac OS X 10.3.3, Network Browser worked in a substantially different way. In particular: (a) mounted servers did not appear on the Desktop on in Finder window sidebars; (b) the login procedure did not require selecting specific volumes to mount (all volumes mounted automatically); (c) all volumes from a mounted server appeared in a Finder window when you double-clicked the server icon in the Network window; (d) the recommended method to disconnect from a server was to drag the server's icon from the Network Browser window to the Trash.

continues on next page

TAKE NOTE ▶ Connect to Server vs. Network: What's the Difference? *continued*

However, there were so many bugs and problems with this method that Apple abandoned it in Mac OS X 10.3.3. Instead, the Network Browser now much more closely mimics how Connect to Server works.

Note: Prior to Mac OS X 10.3.3, if you selected to Show Original for a server alias in the Network window, you were taken to the "original" file stored in /var/automount/Network. In fact, you could go there directly by selecting Go to Folder from the Finder's Go menu and entering the following: /var/automount/Network. In this folder you would find folders representing all of the servers listed in the Network window. In fact, there would likely be folders for recently mounted servers, even if they're no longer mounted. Deleting the files for these no-longer-active servers was recommended to improve the speed of the Finder and solve some potential network connecting problems.

Getting Jaguar's Connect to Server window in Panther. If you want to see the old Jaguar-style Connect to Server window in Panther, you can. In fact, the Panther version is even better than the original Jaguar version: It adds a Show pop-up menu from which you can select to show different types of servers (for example, Web servers, FTP servers, and Telnet hosts). To access this window, follow these steps:

1. Open Script Editor (in the AppleScript folder in /Applications).

2. In the Untitled document that appears, enter the following:

   open location (choose URL)

3. Click the Run button.

The Connect to Server window should now appear. If you wish, select *Save* in Script Editor to save the script so you can more easily get back to this window in the future. For example, if you save it as an application, you can simply double-click the resulting item to instantly access the window. If you place the saved application in the ~/Library/Scripts folder, the script will appear in your Scripts menu with whatever name you assigned to it.

SEE: • **"Take Note: AppleScript," in Chapter 4, for more details on using AppleScript and the Scripts menu.**

Connect to Server

For servers and shared computers not listed in Network Browser (or even ones that are), from the Finder's Go menu select Connect to Server (or press Command-K). The Connect to Server window will appear.

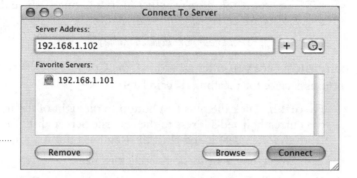

Figure 8.42

The Connect to Server window.

The basic activity you perform in this window is entering a server address. You can enter either a local addresses or a remote one (that is, for a server located outside your local network, such as one you access over the Internet). Here are some details.

Local (LAN) connections. Normally, you would use Network Browser to connect to a local address; however, you can do so here as well. Thus, for a local hostname of BobsMac, you would enter BobsMac.local. Alternatively, if you know the device's IP address (provided in the Sharing System Preferences pane if it's a Mac running Mac OS X), you could enter *it* into the Server Address text box instead. For example, if the local address for BobsMac is 192.168.1.112, you could type afp://192.168.1.112 (where *afp* is the protocol; in this example, *afp* tells Mac OS X to connect via Personal File Sharing).

Remote (WAN) connections. To connect to a remote computer, you need to enter its address in the Server Address field. To do so, you will need to know the exact address of the computer (typically supplied by the owner of the computer to which you want to connect). For some types of servers, you also need to know the name of the share point you wish to access.

In the Server Address field, type your information in the following format: {*protocol*}://{*IPaddress or name*}. Mac OS X supports several protocols. For example:

- AppleShare, via AppleTalk or TCP/IP: afp://{*IPaddress or domain name*}
  Note: This is the protocol that Connect to Server assumes by default if you do not enter one.
- WebDAV (Web Distributed Authoring and Versioning), an extension of HTML that provides read/write functionality: http:// {*IPaddress or domain name*}/path/

- SMB/CIFS, the native sharing protocol for Windows: `smb://{IPaddress or domain name}/ShareName/`.

  Note: You may need to provide the Windows Workgroup in the address, such as in the following: `smb://workgroup;{IPaddress or domain name}/ShareName/`.

- NFS exports, a common way that Unix computers share directory trees: `nfs://{IPaddress or domain name}/path`

- FTP: `ftp://{IPaddress or domain name}`

Fortunately, once you enter an address, the Connect to Server window offers some assistance for recalling it again later:

- **Favorites.** Click the plus (+) button to the right of the text box to add the currently listed address to the Favorite Servers list. To remove an item from the list, select it and click the Remove button.

  To connect to a favorite, double-click its name.

- **Recent.** Click the Clock button to the right of the Plus button to bring up a pop-up menu with a list of recently accessed servers. Select the one you want and its name will appear in the Server Address text box.

  Note: Clicking the Browse button opens the Finder's Network Browser window (covered in the previous section).

- **Connect.** To connect to any server entered in the Server Address text box, click the Connect button. This should bring up the Connect window.

Connect to Server: the Connect/Login window

If all goes well after clicking Connect, a Connect/Login window will appear. In this Connect/Login window, you decide whether to log in as a guest or as a registered user via two radio buttons. As a registered user, you need to enter the name and password for the account on the shared computer (not the one on the computer you're currently using!).

For registered users, an Options button is enabled. Clicking this button allows you to modify several features. Of particular note, you can select Add Password to Keychain (so that you don't have to enter a password the next time you connect). You also have the options to use a clear-text password and to change your password.

Note: If you're connecting to a Windows computer via SMB, you may be asked to provide the workgroup name of the computer and, possibly, the name of the share you're trying to access.

When finished, click the Connect button. The volumes window should now appear.

Connect to Server: the Volumes window

After you click Connect in the Connect/Login window, the Volumes window appears. This window lists all volumes, shares, and user directories that you can access.

If you connected as a guest, all you will see are the names of users with accounts on the computer (if they have enabled file sharing). If you select a user, you will have access to that user's Public folder (the only type of access a guest is allowed).

If you're a nonadministrative registered user, the procedure is the same. However, selecting your own account provides you with full access to your Home directory. In addition, if an administrator of the remote computer has used a utility like SharePoints to set up additional shares, these directories will also be listed.

If you're an administrative user of the computer to which you're connecting, you'll also see the names of all currently mounted volumes and partitions. This, of course, means you'll see the volume to which you're connected. However, if the startup drive has been partitioned or if other drives are connected, these volumes will be listed as well. If you select a volume (as opposed to a user account), you will have the same access to items on that volume as if you were logged in locally as an administrative user. For example, you'll be able to access the Applications folder, the root-level Library folder, and so on. Note that administrative users of a computer will not see custom share points when connecting; this is because they can access the entire enclosing volume.

You can connect to more than one volume or account (by Command-clicking them); however, you should not connect to both your Home directory and the volume that contains that directory at the same time. Doing so would allow you to try to move a file from a folder in your Home directory to the same folder on the full volume, potentially resulting in the loss of the file.

Once you have selected a share (a user folder, share point, or volume), click OK.

Note: It's possible—especially when attempting to connect via FTP—that you won't see any volumes listed in this window, or that the window won't even appear. If this happens, make sure you entered the address, name, and password correctly. If you did, for FTP, try a third-party FTP utility, such as Fetch or RBrowser. If that fails to work, the problem is probably at the server end (in which case, you have to wait for the server administrator to fix the problem).

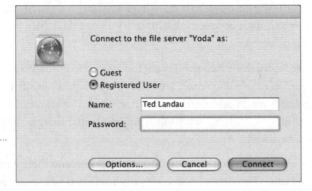

Figure 8.43

Connect to Server: the Connect/Login window.

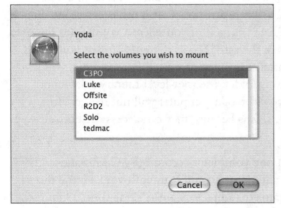 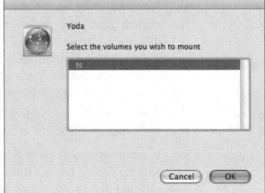

Figure 8.44

Connect to Server: (left) the Volumes window after I logged in as an administrator (tedmac) (showing all mounted volumes) versus (right) the Volumes window after selecting Guest from the Login window.

Connect to Server: connection completed

After you click OK in the Volumes window, each selected item will show up as a separate volume in the Finder's Computer window, on your Desktop (if you have chosen to show connected servers on the Desktop via the Finder Preferences dialog), and/or in Finder sidebars (if you've chosen to display them).

Double-clicking your own User account share opens your Home directory on the shared computer. Double-clicking another user's account share opens that user's Public folder. You will be able to view any files in the user's Public folder, as well as drop files in the user's Drop Box. (As discussed in Chapter 6, you can drop files into another user's Drop Box, but you cannot view its contents.) For drive volumes you access as an administrator, you will be able to access anything there that does not require root access.

Disconnect. When you're finished with a shared volume, you can disconnect from it by dragging its icon to the Trash, clicking the Eject icon next to its name in Finder window sidebars, or selecting the volume in the Finder and then choosing Eject (Command-E) from the File menu. You can also select the Eject command via the contextual menu or the Action menu for the server icon.

Before you do so, you may wish to make an alias of the server icon via the Finder's Make Alias command (Command-L). You can then use this alias as a shortcut to connect to the server.

SEE: • **"Take Note: Connecting to Servers via Aliases and Location Files," below, for more details.**

• **"Troubleshooting Network Browser and Connect to Server," at the end of this chapter, for advice on what to do if you cannot connect or disconnect successfully.**

TAKE NOTE ▶ Connecting to Servers via Aliases and Location Files

If you expect to access the same server(s) repeatedly, you can speed things by creating a file that mounts the server automatically when you double-click it in the Finder. This probably isn't necessary for servers that would normally appear in Network Browser; however, it can be useful otherwise. You can use two approaches: aliases and (for AppleTalk servers) AFP Internet Location files.

Aliases. The basic idea is to make an alias of a server or share to which you're already connected. Once you've done this, double-clicking the alias will mount the volume automatically. Here's how to set this up:

1. Connect to the volume or share via the Connect to Server window.

2. When the Connect/Login window appears, click the Options button and choose Add Password to Keychain. Click OK.

   Note: If you skip this step, double-clicking the alias you create will take you back to the Connect/Login window rather than mount the volume immediately—still faster than going back to the Connect to Server window, but I prefer the express route.

3. Enter your name and password, then click Connect.

4. Mount the volume as usual.

5. In the Finder, press Command-Shift-C to go to the Computer window.

continues on next page

TAKE NOTE ▶ Connecting to Servers via Aliases and Location Files *continued*

6. Hold down the Option and Command keys, and then click and drag the server's icon to the Desktop. This step creates an alias to the server.

If the server icon already appears on the Desktop (because you have chosen to show mounted servers on the Desktop), you can make an alias to the server directly by selecting the icon and choosing Make Alias from the Finder's File menu.

Now after you disconnect from the volume, you can reconnect at any time (assuming that the volume remains on the network) simply by double-clicking the alias. If you would rather connect directly to a certain directory on that volume, you can create an alias to that directory (rather than to the main volume).

Note that you can even use this tip to connect to multiple different iDisks at the same time. If you do, however, be aware of a potential problem: If you use an alias to connect to an iDisk, then connect to a second iDisk (while the first iDisk is still mounted), and then disconnect the *first* iDisk, your alias file may update automatically to point to the second iDisk. There's no work-around for this problem other than avoiding connecting to multiple iDisks at the same time.

AFP Internet Location files. Although aliases usually work well, there are some drawbacks. First, some servers do not allow you to add your password to the Keychain, forcing you to enter it every time you connect. Second, aliases to iDisks have a habit of reassigning themselves and no longer working (as discussed in the previous paragraph).

For these cases, an alternative solution is to use AFP (Apple Filing Protocol) Internet Location files. These files allow you to include the server address, user name, password, and even a volume or share name. The location file then connects automatically when you double-click it.

Unfortunately, creating a location file is not quite as convenient as creating an alias. The easiest method is to use a text editor such as TextEdit and follow these steps:

1. Open TextEdit, and create a new blank document.

2. Type the address of the server, using one of the following formats (substituting the specifics for your server):

AppleShare servers: afp://*username:password*@{*IPaddress or domain name*}/

Specific volumes on AppleShare servers: afp://*username:password*@{*IPaddress or domain name*}/*volume*

Specific share points on AppleShare servers: afp://*username:password*@{*IPaddress or domain name*}/*sharename* (if the share name has a space, replace the space with *%20*)

Note: You used to be able to mount an iDisk using the following command: afp://.*MacUsername*:.*MacPassword*@idisk.mac.com/.*MacsUsername*. However, Apple has dropped AFP support for iDisks, and they will now only mount via the WebDAV protocol.

continues on next page

TAKE NOTE ▶ **Connecting to Servers via Aliases and Location Files**   *continued*

3. Select the entire address in the text window, then drag it to the Desktop or any folder on your drive. An Internet Location file with the extension .afploc is created. This is the same sort of file that is created if you drag a URL from your Web browser to the Desktop.

You can place this file anywhere you like (in the Dock, in a folder, and so on). When you double-click it (or click it in the Dock), it will automatically connect to the server and mount it in the Finder. You can create Location files for every iDisk and server you access. You can even put all of these location files in a folder and drag the folder to the Dock to have a pop-up menu of all the servers you use frequently.

Note: Using a similar method, you can create location files for services other than AFP, such as FTP.

SEE: • **"Take Note: Mounting and Working with iDisks," earlier in this chapter, for more on iDisks and WebDAV.**

• **"Take Note: Location Files and Browser Links," later in this chapter, for related information.**

TAKE NOTE ▶ **Connecting to Servers at Startup**

Mac OS 9 and earlier included an option to log in to AppleShare servers automatically at startup. Mac OS X does not include such an option directly; however, you can accomplish the same thing by using AFP Internet Location files.

After you create a location file for a server, using the instructions in "Take Note: Connect to Servers via Aliases and Location Files," open the Accounts System Preferences pane. Click the Startup Items button for your account, and drag the location file into the list that appears. It's probably best to drag the file to the end of the list so that it loads last.

The next time you log in, the server will be mounted automatically.

Sharing via Target Disk Mode

If you have two or more computers connected on a local network, enabling File Sharing is a convenient way to transfer files. You can use this method to transfer files from a desktop computer to a laptop before going on a trip, for example.

However, if the two computers are physically next to one another, you can use a method that transfers data at a much faster speed: FireWire Target Disk mode. This method requires that both computers have a FireWire port. In Target Disk mode, one Mac acts as though it were an external FireWire hard drive mounted by the other computer. You can then transfer files between the two computers at the same speed as if you had actually attached an external FireWire drive—which is significantly faster than the Ethernet connection used by File Sharing.

Note: This method is entirely different from connecting two computers over a FireWire IP network, as described in "Setting Up System Preferences: Network" and "Take Note: Setting Up and Using Internet Sharing and File Sharing," earlier in this chapter.

Mounting the drive

To use Target Disk mode to mount a drive, follow these steps:

1. Turn off the computer you want to use as an external drive (the target Mac).

   Make sure that you actually shut down the target Mac; a warm restart is not recommended.

2. If you haven't already, turn on the main computer, and log in to your account.

3. Connect the two computers via a standard FireWire cable.

4. Turn on the target Mac and hold down the T key until the FireWire symbol appears on its screen. At this point the target computer should be mounted and accessible on the main computer.

Target Disk mode fails to work. Under Mac OS X 10.2 or later, a computer may not mount via Target Disk mode if you connect it to the source machine prior to starting Target Disk mode. The solution is to start Target Disk mode *before* connecting the machine to the source computer (or disconnect and reconnect the FireWire cable, if Target Disk mode is already running). This is true even though connecting prior to starting Target Disk mode actually should work and remains Apple's overall recommended procedure. This is a bug that Apple may eventually fix.

Unmounting the drive

To stop using Target Disk mode, follow these steps:

1. On the main computer, drag the mounted computer or drive to the Dock's Trash icon (which will change to an Eject symbol), or select the mounted volume and press Command-E to unmount it.

2. Press the Power button on the target Mac to turn it off.

3. Disconnect the FireWire cable.

It's important not to turn off or disconnect the target computer before you unmount it. Doing so risks damaging the data on your drive.

TAKE NOTE ▶ File Sharing: It's Your Choice

When Apple dropped the floppy-disk drive from the original iMac back in 1998, there was concern about how users would transfer files between computers—since at that time, the most common way to do so (at least for small files like word-processing documents) was via a floppy disk or (perhaps) a Zip disk (if you had a Zip drive).

Mac OS X offers a multitude of choices for sharing files (most of them far more convenient and faster than a floppy disk). The following summarizes your more common options (more details on these and other options are discussed elsewhere, primarily in this chapter and in Chapter 6). Specifically, to transfer a file to another computer, use any of the following:

- Burn the file to a CD-R or DVD-R (assuming you have a CD-RW or DVD-RW drive).

- Put the file on a portable FireWire hard drive (an iPod, for example). Connect the drive to the destination computer to transfer the file.

- If two computers are within close physical proximity of one another, you can connect them via FireWire Target Disk mode—in essence, setting up one computer to act as an external drive connected to the other.

- Send the file as an attachment via email.

- Enable Personal File Sharing in the Sharing System Preferences pane, and make the file available in your Public folder.

- Set up Web Sharing in the Sharing System Preferences pane, and make the file available via a personal Web site.

- Enable FTP access, allowing other users to access your data via an FTP client.

- Use Bluetooth for supported devices in close proximity to each other.

- Use iChat, Mac OS X's implementation of instant messaging. When a chat window for a Buddy is open, you can exchange files by choosing the Send a File command from iChat's Buddies menu. Because iChat supports Rendezvous, you don't even need to be connected to the Internet—two Macs connected locally can use iChat to communicate by using the Login to Rendezvous command in the iChat menu.

SEE: • Chapter 11 for more on iChat.

Network Security

Historically, personal computers have not needed much in the way of protection from network attacks, hackers, and the like—primarily because they were connected to the Internet either via a dial-up connection (making the computer difficult for a hacker to nail down and preventing high-bandwidth data transfers) or via a company network (which was protected behind an industrial-strength firewall managed by an IT person).

The widespread use of broadband connections for home use, however, means that more and more computers are permanently connected to the Internet, which means more availability and greater bandwidth. In addition, computer users are becoming more and more Internet-savvy, and the increased bandwidth has led many people to use the various sharing technologies discussed in this chapter, creating more openings for malicious people to try to exploit.

Traditionally, Mac OS computers have been among the least vulnerable to security breaches. Mac OS X continues this trend. Although Mac OS X's Unix base has the potential to be more vulnerable than the classic Mac OS—if only because hackers have spent many more hours trying to break into Unix servers than Mac servers—Mac OS X ships with most remote services (File Sharing, FTP Access, Remote Login, Web Server, and so on) disabled. Thus, you're not vulnerable unless you choose to be. If you *do* decide to enable any sort of sharing, you will likely want some firewall protection.

There are three types of network protection you need to be concerned about: (a) protection of information you *send* over the Internet (typically via email or to a Web site); (b) dangers lurking in material you *receive* via email (such as email that contains a virus or HTML-formatted email with code that attempts to upload data from your Mac); and (c) unauthorized access to your computer (such as by a hacker attempting to gain access via an Internet connection). This section presents an overview of the tools available to protect against all of these dangers.

Note: This section is about protecting your Mac from the dangers present when connected to the Internet and/or a network. For protection of your Mac and its data from people who have physical access to your Mac, check out "Take Note: Securing Mac OS X," in Chapter 10.

Security updates

Your first line of defense should be to make sure you're using the latest version of Mac OS X. Apple has gotten much better at responding rapidly to security issues that affect the OS. As one example, Apple released a security update for Panther less than a week after its release. These security updates most often fix newly identified problems with Mac OS X's underlying Unix software. For more details on available updates, as well as what each update fixes, check out the following Web site: www.info.apple.com/usen/security/security_updates.html.

Note: A security update typically does not change the build number for Mac OS X (as a standard Mac OS X update does).

SEE: • "Take Note: About This Mac," in Chapter 2, and several sections in Chapter 3 for more on build numbers.

Network Address Translation and security

Earlier in this chapter, I discussed Network Address Translation (NAT) in the context of Internet routers. In addition to its value in sharing a single Internet connection among multiple computers, NAT offers a weak form of security protection. Because all data coming into your network must pass through the router, which then directs it to the appropriate computer, computers behind the router are not exposed to the Internet directly. What's more, since only data that has specifically been requested by a computer behind the router actually makes it past the router, hackers will generally not be able to reach any of your computers. (The exception, of course, being ports that you have specifically opened using port mapping.)

SEE: • "Network Address Translation" and "Internet routers and port mapping," earlier in this chapter, for more details.

Firewalls

The single best form of protection is a firewall. As explained earlier in the chapter, a firewall sets up a barrier between your computer and the outside world. The main job of a firewall is to prevent contact with your computer that you did not initiate. For example, when you attempt to load a Web page, the data for that page is sent to your Mac. This does not typically trigger a firewall reaction, because it is understood that you initiated the request when you clicked a link, or entered a URL, to load that page. On the other hand, if an attempt is made by a computer outside your firewall to send data to your hard drive that has not specifically been requested (other than legitimate access to Sharing Services that you've enabled), the firewall should block the data before it reaches your computer. (A firewall can also block unauthorized data going the other direction—such as covert attempts by software on your computer to connect to the Internet and send data. However, most users don't take advantage of this ability because setting it up is not a trivial task.)

If the firewall detects anything it believes is malicious, it blocks it. Depending on the firewall in use and your settings, it may or may not alert you of this block. In any case, the system log, which you can access from Console, should list any firewall-generated activity (if you're using Mac OS X's "built-in" firewall.

Under Mac OS X, you have several potential firewall options:

- The Firewall screen of the Sharing System Preference enables the firewall protection built into Mac OS X.

  SEE: • "Firewall," earlier in this chapter, for details.

- The Firewall screen is actually a front end to the robust Unix firewall software ipfw. A few shareware utilities, such as the excellent BrickHouse, allow you to more fully customize and configure ipfw.

- There are a number of firewalls available for Mac OS X that are completely independent of ipfw. The best example of such is Symantec's Norton Personal Firewall. Its most recent 3.0 version has includes some very cool features, such as one that allows you to visually track an intruder. The Norton Internet Security package includes Personal Firewall and Norton Privacy Control—that latter of which is one of several available utilities that include parental controls for Web access as well as the ability to block ads that may attempt to obtain data from your drive (typically via JavaScript).

Remember, a firewall's protection need not be "all or nothing"—that is, it's not as simple as an On/Off switch. Occasionally, you will want to allow certain types of data or access that would otherwise trigger a block, but still prevent other types of access. This is exactly what Sharing's Firewall screen does when the firewall is enabled but you activate Personal File Sharing: The firewall is active, but it lets Personal File Sharing data through.

How does a firewall determine what it will and won't let through? It works by opening and closing what are called *ports*. As discussed earlier, different types of data intended for different services travel through varying ports. By opening some ports and not others, you can achieve a finer level of control over your firewall. (These ports are different from the network ports discussed earlier in the chapter. In this context, a *port* is a particular network interface that deals with a particular type of data.)

Note: If you have an Internet router, you can typically open and close ports through router settings rather than via Mac OS X software (such as ipfw or ipfw-based utilities). As much as possible, create settings only in one location or the other; if not, you run the risk of having contradictory commands that lead to uncertain results. One potential advantage of using router firewall settings over Mac OS X software settings: Router settings affect *all* devices connected to the router as opposed to just one Mac.

SEE: • "Internet routers and port mapping," earlier in this chapter, for more details.

Note: Using default settings, a firewall lets in most or all traffic originating within your local network (LAN), as opposed to traffic from the Internet (WAN). This is typically what you would want. However, using ipfw or a utility such as BrickHouse, you can block local access as well.

Proxy settings (as set via the Proxies screen of Network System Preferences) also serve as a form of firewall protection. However, proxies are typically only used in large network environments. To find out if you need or can use proxies, check with your network administrator.

SEE: • "Proxies," earlier in this chapter, for more details.

Finding the problem port. One caution about using a firewall: You can be overzealous in your firewall protection, blocking things you don't really want to block. For example, if you're having trouble loading some but not all Web pages, the problem may be caused by your firewall. Assuming you know the Web page you want to load is safe, try disabling your firewall temporarily. If the page now loads properly, it means that a firewall setting was blocking the page. If this happens, it generally means there's some port that is closed that you need to open. How do you find out what this port is? The easiest way is to contact the vendor whose service is being blocked. Otherwise, you can use the Port Scan screen of Network Utility. To do so, set the IP address to 127.0.0.1 (which indicates your local machine) and click the Scan button. Now attempt to perform the action that's blocked by the firewall. With a bit of luck, the port in use will appear in the scan at the same time. That's the port you need to have open.

SEE: • "Firewall," earlier in this chapter, for examples of specific port problems.

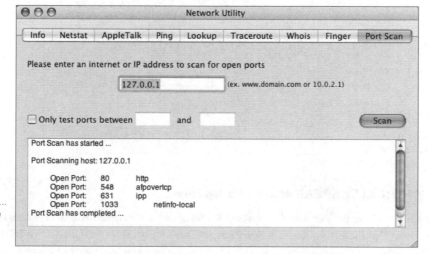

Figure 8.45

Using the Port Scan screen of Network Utility.

Little Snitch and MacScan. Objective Development's Little Snitch is a specialized firewall utility that I have come to rely on. It uses ipfw software but in a different way than most other firewall software. It alerts you every time an application on your Mac attempts to connect to the Internet "on its own." Typical firewall settings often overlook this, because the connection attempt is coming from your Mac rather than the outside. The firewall typically cannot distinguish between a connection attempt made with your awareness versus one that is not. Little Snitch makes this distinction. The goal here is to protect you from any application that might try to upload data that you would prefer kept private (for example, your email address). When Little Snitch detects an attempt, a message appears and you can either deny the connection or allow it. If you repeatedly get a warning for the same connection, you can create a rule that will permanently allow or deny that specific connection.

Note that in many cases, connection attempts are harmless (such as when iTunes attempts to contact its Music Store) and thus should be allowed.

SecureMac.com's MacScan works differently. It scans your drive and locates known examples of any keystroke loggers (which record everything you type), spyware, and Trojan horse software that may have been surreptitiously installed on your drive.

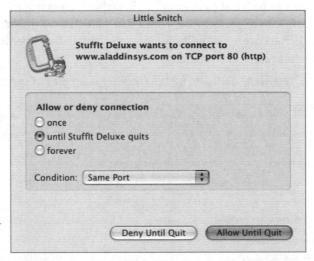

Figure 8.46

A warning message from Little Snitch.

TECHNICALLY SPEAKING ▶ Using ipfw

The Firewall feature of Sharing System Preferences is designed to be easy to use—which leads to some significant limitations. For example, rules only affect TCP ports, not UDP ports. In addition, you can only specifically open a port via a rule; there's no way to close a specific port.

continues on next page

TECHNICALLY SPEAKING ▶ **Using ipfw** *continued*

If you're unsatisfied with the limitations of Sharing's Firewall options, you can explore the full range of functionality available via the ipfw command in Terminal. Using ipfw's arguments, such as add and deny, you can customize your firewall. The output from the man ipfw command will explain exactly how to use ipfw (though not in a very user-friendly way). A friendlier introduction can be found at www.macdevcenter.com/pub/a/mac/2002/12/27/macosx_firewall.html.

Even if you don't intend to use ipfw as your main firewall software, there are two basic commands you should know:

*   sudo ipfw list. The output of this command shows every firewall rule in effect. Changes you make in the Firewall screen of Sharing System Preferences will be reflected here, as will those you make directly using the ipfw command.

    A typical line looks like this:

    02070 allow tcp from any to 80 in

    This means the following: Rule Number 02070 allows incoming TCP transmissions from any IP address to any IP address via Port 80.

*   sudo ipfw −f flush. Use this command to delete all added firewall rules and return the firewall to its default state.

    One occasion where you will find this useful is if you go to Sharing's Firewall screen and get a message that says, "Other firewall software is running on your computer. To change the Apple firewall settings, turn off the other firewall software." This message typically appears because you (or perhaps some third-party software you used) made changes to the ipfw firewall. To avoid potential rule conflicts, Apple turns its own firewall access off. To regain access via Sharing Preferences, and invoke just the rules listed in the Firewall screen, flush the firewall with the above command and then restart the firewall via Sharing Preferences.

Note: Using the ipfw command in Terminal requires root access. This is why all commands are preceded by sudo and will request a password.

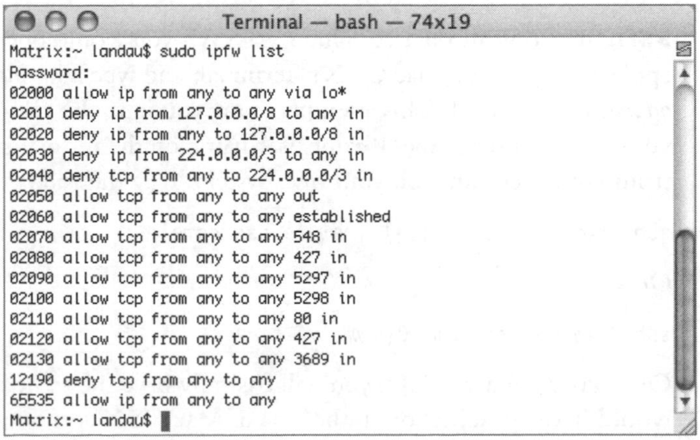

Figure 8.47

The output from the ipfw list *command showing the rules that are in effect when the firewall is enabled via the Firewall screen of the Sharing System Preferences pane of my Mac.*

```
Matrix:~ landau$ sudo ipfw list
Password:
02000 allow ip from any to any via lo*
02010 deny ip from 127.0.0.0/8 to any in
02020 deny ip from any to 127.0.0.0/8 in
02030 deny ip from 224.0.0.0/3 to any in
02040 deny tcp from any to 224.0.0.0/3 in
02050 allow tcp from any to any out
02060 allow tcp from any to any established
02070 allow tcp from any to any 548 in
02080 allow tcp from any to any 427 in
02090 allow tcp from any to any 5297 in
02100 allow tcp from any to any 5298 in
02110 allow tcp from any to any 80 in
02120 allow tcp from any to any 427 in
02130 allow tcp from any to any 3689 in
12190 deny tcp from any to any
65535 allow ip from any to any
Matrix:~ landau$ 
```
Terminal — bash — 74x19

Figure 8.48

The message that
appears in the
Firewall screen of
the Sharing System
Preferences pane if
you have modified
the firewall via ipfw.

SSH and SFTP

It used to be that if you wanted to connect to a Unix-based computer, you used common protocols such as FTP or Telnet. One problem with these methods is that all text, including passwords, is sent as clear text, making it a bit too easy for hackers to grab your address and password. These methods are especially risky in a Mac OS X environment, where knowing your password could give someone administrative access to your computer.

The solution is something called SSH (secure shell), a secure substitute for Telnet, and its file-transfer counterpart SFTP, a secure alternative to FTP. Programs that use the SSH protocol transmit all data in an encrypted format, making it harder to crack. Mac OS X built SSH into its Unix software via the OpenSSH service. You enable both SSH and SFTP access via the Remote Login service in Sharing System Preferences' Services screen.

Note: Enabling FTP Access in the Sharing System Preferences (as described earlier in this chapter) is not required to enable SFTP. Conversely, enabling FTP Access does not enable SFTP; only Remote Login does this. Enabling FTP Access enables the less secure FTP protocol.

SSH. To access another computer via SSH, you would open a command-line application, such as Mac OS X's Terminal, and type ssh *{domain name or IP address of server}*. This attempts to log you in to the remote computer using your current user name. If your user name on the remote system is different from your user name on your own system, type the following instead:

ssh *{name of server}* -1 *{remote username}*

Or

ssh *{remote username}*@*{name of server}*

Once connected via SSH, you will basically have the same capabilities you would have via Telnet or, in the case of Mac OS X computers, via Terminal if you were logged in locally.

Should you want to enable the less secure Telnet protocol on your Mac, you can do so by opening the file /etc/inetd.conf in a text editor (or via pico or vi in Terminal), and then deleting the # symbol in front of the #telnet, #shell, and #login lines of this file. Anyone can then use the `telnet` command to access your Mac. Otherwise, for a computer running Mac OS X 10.2 or later, Telnet is inaccessible altogether; you can only use SSH.

SEE: • "Modifying invisible unix files from Mac OS X applications," in Chapter 6, for related information.

  • "Connect to Server" in the "Terminal's menus" section of Chapter 10, for related information on a simpler method for connecting via SSH.

  • "Take Note: Editing Text Files via Terminal," in Chapter 10, for details on editing Unix files.

SFTP. As a secure alternative to FTP, SFTP can be used in two ways. If you're a fan of the command line, you can use the `sftp` command in Terminal. However, a much easier way is to use a dedicated SFTP client, such as RBrowser, Research Systems Unix Group's Fugu, or Panic's Transmit. These clients allow you to work with files much as you would in the Finder, via drag and drop. You would simply enter the IP address of the remote computer and then provide your user name and password (for the remote computer, not your own).

Security issues with SSH. One thing to be aware of with SSH is that an admin user connected to your Mac via SSH has unfettered access to your system. For example, an admin user could enable the root user via SSH and then log in to any other sharing services as the root user. Or the user could simply use the `sudo` command to execute nearly any command over SSH. The point here is that if you decide to enable Remote Login (SSH/SFTP), you should be extremely careful who (if anyone) has administrative-level accounts.

Note: The `telnet` and `ftp` commands still work in Terminal in Mac OS X to access other servers from your Mac. The restrictions described here are for accessing your Mac from other locations. Type `man telnet`, `man ftp`, `man ssh`, and/or `man sftp` to get more information about the usage of these commands.

Note: Sometimes the term *telnet* is used generically to indicate a remote terminal connection, whether by the actual Telnet protocol or by SSH.

VPN

A VPN (or *virtual private network*) is a type of security connection used mainly by large companies. The idea is to provide a secure way for employees to connect to the mother ship when they're on the road. Mac OS X has a built-in client for one form of VPN, Microsoft's Point-to-Point Tunneling Protocol (PPTP). Using Internet Connect, you can connect to a PPTP VPN.

SEE: • "VPN connections," earlier in this chapter, for more details.

Web and email security

When you send private information to a Web site, such as a credit card number to make an online purchase, you want that transmission to be protected from snoopers who might try to steal the information. With most Web browsers, you're made aware that your data is protected by a message that appears stating that the page you are entering is secure. There may be a graphical indication as well, such as the locked padlock icon that appears in the lower left corner of Internet Explorer windows when connected to a secure server. In such cases, the Web page is likely using SSL (Secure Socket Layer) technology, a form of encryption. You should never send private information over the Web unless the connection to the Web server is secure.

Some email programs, such as Apple's Mail and Microsoft's Entourage, also include SSL options that you can enable for sending and receiving email (check the options in the Accounts screen for each email account). In general, using these options only works if the mail server you're contacting is set up to use SSL.

Web browsers also include numerous other security-related features, typically accessed from the Preferences window. For example, go to Safari's Preferences and select the Security icon. From here, you can turn off Java and JavaScript as well as block pop-up windows. You can also restrict access to cookies. Email clients generally offer similar security measures, such as those noted in the next section, on SPAM.

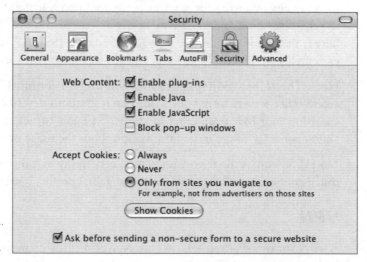

Figure 8.49

Safari's Security Preferences settings.

Cookies. Cookies are a technology used by Web sites primarily to track your previous visits. They can be used to remember a password for the site or to keep track of when you last visited the site (helpful for forums that track "new" posts). This information is stored in a cookie file on your drive. The potential risk of cookies is that a site could use them to place data on your hard drive that might allow them to have otherwise unauthorized access to your drive. No legitimate well-known sites do this. However, if you're browsing the backwaters of the Web, you might want to refuse to accept cookies.

Although you can turn all of these features off to gain security, you're likely to end up blocking features you may actually want to use in the process. Thus, be prepared to turn one or more of these features back on, at least temporarily, if a problem loading a page occurs.

Spoofing. Have you ever gotten an email that purports to come from eBay or AOL or some similar service—that includes a request to go to a Web site to update or confirm your confidential account information? If so, be wary!

In many cases, despite the legitimate look of the email, it is a fraud, a sneaky attempt to get you to divulge your password or credit card information to the perpetrator. Be especially wary of email that comes from a domain that's slightly different from a company's typical domain. For example, *apple.com* is the domain of Apple; *apple.{somedomain}.com* is not. In some cases, the Web URL or email address may look exactly like the legitimate URL or address (for example, it may be www.ebay.com for eBay) and yet still be a fake. These phony addresses and URLs are said to be *spoofs*.

To determine whether a suspicious email is legitimate, check its full header. To do this in Mail, for example, select the message and from the View menu select Show All Headers. The From, Reply-To, and Return-Path lines, in particular, should indicate if the supposed source is the true sender.

A way to check whether a Web URL is a spoof is to do the following:

1. Go to the suspect page (but do not enter any of the requested info!).

2. Enter the following JavaScript code in the Address text box of your browser:

    ```
    javascript:alert("The actual URL is:\t\t" + location.protocol +
    "//" + location.hostname + "/" + "\nThe address URL is:\t\t" +
    location.href + "\n" + "\nIf the server names do not match, this
    may be a spoof.");
    ```

3. Press Return. A dialog should appear that lists both the address URL and the true *actual* URL. If the domains are not the same, play it safe and assume the address is a spoof. Close the Web page immediately!

To do this spoof checking in the future without having to retype the JavaScript code, make it a bookmark. Such JavaScript bookmarks are often referred to as *bookmarklets*. For example, if you are using Safari, drag the icon for the JavaScript text from the Address text box to the Bookmark bar below; rename the bookmark SpoofCheck when prompted. Now, whenever you want to run a check on a currently loaded Web page, just click the SpoofCheck bookmarklet.

Spam

Spam may not always present a security issue; however, it is always an annoyance. *Spam* refers to the junk email you receive, be it about pornography, Viagra offers, or con artist scams. Usually, it's just an annoyance, as you try to wade through dozens (or even hundreds) of unwanted email messages each day. Occasionally, however, it may raise serious security issues, because some of these messages may contain viruses (as discussed next) or include HTML/JavaScript code that tries to perform surreptitious actions behind your back.

You typically have two goals when it comes to spam: keeping it to a minimum, and quickly separating it from "legitimate" email. Here are a few guidelines for achieving these goals:

- To automatically separate spam from real email, you can use a spam filter. These filters sort spam into a separate folder so that it doesn't clutter up your main mailbox and can be deleted more easily. The dilemma with spam filters is a classic signal-detection problem: The better the filter gets at correctly identifying spam as spam, the more likely it will sometimes falsely identify a legitimate email as spam. There's no easy way to avoid this problem, and no spam filter is perfect; however, some are much better than others. Entourage X includes a spam filter that works very poorly in my experience (an updated version of Entourage included as part of Office 2004 is expected to have an improved junk mail filter). In contrast, the junk mail filter built into Mac OS X's Mail application is one of the best I have ever seen. There are also third-party spam filters that can work with an assortment of email applications. In general, the ones that claim to use "Bayesian logic" work best; Michael Tsai's SpamSieve is one example.

- Most spammers get your email address because you have either posted it someplace public or sent it to someone who sells it to a spammer. Your best defense against spam is to be vigilant about providing public access to your email address. For example, don't include your address with postings on online forums, and don't register for anything that requires that you provide your address—unless you're confident your privacy will be maintained. I actually use a phony email address in some cases—where privacy is not assured and a real email address is not required for what I want to do.

- If you have your own Web page, putting your email address on the page (so that visitors can contact you) is asking for spam. Many spammers use automated "crawlers" or "spiders" that scour Web pages for email addresses. However, if you want visitors to your site to be able to contact you, you have no choice but to provide your address. Still, there are some precautions you can take. One technique is to create an encoded email address that gets decoded when someone clicks the email link. Several Mac OS X utilities, such as RAILhead Design's SpamStopper, can automate setting up such a link, using either HTML or JavaScript. When you use an encoded email address, most crawlers will not be able to grab your true address.

- If you get a spam message that instructs you to send a message back if you wish to be removed from the spam list (presumably so that you no longer get spam from this source), you may not want to do so. The reason is that when you send a message back, you're telling the spammer that you actually opened and read the email. For the unscrupulous spammer, rather than removing you from the list, this just encourages him to send you more spam or sell your email address to other spammers as a "confirmed" address. Recent legislation to require legitimate "remove" options in spam have increased the likelihood that the option now works as intended, but I still avoid it unless I know the origin of the email and I am confident it's legitimate.

- Some spam, especially spam sent as HTML rather than plain text, may include code that attempts to automatically send a message back to the sender when you open it (thus verifying that your email address is "real" and allowing the spammer to sell it to other sellers as a "good" address). You can often prevent this by using an email option, available in some email clients, that prevents HTML code (and graphic images) in email messages from being rendered—or that prevents online access to links within email messages. To select such an option in Mac OS X's Mail application, for example, uncheck the "Display images and embedded objects in HTML messages" option (found in Viewing preferences). Alternatively, a firewall that has been configured to detect this sort of activity (for exam-ple, set up via a utility such as Little Snitch) can help out here, as discussed in previous sections.

- Some email programs, such as Mac OS X's Mail, give you the ability to bounce email from a specific address. For example, if you get frequent email "newsletters" from a company, and you don't want them (and you can't find a place to tell the company to stop), you can select Bounce from the Message menu in the Mail application. The sender then receives a "bounce" email indicating that your address is not valid (sort of a "white lie"). Hopefully, this will discourage further emails from being sent to you. However, this will not work for most spam, as the return address for most spam is itself not valid; so your bounce message will get bounced back to you!

Viruses

Because many viruses arrive at your computer via email messages or downloaded files that you deliberately permit past your firewall, a firewall doesn't necessarily protect against computer viruses. As a result, it's wise to have some sort of antivirus software on your computer. The two best such programs in my experience are Symantec's Norton AntiVirus and McAfee's Virex (the latter is included free with a .Mac account). That said, there are currently no known viruses that target Mac OS X. Your vulnerability to and involvement with viruses will stem more from your exposure to Microsoft Word/Excel macro viruses and your Mac's potentially passing viruses to PC users via email.

Note: Many claims of potential virus attacks are actually hoaxes. There are several Web sites where you can learn more about viruses, both real and false. Symantec's SARC site (www.sarc.com) is a good place to start.

Troubleshooting Networking

I've divided the troubleshooting tips in this section into separate categories, such as wireless connections and modem connections. This division is difficult to achieve cleanly, however, because categories overlap—for example, you can connect to the Internet via a dial-up modem, which may be part of an AirPort Base Station. Thus, if you don't find the answer you seek in one of the sections below, try the one that seems next closest.

To help you get started, here are some general guidelines:

- If you're having trouble with File Sharing or Web Sharing over the Internet, you should troubleshoot your network and Internet connections first. If all seems well, then troubleshoot File Sharing or Web Sharing.

- If your problem is limited to your Internet connection, concentrate on Internet troubleshooting, because services such as File Sharing and Web Sharing are not relevant to getting on the Internet.

- If you have a working Internet connection but are having problems with your Web browser or email client, your problem is most likely with the browser or client. Focus your troubleshooting on the application's settings.

Checking the basics

Regardless of the specific likely source of your networking problem, it often pays to start with these basic steps:

- **Check your hardware connections.** Disconnect and reconnect all cables (Ethernet cables, modem cables, power cables, and so on). Make sure that all needed hardware is on and connected properly.

  To test whether a problem is with a cable or the Mac, try swapping: Connect a suspected defective cable to another Mac, for example, and see whether the problem still occurs. Alternatively, try a new cable with the problem Mac.

- **Check the Network System Preferences settings.** In the Network System Preferences pane, check and double-check that you've entered all of your settings correctly. A single incorrect number or letter can prevent you from accessing the Internet. Having AppleTalk disabled will prevent any AppleTalk connections.

  Be sure to go to the Network Status screen. If there's a basic problem with your connection (such as a cable that's not plugged in), you'll find a message here indicating the problem.

  Note: If you maintain a local network and assign IP addresses manually, make sure that no two devices have the same address. If a conflict does exist, you should get an IP Configuration error message when you start up (or wake up) a Mac with a conflicting address.

- **Switch Locations and Network Port Configuration settings.**
  Changing Locations and/or Network Port Configuration settings in the
  Network System Preferences pane may clear up an assortment of connec-
  tion problems. I give specific examples in the sections that follow.

  SEE: • "Setting Up System Preferences: Network," earlier in this chapter,
  for information on how to determine your correct settings and
  switch locations.

Diagnosing Internet problems with Network Utility

Apple's Network Utility (located in /Applications/Utilities) can help you diagnose various Internet problems. You can use it to check whether a failure to
get to a Web site is due to a problem with the site or a more general Internet-
connection problem. Although the scope of all that Network Utility can do is
too broad to cover here, the following provides a brief overview:

SEE: • "Technically Speaking: Terminal Commands to Monitor and Improve
Performance," in Chapter 10, for more on commands accessed from
Terminal that overlap with what you can do via Network Utility.

Info. This screen provides information about your local network connections.
The pop-up menu allows you to choose which network port the information
refers to (en0 is the built-in Ethernet port; en1 is your AirPort card, if applicable,
or a second Ethernet card; fw0 is for the FireWire port). The hardware address
is the unique number (the media access controller, or MAC, address) that
identifies your computer. Your IP address is either your local IP address (if
you're using an Internet router) or the IP address assigned to you by your ISP.

The Transfer Statistics section of this screen provides information about
errors that occur during transfer over the network. A high number of errors
indicates a problem with your network connection.

Netstat. To get various types of feedback about your network, including
summaries of the different types of network traffic (TCP, UDP, IP, and so on),
select an option here and click the Netstat tab. This is fairly technical stuff
that most users will rarely (if ever) need.

For more details about this command, enter man netstat in Terminal. Note:
You can similarly use the man command in Terminal to get more information
about most of the other commands cited in the next sections (for example,
appletalk, ping, and so on).

AppleTalk. AppleTalk can be used to get diagnostic information for troubleshooting AppleTalk connections. I discuss this elsewhere in the chapter.

SEE: • "Troubleshooting AppleTalk connections," later in this chapter, for
examples of using the options in Network Utility's AppleTalk screen.

Ping. Ping is one of the most useful tools for testing an Internet connection. If you type the IP address or domain (for example, macfixit.com) of a remote server and click the Ping tab, Network Utility will send a special signal to the server and request a response. If the server answers, you know that your Internet connection is functioning properly. If it doesn't, try several others; some servers don't return ping requests, and a remote server may simply be having problems. All you need is a single successful ping result to verify your connection.

If you cannot get the Web page of a certain site to load, and you can't ping to that site—but other sites load and ping successfully—this suggests that the Web site is temporarily unavailable. That is, the problem is at the site's end, not yours. In such cases, there is little you can do except wait for the site's Webmaster to fix the problem.

If you cannot ping any site successfully, there's likely a connection problem on your end. Note that some servers have disabled ping responses, meaning that even if your network connection is working fine, you'll never get a response to a ping to that server. Thus, if you don't get a response from a particular server, be sure to try a number of other servers before deciding that your network connection isn't working properly.

Note: Pinging a site is a quick way to learn its numeric IP address. For example, when I pinged macfixit.com, I quickly learned its IP address: 66.179.48.115. Entering this address in a Web browser loads the Web site just as well as the domain name.

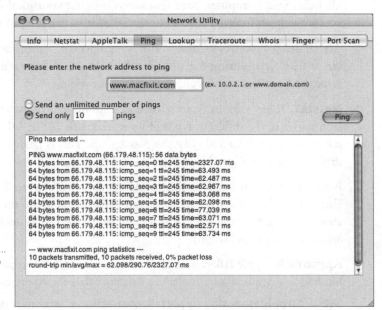

Figure 8.50

A successful ping to a remote server using Network Utility.

Lookup. I discuss this elsewhere in the chapter.

SEE: • "Troubleshooting Web Browsers," later in this chapter, for an example of using Lookup.

Traceroute. Traceroute is similar to ping. In addition to indicating a successful connection, it displays all of the routers and computers your connection must pass through on its way to the destination computer. If there's a problem with your connection to a remote server, knowing at exactly what point the stoppage occurs can help determine the cause. (For example, a stop at the start indicates a problem at your end; a stop at the end indicates a problem at the destination end; a stop in between indicates a problem elsewhere on the Internet that is preventing a connection.)

Note that some Internet routers do not allow traceroutes to function properly. Specifically, when starting a traceroute, you'll see a response from the router itself but not from any device beyond the router. If you attempt a traceroute and it "dies" at the router, keep this fact in mind—it may not be a symptom of a network problem.

Whois and Finger. These screens are useful for searching for information about a Web address (Whois) or an email address (Finger). For example, you can use Whois to find out the administrative and technical contact persons behind any Web site.

Port Scan. I discuss this elsewhere in this chapter.

SEE: • "Firewalls," earlier in this chapter, for an example of using Port Scan.

An alternative to Network Utility is the shareware program IPNetMonitor X (from Sustainable Softworks). It includes features that go beyond what Network Utility can do.

Troubleshooting AppleTalk connections

If you're having trouble accessing AppleTalk devices via Personal File Sharing (or if other users are having trouble accessing your computer via AppleTalk), the following steps will be useful in helping you isolate the cause of the problem.

Make sure that AppleTalk is active—and only on a single port.
Make sure that you have enabled AppleTalk on at least one of your active network ports. The way to do this is to check your port configurations in the Network System Preferences pane. Check the AppleTalk screen for the desired configuration and make sure that Make AppleTalk Active is checked.

Starting with Mac OS X 10.2, AppleTalk can only be enabled on one port at a time. Thus, for example, you cannot enable AppleTalk simultaneously for both AirPort and Ethernet. If you try, you will get an error message.

If you require AppleTalk to be active on multiple ports at different times, the best solution is to create multiple Locations (as described earlier in this chapter), each with AppleTalk active on a different port. Switch Locations when you need to use AppleTalk on a different port.

If you're using an older version of Mac OS X, you may be able to enable AppleTalk on two or more ports at one time. However, you should not do so because it's likely that some or all AppleTalk-connected devices will not work. See the following Apple Knowledge Base article for details: http://docs.info .apple.com/article.html?artnum=106614.

If the Network System Preferences pane claims that AppleTalk is active for your selected port, but it's not working, proceed to the next sections of this chapter.

Enable AppleTalk in Directory Access. I discuss this elsewhere in the chapter.

SEE: • "Connect to Server vs. Network Browser: What's the Difference?," earlier in this chapter.

Use Network Utility or Terminal to determine whether AppleTalk is active and Mac OS X can see AppleTalk devices. If AppleTalk appears to be enabled on the desired port, but you're still having problems, the Network System Preferences pane may be displaying AppleTalk information incorrectly. To get feedback about AppleTalk, you can use the AppleTalk screen of Network Utility or employ Terminal commands.

• **appletalk –s.** To confirm which port is using AppleTalk and whether AppleTalk is active, type appletalk –s. The active AppleTalk interface will be listed, along with other information about the port (network number, node ID, and current zone) and some statistics on AppleTalk traffic.

  The interface designations provided by appletalk -s correspond to specific ports on your Mac:

  en0: This corresponds to the built-in Ethernet port.

  en1: This corresponds to the AirPort card (if no AirPort card is installed, it refers to the second Ethernet port).

  en2: This corresponds to the second Ethernet port (or third Ethernet port, if an AirPort card is installed).

  Alternatively, if you select "Display AppleTalk statistics and error counts" in Network Utility and then click the Get AppleTalk Information button, you will get essentially the same output.

• **atlookup.** To confirm that your Mac is actually seeing connected peripheral devices (such as printers) via AppleTalk, type atlookup. You should get a list of all AppleTalk-connected devices. If the command does not list any peripheral devices (listing nothing or only your own computer), this generally means that AppleTalk is active and that you are connected to an active AppleTalk network, but that the other devices on the network are not communicating properly (or that there are no other AppleTalk devices on the network). The problem is not with your computer.

Alternatively, if you select "Display all AppleTalk zones on the network" in Network Utility and then click the Get AppleTalk Information button, you will get essentially the same output as with `atlookup`. The additional options in the AppleTalk screen of Network Utility match other variations of the `appletalk` and `atlookup` commands (check the `man` output in Terminal for details).

If, when using either command, you get a message that states, "The AppleTalk stack is not running," either AppleTalk is disabled or the port on which it is enabled has not experienced any network activity (so AppleTalk has not been initialized on that port). If you connect an Ethernet cable directly to an AppleTalk device or try to initiate a direct AirPort connection to another AirPort device, this action should initiate AppleTalk traffic on the port. If you run the command again and still get an error, AppleTalk is simply not active. You will need to reset AppleTalk, as described next.

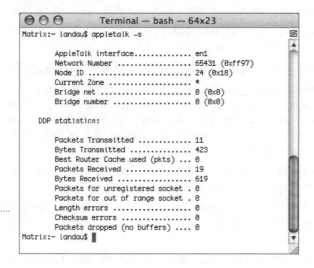

Figure 8.51

Output from `appletalk —s` *in Terminal.*

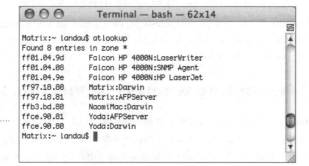

Figure 8.52

Output from `atlookup` *in Terminal.*

Reset AppleTalk connections. If you've checked every aspect of your AppleTalk connection and still aren't getting connectivity, try the following steps to reset your AppleTalk settings. After each step, test your AppleTalk connection. After you have regained connectivity, you can ignore the subsequent steps.

1. In the AppleTalk section of the port for which AppleTalk is active in the Network System Preferences pane, disable Make AppleTalk Active. Click the Apply Now button, and then re-enable AppleTalk by reselecting the option. Click the Apply Now button again.

2. Log out and then log back in.

   Sometimes, the AppleTalk settings in the Network System Preferences pane don't "take" until you do this.

3. Create a new location (using the steps outlined earlier in the chapter), switch to that location, and then switch back to your original location.

   The simplest way to perform a location swap is to create a new location that has no active ports (name it Nothing Active, for example) and then switch to it. Wait a few seconds and then switch back to the location that's giving you problems. With luck, the problem will be gone.

4. Create a new Location, and set it up with the same network settings as the original Location.

   If the new Location works properly, delete the original Location item.

5. Assuming you got the "stack not running" error in Terminal (as described in the previous section), type `sudo appletalk -u en0` (that's a zero at the end), entering your password when asked. Next, type `appletalk -s`. If this fix worked, you should get a screen full of AppleTalk info instead of the error message.

   Note: Enter en1 or en2, as appropriate (instead of en0), depending on the port identified as using AppleTalk.

6. Zap the PRAM on your Mac by restarting and holding down Command-Option-P-R until you hear three chimes. Thereafter, your Mac will start up normally.

   Some AppleTalk settings are stored in PRAM. Thus, if your PRAM gets corrupted, it can cause problems with AppleTalk connections.

7. Delete the Network Preferences file, or all files in the SystemConfiguration folder, as described in "Take Note: Deleting SystemConfiguration Folder Files," later in this chapter.

Troubleshooting wireless connections

If you have a wireless or AirPort network for local networking or Internet access, and you are having connection problems, the following suggestions can help you isolate the problem. If you use AirPort or a wireless Internet router for Internet access and are having connection problems, try the steps suggested here before troubleshooting your Internet connection itself.

Note: To help in your diagnosis, first try to determine whether the problem affects all wireless clients or just some. Similarly, does the problem prevent Internet access only, or does it prevent all wireless access (for example, Internet and file sharing)? The answers to these questions will help you locate the specific cause. For example, if a problem affects all clients, it is most likely with the Base Station software or hardware; if it is instead with just one client, it is most likely with that client's software or hardware.

Switch Locations. From the Network System Preferences pane, switching to a new Location and back again—or creating and using a replacement Location—can fix a variety of AirPort-related problems:

- It may allow you to choose Turn AirPort On from the AirPort menu, which would not work before.

- It may get an AirPort network to appear in the AirPort menu or Internet Connect application, when it would not show up before.

- It may get AirPort to be listed in the Show pop-up menu in the Network System Preferences pane when it was not present before, even though it was enabled in the Network Port Configurations section.

Figure 8.53

The Locations pop-up menu in the Network System Preferences pane. See also Figure 8.19.

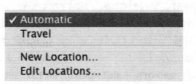

Check Network Port Configurations. You might think that the most reliable way to set up a Location for AirPort would be make it the only port configuration enabled in the Network Port Configurations section. However, I've encountered cases in which an AirPort connection would not work unless Ethernet was also enabled.

This situation leads to another variation on this theme: The problem may be specific to how you set up Network Port Configurations in the Network System Preferences pane. For example, if you have two ports enabled, and the port you want to use is listed second in the Network Port Configurations list, the connection may not work. More specifically, if Ethernet is at the top of the list (especially if you have an Ethernet cable that does not lead to an active network connected to the Mac's Ethernet port), the Mac may not make the AirPort connection. The solution is to switch the order of the network ports, placing AirPort at the top.

The same solution applies if Internet Connect claims you have a valid AirPort connection, but you cannot access the Internet.

Restart the Mac. As is the case with a variety of symptoms, restarting the Mac may get AirPort working properly again. Restarting is especially likely to be helpful if your Mac can locate a network, but, when you select to join it, you get an error message that says, "There was an error attempting to join the network {*name of network*}."

Unplug the AirPort Base Station (or wireless router) and plug it back in. This can fix an assortment of ills, such as renewing a dead DHCP lease issued from your ISP.

There is also a reported problem when using some versions of AirPort Extreme Base Station firmware, where a Mac with an AirPort card spontaneously loses contact with the Base Station; contact typically returns again in a few minutes. Unplugging and then replugging the Base Station can speed recovery.

Downgrading or upgrading to a different version of the Base Station firmware is the long-term fix. After doing this, I would again unplug the Base Station; leave it unplugged for at least 20 minutes and then plug it back in. Check Apple's discussion boards for the latest specific advice.

Check software versions. The preceding firmware problem aside, it's generally advised that you use the latest available versions of software for your Base Station and AirPort cards. As one particularly nasty example, if you install an AirPort Extreme card in your Mac, without first updating to an Extreme-compatible version of the AirPort software (as included on the CD that comes with the Extreme card), you can get a kernel panic on startup.

Remove wireless from the equation. If you're having trouble connecting to an AirPort or wireless network, and you're also set up to connect via Ethernet, switch to Ethernet (adding the cable, if needed) to see whether you can connect.

If you are able to connect, you know that you have a wireless connection problem. However, if you aren't able to connect via Ethernet, either, you have a more general connection problem—one that is not specific to your AirPort connection.

Conversely, if you're able to connect to other local computers via AirPort but can't get Internet access via AirPort, this confirms that the problem is not with the AirPort Base Station directly but rather with the Internet settings or connection.

SEE: • "Troubleshooting routers," later in this chapter.

Check that your AirPort card(s) are seated properly. If the problem appears to be with AirPort, but with only one Mac or Apple laptop, check to see that the computer's AirPort card is installed and seated properly. This procedure is an especially important first step for PowerBooks and iBooks, because the added movement and bumping that occur with a laptop are more likely to cause an AirPort card to come loose than on a desktop Mac.

Check that your AirPort card is active. Launch Internet Connect and verify that your AirPort card is active. If it is, the Internet Connect window should read AirPort Power: On. If not, click the Turn AirPort On button.

Alternatively, if you launch Network Utility and select Ethernet Interface (en1) (or whichever interface corresponds to AirPort) from the pop-up menu in the Info screen, you can check the AirPort connection. Note: You can tell which setting is for a wireless connection by looking at the last line, which will read Model Wireless Adapter (802.11) or something similar. If the Link Status line states Active, your AirPort connection is working.

SEE: • "Diagnosing Internet problems with Network Utility," earlier in this chapter.

Check for AirPort signal-level strength and channel interference. As signal strength weakens, your AirPort connection will slow. Thus, a Web page that takes a few seconds to load when the connection is at full strength may take a minute or more to load when strength is reduced. If signal strength gets too low, you lose the connection altogether—even if all settings and connections are correct. Thus, it is desirable to keep the signal as strong as possible. You can check the signal level via either the AirPort menu bar icon or the Signal Level graph in Internet Connect.

To increase the signal strength of your AirPort connection, try one or more of the following:

- In the simplest cases, a weak signal level may mean that your computer is too far from the Base Station, or that the Base Station is not facing in an ideal direction. Moving your Mac closer to the Base Station and/or rotating the Base Station slightly may fix this.

- The cause of the weak signal may be wireless channel interference. More specifically, the technology behind AirPort and wireless networking uses a narrow range of radio frequencies around 2.4 GHz range. Unfortunately, that range is close to that used by many wireless telephones and other consumer wireless devices (as well as being identical to the range of frequencies used by Bluetooth). Some users have reported problems with their AirPort and wireless connections when in the vicinity of other consumer wireless devices. If you experience such problems and verify the cause, the obvious solution is to avoid such wireless devices or turn them off (including Bluetooth if you're not using it) when you're using your AirPort connection.

- If you are using an AirPort Base Station, launch the AirPort Admin Utility and select different channels from the Channel pop-up menu until you find one that provides better connectivity. Each channel has a slightly different transmission frequency. If you're in the vicinity of other AirPort networks, and these networks are using the same AirPort channel, your connection reliability and data-transfer rates can vary greatly depending upon the channel you select. Client computers connecting to the router or Base Station will switch to the appropriate channel automatically. Note: Non-AirPort wireless routers typically also offer ways to change channels.

- Enable Use Interference Robustness in the AirPort menu. This option is used to minimize connection problems due to interfering devices nearby (such as a microwave oven, a cordless phone, or anything else using the 2.4 GHz band). However, enabling this option is likely to reduce the overall range of your AirPort connection—which means you shouldn't use it unless you're already having connection problems. To use this feature, the Enable Interference Robustness option must also be enabled in the Wireless Options screen of the AirPort Admin Utility.

Do general AirPort troubleshooting. If all else seems well, it's time to recheck your initial AirPort setup. If even this fails to locate a solution, you may need a hardware replacement or repair; contact Apple for advice.

SEE: • **"Take Note: Setting Up an AirPort Base Station and Network," earlier in this chapter.**

   • **"Troubleshooting Sharing," later in this chapter, for related information.**

Troubleshooting routers

If you're using a router, wireless or wired, checking whether it's the cause of an Internet-connection problem is one of the first things you should do. If you have set up your router incorrectly, or if your ISP has taken steps to prevent the use of such routers, no amount of other troubleshooting will solve your connection problems.

A first step is to reset your router. You typically do this by turning it off (unplugging it if necessary) for a few seconds and then turning it back on (or plugging it back in). Sometimes, this alone will fix a problem. Alternatively, if the router has a reset button, use that.

Otherwise, the best way to determine whether the router is the problem is to disconnect the router and set up your computer to access your ISP directly. For most dial-up modem connections, this procedure means connecting the phone wire to the phone port on the Mac (so as to access the internal modem). For broadband connections, connect your broadband (cable/DSL) modem directly to your Macintosh via the Ethernet port.

You will likely have to change the settings in the Network System Preferences pane to reflect this change. For example, if you had been using a manual Ethernet setting to connect your Mac to your router (probably with an IP address such as 192.168.1.101), you may need to shift to DHCP (if that's what your cable or DSL modem setup requires), or—if you have a static IP address—you may need to enter that. To make it easier to switch back to the "router" configuration later, set up a separate location with these alternative settings in advance of any problems. This allows you to switch back and forth easily.

If, after connecting directly, you're able to establish a working Internet connection, the problem is not with your computer or with the connection itself, but with your router or the way you have your Mac configured to access the router. In such cases, consider the following:

Check router TCP/IP settings. I'm assuming you already checked the TCP/IP settings in Network System Preferences. However, with a router, you also need to check whether the router's TCP/IP settings are correct.

SEE: • "Configuring a router," earlier in this chapter.

Check for firmware updates. The router may need a firmware update to correct some bug; check with the vendor to see whether a newer version is available. One firmware version of Apple's AirPort Base Station, for example, had a problem connecting to Comcast's cable Internet services. The fix required an update to the AirPort Base Station firmware.

Check for the MAC address and other ISP/router interaction problems. The cause of a problem may be the interaction between your ISP and your router. For example, some broadband ISPs check the MAC address of the computer before allowing a connection. If the ISP is looking for the MAC address of your Mac and instead finds the MAC address of your router, the connection will fail. One solution is to contact your ISP and request that it update the MAC address in its database. Otherwise, your router may include a feature called Mac Address Cloning, which allows you to enter the MAC address of your computer in a special field in your router's software. The router sends this address to the ISP, fooling the ISP into thinking that the router has the MAC address it's seeking.

SEE: • "Using a Router" and "Take Note: What Are the TCP/IP Settings?" for related information.

If you still can't connect to the Internet, even after taking the router out of the equation, the router is not the direct cause. In this case, proceed with the troubleshooting advice in the following sections. You can reconnect your router after you have determined the cause and solution.

TAKE NOTE ▶ 169.254.x.x and 192.42.249.x IP Addresses: DHCP and AirPort

Both the 169 and 192 IP addresses described here are indications that something has gone wrong with your AirPort and/or DHCP connection.

- **169.254.x.x.** If you're connecting to the Internet via a DHCP server or using dynamically assigned DHCP IP addresses to route connections via a router, you may find an IP address in the 169.254.x.x range (169.254.0.0 to 169.254.254.255) in your Mac's TCP/IP settings. This address is used when the DHCP server fails to make a connection.

  You may see this address, for example, if the cable service is down when you're trying to connect to the Internet via a cable modem. Or you may see it on a computer attempting to connect to an AirPort Base Station if the computer has not connected to the Base Station or is unable to do so.

- **192.42.249.12.** This address is assigned to Graphite Base Stations. If you update the Base Station software, it will also revert to this address. This situation is perfectly normal. Note: 192.42.249.13 is assigned after a hard reset of the Base Station. You then need to re-enter your previous settings.

  The 192.42.249.12 address also occurs, however, if you're trying to connect from a Base Station to an ISP via DHCP, and it cannot make a connection. The likely cause may be at your ISP's end, or it may be with your Internet settings. To check and/or change the Base Station settings, use AirPort Admin Utility. An update to the AirPort software or firmware may also solve this problem.

For more specific guidance on exactly what to do to fix these errors, check the following Apple Knowledge Base documents: http://docs.info.apple.com/article.html?artnum=58618 and http://docs.info.apple.com/article.html?artnum=58619.

SEE: • "Take Note: Setting Up an AirPort Base Station and Network," earlier in this chapter.

Troubleshooting dial-up modems

Despite the proliferation of broadband, dial-up connections are still the most common way for home users to access the Internet. These days, most dial-up connections are made via the internal modem included with every Mac. If your modem fails to connect (or if it appears to connect but no Internet applications can access the connection), and the advice in the preceding sections didn't solve your problem, here are some additional steps specific to standard dial-up modems.

Check your Modem screen settings. In addition to verifying that the TCP/IP and PPP settings are correct in the respective screens in the internal-modem configuration of Network System Preferences (you did that already, right?), make sure that the settings are correct in the Modem screen. If you don't have the correct modem model selected, for example, you may experience poor connections, or you may not be able to connect at all. In addition, make sure that you've selected the correct dialing method (tone or pulse).

Finally, some phone systems that include voicemail beep when you have messages instead of providing the standard dial tone. If you use such a system, uncheck the "Wait for dial tone before dialing" check box.

SEE: • "Take Note: Modem Scripts and Terminal Scripts," earlier in this chapter.

Check Network Port Configurations and Location settings. I discussed the troubleshooting value of switching Locations and Network Port Configuration settings in previous sections of this chapter. Here is yet one more variation on the theme.

Once, when my cable modem went down, I decided to use my internal modem via a dial-up ISP account that I maintained for just such emergencies. It seemed to work OK—Internet Connect indicated that I had successfully connected. But no services worked. I couldn't load Web pages or get email. It turned out that the problem was caused by a glitch in how network ports work. Even though I was dialing in to my ISP using the modem, the network software was still trying to connect through the Ethernet port to the nonfunctional cable modem.

The reason for this is that Mac OS X considered my Ethernet connection to have priority over my modem: Because it detected a valid connection to the cable or DSL modem, it refused to let the dial-up modem provide Internet access—despite the fact that an apparently good dial-up connection had been made.

The solution is to do one of the following:

- Temporarily move Internal Modem to the top of the ports list in the Network Port Configurations screen (accessible from Network System Preferences' Show pop-up menu). You can change the order back when the cable modem is working again.

- Create a separate Location for the modem in which only the Internal Modem setting is active. Switch to this Location.

- Unplug the Ethernet cable (that goes to your cable modem) from your computer.

Use Internet Connect's Connection Log. If you're having trouble figuring out why your modem connection is not working, checking the error messages in the Connection Log may provide a clue. To do this, follow these steps:

1. Launch Internet Connect.
2. From the toolbar click the Internal Modem button (if it's not already selected).
3. From the Window menu choose Connection Log.

You can view information about past connection attempts, or you can use Internet Connect to attempt a dial-up connection and watch the log generate in real time. Even if *you* aren't able to identify the problem, if you end up contacting your ISP for technical support, this log may be useful.

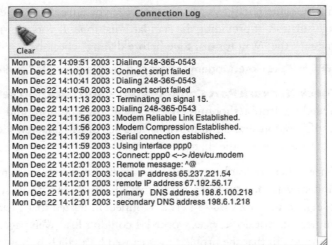

Figure 8.54

An example of the output that appears in the Connection Log, as selected from the Window menu of Internet Connect.

Use verbose logging. If the standard Connection Log doesn't provide enough helpful information, you can enable a more detailed logging procedure called *verbose logging*. To do so, follow these steps:

1. Open the Network System Preferences pane.

2. From the Show pop-up menu, choose the modem configuration you have set up (for example, Internal Modem).

3. Click the PPP button to access the PPP screen.

4. Click the PPP Options button.

5. In the Options screen (see Figure 8.16), check the "Use verbose logging" box.

6. Click OK.

7. Click the Apply Now button to apply your new settings.

    If you already had an Internet Connect window open, this step will generally cause it to close and then reopen.

From this point on, when you choose Connection Log in Internet Connect, the log will contain much more detail about every step of the connection process.

Deselect echo packets. In some cases, the PPP connection to the Internet will not succeed if a PPP server does not reply to LCP Echo packets. The solution is to deselect "Send PPP echo packets" from PPP Options in the PPP screen of the Internal Modem settings of the Network System Preferences pane.

Deselect error correction. Deselect "Enable error correction and compression in modem" from the Modem screen of the Network pane of System Preferences if a modem connection cannot be established or is unreliable. Note: One major cause for this problem was fixed in Mac OS X 10.2.5.

Deactivate phone-line features. Many phone lines have features such as call waiting that can cause frequent disconnects. If you have such features, check with your phone company about how to disable them when you're online.

End hanging disconnects. After selecting to disconnect from your modem, you may occasionally find that the Mac declines your request and remains connected. This "hanging disconnect" can be solved by quitting certain background processes (pppd, modemd, AppleModemOnHold) in Terminal or Activity Monitor. A simpler solution is to get a freeware application called End Hanging Disconnect (from Useful Software) and run it. Otherwise, the only solution is to restart your Mac.

Check your phone line. Unplug your modem and hook a telephone up to it to verify that you have a dial tone and can dial out. This step will also allow you to figure out whether other phones in the house are in use or off the hook, thus preventing your Mac from connecting.

Have your phone line checked. If you are able to connect only intermittently and experience frequent dropped connections, it's possible that the phone lines in your home, or in the area around it, are simply of poor quality. You can contact your phone company to check your phone line quality.

Contact your ISP. If you've gone through every step mentioned here and *still* can't access the Internet, it's probably time to contact your ISP and see whether it can figure out the problem.

Troubleshooting DSL, cable, and PPPoE connections

Broadband connections are the fastest-growing type of Internet connection. They tend to be more reliable than dial-up modem connections, they are much faster, and they are generally available 24/7. Whenever your Mac is on, you're on the Internet (or can get on immediately without having to wait through a lengthy connection/login procedure). Things can still go wrong, however. If the more general advice in the preceding sections didn't help, here are some additional steps specific to standard broadband modems.

Reset your modem. Turn your DSL or cable modem off (or unplug it), and leave it off for 2 to 3 minutes. (If your DSL or cable modem has a reset button, press it first.) After turning it back on, wait a few minutes for it to resynchronize with your ISP, if necessary. Many times, this step will fix a finicky Internet connection.

Restart your Mac. If the reset alone had no beneficial effect, shut down your Mac and restart it.

Fix "configd not available" error. If the system configuration server process (configd) on your Mac unexpectedly quits, DHCP and BootP choices may not be available in the TCP/IP screen and/or you may not be able to change any other settings in the Network System Preferences pane. If this happens, the following alert message will appear when you click the Apply Now button: "The System Configuration server (configd) is not available." The solution is to restart your Mac.

Make sure your computer is properly connected to the DSL or cable modem. Most broadband modems have an indicator light (or lights) that verify that your computer is connected properly. If these lights aren't on, recheck the connecting cable and try a different cable, if possible.

Use Internet Connect's Connection Log for PPPoE connections. If your ISP uses PPPoE, you can use the Connection Log that Mac OS X keeps in order to see detailed information about your connection attempts. The log often includes error messages that indicate the source of the problem, which hopefully provides direction as to the solution. To set this up, click the Built-in Ethernet button (used for PPPoE) from Internet Connect's toolbar before opening the Connection Log.

Fix automatic PPPoE connection failures. If you click the PPPoE Options button (located in the PPPoE screen of the Ethernet port of the Network System Preferences pane), an option called Connect Automatically When Needed appears. If you enable this option, PPPoE should automatically make a connection when you launch an application, such as a Web browser, that requires an Internet connection. This may fail to work if you manually disconnected the last time an automatic connection occurred. Automatic connection is also disabled after three failed connection attempts. The solution is to manually start your PPPoE connection and (if needed) re-enable the automatic option.

Contact your ISP. In my experience, 99 percent of broadband problems (beyond those fixed by resetting your modem) are not your fault—and you cannot fix them. This is especially true of problems that occur spontaneously (that is, when you haven't made any changes or additions to your Mac setup). In such cases, the first thing I recommend to do is contact your broadband ISP. The ISP will often inform you that there's a temporary problem with the service in your area and that it's working to fix the problem. In such cases, there's nothing to do but wait. Occasionally, the ISP may need to *reprovision* your modem (a technique the cable company can perform via the Internet). This task is usually accomplished within a few hours of your call. As a last resort, the ISP may need to make a service call to check your connection or replace your modem.

Note: If your modem is connected via a router or any sort of wireless connection, some broadband ISPs will refuse to help you with potential router-related problems, claiming they don't support or (in some cases) even permit their use. If this happens, temporarily removing your router from your setup may facilitate getting help from your ISP. The fact that you use a Mac may make matters worse, as many ISPs are less skilled in dealing with Mac setups than with Windows PC setups. If your ISP proves unhelpful, and the advice in this book is not sufficient to solve your problem, you may want to seek help from a consultant or other technical support professional.

Optimize your broadband network. Software such as Broadband Optimizer (a startup item) and MOX Optimize (an application from Infosoft) allow you to increase the memory buffers used for TCP transfers, so that data comes in bigger chunks at a time. Ideally, this should result in faster transfers when using a broadband connection, which should translate into faster loading of Web pages, downloading of files, and so on. To confirm that this "optimization" has occurred, type the following command in Terminal before and after enabling the optimizing: sysctl -a. From the long list of output, check the values (##) in the following four items; they should change after optimizing:

```
net.inet.tcp.sendspace: #####
net.inet.tcp.recvspace: ##
net.inet.tcp.delayed_ack: ##
net.inet.udp.recvspace: ##
```

TAKE NOTE ▶ Deleting SystemConfiguration Folder Files

In the /Library/Preferences folder in Panther is a folder called SystemConfiguration. Inside this folder are a number of .plist files. Most of them have to do with networking settings. These include NetworkInterfaces.plist, com.apple.airport.preferences.plist, and preferences.plist. If you're having networking-related problems, deleting one or more of these files (or even the entire folder) may fix them. Any administrator has access to these files.

If you delete these files, new default copies are created—which means you lose your customized settings. For that reason, it's best to save a copy of the original files in another location before deleting them. If it turns out that removing them has no effect, you can replace the new copies with the originals rather than re-create your custom settings. Even better, make a backup copy of this folder when everything is working properly; if you have problems later, you can replace the problem copy with the good backup. You can store the backup copy anywhere you're able to access, ideally somewhere in your Home directory.

Note: If you're reinstalling Mac OS X—and choose not to select the Archive and Install option to preserve network settings, as described in Chapter 3—saving a copy of this folder will still allow you to preserve network settings. Just replace the newly installed copy with the copy you saved (this assumes that both the pre- and post-reinstalled versions of the OS use the same format for these files—which is not the case when going from Jaguar to Panther, as noted below).

continues on next page

TAKE NOTE ▶ Deleting SystemConfiguration Folder Files *continued*

The following represents some more specific information and advice regarding the SystemConfiguration folder.

preferences.plist. If you cannot connect to the Internet from your Mac, and you are able to verify that your Internet connection is functional (perhaps because you can connect to the Internet via a second Mac), the problem could be that the preferences.plist file has become damaged. This preferences file can cause a number of networking problems, including network loss after sleep, an inability to log in, and even an inability to start up.

SEE: • "Take Note: Miscellaneous Crashes," in Chapter 5, for details.

In such cases, assuming you can log in, you should go ahead and remove or delete this file—though not until after you've saved a copy of all of your settings (so that you can re-create them more easily). After deleting the file, log out (or restart) and log back in. Reenter your network settings. Now try to connect to the Internet as you normally do. Assuming the problem was with the preferences.plist file, you should now be able to connect.

NetworkInterfaces.plist and com.apple.airport.preferences.plist. If just deleting the preferences.plist file fails to work, you may have success if you additionally delete NetworkInterfaces.plist and (if the problem involves an AirPort connection) com.apple .airport.preferences.plist. After doing this, again open the Network System Preferences pane and reenter your settings.

Good preferences, bad connections. In some cases, the preferences.plist file is in good shape and your connections are correct, but for some reason Mac OS X just gets "confused" (for lack of a better term). In these situations a simple restart will often solve the problem. However, you may be able to avoid restarting by resetting the interface/port used for the connection having problems. To do so, follow these steps in Terminal:

1. Type ifconfig -a, then locate the interface that is giving you problems.

   This interface will likely be en0 for the internal Ethernet port or en1 for an AirPort card. If the Terminal output indicates that the port in question is inactive (when you believe it should be active), move on to step 2.

2. Type sudo ifconfig en0 inet up (or replace en0 with en1, if applicable).

3. Type ifconfig -a, and look at the interface entry. The port should be active, and various data should now be listed for it. If so, networking should work.

The Jaguar way. In Jaguar, these files end in .xml rather than .plist, and are located in /var/db/SystemConfiguration. The files are owned by root, which means that you cannot simply drag them to the Trash to delete them. In addition, because they're located in the invisible /var folder, you can't easily browse to them from the Finder. You can always use Terminal to locate and delete the files (as described in "Using Unix to delete files," in Chapter 6). Or you can select Go to Folder from the Finder's Go menu, and then type /var/db/SystemConfiguration to reveal the files in a Finder window. However, you will still need to use one of the utilities for working with root-owned files (as covered more generally in "Item cannot be placed in Trash or Trash cannot be emptied," in Chapter 6).

TAKE NOTE ▶ Network Connection Setting Causes Stall at Startup

If your network is set up to access the Internet via a cable or DSL modem, and that connection is not working at startup, you will get a significant delay at startup, most notably at those points where the network is accessed (when "Initializing network" and "Configuring network time" appear onscreen). If this happens, try these solutions:

• Make sure that your cable modem connection is working. If it's not, use the advice in this chapter to determine whether the problem is something you can fix (such as a domain name entered incorrectly in the TCP/IP settings) or something that the ISP needs to fix.

• As a temporary work-around until your Internet connection is fixed, disconnect the Ethernet cable from the Mac. Doing this should eliminate the startup delay.

I have used this slowdown as a diagnostic tool to quickly determine whether a change I made helped or hurt my attempt to fix a connection problem. If I restart and get this delay, I know that I still have problems.

Note: Using manually assigned IP addresses instead of DHCP for a local network can help avoid this type of network stall at startup.

SEE: • **"Take Note: What Are the TCP/IP Settings?" earlier in this chapter, for related advice.**

• **"Startup items" and "Blue-screen crashes and stalls," in Chapter 5, for related information on startup problems related to network settings.**

Troubleshooting Internet Applications

In this section, I cover the more common problems that can occur with Internet applications—primarily Web browsers and email clients.

Troubleshooting Web browsers

If you're having problems browsing the Web, consider the following.

Fix page-loading problems. You may find that you can't access a certain Web site but *can* access others—a symptom that may be accompanied by an error message like one of the following: "The specified server could not be found" or "A connection failure has occurred." If the problem truly is limited to a specific site, the cause most likely lies with the site itself, not your connection.

If these messages appear for all sites you try to reach, however, you probably don't have a successful Internet connection. In this case, first go back to the preceding sections of this chapter for advice.

The same logic holds true if a particular site loads significantly more slow than most other sites—even if you don't get any error messages.

If you get a "404" or "Page not found" error message when trying to load a Web page, this means that the browser was unable to find that particular page; however, since these particular errors are returned by the Web server itself, it means you've at least succeeded in connecting to the server (or *a* server), so the problem is not connection-related. If other pages from the same site load successfully, you may have simply entered the URL incorrectly. Otherwise, the Web-site administrator may have deleted the page or changed its URL.

The next section, on DNS-related problems, covers another cause of these symptoms.

SEE: • **"Diagnosing Internet problems with Network Utility," earlier in this chapter, for related advice.**

• **"Maximizing Performance," in Chapter 6, for related information on Internet application performance.**

Figure 8.55

Three Web browser error messages: (top) the message that may appear if your Internet connection is broken; (middle) the message that may appear if you typed a Web address incorrectly or the site's server is down; (bottom) the message that may appear for any of the cited reasons.

Fix DNS-related problems. You may have a valid connection to your ISP and the Internet, yet still have trouble accessing some or all Web sites by domain name. In such cases, you may be able to ping an IP address but cannot ping or browse the corresponding domain name. Assuming the problem doesn't originate with Web pages that are not loading, as covered in the previous section, the problem is most likely with your DNS settings or the DNS lookup. (*DNS* refers to the process by which domain names are converted into numeric addresses.)

SEE: • **"Take Note: What Are the TCP/IP Settings?" earlier in this chapter.**

Another symptom of DNS problems is significant delays before a Web page will begin to load (however, the page then loads at normal speed).

If you suspect you have a DNS problem, try one or more of the following:

- **Use an IP address to diagnose a DNS problem.** One way to confirm that a problem is specific to domain *names* (rather than an Internet connection problem in general) is to attempt to load a Web page in a browser via its numeric IP address instead of its domain name. If, for example, Apple's IP address (for example, http://17.254.0.91) works just fine, but www.apple.com does not, you have a DNS problem.

  Of course, you need to know the numeric IP address of the problem Web site to test this out. Assuming you can get to the Web site (which may not be the case), you can obtain the IP address via the Ping screen in Network Utility (as described earlier in this chapter, in "Diagnosing Internet problems with Network Utility").

  If this happens with almost all sites that you try, you probably have a DNS problem on your end. If it only happens with one specific site, the source of the problem is likely at the site's end (which you cannot fix; you just have to wait and hope that they fix it).

  Note: Sites may have more than one IP address, and the addresses may change over time. The above IP address for www.apple.com worked at the time of this writing; however, it may not by the time you read this.

- **Check that your Domain Name Server is listed correctly.** A DNS problem at your end may mean that your DNS server information, as listed in the Network System Preferences pane, is incorrect. To check, open the Network System Preferences pane and click the TCP/IP screen for the port you use to access the Internet. Verify that the values entered in the Domain Name Servers box, if any, match the settings given to you by your ISP (or that the box is blank, if your ISP has instructed you to leave it blank). Because domain-name servers convert domain names to numerical IP-address equivalents, mistakes in this setting may prevent you from accessing domain names.

  Note that if you switch network locations in Mac OS X, and the location contains multiple network configurations (modem, Ethernet, and AirPort), it generally takes a few seconds for Mac OS X to determine which of the configurations it will use. During this delay, you will not be able to resolve domain names properly. This is a good reason to disable unused network interfaces and configurations in the Network Port Configurations section.

  SEE: • The "Domain Name Servers" section of "Take Note: What Are the TCP/IP Settings?" earlier in this chapter, for important related information.

- **Use Network Utility's Lookup screen or Terminal's host command.** If the DNS problem is specific to just one Web site, sometimes you can fix it by "waking up" the lookup for that domain.

One way to do this is via Network Utility. To do so, go to the Lookup screen of Network Utility; type the name of the problem domain (for example, www.macfixit.com); and click Lookup (typically with Default Information selected from the pop-up menu). The numeric address will be listed in the output as follows:

```
Name: www.macfixit.com
Address: 66.179.48.115
```

If this fails to work, enable the "Use 'dig' in place of 'nslookup' " option and try again. If this works, you should see output that includes two lines that look something like the following:

```
;; ANSWER SECTION:
www.macfixit.com.2190 IN A 66.179.48.115
```

In the above example, 66.179.48.115 is the numeric IP address for www.macfixit.com.

Alternatively, you can use the host command in Terminal. In particular, for the MacFixIt example, you would type the following:

```
host -a www.macfixit.com
```

This would result in output that looked something like this:

```
www.macfixit.com        844 IN  A       66.179.48.115
```

- **Renew your DHCP lease.** If your ISP uses DHCP to provide you with an IP address, this means procuring a new dynamically assigned IP address from your ISP. Doing so may help with DNS issues (in fact, it may also help connection problems that extend beyond DNS issues). To do this, click the Renew DHCP Lease button in the TCP/IP screen of the Ethernet or AirPort section of the Network System Preferences pane.

  SEE: • **"Ethernet (including cable and DSL Internet)," earlier in this chapter, for more details.**

  There are also shareware utilities, such as Kristofer Szymanski's Cocktail, that include an option to renew your lease.

  Note that if you use a router, this approach won't work—you need to request a new DHCP lease using the router itself. Your router's internal software may include an option to renew the lease.

- **Flush the lookupd cache.** The lookupd daemon maintains a cache on your hard drive of recently accessed information of all sorts (not just for domain names). If the cache becomes corrupt, this can cause DNS-related symptoms. The solution here is to flush the cache. To do so, launch Terminal and type the following:

```
lookupd -flushcache
```

Note: The lookupd -statistics command provides a summary of lookupd information. Use this command before and after a flushcache command to confirm that the cache has actually been emptied. If the cache did empty, the number in the Total Memory line of the output (for example, # Total Memory: 58448) should be substantially lower.

In most cases, flushing the cache will fix the lookupd problem. In rare circumstances, however, you may need to kill the lookupd process altogether from Terminal (it will be restarted automatically). The cache gets flushed as part of this process, but other settings are set to a default as well.

SEE: • "Killing processes from Terminal" and "Technically Speaking: Kill Signals," in Chapter 5, for details.

Solve Java problems. If you're having trouble using Java (either running an applet within a Web browser or running a stand-alone Java application), make sure you're using the latest update of Apple's Java software. The initial implementations of Java for Mac OS X had numerous bugs, which continue to be fixed in updates.

Delete corrupt browser preferences. This troubleshooting mainstay from the Classic Mac OS is still valid in Mac OS X. As is the case with any application, a corrupt preferences file (and sometimes, even a corrupt bookmarks or favorites file) can prevent a Web browser from working properly. In such cases, deleting the corrupt file solves the problem. To locate the file for your browser, see "Take Note: Web Browser Settings and Favorites Files," later in this chapter. As is the case anytime you delete preferences files, it's a good idea to back up the file before deleting it: If deleting the file doesn't solve the problem, you can replace the newly created default file with your backup. This avoids unnecessarily losing all of the information contained in the deleted file (such as your list of Favorites).

Delete Internet-related cache files. Web browsers maintain cache files that help speed the reloading of recently viewed pages. Unfortunately, a corrupt cache file can cause problems in loading pages.

For example, for Internet Explorer, you enable the cache by selecting either "Once per session" or Always from Explorer's Cache settings in the Advanced section of its Preferences. After doing this, Explorer stores its cache files in ~/Library/Caches/MS Internet Cache. All of the files here end in cache.waf. Enabling this cache may or may not improve the loading of Web pages; experiment to see which method works best for you. More important, deleting these cache files may clear up problems with pages that will not update or load properly. To do so, simply click the Empty Now button in the Preferences dialog. You can similarly delete Explorer's record of recently visited sites by clicking Clear History.

Note: These caches are separate from the download cache that Explorer maintains for files that are downloaded to your drive. The download cache file is stored in ~/Library/Preferences/Explorer/Temporary Files. There is no way to empty or delete this file from Explorer's Preferences dialog. If you want to delete it, possibly because the file has gotten very large, quit Internet Explorer and then drag the file to the Trash.

For Safari, you can more simply select Empty Cache from the Safari menu.

Note: There are numerous utilities, such as Cocktail, that delete the cache files listed here as well as other ones.

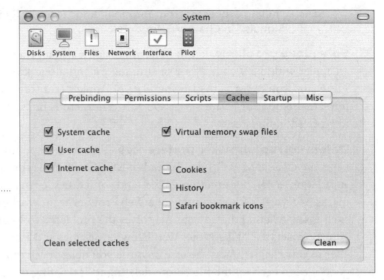

Figure 8.56

Cocktail's options to delete Internet cache files, as well as your browser's Cookies and History files.

Make your browser compatible. If you are using a browser other than Internet Explorer or Netscape (and its derivatives), you may have problems loading certain pages that only work with one or both of these standard browsers. In some cases, alternative browsers, such as Apple's Safari, can mimic the settings of these default standard browsers, allowing problem Web sites to work properly.

SEE: • "Take Note: Troubleshooting Safari," below, for details.

In general, if a page does not load or work in one browser, try another.

TAKE NOTE ▶ Troubleshooting Safari

Apple's Safari is now the default browser installed with Mac OS X, replacing Internet Explorer. With that in mind, here's a brief collection of troubleshooting tips specific to Safari (some of which admittedly overlap with the discussion in the main text):

Installation advice. Do not attempt to install Safari by dragging a copy of the application from one volume to another. Always use the Installer. Otherwise, Safari is likely to not work properly.

Reinstallation advice. If you have more than one version of Safari on your drive, and you run the Safari Installer, it will upgrade the first copy it finds. This may not be the copy you use. The easiest way to avoid this is to delete all but one copy of Safari from your drive.

continues on next page

TAKE NOTE ▶ Troubleshooting Safari *continued*

Using the Debug menu; mimicking other browsers. Safari has a hidden menu that adds several technical features to the browser—one of which allows Safari to mimic a different browser, possibly getting Web pages to load that would not otherwise. To do so, follow these steps:

1. Enable Safari's Debug menu—either by using a utility like Gordon Byrnes's Safari Enhancer or by opening the ~/Library/Preferences/com.apple.Safari.plist file in Property List Editor and changing the `IncludeDebugMenu` property value from No to Yes. If this property does not exist, you will need to add it. You can instead launch Terminal and type `defaults write com.apple.Safari IncludeDebugMenu 1`.

2. Launch Safari, select the Debug menu, and choose User Agent. Now select the desired browser from the hierarchical menu. Safari will identify itself as the desired browser when it connects to Web servers.

If this does not allow the problem pages to load, disable Web Content options (as described later in this sidebar) or try using another browser.

Deleting the Times RO font. Although Mac OS X neither requires nor installs the Times RO font, certain third-party applications may install it. The problem is that after this font is installed, Safari may not load (or may only partially load) some Web pages. The solution is to uninstall the font.

Getting a longer Downloads list. Safari maintains a longer list of downloaded files than it shows in its Downloads window. To access the complete list, open the Downloads.plist file in ~/Library/Safari/. This folder is also the location of the files that contain the Bookmarks and History lists.

Using the Activity window. From Safari's Window menu select Activity to reveal a list of all links (for example, to other Web pages, image files, and so on) for the currently displayed page. Double-click any link to load it. If you're having trouble accessing a specific component of a Web page (for example, an image will not load), select this window. It should indicate which links are causing the error. Try double-clicking these links. If you're lucky (this works for me maybe 50 percent of the time), the linked items will now load—problem solved!

Reimporting bookmarks. The first time you launch Safari, it automatically imports bookmarks from Internet Explorer and Netscape Navigator. It never does this again. The problem is that if you still use Explorer and continue to add bookmarks, at some point you might want to reimport your updated list. One way to do this is to delete the com.apple.safari.plist file in ~/Library/Preferences (while Safari is not open). Safari should reimport bookmarks on its next launch. However, this also eliminates any preferences changes you've made via Safari's Preferences command. For a more elegant solution, follow these steps:

1. Open the com.apple.Safari.plist file in Property List Editor and locate the property called IEFavoritesWereImported. Note: There's a related one for Netscape called NetscapeAndMozilla-FavoritesWereImported; however, I'm only concerned with Explorer here.

continues on next page

2. You have two equally good options at this point: Either select the IEFavorites property and click the Delete button, or access the pop-up menu in the Value column for the IEFavorites item and change Yes to No.

3. Save your changes and close the document. The next time you launch Safari, it will import Explorer's current bookmarks, and the IEFavoritesWereImported property will be re-added (if you deleted it), and its value set to Yes. If you previously imported bookmarks from Explorer and did not delete them, the newly imported URLs will merge with the existing list.

Note: Safari may only partially import bookmarks from Explorer, stopping at some point in the process as if there were a maximum number of bookmarks that can be imported. If this happens, you can work around the problem by deleting all of the successfully imported bookmarks from Explorer and repeating the above procedure with the .plist file. The remaining bookmarks should now import. Save a copy of the ~/Library/Preferences/Explorer/Favorites.html file before doing any of this (and use it to replace the active copy when done with the import), if you want to preserve in Explorer the bookmarks you will be deleting.

QuickTime Plug-in. The QuickTime Plug-in.plugin file is located in /Library/Internet Plug-Ins. Obviously, you need it to play QuickTime movies in Safari. It is also used to provide support for an assortment of other file types, such as sound files (for example, AIFF and MP3) and graphic files (for example, PICT and TIFF). You can see the full list of supported (MIME) file types, as well as enable and disable the ones you want, by accessing the QuickTime System Preferences pane and clicking the "MIME settings" button in the Plug-In screen.

Solving unexpected quits (and other problems). If Safari crashes frequently, try any (or all) of the following to get it working again:

- **Use the Empty Cache or Reset Safari commands.** You may be able to use one of these commands (which you access from the Safari menu) to fix unexpected quit problems and an assortment of other glitches (such as pages' loading incorrectly or with missing content).

  The Empty Cache command does just what its name implies and is the more benign option. It deletes the files stored in ~/Library/Caches/Safari.

  The Reset Safari command zaps just about everything Safari-related (cache, cookies, and so on), restoring Safari to its state upon installation. The only thing you don't lose is your bookmarks file. Note: If you want to save your cookies (which may store items such as passwords for a Web site that you select to keep remembered) so that you can restore them—in case it turns out that deleting cookies does not fix the problem—save a copy of the ~/Library/Cookies/Cookies.plist file. To restore your cookies, drag the copy back to the Cookies folder and allow it to replace the newly created file.

  Utilities such as Safari Enhancer provide another means of deleting these files, including some that the Reset command may not remove (for example, the com.apple.Safari.plist file).

continues on next page

> **TAKE NOTE** ▶ **Troubleshooting Safari** *continued*
>
> - **Disable Web Content options.** Safari may crash when trying to load certain Web pages, especially ones that use Java or JavaScript. To determine whether this is the cause, go to the Security pane of Safari's Preferences and uncheck the three Enable items in the Web Content section (for example, Enable Java).
>
> - **Delete the QuickTime Plug-in plist file.** Quit Safari and then delete the com.apple .quicktime.plugin.preferences.plist file in ~/Library/Preferences. Now restart Safari. This is a confirmed cause and solution for one type of Safari crash.
>
> - **Remove third-party plug-ins.** Remove third-party items located in /Library/Internet Plug-Ins and ~/Library/Internet Plug-ins. If this eliminates the symptom, use trial and error to determine the offending plug-in. If the removal has no effect, return the plug-ins to their respective folders.
>
> - **Try general troubleshooting.** Try more general troubleshooting fixes for unexpected quits, as described in Chapter 5.
>
> **SEE:** • **"Technically Speaking: Internetconfig Preferences," earlier in this chapter, for related information regarding unexpected quits in Web browsers.**

Figure 8.57

Safari's (left) Activity window and (right) "secret" Debug menu.

TAKE NOTE ▶ Location Files and Browser Links

A Web page may include several types of links. Most will link to other Web pages (using the http:// protocol). Others may open your email application and open a message to a particular address (using the mailto:// protocol). Homemade Web pages may even have links to files on your Desktop (using the file:// protocol).

If you click a link in Safari and then drag it to the Desktop, an Internet Location file will be created. This file is simply a marker that, when opened, performs the same action that would occur if you had clicked the link on the Web page—that is, it goes to the selected Web site, email address, or file on your drive.

Each of these different location files has its own file extension. These extensions are hidden in the Finder (unless you enabled the Finder's "Show all file extensions" option). For example, the extension for http links is *.webloc;* the one for email addresses is .mailloc; and the one for files on your drive is .fileloc. If the link is an FTP site, an .ftploc file is created. If the link is a server address (using the afp:// protocol), the file will have an .afploc extension. (I covered .afploc files earlier in this chapter in their capacity to quickly access File Sharing servers.)

Note: These location files can be created any time the selected text is dragged to the Desktop or a Finder window. For example, if you select a URL from a text document in AppleWorks or from Safari's Address text box and drag it to the Desktop, a .webloc (Web Internet Location) file will be created. This is similar to creating text clippings (which have a .textClipping extension) and graphic clippings (which have a .pictClipping extension).

Note: If you select and drag a URL from Safari's Address text box to create a .webloc file, the file's name will be the URL (for example, http://www.apple.com). However, if you select and drag the mini-icon to the left of the URL, the file's name will be the title of the Web page that appears at the top of the Safari window (for example, Apple).

Note: If the extension is not visible in the Finder, and you don't want to enable the Finder preference to make it visible, the extension for a given file can always be viewed via the Name & Extension field of the Get Info window for the file.

Note: If you drag the icon of a location file to a Terminal window, the pathname of the file *will not* appear (as is typical, and explained more in Chapter 10). Instead, you get the "path" for what the file represents. Thus, for a .webloc file, what appears will be the http URL that the .webloc file represents.

SEE: • **"Take Note: Connecting to Servers via Aliases and Location Files" and "Technically Speaking: Internetconfig Preferences," earlier in this chapter, for related information.**

Figure 8.58

The (left) Finder icon and (right) Get Info window for a .webloc file for Apple's home page (www.apple.com).

TAKE NOTE ▶ Web Browser Settings and Favorites Files

If you've decided that you need to delete or replace your browser's preferences files, you need to know where to find them. Here are the locations of preference, bookmarks, and favorites files for the most common Mac OS X Web browsers:

Camino (formerly Chimera)

- Preferences: ~Library/Application Support/Camino/Profiles/default/*xxxxx*.slt/user.js
- Bookmarks: ~Library/Application Support/Camino/Profiles/default/*xxxxx*.slt/bookmarks.xml

   (Note that if you previously used Chimera, the above paths may say *Chimera* instead of *Camino*. In either case, *xxxxx* is a string of characters that differs for each user.)

iCab

- Preferences: ~/Library/Preferences/iCab Preferences/iCab Preferences
- Favorites: ~/Library/Preferences/iCab Preferences/Hotlist.html

Internet Explorer

- Preferences: ~/Library/Preferences/ com.apple.internetconfig.plist
- Favorites: ~/Library/Preferences/ Explorer/Favorites.html
- Toolbar Preferences: ~/Library/Preferences/ Explorer/Language.Toolbar.xml

Mozilla

- Preferences: ~/Library/Preferences/org.mozilla.Mozilla.plist
- Favorites: ~/Library/Mozilla/Profiles/default/bookmarks.html

continues on next page

TAKE NOTE ▶ Web Browser Settings and Favorites Files *continued*

OmniWeb

- Preferences: ~/Library/Preferences/com.omnigroup.OmniWeb.plist

- Favorites: ~/ Library/Application Support/OmniWeb/Bookmarks.html

Opera

- Preferences: ~/Library/Preferences/Opera Preferences/Opera Preferences

- Favorites: ~/Library/Preferences/Opera Preferences/Bookmarks

Safari

- Preferences: ~/Library/Preferences/com.apple.Safari.plist

- Bookmarks: ~/Library/Safari/Bookmarks.plist

Note that Internet Explorer uses Apple's InternetConfig preferences file (com.apple
.internetconfig.plist) to store some of its settings; unfortunately, deleting the com.apple
.internetconfig.plist file also deletes various settings that affect most other browsers,
including Safari.

TAKE NOTE ▶ Troubleshooting Downloading Files

Besides surfing, the thing you're mostly likely to do with your Web browser is download software. Here's a brief collection of tips to assist you when you run into trouble with a download:

- If the download attempt results in text appearing in your browser window, rather than a
  file in your normal download location, it simply means the Web server is configured
  improperly. Depending on your browser, a work-around is usually available. In Internet
  Explorer, for example, you can hold down the Option key when clicking the download link.
  If that doesn't work, try Control-clicking the download link to bring up a contextual menu.
  From the menu, choose Download Link to Disk. This command brings up the Save dialog.
  Click Save, and the download should proceed.

- If the preceding technique does not work, or if you get error messages indicating that
  you're missing a plug-in or other software needed for the file to download, it's time to visit,
  and possibly edit, the File Mappings and Protocol Helpers settings.

  SEE: • "Technically Speaking: Internetconfig Preferences," earlier in this chapter, for
      more details.

- Many Web downloads use the FTP protocol. You will know that this is the case for a specific
  download if the URL of the link to download the file begins with ftp:// instead of http://.
  In such cases, using passive (PASV) mode can be the ticket to preventing download problems. Fortunately, most Web browsers use passive mode automatically. If problems occur,
  you can ensure that this mode is in use by going to the Network System Preferences pane,
  clicking the Proxies screen for the Network port used for Internet access, and making sure
  the Use Passive FTP Mode (PASV) box is checked.

continues on next page

TAKE NOTE ▶ Troubleshooting Downloading Files *continued*

Note: With Apple's Safari Web browser, if you enter the address of an FTP server as a URL, the FTP site mounts as a volume on your Desktop rather than as a Web page. Thus, it works the same as if you had entered the address in the Finder's Connect to Server window. If an ftp site does not mount as expected, delete ~/Library/Preferences/ com.apple.LaunchServices .plist and try again.

Note: If you enter an FTP URL in Safari that points directly to a file on a server, the file will be downloaded immediately, and the server won't be mounted as a volume.

Note: I have occasionally had problems downloading software from the members-only Apple developer site at http://connect.apple.com/. In such cases, the solution was to turn off the Firewall in Sharing System Preferences or enable FTP Access in the Firewall's Allow list. Otherwise, downloads kept getting stuck when the server tried to enable FTP passive mode. I've also encountered a related problem in which software from this site would not download using Safari but worked with Internet Explorer.

• If you still have problems with FTP downloads via a browser, you can instead try using an FTP client, such as Fetch, RBrowser, or Transmit. To do so, launch the FTP client and enter the domain name from the file's URL (the portion between ftp:// and the first slash) where the client asks for an address. Assuming the FTP server is a public server, no password will be needed. Once you're connected, you can navigate to the directory that contains the file you want to download. (Some FTP clients let you simply paste the entire URL into the Server field; they automatically access the appropriate directory and download the file without any further navigation from you.)

• If a download aborts prior to completion, try again. In some cases, you may be able to pick up where you left off, avoiding having to re-download the data already received. In Internet Explorer, double-click the name of the file in the Download Manager window and click the Reload button. This sometimes (but not reliably) completes a partial download. (For it to work, you must do so prior to quitting Explorer.) For other browsers and for FTP clients, check their documentation for specific details.

If you use Mac OS X's Software Update to download software, it should also correctly resume an interrupted download the next time you try.

Troubleshooting email

Assuming your network connection is working, most email problems can be traced to incorrect email settings or problems with your ISP's email server.

Checking your email settings. If you're using an email client such as Mac OS X's Mail or Microsoft's Entourage and are having problems sending or receiving email from one or more accounts, compare the settings you entered in your email client's Preferences dialog or Account Setup screen with the settings provided by your ISP or email provider. At the very least, you will need to know your user name, password, and the mail server addresses—including whether you're using a POP or IMAP server for receiving mail.

POP servers download email to your drive—providing you with a permanent copy that you can read even when you're offline. With IMAP, email is stored on and accessed from a server (until and unless you specifically copy it to your hard drive). The advantage of IMAP is that you can access your email, even messages you have already read, from any computer. The disadvantage of IMAP is that you need to have an active connection to access your previously read email (unless you have stored a copy of the email offline).

If you're using Web-based email (such as Yahoo) instead of an email client, the situation is usually simpler. You need only enter your name and password in fields on a Web page to access your email. If you're using AOL, you need to set up and access your email directly from the AOL software.

Figure 8.59

Email Accounts window in Mail, showing servers for incoming (POP) and outgoing (SMTP) mail.

Storing messages on a POP server. What if you check and download your email at work, on a POP account, but also want to download those messages on your home computer? You can do so, in Mail for example, by clicking the Advanced button for the account in the Accounts screen of Mail's Preferences. From here, enable the "Remove copy from server after retrieving a message" option. From the pop-up menu, select the desired interval for doing so (for example, "After one week"). Downloaded email will now stay on the server for the selected interval before it gets removed. Thus, if you selected a one-week interval, the email you downloaded at work during the day will still be available for you to download again once you get home. At any time, you can click the "Remove now" button to instantly remove all previously downloaded mail from the server (your local downloaded copies are not affected). To always have email immediately deleted from the server when you download it, select "Right away" from the pop-up menu. Note: These settings are not relevant for IMAP accounts.

Skipping messages that are too large. If you don't want your email program to get bogged down downloading large attachments sent to your POP account, most email programs allow you to automatically skip messages that are over a user-specified size. Again, in Mail, this option is located in its Advanced Preferences screen. Note: These settings are not relevant for IMAP accounts.

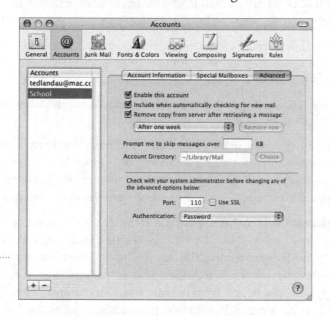

Figure 8.60

The Advanced settings for a POP account in Mail.

Authentication and sending email. Many email providers, in an attempt to block spammers from using their servers, require special procedures for sending email. For example, you may need to check to receive new email before you can send email. Or you may need to enable an SMTP authentication option. Thus, if you get an error when trying to send email, check for new email first, and then try again to send. Otherwise, check with your ISP concerning other authentication options that may be in use and how to enable them in your specific email client.

Spam blockers. Some ISPs and individual users institute protections against receiving spam—which can result in an email you send to them getting bounced back. For example, Apple states that its .Mac service will refuse messages sent to it if the DNS server(s) for the email address provider are not available or are incorrect. The sender will get an error that says, "Cannot resolve PTR record…"

SEE: • "Web and email security" and "Spam," earlier in this chapter, for related information.

Firewall block. If you're running any firewall software, it may block sending and receiving of email (although this is rare, because most firewalls are configured to allow email). To determine whether this is the case, turn the firewall software off.

Pinging the email server. If you're having trouble sending mail and your email client returns an error such as "Cannot contact server," use Network Utility to ping the SMTP server address listed in your email Preferences (this is the server that's used to send mail).

If you cannot retrieve mail (and your email client tells you that it cannot contact the server), ping the POP or IMAP server that you access to receive mail.

If you have Internet access (for example, you can successfully surf the Web) but the server does not respond to your ping, the problem may simply be that your email server is having problems. Contact your ISP for details.

SEE: • "Diagnosing Internet problems with Network Utility," earlier in this chapter, for more on using ping.

Over the past year, .Mac's mac.com email server has been hampered by periodic server failures. During these periods—which have occasionally lasted for days—users have been unable to send or receive email. There's little you can do in such situations except wait for the problem to be fixed.

Problems with attachments. Attachments that cannot be opened by the recipient represent one of the more common email problems—especially if you're a Mac user sending files to a PC user. The solution, in brief, is to make sure that the compression and encryption processes used for the attachment can be decoded by the recipient machine. For example, when sending a file to a PC via Entourage v. X, select the pop-up menu below the Attachment box in the message window. In the mini-window that appears, from the "Encode for" options select "Any computer (AppleDouble)" or "Windows (MIME/Base64)." Then, from the Compression options select None. Also make sure documents have the appropriate filename extension (for example, Word documents should end in .doc).

When receiving files from Microsoft Exchange or Microsoft Outlook, the attachment may be named winmail.dat and/or have a MIME attachment type of application/ms-tnef. To read or use these files, get a utility called TNEF's Enough (from Josh Jacob).

Problems with accounts. If you use Entourage and are unable to access your mail or have other serious problems, hold down the Option key when launching the application. A window will appear from which you can select to rebuild the Entourage database. This often fixes the problem.

For similar problems in Mail, select the problem mailbox and then select the Rebuild command from Mail's Mailbox menu. Otherwise, try restoring Mail's preferences file, com.apple.mail.plist, from a recent backup (if you have one).

These rebuilds should also reduce the size of your email database files, especially if you have deleted large amounts of email since the last rebuild.

Corrupt messages. Occasionally, an email message will arrive corrupted or otherwise conflict with your email application, causing it to freeze or crash when you attempt to access or read the message. This may also appear to prevent you from deleting the email (since attempting to do so results in a crash). The quickest solution here is to select multiple messages for deletion (typically by making a selection that brackets the corrupt message). Because this does not cause the corrupt message to be displayed, the crash should not occur—and you can now delete the selected emails.

Junk mail filtering fails. Occasionally, the junk mail filter for Mac OS X's Mail application can stop working. That is, junk mail is no longer recognized as junk. If this happens, select Preferences from the Mail menu and click the Junk Mail icon in the toolbar. From the screen that appears, click the Reset button. After resetting, all your previous junk mail rules will be lost. You will need to "retrain" the filter. However, the filter should start working again.

Note: This symptom was especially common after selecting a completely blank message (no sender, no subject, no text) and clicking the Junk button in the toolbar. To avoid this result, send such messages directly to the Trash, rather than treat them as junk. In any case, this bug has supposedly been fixed in Mac OS X 10.3.3.

Backing up. It's always a good idea to maintain a backup of your email, especially if you don't maintain frequent backups of your entire drive. To back up the email for Mac OS X's Mail, make a copy of the Mail folder in ~/Library. For Entourage, back up ~/Documents/Microsoft User Data/ Office X Identities.

Mac OS X Mail's Activity Viewer. If you're having problems sending or receiving email using Mac OS X's Mail, and none of the above advice helps, select Activity Monitor from Mail's Window menu to get detailed feedback on what's happening when Mail is attempting to send or receive email (especially useful if you're receiving email from more than one account at a time). If something goes wrong, messages here may help to diagnose the problem. Stop buttons here also allow you to terminate a hung connection (such as when an attempt to get mail from an IMAP server remains hung in the "fetching headers" stage).

More help for Mac OS X's Mail. If you're using Mac OS X's Mail application and are having trouble configuring accounts, sending email, or receiving email, be sure to check the Help files for Mail; they're quite good. Alternatively, you can get the same information from Apple's Knowledge Base documents—in particular, the following two articles: http://docs.info.apple.com/article.html?artnum=135112 and http://docs.info.apple.com/article.html?artnum=135113.

SEE: • "Web and email security," earlier in this chapter, for related information.

> **TAKE NOTE ▶ Troubleshooting Web Browsing and Email: Beyond Mac OS X**
>
> I know—I haven't even touched on many Web- and email-related problems. The reason is that most of these aren't specific to Mac OS X (such as problems with browser bookmarks, getting JavaScript to work, emailing attachments, or understanding MIME types) or *are* specific to particular applications (like Internet Explorer or Entourage). To keep this volume from becoming unmanageably large, I've omitted coverage of those problems. For more information on these matters, check out my previous troubleshooting book *Sad Macs, Bombs, and Other Disasters*. It includes three hefty chapters that cover file sharing, networking, the Internet, Web browsing, and email. Although the emphasis is on Mac OS 9, much of the information on Web and email topics is general enough to apply to Mac OS X as well.
>
> As a help, I have posted one chapter from that book, titled "Road Service for the Infobahn: The World Wide Web, Email and Beyond," on my Web site at www.macosxhelpline.com.

Troubleshooting Sharing

If you've worked through the troubleshooting advice in the preceding sections, chances are good your network connections are working, and you shouldn't have any problems getting Sharing services to work. If you do have a problem, however, the following sections should provide the solution.

Checking the basics

For starters, consider these two basic steps:

- **Restart sharing service.** *On a host/server computer:* If any changes have been made to the Sharing, Accounts, or related settings (such as to change privileges settings for any items), you may need to stop and restart the relevant sharing service (for example, Personal File Sharing) from the Services screen of the Sharing System Preferences pane, before the changes take effect.

  Even if you haven't made any changes, this is worth a try if you're having sharing-related problems. The problem may be that some underlying Unix software has crashed. Restarting the sharing service will typically fix this.

  Note: Doing this restart requires physical access to the host machine. If you're on the client machine but have access to the host machine (for example, both are in the same room), this probably won't present a problem. If, however, you're dealing with a remotely connected host computer, you will need to contact someone who has access to it.

- **Log out and back in; restart.** *On either a host/server or client/connecting computer:* Log out of your account and then log back in again. If this fails to fix the problem, restart your Mac.

If you still have a problem, consider these additional basic tips:

Make sure that the server you want to locate is active, is on the network, and has the desired sharing service enabled. Before you can connect to a host computer, that computer must be active (that is, not asleep or turned off), must be on the network (for example, connected to a router for a local connection or to the Internet for a remote connection), and must have the desired sharing service enabled (for example, as set in the Services screen of the Sharing System Preferences pane). All of these issues are covered earlier in this chapter.

Note: To avoid a host computer's going to sleep unintentionally, temporarily set sleep to Never in the Energy Saver System Preferences pane whenever sharing services are in use. You don't need to do this for the client computer; in most cases, the client computer can sleep without affecting a connection.

Make sure that the client is using the correct protocol and application. If you're a client computer, make sure you are using the correct protocol and application for connecting to a host. As described earlier in this chapter, Mac OS X provides several methods for sharing files over a network or the Internet. Each method is accessible only when you use certain applications or protocols. For example:

- **Personal File Sharing.** The connecting user (client) must be using a Mac OS computer that supports File Sharing. In some cases, the connection may need to be made through TCP/IP (when AppleTalk will not work, for example).

- **Web Sharing.** The connecting user can only access your computer via a Web browser.

- **FTP.** The connecting user must use a dedicated FTP client, a Web browser, or a terminal shell that supports the ftp command (such as Mac OS X's Terminal application).

- **Remote Login/Terminal access.** The connecting user must be using a Terminal-like application and SSH to connect. Again, Mac OS X's Terminal works here.

Make sure that the client has an account with the correct permissions. If, when attempting to connect to a host, you get to a point where you're asked to enter your name and password as a registered user, but doing so leads to a "Login failed" or similar error message, it could be for one of the following reasons: The password may have been changed; you may be entering the wrong password; or the account may have been deleted (or modified in some way that prevents you from logging in successfully) since you last accessed it.

Make sure that Internet router or firewall settings are not blocking access. The settings used to prevent unwanted access to your computer sometimes prevent intended access as well. For example, if you use a router, make sure the port to your computer from your router is open, so that the computer can be accessed for sharing. Similarly, make sure the Firewall settings in the Sharing System Preferences pane are not blocking the needed access.

SEE: • "Using a Router," "Troubleshooting routers," and "Network Security," earlier in this chapter, for more details on these issues.

Make sure the computers have correct IP addresses. The exact IP address you need depends on whether you're having problems with a local (LAN) or an Internet (WAN) connection.

For a LAN connection over TCP/IP, both computers must have an IP address. Depending on your setup, you may need its local address, not its Internet address. Otherwise, if a computer typically connects to the Internet via PPP or DHCP and has not yet connected to the Internet, it may not have an IP address at all. A solution here is to assign the computer an IP address. To do so, you can set up an Ethernet port to be used just for sharing. Set this port to be configured manually (by creating a new port or a new location). Then assign an IP address in the TCP/IP settings; this address should be a local private address, such as one in the 10.0.0.1 to 10.0.0.255 range or in the 192.168.1.xxx range. The subnet mask should be 255.255.255.0.

For WAN connections, similarly make sure you are using the correct IP address for the computer to which you're trying to connect. For example, for dynamically assigned IP addresses, make sure you're not using an expired address. If you will be trying to connect to your home or office computer while on the road, a utility called Ipanema (from If Then Software) can automatically email your current IP address each day, allowing you to track potential changes to your home/office computer's address.

SEE: • "Take Note: What Are the TCP/IP Settings?" earlier in this chapter, for more on IP addresses and related information.

Troubleshooting Network Browser and Connect to Server

This section describes an assortment of problems and solutions related to connecting to servers via either the Network Browser or the Connect to Server command.

Finder freeze/hang. In several of the situations described below (for example, unexpected disconnect, disconnect fails, alias could not be opened), the Finder may hang or freeze when you try to access an open window for the problem server or double-click an (alias) icon of the server. The primary symptom is a spinning beach-ball cursor (just in the Finder) that continues indefinitely. Sometimes, if you wait long enough, the Finder unhangs itself and an error message appears. If so, follow the advice for that message (as described below). Otherwise, if the freeze persists, relaunch the Finder (for example, by holding down the Option key and selecting the Dock menu for the Finder, and then selecting Relaunch). If even this fails, it's time to restart the Mac.

If the hang recurs when accessing the server after a restart, the source of the problem is most likely on the host machine. A common fix is to restart Personal File Sharing on the host/server computer (assuming you have access to it).

Network command dimmed. If the Network command is dimmed in the Go menu, the Network icon in the sidebar will likely still work. Use it, instead of the Go menu command, to get to the Network Browser window. Otherwise, relaunch the Finder (for example, by holding down the Option key and selecting the Dock menu for the Finder, and then selecting Relaunch); the Network command in the Go menu should now be active.

Server does not appear in Network Browser window. Occasionally, you may have a problem in which one or more local servers that you know have been set up correctly do not appear in the Network Browser. If this happens, here's what to do:

- Assuming you know the server's IP address, enter it in the Address text box of the Connect to Server window and try to connect this way.

- Often, although Computer A can't locate Computer B, Computer B can locate Computer A. Thus, if you have access to both computers, you can make the File Sharing connection go the other way (assuming you have an account set up to do so). If all you want to do is copy files back and forth, the direction of the connection shouldn't matter.

- If two servers on your local network have the same name, only one (or none) of them may appear in the Network Browser. The solution is to change the name of one. If you don't have the needed access to do this, contact the person who does.

- Make sure the needed service (such as AppleTalk for AppleTalk-connected servers) is enabled in Directory Access. If the needed service is already enabled, disable it and re-enable it to restart the service in the Directory Access application.

Note: A crash of the DirectoryService process on your Mac may prevent servers from appearing in the Network window. In this case, restarting your Mac may be the simplest solution. If you want to check whether or not a crash has occurred, you'll typically find a message noting such a DirectoryService quit in the log files (either console.log or system.log) accessible via Console.

SEE: • **"Directory Access," in Chapter 4, for background information on this application.**

• **"Take Note: Connect to Server vs. Network: What's the Difference?" earlier in this chapter, for more specific advice (especially regarding accessing AppleTalk servers).**

- Otherwise, it's time to check the basics (for example, is the computer on and awake; is it connected to the network; is Sharing enabled; did you restart Sharing; and more), as described earlier in this section.

Alias could not be opened. You click to connect to a server via the Network Browser or an alias (or location) file that you created for a server. Instead of connecting or getting a login window, however, you get an error message that says, "The alias could not be opened, because the original item could not be found." If this happens, simply try again; the connection may succeed. Otherwise, if using the Network Browser, trying going to the Browser window via a different method (such as via the Computer window instead of the Finder sidebar); try again. If this, too, fails, it's time to check the basics, as described above.

Connection failed or timed out. After you click the Connect button (most likely when using Connect to Server to connect to a remote server), you may get a message that says, "Contacting {*address*}. Timeout in *xx* seconds." This means that Mac OS X cannot locate the selected server. If it cannot do so before the timeout expires, the connection will fail (the message will change to Server Connection Time Out). The most likely cause is that either the server you want to access is not currently on the Internet or you're not on the Internet. Check the basics, as described above.

More generally (either with Connect to Server or the Network Browser), you may get a message stating, "Connection failed," followed by either a generic message (that is, "No response from the server. Please try again") or a more specific message explaining the reason for the failure. Or you may get no message at all—but still a connection fails. Here's what may be going on and what to do about it:

- **You may not have waited long enough.** Wait at least 30 seconds before you assume you have a problem. Especially if you are opening a window from a server for the first time after making a connection, it may take a few seconds before the contents of the window appear. Until this happens, the Finder window may erroneously say that there are zero items in the window.

- **You may have selected a connection method that's not working for a reason you cannot diagnose.** To work around this, if possible (for example, for a server listed in the Network Browser window and for which you know its address), switch from using the Network Browser method to the Connect to Server method to connect. Or vice versa. Often one method works when the other does not.

- **There's some other unspecified network-related problem.** Check the basics (such as for the Network System Preferences settings), as described above. If everything you check appears to be OK, restarting the Mac may help clear up any temporary glitches.

- **You're using Connect to Server and the address you entered in the Server Address text box does not exist (because you mistyped it, for example).** The fix is to find the correct address and use it.

- **You're attempting to connect to a Mac running Mac OS 9.** Although this should work, assuming sharing is enabled on the Mac OS 9 machine, I have seen it fail. In this case, the easiest work-around is to reverse the connection attempt (that is, connect to the Mac OS X machine from the one running Mac OS 9).

- **You're using an HTTP address to connect to a server, and the server does not use WebDAV.** The solution here is to use a Web browser to connect to the server.

   SEE: • "Take Note: Mounting and Working with iDisks," earlier in this chapter, for more on WebDAV.

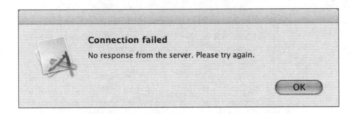

Figure 8.61

Examples of messages that may occur when attempting to connect to a server fails.

Host (or client) unexpectedly disconnects. As described earlier in this chapter, if the owner of a host machine decides to turn off Personal File Sharing while other users are connected to it, the other users will typically get a warning message alerting them of the impending disconnect. If the owner decides to bypass this warning or otherwise causes a disconnect to occur (for example, by changing network settings, allowing the computer to go to sleep, or disconnecting from the network), the connected users will likely get a message like the following: "The connection to this server has been unexpectedly broken or shut down. The file server has closed down." Or, you may get a Server Disconnect Confirmation message, asking if you're sure you want to disconnect (although you really have no choice here).

If a window to the now-disconnected server is still open, or an alias to the server remains in the Network Browser window, you may also get an error message (such as "No file services are available at the URL") if you try to use the window or icon to access the server. Or icons may vanish as soon as you select them. Otherwise, you may get a Finder freeze, as described above.

A similar situation can occur if the client causes an unintended disconnect. For example, this may happen if the client's Ethernet cable accidentally comes loose, or if the client computer is a laptop connected via AirPort and moves out of AirPort range. The problem may remain even after you reconnect the cable or move back in range.

If the problem is a disconnect at the host end, the obvious solution is for the host to reconnect. For persistent problems at the client end, logging out or restarting the Mac should fix things.

SEE: • **"Stopping File Sharing with users connected" in "Personal File Sharing," earlier in this chapter, for related information.**

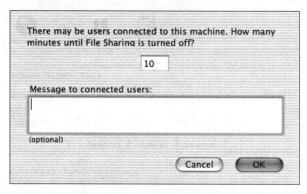

Figure 8.62

Two examples of warning messages that occur on the host computer when attempting to stop Sharing or to shut down with users connected.

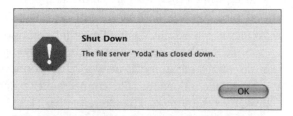

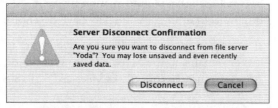

Figure 8.63

Two examples of messages that occur on the client computer if a successful connection is unexpectedly broken (such as because the host server shuts down).

Disconnect fails. Occasionally, especially when using the Network Browser in versions earlier than Mac OS X 10.3.3, you may be unable to disconnect from a server. Typically, you drag the server icon from the Network window to the Trash and all appears to go well; however, you remain connected. If this happens, try the following until something works:

- Select the server and use the Finder's Eject (Command-E) command. I have found this to be more reliable than dragging the item to the Trash.

- Go to the Network System Preferences pane and select a different location or create a new one if necessary. In this new location, turn off the port to which you're currently connected to the network (for example, turn off AirPort if that's what you're using). This should break the connection to the server. Now you can return to your initial location.

- Physically disconnect from the network. For example, for an Ethernet connection, remove and then replace the Ethernet cable.

- If it additionally appears that the Finder has frozen as a result of your disconnect attempt, relaunch the Finder (via the Relaunch command available when you hold down the Option while accessing the Finder's Dock menu). If that fails, restart the Mac. Simply logging out and back in again, or putting the Mac to sleep, is not likely to be sufficient.

SEE: • "Using Network and Connect to Server" and "Take Note: Connect to Server vs. Network: What's the Difference?" earlier in this chapter, for related information.

Miscellaneous other Sharing problems

If you're still having problems with Sharing features, consider the following, more specific, problems and solutions:

Sharing turned off at startup. Personal File Sharing is disabled at startup if you're not connected to a network (for example, via an AirPort card or network cable). The solution is to connect to a network and re-enable File Sharing in the Sharing System Preferences pane.

More generally, Sharing requires software in the Extensions and StartupItems folders of the /System/Library folder. For dealing with startup issues that may cause problems here, see Chapter 5.

Internet Sharing disconnected, turned off, or blocked. If Internet Sharing is not running as expected, there could be several possible causes, including the following:

- If you change your Location in Network System Preferences while Internet Sharing is on, shared computers will no longer be able to connect. The solution is to stop and restart Internet Sharing.

- Internet Sharing will be turned off whenever you restart or shut down your Mac. You must restart Internet Sharing each time the computer is restarted.

- Turning on the firewall may block the use of Internet Sharing. If this happens, the solution is to turn the firewall off *before* starting Internet Sharing. In some cases, I've found that enabling Personal Web Sharing (in Sharing's Services screen) can get Internet Sharing to work with the firewall running when it would not otherwise work with the firewall on.

SEE: • "Internet," and "Take Note: Setting Up and Using Internet Sharing and File Sharing," earlier in this chapter, for related information.

Sharing and configuration priority glitches. In general, the port you intend to use for Internet Sharing should be the one at the top of the list (highest priority) in the Network Port Configuration screen of the Network System Preferences pane. Otherwise, Internet Sharing may not work. This is especially true for sharing over FireWire or sharing an AirPort Internet connection with wired Ethernet clients.

Similarly, for File Sharing, if a server is accessible only over wired Ethernet, and you have AirPort listed as your top preferred network port, you may not be able to connect to the server. The simplest solution here is to move Built-In Ethernet up to the top port in Network System Preferences' Network Port Configuration list—at least temporarily.

Problems making an SMB connection and/or copying files via Windows Sharing. If an attempt to copy a file to a Windows PC via the SMB protocol results in a corrupt file or a failure to copy (often with some error message), or if you're having any problems connecting to a Mac from a PC, try one or more of the following:

- Turn Personal Windows Sharing off and back on again.

- Disable and re-enable the SMB service in the Directory Access application. In addition, if your network uses a WINS Server, make sure you entered it in the SMB settings in Directory Access. (To access these settings, double-click the SMB service item in the Directory Access list.)

- Go to the Accounts System Preferences pane and change your password. If you like, change it back again to the original password. The important thing is to get the Mac's "attention" by making the change.

- Use a utility such as Cocktail to delete Sharing-related cache files.

- Do not use any of the following characters in the name of a file you want to copy to a PC: < > / \ | * ? ".

- When viewed from a Mac, files copied from a Mac to a Windows PC may copy correctly yet not appear in the Finder immediately. Creating an empty folder on the Windows computer may force the Finder to update and show the copied items. Otherwise, relaunching the Finder or logging out and logging back in should do the trick.

SEE: • "SMB," in "Directory Access," in Chapter 4, for related information on using Directory Access (which can help if the PC does not show up in the Connect to Server or Network Browser windows).

USB printer utilities not available via AirPort Extreme. USB printer utilities that may be used when a printer is directly connected to a computer via a USB port cannot be used when the printer is connected to the USB port on the AirPort Extreme Base Station.

SEE: • "Changing printer configurations (Show Info)," in Chapter 7, for related information.

9

The Classic Environment

Perhaps you're a recent Mac convert and Mac OS X is the only Mac OS you've ever used. Or perhaps you're an old-timer but have been using Mac OS X for several years and have made the transition so completely that you never need to run anything other than Mac OS X software anymore. If you fit into either of these categories, you may be able to skip this chapter.

If, on the other hand, you just upgraded to Mac OS X and still want and need to use Mac OS 9 applications, or you occasionally need to use Mac OS 9 applications but your brand-new Mac doesn't boot in Mac OS 9, this chapter is mandatory.

The solution for those who are using Mac OS X but still have a need for Mac OS 9 is to use the Classic environment (also referred to simply as Classic). Via the Classic environment, you can run most Mac OS 9 software while you're booted from Mac OS X.

Once you've launched the Classic environment (as described briefly in Chapter 2 and covered more later in this chapter), Mac OS 9 applications will run almost as though you had started up from Mac OS 9. You can switch between the Classic environment and Mac OS X fairly seamlessly. You can also run Mac OS 9 Internet applications and print from Classic.

However, because you didn't really start up from Mac OS 9 (that is, you're still running Mac OS X), Classic is at times a less-than-perfect substitute. That said, it still works remarkably well. The Classic environment—what it is, how it works, and what to do when it doesn't work—is the subject of this chapter.

SEE: • Chapter 3—especially "Will you be installing Mac OS 9?" and "What About Mac OS 9?"—for more about the requirements and limitations of installing, booting from, and using Mac OS 9.

In This Chapter

What Is the Classic Environment?

As discussed in Chapter 1, Mac OS X is such a fundamentally different operating system from Mac OS 9 that Mac OS 9 applications simply do not run in Mac OS X (and vice versa). Thus, it may initially appear that your investment in Mac OS 9 software goes down the drain when you move up to Mac OS X. Anticipating that users would not welcome such obsolescence, Apple provided two solutions: Carbon applications and the Classic environment.

I explained the significance of Carbon applications in Chapter 4. Briefly, Carbonizing a Mac OS 9–only application allows it to run in Mac OS X. Carbonizing an application is a developer's alternative to writing a Cocoa-based Mac OS X application from scratch. In many cases, a Carbonized application will run in both Mac OS 9 and Mac OS X, making these applications the lone exceptions to the rule stated in the previous paragraph. However, some Carbonized applications only run in Mac OS X. In either case, Carbon applications don't provide a perfect solution: They don't always take full advantage of Mac OS X features, and they often run more slowly than their Mac OS 9 counterparts. Still, they remain an excellent compromise. If all Mac OS 9 software were Carbonized, there would be no need for another solution to the Mac OS 9 compatibility problem.

Unfortunately, thousands of existing applications written for Mac OS 9 will never be Carbonized—or at least not for a long time (for example, Mac users had to wait almost three years for a Mac OS X version of QuarkXPress). For these programs, Classic provides a solution by letting you run Mac OS 9 applications *within* Mac OS X.

Some of you may have been using Macs long enough to remember the transition from the 680x0 processors to PowerPC processors. The Mac OS ran PowerPC–native applications faster but emulated the older 680x0 processors so that nonnative applications could still be used just like any other applications. In everyday use, PowerPC and non-PowerPC applications looked and functioned identically. Running the Classic environment under Mac OS X is not exactly the same experience, but it's still a useful metaphor for understanding what's going on. At times, you may not even be aware of the shift from Classic to Mac OS X and back.

At the simplest level, the Classic environment is a Mac OS X *application* that runs in the background and provides what is called a *hardware abstraction layer*. Then it boots up a slightly modified version of Mac OS 9 that runs (invisibly) on top of this layer. Classic applications run inside Mac OS 9 just as if they were on a Mac running only Mac OS 9. The main caveat is that Classic applications must be compatible with Mac OS 9.1 or later to be compatible with the Classic environment. In fact, running Classic in recent versions of Mac OS X may require Mac OS 9.2 or later. (Mac OS 9.2.2 was the most recent version as of this writing.)

The following defines some terms that will be used throughout the chapter:

- **Classic Mac OS or Mac OS 9.** Versions of the Mac OS that preceded Mac OS X; usually Mac OS 9.1 or later.

- **Classic environment, or Classic.** The Classic environment in Mac OS X.

- **Mac OS 9 in Classic.** The version or copy of Mac OS 9 that's running in the Classic environment.

- **Classic applications.** Applications written for Mac OS 9 or earlier.

What hardware and services does the Classic environment support?

Although the Classic environment actually runs a copy of Mac OS 9, it does not necessarily support all the same hardware, services, and input/output devices and protocols that Mac OS 9 would support on the same hardware. Classic directs all in/out operations from Mac OS 9 in Classic *through* Mac OS X, rather than communicating with the hardware directly. When you print from an application in Mac OS 9, for example, your data does not go directly to the printer; instead, the data is sent through Mac OS X, which then sends it to the printer. Thus, if Mac OS X does not support certain hardware or protocols, Classic does not, either. Likewise, some devices (such as internal modems) are not accessible to the Classic environment at all.

On the other hand, Classic can support hardware-related features that Mac OS X does not support directly, as long as the needed information is passed to the Classic environment For example, you can still use Mac OS 9's Chooser to select a printer in Classic that is not yet supported for printing in Mac OS X. You can also use USB printer sharing in Classic.

The Classic environment *does* support the following:

- USB
- IDE
- Built-in audio/sound
- Disk images
- Ethernet
- SCSI
- FireWire
- Built-in video

The Classic environment *does not* support the following:

- ADB, except for the primary keyboard and mouse, and only when used from a built-in ADB port. (Note that some crashes within Classic will require you to reboot Classic to regain the use of ADB.)

- LocalTalk.

- Internal floppy drives. External USB floppy drives will work, however.

- Built-in serial ports.

- Infrared ports.

- PCI/PC Cards (including audio, video, and SCSI cards) that are not supported by Mac OS X.

- Modem-based applications (such as AOL, Z-term, and most fax software) that cannot access the modem directly from within Classic. PPP connections (in fact, all network connections) must be made under Mac OS X and then funneled to Classic applications.

General problems running applications in the Classic environment

The main advantage of the Classic environment is obvious: It lets you upgrade to the latest and greatest Mac OS while continuing to use most of the Mac OS 9 applications that won't run in Mac OS X. There are some downsides, however:

- You're more likely to encounter compatibility problems because everything you do in Classic is funneled first through Mac OS 9, then through the Classic environment bridge, and finally through Mac OS X before reaching your Mac's hardware.

- Applications often run significantly slower in Classic than if you had booted into Mac OS 9.

- Classic applications do not take advantage of the advanced memory and processing capabilities of Mac OS X. Applications running in Classic behave (or misbehave) just like applications under Mac OS 9. Although the Classic environment itself takes advantage of protected memory under Mac OS X (because it is simply an application), everything running *within* the Classic environment does not.

Bottom line: If there's a way to accomplish what you want to do without using Classic, you're almost always better off doing so. Otherwise, depending on what you want to do, using Classic can be anything from a barely adequate to a perfectly fine alternative.

SEE: • **"Troubleshooting the Classic Environment," later in this chapter, for more specific information.**

How to Install and Configure Classic

Guess what? You don't have to do anything to install Classic. The needed software was installed when you installed Mac OS X (or, on newer Macs, when you took your computer out of the box). As long as a version of Mac OS 9 is available somewhere on a mounted volume, you should be able to use Classic almost instantly. All currently shipping Macs come with both Mac OS X and Mac OS 9 preinstalled. Still, before you launch Classic for the first time, you need to consider several issues.

Note: With the release of Mac OS X 10.2/10.3 and the shift to Macs that can no longer boot in Mac OS 9, Apple has changed the accessibility of Mac OS 9. Prior to Jaguar, Mac OS X shipped with a Mac OS 9 Install CD. Jaguar and later versions of Mac OS X no longer include this. New Macs similarly no longer come with a Mac OS 9 CD. For these systems, the only way to reinstall Mac OS 9 (without obtaining a Mac OS 9 CD or doing hacks that Apple does not support) is via the Software Restore discs that come with your Mac.

SEE: • Chapter 3 for more details on using Software Restore.

Do you have enough RAM?

Classic uses a lot of memory. If you intend to run Classic often, you will almost certainly need more RAM than the minimum Apple recommends for Mac OS X. I recommend having at least 256 MB of RAM, and more if you can afford it. As a bonus, you'll find that almost everything in Mac OS X is faster with more RAM.

Do you have the right version of Mac OS 9?

As explained earlier in this chapter, to use Classic, Mac OS X requires at least Mac OS 9.1 and probably Mac OS 9.2 or later. In general, if you're using the latest version of Mac OS X (which you should be), make sure that you're also using the latest version of Mac OS 9. You can check what version of Mac OS 9 is installed by choosing About This Computer from the Apple menu while you're booted in Mac OS 9. Or, if you're running Mac OS X, select the Startup Disk System Preferences. It will list the Mac OS 9 version number for every volume that can boot from Mac OS 9.

If Classic is already running, the Memory/Versions tab of the Classic System Preferences will also indicate which version of Mac OS 9 is in use.

Customizing for booting from Mac OS 9 vs. using Classic

When you launch the Classic environment under Mac OS X, you actually start up a copy of Mac OS 9 from a System Folder on your hard drive. Likewise, if you have a Mac that can still boot from Mac OS 9, you may want to boot directly into Mac OS 9 at times. To handle this, I recommend that you maintain two Mac OS 9 System Folders: one for booting into Mac OS 9 and a slimmed-down version for Classic. (For recommendations about *how* to slim down the folder, see "Optimizing Mac OS 9 for the Classic environment," later in the chapter.) Because Classic does not support or need all of the files included in a full installation of Mac OS 9, parts of Mac OS 9 are not functional under Classic—particularly with respect to items in the Extensions and Control Panels folders. In fact, parts of Mac OS 9 are dysfunctional under Classic—meaning they can actually cause problems.

As an alternative to maintaining two System Folders, you could use Extensions Manager to create two Mac OS 9 startup sets: one containing your full complement of startup files and another containing just those you need for Classic. Then you can choose the appropriate set depending on whether you're booting Mac OS 9 by itself or within the Classic environment. I find this method to be less convenient than the two–System Folder approach, however. In addition, because Mac OS X modifies the System Folder used in Classic by installing extra and updated startup files and by altering preferences files, having two different Mac OS 9 System Folders allows your "full" version of Mac OS 9 to be free of the potential conflicts these Classic files may cause when booting from Mac OS 9.

At this point, you may be wondering why you would ever want to boot into Mac OS 9 after upgrading to Mac OS X. The answer (as detailed elsewhere in this chapter) is twofold: (1) You may need to boot from Mac OS 9 occasionally to run applications that don't run in either Mac OS X or the Classic environment; and (2) certain troubleshooting techniques may require booting from Mac OS 9 (such as to run a firmware update), or booting from Mac OS 9 may at least make it easier to accomplish some tasks.

Can you have multiple Mac OS 9 System Folders on the same volume?

Since the release of Jaguar, Mac OS X *directly* supports having multiple Mac OS 9 System Folders on the same volume. Although you could do this in earlier versions of Mac OS X, it was more cumbersome.

In brief, the Classic Systems Preferences pane lists all valid Mac OS 9 System Folders on all mounted volumes. When you initially launch Classic System Preferences, it checks for Mac OS 9 System Folders and adds any new ones to its previously created list. To see all System Folders for a given volume, click the disclosure triangle next to the volume name in the scrollable text window of the Start/Stop tab of the Classic System Preferences pane. Their names will appear.

To choose the System Folder you want, simply click it. You will continue to use this one until you select a different one.

Why would you want to have two separate Mac OS 9 System Folders? So that you can set up one System Folder for Classic and the other as a boot folder. If your Mac cannot start up in Mac OS 9, this is obviously of less concern.

Should you partition your drive?

If you plan to maintain two Mac OS 9 System Folders, I recommend keeping them on separate volumes. If you only have one hard drive, you can do this by dividing the hard drive into separate partitions. Each partition acts as a separate volume, with its own icon listed on the Desktop.

Typically, when you partition a drive, you're required to erase the drive. Thus, it's best to do this right away—say on the day you unpack your new Mac! As discussed in Chapter 3, you can use third-party software to partition a drive *without* erasing—with some limitations. Otherwise, you'll need to back up all of your data before partitioning the drive and then restore it afterward.

In the most common setup, you divide your drive into two partitions. One partition contains Mac OS X and a customized Mac OS 9 System Folder used for the Classic environment. The other partition contains a separate full Mac OS 9 System Folder that you use when you boot directly into Mac OS 9 (or any other OS version that your Mac can use, should you want). A less common alternative is to have three partitions: one for Mac OS X and one each for the two Mac OS 9 Systems.

SEE: • "Take Note: Why and How to Partition," in Chapter 3, for more details.

Optimizing Mac OS 9 for the Classic environment

Before using the Classic environment for the first time, you can take several steps to improve its speed and stability—steps that work best if you perform them *before* you launch Classic for the first time. In some cases, this may only be possible if you boot from Mac OS 9 to make the change. If you have a Mac that cannot boot from Mac OS 9, you'll have to make the changes (if needed) by launching Classic. Similarly, some of the recommendations (for example, steps 2 through 4 below) are only important if you're using a Mac OS 9 System Folder that you previously used as your Mac OS 9 startup folder (for example, before upgrading to Mac OS X). With these caveats in mind, here's what you can do (ideally while still booted from Mac OS 9) to make Classic speedy and stable:

1. Make sure that you have Version 9.2.1 or later of the Startup Disk control panel before using that copy of Mac OS 9 in the Classic environment.

   If you don't have this version, you can obtain it via the Software Update control panel or by downloading it from the Apple Web site. If you've updated to the latest version of Mac OS 9 (as recommended earlier in the chapter), this step should already be done. If you're using an early version of Mac OS 9, you may have to download and run a sequence of updaters to get to 9.2.2.

2. In the Appearance control panel, make sure that any Soundtrack sounds are disabled.

3. Inside the Preferences folder within your System Folder delete the Navigation Services folder.

4. From the same folder, remove the Hosts file.

5. Disable unneeded startup files.

   Veteran Mac users may remember the days of 16 MB of RAM, when they tried to trim down their startup files (extensions and control panels) to the bare minimum. Ironically, those days are back with the Classic environment. Just as the Classic Mac OS uses RAM at startup, the Classic environment takes a big chunk of RAM when you use it, and the more startup files you have enabled, the more RAM the Classic environment uses. In addition, extensions and control panels (especially third-party ones) are much more likely to cause problems in Classic than in Mac OS 9 itself. Therefore, you can reduce how much RAM Classic uses—and reduce the chance of conflicts—by cutting down on startup files.

   Ideally, you want the copy of Mac OS 9 that Classic uses to be as lean and mean as possible: This enables it to run faster, use less memory, and be more stable. This means disabling all extensions and control panels that you do not absolutely need, typically by using Extensions Manager.

   In fact, beyond the obviously essential files such as System and Finder, very few things are absolutely *required* by Mac OS 9 when you use the Classic environment. If you open Extensions Manager, choose the As Items view option, and click the Package column to sort by package name, you will see several items that are part of the Classic compatibility environment. These items are the only ones specifically required for Classic.

   Although it's beyond the scope of this book to provide a complete list of the startup files in a Mac OS 9 System Folder (not to mention discussing whether you should disable them for use in Classic), several other resources do provide information on startup files: Extension Overload, for example.

In some cases, Mac OS X may alert you to a problem with startup files when you first launch Classic. For example, I once received the following message: "The version of QuickTime installed in the Mac OS 9 system folder used by Classic is not recommended." It advised me to install a newer version of QuickTime.

6. Install any additional necessary startup files.

Some applications and/or hardware that you will be using in the Classic environment may require startup files (extensions or control panels) to function properly. If so, this step is a good time to install them, because they may not install properly when you're using the Classic environment. If you use Microsoft Office 98 or 2001, for example, you should run each of the Office applications once so that Office will be able to install and configure its System Folder files. While you're using the Classic environment, if you ever get an error message stating that a Classic application will not run because you're missing certain files, there's a good chance you need to boot into Mac OS 9 and reinstall the application to get the necessary startup files installed.

7. Launch Classic and allow it to modify the System Folder at launch (if and when asked).

SEE: • "Launching Classic," later in this chapter, for more details.

TAKE NOTE ▶ Control Panels and Extensions in Classic vs. Mac OS X

Many Mac OS 9 control panels and extensions continue to work when run from Classic; however, they only affect the Classic environment. For example, menu modifiers such as ACTION Menus work in Classic, but you will only see your custom menus when a Classic application is active.

Many other control panels and extensions, however, *do not* work in Classic. They're either disabled automatically when Classic launches or ignored (if you do try to use them). In some cases, they can even cause startup conflicts. ACTION GoMac and RAM Doubler are two such files. As suggested in the main text, the best way to avoid problems with these extensions is to disable them.

The following are some general guidelines that should help you figure out what does and doesn't work:

• Classic settings that conflict with Mac OS X (such as appearance, virtual memory, and some File Sharing settings) are ignored or refused. These settings are handled entirely by Mac OS X.

In some cases, these control panels import settings from Mac OS X. For example, if you open the File Sharing control panel in Classic, you should find that your Computer Name is the same one as that listed in Mac OS X; the only difference is that the word *Classic* is appended to this one (for example, MatrixClassic).

Software Update also no longer runs in Classic; updates are handled by Mac OS X's Software Update instead (as detailed in "Problems installing software," later in this chapter).

continues on next page

TAKE NOTE ▶ Control Panels and Extensions in Classic vs. Mac OS X *continued*

- Similarly, the Mac OS 9 control panels that handle networking settings (AppleTalk, Modem, Remote Access, and TCP/IP) are no longer used in the Classic environment. Instead, the Classic environment uses whatever networking protocols and connections Mac OS X provides. This means that you must establish your network, AirPort, or dial-up connections under Mac OS X; your Classic applications will be able to use them just as any Mac OS X application would.

- Mac OS X applications use the Internet settings in Mac OS X's System Preferences window, whereas Classic applications use the settings in the Mac OS 9 Internet control panel (which you can also configure by using the Internet Config utility). This means that if you click a URL or email address in a Classic application, it may open in a different browser or email client than it would if you clicked the link in a Mac OS X application, depending on whether the two settings are different.

Exactly what happens when you try to access a control panel that does not function in Classic (such as TCP/IP or Memory) depends on how the Classic System Folder was installed (for example, from a Mac OS 9 Install CD versus preinstalled with the Mac you purchased) and the version of Mac OS X you're running.

In older Mac systems, you can open these Mac OS 9 control panels in Classic. However, most changes are prohibited. The control panel just lists the settings that you created in Mac OS X. In some cases, the control panel may open and allow you to make changes, but the changes will be ignored.

In more recent Mac systems, you can't even open these control panels. If you try, you get an error message like the following: "The application {*name of application*} is not supported by Classic" or "That application or control panel is not supported by Classic."

In the most recent Mac systems, these control panels are not installed to begin with, so you won't even be able to try to open them. However, they may be present, even in these recent systems, if you separately installed Mac OS 9 from a Mac OS 9 Install CD or if you upgraded your software from an older version (where these control panels were present).

SEE: • **"Startup conflicts," later in this chapter, for how to disable startup files and resolve potential extension conflicts.**

  • **"The Jaguar Way: Network and Internet Connections in Classic," later in this chapter, for related information.**

Figure 9.1

The error message that appears when you attempt to open a control panel or application in Classic that cannot run in Classic.

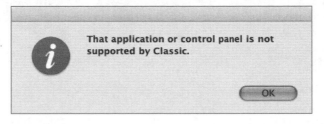

Using Classic

After you've installed and optimized the Classic environment and Mac OS 9, you're ready to use your Classic applications from Mac OS X. The following sections explain what to do after you start up from Mac OS X.

Overview

To launch Classic, monitor its status (once launched), and modify its settings, you use the Classic System Preferences pane. This pane includes three main tabs, each of which accesses a different screen: Start/Stop, Advanced, and Memory/Versions. I gave a brief overview of these screens in Chapter 2; the following provides a more detailed description (with more details to follow in the remaining sections of the chapter):

Start/Stop. From this screen you select which Mac OS 9 System Folder you want to use to run Classic (if more than one System Folder is available). You can also use this screen to start or stop Classic (via the Start/Stop, Restart, and Force Quit buttons).

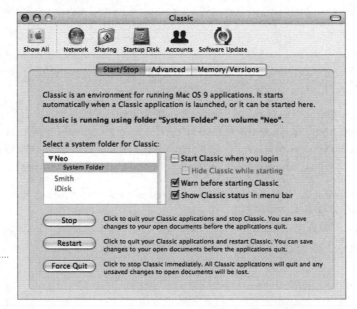

Figure 9.2

The Classic System Preferences pane's Start/Stop screen.

This screen also includes four options with check boxes:

- **"Start Classic when you login."** If you select this option, Classic starts automatically each time you log in.

  Note: If you place a Classic application in your Startup Items list in the Accounts System Preferences pane, this will also cause Classic to launch automatically when you log in.

- **"Hide Classic while starting."** If you chose to start Classic at login in the above option, this suboption hides the Classic startup window that would otherwise appear.

- **"Warn before starting Classic."** If you enable this option, a message will appear if you launch a Classic application when Classic is not running. The message states, "Classic is starting" and gives you two choices: Don't Start, or Start Classic. If you don't make a choice within 30 seconds, Classic starts by default.

  Note that the warning appears only when Classic is launched by launching a Classic application from the Finder. If you launch Classic by clicking the Start button in the Classic System Preferences pane or via the Classic status menu (discussed below), you won't get this warning.

  The advantage of this option is that if you launch a Classic application in error, the warning eliminates the need to either cancel an in-progress launch of Classic (via the Stop button in the Classic startup window that appears) or wait for Classic to finish launching and then quit it. Apple cautions that clicking the Stop button while Classic is launching can cause unspecified problems; however, I've never encountered any when doing so.

Figure 9.3

The warning message that appears if you launch a Classic application before starting Classic—when the "Warn before starting Classic" option is enabled.

- **"Show Classic status in menu bar."** This option is new in Panther. It places a Classic menu extra on the right side of the menu bar. From here, you can start, restart, or stop Classic, eliminating the need to access the Classic System Preferences pane. The Restart option can be useful if you're having problems with Classic that you believe might be fixed if you quit and immediately restart Classic.

  This menu and its icon also tell you whether Classic is currently running (or sleeping)—useful since the icon that appears in the Dock while Classic is launching disappears once the launch is complete. Thus, without the menu there's no easy visual feedback to let you know whether Classic is running.

Figure 9.4

The Classic menu as it appears when Classic is running.

Finally, this menu includes an Apple Menu Items command. If you select this command, a hierarchical menu appears listing all of the items in the Mac OS 9 Apple menu. This is useful because the only other way to access this menu is to launch a Mac OS 9 application, make it the active application, and then access the Classic Apple menu.

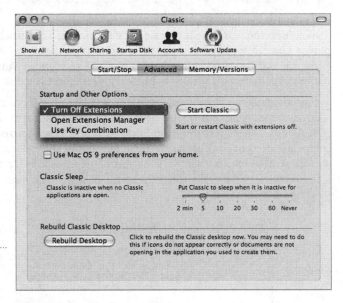

Figure 9.5

The Classic System Preferences pane's Advanced screen.

Advanced. The Advanced screen contains three sections, each of which includes features used primarily for troubleshooting problems with Classic. I discuss these in more detail later in the chapter (primarily in "Troubleshooting the Classic Environment"); in brief, they are the following:

- **Startup and Other Options.** The pop-up menu here allows you start Classic with extensions off, with Extensions Manager open at startup, or with other special startup key combinations.

  This section also includes the "Use Mac OS 9 preferences from your home" option.

  SEE: • "Startup conflicts," later in this chapter, for more on these startup options.

  • "Take Note: Use Mac OS 9 Preferences from Your Home," below, for more on this option.

- **Classic Sleep.** This is where you select the time interval at which you want to put Classic to sleep. This is separate from the overall sleep as set in Mac OS X's Energy Saver System Preferences pane.

  Classic sleep is invoked after the specified period of time—*if* the Classic environment is running but no Mac OS 9 applications are open. This quits most of the resources used by Classic so that it uses very little memory and CPU activity until you wake it up again by accessing a Classic application. Apple advises letting Classic go to sleep, rather than quitting and restarting Classic, if you still intend to use Classic but not for an extended period of time.

  How can you tell if Classic has gone to sleep? When Classic is asleep, the first item in the Classic menu changes from "Classic is running" to "Classic is sleeping."

- **Rebuild Classic Desktop.** Clicking the Rebuild Desktop button performs what would otherwise require holding down the Command-Option keys at Mac OS 9 startup. This rebuilds the database files that match the correct icons to files and determine which applications launch when you double-click a document file. This is useful if Mac OS 9 icons are incorrect or if double-clicking a document does not open the expected application.

TAKE NOTE ▶ Use Mac OS 9 Preferences from Your Home

In the Advanced screen of the Classic System Preferences pane is an option called "Use Mac OS 9 preferences from your home." Click its check box to enable this feature.

This option allows each user to have his or her own settings for the Classic environment. When this option is turned on and the Classic environment is started up for the first time, a Classic folder is created in the Library folder of the user's Home directory (for example, ~/Library/Classic). This folder contains subfolders for Apple Menu Items, Favorites, Startup Items, and so on; it also contains its own (Mac OS 9) Preferences folder. From this point on, when you launch Classic, these files will be used in lieu of the ones in the Mac OS 9 System Folder itself.

The first time you launch Classic after this feature is enabled, you will also get the following message: "Would you like to copy the contents of the folders in the Mac OS 9 System Folder you selected to the folders in your home?" Click the Copy Contents button (assuming you want to do so). Otherwise, click Leave Empty.

In either case, you'll use the folders created in your Home directory. To stop using these folders, you need to disable the option in the Classic System Preferences pane.

Not only does this arrangement allow each user to maintain separate settings for Classic, but when using the same Mac OS 9 System Folder for Classic and for booting into Mac OS 9, it allows a user to have one set of preferences for Classic use and another for booting into Mac OS 9 (assuming your Mac can boot from Mac OS 9). With this option enabled, the files in the Home folder are used when running Classic, while the files in the Mac OS 9 System Folder itself are used when booting from Mac OS 9.

continues on next page

TAKE NOTE ▶ **Use Mac OS 9 Preferences from Your Home** *continued*

Note: This option may be dimmed if you're not an administrator and limitations have been set (via the Accounts System Preferences pane) that would prohibit using this option. In contrast, this option is automatically selected (and cannot be deselected) if your computer is part of a managed workgroup connected to a Mac OS X Server.

Clean install of Mac OS 9. If you do a clean reinstallation of Mac OS 9 (that is, one in which you replace the System Folder) in an attempt to resolve problems with the OS, the Mac OS 9 files in your Home folder remain unchanged. Thus, if they are the source of the problem, the clean install will have no effect. To address this, empty the contents of the ~/Library/Classic folder when Classic is not running. Now, after doing the clean install of Mac OS 9, launch Classic. You will again be asked if you want to copy the contents to your Home directory. Do so.

See the following Apple Knowledge Base documents for more information on this feature: http://docs.info.apple.com/article.html?artnum=107184 and http://docs.info.apple.com/article.html?artnum=107398. For details on doing a clean install of Mac OS 9, see this document: http://docs.info.apple.com/article.html?artnum=107383.

Figure 9.6

The message that may appear when you first launch Classic after enabling the "Use preferences from home folder" option.

Classic has created folders in your home.

These folders were created in your home: Apple Menu Items, Preferences, Internet Search Sites, Favorites.

Would you like to copy the contents of these folders in the Mac OS 9 system folder you selected to the folders in your home?

[Leave Empty]   [Copy Contents]

Memory/Versions. This screen made its debut in Mac OS X 10.2. The Active Applications list provides a graphical display similar to what you would see in the About This Computer window when you boot in Mac OS 9, including the name of each Classic application or process that's running and each application's memory usage.

How much memory an application is currently using, as well as how much has been assigned, is depicted in the bar graphs in the Memory Use section of the Active Applications list. The bar length indicates what has been assigned; the shaded area represents how much is in use.

The bottom of the screen lists which versions of Mac OS 9 and Classic (Classic Support, Classic Enabler, and, most critically, Classic Environment) are in use. Classic Environment refers to the overall version of the files that are typically added to the Mac OS 9 System Folder when you first launch Classic.

There are two other options of note:

- **Show background applications.** If you check this box, the list will also show background processes running in Classic that are not otherwise accessible from the Finder. Classic Support is one such process.

- **Adjust Memory.** If you hold down the Option key when you select Memory/Versions, an additional button will appear in the lower right portion of the window: Adjust Memory. If you click this button, a slider appears that allows you to adjust the amount of Application Memory versus Temporary Memory available to Classic applications.

In brief, with Application Memory, the amount of memory in use by an application cannot be increased or reduced while the application is running. This is the traditional way Mac OS 9 has worked. Via Temporary Memory, however, an application may use otherwise unused memory on a temporary basis (if the memory is later needed by another application, temporary memory is purged). Thus, if temporary memory is available, you may see the memory allocation of a given application increase and decrease over time. You can adjust the minimum and maximum allocation to temporary memory from a minimum of about 48 MB to a maximum of 512 MB.

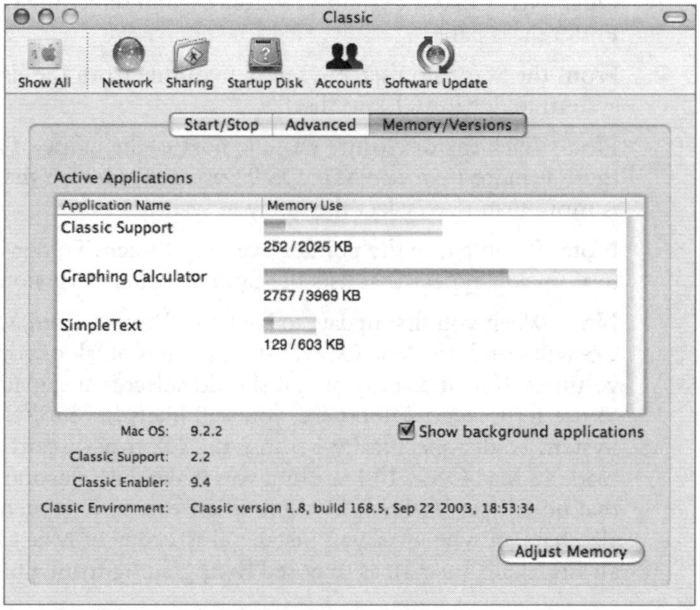

Figure 9.7

The Classic System Preferences pane's Memory/Versions screen.

Except for unusual circumstances, I would leave this Adjust Memory setting alone. If you do decide to change it, there's no hard-and-fast rule as to whether an increase or decrease is best. In general, you may need to increase the amount allocated to temporary memory if you usually work with a small number of Mac OS 9 applications open at once but find that one or two of these applications occasionally require an unexpectedly large memory allocation.

You can always return to the default settings by clicking the Default button. You need to quit and relaunch Classic before any change here takes effect.

SEE: • "Memory problems," later in this chapter, for related information.

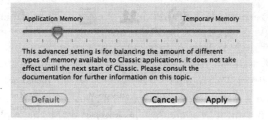

Figure 9.8

....

The Adjust Memory setting.

Selecting the Classic environment volume

Before you launch Classic for the first time, you need to select the Mac OS 9 volume you want to use for Classic. This step is especially important if you have more than one potential Mac OS 9 System Folder. To make this choice, follow these steps:

1. Open Mac OS X's System Preferences, and select the Classic System Preferences pane.

2. From the Start/Stop screen, select a volume from the list in the "Select a system folder for Classic" list.

   Note: Click the disclosure triangle next to the name of a volume to see if there is more than one Mac OS 9 System Folder on the volume. If there is more than one, select the one you want.

   Note: If you pause the pointer over any System Folder item in the list, a tool tip will appear that lists the System Folder's version of Mac OS 9.

   Note: When you first update to Jaguar or Panther from Mac OS X 10.1, the OS will search for Mac OS 9 System Folders on all of your locally mounted volumes. If it finds only one, it should select it automatically as the folder to use for Classic. Otherwise, you will likely have to select a Mac OS 9 System Folder specifically, because the OS may discard any selection you made in Mac OS X 10.1.x. Until you make this selection, the OS will claim that no Classic System is available when you try to launch Classic. This may also happen whenever you install a fresh copy of Mac OS X (such as via an Erase and Install), as opposed to upgrading from a previous version.

Figure 9.9

....

The tool tip that appears in the list of Mac OS 9 System Folders in the Start/Stop screen of the Classic System Preferences pane.

Classic is running using folder "System Folder" on volume "Neo".

Select a system folder for Classic: Searching for new folders...

▼ Neo
    System Folder   Start Classic when you login
                                         Hide Classic while starting
Smith   Volume: Neo   efore starting Classic
iDisk   Location: /Volumes/Neo/System Folder
                                         Version: Mac OS 9.2.2   Classic status in menu bar

Launching Classic

This section explains how to launch Classic and what you need to be aware of when doing so.

Selecting a launch method. You can launch the Classic environment under Mac OS X in three ways:

- **Manually.** Click the Start button in the Start/Stop screen of the Classic System Preferences pane.

- **At login.** In the Start/Stop screen of the Classic System Preferences pane, check the "Start Classic when you login" checkbox. Now whenever you start up your Mac in OS X, Classic will launch automatically when you log in.

- **By launching a Classic application.** If Classic is not running, and you try to launch a Classic application, the Classic environment will load automatically; once it has completed loading, the application will launch.

Overall, the preferred option is to launch Classic manually. Occasional problems have been reported with both of the other options, though Apple has fixed most of these in more recent versions of Mac OS X.

SEE: • "Copy/Paste problems," later in this chapter, for an example of a problem that may occur from an automatic launch of Classic.

Launching Classic for the first time, or for the first time since upgrading Mac OS X. When you boot into Mac OS X and start the Classic environment for the first time, you will likely get the following message: "Classic needs to update files in 'System Folder' on {*volume name*}. These files will not affect starting your computer from this system folder." You can select from two choices: Quit or Update.

This message will appear unless the items were already added when Mac OS X was first installed. You will also get this message after updating to a new version of Mac OS X, if any of the relevant Classic items have been updated.

These files are needed for Mac OS X compatibility with Classic. You *must* select Update or you will not be able to use the Classic environment—even if you're using what is otherwise the latest available version of Mac OS 9. If your Mac can boot from Mac OS 9, the addition of these files will not prevent Mac OS 9 from booting.

The required files, often referred to as the Classic Support files, include the following files located at the root level of the Mac OS 9 System Folder:

- Classic
- Classic Support
- Classic Support UI

Other added or updated support files are in the Mac OS 9 Control Panels and Extensions folders. These include General Controls, Startup Disk, AppleScript, Classic RAVE, File Sharing, Network Setup Extension, PrintingLib, and more.

SEE: • **"Technically Speaking: The Mac OS X Storage Location of Classic Support Files,"** below, for more details.

• **"Problems installing software,"** later in this chapter, for related information.

Figure 9.10

The message that appears the first time you launch Classic or after you update Mac OS X (if the update also includes files for updating Classic).

TECHNICALLY SPEAKING ▶ The Mac OS X Storage Location of Classic Support Files

Go to /System/Library/CoreServices. Here you will find an application called Classic Startup. This is the file that's launched when you start Classic.

Select the contextual menu for this application and choose Show Package Contents. Navigate to the Contents/Resources directory.

If you're using Jaguar, you will find a folder here named UniversalForks. If you're using Panther, the folder remains, but you won't see it because its invisible bit has been set. To access this folder in Panther, you need to either use Terminal or temporarily make invisible files visible in the Finder (using a utility such as mac4ever.de's InVisibles, as described in Chapter 6).

Once you can access this folder, open it. Here you will find all the files that are added or updated to the Mac OS 9 System Folder when you first launch Classic. When I just checked, my copy of this folder had 30 items in it, including such files as Classic Support, Extensions Manager, QuickTime Player and Script Editor, and USB Printer Sharing Extension.

Also from within the Resources folder, check the localization folder for the language you use. Thus, for English systems, open the English.lprog folder. Inside here, open the SystemFiles folder (which is also invisible). Here you will find copies of some of the same files that are included in UniversalForks. These have presumably been localized for the selected language. Some of the files (14 of UniversalFork's 30 items on my Mac) will be at the root level of this folder. The remaining files can be found in the invisible OptionalFiles folder inside the SystemFiles folder. This folder contains files that are needed only if older versions of these files are already installed.

continues on next page

> **TECHNICALLY SPEAKING ▶ The Mac OS X Storage Location of Classic Support Files** *continued*
>
> It is from these folders that Mac OS X obtains these files and transfers copies of them to the Mac OS 9 System Folder as needed. Because Apple has stopped updating Mac OS 9 (Mac OS 9.2.2 is likely to be the last official version), this is now the only way that files newer than those included in Mac OS 9.2.2 will be added.
>
> One bonus of this setup is that you can easily copy and move these files yourself. Thus, if you believe that one of these files in a Mac OS 9 System Folder is damaged or missing, and you want to replace it, you can do so even though Mac OS X may not replace the file automatically when Classic is launched.

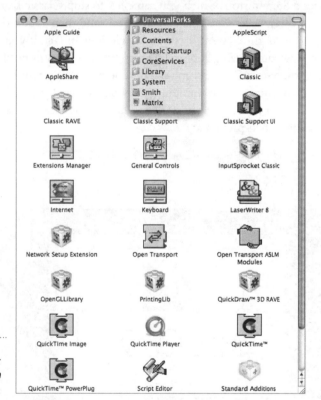

Figure 9.11

The UniversalForks folder in the Classic Startup application package.

Launching Classic after downgrading Mac OS X. If you reinstall an older version of Mac OS X (such as by reinstalling Mac OS X 10.3.0 via the Installer's Archive and Install option after having previously updated to Mac OS X 10.3.2), it's possible that the Classic System Folder will have newer versions of its components than the ones installed by the OS version you're now running. If so, you will get a message when you launch Classic that says something like the following: "Your selected System Folder has been modified by a newer version of Classic, you can use the older enabler but this would be an unsupported configuration." Solutions include (1) updating Mac OS X back to the version you were using previously; (2) reinstalling Classic from the Restore CD/DVD that came with your Mac; or (3) remove the newer files from the Classic System Folder (as listed in "Launching Classic for the first time, or for the first time since upgrading Mac OS X") so that the older files get installed the next time you launch Classic.

After launching Classic. Whichever launch method you use, when Classic starts to load, a window will open with a title that states, "Classic starting up using {*System Folder*} on {*Volume Name*}," where *System Folder* is the name of the Mac OS 9 System Folder being used by Classic and *Volume Name* is the name of the volume on which that System Folder is located. This window also includes a Stop button, which you can click to stop Classic from loading. It's safer, however, to let Classic load completely and then shut it down from the Classic pane of the System Preferences window. In fact, if you click the Stop button, a warning dialog appears, stating, "It's best to wait until Classic finishes starting, then stop Classic using the Classic pane of System Preferences." To avoid this dilemma when unintentionally double-clicking a Classic application, check the "Warn before starting Classic" box in the Classic System Preferences pane, as described previously.

Figure 9.12

The window that appears when Classic is loading (after clicking the disclosure triangle to expand the window).

Figure 9.13

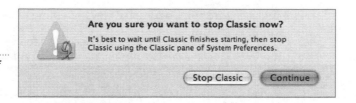

The message that appears if
you click the Stop button
while Classic is loading.

Figure 9.14

The Classic Dock icon that appears
while Classic is loading.

In the Classic startup window, you will also see a disclosure triangle in the lower left corner with the words "Show Mac OS 9 startup window." If you click this triangle, the window expands to show what looks like a Mac OS 9 startup screen. You will see the Mac OS 9 graphic, just as though you were booting into Mac OS 9; eventually, extensions and control panels will appear across the bottom of the window, just as they do when Mac OS 9 is booting up. As mentioned earlier in this chapter, this is exactly what is happening: An entire iteration of Mac OS 9 is being loaded. But because the Classic environment is simply an application running on Mac OS X, you can do other things on your computer while it loads!

Another way to tell that Classic is launching is that the Classic Startup application icon (a gray Mac OS face with a *9* overlaid on it) will appear in the Dock; as Classic loads Mac OS 9, the *9* "fills up" with orange, indicating the progress of Mac OS 9 loading in Classic. (If you're running Jaguar or earlier, you'll just see a gray Mac OS face with an orange *9*, without the animation.) In addition, the Classic System Preferences pane and the Classic menu (if enabled) will state that Classic is starting.

After Classic has launched. After Classic is fully loaded, you will notice…well, you won't notice anything. Unfortunately (or fortunately, depending on your point of view), the Classic icon disappears from the Dock and there is no other immediate feedback that Classic has launched and is running.

The quickest way to check on Classic's status at this point is to check the Classic menu (enabled via the Start/Stop screen in the Classic System Preferences pane). The Classic menu icon changes slightly after Classic has finished launching (the background to the left of the *9* fills in). In addition, the top line of the menu will read, "Classic is running."

The following are some additional ways of telling whether the Classic environment is running:

• If a Classic *application* is running, its icon will appear in the Dock, just like the icon of any other application.

• If you go to the Classic System Preferences pane, it will state, "Classic is running." In addition, the Start button will change to Stop, and the Restart and Force Quit buttons will be available. If you go to the Memory/Versions tab and enable "Show background applications," you will see that the Classic Support process is running.

• If you go to the Force Quit window (for example, by selecting Force Quit from the Apple menu), Classic Environment will be listed as one of the applications you can force quit. Quit this to quit Classic and all open Classic applications.

  Also note that if you go to the Force Quit window while Classic is launching, Classic Startup will also be listed. It disappears when Classic is finished launching (just as the Classic Startup icon disappears from the Dock).

  In addition, each open Classic application will be listed in the Force Quit window.

• In Activity Monitor, the Classic environment shows up as TruBlueEnvironme (in Jaguar) or typically as *(null)* in Panther. From Terminal, the top command lists the Classic environment as TruBlueEnv. Unlike in the Force Quit window, individual applications opened in Classic are not listed in these two locations.

• Several shareware or freeware utilities maintain a Classic icon in the Dock and provide visual cues about whether Classic is running from the Dock. One such application is Northern Softwork's Classic Toggler.

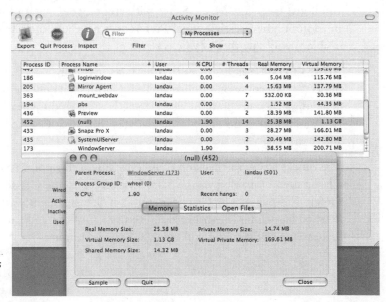

Figure 9.15

Activity Monitor lists (null), which means Classic is running.

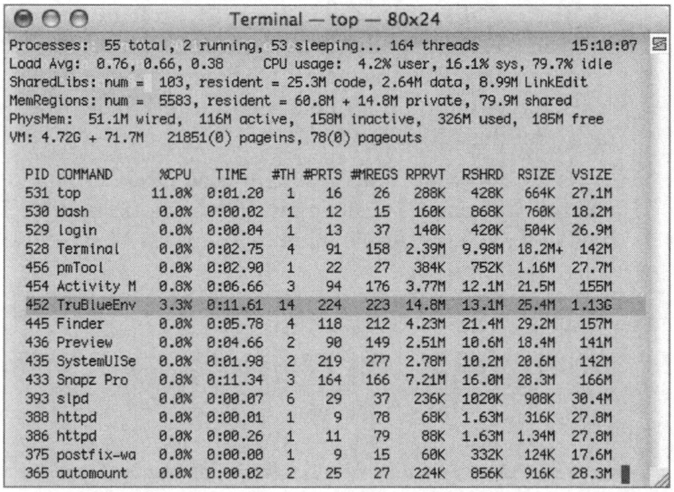

```
  ● ○ ○              Terminal — top — 80x24
Processes: 55 total, 2 running, 53 sleeping... 164 threads        15:10:07
Load Avg: 0.76, 0.66, 0.38    CPU usage: 4.2% user, 16.1% sys, 79.7% idle
SharedLibs: num = 103, resident = 25.3M code, 2.64M data, 8.99M LinkEdit
MemRegions: num = 5583, resident = 60.8M + 14.8M private, 79.9M shared
PhysMem: 51.1M wired, 116M active, 158M inactive, 326M used, 185M free
VM: 4.72G + 71.7M   21851(0) pageins, 78(0) pageouts

PID COMMAND      %CPU  TIME    #TH #PRTS #MREGS RPRVT  RSHRD RSIZE  VSIZE
531 top          11.0% 0:01.20  1   16    26   288K   428K  664K   27.1M
530 bash          0.0% 0:00.02  1   12    15   160K   868K  760K   18.2M
529 login         0.0% 0:00.04  1   13    37   140K   420K  504K   26.9M
528 Terminal      0.0% 0:02.75  4   91   158   2.39M  9.98M 18.2M+ 142M
456 pmTool        0.0% 0:02.90  1   22    27   384K   752K  1.16M  27.7M
454 Activity M    0.0% 0:06.66  3   94   176   3.77M  12.1M 21.5M  155M
452 TruBlueEnv    3.3% 0:11.61 14  224   223   14.8M  13.1M 25.4M  1.13G
445 Finder        0.0% 0:05.78  4  118   212   4.23M  21.4M 29.2M  157M
436 Preview       0.0% 0:04.66  2   90   149   2.51M  10.6M 18.4M  141M
435 SystemUISe    0.0% 0:01.98  2  219   277   2.78M  10.2M 20.6M  142M
433 Snapz Pro     0.0% 0:11.34  3  164   166   7.21M  16.0M 28.3M  166M
393 slpd          0.0% 0:00.07  6   29    37   236K   1020K 908K   30.4M
388 httpd         0.0% 0:00.01  1    9    78   68K    1.63M 316K   27.8M
386 httpd         0.0% 0:00.26  1   11    79   88K    1.63M 1.34M  27.8M
375 postfix-wa    0.0% 0:00.00  1    9    15   60K    332K  124K   17.6M
365 automount     0.0% 0:00.02  2   25    27   224K   856K  916K   28.3M
```

Figure 9.16

Terminal lists TruBlueEnv, which means Classic is running.

Quitting Classic

To quit Classic at any time, select the Stop or Force Quit buttons from the Start/Stop screen of the Classic System Preferences pane. Alternatively, from the Classic menu select Stop Classic.

In addition, shareware utilities such as Classic Toggler include options for starting or quitting Classic from their Dock icons.

The look and feel of Classic

If you launch a Classic application in the Classic environment, it appears to launch just like any Mac OS X application. The application's icon bounces in the Dock as it is loading and remains there as long as the application is running. There are, however, some differences.

Menu bar. When a Classic application is active, all menus and the menu bar switch to the Mac OS 9 Platinum appearance (gray with black text), and you see a menu bar arranged exactly as it would be in Mac OS 9. Two things occur as a result of this:

- All of the Mac OS X additions to the menu bar, especially those at the right end (Date & Time, Volume icon, AirPort signal strength, Displays, and so on) vanish and are replaced by whatever Mac OS 9 would place there.

- The Apple menu shifts to the Mac OS 9 Apple menu. From here, you can choose Mac OS 9 control panels, the Chooser, and any other items from the Mac OS 9 Apple menu. Note: If you have enabled the Classic menu, you can also choose Apple menu items from the Classic menu, even with no other Classic applications open or even with the Classic environment itself not currently running (Classic will launch when you select an item, if necessary).

Note: As an alternative to the Apple Menu Items item in the Classic menu, you can drag the Apple Menu Items folder from the Classic System Folder to the Dock to create a Dock icon for the folder. You can then access items within the Apple Menu Items folder via the hierarchical menu for this Dock icon.

Note: The Recent Items listing in Mac OS X's Apple menu will list recently launched Classic items. However, the similar Recent Items listings in the Classic Apple menu will not list Mac OS X items.

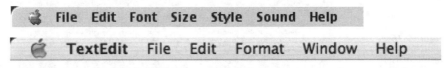

Figure 9.17

The menu bar in Mac OS X when (top) a Classic application (SimpleText) is active and (bottom) a Mac OS X application (TextEdit) is active.

Figure 9.18

The Apple menu in Mac OS X when (left) a Classic application is active and (right) a Mac OS X application is active.

Windows. Windows in Mac OS X–native applications use the Aqua interface, as described in Chapter 2. Windows in Classic applications look and act as they do in Mac OS 9, using the Platinum appearance. You can even use the WindowShade effect with Mac OS 9 windows—where double-clicking the title bar "rolls up" the window—even though this feature is not included as part of Mac OS X.

Similarly, Open and Save dialogs in Classic applications work as they do in Mac OS 9.

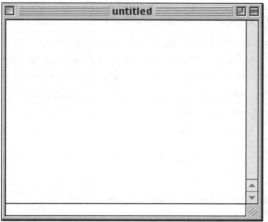

Figure 9.19

A document window of a Classic application.

Figure 9.20

A document window of a Mac OS X application.

Fonts. Classic applications typically only access fonts in the Mac OS 9 Fonts folder. In particular, they will not access fonts in the various Library folders of Mac OS X. On the other hand, Mac OS X applications do recognize fonts placed in the Mac OS 9 System Folder that Classic uses.

In addition, Mac OS X does not permit you to add fonts to or remove fonts from a font suitcase file, as you can in Mac OS 9, even when you're accessing these files with Classic running. Third-party utilities such as Extensis Suitcase can work around most of these limitations.

SEE: • Chapter 4 for more information on fonts.

TAKE NOTE ▶ File Navigation in Open and Save Dialogs

Classic applications running in the Classic environment may use either of the two types of Open and Save dialogs used in Mac OS 9: The first type is the older small, white Standard File Package dialog (also called a *modal* dialog because you can't do anything else on your computer—including moving or resizing the dialog—until you dismiss it by opening or saving a file, or canceling). The second type is the newer Navigation Services dialog. These gray dialogs can be resized and moved, and they offer a few more menu and button options. In addition, they are only modal for the application in which they were opened. Thus, if you're using Microsoft Internet Explorer, for example, and choose its Save As command to open a dialog, you can still switch to another application and use it while the Internet Explorer dialog remains open.

continues on next page

TAKE NOTE ▶ **File Navigation in Open and Save Dialogs** *continued*

The Open and Save dialogs used by Mac OS X applications differ from either Mac OS 9 type (although they, too, are called Navigation Services dialogs) in that they have the Aqua appearance. In addition, each document gets its own Save dialog. If you have several documents open in a native application and use the Save or Save As command, the resulting dialog is attached to the currently active document. You can switch to other applications, or even to other documents within the same application, while the dialog remains open.

Note: Carbon applications running native in Mac OS X may use either Mac OS 9 or Mac OS X dialogs, depending on how the developer wrote the application.

SEE: • "Opening and Saving: Saving Files," in Chapter 6, for additional information.

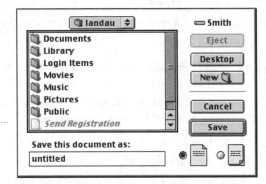

Figure 9.21

A Mac OS 9 Standard File Package Save dialog.

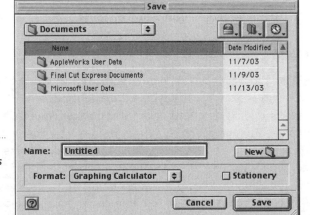

Figure 9.22

A Mac OS 9 Navigation Services Save dialog. Some Mac OS X Carbon applications may also use this.

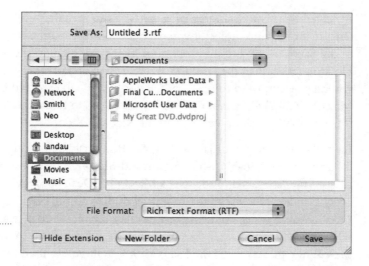

Figure 9.23

A Mac OS X Save
dialog.

Desktop Folders in Mac OS 9/Classic vs. Mac OS X

If you routinely save files to the Desktop, and you boot back and forth
between Mac OS X and Mac OS 9, you may notice that files saved to the
Desktop in Mac OS 9 are no longer on the Desktop when you boot into
Mac OS X, and vice versa. This is because the Desktop is handled differently
by Mac OS X and Mac OS 9.

Booting from Mac OS 9. The Classic Mac OS was designed as a single-
user environment—that is, one in which everyone shares the same files and
folders. (Mac OS 9 did introduce a Multiple Users feature, but that's another
story.) In Mac OS 9 and earlier, every hard drive or volume contains an invisible
folder called, appropriately enough, Desktop Folder. If you have more than
one volume mounted, there is thus more than one Desktop Folder available.
Any items from a volume that are moved to the Desktop are stored in the
Desktop Folder for that volume. However, the contents of all Desktop Folders
are visible together on what seems to be the sole Desktop of Mac OS 9.

Booting from Mac OS X: Desktop files and screen captures. In Mac
OS X, every user has his or her own Desktop Folder. This folder, called
Desktop, is located at the root level of each user's Home directory (/Users/
user name/Desktop). When you log in to your Mac OS X account, anything
you place on the Desktop is placed in your private Desktop folder. If someone
else uses another account to log in to your computer, that person will never
see—or even be able to access—the contents of your Desktop.

This also means that files saved to the Mac OS X Desktop do not appear on
the Mac OS 9 Desktop when you're booted from Mac OS 9, and vice versa.

A related issue is that some Classic applications save files to the Desktop by default (or by your choice, if you click the Desktop button or pop-up menu in the Save dialog), but they will most likely save them to the Mac OS 9 Desktop rather than the Mac OS X one. If you do not realize this situation, you may be surprised to find that the document you expected to see on your Mac OS X Desktop is not there. The solution is to locate the document on the Mac OS 9 Desktop rather than the Mac OS X one.

A similar issue occurs in Jaguar (but not Panther) when taking screen captures by using Command-Shift-3 or Command-Shift-4. In Mac OS X, the resulting capture files are saved to the user's Mac OS X Desktop. In Mac OS 9, however, the files are saved to the root level of the volume that contains the Mac OS 9 startup System Folder. When running Jaguar, if you take a screen capture when a Classic application is active, the files are also saved to the root level of the volume that contains the Mac OS 9 System Folder used for Classic. This has been fixed in Panther: Now, regardless of what application is active, screen captures are saved to the user's Mac OS X Desktop.

SEE: • "Take Note: Screen Captures," in Chapter 2, for related information.

How to access the Mac OS 9 Desktop from Mac OS X. There are two basic ways to access Mac OS 9 Desktop Folders when you're running Mac OS X, depending on which Desktop Folder you want to access and are using with Classic:

- On any volume with Mac OS X installed, you may find an alias called Desktop (Mac OS 9) located at the root level of the Mac OS X volume. This alias is a link to the invisible Desktop Folder on the startup volume. (The folder and its alias only appear if there are items currently in the Desktop Folder for that volume.) Double-click this alias to open and view the otherwise invisible contents of the Mac OS 9 Desktop Folder for the startup volume.

  If there is a separate Desktop Folder on a nonstartup volume with Mac OS X installed, it remains invisible—with no alias to access it. The way to access it is via the Finder's Go to Folder command.

  SEE: • "Take Note: The Location of Desktop Folders," in Chapter 4, for details.

- On volumes that do not have Mac OS X installed, you may find a visible folder called Desktop Folder. This folder contains the Mac OS 9 Desktop items stored on that volume.

Whatever volume contains the Mac OS 9 System Folder that you use for Classic also contains the Desktop Folder where items will go when you save files to the Mac OS 9 Desktop from Classic applications. However, in most cases, when selecting Desktop from the Open or Save dialogs of Mac OS 9 applications running in Classic, you're taken to your Mac OS X Desktop, not the Mac OS 9 Desktop. Thus, you should rarely, if ever, be placing items in a Mac OS 9 Desktop Folder.

SEE: • "Take Note: The Location of Desktop Folders" in Chapter 4, and "'Desktop (Mac OS 9)' file is a symbolic link," in Chapter 6, for related information.

Accessing the Mac OS X Desktop from Mac OS 9. If you boot from Mac OS 9 and need to access your Mac OS X Desktop, locate the Users folder (at the root level of the volume containing Mac OS X). Within it, locate the folder with your Mac OS X user name on it. Inside that folder you'll find your Mac OS X Desktop Folder.

Applications and Documents folders in Mac OS 9/Classic vs. Mac OS X

Mac OS 9 maintains certain applications in the Applications (Mac OS 9) folder. Similarly, it may store the documents you create in its Documents folder. Both of these folders are located at the root level of the Mac OS 9 volume.

There's also a Mac OS X Applications folder at the root level of the Mac OS X volume. In addition, there is a Documents folder in the Home directory of every user. These Mac OS 9 and Mac OS X folders, despite their overlapping names, are separate.

Prior to Mac OS X 10.2, if you saved a document from an application running in Classic, it was saved to the Mac OS 9 Documents folder by default. Starting with Mac OS X 10.2, the default behavior in all cases is to save files to the Documents folder in your Mac OS X Home directory.

Although this consistency is a good idea overall, it can cause problems for Classic applications (such as Microsoft Office 2001) that have data in the now-unused Mac OS 9 Documents folder (because you used these applications prior to installing Mac OS X 10.2). A solution is to drag the files (for example, the Microsoft User Data folder, for Office 2001) to the Documents folder in your Home directory. However, doing this may prevent you from accessing the data when booting from Mac OS 9. If so, putting an alias to the User Data folder in the Mac OS 9 Documents folder should work around the problem.

On the other hand, if you have Microsoft Office for Mac OS X installed, Office will have already placed a User Data folder in the Documents folder of your Home directory. Do not replace it with the Mac OS 9 folder; if you do, you will lose all of the data that the Mac OS X folder contained. If you have Office v. X, of course, you presumably don't need to run Office 2001 from Classic.

In any case, if a file you expect to find on the Desktop appears to be missing, check both the Mac OS 9 and Mac OS X folder locations before assuming it's lost.

Troubleshooting the Classic Environment

Because the Classic environment is actually running a copy of Mac OS 9, many of the same problems that can occur while running Mac OS 9 can occur in Classic. Unfortunately, troubleshooting Mac OS 9 is a topic too large to tackle here. Indeed, I've covered it at great length in a separate book, *Sad Macs, Bombs, and Other Disasters*. However, some troubleshooting issues are specific to interactions among Mac OS 9, Classic, and Mac OS X. I cover a selection of those issues in this section.

One overall advantage of using the Classic environment instead of booting into Mac OS 9 is that Classic acts just like another Mac OS X application. Although a freeze or crash in a Classic application might take down the Classic environment, Mac OS X itself and Mac OS X applications will keep chugging along as though nothing had happened; you can even relaunch Classic while you work on other things. It also means that you can troubleshoot the Classic environment while you're doing other things in Mac OS X; restarting Classic does not take over your whole computer.

Can't select or launch Mac OS 9 from Classic System Preferences pane

As described earlier in this chapter (see "Selecting the Classic environment volume"), any volumes that contain a valid Mac OS 9 System Folder should appear in the Start/Stop screen of the Classic System Preferences pane. Any System Folders on that volume should be selectable as the Classic System Folder.

In some cases, however, a volume with Mac OS 9 on it may not show up in this list or its name may be dimmed (and thus unselectable). Or you may be able to select a System Folder but unable to get Classic to launch successfully. In the last case, in particular, you're likely to get an error message like one of the following:

- "No startup volume. There is no volume with a system folder that supports starting Classic. Please install Mac OS 9.1 or later."
- "You do not have sufficient permissions to run Classic from /System/Library/CoreServices. Please correct permissions and restart Classic."
- "Cannot launch Classic, Classic Boot ROM missing or damaged, reinstall system software."
- "To start Classic, you need Mac OS 9.1 or later installed. See your documentation for instructions on installing this software."
- "The application 'Finder' has unexpectedly quit."

There are several potential causes and solutions:

Make sure Mac OS 9 is on the volume. Make sure Mac OS 9 is actually on the volume you want to select. If Mac OS 9 is not on any mounted volume, you will need to install it, most likely via the Software Restore disc(s) that came with your Mac (as described in Chapter 3).

SEE: • **"Volumes fail to mount when booting from Mac OS 9," later in this chapter, for related information.**

Use Startup Disk to *bless* the Mac OS 9 System Folder. If your Mac can boot from Mac OS 9, the following procedure should get the volume to be selectable from the Classic System Preferences pane:

1. From the Mac OS X Startup Disk System Preferences pane, select the desired Mac OS 9 volume as the startup volume.

2. Do not select to Restart. Instead, switch to the Classic System Preferences pane.

3. Before the Classic pane appears, a dialog will drop down asking whether you want to change the startup disk. Click the Change button. This "blesses" the Mac OS 9 System Folder.

4. When the Classic pane appears, you should be able to select the desired volume. Do so.

5. Return to the Startup Disk pane to change the setting back to your normal Mac OS X startup volume.

Delete the ByHost Classic file. If you can't start up from Mac OS 9, the prior suggestion won't work because the volume won't be listed in the Startup Disk System Preferences as a Mac OS 9 volume. In this case, go to the ~/Library/Preferences/ByHost folder and look for a file called com.apple.Classic.###.plist, where ### represents a series of numbers and letters (which is technically your Mac's MAC address). Delete this file. Return to the Classic System Preferences pane. The missing or dimmed volume/partition should now be selectable. If not, log out and log back in, and then check again.

Repair Permissions. If you get the "You are running Classic without supervisor (root) privileges" error when launching Classic and you're running Mac OS 10.2 or later, the solution is to select to Repair Disk Permissions from the First Aid section of Disk Utility. After permissions are repaired, Classic should launch.

If you get the "You do not have sufficient permissions…" error, you should select Disk Utility's Fix Mac OS 9 Permissions command.

SEE: • **"Permissions settings and running Classic," later in this chapter, for more details.**

Don't use newer Classic with older Mac OS X. After you've updated a Mac OS 9 System Folder with Classic files for Mac OS X 10.2 or later, you should no longer use it for running Classic from Mac OS X 10.0 through 10.1.5. If you try, you will get the following error message: "The application 'Finder' has unexpectedly quit." The same principle may apply when updating to Panther (Mac OS X 10.3) from Jaguar (Mac OS X 10.2).

SEE: • "Take Note: Blessed Systems and Starting Up," in Chapter 5, for more on this issue.

• "Launching Classic and Fast User Switching," later in this chapter, for a related issue.

Startup conflicts

Just as Mac OS 9 loads files at startup (mainly in the Extensions and Control Panels folders of the Mac OS 9 System Folder), so does the Classic environment. And just as you can watch those file icons appear across the bottom of the startup screen as they load into Mac OS 9, you can also watch them come up in the Classic Startup window as the Classic environment loads. Because of this similarity, Classic is susceptible to the same startup-file conflicts (often called *extension* conflicts) that can occur when booting from Mac OS 9. These conflicts can lead to anything from a minor problem when accessing a command in a certain Classic application to a fatal crash as Classic attempts to load. The following are some things you can try if you encounter such problems.

Start up with extensions off. The surest way to minimize such problems is to use a slimmed-down and optimized Mac OS 9 System Folder for Classic, as I recommended earlier in this chapter. If problems persist, you will want to determine whether an extension is causing the conflict.

The most direct way to do this in Classic is via the settings in the Advanced screen of the Classic System Preferences pane. In particular, you can choose the Turn Off Extensions option from the Startup and Other Options pop-up menu before starting or restarting Classic—the equivalent of starting up Mac OS 9 with the Shift key held down. If you have problems getting this option to work, you can choose the Use Key Combination option instead and make the Shift key the key to use at startup. This method, too, should launch Classic with all extensions disabled. In either case, if the problem no longer occurs, a startup file was the cause.

Note: To use these startup options, you must start Classic via the Start Classic button located in the Advanced screen; other methods for starting Classic, described earlier in this chapter, will start Classic normally.

Note: In a few cases, enabling the Use Key Combination option may cause problems for Classic applications that require other keyboard input before Classic finishes starting up. If this happens, select another option from the pop-up menu instead. Alternatively, at any time during the launch of Classic, if you press and release the keys listed in the Use Key Combination option, the keys are no longer seen as pressed.

Figure 9.24

....

The Startup and Other Options section of the Advanced screen of the Classic System Preferences pane—after selecting the Use Key Combination option from the pop-up menu. See also Figure 9.5.

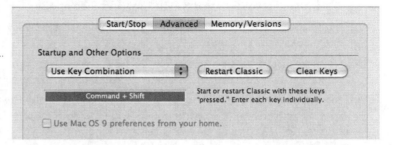

Delete or replace Classic files. The next step is to figure out which startup file(s) are responsible for the conflict. One frequent cause of such conflicts is one of the files that Mac OS X installs in your Mac OS 9 System Folder for Classic compatibility. The most likely culprits are the Classic files installed at the root level of your System Folder: Classic, Classic Support, and Classic Support UI. Try moving these files to the Trash, emptying the Trash, and then starting up Classic normally. Mac OS X should ask you for permission to add these files back to your System Folder; allow it to do so. If your Classic startup conflict is gone, the problem was most likely that one of those files was corrupted; thus, replacing them with new copies solves the problem.

Check the Startup Items folder. If you have aliases to servers in the Startup Items folder (in your Classic System Folder) and those servers are not accessible to mount, Classic will fail to launch successfully. Instead, it will hang indefinitely at the point where it tries to mount the servers.

Isolate the startup-file conflict. If none of the preceding suggestions work, you'll need to hunt down the startup file(s) that are causing the problem. Those of you who have isolated startup-file conflicts in Mac OS 9 know the procedure well—though straightforward, it's also tedious and time-consuming!

SEE: • "Take Note: Isolating Startup-File Conflicts," below, for details.

TAKE NOTE ▶ **Isolating Startup-File Conflicts**

When a startup file doesn't load properly, conflicts with another file during startup, or conflicts with other software used after startup is complete, you have a startup-file conflict. To track down the offending file or files, follow these steps:

1. If your problems began recently, chances are good that a newer startup file is causing the problem, so disable files that you recently installed and see if the problem goes away.

   If it does, you can add the newer files back one at a time until you find out which one (or more) caused the problem.

   To disable a file, drag it out of the Mac OS 9 System Folder (the one used by Classic) and restart Classic. Alternatively, you can use Extensions Manager, as described in the following step.

   If testing newly added files does not solve the problem, the cause is likely third-party shareware extensions or control panels added to your System Folder. One or more of those files may not be compatible with Classic or is conflicting with other files.

2. Launch Classic with only the startup files that came with Mac OS 9 enabled.

   To start up with just Apple's Mac OS 9 files enabled, from the Startup and Other Options pop-up menu in the Advanced tab of the Classic System Preferences window, choose Open Extensions Manager. Then click the Start/Restart Classic button to the right of the menu. This action causes Extensions Manager to open as Classic launches. When Extensions Manager opens, from the Selected Set pop-up menu choose Mac OS 9 All, then click Continue.

   If the conflict no longer occurs, one of the non–Apple Mac OS 9 files you disabled was the cause.

If the problem persists, you can restart Classic with Mac OS 9 Base selected in Extensions Manager. This method enables an even smaller set of Apple startup files—just those considered essential. If the conflict no longer occurs, one of the Apple files you disabled was the culprit. The chances are quite slim that Mac OS 9 Base will find the culprit if Mac OS 9 All does not, however.

Note: In versions of Mac OS 9 prior to Mac OS 9.2.1, selecting Mac OS 9 Base or Mac OS 9 All in Extensions Manager disabled the required Classic compatibility files (such as Classic Support UI). If this occurred, you would need to create a custom set that added these files to the Base or All sets. Fortunately, you can prevent this hassle simply by making sure you're using the latest version of Mac OS 9.

After you've determined whether the offending file is an Apple file, you will likely need to determine which of the numerous possible files is the culprit. This process can be tedious. Here are two suggested ways to go about it:

- **Extensions Manager.** Use Extensions Manager to enable and disable files selectively, restarting Classic each time. The recommended approach is to disable half of all files the first time. If the remaining files still produce the conflict, disable half of those files. Keep doing this until the problem no longer occurs. At that point, shift to the group you just disabled and continue the process. Eventually, you will be left with just one file: the culprit.

continues on next page

TAKE NOTE ▶ Isolating Startup-File Conflicts *continued*

- **Conflict Catcher.** If that process sounds too tedious (which it is!), you can try Casady & Greene's Conflict Catcher. (Unfortunately, Casady & Greene recently went out of business, so this product is no longer being marketed. However, if you have or can obtain a recent version of Conflict Catcher, it still works fine in Classic.) This utility automates the process. In fact, Conflict Catcher works even better in the Classic environment than it does in Mac OS 9. When you're using Classic, you don't have to restart your machine to perform testing; you simply reload Classic. In addition, you can work on other things during the process. Conflict Catcher 9 also allows you to maintain separate extension sets for launching Classic versus booting in Mac OS 9—helpful if you're using the same Mac OS 9 System Folder for both.

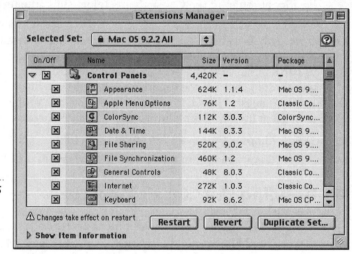

Figure 9.25

You can use Mac OS 9's Extensions Manager to help diagnose extension conflicts.

Font conflicts

As discussed earlier in the chapter, Mac OS X uses fonts from the Fonts folder within the Classic System Folder—and because it does, Classic fonts can cause problems for Mac OS X, including an inability to start up, even if you've never launched Classic.

Isolating a problem font can be time-consuming task. In general, suspect older fonts, especially bitmap fonts and fonts in font suitcases. To test a suspected font, remove it from the Mac OS 9 System Folder that Classic uses, and restart Mac OS X. If the suspected font problem is preventing Mac OS X from starting up and your Mac can boot from Mac OS 9, boot from Mac OS 9 or from a bootable Mac OS 9 CD, and remove the font from the System Folder.

Alternatively, if the problem is specific to running Classic, you can use Conflict Catcher to isolate problem fonts in the same way you use it to isolate problems with startup files.

Following are some examples of problems (in both Classic and Mac OS X itself) that can occur due to fonts in the Mac OS 9 System Folder:

- Having too many fonts in the Classic System Folder can cause startup problems for Mac OS X. In general, keep fonts in the Classic System Folder to a minimum. If the folder contains fonts you no longer need in Classic but want to use in Mac OS X, move them from the Fonts folder in the System Folder to the Fonts folder in your Home directory's Library folder. Mac OS X will still be able to use these fonts; however, they'll no longer be available in the Classic environment.

- Similarly, some applications may run exceptionally slowly in Classic if too many Classic fonts are present. I encountered this problem with Adobe GoLive 4.x and 5.x. I found that reducing the number of fonts (especially PostScript fonts) in the Classic Fonts folder substantially improved GoLive's responsiveness.

- Certain fonts in the Classic Fonts folder may cause Mac OS X applications, especially Carbon ones, to crash on launch. Classic does not need to be running for this problem to happen. Crashes logged by Console will most likely have the following text at the top line of the list: "#0 ... In FindTablesInNFNT." Fortunately, most of the problems that produced this symptom have been eliminated in recent versions of Mac OS X.

    SEE: • **Chapter 4 for more information on fonts.**

    • **Chapter 5 for more information on startup problems.**

Rebuilding the Classic Desktop

Just like Mac OS 9, the Classic environment occasionally loses track of which documents should be opened with which applications, or which applications are on your hard drive. Potential symptoms of this problem include documents' failing to launch with their creating application when double-clicked in the Finder, as well as documents with incorrect icons. As in Mac OS 9, the most common solution is to rebuild the Desktop. When booting in Mac OS 9, you typically do this by holding down the Command and Option keys at startup (as mentioned in the previous section).

One advantage of working with Classic, however, is that you don't have to start or restart Classic to do a rebuild. Instead, simply go to the Advanced screen of the Classic System Preferences pane and click the Rebuild Desktop button. A small window appears from which you can select to rebuild the Desktop for any or all mounted volume(s).

A progress bar will appear, indicating when the rebuild is complete. If you selected more than one volume, the Desktop for each volume will rebuild sequentially.

Note: If you instead choose to rebuild the Desktop by holding down the Command and Option keys at Classic startup (the traditional required method when booting from Mac OS 9), the Desktops of multiple volumes will be rebuilt in parallel, potentially saving some time.

Note: When you select to rebuild the Desktop, you are selecting to rebuild two invisible files at the root level of the volume: Desktop DB and Desktop DF. During the rebuild process, two temporary additional files are created: "Desktop DB – for rebuild" and "Desktop DF – for rebuild." These files should be automatically deleted when the rebuild is complete. If, for some reason, they are not deleted, you can delete them manually (see Chapter 6 for how to locate and delete invisible files).

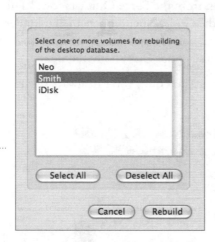

Figure 9.26

The window that appears when you click the Rebuild Desktop button in the Classic System Preferences pane.

THE JAGUAR WAY ▶ Rebuilding Multiple Desktops

In Jaguar, one disadvantage of using the Rebuild Desktop button in the Classic System Preferences pane is that if you have more than one volume, only the volume with the copy of Mac OS 9 that Classic is using will be rebuilt. There is no option to select which volume(s) to rebuild, as there is in Panther.

Thus, if you have multiple Mac OS 9 volumes, a potentially better approach is to hold down the Command and Option keys as Classic launches (just as you would when booting in Mac OS 9), or have the Command and Option keys selected automatically via the Use Key Combination option in the Advanced screen of the Classic System Preferences pane. Both methods bring up dialogs for each partition or volume, asking whether you really want to rebuild your Desktop. This procedure will rebuild the Desktops of multiple volumes in parallel, making the rebuild potentially faster than the sequential rebuilding that would occur if your booted from Mac OS 9.

Classic application freezes

If a Classic application freezes, and you cannot seem to quit it by using the standard Quit command (either by choosing it from the application's File menu or by pressing Command-Q), you can still likely force-quit the application. To do this, either (a) access the Force Quit window by holding down Command-Option-Escape and selecting to force-quit the Classic application, or (b) Option-Control-click the Dock icon for the Classic application and select the Force Quit command from the menu that appears.

Force-quitting a Classic application may cause the entire Classic environment to quit. In fact, you may get the following warning when you attempt to force-quit a Classic application from the Force Quit window: "This may cause all applications running in the Classic Environment to quit immediately." However, in Mac OS 10.1.3 or later, you can potentially quit an individual application without bringing down the entire Classic environment.

If the Classic environment does quit, you can always relaunch it immediately, if desired.

Figure 9.27

The warning that appears when you attempt to force-quit a Classic application.

Even if the Classic environment doesn't quit after you force-quit an application, I recommend saving any unsaved work in other Classic applications and selecting to restart the Classic environment (for example, via the Restart Classic command in the Classic menu) to prevent further problems.

Sometimes, force-quitting an application doesn't work—especially if the problem occurs while the application is launching (that is, the Dock icon continues to bounce endlessly, but the application never opens). If you Control-click the application's icon in the Dock, the pop-up menu may say that the application is not responding. In this and similar cases, follow the advice in the following section, "Classic environment freezes."

SEE: • "Force-quitting," in Chapter 5, for more details on how to force-quit applications in Mac OS X.

Classic environment freezes

As is true when you're booted from Mac OS 9, a freeze of even one open application in Classic often freezes the entire Classic environment. Symptoms of this problem in Classic include the following:

- You can't launch Classic applications, even though the Classic pane of the System Preferences window says, "Classic is running."
- A blank menu bar appears when you attempt to bring a Classic application to the foreground.

If either of these symptoms occurs, try force-quitting from any Classic application. If you're unable to do so, try stopping Classic by selecting Stop Classic from the Classic menu or the Classic System Preferences pane. If none of these methods work, you will need to force-quit the Classic environment. To do this, try one or more of the following techniques until you're successful:

- In the Classic System Preferences pane's Start/Stop screen, click the Force Quit button.
- With a Mac OS X application active, from the Mac OS X Apple menu, choose Force Quit. Then, in the Force Quit window that appears, select Classic Environment and click the Force Quit button.
- Open Mac OS X's Activity Monitor utility, select the *(null)* process, and from the Process menu choose Quit. Then select to Force Quit.

  Note: Technically, a process named *null* could represent something other than the Classic environment. If so, you probably do not want to quit it. However, if Classic is running, and only one null process is listed, it's virtually certain to be Classic. If you're still not convinced, you can use the top command in Terminal instead, as described next. Why, you may ask, did Apple shift to listing Classic as null here? I don't know. In fact, I am aware of some instances where the older TrueBlueEnvironme terminology shows up in Panther instead of null. Hopefully, Apple will get this all straightened out in a future update.

- Use the top command in Terminal to identify the process ID number (PID) of TruBlueEnv, and then type kill {PID#} to kill the Classic process. Alternatively, type killall TruBlueEnv.

SEE: • See "Killing process from Terminal," in Chapter 5, for more details.

If none of these methods work, restart your Mac.

Finally, as suggested earlier in the chapter, having Classic launch automatically at startup (via the Classic System Preferences setting) can trigger freezes in certain situations that would not occur if you launched Classic manually after startup was complete. To avoid this, disable the automatic option and instead launch Classic manually.

The "Classic Environment is Not Responding" message. An Apple document states, "After clicking Stop in the Classic pane of System Preferences, an alert box appears with this message: '*The Classic Environment is Not Responding. You may click Cancel and attempt to save any changes to open documents...*' If the Classic pane of System Preferences states that 'Classic is not running,' then your stop attempt was successful." To get rid of the inaccurate message, click Cancel. To get rid of the inaccurate message, click Cancel. The latest word from Apple is that this problem has been fixed in recent versions of Mac OS X.

SEE: • Chapters 2 and 5 for more information on Activity Monitor and on restarting your Mac after a freeze.

• Chapter 10 for more information on Terminal.

Problems launching applications

In theory, Classic applications load in the Classic environment, and Mac OS X–native applications open in Mac OS X. In practice, however, what *should* happen and what actually does happen don't always coincide.

"Cannot be used in Classic" error. Occasionally, if you attempt to launch a Mac OS X application (especially from the Dock while Classic is running), the application may attempt to launch in Classic. If it can't do this, you will get the following error message: "This version of {*application name*} cannot be used in the Classic Environment."

This situation can also occur if you double-click a document for which you have both a Classic and a Mac OS X version (for example, if you have two copies of Internet Explorer—one for each OS—and you double-click an Internet Explorer document). This problem is caused by a bug in Mac OS X. If you click OK and attempt to relaunch the application, it will usually launch normally. Sometimes, however, you may need to make sure that you're not actually "in" the Classic environment by switching to a Mac OS X application first.

Wrong version accessed. When you have both Classic and OS X versions of the same application on your drive, the Mac OS 9 version may open in error.

If you have both variants of the same Web browser, for example, and you don't have the Mac OS X version running, clicking a URL from within a Classic application (such as a Classic email client) will likely launch the Classic version of the Web browser instead of the Mac OS X version. This is caused by the way the Classic environment looks for applications to open files: First, it looks to see whether the appropriate application is already running, and, if it does not find the application open, it tries to launch it. In such cases, Classic may see only the Mac OS 9 version (not recognizing a Mac OS X package .app file as being a legitimate application) and thus launch it. The solution is to keep the Mac OS X version of your Web browser running or to launch it before clicking a URL.

A similar problem can occur if you have both the Mac OS 9 and Mac OS X versions of StuffIt Expander. The Mac OS 9 version may launch when you expect the Mac OS X version to be used. The solution is easy—because StuffIt Expander 6.0.1 or later is a Carbon application that will run in both Mac OS X and Mac OS 9, simply delete all earlier versions from your drive.

SEE: • "Understanding Image, Installer Package, and Receipt Files" in
          Chapter 3.

        • "Document opens in the 'wrong' application," in Chapter 6, for
          related information.

When you want to use the Classic version instead. Finally, you may occasionally want to open a Carbon application in Classic rather than in Mac OS X. (Perhaps you have an application that has a spelling-checker that works in Mac OS 9 but not in Mac OS X, so you prefer to use the Mac OS 9 version.) If you open the Get Info window for certain Carbon applications, there may be an "Open in the Classic environment" check box. If so, enable this option, and the application will always load in the Classic environment.

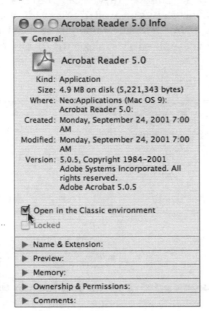

Figure 9.28

The "Open in the Classic environment" option in the Get Info window of a Carbon application.

TAKE NOTE ▶ Applications Packages Containing Two Application Versions

Some application packages—AppleWorks 6 being a prime example—work in both Classic and Mac OS X by maintaining two separate versions of the application within the application package file. The appropriate "inside the package" application for the current OS gets launched when you double-click the package icon. Unlike what occurs in applications that consist of a single Carbonized version that can run in either Mac OS X or Classic, however, the Get Info window for these dual-application packages does not include the "Open in Classic environment" check box. When you're running Mac OS X, AppleWorks 6, for example, will always launch its Mac OS X version, even if Classic is running. The Mac OS 9 version will launch only if you boot from Mac OS 9.

What can you do when you want to force the Classic version to be used when you're running Mac OS X? Follow these steps, using AppleWorks as an example:

1. Open the AppleWorks package via the Show Package Contents command in the contextual menu.

2. Navigate to the MacOS Classic folder, and open it.

You will see the Classic AppleWorks icon.

3. Double-click the icon to launch AppleWorks.

Note: If you plan to use the Mac OS 9 version frequently, you can drag the Classic AppleWorks icon to the Dock so that it will always be available. Similarly, dragging the Mac OS X version of AppleWorks (located in the MacOS folder) to the Dock ensures that the Mac OS X version gets launched (in case an error results in the Classic version's being launched instead).

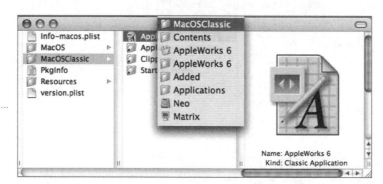

Figure 9.29

The Classic version of the AppleWorks application in the AppleWorks package.

Mac OS X error message appears when you launch documents in Mac OS 9. Occasionally, when you're booted in Mac OS 9 (only possible on older Macs that can still boot from Mac OS 9), an error message may appear when you double-click a document, saying that you need to be running Mac OS X to use the software you just tried to launch. Or you may get a more general error message that indicates that the file cannot be opened.

This message occurs, as you would expect, when you try to launch a Mac OS X application in Mac OS 9. It also occurs if you double-click a document that was created with a Mac OS X application (because the Mac OS will attempt to launch the application that created the document—in this case, a Mac OS X application—in order to open it).

The problem is that this message may also appear when you're trying to open a document that *should* launch a Mac OS 9 application, especially if you also have a Mac OS X version of the application installed. This has been known to occur after Microsoft Office X has been installed. In this case, when you boot in Mac OS 9 later and double-click an Office document—even one that you created and saved in a Mac OS 9 version of Office (such as Office 2001)—Mac OS 9 may attempt to launch the Mac OS X version. You receive an advance warning in the form of the document's icon shifting to the Mac OS X version.

There are a variety of work-arounds for this problem. I recommend that you rebuild the Desktop when you boot in Mac OS 9 (by holding down the Command and Option keys at Mac OS 9 startup, similar to the technique described in "Rebuilding the Classic Desktop," earlier in this chapter). If that technique alone does not work, first compress the Mac OS X version of the application (using a program such as DropStuff), and then rebuild the Desktop. You can then decompress the compressed application.

Problems installing software

Although Classic software installers will run in the Classic environment, they won't necessarily work properly. Due to Mac OS X's use of permissions, Classic installers, if not written properly, can try to install into or write to directories for which the user does not have enough privileges. To make things worse, the error messages that result are not always clear. If you get strange errors when you're trying to install Classic software, try rebooting into Mac OS 9 and then running the installer again. In fact, it's probably a good idea to always boot into Mac OS 9 when you're updating or installing Classic software.

Current Macs, however, cannot boot into Mac OS 9. For these newer Macs, the main solution (other than giving up on using the software) is to install the software on a Mac that *can* boot in Mac OS 9 and then copy the software from that Mac to your Mac OS X Mac. Or, more conveniently, you can boot from a Mac that *can* boot in Mac OS 9 and connect the newer Mac to the old one via FireWire Target Disk mode. You can now directly install the software onto the newer Mac.

SEE: • "Sharing Via Target Disk Mode," in Chapter 8, for details on this option.

One potential problem with the Target Disk method is that if the installation places software in the System Folder, it will likely place it (incorrectly for your purposes) in the System Folder on the Mac currently running Mac OS 9 rather than on the Target Disk. Actually, this is a potentially relevant issue with any method of installing and transferring Mac OS 9 software. The only solution is to determine (either by checking the software's documentation or by checking the Mac OS 9 drive for recently added files) where all installed files are located—and making sure you transfer them to the desired location if needed.

Software Update. In Mac OS X 10.1, you could run the Mac OS 9 Software Update control panel from Classic. Neither Jaguar nor Panther supports this. If you select the panel (assuming it's even present in your Mac OS 9 System Folder), you get the following error message: "That application or control panel is not supported by Classic." Any needed updates for Classic files are now handled via Mac OS X updates and get added to the Mac OS 9 System Folder the next time you launch Classic (as described more in "Launching Classic for the first time, or for the first time since upgrading Mac OS X," earlier in this chapter).

Alternatively, if your Mac can boot from Mac OS 9, you can do so and still run Software Update from there.

"QuickTime version not recommended" error. In at least one case, you will not be able to update Mac OS 9 using the just-described Software Update method. In particular, if you have an older version of QuickTime in your Classic System Folder, you may get a message such as the one shown in **Figure 9.30** when you launch Classic. The solution is to follow the message's advice and download the latest Mac OS 9 version of QuickTime. To complete the upgrade, run the downloaded QuickTime Updater in Classic.

Figure 9.30

If you're using an older version of the QuickTime software, a message such as this one may appear when you launch Classic.

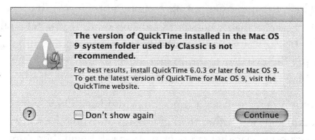

The version of QuickTime installed in the Mac OS 9 system folder used by Classic is not recommended.

For best results, install QuickTime 6.0.3 or later for Mac OS 9. To get the latest version of QuickTime for Mac OS 9, visit the QuickTime website.

☐ Don't show again   (Continue)

Installing files that should install in the System file. In Mac OS 9, certain files, such as keyboard layout and sound files, get installed directly in the System file (located in the System Folder). To add one of these files to the System file, you would just drag the file to the System file icon. You can also double-click the System file icon to reveal a window that shows all of these user-installable files.

Unfortunately, none of this works in Mac OS X. The System file cannot be opened and files cannot be installed in it. Starting in Panther, however, there is a work-around: Place the files that would have gone in the System file in the Appearance folder instead. They will now work correctly in Classic.

Volumes fail to mount when booting from Mac OS 9

A volume that was formatted when installing Mac OS X will not mount when booting from Mac OS 9 if the Mac OS 9 disk drivers were not installed. If this happens, the obvious solution is to install them. Here's how:

- One way you can do this is by booting from the Mac OS X Install CD. Once you've done this, from the Select Destination window select Erase and Install. This also automatically adds the Mac OS 9 drivers (assuming your Mac can boot from Mac OS 9) when you erase and reformat the drive.

- Otherwise, you can install the drivers via Disk Utility. You do this by accessing the Partition or Erase screen of Disk Utility and enabling the Install Mac OS 9 Drivers option when formatting or erasing a drive. In Panther, this option only appears if your Mac is capable of starting up from Mac OS 9.

- The obvious downside of the above solutions is that you need to erase your drive (and then to restore its contents) to fix the problem. An alternative solution avoids this hassle—but you can only take advantage of it if your Mac can still boot in Mac OS 9. (You can use a Mac OS 9 Install CD if no hard drive with Mac OS 9 installed is available.) To install the drivers, launch Drive Setup, select the name of the volume that's refusing to mount, and from the Functions menu select Update Driver.

SEE: • Chapter 3, especially "Take Note: Why and How to Partition," for more on Erase and Install, using Disk Utility from the Installer, and other issues regarding installing Mac OS X.

Copy/paste problems

Classic and Mac OS X share the Clipboard—which means you can cut and paste between Classic and Mac OS X applications just as you can between two applications in Mac OS 9. Mac OS X and Classic applications don't always use the same data types for Clipboard content, however, so some copy/paste operations between Classic and Mac OS X applications fail. The Mac OS 9 Clipboard may not recognize the format of a particular clip from Mac OS X, for example; thus, you lose the clip's formatting when you paste the clip into a Mac OS 9 application. Typically, you can prevent this problem by dragging the content directly from one application to the other, or from one application to the Desktop, and then from the Desktop to the second application.

Can't copy and paste from Classic to Mac OS X. Some older versions of Mac OS X have a bug that prevents you from pasting a Clipboard selection from an application running in Classic to a Mac OS X application. In the less serious form of this problem, you may have to copy and/or paste multiple times before the procedure works. In the more annoying form, it never succeeds.

You may even get a persistent spinning cursor when you attempt to paste the item. Following are some work-arounds for this symptom; try each fix in turn until one works:

- Update to the latest version of Mac OS X: It should fix this bug.

- Restart Classic via the Restart button in the Classic System Preferences pane.

- Deselect the "Start Classic when you login" option and manually launch Classic instead. This often prevents the problem.

- Quit Classic and delete the following files from the Classic System Folder: Classic (located at the root level of the System Folder) and Classic RAVE (located in the Extensions folder of the System Folder). When you relaunch Classic, Mac OS X will ask you whether it can add files to the System Folder to replace the two you just removed; allow it to do so.

- Delete the Finder preferences file located in the /Library/Preferences folder of your Home directory: com.apple.finder.plist. Then immediately relaunch the Finder (for example, by holding down the Option key when accessing the Finder's Dock menu and selecting Relaunch).

Memory problems

For Mac OS X applications, there is no need (or option) to separately set the memory allocation for each application. However, the issue remains relevant for Mac OS 9 applications run via Classic.

Application memory. Although Mac OS X allocates RAM dynamically to Mac OS X applications and the Classic environment itself, Classic applications use memory just as they do when you're booted in Mac OS 9. Each application can use only as much RAM as you have allocated to it in its Get Info window. If an application is having memory-related problems, you may need to allocate more memory to it. To do so, follow these steps:

1. Quit the application, and then select its icon in the Finder.
2. From the File menu choose Get Info (or press Command-I).
3. In the Get Info window, click the disclosure triangle next to the Memory item to reveal its contents.
4. Increase the application's Preferred Size. I recommend starting with an increase of 25 to 50 percent. Do not change the Minimum Size.
5. Close the Get Info window.
6. Relaunch the application.

To view the current memory allocation for each process and see how much of its allocated memory is actually in use, go to the Memory/Versions tab of the Classic System Preferences pane. The Memory Use bar next to each process name represents the memory allocation (which may be less than the preferred size, if insufficient memory is available to allocate the preferred size). The shaded portion of the bar represents the amount of allocated memory currently in use. If an application doesn't appear to ever use its allocation (and its preferred size was increased from its default setting), you can try reducing the size again if you want to free up more memory for other Classic applications. To do so, follow the same steps as above, except decrease rather than increase the preferred size.

If none of this seems to help and you're still having memory-related problems, you can experiment with the Adjust Memory setting accessed from the Memory/Versions screen of the Classic System Preferences pane, as described earlier in this chapter in "The Classic System Preferences Pane: An Overview."

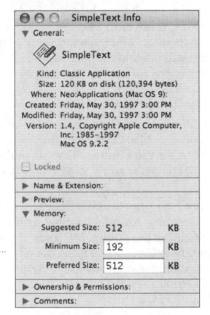

Figure 9.31

The Memory options of the Get Info window for a Classic application.

Virtual memory. Because Mac OS X handles all memory management, the Classic environment always operates as though virtual memory is disabled. As a consequence, Classic applications that require virtual memory (and there are only a few that do) will not function properly in the Classic environment. Unfortunately, there's no work-around for this problem right now—other than to boot into Mac OS 9, if possible, to use the applications.

Printing problems

Printing in Classic is very similar to printing in Mac OS 9. To enable printing, open the Chooser (from the Classic Apple menu, which is accessible when a Classic application is active), select a printer type (for example, LaserWriter) from the left side of the window, and then select a printer name (or port) from the right side. For AppleTalk printers, you may also need to select an AppleTalk Zone. You are now ready to print from a Classic application.

For LPR and PostScript USB printers, you need to use the Mac OS 9 Desktop Printer Utility, as you would if booted in Mac OS 9.

There are, however, some special considerations when printing from Classic:

- In many cases, Classic will be able to access the printer drivers in Mac OS X (via the Chooser), eliminating the need to manually install them in the Classic System Folder. The needed file will be placed in the Printer Descriptions folder inside the Extensions folder in the Mac OS 9 System Folder when you set up the printer in the Chooser.

  If the Mac OS 9–specific printer drivers were not preinstalled as part of Mac OS 9, you may need to install them before using the Chooser. If your printer requires a PPD file or driver in Mac OS 9, and you don't have it installed, you'll need to install it before you can print. If all that's required is a PPD file, you can install it while running Mac OS X by dragging the file to the Printer Descriptions folder. However, if you need to run an Installer utility, you may have to boot from Mac OS 9 to do so. If your Mac cannot boot from Mac OS 9, contact the printer vendor for advice.

  Note: No matter how the printer drivers are installed or accessed, the Classic environment still uses Mac OS X's printing software to contact the printer after you click the Print button. Thus, if you're having problems printing in Mac OS X, you're likely to have printing problems in Classic as well.

- If you select a PostScript laser printer in the Chooser, a Setup button typically appears. If you select this, you are presented with various options for setting up and configuring the printer. However, if you're accessing the printer drivers from Mac OS X when using the Classic environment (as just described), you should instead enter these settings via the relevant options in Mac OS X's Printer Setup Utility (as described in Chapter 7) rather than from Mac OS 9's Chooser.

- Although Mac OS X supports non-AppleTalk serial-port printers, you cannot print to such printers from within Classic because Classic cannot access serial ports through Mac OS X. Similarly, you cannot print to LocalTalk-connected printers from Classic.

- Classic does not support Mac OS 9 desktop printers, nor does it use the Mac OS X print queue. To monitor your Classic print jobs, you must use the PrintMonitor application (located in the Extensions folder of the Classic System Folder).

- Do not attempt to print from a Classic application to a USB printer while that printer is currently printing a document from a Mac OS X application. Otherwise, you may get an error that says the printer is not responding.

If you're still having problems getting documents to print in Classic, here are a few more things to consider.

PrintMonitor memory. You can solve some Classic printing problems by increasing the memory of the Classic PrintMonitor application (which is located in the Extensions folder of the Mac OS 9 System Folder). To do this, open the Get Info window for the application, from the pop-up menu choose Memory, and replace the Preferred Size setting (probably 300 KB by default) with a larger value (perhaps double or triple its initial size).

Background printing. Background printing is a Mac OS 9 feature of the LaserWriter driver (selected in the Chooser). If the feature is enabled, it may prevent printing from within the Classic environment. To work around this problem, disable background printing. To do so, follow these steps:

1. From the File menu of a Classic application, choose Print to open the Print dialog.

2. From the pop-up menu in the Print dialog, choose Background Printing.

3. From the "Print in" options that appear, choose "Foreground (no spool file)" rather than the default Background.

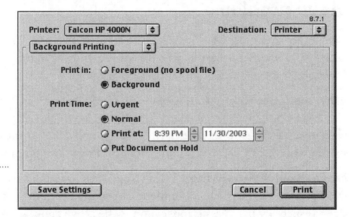

Figure 9.32

The Background Printing options in the Print dialog.

AppleTalk and printing. To print to AppleTalk-connected printers, make sure that AppleTalk is listed as Active in the Chooser. Beyond that, all relevant settings are handled by Mac OS X, not Classic, software. In particular, enable AppleTalk for the desired port via the Network System Preferences pane. Note: In Mac OS X 10.2 and later, AppleTalk can be active for only one port at a time.

SEE: • "Internet connection problems," later in this chapter, for more details.

   • Chapter 8 for much more on configuring network settings.

Printing in Mac OS X with Classic active. If you're having general problems printing in Mac OS X while Classic is active, be aware that some printers will not print when Classic is running. In this case, the solution is to quit Classic before attempting to print.

SEE: • Chapter 7 for more general information on troubleshooting printing problems.

> **TAKE NOTE** ▶ **Saving as a PDF File to Print in Classic**
>
> In some situations, a document refuses to print in Mac OS X but *will* print in Mac OS 9. For example, some USB printers are supported in Classic but don't work under Mac OS X—which means that if you're using a Mac OS X application, you won't be able to print.
>
> The solution is to do one of the following:
>
> • In the Print dialog of the Mac OS X application, click the Save As PDF button instead of the Print button. This converts the file to a PDF document.
>
> • From the pop-up menu in the Mac OS X Print dialog, choose Output Options and then check the Save as File box, choose PDF from the Format pop-up menu, and save the file.
>
> In either case, assuming that you have a version of Adobe Acrobat that opens in Classic (Acrobat 4.x or the Classic version of Acrobat 5.x, for example), you can open the resulting PDF document in Classic and print from there.

Sleep problems

The ability to put the Mac to sleep is a great energy-saving feature. It works in Mac OS X whether or not Classic is running. However, the combination of Classic and sleep presents a few special problems.

Slow wakeup. Waking from sleep is dramatically faster in Mac OS X than it is in Mac OS 9. However, if Classic is running and a Classic application is active, wakeup time can slow dramatically. To speed up waking from sleep, be sure to switch to a Mac OS X application before putting your computer to sleep.

Wake-from-sleep crashes. Numerous users have reported crashes waking from sleep if the Classic environment is running when the computer is put to sleep (especially if a Classic application is the active application). The reported crashes range from mild (the Finder and Classic quits) to serious (kernel panics). Although Apple has apparently fixed many of the causes of this problem in its most recent Mac OS X updates (and the problem may affect some Mac models more than others), if you experience problems on waking your computer, it may pay to make sure that Classic is stopped before putting your Mac (or letting it go) to sleep—or at least make sure that a Mac OS X application or the Mac OS X Finder is the active application.

Putting Classic to sleep. As covered earlier in this chapter (the "Overview" section of "Using Classic"), the Advanced screen of the Classic System Preferences pane includes an option to put Classic to sleep when it's inactive for a specified time. This is separate from the overall computer sleep, as set in the Energy Saver System Preferences pane. As may happen with the more general sleep, you may find that a freeze or a crash is more likely when Classic wakes from sleep than if it does not go to sleep at all. This symptom is increasingly rare in more recent Mac OS X versions. Still, if this happens to you, the workaround is to set the sleep time in the Classic System Preferences pane to Never.

SEE: • **Chapter 5 for more on dealing with crashes.**

Internet connection problems

In Panther, Classic automatically adjusts its Internet connectivity settings to match the settings in use in Mac OS X. For example, suppose you have both an AirPort connection and a wired Ethernet connection—and you're currently using AirPort to connect to the Internet. In this case, Classic will also use AirPort to connect to the Internet. If, via Mac OS X's Network System Preferences pane, you switch to the wired Ethernet connection for Internet access, Classic will do the same. You will not need to adjust any settings in Classic for this to happen. You don't even have to quit and restart Classic for the change to take effect. In essence, you just launch Classic once, and everything works!

SEE: • **"The Jaguar Way: Network and Internet Connections in Classic," below, for problems with Internet connections in Classic, specific to Jaguar.**

THE JAGUAR WAY ▶ Network and Internet Connections in Classic

Jaguar does not handle changes to Classic environment network connections as elegantly as Panther. More specifically, when setting up a network connection for Mac OS 9, Jaguar creates a new configuration named Classic for use by the TCP/IP control panel. This configuration is used to funnel all TCP/IP traffic in Classic through Mac OS X.

Normally, this situation works wonderfully, allowing you to access the Internet via Classic applications without requiring that you manually enter any settings in Classic. Occasionally, however, Mac OS 9 Internet applications may fail to work even though Mac OS X applications are connecting to the Internet with no problems. This is most likely to happen if you switch your method of connecting to the Internet (such as going from AirPort to Ethernet).

Mac OS X is able to detect that the switch has occurred and will automatically shift to the correct network settings (as explained more in Chapter 8), whereas the settings in Mac OS 9's TCP/IP control panel remain static.

To elaborate, when Mac OS X creates the Classic configuration in TCP/IP, it chooses the first type of connection specified in the Network Port Configurations section of Mac OS X's Network System Preferences pane. If your first setting is AirPort and your second is Ethernet, Classic's TCP/IP setting will be AirPort. As long as Mac OS X is connected to the Internet via an AirPort connection, everything is fine. The problem occurs if you switch from an AirPort connection to an Ethernet connection, or if AirPort is not available. Mac OS X will detect the change and switch automatically, but Classic will continue to think that it should be using an AirPort connection. If no AirPort connection is available, the connection will fail.

continues on next page

THE JAGUAR WAY ▶ **Network and Internet Connections in Classic** *continued*

Unfortunately, this problem has no permanent fix—other than to upgrade to Panther. If this bug bites you, the work-around is to delete the TCP/IP Preferences file in the Mac OS 9 System Folder before you launch Classic. When you launch Classic, Mac OS X will create a new configuration that corresponds to the current Mac OS X connection. If you switch connection types again, the problem will reappear.

The TCP/IP Preferences file. In Jaguar, when you first launch the Classic environment, Mac OS X alters the configuration setting for Mac OS 9's TCP/IP control panel. These settings are stored in the TCP/IP Preferences file, located in the Preferences folder of the Classic System Folder. This preferences file is no longer used for Classic in Panther. In fact, even if you delete the file in Panther, network connections in Classic will still work. For those still using Jaguar, note the following about this preferences file:

- **Additional configurations.** If you boot into Mac OS 9 by using the System Folder used for Classic, you may have created additional TCP/IP configurations for accessing the Internet from Mac OS 9. If you delete the TCP/IP Preferences file, all of these additional settings will be deleted. To prevent this problem, save a copy of the preferences file outside the System Folder before you delete the file. When you're booted from Mac OS 9, you can drag the copy back into the Preferences folder to restore your additional settings.

- **Corrupt TCP/IP preferences.** More generally, Mac OS 9's TCP/IP Preferences file seems to corrupt much more often in Classic that it does in Mac OS 9. Problems with the TCP/IP Preferences file can even prevent Classic from starting up (or cause it to take an unusually long time to start up). If you're having Internet connection problems or startup crashes in Classic, throw away the TCP/IP Preferences file and launch the Classic environment again.

SEE: • "Take Note: Control Panels and Extensions in Classic vs. Mac OS X," earlier in this chapter, for related information.

• Chapter 8 for more information on troubleshooting Internet problems.

Permissions settings and running Classic

In early versions of Mac OS X 10.2 (Jaguar), the permissions for the Mac OS 9 System Folder could be set so that only the System Folder's owner—typically the initial administrative user (that is, you if you own the Mac in question)—had Read & Write or even Read Only access to the folder. This restriction prevented other users from starting up Classic from that folder. If they tried, the following error message would appear: "You do not have sufficient permissions to run Classic from the selected System Folder."

The main way to solve this problem is by updating to Mac OS X 10.2.3 or later. If similar problems occur in Panther, the likely solution is to launch Disk Utility and from the File menu select the Fix OS 9 Permissions command.

SEE: • "Performing repairs with Disk Utility (First Aid)," in Chapter 5, for more information.

The "manual" solution is for the administrative owner to change the System Folder's permissions, via the Ownership & Permissions section of the folder's Get Info window. For example, starting in Mac OS X 10.2.4, an administrative user can set permissions for files used by the Classic environment so that all System files and local applications used by the Classic environment are protected from being disabled, moved, renamed, or deleted by users who do not have administrative privileges. Nonadministrative users will still be able to launch Classic. To do this, set the permission settings for the Mac OS 9 System Folder and Applications (Mac OS 9) folder as follows:

- Owner: system
- Access: Read & Write
- Group: admin
- Access: Read & Write
- Others: Read only

In Panther, these should be the default settings.

Accounts preferences. When attempting to use certain control panels in Classic under Mac OS X 10.2.4 and earlier, users may receive an alert message with error code 1016. This message indicates that an administrative user has restricted access to the item for that user (via the Limitations option in the Accounts System Preferences pane). If an administrative user has purposely restricted access, nothing needs to be done. Otherwise, you may wish to modify this setting.

In any case, updating to Mac OS X 10.2.5 eliminates the error message (though not the intended restriction).

SEE: • "Accounts" in the "System" section, in Chapter 2, for more details.

Using preferences from your Home folder. You can also limit users' ability to modify files in the Classic System Folder by enabling the "Use Mac OS 9 preferences from your home" option, in the Advanced screen of the Classic System Preferences pane, for each user. See the following Apple Knowledge Base document for details: http://docs.info.apple.com/article.html?artnum=25422.

SEE: • The "Overview" section of "Using Classic," earlier in this chapter, for more details on using this option.

   • "Ownership & Permissions," in Chapter 4, for more details on setting permissions.

Classic Quick Fixes

Following are brief descriptions of an assortment of problems related to the use of Classic, as well as their known solutions and fixes. Some of these may apply only to specific versions of Mac OS X or Classic and may get fixed in subsequent updates to Mac OS X.

Files locked in Mac OS 9

When you're booted in Mac OS 9, you can lock files via the Locked check box in the Get Info window for the file. This Locked/Unlocked setting carries over to Mac OS X. If you try to throw away a file that was locked in Mac OS 9, Mac OS X will not let you do so. In fact, it will most likely not even allow you to place the file in the Trash, claiming you don't have "sufficient privileges."

In most cases, you can still delete the file in Mac OS X by opening the Get Info window for the file and unchecking its Locked check box. If that doesn't work, you'll need a more industrial-strength Trash removal solution, as described in Chapter 6.

SEE: • Chapter 6 for much more information on problems with deleting files, locked and otherwise.

Figure 9.33

The Locked check box in a Get Info window when (left) booting from Mac OS 9, and (right) booting from Mac OS X.

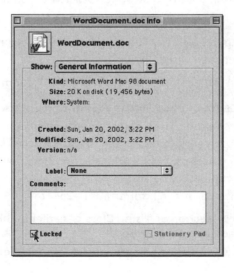

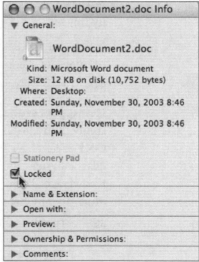

Clipping files in Mac OS 9 vs. Mac OS X

A text clipping file is created when you drag a selection of text from a document to the Desktop. Typically, double-clicking these files opens a window displaying the text contents.

Opening clipping files created in Mac OS X when you're booting from Mac OS 9. If you create a clipping file in Mac OS X, the file will not open when you're booted in Mac OS 9. Double-clicking it in Mac OS 9 instead results in an error message that says, "This file is used by the System Software. It cannot be opened."

The solution is to use a utility that allows you to change the creator of a file, either in Mac OS X (by using a utility such as Gideon Softworks' FileXaminer) or in Mac OS 9 (by using a utility such as Objective Development's Little Snitch). Simply change the creator of the clipping file from MACS to drag, and the file should open in Mac OS 9 as expected.

You can open Mac OS 9–created clipping files in Mac OS X without modifying the files' attributes.

Note: Depending on what you drag to the Desktop, you may create different types of clipping files, such as picture clippings and Internet-address clippings.

Clipping files with long names. Sometimes, a text clipping created in Mac OS X has a name with more than 31 characters. Because Mac OS 9 does not support filenames of this length, if you try to copy one of these clippings to another Mac or a file server running Mac OS 9 or earlier, you will get an error. The solution is to rename the clipping file with a shorter name.

Disappearing pointer

Sometimes the pointer disappears when you're using a Classic application. There are two quick ways to fix this problem:

- Press Command-Tab to switch to a Mac OS X application, then click somewhere in the application. When you switch back to the Classic application, the pointer should be visible.

- Move the (invisible) pointer all the way to the edge of the screen so that when you click, you are clicking the Desktop. Making the Desktop active effectively takes you out of Classic. Then switch back to the Classic application.

Classic application and folder names

If a Classic application and its enclosing folder have the same name (such as Claris Emailer), the application may not launch in Classic. The solution is to rename the application or the folder so that they have different names.

"The operation could not be completed" message

Occasionally, when trying to eject a CD or unmount a disk-image file, you may get the following error message: "The operation could not be completed because the disk is in use." This occurs even though nothing on the CD or image appears to be in use. In such cases, quitting Classic should allow the image or CD to unmount or eject.

SEE: • Chapter 6 for more information on "in-use" error messages and ejecting discs.

Classic and mounting CDs

In certain cases, especially with copy-protected CDs and CDs that contain both audio and data partitions, a Mac OS Classic application may not recognize that a CD has been inserted and mounted. The solution is to mount the CD before launching the Classic environment. If this does not succeed (perhaps because you need to mount multiple CDs to do an installation), the solution is to boot in Mac OS 9, if possible. Otherwise, contact the manufacturer of the CD for a possible upgraded version.

SEE: • "Problems installing software," earlier in this chapter, for related information.

Launching Classic and Fast User Switching

You will be unable to launch Classic (and thus unable to run applications that require Classic) if you have enabled Fast User Switching and another currently logged-in user is currently running Classic. Only one logged-in user at a time can run Classic.

SEE: • "System," in Chapter 2, for a description of the Fast User Switching option, as enabled from the Accounts System Preferences pane.

If you try to launch Classic when another user is running it, you will get an error message describing the problem. After dismissing the error message, you may also get a message saying that Classic has unexpectedly quit.

One way of solving the problem is by simply asking the other logged-in user to quit Classic—assuming that person is available to do so. Otherwise, if your account has administrative access, launch Activity Monitor and quit the Classic (null) process, from the Other User Processes listing. You should now be able to launch Classic.

Figure 9.34

*The message that appears if
you try to launch Classic
when another logged-in user
is already using it.*

Booting from Mac OS 9 on Macs that cannot boot from Mac OS 9

When I heard that Apple was going to drop the ability to boot in Mac OS 9 from new Macs shipping in 2003, my first reaction was that within a week a shareware author would have released some hack to work around the restriction. I was wrong. As of this writing, such a hack still does not exist.

However, it is still technically possible to boot from Mac OS 9 on at least some new Macs. The trick is to have an updated version of the Mac OS ROM file (version 9.8.1 or later) that resides in the Mac OS 9 System Folder. The problem is that Apple restricts access to the updated version of this file to Apple Service Providers. Even with this ROM file, users report problems with some Classic features.

10

Unix for Mac OS X Users

As first mentioned in Chapter 1, the core of the Mac OS X operating system is an operating system whose origins predate the Mac itself: Unix.

SEE: • **Chapters 1 and 4 for a general background on Unix in Mac OS X.**

For the majority of Mac users, the fact that Unix exists on the Mac is about as relevant as the fact that REALbasic exists as a programming language for Mac OS X. You don't need to bother with either just to use a word processor or a Web browser.

Troubleshooters, on the hand, don't have that luxury. When things go wrong and the standard Mac OS X techniques don't work, your ability to use Unix commands may represent your best or only chance of solving the problem. That's why I've peppered the preceding chapters with tips that demonstrate these commands' effectiveness. In case you missed them along the way, here are just a few prime examples:

- **"Technically Speaking: More About Disk Utility's Image and Restore Features," in Chapter 3**
- **"Technically Speaking: Restoring and Replacing NetInfo and Directory Access Data," in Chapter 4**
- **"Technically Speaking: Connecting Remotely to a Frozen Mac: Killing Processes, Running Sync Processes" in Chapter 5**
- **"Killing from Terminal" and "Technically Speaking: Kill Signals," in Chapter 5**
- **"Viewing default permissions in Terminal," in Chapter 5**
- **"Using Unix to delete files," in Chapter 6**
- **"Modifying invisible Unix files from Mac OS X applications," in Chapter 6**
- **"CUPS," in Chapter 7**
- **"Technically Speaking: Using ipfw," in Chapter 8**

For those users with little or no background in Unix, and who may have felt a bit mystified by what was actually going on in the above examples, this is the chapter that explains all the basics.

In This Chapter
. . . .

Understanding the Terminal Application

The typical way to issue Unix commands is by typing text in a terminal application. Mac OS X provides such an application, called—appropriately enough—Terminal. Terminal has a command-line interface (CLI) as opposed to Mac OS X's more familiar graphical user interface (GUI). To be fair, though, Terminal does offer some handy GUI tools for working with the CLI via its menu bar items.

The Terminal application is located in the Utilities folder of the Applications folder. When you launch Terminal, a window opens into which you enter typed commands. From this window, Terminal accepts only text input and produces only text output, making almost no use of the mouse.

What exactly does Terminal do?

Terminal is your window to the Unix world. Via Unix commands entered in Terminal, you can do almost anything in Mac OS X that you could do from a standard Unix (that is, non-Mac) machine. This includes creating and running Perl scripts (often used in conjunction with Web sites); setting up cron events (such as maintenance tasks); accessing FTP, Telnet, or Apache Web server software; and setting up your own mail server. It's no wonder that many advanced computer users have been almost drooling at the prospect of what can be done with Mac OS X's combination of Unix and a traditional Mac interface.

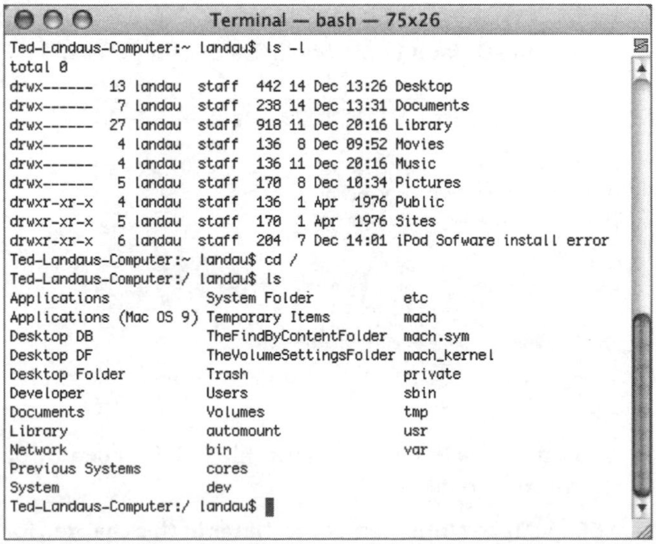

```
Terminal — bash — 75x26
Ted-Landaus-Computer:~ landau$ ls -l
total 0
drwx------   13 landau   staff    442 14 Dec 13:26 Desktop
drwx------    7 landau   staff    238 14 Dec 13:31 Documents
drwx------   27 landau   staff    918 11 Dec 20:16 Library
drwx------    4 landau   staff    136  8 Dec 09:52 Movies
drwx------    4 landau   staff    136 11 Dec 20:16 Music
drwx------    5 landau   staff    170  8 Dec 10:34 Pictures
drwxr-xr-x    4 landau   staff    136  1 Apr  1976 Public
drwxr-xr-x    5 landau   staff    170  1 Apr  1976 Sites
drwxr-xr-x    6 landau   staff    204  7 Dec 14:01 iPod Sofware install error
Ted-Landaus-Computer:~ landau$ cd /
Ted-Landaus-Computer:/ landau$ ls
Applications             System Folder           etc
Applications (Mac OS 9)  Temporary Items         mach
Desktop DB               TheFindByContentFolder  mach.sym
Desktop DF               TheVolumeSettingsFolder mach_kernel
Desktop Folder           Trash                   private
Developer                Users                   sbin
Documents                Volumes                 tmp
Library                  automount               usr
Network                  bin                     var
Previous Systems         cores
System                   dev
Ted-Landaus-Computer:/ landau$ █
```

Figure 10.1

A Terminal window.

Terminal is also a potentially dangerous tool, especially if you're not familiar with how to use it. A small error could result in your deleting a good portion of the data on your drive without even getting a warning about the trouble that's about to occur. Thus, if you're new to Terminal, it pays to enter the pool at the shallow end, which is what we do in this chapter.

For starters, we'll take a look at the part of Terminal that's most Mac-like: the menu commands, as accessed from the menu bar at the top of the screen (or via their Command-key equivalents). Admittedly, for the troubleshooting focus of this book, most users will never need to access any of these menu options: The default settings work just fine, and you can go directly into entering commands in the main window. Thus, you may decide to skip the next two sections (although I thought I would still check out the sidebars). For those who would instead prefer to have an overview of the menu commands, these sections provide it. The remaining sections of the chapter explore how to use the Terminal main window itself.

Terminal's menus

After launching Terminal, its menus appear in the menu bar at the top of the screen. The following describes these menus.

Terminal. The main points of interest in this menu include the following:

- **Preferences.** This command opens a window from which you can select several options. The first options modify what happens when you open a new Terminal window.

  For example, if you want Terminal to open in a shell other than the default shell, you would select "Execute this command" and enter the path to the shell in the text box.

  SEE: • "Technically Speaking: What's a Shell?" and "Take Note: Changing the Default Login Shell," below, for details.

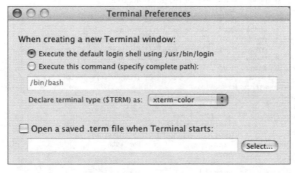

Figure 10.2

Terminal's Preferences window.

  You can also select a saved .term file to be opened by default when Terminal launches.

  SEE: • "Take Note: .Term Files," later in this chapter, for details.

Finally, you can declare your terminal type ($TERM) here. Unless you need to have your Mac emulate a specific terminal (a throwback to the days before desktop computers replaced terminals) other than the default, you don't need to make any changes here. (However, see "Scrollback," a bit later in this chapter, for one reason to use this option.)

- **Window Settings.** This command is one of several menu commands you can use to access Terminal's Inspector window.

SEE: • "Terminal Inspector," later in this chapter, for details.

TECHNICALLY SPEAKING ▶ What's a Shell?

A *shell* in Unix refers to a command-line interpreter: When you type a command (such as 1s), the shell determines the response to that command.

The Mac OS's graphical interface typically only includes one "shell": the Mac OS itself. However, you can think of different versions of the Mac OS as different shells. Thus, if you have both Mac OS 9 and Mac OS X on your Mac, and you shift between them, commands will work differently. Command-N, for example, creates a new folder in Mac OS 9 but opens a new Finder window in Mac OS X. Changing shells in Unix can have the same effect.

For the basic Unix commands described in this chapter, all shells work pretty much the same—just as many Mac OS commands do the same thing whether you're in Mac OS 9 or Mac OS X.

In Panther, Terminal defaults to the *bash* shell (which stands for *Bourne-again shell*). Other shells available from Terminal include the following: *tsch* (known as the *terminal-based C shell*), which was the default shell in Jaguar and earlier; *csh* (called the C shell); and *sh* (called the Bourne shell). The sh and bash shells are preferred for running shell scripts (such as the .command files you can create, as described later in this chapter).

You can change to a new shell simply by typing its name in the Terminal window and pressing Return. For example, to shift to the csh shell, type csh and press Return. To revert to the preceding (parent) shell, type exit and press Return again.

Note: When you use the su command to get root access, you similarly temporarily shift to a new shell.

If you want to have two shells open at once, it's simple: Just open another window (by selecting New Shell from Terminal's File menu). If you want the shell to be different from the default shell, type the command for the desired shell in the new window.

If Active Process Name is enabled in the Window section of the Terminal Inspector (as described in "Terminal Inspector," in the main text), the title bar will indicate which shell is currently active in that window.

continues on next page

TECHNICALLY SPEAKING ▶ **What's a Shell?** *continued*

Technical note regarding tcsh. Apple has the following to say about tcsh (in the Apple Knowledge Base article http://docs.info.apple.com/article.html?artnum=107106):

Terminal in Mac OS X 10.2 (and later) defaults to industry-standard settings for tcsh, rather than to the highly customized default set used in version 10.1.5 or earlier. This change brings the default behavior of Terminal in line with other UNIX operating systems.

If you used these customized settings from Mac OS X 10.1.5 or earlier and want to get them back (or otherwise customize them), and you're comfortable working in Terminal, go to the following directory (using the Finder's Go to Folder command): /usr/share/tcsh/examples/. Once there, open the read-me file to obtain additional information, such as how to set up an aliases.mine file for custom aliases.

Environment and shell variables. You can view the system default shell by typing env (for *environment*) in any Terminal window. From the several lines of output that appear, check the SHELL line to see the default. This command also gives you a host of other basic environment information, such as OSTYPE (darwin) and HOSTTYPE (macintosh), and the PATH listing.

In Panther, for example, the env command lists bash (/bin/bash) as the system default shell for accounts created in Panther but lists tcsh as the default shell for accounts carried over from Jaguar (as described in "Take Note: Changing the Default Login Shell," elsewhere in this chapter).

There is a distinction between shell variables (which are not inherited by programs, such as subshells) and environment variables (which are inherited). The set command is for shell variables. The setenv command (in tcsh) and the env command (in bash) are used to modify environment variables. If you just type set with no arguments, you get a list of its variables. Similarly, if you just type setenv or env with no arguments, you get a list of their variables.

continues on next page

Figure 10.3

Output from the env *command: The default shell name is listed in the* SHELL *line. On this Mac (upgraded to Panther from Jaguar), it's* /bin/tcsh.

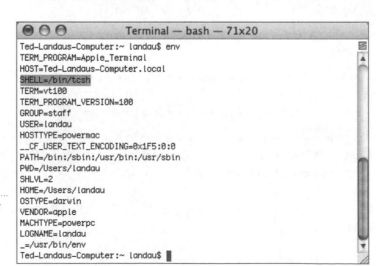

```
Ted-Landaus-Computer:~ landau$ env
TERM_PROGRAM=Apple_Terminal
HOST=Ted-Landaus-Computer.local
SHELL=/bin/tcsh
TERM=vt100
TERM_PROGRAM_VERSION=100
GROUP=staff
USER=landau
HOSTTYPE=powermac
__CF_USER_TEXT_ENCODING=0x1F5:0:0
PATH=/bin:/sbin:/usr/bin:/usr/sbin
PWD=/Users/landau
SHLVL=2
HOME=/Users/landau
OSTYPE=darwin
VENDOR=apple
MACHTYPE=powerpc
LOGNAME=landau
_=/usr/bin/env
Ted-Landaus-Computer:~ landau$
```

Terminal — bash — 71x20

TECHNICALLY SPEAKING ▶ What's a Shell? *continued*

In some cases, as when changing the PATH setting, the shell-versus-environment distinction is not critical. Changing the PATH setting via the set command (as described later in this chapter in "Unix: Executing Commands"), for example, changes it for both the shell and environment variable settings. In addition, environmental variable changes made via a configuration file at login generally get passed to opened subshells.

TAKE NOTE ▶ Changing the Default Login Shell

In Panther (Mac OS X 10.3), Terminal defaults to the bash shell. Prior to Panther, Terminal defaulted to the tsch shell. To change the default login shell:

1. From Terminal's Terminal menu, select Preferences.

2. From the "When creating a new Terminal window" option, switch from the default choice ("Execute the default login shell using /usr/bin/login") to "Execute this command."

3. In the text box, enter the complete path to the shell of your choosing. The shells you can use (for example, tcsh, bash, csh, and sh) are located in Unix's /bin directory. Thus, to select tcsh as the default shell, enter the following: /bin/tcsh. By default, the text box contains the path for the bash shell: /bin/bash.

Now, whenever you launch Terminal, it will use tcsh instead of bash. Note: This will not change the SHELL listing the env command's output.

Bash or tcsh: Which should you use? Which is used in this book? Perhaps it's just that I got used to tcsh as the default choice prior to Panther, but I prefer it to bash. Because I find it a bit more user-friendly (if you can use such a term to describe Unix!), I've made tcsh my default shell in Panther. Although the bash shell is better for creating shell scripts, this has never been an issue for me. In any case, you can still create a shell script in bash and keep tcsh as your default shell.

However, in keeping with Apple's shift, the examples in this chapter refer primarily to bash—though I may on occasion refer to tcsh. With regard to the topics covered in this book, their differences are mostly minor to nonexistent. In the few cases where there are significant differences between the two shells, such as when using the alias command or setting up shell configuration files, I describe the "rules" for both shells.

Note: If you try a command listed in this chapter and it doesn't work as expected, it's probably because it only works in one shell (and I perhaps forgot to specify this). Thus, if you're using bash, switch to tcsh and try the command again. It should now work.

Why is tcsh my default in Panther? Despite the fact that bash is supposed to be the default shell in Panther, you may find that tcsh is your initial default. This happens if you upgraded from Jaguar. In this case, Panther retains tcsh as the default in all upgraded accounts. If you create an account for a new user after upgrading to Panther, however, bash will be the default for that user.

SEE: • "Technically Speaking: What's a Shell?" above, and "Using shell configuration files," elsewhere in this chapter, for more details.

File. This menu includes the typical New, Open, Save, and Print commands, plus a few more unusual ones. The most important ones for you to know include the following:

- **New Shell.** This command opens a new Terminal window.
- **Connect to Server.** New in Panther, this command provides a convenient way of accessing another computer via Terminal. For example, if a user has enabled Remote Login in their Sharing System Preferences pane and you have an account on that Mac, you can log in by selecting Connect to Server. You can also use this command to log in to any Unix server for which you have remote-login access. To do so, follow these steps:

  1. Select Connect to Server. From the window that appears, in the Services column select Secure Shell (ssh).
  2. At the bottom of the Server column, click the plus (+) button.
  3. Enter the IP address of the computer to which you want to connect. Click OK. Then select the IP address in the server list.
  4. Type your account name (on the target computer) in the User text box.
  5. Click Connect. A Terminal window will open. If the connection is successful, you will be asked for your password. If you give the correct password, you will be logged in to your account on that computer.

  Note: After doing this, your login information is saved in the pop-up menu at the bottom of the window. The next time you want to access that computer, just select it; no need to re-enter your name. To enter a new name, delete any name in the User text box and reselect the IP address listed in the Server column; then enter a new name.

- **Save.** Use this command or the Save As command to save a Terminal settings (.term) file.

  SEE: • "Take Note: .Term Files," later in this chapter, for more on the Save command, as well as the Open, Library, and Use Settings As Defaults commands, also in the File menu.

- **Save Text As.** Use this command as well as the Save Selected Text As command to save the text in a Terminal window to a text file.

- **Send Break (Ctrl-c).** Use this command (or the Send Reset and Send Hard Reset commands, if needed) to stop a process that appears to be hung.

  SEE: • "Take Note: Unix Problems and How to Fix Them," later in this chapter, for more information.

- **Secure Keyboard Entry.** Use this command to ensure that other applications on your computer (or on any computer on your network) cannot detect or record what you're typing. If you're worried about someone trying to steal your password, for example, you should use this command.

- **Show Info.** This command opens the Terminal Inspector (as does the Set Title command).

  SEE: • "Terminal Inspector," later in this chapter, for details.

Edit. This menu includes the typical Copy, Cut, and Paste commands, as well as a Find command. The Paste Escaped Text command adds a backslash in front of any spaces in the copied selection when pasting it so that the text is treated as a single selection (rather than multiple commands) when pasted into Terminal.

SEE: • "Take Note: Spaces in Pathnames," later in this chapter, for details

Scrollback. This menu provides commands (such as Line Up and Page Up) for navigating the text output in the Terminal window.

Note: When using these commands (or the scroll bars on the side of the window) to scroll back, you may note that the previous output *does not* appear—especially if you're viewing man output, for example. To work around this problem, use the up (and down, for scrolling forward again) arrow keys on the keyboard. You can also work around the problem by accessing Terminal's Preferences, and then from the "Declare terminal type ($TERM) as" pop-up menu, select vt100. Once you've done this, all of the Scrollback commands should work as expected.

You can use the Clear Scrollback (Command-K) command to "erase" the window's currently displayed text. Note: Typing clear in the Terminal window accomplishes the same thing.

Font. This menu provides commands for customizing the size and look of the text in the Terminal window. The Show Fonts (Command-T) command opens a Font window similar to that described for TextEdit in Chapter 4.

Window. This menu includes commands for minimizing and enlarging a window as well as for rotating among windows or selecting a specific window (if you have more than one window open).

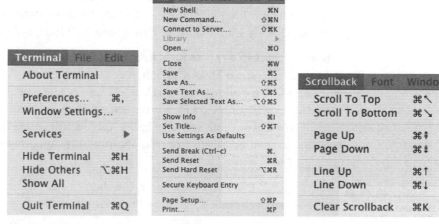

Figure 10.4

Terminal's (left) Terminal, (middle) File, and (right) Scrollback menus.

Terminal Inspector

You can open Terminal Inspector in any of the following ways: (a) by typing Command-I, (b) by selecting Show Info from the File menu, or (c) by selecting Window Settings from the Terminal menu.

The different screens in Terminal Inspector are accessed via the pop-up menu at its top. The choices are Shell, Processes, Emulation, Buffer, Display, Color, Window, and Keyboard. Any changes you make in the Inspector only affect the current shell window—unless you click the Use Settings as Defaults button.

The following Inspector settings and options are the ones I use most; feel free to experiment with others to discover your own preferences.

Processes: Prompt before closing window. See "Quitting Terminal," later in this chapter, for coverage of this selection.

Emulation: Option click to position cursor. From the Terminal Inspector pop-up menu, select Emulation and then enable the "Option click to position cursor" option. Why? Consider this: When typing in a shell window, if you discover a typo ten letters back, you would normally press the Delete key ten times and then start over from that point. However, with the Emulation option enabled, you can Option-click to any location in the command line and instantly fix the typo. Once you've made the correction, Option-click back to the end of the line to return to your previous location.

Buffer: Unlimited scrollback. From Inspector's menu, select Buffer. Then, from the Buffer Size option, you can adjust the size of the scrollback buffer. This is especially relevant when you select a command that produces a large amount of output that quickly scrolls through your window. When the scrolling stops, you may want to scroll back to the beginning of the output. If the scrollback buffer is too small, the initial output will have disappeared. The default setting is for 10,000 lines—adequate for most situations. However, you may occasionally want to change that setting to "Unlimited scrollback."

Display: Enable drag copy/paste of text. From Terminal Inspector's pop-up menu, select Display and then enable the "Enable drag copy/paste of text" option. This allows you to select any text in a Terminal window and drag it to the current command line—convenient when you want to reuse a long selection of text without retyping it. You can even drag text from one shell window to another—or from any application that supports dragging of text.

Color: Transparency. From Terminal's Inspector's pop-up menu, choose Color. From the options that appear, use the Transparency slider to adjust the transparency of Terminal's windows to your liking.

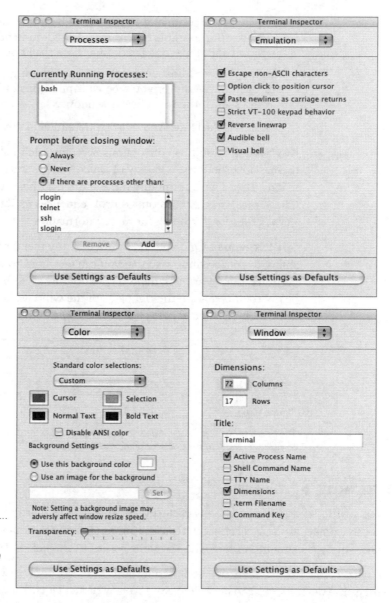

Figure 10.5

Four views of Terminal Inspector: (top left) Processes, (top right) Emulation, (bottom left) Color, and (bottom right) Window.

Window: Title. When you initially launch Terminal, it opens a shell window, which likely reads something like the following: "Terminal – bash – 80x24." To customize this title, open Terminal Inspector and from the pop-up menu select Window. From here, choose the options you wish to display.

- Active Process Name should be selected by default. If it's not, it's a good idea to select it because it identifies the active shell. Further, should you ever change your shell (such as typing the csh command to go from bash to csh), the change is instantly reflected in the title. In fact, if you enter certain shell-modifying commands, such as su, the command name will temporarily appear in the title as the active process.

- If you select Command Key, you will be told which Command-key shortcut (for example, Command-1 or Command-2) to type to make that window the active one (assuming more than one window is open).

- In the Title text box, enter text of your choosing—for example, Command & Control. Whatever you type will appear, instead of the word *Terminal*, at the start of the title of each window.

SEE: • "Take Note: What Is a Shell?," earlier in this chapter, for more details.

Keyboard. I don't use the options here, but I felt I should at least mention them. Most shells use a variety of keyboard shortcuts for common commands. If you wish to modify these shortcuts, this is where you would do so. Check out "Creating custom control sequences in Terminal," in the Help Viewer files for Terminal, for more information.

Split window. One option not listed in any menu or Inspector option is the ability to split a window so that you can view and compare two sections of the Terminal output at the same time. To do this, click the torn-square icon just below the title bar on the right side of the window. To revert to a single window, click the solid square icon in the lower of the two panes.

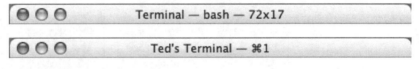

Figure 10.6

The title bar of a Terminal window (top) before and (bottom) after making customized changes in the Window section of the Inspector.

TAKE NOTE ▶ .Term Files

If you customize a Terminal window via Inspector and want to save these changes as defaults, you can usually do so by clicking the Use Settings As Defaults command in Terminal's File menu—or by clicking the button with the same name in Terminal Inspector.

But what if you want to save several different sets of settings, none of which you necessarily want as the default? You can do so. You can save any particular customization (font size, color, transparency, and so on) via a Terminal settings (.term) file.

To do so, make all of the changes you wish to save, and then select Save from Terminal's File menu. This creates a file of the current settings; the file will have the name you selected and a .term extension appended to it. From options in the Save window you can also select (a) whether to open this .term file when launching Terminal (which overlaps with the setting in Terminal's Preferences window); (b) whether to save all currently open windows or just the active (main) one; and (c) additional options (again overlapping with preferences settings) for which shell and command to execute when opening the file.

continues on next page

TAKE NOTE ▶ **.Term Files** *continued*

If you do not select to open the saved .term file by default when Terminal starts up, you can always open later it by selecting the Open command from Terminal's File menu.

Terminal is supposed to save .term files in ~/Library/Application Support/Terminal. However, when I tried this, Terminal instead elected to save the file in my Documents folder. If this happens to you, you can create your own Terminal folder in the Application Support folder and save the .term file there (or move any existing file there). After doing so, quit and relaunch Terminal. You will now see that the Library command in Terminal's File menu is no longer dimmed. Select it, and you'll be able to access a hierarchical menu listing all .term files in the Terminal folder. When you subsequently elect to save a new .term file, it should now go to the Terminal folder by default (rather than the Documents folder).

The .term file is a text file (in XML format). Therefore, you can open it in a text editor and add Unix commands to it. A popular use here would be to connect to a remote server via ssh on launch. The added commands run when the .term file is opened. For more details, see the following Apple Knowledge Base article: http://docs.info.apple.com/article.html?artnum=86134.

These .term files have a significant limitation: If set to run automatically when Terminal launches, a .term file only affects the initial shell window. To see what I mean, make a change to your default settings (such as choosing a larger font) and then save the change as a .term file (via the Save command). In the Save dialog, enable the "Open this file when Terminal starts up" option, then quit and relaunch Terminal. The window will indeed open in the modified font. But now select Command-N to open a second Terminal window. The second window will use the default font, *not* the one in the .term file. Sometimes this may be what you want: For example, if you're using the .term file to connect to a remote server, you may not want this action performed with each new window you open. However, if you do want to repeat the action, you can always use the Open command to select the .term file and run it a second time. And for something like a font change, if you really wanted that to occur in every shell window, you could select it as the default font. Still, there are commands, beyond what can be set via Terminal's menus, where it would be more convenient if the commands were run automatically with each new window.

Although there's some overlap in function, a .term file is not the same as a shell script, a .login file, or a .tcshrc/.cshrc file. A .term file is primarily a way to select customized window settings, which would otherwise be set via Terminal's menu commands. A .term file, for example, is what you would use to change default settings for text color and font. A .term file is a Mac feature. The other types of files modify the Unix command-line environment, and are Unix features.

SEE: • **"Using shell configuration files" and "Using a shell script," later in this chapter, for explanations of these other types of files.**

Launching Terminal

When you launch Terminal, a window opens that says, `Welcome to Darwin!` The next line is the command-line prompt—which in the bash shell typically reads as follows:

`computer_name:~ user_name$`

For example, on one of my Macs, which is named Yoda, when the logged-in user is tedmac, the command-line prompt reads as follows:

`Yoda:~ tedmac$`

In the tcsh shell, in contrast, the general format for the command-line prompt will typically read as follows:

`[computer_name:~] user_name%`

In either case, `computer_name` is the name of your Mac (as listed in the Sharing System Preferences pane), and `user_name` is the short name of the currently logged-in user (as set up in the Accounts System Preferences pane). If you're connected to a server, the name assigned to your computer by the server will appear instead of your local names.

The symbol and/or text that appears after the colon represents the name of the directory at your current location—which in this case is the root level of your Home directory. The tilde (~) is a standard Unix abbreviation for this location. This is the default location when you open a new shell.

The % and $ symbols indicate that Terminal is ready to accept your typed input. The symbol may be different (perhaps a #), or absent, in other shells.

Quitting Terminal

To log out of a Terminal session, type `logout`. However, you do not need to log out before quitting Terminal. When you quit Terminal (by pressing Command-Q) or even simply close a shell window, Terminal logs you out. Depending on the option selected in the Processes item of the Inspector window, you may get a Close Window dialog with the following warning: "Closing this window will terminate the following processes inside it..." (followed by a list of processes). If you get this dialog, click the Terminate button to close the window and truly log out.

To prevent the Close Window dialog from appearing, select Never from the "Prompt before closing window" section of the Processes screen of the Inspector window. However, with certain processes active and Never selected, Terminal will refuse to quit when you select Quit from the File menu. If this happens, you can still force-quit Terminal by selecting Force Quit from the Apple menu.

You can avoid this hassle, however, by closing all Terminal windows before choosing Quit or by not using the Never option. If you type logout when done with a shell window, this also avoids any possible hassle with a Force Quit or having active processes open when trying to quit Terminal.

Figure 10.7

An example of the Close Window message.

Close Window

Closing this window will terminate the following processes inside it: bash, tcsh

Cancel   Terminate

TAKE NOTE ▶ Learning What Commands Do

To get more information about almost any Unix command, you have three main options from within Terminal:

man. Type man (for *manual*), followed by the name of the command. To learn more about the ls command, for example, type man ls. You will be provided with details on the various options available for use with the ls command.

You can even type man man to find out about the man command itself.

The output of man requests often assumes you already know a good deal about how Unix commands work. Don't expect a tutorial! However, even Unix novices can usually glean some useful information from the output—especially about the various options that work with a command. Unlike the Mac, which has menus and check boxes, Unix gives you no easy way to guess what options are available. Without the man command to tell you what your options are, you might never know.

continues on next page

Figure 10.8

The initial output that appears if you type man ls.

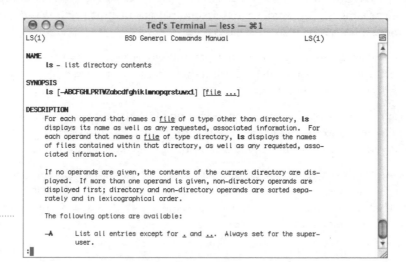

TAKE NOTE ▶ **Learning What Commands Do**   *continued*

Most man output exceeds what can fit on a screen. To see more, just keep pressing the Return key. If you want to exit before the output is complete, press the Q key.

Apple maintains an HTML version of all of Mac OS X's man pages, viewable from your Web browser, located at the following address: http://developer.apple.com/documentation/Darwin/Reference/ManPages/.

Several Aqua-based utilities, such as Carl Lindberg's ManOpen and computer-support.ch's Xupport, provide access to the man output from the Finder.

apropos. To search for a command by keyword, enter apropos {*keyword*}. For example, to get a list of commands that include the word *Apple* in their names, or that directly refer to Apple, you would type apropos Apple. If the resulting list includes the command you seek, you can then use the man command to get more information about it.

Usage. Many Unix commands only work correctly if an option is added to the command. For example, the remove (rm) command only performs an action if you specify what you want removed. In this case, if you type rm—and nothing else—you get a usage summary of how the command works. Try this for the Apple-created diskutil command, for an even better example. The usage output is much shorter than the man information, but it can be a convenient reference if you already know the basics of how the command works. In some cases, where no man output exists for a command, there is still a usage summary available. So if you are looking for help, try both.

TAKE NOTE ▶ **Unix Problems and How to Fix Them**

If you thought some of the error messages in Mac OS 9 and Mac OS X were too cryptic, you won't find any relief with Unix's error messages. They're usually worse.

Unix error messages. When Unix doesn't like what you've typed, it will often give you an error message—most commonly for incorrect commands. The causes can range from typographical errors (such as a misspelled word) to nonexistent paths and attempting to use an option that requires more information than you've provided.

If Unix has a good guess as to what went wrong, it may prompt you with its guess about the solution (for example, revising the input) and then ask, OK? If you like its guess, type y (for *yes*). Of not, simply press Return (for *no*).

Other error messages simply provide an indication of what went wrong. For example, if you mistyped a name, Unix might say, No such file or directory. This is your clue to make sure you didn't type the name incorrectly or attempt to access a nonexistent file.

In other cases, Unix may offer a brief summary of the format of the command and some common options. This is essentially the same as the usage summary described in "Take Note: Learning What Commands Do." If you get this usage feedback, it usually means you used an invalid option or typed something incorrectly.

continues on next page

TAKE NOTE ▶ Unix Problems and How to Fix Them

Stopping Unix. Sometimes, after typing a command, you may find yourself waiting indefinitely for the command-line prompt to reappear. This may be exactly what's supposed to happen: It means Unix has entered a mode in which the command line won't return unless you specifically instruct it to. Typically, typing q or exit will bring the prompt back.

Other times, it may just mean that Unix is doing some intensive processing: The command line will return when it's finished; you just need to be patient.

If neither of the above is the case, you may have the Unix equivalent of a freeze. To fix this, press Control-C or Command-period. This halts whatever process is in progress but allow you to enter further commands. Selecting the Send Break command in Terminal's File menu is the same as pressing Control-C. If none of this works, from the File menu you can select Send Reset or Send Hard Reset, as needed.

You can use the same commands if the output from some earlier command continues to scroll and scroll, with no end in sight. At least one of these commands should bring the scrolling to a halt.

As a last resort, you can always close the window or quit Terminal.

To prevent such freezes or excessive scrolling from occurring the next time, make sure that you typed the initial command correctly. If you're not certain, use man to check the manual for the problem command to make sure you're using it correctly. Some commands normally produce an excessive amount of output; these usually have options to restrict the output as needed. If this still fails to turn on any light bulbs, you'll probably need to consult a book on Unix or seek other outside help.

```
Ted-Landaus-Computer:/ landau$ sp
-bash: sp: command not found
```

```
Ted-Landaus-Computer:/ landau$ cd ~/Dcouments
-bash: cd: /Users/landau/Dcouments: No such file or directory
```

```
Ted-Landaus-Computer:/ landau$ cp
usage: cp [-R [-H | -L | -P]] [-f | -i | -n] [-pv] src target
       cp [-R [-H | -L | -P]] [-f | -i | -n] [-pv] src1 ... srcN directory
```

Figure 10.9

Three examples of the feedback Unix provides when something goes wrong: (top) for typing a nonexistent command; (middle) for entering a nonexistent pathway; and (bottom) for entering a command without its required additional parameters.

Unix: Listing and Navigating

In the remaining sections of this chapter, you'll find out about an assortment of Unix commands and files essential to troubleshooters. I'll start here by describing the basic commands used to list the contents of a directory (folder) and then show you how to navigate to any directory you want.

The ls command

The ls (*list*) command lists the contents of the current directory location. When you first launch Terminal, you arrive by default at the root level of your Home directory (~). Thus, typing ls gives you a list of items in your Home directory. You can compare this list by typing open . in Terminal to open a window for the current directory (Home) in the Finder. The items you see in the window should be the same items that are listed in Terminal.

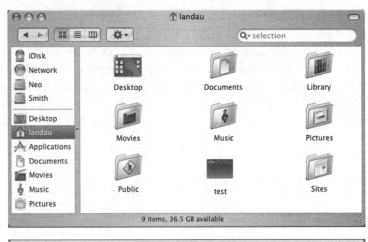

Figure 10.10

The items in your Home directory, as viewed in (top) the Finder and (bottom) the Terminal.

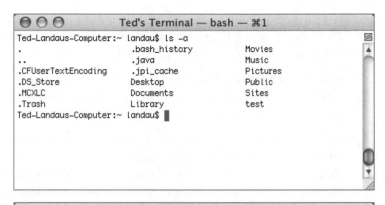

Figure 10.11

The same Home directory, as listed after typing (top) ls -a and (bottom) ls -l.

Options. Most Unix commands have options that can be appended to them (see also "Take Note: Learning What Commands Do," earlier in this chapter). These options usually start with a hyphen, followed by an uppercase or lower-case letter. The ls command has three notable options:

• **-a.** With this option, the output of the ls command includes items that are normally invisible (for example, ones that start with a dot). Typing this command for your Home directory, for example, will reveal the .Trash directory, which is where most of your files go when you drag them to the Trash.

• **-l.** This option outputs the *long* form of the directory listing. Each item is listed in its own row, followed by an assortment of additional information, including each item's permissions settings, owner, and group name. If you've read earlier chapters of this book (especially Chapters 4 and 6), you know what these permissions are used for. I also review the topic as it applies to Terminal in "Unix: Modifying Permissions," later in this chapter.

• **–F.** With this option, directory names end in a trailing forward slash (/). Thus, a directory named Documents would appear as Documents/ when you type ls –F. This makes it easy to distinguish between files and directories—a distinction you can't make based on the output of a basic ls command.

You can combine options in the same line, using only one hyphen if desired. Thus, to get a list that both includes invisible items and is in the long form, you could type either ls -a -l or ls -al.

ls of any directory. If you want to see a list of items in a location other than your current one, you can type ls followed by the desired options and then the absolute or relative path to the directory you want to view.

Suppose, for example, you wanted to view the contents of the Documents directory of your Home directory. Assuming you're still in your Home directory, you could simply type ls Documents. This is what's known as a *relative-pathway command.* Unix assumes you're starting your path at your current directory location; thus, it looks for a directory called Documents in your Home directory.

Suppose, however, you wanted to see the contents of the root-level Applications folder. The simplest way to do that would be to type the *absolute pathway*—that is, the pathway that starts at the root level of the volume itself. In this case, you would type ls /Applications. The initial slash instructs Unix to start the path at the root level of the volume.

By the way, Unix commands are almost always case sensitive. Thus, typing ls /Applications is not the same as typing ls /applications. If the name of the folder is Applications, using the lowercase *a* to begin its name will result in an error.

SEE: • **"The cd command and related commands,"** later in this chapter, for more on pathways and navigational commands.

• **"Take Note: Finder Folders vs. Unix Directories,"** in Chapter 4, for background on absolute and relative pathnames.

TAKE NOTE ▶ Unix Shortcuts

Having to type a long pathname and/or a string of command options can get to be a pain—especially when one typographical error can ruin the entire line and force you to start over. That's one of the reasons why a Mac-like interface is often preferred. Still, Unix offers a variety of shortcuts to help reduce typing. The following are the ones I use the most:

• **History.** Press the up arrow key at any point to make the last command you typed appear. You can then keep pressing the up arrow key to retrace your history for as many commands as Terminal tracks. You can use the down arrow key to return to your starting point. When you find the command you want to use again, simply press Return, and it will execute. To modify the command, press Delete to backspace the needed number of characters, then type in the new characters and press Return.

continues on next page

TAKE NOTE ▶ **Unix Shortcuts** *continued*

If you type the `history` command in Terminal, you'll get a list of all commands entered since the shell was started, numbered sequentially and beginning with *1* for the first command entered. To re-enter a command from the list, type `!n`, where *n* represents that command's number in the history list. Thus, to re-enter the third command in the list, you would type `!3`. As an alternative method, you can type `!!` in order to re-enter the most recently used command.

- **Wildcards.** The asterisk (*) is a wildcard character—which means it provides a match for any number and sequence of characters. For example, suppose you're in your Documents directory and want to delete (remove) every item that ends in .html. Instead of typing each item separately, you could simply type `*.html` just once following the remove (`rm`) command. The asterisk instructs Unix to match every file that ends in .html, no matter what precedes it.

  The question mark (?) is also a wildcard, except that it can only substitute for a single character. Suppose, for example, you wanted to match every file ending in .dmg or .img. You could type `*.?mg`. This command matches every file, no matter what precedes the period, as long as it ends in a period followed by any single character followed by *mg*. Assuming that no files end in some other combination of a character plus *mg*, this command would do the trick.

- **Tab.** Whenever you start to type a pathname, pressing the Tab key fills in the remainder of the item name that matches what you're typing.

  For example, if you type `ls ~/Do` and then press Tab, Unix will fill in the rest of the name (*Documents*) for you—a great time-saver for long filenames or names you can't remember precisely.

  If there's more than one matching item in a given directory (for example, if you type `ls ~/D` and Tab, the *D* could represent either *Desktop* or *Documents*), you will hear a beep or be presented with a list of all possible matches. In either case, continue to type letters, pressing the Tab key after each, until you have a unique match.

- **Dragging a Finder icon.** This last trick is not a Unix one, exactly, since it depends on the Mac OS; however, it makes working in Terminal a bit easier. If you drag a Finder icon to the Terminal window, it pastes the pathname of the icon into the current command line. Alternatively, numerous Aqua-based utilities allow you to select an item and copy its Unix pathname to the Clipboard. Sebastian Krauss's Locator is one such utility: Once the item is in the Clipboard, Locator lets you paste the pathname into Terminal.

  Thus, to list the contents of a particular directory in Terminal, including invisible items, type `ls -a` followed by a space, and then drag the Finder icon of the directory you want to list to the Terminal window. Its pathname will be added to the line. Press Return, and the directory list will appear.

- **Dragging text.** If you checked "Enable drag copy/paste of text" from the Inspector, as described in "Terminal Inspector," earlier in this chapter, you can drag any selected text to the current command-line location.

TAKE NOTE ▶ Spaces In Pathnames

When you type pathnames, Unix interprets a space as being the start of a new name. Thus, if you type Research Report as the filename to be used with some command, such as cp or rm, Unix will think you're referring to two separate file or directory names—one called Research and another called Report—rather than a single item called Research Report. To instruct Unix to include the space as part of a single name, you have two options:

- You can place a backslash before the space—that is, type Research\ Report.

  Preceding a character with a backslash (\) negates any special meaning it may have. Thus, preceding a space with a backslash says, "Treat the space as a space, not as a name divider."

- You can put the name in quotes (ideally single quotes, though double quotes usually work as well)—that is, type 'Research Report'. Putting a pathname in quotes tells Unix to treat everything within quotes exactly as typed. This means that a space is treated as part of the name and not as a separator.

Note: If you copy the name of a file in the Finder (or copy any text), you can make sure the text is pasted with backslashes as needed by selecting Paste Escaped Text from Terminal's Edit menu. This eliminates the need to enclose the pasted text in quotation marks. Unlike dragging an icon from the Finder, however, this does not copy the full pathname.

Auto-filling a pathname. To make sure you're entering a pathname correctly, with spaces treated as spaces, use the Tab key to complete a name or drag the Finder icon for the item to the command line, as explained in "Take Note: Unix Shortcuts," earlier in this chapter. These techniques automatically fill in the pathname, correctly adding backslashes in front of each space as needed.

SEE: • "Unix: Copying, Moving, and Deleting," later in this chapter, for more on the rm command.
- "Take Note: Using rm: Risk Management," later in this chapter, for a warning about how errors involving spaces in pathnames combined with the rm command can lead to disaster.

The cd command and related commands

Sometimes, it's not enough to list the contents of a directory; sometimes you need to *go* to the directory. Among other things, moving to the desired directory can simplify working with items there. For example, when you're at a directory, just typing ls yields a list of its contents; you no longer need to enter the directory's path each time.

To move to a different directory, you use the cd (*change directory*) command. To move to the Applications folder, for example, you would type cd /Applications.

The following are some further examples of using the cd command and the related pwd command:

- To determine what directory you're in, type pwd (*print working directory*).
- To move to the root level of the volume, type cd /.
- To return to your Home directory quickly, type cd with no path specified.
- Use the ~ symbol to indicate an absolute path to your Home directory. Thus, to go to the Documents directory in your Home directory, no matter where you're located, type cd ~/Documents.
- You can use relative pathways to navigate. This method saves time, because you don't have to type the longer absolute path. Thus, if you want to move to the Documents directory and you're in your Home directory, just type cd Documents.
- You can use dots in pathnames to assist in navigating. For example, if you're in the Documents directory and want to return to your Home directory, you can simply type cd to get there. However, there's a more general shortcut you can use to go up a level, regardless of where you're located: Simply type cd .. and press Return. To go back more than one level, you can type this command multiple times. Or, to go back two levels with one command, type cd ../.. and press Return.

  A single dot refers to the current directory. Thus, cd ./Documents tells Unix to go to the Documents directory within whatever directory you're currently in. In most cases, the single dot is not needed; simply typing cd Documents would have worked just as well. However, the dot is necessary for some commands other than cd. For example, as explained in "Unix: Executing Commands," later in this chapter, you may need the single dot when you're trying to execute a command located in the current directory.

Many of the examples described here apply just as well to Unix commands other than cd. Thus, the use of the dot shortcuts would work the same when entering a pathname for ls as for cd.

Unix: The sudo and su Commands

If you type a command in Unix and get a "permission denied" or "operations not permitted" error message, you probably need root access to do what you were trying to do. There are two means of obtaining this type of access: the su command and the sudo command.

Using su. To get root access, type su, then press Return. You will be prompted to provide the root password. Once you've done so, the prompt will change to something like the following (note that the computer and user names are from my own Mac; I was located in my Home directory, called tedmac, when I typed the su command):

```
Yoda:/Users/tedmac root#
```

You are now a root user and will remain so until you type exit or logout.

Note: The password you provide here is the root user password, not your administrative password. This is the password you set in NetInfo Manager when you enable the root user. Still, you need to be an administrator for the root user password to work. If, after entering a correct password, you get a message that says, Sorry, this probably means that root user access has not been enabled for your Mac. To remedy this, launch NetInfo Manager and enable root access, as described in Chapter 4. Alternatively, you can enable root access in Terminal simply by setting a password for it. To do so, type sudo passwd root. Give your administrator's password when asked. You will then be prompted to enter a new password for the root user.

Note: After using su to change to the root user, your Home directory (in Terminal) changes to that of the root user. This means that shortcuts (such as the ~ symbol) that indicate a Home directory now refer to a different Home location. To avoid errors when typing commands that include pathnames, you may thus want to enter the absolute path for a file rather than one that includes the ~ symbol or other shortcuts.

Using sudo. Alternatively, to get *temporary* root access, you can type sudo followed by the name of the command you wish to execute with root access, all on the same line. For example, to delete a file that requires root access to do so, you would type the following:

sudo rm *filename*

You will now be asked for your administrator's password, *not* the root user's password. In this case, you retain root access only for the command(s) on that line; you do not need to type exit to return to your previous status. Also, unlike sudo, this command works regardless of whether you've enabled root access in NetInfo Manager.

Once you've executed the sudo command, you can continue to use the command for 5 minutes without having to re-enter your password. Once that period has elapsed, you will be asked to re-enter your password. There are, however, ways to extend or reduce this time limit—most notably, typing sudo -v to extend sudo privileges for an additional 5 minutes, or typing sudo -k to immediately revoke sudo privileges (called *killing,* or invalidating, the timestamp).

Finally, you can use a variation of the sudo command to mimic the effect of the su command. To do so, type sudo –s; no additional input is needed on the line. This gives you sustained root access via your administrator's password rather than the root user password.

Type man sudo for details on these and other sudo command options.

Note: Although sudo works with almost all common Unix commands, you cannot combine sudo with the cd command to move to a directory for which you do not have permission.

Which to use? In general, you should use sudo rather than su so that root access remains as limited as possible. Even if you have the best of intentions, mistyping a command while having root access can have devastating consequences—sometimes wiping out the files the OS needs to work or deleting an entire Home directory. With the more limited sudo command, the risks are minimized because you are not "permanently" given root access.

The main reason to consider using su is if you need to retain root access over a series of commands, especially if you need to do so for more than 5 minutes. However, even in this case, you could use sudo −s instead of su. And with sudo −s, you don't need to first enable the root user in NetInfo Manager.

The sudoers file. The list of users who can use the sudo command, the time limit for re-entering your password (5 minutes by default), and other sudo-related options (such as a list of all user categories that can use the sudo command) are maintained in a file called sudoers (located in the /etc directory).

You can modify this file (in a text editor) to change how sudo works. For example, if you change the value of timestamp_timeout from 5 to 0, sudo will ask for a password every time you use it (eliminating the 5-minute grace period). Type man sudoers in Terminal for more information about this file.

Note: Opening and editing this file requires root access. In fact, the default setting is for the owner of the file (System) to have Read Only access (so even the root user can't modify the file without first changing its permissions!). Don't modify this file unless you're confident that you know what you're doing. Making a mistake here could prevent you from using sudo altogether.

Figure 10.12

Using the sudo *command: Without* sudo, *the attempt to list the contents of a restricted directory fails. With* sudo, *the* ls *command succeeds.*

```
Ted-Landaus-Computer:/var landau$ ls cron
ls: cron: Permission denied
Ted-Landaus-Computer:/var landau$ sudo ls cron
Password:
tabs
Ted-Landaus-Computer:/var landau$ ▌
```

SEE: • "Root Access," in Chapter 4, for much more information on this topic.

• "Using Panther's Finder Authenticate method," in Chapter 6, for a separate method of temporarily having privileged access in the Finder.

TAKE NOTE ▶ **Securing Mac OS X**

The su and sudo commands are intended to guard against unauthorized access to your Mac.

If your Mac is in your home, and only you and your family have access to it, your main security concern is that a thief might steal your Mac, not that an unauthorized user might gain access to your data. Although it's possible that your Mac's security could be breached via an Internet connection, it's doubtful that anyone would try—unless you have valuable information on your computer that some unscrupulous person knows about.

If you're in a more public environment, such as a university, data security is of greater concern. This book is geared toward users with more modest security concerns—which explains why I've been fairly lenient in my attitude toward root user usage, for example. Still, it's worth knowing what security options are available. The following reviews some data-security tips introduced elsewhere in this book:

- Creating separate user accounts represents the most basic form of security; for more on this, see Chapter 2.

   Tip: It's more difficult for people to log in illegally if they don't know the names of the valid accounts. You can hide these names by selecting "Name and password" from the "Display Login Window as" options in the Login Options section of the Accounts System Preferences pane (rather than using the "List of users" option). You can also download a utility from Apple's Web site called HideorShowPreviousLogin. Running this turns off the feature in which the name of the last person to log in is shown in the Login window by default.

   Obviously, if security is a concern, you don't want to enable automatic login.

   SEE: • "System Preferences," in Chapter 2, for coverage of the Accounts System Preferences pane.

- You can disable the root user if you have enabled it, using NetInfo Manager, as covered in Chapter 4. This makes it more difficult for someone to get unauthorized root access. In most cases, the sudo command, which does not require that the root user be enabled, will be sufficient for your root user needs in Terminal.

   You can always re-enable the root user temporarily if you need to, such as to log in as root from Mac OS X.

   Actually, if you've never enabled the root user, you should do so, and then enter a password (and then disable the user if you wish). Otherwise, by default there is no password for the root user, which itself is a security risk.

- You can encrypt your Home directory (via Panther's FileVault option) and/or require a password when waking up the computer from sleep (or a screensaver). To select these and related options, go to the Security System Preferences pane.

   SEE: • "System Preferences," in Chapter 2, for coverage of the Security System Preferences pane.

continues on next page

Unix: Modifying Permissions

Ownership and permissions in Unix refer to what are in essence the same settings you access via the Ownership & Permissions section of a file's Get Info window in the Finder. Changing the settings in Get Info modifies the underlying Unix settings. The main difference is that you have access to settings in Terminal that are not available via the Get Info window. You can also access these additional settings via third-party utilities such as Rainer Brockerhoff's XRay and Gideon Softwork's FileXaminer. In general, I find these utilities to be more convenient and less time-consuming than going to Terminal, but for those who prefer not to invest in additional shareware, Terminal is the way to go.

I've discussed changing permissions settings in several other chapters of this book; the focus of *this* section is the basics of viewing and modifying these settings in Terminal.

SEE: • **"Ownership & Permissions," in Chapter 4, "Opening and Saving: Permissions Problems," in Chapter 6, and "Copying and Moving: Problems Copying and Moving Files," in Chapter 6, for more background on these topics.**

Unix assigns a minimum of nine permissions settings (or bits) to each item: a *read* (r), *write* (w), and *execute* (x) value for each of three categories—the *owner* of the item, the *group* assigned to the item, and *everyone else*. Each of these settings can be either *on* (you have the needed permission) or *off* (you don't). In brief, r refers to the ability to open and view a file; w refers to the ability to modify a file; and x refers to the ability to execute or run a program.

These settings are also used for directories and folders (in addition to individual files), but they have slightly different meanings in that context. For example, you can't *run* a directory, so the execute bit takes on a different meaning. The execute permission needs to be enabled for a directory before the r and w settings have an effect. In fact, when it's used with directories, the x bit is more often called the *search* bit than the *execute* bit, because it needs to be on before you can search or view the contents of the directory.

```
drwxrwxr-x   3 root    admin    102  7 Dec 13:19 Stickies.app
drwxrwxr-x   3 root    wheel    102  7 Dec 13:19 System Preferences.app
```

Figure 10.13

The view from Terminal of permissions settings for two files in the Applications folder (Stickies and System Preferences). Note that even though they're applications, Terminal correctly shows the files as directories. Compare the permissions, owner, and group settings here to those shown in Figure 10.11 (bottom), for items in a Home directory.

In Terminal, when you use the `ls -l` command to view a list of directory contents, you see the permissions settings for each file in the column on the far left. A `drwxrwxr-x` listing would be a common setting for applications located in the Mac OS X Applications directory, for example. Here's what this permissions listing means:

- **d.** The initial d means that the item is a directory (or folder in Mac OS X jargon). In this example, it may seem odd that applications are considered to be folders. Remember, however, that most Mac OS X applications are really .app packages, which are simply special types of folders. If an item is a single file instead of a folder, the initial character would be a hyphen (-).

- **owner rwx.** The first trio of rwx refers to the owner's permissions. In this case, the owner of the application has read, write, and execute permissions. As indicated in the columns to the right, for applications installed by Mac OS X, the owner is *root*.

- **group rwx.** The second rwx refers to the permissions for the members of the listed group. As indicated in the group column, for most applications installed by Mac OS X, the group is *admin*. Because all administrative users are in the admin group, they all have the same access to the items in this directory as does the owner. Note: For most files in your Home directory, the owner will be you, and the group will be one with the same name as your owner name or one named *staff*.

- **everyone r-x.** The third trio, r-x (for *everyone else*), means that all other users can access and execute the application but cannot modify it.

The precise implication of having no modify access can get a bit tricky. (Can you move the application out of the Applications directory without modify access? Can you modify a text file within the .app package? Can you delete the application?) What you can or cannot do is determined by a combination of the permissions settings for the item itself and for its enclosing directory or directories. I cover most of the specifics in Chapter 6. In this chapter, my focus is not on the nuances of what these settings mean but how to use Unix commands in Terminal to edit these settings.

The chmod command

You use the chmod (*change mode*) command to change permissions (also called *mode bits*). At any time, you can use the ls -l command to examine the current settings and confirm that your intended change was made.

Note: The following examples assume you're in the parent directory of the item you want to modify; thus, you only need to enter the name of the item. Otherwise, you would need to include a relative or absolute pathname for the item.

You can use the chmod command in two ways:

Octal method. The first method requires entering numbers to indicate the permissions settings you want to use. This method is called the *octal* method, because it has eight possible values (0 to 7). A 0 implies no access, while 7 indicates all access (rwx) for the indicated category of user (owner, group, or everyone).

Each type of access (r, w, and x) has an associated numeric value: x is assigned 1, w is assigned 2; and r is assigned 4. If you want to assign more than one type of access (such as both read and write) to a given category of user, you add the numbers for each individual access type.

Thus, the octal notation for read and write but not execute access (rw-) is *6 (4 + 2)*. The octal notation for complete access (rwx) is 7 *(4 + 2 + 1)*. And so on.

When using this form of the chmod command, you enter three of these numeric sums, one each for owner, group, and everyone—in that order. Thus, the octal notation for rwx access for owner and group, but r-x access for everyone else, is 775. To set this permission for an item called test.app, for example, you would type the following:

```
chmod 775 test.app
```

A minor disadvantage of the octal method is that, if you want to make a single modification (perhaps removing write access for the group), you still need to re-enter all the octal values. Thus, to make the cited group assignment change for test.app, you would need to type the following:

```
chmod 755 test.app
```

Symbolic method. In the *symbolic* method, you use an equation format that describes what you want to do. The equation has three parts:

- First, you pick which category of user the change will affect (*u* equals user, which is the same as owner; *g* equals group; and *o* equals other, which is the same as everyone).

- Second, you indicate whether you want to add (+), remove (-), or set (=) a permission for that user category.
- Third, you select one or more permission types (r, w, and/or x).

Again, suppose that you want to change the permission of the test.app item from rwxrwxr-x to rwxr-xr-x. With symbolic notation, you would type the following:

chmod g-w test.app

This command says, "For just the group setting, remove the w access."

Another example: To set rwx access for group and other, overwriting the current settings, you would type the following:

chmod go=rwx test.app

Special-mode bits. In addition to read, write, and execute, you may encounter some less well-known modes: the sticky bit, SetUID, and SetGUI.

SEE: • **"Sticky bits and the Drop Box" and "Technically Speaking: SetUID and SetGID," in Chapter 6, for more information on these settings.**

You can use the chmod command to change these special-mode settings. To do so via the octal method, you add a fourth digit in front of the initial three: 1 enables the sticky bit; 2 enables the SetGID bit; and 4 enables the SetUID bit.

Suppose, for example, you wanted to enable the sticky bit for a directory called myitems that currently has rwxr-xr-x access. To do so without changing existing rwx permissions, you would type the following:

chmod 1755 myitems

If you use ls -l to see the permissions settings after making this change, you will see that it now reads rwxrwxrwt. The t at the end, rather than an x, indicates that the sticky bit has been enabled.

As another example, to enable the SetUID bit for a file called myfile, precede the standard octal notation with a 4. That is, type the following:

chmod 4755 myfile

If you now use ls -l to see the permissions settings for the file, it will read rwsr-xr-x. The s at the end of the first trio of letters indicates that SetUID has been enabled for the owner (SetUID always applies just to the owner).

For those who prefer to use the symbolic method, you can make the same changes, though I'll omit the details here.

Viewing Terminal commands and output via GUI utilities. A reminder: If you don't want to bother with any of these techniques, you can use an Aqua-based utility such as XRay instead. A convenient tutorial feature of XRay is that it shows the ls command info (such as rwxrwxrwx) and chmod command input (such as chmod 777) for whatever change you make. You can then use this information to compare the changes you make in XRay with what you would have done in Terminal.

The chown and chgrp commands

Although the previously described methods allow you to edit the *permissions* of the owner and group of a given item, they don't actually change the owner or group themselves. To do that, you must use the chown (*change owner*) and chgrp (*change group*) commands.

The format is quite simple: You just type the command, the new owner or group, and the pathname of the item to be changed. To assign the group named *staff* to an item called testfile, for example, type the following:

chgrp staff testfile

Similarly, to change the owner of an item called test.framework from root to yourself (*yourname*), you would type the following:

chown *yourname* test.framework

OK, it's not quite *that* simple. You can't change the group assignment of an item unless you own that item. A greater obstacle is that no one but the root user can change an item's owner. In fact, you can't even change the ownership of a file you own. Thus, typing this chown command will lead to an "operation not permitted" error.

True, as I discussed in Chapter 6, copying a file from one directory location to another may modify the ownership of the file. But that's a separate issue from modifying the permissions of a file directly.

The solution—assuming you're an administrative user—is to use the sudo command, as described earlier in this chapter, to get temporary root access. To do so, type the following:

sudo chown *yourname* test.framework

Enter your password when requested, and the change should be made. If not, you can try using the su command alternative to get root access and then separately entering the chown command. I've seen a few instances in which this succeeded when sudo did not.

Be aware that changing the ownership or group of an item could mean that you can no longer modify or even access the item via the Finder. For example, for a document that is owned by root, where the group is admin and has read and write access, if you change the group to one to which you do not belong, you will no longer be able to edit the item or even open it in the Finder. To regain access, you would have to modify permissions again (or possibly access the file with root access).

> SEE: • "Root Access," in Chapter 4, for related details.
>
> • "Ownership & Permissions," in Chapter 4, for how to make these changes from the Finder.

The chflags command

The chflags command is used to change flags, which are similar to Finder attributes. You can thus use this command to modify such attributes (bits) as whether a file is locked or unlocked, visible or invisible.

For example, if you type chflags nouchg *myfile*, you're turning off (no) the immutable flag (uchg) for the file named *myfile* (though, again, you can do the same thing via a utility like XRay).

Modifying the immutable flag is similar to locking and unlocking files from the Finder's Get Info window. Sometimes, however, the Finder may indicate that a file is unlocked even though this flag is set. That's when you may need to use this command.

> SEE: • "Using Unix to delete files," in Chapter 6, for more details on using this command.

```
Ted-Landaus-Computer:~ landau$ ls -l TEST
-rw-r--r-- 1 landau  staff  0 13 Dec 15:15 TEST
Ted-Landaus-Computer:~ landau$ chmod ugo+x TEST
Ted-Landaus-Computer:~ landau$ ls -l TEST
-rwxr-xr-x 1 landau  staff  0 13 Dec 15:15 TEST
Ted-Landaus-Computer:~ landau$ █
```

Figure 10.14

Examples of some permissions commands: (top) using chmod to give execute (x) access to owner (u), group (g), and others (o) for the file called TEST; (bottom) using chgrp to change the group of the TEST file from staff to admin.

```
Ted-Landaus-Computer:~ landau$ ls -l TEST
-rwxr-xr-x 1 landau  staff  0 13 Dec 15:15 TEST
Ted-Landaus-Computer:~ landau$ chgrp admin TEST
Ted-Landaus-Computer:~ landau$ ls -l TEST
-rwxr-xr-x 1 landau  admin  0 13 Dec 15:15 TEST
Ted-Landaus-Computer:~ landau$ █
```

Figure 10.15

Using the mv command to rename a file: TEST is changed to testy.

```
Ted-Landaus-Computer:~ landau$ ls
Desktop      Library      Music      Public      TEST
Documents    Movies       Pictures   Sites
Ted-Landaus-Computer:~ landau$ mv TEST testy
Ted-Landaus-Computer:~ landau$ ls
Desktop      Library      Music      Public      testy
Documents    Movies       Pictures   Sites
Ted-Landaus-Computer:~ landau$ █
```

Unix: Copying, Moving, and Deleting

In most cases, when you want to copy, move, or delete files, you will do so in the Finder. Occasionally, however, the Finder may not carry out the operation successfully; in such cases, you may find that using Terminal solves the problem. In addition, if you're already working in Terminal, you may sometimes find it more convenient to stay within Terminal to perform these actions.

Remember that any changes you make in Terminal affect the location of these files in the Finder as well: These are two interfaces to the same environment, not two parallel universes.

SEE: • Chapter 6, for several examples of using Unix to copy, move, and delete files for troubleshooting purposes.

The cp command

The cp (*copy*) command is (almost) the equivalent of the Mac's Copy command. It creates a copy of the file without deleting or modifying the original. A simple format for this command is as follows:

`cp `*`oldfilename newfilename`*

This example assumes that you're in the directory of the old file. In this case, a new copy of the original file is created in the same directory.

Note: A limitation of the cp command is that it does not copy the resource fork portion of a file (if present), as explained in "The CpMac and MvMac Commands," later in this chapter.

Copying to a different location. If you want the new file to reside in a different directory than the old file's, you need to specify its path. Thus, if you're at the root level of your Home directory and want to copy a file called report.doc to your Documents directory, where you want it listed as report42.doc, you would type one of the following:

`cp report.doc Documents/report42.doc`

or

`cp report.doc ~/Documents/report42.doc`

or

`cp report.doc /Users/`*`yourusername`*`/Documents/report42.doc`

Copying with the same name. If you're content to have the name of the new file be the same as that of the original, you can leave off the filename in the second path. Thus, to move a file called song.mp3 from the root level of your Home directory to your Music directory, you could type the following:

```
cp ~/song.mp3 ~/Music/
```

Batch copying. You can combine the `cp` command with wildcard notation (such as an asterisk) to copy several files at the same time. Thus, to copy all files at the root level of your Home directory that end in .mp3 to the Music directory, you could type the following:

```
cp ~/*.mp3 ~/Music/
```

This represents a case where using Terminal is easier than using the Finder—that is, selecting and copying the same batch of files in the Finder would not be as simple.

Copying directories. So far, I've been talking about copying files. If you try to use the `cp` command to copy a directory—one called testfolder, for example—it will fail. You will get the following error message: **cp: testfolder/ is a directory (not copied).**

To solve this problem, you need to type cp –R, followed by the pathname(s). The –R option is the recursive option. (Note: Using an uppercase or lowercase *R* works equally well here, though don't count on this being the case for all commands.) Thus, to copy testfolder for the current directory to the Documents directory, you would type the following:

```
cp -R testfolder ~/Documents/testfolder
```

In this case, you should end the second path with the desired name of the new directory—even if it's the same name as the original. If you're using wildcards in the name of the first path, however, you can just specify the destination directory in the second path. Thus, the following command copies all items, files, or directories in the current directory that begin with *test* to the Documents directory without changing any names:

```
cp -R test* ~/Documents/
```

Similarly, to copy an application, such as TextEdit, from the main Applications folder to the Applications folder in your Home directory, you would enter the following:

```
cp -R /Applications/TextEdit.app ~/Applications/TextEdit.app
```

Note: The -R option was necessary here because, as discussed in Chapters 3 and 4, applications such as TextEdit are actually packages, which Unix sees as folders. In addition, you need to use the .app extension because the full name of these applications includes that extension, even if it's not seen in the Finder.

In one example of how the cp command could help in troubleshooting, I once ran into a situation where I couldn't copy an application from a CD to my hard drive using the Finder. I kept getting a –50 error (which I later discovered was due to an oddity with one of the files inside the .app package). Using the cp command succeeded where the Finder failed.

The mv command

The mv (*move*) command follows almost exactly the same structure as the cp (*copy*) command. The main difference is that mv deletes the original file, so that only the moved version remains. As its name implies, you appear to move the file to its new location rather than copy it. Thus, if you wanted to move the previously cited report.doc file, instead of copying it to the Documents directory (and changing its name at the same time), you would type the following:

```
mv report.doc Documents/report42.doc
```

You can also use the mv command to rename a file without moving it. That is, if you left off Documents/ from the above command, it would simply rename report.doc to report42.doc, leaving the renamed file in its original location rather than moving it to the Documents folder.

The mv command works equally well with files and directories. Like the cp command, it can be used to move multiple items. Unlike the cp command, it doesn't need a –R option.

Note: A limitation of the mv command is that it does not copy the resource fork portion of a file (if present), as explained next in "The CpMac and MvMac Commands."

SEE: • "Opening and Saving and Permissions Problems," and "Copying and Moving: Permissions Problems," in Chapter 6, for a discussion of how moving versus copying may affect permissions.

The CpMac and MvMac commands

As an alternative to copying files with cp, Apple includes a command in /Developer/Tools (installed with the Developer Tools software) called CpMac.

For moving files, Apple similarly provides an alternative to the mv command: MvMac.

Note: If the CpMac or MvMac command does not run if you type just its name in Terminal, you need to enter its full pathname. For example, to copy the TextEdit application, as cited above, you would type the following:

```
/Developer/Tools/CpMac –rp /Applications/TextEdit.app
~/Applications/TextEdit.app
```

Copying and moving, and the problem with resource forks.
Why did Apple bother with these commands? Why aren't cp and mv sufficient? The following explains why.

Many Mac files are composed of two forks: a resource fork and a data fork. Note: You cannot tell if a file has both forks just by looking at the file in the Finder; this is a "behind the scenes" characteristic.

The resource fork is limited mainly to older Carbon applications (usually imported from Mac OS 9) that do not use the package (.app) format, as well as document files created by many applications in Mac OS 9. Most other Mac OS X files do not include a resource fork.

Files created in the Unix environment never have resource forks; every Unix item consists only of a data fork. Consistent with this, the cp and mv commands copy only the data fork of an item. Thus, they will not successfully copy files that contain a resource fork.

The CpMac and MvMac commands solve this dilemma by copying both the data and resource forks, if present, of a file.

If you're uncertain whether a file contains a resource fork, don't worry. You can test it out by using the cp command. If it fails to work, just delete the resulting partial copy and try again with the Apple-supplied command.

SEE: • "Unix: Executing Commands," later in this chapter, for more on how to run the commands in the Developer directory.
• "Technically Speaking: Type/Creator vs. Filename Extensions," in Chapter 4, for background information on resource and data forks.

The ditto command

There are times when even the CpMac command is not sufficient to copy a file or directory exactly the way you would like. The problem is that CpMac does not necessarily copy permissions and links accurately. This can be a real problem if you're trying to make an exact duplicate backup of a Mac OS X volume. In such cases, you can use the ditto command—which *does* copy permissions correctly, maintaining the same settings as the original file(s); it can even preserve resource fork information.

The man entry for ditto states the following:

> *The ditto command overwrites existing files, symbolic links, and devices in the destination when they are copied from a source. The resulting files, links, and devices will have the same mode, owner, and group as the source items from which they are copied. ditto preserves hardlinks present in the source directories and preserves setuid and setgid modes. Finally, ditto can also preserve resource fork and HFS meta-data (e.g., Type/Creator) information when copying files within or between file systems.*

In other words, ditto copies everything exactly and correctly, which is why it's useful for volume backups. As I mentioned above, it will even preserve resource fork data, via its -rsrcFork option.

The ditto command requires root access when you're using it to back up an entire volume, because this involves copying files that you would otherwise not have permission to copy. To get this access, use the sudo command. Since there's no harm in using sudo, even if it's not required, I typically use it whenever I employ the ditto command. For example, to copy a folder called BackUps in your Home directory to an external drive called BackupDrive, you could enter the following:

```
sudo ditto -rsrcFork ~/BackUps /Volumes/BackupDrive/BackUps
```

No -R option is needed because ditto automatically copies a directory and its contents, if indicated.

When this type of industrial-strength copying is not essential, CpMac and cp are simpler to use. The ditto command is used primarily for volume backups. Another command to consider using for volume backups is asr.

SEE: • "Backing up Mac OS X: utilities for volume backups," in Chapter 3, for more on ditto, asr, and related commands.

The rm command

The rm (*remove*) command deletes files and directories. To use it, type rm plus the name of the item(s) you want to delete. If you want to delete a directory (and all of its contents), add the –R option. Thus, to delete a song.mp3 file from your Desktop, you would type the following:

```
rm ~/Desktop/song.mp3
```

To delete the Music directory and its contents from your Home directory, you would type the following:

```
rm -R ~/Music
```

You can remove multiple items by typing them individually (separated by a space) or by using a name with a wildcard. You could thus delete both of the preceding files with one remove command. To do so, type the following:

```
rm -R ~/Music ~/Desktop/song.mp3
```

Remember that you can also add a pathname by typing rm followed by a space, and then dragging the Finder icon(s) of the item(s) you want to delete to the Terminal window.

When combined with the sudo command, the rm command can be used to delete files that are owned by root. But again: Be careful!

SEE: • "Take Note: Using rm: Risk Management," below, for the risks involved with the rm command and ways to minimize them.

• "Using Unix to delete files," in Chapter 6, for practical examples of using the rm command for troubleshooting.

The rmdir and mkdir commands. If a directory is empty, you can use the rmdir command to delete it. If you want to create a new directory, use the mkdir command. In both cases, follow the command with the pathname of the directory you want to delete or create. Thus, to create a directory called mp3files in your Home directory, you would type the following:

```
mkdir ~/mp3files
```

A newly created directory should have the default permissions for the folder that contains it. For any location in your Home directory, this will typically be rwxr-xr-x.

TAKE NOTE ▶ Using rm: Risk Management

You can delete a file via the rm command, even if the file is not in the Trash. In fact, unlike the Finder, there is no "interim" place for a file to be placed when you delete it. You can't "remove it from the Trash" if you change your mind—instead, the file is deleted immediately. As you can imagine, this makes rm a potentially dangerous command—one with the ability to delete a file anywhere on your drive instantly. Even worse, most Mac OS X utilities that claim to be able to undelete files (such as Symantec's Norton Utilities UnErase) are not able to undelete files deleted via the rm command.

Combined with the -R option (which provides a way to delete files within folders, as described in the main text), the rm command becomes even more dangerous. Normally, rm will not delete a folder that contains files or folders. However, the -R option instructs the OS to override this restriction, deleting all listed files and folders, as well as all the files and folders contained within the listed folders.

Thus, you should be very careful when using the -R option: It can irrevocably delete everything in the directory you select—which means that even a simple typing error can have devastating consequences, especially if you invoked the rm command via the sudo command for root access.

Inadvertent spaces in pathnames represent the biggest potential source of problems. Suppose, for example, you wanted to delete your entire Applications folder (not that I recommend doing this): To do so, you would type rm -R /Applications, with no space between the forward slash (/) and the A. If, however, you accidentally placed a space there—that is, typing rm -R / Applications—Unix would interpret the forward slash and Applications as two separate items. Since the / character by itself refers to the root level of your volume, you would be requesting that the entire contents of your drive be deleted!! As I said, be *very* careful.

continues on next page

TAKE NOTE ▶ **Using rm: Risk Management** *continued*

Even Apple is not beyond making an error here. As I noted in "Updating Mac OS X," in Chapter 3, Apple made an error of this type in a script file inside an iTunes Updater package back in the days of Mac OS X 10.1. Before Apple caught and corrected this mistake, hundreds of users ran the Updater and wound up deleting entire volumes.

If you need to use the rm command, there are several things you can do to minimize the risk:

- **Auto-fill a pathname.** Use the Tab key or drag the Finder icon of the desired item to the command line to automatically fill in the pathname, as described in "Take Note: Unix Shortcuts" and "Take Note: Spaces in Pathnames," earlier in this chapter. This minimizes the chance of inserting an inadvertent space in the command.

  For example, to delete a file you're having problems deleting from the Finder, type sudo rm -R followed by a space. Then drag the icon of the problem file to the command line and (after the pathname appears) press Return.

- **Use quotes.** Putting a pathname in quotes similarly prevents a space in a pathname from being treated as a separator (as covered in "Take Note: Spaces in Pathnames," earlier in this chapter).

  If a space is typed intentionally within quotes, this is what you want. If a space is typed unintentionally, the intended file will not be deleted, but at least no unintended files will be deleted, either.

- **Use -i option with rm.** If you type sudo rm -Ri *pathname*, the use of the -i option results in a confirmation request appearing before anything is deleted. The following output will appear after you press Return:

  remove *pathname/filename*?

  Type y for *yes* or n for *no*. You can still end up in trouble here by saying yes when you should have said no. However, at least the command shows you what it intends to delete and gives you a chance to back out if you realize you made a mistake.

  Even better, you can modify your environment so that typing rm is automatically treated as typing rm -i. This way, you don't have to remember to type the i. To do this, add an alias to your .profile or .cshrc file, as explained in "Using shell configuration Files," later in this chapter.

continues on next page

Figure 10.16

Using the rm command to delete the testy file.

```
Ted-Landaus-Computer:~ landau$ ls
Desktop          Library          Music          Public          testy
Documents        Movies           Pictures       Sites
Ted-Landaus-Computer:~ landau$ rm testy
Ted-Landaus-Computer:~ landau$ ls
Desktop          Library          Music          Public
Documents        Movies           Pictures       Sites
Ted-Landaus-Computer:~ landau$ █
```

> **TAKE NOTE ▶ Using rm: Risk Management** *continued*
>
> Note: If you have a large number of files to delete, the repeated requests for confirmation can become annoying. Depending on a file's permissions, you may be asked for a confirmation, even if you don't use the -i option. In such cases, you may want to actively *prevent* confirmation requests. To do so, use the -f option. The -f option acts as the opposite of -i, instructing Unix to remove the indicated files without prompting for confirmation, regardless of the file's permissions. Use this option with care, though, as it removes a protection against deleting files in error.
>
> • **Use Data Recycler X.** Prosoft Engineering's Data Recycler X is a third-party utility that can undelete files you've deleted by selecting Empty Trash from the Finder, as covered more in Chapter 6. A unique capability of Data Recycler X is that it also allows items deleted via the rm command to be recovered. It does this by replacing the standard rm command with a new one that works with the Data Recycler X software to preserve files deleted in Terminal in the same way it preserves those deleted from the Finder. This may not work if you deleted the very software needed for Data Recycler to work. Otherwise, however, it's a good protection.
>
> **SEE:** • **"Using Unix to delete files," in Chapter 6, for related information.**

Unix: Executing Commands

When you type 1s, cp, or most of the other commands discussed in this chapter, you're executing (or *running*) a built-in Unix program. However, you're not limited to what's "built in." Just as you can add software beyond what ships with the Mac OS, you can add new software to run in Unix.

Note: To see a full list of all commands available for you to run in Unix, launch Terminal and hold down the Escape (esc) key for about 3 seconds. A line will then appear that states the following:

`Display all ### possibilities? (y or n)`

In the above output, ### represents the number of commands available. Type y to view the list.

To run a built-in Unix program, you don't need to precede the name of the file with any special command. To run the 1s command, for example, you don't need to type run 1s or anything like that. Neither do you need to include the relative or absolute path to where the 1s command file resides. That is, you don't need to type /bin/1s, just 1s. In general, Unix understands that you want whatever you type as the first term in a line to be treated as a command to be run and executed.

For commands to run in this manner, two conditions must be met:

- The execute (x) bit must be enabled for the item to be executed.
- The file must be in a directory that Unix searches when it looks for commands that match what you type.

When you type a command such as ls, the OS checks specified directories for executable files. If it finds a file that matches the name you typed, it executes and runs the file. Two of the directories where Unix looks, for example, are the /bin and /sbin directories (both at the root level of the startup volume). Thus, all commands in these directories will work as described, just by your typing their names. Commands such as ls, cp, and kill are stored here.

PATH. To see a complete list of all directories searched by a Unix shell, type env. In the output that appears, examine the PATH line. All the searched directories are listed and separated by colons.

SEE: • "Technically Speaking: What and Where Are the Unix Files?," in
            Chapter 4, for more information on /bin, /sbin, and related directories.

You can also use the echo command to see a PATH listing. In its simplest form, echo prints to the screen whatever text follows the command. Thus, typing echo ls generates an output line that simply reads ls.

You can use echo in combination with the dollar sign ($), however, to print the value of a variable. Thus, if you type echo PATH, you simply get the word PATH as output. But if you type echo $PATH, you get a list of all directories searched by the shell, just as would appear in the PATH line of the env output. A colon separates each path.

Figure 10.17

The output from the echo *$PATH command. Note that it's the same as the listing in the PATH line in the output from the env command that follows.*

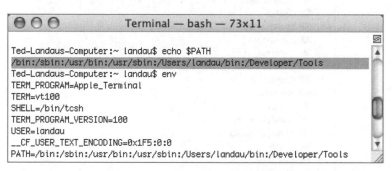

```
Ted-Landaus-Computer:~ landau$ echo $PATH
/bin:/sbin:/usr/bin:/usr/sbin:/Users/landau/bin:/Developer/Tools
Ted-Landaus-Computer:~ landau$ env
TERM_PROGRAM=Apple_Terminal
TERM=vt100
SHELL=/bin/tcsh
TERM_PROGRAM_VERSION=100
USER=landau
__CF_USER_TEXT_ENCODING=0x1F5:0:0
PATH=/bin:/sbin:/usr/bin:/usr/sbin:/Users/landau/bin:/Developer/Tools
```

Note: When searching for a command, Unix searches directories in the order listed in PATH. This means that if, for some reason, you have two executable files with the same name in two different directories, Unix will execute only the one it finds in the first directory it searches, ignoring the other. If the two command files perform different functions, this could be a problem. The simplest solution is to rename one of the files. Most Mac OS X users, however, will never encounter this problem.

Developer/Tools. If you installed the Developer software, you have a Developer directory at the root of your drive. Inside this directory is a Tools directory, which contains a collection of Apple-supplied Unix commands. The CpMac and MvMac commands (discussed earlier in "The CpMac and MvMac commands") are two such commands.

SEE: • **"Take Note: Developer Software," in Chapter 2, for more details on the Developer (Xcode) Tools software.**

All the commands in the Tools directory have their execute bits set so that they have no problem meeting the first criterion cited above. Still, if you type just CpMac followed by the pathname(s) of the file(s) you want to copy, the command will not work (assuming the Tools directory is not in your PATH list, which it is not by default). Instead, the following error message appears: CpMac: Command not found. This is because Unix does not check the Tools directory for commands.

Note: The PATH listing in **Figure 10.17** includes /Developer/Tools; this is because I separately added it to the PATH listing (as described later in this chapter under "Using shell configuration files").

So how do you get a command like CpMac to run? There are several options. Some details are beyond the scope of this book, but the following sections should provide enough information for you to accomplish your goal.

Figure 10.18

The Developer/Tools directory, as viewed from the Finder.

Typing the absolute or relative pathname

If you type a correct absolute or relative pathname for a command, Unix will execute it—even if that command doesn't reside in one of the default directories that Unix searches.

Thus, to run the CpMac command from any directory location, type the following:

/Developer/Tools/CpMac

If you're in the directory that contains the command file (/Developer/Tools, in this example), you can take a shortcut and just type the following:

./CpMac

TAKE NOTE ▶ Opening Mac OS Applications from Terminal

You can open almost any Mac OS application via Terminal: The application will launch, just as if you had double-clicked it in the Finder. To do this, type the following:

open *pathname*

Thus, to launch Mac OS X's Calculator, you would type:

open /Applications/Calculator.app

Or, even simpler, just type this:

open -a Calculator

The -a option tells the open command to search all the Applications folders on your drive for a match for the name given (in this case, *Calculator*). One possible glitch here: When I tried this, Terminal tried to launch the version of Calculator it found in my Mac OS 9 Applications folder. A work-around is to instead type:

open -a Calculator.app

There's usually no advantage to opening a file with the open command rather than double-clicking it from the Finder; however, if you're already working in Terminal, it may be more convenient.

Opening applications by selecting the "application" within the .app package. If (from the contextual menu or the Action menu) you select Show Package Contents for an application package and navigate to Contents/MacOS, you will typically find the actual application file.

In some cases, primarily for Carbonized applications, it will be a "true" Mac OS application. AppleWorks 6.x is one application that works this way. If you double-click such files, they open just as if you had double-clicked the application packages themselves.

continues on next page

TAKE NOTE ▶ Opening Mac OS Applications from Terminal *continued*

Most Mac OS X applications, however, work a bit differently. In these cases, when you navigate to the application package's MacOS folder, you'll still find a file with the name of the application there. However, the file will have either a blank document icon (typically the case in Jaguar and earlier versions of Mac OS X) or the exec icon that represents a Unix executable file (typically the case in Panther).

SEE: • **"Take Note: Unix Executable Files and TerminalShellScript Files," below, for details.**

In Panther, if you double-click these application executable files, Terminal launches and executes a command. The result is that the application launches in the Finder, again just as if you had double-clicked the application package icon. Note: When Terminal launches in this situation, it opens a separate shell specific to that application; if you close this shell window, the application quits as well.

In Jaguar, however, if you double-click the document icon, you get the following error message: "There is no default application specified to open the document." The Calculator application is an example of this. All Cocoa and some Carbon applications work this way. Despite this error, these documents are still the same Unix executable files that are in Panther. Thus, you can still use them to launch the application. However, you must do so manually by entering a command in Terminal. For example, to launch the Calculator application this way, you would type the following:

```
/Applications/Calculator.app/Contents/MacOS/Calculator &
```

The ampersand symbol is needed if you want Terminal's command-line prompt to return after launching the application. It tells Unix to run the application in the background. Just press Return in Terminal and the prompt should reappear. Otherwise, the prompt will not return until you quit the application.

Opening applications as root. Why bother with opening an application via its executable file in the package? As briefly discussed in Chapter 4 (under "Root Access"), you can use the sudo command to open applications as root. However, you cannot do this simply by using sudo in combination with open. If you try, the application opens, but not with root access. For Cocoa applications (and the Carbon ones that work similarly), you can work around this restriction by typing the following command (all in one line), modified for the application you want to open:

```
sudo -b /Applications/TextEdit.app/Contents/MacOS/TextEdit
```

This opens the Unix executable file directly, allowing the sudo option to work. The -b option here serves a similar function to the ampersand in the previous example (which doesn't work with sudo).

continues on next page

TAKE NOTE ▶ Opening Mac OS Applications from Terminal *continued*

For Carbon applications that won't work via this method (that is, ones that don't use the package format), there's still a way to use sudo to open the application with root access. To do so, type the following on one line (assuming the application you want to open is in the main Applications folder):

```
sudo -b /System/Library/Frameworks/Carbon.framework/Versions/Current/Support/
LaunchCFMApp '/Applications/{name of application}'
```

This in essence launches the LaunchCFMApp application with root access. By using the pathname to the actual application (in quotes, if needed, to handle spaces in its name) as an argument, the named application is indirectly launched with root access.

Note: You can use the Pseudo utility (from Brian R. Hill) to duplicate using sudo in this manner, thus eliminating the need for Terminal.

SEE: • **"Take Note: Editing Text Files via Terminal," later in this chapter, for related information.**

TAKE NOTE ▶ Unix Executable Files and TerminalShellScript Files

There are files you can access from the Finder (without having to delve into a package) that typically launch Terminal when double-clicked. I covered one such file type earlier in this chapter: the .term file (see "Take Note: .Term Files"). This sidebar focuses on the two other major types:

Unix software. These files are, in essence, executable files designed to run in Unix. Thus, for example, if you install the Developer software, all the items in the /Developer/Tools folder will be listed as Unix executable files. Similarly, all of the commands in Unix's invisible /bin folder are also of this type. These files all have an icon that looks like a Terminal window with *exec* printed on it. If you access the Get Info window for these files, you will see that their Kind is listed as Unix Executable File.

If you double-click these files, they typically launch Terminal and execute. However, most commands require additional arguments to work. For example the cp (or CpMac) command requires that you indicate *what* you want to copy. When you just double-click the cp icon from /var (or the CpMac icon in /Developer/Tools), you get the same usage summary that would appear if you typed cp (or CpMac) while already in Terminal. Nothing will be copied. In contrast, typing the ls command yields a list of the items in the current directory (because ls doesn't require additional arguments). However, once you've executed a command, you will be logged out—which means you couldn't execute additional commands without opening a new shell. Overall, double-clicking these files from the Finder is usually not very useful. One potential exception is when opening files in an .app package (as described in "Take Note: Opening Mac OS Applications from Terminal," above).

continues on next page

> **TAKE NOTE** ▶ **Unix Executable Files and TerminalShellScript Files** *continued*
>
> In a few cases, you will not be able to directly open an executable file in the Finder, getting the following error message instead: "There is no default application specified to open the document." This happened to me, for example, when I tried to open executable files inside frameworks (located in the /System/Library/Frameworks folder). This is almost always what happens in Jaguar (where these files are not identified as executable files and have a blank document icon); it only rarely happens in Panther. If you want to execute these files, you can work around the error message (as described in "Take Note: Opening Mac OS Applications from Terminal").
>
> **TerminalShellScript files.** Terminal shell scripts are similar to Unix software. However, rather than containing any compiled program code, they mainly contain a series of Unix commands in plain text. You can quickly see the difference by comparing a shell script and an executable file in a text editor, such as TextEdit. Terminal shell scripts often have a .command extension and have a Kind of TerminalShellScript in the Get Info window.
>
> **SEE:** • "Using a shell script," later in this chapter, for more details.

Figure 10.19

The icons of (left) a Unix executable file and (right) a TerminalShellScript file.

Using your Home bin directory

As a rule, I recommend that you don't add files to the root-level Unix directories (such as /bin) because they may end up being eliminated in a Mac OS X update or otherwise cause problems. In addition, you need root access to add files here, which makes it less convenient. Thus, although moving the CpMac file to the /bin directory would allow CpMac to run without your having to type its pathway, I would not move it there.

Fortunately, an alternative exists that accomplishes almost the same goal, but without the risks or hassles: Move CpMac (or whatever software you wish) to the bin directory in your Home directory. The main glitches here are that (a) if you check your PATH listing, you will likely not find an entry for this directory; and (b) you will not find a bin directory in your Home directory. Thus, to use this bin option, you must first set it up. Here's how:

1. Create a bin directory in your Home directory. You can do this via either the Finder (by pressing Command-Shift-N while in your Home directory and naming the folder *bin*) or Terminal (type mkdir ~/bin).

2. Add the ~/bin directory to your PATH listing via a set path command in the shell configuration file for your shell type. This is necessary to make the PATH change permanent (so that you don't need to re-enter the set path command every time you launch Terminal).

> **SEE:** • "Using shell configuration files," later in this chapter, for details on how to do this.

3. Copy or move the CpMac file (and any other similar Unix command tools you wish to use) from their location in /Developer/Tools to the newly created bin directory.

   Again, you can do this via the Finder or Terminal. To copy just the CpMac command via Terminal, type the following (and note the space prior to the ~):

   ```
   cp /Developers/Tools/CpMac ~/bin/
   ```

4. Before trying to use the command, open a new shell window in Terminal (by pressing Command-N), or just quit and relaunch Terminal.

   Type CpMac.

   The command should now execute correctly. In this case, since you didn't specify any files, you'll just get the usage summary.

Using other directories

Perhaps you would rather not copy files from one location to another (for example, from /Developer/Tools to ~/bin). If so, there's an alternative that still allows you to run a command in /Developer/Tools, for example, by just typing its name: You simply instruct Unix, via your shell configuration file, to add the relevant directory (/Developer/Tools, in this case) to the PATH list. This is what I did and why Developer Tools is listed in the PATH listing in Figure 10.17.

> **SEE:** • "Using shell configuration files," later in this chapter, for details on how to do this.

Multiple users and /usr/local/. A limitation of both prior solutions is that the Developer Tools commands still won't work via just their names when someone other than you logs in. If access by multiple users is important, you could repeat the same procedure (for example, modifying PATH listings) for each local user on your drive.

A potentially less tedious method, though it requires manipulating the root-level Unix directories, is to create a bin directory in the /usr/local/ directory. Files placed here are accessible to all local users. Actually, a bin directory (as well as others) may have already been created here if you previously ran installers for third-party Unix software. However, at least on my Mac OS X systems, these directories are not included in the PATH listing by default. Thus, you may still need to add this directory to the PATH listing of each user to run software installed in /usr/local—but at least you don't have to create and set up a separate bin directory for each user.

Note: Changes that you make in locations such as the /usr folder may be eliminated when you upgrade to a new version of Mac OS X. To protect against losing all of your work, make sure you've made backup copies of whatever files you modified or moved.

> **TAKE NOTE** ▶ **Installing Third-Party Unix Software**
>
> Some Unix software for Mac OS X includes an Aqua-based Installer utility. In such cases, the Unix software is likely to be installed in the /usr/local directory, especially /usr/local/bin. The psync software, noted in "Backing up Mac OS X: utilities for volume backups," in Chapter 3, is one such example.
>
> **Fink.** Other Unix software may come without the benefit of an installer. Because the software may include a host of files that need to be installed in a variety of locations, it can be tedious to manually install it all.
>
> A solution is to get and install Fink (by the Fink Project), software designed to help you install other Unix software. Note: Fink itself is installed in a directory named *sw*, created and located at the root level of your startup volume (see http://fink.sourceforge.net/faq/general.php for more background).
>
> **X11.** Although Unix is essentially a text-only command-line system, there is a way to run a graphical user interface on Unix: It's called the X Window System, commonly referred to as X11. Apple has created a version of X11 designed especially run on a Mac OS X implementation of Unix. It features a level of integration with Aqua not available in non-Mac systems. With X11 installed, you can then install and run application software designed for X Window environments.
>
> **SEE:** • "Terminal and X11," in Chapter 2, for more details.

Creating an alias

In Unix, the `alias` command is used to create a shortcut for another (usually longer) command. Suppose, for example, you don't want to make any of the changes described in the preceding sections for getting a command to run. Instead, each time you want to run the `CpMac` command, you're willing to type `/Developer/Tools/CpMac`. However, because you use this command frequently, you eventually decide that you would prefer to invoke it with less typing. The solution is to create an alias using the `alias` command, which works a bit differently depending upon which shell you're using. In particular:

- In the default bash shell, you would type

    `alias CpMac=/Developer/Tools/CpMac`

- In tcsh or csh, you would type

    `alias CpMac /Developer/Tools/CpMac`

The only difference is that bash requires an equals sign (=), whereas the tcsh and csh shells work with just a space. The following examples use the bash shell.

In either case, when you next type `CpMac`, it will act as an alias for the longer command.

The name you choose for the alias does not need to be similar to that of the original command; it can be anything you want. For example, you could type the following:

```
alias cp2=/Developer/Tools/CpMac
```

Now when you type cp2, it will invoke the CpMac command.

Overriding existing commands. You can also use an alias to modify the meaning of an existing command. If you almost always use ls -al (to list the contents of a directory in the long form with invisible files included) rather than just ls, you could type the following:

```
alias ls='ls -al'
```

The single quotation marks are used to make sure that the space before the hyphen is correctly interpreted. They are not always required, but I would use them to be safe.

Now whenever you type just ls, Unix will interpret it as ls -al. If you later want to invoke the original ls command while maintaining the alias, type \ls. The backslash tells Unix to interpret the command literally—meaning without substituting any potential alias. If you want to delete the alias and revert to the default use of the command, type unalias ls.

Alternatively, instead of changing the meaning of ls, you can create a new alias name, such as lls, for ls –al by entering the following:

```
alias lls='ls -al'
```

In fact, Unix experts advise against using the name of a built-in command for an alias, since this can cause problems for other programs that invoke the command and expect it to work in the standard way. If you're concerned about this, using lls would be preferable to ls in the examples above.

Aliases vs. aliases. In Unix, an *alias* (as described here) has an entirely different meaning than the same term in Mac OS X. The Unix equivalent of a Mac OS X alias is a symbolic link.

SEE: • "Aliases and Symbolic Links," in Chapter 6, for more information on this distinction.

Aliases are not saved. One limitation of aliases is that they're forgotten as soon as you close the shell window. This means you have to re-create them each time you launch Terminal—or even open a new shell window.

There are, however, ways to circumvent this limitation—ways of not only preserving the aliases you've created but of automatically running any command (or sequence of commands) in Terminal. These impressively flexible methods are described in the next two sections of this chapter.

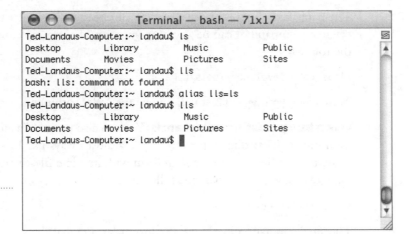

Figure 10.20

After creating lls as an alias, the command works.

Using shell configuration files

Shell configuration files refer to files that are accessed when launching Terminal or when logging into and/or opening a new shell. Settings and commands, as listed in these files, are executed—modifying what would otherwise be the default behavior of the Terminal window.

.term files vs. shell configuration files. I've already described a Mac OS X–specific method for modifying a shell: the .term file. However, when selected to run automatically when Terminal launches, this file only affects the initial shell window. Although you can add Unix commands to a .term file, the method for doing so is not quite as convenient as the other techniques described here. These .term files are primarily intended to be used for changes made via (Mac OS X) menu commands in Terminal. Overall, I recommend that you do not use .term files as a substitute for shell configuration files.

SEE: • "Take Note: .Term Files," earlier in this chapter.

Logging in vs. starting a new shell. When you open a new shell window and see the Welcome to Darwin message, you are said to have logged in to the shell. In this case, you're logging in and starting a new shell at the same time. In contrast, if you type the name of a shell while in a shell window (for example, typing bash while in a tcsh shell), you open a new shell (referred to as a *subshell,* or as a child to the parent shell) but you do not re-log in.

This distinction has consequences for the different configuration files described below. Some files work whether you're logging in or just opening a new shell. Others only work in one situation or the other.

.cshrc and .tcshrc configuration files. For the tcsh and csh shells, your personal shell configuration files are called .tchsrc and .cshrc respectively. The period at the beginning of their names keeps these files invisible in the Finder.

These .tcshrc and .cshrc files do not exist by default in your Home directory. If you want a shell configuration file customized with your own commands, you must create it yourself and save it to the root level of your Home directory.

The tcsh and csh shell configuration files run each time you open a new shell or subshell of the appropriate type. In Terminal, this means that such files are run each time you open a new tcsh or csh window, or enter the appropriate shell command in an existing window.

More specifically, a .cshrc file runs when either a new csh or tcsh shell is opened. A .tcshrc file will only run when opening a tcsh shell (and is the only file run when opening a tcsh shell, should you have both a .tcshrc and a .chsrc file in your Home directory). Overall, because it works for both types of shells, I prefer to use a .cshrc file rather than a .tcshrc file, even for tcsh shells. The only potential glitch here is that you cannot use a command in a .cshrc file that only works in the tcsh shell.

.login and .logout files for csh/tcsh. If there is a .login file at the root level of your Home directory, Terminal will find it and execute the commands contained in the file, as appropriate, whenever you open a new window for a csh or tcsh shell. A .login file, however, is not executed if you open a subshell, as this does not represent a new login. As .cshrc and .tcshrc files are also run at login, you probably won't need to use a separate .login file, certainly not for the relatively simple troubleshooting-related examples described in this book.

Similarly, you can create a .logout file in your Home directory. It will be executed whenever you enter the logout command. This, too, is rarely needed in a Mac OS X Unix environment.

bash configuration and login/logout files. In the tcsh shell, a .tcshrc or .cshrc configuration file is conveniently executed both at login and whenever a new subshell is otherwise opened. There is no comparable file in bash. For this shell, you have to choose between a file that only runs at login and one that only runs when opening a subshell, not both. In the examples described here, where subshells are rarely used, it's much more important to have the file run at login (for example, when a new window is open in Terminal). Thus, I focus almost exclusively on such files. To have a file run at login for bash, name it .profile, .bash_profile, or .bash_login. For simplicity, I use just the name .profile in the examples later in this chapter.

If you do need a configuration file that runs when opening a subshell in bash, create a file called .bashrc. And here's a neat trick: If you want the commands in this file to also run at login (mimicking the way the .cshrc file works), create a .profile file and add the following line to it:

```
. .bashrc
```

Finally, should you want a file that runs at logout, create a file called .bash_logout.

Again, none of these files exist by default in your Home directory. You must create them yourself, as described next.

TECHNICALLY SPEAKING ▶ System-Wide Shell Configuration Files

Unless you override it via Terminal's Preferences settings, the default login shell uses the instructions in /usr/bin/login.

If you're using the tcsh or csh shells, there are also default *system-wide* .login, .logout, and .cshrc files located in /private/etc, specific to those shells. They are called csh.login, csh.logout, and csh.cshrc, respectively.

If you're using bash, there are system-wide bashrc and profile files in the same /etc directory.

Although you can edit these files to make system-wide changes (that is, changes that would affect all users of your Mac), I prefer to create user-specific files, as described in the main text. Among other things, this avoids having to modify files owned by root, and it retains the defaults as a reliable unmodified fallbacks.

Creating and using a shell configuration file. We now return (finally!) to the issue of how to permanently save commands using a shell configuration file. For the purposes of our discussion, I'll be creating a .profile file to run in a bash shell (because bash is the default in Panther). If you're using a tcsh shell, create a .cshrc file instead. Aside from the name change, the steps are almost identical; where differences do occur, I make note of them. Here's what to do:

1. Create the shell configuration file (for example, .profile).

    You can't do this directly in the Finder because it will not let you create a file that begins with a period (since such files are invisible there). Given that you're using Terminal anyway, the simplest solution is to use Terminal to create the file. To do so, first make sure you're at the root level of your Home directory (type cd and press Return to take you there). Next, type the following:

    touch .profile

    If you now type ls —a, you will see that the file is there.

    Note: An alternative solution is to open a file in a Mac text editor such as TextEdit. You can then enter the commands in the file (as described in step 3) and save the file as profile. Next, launch Terminal and use the mv command to rename the file: mv profile .profile. Although TextEdit does not provide an option to save files in Unix format (as described for TextWrangler and BBEdit, in step 2), I've found that TextEdit's plain-text files do work. You could also do all of this in Terminal, using a Unix text editor such as pico, but I prefer the easier-to-use Mac interface for text editing.

SEE: • "Take Note: Editing Text Files via Terminal," below, for more details on this subject.

2. Open the .profile file in a text editor.

To do so, use a utility such as Bare Bones Software's TextWrangler (or its freeware cousin, BBEdit Lite, if you can still obtain this now-defunct program). These utilities include an Open Hidden command that you can use to locate and open invisible files such as .profile. Note: When using Open Hidden, you should select All Files from the Enable pop-up menu that appears in the Open dialog.

These utilities can also make sure that line breaks are created using a format that Unix understands (as opposed to a Mac format that might cause trouble when Unix tries to access the file). To make sure this option is enabled, in the Save dialog click the Options button and access the Line Breaks pop-up menu. Make sure Unix is the selected item.

Note: If Unix is not the default choice for the program, you can make it the default by going to the Text Files: Saving Preferences screen and clicking the Unix radio button for Default Line Breaks. Once you've done this, Unix will be the default choice for all subsequently opened documents.

3. Add commands to the .profile file. To add a command to this file, simply enter it as you would in Terminal. You can add as many commands as you like. The following are examples of some useful commands you may wish to add:

- **alias commands.** To save the alias that makes lls the equivalent of ls –al, enter the following:

  `alias lls='ls -al'`

  To make sure that every time you type rm, you're asked for confirmation before anything is deleted (as described in "Take Note: Using rm: Risk Management," earlier in this chapter), enter the following:

  `alias rm='rm -i'`

  Note: If you ever want to override the -i option when deleting files, you can add the -f option to the command in Terminal. For example, to delete a folder full of files without getting the confirmation requests, you would type rm -Rf {*foldername*}.

  Alternatively, consider adding this more advanced rm alias:

  `alias rm='mv \!* ~/.Trash'`

  This will cause any files you selected for deletion to be moved to your Trash folder instead, just as if you had dragged them to the Trash via the Finder. You can then later decide if you want to use the Finder's Empty Trash command to truly get rid of them.

  Note: As explained earlier in the chapter, if you're working with a .cshrc file, use a space instead of the equals sign for the above alias commands.

- **set path commands**. To set your Home bin directory to be searched for commands by default (as noted in "Using your Home bin directory," earlier in this chapter), enter the following:

  PATH=$PATH:$HOME/bin

  To set the entire Tools directory in the /Developer folder to be searched for commands by default, enter the following:

  PATH=$PATH:/Developer/Tools

  Note: if you are working with a .cshrc file, use these commands instead:

  ```
  set path=($path ~/bin)
  set path=($path /Developer/Tools)
  ```

4. Save the file. How you do this depends on what editor you're using, For Mac applications, simply select the Save command (making sure you save the document with Unix line breaks, if this option is provided).

That's it. To test out your newly created file, open a new shell (by typing Command-N in Terminal). All of the commands you included in your .profile file should now be in effect. Congratulations!

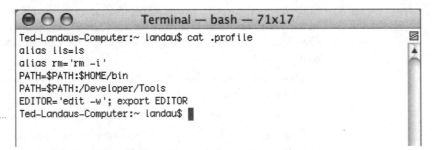

Figure 10.21

The contents of my .profile file.

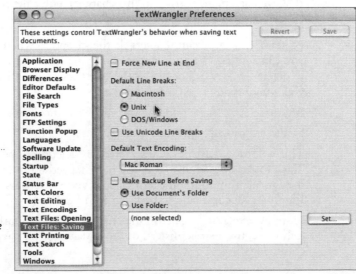

Figure 10.22

When using a utility such as TextWrangler for creating shell configuration files, make sure you have set files to be saved with Unix line breaks.

TAKE NOTE ▶ Editing Text Files via Terminal

Suppose you want to edit a text file, such as a .profile file. As suggested in the main text, one way to do so is to avoid Terminal altogether and instead open the text file in a Mac OS X text editor such as TextEdit or TextWrangler.

Using the open command. Assuming you're starting in Terminal, you can switch from Terminal to a Mac OS X application without having to go to the Finder by using the open command in Terminal.

SEE: • **"Take Note: Opening Mac OS Applications from Terminal," earlier in the chapter, for more on the open command.**

This is because the open command can open documents as well as applications. For example, type the following:

```
open ~/Documents/report.txt
```

This opens report.txt in the default application (as if you had double-clicked it in the Finder). In this example, it will most likely launch TextEdit, because it's the default application for .txt files (unless you changed it via the Finder's Open With option).

Alternatively, you could type the following:

```
open -e ~/Documents/report.txt
```

The -e option forces the document to open in TextEdit, even if it is not the specified default. Thus, to go directly from Terminal to editing the .profile file in TextEdit, you would enter the following:

```
open -e .profile
```

This has the bonus of allowing you to open invisible files in TextEdit, eliminating the need to change the name of the .profile file (as suggested in the main-text example).

Finally, you can also choose to open a document in any specified application; for example, you could type the following:

```
open -a {application pathname} ~/Documents/report.txt
```

In this case, the document will be opened in whatever application you specified in the pathname. For example, to open it in AppleWorks, you would specify '/Applications/AppleWorks/AppleWorks 6.app' as the pathname.

Creating a text file in TextEdit. If you want to create a new Unix-compatible text document in TextEdit (as opposed to opening an existing document), make sure the new document uses plain text format rather than rich text. Because rich text is enabled by default, you will probably need to select Make Plain Text (Command-Shift-T) from the Format menu before saving the document. If you don't, the document will be saved in rich text format (with a .rft extension) and cannot be used with Unix (for example, it would not work as a .profile file or a shell script). In addition, plain text files are saved with a .txt extension by default. For a .profile file, eliminate the extension. If you want to use the file as a shell script, you can change the extension to .command.

TAKE NOTE ▶ Editing Text Files via Terminal *continued*

Using TextWrangler's edit command. With BareBones' TextWrangler word processor, you have the option of installing an edit command when you first launch the application. (It gets installed in the /usr/bin directory.) If you fail to install it at this time, you can install it at any later time via the "Install 'edit' tool" button in TextWrangler's Application Preferences. If you own this software, you should install this command: It offers some convenient and powerful options. (Note: BareBones' BBEdit—but not BBEdit Lite—installs a similar command called bbedit.)

Once installed, edit works just like any other command in Terminal. Type edit plus arguments to use it. Type man edit to get full details on its use. Here are the essentials:

- If you type edit *{text document name}*, the selected text document will open in TextWrangler.

- If you type edit -w *{text document name}*, the selected text document will open in TextWrangler, and the command-line prompt will not return (for example, edit remains open in Terminal) until you close the document. This allows TextWrangler to mimic the behavior of Unix editors such as pico and vi.

- If you type any command that produces output and add | edit to the end of it, this pipes the output of the command to TextWrangler. For example, suppose you wanted a text copy of the output of an ls command. To obtain it, you would type the following:

ls | edit

Note: The | symbol in the above command invokes the *pipeline* feature of Unix. In essence, this says to use the output of the first command as the input for the second command. In this case, since edit opens up an untitled document in TextWrangler, the output of ls pipes into the untitled document as input.

continues on next page

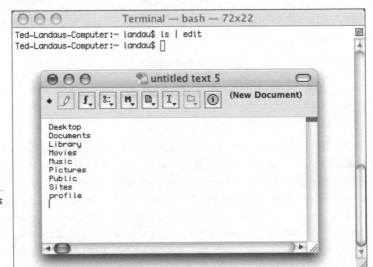

Figure 10.23

Using TextWrangler's edit *command to pipe the output of an* ls *command to a TextWrangler document.*

TAKE NOTE ▶ Editing Text Files via Terminal *continued*

- If you want TextWrangler to be your default text editor (that is, opened any time another Unix command would cause the default Unix text editor to open), you can add the following line to your .profile file:

`EDITOR="edit –w"; export EDITOR`

Note: If you're working with tcsh and a .cshrc file, add the following command instead:

`setenv EDITOR "edit –w"`

Note: Adding this command will cause problems for a few commands that launch text editors, such as `crontab`. See the man pages for the edit command for a potential work-around.

Using pico, vi, or emacs. If you wish, you can avoid Mac OS X applications altogether and edit files directly in Terminal. Mac OS X comes with several different Unix text editors, including vim (vi in Jaguar and earlier), emacs, and pico. If you choose any of these, be sure to check out the text editor's man pages to find out how to use it. The pico editor is the most user-friendly for non-Unix folks.

For starters, to open any text file in pico, type `pico` *filename*. To open the file with root access, precede the command with `sudo`. Press Control-X to exit from pico.

The vim editor is the default text editor in Terminal. If you find yourself in vim and want to get out, type `:q`.

You can change the default editor from vim to pico, using the same `sentenv` command that I used to set TextWrangler as the default editor. To do so, add the following to your .profile file:

`EDITOR=pico; export EDITOR`

Note: If you're working with tcsh and a .cshrc file, add the following command instead:

`setenv EDITOR pico`

To see what effect this addition has on your .profile or .cshrc file, type `crontab –e` before and after making the change (also open a new shell window after making the change). The `crontab –e` command opens your crontab file (or a blank file, if no crontab file exists) in the default text editor. Before the addition, the command will open the crontab file in vim. After the change, it will open in pico.

SEE: • **"Modifying invisible Unix files from Mac OS X applications," in Chapter 6, for related information.**

   • **"Technically Speaking: Terminal Commands to Monitor and Improve Performance," later in this chapter, for more on crontab.**

Using a shell script

A shell script is a text document that contains one or more Unix commands. When you run the script, the commands are executed. A shell script is not limited to any particular length, so you can use it to carry out what would otherwise require a long sequence of commands—which means it can save you from having to repeatedly re-enter the same series of commands at the command prompt. Think of it as the Unix equivalent of macro utilities, like QuicKeys X, in Mac OS X.

Shell scripts can also get much more elaborate than just a string of commands that mimic what you might type in Terminal. For example, similar to how utilities such as QuicKeys work in the Aqua environment, you can add conditional statements to make the script perform different actions depending on what it finds when executing. For our purposes, however, I'm going to skip these complexities. Instead, let's walk through the creation and use of a simple example, which is based on the following sequence of Unix commands (as first described in Chapter 6):

```
sudo rm -R ~/.Trash/
sudo rm -R /.Trashes/
sudo rm -R /Volumes/volumename/.Trashes/
```

SEE: • "Technically Speaking: More Trash Talk," and "Using Unix to delete files," in Chapter 6, for more details.

The third line refers to an additional mounted volume beyond the startup volume, named *volumename*. If you have no such volume, you can omit that line. If you have more than one such volume, you need a separate line for each one.

This sequence makes sure that everything in your Trash bin is deleted, regardless of where the Trash items are stored—a useful thing to try if you're having problems emptying the Trash from the Finder. However, if you use this sequence often, you would probably like to invoke it without having to retype the entire sequence each time—not only saving time but preventing problems that could result from mistyping it. A shell script accomplishes these goals.

Creating a shell script. To create a shell script for the above commands, follow these steps:

1. Create a new blank document in a text editor. For this example, I'll assume you're using a Mac OS X editor, such as TextEdit, BBEdit Lite, or TextWrangler.

    SEE: • "Creating a shell configuration file" and "Take Note: Editing Text Files via Terminal," earlier in this chapter, for more details on how to use text editors, including TextWrangler and TextEdit, with Unix.

2.   For the first line, type #! /bin/sh.

   This line is optional if you want to use the default shell (bash). Otherwise, you will need to enter the path of the shell you want to use. Both sh and bash are shells commonly used for scripts. Apple primarily uses sh shells in its Mac OS X scripts, so I'm conforming to its example. Either alternative will work for the shell script in this example.

3.   Type the sequence of sudo rm commands, pressing Return at the end of each line, including the last line.

   Remember: You may need to type several variations of the last line, one for every partition or volume that you have mounted. Substitute the actual volume name where *volumename* is located in the command. If you're unsure what volumes are available, type 1s /Volumes to get a list.

   Note: If the script does not work when created as just described, try ending every line but the first (#!) line with a semicolon. With the semicolon, you should not need to press Return at the end of each line (though it won't cause a problem if you do); the semicolon is interpreted as a Return character. Some combinations of shell scripts and shell environments work better with this format.

4.   Save the file—for now, anywhere in your Home directory; the root level is fine. Later, I'll describe how to move the file to your Home bin directory, if you created one.

   Ideally, the file's name should end in .command—for example, deletetrash .command. The .command extension is needed to run the command from the Finder via a double-click. Even without this extension, however, you could still run the command by opening it from within Terminal (as I explain in the next section, "Running a shell script").

   If you're using TextEdit, make sure you save the file as plain text (via the command in the Format menu). Also, after adding the .command extension, when you select to Save, you will be asked if you want to append the .txt extension anyway. Select Don't Append.

Figure 10.24

The message that appears when you save a plain text file ending in .command in TextEdit.

5.   Using the chmod command (in Terminal) or a utility such as XRay (in the Finder), change the permissions of the file so that the execute (x) permission is enabled for owner, group, and other (referred to as *world* in XRay). Note: This is one permissions change that cannot be done from the Get Info window for the file.

For example, if you're using Terminal and are in the same directory as the deletetrash.command file, type the following:

```
chmod ugo+x deletetrash.command
```

SEE: • **"The chmod command," earlier in this chapter, for details on using this command.**

• **"Technically Speaking:"How Mac OS X Selects a Document or Application Match" and "Copying and Moving: Permissions Problems with Copying and Moving Files," in Chapter 6, for more information on using XRay and similar utilities.**

6. Return to the Finder. If you want the script to launch and execute automatically when you double-click it in the Finder, you may have one more step to go. Do one or both of the following, as appropriate:

If you did not add the .command extension to the end of the file's name, open the Get Info window for deletetrash.command, and in the "Open with" section, select Terminal as the application. (You may choose to do this, even with the .command extension added, in case you might later want to remove the extension.)

If you used TextWrangler or BBEdit Lite, you need to delete the file's creator. You can skip this step if you used TextEdit or a Unix text editor.

To do this using XRay, go to the Type, Creator, & Extension section and, from the Creator pop-up menu, select "No specific creator" (which leaves a blank creator code). If you use FileXaminer and installed its contextual-menu items, you will find an item called Clear Type and Creator. Use it for the deletetrash.command file. Without this modification, the file would open in the text editor (for example, BBEdit Lite or TextWrangler) rather than Terminal, even with the .command extension.

Alternatively, you can do this in Terminal via the Developer Tools' SetFile command. To do so, enter the following:

```
/Developer/Tools/SetFile -c "" pathname
```

In the above, *pathname* is the relative or absolute pathname for the deletetrash.command file.

Note: To later re-edit this script file, you can still open it in a Mac OS X text editor, but you will have to use the application's Open command (or drag and drop the file to the editor's icon) rather than double-clicking it in the Finder.

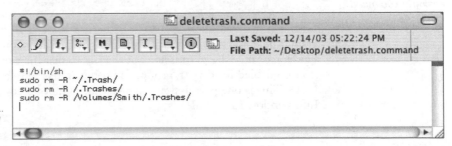

Figure 10.25

The completed shell script.

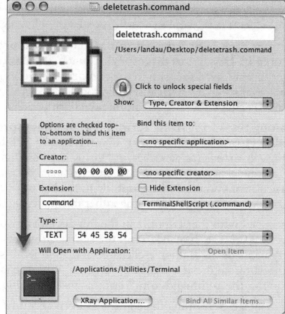

Figure 10.26

How a .command file's settings appear in XRay after making the changes to make it a double-clickable shell script: (top) Permissions screen; (bottom) Type, Creator & Extensions screen.

Running a shell script. You can run a shell script by doing any of the following:

- **Double-clicking the script file.** When you double-click a shell script file in the Finder (assuming you set it up as a .command file, as described in the previous section), the file will launch in Terminal in its own window (even if Terminal is already launched and a shell window is open), carry out the designated commands, and log out.

  Note: In the deletetrash.command example, Terminal should ask for your password before executing (because you're asking to run it as root).

  Note: If you get an error message that says, "No such file or directory," one or more of the Trash directories is empty. You can ignore this message. The script will still empty the other Trash directories.

Note: After running this command, when you later drag items to the Trash in the Finder, you may get a message that says, "The item will be deleted immediately." If this message persists and you want to get rid of it, log out and log back in.

- **Dragging the script file icon to the Terminal icon.** Dragging the file icon to the Terminal icon will similarly launch the script. You only need to do this if you *did not* set the file to be double-clickable.

- **Using Terminal's New Command menu item.** You can run any command, shell script or otherwise, via the New Commands item in Terminal's File menu. In the window that appears when you select the command, type the pathname to the command file in the text box. For the delete-trash example (assuming you saved the file at the root level of your Home directory), type ~/deletetrash.command. Then click the Run button.

  Optionally, if the script produces output that you want to view in Terminal, check the "Run command in a shell" box before clicking Run.

- **Executing the script from Terminal's command prompt (script *not* stored in Home bin directory).** Launch Terminal, and after the prompt appears, type the path to the command. If you saved the file in the root level of your Home directory, for example, you would type ~/deletetrash.command. The command will run.

- **Executing the script from Terminal's command prompt (script stored in Home bin directory).** If you created a ~/bin directory for running commands (as described in "Using shell configuration files," earlier in this chapter), you can run these scripts a bit more conveniently. In particular, if you move the script file to the bin directory, you can run the script just by typing its filename rather than entering its full pathname.

  For example, with the script file in the bin directory, you would only have to type deletetrash.command to run the script. Used this way, you may no longer care if the file is double-clickable in the Finder. If so, you can eliminate the .command extension from its name. With the extension gone, you can run the command from Terminal just by typing deletetrash.

  One advantage of running the command from Terminal (rather than the Finder)—whether or not the file is in the bin directory—is that after the command is completed, you're not logged out. Thus, you can continue typing commands after the script is run without needing to open a new shell window. If the shell script deleted a file, for example, you can continue to work in Terminal, just as though you had deleted the file with an rm command rather than via the script.

  However, even though you're not logged out, Terminal treats the script as an independent subprocess that opened and closed after it ran. The running of the script is described as a *child* of the initial *parent* process. After the script has run, you're back at the parent level. An important implication of this is that any changes made by the script that would get undone when you exited a shell will also be undone after the script is run. Therefore, you cannot use a shell script in this way to run a list of alias commands. The aliases will be forgotten after the script is run, just as they would be after you exited a shell or logged out.

Fortunately, there's a way to preserve the results of alias commands (or other commands with the same problem) *after* a script is run: You can use the source command.

• **Using the source command.** Suppose you created a shell script, called loadaliases, to run a list of alias commands, such as the alias lls=ls –al command mentioned earlier in this chapter. That text might look like the following:

```
#! /bin/bash
echo 'enable aliases'
alias lls='ls –al'
```

The script could continue with as many additional alias (or other) commands as you wanted to include.

(The echo line is optional here. It provides feedback when you execute the shell, so that you can tell that it ran successfully. This is desirable because an alias command doesn't produce any immediate output on its own.)

You can create and run this shell script via the methods just described. Suppose, for example, you placed it in your Home bin directory: When you type loadaliases in Terminal, the script will run successfully. However, when you next type lls, the alias will not execute. As just noted, this is because the alias change is not preserved after the script is run and its shell is exited. To solve this problem, use the source command: source *pathname*. In this case, you would type the following:

```
source ~/bin/loadaliases
```

Note: In some shells, you use a dot (.) rather than the word source (that is, type . ~/bin/loadaliases).

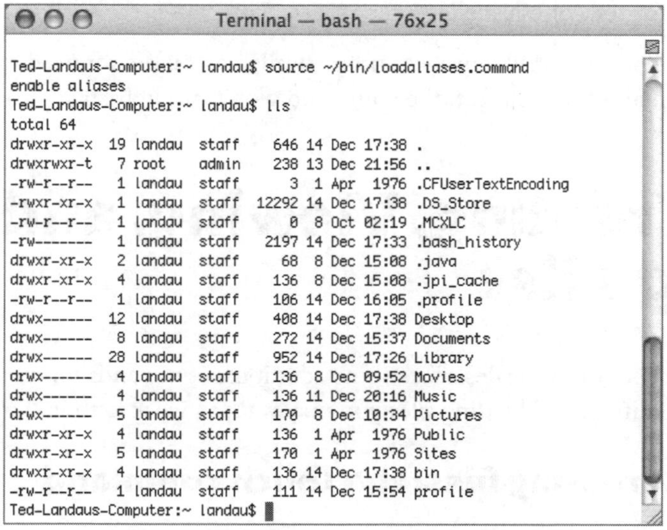

Figure 10.27

Running the load-aliases shell script (described in the main text) via the source command preserves an alias command contained in the script. In this case, lls becomes an alias for ls –al.

```
Ted-Landaus-Computer:~ landau$ source ~/bin/loadaliases.command
enable aliases
Ted-Landaus-Computer:~ landau$ lls
total 64
drwxr-xr-x  19 landau  staff    646 14 Dec 17:38 .
drwxrwxr-t   7 root    admin    238 13 Dec 21:56 ..
-rw-r--r--   1 landau  staff      3  1 Apr  1976 .CFUserTextEncoding
-rwxr-xr-x   1 landau  staff  12292 14 Dec 17:38 .DS_Store
-rw-r--r--   1 landau  staff      0  8 Oct 02:19 .MCXLC
-rw-------   1 landau  staff   2197 14 Dec 17:33 .bash_history
drwxr-xr-x   2 landau  staff     68  8 Dec 15:08 .java
drwxr-xr-x   4 landau  staff    136  8 Dec 15:08 .jpi_cache
-rw-r--r--   1 landau  staff    106 14 Dec 16:05 .profile
drwx------  12 landau  staff    408 14 Dec 17:38 Desktop
drwx------   8 landau  staff    272 14 Dec 15:37 Documents
drwx------  28 landau  staff    952 14 Dec 17:26 Library
drwx------   4 landau  staff    136  8 Dec 09:52 Movies
drwx------   4 landau  staff    136 11 Dec 20:16 Music
drwx------   5 landau  staff    170  8 Dec 10:34 Pictures
drwxr-xr-x   4 landau  staff    136  1 Apr  1976 Public
drwxr-xr-x   5 landau  staff    170  1 Apr  1976 Sites
drwxr-xr-x   4 landau  staff    136 14 Dec 17:38 bin
-rw-r--r--   1 landau  staff    111 14 Dec 15:54 profile
Ted-Landaus-Computer:~ landau$
```

The source command runs the script in the current shell rather than in a separate subshell, preserving the changes. Try it!

One potential glitch here: The source command only works as described if the script is written in a shell that's compatible with the one that's active in the Terminal window. For example, the default bash shell in a Terminal window will correctly run scripts as source if they're written in the sh or bash shells but not if they're written using the tcsh or csh shells. The opposite is true for Terminal windows using the tcsh and csh shells.

In my view, a far better way to deal with this alias issue is to include the commands as part of a configuration file, such as .profile, as described above. (In fact, these files are often called *source* files for this very reason.) However, I wanted you to be aware of this alternative option.

Bottom line: This introduction should help you see how even simple shell scripts can be extremely valuable tools. Even if you only use Terminal occasionally, turning sequences of commands into scripts can save time and eliminate the need to remember what to type.

AppleScript and shell scripts. AppleScript includes a do shell script command that lets you run shell scripts via AppleScript. See the following Apple document for more details: http://developer.apple.com/technotes/tn2002/tn2065.html.

SEE: • "Take Note: AppleScript," in Chapter 4, for more on AppleScript.

The rehash command. When you execute a command while a shell is open, the shell typically looks for the command in a cache it maintains, which is quicker than having to search all the locations in PATH. If you created a new command, via any of the methods described here, the command may not work initially because it has not yet been added to the cache. To remedy this, for tcsh or csh shells, enter rehash. This causes the shell to re-create its cache.

The bash shell rehashes automatically, so you do not need to use this command there. In fact, the command won't run in bash.

Unix: Creating, Viewing, and Finding Files

The following describes some additional commands for creating, viewing, editing, and locating files you may want to work with in Terminal.

Creating files: the touch command

To create a new blank document file or to update the modification time of an existing file, type the following:

touch *filename*

If no file with your selected name exists in the current location, Unix creates one (a simple text file). This command is especially useful for creating documents whose name begins with a period (since the Finder won't let you do this).

If the file already exists, Unix updates the "last modified" time for the file to the current time.

As always, you can type a relative or absolute path to the file to create or modify a file in a location other than the current one. Alternatively, you can use text editors to create and edit documents.

SEE: • "Take Note: Editing Text Files via Terminal," earlier in this chapter, for more details.

Viewing files: the head, tail, cat, more, and less commands

If you want to view the contents of a text file related to troubleshooting, you can easily use Mac applications such as TextEdit and Property List Editor. If you're working in Terminal, however, it may be more convenient to examine a file's contents directly from that application. If you need to view the file's contents without editing it, you can use any of the following commands.

head and tail. These commands output the first and last 10 lines of a file, respectively. You can request to see more or fewer than 10 lines by adding a number option to the command. For example, to see the first 20 lines of a file called mydoc.txt, located in the current directory, you would type the following: head –20 mydoc.txt.

cat. Use the cat command, followed by a filename, to view an entire file (as long as it doesn't exceed Terminal's scrollback buffer). For example, type cat mydoc.txt to view the contents of the file.

more. Use the more command for long files, especially ones that exceed the scrollback buffer. The output of this command resembles that of the man command—that is, it stops when the screen is filled. To see more of the file, you need to keep pressing the Return key (to advance line by line) or the spacebar (to advance screen by screen). Type q at any point to quit the output display and return to the command prompt.

less. Yes, there is a matching less command. Contrary to its name, though, it actually provides more options than the more command. For starters, you remain in a separate process after entering the less command (where you can issue further commands) until you quit the less command by typing q. For example, if you type less mydoc.txt, the initial part of the document will appear. Pressing D advances the document approximately one-half screen at a time. (You can also press the Return key to advance line by line). Press B, and the document will scroll backward; press V, and the entire document will open in the default text editor (where you can modify it). Type man less to reveal additional details about using the command.

SEE: • **"Take Note: Editing Text Files via Terminal," earlier in this chapter, for more on editing files.**

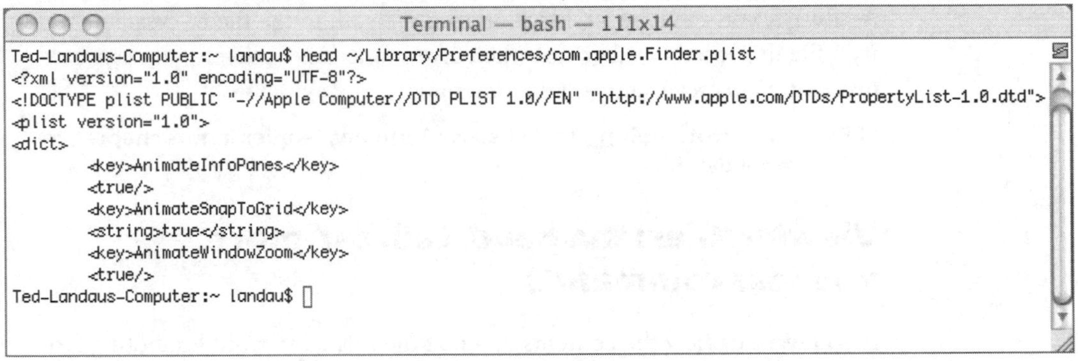

```
Terminal — bash — 111x14
Ted-Landaus-Computer:~ landau$ head ~/Library/Preferences/com.apple.Finder.plist
<?xml version="1.0" encoding="UTF-8"?>
<!DOCTYPE plist PUBLIC "-//Apple Computer//DTD PLIST 1.0//EN" "http://www.apple.com/DTDs/PropertyList-1.0.dtd">
<plist version="1.0">
<dict>
        <key>AnimateInfoPanes</key>
        <true/>
        <key>AnimateSnapToGrid</key>
        <string>true</string>
        <key>AnimateWindowZoom</key>
        <true/>
Ted-Landaus-Computer:~ landau$ []
```

Figure 10.28

Output from the head command.

Finding files: the find and locate commands

Similar to using Find in the Finder, Unix has its own commands to help you find items from within the Terminal application.

find. In its basic form, the find command displays a list of every item in the directory you specify. Thus, to display a list of *all* files and directories in the Applications directory, including items contained within subdirectories, type the following:

find /Applications

Because .app packages are considered to be directories in Unix, the resulting list will include the items within every .app package—probably much more than you want to see, which limits the usefulness of the command. In fact, you'll likely want to press Command-period to halt the scrolling output that results from the command.

You can get less output by limiting the scope of your search. For example, if you knew the item you wanted was in the Utilities folder inside the Applications folder, you could type /Applications/Utilities as the path-name, instead of just /Applications.

To further limit (or extend) your search, you can use wildcards in any part of the search term. Thus, you could type /Applications/Utilities/Air* as the pathname for the find command. With this expression, the command would match any item at the root level of the Utilities directory whose pathname (starting from the Utilities directory) begins with the word *Air*. In other words, it would match AirPort Admin Utility.app and AirPort Setup Assistant.app. However, it would also list all of the items *within* these two packages as matches. For example, /Applications/Utilities/AirPort Admin Utility.app/Contents/ Info.plist would be a match because AirPort Admin Utility.app matches the wildcard for the pathname.

You can also use the find command to limit matches to items where the search term is in the actual filename (that is, the search term must be in the very last segment of the pathname). This more limited search will probably yield results closer to what you typically want. To perform this type of search, you need to use the -name option. You combine the -name option with the filename (or part of a filename, with wildcards added) that you're seeking. Thus, to find every filename in the /Applications directory that contains the word *Chess*, type the following:

```
find /Applications -name "*Chess*"
```

Similarly, to find all filenames that end in .mp3 in your Home directory, type the following:

```
find ~ -name "*.mp3"
```

You can also use the Finder's Find command to perform a similar search, but the results won't be the same: The Finder's Find command does not list files contained within packages; the Unix find command does.

The following represents some further advice about using the find command:

- If you plan to use wildcards with the -name option, the filename should be in quotes.

- Without wildcards (and without the –name option), the find command will only find exact matches. For example the full name of the Chess application is Chess.app—even though all you see in the Finder is the word *Chess*. Thus, the application itself will not appear as a match in a search for the exact term *Chess*. A search for Chess.app or Chess*, on the other hand, *would* yield a match.

- Remember that Unix is case sensitive. Thus, in the Chess example, if I had wanted to search simultaneously for *Chess* and *chess*, it would have been better to search for *hess*.

- If you get "permission denied" messages for certain directories, and you believe that the item you're searching for does exist in those directories, you'll need to search again with root access (by preceding the find command with sudo).

The find command includes numerous options not described here. You can check out man find to see the full range of this command, but I don't recommend it. The rules that determine what output you get with find can be confusing even to experts. And no matter what you do, you'll often fail to turn up the item you're seeking. If you're unable to get the find command to yield the desired results using the advice presented here, you can try using the locate command instead. It works similarly to the find command but includes fewer options and is usually easier to use. Otherwise, search via Mac OS X and bypass Terminal altogether.

Figure 10.29

Output from the *find* command with the *-name* option selected.

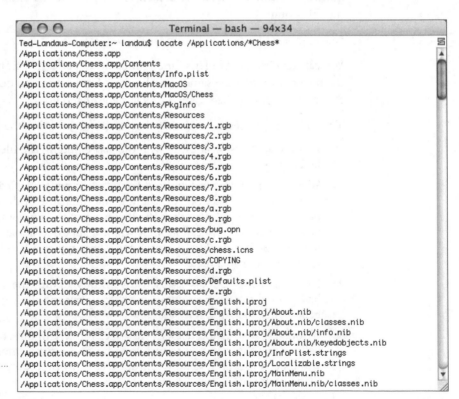

Figure 10.30

Output from the *locate* command.

locate. The `locate` command also finds (or *locates*) files. Since there are no options to select, it's simpler to use. In its basic format, you simply type the following:

`locate` *searchterm*

For example, if you type `locate /Applications/*Chess*` (or even just `locate /Applications/Chess`), you will get a list of all items (in the database that the `locate` command searches) that include the term *Chess* in the segment of their pathname that immediately follows the Applications segment.

Note: When you use the find command with just a single argument, the procedure is called *fast-find*, and it works almost the same as `locate`. The `locate` command was created as an addition for Unix variations that did not include the fast-find feature. In Terminal's shells, both fast-find and `locate` are included, so you get your choice. Thus, typing find `/Applications/*Chess*` will produce the same result as the `locate` command.

Recall that typing find `/Applications -name "*Chess*"` yields a different and smaller subset of results. It lists just those items with *Chess* as part of the final file- or folder name in the path. Thus, the item /Applications/Chess.app/ Contents will be a match for /Applications/*Chess* when you use `locate` but not when you use find with the `-name` option. You can get the `locate` command to provide results similar to the just-cited find command by typing `locate *Chess`.

The following represent a few items of interest about how `locate` works:

- The `locate` command (as well as the fast-find variation of the find command) searches a database that is updated periodically (via a cron job, as described in "Technically Speaking: Log Files and Cron Jobs," in Chapter 4). This database will likely include information about any volume that was mounted at the time of the most recent update. In contrast, the find command, used with options such as `-name`, performs a real-time search of the current entire contents of the startup volume.

  As a result, the `locate` command is typically much faster than the find command, especially for large volumes filled with files. However, it also means that `locate` may not match an item if the item was added after the last update to the database. You can update (or create, if the database does not yet exist) the database at any time by typing the following:

  `sudo /usr/libexec/locate.updatedb`

  Note: An update may take several minutes to complete.

- There are minor differences in the way the `locate` command works, depending on whether you're in a tcsh or a bash shell (for example, the effect of the presence or absence of quotation marks and wildcards is a bit different in the two shells). The examples in this section were all done while running the bash shell. If something doesn't work exactly as described in this chapter, check which shell you're using. Exact details of how these commands work, for any shell, may also change in future upgrades to Mac OS X if an updated version of the command software is included in the Mac OS X upgrade.

- A command with no wildcards or other special characters is interpreted the same as if asterisks surrounded the search term. Thus, locate 'Chess' yields the same results as locate '*Chess*'.

- If you type locate /Applications*Chess (note the lone asterisk!), you'll only get a single match—that is, to the only file in which Chess comes at the very end of its pathname:

  /Applications/Chess.app/Contents/MacOS/Chess.

  This is one place where the fast-find version of the find command works differently from locate. If you type find /'Applications*Chess', you won't get a match.

- Sebastion Krauss's Locator is a third-party Mac OS X utility that serves as a graphical front end for Unix's locate command. If you want to get the benefits of locate without using Terminal, this is the way to go. I use Locator, for example, whenever I want to search the contents of packages (because Mac OS X's Find options don't do this, unless you're actually within a given package and use the search box in a Finder window).

  SEE: • "Technically Speaking: Inside Packages," in Chapter 3.

Beyond the Basics

This chapter is obviously not the last word on everything that might be said about using Unix in Mac OS X. For those who want to know more, the following information should set you on the right path.

Front-end Mac utilities and back-end Unix commands

Mac OS X software and Unix commands interact in several significant ways. The following describes some of those interactions.

Mac OS X front ends for Unix commands. When you're using Terminal, it's easy to forget that you're running Mac OS X (with a mouse/window interface) rather than a machine that only runs Unix. Mastering the use of Terminal is as difficult (or easy, depending on your bias) as mastering Unix itself. For those who would prefer to skip this mastery, Mac OS X offers an out: Many of its utilities and System Preferences provide indirect access to Unix commands via the traditional Mac-like menu and window GUI. For example, when you modify the Firewall settings in the Sharing System Preferences pane, you're really accessing Unix's ipfw command. You could do the same thing in Terminal by typing ipfw and adding the appropriate options. The ipfw command even provides access to options not available from the Sharing System Preferences pane. However, learning how to use ipfw is more of hassle for most users than learning how to use Sharing.

In addition, where Apple has left off, third-party developers have kept going. There are numerous third-party utilities (such as the ones mentioned in "Maximizing Performance" in Chapter 6) that similarly give an Aqua interface to Unix commands. The front-end utilities mentioned most frequently in these pages are for modifying permissions, such as XRay and FileXaminer. The third-party utility SharePoints (by HornWare) is another great example of a front-end utility: It provides access to personal file-sharing features not available via the Sharing System Preferences pane.

Unix back ends for Mac OS X software. Conversely, there are some commands that were specifically created (typically by Apple) to serve as the underlying software of a Mac OS X utility. They have no general Unix function and would never be found on a non-Mac Unix machine. These specially created Unix commands are more commonly referred to as back ends to the Mac OS X software. This is the case for the asr, diskutil, and hdiutil commands, for example, which serve as back ends for Apple Software Restore, Disk Utility, and DiskImageMounter (formerly Disk Copy).

Unix commands created for Mac OS X. Finally, there are Unix commands created by Apple (or carried over from NextStep software) that are designed specifically to work with Mac OS X (Darwin) but have no direct match to corresponding Aqua-based software. As with the previous similar category, these commands would not be found in a non-Mac Unix system. Some of these commands are included as part of a basic Mac OS X installation. Others are only available if you install the Developer Tools software. Examples of such commands include lsbom and CpMac.

To Unix or not to Unix: That is the question. You may well ask: Why bother with a Unix command when you can use an Aqua alternative instead? In many cases, there *is* no good reason. Unless you simply prefer the Terminal environment, the Aqua alternative is usually the better choice. However, the Aqua software is often only a subset of what's available via the Unix command. To access the full range of options (assuming you need them), you must use the Unix command. You may also run into troubleshooting situations (such as when connecting to a Mac via SSH) in which using Unix is your only option. And, if you're willing to learn the basics of Unix, there are some situations where using Terminal is simpler and faster than accessing Unix commands from the Aqua interface.

Knowing how to use commands in Terminal frees you from dependence on Aqua-based utilities. If you can use Terminal, you can do anything that can be done with Unix on a Mac. Conversely, using Mac OS X front ends and other utilities frees you from having to learn how to use Unix and typically represents a more user-friendly solution. Take your choice.

Running Mac OS X software from Terminal

The following list represents my choice of the Mac-specific Unix commands— as well as some general Unix commands (which serve as back ends for Mac OS X System Preferences and utilities)—that are of the most use to troubleshooters. Many of these commands are also mentioned in earlier chapters.

Some of these commands require root-user status to run; in those cases, you must precede the command with sudo. I include examples of what you can accomplish with these commands that you *cannot* do from Mac OS X directly. Finally, you can type either man *{name of command}* or just the command name to get more details on how to use each.

- **appletalk.** You can use this command to enable or disable AppleTalk. You can do this from the Network System Preferences pane as well; however, you have more options here. For example, you can type appletalk -n to find out the AppleTalk interface (typically en0), Network Number, Node ID, and Current Zone. (In Panther, most or all of this information is now available from the new AppleTalk tab of Network Utility.)

  The appletalk command is also useful for enabling AppleTalk in cases where turning it on from the Network System Preferences pane does not appear to work.

  SEE: • Chapter 8 for more on using this command to enable AppleTalk.

- **asr.** This is the back-end software used by the Apple Software Restore utility as well as the Restore functions in Panther's Disk Utility, as described in Chapter 3. It provides options not available via the Aqua version of either utility. It not only restores software from existing images, but it can also be used to create new images for a subsequent restore. For example, you can clone an entire volume using a command like the following:

  ```
  sudo asr -source /Volumes/Classic -target /Volumes/install
  ```

  Although the Restore features in Panther's Disk Utility can now similarly clone a volume, the asr command offers more options.

  SEE: • "Technically Speaking: More About Disk Utility's Image and Restore Features," in Chapter 3, for more details.

- **bless.** Running this command enables a volume to be used as a startup volume. In most cases, such as when you install Mac OS X on a volume using the Installer utility, running this command is not required (because the Installer does the work for you). However, if you're having trouble getting a volume to boot, this could be the fix. One way to bless a volume with Mac OS X installed is to bless the CoreServices folder on the volume. Thus, for an external volume named HardDisk2, you would type the following:

  ```
  bless —folder /Volumes/HardDisk2/System/Library/CoreServices
  ```

If you want the volume to be the default startup drive (that is, so that the Mac will attempt to boot from this drive at the next startup), add -setOF at the end of the above command. Presumably, you can duplicate the effect of the -setOF option by selecting the volume in the Startup Disk System Preferences pane.

SEE: • "Take Note: Blessed Systems and Starting Up," in Chapter 5.

• **chmod, chown, and chgrp.** As discussed earlier in this chapter, these commands are the more full-featured Unix equivalents of what you otherwise do via the Ownership & Permissions settings in a file's Get Info window.

• **cupsd.** This is the basic CUPS software command. It serves as the back end for many of the features in Printer Setup Utility.

SEE: • "CUPS," in Chapter 7, for more information.

• **defaults.** This command is used to modify the defaults for Mac OS X software. (In this context, *defaults* is synonymous with *preferences*.) Thus, this command duplicates what you can do via Property List Editor or (in a more limited way) by using the Preferences dialog for the relevant software.

Note: To make sure that changes you make are not "undone," do not modify the defaults of a currently running application.

SEE: • "Modifying a .plist file," in Chapter 4.

• **diskutil.** You can use this command to verify, repair, mount, and erase volumes, as you would otherwise do via Disk Utility. You can also use it to unmount, mount, rename, or eject drives and partitions. There is no manual (man) entry for this command, but you can get a summary of its options by just typing the command and pressing Return.

This command has some options that are not included in Disk Utility, such as to check RAID sets for errors, and to repair a damaged set.

Note: To use diskutil, you use a device name, not a disk or volume name. Type diskutil list to find the device name for a volume. For example, when I did this, included among the output was the following line, which describes a currently mounted nonstartup partition:

```
9:   Apple_HFS Solo     10.0 GB       disk0s9
```

This indicates that disk0s9 is the device name for the volume called Solo. Note: The Unix commands mount and df will similarly provide this device information.

To unmount a mounted partition or volume (other than the startup volume, which cannot be unmounted), you would type diskutil unmount {*device name*}. To remount it, use the mount option.

Note: disktool is a related command that can also be used for mounting and unmounting volumes.

SEE: • "Performing repairs with Disk Utility (First Aid)," in Chapter 5, for more on enabling journaling and other Disk Utility features.

- **ditto.** This is one of several commands that can be used to copy a bootable volume to a backup.

  The third-party utility Carbon Copy Cloner (from Mike Bombich) relies on the ditto command as its back end.

  SEE: • **"Unix: Copying, Moving, and Deleting," earlier in this chapter, for more on ditto and related commands like CpMac and MvMac**

  • **"Backing up Mac OS X: utilities for volume backups," in Chapter 3, for still more information.**

- **drutil.** This command accesses the DiskRecording framework to interact with CD and DVD burners. One interesting option here is bulkerase. With this option, after an initial -RW disc is erased, the Mac will eject the disc and prompt to insert another one. The next inserted disc will also be erased. This will continue until you terminate the process. You can type man drutil to get more details.

- **fsck_hfs.** This command is virtually identical to selecting to repair a disk via Disk Utility's First Aid option. Unlike First Aid or diskutil, however, it may be usable on the current startup volume.

  SEE: • **"Running fsck_hfs via Terminal," in Chapter 5, for more details on using this command.**

- **hdiutil.** This is the back end for Mac OS X's DiskImageMounter background utility, as well as the source for Images functions in Disk Utility. Prior to Panther, this command served as the back end for Disk Copy. Most of what you can accomplish here can be at least as easily accomplished by using Disk Copy (in Jaguar) or Disk Utility (in Panther). Still, there are some options and features available only via hdiutil.

  For example, you can create a sparse image with Disk Utility in Panther, but you have more options for doing so with hdiutil. The following provides a brief look:

  ```
  hdiutil create ~/Desktop/testcase -size 800m -type SPARSE -fs
  HFS+ -volname testcase
  ```

  The above command creates a disk image on your Desktop named testcase.sparseimage. If you double-click the file, it will mount an image called *testcase* (this is what the volname option establishes). The image will be in HFS Plus format. The testcase volume will be able to hold a maximum of 800 MB of data (as specified by size option). Most important, the —type SPARSE option means that the testcase.sparseimage file will start off at a minimal size (much smaller than its 800 MB limit) and grow as needed to accommodate what you add with the mounted image.

  Note: Apple's man entry for hdiutil states the following:

  > *Specifying SPARSE creates a read/write image which starts small and grows as more data is written to it. The default is to grow one megabyte at a time. SPARSE images (and shadow files) are designed to be used during intermediate steps in the process of creating other images when final image sizes are unknown. Such growable files should not be used for persistent storage because their internal structure exacerbates any fragmentation introduced by the filesystem.*

An alternative is to create an image with the –stretch option. This creates an image of a fixed size, but it can later be changed via the hdiutil resize command or by using the Convert command in Disk Utility.

Another intriguing option is -shadow. The man entry says this about the option:

> *This option prevents modification of the original image and allows read-only images to be used as read/write images. When blocks are being read from the image, blocks present in the shadow file override blocks in the base image. When blocks are being written, the writes will be redirected to the shadow file.*

You can also use the segment option to divide a single image file into multiple segments. This is especially useful if, for example, you need to divide a large image file over several CDs. In Jaguar, Disk Copy included a segment capability, but this option is not included in Disk Utility in Panther.

Finally, the makehybrid option can be used to create a disk image in hybrid formats such as an HFS+, ISO9660, and Joliet hybrid. The image can later be burned to a CD, enabling audio CD tracks and computer data to exist on the same CD.

SEE: • "Backing up Mac OS X: utilities for volume backups," "Bootable CD," "Technically Speaking: More About Disk Utility's Image and Restore Features," and "Technically Speaking: Internet-Enabled Disk Images," in Chapter 3, for more on hdiutil options.

- **id.** This command gives basic ID information about your account: your user ID (and name), your group ID (and name), and the other groups to which you belong. This information is otherwise available via NetInfo Manager.

- **ifconfig.** This is a non-Apple Unix command that's used to configure network settings. It overlaps some with the settings in the Network System Preferences pane.

  SEE: • "Take Note: Deleting System Configuration Folder files" and "Technically Speaking: Ethernet Speed, Duplex, and MTU Problems," in Chapter 8, for examples of using this command.

- **installer.** This command can be used instead of Mac OS X's Installer utility to install .pkg files. Personally, I've never had a need for this utility, much preferring to use Installer instead. However, if you do decide to use the installer command, note that it does not issue a restart command automatically like the Installer utility does. Thus, for software that requires a restart, type either /sbin/reboot or /sbin/shutdown –r after the installer is finished.

- **ipfw.** This is the back end for the firewall available via the Firewall tab of Sharing System Preferences. Third-party utilities such as Brian R. Hill's BrickHouse are also based on this ipfw software.

  SEE: • Chapter 8 for more on using this command to enable some settings that cannot be configured via Sharing.

- **kill and killall.** These commands provide alternatives to Mac OS X's Force Quit command and the Force Quit option in Activity Monitor.

  SEE: • "Force quitting," and (especially) "Technically Speaking: Kill Signals," in Chapter 5, for more information.

- **locate.** As mentioned earlier, locate is an alternative to the Finder's Find command. However, the Finder's Find command is not a front end for locate; they work by separate means. Instead, the third-party utility Locator is a front end for locate.

- **lpr.** This command, followed by the pathname of a document, prints a document to the default printer just as if you had opened it and selected Print from the application showing the document.

  SEE: • "Technically Speaking: Creating a PostScript File for Printing," in Chapter 7.

- **lsbom.** This command lists the contents of a binary *bom* (bill of materials) file in text form. These bom files are often included in .pkg files and list the contents of all items installed by the .pkg file.

  SEE: • "Technically Speaking: Repair Disk Permissions and Receipts," in Chapter 5, for an example of how to use this command.

- **niutil.** The niutil command is used to modify data in the NetInfo database. Related commands include nicl, niload, and nireport. In most cases, you can duplicate the actions of these commands by using NetInfo Manager. However, if a problem with the database is preventing a successful startup, using these commands from single-user mode may be needed.

  Note: The Jaguar version of NetInfo Manager includes Save Backup and Restore From Backup commands in its Management menu. These commands have been dropped from Panther, which means you must use Terminal to perform these operations. (Don't be disappointed: The NetInfo Manager menu commands rarely worked properly!)

  SEE: • "NetInfo and NetInfo Manager" and, especially, "Technically Speaking: Restoring and Replacing NetInfo and Directory Access Data," in Chapter 4, for more details.

- **nvram.** This command can be used to modify Open Firmware variables. It provides an alternative to accessing Open Firmware via holding down the Command-Option-O-F keys at startup.

  Type nvram -p to get a list of most Open Firmware variables and their current settings. As one interesting example, the boot-screen variable is what determines the graphic image displayed at startup.

  I'm not going to delve into using this command in Terminal because in my experience, it's rarely needed. I would rather work in Open Firmware directly. In any case, you should only make changes to Open Firmware if you know exactly what you're doing: Mistakes can lead to startup failures or even a complete inability to start up your Mac again! If trouble occurs, try resetting the PRAM (Command-Option-P-R at startup) and/or NVRAM; this should reset most Open Firmware values to their default states and allow startup to proceed.

  SEE: • "Technically Speaking: Open Firmware Commands," in Chapter 5, for more on Open Firmware commands.

- **plutil.** With this command, you can check if the content of a property list file uses the proper syntax. To use it, type plutil followed by the pathname of the desired file. If a problem is reported, you should probably trash the file. This command won't detect every possible type of corruption, but it is a good start. Alternatively, Preferential Treatment is an Aqua-based utility that employs this command. It can check all of your preferences files with one mouse click. I recommend reading the utility's Help file for a good overview of the issues involved here.

    SEE: • "Deleting or removing preferences," in Chapter 5, for more on this topic.

- **pmset.** You can use this command to modify the power-management settings, otherwise accessed from the Energy Saver System Preferences pane.

    SEE: • "Technically Speaking: Hard-Drive Sleep," in Chapter 2, for an example of using this command.

Figure 10.31

Usage summaries of two of the commands listed in "Running Mac OS X Software from Terminal": (top) defaults *and (bottom)* pmset.

- **reboot (and shutdown).** These commands duplicate what you can do by selecting Restart and Shut Down from the Apple menu. In particular, to shut down immediately, almost no matter what's going on at the moment, you would type the following:

```
shutdown -r now
```

- **screencapture.** This command duplicates what you can do via Command-key sequences (such as Command-Shift-3 and Command-Shift-4). I see no advantage to using Terminal for this, unless the Command-key equivalents are not working for some reason.

    SEE: • **"Take Note: Screen Captures," in Chapter 2, for related information.**

- **SetFile.** This is one of about two dozen Unix commands included in the /Developer/Tools directory (if you installed the Developer software). With this command, you can lock and unlock files, change a file's visibility, and modify file attributes that you would otherwise access from the file's Get Info window or via a third-party utility such as XRay or FileXaminer.

    For example, to make a currently visible file (as an example, a file called ReadMe located on your Desktop) invisible (by enabling its invisibility bit), type the following:

```
SetFile -a V ~/Desktop/ReadMe
```

    You will need to relaunch the Finder to make the file vanish. To restore the file's visibility, use the same command—but use a lowercase v instead of an uppercase one.

    Note: GetFileInfo is a related command that displays but does not modify these settings. The chflags command, covered in the main text of this chapter, is a non-Apple Unix command that has some overlap with SetFile.

    SEE: • **"Unix: Executing Commands," earlier, for more on how to run software located in the /Developer directory.**

    • **"Take Note: Developer Software," in Chapter 2, and "The Mac OS X Install CDs or DVD," in Chapter 3, for more on the Developer software.**

    • **"Invisible Files: Making Invisible Files Visible (and Vice Versa)," in Chapter 6, for more on invisibility.**

- **softwareupdate.** This is a simple and largely unnecessary command, unless you prefer to do from the Terminal what you can otherwise do from Mac OS X itself. In this case, the command checks for and allows you to install software updates that you would otherwise get via the Software Update System Preferences pane.

    For example, type softwareupdate -l to get a list of all currently noninstalled updates (that is, the same list you would get by running the Software Update application).

    About the only case where I could imagine preferring this command over the application is if you wanted (or needed) to update software over a network. For example, you could use ssh to log in to another user's computer (assuming you had permission) and use softwareupdate to update that computer.

- **srm.** This command duplicates the effect of the Secure Empty Trash command in the Finder. That is, it overwrites all blocks that contain the to-be-deleted file with random data (so as to make it almost impossible for someone to later recover the deleted information). The srm command offers additional options not available from the Finder. For example, you can choose between -s (which only overwrites with a single pass) and -m (which overwrites with seven passes, which is what the Finder command does). A -z option zeros all data blocks after overwriting them with random data, for even more security.

- **sw_vers.** This is a substitute source of the information otherwise available from the Apple menu's About This Mac command. It tells you the product name (Mac OS X), product version (for example, 10.3.2), and build version (for example, 7D24) of your current startup system.

- **SystemStarter.** This command allows you to restart all items in the /System/Library/StartupItems and /Library/StartupItems folders—useful when doing so will fix a problem that would otherwise require a true restart, thereby saving you some time and inconvenience.

    SEE: • "Technically Speaking: SystemStarter," in Chapter 5, for more details.

- **tiff2icns.** This command allows you to take any TIFF graphic image and convert it to an icns file suitable for using as a Finder icon. Using it is quite easy: Just type tiff2icns {*filename*.tiff}. This creates an icns file named *filename*.icns at the same location as *filename*.tiff.

- **top.** This command overlaps with the information available via Mac OS X's Activity Monitor. It provides details about memory and CPU usage of all currently running processes.

    SEE: • "Technically Speaking: Terminal Commands to Monitor and Improve Performance," below, for more information on top and other performance-related Unix commands.

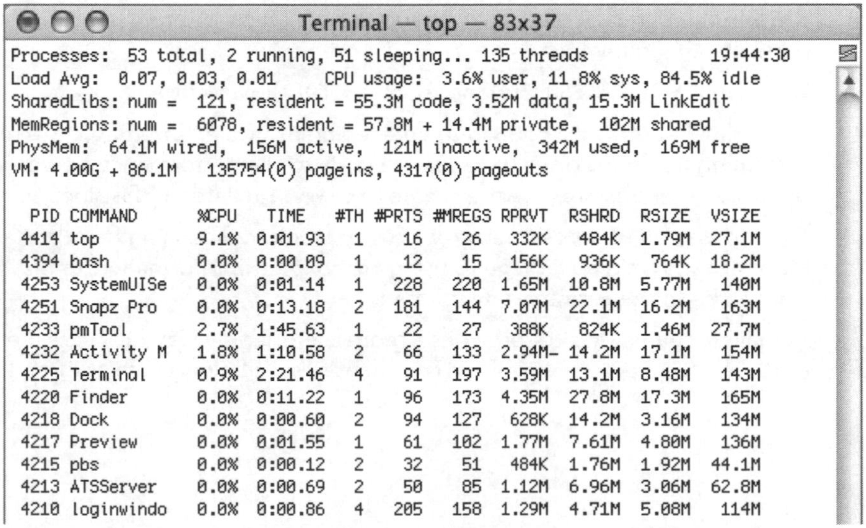

Figure 10.32

The top display in Terminal.

```
 ● ● ●                  Terminal — top — 83x37
Processes:  53 total, 2 running, 51 sleeping... 135 threads          19:44:30
Load Avg:  0.07, 0.03, 0.01     CPU usage:  3.6% user, 11.8% sys, 84.5% idle
SharedLibs: num =  121, resident = 55.3M code, 3.52M data, 15.3M LinkEdit
MemRegions: num =  6078, resident = 57.8M + 14.4M private,  102M shared
PhysMem:  64.1M wired,  156M active,  121M inactive,  342M used,  169M free
VM: 4.00G + 86.1M   135754(0) pageins, 4317(0) pageouts

  PID COMMAND      %CPU   TIME   #TH #PRTS #MREGS RPRVT  RSHRD  RSIZE  VSIZE
 4414 top          9.1%  0:01.93  1    16    26   332K   484K   1.79M  27.1M
 4394 bash         0.0%  0:00.09  1    12    15   156K   936K   764K   18.2M
 4253 SystemUISe   0.0%  0:01.14  1   228   220   1.65M  10.8M  5.77M  140M
 4251 Snapz Pro    0.0%  0:13.18  2   181   144   7.07M  22.1M  16.2M  163M
 4233 pmTool       2.7%  1:45.63  1    22    27   388K   824K   1.46M  27.7M
 4232 Activity M   1.8%  1:10.58  2    66   133   2.94M- 14.2M  17.1M  154M
 4225 Terminal     0.9%  2:21.46  4    91   197   3.59M  13.1M  8.48M  143M
 4220 Finder       0.0%  0:11.22  1    96   173   4.35M  27.8M  17.3M  165M
 4218 Dock         0.0%  0:00.60  2    94   127   628K   14.2M  3.16M  134M
 4217 Preview      0.0%  0:01.55  1    61   102   1.77M  7.61M  4.80M  136M
 4215 pbs          0.0%  0:00.12  2    32    51   484K   1.76M  1.92M  44.1M
 4213 ATSServer    0.0%  0:00.69  2    50    85   1.12M  6.96M  3.06M  62.8M
 4210 loginwindo   0.0%  0:00.86  4   205   158   1.29M  4.71M  5.08M  114M
```

TECHNICALLY SPEAKING ▶ **Terminal Commands to Monitor and Improve Performance**

You can view (and, in some cases, modify) a variety of important performance measures via Unix commands entered in Terminal. The following are some examples:

top. When in Terminal, type top and you'll get a list of the currently running processes, sorted in the order of their PID numbers (with the largest number at the top). You will only see as many processes as fit in the window. To see more, enlarge the window; you cannot scroll the list. The list is constantly updated, in real time, to reflect changes in the data. To exit this display, type q (for *quit*).

Note: In Panther, when you quit top, the list vanishes. In Jaguar, the display remains (though it's no longer updated).

Each column provides information about the specific processes. The PID column, for example, gives the Process ID number for a process; the Command column displays the name of each process; and the %CPU column indicates current CPU use.

At the top of the top display are some important numbers not specific to an individually listed process:

- **Load Avg** is an indication of CPU use. The three load average numbers represent the most recent average and the two averages from minutes before. Generally, the load should stay below 2.0. If it gets higher and stays there, and performance slows, you may be trying to do something beyond what the processor can handle. If that task is essential to your work, you may need to upgrade to a faster processor. Otherwise, you need to try to do less at the same time.

- **CPU usage** numbers provide a different perspective on how the CPU is being used. These numbers indicate how much of the CPU is allocated to the system (kernel) versus the user versus how much is not currently being used (idle). Be especially on guard as the idle percentage approaches 0, which is likely to correlate with performance slowdowns.

- **VM** (virtual memory) gives an indication of the Mac's memory use. The VM line looks something like the following:

  ```
  VM: 3.19G + 50.7M 25092(0) pageins, 24969(0) pageouts
  ```

  If the initial number (3.19 GB in the preceding example) is getting close to the size of your remaining free hard-drive space, you're likely to see performance slowdowns. For further details on memory use, see the coverage of vm_stat, later in this sidebar.

  The top display is Unix's version of Activity Monitor. Given Panther's beefed-up Activity Monitor, I see little advantage to using top to get this information, unless you specifically want to be in the Terminal environment.

  Actually, Activity Monitor provides a more user-friendly way to access the same information available from several of the commands listed below (such as df and vm_stat).

continues on next page

TECHNICALLY SPEAKING ▶ Terminal Commands to Monitor and Improve Performance *continued*

crontab (and periodic). The `crontab` command is used to view and potentially modify the maintenance *cron jobs*. These are the jobs that clean up log files, update the locate database, and more.

SEE: • "Technically Speaking: Log Files and Cron Jobs," in Chapter 4, for more background information.

There's a system `crontab` file that is run by default. It is located in the /etc directory. To view its contents, type the following:

`cat /etc/crontab`

The key section of its output will look like this:

```
#minute hour    mday    month   wday    who     command
#
#*/5    *       *       *       *       root    /usr/libexec/atrun
#
# Run daily/weekly/monthly jobs.
15      3       *       *       *       root    periodic daily
30      4       *       *       6       root    periodic weekly
30      5       1       *       *       root    periodic monthly
```

The last three lines indicate which commands will be run and how often they will be run. Note: Lines preceded by # are comments lines and are not executed.

The first five columns indicate when the script should be run: minute, hour, day of month, month, and day of week (where 1 = Monday). An asterisk means to ignore that parameter. In this case, the first line indicates that the command `periodic daily` will be run at 3:15 a.m. every day. The latter two lines indicate that `periodic weekly` will be run at 4:30 a.m. on the sixth day of the week, and that `periodic monthly` will be run at 5:30 a.m. on the first day of the month.

In these commands, `periodic` is actually the name of the program that is run. The `daily`, `weekly`, and `monthly` terms refer to the scripts that the `periodic` command uses to determine exactly what actions are taken. The scripts are located in the /etc/periodic directory. For example, for the weekly script, open up the weekly directory in the periodic directory. Any script files here are run weekly (you could even add your own, if you are sufficiently skilled in Unix to tackle the task). There should be at least one file here by default: 500.weekly. You can open this file in a text editor to view its contents—though unless you're skilled in reading Unix scripts, it may not be too meaningful.

continues on next page

TECHNICALLY SPEAKING ▶ **Terminal Commands to Monitor and Improve Performance** *continued*

You can also run these scripts yourself, at any time you want, by using the `periodic` command. This can be especially useful if you don't leave your computer on at night when a cron job would automatically run. For example, to run the weekly script, type the following:

```
sudo periodic weekly
```

Note: The following command does the same thing:

```
sudo sh /etc/weekly
```

Third-party utilities, such as Brian R. Hill's MacJanitor and Atomic Bird's Macaroni, can do this as well, bypassing the need to use Terminal.

Note: You can create and edit your own crontab file, so as to run commands in addition to the ones in the system crontab. This personal file is stored separately from the system crontab and is accessed only for your account. Doing this is much preferred to editing the system crontab. To edit your own crontab file, type the following:

```
crontab -e
```

This opens your crontab file (creating one, if none exists) in the default Unix text editor. If you're unfamiliar with working in a Unix text editor, an easier alternative is to use the utility CronniX (by Kochund Schmidt Systemtechnik GLR). This allows you to edit your crontab file (or any other, for that matter) via a Mac interface.

If you have a crontab file and simply want to view its contents, type the following:

```
crontab -l
```

To delete an existing crontab file, type the following:

```
crontab -r
```

As an administrator, you can view the crontab file of any user. For example, to view the crontab file of the root user, if one exists, type the following:

```
sudo crontab -u root -l
```

Finally, you may still be wondering what's with the line that reads as follows:

```
#*/5    *       *       *       *       root    /usr/libexec/atrun
```

Here's what Apple has to say about it (in a man file):

at, batch, atq, atrm are all disabled by default on Mac OS X. Each of these commands depend on the execution of atrun which has been disabled due to power management concerns. Those who would like to use these commands, must first re-enable /usr/libexec/atrun by removing the leading '#' from the atrun line in the file /etc/crontab.

continues on next page

TECHNICALLY SPEAKING ▶ **Terminal Commands to Monitor and Improve Performance** *continued*

df. The df -h command tells you the amount of space used by every volume on your drive. The first row is for your Mac OS X startup volume. The various columns indicate the volume's capacity in terms of the amount used, the amount available, and the percentage of capacity used. Note: The -h option formats the listing in "human readable" form.

The first column is the filesystem name of the volume, such as /dev/disk0s10 (these names may be required when referencing the volume via certain other Unix commands, such as hdiutil). The last column ("Mounted on") lists the names and *mountpoints* of volumes (the name is the volume's name as displayed in the Finder; the mountpoint is the point on the filesystem at which the volume is mounted). The exception is the name of the startup volume, which is listed simply as /.

fstat. This command provides a list of currently open files—that is, ones that the Finder says are "in use." From the output that appears, the Name column gives the name of the open file, while the CMD column displays the command name of the process using the file. This information can be useful, for example, in identifying a file that cannot be deleted because it's in use.

SEE: • "Using Unix to delete files," in Chapter 6, for more details

fs_usage. The fs_usage command is useful for diagnosing problems with file usage in real time, providing a constantly updated running list of all filesystem activity. Each time a process is "used," it gets listed. This can be helpful in nailing down the cause of problems that appear linked to a specific process but you're not sure which. For example, suppose a logout fails due to some process not quitting. The fs_usage listing should allow you to see which process is stalling the logout. Similarly, if a strange noise or visual artifact occurs about every 30 seconds, the fs_usage listing should allow you to see what process is being used at approximately the same interval, and is thus the likely culprit. fs_usage must be run as root.

You can press Control-C to halt the output at any point.

To view the entire list of output, you may prefer to have it stored in a text file so that you don't have to scroll back through the Terminal screen. To store it in a text file, type the following:

sudo fs_usage -w -w > fsoutput.txt

At this point, no text will appear in Terminal. Instead, it's accumulating in fsoutput.txt. To stop the output, press Control-C. Then type open fsoutput.txt to view the file in TextEdit.

Note the following from the man entry for fs_usage:

The output presented by fs_usage is formatted according to the size of your window. A narrow window will display fewer columns of data. Use a wide window for maximum data display. You may override the window formatting restrictions by forcing a wide display with the -w option. In this case, the data displayed will wrap when the window is not wide enough.

continues on next page

TECHNICALLY SPEAKING ▶ **Terminal Commands to Monitor and Improve Performance** *continued*

Note: The > symbol in the command line above is an example of Unix's *file redirection*. It instructs the system to direct the output of the fs command to the file named fsoutput.txt. This serves a similar function to the pipe feature described in "Take Note: Editing Text Files via Terminal," earlier in this chapter.

netstat. The netstat command gives you a quick indication of whether your network connection is performing up to par. For starters, type netstat -i. In the listing that appears, you will get a separate line for all network connections. For your Internet connection, look for the address that represents your current IP address (as listed in the Network or Sharing System Preferences panes). If the incoming packet count (Ipkts) for that line is 0, you probably don't have an active connection. If your error counts (Ierrs and Oerrs) are greater than 1 to 2 percent of the total number of packets listed, there is likely to be some problem with your connection (perhaps a network difficulty at your ISP's end).

Type netstat -i 10, and the display is updated every 10 seconds. This technique allows you to perform diagnostic tests. For example, you could start your browser to see whether the error counts change as the browser attempts a connection.

The Netstat tab of Network Utility (included in the Utilities folder of Mac OS X) offers functionality similar to Unix's netstat command's.

SEE: • **Chapter 8 for more information on networking issues.**

renice. Mac OS X's preemptive multitasking attempts to allocate the processor's attention such that the most important tasks get the most attention (generally giving greater attention to a foreground application than a background one, for example). Tasks that get the greatest attention are completed the most quickly. One way the OS makes these decisions is by assigning each process a priority ranking. When two processes are competing for the CPU's attention, the one with greater priority receives greater attention.

SEE: • **"Mach," in Chapter 4, for more background on preemptive multitasking.**

On occasion, however, you may want to override the OS's default priorities. Some users have found, for example, that they can give Microsoft Virtual PC a speed boost by assigning a higher priority to it. To do this, you use Terminal's renice command. The default nice level for most applications is 0. The potential range is between –20 and +20. To increase an application's priority, you lower its nice level from 0 to a lower number. (The lower the number, the more attention a process gets.) There are limits, of course. If you give everything a score of –20, for example, you won't be increasing the performance of anything. The benefits are always relative to the priorities assigned to other processes.

continues on next page

TECHNICALLY SPEAKING ▶ Terminal Commands to Monitor and Improve Performance *continued*

To change a nice value, type sudo renice {*nice #*} {*pid*}, where {*nice #*} is an integer from –20 to +20 and {*pid*} is the process ID number of the process you want to change. (You can determine a process pid from the top command or from Activity Monitor.) Unfortunately, these changes may not be saved after you quit the application and/or restart the Mac. Thus, you may need to re-enter your change each time you use the application.

Northern Softwork's Renicer, Ryan Steven's Nicer, and La Chose Interactive's Process Wizard are examples of Aqua-based utilities that allow you to modify the nice level of a process, bypassing the need to use Terminal.

ps. The ps command displays "process status." This overlaps some with the top command, but with two significant differences: (1) it is not updated in real time; and (2) it can provide a more complete list of all active processes (you'll likely need to scroll back through the Terminal window to see the complete listing). Thus, it provides a snapshot of all active processes at a moment in time. The best variations of this command to get the complete list are either ps –aux or ps –auxc.

tcpdump. This command performs a *packet analysis*. Utilities that do this are often called *packet sniffers*. Although there are Mac OS X utilities that do this (for example, WildPacket's EtherPeek), for the price (free!) tcpdump can't be beat. In essence, what a packet sniffer does is report all incoming and outgoing traffic on your Internet connection. If you suspect a hacker is trying to bust through your firewall, for example, the tcpdump output should provide the evidence. The command must be run with root access, so precede the command with sudo. Type Command-period, if needed, to stop the output.

The problem with the command is that its output is so overwhelming and obscure that anyone new to packet analysis will have a difficult time deciphering what they're seeing. Check man tcpdump to learn more, especially about all the optional arguments that are available.

update_prebinding (optimize). When you run a Mac OS X update via the Installer utility, at some point, the Installer typically says that it's optimizing the software. What the Installer is doing at this point is running the Unix update_prebinding command. To explain the process in relatively nontechnical language, the command updates the linkage among applications and the shared library files that may be required to run them. Whenever a new application is installed, this information map needs to be updated. If the information is not updated, the resolving of these links is calculated when you launch the application, which takes added time and thus slows performance. Installers perform this task because updating this map is desirable following the installation of new software.

continues on next page

TECHNICALLY SPEAKING ▶ **Terminal Commands to Monitor and Improve Performance** *continued*

If you add applications to your drive by any method that does not do this updating (which would be the case for most applications that don't use Apple's Installer utility), running the update_prebinding command yourself could increase the speed of Mac OS X. However, as mentioned in Chapter 6, starting in Mac OS X 10.2, the need to separately run the update_prebinding command has largely been eliminated. The optimizing is done "on the fly," as needed, when an application is launched.

Xoptimize is an Aqua-based utility that duplicates the function of the update_prebinding command.

SEE: • **"Optimizing Mac OS X volumes," in Chapter 5, for related information.**

vm_stat. The vm_stat command provides a more focused look at Mac OS X's memory use than that provided by top. Of particular interest is the number of pageouts (also listed in the top display). The pageout value is an indication that physical memory is being paged (swapped) to the swapfile on your drive. The higher the number of pageouts, the greater the disk access and the worse your Mac's performance is likely to be. A performance problem is especially indicated if your pageouts increase over time.

If pageouts equal 0, you're not using the swapfile at all—ideal, since any use of the swap file is likely to slow performance. As long as the pageout number is near 0 and relatively stable, you needn't be too concerned about memory use, even if other statistics indicate that your memory use is at or near 100 percent.

SEE: • **"Not enough memory" and "Technically Speaking: Dividing Up Mac OS X's Memory," in Chapter 4, for more background information on memory.**
  • **"Technically Speaking: Swapfiles and RAM Disks," in Chapter 6, for related information.**
  • **"Utilities for monitoring and improving performance," in Chapter 6, for information on using Activity Monitor and other utilities as alternatives to these Unix commands.**

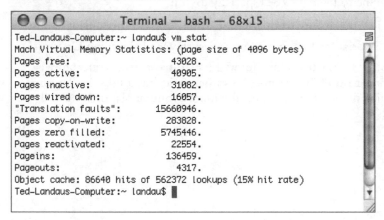

Figure 10.33

The output of two of the commands listed in "Technically Speaking: Terminal Commands to Monitor and Improve Performance": The df command (top) lists mounted volumes and/or partitions (the last item in the list is a network-mounted volume; "volumes" with a capacity of 100 percent can be ignored in most cases); and (bottom) the vm_stat command indicates memory usage.

Unix information beyond this book

If you're motivated to learn still more about Unix, many resources are available.

Books. There are numerous books on Unix that are worth reading. Some are specific to Unix's implementation on Mac OS X. Others are more general. Some are for beginners. Others are for advanced users. Here are four of my favorites:

- *Unix for Mac OS X: Visual QuickPro Guide,* by Matisse Enzer (Peachpit Press, 2002). If you're new to Unix, this book is a good place to start your journey.

- *Mac OS X Panther in a Nutshell*, by Jason McIntosh, Chuck Toporek, and Chris Stone. (O'Reilly, 2004). This has the most complete listing of all Unix commands, including ones just found on Mac OS X systems, that I have seen anywhere.

- *Mac OS X Unleashed, Third Edition*, by John Ray and William C. Ray (Sams Publishing, 2003). If you want to learn how to do almost any advanced Unix procedure on Mac OS X, such as setting up a Web or FTP server, this is the book you want.

- *Unix Power Tools,* 3rd Edition, by Shelley Powers, Jerry Peek, Tim O'Reilly, and Mile Loukides (O'Reilly, 2002). This book is an exhaustive resource of just about every imaginable Unix tip and trick. It is not a Mac OS X–specific book.

Web sites. Numerous online tutorials and reference databases are available. I have found the following to be especially useful:

- UNIX Reference Desk (http://ihome.ust.hk/~chxw/unix/unixdesk.htm).

- UNIX Tutorial for Beginners (www.ee.surrey.ac.uk/Teaching/Unix).

- Carbonized Interactive Unix Tutorial (www.macinstruct.com/tutorials/unix/x/index.html). This tutorial is rather basic, but it uses the Terminal application in Mac OS X, unlike the more common platform-neutral tutorials.

11

Troubleshooting the iApps

Most of this book is concerned with Mac OS X as an operating system—specifically, how to solve problems with the operating system and with applications in general. This chapter is the exception: It focuses on a specific collection of applications included as part of Mac OS X that are referred to as the *iApps*—because their names all begin with *i*.

The core of the iApps is a suite of excellent and popular multimedia applications, typically referred to as the iLife applications: iTunes, iPhoto, iMovie, and (if your Mac comes with a SuperDrive) iDVD. Also included in the more general category of iApps are iCal (Mac OS X's calendar program), iSync (Mac OS X's synchronization utility), and iChat (Mac OS X's instant messaging and conferencing application). Closely related to iTunes is the iPod and its associated software. Finally, even though its name doesn't begin with an *i*, Mac OS X's Address Book utility works closely with several of these applications.

Although space constraints prevent me from going into detail about the use of each of these applications, this chapter covers their basic functionality and the problems you may experience when using them.

Tip: One of the first things you can do to avoid problems with your iApps is to make sure you have the latest versions installed. Updates are listed in Software Update and on Apple's Web site.

In This Chapter

TAKE NOTE ▶ **iLife '04**

In January 2004, Apple released iLife '04, which is made up of iTunes 4.2 (the version covered in the main text); updated versions of iPhoto, iMovie, and iDVD (all now at version 4); and a new program called GarageBand. Although these programs are included free on all new Macs, as of this writing they had not been added to the retail version of Panther. In addition, iTunes is the only component that is still available as a free download.

This chapter is mainly based on the versions of the software that originally shipped with Panther. However, even if you're using the new '04 versions, most of the information presented in the main text remains accurate. None of the programs received a major overhaul. Each program has a few new features (most of which are noted here or in the main text). In addition, a few of the bugs in the previous versions have been fixed.

Here are the highlights of what's new and what you need to know:

- **iPhoto 4.** This update offers significantly improved performance. You can now have a library of as many as 25,000 photos and view each one almost instantly.

    You can now use Smart Albums (similar to iTunes' Smart Playlists) to automatically add photos to an album based on criteria you set. Troubleshooting tip: If a photo is contained within a Smart Album, you will not be able to delete the photo from iPhoto until you remove it from the Smart Album. To do so, change the criteria used to define the album or edit the photo, so that the photo no longer meets the album's criteria.

    In addition: With iPhoto 4, you can use Rendezvous to share photos with other users on your local network. Organize your photos by time or rating. Directly edit a photo while going through a slide show via onscreen controls. iPhoto 4 also includes enhanced options for adding music and transitions to slide shows.

- **iMovie 4.** This update offers *nondestructive editing*—which means you can trim clips directly in the Timeline without deleting the original footage.

    In addition: You can also edit multiple clips simultaneously. Audio options have been enhanced with improved audio-video syncing and new sound effects. Rendering performance is faster.

- **iDVD 4.** This update features a new DVD Map view (the Map button is between the Motion and Preview buttons on the main screen), which displays an organizational diagram of your entire project.

    In addition: An AutoPlay feature enables a movie or slide show to begin playing as soon as you insert the DVD—that is, even before the menus appear. There are 20 new themes. A DVD can now contain up to 2 hours of material.

- **GarageBand.** This amazing new program amounts to your own personal recording studio. Use the built-in loops to add percussion and rhythm backgrounds. Then select from an array of real and software instruments to add your own melody lines (using instruments you connect to your Mac). You can even add your own voice track, using either the microphone built into most Mac models or an external mike. Use multiple tracks to create a complete multi-instrument composition. In addition, you can edit each track in a seemingly infinite number of ways. A brief summary cannot begin to capture the breadth and depth of this program. You have to see it to believe it!

continues on next page

TAKE NOTE ▶ iLife '04 *continued*

For a more complete overview of the suite of software, see the following Apple Web page: www.apple.com/ilife. For information on iTunes 4.5, separately released in April 2004, see: www.apple.com/itunes/download.

Troubleshooting tip: iLife and your hardware. The single most important piece of advice I can offer regarding iLife is this: Get the most Mac you can afford! The faster your CPU, the more RAM you have installed, the larger and faster your hardware, the better the software will run. Apple's minimum requirements should be taken with a grain of salt. The programs will run with the minimum—but not necessarily well. For example:

- **GarageBand** is the iLife component most likely to have processor- and memory-related problems.

  For starters, the maximum number of Software Instrument tracks a song can contain is directly related to the amount of RAM in your Mac. The more memory, the more tracks.

  In addition, the more tracks and instrument effects you use, the greater the demand on the processor. Having more than one note play at a time on a track also increases the processor load.

  If the load gets too high, GarageBand cannot read and/or write data quickly enough to keep pace with the song that's playing. This is such a critical issue that the triangle at the top of the playhead changes color (from white to orange to red) to indicate the demand on the processor. In my experience, a red triangle is an all-too-frequent occurrence. If it stays red too long, you will likely get a System Overload or "Disk is too slow" error. The song will stop playing. If this happens, try one or more of the following:

  Quit other open applications to free up memory and processor access for GarageBand. Quit and reopen GarageBand itself.

  Go to GarageBand's Preferences. Click the Audio/MIDI button, and from the Optimize section select Better Performance. Click the Advanced button and lower the limits for Maximum Number of Tracks and Voices Per Instrument.

  Simplify the song: Mute, delete, or combine tracks as practical.

  Do not use FileVault.

  Add more memory to your Mac, get a CPU upgrade, or get a new faster Mac.

  Note: If you have multiple users logged in, only one user can use GarageBand at a time.

  See the following Web page for more GarageBand tips: www.apple.com/ilife/garageband/hottips.

- For **iDVD**, Apple advises that you have at least 10 GB of hard-disk space available before burning a DVD. Otherwise, you may get a "Multiplexer preparation" error.

Troubleshooting iTunes

iTunes is Mac OS X's audio hub: It plays audio files and CDs, converts audio files from one format to another, organizes music, connects to Apple's iPod portable music player, and even allows you to purchase new music (via the iTunes Music Store). In addition, it serves as a music library for other users in your household (via iTunes Sharing) and for the other iLife applications, iPhoto, iMovie, and iDVD.

iTunes basics

Even if it didn't offer features for sharing and purchasing music, as well as interacting with the other iLife apps, iTunes would still be a full-featured music center. With it, you can play your favorite CDs, listen to audio files located on your hard drive (generally referred to as MP3s, though iTunes supports a number of other audio file formats as well), create MP3s from your CD collection, and listen to *streaming audio*—that is, live audio broadcast over the Internet. When listening to audio from your hard drive, you can create playlists that contain any combination and order of songs—and in doing so, become your own DJ! You can even burn your own audio CDs for use in the CD player in your home or car.

SEE: • "Take Note: Burning CDs (and DVDs)," in Chapter 6, for more on CD and DVD burning.

The column on the left side of the main iTunes window displays the Source list with the currently selected source item highlighted ("60's Music" in **Figure 11.1**). The central section of the window contains the contents of the selected audio source (the song list with columns for name, time, artist, and so on). Playback and volume controls are in the upper left, information about the current track (such as remaining time) is in the upper center, and a Search text box and a Burn Disc button are in the upper right. Along the bottom are a row of buttons for features such as creating a playlist, turning shuffle on or off, accessing the Equalizer window, ejecting a disc, and more. If you place the pointer over any item, a yellow tool tip describing its function will appear.

If you double-click any item in the Source list, including the Music Store, a separate window opens for that source.

To begin playback, select a source, select a song, and then click the Play button. Alternatively, you can double-click a song in the song listing. You can adjust the volume using the volume slider and, if desired, click the Equalizer button to apply one of a number of EQ settings. The right- and left-arrow buttons skip forward or back one track, respectively; if you hold the mouse button down on either arrow, you'll "scan" through the current song instead. Finally, the Play button doubles as a Pause button: Click it once to pause playback, and again to resume.

Play controls and volume slider   Current track info: song, album, and artist rotate into view

Source
list

Create a
playlist

Turn shuffle off or on   Artwork   Open the Equalizer window   Eject disc

Repeat   Visualizer

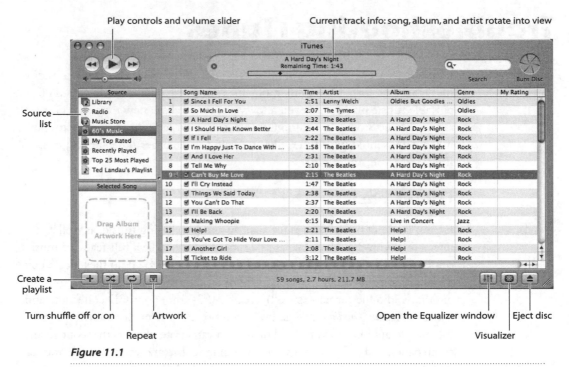

Figure 11.1

The main iTunes window.

Those are the basics of playback; however, there are a number of other playback features that aren't immediately obvious:

Browsing. When a music library, rather than a playlist, is selected in the Source
list, the icon in the upper right of the iTunes window shifts from Burn Disc to
Browse. By clicking the Browse button, you can change the song list to a file
browser that lets you browse by genre and/or artist, and then by album, allowing you to restrict playback to a certain type of music, a single artist, or even a
single album.

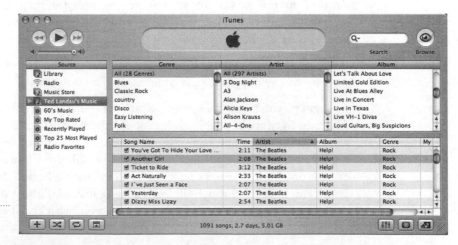

Figure 11.2

*iTunes' Browse
mode.*

Playback modes. In the lower left portion of the iTunes window is the Shuffle control button (the one with two arrows crossing, as seen in Figure 11.1). Clicking this button turns it blue, meaning that random-shuffle playback is enabled. Just to the right is the Repeat control (two arrows forming a circuit): A single click enables Full Repeat mode, meaning that once the current playback selection (your Library, a playlist, an album, and so on) finishes, it will repeat. A second click switches to Single Repeat mode, which repeats the currently playing track over and over. A third click disables Repeat mode.

iTunes visuals and artwork. If you click the Visualizer button (in the lower right portion of the iTunes window; the button that looks a bit like an asterisk), iTunes' Visualizer activates to provide a graphics display that changes in time to the beat. If you click the Artwork button (fourth button from the left in the bottom left corner of the iTunes window), an artwork panel is displayed below the Source list: If the currently playing track has embedded artwork, it will be displayed. Many tracks purchased from the iTunes Music Store contain artwork (primarily the CD cover); you can also drag your own artwork into the artwork panel.

Enabling and disabling tracks. Each song in the Song list has an associated check box. If its box is checked, the song will be available for playback; if it's not checked, the song will be skipped.

Columns and sorting. You can add or remove columns in the Song list by opening the View Options dialog from the Edit menu, and then enabling or disabling the appropriate column types. (You can also Control-click any column head to bring up a list of possible columns. Select one to switch its current status—viewed or not.) When you click a column name in the Song list, songs will be sorted by that column. For example, to group songs by album, click the Album column head.

Searching. By typing words into the Search field in the upper right side of the iTunes window, you instruct iTunes to find—in real time—all music files that contain those words in its artist, composer, album name, or song name. For example, if you type *door*, iTunes will find all songs that contain the word *door* in their titles, as well as any songs by The Doors or Three Doors Down. The songs it finds are listed in the Song list. (The Search field is in effect a filter that determines which audio files are visible.) If you click the magnifying glass on the left side of the Search field, you can elect to search only one of the available fields rather than all of them.

Help. For more details on iTunes' features, check out iTunes and Music Store Help and Keyboard Shortcuts from iTunes' Help menu.

TAKE NOTE ▶ The iTunes Library and iTunes Music Folder

The Library item in iTunes' Source list represents the collection of audio files located on your hard drive (or on a connected volume) and accessed by iTunes. Although you can create *playlists*, which are individual subsets of audio tracks, the Library always shows *all* files—providing, in effect, a database of your music.

By default, iTunes' main files are located in a folder called iTunes, located in the Music folder in your Home directory (~/Music/iTunes). Inside this folder is the Library database, called iTunes *x* Music Library (where *x* is the version of iTunes you're running—for example, iTunes 4). There's also a folder here called iTunes Music: This is where the actual music and audio files are stored. You can change the location of the iTunes folder—for example, to store music files on a second hard drive (to conserve space on your boot volume) or to store files in a public directory (to make them available to all users).

SEE: • "Moving your iTunes Music folder to a different folder or volume," later in this chapter.

Although you *can* use the iTunes Music folder to store music files, iTunes doesn't *require* that you do so. Audio files created in iTunes—for example, files created from audio CDs or songs downloaded from the iTunes Music Store—are automatically placed inside the iTunes Music folder. However, files not created or downloaded by iTunes may reside elsewhere. You determine where they're placed by adjusting the following setting in the Advanced section of iTunes' Preferences: "Copy files to iTunes Music folder when adding to library." When you double-click an audio file to play it in iTunes or drag it into the main iTunes window, the file's information is automatically added to your Library. If the above option is enabled, a copy of the file is placed in the iTunes Music folder (you can later delete the original, if desired). If it is not enabled, the file remains in its original location; if you delete it, iTunes will no longer be able to find it.

You determine how files are organized *within* the iTunes Music folder by adjusting another setting in iTunes' Advanced preferences: "Keep iTunes Music folder organized." If this option is disabled, files are stored loosely. If the option is enabled, iTunes examines each file's *ID tags* (which include such information as the file's name, artist, and so on) and creates folders for each artist, subfolders for each album, and so on—in an effort to organize your music files.

If you previously chose *not* to keep the iTunes Music folder organized but later decide to take advantage of this feature, selecting Consolidate Library from iTunes' Advanced menu will place copies of every file in your Library in the iTunes Music folder—making your iTunes Music folder look like you had the Organize option enabled from the start.

If you need to locate a particular audio file on your hard drive, you can select it from the song list, and then from the File menu choose Show Song File.

"Ripping" (converting) audio

If you're playing a CD via iTunes, it's obvious where your music is coming from. But where do you get *other* music to put on your computer (and, if you have one, onto your iPod)? One way is to purchase music from the iTunes Music Store (discussed later in this chapter) or another online music service; the music is generally downloaded in the appropriate format. Many users also—rightly or wrongly—download music files from free file-sharing services (shared by other users over the Internet).

You can also copy (or *import,* as it's called in iTunes) music from a CD to your hard drive. *Ripping* is the common term for copying music from a CD and converting it to a file format that can be stored on your computer and played back later. As I mentioned earlier, iTunes includes everything you need to rip your own CDs. To do so, simply follow these steps:

1. Place an audio CD in your drive and wait for it to appear in the Source list (in iTunes' main menu).

2. Click the CD to view the song list: If, in the On CD Insert pop-up menu in iTunes' General Preferences, you've selected Show Songs, iTunes will connect to the Internet and get the names of the tracks on the CD. It does this by connecting to an Internet CD database and matching identification codes on the CD.

3. To import the CD, click the Import button (in the upper right portion of the iTunes window; it becomes the Browse button when viewing your Library). If you don't want to import all of the songs on the CD, uncheck the unwanted songs in the song list and then click the Import button.

iTunes automatically imports songs using the MP3 file format. However, you can customize both the format and settings for ripping via the Importing pane of iTunes' Preferences.

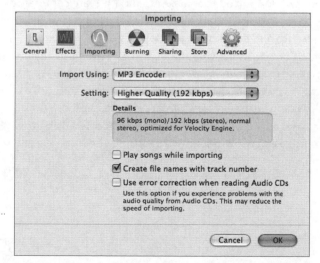

Figure 11.3

iTunes' Preferences window, with Importing selected.

For example, from the Import Using pop-up menu, you can choose among AAC, AIFF, MP3, and WAV formats. From the Setting pop-up menu, you can choose among a few different quality settings for each format (or choose Custom to create your own settings). The Details box displays a summary of the current settings.

Note: In Mac OS X 10.3.2 and later, iTunes will continue importing songs from a CD even if you switch to another account, via Fast User Switching, while the import is in progress.

TAKE NOTE ▶ **Audio File Formats**

When you import files from CDs, iTunes uses the settings chosen in the Importing pane of iTunes' Preferences. You can choose among four encoding formats: AAC, AIFF, MP3, and WAV. Since the differences between these file formats are a bit of a mystery to most users, the following provides a quick summary.

AIFF and WAV. These *uncompressed* encoding formats are basically identical—except that AIFF is a Mac file format, and WAV is a Windows file format. Files typically appear in one of these formats on an audio CD mounted in the Finder. Extracting audio in these formats produces files of the same size as the original music files on the CD—basically, around 10 MB per minute of music. For both AIFF and WAV files, iTunes is set to "automatic"—meaning it figures out the settings of the original music file and imports using those same settings. Unless you're specifically trying to create a mono version of a stereo song, you should leave these settings alone.

You would generally use the AIFF or WAV formats to make an exact copy of an audio CD. You would extract AIFF or WAV versions of the songs on the CD, and then burn them to a blank CD. Or, if you're a die-hard audiophile who refuses to listen to compressed audio (more on that in a second), you would import CDs in AIFF or WAV format to have the highest-quality audio files on your hard drive.

AAC and MP3. The other two supported formats, AAC and MP3, are *compression* formats. When importing using one of these formats, for each fraction of a second of audio, iTunes uses a process called *perceptual encoding* to estimate which parts of the spectrum the human ear won't be able to hear at all, or won't miss very much, and then discards that information. It then creates a new, much smaller audio file that is saved to your hard drive and added to your iTunes Library. The result is that you can store much more music on your hard drive (or iPod) than you would had you imported using *uncompressed* formats (such as AIFF or WAV). For example, a song that may have required 65 MB of hard-drive space if imported using the AIFF format may require as little as 3 or 4 MB using a low-quality MP3 format.

continues on next page

TAKE NOTE ▶ **Audio File Formats** *continued*

The drawback to AAC and MP3 is that in order to compress files so dramatically, they *lose* data. Granted, the perceptual encoding process described above ensures that much of what is lost you'll never miss. However, if you have good ears and good audio equipment (for example, great speakers or headphones connected to your Mac), you may be able to hear a difference between the original CD and the compressed versions on your hard drive. This is where iTunes' Importing settings come in. The AAC and MP3 encoders both have a Settings dialog that allows you to decide how much of a trade-off you're willing to make between sound quality and file size. If you choose AAC or MP3 as the encoder, and then choose Custom from the Settings pop-up, you'll be presented with a dialog that allows you to customize the AAC or MP3 settings. The most important of these is the *bit rate*, which tells iTunes how much data you want to be used to represent each second of audio—the higher the bit rate, the better the quality but the larger the file.

Unfortunately, I don't have enough space to describe each setting for AAC and MP3 files. Your best bet is to play around with them, importing songs using each, until you find the best settings for you. If you have a small hard drive (or iPod), you may want to use lower-quality encoding in order to fit more music. On the other hand, if you have a huge hard drive with lots of free space, you may be more willing to use higher-quality encoding.

So what's the difference between MP3 and AAC? AAC is a newer encoder that uses Apple's QuickTime 4 technology. It's not as widely used as MP3, but it works with iTunes and Apple's iPod. AAC is designed to offer better sound quality than MP3 at lower bit rates, whereas many users feel that MP3 files sound better at higher bit rates. In general, I would say that if you're looking for small file size, use AAC as the import format, with a 128k or 160k bit rate. If you're looking for better sound quality and don't mind larger files, use AAC at 192k or MP3 at 192k or higher.

Creating playlists

Once you've downloaded and/or imported songs into your iTunes Library, you'll probably want to listen to them as you would albums—that is, as smaller subsets of songs. You can do this by creating playlists; iTunes features two types: standard and smart.

Standard playlists. A standard playlist is created manually: You simply click the plus (+) button in the lower left corner of the iTunes window (or from the File menu choose New Playlist), and a new untitled playlist appears in the Source list. After giving the playlist a name, you add songs to it by simply dragging them from the Library's song list. You can re-create single albums (by dragging all of the songs from a particular album) or your own "mix" playlists. Basically, you decide exactly what songs should be in a playlist. When you click the playlist, its contents are displayed in the song list. You can drag songs up or down to change their play order, and you can delete songs by selecting them and pressing the Delete key.

Smart playlists. Smart playlists are, well, *smart*. Instead of choosing which songs you want your playlist to include, you tell iTunes what *kinds* of songs to include and iTunes automatically populates the playlists with every song that fits your criteria. To create a new smart playlist, hold down the Option key and click the New Playlist (+) button in the lower left corner of the iTunes window (or from the File menu select New Smart Playlist). You'll notice that the new, untitled, playlist has a different icon than the one displayed by standard playlists.

Once you've assigned a name to your smart playlist, select it in the Source list, and from the File menu choose Edit Smart Playlist (or press Command-I). A dialog will appear that lets you choose specific settings for the playlist. Under "Match the following condition," you can choose the criteria to be used to populate the playlist. For example, you could choose songs that you've rated as more than four stars, songs from 1960 to 1969, songs from the folk genre—you can use any criteria that iTunes tracks. If you click the plus button to the right of the "conditions," you can add additional criteria to fine-tune your playlist. If you want to limit the number of songs in the playlist, you can check the "Limit to" box and specify a number of songs/minutes/MB and designate how to choose those songs. If you want iTunes to update the playlist on the fly (for example, adding new songs to the playlist as you add new files to the iTunes Library), be sure to check the "Live updating" setting.

Figure 11.4

The settings for an iTunes smart playlist.

Smart playlists are one of iTunes' shining features. With a bit of creativity, you can use smart playlists to create an infinite number of unique playlists to satisfy any music mood you might be in. You can even burn smart playlists—just like standard playlists—to CDs for listening at home or on the go.

Listening to Internet radio

With iTunes, you can listen to Internet streaming radio—that is, radio stations broadcast over the Internet. You can browse a built-in list of stations or connect directly to a known station.

To browse stations, click the Radio item in the Source list. The song list changes to a list of available stations, organized by music type. Click the disclosure triangle next to a genre to reveal available stations in that genre. Double-click a station to connect to it (or select it and click the Play button).

To connect to a known station, from the Advanced menu choose Open Stream and then enter the station's address.

iTunes basics: tips and fixes

The following are a number of iTunes tips and fixes that should help you get the most out of the application, as well as overcome trouble, should you encounter any.

Backing up your iTunes music and Library. To prevent losing music you have downloaded and avoid re-ripping the music you transferred from CDs, you should back up your MP3s by copying them to an external hard drive or burning them to CDs or DVDs. Ideally, you should copy the entire ~/Music/iTunes folder. At the very least, copy the music files in ~/Music/iTunes/iTunesMusic.

Note: Some users who previously used iTunes 2 or iTunes 1 may find that their iTunes folder is located at ~/Documents/iTunes.

SEE: • "Backing Up and Restoring Mac OS X Volumes," in Chapter 3, for more general advice on backing up.

Making batch changes to iTunes songs. Suppose you have a collection of several dozen songs, all of which you want to apply the same change to (perhaps changing the genre from Rock to Oldies). You can do this in one step by selecting all the songs in the Library list and then selecting Get Info (Command-I). This brings up the Multiple Song Information window: Any changes you make here will simultaneously affect all selected items.

Of course, to make changes to a single song, select Get Info for that song. A somewhat different set of editing options appears.

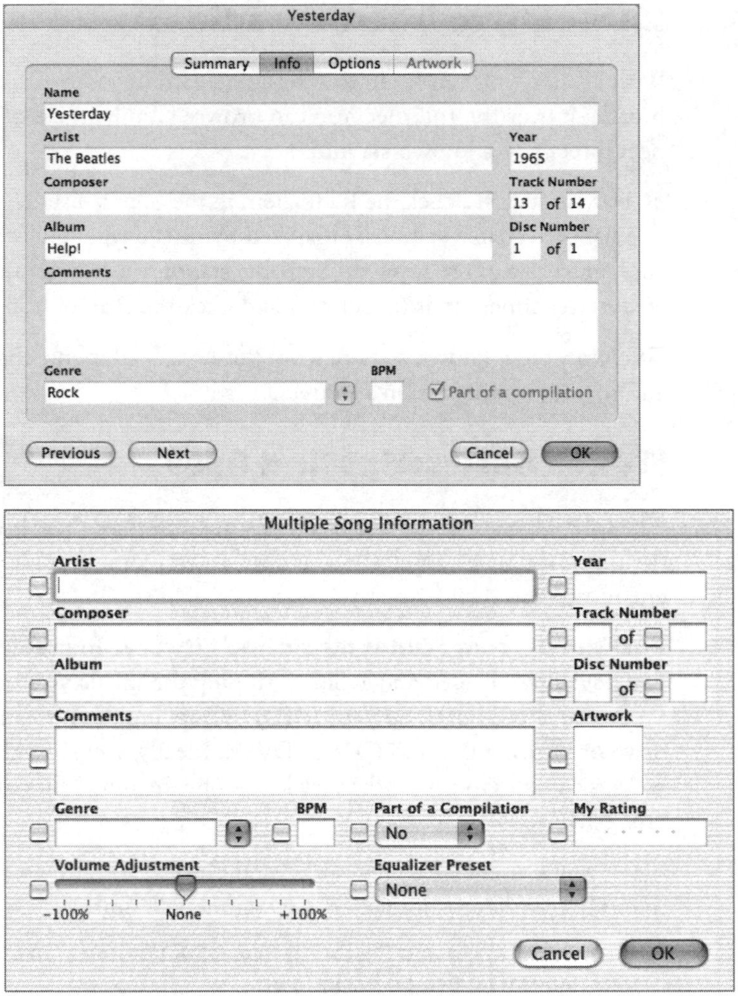

Figure 11.5

The Get Info settings for (top) a single song and (bottom) a selection of multiple songs.

Moving your iTunes Music folder to a different folder or volume.
If you decide that you would rather have your iTunes folder in a different folder or on a volume other than the startup disk (say because you want to make your music available to other users, save space on your startup volume, or ease backups), follow these steps.

1. Copy the iTunes Music folder from your startup drive to the alternative volume.

2. From iTunes' menu, select Preferences, and click the Advanced button.

3. Click the Change button next to the iTunes Music Folder Location box.

4. From the window that appears, navigate to the *new* iTunes Music folder location, then click Choose.

Note that if you move your iTunes Music folder to another volume, that volume must be connected and mounted for iTunes to play your music files.

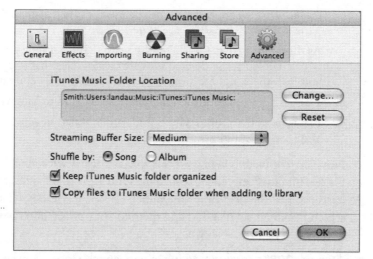

Figure 11.6

iTunes' Preferences window, with Advanced selected.

Accessing another user's iTunes music. If another user has placed his or her iTunes Music folder in a public location (for example, his or her own Public folder or the Shared folder), you can add that user's music to your iTunes Library list by following these steps.

1. From iTunes' menu, select Preferences, and click the Advanced button.

2. Uncheck "Copy files to iTunes Music folder when adding to library" and click OK.

3. From the File menu choose Add to Library.

4. Navigate to the other user's iTunes Music folder; highlight it, and click the Choose button.

The contents of the user's iTunes Music folder will be added to your Library list.

Reconnecting to or re-creating the iTunes Library. If you launch iTunes and no songs or playlists are listed, it typically means one of two things: iTunes has lost track of where your iTunes folder is located or the Music Library data has become corrupt. In either case, this can usually be fixed.

To check for and fix the former cause, locate and reselect the "disconnected" iTunes Music folder via the Change button next to the iTunes Music Folder location box located in the Advanced section of iTunes Preferences.

For the latter cause, you will need to re-create your iTunes Library. This will likely mean all your custom playlists will be lost, but your songs will be saved. To re-create the Library, do the following:

1. Quit iTunes if open. Locate your iTunes folder. Unless you moved it from its default location, it will be in either ~/Documents or ~/Music.

2. From within the folder, delete iTunes 4 Music Library, iTunes Music Library.xml, and any other files (not folders) that may be in the iTunes

folder. Whatever you do, do not delete the folder named iTunes Music. This is where your songs are stored.

As discussed earlier (in "Take Note: The iTunes Library and iTunes Music Folder"), the deleted files are catalog files that keep track of where and how the songs are stored. They do not actually contain the songs.

3. Launch iTunes. From the File menu, select Add to Library.

4. Navigate to the iTunes Music folder mentioned in step 2. Click Choose. Your songs should now reappear.

Note: To ease the rebuilding process, you can also delete your iTunes Preferences file (~/Library/Preferences/com.apple.iTunes.plist). This resets iTunes preferences, so that the next time you launch iTunes, it will ask whether it should search for all music files and add them to your music library, bypassing the need for steps 3 and 4 above.

"Error -208" message. If, when you launch iTunes, you see the message "Error -208 Cannot Open iTunes Music Library," your iTunes Music Library file may be corrupt. To fix this, follow the steps to re-create the iTunes Library, as described in the previous section.

iTunes Library 32,000-song limit. Versions of iTunes prior to iTunes 4 have a limit of 32,000 songs/audio files. If you have more than 32,000 audio files, you can get around this limit by creating multiple iTunes Music Library files, as described in the following Apple Knowledge Base article: http://docs.info.apple.com/article.html?artnum=61585. An easier solution, however, is to simply update to iTunes 4 or later.

iTunes text is rough or jagged. After updating to iTunes 4, you may notice that the text in your iTunes windows appears jagged and difficult to read. This is caused by an anti-aliasing glitch between iTunes 4 and Mac OS X—namely that Mac OS X's font-smoothing setting is set lower than the default text size for iTunes. You can solve this problem in one of two ways:

- **Increase the size of text in iTunes.** In iTunes' Preferences, click the General button in the toolbar. Then choose Large in the pop-up menus for Source Text and Song Text. Click OK to save the changes. The text in iTunes' windows will now be a bit larger and thus smoothed by the OS.

- **Change the font size at which the OS smooths text.** Open the Appearance System Preferences pane. Choose 10 from the pop-up menu in to "Turn off text smoothing for font sizes _ and smaller." The allows the default text size in iTunes to be smoothed. You will need to quit iTunes and relaunch it for the change to take effect.

Sound fluctuation with iTunes 4.0. If you're using iTunes 4.0 and have enabled any of the options in the Effects section of iTunes Preferences, you may hear fluctuations in the sound level or distortion of the audio. This bug is fixed in iTunes 4.0.1 and later.

AAC files won't play. Although iTunes generally supports the AAC file format, you may find that some AAC files won't play on your computer. There are a couple of reasons why this might happen:

- Some AAC files simply don't work with iTunes. If an AAC file won't play in iTunes, chances are it wasn't created in iTunes or QuickTime, or it wasn't purchased from the iTunes Music Store.

- A song was purchased from the iTunes Music Store, but your computer is not authorized to play it. To authorize a purchased song for your computer, double-click it; you'll be asked to provide the Apple ID and password of the person who purchased it.

SEE: • **"iTunes Music Store," later in this chapter, for more details.**

Song titles include strange characters. If you've obtained MP3 files from sources other than your own CDs or the iTunes Music Service, some song titles may include strange characters—occasionally making the titles undecipherable. This generally happens when files are created in an application that uses a different system for titling songs. It may also be indicative of songs with titles in non-Roman-character languages.

To update the titles, you can use iTunes' ID3 Tag feature. To do so, follow these steps.

1. Select the songs with titles you wish to update, and from the Advanced menu choose Convert ID3 Tags.

2. Enable the "ID tag version" option, and from the pop-up menu select the desired version. Click OK. If appropriate, also select "Translate text characters" and choose an option from among the three choices presented.

3. If you're uncertain which option you should select, you can try different ones, varying your selection until you find the combination that best fixes your filename problems.

If converting ID3 tags doesn't fix song names, you can always edit song information manually by selecting a track and then choosing Get Info from iTunes' File menu.

"Unsupported Compression Scheme" error message. If you use a proxy when accessing the Internet, inserting a CD while iTunes is running may prompt an error message about an Unsupported Compression Scheme to appear. What's actually happening is that iTunes is attempting to connect to the online CDDB (CD Database) to retrieve information about the CD (track names and so on), but your proxy server is not properly passing CDDB data. This usually occurs with nonstandard proxy servers. If you can contact the proxy server administrator, you can request that a more standard proxy be implemented, but an easier solution is usually to simply avoid using the proxy server (if possible).

iTunes Radio cannot connect. If you're using iTunes behind a firewall, you may find that you cannot connect to iTunes Radio (streaming audio) stations. This is because streaming audio uses ports that most firewalls close by default. Unfortunately, each station/stream can choose its own port, so it's difficult to suggest which ports you'll need to open.

If you are able to figure out which port(s) you need to open for a particular station or stream, you can open them in your firewall. If you're using a hardware or third-party firewall, check with the documentation for the firewall for how to open those ports. If you're using Mac OS X's Firewall, as accessed from the Sharing System Preferences pane, you can open the needed ports by creating a new rule.

SEE: • "Firewall" in "Setting Up System Preferences: Sharing," in Chapter 8, for details on how to create a new rule to open a port.

Streaming performance. The Advanced pane of iTunes' Preferences includes a pop-up menu for Streaming Buffer Size. To get the best performance out of streaming audio (for example, from Internet radio or iTunes Music Store), select Small if you're using a DSL/cable modem or Large if you're using a dial-up modem. The default setting is a compromise: Medium.

Playlist too big to fit on disc. Beginning in iTunes 4.1, if the playlist to be burned to a disc contains more songs than will fit on the disc being used, iTunes will ask you to insert additional discs as needed. Older versions of iTunes will only burn as many as will fit on one disc. In these cases, you will need to create several smaller playlists, each containing only as many songs as will fit on the media being used.

After selecting a playlist, you can see the total size of the songs to be burned by looking at the bottom edge of the iTunes window. A CD-R or CD-RW will generally hold about 650 MB, whereas a DVD-R or DVD-RW will hold about 4.7 GB.

Problems burning CDs. For other problems with burning CDs, see "Take Note: Burning CDs (and DVDs)," in Chapter 6.

Apple's Tips page. Apple has an "iTunes Tips and Tricks" document in its Knowledge Base that offers a number of useful tips. You can read it at the following address: http://docs.info.apple.com/article.html?artnum=93120.

iTunes Music Store

From the iTunes Music Store, you can purchase and download music from thousands of artists from directly within iTunes. Music is encoded in AAC format at a 128k bit rate, so quality is quite good considering the small file sizes. In the Source list, click Music Store, and the song list will change to the Store.

To purchase music from the iTunes Music Store, you need an Apple ID and account. You can set one up on the online Apple Store (http://store.apple.com), or you can create one from within iTunes by clicking the Account button just below the Search/Browse area in the upper right corner. Starting with iTunes 4.2, you can also use the Music Store via your AOL account.

Note: When you set up your account, one of the options is 1-Click ordering, which allows you to purchase and download a song with a single click.

Figure 11.7

The iTunes Music Store main screen (top); an album selected in the Music Store (bottom).

The iTunes Music Store storefront, if you will, presents special promotions, new releases, and other items of interest. However, most users will find the Search Music Store field to be the most-used feature; it works just like the regular iTunes Search field, only it searches the iTunes Music Store for available music that you can purchase. In addition, if you click the magnifying-glass icon on the left of the Search field, you can choose Power Search, which lets you search by song, artist, album, genre, and composer simultaneously. You can also click the Browse button, which works just like the Browse function when viewing your own iTunes Library.

When you find a song you like, you can double-click it (or select it and click the Play button) to play a 30-second preview. Click the right arrow next to the artist name to view that artist's page, or click the arrow next to the album name to view that album. (The Left/Right/Home buttons at the top of the Store pane work like the Back/Forward/Home buttons in your Web browser.) To buy a song, scroll to the right and you'll see the price as well as a button. If you have 1-Click ordering enabled, the button will say "BUY SONG"; clicking it purchases the song and downloads it to your computer. If you don't have 1-Click ordering enabled, the button will say "ADD TO CART." Once you've selected all the songs you want to purchase, you can view your cart and then purchase them all in one transaction.

Once you've purchased music from the iTunes Music store, a new playlist is created called Purchased Music. Although all of your purchased music is automatically added to your main Library, this playlist contains *just* your purchased music. It provides a convenient way to see what you've bought, which can be very useful if you want to back up those files (see below).

Music purchased from the iTunes Music Store has two restrictions. First, you can only burn an audio CD from a playlist containing purchased music ten times without altering the playlist somehow. This is Apple's way of preventing people from mass-producing audio CDs from purchased music.

Second, although you can transfer purchased music files to any number of iPods that connect to your Mac, you can only listen to purchased music on *three* computers, including the one used to purchase the song. When a user of another computer attempts to play any purchased song—via iTunes Sharing (discussed below) or by copying the song to the computer and then adding it to a user's iTunes Library—he or she will be required to provide the Apple ID and password of the person who purchased the song. This has two consequences: First, it means you need to trust the person who wants to play the song enough to give him or her your Apple ID and password (which theoretically allows that person to access your Apple Store account as well as other confidential information). Second, it means that Apple can enforce the three-computer policy. When a user provides your ID and password, his or her computer will access the iTunes Music Store over the Internet. If you haven't already reached the three-computer limit, that person's computer will then be "authorized" to play your purchased music. If three computers are already authorized, that user will be prevented from playing any such songs.

There is one other consequence of this authorization process. Apple authorizes *computers*, not users, and that authorization remains in place for each computer until you manually *deauthorize* it. Thus, if you sell your Mac, or one of the other two authorized computers is sold (or otherwise changes hands), you need to make sure that you deauthorize those computers as well. You can do this by opening iTunes on the computer, and from iTunes' Advanced menu choose Deauthorize Computer. If you don't do this, that computer will continue to be authorized, and you won't be able to authorize another computer to take its place.

iTunes Music Store: tips and fixes

The following represent a number of iTunes Music Store tips and fixes for getting the most out of the store and solving some of the most common problems that can occur.

Backing up purchased songs. Even if you don't back up your entire iTunes music library, you may want to back up songs you've purchased through the iTunes Music Store, since Apple does not allow you to re-download songs (if you lose a song, Apple asserts that you must buy it again). Assuming your Mac has a CD-RW drive or SuperDrive, the easiest way to back up these songs is to burn a data CD or DVD. To do so, follow these steps:

1. Open iTunes, and from the iTunes menu choose iTunes Preferences.
2. Click the Burning button in the Preferences toolbar.
3. Next to Disc Format, select Data CD, then click OK. Note: Files purchased from the iTunes Music Store cannot be burned to MP3 CD format.
4. If you still have the Purchased Music playlist that was created automatically the first time you purchased music, select it. If not, create a new playlist, include all of your purchased songs in it, and then select it.

   Make sure all of the songs in the selected playlist are checked.
5. Click the Burn Disc button in the upper-right corner of the iTunes window.
6. Insert a blank disc (CD-R, CD-RW, DVD-R, or DVD-RW), then click the Burn Disc button again.

Can't purchase or play songs. If you find you're unable to purchase music from the iTunes Music Store or play previously purchased music, it might be because the Shared user folder (/Users/Shared) is missing. (iTunes uses this folder to keep track of certain data on purchased music.) If this is the case, you can re-create the folder by following these steps (which require administrative access):

1. In the Finder, navigate to /Users; assuming the Shared folder does not exist, proceed to the next step.
2. From the File menu, choose New Folder.

3. Name the new folder Shared.

4. Select the new folder, and from the File menu choose Get Info.

5. Click the disclosure triangle next to Ownership & Permissions to reveal that section.

6. If the padlock icon is locked, click it to unlock it.

7. Using the pop-up menus, change the access for Owner, Group, and Others to Read & Write.

8. Close the Info window.

The next time you launch iTunes, you should be able to purchase music and play purchased music.

Can't play purchased songs. If you find yourself unable to play previously purchased music, and iTunes doesn't even prompt you to enter an Apple ID and password, the problem could be that the permissions on your hard drive are set incorrectly. To fix this, quit iTunes, open Disk Utility, and from its First Aid tab select Repair Disk Permissions.

Can't connect to Music Store or play purchased songs. If attempting to connect to the Music Store or play music purchased from the Music Store results in a -9800, -9814, or -9815 error, the cause is most likely that the date and time on your Mac are set incorrectly. Quit iTunes and then set the correct date and time in the Date & Time pane of System Preferences.

Errors downloading songs. If you purchase songs from the iTunes Music Store but experience errors when iTunes attempts to download them (such as error -35, error -5000, or a more generic one like the following: "There was an error in the Music Store"), your iTunes Music folder is probably missing (or its alias is broken, if you've moved it), or the permissions on the iTunes Music folder are incorrect.

The first thing to do is verify that the iTunes Music folder exists at ~/Music/ iTunes Music. If it does not (and you haven't moved it elsewhere, meaning it doesn't exist on your Mac), you must create it. To do so, follow these steps:

1. Launch iTunes, and from the iTunes menu choose iTunes Preferences.

2. In the Preferences toolbar, click the Advanced button.

3. In the "iTunes Music folder location" section, click the Change button.

4. Navigate to the location you want to use for your iTunes Music folder. (The default location is inside ~/Music, and unless you have reason to place it elsewhere, this is the location I recommend.)

5. Click the New Folder button to create a new folder. Name the folder iTunes Music, then click the Create button.

6. After creating the new folder, select it in the dialog and click the Choose button. The "iTunes Music folder location" box should now show your new folder.

7. Click OK in iTunes Preferences, and you'll see the following message: "Changing the location of the iTunes Music Folder requires updating the location of each of the songs in your music library. This update will not move or delete any of your song files." Click OK.

8. From iTunes Advanced menu, choose Consolidate Library, and the following message will appear: "Consolidating your library will copy all of your music into the iTunes Music folder. This cannot be undone." Make sure the hard drive hosting your iTunes Music folder has enough room to hold all of your MP3s, then click the Consolidate button.

Figure 11.8

iTunes' Advanced menu.

If the iTunes Music folder exists elsewhere, but you have not placed an alias to it in ~/Music, do so. If you previously created an alias to your iTunes Music folder in ~/Music, verify that the alias works properly; if it doesn't, replace it with a valid alias.

If you have a valid iTunes Music folder, and you still experience these errors, you should verify that permissions are set correctly for that folder. To do so, follow these steps (your account must have administrative access):

1. Select your iTunes Music folder in the Finder, and from the File menu select Get Info.

2. Click the disclosure triangle next to Ownership & Permissions to reveal that section.

3. If the padlock icon is locked, click it to unlock it.

4. Using the pop-up menus, change Owner Access to Read & Write, Group Access to Read Only, and Others to Read Only.

5. Click the "Apply to enclosed items" button.

6. Close the Info window.

Can't burn Music Store songs to CD. If you try to burn a playlist to a CD in MP3 format, and that playlist only has songs you purchased from the iTunes Music Store, you'll get the following message: "None of the items in this playlist can be burned to disc." Likewise, if the chosen playlist includes both purchased songs and your own songs, the CD will be burned, but iTunes Music Store songs will be "grayed out" and will not be copied to the CD.

The reason for this is that the songs you purchase from the iTunes Music Store are in AAC format, not MP3 format. AAC files can be converted to standard Audio CD format but not to MP3 format.

There is a work-around for this—but you must first burn your iTunes Music Store songs to CD in Audio CD format. Once you've done this, you can rip them *back* into iTunes using iTunes' MP3 encoder (at which point they'll be in MP3 format and can be burned to MP3 CDs). Note, however, that this procedure significantly reduces the sound quality of your song files. Because AAC files are already compressed, when you convert them to Audio CD and then to MP3, you're adding another level of compression. The result is an audio file that's been compressed twice.

Music Store previews are choppy. If song previews from the iTunes Music Store are choppy or distorted, the problem could be your Internet connection. Apple recommends a connection speed of at least 128 Kbps (more than twice that of a dial-up modem) for best results. However, you can improve performance over slow connections by opening iTunes Preferences, clicking the Store item in the toolbar, and then enabling the "Load complete preview before playing" option. This downloads the entire preview before playing it, instead of playing it as it downloads (streaming).

Hiding the Music Store. Although it's not really a troubleshooting issue, many users want to hide the iTunes Music Store—for example, to prevent their children from accessing it, to leave more room for their own playlists, or even to remove the temptation to buy more music! To do so, open iTunes Preferences, click the Store item in the toolbar, and simply uncheck the Show iTunes Music Store option.

Blocking the Music Store. If you want to block all access to the iTunes Music Store, you must block traffic to and from phobos.apple.com. Many Internet routers will allow you to "blacklist" particular hosts for your entire network. You can also add a rule to Mac OS X's built-in firewall using Terminal or a utility like Brian R. Hill's BrickHouse that blocks traffic to and from this host; this would prevent any user of your Mac from accessing the Music Store.

SEE: • Chapter 8 for more on firewalls.

Proxy Servers and the iTunes Music Store. If your network requires you to use a proxy, note that not all proxy servers work with iTunes. According to Apple, Web (HTTP) and Secure Web (HTTPS) proxy servers work fine. However, SOCKS proxy servers and proxy servers that require authentication (a name and password) will not work. In addition, the "Bypass proxy settings for these Hosts & Domains" setting in the Proxies screen of Network System Preferences in Mac OS X does not work with the iTunes Music Store.

iTunes Sharing

New to iTunes 4, iTunes Sharing lets you share your music library with other local iTunes users (that is, other iTunes users connected to your local network). Specifically, when you have iTunes Sharing enabled, anyone located on the same *subnet* of your network can play music from your Library and access (but not modify) your playlists.

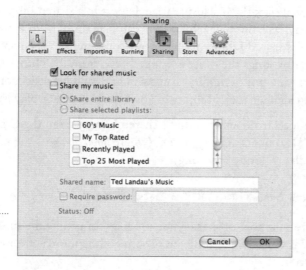

Figure 11.9

iTunes' Preferences window, with Sharing selected.

Allowing your music to be shared. To enable iTunes Sharing, follow these steps:

1. Open iTunes Preferences and from the Toolbar click the Sharing button.

2. Check the box next to "Share my music."

3. Select either the "Share entire library" option (making your entire Library and all playlists available to other local users) or the "Share selected playlists" option (making only those playlists you select accessible).

4. Enter a name for your shared music in the "Shared name" field. This is how the shared music will be displayed in other users' Source lists.

5. If you want to require a password for users to access your iTunes music over the network, check the "Require password" box and enter a password.

A maximum of five other users can access your iTunes Library simultaneously; if a sixth user attempts to connect, he or she will be prevented from doing so. However, to prevent people from monopolizing your connections, if five users are connected and one of them has not played a song from your Library within 30 minutes, that user will be automatically disconnected when another user tries to connect.

Accessing music shared by others. To connect to other users' shared Libraries, follow these steps:

1. Open iTunes' Preferences, and from the toolbar click the Sharing button.
2. Check the box next to "Look for shared music."

When your Mac is connected to the local network and detects shared iTunes Libraries, those libraries will show up in the Source list (as seen in **Figure 11.2**). If you click the disclosure triangle next to a shared Library, you'll see all shared playlists from that Library. You can play songs from any shared playlist or from the shared Library itself; if your computer has been authorized, you can even play songs the other user purchased from the iTunes Music Store. However, you cannot modify shared Libraries and playlists, nor can you copy files from another user's Library to your own Library or playlists.

To disconnect from another user's shared Library, from the Controls menu choose "Disconnect {*library name*}" (where *library name* is the name of the shared Library you're accessing).

iTunes Sharing: tips and fixes

Below are a number of sharing tips and fixes for getting the most out of iTunes Sharing, as well as for getting out of some of the more common trouble you may encounter.

Can no longer share your music library over the Internet. If you update your iTunes to version 4.0.1 or later, you will find that you can no longer share your iTunes music over the Internet. Apple removed this ability in version 4.0.1; you can only share your music with other users on a local network (more specifically, to users on the same subnet of a local network). To share music over the Internet, both users must be using iTunes 4.0.

"Shared music library not compatible" error. If you try to access an iTunes Library being shared by another iTunes 4 user and get an error stating, "The shared music library {*library name*} is not compatible with this version of iTunes," the problem is that you and the person sharing the library are using different versions of iTunes 4 (for example, 4.0 and 4.0.1). The solution is to update the earlier version to match the newer version.

Music Sharing not working due to firewall. If you're using iTunes behind a firewall and attempt to share your music, other computers will be able to see your iTunes Sharing name but won't be able to access your shared playlists. The iTunes application gets stuck at the message "Loading *iTunes sharing name*." This is because iTunes Music Sharing uses a port (3689) that most firewalls close by default. If you have Mac OS X's Firewall enabled in the Sharing System Preferences pane, the solution is to go to the Firewall screen and either turn off the Firewall or enable the iTunes Music Sharing rule.

SEE: • "Firewall" in "Setting Up System Preferences: Sharing," in Chapter 8, for details on how to enable the iTunes Music Sharing rule.

iTunes and other iLife applications

The iTunes Library doesn't appear in other iLife applications.
You may find that your iTunes Library does not appear in iDVD, iMovie, or iPhoto. Assuming you've installed current versions of all four applications, make sure you've opened iTunes at least once. If your iTunes music is still not available in the other apps, you may need to re-create iTunes' Music Library file. To do so, follow these steps:

1. Quit iPhoto, iMovie, iDVD, and iTunes.
2. In the Finder, navigate to your iTunes Music Library folder (located by default at ~/Music, though you may have relocated it manually).
3. Delete the file iTunes Music Library.xml (or move it to the Desktop).
4. Open iTunes.
5. Create a new playlist(s).
6. Quit iTunes.

The next time you open iPhoto, iMovie, or iDVD, your iTunes music should be available.

Can't see all iTunes songs in iMovie. Many iMovie 3 users have reported that they can only access a portion of their iTunes music from within iMovie. A solution that seems to work for most people is to quit both iTunes and iMovie, and then delete the iTunes preferences file (~/Library/Preferences/com.apple .iTunes.plist). The next time you launch iTunes, you'll need to reset some of your preferences, but all of your music and playlists will be intact. Even better, you should now be able to access all of your iTunes music from within iMovie.

Troubleshooting the iPod

If you've watched TV, read a magazine, or even just walked down the street in the past couple years, you're familiar with the svelte white-and-chrome iPod (or its newer multicolored sibling, the iPod mini), Apple's hard-drive-based portable music players. Depending on the size of your iPod—4, 5, 10, 15, 20, 30, or even 40 MB—and the encoding method you use for your audio files, you can store days or even weeks of continuous audio. (The 40 GB model, for example, can store as many as 10,000 songs at a 128k bit rate—enough to play 24 hours a day for almost a month!)

What makes the iPod really stand out, though, is its integration with iTunes and the Mac OS. You simply connect it to your Mac—on older models, via a standard FireWire cable; on newer models, via a special "dock" or the dock cable—and iTunes launches; your music (including custom playlists) is transferred (in a matter of seconds or minutes); and the battery charges. Accessing your music on the iPod is as simple as using the circular scroll ring (either a touchpad or a mechanical wheel, depending on the model) to navigate to a menu item, and then pressing the Enter button in the middle of the ring to select that item. Pressing the menu button moves you back to the previous menu. It's as simple as that—and it's one of the reasons why the iPod is the most popular hard-drive-based player on the market.

However, the iPod can do a lot more than simply play music. You can customize what music and which playlists are stored on it. In addition, it can store your calendar, contacts, and notes and other text information. You can even use it as an alarm clock. In addition, you can use it as an ordinary external FireWire drive, including (with some difficulty) getting it to work as a bootable drive!

Adding music to an iPod

With iTunes open when an iPod is attached, the iPod appears in the Source list. If this is the first time your iPod is attached to your Mac, all of your iTunes' music and playlists will be copied to the iPod.

By selecting iPod from the Source list and clicking the iPod Eject button in the lower right (or choosing Eject {*iPodName*} from the Controls menu), the iPod disconnects from iTunes, and you can physically disconnect it from your computer. Each time you reconnect your iPod, iTunes compares its Library and playlists, and updates the iPod's music files to reflect any additions, deletions, or changes.

Note: If the iPod does not appear in iTunes after connecting it to your Mac, you may need to restore or reset the iPod, as covered later in this chapter.

iPod Preferences. You can modify the default automatic updating as well as other iPod-related settings via the iPod Preferences window in iTunes. The window is accessible when an iPod is connected and the iPod is selected in the Source list. To open it, click the iPod button in the lower right.

- The default selection at the top of the iPod Preferences window is "Automatically update all songs and playlists." This results in the behavior I just described.

- Alternatively, you can choose "Automatically update selected playlists only," and then check the boxes next to the playlists you want copied to the iPod. Only those playlists, and the audio files contained in them, will be copied.

- Finally, you can choose "Manually manage songs and playlists." If this option is chosen, you simply drag songs from your iTunes Library to the iPod icon in the Source list. If you drag a playlist to the iPod, that playlist and its songs will be copied.

Note that by updating automatically, your iPod will only contain songs that are currently in your iTunes Library. If you want to keep *different* songs on the iPod—songs that aren't in your iTunes Library—you'll need to use the "Manually manage songs and playlists" option.

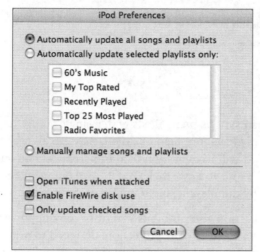

Figure 11.10

The iTunes' iPod Preferences window lets you customize your iPod syncing.

In the lower part of the iPod Preferences window, there are three check boxes:

- If you uncheck the "Open iTunes when attached" box, you will need to manually launch iTunes in order to update your iPod. This can be useful if you don't change your iTunes Library often but frequently connect your iPod to your Mac, such as to recharge the iPod's battery.

- The "Enable FireWire disk use" option allows you to use your iPod as a FireWire hard drive (see below).

- The "Only update checked songs" option will only copy songs to your iPod that are checked in the iTunes Library or in individual playlists, regardless of your update settings. In other words, iTunes will use the "all songs and playlists/selected playlists/manually" update setting but will only copy songs in your Library (or in selected playlists) that are checked.

iPod settings. The iPod itself has Preferences settings that you access via the Settings menu on the iPod. These include, for example, the Shuffle, Repeat, Sound Check, and Sleep Timer settings. Because these are not Mac OS X–specific features, I won't be covering them in this book. For more help with these features, search Apple's Knowledge Base documents at http://docs.info.apple.com.

Multiple iPods, multiple Macs. You can sync an iPod with just one particular computer. The iPod is said to be *linked* to that Mac. If you connect it to another computer, when iTunes is launched, a dialog will appear asking you if you want to associate the iPod with that computer, wiping out the iPod's music content and replacing it with the iTunes Library of the new computer!

If you say OK here by mistake, you will erase all the music on your iPod, so be careful! This feature also means there's no way to copy songs from different iTunes Libraries (from different Macs) to the same iPod.

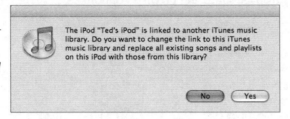

However, you can sync as many iPods with a single computer as you like. If you or your family has more than one iPod, they can all use the same iTunes Library. Each iPod will have its own iPod Preferences. The only caveat is that you need to make sure you give each iPod its own unique name. You can change an iPod's name by double-clicking it in iTunes' Source list.

The iTunes application also prohibits you from copying music from an iPod to a Mac. This is a form of copy protection, designed to prevent an iPod owner from using the iPod to transfer music to a friend's computer. While I am by no means suggesting that you break any copy-protection laws, it must be noted that this is a very weak form of copy protection. For starters, you could obviously transfer music to a friend via an external hard drive, a burned CD, or any other portable media. Second, you can even use your iPod to transfer music files; there are two ways to do this:

- You can access and copy the invisible music files on your iPod. Once you've done this, you can install them in the iTunes Library just as you would any other music you added to your hard drive.

  SEE: • "Take Note: Where Is My Music?" below.

- You can use a third-party utility that permits iPod-to-Mac copying. My preferred choice here is a utility called iPod Access (from Findley Designs). Others include Sci-Fi Hi-Fi's PodWorks and KennettNet's PodUtil. These automate and simplify the procedure, allowing you to restore both songs *and* playlists from your iPod to iTunes.

Insufficient space on an iPod. If you have too much music in your iTunes Library to fit on your iPod, and you try to update your iPod using the "Automatically update all (or selected) songs and playlists" options, you'll get an error that your iPod isn't big enough. In this case, iTunes will copy as much music as will fit, but you have no control over which particular music gets copied. If you want to decide which music to copy to the iPod, you have several options:

- You can use the "Manually manage songs and playlists" option. With this option activated, you simply drag songs and playlists until the iPod is full. Note: The bottom of the song list for the iPod shows how much free space you have.

- You can delete songs from the iPod by selecting them in the song list or selecting playlists from the iPod Playlist menu in the Source list, and pressing the Delete key.

- You can use the "Automatically update selected playlists only" option, and then choose as many playlists as will fit on your iPod. You can also take advantage of Smart Playlists—limiting Smart Playlists by size so that they only contain a specific number of songs, or a limited number of megabytes of music. Note: In iTunes 4.2 or later, if your iPod does not have enough space to hold your entire Library, iTunes will automatically create a playlist that will fit on your iPod. See this Apple Knowledge Base article for more details: http://docs.info.apple.com/article.html?artnum=93656.

Music purchased from iTunes Music Store won't play on iPod. If you have an older iPod, and songs purchased from the iTunes Music Store and transferred to your iPod will not play, the problem is most likely an out-of-date version of the iPod software. iTunes Music Store tracks are encoded in AAC format, which is only supported by iPod Software 1.3 and later.

To fix this, install the latest version of the iPod software, as described in "Updating and restoring the iPod software," later in this chapter.

Artist names that begin with *The* appear alphabetized under *T*. If you've updated your iPod to iPod Software 2.0 or later, from a 1.x version, artists whose names begin with *The*—The Beatles, The Doors, The Cure, and so on—may appear under the letter *T* in the artist list. In iTunes, in contrast, the same artists are "correctly" alphabetized by the second word in their name (ignoring the "The").

To fix this, you need to reset your iPod, as described in "Reset the iPod" later in this chapter, to force it to use the iTunes method of alphabetizing.

TAKE NOTE ▶ Where Is My Music?

If you put your iPod into FireWire disk mode and open it in the Finder, you may find yourself asking, "Where is all my music?" This is because at first glance, it doesn't appear to be on the iPod. Your music is actually stored in a number of *invisible* folders on the iPod. Apple did this to prevent music piracy—the theory is that if you can't find the music on your iPod, you won't be able to connect it to a friend's computer and give him or her copies of it.

However, there are some legitimate reasons for accessing the music stored on your iPod from the Finder. For example, what if your Mac's hard drive crashes and you lose all of your iTunes music? Or what if you're desperate for some free hard-drive space, so you delete a few music files? You would think you could later simply restore that music from your iPod to your hard drive. However, because the iPod doesn't normally allow you to copy music *to* your Mac, to do so you need to access these hidden folders.

continues on next page

TAKE NOTE ▶ **Where Is My Music?** *continued*

The iPod stores your music in an invisible folder called Music, inside another invisible folder called iPod_Control. Inside the Music folder are *more* invisible folders that contain individual song files. Unlike songs stored on your hard drive, which (if you've selected "Keep iTunes Music folder organized" in iTunes' Preferences) are neatly stored in hierarchical folders in the format Artist/ Album/Song, music on your iPod is stored randomly in a series of folders called F00, F01, F02, and so on. This, again, is to make it difficult to find and copy songs from your iPod to a computer.

So how do you get music files from your iPod to your computer? You can do so in any of the following ways:

- You can use a utility, such as Marcel Bresnik's TinkerTool, that makes invisible files visible in the Finder.

  SEE: • "Invisible Files: Making Invisible Files Visible (and Vice Versa)," in Chapter 6, for details.

- You can use Terminal to see your music folders. For example, type cd /Volumes/iPodname/ iPod_Control/Music/F00 and then press Return. Now type ls and press Return again. This will list all the music files in the F00 folder. You can now use the cp (*copy*) command to copy them to your hard drive.

  SEE: • Chapter 10 for more on using Terminal and Unix commands.

- You can use a third-party utility, such as iPod Access, as described in the main text.

  SEE: • "Multiple iPods, multiple Macs," earlier in this chapter.

Using calendar, contacts, and notes on an iPod

In addition to storing music, you can use your iPod as a limited PDA: You can store calendars, contact info, and even text notes on it—and view this info on the iPod's screen. You won't be able to edit or add information—the iPod has no way to easily input text—but for those times when you need a phone number or address, need to check your schedule, or want to bring some text information along with you, the iPod is more than adequate and saves you from having to carry an additional gadget.

Calendars and contacts. You can store calendar and contact information on your iPod in one of two ways:

- When the iPod is mounted as a FireWire drive, you can drag iCal (ICS) files to the Calendars folder at the root level of the iPod, and drag vCard files to the Contacts folder. Most contact and calendar applications let you export calendars in ICS format and contacts in vCard format. These calendars and contacts will then be accessible from the Contacts and Calendars items, respectively, in the iPod's main menu.

- If you use iCal and Address Book, the easier way is to use iSync, as described later in this chapter. Using iSync doesn't require FireWire Disk use, and, even better, it means that iSync will automatically sync your iPod to contain the latest contact and calendar info. These calendars and contacts will again be accessible from the Contacts and Calendars items, respectively, in the iPod's main menu.

iPod Note Reader. With iPod 2.x software, you can store text notes on your iPod. To do so, first enable FireWire disk use in iPod Preferences in iTunes. Then copy your text notes to the Notes folder at the root level of the iPod. The notes will now be visible via the Notes item in the iPod's main menu. For more information on the iPod's Note Reader, check out the following PDF file: http://developer.apple.com/hardware/ipod/ipodnotereader.pdf.

Using an iPod as a FireWire drive

Figure 11.12

The Eject button for an iPod in a sidebar.

In addition to being an impressive music player and limited PDA, the iPod can also serve as a FireWire hard drive. To have it do so, check the "Enable FireWire disk use" option in the iPod Preferences window, as described in the previous section.

Your iPod will now appear on the Desktop as a mounted volume. You can open it just like any other hard drive, copy files to and from it, and even run applications from it. This makes the iPod an excellent means of transferring documents and other data.

When you use your iPod as a FireWire drive, it is still updated by iTunes when you connect it (unless you have the "Manually manage songs and playlists" option enabled). However, keep in mind that when you store other data on your iPod, this takes away from the amount of space available for storing music. In addition, it means you must manually eject the iPod before disconnecting it—either by clicking the iPod Eject button in iTunes or by ejecting it from the Finder. Without the "Enable FireWire disk use" option enabled, the iPod automatically unmounts when you quit iTunes.

Disconnect advice. When your iPod is connected to the Mac and mounted, the "Do not Disconnect" screen appears on the iPod. Follow its advice. To disconnect the iPod, do one of the following:

- Drag the iPod's icon on the Mac to the Trash.
- Click the iPod's icon on the Desktop and from the Finder's File menu choose Eject, or click the Eject button next to the iPod icon in the sidebar of a Finder window.
- Launch iTunes and click the button to eject the iPod at the bottom of the window.

The iPod's screen should now change to OK to Disconnect. Now you can disconnect.

If you fail to follow this procedure, an error message will appear on the Mac, warning you that the "disk has stopped responding" or that the "storage device that you just removed was not properly put away." The message will further warn that data on the device may have been damaged. Actually, it's unlikely that any damage has occurred. Regardless, your next step should be to reconnect the iPod and then disconnect it properly. If all seems well with the iPod at this point, it should be fine.

Note: If you unmount an iPod but do not disconnect it from the Mac, you should also be able to remount it by launching Disk Utility, selecting the iPod, and clicking the Mount button.

If you try to reconnect an iPod immediately after having one of these disconnect problems, it may appear to connect properly but not show up in the Finder. In such cases, relaunching the Finder typically fixes the problem.

Once disconnected from the Mac, the iPod will automatically shut itself off after 2 minutes of inactivity. To immediately shut the iPod off, prior to its sleep time, hold down the Play/Pause button for a few seconds.

The iPod and Mac sleep. When your iPod is connected to your Mac as a FireWire drive, I advise either not letting your Mac go to sleep or disconnecting the iPod before sleep begins. The main reason for this is that I've found that the iPod may not automatically remount, or may otherwise exhibit odd symptoms, after the Mac wakes from sleep. Some reports indicate that the iPod's battery may discharge if the iPod remains connected to a sleeping Mac. In some cases, your Mac may freeze if it goes to sleep while an iPod is connected, requiring a restart to get the Mac working again.

iPod as a bootable drive. Apple concedes that you can install Mac OS X on an iPod and use it as a bootable drive—a potentially great troubleshooting feature since it provides you with a portable emergency startup disk (for booting a Mac that will not otherwise start up from its internal drive) without needing to purchase an additional device. However, Apple also lists this feature as *unsupported*—and most recently directly warns that "you shouldn't use the iPod as a startup disk." In addition to meaning that Apple will not assist you if you have trouble with this option, it also means (at least with the current software) that you can anticipate having trouble. For starters, the iPod mini will currently not work as a bootable drive, even if you succeed in installing system software on it. In addition, for the standard size iPod, expect one or both of the following problems:

- When starting up from a Mac OS X Install CD, the iPod is not listed as a device on which you can install Mac OS X.

  If this happens, you can work around the failure by bypassing the Installer and instead installing a backup copy of a bootable volume to the iPod via a utility such as Dantz Retrospect or Mike Bombich's Carbon Copy Cloner (as described in Chapter 3). This is not as convenient as using the Installer, but it works.

Note: I did not have this symptom with Mac OS X 10.1; however, I started seeing it in 10.2. I had success once again when trying to install Mac OS X 10.3 on my iPod.

- Assuming you succeeded in getting Mac OS X to install on your iPod, you may have a problem when later trying to install an updated version of the iPod software. In particular, the iPod update may fail, typically with an error message appearing. Exactly what the error message says may vary depending on the version of the OS you're running; but the net result is that the update will not install.

The main solution here is to select the Restore rather than the Update option from the Updater utility (as described in the next section). This erases all of the data on the iPod, including system software, but it succeeds where the Update failed. You can now reinstall Mac OS X (assuming you can get the Installer to work) and read your music files from your iTunes Library.

If you would prefer not to Restore, you can try simply removing all traces of Mac OS X (including invisible Unix files) from the iPod. However, I have not found this to work reliably; the Update may still fail. Restoring is a safer bet.

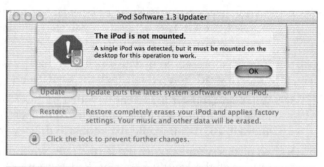

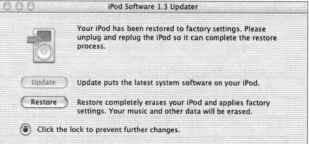

Figure 11.13

The iPod Software Updater application: (top) a message that may appear after trying to update an iPod that has system software installed on it; (bottom) the message that appears after successfully restoring an iPod.

Updating and restoring the iPod software

Apple periodically releases updates to the iPod software. This is completely separate from the music files placed on your iPod via iTunes. You will typically be notified of these updates when you run the Software Update application. Otherwise, you can always download the latest version of the updater from Apple's Web site at www.apple.com/iPod. When you download and install the update package, an application called iPod Software Updater is installed in your /Applications/Utilities folder and automatically launched. You have two options here: Update and Restore.

Updating the iPod. To update your iPod's software, follow these steps:

1. With the iPod connected to your Mac, launch the iPod Software Updater (if it's not already automatically launched). Your iPod should be listed in the iPod Updater window.

2. Click Update. If the Update button is dimmed, click the padlock icon to authenticate; provide your administrator's name and password when prompted.

3a. If you're updating iPod 2.0 or later, the update procedure is complete. Quit the Updater application.

3b. If you're using an iPod software version prior to 2.0, disconnect the FireWire cable from your iPod and then reconnect it. A progress dialog will appear on the iPod's screen; once it finishes, the iPod will be updated.

Note the following issues regarding updating an iPod:

- If you already have the same or a newer version of the iPod software installed, the Updater application will alert you and refuse to update. The Update button will be dimmed even if the padlock icon is unlocked.

- If you choose not to update when the Updater is launched, quit the application instead. You can relaunch the Updater and update at any future time.

- When an Updater is present in your Utilities folder, but you have not yet installed the update, iTunes will detect the Updater when you launch iTunes and will ask if you would like to install the new version of the software.

- As of this writing, older iPods (the ones without a dock connector) cannot install the latest versions of iPod software (2.x). Instead, they must use a 1.x version of the software. These 1.x versions do not include On-the-Go playlists (the ability to create a playlist directly on an iPod) or several other new features available in the 2.x versions.

Restoring the iPod. If the update procedure does not work, you may need to restore your iPod. Be aware that restoring your iPod erases the hard drive completely and then restores it to its original factory configuration, using the version of the software included with the Updater application. Thus, you will want to make sure that any files on your iPod are backed up before you attempt a restore.

To restore your iPod's software, follow these steps:

1. Launch the iPod Software Updater application.

2. Click Restore. If the Restore button is dimmed, click the padlock icon to authenticate; provide your administrator's name and password when prompted.

3. If you're using an iPod software version prior to 2.0, disconnect the FireWire cable from your iPod and then reconnect it. A progress dialog

will appear on the iPod's screen; once it finishes, the iPod will be restored. Otherwise, just continue to step 4.

4. The iTunes Setup Assistant will appear. Provide a name for your iPod and then select your iPod updating preference.

5. Allow iTunes to update your iPod's contents, then quit iTunes.

6. Disconnect the iPod from your computer and quit the iPod Software Updater.

7. Your iPod will show its setup screen; select a language using the scroll wheel and click the Select button.

iPod: problems starting up

The iPod is a rugged, reliable device. Still, you may occasionally hit a snag in which the iPod does not start up as expected. When this happens, you'll get an error message of some sort; the iPod may be unresponsive to its buttons and scroll wheel; or it may appear completely dead. In some cases, you may not even be able to get it to mount or be recognized when connected to a Mac. In such cases, try the following:

Turn the Hold switch on and off. If you have one of the newer iPods with the touch-sensitive controls, under certain circumstances, waking the iPod from sleep results in the controls' being unresponsive. Specifically, if the iPod is asleep with the Hold switch in the On position, and you wake it by turning the Hold switch off while touching one of the other controls, the iPod's touch-sensitive controls may not respond. The reason for this is that the iPod recalibrates its touch-sensitive controls whenever you turn the Hold switch off; if you're touching any of the controls when this recalibration occurs, the iPod doesn't recalibrate properly.

To fix the problem, turn the Hold switch on and then off again.

Reset the iPod. If your iPod won't respond to any buttons or the scroll wheel, the first thing to do is to make sure the battery isn't simply dead. Plug it into your computer or the power adapter, and see if it responds.

If it doesn't respond, you probably need to reset the iPod. To do so, follow these steps:

1. Connect the iPod to the iPod power adapter or your computer via the FireWire/dock cable or the iPod dock.

2. Slide the Hold switch to the On position (the switch shows a bright orange color) and switch it back to Off.

3. Press and hold the Play/Pause button and the Menu button simultaneously until the Apple logo appears.

All of your data (music, playlists, contacts, and so on) is saved. A few preferences set using the iPod's Settings menu, however, may be lost.

Note: The procedure for resetting an iPod mini is a bit different. See the following Apple Knowledge Base article for details: http://docs.info.apple.com/ article.html?artnum= 61705.

Update and/or restore the iPod. If even the reset procedure described above doesn't bring your iPod back to life, you may need to update or (more likely) restore your iPod's operating software.

SEE: • "Updating and restoring the iPod software," earlier in this chapter, for details on how to update and restore.

Place iPod in Disk Mode. If the Apple logo appears when you turn on the iPod and then refuses to go away, you need to update or restore the iPod. However, with an Apple logo freeze, it's unlikely that the iPod will mount or otherwise respond when you connect it to a Mac (especially if you haven't enabled FireWire disk use in iTunes' iPod Preferences). To work around this problem, you need to "manually" put your iPod in FireWire disk Mode. To do so, follow these steps:

1. Slide the Hold switch to the On position (the switch shows a bright-orange color) and then switch it back to Off.

2. Hold down the Play/Pause and Menu buttons simultaneously until the Apple logo appears.

3. As soon as you see the Apple logo, press and hold the Previous/Rewind and Next/Forward buttons simultaneously until either a FireWire logo or the "OK to disconnect" logo appears.

   Repeat steps 1 through 3 if they did not succeed the first time.

4. Connect the iPod to your computer via the FireWire/dock cable or the iPod dock.

5. At this point, a message may appear stating that the volume could not be mounted and asking if you want to initialize it. Clicking OK will erase all of the data on your iPod—but your data is probably hosed at this point anyway. So click OK and then choose the Mac OS Extended /HFS Plus format.

6. The iPod should appear in iTunes and/or mounted in the Finder.

7. Update or restore your iPod, as appropriate. If you erased the iPod's data, only a Restore will work. You may also need to reset the iPod to get it working normally again. All of these procedures are described earlier in the chapter.

If your iPod is still not up and running, it's time to consider getting it repaired. You can take it to an Apple Store or visit Apple's online repair page at http:// depot.info.apple.com/ipod.

Note: The procedure for using Disk Mode on an iPod mini is a bit different. See the following Apple Knowledge Base article for details: http:// docs.info.apple.com/article.html?artnum=93651.

"Disk scan" icon appears when iPod is turned on. If, when you turn on your iPod, a screen with a disk and a magnifying glass appears, this means that the iPod has found a problem with its hard drive and is in the process of examining and, if possible, repairing it. Once the procedure is complete (which can take as long as 20 minutes, so be patient), one of the following icons will appear:

- **Disc with check mark.** No problems were found.

- **Disc with right arrow.** Serious problems were found but repaired. You should restore your iPod using the procedure described above under "Updating and restoring the iPod software."

- **Disc with alert symbol (exclamation point).** Diagnostics failed and will be repeated the next time you turn the iPod on.

- **Disc with "x" symbol.** Diagnostics were canceled by the user and will be repeated the next time you turn on the iPod. You can cancel diagnostics by holding down the Enter key for 3 seconds or longer.

- **iPod with alert symbol.** iPod is damaged and cannot be repaired. You most likely will need to get the iPod serviced by Apple.

Folder with alert symbol appears when iPod is turned on. If you see a folder with an alert symbol (exclamation point) when you turn on your iPod, this can indicate any of the following problems:

- **Near-dead battery.** To fix this, connect your iPod to the power adapter or to your computer to charge it.

- **iPod needs to be reset.** Your iPod may simply need to be reset. To do so, use the procedure described previously in "Reset the iPod."

- **Hard drive has been reformatted or erased.** If you erased or reformatted your iPod from the Finder, the iPod software may be missing and/or you may have chosen an incorrect hard-drive format. Reformat the iPod in the Finder as Mac OS X Extended (HFS Plus) format and restore the iPod using the procedure described previously in "Updating and Restoring the iPod Software."

- **Incorrect iPod software version.** You may have installed a version of the iPod software that is too old for your iPod. To remedy this, update your iPod's software using the procedure described previously in "Updating and restoring the iPod software."

- **Serious damage.** Your iPod may have a hardware failure or other serious damage that requires service.

Figure 11.14

Examples of iPod error screens: (left) Disk Scan Failed icon; (right) folder with exclamation point icon.

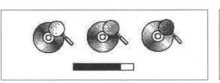

Troubleshooting iPhoto

iPhoto is the image spoke of Apple's digital hub. It allows you to organize, edit, and share your digital images, and is one of the most widely used and praised iApps. However, it's also one of the most widely criticized—primarily due to a few quirks as well as its potential (prior to iPhoto 4.x) for slow performance once you've acquired a large number of photos.

The first time you launch iPhoto, you'll see a "welcome" screen asking, "Do you want to use iPhoto when you connect your digital camera?" If you click Use iPhoto, iPhoto will launch whenever you connect your digital camera to your Mac. If you click Use Other, you can import photos from your camera using your camera's software or a digital-media reader, or by importing them manually (I talk about importing photos below). You can hold off on making a choice by clicking Decide Later.

Figure 11.15

iPhoto's initial setup screen.

The main iPhoto window has five distinct areas: the Library/Album list in the upper left portion; the main image-viewing pane; the information box just below the Library/Album list; the *control bar* items, which are listed horizontally below the information box and image-viewing pane; and the *action bar* along the bottom of the window. In many ways, iPhoto looks much like iTunes; it works similarly as well.

Library/Album list and main image-viewing window. The Library/Album list on the left side of the iPhoto window provides quick access to your Photo Library (the main library containing all of your images), as well as any albums you've created.

- **Photo Library.** Select Photo Library to see all of your photos in the viewing window to the right.

- **Last Import.** Select Last Import to view only those images you added to your Photo Library during the most recent import. Select any listed album, and the viewing pane shows just the images it contains. (For more about creating albums, see the discussion of Organize mode a bit later in the chapter.)

- **Trash.** The Trash item is the last item in the Library/Album list. It contains any images that you've deleted from your main Photo Library.

The only time a photo is moved to the iPhoto Trash is if you delete it from your main Photo Library; deleting an image from an album *does not* move it to the iPhoto Trash. This is because when an image is added to an album, iPhoto references that photo from your main Photo Library; deleting an image from an album simply deletes the reference. The photo itself remains in your Photo Library. This also means that to permanently delete an image from iPhoto, you need to delete it from the Photo Library.

The iPhoto Trash works independently of Mac OS X's Trash. To empty the iPhoto Trash, you must choose Empty Trash from iPhoto's File menu.

Figure 11.16

iPhoto's main window with Organize selected in the control bar.

Information box. Just below the Library/Album list is the information box, which displays information about whatever item is selected—an item from the Library/Album list or a photo in the viewing window. In the case of an album, it allows you to rename the album. In the case of an image, it lets you rename the photo as well as change the date. (If you change the name or date on a photo, that information is changed everywhere that photo occurs within iPhoto—that is, in the main Photo Library as well as in any albums.)

Control bar. The control bar provides a few important controls that let you work with albums and photos.

At the far left, the plus (+) button adds a new album to the Library/Album list. The Play button (the one with the side-facing triangle) starts a full-screen slide show using whichever album is selected above, including the main Photo Library.

Note: You can access settings for the slide show in Organize mode, discussed a bit later in the chapter.

The Information button (the one with the lowercase *i*) toggles the information area between three modes: Hidden, Information, and Information and Comments. When the Comments field is visible, you can add comments to any photo or album. The button to the right of the Information button is the Rotate button: Selecting an image (or multiple images) and then clicking this button rotates the image(s) 90 degrees. The default rotation direction, clockwise or counterclockwise, is configurable in iPhoto Preferences; holding down the Option key as you click the button temporarily switches the direction of the rotation.

The middle of the control bar is occupied by four buttons that allow you to switch between iPhoto's four *modes*: Import, Organize, Edit, and Book. I talk about each mode below.

The slider at the right end of the control bar designates the size of images in the viewing window. If the slider is all the way to the right (largest), you'll only be able to view an image at a time, and it will fill the viewing window. If the slider is all the way to the left, images will be quite tiny—you will be able to see many of them, but they may be too small to differentiate. You can choose any size in between to find one that offers you the best compromise between detail and number.

Action bar. The lower bar, which I call the *action bar*, changes depending on the mode selected on the control bar (Import, Organize, Edit, or Book), providing options specific to each view. I'll discuss these options when I discuss each mode.

TAKE NOTE ▶ The iPhoto Library

Like the iTunes Library, the Photo Library item in iPhoto represents your iPhoto image library. This library is a folder located in your Home directory at ~/Pictures/iPhoto Library. Unfortunately, unlike in iTunes, this folder is not organized in a way that will make immediate sense to most people. Photos are organized in folders by year; within each year folder are month folders, and within each month folder are day folders. Within each of *those* folders are loosely stored images, a folder called Thumbs that stores thumbnails for these images, and a folder called Data that iPhoto uses to store data for keeping track of image information and changes made to those images.

Original vs. cropped images. If you make any changes to a photo via Edit mode, an additional folder will be added to that day's folder, called Originals. iPhoto makes a copy of the original image and moves it into this folder before making changes to the image. This is how iPhoto allows you to revert to the original photo if you decide you aren't happy with your edits.

continues on next page

TAKE NOTE ▶ The iPhoto Library *continued*

Back in the main iPhoto Library folder, there's a file called AlbumData.xml and a folder called Albums. These two items contain all the information about albums that you create in iPhoto. Apple has a bit of information about this organizational structure at the following address: http://docs.info.apple.com/article.html?artnum=61262.

Backing up your iPhoto Library. If you want to back up your iPhoto Library, you can periodically copy it to another hard drive or burn it to CD or DVD. You can also use a dedicated backup utility to back it up regularly.

Moving your iPhoto Library to a different volume. If you decide you want your iPhoto Library on a volume other than the startup disk (perhaps because your startup disk is getting low on space, or you want to put your iPhoto Library on an external FireWire drive so that you can take it with you), you can follow these steps to do so:

1. Navigate to your Pictures folder in the Finder (~/Pictures).
2. Drag the iPhoto Library folder to the destination volume, and wait for the copy to complete.
3. Rename the iPhoto Library on your startup disk (the original library) to something like Original iPhoto Library.
4. Launch iPhoto; you'll see an error message dialog that your Photo Library cannot be found.
5. Click the Find Library button in the alert dialog.
6. Navigate to the iPhoto Library on the alternative drive (in other words, find the "new" Library you just copied).
7. After you've selected the new iPhoto Library folder, click the Open button.

Your new iPhoto Library, located on a different volume than your startup disk, should now be used whenever you launch iPhoto. After verifying that everything is working properly, you can delete the "Original iPhoto Library" by dragging it to the Trash.

Note: if you place your iPhoto Library on a different volume, you must make sure that volume is accessible before you launch iPhoto or any other iLife application that accesses your iPhoto Library. For example, if you place your iPhoto Library on an external FireWire drive, make sure the drive is connected and mounted in the Finder.

Using multiple iPhoto Libraries. If you have so many photos that iPhoto is starting to slow down, one solution is to have more than one iPhoto Library. You can do this manually, or you can use a third-party utility. To manually use multiple libraries, follow these steps:

1. Make sure iPhoto is not currently running.
2. Navigate to your current library at ~/Pictures/iPhoto Library.
3. Rename the iPhoto Library folder; use something meaningful that will allow you to differentiate between libraries once you have more than one (for example, Original Library or Library #1).

continues on next page

TAKE NOTE ▶ **The iPhoto Library** *continued*

4. Launch iPhoto. You'll get a message stating that iPhoto cannot find your Photo Library and presenting you with three options: Quit, Create Library, or Find Library. Click Create Library, and iPhoto will launch using a brand-new Photo Library. The new library will be located at ~/Pictures/iPhoto Library, just like your original.

5. After working with your new Photo Library, quit iPhoto, and then rename the *new* iPhoto Library folder.

6. If you want to create more iPhoto Libraries, repeat steps 4 and 5 as necessary.

Now whenever you launch iPhoto, you'll see the "Photo Library was not found" dialog. From this point on, click Find Library and then choose whichever library you want to use.

If you want to automate this process, a number of utilities have sprung up to make it easier. Some of the most popular are BubbaSoft's iPhoto Buddy, Scruffy Software's iPhoto Librarian, Brian Webster's iPhoto Library Manager, and Lue Regnault's MorePhotoLibs.

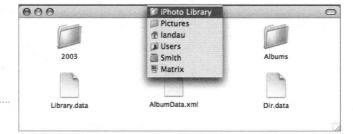

Figure 11.17

The iPhoto Library folder.

Import mode: importing photos into iPhoto

When you click the Import button in the control bar, most of the iPhoto window continues to look the same; the action bar, however, changes to Import mode for bringing photos into your Photo Library. There are several ways to do this; you can choose the one that works best for you. If a photo is in JPEG (.jpg) format when you import it, it will remain in that format. However, images that you import in other formats (GIF, TIFF, PICT, and so on) will be converted to JPEG.

Figure 11.18

The bottom portion of iPhoto's main window as it appears after you click the Import button.

Importing directly from a digital camera. You can import your photos directly from your digital camera by connecting your camera to your Mac (usually via a USB cable), launching iPhoto, and clicking the Import button from the navigation bar. The action bar at the bottom of the window will switch to Import mode. Assuming your camera is supported, iPhoto will display the model, along with the number of photos it currently contains. Click the Import button, and iPhoto will copy photos from your camera to your iPhoto Photo Library. During the transfer, the small preview window displays images of the photos being transferred; the progress bar shows how many photos remain to be transferred. Once importing is complete, the new photos will be added to your Photo Library. If you have chosen to view Film Rolls (from the View menu), the newly imported photos will be listed within a new roll called "Roll *number*" whose name includes the import date.

The Import function provides an "Erase camera contents after transfer" option; however, if iPhoto runs into a problem when attempting to add the imported photos to your Library—but *after* the photos have been deleted from your camera—you could lose your photos. Thus, I recommend *not* using this option. Once you're sure that your photos have been imported successfully, you can delete them from your camera manually (using whatever procedure your camera uses to delete photos).

Importing via the Finder. If you have an image, or a folder full of images, already on your Mac, you can import them into iPhoto by choosing Import from the File menu and then navigating to an image or folder of images. Even easier, you can simply drag photos or a folder of photos into the iPhoto image pane in either Import or Organize mode. The photos will be added to your Photo Library.

When you import images into iPhoto from the Finder, the original photos aren't modified. Instead, a copy of each photo is created in your iPhoto Library folder. The original photos remain untouched.

Each time you drag an image file, or folder of images, into iPhoto, a new "roll" is created. Thus, if you want a group of images to appear in the same roll, be sure to either drag them at the same time or place them in a folder and then import that folder. When you import a folder, the new "roll" is given that folder's name. If, instead of dragging a folder or group of images to the iPhoto image pane, you drag them into the Library/album list, they will be added to your Library as usual, but in addition, a new album containing those images will be created (see "Organize mode: arranging and sharing your photos," a bit later in the chapter).

Although iPhoto supports a wide range of digital cameras, it does not support every model on the market. A list of supported cameras is available at www.apple.com/iphoto/compatibility/camera.html. If your digital camera is not supported, you can take advantage of the above process to import your photos into iPhoto. Chances are, your camera uses some form of removable digital media (CompactFlash, Memory Stick, Microdrive, MultiMedia Card, Smart Media, Secure Digital, and so on). Thus, you can purchase an inexpensive digital-media reader (USB, FireWire, or PC Card) to mount the digital media in the Finder.

TAKE NOTE ▶ iPhoto Image Formats

iPhoto supports a number of image formats, but the support varies depending on whether you're importing, exporting, or editing.

iPhoto can *import* any photo format supported by QuickTime, including BMP, GIF, FlashPix, JPEG/JFIF, MacPaint, PICT, PNG, Adobe Photoshop, SGI, Targa, and TIFF.

iPhoto can *export* photos as JPEG, PNG, or TIFF images.

Finally, when editing a photo within iPhoto (including rotating it), GIF images are converted to JPEG images. All other images retain their original file formats.

Import warning. If you try to import formats other than the ones noted above (including non-graphic files, graphic files in an unsupported format, and damaged files), you will likely get a warning message when you try to import the file(s).

CMYK photos don't print properly. iPhoto can import photos created or edited using other photo and graphics applications; however, if photos have been saved using the CMYK format, you should convert them to RGB format before importing them. CMYK photos will not print properly from iPhoto (either directly to a printer or when ordering prints or books).

Importing using Image Capture. You can also import photos directly from your digital camera to your hard drive using Mac OS X's Image Capture application—you can then later import them into iPhoto via the Finder. Although most users will be content with using iPhoto, Image Capture offers a few features not otherwise available. For example, you can view all images on your camera before downloading, choose where to save images, and even *selectively* download only certain images. You can even automatically process images—to build a slide show, build a Web page, crop or fit to a specific size, or process with another application or AppleScript. There's not enough space to discuss all of Image Capture's features here, but be aware that it's an option.

Organize mode: arranging and sharing your photos

iPhoto's Organize mode is the application's main mode—if only because it provides you with most of iPhoto's arrangement and sharing options.

When in Organize mode (see **Figure 11.16**), you can browse through your photos (either in your main Photo Library or in albums). You can also create new albums by clicking the "Create a new album" button (the + button under the Library/album list) and then dragging photos from your Library or other albums into the new album. When viewing an album, you can rearrange the order of photos by dragging them around the viewing pane. You can also rotate photos by selecting them in the viewing pane and then clicking the Rotate button.

However, Organize mode also provides you with the many options shown in the action bar at the bottom of the iPhoto window. What follows is a brief overview of each option:

Print. Clicking the Print button is the same as choosing Print from the File menu. Instead of the standard Mac OS X Print dialog, iPhoto presents a simplified version that allows you to choose the printer, printer presets (if any), iPhoto printing styles (contact sheet, greeting card, full page, and so on), margins, and number of copies. If you would rather use the standard Mac OS X Print dialog, click the Advanced Options button at the bottom of the iPhoto dialog.

Slideshow. The Slideshow button lets you set your preferences for the iPhoto slide show (accessed via the Play button). You can choose the duration of each slide, the order of slides (random or sequential), to repeat or not, and which music to use, if any. If you choose to use music, you can select a song from your iTunes Library or from any playlist (you can even search for a song if your iTunes Library is large). Starting in iPhoto 4.x, you are no longer limited to one song per show.

Email. The Email button lets you quickly email photos. If you select one or more photos in the viewing pane and click the Email button, a dialog appears asking what size you want to use for the photos and whether to include photo titles, comments, or both. When you choose a size, you're shown the total size of the files to be sent. Click Compose, and iPhoto creates resized versions of the selected photos and then opens a new email message with those versions enclosed as attachments. Note: You can choose your preferred email client in iPhoto preferences.

Order Prints and Order Book. The Order Prints and Order Book buttons allow you to order professionally printed prints and books from your photos. To order prints, select a group of photos in the viewing pane (use the Command key to select multiple photos) and then click Order Prints. A window will appear that allows you to select how many of each size of each print you want to order. If you have 1-Click ordering enabled, you can simply click Buy Now to order. If not, you'll be asked to provide your personal and credit card info. Either way, iPhoto will connect to Apple's iPhoto ordering service via the Internet and upload your photos and order information.

When ordering photos, Apple recommends certain resolutions and certain aspect ratios to get good results. See the following Knowledge Base articles for more information: http://docs.info.apple.com/article.html?artnum=93279 and http://docs.info.apple.com/article.html?artnum=93288.

The Order Book button does the same thing as Book mode, discussed below, except that it immediately assembles the book without giving you a chance to work on it. It's basically a shortcut to the Order Book button in Book mode.

HomePage. If you have a .Mac membership, HomePage lets you publish photos as a Web page to your iDisk's Sites folder. Select a group of photos and click the HomePage button to bring up the Publish HomePage dialog. You'll be able to edit the title, as well as captions for each picture, and decide on the layout and frames (if any) you want to use. You can also place a link to email you, and a counter, on the page. Click Publish to publish your photo page; you will be provided with the URL, which you can then share with others.

Note: iPhoto will use the iDisk belonging to the .Mac account entered in the .Mac panel of System Preferences.

.Mac Slides. If you have a .Mac membership, you can publish photos as a .Mac slide show to your iDisk. Simply select a group of photos, click the .Mac Slides button, and iPhoto will create resized versions of your photos and upload them as a slide show to your iDisk. You will also be given the option to "Announce" your slide show; your preferred email account will open with a new email explaining how to view your slide show.

Note: The images are stored in a folder named Public, located in the Pictures/Slide Shows folder.

You (or another Mac OS X user) can also view the slide show as a screen saver. To do so, follow these steps:

1. Access the Desktop & Screen Saver System Preferences pane.

2. Click the Screen Saver button.

3. From the Screen Savers list select .Mac.

4. Click the Options button. From the dialog that drops down, enter your .Mac name in the .Mac Membership Name field.

5. Click OK. Your account list is added to the list at the top of the Options dialog and automatically selected.

   SEE: • ".Mac," in Chapter 8, for more on setting up and using .Mac.

Desktop. If you select a photo and click the Desktop button, Mac OS X will use the photo as your Desktop background.

iDVD. Clicking the iDVD button launches iDVD—provided it's installed on your Mac—and creates a new photo DVD project using the selected pictures.

Burn. The Burn button lets you burn the selected photos to a CD.

Edit mode: fine-tuning your photos

Although iPhoto isn't a full-featured graphics application like Photoshop, it does provide limited but effective editing functionality. To switch to Edit mode, either select a photo in the viewer pane and click the Edit button (in the control bar) or double-click a photo. Depending on which option you've chosen in iPhoto Preferences, the photo will appear in the main iPhoto window and the action bar will switch to Edit mode, or the photo will open in a new editing window. One advantage of the "separate window" setting is that it provides you with a few extra options, such as custom constrain settings.

Note: You also have the option, via iPhoto Preferences, to open the photo in another application—which means you can actually do your editing in Photoshop, GraphicConverter, or another application.

Figure 11.19

The bottom of iPhoto's main window after selecting the Edit button.

Edit mode gives you a few helpful editing tools. You can use the mouse to select an area of the photo; clicking the Crop button then crops the photo accordingly. You can use the Constrain pop-up menu to select a specific size or aspect ratio for cropping. And you can press the Control key to toggle between cropped and original views of the photo.

The Enhance button automatically adjusts the color and contrast of the photo to match what iPhoto thinks it should be. On some photos, this feature works great; on others, it has little effect; and on still others, it makes the image worse. Try it out; if you don't like the result, from the Edit menu select Undo.

If someone in your photo has red-eye, select an area around the eyes and then click the Red-Eye button. iPhoto will automatically fix it, which works quite well. You can also use the Retouch feature to "brush out" facial blemishes, cuts, bruises, and so on. Edit mode also includes a B & W button and (in iPhoto 4.x or later) a Sepia button, for converting a color image to black-and-white or sepia tones. Finally, you can manually adjust brightness and contrast using the sliders on the right side of the action panel.

You can always undo your last edit, so feel free to experiment. In addition, as mentioned in "Take Note: The iPhoto Library," whenever you make a change to a photo, iPhoto saves the original. Thus, if at any time you decide you want the original photo back, you can simply choose Revert to Original from the File menu, and iPhoto will delete the edited photo and restore the original.

One last note about editing photos: If you edit a photo in your main Library or in any album, those edits will be reflected everywhere the photo occurs. In other words, if you have the same photo in three albums, changes to that photo in one album will also be reflected in the other two albums.

SEE: • "Take Note: The iPhoto Library," earlier in this chapter, for related information.

Book mode: publishing your work

Book mode lets you assemble and order a bound, printed book from an album of pictures. You first select an album from the Library/album list—iPhoto will include all photos from the album in the book, so you may need to create a new album with fewer pictures if you don't want to use all of them. The action bar at the bottom of the iPhoto window then switches to Book mode: Choose a book theme and which options (guides, titles, comments, page numbers) you want shown. For each page, provide captions (if desired) and select a design (cover, introduction, one photo per page, two photos per page, and so on). If you select a page and then check the Lock Page box, that page will not be affected by changes you make to the surrounding pages. Finally, you can click the Preview button to see a preview of your book. When you click the Order Book button, you'll be presented with a dialog in which to place your order (much like when ordering prints).

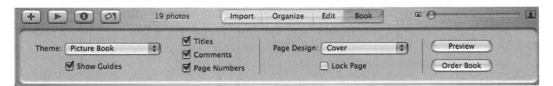

Figure 11.20

The bottom of iPhoto's main window after selecting the Book button.

TAKE NOTE ▶ Making Sure Your Book and Prints Look the Way You Want

When you create an iPhoto book or order prints, it seems fairly straightforward: What you see onscreen and print out should represent how the book will look when printed, right? Not necessarily.

Books. If your photos are too large to fit on a printed page, iPhoto scales them down to fit on the "page" in iPhoto. However, when you send the photos to Apple for processing, they don't always get scaled properly. If this happens, you'll get an email from Apple telling you that your book couldn't be printed. You must then go through a lengthy procedure, possibly via the telephone, to get your book right before sending it again.

continues on next page

TAKE NOTE ▶ **Making Sure Your Book and Prints Look the Way You Want** *continued*

To avoid this situation, follow the steps outlined below to see *exactly* what your book looks like *before* you send it:

1. Make sure that 1-Click ordering is disabled. To do this, access any ordering screen (for example, by selecting a picture in Organize mode and then clicking the Order Prints button). Click the Account Info button and then disable 1-Click ordering. After you've disabled it, cancel the order to get back to the main iPhoto window.

2. Select the album you wish to print as a book, and click the Order Book button.

3. When the Assembling Book progress bar finishes, you'll see the Order Book screen. Click the Cancel button to cancel the ordering process.

4. Launch Preview or Adobe Reader, and from the File menu choose Open.

5. In the Open dialog, in the "Go to" field, type /tmp and click Open. The dialog will show you the contents of the invisible tmp folder on your hard drive.

6. Select the iPhoto folder in the dialog, and you'll see a file called "Book-#######.pdf" where ####### is some string of numbers. This is the actual PDF file sent to Apple, which is then used to print your book. Select it and click Open.

Carefully examine each page of the book in Preview or Adobe Reader:

- If any images are cut off or misaligned, it could be because they are too large. You may need to resize them using a third-party graphics application like GraphicConverter or Photoshop.

- If text (such as captions or titles) is cut off or doesn't appear, it could be that you're using a font that is not supported by iPhoto. According to Apple, you should only use the following fonts in iPhoto books: Helvetica, Helvetica Neue, Century Gothic, Papyrus, Gill Sans, Markerfelt, Baskerville, and Brush Script. In addition, you should use the "plain" version—avoid using bold, italic, or other styles.

  To select a different font, from the Edit menu choose Font, and then from the submenu choose Show Fonts.

- Don't use page numbers in a Photo Book if many overlap with photos. If you've chosen to show page numbers in a Photo Book, but your photos are big enough that they cover the page number on more than half of the book's pages, your order will be rejected by Apple. The solution is to simply disable page numbers in the book.

Follow the above steps again after you've edited the book. Once the book looks fine, restart the order process and order your book.

Note: Although iPhoto's Book feature allows you to include photos that use any aspect ratio, Apple recommends using only the 4:3 ratio for photos added to a book. To change a photo's aspect ratio, select the photo in an album, click the Edit button, and from the Constrain menu select either "4x3 (Book, DVD)" or "4x3 Portrait (Book)."

Prints. A cropping problem may occur when ordering single prints. Photos are automatically cropped by the printing service to fit the dimensions of the print size you selected. To prevent unexpected surprises when you get your prints back, crop the photo yourself to fit the dimensions of the photo size prior to sending it to Apple. Use the Constrain pop-up menu to select the desired aspect ratio.

Exporting photos

iPhoto also has an export feature, hidden away in the File menu. If you select a group of pictures or an album, and from the File menu choose Export, you'll be presented with a dialog offering three choices: File Export, Web Page, and QuickTime.

- **File Export** exports the selected photos as files. You can choose the image format (JPEG, TIFF, or PNG), the size (if you want them resized), and the naming convention (the filename from the Finder, the iPhoto photo title, or names based on the album name).

- **Web Page** creates a Web site that you can later upload to your Web server (or your iDisk Sites folder) and access via a Web browser. You can choose the title, layout, site colors, and image and thumbnail sizes.

- **QuickTime** saves the photos as a slide show in QuickTime movie format. You choose the movie screen size, duration of each slide, background, and whether to add music.

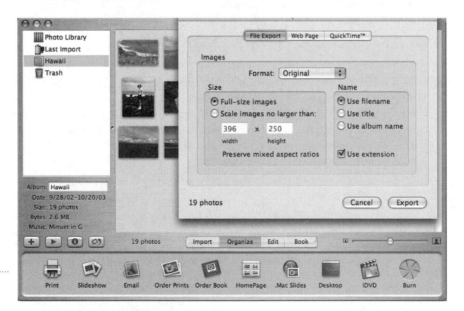

Figure 11.21

iPhoto's Export Photos dialog.

Solving iPhoto problems

The following represents a collection of common iPhoto problems and some suggestions for avoiding or solving them.

Don't modify the iPhoto Library from the Finder. In general, to avoid an assortment of problems, do not change anything inside the iPhoto Library folder via the Finder. Only use the iPhoto application to make changes to the folder's contents.

When a problem occurs despite your following this advice, you may need to make an exception to the rule to fix the problem (as evidenced in a few of the items that follow).

iPhoto performance slows. This is probably the No. 1 complaint about iPhoto. The more photos you add to your iPhoto Library, the slower iPhoto runs. Unfortunately, there's not a lot you can do about this. However, here are a few tips:

- **Disable drop shadows.** In iPhoto Preferences, switch the Appearance setting to No Border. Showing borders seems to slow things down a bit, and if you have a lot of photos, showing drop shadows can *really* slow things down.

- **Hide rolls.** When viewing your Photo Library, use the File Rolls option from the View menu; this groups your photos by roll. You can then use the disclosure triangles next to the roll names to hide any rolls you aren't currently using—which can dramatically speed iPhoto's performance.

- **Use multiple iPhoto Libraries.** If your Photo Library is very large, but most of those photos are ones you don't access frequently, you may want to consider having multiple Photo Libraries. For example, you can keep older photos in one library and newer, frequently accessed photos in another.

SEE: • "Take Note: The iPhoto Library," earlier in this chapter, for more details on this option.

Note: Updating to iPhoto 4 largely eliminates this slow-performance problem (as described in "Take Note: iLife '04," earlier in this chapter).

iPhoto Library disappears or becomes inaccessible. Although this is rare, some users have experienced problems in which their iPhoto Library "disappears"—that is, iPhoto doesn't show any photos in its Photo Library. However, if you look in your iPhoto Library folder in the Finder, all the photos seem to be there. If this happens to you, try the following procedures (in the order listed here) until one works:

- Quit iPhoto and then delete the iPhoto preferences file (~/Library/Preferences/com.apple.iPhoto.plist). Now relaunch iPhoto and see if your photos reappear.

- Quit iPhoto and then drag your iPhoto Library folder onto the iPhoto icon while holding down the Option and Command keys. This forces iPhoto to use the selected Library.

- Restore your iPhoto Library from a backup, as some of your data may be damaged.

- If you don't have a recent backup, iPhoto has a built-in "rebuild Library" feature. To access this feature, hold down the Shift and Option keys when launching iPhoto. You'll see an alert, warning you that you may lose data by using this procedure if there are any damaged photos or data files, but if the above procedures didn't help, this is better than nothing. Note that you *will* lose photo rolls and date information.

- If all else fails, some users have had excellent results with the freeware utility iPhoto Extractor (from Sean Butler). Try it.

iPhoto Library doesn't appear in other iLife applications. You may find that your iPhoto Library does not appear in iMovie or iDVD. Assuming you have the latest versions of all three applications, make sure that you've opened iPhoto at least once. In addition, make sure that your iPhoto Library hasn't been moved; it should be in ~/Pictures/iPhoto Library. Finally, if all of the above are as they should be, you may need to re-create iPhoto's album file. To do so, follow these steps:

1. Quit iPhoto, iMovie, iDVD, and iTunes.
2. In the Finder, navigate to ~/Pictures/iPhoto Library.
3. Delete the file AlbumData.xml (or move it to the Desktop).
4. Open iPhoto.
5. Create a new album (or albums).
6. Quit iPhoto.

When you open iMovie or iDVD, your iPhoto albums should now be available.

"iPhoto Library not found" error message appears. You may get a message that says: "Your Photo Library was not found. Do you want to find your Photo Library? iPhoto can't continue without a Photo Library. Make sure the disk containing your Photo Library is connected." If so, it may indeed mean that your iPhoto Library is on a volume not currently mounted. The solution, of course, is to mount the needed volume.

However, the symptom can also occur due to some unexpected causes. In particular, it can happen if you select iPhoto as the scanning destination in Image Capture. Whatever the cause, the solution is the same: Click the Find Library button and locate the desired iPhoto Library folder. Select the folder and click Open.

Warning icon appears. When building a book or ordering prints, Apple states that the following will occur: "A warning icon (an exclamation point inside of a yellow triangle) will appear next to pictures whose resolution may be too low for a quality print at a given size or next to a text caption when entered text overruns the border." For pictures, if the picture has been cropped, reverting to the original may help (use the Revert to Original command in the File menu). Otherwise, print at a smaller size. For fonts, selecting a different font may help. See the following Apple Knowledge Base document for additional advice: http://docs.info.apple.com/article.html?artnum=61025.

Figure 11.22

Warning icons visible in iPhoto's Book mode.

Duplicate photos imported. Normally, when you attempt to import photos into iPhoto that have already been imported, an alert will appear informing you of this fact. However, if the time/date settings on your camera change between the two imports, iPhoto will assume that the photos are actually different. The solution is to make sure that your camera's date/time settings are correct when you take pictures.

In general, whenever the date and/or time on your camera is incorrect, you may wind up with duplicate imported pictures.

"Unrecognized file type" error. When importing photos, you may get an error message listing files that cannot be imported because "they may be an unrecognized file type or the files may not contain valid data." There are a couple of possible reasons for this. The first is because some of the files may actually not be recognized as valid image files (because they aren't images, or because they're damaged). The other reason is that your hard drive may be full. Check to see if your hard drive has enough free space before importing.

SEE: • "Take Note: iPhoto Image Formats," earlier in this chapter, for more details.

Rotated photos not rotated when opened in other applications.
If you rotate a photo in iPhoto and then later drag that photo to another application (such as a word-processing document, an email message, or another graphics application), you'll find that the document "loses" its rotation (that is, it appears in its original orientation). The reason for this is that iPhoto's Rotate command doesn't actually edit the photo; rather, it simply changes the way iPhoto presents the photo for viewing. If you want to use the rotated version of the image in another application, you need to export the photo from iPhoto. To do so, follow these steps:

1. Select the desired photo in an Organize or Edit window in iPhoto.
2. Rotate the photo to the desired orientation using iPhoto's Rotate command.
3. From the File menu choose Export and then click the File Export button.
4. Select your desired export options, and then click Export (provide a name and location for the exported photo when prompted).
5. Open the exported version of the photo in the other application or drag it into the desired document.

Page Setup "Scale" setting does not affect printout. If you attempt to print a photo from within iPhoto, and you change the Scale percentage in the Page Setup dialog, you will find that the photo is printed at its original scale. The reason for this is that iPhoto does not honor the Page Setup Scale setting. To change the size of printed photos, you must access the standard Print dialog and do the following:

1. From the Presets pop-up menu in the Print dialog, choose Standard.
2. From the Style pop-up menu choose Standard Prints.
3. Select the desired printout size next to Size.

Alternatively, you can bring up the Print dialog and click the Preview button to create a preview of the printout in the Preview application. You can then use the Preview application's Page Setup dialog to choose a Scale percentage and then print directly from Preview.

iPhoto fails to recognize newly formatted Memory Stick. If your digital camera has Memory Stick memory and you use the camera's Format/ Erase feature to erase a Memory Stick and then immediately connect your camera to your Mac, neither iPhoto nor Image Capture will recognize it. The reason for this is that until you actually take a picture, a newly formatted Memory Stick does not have the proper format for your Mac to recognize it as photo media. Once you take a picture on the newly formatted Memory Stick, your Mac will recognize it.

HomePage captions limited to 40 characters. If you create a photo album using the online .Mac HomePage feature, you can add photo captions of as many as 80 characters. However, if you use iPhoto to publish a photo album to .Mac, photo captions are limited to 40 characters. If you prefer to use iPhoto to publish photo albums, the good news is that you can later log in to the .Mac Web site and edit your photo album captions, and you'll have the ability to use longer captions.

Can't access HomePage or .Mac Slides features. If you attempt to use the HomePage or .Mac Slides features of iPhoto, you may get the following error message: "A connection could not be established at this time. Please ensure your network connection is active and try again." The cause could be that your computer's date and time are set incorrectly. Check to make sure your date and time are correct in Date & Time System Preferences, and then try again.

Can't order photos from within iPhoto. If you attempt to order photos from within iPhoto, you may get the following error message: "There was an error while accessing your account information. Please check your network connection and try again." The cause could be that your computer's date and time are set incorrectly. Check to make sure that your date and time are correct in Date & Time System Preferences, and then try again.

1-Click password doesn't work in iPhoto. If you have a 1-Click account with Apple that has a long password, it may not work when used with iPhoto's 1-Click ordering system. Although the online Apple Store allows 1-Click passwords of as many as 32 characters, iPhoto limits 1-Click passwords to 30 characters. The easiest solution is to go to the online Apple Store and edit your password so that it has 30 characters or less.

Corrupt photos or thumbnails. Occasionally, a photo or a thumbnail of a photo may become corrupt. This can lead to crashes when accessing the photo or its thumbnail. Deleting the corrupted file and reimporting the photo (or re-creating the thumbnail) will fix the problem. If you need help with exactly how to do this, I suggest getting *iPhoto 4 for Mac OS X: Visual QuickStart Guide,* by Adam Engst (Peachpit, 2003). In particular, check out Chapter 7, on troubleshooting. It includes tips on this and an assortment of other problems.

Troubleshooting iChat and iChat AV

iChat is Apple's instant-messaging and conferencing client. With it, you can communicate over the Internet with other users (both Mac users and users of other platforms). The original version allowed you to communicate via text messaging using a .Mac or AOL Instant Messenger (AIM) account. The newer version, iChat AV (included with Panther or available as a separate purchase for Jaguar users), lets you communicate via audio and video as well.

The version of iChat AV that originally shipped with Panther can only be used to videoconference with other Macs running iChat AV. However, starting with iChat AV 2.1 (update available from Apple's Web site), you can videoconference with PC users running AOL Instant Messenger 5.5 for Windows.

This section assumes you're using iChat AV. However, the older iChat works almost identically for text messaging.

To use iChat, you need an account. If you're a .Mac member, you can use your .Mac account name as your iChat user name (in the form *username*@mac.com). Otherwise, you can get an iChat-only .Mac user name, or you can use an AOL Instant Messenger (AIM) account, which you can sign up for at www.aim.com. Note that if your .Mac password is longer than 16 characters, you can't use it to log in to iChat; the solution is to change to a shorter password.

When you first launch iChat, you'll be asked to set up iChat. Enter your first and last name, select the account type, and provide your user name and password. (If you want an iChat-only .Mac account, click the Get an iChat Account button.) After you click Continue, you'll be asked whether you want to enable Rendezvous messaging. This allows you to communicate with other iChat users on your local network, even if you aren't connected to the Internet. I generally recommend enabling the "Use Rendezvous messaging" option.

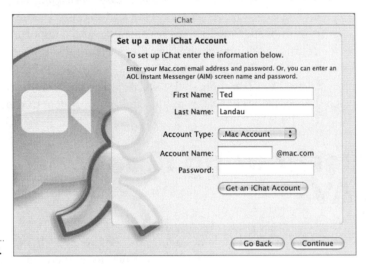

Figure 11.23

iChat's setup screen.

Figure 11.24

iChat's Buddy List window.

If you have a compatible video camera connected to your Mac—such as Apple's iSight or a digital video (DV) camcorder—the next screen allows you to configure iChat for use with the camera.

Chatting: text, audio, and video

Depending on your setup, you can initiate a text chat, an audio-only chat, or an audio-video chat.

When you first launch iChat, you may automatically log in to your accounts or you may be listed as offline. Which option occurs depends on the setting you select in the General section of iChat's Preferences. In particular, to automatically log in, check "When iChat opens, automatically log in" from the Settings options.

From the same Settings options, select "Show status in menu bar." From the menu that appears, you can modify your iChat status. There are, in essence, three status options: Offline (you're not connected), Away (you're connected but away from your desk and thus not replying to requests), and Available (you're at your desk and ready to use iChat). You can set up a chat if you're listed as Away but not if you're listed as Offline.

If you click your own picture at the top of your Buddy List or Rendezvous window, a menu that includes all your recently used pictures drops down. Select one, if you wish, to switch to that picture. If you instead select Edit Picture, you're presented with a dialog in which you can either choose a different picture from your hard drive (by clicking Choose) or take a picture (Video Snapshot) using a connected video camera.

If you click the status item (for example, Available, Away, Offline) below your name at the top of your Buddy List or Rendezvous window, you can change both your online status and the status message that other users see for you. Choose Custom to create your own status message. Select Edit Status Menu to edit any of your custom changes.

Note: iChat's Preferences and menus include many more options than there's room to cover here. I recommend exploring them on your own to see what is available.

Text chat. To initiate a text chat with another user, from the File menu choose New Chat with Person, and then enter that person's .Mac or AIM address. Once the person accepts, a new iChat window opens, and you can communicate by simply typing a message and pressing Return to send it. You can read the other person's messages in the same window.

However, if you plan on communicating with that user in the future, a better option is to make that user a *buddy*. To do so, click the plus (+) button in the Buddy List window. This brings up a list of all contacts in your Address Book application's database. If the person is already in your Address Book, simply choose his or her name and click Select Buddy. Otherwise, click New Person and enter his or her information. That person is now added to your Buddy List: You can see when he or she is online and determine that person's current status (Available, Away, and so on). To initiate a text chat, double-click a name in the Buddy List. Alternatively, select a name and click the A (text) button at the bottom of the window.

To send a file to someone with whom you're chatting, after first sending a text message, simply drag the file into the chat window. (You can also select Send File from the Buddies menu.) Once the recipient accepts the file, it will be transferred to the folder designated as that person's Downloads folder in Internet or Safari Preferences.

Audio chat. A Telephone icon next to a buddy's name indicates that the user has a microphone connected and can participate in an audio conference (which works like an Internet telephone)—assuming you have audio capability as well. If you have an iSight camera, you can use its built-in microphone, bypassing the additional video option. Macs with internal microphones will also work.

To initiate an audio chat, click the Telephone icon next to a buddy's name. That person will get a message that you're trying to initiate a chat. If the other user accepts, you can start talking. If that user rejects your invitation, you'll see a message indicating as much.

Note: You can alternatively select a name and click the Telephone icon at the bottom of the window: This will start an audio chat using an iSight camera, even though the Telephone icon is not listed next to the person's name.

Video chat. A camera icon next to a buddy's name indicates that he or she has a video camera connected and can engage in a video chat—again, assuming you have similar video capability, such as an iSight camera or any compatible digital video camera (connected via the FireWire port).

To initiate a video chat, click the Camera icon next to a buddy's name. Alternatively, select a name and click the Camera button at the bottom of the window. That person will get a message saying that you're trying to initiate a chat. If your buddy accepts, you can start talking. If your buddy rejects your invitation, you'll see a message indicating as much.

If you have a video camera, but the other person only has a microphone, you can instead select Invite to One-Way Video Chat from the Buddies menu: Even though that person can only *talk* to you, he or she will be able to *see* and hear you just fine.

If you click the Camera icon next to your picture, it opens a window that allows you to preview your appearance on camera.

Note: What *you* see is actually a mirror image of yourself. However, the user on the other end of the chat sees your image correctly (for example, text will be readable). This is not a bug; Apple assumes that people are more familiar with seeing themselves in mirror image.

To use the audio chat mode, Apple recommends a 56K or faster modem connection; however, for video chats, you need at least a DSL or cable modem connection. In addition, you need a Mac with a 600 MHz G3 processor (at minimum) to do any audio or video chatting. Apple provides the following examples of quality versus requirements:

	Standard Quality	Enhanced Quality	High Quality
Window size	352x288 to full screen	352x288 to full screen	352x288 to full screen
Video resolution	176x144	176x144	352x288
Frames/second	15	30	20/30
Processor req'd	>600 MHz G3	>1 GHz G4	>Dual 800 MHz G4 or any G5
Bandwidth needed	100–500 Kbps	100–500 Kbps	>500 Kbps

Solving general iChat problems

In this and the following two sections, I cover common iChat problems and their solutions, This section covers iChat issues that generally affect both iChat and iChat AV. The other two sections cover iChat AV–specific issues and issues with Apple's iSight or digital video cameras.

"Could not connect to Rendezvous" error. If you get this error message, or if you can't connect to a buddy in your Rendezvous Buddy List (even though you know you're connected to a local network), there are three possible causes.

- **You don't have Mac OS X's BSD Subsystem installed.** This should only be an issue if you manually installed Mac OS X, chose a Custom installation, and specifically deselected the BSD Subsystem.

- **One of the services Rendezvous uses has quit (usually accidentally or unexpectedly).** Restarting your Mac will generally solve this problem.

- **Mac OS X's Firewall is blocking the port needed for iChat to communicate over a local network (port 5298).** If you have Mac OS X's Firewall enabled in the Sharing System Preferences pane, the solution is to go to the Firewall screen and either turn off the Firewall or enable the iChat Rendezvous rule.

SEE: • "Firewall" in "Setting Up System Preferences: Sharing," in Chapter 8, for details on how to open this iChat Rendezvous port.

Can't send or receive files via iChat when Firewall is active. Similar to the previous problem, if Mac OS X's built-in firewall is active, you will not be able to send or receive files to and from other iChat users. If you're only sending or receiving a single file, you can simply turn the Firewall off in the Sharing System Preferences pane, and then turn it back on after sending or receiving the file. If you want to be able to send and receive files at will, you should open the necessary port (5190) in Sharing's Firewall.

SEE: • "Firewall" in "Setting Up System Preferences: Sharing," in Chapter 8, for details on how to create a rule to open this port.

iChat and routers. iChat AV works seamlessly with most Internet routers, including Apple's own AirPort Base Stations. However, in some cases, you may get a "network timeout" or "user did not respond" alert message when attempting to use iChat AV with a Mac connected via a router. If this happens, check to see if there is a newer version of the router firmware that may fix the problem. Otherwise, you will likely need to access the router's Port Forwarding feature and open the same 5298 port noted above.

SEE: • "Firewall" and "Using a Router," in Chapter 8, for more details.

Can't send a file until a text message is sent. If you try to send an attachment to someone via iChat without first sending a text message, an error beep will sound (though there's no error box describing the error). iChat requires you to first send a text message to the other user to establish the chat connection; you can then send the file.

Unable to chat with AIM users. Some AIM users may not be able to communicate with iChat because of an incompatibility with older versions of AIM. The solution is to make sure that AIM users update to version 4.5.651 or later for Macs and version 4.8.2790 or later for Windows.

iChat problems with proxies. If your Internet connection uses a proxy server, you must set up iChat for proxy use separately from Network System Preferences. In iChat Preferences, go to the Accounts panel and then click the Server Settings button.

Note: iChat supports SOCKS 4, SOCKS 5, and HTTPS proxies; however, it does not work with proxy servers that require a name and password.

Adding a new user to chat. If you have an active chat session with someone, you can add people to the chat if you wish. To do so, click the plus (+) button at the bottom of the Participants list that is to the side of the chat window. If the list is not visible, select Show Chat Participants from iChat's View menu.

Additions to Buddy List fail to "stick." The AOL Instant Messenger network limits the number of AIM buddies any user can have. According to Apple, the stated limit is 150 buddies. If you try to add more, you may find that after quitting iChat and later reopening it, the most recently added buddies (those over the limit) either show up incorrectly or don't show up at all. You'll need to delete one or more buddies from your Buddy List in order to add more.

iChat status doesn't change when using custom status messages. If you're using a custom Away status message and decide you want to change your status to Available but retain the same custom status message (or vice versa), you'll find that after typing in the custom status message, your status will revert to the previous value (for example, Away). The reason for this is that iChat associates custom status messages with a particular status—that is, you cannot use the same custom status message for both Away and Available. If you want to change a custom status message from one status to another, you need to choose Edit Status Menu from the Status pop-up menu, delete the custom status message from its current status, and then add it to the other.

Can't eject a disk after sending a file via iChat. If you send a file located on a nonboot volume (that is, any volume or disk other than the Mac OS X startup disk) to another user via iChat, you may not be able to eject or unmount that volume. You're likely to get an error to the effect that the disk is "in use." The work-around is to copy files to the startup volume *before* sending them via iChat. Otherwise, you will have to quit iChat and possibly even log out before you can eject/unmount the volume.

Solving AV problems with iChat

Videoconferencing requires open ports. If you're using iChat AV from behind a firewall, you may find that you can't establish a videoconference with another user outside the firewall. This is because iChat AV uses ports that most firewalls close by default. If you turned on the Firewall in the Sharing System Preferences pane, you will need to either turn it off or open the needed ports (5060, 5190, 5297, 5298). You should then be able to videoconference with users outside your firewall.

SEE: • "Firewall" in "Setting Up System Preferences: Sharing," in Chapter 8, for details on how to open these ports.

If you're using a hardware router or third-party firewall, you need to open ports 5060, 5190, 5298, 5353, and 5678, plus Ports 16384–16403. Check the firewall's documentation to find out how to open these ports.

SEE: • "iChat AV and UDP ports" in "Firewall," in Chapter 8, for more details.

Poor AV quality over AirPort, part I. If you attempt to audio- or videoconference over a wireless/AirPort connection, you may experience jumpy or choppy audio and/or video. You might even get a message stating that "no packets have been received for the last 10 seconds," followed by a disconnection of your audio- or videoconference. This is generally caused by packet loss, a symptom of a weak wireless connection.

If you open iChat AV's Connection Doctor—which you access from the Video (or Audio, if no camera is connected) menu—you can verify packet loss by looking at the Quality section. If one or both of the Video and Audio meters show less than 100 percent, you're probably experiencing packet loss. If possible, connect your Mac to your network or Internet connection via a wired (Ethernet) connection, and try again. If the Quality meters show 100 percent, the problem was a less-than-ideal AirPort connection. If the Quality meters still show packet loss, the problem is most likely with your Internet connection (or a problem with your local network, if you're conferencing with another local user).

Poor AV quality over AirPort, part II. If you have an iBook and are using iChat AV to audio- or videoconference over an AirPort connection, *and* are using the book's internal microphone, you may hear popping noises or severe interference. According to Apple, the iBook's AirPort signal can interfere with its internal microphone. The solution is either to use an external microphone (USB, FireWire, or the microphone built into Apple's iSight camera), or to connect via Ethernet.

Poor audio quality, general. If you find that your video chats provide poor audio quality, many users have found success in opening iChat Preferences, clicking the Video button, and changing the Bandwidth Limit pop-up menu to 500 Kbps. This limits the amount of bandwidth used by the video portion of AV chats, freeing up more bandwidth for the audio portion. You may also want to experiment with different values here until you find the one that works best for you.

Audio chats lag or go silent. Some users experience problems in which audio gets choppy and may even halt. One solution that works surprisingly well is for both chat participants to click the Mute button in the Chat window (to mute sound), and then click it again to unmute. This forces iChat to "resync" audio and often fixes the problem immediately.

CRT iMac microphones. The built-in microphones on some CRT-based iMacs do not provide enough gain for iChat AV. Apple suggests using an external microphone or, if you're using Apple's iSight camera, iSight's own microphone. You can select among multiple microphones via the Microphone pop-up menu in the Video section of iChat AV's Preferences.

Disconnecting USB microphone crashes iChat AV. If you disconnect your USB microphone while iChat AV is running, iChat AV may crash. Unfortunately, the only solution seems to be to quit iChat before unplugging the microphone.

No sound from left speaker on PowerBooks and iBooks. If you have a PowerBook or iBook with stereo (left and right) speakers, only the right speaker will provide sound. This is to prevent audio feedback, since the microphone on these computers is located near the left speaker. This doesn't affect sound quality, since iChat AV audio is transmitted in mono. However, if you wish to hear the audio better, you can connect external speakers or headphones to your PowerBook or iBook.

Solving iSight and other camera problems

iSight microphone not recognized. If you connect an iSight video camera to your Mac while iChat AV is running, the iSight's microphone may not be recognized by iChat AV. Quitting iChat AV and relaunching it generally fixes the problem.

"Your camera is in use by another application" message. If you try to use iChat AV with an iSight camera but get an error message that the camera is in use by another application, first quit all other applications that might be using iSight, then quit and relaunch iChat AV. If that doesn't fix the problem, quit iChat AV, unplug the FireWire cable from the iSight and your Mac, and then reconnect everything and launch iChat AV again. The camera should now work normally.

Connecting iSight and DV cameras simultaneously freezes video editing software. If you connect both an iSight camera and a digital video (DV) camera to your Mac at the same time, video editing applications (iMovie, Final Cut Pro, Final Cut Express, and so on) may freeze. This is a known bug, and Apple recommends disconnecting your iSight camera before launching any video editing applications.

DV camera not recognized on G3. iChat AV does not support digital video (DV) cameras on Macs with a G3 PowerPC processor (older iMacs, iBooks, and PowerMac G3 computers). To use iChat for videoconferencing on these computers, you need to use a dedicated USB or FireWire video camera, such as Apple's iSight.

Troubleshooting iCal

iCal is Apple's take on the electronic calendar and "to do" list. Via an onscreen calendar, it allows you to schedule events and keep track of tasks, schedule reminders, and publish your events and tasks to the Internet for other users to view. You can also subscribe to other users' calendars, making it a great way for families and small businesses to coordinate schedules.

When you launch iCal, you'll see the main window with the Calendars list and monthly calendar on the left, the current calendar view in the middle, and your To Do Items on the right.

You can hide or show the monthly calendar using the Calendar button in the lower left corner of the window. You can hide or show To Do Items by clicking the Thumbtack button in the lower right corner or by choosing Show/Hide To Dos from the Window menu. You can switch the current calendar view between Day, Week, and Month views, as well as advance the calendar forward and backward in time, using the View menu or the buttons at the bottom of the main window.

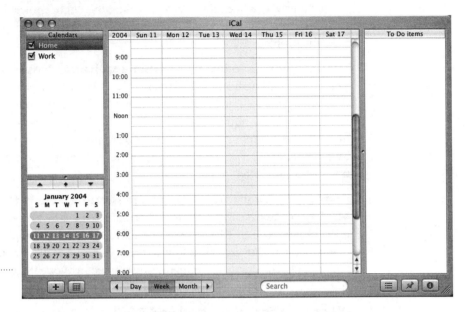

Figure 11.25

The main iCal window.

You can create as many independent calendars as you like. By default, iCal provides you with Home and Work calendars. Clicking the plus (+) button in the bottom left portion of the window (or choosing New Calendar from the File menu) creates a new calendar. Selecting a calendar in the Calendars list and pressing the Delete key (or choosing Delete from the Edit menu) deletes it. If you select a calendar and click the Info button (the lowercase *i* button in the lower right corner of the main window), an information drawer will appear. You can edit the calendar name, provide a description, and change the calendar's color scheme.

Creating, deleting, and editing events and To Do items

This section explains how to create a new event, edit an existing event, and create and edit To Do items.

Creating a new event. To create a new calendar event, follow these steps:

1. From the Calendars list select a calendar (to determine *which* calendar the event will be part of).

2. From the File menu choose New Event, or drag the pointer across the time span of the event (for example, from 10 a.m. to 11 a.m.). A new event is created with the name highlighted.

3. Type the name of the event and press Return to enter it.

Deleting an event. To delete an event, select it in the calendar and either select the Delete command in the Edit menu or press the Delete button on the keyboard.

Editing an event. You can edit an event in two ways:

- To change the time or duration of the event, you can simply drag the event to another time slot, or click the top or bottom edge of the event and drag it to extend or reduce the duration.

- To get much more control over the event, click the Info button in the bottom right corner of the main window (or choose Show Info from the Window menu).

  As shown in **Figure 11.26**, the Info (New Event) window allows you to change the time and date (or set the account as an "all-day" event); the repeat status (whether or not the event repeats, and the schedule); whether to set up a reminder alarm, and what type (a pop-up message, audio, sending an email, or opening a file); which calendar the event should belong to; a URL to associate with the file; and any notes you want to include with the event. You even have the option to add *attendees* to the event. You can type in the names of people who will be attending the event. However, if you open Address Book, you can drag contacts to the "attendees" space to add them to the event. In fact, once you've added attendees, if you click the "attendees" label, you can choose Send Invitations to have email invitations sent to all attendees.

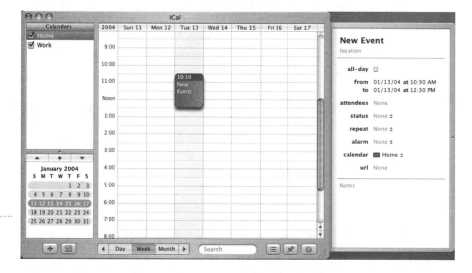

Figure 11.26

Editing an iCal event using the Info window.

Create and editing To Do items. Creating a new To Do item works in much the same way as the above. However, the info drawer contains a few different options. You can assign one of three priorities, set a due date, and "check off" the task once it's completed.

Importing and exporting calendars

iCal can import calendars from other applications, as well as export its own calendars.

Importing calendars. If you're just starting to use iCal and have information stored in another calendar application, iCal can import a number of calendar standards. From the File menu select Import; iCal presents a dialog asking which type of calendar you wish to import: iCal (iCalendar format) file, vCal (vCalendar format) file, or Entourage data. If you have Microsoft's Entourage installed, choose Entourage and iCal will automatically launch Entourage and import calendar information from it. Otherwise, choose iCal for data stored in the iCal format or vCal for vCal format, and then navigate to your calendar file.

One of the most popular "switches" is to convert from the Palm Desktop application, used by many handheld organizers, to iCal. To do this, launch Palm Desktop and from the File menu choose Export. In the resulting dialog, choose vCal as the export format and then save the vCal file to your hard drive. Using the procedure described in the previous paragraph, import this vCal file, and all of your calendar info will appear in iCal as a new calendar.

SEE: • "Troubleshooting iSync," later in this chapter, for more information on syncing your Palm handheld with iCal.

Exporting calendars. iCal can also export its own calendars in the .ics format. Saved calendars will have the .ics extension in their names. To export a calendar, from the File menu choose Export and then choose a location to save the .ics file. You (or any other user) can then import that calendar into iCal or another calendaring application.

Publishing and subscribing to calendars

In addition to exporting calendar files, you can publish your iCal calendars over the Internet and allow other users to *subscribe* to them: Those users won't be able to change a published calendar, but they will be able to view it and, if you allow them, be reminded by your reminders. You can also subscribe to calendars that others have published.

Publishing calendars. To publish a calendar, follow these steps:

1. Select the calendar you wish to publish from the Calendars list, and from the Calendar menu choose Publish.

2. In the resulting dialog, provide a name for the published calendar and then choose your publishing options.

   You can choose to have the published version automatically updated with any changes you make in iCal, as well as whether your To Do items are included and whether your notes are included in the published version.

3. Choose whether to publish the calendar to .Mac or to a WebDAV server.

If you choose .Mac, iCal will use the .Mac account set up in the .Mac panel of System Preferences.

If you choose WebDAV server, you'll need to provide the URL, login name, and password to connect to the server.

In either case, once the calendar has been published, iCal will provide you with the URL to provide to other users who want to subscribe to your calendar. You'll also be provided with a standard HTTP URL that allows anyone to view your calendar in a Web browser—generally in the format http://ical.mac.com/*username/calendarname*. Once a calendar is published, a Broadcast icon will appear next to the calendar name in the Calendars list.

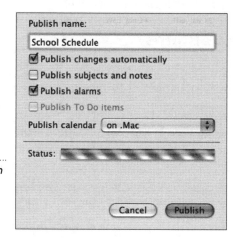

Figure 11.27

iCal lets you publish your calendars to the Internet for other users to view them.

If you decide that you no longer want others to view your calendar, select it in the Calendars list and from the Calendar menu select Unpublish. You can also change the location where the calendar is published by selecting Change Location from the Calendar menu (or by opening the Calendar info drawer and clicking the "published" line).

Subscribing to calendars. Just as other users can subscribe to your calendars, you can subscribe to the calendars of other users. There are a couple of ways to do this:

*   The first way is to choose Subscribe from the Calendar menu, and then enter the calendar URL in the resulting dialog. Choose whether or not to remove alarms and/or To Do items.

*   The other way is to click a *webcal* URL (a URL that takes the form webcal://*serveraddress/calendaraddress*) in an email or a Web browser. The same dialog will appear, with the URL already entered. In either case, click Subscribe and the calendar will show up in your Calendars list (with an arrow next to it).

    Where do you get webcal URLs? The most obvious source is other iCal users who have published their calendars. However, Apple provides a huge library of published calendars—holidays, sports schedules, concert dates, TV schedules, and more—to which iCal users can subscribe. To access these calendars, either choose "Find shared calendars" from the Calendar menu (which will open the calendar library in your Web browser) or switch to your Web browser and surf to www.apple.com/ical/library. Click a calendar link in your browser to subscribe.

Refreshing calendars. To refresh a calendar (to see if any changes have been made to it), select it and from the Calendar menu choose Refresh (or "Refresh all" to refresh all calendars).

Unsubscribing from calendars. To unsubscribe from a calendar, select it and from the Calendar menu choose Unsubscribe.

Solving iCal problems

Although the most commonly reported iCal problem is sluggish performance (which I can't help you with but which Panther improves dramatically!), there are a few known issues you can avoid or fix by using the following tips.

iCal crashes on launch. One of the more common problems with iCal is caused by a font conflict. iCal requires the TrueType version of the HelveticaNeue font (/Library/Fonts/HelveticaNeue.dfont). If you remove this font (some users remove it to substitute a PostScript version), iCal will crash on launch. To reinstall it, log in to an admin-level account and drag the font back to /Library/Fonts.

Login crash caused by iCal. If your Mac crashes *after* you log in but *before* the login process is complete, the culprit may be a loginwindow process crash triggered by a corrupt com.apple.scheduler.plist file, which is used by iCal and located in ~/Library/Preferences. Log in as root or using Single User mode at startup, and delete the file to fix the problem.

Can't edit published calendars if original is deleted. If you deleted a local copy of a calendar that you published on .Mac, changed computers recently, or had to reinstall Mac OS X, you won't be able to use iCal to change the published copies of your calendars. However, the calendar will still be visible to users who have subscribed to it.

To make changes, you will need to re-create the calendars and republish them, using the same calendar names you used the first time you published them. Newly published calendars will replace previously published calendars that have the same name. You can now edit the calendar.

Alternatively, you can simply remove the calendar from .Mac. You would think you could use iCal's Unpublish command here, but that won't work if the original calendar file is no longer present. Instead, to remove published calendars from .Mac, follow these steps:

1. From the Finder's Go menu choose iDisk. Your iDisk will appear in the Finder. If your iDisk is already mounted, you can skip this step. If you're

using a local copy of iDisk, remember that it needs to sync with the online copy before the change will take effect.

SEE: • ".Mac," in Chapter 8, for details.

2. From the Go menu choose Go to Folder.

3. Type the following: /Volumes/*membername*/Sites/.calendars/ (where *membername* is your .Mac account name).

4. In the window that appears, drag the calendars you no longer want published to the Trash.

Can't send invitations or reminders via email client selected in Internet System Preferences. If you try to send an email invitation to an iCal event or enable email reminders, Mail opens—even if you have a different email client selected in Internet System Preferences. Unfortunately, iCal only support's Apple's Mail email client, in conjunction with Address Book, for sending email invitations.

You can get third-party software that modifies the scripts iCal uses so that it can access other email programs, such as Entourage (for example, get ZappTek's iCal via Entourage). However, undoing this change requires reinstalling iCal or restoring it from a backup.

Invitees aren't notified if you delete an event. If you delete an event after previously inviting others via iCal's Invite feature, invitees will not be automatically notified. You'll need to notify them of the "cancellation" manually.

"This invitation is not correct" alert. If you receive an iCal invitation in Mail and receive an alert stating, "This invitation is not correct," the problem is that you haven't specified your *own* card in Address Book. You need to create an Address Book entry for yourself and then from the Card menu choose This Is My Card. Make sure that all of your email addresses are listed in the card's contact info area.

Can't export a calendar by dragging it to the Finder. If you're one of the few people who actually reads the help files for applications, you may have read that you can export an iCal calendar by dragging it to the Finder. Unfortunately, this is an error in iCal Help. This feature isn't actually available at this time (version 1.5.2 at the time of this writing). To export a calendar, you need to select its name and from the File menu choose Export.

iCal can't read Entourage .ics files. Even though iCal and Entourage both support the iCalendar (.ics) standard, their .ics files are not compatible with each other. Apple claims it is "investigating this issue." However, you can import Entourage calendars using iCal's Import command (from the File menu); simply select the Import Entourage Data option in the Import dialog.

Alarm fails to go off as scheduled. A previously set alarm will likely not go off within the first hour after turning your computer on. Nor will it go off if your computer is asleep.

Troubleshooting iSync

iSync allows you to synchronize your iCal data (calendars and To Do items) and your Address Book contacts between your Mac and any number of devices, such as handheld computers (for example, Palm handhelds), mobile phones, and iPods. The only requirement is that the device be iSync-compatible. For a full list of supported devices, visit the following Web site: www.apple.com/ isync/devices.html.

In addition, if you're a .Mac member, you can sync your calendars, contacts, and even your Safari bookmarks between multiple Macs via the Internet. Once you've synced your data via .Mac, you can also access your calendars and bookmarks from any computer using a Web browser.

Note: Synchronizing your calendar(s) via iSync is independent of publishing calendar(s) via iCal as described in the previous section. Whenever you iSync, it updates the calendars on all synced devices. However, to update a published calendar, you need to update it from within iCal.

SEE: • ".Mac," in Chapter 8, for more on this service.

iSync Preferences. If you select Preferences from the iSync menu, it opens a dialog with three options:

- **"Show iSync in menu bar."** This enables a menu from which you can check when the last sync occurred or initiate a new sync. You can also launch iSync from the menu.

- **"Display Palm HotSync warning."** If you're syncing to a Palm OS device, enabling this option warns you, when selecting to sync, that syncing with a Palm requires that you use the HotSync application or button on the device cradle, not the Sync Now button in iSync.

   SEE: • "Syncing with Palm devices," later in this chapter.

- **"Show Data Change alert when {*percentage pop-up menu selection*}."** If you enable this option, you will be notified before syncing if the upcoming sync is going to change more than the specified percentage of data on your Mac. This can prevent you from accidentally deleting information. For example, if you accidentally erased your .Mac contacts when you first synced from another computer, the next time you synced this computer, iSync might think that you wanted to delete all of those contacts on all registered computers. This option would notify you first, giving you an opportunity to avoid such a disastrous sync.

iSync Log. The iSync Log, viewable by choosing Show Logs from the Window menu, displays a history of every sync operation. Clicking the disclosure triangle next to a particular sync provides you with details of that sync, including how many changes were made to which devices and any problems encountered.

If you ever have a failure after selecting to Sync, checking the Log files is a good first step. The log should indicate the nature of the error, hopefully facilitating your ability to fix the problem.

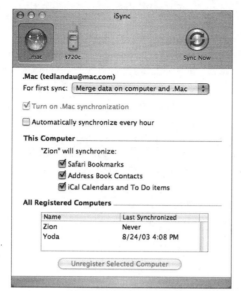

Figure 11.28

The main iSync window, with the .Mac drawer shown.

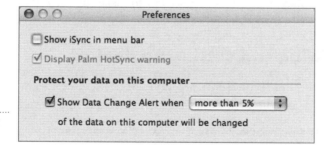

Figure 11.29

iSync's Preferences dialog.

iSync and .Mac

When you first launch iSync, you'll see a rather sparse window with two buttons, .Mac and Sync Now. At this point, your only options are to sync your contacts, calendar(s), and Safari bookmarks via .Mac.

Assuming you have a .Mac account, if you click the .Mac button, a dialog will slide down, revealing the .Mac Sync settings. First, you choose which of the following actions you want iSync to take on the first sync:

- Merge data on computer and .Mac
- Erase data on .Mac then sync
- Erase data on computer then sync

After the first sync, these options are replaced by a status line that tells you when the last synchronization occurred.

From the settings dialog, you can choose how you want iSync to, well, sync:

- If you want all of your info synced automatically, for example, check the "Automatically synchronize every hour" box.

- The This Computer section lets you decide which information—Safari bookmarks, contacts, and calendar/To Do items—should be synced to .Mac.

- If you've set up iSync on different computers to sync with this .Mac account, the All Registered Computers list lists all syncing computers, along with the last time they were synced. Note that iSync can't synchronize two computers if they have the exact same name (as set in the Sharing pane of System Preferences). To disallow a computer from syncing, select it in the list and then click Unregister Selected Computer.

- To temporarily prevent .Mac from syncing with your computer, uncheck the "Turn on .Mac synchronization" check box.

Once you've selected your preferred sync settings, click the Sync Now button to start the process; if you've opted to automatically sync every hour, you don't have to do anything.

If you have several computers, such as one at work and another at home, using .Mac with iSync is a great way to make sure that items such as browser bookmarks are always the same on all computers.

Adding and setting up devices

If you want to sync with a supported device such as a Palm handheld, an iPod, or an iSync-compatible phone, you need to add it to iSync's device list.

Adding a device. To add a device, follow these steps:

1. Make sure the device is connected to your Mac. For an iPod, connect to a FireWire port. For USB-equipped Palms and mobile phones, connect to a USB port.

    If your USB device requires a special software driver—some (not all) Motorola phones, for example, require a driver to connect via USB—make sure that driver is installed. Connecting a Motorola phone via USB also requires a special USB cable (which you purchase from Motorola). This is because the mobile phone itself does not have a standard USB port.

    For Bluetooth-enabled phones and handhelds, "pair" the device with your Mac.

    SEE: • "Syncing with Bluetooth devices," later in this section.

2. Launch iSync.

3. From the Devices menu choose Add Device. iSync will scan your Mac's ports and connections and present you with a list of the compatible devices it finds.

4. In the Add Device dialog, double-click the device you want to add. The device will be added to the iSync window.

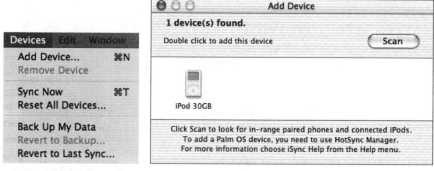

Figure 11.30

iSync's (left) Devices menu and (right) Add Device dialog.

If you have problems adding a device (assuming it's an iSync-compatible one), make sure all Bluetooth devices have been paired with your computer and that all USB mobile phones are listed in the Network Port Configurations section of your Mac's Network System Preferences pane.

SEE: • Chapter 8, for advice on solving network-related problems.

Removing a device. If you decide to remove a device, click its icon in the iSync window and from the Devices menu choose Remove Device.

Device settings. Each device has its own customizable settings, similar to the settings options described for .Mac in the previous section. To access a device's settings, click its icon (at the top of the iSync window). A Settings dialog will drop down. The various settings will differ slightly according to device type; however, they generally allow you to enable and disable syncing, and decide whether you want to sync contact, calendars, or both. Of particular note are the following settings:

• **Contacts.** From the Contacts section, you can choose to sync all Address Book contacts or just those in a particular group.

   SEE: • "Take Note: Address Book Groups and iSync," below, for more details on using groups with iSync.

   For some phones, iSync will give you the option to only sync contacts with phone numbers. If your iSync doesn't give you this option for your phone, you can make a group in Address Book called *phone contacts*, drag all contacts with phone numbers into the group, and then in iSync choose your phone contacts group from the Synchronize pop-up menu.

• **Calendars.** The Calendars section lets you choose to sync all or selected iCal calendars. Some devices also give you the option to only sync calendar information for a selectable period of time (for example, the next four weeks). Finally, if you sync more than one calendar with your phone or Palm, you can choose which calendar events *created* on the device will be placed when you sync.

TAKE NOTE ▶ Address Book Groups and iSync

To create a new group in Address Book, select New Group from Address Book's File menu. Give the new empty group any name you want by replacing the default Group Name in the Group column.

Alternatively, you can select a group of existing contacts and select New Group from Selection. This immediately populates the new group with the contacts you selected.

Groups in Address Book play an important role in iSync. In particular, suppose you want to sync the contacts on your mobile phone. However, you have hundreds of contacts in Address Book and only a dozen or so that you keep on your phone. How can you sync the phone so that its contacts get copied to Address Book, without having all of Address Book's contacts copied to your phone? The answer is, by creating groups. To do so, follow these steps:

1. Create an empty group in Address Book and name it for your phone (for example, Motorola).
2. Launch iSync and double-click the icon for your phone.
3. From the Contacts section of the settings options, select the Synchronize pop-up menu. The default choice is "All contacts." From the pop-up menu, select the name of your newly created group.
4. Click the Sync Now button. The contacts on your mobile phone will be copied to the group in Address Book. No Address Book contacts will be copied to the phone.

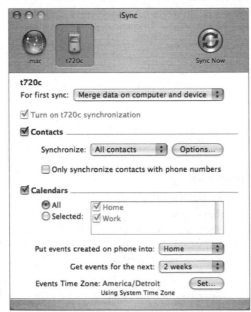

Figure 11.31

The main iSync window showing the Settings options, with a mobile phone selected.

Syncing devices

In most cases, once you've selected the settings for a device, syncing the device is as simple as clicking the Sync Now button in iSync. However, some devices require additional considerations. For additional help, check out the "Setting up computers with devices" section of the iSync Help files included with Panther.

Syncing with Palm devices. Before you add a Palm handheld to your list of iSync devices, you need to install the Palm Desktop software 4.0 or later (which should have come with your handheld). In addition, you need to install the iSync Palm Conduit 1.2 or later, available from www.apple.com/isync/download/index.html#palm.

To choose what information is synced with your Palm handheld, instead of clicking the Palm icon in the iSync window, launch the Palm HotSync Manager and from the HotSync menu choose Conduit Settings. Double-click iSync Conduit, and then check the box next to "Enable iSync for this Palm device."

Some caveats to consider with Palm handheld syncing:

- When syncing with a Palm OS device, you must initiate the sync via the HotSync feature of the Palm device, not the Sync Now button in iSync. For faster syncing, make sure the HotSync Progress window is kept in front.

- Because neither iCal nor Address Book provides a notes application or functionality, your Palm Notes will still sync with Palm Desktop.

- Certain options in iCal for "repeating" events do not transfer properly to Palm handhelds. For details, see http://docs.info.apple.com/article.html?artnum=93172.

- If you're sure the Palm device is set up correctly and you're still having problems getting the device to sync, force iSync to do a *slow sync*. To set this, click the iSync device icon in iSync to access its settings. Check the "Force slow synchronization" box. Now sync the Palm as usual.

Syncing with Bluetooth devices. If your Mac has Bluetooth functionality (either built in or via a USB Bluetooth adapter) and you plan on syncing with a Bluetooth-enabled device, such as a Palm handheld or mobile phone with built-in Bluetooth, before you can add the device in iSync you need to pair the device with your Mac.

SEE: • "Bluetooth," in Chapter 8, for more details on pairing a device and other Bluetooth-related features.

Likewise, if you want to use iSync to sync with a Bluetooth-enabled Palm device, you need to first disable the Palm conduits and install the iSync Palm conduit, as described above.

Syncing with an iPod. As mentioned earlier in the chapter, you can drag vCard files into the iPod's Contacts folder, and iCal/.ics files into its Calendars folder, to add them to the iPod's Contacts and Calendars features. However, if you plan on using iSync for contact and/or calendar synchronization with your iPod, you should not use this manual method. The data will not be synchronized by iSync, nor will iSync delete the data. If you want such data to be synchronized, you'll need to add the data to iCal and/or Address Book on your Mac, and then delete the duplicate vCard and .ics files from the iPod.

Undoing changes after syncing

iSync provides several methods of undoing the changes that occur after selecting to sync devices. You can use these methods to recover from accidentally deleting or overwriting data during syncing. Note that all of the commands for these options are located in the Devices menu (see **Figure 11.30**).

Backing up and restoring data. When you choose Back Up My Data from the Devices menu, iSync creates a local copy of all of the data from the most recent sync. This data is stored in ~/Library/Application Support/ SyncService/Backup Data. Although you won't be notified that the backup was successful, you can check the modification dates on the folders and files in this folder to confirm that the backup did indeed occur.

To restore data, choose Revert to Backup from the Devices menu. With this command, your local data will revert to its state when you last used the Back Up My Data command, and iSync will replace the contents of connected devices to reflect that data. If you sync with .Mac, your .Mac data will also revert, so that the next time any *other* of your computers are synced with your .Mac account, they too will sync to the reverted data.

Resetting. The Reset All Devices command, available from the Devices menu, erases all of the data in all connected devices (mobile phone, iPod, Palm, and so on) and replaces it with the current data in Address Book and iCal (if you select This Computer from the pop-up menu) or with your .Mac data (if you select .Mac from the pop-up menu). After making your selection, click the Reset All button.

This can be a useful option if you're having trouble with the data in one of your devices; however, it can also result in data loss if you're not careful. Before using Reset All, make sure that any new information added to a connected device has been synced or added to Address Book or iCal as well.

In addition, Apple warns that on some devices, a Reset command will erase information that is not synced by iSync, such as voice dial tags, speed-dial info, and custom-ring tags that are attached to contacts. In essence, any information stored on the device but not also stored on your computer will be lost. Thus, use this option with caution!

Reverting. If you choose Revert to Last Sync from the Devices menu, your local data will revert to the state it was in just prior to the most recent synchronization, and your connected devices will be synced accordingly.

How, you may ask, does iSync know the state of your data prior to your most recent sync? The way it knows this is that each time you perform a sync, iSync automatically saves a copy of your Address Book, iCal, and Safari bookmark data, specifically for use by the Revert command, in ~/Library/Application Support/SyncService/LastSync Data.

You cannot do this to undo changes made to devices other than your local computer (for example, you cannot revert the data on a mobile phone that was just synced).

Solving iSync problems

This section lists a number of common problems that may occur with iSync, along with their solutions. Apple has also documented a number of specific issues that may occur with certain devices (particular phone models, for example). You can find out more about these issues by visiting Apple's Knowledge Base at http://kbase.info.apple.com and doing a search for "iSync." Also check out the Help files for iSync included with Panther. As is generally true for Panther, the Help files are considerably improved from those available in previous versions of Mac OS X.

Solving synchronization conflicts. If you're syncing multiple devices and/or computers and you've made changes to the same item in more than one location (and the changes are not the same), iSync will prompt you via a dialog to indicate which data should be used when syncing. Select the source you wish to use.

Syncing devices to just one computer. If you add a device, such as a mobile phone, to more than one computer, the device may not sync correctly.

Synchronization fails due to incorrect computer date. If your computer's date is incorrect—more specifically, if the date is set to a year before 2001—iSync will not be able to connect with Apple's .Mac servers. If you click the .Mac button in iSync, you'll get the following error message: "A network error interrupted the connection to .Mac." Likewise, if you click the Sync Now button, you'll get this error message: "Unable to get data from the server: A network error interrupted the connection to .Mac." The solution is to make sure your computer's date is set correctly in Date & Time System Preferences.

Syncing large amounts of data fails with some phones. When syncing data with some mobile phones—the Sony Ericsson P800 and Nokia x650 are two examples—you may get an error stating that some data will not fit. This often occurs because you're trying to synchronize more data than the phone's memory can hold. The solution is to sync less data, which you can do by choosing to sync fewer iCal calendars or creating a smaller group of contacts in Address Book and then only syncing that group.

Can't sync to Motorola mobile phone because "device is unavailable." If, when you attempt to use iSync to synchronize data with a Motorola phone, you receive this error message, make sure your phone isn't locked (the phone's screen will show a "locked" message or a padlock icon if it is). If it is, unlock the phone and then sync again.

iPod fails to Sync if iSync.vcf file removed. iSync stores its iPod settings on your iPod in a file called iSync.vcf. If you mount your iPod in the Finder and delete this file, iSync will think that your iPod has never been synced before and re-sync all of your data from iCal and Address Book.

Using iSync to synchronize calendars fails to update published calendars. If you've published an iCal calendar to .Mac, you won't be able to use iSync's iCal synchronization feature to update those calendars. You must instead use the Update command in iCal's Calendar menu. Note: The calendar's Inspector window includes an option to update the published version automatically when changes are made.

Restoring Palm HotSync conduits. When you install the iSync Palm Conduit, it automatically disables certain Palm HotSync conduits—that is, those that would conflict with iSync. If at some point you decide to use Palm Desktop instead of iCal and Address book, you'll need to disable the iSync conduit and re-enable the Palm conduits. To do this, move the Apple conduit from /Library/Application Support/Palm HotSync/Conduits to /Library/Application Support/Palm HotSync/Disabled Conduits, and then move the contents of /Library/Application Support/Palm HotSync/Disabled Conduits to /Library/Application Support/Palm HotSync/Conduits. You'll then need to launch the Palm HotSync Manager and configure each of the restored Palm conduits.

Troubleshooting iMovie

iMovie is Apple's "consumer" movie editing application. (Final Cut Express and Final Cut Pro are Apple's professional-level editing applications.) It is included free with Mac OS X.

iMovie overview

To create a movie, you can import video directly from a digital camcorder or existing movie files, include music from your iTunes Library, and even use images from your iPhoto Library. You can edit your movies and save them as movie files or export them to iDVD for use in iDVD projects.

The first time you launch iMovie, you're given the option to open an existing project or create a new one. Unlike with most applications, when you create a new movie project, you need to save the file *before* you start to work on it; the default location is your Movies folder inside your Home directory. On subsequent launches, iMovie opens the project you were using most recently.

The main iMovie window includes three distinct sections:

Viewing screen and basic controls. The upper left portion of the iMovie window is the viewing area. Like a TV screen, it lets you view video as it is imported and preview the current status of your iMovie project.

Directly below the screen are the basic controls for viewing the video:

- **Scrubber bar.** Directly below the viewing area is a scrubber bar. Similar to the timeline viewer described below, you can use this to drag a pointer to any location in the current clip. You can also use the crop markers to define a section of a clip to be cropped.

  Note: If a specific clip is not selected in the clip/timeline viewer below, the entire movie is "listed" in the scrubber bar (rather than a single clip).

- **Playback buttons.** Click the Play button (the large triangle button) to play the clip currently in the viewer. Use the Play Full Screen button (button with the Play symbol within the screen symbol) for full-screen playback (press the Escape key to stop full-screen playback). The Rewind button takes you to the beginning of the selected clip.

- **Volume slider.** Use this to adjust playback volume.

- **Camera/Scissors switch.** This switch lets you toggle between Import (camera) and Edit (scissors) modes. Use Import mode when a camera is connected to the Mac and you're importing video; use Edit mode when editing an already imported clip.

- **Clip/Timeline Viewer switch.** This switch toggles the viewer below between Clip versus Timeline modes (as described next).

Clip viewer and timeline viewer. The lower part of the iMovie window contains either the clip viewer (which shows you the times and arrangement of individual movie clips) or the timeline viewer (which lets you view and edit your project on a timeline).

When you use the timeline viewer, the area below the viewer provides a few timeline-related controls:

- The *zoom control* lets you choose how much of the timeline you see at any one time.

- The *speed slider* controls how quickly a particular part of the timeline plays.

- The *volume slider* (or the adjacent % field) allows you to specify different volume levels for each clip in your project.

Finally, you can view *available drive space* just below the viewer. The size of the Trash's contents is also shown.

Action pane. The right-hand pane of the iMovie window (which I call the Action pane) shows various options for adding content to or enhancing the content of a movie. The options that appear here depend on which mode is selected from the row of buttons below the pane: Clips, Photos, Audio, Titles, Trans (transitions), Effects, and iDVD.

SEE: • "Editing Video," below, for a brief description of each of these modes.

The following sections provide additional details about iMovie's basic functions. The last part looks specifically at solving iMovie problems.

Figure 11.32

The main iMovie window: The initial part of the selected clip is set to be cropped in the scrubber bar; the timeline viewer is shown in the lower part of the window; Clips is selected in the Action pane.

Importing video

There are a number of ways to import video into iMovie:

*   To import directly from an existing movie file on your hard drive, from the File menu choose Import and then navigate to that file.

*   If you have a DV camera with a FireWire port, connect the camera to your Mac via a FireWire cable. Place your camcorder in Playback mode (often called VCR or VTR mode), and then place iMovie in Camcorder mode (via the Camera/Scissors switch below the main viewing area). To import an entire video, simply click the Import button. If you've enabled the "Automatically start new clip at scene break" option in iMovie Preferences, iMovie will create a new clip each time it detects a scene break—most DV cameras

insert a scene break each time you pause or stop recording. Note: With iMovie 4.x, you can also record from an iSight camera.

- To import selections of video, use the playback controls beneath the viewing window to find the beginning of the section to be imported, then click the Import button (or press the spacebar); click it again to stop importing. iMovie shows the tape counter from your DV camera at the top of the viewing window.

Note: By default, newly imported clips are placed in the Clips pane. However, you can choose, via iMovie Preferences, to instead have them added directly to the movie timeline.

TAKE NOTE ▶ iMovie Projects

When you create a project in iMovie, it's saved in an iMovie project folder. By default, the project folder is saved inside your personal Movies folder. However, as discussed in the main text, you can choose to save your project folder anywhere. The important thing is that you keep the folder intact because it contains all of the data needed for your project.

The folder itself contains a few files and folders: a filename after your project, a folder called Media, and a file called *projectname*.mov, where *projectname* is the name of your iMovie project. The project file contains a complete map of your project—which clips are used, in what order; using which transitions and effects; titles; and so on. The Media folder contains all of the imported video clips and other data files for your project. Finally, the .mov file is the currently rendered version of your movie (sort of a "draft" version). This is what iMovie uses to play the movie in the viewing area (you can double-click this movie file in the Finder to play it in QuickTime Player).

If you delete a project folder, or any file within it, that project will no longer be usable, so keep it safe. On the other hand, to get rid of a project, simply drag the project folder to the Trash.

Editing video

Apple has made editing video in iMovie extraordinarily simple. You just drag clips from the Clips pane to the clip viewer at the bottom of the window. To rearrange clips in a movie, simply drag them around in the clip viewer.

Figure 11.33

iMovie's clip/timeline view in Clip Viewer mode.

You can trim a particular clip in the scrubber bar: To do so, use the two crop markers (found on the lower left edge of the scrubber bar below the viewer) to enclose the section of the clip to be cropped—that section will be highlighted yellow (instead of blue) on the bar. Now press the Delete key to cut the enclosed section. This change will be reflected in the clip/timeline viewer at the bottom of the window. You can also use the timeline viewer to fine-tune your movie's audio and video tracks as well as to add audio tracks.

Note that for many editing actions, after you apply the action, the clip(s) will need to be *rendered*, meaning that the action (transition, effect, title, and so on) will need to be digitized into the existing video. Because this takes some time, the bottom of the clip image (in Clip Viewer mode) or video track (in Timeline Viewer mode) displays the progress of the current render. Once rendering is complete, you'll be able to play the finished clip in the main viewing area.

Other editing functions are available via the various editing modes you access from the Action pane buttons:

Clips. The Clips pane lists all of the video clips imported into the current project.

Photos. You can use this pane to access any photo in your iPhoto Library for use in your iMovie project.

If the Ken Burns Effect is unchecked, you can use a static picture in your project. With the Ken Burns Effect enabled, you can pan and zoom around a photo, just as you see on TV (the effect is named after documentary film-maker Ken Burns, who uses such an effect frequently). When you're satisfied with your photo, drag it from the photo list to the clip viewer to add it to your project.

Audio. The Audio pane works much like the Photos pane. You can select any playlist from your iTunes Library and then choose a song. To add the song to your project, drag it to the timeline's audio track or click the Place at Playhead button.

The Audio pane also lets you record audio via your Mac's built-in micro-phone (if applicable) or an external mike. Click the red Record button to begin recording, and a new audio track will be added to the timeline. Click the button again to stop recording.

Titles. Using the Titles pane, you can add titles, credits, or any other text to your iMovie project. When you've completed your creation, drag the title from the list to the beginning of any clip in the timeline; make sure the clip you choose is longer than the duration of the title.

Figure 11.34

Two examples of iMovie panes: (left) Photos and (right) Titles. See Figure 11.32 for the Clips pane.

Trans(itions). You can apply transitions between clips using the Transitions pane. Select a transition from the list, and then choose a speed (you're actually choosing the duration of the transition). Once you're satisfied, drag it from the transition list to the divider between two clips—the transition will be rendered using those two clips.

Effects. iMovie comes with a number of built-in video effects that you can apply to clips via the Effects pane. To do so, select the clip to which you want the effect applied, then select an effect from the list and choose your desired settings. (Each effect has its own settings; the Effects pane will change to reflect this each time you select a different effect.) If you're happy with the result, click Apply.

Note that if you apply an effect to a clip, any transitions you previously applied to that clip will be deleted; you must reapply the transition after the effect has been rendered.

iDVD. If you plan to export your iMovie project to iDVD for burning to a DVD, the iDVD pane lets you add chapter markers to your movie. As with the chapters in a commercial DVD, these markers allow viewers to use their DVD players' Forward and Reverse buttons to skip between "scenes" or to go directly to a particular chapter. When you export your project to iDVD, iDVD automatically creates menus and buttons for these chapter markers.

To add a chapter marker, move the scrubber (either in the clip/timeline viewer or in the main viewing area) to the spot at which you want the marker to appear; then click Add Chapter in the iDVD pane. You can even name the chapter; iDVD will use this name when creating your DVD.

iMovie plug-ins

A number of third-party developers offer plug-ins that enhance iMovie. Most work by simply dropping the plug-in file into ~/Library/iMovie/Plug-ins. If iMovie is running, you'll need to quit it and then relaunch it for the plug-in to take effect. These plug-ins usually provide additional transitions and effects, which will be available from the standard Transitions and Effects panes.

Exporting iMovie projects

When you've finished producing your movie, you can export it in a number of ways.

Note: If you have upgraded to iMovie 4, all export options are accessed from a Share command in the File menu, rather than as described below. After selecting Share, you will have access to a toolbar from which to can select to export via Email, HomePage, Videocamera, iDVD, QuickTime, or Bluetooth.

Exporting to iDVD. To export to iDVD, from the File menu choose Export, and from the pop-up menu in the dialog that appears choose To iDVD. In the dialog that appears click the Export button. iDVD will open with a new project, containing your movie, ready to go.

Alternatively, you can select iDVD from the Action pane buttons on the right side of the iMovie window and click the Create iDVD Project button that appears.

Note: The Export To iDVD options only work with iDVD 3 and later. If you're still using iDVD 2, here's how to export video that can be used with iDVD 2:

1. From the File menu choose Export To QuickTime (rather than Export To iDVD).

2. From the pop-up menu choose the Full Quality DV option.

3. Click Export; give the movie a name and save it to your hard drive.

4. Copy the exported movie to a new iDVD 2 project folder.

Exporting to QuickTime. If you want to create a movie file to post on the Web, burn to a data CD, or keep on your hard drive, choose Export from the File menu and select To QuickTime from the pop-up menu in the dialog that appears.

A Formats pop-up menu will appear, allowing you to choose the type of QuickTime file/movie you want to produce: Web (creates a small, low-quality QuickTime .mov file); Email (creates a smaller but even lower-quality file); Web Streaming (creates a file suitable for a QuickTime Streaming Server); CD-ROM (asks you to insert a blank CD and creates a CD containing the movie that will be playable on any Mac or Windows computer via QuickTime); and Full Quality DV (provides the highest-quality QuickTime .mov file, but that file will be very large). Finally, you can select Expert Settings, which allows you to choose from a number of different AV formats, including some audio-only formats (so that you can export just the audio from a movie).

When finished, click the Export button. You will be prompted to name the file and indicate the location for the file to be saved. If you selected Expert Settings, there will also be an Options button. Select this for additional options, such as compression quality, target size, and audio quality.

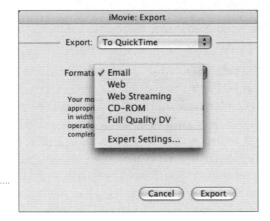

Figure 11.35

iMovie's Export to QuickTime dialog.

Exporting to Camera. To export your movie back to your DV camera, first make sure your camera is connected and in VTR (VCR) mode. Once you've done this, from the File menu select Export, and from the pop-up menu in the dialog that appears select To Camera. From the options that appear, you can tell iMovie how long to wait before it starts sending data, as well as how many seconds of black screen to send before and after the movie. Click the Export button and iMovie will automatically put your DV camera in Record mode and send your finished movie to the camera.

Solving iMovie problems

The problems most users experience with iMovie seem to be more performance related than those seen with the other iApps. Typical specific symptoms are that iMovie's response to commands is too slow or movies are too choppy. There is no surefire cure for this. To try to improve iMovie's performance, do one or more of the following : (a) rebuild your project (as described in

"'Your iMovie project is unreadable' message" below); (b) remove plug-ins in ~/Library/iMovie/Plug-ins; (c) store your project in a folder not protected by FileVault; (d) gain free memory by quitting all open applications; (e) defragment your drive; (f) buy a faster Mac. See this Apple Knowledge Base document for further advice: http://docs.info.apple.com/article.html?artnum=93699.

The following represent some of the more common *nonperformance* issues with iMovie.

DV camera (camcorder) not recognized by iMovie. If your DV camera isn't recognized, make sure of the following:

- The camera is compatible with iMovie. Apple has a list of compatible cameras at www.apple.com/imovie/compatibility/camcorder.html.
- The camera is turned on and connected via FireWire. iMovie does not support USB.
- The camera is set to VTR/Camera mode, not "record/on" mode.

See the following Apple Knowledge Base article for more advice on this matter: http://docs.info.apple.com/article.html?artnum=43000.

"Found files that don't belong" message. If iMovie finds files in a project's Media folder that don't correspond to any part of the project, you'll receive the following error message: "Found files that don't belong in project folder. Okay to move them to Trash?" These files are usually files that were accidentally moved to the Media folder by the user, or files created when iMovie crashed during rendering. Generally it's OK to click the Trash Unused Files button to move these files to the Trash. If you instead click Leave Files Alone, iMovie will leave them in the Media folder, but you will get the above-described error each time the affected project is opened in iMovie.

"Your iMovie project is unreadable" message. If your iMovie project becomes damaged or corrupt, you may be unable to open it in iMovie, instead seeing this message. It's sometimes possible to recover a project by following the steps outlined below:

1. Create a new project in iMovie.
2. Navigate in the Finder to the Media folder of the original (damaged) project.
3. Drag the contents of that Media folder from the Finder into the iMovie Clips Action pane of the new project.
4. Re-create the original project by dragging clips from the Clips Action pane to the timeline.
5. Save the new project. You can now delete the original Media folder in the Finder.

Alternatively, if you're using iMovie 3 or later, try the following:

1. Create a new project in iMovie.

2. Navigate in the Finder to the project folder of the damaged iMovie project.

3. Drag the file reference.mov from the damaged project folder to the timeline of the new iMovie project. This should import the original project contents as a single clip.

4. Save the new project.

Third-party iMovie plug-ins can cause iMovie to crash. If you're experiencing unexpected quits with iMovie, the cause could be an incompatible third-party iMovie plug-in file. A related symptom that often has the same cause is a message that states, "Something is wrong with the plugin Localized.rsrc," when you launch iMovie.

To diagnose and fix this, remove all plug-ins by following the steps outlined below:

1. Quit iMovie.

2. In the Finder, navigate to ~/Library/iMovie/Plug-ins.

3. Drag any files in this folder to the Desktop.

4. Launch iMovie.

If the symptoms have disappeared, isolate which plug-in was the cause and contact the vendor for further advice. The solution is usually to get a newer version of the plug-in.

Toast Video CD Export plug-in causes iMovie to crash. If you've installed Toast, the third-party CD-burning software from Roxio, you may have also installed the Toast Video CD Export plug-in for iMovie. This plug-in is an occasional source of problems—in particular, causing a crash when selecting iMovie Help. Unfortunately, this plug-in is typically installed directly inside the iMovie application package. Thus, the advice in the previous section will not work. Here's how to delete it:

1. Quit iMovie.

2. In the Finder, select Get Info for iMovie.

3. Click the disclosure triangle next to Plug-ins.

4. Find the Toast Video CD Export plug-in in the Plug-ins list, and then uncheck it to disable the file. Or click the Remove button to delete it completely.

5. Launch iMovie and see if the problem has disappeared.

Third-party QuickTime codecs cause iMovie to crash. If you've installed any third-party codecs for QuickTime, they can potentially cause iMovie to quit unexpectedly. To see if these codecs are responsible for problems, follow these steps:

1. Quit iMovie.
2. In the Finder, navigate to /Library/QuickTime; if any files exist in this folder, drag them to the Desktop.
3. In the Finder, navigate to ~/Library/QuickTime; repeat the above procedure.
4. Launch iMovie and see if the problem has disappeared.

If this fixes the problem, isolate which codec is the cause, and contact the vendor for further advice.

After reinstalling Mac OS X, the iMovie icon is generic and iMovie may not launch. If for some reason you reinstalled Mac OS X and are now experiencing problems with iMovie (for example, it won't launch, or its icon becomes generic), drag the damaged iMovie application to the Trash and then reinstall iMovie (via the Panther or iLife CDs).

Changing display resolution quits iMovie. If you change your monitor resolution to 640 by 480, iMovie immediately quits. The reason for this is that iMovie requires a minimum resolution of 800 by 600 and thus automatically quits if it detects a lower resolution. The solution is to adjust your screen resolution to at least 800 by 600 and then relaunch iMovie.

Moving iMovie projects to a different volume. If your boot drive is low on space, you may want to store your projects on another volume. When creating a new project, you can simply choose a different volume as the save location. However, if you want to move an existing project, you need to use the following procedure:

1. Quit iMovie.
2. Drag the existing project folder from its current location to the desired location on the alternative volume. Make sure you drag the *entire* project folder, not just the project file.
3. Launch iMovie and open the project from the new location.

Note that you should always store iMovie projects on hard drives, rather than on slower media such as Zip/floppy drives, CD-RWs, or USB devices. In addition, iMovie requires that projects be stored on HFS (Standard or Extended/Plus) volumes. You cannot use projects stored on volumes formatted as UFS, or any Windows file system.

"Disk responded slowly" alert message. If you use the audio recording feature of iMovie—for example, to record a voice-over—you may get the following message:

The disk responded slowly. It may have been interrupted by something, or it may not be fast enough for your movie. If you have a lot of audio clips, you might try muting the audio tracks to see if helps playback speed.

The problem here is that your hard drive is having trouble keeping up with iMovie. This doesn't mean, however, that your hard drive is inherently too slow. Rather, it's more commonly due to factors such as having too many applications open or virtual memory paging to disk too often. To fix this, try quitting open applications and don't switch to other applications when iMovie is recording.

Another cause may be that your hard drive is extremely fragmented, causing hard-drive access to slow down. The solution would be to defragment your hard drive (as described in Chapter 5).

Graphics import as blank clips. If you import PICT files into iMovie, they may appear as blank (white) clips after being rendered. The solution is to first convert the images to JPEG or TIFF. You can do this fairly quickly by opening them in Apple's Preview application and then choosing Export from the File menu.

Can't use 16:9 video clips in iMovie. If you have video clips formatted with a 16:9 aspect ratio, you'll find that you cannot import them into an iMovie project. This is because iMovie does not support 16:9 video. Thus, you'll need to either reformat the video clips outside of iMovie or use one of Apple's higher-end video products, Final Cut Express or Final Cut Pro.

Exported projects don't sync audio and video. Projects exported from iMovie to iDVD or QuickTime using 12-bit audio may not synchronize audio and video properly. This problem is most pronounced with movies that are more than 20 minutes long. The solution is to use 16-bit audio in your iMovie projects.

If your movies already have 12-bit audio, Apple suggests exporting them back to your DV camcorder with 16-bit audio enabled on the camcorder, and then reimporting them back to iMovie.

Can't export to iDVD. If you're using iMovie 3 but don't have iDVD 3 installed (for example, your Mac came with iDVD 2, but you haven't upgraded to iDVD 3), you will not be able to use the Export to iDVD option. You need to upgrade to iDVD 3 to use this option. Of course, upgrading to the iLife '04 versions of these applications will also work.

More iMovie help. For help with an assortment of basic troubleshooting issues, be sure to check the Troubleshooting section of iMovie Help (as selected from iMovie's Help menu). Among the topics covered there are questions like the following:

- **Why do I hear an alert sound when importing video?** Answer: The "Filter audio from camera" option in iMovie's Preferences is disabled. To fix this, enable it.

- **Why do I get a message about files not belonging in my project?** Answer: This message may appear if iMovie crashed or was force-quit while iMovie was rendering a file—or if you added files to the Media folder from the Finder. If you're sure you don't need the files, select Trash Unused Files.

- **Why don't I see any photos in the Photos pane?** Answer: Make sure you're using iPhoto 2 or later with at least one picture in the Library. If you are, and you still see no photos, quit iMovie, launch iPhoto, create a new album, quit iPhoto, launch iPhoto again, and delete the album you just created. Now launch iMovie; Photos should now appear in the Photos pane.

Troubleshooting iDVD

iDVD is Apple's DVD-creation software. You can create custom DVDs using movies from iMovie, stand-alone video clips, and even photos. You then create your own DVD menus and burn your DVD content to a disc that can be played on any standard DVD player.

You only get iDVD for "free" with Macs that come equipped with an internal, Apple-branded SuperDrive. It is not a standard part of Mac OS X. Otherwise, you can purchase iDVD as part of the iLife suite of software.

Note: You can get iDVD to install from the iLife disc and run on a Mac that does not have a SuperDrive. However, to burn a completed project to a DVD, you will still need to transfer the project to a Mac with a SuperDrive. To get iDVD 3 to install on a non-SuperDrive Mac, follow these steps:

1. Insert the iLife DVD and click once on the Install icon alias. From the File menu, select Show Original (Command-R).

2. From the window that opens, double-click the Packages folder.

3. From the new window that opens, double-click the iDVD.pkg file. The Installer should launch, and iDVD should now install.

Note: With iLife '04, you can install iDVD 4 on any Mac simply by launching the Installer and selecting the Customize option. From the screen that appears, select to install iDVD.

iDVD overview

When you launch iDVD for the first time, the initial screen gives you three options: Open Tutorial, Open Project, and New Project. I highly recommend choosing Open Tutorial if you've never used iDVD before. If you choose New Project, iDVD will ask you to name the project and choose a location to save it to (it's saved in Documents by default). In the future, iDVD will always open the last project on which you were working, assuming it is still available. Choose Open Project to reopen a project other than the one that opens by default.

Figure 11.36

iDVD's main window.

iDVD opens a new project using its default settings. The screen area in the main window lets you view your project in action as well as edit it. The window provides only a few options, via buttons along the bottom:

- **Customize** opens iDVD's Customize pane, which is where most of your project-editing tasks will occur.

- **Folder** adds a link for a folder on the currently viewed screen.

- **Slideshow** adds a link for a slide show of images (typically taken from your iPhoto Library) on the currently viewed screen.

- **Motion** lets you preview menus that you create containing motion, as well as listen to background music.

- **Map** is new in iDVD 4.x. As mentioned in "Take Note" iLife '04," earlier in this chapter, it displays a diagram of your entire project, which you can use to navigate to a specific location.

- **Preview** switches iDVD to Preview mode—that is, a DVD Player remote appears, and you can preview your project (which appears just as it would to someone who popped your finished disc into a DVD player).

- **Burn** allows you to burn your DVD to disc. However, before you do that, you're going to want to edit and customize your DVD, as briefly explained in the next sections.

The following iDVD sections assume you're familiar with how iDVD works and are mainly seeking troubleshooting help. The coverage of basic iDVD features is intended only as a brief reference.

TAKE NOTE ▶ iDVD Projects

When you create a project in iDVD, it's saved in a file called *projectname*.dvdproj. This file is actually a *package* (as explained in Chapter 3). If you look inside the package, you'll find a folder called Resources that contains a file called ProjectData—which contains the map of your project, including a catalog of all audio, video, menus, and other settings—and a bunch of folders that contain the actual data: Audio, Menu, MPEG, Overlay, Slideshow, and Thumbnails.

However, unlike iMovie project folders, iDVD packages don't actually contain all of the files used in the project. If you've used photos, movies, audio, and so on in your project, those files still exist wherever they resided before you used them in your project. For this reason, you can't move your iDVD project to another computer simply by copying the project file. You must also copy over all of the accompanying support files. Thus, I recommend storing all of your project files in the same folder when creating the project.

Editing a DVD: Customize

You aren't limited to iDVD's default DVD design—not by a long shot! When you click the Customize button, the Customize drawer slides out, offering six editing panes: Themes, Settings, Audio, Photos, Movies, and Status.

Note: In iDVD 4.x, the Audio, Photos and Movies options have been replaced by a Media option. You then select Audio, Photos, or Movies from the pop-up menu that appears after selecting Media.

Themes. From the Themes pane, you can choose one of a number of themes for your DVD. A theme consists of a coordinated set of background, buttons, menus, music, and so on. The pop-up menu lets you browse them by group: All, New Themes (themes added to recent versions of iDVD), Old Themes (themes that came with the original version of iDVD), and Favorites (themes you've modified or created and saved for future use). If you see a theme with a tiny Person icon, that theme contains animated features.

Click any theme icon, and your project will instantly switch to that theme. If a theme contains motion elements, click the Motion button in the main window to view them.

 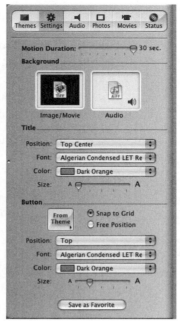

Figure 11.37

iDVD's Customize drawer lets you customize the look of your DVD creation: (left) the Themes pane; (right) the Settings pane.

A quick note about terminology: In iDVD, the term *menu* has two distinct meanings: As in all of Mac OS X, it can refer to a drop-down menu available via the menu bar; however, it can also refer to the graphical system for navigating a DVD (which the user employs when playing the DVD on a standard DVD player). I differentiate between the uses when there's any chance of confusion.

In addition to design elements, many iDVD themes contain *drop zones*—areas of a theme into which you can (guess what?) *drop* movies or photos. For example, iDVD's Projector theme has a drop zone on its main screen into which you can drop a photo or movie. That photo or movie then becomes part of the background of your project's theme. You can even drop a group of photos; iDVD will rotate through them (click the Motion button to view this animation). Although drop zones represent a very cool feature, you need to be careful to drag your movies or photos into the correct positions. For example, if you want the movie to serve as one of the actual video portions of your DVD, you must make sure that you *don't* drop it into a drop zone, but instead drop it into the main menu area.

SEE: • "Movies," later in this section, for further details.

Settings. The Settings pane lets you customize the settings for almost everything on your DVD. In fact, even though it's the second pane in the list, most people will end up using it *after* the Audio, Photos, and Movies panes, because it lets them edit buttons, text, and so on for each menu.

For each menu screen, you can remove any custom image, movie, and or audio you may have added. If the menu includes animation (for example, built into the theme or added to a drop zone), you can use the Duration slider to determine how long that motion lasts before repeating. Via the Title (called Text in iDVD 4.x) section options, you can edit the position, font, color, and size of each menu screen's title. Via the Button section options, you can make similar editing changes for buttons on the menu screen.

Once you've completed your changes, clicking the Save as Favorite button will save your settings as a new theme. A dialog will appears asking you to name the new theme.

TAKE NOTE ▶ **Theme Favorites and Third-Party Themes**

When you modify your theme settings via the Settings pane, you can save the current settings by clicking the Save as Favorite button. What this actually does is create a *new* theme inside /Library/iDVD/Favorites (if you chose the "Shared for all users" option) or ~/Library/iDVD/Favorite (if you didn't). If you want to use your custom theme on another Mac, you can copy the theme file to the same location on that computer. Likewise, if you want to share your custom theme with friends, you can simply give them a copy of that theme file, and they can place it inside their Favorites folders.

Along those lines, you can find lots of third-party themes—some free, some shareware, some commercial—on the Internet. If you find one you like, simply quit iDVD and place the theme file inside one of the folders mentioned above. The next time you launch iDVD, the theme will be available from the Themes pane.

Audio. The Audio pane lets you add an audio track from iTunes to a menu screen or slide show. The box at the top displays all of your iTunes playlists, and the list beneath it shows all tracks in the selected playlist. You can also sample the selected song and search for a particular song, using the controls at the bottom of the pane.

To add a song to a menu, simply drag it to an open area in the screen. To add a song to a slide show, switch the main screen to the Slideshow settings and then drag the song to the Audio icon. You can also drag audio files to iDVD from the Finder.

Photos. The Photos pane works much like the Audio pane. Your iPhoto Library and any albums are listed at the top, and photos in the chosen album are shown at the bottom. You can add a group of photos to a drop zone in a menu, or in a slide show's or folder's screen (which appears when you double-click a Slideshow of folder's button). You can also drag photos to iDVD from the Finder.

Movies. The Movies panes is the third of the media panes. Your Movies folder is listed at the top, and any movies contained in it—including iMovie projects (whose thumbnails include the iMovie icon)—are shown below.

Note: If you want iDVD to look in other folders as well, open iMovie's Preferences, click the Movies button, and then add folders via the "Look for my movies in these folders setting." To preview a movie, select it and click the Play button.

You can drag a movie to a drop zone to animate the menu or to the main menu area to add it as a "feature" for the DVD. You can also drag movie files from the Finder. If you drag a movie to the menu area, iDVD creates a menu button for you. If the movie already contained chapter marks (such as from an iMovie project for which you created chapter marks, as discussed in the iMovie section earlier in this chapter), iDVD adds a second menu button, called Scene Selection, which works just like the Scene Selection button on commercial DVDs.

Status. The Status pane shows you the status of your DVD. If you're doing something that requires that video be encoded, the Encoder Status option in the pop-up menu shows you the process of the encoding. If you choose DVD-ROM Contents from the pop-up menu, you'll see all the files that will be available when the resulting DVD is used in a computer's DVD-ROM drive. You can even create new folders by clicking the New Folder button (to rename the folder, double-click its name). You can move files and folders around by dragging and dropping them.

Editing a DVD: Folder and Slideshow

You use the Folder and Slideshow buttons to add content—generally *after* choosing a theme.

Folder. If you plan to use a single movie for your DVD, you won't need the Folder button. However, if you want another "screen" of options—for example, like a commercial DVD's Special Features screen—you must add a folder to your DVD. Click the Folder button, and a new folder button/menu item will be added to the menu screen.

If you double-click the new folder's icon or label, the screen will change to display that folder's menu (rather than the DVD's main menu). You'll now see a left-pointing arrow, indicating how to get back to the main menu. This folder is basically a subscreen that can do anything your main screen can.

To delete a folder from a menu, click once on its icon or label and press the Delete key.

Slideshow. The Slideshow button adds a Slideshow button/menu item to the menu screen. When you double-click the icon/label for the slide-show item, the screen area changes to a slideshow editor. Drag photos from the Finder or the Photos panel to add them to the slide show. Options here include the ability to set the duration for which each photo is displayed (or choose Manual for no automatic advance) and the ability to add an audio background to the show (just drag an audio file to the Audio pane to do so).

Figure 11.38

The iDVD slide-show editor, which you access by double-clicking a Slideshow button on the project window.

You can also select the "Add original photos on DVD-ROM" option, which allows people using the DVD you created to access the original photos—a nice feature if you're sharing the DVD with relatives or friends.

To see what your slide show will look like, click the Preview button. When you're finished, click the Return button to go back to the previous menu.

Note: Slide shows, by default, fill the entire screen. However, since most TVs end up cropping the edges of images, you may not be able to see the entire image during a slide show viewed on a TV. To avoid this problem, from the iDVD menu select iDVD Preferences, click the Slideshow button in the Preferences toolbar, and then check the box next to "Always scale slides to TV Safe area."

To delete a slide show from a menu, click once on its icon/label and press the Delete key.

Burning a DVD

When you've finished creating your DVD, you're almost ready to burn it to disc. Before you do so, however, click the Preview button to thoroughly test it out. Make sure all the buttons work and that everything is viewable. In addition, if your DVD will be viewed on a TV, from the Advanced menu choose Show TV Safe Area. Since many TVs crop the edges of video, this allows you to view your DVD using the worst-case-scenario, cropped-TV view.

When you're ready to burn your DVD to disc, click the Burn button. It then becomes a Burn *icon*, which you must click again. You will then be asked to insert a blank DVD-R, at which time iDVD will encode your DVD and burn it to the disc. This process takes a bit of time, so you may want to find something else to do in the interim. Unless you have one of the most recent super-fast Macs, I don't recommend doing anything else on the computer while iDVD is doing its thing.

When the DVD is finished, iDVD will eject it. You can now play it on any computer that plays DVDs or any standard DVD player.

Cleaning up

iDVD projects can take up a lot of space, especially if they contain a lot of raw video or iMovie projects. Some people delete iDVD projects after they've been burned to DVD, but many people like to keep them around. If you want to keep them handy, there is a way to reduce the amount of hard drive space they occupy: From the iDVD menu select iDVD Preferences. Click the General button and check the box next to "Delete rendered files after closing a project."

Now, when you click the Burn button and burn your project to DVD, iDVD first encodes it into a format used for DVD discs. It then burns that data to the DVD. After burning, iDVD deletes the encoded files, freeing up quite a bit of space. If this option is unchecked, iDVD keeps both the original project files *and* the encoded DVD files on your hard drive. The drawback of checking this option is that if you ever decide to burn another copy of a project, you'll have to wait for iDVD to re-encode the entire project again.

Solving iDVD problems

This final section lists the most common problems users have with iDVD—and some suggested solutions.

Can't install iDVD from iLife CD because of "newer versions." If you previously installed iMovie 3, iPhoto 2, and/or iTunes by downloading them over the Internet, and you then purchased Apple's iLife DVD (which includes all three applications plus iDVD), you may find that you cannot install the iLife package because the installer detects "newer" versions of the iLife applications. This may occur even if you don't have iDVD installed, or if your version of iDVD is clearly older than the one on your Mac (for example, version 2).

Chances are, the versions of iMovie, iPhoto, and/or iTunes you installed really *are* newer than those on the iLife DVD. Because the most common reason for buying iLife is to obtain iDVD 3, this is clearly a problem in need of a solution. Here are two:

- **Access the iDVD Installer package directly.** To do so, follow these steps:

  1. Insert the iLife DVD in your CD/DVD drive.

  2. From the Go menu choose Go to Folder.

  3. In the dialog that appears, type /Volumes/Install DVD/Installer/ Packages and click the Go button.

  4. Double-click the iDVD.pkg file to launch the Installer utility and install iDVD.

- **Delete receipts.** From the Finder, go to /Library/Receipts and delete the iDVD.pkg, iMovie.pkg, iPhoto.pkg, and iTunes.pkg files. These files tell the installer that each application has already been installed; by deleting them, the installer will think that you haven't installed them yet and will let you use the iLife DVD to do so.

Of course, upgrading to iLife '04 should also bypass this problem.

Restoring iDVD. Unless you obtained iDVD by purchasing Apple's iLife bundle, it came preinstalled on your hard drive. Because iDVD cannot be downloaded for free from Apple, if you ever need to reinstall it, you'll need to use the Apple Software Restore CD or DVD that came with your computer. To do so, use the Software Restore CDs or Software Restore feature on the Install DVD that came with your Mac.

SEE: • "Using Software Restore," in Chapter 3, for more details.

"Projects were found validating your project" message. If, after clicking the Burn button, you get a message stating, "Problems were found validating your project. A DVD must have at least one video track or one slideshow," you may have accidentally dragged all of your photos and/or videos to drop zones rather than to menus. As described earlier in the chapter, if you drag photos or movies to drop zones, they become part of the theme background rather than part of the slide show or a movie. If you don't have at least one actual slide show or movie in your project, iDVD will not be able to validate the project. The above error message is the result. The solution is to add a slide show or movie to your project, being careful not to place it in a drop zone.

Can't burn DVD on computer without a SuperDrive. Under iDVD 3.0 and earlier, you couldn't even launch iDVD unless your Mac had a SuperDrive. Beginning with iDVD 3.0.1, you can actually use iDVD to create a project on any Mac, but you won't be able to burn the resulting DVD unless your Mac has a built-in SuperDrive. How to install iDVD on a Mac without a SuperDrive is described at the start of the iDVD section of this chapter.

Note: A DVD-R drive that uses the same drive mechanism as Apple's SuperDrive may be able to work with iDVD if you get a third-party patch. Check online for the latest status of such hacks.

Can't remove iDVD themes. iDVD 2 allows you to save custom iDVD themes as Favorites. However, it doesn't allow you to delete or remove these themes from within iDVD. To delete a custom/favorite theme, quit iDVD, go to ~/Library/Favorites, and drag the theme you want to delete to the Trash. The next time you launch iDVD, the theme will no longer appear.

Chapter submenus not created when importing movies. When you import a movie to iDVD that includes chapter markers, iDVD automatically creates a submenu containing buttons for each chapter. However, you can modify this default behavior by selecting Preferences from iDVD's iDVD menu, clicking the Movies button, and making a different selection from the "When importing movies" choices. If you select "Ask each time" and import a movie that's more than 60 minutes long, no chapter menus will be created. The simple solution is not to select this choice for long movies.

Eliminating the Apple logo watermark. To get rid of the Apple logo watermark that appears on all iDVD screens, select Preferences from the iDVD menu. From the General section, deselect the "Show Apple logo watermark" option.

Characters you assign to a DVD name don't appear on the burned DVD. DVD names can only include the letters A through Z, the numbers 0 through 9, and the underscore character. Spaces in names will be replaced by the underscore character. All other nonalphanumeric characters will be ignored.

iDVD Dock icon stops working after upgrading to iDVD 3. Unlike the case in most Mac OS X applications, if you upgrade from iDVD 2 to iDVD 3, the existing iDVD icon in the Dock no longer functions. The solution is to drag the iDVD icon out of the Dock, go to the /Applications folder, and drag the new iDVD icon to the Dock.

Index